Also by Carolyn Burke

Becoming Modern: The Life of Mina Loy

Lee Miller

Lee Miller

A Life

Carolyn Burke

Alfred A. Knopf   New York · 2005

Library of Congress Cataloging-in-Publication Data
Burke, Carolyn.
Lee Miller : a life / Carolyn Burke.
p.   cm.
ISBN 0-375-40147-4 (alk. paper)
1. Miller, Lee, 1907–1977.   2. Photographers—United States—Biography.   3. Models
(Persons)—United States—Biography.   I. Title.
TR140.M55B87 2005
770'.92—dc22
[B]   2004043844

Manufactured in the United States of America

First Edition

For Valda

I want to have the utopian combination of security and freedom, and emotionally I need to be completely absorbed in some work or in a man I love. I think the first is to take or make freedom, which will give me the opportunity to become concentrated again & just hope that some sort of security follows & even if it doesn't the struggle will keep me awake and alive.
                    —Lee Miller to Aziz Eloui Bey, November 17, 1938

I keep saying to everyone, "I didn't waste a minute, all my life—I had a wonderful time," but I know, myself, now that if I had it over again I'd be even more free with my ideas, with my body and my affections.
                    —Lee Miller to Roland Penrose, September 9, 1947

Contents

Part Three: **Madame Eloui Bey**

Part Four: **Lee Miller, War Correspondent**

Part Five: **Lady Penrose**

Introduction

Lee Miller was one of the most remarkable, and underrecognized, photographers of the last century. At their best, her images put head, eye, and heart on one line of sight—to borrow a phrase from her friend Henri Cartier-Bresson. Like him, Lee Miller captured those decisive moments when reality seems to compose itself for the camera, when the visual world speaks. But because she did not pursue a conventional career, her reputation, until recently, has been eclipsed by her legend, and the famous men who helped construct it.

While it is true that Lee Miller's early work in Paris recalls that of her lover Man Ray, it was uniquely her own—full of startling perspectives and witty surprises. In Egypt, her home in the mid-1930s, her unforced Surrealist eye saw familiar and unfamiliar sights through the skewed lens of her expatriation. In the 1940s, her World War II coverage for *Vogue* conveyed the urgency of combat, the horror of the death camps, and the war's impact on ordinary lives—the collateral damage that gripped her long after it came to a close.

That Lee Miller was also one of the most beautiful women of the twentieth century has made it difficult to evaluate her work in its own right. Her astounding good looks seem to get in the way. For many, her beauty is at war with her accomplishment, as if the mind resists the thought of a dazzling woman who is a first-rate photographer.

One might even say that there are too many portraits of Lee Miller by better-known artists. Edward Steichen launched her as a model; Man Ray photographed her, whole and in parts, as his perversely enchanting muse; Jean

Cocteau cast her as the spellbinding classical statue in his film *Blood of a Poet;* Picasso painted six portraits of her as a Provençal wench whose bare breasts inspire reveries of sexual freedom; Roland Penrose charted his erotic relations with her in a series of paintings that range from ecstatic to melancholy.

Mesmerized by her features, we look at Lee Miller but not into her. We think of her as a timeless icon. To this day, her life inspires features in the same glossy magazines for which she posed—articles explaining how to re-create her "look." This approach turns the real woman into a screen on which beholders project their fantasies. Looking at her this way perpetuates the legend of Lee Miller as "an American free spirit wrapped in the body of a Greek goddess" (in the words of her friend John Phillips) while underplaying her élan, the imaginative and moral energy that magnetized those who knew her, often to their cost.

In Lee Miller's time, her admirers were equally spellbound by her beauty, but they also saw her as an incarnation of the modern woman—in the United States of the twenties, as a quintessential flapper; in Paris of the thirties, as a subversive *garçonne* or a maddeningly free *femme surréaliste*—one who sparked creativity in others but played the role of muse only when it suited her, and sought, despite her lovers' objections, to keep her energy for herself.

Breaking free of conventional roles for women, whether in traditional or avant-garde circles, Lee Miller stirred up trouble for herself and those who loved her. Like screenwriter Anita Loos and actress Louise Brooks (whose careers she followed), she helped reshape women's aspirations through her embrace of popular culture, starting with her appearances in *Vogue* after her accidental discovery, in 1927, by Condé Nast. At the same time, she pursued a self-directed training in art, stage design, photography, and, later, politics, all of which inform the incisive dispatches she wrote in the 1940s in her unexpected, and defining, role as *Vogue*'s war correspondent.

Lee Miller's movement from model to combat photojournalist is perhaps the most remarkable metamorphosis in a life full of self-reinvention. "Who else has written equally well about GIs and Picasso?" the head of U.K. *Vogue* asked when she returned to London after the war. "Who else can get in at the death in St.-Malo and the rebirth of the fashion salons? Who else can swing from the Siegfried line one week to the new hip line the next?"

Two portraits of Lee Miller, emphasizing hats rather than hemlines, suggest her significance in her own time. The first, a drawing by Georges Lepape, appeared on the cover of *Vogue* a month before her twentieth birthday. Posed against Manhattan's night sky, she stares into the future from beneath her helmetlike cloche hat—the incarnation of what it meant to be "moderne."

Nearly two decades later, *Vogue* ran a striking shot of Lee Miller in uniform wearing a U.S. Army helmet: one can read in her eyes the imprint of the wounded and dying soldiers she had just photographed, for her first illustrated report on the Normandy invasion. These images suggest her exceptional range.

The woman who inspired artists to depict her as the quintessential flapper became the photographer whose war images, like those of her colleague Margaret Bourke-White, still have the power to set our hair on end.

Yet if I were to choose one image to represent her, it might be the self-portrait she called *LM* par *LM*—Lee Miller *by* Lee Miller. Taken after she moved into her Montparnasse studio in 1930, near Man Ray's yet at a slight distance, it differs from his better-known portraits of her in its unposed quality, the way it reveals how it felt to be alone with herself. *LM* par *LM* lets us see the softness she rarely showed to others, since even then, she behaved as if she were one of the guys, an American *garçonne*.

Reading Lee Miller's letters, one learns that her sense of herself, shaped by psychic wounds sustained in childhood, was far from confident. Beneath her defiant pose, she experienced the doubts that were papered over in her ever-expanding search for freedom. The unstable balancing act between her quest for fulfillment, personal and creative, and her need for love registered in the alcoholism and depression of her later years, when early trauma and the aftereffects of combat returned to haunt her.

Lee Miller's life can be seen as segmented—a set of phases through which she moved as if going from one role to another in a number of wildly different movies. When one stands at a distance from the ways she caught the world's attention—as *Vogue* model, avant-garde muse, stylish portraitist, photojournalist, and unexpectedly, gourmet cook—her restless desire for change occupies the foreground.

But if one changes the focus to see her close-up, themes emerge from beneath the surface of her variousness. Continuities reveal themselves. To borrow a metaphor from photography, the biographer needs a set of different lenses, focused now at a distance for the big picture, now at close range for detail. A flexible vantage point helps us grasp a life in its multiple contexts, but also to feel the subject's inwardness, the emotional and aesthetic imperatives at work even as she seized each chance to reinvent herself.

To understand someone who met the world visually, we must also look through her eyes—and in the case of Lee Miller, note her compositions' expressive use of space. In each phase of her work, she took photographs characterized by her feel for the medium as a way to speak bodily truths that otherwise remain silent. Her archive guides us in this reading, one that tells the tale of a life that was multiple, yet marked by fault lines revealed at times of stress, leaving traces on her most mysteriously moving photographs.

At the same time, she was extraordinarily able to respond to what came her way, to meet reality on its own ground. Lee Miller's gift for being in the moment created compositions that say, simply, this is how it was—as if in the onrush of life, she caught the essence of each scene or person in her viewfinder. Her images have the feel of fortuitous encounters.

Appropriately, it was chance, or synchronicity, that brought us together. I met Lee Miller in 1977, when I happened to sit beside her at a public event in Paris. We began to talk. The conversation continued the next day. She told me about her life in Poughkeepsie, Manhattan, Paris, and Egypt, then about the war and its aftermath. I knew right away that I wanted to write about her after the completion of my project at that time, a life of her friend Mina Loy. Years later, seeing Lee's war images—in which her surrealist imagination meets a shattered reality head-on—impelled me to pursue the idea. The encouragement of her son, Antony Penrose, who opened the Lee Miller Archive to me, made it possible for me to do so.

Since then, I have interviewed scores of her friends, family, and associates, many of whom are still puzzled by her life's discontinuities; worked in archives in the United States, Britain, and France; read widely on all areas of her life; and corresponded with specialists on related projects—often returning to the Lee Miller Archive to verify details and refine interpretations. It has been moving to handle the diverse documents held there and encountered elsewhere—a favorite book from her childhood, *The Goop Directory*; a notebook filled with adolescent musings; emergency guides to London during the Blitz; the yellow cotton Jewish star she took as a souvenir after the liberation of Paris—and to pore over her correspondence, the eloquent, teasing letters she signed "Lovelee." As I pieced together her life from these materials and from work by others, it sometimes felt as if I were assembling a puzzle from which pieces were missing.

Eerily, it seemed as if Lee Miller's past had entered my present when I read in a 1937 letter to Roland Penrose that she saw her life as a jigsaw puzzle, one whose pieces "don't match in shape or design"; trying to compose a new shape with these mismatched bits, she wondered if she were "ever meant to fit together." This metaphor (Miller loved puzzles of all kinds) recurs in descriptions of her state of mind: "I feel about as popular as a leper and as rational as a scattered jigsaw puzzle," she wrote in 1945, when in despair about the future of Europe, and her own.

It was difficult to understand her turn to gourmet cooking in the 1950s, after she settled in London, married Penrose, and stopped working as a full-time photographer. Lee chose cookery "for therapeutic reasons," her friend Bettina McNulty explained, "to put her wartime experiences behind her and to share the results of her efforts with her wide circle." After trying her more outrageous Surrealist-inspired recipes, I understood that cooking provided some of the sensual and artistic immediacy she had found in photography. An intensely social person, Lee created in her kitchen a vibrant conviviality, a world she sustained and, to some extent, composed to her liking—though when dinner finally appeared, she and her guests were often in their cups.

In the end, Lee Miller could not fit the pieces of her life into a coherent pattern. Few of us can. It is the work of the biographer to complete the pattern while indicating the convergences and discrepancies, the matching up of the scattered bits. Looking when possible through her eyes—in the case of a great photographer, a transformative experience—this life of Lee Miller relates her baffled search for integration within herself, with those she loved, and with her time, even as she took every opportunity to defy and confound its conventions. Despite her attitude toward photography (she believed, as did many of her contemporaries, that it was a technique, not an art), Lee Miller produced a body of work that continues to surprise us, revealing moments of composure in the midst of chaos, boldly aligning head, eye, and heart.

Part One

Elizabeth

Florence, Erik, Elizabeth, John, and Theodore Miller, 1914 (Theodore Miller)

Chapter 1

A Poughkeepsie Girlhood

(1907–15)

On April 23, 1907, Theodore Miller entered the birth of his daughter, Elizabeth, in his diary, noting the time of day (4:15 p.m.), the place (the Miller home, 40 South Clinton Street, Poughkeepsie, New York), her weight (seven pounds), and the names of those in attendance (Dr. Gribbon and Nurse Ferguson). His firstborn, Elizabeth's brother John, had come into the world two years earlier, but the little girl—Li Li, then Te Te, Bettie, and in her twentieth year, Lee—would always be her father's favorite. Her blue eyes and blond curls enchanted him. Whatever name she went by, she was his Elizabeth, whose growth he would continue to document, one might almost say obsessively.

By the time Elizabeth was born, Theodore Miller was the superintendent of Poughkeepsie's largest employer, the DeLaval Separator Company (its machines separated heavier liquids from lighter ones). An ambitious man of thirty-five who was on his way to becoming one of the town's elite, he had married three years earlier after securing his position at DeLaval's recently enlarged plant on the bank of the Hudson River. Florence Miller, his wife, is not mentioned in the diary entry, as if her part in the arrival of their daughter could not be reckoned among the facts and figures that gave him his grip on the world. Perhaps it was taken for granted. Like most men of his time, Theodore believed that a woman's place was at home, a man's with the new world of science and technology—the forces that enabled entrepreneurs like himself and the country as a whole to move forward.

Theodore always said that he came of a long line of mechanics. A tall, erect man with penetrating blue eyes, he might have stepped out of a Horatio Alger novel. Born in 1872 in the aptly named Mechanicsville, Ohio, he grew up in Richmond, Indiana, at that time the largest Quaker settlement in the country. Although the Millers were not Quakers, he thought well of this sect despite his opposition to formal religion and, in adulthood, his atheism. More important to him than the Society of Friends and the Inner Light were facts. As a youth he had worked in a roller-skate-wheel factory, then a machine shop where he operated lathes. Earning his qualification in mechanical engineering through a correspondence course reinforced the idea that hard work led not only to self-improvement but also to material rewards.

When telling his children about his rise in the world, Theodore emphasized the Miller self-reliance. His ancestors included Hessian mercenaries who had fought for the British in the Revolutionary War; his father was famous as the man who laid seven thousand bricks a day when helping to build Antioch College; his older brother, Fred, was an engineer widely known as the editor of the *American Machinist*. Theodore's career illustrated the belief that a self-confident man could try his hand at anything. In his twenties he had worked in New Jersey at a U.S. Navy shipyard, in Brooklyn at a typewriter factory, in Mexico at the Monterrey Steel Works, and in Utica, New York, at the Drop Forge and Tool Company, where he became general manager. So intent upon making his way that he did not think about marriage until he turned thirty, he then proposed to Florence MacDonald, the fair-haired Canadian nurse who had cared for him during his treatment for typhoid at Utica Hospital.

It was typical of their union that the children heard more about the Millers than about the MacDonalds. Florence told them little of her background except that her people were Scots-Irish settlers from Brockville, Ontario, where she was born in 1881, and that her parents had died when she was a girl, after which she went to live with relatives. Only later did they learn that the MacDonalds had been defeated by their hard, rocky land, and that Florence had had little education apart from nurse's training. Then, nursing was one of the few paths open to women from poor families. There were more opportunities in the United States than at home but the work required dedication. Florence would have earned little more than room and board at the training hospital in Utica—except for the hope that once certified, she could work anywhere. Theodore Miller may have won her heart, but he was also a good catch.

Their life together as members of Poughkeepsie's bourgeoisie began when they married in 1904, after he had settled into his position at DeLaval. It would have required an adjustment on Florence's part to manage a household staffed with servants, including some from the town's black community. In the few family photographs taken before 1904 Florence is a shy, slender young woman. She was happy to trade her white cap and nurse's uniform for the large-brimmed hats and flowing gowns of the 1900s, to collect bric-a-brac for her new house, and in time, once her children were at school, to educate herself.

Although Florence took her turn giving the tea parties expected of the Poughkeepsie ladies with whom she mingled, some insecurity prevented her from enjoying these occasions. She fussed about details. Unsure which of Poughkeepsie's many Protestant churches to attend, she tried them all. Traces of her time as a nurse were still discernible in her bathroom, where white tiles and a doctor's scale implied that cleanliness was next to godliness. Florence retained a horror of germs and a reverence for doctors. She was also in awe of her husband, who was nearly ten years older and the mainstay of their comfortable life.

The Millers often told their children a story from their early days in Poughkeepsie. Because of Theodore's position, the local chapter of the Daughters of the American Revolution invited his bride to join this ultraconservative organization. Florence filled in the genealogical forms required of new members. Her husband's Hessian forebears, who had fought against the revolution that gave the group its name, raised a few eyebrows, but as soon as the membership committee saw that she was Canadian, the invitation was withdrawn. Having been treated as less than loyal Americans, the Millers turned the incident into a joke. And since it was impossible to infiltrate the old families whose cupolaed mansions overlooked the Hudson, they made the best of the matter by establishing themselves as citizens of the new century.

Depending upon whom you were talking to, Poughkeepsie in the 1900s was either a declining regional capital or an industrial center ready to take advantage of its strategic location. Both accounts were accurate. To the town's more progressive citizens, its values seemed Victorian. Yet at the same time, institutions like Vassar College—located two miles east of town—were trying out new ideas about women's social and intellectual potential, and forward-looking businesses like DeLaval, a Swedish firm, were rethinking the relations between civic and professional life. Many Poughkeepsians believed they lived at the center of things. The New York Central's trains sped north along the Hudson to Albany and south to New York City, the bridge across the river encouraged trips west to New Paltz and the Catskills, the Dutchess Turnpike ran east past rich farmlands to Connecticut.

Since the eighteenth century, the "river families," the old guard of Dutchess County, had looked down from their hilltop estates on the villages along the Hudson's shores as if they were the fiefs in some American version of feudalism. Poughkeepsie, a town of twenty-four thousand when Elizabeth was born, had always been something of an exception. Its inhabitants prided themselves on their town's history as a seventeenth-century Dutch settlement and an early state capital, the site of New York's ratification convention for the U.S. Constitution, and from the 1860s on, the hub of swift railroad connections to the north and west. Although the symbol of the new century, the Twentieth Century Limited, flew past Poughkeepsie on its way from New York to Chicago, the city's position halfway between New York and Albany was thought to ensure its influence—provided the town fathers could agree on what was meant by progress and how to go about implementing it.

Prominent Poughkeepsians looked to technology as the way to be "up-to-date." At a time when civic leaders all over the United States indulged in boosterism to enhance their town's reputation at the expense of neighboring ones, they proclaimed Poughkeepsie's superiority over its rivals, Syracuse and Albany. Yet in reality it had grown very little since the 1870s, a number of businesses having failed or gone elsewhere. Industries clustered along the Hudson in former times had included shipbuilders, dye mills, a brewery, and an ironworks, many of which had been replaced by larger, more modern concerns like DeLaval and Queen Undermuslins, a manufacturer of women's underwear. What was good for these businesses was good for Poughkeepsie, town officials said, as were recent municipal gains like electric lights, telephones, and macadam paving. But there were those who said that they had been right to decline Thomas Edison's offer to make Poughkeepsie the first fully electrified American city, after which he bestowed the honor upon Newburgh.

In Theodore Miller's espousal of modern technology, he spoke for the "progressives," those who favored any and all improvements. His credentials— a professional engineer's license, membership in the American Society of Mechanical Engineers, and his new post—so impressed members of the town's preeminent social group for men, the Amrita Club, that they made him a member within months of his arrival in 1903. There he met local aristocrats like the Roosevelts and those who were on their way to positions of influence in banking, commerce, and politics. By the time Elizabeth was born, Theodore was known as the forward-looking manager of DeLaval's large workforce or, alternately, as its benevolent dictator.

DeLaval had opened the plant in 1892 for the manufacture of its centrifugal cream separator (which separated cream from milk), then enlarged it the year before Miller was hired to quell labor unrest. A history of Poughkeepsie published in 1905 hails DeLaval as the town's most advanced industry, functioning with electricity "driven by a dynamo driven by the only turbine engine so far installed in the city." Over the years, new applications were developed for DeLaval's machines. Theodore oversaw the production of machinery designed to clean industrial oils and varnishes, prepare blood plasma, and perform other tasks based on the principle of separating solids from liquids. The company was known as a good place to work. Theodore paid higher wages than were being paid in the rest of the county, instituted a forty-eight-hour workweek, and set up employee benefits including a restaurant, insurance, and profit sharing. To a labor force that had known harsh conditions elsewhere, he seemed a humane employer.

Nonetheless, good labor relations depended upon the employees' knowing their place. The noblesse oblige attitude that prevailed in social circles—the river families' distant patronage of their inferiors—operated at DeLaval. Theodore's position, which would lead to his serving on the boards of civic institutions, planning commissions, and local banks, presupposed absolute control of his workers. The women employees whom he fondled did not complain of harassment, the members of ethnic groups—Italians, Poles, and other minorities, mostly Catholic—did little in the face of the "Wasp" values that kept them from advancing, and the few members of the town's black community thought themselves lucky to have jobs. Theodore's strict rule over his five hundred employees was taken for granted.

In this respect his ideas about the workforce were only somewhat more liberal than those of his cronies at the Amrita Club, which barred from membership Jews, Catholics, and blacks. Members invited their wives and daughters to a New Year's Day tea dance, but the rest of the time women were excluded. Much of Poughkeepsie's growth was decided at the Amrita Club's dinner table, which was served by the best cook in town. Like the rest of Dutchess County, the city fathers were Republicans, but in this respect as in others (such as his atheism), Theodore demonstrated his independence of mind by voting Democratic. Despite these eccentricities, his preeminence was not disputed.

During the last decades of the nineteenth century, civic leaders had sought to express the town's standing in monumental public buildings. In 1912, when the Amrita Club's elegant new premises were completed, members concluded that they too belonged to the country's elite—since McKim, Mead and White, the architects of New York's Harvard Club, had designed their Colonial Revival headquarters. The new building, the mayor declaimed, symbolized "the orderly progress of a community" by incorporating modern conveniences into a design recalling the town's colonial beginnings. Poughkeepsie was "the 'City Beautiful,'" according to the board of trade. Greek Revival banks, Gothic churches, and Renaissance palazzo department stores lent a sense of history; the mansard roofs of Vassar's Main Building evoked the Tuileries Palace, the Eastman Business College's turrets recalled Oxbridge. Young men entering the portals of the new YMCA, whose façade evoked a Medicean palace, would emerge "the better for that beauty," the town fathers told themselves.

The young men of the day, most of whom hoped to make their way as Theodore Miller had, no doubt felt the better for time spent out of doors rather than inside the edifices intended to civilize them. Few could afford the train trip to New York, where increasingly people of Miller's standing would go for entertainment; many were intimidated by the idea of the big city. Young people took part in a round of local activities that began in autumn with trips to apple orchards for cider, winter carnivals, ice skating and boating on the frozen Hudson, fishing in April when the shad ran downriver, and in warmer months, garden parties and socials beneath the flowering fruit trees or among the azaleas.

The social calendar peaked in June when rowing crews from the Ivy League colleges came to train for the Intercollegiate Regatta. Poughkeepsians spoke proudly of having won out over Saratoga Springs, the home of the regatta until 1898—when the broad four-mile stretch of the Hudson north of town was deemed more appropriate than Lake Saratoga. Thousands of rowing enthusiasts came by train to stroll along the river, watch the rowers, and boost the local economy. The crews and their supporters occupied all the rooms in the area. Young men in boater hats strolled around town in the company of ladies with upswept hairdos; romances flourished. For a month the river was a watery stage crisscrossed by ferryboats full of rowing buffs and lined by viewing stands on specially fitted railroad cars.

This spectacle enchanted the local girls and decided the futures of a number of Vassar students, some of whom settled in Poughkeepsie. Elizabeth Miller had no such fate in mind for herself. She would always refer to her hometown as "P'ok"—as in *poke,* to prod, pry, or meddle, and *pokey,* as in cramped, frumpy, or, in slang, a prison—and she would do anything to *épater* the local bourgeoisie. Once she knew something about the Old World always being evoked in "P'ok," Europe became her destination. By the end of her life, when she had lived abroad for fifty years, she had assimilated the Surrealists' antibourgeois stance and accepted her odd status as the wife of Sir Roland Penrose—this after having been born into privilege, American style, and turning her back on what Poughkeepsie had to offer.

Yet the geography of Lee Miller's escapes—to New York, Paris, Cairo, and then to the movable country of the avant-garde—was mapped onto the landscape of Dutchess County as its opposite. Despite her hometown's narrowmindedess, it amused her to sign her name (as she did on a Caribbean cruise) as Lady Penrose of Poughkeepsie, New York.

∞

The Millers lived until 1912 in the comfortable frame house on South Clinton Street where Elizabeth was born. Theodore liked the location near the center of town, Florence walked to the local shops beneath the flowering cherry trees and Japanese maples that lined the street, an Italian organ-grinder played his spirited tunes outside their door, and the fife-and-drum band passed, waving banners, on the Fourth of July. After the birth of Elizabeth's younger brother, Erik, in 1910, her parents talked of moving to the country. Wherever they lived, Elizabeth always saw Erik as *her* playmate, a loyal sidekick ready to do her bidding. The Millers arranged to limit their family to the three children, another choice thought by some to show a progressive spirit.

Yet each parent's marked attachment to the child of the opposite sex struck some of their contemporaries as unusual. Florence preferred her firstborn. She dressed John in girls' clothing and tied bows in his hair until he was six, when she reluctantly agreed to trim his curls—a year after Theodore had himself cut Elizabeth's long fine hair and commemorated the event with before-and-after photographs. In a kind of reversed symmetry, Elizabeth often wore boys' clothing. Theodore so obviously preferred his daughter that John not unreasonably formed the opinion that girls had all the luck: they won their fathers' attention and didn't have to do chores. The two older children would share little except a passionate interest in machinery and what the family called their strong-mindedness. In most respects, they were opposites.

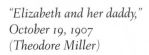

"Elizabeth and her daddy,"
October 19, 1907
(Theodore Miller)

From an early age Elizabeth disdained dolls, except when required to pose with one for Theodore, who used his camera to document her childhood on all occasions. He photographed himself holding John while both watched Florence with three-week-old Elizabeth, his little girl swathed in stiff white garments ("Elizabeth as a starched daisy"), himself holding her aloft at six months ("Elizabeth and her daddy"), John and his sister eating "in their pelts" on a hot day. No one thought much of his nude photos of Elizabeth at eighteen months, although it must have been hard to make her sit still on her wicker chair for both profile and rear views. The family albums hold many more shots of Theodore's daughter, all meticulously captioned in purple ink, than of his sons.

Theodore had many more occasions for picturesque shots after their move in 1912 to Cedar Hill Farm, four miles south of town. The property, which covered 165 acres, became a vast playground for the children. They lived first at Cedar Hill cottage, then in a two-story frame house. Over the next eight years, as Elizabeth grew up, her father enclosed the porch, added rooms, and built a playhouse behind the house with a bronze bell in the belfry to summon the children. Theodore's code worked according to birth order, one ring repeated three times for John, two rings for Elizabeth, three for Erik. Once Theodore gave John his own tools, the playhouse became John's shop. The younger children watched him build a locomotive that ran on a track equipped with a switch to avoid collisions and that had eight brass wheels that Theodore had specially cast. They sustained skinned knees from the inevitable wrecks as the train raced on its wooden tracks down the hill behind the house, across the flat land, and up the opposite hillside. Until John transferred his love of trains to airplanes, all three looked forward to their future as engineers.

Elizabeth habitually played boys' games. Delighted when John allowed her to ride his train, she developed such an interest in locomotives that she disappeared one day when the family was about to begin a train trip. Her parents worried until the conductor appeared to explain that she had gone to inspect the engine. Much of her play involved tinkering with things and taking them apart out of curiosity, a trait encouraged by her father. With John and Erik she built a waterwheel beside the stream that ran through the property—where they picnicked, swam, and picked watercress in the summer. She learned the rudiments of photography from Theodore, who gave her a box camera—at a time when Kodak ads enticed young customers to adopt the Brownie as the latest, and most creative, kind of toy. She climbed trees, camped, went riding and fishing with white bows in her flyaway blond hair—her mother's attempt to keep her from being a tomboy.

The children saw their father as a cross between a wizard and an inventor. While remodeling the farmhouse, he added running water, a heating system, and electricity, but what impressed them even more were gadgets of his own design: a new kind of nutcracker, a light that came on when the cupboard was opened, a sealed photo lab set up in a converted bathroom. Theodore taught John to use either hand for certain tasks to make him ambidextrous and encouraged the children to write with both hands, as he did—an interest adopted by Elizabeth, with the result that her handwriting varies as much as his does. Theodore's respect for facts—the time, the weather, one's digestion, or how one had slept—implied that such matters were bedrock. What counted was what one could measure or record.

Inventors were national heroes while the Miller children were growing up. The proximity of Locust Grove, the richly landscaped property that had been the home of Samuel Morse, maintained its owner's reputation as an American Leonardo. That the inventor of the telegraph and Morse code had also been a leading nineteenth-century artist and an agriculturalist provided another example of masculine omnicompetence. His Italianate villa, said to be connected telegraphically to the major sites of North America, sat at the end of a curving drive that led to a romantic "French" garden. Locust Grove was more patrician than Cedar Hill Farm, and Theodore Miller was a man of the new age. Yet in some ways his vision of a healthy setting for his children's development harked back to the values with which his generation had been raised.

Since Theodore spent his days at the DeLaval plant, it made sense to have the property farmed by others. Through Florence's relatives, Theodore contacted the man his children would call Uncle Ephraim Miller, though he was not a relative. Ephraim traveled from Canada to Poughkeepsie with his wife, four daughters, and livestock to run the farm, which he did in the manner current in his homeland. They made all their own food except for staples, used flails to harvest grain, and lived according to the tenets of his Methodist faith. The girls played enthusiastically with Elizabeth and her brothers except on Sundays, when they walked the four miles to town to attend church. Theodore disapproved of what he called Ephraim's backwardness—his lack of interest in modern equipment—but until some years later, when he replaced Ephraim with a more forward-looking manager, the children had playmates with whom they formed an extended family.

During the long winters, when the family was often snowbound, Florence read them instructive stories like Margaret Sidney's *Five Little Peppers and How They Grew*. They were better off than the fatherless Pepper children, yet it sometimes seemed as if their home on Cedar Hill Farm resembled the little brown house of this impoverished but cheerful group. At first, before Theodore added a bathroom, they too heated water on a coal stove and bathed in the kitchen. Unlike the Pepper parents, however, their father was a force to be reckoned with, and their mother was not obliged to take in sewing. Nor could anyone imagine Elizabeth imitating industrious Polly Pepper by coaxing cakes out of brown flour and old raisins. The Peppers' rags-to-riches saga (a millionaire railroad director, Mr. King, becomes their benefactor) sketched out an alternative to the Horatio Alger model, one in which all were so unvaryingly kind that their elevation to a more aristocratic way of life did little to change them.

Elizabeth preferred a series in a different vein, the Goop books. Ostensibly created to tell children what not to do, Gelett Burgess's unruly Goops sent up the moralism of nineteenth-century children's stories and, in the process, made bad behavior look delicious. (Burgess betrayed his sympathy for his big-headed imps in one series title, *Goops and How to Be Them.*) Infantile crimes like Talking While Eating, Whining, Sulking, and Not Minding Mother were portrayed as reprehensible, yet one guesses from the subtitle of a later edition, his manuals "for impolite infants, depicting the characteristics of many naughty and thoughtless children," did more to inspire Goop-emulation than to persuade children to its opposite. *The Goop Directory,* which Elizabeth kept in her adult library, attributed infantile indiscretions to familiarly named children: one Eliza Puddingfoot, found guilty of Cheating at Play, is shunned by all but so dominates the illustration that one cannot feel sorry for her.

Unlike the recently departed Mr. Pepper, Theodore was a major presence in the children's lives. He interested himself and them in pastimes befitting a man of his position—like Teddy Roosevelt, he disappeared for several weeks each fall to hunt deer and bear, which he brought home as trophies. He was gregarious and loved to travel, at first by train, then in the big Buick sedan he bought in 1917. The children peered through its cut-glass panels as they toured with their parents during summer holidays, when they went to the mountains and seashore, or to visit their prosperous Uncle Fred, whose island estate on the Delaware River impressed them more than Morse's house at Locust Grove.

The Millers also attended performances at Poughkeepsie's Collingwood Opera House, where under the auspices of high culture, they saw everything from farce to vaudeville. The children were taken there to experience the novelty of the day, the "motion pictures" used as curtain-raisers before more high-class events. They were also initiated into Theodore's passion for the stereoscope—a photographic camera and viewer that purveyed with a startling depth and detail images of exotic places, technological marvels, and humorous or titillating scenarios. What the children did not see, presumably, were the stereoscopic poses of naked women widely available at the turn of the century and still popular at gentlemen-only venues like the Amrita Club. It was one thing to gaze at the prickly texture of pineapple plants in Hawaii and quite another to contemplate bare-breasted harem girls recumbent on their couches.

Theodore often told the children about his upbringing. As a boy he had never defied his father. He saw himself as a strict but reasonable parent: if the children talked back or otherwise misbehaved, they were sent to their rooms. Elizabeth's remarks about Erik's table manners resulted in angry retorts by Florence, who told her not to criticize the little boy, then sent her upstairs to con-template her goopishness: she had not only hurt her brother's feelings but set a bad example. Theodore told the children that they could do as they pleased as long as it didn't harm anyone. Good behavior was based on ethical princi-ples. In his view his large collection of books on atheism made more sense than the Bible. Organized religions produced fanatics who believed in mira-cles or unyielding throwbacks like Uncle Ephraim. As a concession to Flo-rence the family attended the Unitarian church, which had the merit of not greatly challenging Theodore's outlook while also maintaining contact with Protestant doctrine.

In later years Theodore met once a week with the Episcopalian minister, to whom he referred as his spiritual adviser, but as if to balance his influence, often invited him to dinner with the head of Vassar's astronomy department. Since his sister Elizabeth had married a Quaker missionary, Theodore made an exception for this sect. Little Elizabeth listened attentively to her aunt's stories of life in Japan when the Binfords came to visit, and dressed for photo sessions in the kimono and obi brought as gifts, along with swords and armor for her brothers. These glimpses of other lives, combined with evenings spent looking through the stereoscope viewer at faraway lands—Hawaii, India, or Japan, where the Binfords lived—inspired a precocious wanderlust.

John lost interest in trains after his father took him to see Glenn Curtiss, a contemporary of the Wright Brothers who in 1910 landed his flying machine near their farm to refuel. The experience so impressed the little boy that he vowed to become a pilot. Elizabeth, still enchanted by terrestrial engines, dis-covered a source of inspiration other than her father in an equally unlikely place. Decades later, recalling her first motion picture—"a thrill-packed reel of a spark-shedding locomotive dashing through tunnels and over trestles"—she could still feel its dizzying speed and see the "head of the train glar[ing] at its own tail" as it curved around a chasm. "Nothing whatever stayed still," she wrote, "and I pulled eight dollars worth of fringe from the rail of our loge, in my whooping, joyful frenzy."

What inspired her rapture was not the film's engineer but a character who documented their ride as it happened—"the intrepid cameraman himself who wore his cap backwards, and was paid 'danger money.'" In this retrospective account of her seven-year-old self, the child's identification with her on-screen hero is one with an intoxicating sense of forward motion. It is an intense vis-ceral memory for a little girl who years later as a photographer would neither stay still nor receive her due in fame or "danger money."

∞

Something of a spark-shedding locomotive herself, Elizabeth led an untrameled life compared to other girls. Brought up as her daddy's darling, she was used to roaming over the farm, alone or with her brothers, and to getting her way. She was also confident in her powers of judgment and determined to discover how things worked, especially if they were men's business. Above all, she was drawn to the conjoining of motion and materiality in machines—whether DeLaval's separators, which broke matter into its constituent parts, the locomotives of the New York Central line, or her father's well-appointed touring cars. These engines stirred the little girl's imagination—in which she too was full of energy and sufficient unto herself, like the train curling back on its own beginning. Recalling the ourobouros (the snake biting its tail—an archetype of nature's continuity), this strong figure conveys the child's sense of autonomy.

From her mother's perspective, however, Elizabeth was unladylike. Florence wanted her to look more like the girl of the family. After her marriage Florence had cut a fashionable figure—until three pregnancies and the Millers' removal to the farm combined to increase her girth. When Elizabeth was little, Florence dressed her as a small version of herself in a miniature nurse's uniform. On the principle that while her behavior was unruly she could at least dress properly, for special occasions Elizabeth wore white lace frocks and embroidered jackets, or a white alpaca coat with matching muff, gloves,

Elizabeth on her fourth birthday
(Theodore Miller)

hat, and hairbow. In photo albums she appears alternately in her overalls and gumboots and in the delicate feminine garments of her mother's choosing.

While Elizabeth's early life was happy, it is hard to know what to make of her parents' relationship. On the one hand, Theodore was as much a domestic tyrant as an industrial one; Florence deferred to him, tacitly accepting his liaisons with other women. On the other hand, she was not without influence. After he initiated her into his passion for photography, Florence agreed to pose in the nude. This unusual request seems not to have alarmed her, no doubt because he explained that such portraits were "Art." They were for his own enjoyment, and nudism was, in any case, a progressive practice. Such things were taken for granted in the family.

Theodore regularly made trips to DeLaval's home office in Stockholm. One winter, after his return, the neighbors thought he had gone mad when they saw him sliding down the snow-covered hills on a pair of curved boards; until then, skis were unknown in Poughkeepsie. The children caught on quickly after he made skis for them by steaming boards to turn up the ends. In addition to the skis, he came home with great respect for Swedish manufacturing. In Stockholm DeLaval was thought a genius, in the same company as Alfred Nobel. Theodore also looked with interest on the early stages of the Swedish social welfare program and the gradual rise of the Social Democrats, although their policies regarding workers' rights differed from his own. Although Sweden had come late to modernization, its industrial breakthrough predisposed him in the country's favor.

When Swedish friends visited Poughkeepsie, they often brought presents for the Miller children. Family photos show Elizabeth dressed as a Swedish girl or holding a Swedish doll. During the Millers' visit to Sweden in July 1913, they spent several idyllic days at a DeLaval associate's summer home on Lake Mälaren with an attractive young couple, the Kajerdts, who later came to the United States to work with the company's American branch. When in Poughkeepsie, the couple often visited the Millers. Astrid Kajerdt (who had no children of her own) took a fancy to Elizabeth, whose blond good looks may have reminded her of home. Her affection was reciprocated—so much so that Elizabeth looked forward to staying with the Kajerdts in Brooklyn while Florence recovered from an illness.

Mrs. Kajerdt wrote to Florence about Elizabeth's impressions—when they went into the subway she asked whether night had fallen—and her ability to "take things so natural and feel quite at home with everything and everybody." They fed the squirrels in the park, rode on a merry-go-round, and inspected Abraham and Straus's toy department. Elizabeth made new friends—the boy upstairs and Mrs. Kajerdt's brother-in-law, "Uncle Bob," who took his meals with the family. Everyone enjoyed her, Astrid wrote: "It is strange how a child can make you young again. She really is the most important person in the house at present, but I will try my best not to let the gentlemen spoil her."

This visit marked the end of Elizabeth's sense of security and, in some ways, her childhood—at the age of seven. One day when Astrid went shopping, she left the girl in the care of a male friend, "Uncle Bob" or a nephew who was also staying with the Kajerdts on leave from his tour of duty as a sailor. The details of what happened are unclear. Mrs. Kajerdt's correspondence ended abruptly; Theodore's diaries are mute on the subject even though Elizabeth was rushed to Poughkeepsie. At nine her brother John did not know the word *rape,* but he later surmised that Elizabeth's caretaker had raped her during Mrs. Kajerdt's absence. Given the secrecy surrounding such matters it is no wonder that John had to piece together the story, which was never explained.

For Elizabeth the experience was so unexpected, so traumatic, and so impossible to process that its impact must be inferred from the patterns of her later life. During rape, integrity is ruptured, trust in the world undone. The act deprives the victim of her autonomy whether or not she can defend herself. Often a kind of numbing ensues. The helpless person may experience an altered state of consciousness in which the attack seems unreal: "as though she is observing from outside her body, or as though the whole experience is a bad dream from which she will shortly awaken." Judging by Lee Miller's adult life, she never quite awoke from this nightmare. The damage done to her seven-year-old self stayed with her, even though she later made use of her ability to observe as if objectively what was happening to her body.

If rape is also understood as a violation of inwardness, "the most sacred and private repository of the self," its impact on a young child—whose self is a work in progress—is all the more terrifying. Maya Angelou, raped by a family friend at about the same age, called the episode "a breaking and entering when even the senses are torn apart." Decades later, Lee Miller put her outraged emotions into her compositions—where enigmatic doorways hint at damage to the house of the self, or look to a space beyond loss and trauma.

∞

Although there are many uncertainties about this turning point in Elizabeth's life, its impact is apparent in Theodore's photographs. In one of them, most likely taken before her stay in Brooklyn, she stands between John and Erik, with her parents planted protectively behind them. Wearing a white summer dress, matching shoes and stockings, and a large bow in her hair, she smiles confidently. The embrace of her family is taken for granted. In another photo, made less than a year later, Elizabeth stands alone with one arm propped against the support of the playhouse. She wears shapeless overalls, her hair is slicked back and bowless, her expression at once depressed and angry. Barely eight, she seems quite unlike her self from the previous year. Much later, John observed that his sister never fully assimilated the trauma. "It changed her whole life and attitude," he reflected—adding as an afterthought, "she went wild."

After her return home Elizabeth's recovery was still uncharted. Reestablishing a sense of trust after rape depends to a large extent on family members' attitudes. Nothing in Theodore's commitment to the certainty of facts could have prepared him for this emergency, nor did nurse's training at the turn of the century include advice on the subject. The Millers turned not to a spiritual adviser but to a doctor, probably a psychiatrist. They understood him to say that they must tell Elizabeth that the damage was not permanent, since sex was one thing and love another. This applied Freudianism sounded up-to-date, but had the effect of separating body from spirit, the senses from the emotions.

The task of attending to their daughter's physical condition fell to Florence, who realized that the rape had not only changed Elizabeth's attitude but had left her with a disease, which was soon diagnosed as gonorrhea. In the first decades of the century, public health officials warned that an epidemic of such complaints threatened the country; Dr. Prince Morrow, an expert on "the diseases of vice," warned that syphilis and gonorrhea had invaded the habitations of virtue. Although polite discourse did not permit discussion of such matters, sexually transmitted diseases constituted a grave problem—both ethically, since innocent females contracted these diseases unknowingly, and in their effect on the body politic. Gonorrhea was, Morrow believed, the single most powerful factor in depopulation: 50 percent of infected women became sterile. Moreover, the treatments then available could have disastrous consequences. "The flower of our land, our young women," another expert wrote, "are being mutilated and unsexed by surgical life-saving measures because of these diseases."

Since no one in Poughkeepsie could know the cause of Elizabeth's illness, her case had to be handled discreetly—which meant continued isolation during her recovery. Florence took her to Vassar Hospital several times a week for the next year. Before sulfa drugs, the treatment for gonorrhea in females consisted of an antiseptic sitz bath followed by the "irrigation" of the bladder with a solution of potassium permanganate (the ominous-sounding equipment included a glass catheter, douche can, and rubber tubing), after which the patient was douched with a mixture of boric acid, carbolic acid, and several oils. As if this were not enough, the cervix had to be probed twice a week with cotton-wool swabs to remove secretions, then daubed with a solution of "picric acid in glycerine."

Florence administered these treatments in her immaculate white bathroom. Although the boys were not supposed to know what was happening, John heard his sister cry out when their mother performed the irrigations, and he watched her sterilize the fixtures to keep the disease from spreading. Whatever Elizabeth touched, bathtub, basin, or toilet seat, had to be scoured with dichloride of mercury, a strong disinfectant. It is not difficult to imagine the effect of this routine on the little girl, or to understand how her mother, rather than comforting her, unwittingly made the situation worse.

In the cases with the best outcomes, trauma victims undergo stages in recovery. Regaining a sense of control over one's body is vital, but daily irrigations and frequent "inoculations" over the course of the year must have made it seem—to a seven-year-old—that she would never regain the freedom she had enjoyed before the attack. Nor would the capacity for trust be reestablished, since the rape occurred at the home of friends. It is likely that Elizabeth learned to dissociate herself from the event (since her father had said that sex was separate from love) and from its aftermath, the feelings of guilt, blame, and anger. Whatever Florence actually said, the treatments she administered made her daughter feel that she had been contaminated. In the parlance of the day, she was "damaged goods." It is from this time that Lee's tendency to see herself as split between good and bad selves may be dated.

One morning in 1915, two weeks before Elizabeth's eighth birthday and Theodore's next trip to Sweden, he announced that he would be taking a different kind of portrait, to be called "December Morn"—although it was April. Thinking perhaps that he was carrying out the doctor's orders or hoping to make his daughter feel more comfortable with her body, perhaps wanting to mark the close of this horrible year, he told her not to dress up. She was to pose outside in her birthday suit. In this photo the child stands naked, except for her slippers, in the snowbanks beside the house. Trying not to shiver, which would have spoiled the picture, she looks ill at ease, yet somehow proud of herself.

Today, Theodore's blend of therapy and "Art" seems peculiar—especially when one realizes that his inspiration was Paul Chabas's *September Morn*, a painting of a nubile nude emerging from a pool that provoked a national scandal when it was shown in New York the year before. For a time, this titillating artwork (now owned by the Metropolitan Museum) was as famous, or notorious, as the *Mona Lisa*.

From our perspective, we wonder whether Theodore, too, saw his daughter as damaged goods—her innocence despoiled yet preserved in his imagination, her image held for his private view in stereoscopic slides and annotated

December Morn, *April 14, 1915*
(*Theodore Miller*)

albums. Then, the family accepted his hobby as a form of art. Florence, who often supervised photography sessions, did not object to their effect on Elizabeth. And despite her many lovers in later life, Lee would always rely on her father. Erik observed: "He was the only man she could feel comfortable with and really love."

The Millers, 1920 (Theodore Miller)

Chapter 2

Never Jam Today

(1915–25)

If Theodore hoped to reassure Elizabeth by casting her as his prepubescent muse, this peculiar "treatment" deepened their bond while further objectifying her. The rape and its aftermath, occasional bouts of gonorrhea, became an unmentionable part of her life. During a flare-up twelve years later, she wrote obliquely of their impact in a journal addressed to an imaginary reader—who is asked to sympathize, yet held at arm's length. Her confession, she noted with the self-absorption of a nineteen-year-old, was "something to hand down to posterity."

"Of my dark and supposedly lurid past," she began, "I will say almost nothing. . . . I will content myself this time in saying that anything you hear about me is probably true." Her "sordidly experienced life" could be seen as a pattern initiated by a random cause—just as in novels, events resulting "from the circumstantial placing of individuals" could generate a "natural and probable occurrence." This pattern, she went on, has been "true to life—to *my* life!"

But generalities offered little comfort: she could not bring herself to name her distress. And the effort to accept objective theories about the "circumstantial placing of individuals" was so great that after formulating this account, Elizabeth burst into tears. "I was the nearest to suicide I have ever

been," she wrote later—overwhelmed by a sense of "sheer hopelessness, activated by that swollen awkward feeling which ha[s] followed me from childhood." This awkward feeling suggests the stored bodily memory of the rape
and the ensuing treatments—a discomfort that sometimes surfaced like a
threat to her being.

∞

From the end of Elizabeth's childhood at seven to her departure from home at
nineteen, her moods dominated the household. Florence often lost patience
with her; Theodore usually responded by taking his daughter's side in family
squabbles. Her wishes were indulged, her health constantly monitored. While
John was given tasks like mowing the lawn as well as his daily chores, Elizabeth was treated like a princess. The little boy couldn't understand why she
didn't have to do women's work but could spend her time reading, drawing,
and looking at albums of film stars or dreaming about the scripts in which she
would shine as an actress.

The few girls who lived nearby, most of whom attended a Vassar prep
school called Putnam Hall, were invited to keep Elizabeth company. When
she had recovered from the trauma, her parents sent her to Governor Clinton
School to start first grade, where she chose as her best friend a lively eight-
year-old named Miriam Hicks, nicknamed Minnow. Elizabeth took to running
away as an alternative to venting her temper at home. On these occasions her
father drove straight to Minnow's house and waited outside until her mood
had changed.

One wonders what Theodore made of Elizabeth's turn from boys' games to
more "feminine" activities—whether he saw it as natural or as a consequence
of her precocious sexual knowledge. (Typically, he did not commit thoughts or
feelings to paper but made factual notes, such as "Elizabeth had tantrums,
threw things in her room.") The psychiatrist the Millers consulted may have
said that they could expect a stormy period right through her adolescence. The
trauma had sexualized her at an early age—seven being considered the start of
latency, a period in child development when eros is thought to lie dormant.
From this perspective, her tantrums expressed her buried rage. But the
episode was never mentioned, except when Theodore repeated the doctor's
remark that sex and love were not the same.

Florence continued to practice the pastimes befitting a woman of her station: bridge, gourmet cooking, and churchgoing. She enrolled Elizabeth at
Sunday school, for piano lessons, and for dance classes at Miss Rutherford's,
where the offspring of the local elite studied tap, ballet, and ballroom dancing.
For the next three years her mother also took her to New York for treatments
with a Dr. Robinson. (Theodore's diaries record the dates of these trips but

nothing more.) In order to keep watch on Elizabeth, Florence chose not to accompany her husband on his next trip to Sweden.

Under her mother's attentive eye, the little girl indulged in pastimes like jewelry making and other crafts, and with her brothers, enjoyed the pleasures of country life. She rode Ginny, the donkey, around the farm, lolled in the hammock or swung on the swings Theodore hung from the birch trees, and camped, swam, and fished with John and Erik during the summer. In winter months she skated on the frozen pond or at nearby Lake Upton—activities recorded by Theodore, whose desire to document the children's days was accepted as something fathers did, like hunting and fishing.

Theodore's fascination with the camera and his love of gadgets came together in his passion for photography. In these years, he initiated his family into a pastime that had, for the past decade, been encouraged by Eastman Kodak, the pride of Rochester. Kodak urged middle-class families to record their lives: "Bring your vacation home in a Kodak," the company exhorted; "There are no Game Laws for those who hunt with a Kodak," proclaimed an ad aimed at outdoorsmen. The "better" magazines all featured well-dressed women photographing foreigners encountered on their holidays or memorializing Christmas at home; the Kodak Girl, a subdeb version of modern womanhood, appeared with her camera in publicity campaigns emphasizing her sense of adventure—but also her amateur status.

While Theodore often used a box camera, he preferred the stereoscope, which took a pair of pictures set slightly apart so that the two images formed one when seen through a viewer. In 1916, he began experimenting with techniques for projecting the twin images on a screen, using a revolving shutter to get "the true stereoscopic effect, the important point being to get both projections focused alike." Although John continued to prefer airplanes to photography, Elizabeth and Erik loved to watch images of themselves appear as if by magic as Theodore took prints from the

Publicity card for the Kodak Girls, Eastman Kodak's role models for budding female photographers

chemical bath in his darkroom. They enjoyed their closeness to him in this private space, and at night, when he entertained the family with slide shows of faraway lands shown in deep perspective.

Peering intently through the stereoscope viewer, Lee got her eye in at an early age. Some of these devices were held like opera glasses. Others enhanced the sense of a theatrical experience by shielding the spectator's eyes under a slight overhang: one entered this private space to gaze at the Eiffel Tower or the fronds of date palms beside the Pyramids. The stereoscope, a pastime combining home entertainment with educational instruction (commercial slide sets included courses of study), gave the little girl a precocious visual training and the desire to visit the foreign lands at which she gazed.

Formal education did not interest her, however, nor could she accept the discipline required at local institutions of learning. From an early age, Elizabeth picked up information by more amusing methods, like the stereoscope, her stamp collection, and the chemistry set Theodore gave her one Christmas, with which she performed a series of disastrous experiments. Since she wanted to be entertained while learning, the regimented teaching methods at Governor Clinton did not suit her. Teachers thought her more than a little spoiled; classmates called her a show-off. As she grew up, Elizabeth took delight in being provocative. One afternoon she had her braids cut off, then appeared at school with a fashionable bob. "That one, she had a mind of her own," recalled Miss Freer, whose sixth-grade English classes had the merit of providing her with an excuse to read as much as she liked.

Theodore's interests provided an alternative to formal education. At dinner the family debated the ideas of Henry George, the economic visionary who, he believed, offered the solution to social injustice. Toward the end of the nineteenth century Georgism had influenced a wide range of people, from artists and revolutionaries like Tolstoy and Sun Yat-sen to wheat farmers in the United States, Canada, and Australia. Prominent Americans like William Jennings Bryan favored George's principle of a single tax on landowners, which eliminated taxation on wage earners and the landless. Theodore agreed that the land belonged to the people. Once landowners could no longer profit from speculation, the natural order would be restored, and all classes would benefit.

No one at the dinner table noticed the contradictions between Georgism and the ideas of Henry Ford, another of Theodore's favorites. Although both men rejected the aristocracy of inherited wealth and looked to a more democratic future, their differences were profound. But this was of no concern to Theodore. Ford's vision of motorcars for the multitude was heroic; his mass-production techniques, socially useful. And his recent decision to give factory workers a living wage while reducing their hours had already proved good business practice, since workers could then buy the very Model Ts they were turning out every twenty-four seconds.

The man whose career inspired the whole family was Thomas Edison, the

holder of more than a thousand
patents for his inventions—among
them the microphone, the phonograph, and the incandescent bulb.
The cover of *Success,* an illustrated
magazine that publicized national
heroes, featured a reflective Edison
in the laboratory where he worked
on such projects as a motion picture projector synchronized with a
phonograph—an early form of
"talkies." Edison also devised a new
power source, the alkaline storage
battery. By the mid-1910s, Edison's
batteries were powering submarines, electric motorcars, and
the starter for the Model T.

*Elizabeth learned about perspective by
peering through her father's stereoscope
viewer, shown with his slides of the
Millers and of Lee at twenty-one.*

Another of his projects intrigued Theodore. Edison's workshop had tried to
develop a magnetic separator to extract iron from low-grade ores. Although the
effort had been abandoned, the parallel with DeLaval's use of its separators
was striking.

Theodore, it was generally agreed, was a man of the future. He espoused
health habits considered eccentric by some and progressive by others, such as
birth control, a diet of whole foods, and exposure to the sun's rays through the
practice of nudism—practices in which Florence joined him. While these
opinions made him seem advanced, he also enjoyed the reputation as one of
Poughkeepsie's most influential citizens. The children looked to their father as
the household Edison, whose inventions made life more interesting. His purchase of the first electric blankets seemed to prove his wisdom, especially in
cooler months, when the family still slept on the sleeping porch.

The Millers' lives were not much affected by the hostilities in Europe even
when Poughkeepsie was swept up in the wave of patriotism that overwhelmed
the country after the United States entered the war in 1917. The children followed its progress in the newspaper; each class at Governor Clinton formed a
military company. John used an army manual to drill his company (they took
first prize) and wore his Boy Scout uniform to sell war bonds. Having recently
been subjected to sewing lessons by Florence, Elizabeth knitted socks for the
refugees and posed in her Red Cross nurse's uniform—one of the rare occasions when she could be said to take after her mother. She played war games
with Erik but did not succumb to war fever, nor did she join her parents at victory meetings or the timely performance of George Bernard Shaw's *Arms and
the Man,* held in town at the Collingwood Opera House.

The Collingwood, which combined the functions of civic meeting place and temple of culture, ran anti-German propaganda films on Friday and Saturday nights, when the Millers took the children to Poughkeepsie. These melodramas portrayed the enemy as fiends who took pleasure in ruining the innocent. "Dishevelled girls staggered from the private quarters of the Crown Prince of Germany who raped his way across Belgium," Lee recalled of such programs, "while his officers tortured civilians behind haystacks. The Kaiser himself was busy gloating over Zeppelin raids," she went on, "the chopped-off hands of little children and 'the worse-than-death' fate of nuns and nurses. Oh! how gloaty was the gloating, how lecherous the leer and oh, how pure the innocent."

On December 8, 1917, the Millers took Elizabeth to the Collingwood to see Sarah Bernhardt's latest farewell tour. The experience, her first theatrical event, so marked her imagination that she could still visualize it decades later. With John and her parents she walked through the crowded lobby, past the fountain banked with flowers, and into the vast semidark opera house to their loge. High above them, on the great dome and decorated ceiling representing the firmament, Italianate gods lolled on billowing clouds. Straight ahead loomed the huge stage, framed like an enormous painting by its eighty-foot proscenium arch, and all around, the audience arranged in tiers and balconies. That night the house was full of Vassar girls and soberly dressed notables, whose decision not to wear evening clothes "portended a change of feeling," an onlooker wrote—as if the town agreed "to show Mme. Bernhardt that we are taking the war seriously."

The curtain-raiser, a one-reel silent, starred Elizabeth's hero—the cameraman who took pictures while hanging out the train window to earn his "danger money." Next came the slightly risqué *tableaux vivants,* which featured immobile nudes impersonating abstractions or statuary, with titles like Motherhood, Columbia, and Venus de Milo. A quivering light played over these feminine icons, Lee recalled with a touch of sarcasm, but to her eyes, already accustomed to her father's nude studies, "It was just more ART."

The Divine Sarah, although over seventy and missing a leg, exceeded expectations by enacting the death of Cleopatra on her chaise longue. Then, following the mayor's exhortations on behalf of the Red Cross drive, she leaned against a pillar to play Portia in *The Merchant of Venice.* Watching the actress declaim "was of considerable morbid interest to me," Lee recalled. "Though I understood no French, her Portia, pleading, seemed urgent." Bernhardt had come to the United States to fan prowar sentiment: she represented what the Allies were fighting for, and her transformation from horizontal to vertical seemed miraculous.

The entire audience leapt to their feet at the end of the performance. Everyone applauded as the actress returned again and again to the stage, even though few apart from the Vassar contingent had understood what she said.

This triumph of mind over body, the reviewer wrote, joined with the prevailing spirit of patriotism to inspire all those who were present. At the end of the evening the accompanist played the Marseillaise, the Vassar girls sang from the balcony, and members of the audience wiped tears from their eyes. Bernhardt, "as full of life and as active as many women are at 30," had given Poughkeepsie a triumph.

Elizabeth was ten when she saw this stirring program. Yet in 1956, as she drafted these recollections for a *Vogue* article, "What They See in Cinema," she placed the experience several years before it happened. Given that her memory was excellent, one may suppose that such errors are not accidents. "What They See in Cinema" links visceral memories of that December night in 1917 with other evenings at the Collingwood when she watched the "worse-than-death fate" befall the kaiser's victims—images that must have evoked her own victimization at age seven—while its ironic tone holds the "dishevelled girls" at arm's length, as if the scene were too painful to examine head-on.

That same weekend saw the opening of *Arms and the Girl,* a popular "photoplay" inspired by G. B. Shaw's success. The film met the demand for uplifting entertainment by depicting innocent femininity as a weapon against masculine beastliness: Billie Burke, a guileless American, saves a gallant compatriot from execution by pretending that they are engaged, then marries her "fiancé" on the orders of a cruel German general. Its mixed message implied that while society gave women a limited scope for heroism, feminine virtue would nonetheless triumph.

In the 1910s, photoplays, as movies were called, were *the* modern form of entertainment, combining technical innovations with lively artistic effects. Elizabeth often escaped to the movies with Minnow—who, in addition to sharing her love of the cinema, got free passes from her father. Although Elizabeth would always admire Bernhardt's bravery, it was hard for a young girl to imitate a seventy-year-old tragedienne. But it *was* possible to think of imitating Billie Burke's spirited film heroine, or Geraldine Farrar, who, Lee wrote, "besieged Orleans as Joan of Arc, with noble Wallace Reid by her side." Cecil B. DeMille's *Joan the Woman* (more prowar propaganda) was "as grand as Delacroix," she went on. "It's pretty good going to be awed, educated and entertained simultaneously," she added, recalling her ten-year-old self's enthusiasms.

In 1918, after the armistice, filmmakers returned to less uplifting, but equally entertaining, subjects—like sex. Elizabeth and Minnow admired the former Ziegfeld Follies dancer Mae Murray, who starred in such classic silent films as *Jazzmania* and Erich von Stroheim's *Merry Widow.* Reading about her "bee-stung lips" in the fan magazines, they pursed their own in imitation. Other Hollywood heroines included the diva-turned-film-star Lina Cavalieri, who "thumbed-down handsome gladiators and orgied through ancient history," Lee wrote, and during their teenage years, the young "flappers" Colleen Moore and Louise Brooks.

While the girls also admired noble Wallace Reid and smoldering Rudolph Valentino, their Hollywood pantheon soon included more writers and directors than actors—since they wrote the stories that thrilled the masses. Unchaperoned, Elizabeth and Minnow watched the orgies of destruction in *The Ten Commandments* and *The Last Days of Pompeii,* whose sources in the Bible and in history justified their on-screen saturnalia. Such large-scale misbehavior was inspiring, as was the silent movies' sexual innuendo. The girls practiced lipreading to learn "what the bride really said at the altar." The cinema, Lee observed dryly, "offers us variety in vicarious living."

Rather than act in the movies, the two friends decided to write for them. To this end, they studied *Photoplay,* a popular movie magazine, as if it were a textbook. It was exciting to learn that Wallace Reid had entered a sanatorium after becoming addicted to morphine, and that Valentino had been charged with bigamy following his marriage to Natacha Rambova, who was said to have him under her spell. Another of their heroes, Allan Dwan, who had been an engineer before becoming a director, was known to be practical: "You will never hear Allan Dwan prate about 'My Art,'" *Photoplay* explained. "He believes in the photoplay as an art and as an industry, but he doesn't waste time telling everybody about it."

Elizabeth and Minnow were even more interested in the women who achieved recognition as writers. While the *Photoplay* columnist Adela Rogers St. John had an insider's knowledge of Hollywood, they planned to emulate Anita Loos, who began writing for D. W. Griffiths as a fifteen-year-old and would go on to write the book *Gentlemen Prefer Blondes.* Loos had worked with both Griffiths and Dwan on vehicles for Douglas Fairbanks; her recent successes included *Wild and Wooly, A Virtuous Vamp,* and *The Perfect Woman,* but she was even better known for her dark bob—at a time when most women, especially in Poughkeepsie, had long tresses. Loos became their model. Their scripts, which combined elements of the films they saw and the Hollywood lore they devoured, "were full of naked sinners on bearskin rugs," Minnow mused, but "they made us happy."

Reflecting on her early love of motion pictures, Lee concluded that what had moved her was the occasional "flash of poetry." "Often it is born of motion, alone," she went on. "It might be the way an arm moves, a shadow falls, or some dust settles." This poetic quality was, moreover, an accident: "neither study, sincerity, taste nor trying can synthesize or pin it down."

Years later, as Lee peered through her camera at people, buildings, and landscapes, flashes of poetry often revealed themselves—like a private viewing space, the apparatus itself helped to capture the quality of motion. But as a teenager desperate to escape from Poughkeepsie, she feared that despite her artistic temperament, she had no definable talent. English teachers did little to encourage her desire to write. The few school assignments remaining among her papers include two poems written in completely different styles, as if she were trying on voices just as she tried different kinds of handwriting and different identities: she submitted these verses as "Betty" Miller.

The more traditional of the two, "A Song," exhorts her fourteen-year-old self to "Do good, since thou still liveth, / Love, it is not too late. / Do good, for the joy it giveth, / Put from thy heart all hate." The speaker tells the self straining between contradictory emotions to resolve them in work, the nature of which remains vague, but ends the poem on a positive note: "Live, for thy life's not long / Dream, for thy dreams are real. / On thy lips let there be a song / Of Life, of Work, an ideal." Beneath the moralizing rhymes and antiquated diction, Elizabeth's belief in the reality of dreams—Art?—is discernible to a sympathetic reader.

Her other poem, "Chinese Shawls," abandons Victorian sentiment to focus a self-consciously Beardsley-esque composition—three shawls arranged on "a chest of lacquer red." Their colors—"black, with poison green," "powdered Chinese gold," and "Night-black and paper-white"—suggest a Greenwich Village studio of the 1910s, and since the meter is more relaxed than in "A Song," one may suppose that art for art's sake came more easily than moral uplift.

About this time, Elizabeth also wrote a story, "Distributing Letters," whose characters are Jean, "the pretty and popular daughter" of Judge Ashford; Jean's older brother; and their father. Jean's mother having conveniently died when she was eleven, "Jean was very much spoiled by her father"—who, in spite of being a town notable, "could do nothing with her, for she had a will of her own." Each morning at breakfast she receives anonymous letters from a watchful critic, the most recent of which begins, "At the tennis match your white hat was very smart and becoming, but your new dress would be much better if it were several inches longer." The writer also taxes her with "making eyes," behavior that "marks you as not being well-bred, which is a shame on your father." By the end of the story, Jean's brother realizes that Judge Ashford is the author of these missives and agrees to join him in curing her faults.

In the opinion of Elizabeth's teacher (who gave the story an 83), "Distributing Letters" lacked unity. To a more sympathetic reader, the tale is transparent. At fourteen, Elizabeth felt caught between doing her own looking and being scrutinized for properly feminine behavior. She had a will of her own that she wanted to exercise. But as the daughter of a prominent family, her attempts to be active in the world were proof that she was not what she seemed. A nagging voice insisted that despite the smart white outfit, she was not "well-bred."

∽

Given her lack of success at school, Elizabeth's career as the next Anita Loos seemed uncertain. In the meantime, the local newspapers announced the establishment of a community theater. Although the "little theater" movement had been popular across the country before the war, Poughkeepsie was the first large city to commit resources to this kind of cultural venture. The new Community Theatre planned to produce plays of a high standard (in keeping with its Anglophile spelling), thereby avoiding the "vulgarity of some Broadway successes."

Gertrude Buck, the force behind the project, was an energetic Vassar English professor whose students already staged, directed, and acted in the plays produced in her theater workshop—an innovation at a time when most drama courses consisted of play reading. Her hands-on approach offered a model for the community. The Vassar Brothers Institute trustees gave the use of their premises rent-free, prominent residents became subscribers, and the head of the First National Bank signed on as chairman.

The plan was to present a new play for children on successive Saturday afternoons each month, followed by an adult play in the evening. Elizabeth auditioned and won a part in a stage version of Lewis Carroll's *Alice in Wonderland.* Cast as the absentminded White Queen, whose opening lines— "bread-and-butter, bread-and-butter"—never failed to produce laughter, she had difficulty keeping a straight face at rehearsals, especially when telling Alice that one might have "jam to-morrow and jam yesterday—but never jam *to-day.*" She managed to stay in character and celebrated her fourteenth birthday onstage.

When Elizabeth returned to school on Monday mornings, the White Queen's declaration that she could do sums but could not manage subtraction "under *any* circumstances" may have come to mind. Her scapegrace antics infuriated teachers while entertaining classmates. Cooking class struck her as a particular waste of time. One day as she and Minnow were washing the dishes, she began flicking water at the others. The teacher complained to the principal and had her expelled.

The Millers visited several private schools before choosing the new Quaker establishment, Oakwood, as the institution of learning most likely to instill discipline in their mischievous daughter. Townspeople were proud of having attracted Oakwood to the area: it was thought to cap Poughkeepsie's reputation as a center of learning. The first coeducational boarding school in the United States, Oakwood was run on strict principles. Theodore decided that John and Elizabeth would both board there, even though the school was a short walk from their new house in Kingswood Park. He could afford the fees, and he admired the principal, an ambitious man named William Reagan, who said that the Quaker ethic would benefit both children.

Although classes were coed, boys and girls were allowed to socialize for only one hour on Sundays. Fads like dancing, jazz, and short hair were deemed immoral; swear words and personal adornments were forbidden. The high point of the week came when the whole school assembled to hear Mr. Reagan read aloud from Dickens. No other amusements were allowed. When Elizabeth complained to Theodore, he wrote her a teasing letter: as his "Queen of Hearts" she must maintain her reputation, for it was "the King who suffered for [her] sins or shortcomings." Pleased, nonetheless, by the design she sent him for a perpetual-motion machine, he continued, "The only good thing about the general scheme is that they furnish some mental exercise and teach boys, and on rare occasions girls, to inquire into the whys and wherefores of mechanics."

But Oakwood's curriculum did not provide the mental exercise Elizabeth craved. When she lamented her domestic science class and her cake's failure to rise, Theodore consoled her with the hope that future culinary experiments would be more successful. Two years of Quaker discipline turned Elizabeth into a headstrong sixteen-year-old who spent much of her ingenuity cultivating her reputation as her own perpetual-motion machine. Proud to be known as a bad influence, she used swear words deliberately and devised practical jokes. With her dormitory mates she strewed sugar on the floor outside their room so that they could hear the woman who came to do bed checks, but when "Old Sugarfoot" discovered the ruse and told Mr. Reagan, the principal informed Theodore that Elizabeth was no longer welcome at Oakwood.

One can read equal parts of parental concern, pride, and identification in her father's response to her defiance. Theodore decided to further Elizabeth's education by taking her to Puerto Rico. This trip would not only be a vacation, he told his sister, "but being rather disturbers ourselves, it serve[s] the double purpose of giving the balance of the family a rest." On board their ship, he photographed Elizabeth touring the power plant with the engineer, contacting other vessels from the wireless station, and gazing at flying fish from the bow. Their tour of the island provided more opportunities for lessons: they inspected San Juan's fortress, a factory, a hydroelectric plant, sugar mills, and plantations. While Elizabeth was surprised to see bananas growing upside down, her father noted with approval the use of a centrifugal separator to extract crystallized sugar from molasses and registered their ascent to the island's highest point on his barometer. Theodore photographed everything with both single view and stereoscopic cameras, since he planned to treat the family to a slide show—most of it starring Elizabeth.

Ten days in Puerto Rico may have been meant to compensate in advance for her next school year—at St. Mary's in Peekskill, a Catholic school for girls whose teaching methods were stricter than Oakwood's. Elizabeth begged Minnow to send her reading matter, shared each week's allotment with her roommates, and tried not to finish before the next chapter arrived. As at Oakwood, she became the class ringleader, making outrageous remarks and thinking up practical jokes to inspire her followers. She contrived to have an unsuspecting classmate swallow a capsule containing diagnostic dye; when the girl's urine came out blue, she had hysterics. In May 1924, Elizabeth and two other girls stayed out late and were caught smoking. Summoned to Peekskill by the mother superior, Theodore learned that "Elizabeth had misbehaved," he noted without further comment.

He brought his daughter home to a household in crisis. Florence quarreled with Elizabeth about her future and blamed Theodore for spoiling her. She worried even more about John, who had ended his freshman year at Antioch after one month because, in his view, while the teachers preached socialism, they did not appreciate his thoughts on Henry George. At nineteen John was tall, handsome, and, unlike his sister, well behaved. However, while he was still determined to become an aviator, he also liked to wear women's clothing. Only Erik seemed to be growing up normally. (Looking back at this time, Erik said that he had been fortunate to have been born last, since his parents were too preoccupied with his brother and sister to pay attention to him.)

The children knew that things were wrong with Florence when they heard her crying, yet Theodore said nothing about her distress. What they did not know at the time was that after years of accepting his affairs with other women, she had herself fallen in love and could not decide whether to leave: divorce meant scandal, and she had a lot to lose. In June, Theodore dealt with the situation by giving Florence a new Ford. One morning she prepared breakfast as usual, went into the garage, locked herself in the car, and turned on the engine. Theodore broke down the door in time to save her. As if unable to empathize, he noted only that on her return from the hospital, Florence hurled a chair at their bed and hit the wall, "where a great dent was made in the plaster." When she again threatened suicide, he took her to a New York specialist, then back to the hospital, where she remained until August. His diary records the facts but says nothing about his feelings or those of the children.

Something had to be found to occupy Elizabeth. Theodore gave her a Remington portable and enrolled her at the Eastman Business College, on the theory that if she learned typing, she would never starve. But Eastman, a Poughkeepsie institution with a reputation for turning out good secretaries, was only a stopgap for a lively seventeen-year-old who needed to complete her education. To make matters worse, Minnow had already graduated from high school. Elizabeth did not like to show the frustration she felt beneath her bravado, nor could she admit her fear that she would never find anything meaningful to do.

Florence came home in time to celebrate her twentieth wedding anniversary. A few days before the family picnic intended to symbolize the return of domestic harmony, she began treatment in New York with the well-known Freudian doctor A. A. Brill, which continued several times a week for a year, despite Theodore's objections. Elizabeth stayed at home for the next few months and often accompanied her mother on the train to town. While it was a mixed blessing to travel as her companion, Florence's illness gave both a reason to get away.

Brill had trained with Freud after studying medicine at Columbia University: he returned to the United States in 1912 to start practice as the first American psychoanalyst. By 1924, when Florence became ill, he had translated many of Freud's books and was the best-known specialist in the treatment of nervous disorders. Brill's credentials were impeccable. He taught at Columbia Medical School, ran Bronx Hospital's Department of Neurology, and was said to understand women.

Seeing a psychoanalyst was, nonetheless, an unusual thing to do. Brill may have been the doctor Theodore and Florence consulted after the attack on their daughter. On the other hand, it is unlikely that Brill would have told them that sex and love were two different things. Given the general public's reductive understanding of psychoanalysis, Brill took care to explain that what Freud understood by sex was much broader than people thought. It encompassed what was meant by *love* and *eros,* and while sex was a central part of a relationship, unhappy women lacked love more than they did its physical counterpart.

Brill's methods—he had patients tell their dreams and free-associate—would have been novel for Florence, who was not used to having her thoughts, conscious or unconscious, taken seriously. If she identified her relationship with her daughter as one of the causes of her distress, Brill's views on the anxiety he found to be prevalent in teenage girls may have helped her to understand their difficulties. "It is at these ages," he believed, "that the girl becomes aware of the sex urge but cannot as yet place her emotions properly." Brill may also have helped Florence become aware of her rivalry with Elizabeth, who had become a head-turning beauty—the epitome of the sexually curious, emancipated flapper. One wonders how much of Florence's understanding she shared with her daughter, and whether Elizabeth sympathized with her mother's unhappiness.

In November Theodore agreed that Florence could decide between him and the other man. His willingness to respect her decision may have been exactly what she wanted, since she chose to remain married, and with Brill's advice, found other interests. By the following year, Florence was acting in local theater, reading Shakespeare at Vassar as a special student, and staying overnight in New York to see plays after sessions with Dr. Brill.

Once her mother's condition had stabilized, Elizabeth could return to school—provided one would agree to take her. She completed her last year of formal education as a day girl at Putnam Hall. Hoping that she too might be allowed to do as she wished, she dreamed of living in Europe and, through her reading, explored all possible means of escape.

After school she often browsed through books on subjects as diverse as poetry, drama, graphology, and anthropology at Lindmark's, the used-book shop near the Hudson. Jack Lindmark, the owner, wore knickers to work, he said, because it was easier to squat among his collection of 200,000 volumes in these old-fashioned trousers. Elizabeth and Minnow loved the bookshop's bohemian atmosphere: Lindmark's, a contemporary wrote, was "filled with the sorrowful voice of Ophelia and the sonorous tones of Scrooge mingled with the signs of the Prisoner of Chillon and the merry conversation of Robin Hood." To the girls, what mattered was that Jack and his wife, Ray, were from New York and took an interest in their young clients. They should always wear fine undergarments, Ray teased, since one never knew when one might be in an accident; Jack said that whatever they wore, they were "sitting on a million dollars."

About this time, Elizabeth befriended another pair of local freethinkers, Frank and Helen Stout, whom she met soon after they came to Poughkeepsie to direct the Community Theatre. For some time she had been seeing the latest New York plays with her parents, often reading them in advance at Lindmark's, and while she still dreamed of writing for the movies, she looked to the theater as a mirror of the larger world. The Stouts encouraged her to take drama seriously.

Elizabeth made her adult acting debut in a staged version of *The Girl from the Marshcroft,* by the Swedish novelist Selma Lagerlöf. Lagerlöf, then famous as the first woman to win a Nobel Prize, denounced the narrowness of Swedish folkways in her tale of a country girl "more sinned against than sinning," the *Evening Star* explained. The stage version, featuring authentic Swedish costumes and dances, was faithful to Lagerlöf's ending. After the heroine bears a child to the master of the household where she is in service, a wealthy young man sympathizes with "her struggle against the severe code established for women" and rejects his rich fiancée to wed this modest heroine. Whatever associations this production may have set off in Elizabeth's mind, she brought comic relief to her role as the fiancée's sister, charming the audience with a spirited polka.

Interpretive dance (at that time a branch of "art" theater) attracted girls of Elizabeth's age, since it was said to give grace to one's gestures and improve the figure. Miss Rutherford, whose shapely form proved the theory, told her pupils tales of her life on the New York stage. Before marrying into the old Pough-keepsie family in whose house she taught gymnastics, ballroom dancing, and tap, she had been Marilyn Miller's understudy at the Ziegfeld Follies. The Rutherford Dance Studio was as unusual as its director. On the outside, the house resembled a steamboat, but once inside, ordinary girls became ephemeral creatures in tutus whose reflections multiplied along the ballroom's mirrored walls. Dance, Miss Rutherford explained, was a calling.

In 1923 the opera house reopened as the Bardavon, with a revamped inte-rior and the latest cinematic equipment, after having been bought a few years earlier by a group of businessmen who saw the opportunity to invest in enter-tainment. While its name gestured to Stratford-upon-Avon, the corporation planned to show everything from films and Broadway tryouts to grand opera. The highlight of the season came on January 15 when the Denishawn company presented its free-form dramatic dances (the name amalgamated those of its founders, Ruth St. Denis and Ted Shawn). Few were sure how to describe what they did except to say that these interpretive (or "figure" or "aesthetic") dances were performed barefoot in exotic costumes, and that they resembled moving *tableaux vivants*. The company's style was familiar to Elizabeth from the Hollywood epics she loved, since D. W. Griffiths had employed Den-ishawn dancers to evoke his imaginary Babylons.

That night the program featured one of St. Denis's "music visualizations," as well as a snake-encircled Shawn writhing to Satie in his Cretan "dance-drama," *Gnossienne,* and both principals in Shawn's smoldering *Valse Direc-toire.* The whole company, including several who would go on to establish a unique style of American dance—Martha Graham, Doris Humphrey, and Charles Weidman—performed Shawn's lavishly costumed Toltec spectacle, *Xochitl:* in his huge cape of orange feathers Shawn pursued Martha Graham as Xochitl, the Salome-like dancer whom he all but rapes before claiming her as his empress. Perhaps the most unusual company member that season was a sixteen-year-old named Louise Brooks, whose large dark eyes gave her an exotic look despite her fashionable Anita Loos–style bob.

Up to this point, Elizabeth's dance performances had been restricted to posing in her hootchy-kootchy dress for Theodore and dancing in the chorus of *Kat-cha-koo,* a musical comedy staged in town. She decided to work harder on dance lessons. It was unthinkable to move to New York to study at the Den-ishawn School as Louise Brooks had done before joining the company, but it *was* possible to learn interpretive dance in Poughkeepsie. In June she danced in the Community Theatre's open-air production of *Midsummer Night's Dream,* with the chorus in the airy Grecian garb favored by St. Denis and Isadora Duncan. The following year she went to New York with Florence for the gala in honor of Anna Pavlova at the Metropolitan Opera—where the great ballerina accepted her tributes in a simple white gown.

But to a rebellious seventeen-year-old dreaming of a career in the arts—whether moving pictures, theater, or dance was unclear—swooning divas like St. Denis and Pavlova were passé, the heroines of her mother's generation. Elizabeth wanted to be modern, which meant being active, energetic, unhindered by small-town, middle-class expectations. Women had won the vote in 1920. It remained to be seen what they would do with their freedom.

∞

Elizabeth's teenage years coincided with the first half of the 1920s, when an upheaval in the mores of young people preoccupied the country. Critics blamed this permissiveness on the end of the war, the returned soldiers' hedonism, the movies, and, once Prohibition was enacted, the thrill of clandestine drinking—since to drink meant to break the law and consort with bootleggers and other lowlife. Others pointed to the changes in women's lives. Middle-class girls left home to work in the cities even though their parents could support them; those who stayed home enjoyed greater freedom from surveillance due to the motorcar.

It was more difficult to explain the rise of the flapper. Some said that she had been created by F. Scott Fitzgerald, whose first novel, *This Side of Paradise,* imagined a new kind of American girl based on Zelda Sayre, the southern belle he married soon after its publication in 1920. The cover of Fitzgerald's next book, *Flappers and Philosophers,* showed a puzzled group of citizens watching a barber wielding his shears on the head of a young woman—the rite of passage celebrated in his *Saturday Evening Post* story "Bernice Bobs Her Hair." Fitzgerald's preeminence in the matter was soon challenged by writers like Dorothy Speare, the author of *Dancers in the Dark,* and Warner Fabian, whose 1923 *Flaming Youth* spawned the phrase for this turbulent decade. Some said that the flapper had been created by Hollywood, which not only filmed Fitzgerald's and Fabian's books but churned out sensational dramas of its own, including *Naughty but Nice, Flirting with Love,* and *The Perfect Flapper.*

Wherever the flapper came from, her bold carelessness marked Elizabeth's vision of how she meant to live: this brazen young woman's stance declared, "I do not want to be respectable because respectable girls are not attractive," in the words of Zelda Fitzgerald, its prototype. Yet being a flapper was sometimes only a matter of style. Although Zelda soon announced the demise of the flapper due to the widespread adoption of her accoutrements—short skirt, cloche hat, rolled stockings, one-piece bathing suit, rouge, "and a great deal of audacity"—Elizabeth rebobbed her marcelled waves and had them cut in bangs, like Louise Brooks; later, she and Florence purchased man-tailored flapper outfits and posed in them for Theodore. In these pictures, her mother, caught up in her own way in hopes for greater freedom, seems unaware of the incongruity of dressing like her daughter—who was trying on the flapper's stance along with her clothes.

The flapper's philosophy included flirting, taking life lightly, and refusing to go in for the moral uplift required of girls in previous generations. But it also meant cultivating her mind. Contrary to popular belief, the modern girl was neither flippant nor cynical, Scott Fitzgerald insisted; she was simply intent on exercising her intelligence. Unlike her parents, she understood that "the accent [had] shifted from chemical purity to breadth of viewpoint, intellectual charm, and piquant cleverness." The flapper might not be well educated, but her curiosity attracted her to a range of subjects. "She refused to be bored," Zelda quipped, "chiefly because she wasn't boring."

Yet Hollywood flappers rarely did anything but celebrate their own high spirits. Colleen Moore, the star of *Flaming Youth;* Clara Bow, the "It" girl; and Louise Brooks, the dancer-turned-movie-star, all flaunted their youthful self-assurance in films meant to demonstrate their sex appeal as well as their talent for living. "An artist in her particular field," Zelda reflected, the flapper claimed as her domain "the art of being—being young, being lovely, being an object."

While Elizabeth shared the flapper's talent for being (and being an object), she wanted to be an artist in her own right. Well trained as her father's muse, she would continue in this role when it suited her to collaborate with those whose worship of her beauty conferred on her the power to win their hearts. She would be young and lovely, but on her own terms. And while she often spoke without regard for consequences, her boldness disguised an emotional reticence. Of the consummate flapper, Zelda wrote in 1925, "you always know what she thinks, but she does all her feeling alone." She might have been describing Elizabeth.

Elizabeth and Theodore Miller on the SS Minehaha, New York, May 29, 1925

Chapter 3

Circulating Around

(1925–26)

Elizabeth's year at Putnam Hall passed without incident. She studied French, directed the Drama Society's end-of-year play, and—unexpectedly—passed all her courses, yet showed no interest in college, not even as a place to meet men. Boys her age let her know that in their opinion she had as much "It" as Clara Bow. But eighteen-year-olds were callow. What she wanted was to live in Paris among the bohemians she read about in novels and saw dramatized on Broadway in plays like *Kiki,* the tale of a gamine who becomes a sprightly chorus girl.

As Elizabeth was completing her education, she found inspiration closer to home—in Anita Loos's *Gentlemen Prefer Blondes,* published that spring. Like their counterparts all over the country, Putnam Hall girls did their best to imitate its heroine, Lorelei Lee, whose sugar daddy sends her to Europe to broaden her mind. Lorelei's self-possession is surpassed only by her ability to coax diamonds out of skinflints; the novel ends with her marriage to the millionaire who promises to back her film career. Loos's best seller underscored Zelda Fitzgerald's quip about the flapper's philosophy: girls like Lorelei were "merely applying business methods to being young."

∞

While Lorelei was broadening her mind and portfolio, Elizabeth was plotting her departure from Poughkeepsie. Her French teacher, an impoverished Polish countess known as Madame Kohoszynska, planned to spend the summer in France with her companion. As her chaperones, they could introduce Elizabeth to Europe and settle her in the finishing school in Nice where Madame Kohoszynska was to teach during the summer. Ever indulgent with his only daughter, Theodore agreed.

On May 29, 1925, Florence, Theodore, Erik, and Elizabeth spent the night in a New York hotel before nearly missing her early morning departure on the wonderfully named SS *Minehaha.* Her family watched Elizabeth race up the gangplank, looking fashionable but subdued in her paisley dress, calf-length coat, and cloche hat. Once on French soil, she took charge. Madame Kohoszynska could not manage enough French to order a taxi and, when they settled in Paris, failed to notice the unusual number of men entering and leaving their hotel—which proved to be a *maison de passe,* a hotel used as a brothel. "It took my chaperones five days to catch on, but I thought it was divine," Lee recalled. "I was either hanging out of the window watching the clients," she went on, "or watching the shoes being changed in the corridor with amazing frequency." She had found what she was looking for. "I loved everything," she recalled fifty years later. "I felt everything opening up in front of me."

That summer Paris resembled a series of gleaming stage sets built to display the union of art and industry. The city's historic monuments served as backdrops for the 1925 International Exhibition of Modern Decorative and Industrial Arts, the first major exhibition of Art Deco, as the style came to be known. Its eye-catching pavilions were everywhere. National displays from all of Europe lined the Seine; luxury boutiques stretched from the Left Bank across the Pont Alexandre III, where visitors saw the latest designs in crystal, polished metals, and richly embroidered fabrics. Lalique's glass fixtures shimmered at different spots throughout the city; Sonia Delaunay's Simultanist *robes-poèmes* wed bright primary colors to Cubist shapes (one could order a car to match); Paul Poiret showed his new fashions on three lyrically named barges, *Amours, Délices,* and *Orgues.* "One look at Paris," Lee recalled, "and I said, 'This is mine—this is my home.'"

Showing remarkable self-assurance for an eighteen-year-old, she told Madame Kohoszynska that she would *not* be going to Nice, wired her parents that she wanted to study art in Paris, and, like Kiki, found herself a maid's room. Theodore, who may have seen this as Elizabeth's chance to prove herself, agreed to the plan and upped her allowance by the sum he had been paying the chaperone. *La vie de bohème* was what she had been seeking. Artists were always broke, Lee recalled later, "but it didn't matter. We lived off each other toward the end of the month." Shared resources, casual romances, and "intermingling nationalities" delighted her, and the occasional visiting Americans who hired her as their guide to bohemian Paris took her to the best restaurants—though not in the style of Lorelei's protectors.

Elizabeth also persuaded Theodore to pay her fees at one of the first schools to teach stage design, L'Ecole Medgyès pour la Technique du Théâtre—under the direction of the Hungarian artist Ladislas Medgyès. This decision made sense. Unlike the Montparnasse art academies frequented by most foreigners, the Medgyès School trained students in the applied arts of lighting, costume, and design. Several Medgyès graduates had already distinguished themselves in the New York theater. What Theodore did not know was that in the drama world Medgyès was considered a revolutionary.

His reputation derived in part from his paintings, which combined the intense coloration of the German Expressionists with bright abstract patterning. But Medgyès was also something of a "play-boy," in the view of Frank Crowninshield, the urbane *Vanity Fair* editor who visited the school and met Elizabeth there that autumn. "If you will roll together six of the gayest of contemporary Parisian masters—Picasso, Van Dongen, Laurencin, Cocteau, Pascin and Soudeikin," Crowninshield noted, "you will have Medgyès . . . who thinks of art as a beguiling adventure."

It took an adventurous spirit to pick one's way through the jumble of miniature sets, masks, and marionettes in his studio, where animated conversations went on in several languages. Treating students as apprentice designers, Medgyès put them to work in contemporary productions and encouraged them to approach the stage not as a room with the fourth wall removed, but as an evocation of what one saw with the mind's eye.

For the rest of the year Elizabeth studied with Medgyès and his colleagues, the directors Charles Dullin and Louis Jouvet—both champions of experimental drama. Their teacher, Jacques Copeau, had staged antirealist dramas at his theater, Le Vieux-Colombier, where he used the play of colored lights to sculpt the stage. Medgyès taught his students to evoke form in the same spirit: the bare stage, modeled by shifting lights, he explained, would put the emphasis back on the play. In his ideal theater, shadows would be projected onto screens set at angles, and the impression of depth created through the manipulation of objects backstage. The class admired his model of this dream stage, a five-sided space overarched by a ten-sided dome to reflect light. The problem was not creating new stages, he said, but finding plays that mirrored life—that were "as gay, as sad, as tragic, as alive, as this game we are all playing."

Paris became Elizabeth's university. She learned the cobblestone streets of the Latin Quarter, the patrician St. Germain des Près area, and the historic sites of French drama—the imposing Comédie Française just beyond the arcaded rue de Rivoli, the baroque Opéra sitting like a dowager at the end of its avenue, the colonnaded Odéon Theater near the Luxembourg Gardens, where nannies perambulating their charges mingled with lovers holding hands. The cold, rainy skies did not bother her. There was always a café nearby, a glass of hot wine, an art students' party. That autumn, the Dadaists were reinventing themselves as Surrealists under the leadership of André Breton, Jean Cocteau was memorializing his dead lover in *Orphée*, Picasso was becoming dissatisfied with his fame and his marriage, Gertrude Stein was entertaining in the rue de Fleurus, and Hemingway was completing *The Sun Also Rises*, whose heroine, Brett Ashley, would replace Lorelei Lee as an inspiration for girls like Elizabeth. While she would meet these luminaries in a few years, in 1925 her social world was confined to her fellow students and the drama circles she came to know through Medgyès.

Her teacher envisioned his own theater as a magical space, a scenery-less music hall with sets made of mirrors and actors of spun glass. "Like marionettes, they would be more intelligent than humans," he explained. "They would not mind sacrificing their personal vanity for the artistic effect." To objections that only serious drama suited his futuristic stage, he replied that one could easily create a Chaplinesque aura with props—ladders, platforms, and barrels were all that was needed to make people laugh.

Lee described this period of her life as particularly happy. Medgyès found her employment at the school and recommended her for a job at an "art theater"—as Left Bank venues like Le Vieux-Colombier were called to distinguish them from the commercial theaters. Having already trained her eye with photography, she soon learned to visualize plays onstage and to apply her aptitude for solving technical problems. "Every once in a while I quite surprise myself by my actual intelligence," she admitted, although only one completed project by Elisabeth Miller (her name spelled as if she were French) was listed in the 1926 school brochure. For the first time in her irregular education, she was absorbing what Medgyès called *métier*—a professional attitude toward one's craft—and learning to focus her eye while awakening to the promise of a larger life through art.

With their teacher, Medgyès's students also critiqued the more traditional "well-made plays" at the Right Bank theaters—farces by playwrights like Henri Bernstein, whose *Le Venin* dramatized the passions of a man caught between his wife and his mistress, and Alfred Savoir, whose *Deux Amis* staged the tale of a son who condones his mother's affair with his best friend—because she is "first of all, a woman." In such plays, an observer wrote, sex was just "an appetite in which man is revealed as funny." But Americans in the grip of "the inevitable Puritanism, repression, and sentimentalism" were often disturbed by the Parisian blend of frankness and sensuality.

Like many girls on their own in Paris for the first time, Elizabeth tried to make up for any residual puritanism. Accepting sexual advances proved that she was emancipated; it was sometimes easier to acquiesce than to say no. The following year, looking back on "all the various and nasty affairs" she had had in her teens, Elizabeth concluded that she had "never been . . . really loved." One wonders whether she was thinking of Medgyès, with whom she probably began a liaison despite the difference in their ages—or because of it. Their names for each other suggest a playful complicity. Her teacher was "Maestro," she was "Souris" (Mouse)—though her determination to do as she pleased was hardly mouselike. He admired her mind, she thought, but was particularly fond of her breasts. Although we may conclude that Medgyès abused his position, relations of this sort—combining authority with intimacy—were familiar to her. Their relationship did not strike her as odd.

It was with mixed feelings that Elizabeth read a letter from Florence announcing her arrival in Paris on October 5, 1925. Within a short time, Florence cabled Theodore to come at once, adding "Elizabeth unaware." Elizabeth's behavior changed once he joined them: she and her mother shopped for clothes at the couturiers'; they toured Paris, went to the theater, and dined at fine restaurants. To allay her parents' suspicions, Elizabeth introduced them to Medgyès, who sent flowers to Souris's mother and invited the family to a tea dance. As men of the world, the Maestro and Theodore understood each other.

Theodore left to see his DeLaval associates in Stockholm; Florence took the precaution of staying in Paris until the end of the year. Elizabeth completed her studies with her mother as chaperone while presumably finding time for clandestine trysts. In January, Florence and Elizabeth made the return voyage on the *Suffren*.

Theodore was waiting for them at the French Line pier on January 23, 1926, an unusually cold day even by New York standards. In the time it took to collect their luggage and drive to Poughkeepsie, Elizabeth's spirits sank. The next day she could not get up. When her condition was diagnosed as congested lungs, she stayed in bed for a month, too feverish to interest herself in her father's testimony in Washington in favor of the metric system or his talks at the local YMCA on youth's need to prepare for work. Her father worried about her health—a doctor came daily—but did not connect her collapse to her homecoming after seven months in Paris.

∾

Toward the end of February Theodore wrote in his diary, "Elizabeth has so far recovered as to be up and around the house." What would come next was unclear. Young women of her class did not need to work; her time in Paris had not prepared her for anything, although to her mind it opened the door to a more spacious vision of life.

Hallie Flanagan, director of Vassar's
Experimental Theatre

There was a solution nearby. Poughkeepsie shared Vassar's view of itself as the best women's college in the country. Vassar girls came from good families; their intellectual achievements did not seem to lessen their chances in marriage. Yalies and Harvardians squired these young women around town and sampled cakes with them in the local tea shops. Moreover, in 1926, Vassar's trustees approved a new course of study called Euthenics, which aimed "to raise motherhood to a profession worthy of [woman's] finest talents" by offering classes called Husband and Wife, Motherhood, and the Family as an Economic Unit. While many faculty members argued that Euthenics travestied Vassar's commitment to women's minds, the program reassured parents who looked less than favorably on their daughters' desires for independence.

Vassar was responding to a national change in attitudes. A 1923 survey of its students had shown that in contrast to prewar years, when most looked forward to professions, 90 percent now called marriage the biggest of all careers. Women were marrying more frequently and much younger than in the first part of the century. Popular magazines praised domesticity; newspapers quoted the new experts like psychologist John B. Watson, for whom "sex adjustment" represented a female's best chance for fulfillment. Only a small number of Vassar students hoped to combine work with public service, a vision that Mary McCarthy, a student there in the 1920s, called the Vassar girl's wish "to play a part in the theatre of world events."

While Elizabeth had been studying stagecraft in Paris, Vassar had also begun a program called Dramatic Production, or "D.P." Henry MacCracken, the president, had opposed the Euthenics program, which he saw as a step back from the kind of progressive education he favored. Having lost the war over Euthenics, he planned to inaugurate an opportunity of a new kind, based in the theater. In 1925 MacCracken hired Hallie Flanagan, one of the first women graduates of George Pierce Baker's highly respected Workshop 47 at Harvard, to direct a similar drama program at Vassar. Students would write, stage, and direct their own plays as well as selected classic and contemporary ones; interested townspeople could take part. Flanagan's work at Vassar's Experimental Theatre would contribute to her being chosen by President Roosevelt to head the Works Progress Administration's Federal Theatre Project in the 1930s. In 1925, she was already much admired by theater buffs like MacCracken, who expected her to play a major role in Vassar's modernization.

If nothing else Vassar offered a daily reason to leave home. Because at this point, Elizabeth saw her future in the theater, she summoned the energy to enroll in D.P. as a special student in March—a move that may have exacerbated Florence's unacknowledged rivalry with her daughter since she too was studying theater, in Vassar's program for townspeople. While being the child of a prominent Poughkeepsian may have smoothed Elizabeth's way, it is likely that Flanagan took her on Medgyès's recommendation. Her new student was knowledgeable about trends in European scenography and could provide an introduction to the Maestro, whom Flanagan hoped to meet the following year.

Elizabeth's new teacher, who saw the theater as a progressive social force, urged students to take a professional attitude. Perhaps because she compared her to Medgyès, Elizabeth did not warm to her new mentor, a diminutive redhead who behaved like a powerhouse. Flanagan was, she noted in the diary she began after starting classes, "more interested in Medgyès and what I might tell class of his work—and work with others, than in my studying in her drama production class." Flattered by the attention just the same, Elizabeth accepted her invitation to lecture to the class on the contemporary European theater.

Flanagan also put her in charge of lighting for the workshop's production of *King's Ward*, a romance set in medieval Portugal. Elizabeth researched the settings in Vassar's Gothic library before organizing her crew, including two electricians and six Vassar seniors. The only onstage scenery was a Moorish door; the mood had to be evoked by the lights. Her design, a series of images projected onto a curtain, required long hours in the theater to adjust the lights. "Swearing mentally and spiritually at the false connection on the lighting circuit," Elizabeth wrote, she clambered into the light loft while juggling electric wires "without the slightest knowledge of the system," but with faith in the hereditary Miller ingenuity. The audience applauded the lighting after each performance. Elizabeth wrote that she had acquitted herself "with honour and glory, even though Flanagan gave most of the credit to Medgyès." (She added dryly, "Thank god for any natural cleverness!")

The success of *King's Ward* brought her to the attention of the Vassar Community Theatre leaders Frank and Helen Stout, who greeted her as a peer. They persuaded her to do the lighting for their next play, *Overtones,* and gave her a small part in the production, to be presented at the Women's City and Country Club on March 26. She was suddenly too busy to miss Paris. After the performance she went to sleep in her makeup and awoke at noon the next day, physically and emotionally exhausted.

Campus life did not appeal to her, nor did Vassar students—with the exception of the girls from D.P. with whom she went to New York to see plays. During the week they flocked to her parents' house in Kingwood Park to smoke in her bedroom on the sly, indulge in "lewd conversation," and hear about life in the Latin Quarter. But the glamour surrounding the college in the eyes of new students was not apparent to one who had grown up nearby. A night in a Vassar dormitory after working on a play was a "somber thing," Elizabeth wrote, nor did she like "breakfasting in a noisy gloomy clammy cold dining hall with a hundred other cross sleepy girls." Social pretensions were rife. The next production was "arty in the perfection of manner so pleasing to college dramatic groups." However, of another Vassar proclivity, erotic friendships, Elizabeth noted that a certain M. E. Clifford was "enough to make a lesbian of one." She wondered whether she might herself "go queer."

After her return from Paris, Elizabeth underwent treatment for recurrent gonorrhea—daily douches supervised by her mother and weekly trips to the doctor for inoculations to strengthen her resistance. His "inoculation torture" often produced cramps, fever, and nausea, which reinforced her sense that she was damaged goods; the enforced intimacy of douches in Florence's bathroom led to quarrels and, occasionally, "an almost closeness to mother." However much Elizabeth fancied the idea of herself as sexually free, she had to accept the need, for the moment, of "a virgin life." This condition had the advantage of allowing her to flirt with impunity. Her diary entries for March 1926 note "passionate love proposals" from boys her age, "flirtation and refusal with two Frenchmen," dinner with a seductive friend astounded by her chastity, and telephone sex with a theatergoer named Harold ("Hope he acquired erection," she wrote; "I was sufficiently naked, also soapy and wet").

Harold also accompanied Elizabeth to art galleries in New York and Greenwich Village hangouts like Romany Marie's, where they engaged in "analytical conversation." Despite these efforts, her opinion of his intellect was not high. She gave him some light reading, *Gentlemen Prefer Blondes* and a recent success about a well-mannered adventuress, *The Diary of a Young Lady of Fashion.* Wondering why she was still corresponding with the Maestro, she considered the effect of her beauty on him while imagining his response to a change in her breasts: "Medgyès will be sorely grieved—tho why now should it interest him? thus does my new found virginity affect me!"

Daydreams about Paris and her future there returned to plague her. Since there was no point in confiding in her Vassar friends or in Harold, she scrawled the occasional poem in her notebook. In one of these, distinguished chiefly by its self-deprecation, she dismissed her private "thots" (thoughts) as "callow." The poem, which is addressed to an unnamed but judgmental reader ("you that talk of places far across the sea"), concludes that such a person wouldn't even want "to know / About those most precious thots / Hidden deep below." Despite this inner critic, the last lines express one heartfelt thought: "Would that I might trade my all, for Paris fog and rain!"

Seven months in Paris had made Vassar seem tame and Poughkeepsie unbearable. Elizabeth looked to New York for something more inspiring; as usual, Theodore underwrote the process of exploration. During the winter and spring of 1926 she attended fifteen productions—staged by the Theater Guild, the Moscow Art Theater, the Actors' Theater, the Provincetown Players, and the Metropolitan Opera. She scrutinized the plays she saw for more generous views of life, but also as correlatives of her inner turmoil.

When Elizabeth took the train to New York on days she didn't have classes, there was a price to pay: Florence often accompanied her. Her mother liked to discuss plays, even though they rarely agreed on the merits of contemporary drama's emphasis on psychosocial issues. Florence preferred the classics; Elizabeth worshipped Eugene O'Neill. *Desire Under the Elms,* she thought, dramatized the "inhibitions, repressions, & prohibitions" of the kind she struggled with in private. Plays about the sexual tension of American life made her feel "the squirmings of uncivilized ideas which we are supposed to have outgrown." Although the psychological drama then popular in New York was not poetic in the Medgyès style, such plays, she wrote, left her "nervous, tense, and hard from the unexpected stirring of all my primitive emotions."

Strong emotions dominated the stage that season. One of the first plays Elizabeth saw after her return from Paris was the Provincetown Players' revival of O'Neill's *Emperor Jones.* With a group of D.P. students she met the Provincetown staff—James Light, Eleanor Fitzgerald, and the designer, Cleon Throckmorton. The production's luminescent onstage dome mesmerized the audience and surely brought back memories of Medgyès. The sectioned plaster set, polished until its interior curves reflected light in all directions, created an illusion of deep space in which the actors loomed, especially Charles Gilpin, who as the runaway black prisoner became a larger-than-life silhouette against the glowing sky. But watching demons and nightmares pursue Gilpin through the jungle made Elizabeth feel so tense that she took an early train home and went to bed.

Since discussions with Florence ended in quarrels, she turned instead to the set of monthly diaries she had brought home from Paris—as if primitive emotions could be more readily disclosed to an imaginary confidante. After overindulging at a party with the D.P. group, she confessed (while keeping much hidden): "Bubbles! Bubbles!—they take too many things away at once.—unknowingly—and cigarettes,—cocktails! dope—there'll be a smash up soon." "Bubbles" (champagne), along with cigarettes and "dope" (marijuana), were temporary means of blunting her inner turmoil as she ran back and forth between Poughkeepsie and New York.

Plays dealing with social outcasts deepened Elizabeth's sense of imminent "smash up." The Theater Guild's controversial production of Franz Werfel's *Goat Song* treated the play as an allegory. In this tale of revolt against the old order, an aristocratic couple keep their half-beast, half-human offspring locked up until a group of peasants release the monster. At Romany Marie's, where the D.P. gang repaired after the performance, people said that *Goat Song* staged the conflict between the Apollonian and Dionysian forces. When Elizabeth tried to explain the play's enactment of primitive urges to Florence, who must have felt its resonance, their talks ended in the usual argument.

Ibsen's view of modern life was equally disturbing. The Actors' Theater 1926 production of *Hedda Gabler* presented the heroine as an alarming example of modern womanhood. Hedda's attempts to control those around her through force of will made her a "fiend," a reviewer wrote, even though she "never quite succeeds in guiding the destiny of a man." If *Hedda Gabler* was a warning to headstrong women, Ibsen's *Ghosts,* also at the Actors' Theater, raised the issues of social hypocrisy about venereal disease. *Ghosts,* staged as "a mystery play of sex," urged creative freedom but ended by visiting the sins of the fathers on their sons. It would have been a painful reminder of Elizabeth's condition. Nearly every play that season dealt with sex, although few as darkly as Ibsen.

Despite their differences, Hallie Flanagan recognized her special student's promise. She encouraged Elizabeth to continue in stage design and had her invited to events with Vassar dignitaries—President MacCracken and his guest George Baker, then the head of the Yale Drama School and, she learned, the teacher of her beloved Eugene O'Neill. But while Baker's dinner speech was amusing, Elizabeth felt "uncompromisingly bored" by academic chitchat. She longed to leave "P'ok" to work in an experimental theater of the kind she had discovered in Paris.

That spring, Elizabeth spent as much time as she could with the Provincetown Players, who welcomed her as a neophyte designer. Although the Players no longer ran their theater as a cooperative, the group still refused what they called the crass commercialism of Broadway. The Playhouse, a few steps south of Washington Square at 133 MacDougal Street, retained the sloping floor from its earlier days as a stable. The walls had just been painted a tawny orange brown, and the low ceiling, indigo; cushions were strewn on the wooden benches in a concession to comfort. While the Players still staged experimental work—commedia dell'arte, plays from the Moscow Art Theater, "negro drama"—they tried hard to meet expenses with revivals.

After performances, Elizabeth went upstairs to Christine Ell's restaurant over the Provincetown Playhouse to discuss staging with the set designer, Cleon Throckmorton. Although his name suggests a stage villain, "Throck" was by training a Carnegie Institute engineer. His sets for *The Emperor Jones* had been so successful that he had given up engineering in favor of the theater. (In the 1930s, he would serve under Flanagan as technical director of the Federal Theatre Project.) Throck was artistic yet practical—like her father, or Medgyès.

Like many young women of her time, Elizabeth wanted the social and sexual autonomy reserved for men. Though frowned on in Poughkeepsie, this kind of "free" thinking was rife in Greenwich Village, where psychoanalysis, free love, and self-expression were taken for granted. She spent hours in the cafés frequented by Village celebrities like Jane Heap, Edgar Varèse, and Bobby Edwards, peered into Patchin Place to see where E. E. Cummings lived, and one day at Romany Marie's, teased Edwards into singing all the verses of his off-color "Village Epic." Strumming his ukulele, he crooned, "Way down south in Greenwich Village / There they wear no fancy frillage, / For the ladies of the square / All wear smocks and bob their hair," then intoned, as if specially for her, "Way down south in Greenwich Village / In the Freud and Jung and Brill age / People come with paralysis / For the balm of psychoanalysis." The contrast between New York and Poughkeepsie was obvious.

Elizabeth found some comfort in the privacy of her 1926 notebook, but even there, she still felt the presence of an inner critic. Having partially expressed the "awkward, swollen feeling" from childhood, she wrote, "You who read this may well marvel at lack of emotion," then confessed that she had recopied her first draft because the original "was too laden with excitement to be legible." This process, the recopying or reframing of material "too laden with excitement," would take a different form in photography, where her choices of subject and composition became the means to convey the tensions she felt between depth and surface, inside and outside.

Analyzing the pages of her notebook as an amateur graphologist, she decided that her different styles of writing revealed her contradictions. "Why does my handwriting vary with my mood," she wondered. Did it imply that she was overly imaginative, mentally sloppy, or the sort of person "who never becomes exactly settled in one run of living and thinking?" (Her normally left-leaning hand inclined to the right in these bouts of self-criticism.) The hand revealed the inner self, she thought: "Is it not ironic that I, who expend so much attention on hands and handwriting, should be endowed with this irregular script."

The act of keeping a notebook also concerned her. She used its pages to spare others her "supreme egoism," she wrote, but also to acquire self-confidence—"since there is no opportunity in my daily contacts." Because she found fault with most of her acquaintances, she wondered about her capacity for love. She was romantic, "but sentimental, never." Yet she looked back on her emotional life with regret: "always there has been some ugly animal attachment." (This conviction would have been reinforced by the recurrence of gonorrhea and the treatments required to keep the symptoms under control.) Agreeing with Freud that "all sentimental relations have sex at the bottom," she wished it were otherwise. "I long to be loved, just once, somewhat purely and chastely," she went on, but feared that it was "too late . . . to be anything but an animal with unhealthy desires."

Whatever her shortcomings, Elizabeth believed that she was "different." Yet despite contemporary talk at Vassar and in the press of brilliance in women, she feared that genius was masculine, that "there is none in the feminine sex." Her own gifts lay in some as yet unspecified "artistic-emotional field." "My fingers feel empty with the longing to create," she continued in the purple prose of adolescent diarists. "Void—yet full of yearning," she wondered whether she would ever "attain harmony with the infinite," or instead keep finding that she must "throw my puny self against the inevitable power of things that are."

Despite Elizabeth's success with the Experimental Theatre she had no wish to be remade in the Vassar image. Her time at the college had not inspired her to pursue learning for its own sake—although in later life, Lee often said that she regretted her lack of formal education. Despite her adventures in Paris and New York, she remained a willful, talented, and extremely beautiful young woman with an uncertain future.

In April 1926, Elizabeth persuaded Theodore to pay for training of a practical kind: dance lessons in New York. The decision paid off. The following month she was hired to dance in the chorus of George White's Scandals. With her father's help, she rented a hotel room for late-night rehearsals.

White's revue was known to be faster and livelier than Ziegfeld's Follies, since the Scandals girls performed the latest steps in costumes that stopped just short of nudity. A few years before, the press had made much of their glittering attire, stitched in Paris from designs by Erté: "There were large quantities of gorgeous costumes," a critic wrote, "much of them on the girls of the chorus from the neck up and the shoes down." That year, seventeen-year-old Louise Brooks had been the youngest chorus member and the only trained dancer. At nineteen, Elizabeth fit in, though, like Brooks, she was probably bored by the other chorus girls "mooching around from dressing room to dressing room, talking about men and sex."

Dancing in the chorus of a revue was not the sort of creative activity that put one in touch with the infinite, yet it was a start. Martha Graham had performed in the Greenwich Village Follies before founding her own company; Louise Brooks's nightly appearances in the Scandals had led to film roles. (Showgirls were courted by bachelors who, "finding debutantes a threat, turned to pretty girls in the theater," Brooks recalled.) For those who knew how to capitalize on their natural resources, invitations to Park Avenue parties might lead to lavish wardrobes, screen tests, and financial rewards—or, for the less enterprising, a job modeling something more substantial than a Scandals costume.

To her parents' relief Elizabeth did not follow this course of action. The Millers visited several times a week, often staying the night in her hotel. They worried about her health as well as the somewhat louche atmosphere of the Scandals. In June, when she became ill and spent several days in bed, Theodore enlisted two of her friends to join him in persuading Elizabeth to come home.

After a few weeks' rest she felt well enough to see friends. Harold was good company despite his lack of intellectual powers; there was still a sexual charge between them. They went rowing in Upton Lake on a hot July day. Wanting to show off, perhaps, Harold dove off the side of the boat, then disappeared. Elizabeth went into shock. She waited with her family while the authorities dragged the lake until his body was recovered; efforts to revive him were to no avail. Theodore entered the date in his diary, but said nothing about the effect of this tragedy on Elizabeth. The shock would have reactivated buried feelings of guilt about being sexual, especially when Harold's mother implied that her son's death was Elizabeth's fault.

Elizabeth coped with her emotional distress by looking for another job in New York. Taking the first one she found, she moved back to the city in August to start work as a lingerie model at Stewart & Company on Fifth Avenue—an occupation that was only slightly less risqué than dancing the shimmy in sequins. Florence helped her settle into a rented room on East Fifty-fourth Street. Her obliging parents, resigned to her determination to leave home, accepted the break but did not quite believe in it.

Art Students League class, New York, 1926 (Lee is third from the left in the front row)

Chapter 4

Being in Vogue

(1926–29)

Although Elizabeth was now a New Yorker, her parents oversaw the practical side of her life. Florence visited frequently. Theodore paid the rent and examined her expenses on "bill days," when the Millers often stayed in town to take Elizabeth to the theater. Together they saw the Broadway version of *Gentlemen Prefer Blondes*—whose Lorelei left the stage to wed a tycoon, a case of an actress who kept on playing her role after the show had closed. But unlike her heroine, Elizabeth showed no interest in marriage. Theodore indulged her wish for independence while keeping her on a long leash.

At the end of the summer, reverting to the strategy that had served her in Paris, she told him that she hoped to complete her training in stage design. Since John was to spend the year in New York earning his engineering degree at Pratt Institute, the Millers found them an apartment in a brownstone on West Forty-eighth Street, near Fifth Avenue. From then on, brother and sister led separate lives, meeting at night or on weekend trips to Poughkeepsie. John spent his days at Pratt and after classes with a group of aviators who met in a speakeasy to relate their exploits in the Great War. Elizabeth continued to model while looking for art courses with practical applications.

✿

In 1926, the Art Students League of New York was considered the most progressive school of its kind in the United States. While most American painting academies were nearly as formal as their model, the Académie des Beaux-Arts in Paris, the League attracted young painters interested in modern art. The faculty's preference for representational treatments of American scenes did not blind them to the merits of Cézanne, Matisse, and Picasso: teachers there included Maurice Sterne, Max Weber, and the director, John Sloan, whose canvases throbbed with the rhythms of his favorite subject, Manhattan. Sloan emphasized the basics—line, color, composition, perspective—while warning students against too much devotion to technique. Rather than imitate reality they should paint the idea of it.

Elizabeth began classes in October. Each morning she walked uptown and west along Fifty-seventh Street to the League's gray stone Renaissance building, arriving just in time for Life Drawing and Painting for Women. She returned in the afternoon for Antique Drawing, followed by George Bridgman's Constructive Figure Drawing class, where students drew the live model and learned nearly as much anatomy as if they had been at medical school. In successive classes Bridgman lectured on the head, neck, shoulders, hands, forearms, hips, thigh, knee, and foot, then examined the whole figure. Since Elizabeth considered the hands the most expressive parts of the body, she continued to study handwriting as if it revealed one's inner nature.

During a weekend visit to Poughkeepsie in October, Theodore asked Elizabeth to pose for him. Having seen her model lingerie at Stewart's, he thought that she would be the perfect subject for a new photographic series. They drove to Oak Ridge, found a secluded spot in the woods, and set up the stereoscope camera. Elizabeth took off her clothes. The idea was that he would portray her as a woodland nymph in a modern version of *September Morn*. Judging by the results, she felt uncomfortable. In some photos, she covers her face with her hands; in others she stands stiffly and shields her genitals. After trying different poses—backbends, a frontal stance that offers her body to the camera—she turned to her father with her arms bent behind her head and looked away.

They drove home to continue indoors. Elizabeth stood before a mirror, placed her hands behind her back, and looked at Theodore as if willing herself to be his partner in this enterprise. Later, with him in the darkroom, she would have experienced the sensation of seeing double: herself as aesthetic subject; her body as object of scrutiny for the man in whose eyes she saw herself mirrored. And if she studied these arresting images through his stereoscopic viewer, the distancing effect would have been multiplied by the startling depth

One of Theodore's many stereoscope art studies of his daughter, annotated by her
"me, Lee Miller," Poughkeepsie, 1928 (Theodore Miller)

of field. Perhaps observing her body with detachment gave her a sense of control over the uses to which it had been put—though it also meant experiencing not her inner states but the camera's objectifications.

To us, Theodore's "art studies" are disturbing. While their collaboration indicates a deep trust between father and daughter, his interest seems obsessive, and her stance oddly compliant. Seeing these images, we cannot help asking whether Lee's career was not marked by the need to protect herself against the camera. "This ravishing young woman," a critic writes, "used her camera as a defence against the potentially crushing force of the narcissism pressed upon her." We wonder why a father would take such pictures, why a mother would not intervene, and what long-term effects such sessions would have on a moody nineteen-year-old whose early sexual experience still haunted her.

While there is no evidence apart from these images of what we would call, at best, an overly intimate relationship, it is apparent that Elizabeth coped with the situation by dissociating. In each of these photographs, she distances herself from the use of her body to which her love for her father bound her—a set of responses that look back to her childhood and forward to what would become her way of dealing with those who sought to capture her image, her body, and her trust. Yet at the same time, in these peculiar sessions Elizabeth worked out a compromise: evaluating the modus operandi of those for whom she posed, starting with Theodore, she took what was to be gained and stored it away for future use.

∞

At the League Elizabeth met a number of lively companions, including the sculptor Isamu Noguchi and a young woman who earned her living as a model, Tanja Ramm. The daughter of Norwegian immigrants, Tanja was a year older than Elizabeth but far less worldly. A slender brunette with a piquant expression, she felt awkward about her modest family background and her lack of education. While Tanja admired Elizabeth's insouciance about having been expelled from nearly every school she attended, she was often shocked by her behavior, especially her casual attitude toward alcohol and sex (although Elizabeth's diary ended abruptly before her move to New York, one can assume that the inoculations were a success).

The two women became close despite their differences. To Tanja, her new friend was more like the artists at the League than someone from Poughkeepsie. Tanja's shyness compensated for Elizabeth's boldness: "I was so pure I gave her a good reputation," she remarked years later. Tanja was not so much prudish as cautious, while Elizabeth, who meant to throw caution to the wind, sometimes felt the need to look respectable. Tanja enjoyed the well-mannered college men who took them out—including several Yalies in love with Elizabeth. "Her admirers were legion," she recalled. "One besotted young man told me that she was a cross between Marlene Dietrich and Greta Garbo."

The League failed to hold Elizabeth's interest. Painting required more discipline than she could muster; from her perusal of art history it seemed to her "that all the paintings had already been painted." Most artists looked to the past for the means to depict the present day: what she wanted was a medium that was fast-paced, mechanical, and modern. Elizabeth gradually understood that she lacked the dedication to become an artist. Life in Manhattan had made her lighthearted and streetwise. She was more interested in the city's promise of "fantastic success and eternal youth" (as Fitzgerald wrote in *The Crack-Up*) than in the pursuit of Art.

Elizabeth would have gone on "circulating around," she told an interviewer later, but for an accident—which itself sounds like fiction or Hollywood fantasy: one day she was "discovered" when she stepped into the path of an oncoming car and was pulled back onto the sidewalk by a well-dressed stranger, into whose arms she collapsed. Her rescuer proved to be Condé Nast, the founder of the publishing empire. Elizabeth happened to be wearing an outfit bought in Paris the year before and in her shock began babbling in French. Nast had a closer look, invited her to his office, and asked her to think about working for *Vogue*.

At the time she did not know that Nast, who dressed like a banker, was said to be obsessed with sex, or that his headquarters was "both an escort service and a feudal village." While he preferred women with quick minds, they also had to have "the intangible quality of chic" that in his view character- ized his magazines. Edna Chase, *Vogue's* understanding editor, was accustomed to finding work for the comely amateurs who turned up at Nast headquarters after meeting her employer. By chance, Elizabeth came along at the precise moment when Chase was pondering a new look for the magazine, one that would portray the modern woman's indepen- dence and élan.

A 1928 portrait of Tanja Ramm, Lee, and Florence Miller in similar outfits hints at Florence's ongoing rivalry with her daughter. (Theodore Miller)

What was chic at *Vogue* in the winter of 1927 included short hair, Art Deco, cloche hats, and Cubism, but above all New York itself—"the crowding of Fifth Avenue with motors flashing in the sun, the tumult of the smart restaurants, the anguished haste of dressmakers and modistes, and the sandwiching of picture exhibitions and special matinees for the illuminati between luncheons at Marguery's and first nights of the luscious and glitter- ing . . . reviews." Elizabeth looked as if she were one of the smart set, someone for whom modistes stitched and matinees were arranged. Her features would suit the March issue, on the new Paris fashions. She would make her first appearance in *Vogue* on its cover.

In the twenties it was not yet the practice for magazines to use photo- graphs as cover art. Condé Nast publications featured the work of well-known illustrators like Georges Lepape, who earned as much as $1,000 per drawing. Before the war, Lepape had become famous in Paris for his work on Paul Poiret's fashion albums. His sylphs, garbed in sinuous silk and swirling lamé, had decorated *Vogue* for the past ten years, but their poses now looked too lan- guid to illustrate Nast's belief that times had changed. About this time, *Vanity Fair* announced emphatically: "Women don't faint at the slightest provocation. Most girls, before they are twenty, become interested in the world in general and in some work in particular!"

Lepape's cover presents Elizabeth as one of these "girls"—but also as the spirit of the city that had become her theater of operations. Against the background of Manhattan's night sky she looks straight ahead, a determined figure in a helmetlike cloche. His depiction of her short bob and purposeful gaze brought out an androgynous quality, one that was often present in his illustrations but until then had not found its subject. Unlike the willowy figures of earlier *Vogue* covers, this twenty-year-old is not only interested in the world but prepared to meet it head-on. The image of Elizabeth as unflappable flapper evoked all that was "moderne," the term in use for streamlined furniture and free-spirited behavior alike.

The March *Vogue* actually appeared a month before Elizabeth's twentieth birthday, like an announcement of her emancipation. The issue featured a "confidential guide" to the new French fashions, in which the American reader learned that the Parisienne's approach was not so different from her own. *Vogue* also promised to simplify the job of shopping in Paris by explaining the rituals of its spring season. "It is far better to be too informal than too formal," it told the perplexed. Lepape's image of Elizabeth implied that Paris chic could be naturalized in New York provided one had the right spirit—a blend of determination and insouciance.

∽

Suddenly Elizabeth was in demand with the best-known photographers in New York, all of them Europeans. Nickolas Muray, a Hungarian whose celebrity portraits also earned as much as a thousand dollars a page, had worked freelance for *Vanity Fair* before becoming *Vogue*'s official color photographer. Muray befriended Elizabeth and later helped her start her own career as a studio photographer. In a fashion shot from one of their first sessions, she wears a fur-lined coat that would have suited a Park Avenue matron. Her hands, resting protectively on her hip, say more than her impassive features—appropriately enough for someone who believed that hands reveal character.

Arnold Genthe, a founding member of Alfred Stieglitz's Photo-Secession movement, had photographed many women artists—Isadora Duncan, Ruth St. Denis, Pavlova, Garbo. Genthe was close to Theodore's age when Elizabeth sat for him. Perhaps for that reason her features softened in his presence. He discerned in her something that others failed to see. His portraits of her show not the forthright flapper but the dreamy, vulnerable girl. Elizabeth liked to visit Genthe in his studio. He gave her roses and told her tales of his youth in Germany, where he had studied archeology, languages, and music. From Genthe she learned the range of interests that one could bring to photography and the difference that a trusting relationship made to the final product.

Of the photographers with whom Elizabeth worked after her *Vogue* debut, Edward Steichen was by far the most celebrated. Before the war, Steichen had been a painter. After giving up art for photography, he won fame first as a pic-torialist and a member of the Photo-Secession, then as an modernist whose tightly cropped images showed the influence of his Paris friends—Matisse, Picasso, and Brancusi. (He had brought their works to the United States, to hang at 291, the gallery he founded with Alfred Stieglitz.) Because Steichen had served as a U.S. Army photographer during the war, *Vogue* staffers referred to him as the Colonel. In 1923 he became chief photographer for Condé Nast, with an annual salary of $35,000, to which he added another $20,000 after tak-ing the job of art director at the J. Walter Thompson advertising firm.

When Elizabeth began posing for Steichen, he was the wealthiest artist in America and a celebrity whose glossy portraits of other celebrities summed up the period's love affair with glamour. As photography replaced illustrations in ad campaigns, the public began to think of photographers as heroic figures. They were a new breed of aesthete whose work was practical, and the Colonel was the most admired of all *because* he earned so much money. At work he could be arrogant. "He managed to give the impression that a photographic session in his Beaux Arts studio was the equivalent of an investiture at Buck-ingham Palace," a *Vanity Fair* editor wrote. Those who sat for him were often awed, but some Condé Nast staffers made fun of "this the-Master-is-creating atmosphere."

Steichen liked to present himself as a man of the people. "Big, rugged and bony in build, dressed in a rough tweed suit and a soft blue shirt," a reporter wrote, "he somehow symbolized the simplicity and democracy that is so much a part of him." He had abandoned painting, he explained, to make art that was "of so much greater use than a canvas in a parlor." Living proof that it was pro-ductive to embrace modernity, he opined, "we are living in an age in which all things have to stand the test of usefulness."

It was a philosophy in keeping with Elizabeth's own—in so far as she had one, an amalgam of her father's belief in facts, her own interest in how things work, and Medgyès's machine-age vision of art. At that time, Steichen's approach to design was being hailed as revolutionary. *Vogue* printed Steichen's shots of his fabric patterns under the banner "The Camera Works Out a New Theory of Design." In one photograph, matches arranged in irregular fan-shaped swirls recall Cubism; in another, a shimmering abstraction proves to be made of metal tacks. These designs were "satisfying and effective," *Vanity Fair* observed. Readers should buy the new fabrics "if only to see that good art, when entrusted to the right man, is often inspired by the simplest and most everyday subjects."

For the most part, Steichen's fashion shots rejected the everyday in favor of glamour. He often photographed in Nast's duplex, a thirty-room penthouse on Park Avenue that looked like a stage set. Its gilt-framed mirrors, French antiques covered in pale green damask, and gleaming parquet floors created an opulent background for Steichen's photos of Elizabeth. In one, she turns to reveal the deep V back of an evening dress: posed in front of a costly Louis XV table, she seems to belong in this setting. In others, taken outside to show off her summer frock and picture hat, we see her as the sort of girl who spends her afternoons at garden parties, but in a summery image that ran in the June *Vogue* in 1928, she looks uncomfortable in a broad-brimmed hat and Art Deco dress, perhaps an effect of the "Master-is-creating" atmosphere.

Despite (or because of) the luxurious surroundings in which Steichen worked, Elizabeth often seemed detached from the fantasies to which she lent herself. She became one of his favorite models nonetheless, perhaps because she paid attention to their work together. Photography sessions resembled the-ater rehearsals, with the Colonel as designer and director. When he worked on advertising campaigns for firms like Jergens and Packard, technicians set up the lights and adjusted the cameras; the cameraman took the picture when Steichen snapped his fingers; darkroom assistants printed from the big glass plates; and the Master chose the final product.

It was Steichen, Lee explained years later, who "put the idea into my head of doing photography." A man of her father's generation, the Colonel carried himself with self-assurance and through his commercial work combined Theodore's own passions, business and art. Lee also observed ironically—but with pride—that "she had practically been born and brought up in a dark room." In this account, Theodore's parenting gives birth to her vocation. The "upbringing" begun in her father's darkroom continued in sessions with the Colonel—the most recent in the series of confident, creative men after whom she modeled herself.

In this respect as well, she was a girl of the twenties, who—the *New York Times* argued—liked to "take a man's view as her mother never could." A mod-ern woman preferred men to her own sex, essayist Dorothy Bromley argued in 1927, because "their methods are more direct, . . . their view larger, and she finds that she can deal with them on a basis of frank comradeship." Bromley describes the new feminists as Fitzgerald heroines seeking to reconcile work, self-expression, and marriage. Taking several more steps along this radical path, Elizabeth also adopted a man's view in her dreams of creative and sexual freedom, which at this point meant liberation from the creeds of Poughkeep-sie in particular and puritanism in general. "I wish I had been born a man," wrote a contributor to a feminist symposium published that year in *The Nation.* "I *was* my father," another asserted. Elizabeth would have agreed.

∞

Following her appearance on the cover of *Vogue,* she moved effortlessly into café society—the self-regarding group of artists, patrons, and publishers "which sets the pace in fashion, in genteel living and entertaining," according to the *New York Times*. At Condé Nast's, Elizabeth met the celebrities profiled in his magazines—all those said to be clever, gay, and amusing. What counted in this world was a light touch and some familiarity with cultural fashions, from "modernist" art to the writings of Gertrude Stein and the new dance craze, the Black Bottom.

Since it also helped to be beautiful, Elizabeth and Tanja were always welcome. "We went to many parties at Condé Nast's," Tanja recalled. "He loved to mix the social, business, and theater communities, adding a few young things like Lee and me." At his soirées one saw George Gershwin, Bea Lillie, the Vanderbilts, Fred Astaire, Cecil Beaton, and Steichen. Elizabeth again met Frank Crowninshield, the dapper, knowledgeable editor of *Vanity Fair,* whose magazine conferred celebrity status on Nast's guests—for the most part, people who knew how to present themselves in the influential new media that coincided with the rise of photography.

Nast had been divorced from his wife since the early twenties. A wealthy man, he had his pick of debutantes and professional beauties. The gossip columnists chronicled his appearances in smart restaurants with a different companion each night. Young women whispered that he could be generous to protégées. Elizabeth, already accustomed to overtures from nearly every man she met, dismissed him affectionately as "a harmless old goat"; laughing over her New York adventures one weekend at home, she warned Minnow that in tête-à-têtes, "you had to keep the desk between yourself and Mr. Nast."

Nast often looked uncomfortable at his own parties. The person whose role it was to create the scintillating atmosphere that surrounded him was Crowninshield, who relished the offbeat and the unexpected. Known as "the man-who-knows-more-celebrities-than-anyone-else-in-New-York," he and his reserved employer were opposites. *Manners for the Metropolis,* Crowny's tongue-in-cheek etiquette book, purported to help the newly rich avoid panic "at the mere sight of a gold finger bowl, an alabaster bath, a pronged oyster fork, or the business end of an asparagus."

Crowny's feeling for modern art set the tone for *Vanity Fair.* In its pages he introduced Marie Laurencin, Jacob Epstein, Matisse, Maillol, and Picasso to America. He published new writers like Dorothy Parker, Edna St. Vincent Millay, E. E. Cummings, and Edmund Wilson, and championed some who were already known, including Fitzgerald and Anita Loos—a favorite of his, whose latest book, play, or film *Vanity Fair* always plugged. Crowny also appreciated witty women. He remained friendly with Dottie Parker even after firing her as the magazine's drama critic; they lunched together at the Algonquin Hotel, known to the circle of wits who made it their headquarters as "the Gonk."

Elizabeth met Dottie at the Algonquin group's unofficial annex, Neysa

McMein's painting studio in a dingy brick building on West Fifty-seventh Street. After classes, the more adventurous League students gathered there to drink bootleg gin and mingle with Neysa's bohemian friends, many of them people one read about in the gossip columns. They rehearsed Dottie's latest quips and toasted her *Vogue* captions (e.g., "brevity is the soul of lingerie"). But judging by her recent verse, Parker's reputation as the wittiest woman in New York had not brought happiness. Her subjects—the cynicism of the flapper; the fate of unmarried, divorced, and "career" women; rejection in love—did not inspire younger women to follow in her footsteps.

Elizabeth preferred Neysa McMein, an illustrator whose portraits often appeared in Nast's magazines. Her talent for amusing herself in unusual ways, such as riding in a parade on an elephant, made good copy. One day Neysa, a statuesque blonde, would be judging bathing beauties at Coney Island; the next she might be "opening a new movie house in Toronto or swimming impromptu in the Marne," wrote Alexander Woollcott, another regular at the Gonk. A confident woman with a talent for self-promotion, Neysa had done war posters and fashion drawings, but now specialized in pastels of famous women—Parker, Edna Millay, Helen Hayes. Née Margery, she had changed her name "because some seeress had assured her in sibylline accents that it would bring her luck." Her studio was crowded and noisy, but the guests liked the confusion. Charlie Chaplin might be rehearsing a bit of slapstick while Irving Berlin played the piano; Neysa, her short hair streaked with pastel dust, might suddenly decide to improvise with Chaplin or join Berlin at the keyboard. Unexpected things happened to her, Woollcott thought, because she had "an insatiable, childlike appetite for life."

Neysa, who in some ways resembled Elizabeth, adopted the young woman as her protégée. Elizabeth must change her name as she herself had done, Neysa explained, to ensure the continuation of her good luck. They went over her childhood nicknames before choosing the slightly androgynous Lee—an abbreviated, updated version of Li Li. Her career dated from the day she changed her name, she told Minnow—who recalled years later that "we all started using *Lee,* but it was difficult. We had to think of her as this new person." Once she began working as a photographer, the name proved to be useful. Prospective clients were unsure whether she was male or female—an advantage, she thought, in the early days of commercial photography.

Neysa also explained the lay of the land to Elizabeth during their visits to Long Island's north shore, known as the Gold Coast. So many members of the smart set had weekend houses there that the *New Yorker* illustrator John Held Jr. drew a map showing the residences of local luminaries. Neysa's Port Washington cottage was down the street from Chaplin's grander dwelling and across Manhasset Bay from Fitzgerald's. If Held's tongue-in-cheek Who's Who charted the fluid social worlds on which Fitzgerald had modeled *The*

Great Gatsby, Nast lived in the style of the novel's title character. Soon Elizabeth (the transition to her new name not yet complete) was spending more
weekends at Neysa's or at Sandy Key, Nast's mansion in Stony Point, than in
Poughkeepsie.

By 1927, when Nast bought Sandy Key, his magazines' circulation had
risen, along with the worth of the parent company, and *Vogue*'s European editions had extended his fame. That year, Nast crowned his success by purchasing a country home whose grounds extended from his colonnaded porch to
Long Island Sound. His famous guests sipped cocktails, played tennis, wandered in the gardens, and swam in the huge oval pool while Nast courted
Leslie Foster, the *Vogue* staffer a few months younger than Elizabeth whom he
would later marry.

After her appearances in *Vogue,* Elizabeth had no shortage of beaux. A
rotating crew of suitors took her dancing, sailing, to polo matches, and up in
their two-seater planes—a pastime that earned the approval of her brother.
John, with whom she still shared the apartment, was impressed when she
dated Grover Loening, an aeronautical engineer twenty years her senior. The
U.S. Army had adopted Loening's treatise on military airplanes during the war;
the engineer had recently patented his designs for seaplanes, including the
five-seat Flying Yacht sent on the army's recent Pan-American goodwill flight.
One wonders how he coped with Elizabeth's need for independence, and
whether she saw the similarities between Loening and her father.

That summer she also met Charlie Chaplin. His reputation as a lover of
young women preceded him, as did reports of his superior physical endow-
ment. Two years earlier, when *The Gold Rush* premiered on Broadway, Chaplin had begun an affair with Louise Brooks, who at eighteen was half his age.
Elizabeth's friendship with Chaplin came at a shaky time in his life. When his
"child bride," Lita Grey, sued for divorce in California, threatening to name
prominent actresses with whom he had had affairs, he fled to New York.
Despite the scandal, the public loved him, socialites sought him out, friends
like Neysa helped revive his spirits. In August, after he agreed to pay Lita a
million dollars, the press called him a hero and artists rallied to his defense.
Chaplin took comfort in the news that in Paris, André Breton published a
protest on his behalf entitled "Hands Off Love," signed by artists and intellectuals like Louis Aragon, René Clair, and Man Ray.

Not all of Elizabeth's suitors were older than she. Alfred De Liagre Jr., one
of the Yale men who took Elizabeth and Tanja on double dates, was the son of
a European business executive. Dellie was warm, witty, and imaginative;
within a few years he would become a well-known Broadway director. Although
Elizabeth cared for him, their love affair was punctuated by arguments about
other suitors. They worked out an agreement by which they remained intimate
while she also went out with his friend, a Canadian aviator named Argylle—

another male companion whose independence mirrored her self-image as a free spirit.

$$\infty$$

In 1927 millions looked to aviators as a new breed of hero—modern-day explorers whose flights enacted the aspirations of the earthbound. In May, as Charles Lindbergh prepared for the first nonstop transatlantic flight, the news galvanized the world. Several aviators had already tried to make the trip, in vain. Lindbergh, the twenty-five-year-old dubbed "the flying fool," hoped to advance the cause of aviation by attempting this difficult flight. On May 20, John and Elizabeth joined the crowd at Roosevelt Field in the early morning. They watched the small silver plane race down the runway in the dark, lift into the mist, and clear the obstacles—a tractor and telegraph wires—at the end of the field.

When the news of his landing at Le Bourget reached the United States, the press renamed him "Lucky Lindy." A hundred thousand Frenchmen welcomed the aviator; the press hailed him as a new type of American. On his return to the United States, President Coolidge awarded him the Distinguished Flying Cross, and on June 13, all New York lined up for his reception. Waves of cheering greeted the cavalcade's slow progress up Broadway beneath a snowstorm of confetti. Lindbergh was the most admired person in the world in an era of intense hero worship.

At the same time, the *Little Review*'s Machine-Age Exposition became the sensation of the New York art world. Students at the League flocked to Steinway Hall, one block west of their school, to see the exhibit celebrating "the great new race of men in America: the Engineer." It was vital for modern civilization that this new hero "make a union with the artist," declared Jane Heap, the organizer. She had planned the show, she continued, because machinery had already inspired some artists to turn "the realities of our age into a dynamic beauty."

Steinway Hall in no way resembled an art gallery. Bare posts and girders framed the large open space. Actual machines (a tractor, a machine gun, an airplane engine) and photographs of machines were displayed next to images of grain silos and skyscrapers or juxtaposed with works by artists like Man Ray, Marcel Duchamp, Charles Demuth, and Charles Sheeler. The catalogue used a Fernand Léger design on the cover; the *Little Review* ran his tribute to machines as "the most beautiful spectacles in the world." Heap's landmark exhibition illustrated her belief that machines were the icons of modern life.

From this perspective, photography was clearly *the* modern art. "The moving picture and the snapshot mark the tempo of our time," wrote a *New York Times* critic. A publicity campaign that year claimed that photography could be trusted to deliver the truth, or a version thereof. "Photographs mingle romance and reality; present your wares exactly as they are; yet with a captivating charm that leads to bigger, quicker sales," the Professional Photographers of America told prospective advertisers. While an illustration might be dismissed as "the fanciful dream of an artist," the camera was objective—telling its story "as an unprejudiced eye witness." It was an exhilarating time to think about becoming a photographer, as Elizabeth did while continuing to study art, model for *Vogue,* and conduct her life as actively as if she were a man.

Looking back on her New York years decades later, Lee told an interviewer, "I looked like an angel, but I was a fiend inside." At the time, it distressed her that her life was full of contradictions. A proud young woman whose radiance made people stare when she entered the room, she felt that her inner nature belied what they saw. By 1928, she had all but left Poughkeepsie—having taken a new name, learned the rudiments of art, and assumed the right to sexual freedom. Yet as Lee's remark about the gap between her angelic and fiendish selves implies, she remained in the grip of childhood trauma. Deeply held fears about inside and outside as contradictory realms of experience continued to haunt her. Only in later life did she become aware that she had internalized aspects of the puritanism she claimed to despise.

While Lee did not tell the interviewer about Theodore's passion in those days, she may also have been thinking of the way she was pictured in the many stereoscopic photographs he took of her on weekend visits. It is difficult to contemplate these "art" nudes with equanimity. Just before her twentieth birthday, Theodore photographed Elizabeth gazing at her reflection in a mirror, a pose in which she is both subject and object. She stares at her naked body and at the same time at her father, who is taking the shot. While her expression is vacant, as if her mind were elsewhere, she also participates—gaining some measure of control by helping to stage these scenes with her father. Other shots show her facing the camera with her hands behind her back—a provocative pose but one that diminishes her agency. In still others, she daydreams naked on the living room couch, a lace antimacassar placed anachronistically behind her boyish head.

However *we* respond to such images, whatever we make of Theodore's love for his daughter, and hers for him, we cannot know what happened. Just the same, if their intimacy was unconsummated (as seems likely), a transgression of the boundary that should protect a child from incestuous wishes did take place. A father's expression of his desire—of which he may be unaware—harms a child in a different way, perhaps as much as if the act were committed. The evidence of this harm, which multiplied the effects of Elizabeth's rape at the age of seven, can be seen in Theodore's photographs. Whether or not he was conscious of his motivation, they exploit his knowledge of the rape by putting her on display. Yet it is also true that, over time, Elizabeth became complicit in their sessions and may have taken pride in her dual role as object and collaborator.

Oddly—to us—Theodore continued to do these private studies while also clipping and pasting into his diaries every account of her appearances in *Vogue,* as if there were no contradiction between the two kinds of poses. "June Vogue Contains Two Artistic Photos of Elizabeth Miller," the *Poughkeepsie Star* announced on the society page a month after her birthday—adding, in case anyone didn't know, that she was the daughter of Mr. and Mrs. Theodore H. Miller. The wayward girl who had been expelled from nearly every school she attended had become a celebrity.

By the end of the decade, advertising campaigns with endorsements predominated in women's magazines. Steichen's photographs for Jergens lotion had evolved from images of homemakers peeling potatoes to scenes of upper-class women pouring tea, the implication being that Jergens raised one's social status while softening one's hands. Steichen also used portraits of titled beauties to promote Pond's cold cream as the secret every woman could afford. In the first of this series, the duchesse de Richelieu, who had lived in Baltimore before marrying into one of the oldest aristocratic lines in France, was photographed like a film star combining Old World status with a New World fortune.

It was one thing to associate one's prestige with Pond's and another to appear in the "whisper" campaigns depicting the consequences of failing to use hygienic products. Admen for the mouthwash Listerine produced the slogan "Even your best friend won't tell you"; a copywriter for Absorbine Jr., a liniment company, coined the phrase "athlete's foot"; negative campaigns about the new social sin, body odor, promoted Odorono. Typically, such ads showed one woman whispering to another about the ignorance of a third—the sort who was often a bridesmaid but never a bride because she failed to mask her natural functions.

Madison Avenue presented the female body as a terrain for the projection of fantasized needs. On the one hand, this attention made consumers more health-conscious; on the other, it projected a sanitized image of bodies anxious not to offend. The ad campaign for another new product, Kotex, became the test case for what a critic calls this "WASP vision of a tasteless, colorless, odorless, sweatless world." As an alternative to cloth devices, nurses in French hospitals during the war had used "cellucotton" bandages made of wood fiber. Their innovation, ads claimed, now available commercially, eased the strain caused in "better" households by the postwar shortage of servants. By 1928, Kotex ads also stressed the embarrassment factor. At tea, two women discuss "this grave social offense," while a third seems unaware that Kotex gives "peace of mind under trying conditions."

When Elizabeth's image unexpectedly graced the advertising campaign for the "new, improved" Kotex, she was outraged. The ad, which ran in different versions in *McCall's* and other women's magazines, used a Steichen portrait taken at Nast's penthouse. Her gleaming pearls and columnar white gown seemed to support the claim that "correct appearance and hygienic comfort" could now be combined, thanks to Kotex; readers could assume that she was one of the unnamed consumers quoted saying that the pad could be worn "under the sheerest, most clinging frocks." De Liagre's protest to Condé Nast and Elizabeth's letters to the agency made no difference. She had signed the release form. By 1929, when the ad appeared for the last time, she reversed her position and took pride in having shocked family and beaux alike.

Poughkeepsians, who had long been scandalized by Elizabeth, would have been even more shocked to learn that the notorious spokeswoman for Kotex was also a participant in Theodore's new pastime: group nude shots of his daughter and her friends. Tanja and Minnow were both persuaded to sit for him, with Elizabeth or with other young women, in pairs and trios. "Theodore was always begging us to pose for him in different stages of undress," Tanja

Kotex ad, Delineator, *March 1929*

"I warn women
when they have gowns fitted

says a famous
MODISTE

Sanitary protection can make for embarrassment if the lines of a gown reveal awkward bulkiness beneath . . This new way solves a difficult question

MANY a smart costume has failed in its effect; many a perfect evening has been ruined because of certain outstanding flaws in grooming. Women who have been aware of awkward bulkiness in sanitary protection now welcome the Improved Kotex, which is so rounded and tapered at the ends that it fits with an entirely new security. Now there is no break in the lines of a costume, no need for unhappy self-consciousness.

Kotex deodorizes completely*

And another hindrance to fastidious grooming is finally removed; Kotex deodorizes thoroughly and safely—by a patented process*. Greater softness of texture; marvelous absorbency; instant disposability; the fact that you can adjust the layers of the filler—these things are of great importance for comfort and good health. Cellucotton absorbent wadding, which fills Kotex, actually takes up 16 times its own weight in moisture. That is 5 times more than cotton itself. Kotex scientists have tried every new way to achieve perfection in a sanitary pad. Improved Kotex is the result of their research.

Buy a box . . . 45c for twelve . . . at any drug, dry goods or department store. The Improved Kotex is also available in vending cabinets of restrooms by West Disinfecting Co.

*Kotex is the only sanitary pad that deodorizes by patented process. (Patent No. 1,670,587.)

Use Super-size Kotex
Formerly 90c—Now 65c

Super-size Kotex offers the many advantages of the Kotex you always use *plus the greater protection* which comes with extra layers of Cellucotton absorbent wadding. Disposable in the same way. Doctors and nurses consider it quite indispensable the first day or two, when extra protection is essential. Buy one box of Super-size to every three boxes of regular size Kotex. Its added layers of filler mean added comfort.

K O T E X
The New Sanitary Pad which deodorizes

recalled. Minnow felt pressured, albeit politely: "If you didn't do it, you'd feel prudish," she explained, adding that Florence watched over the proceedings. In some photos, Tanja and Lee recline on the sleeping-porch sofa, warming their limbs in the sun. In others, they tell stories by the fire, or, more provocatively, Lee's head rests on Tanja's thigh. The boldest image in the series treats the two friends as a study in light and dark: arms linked, they strike hip-shot poses on a Navajo rug that looks "moderne," like the arty display of their naked bodies. As a group, however, Theodore's nudes hark back to the prurience of the stereoscope.

While posing for her father's ongoing series, Elizabeth was simultaneously absorbing Steichen's approach to the craft. The Colonel justified "faking," his term for interventions in the photographic process such as marking, shading, or otherwise manipulating negatives, as a means to capture the truth. He had recently renounced art by taking his canvases into the garden and burning them—the sort of gesture that appealed to Elizabeth. After two years of modeling, she announced her intention to become a photographer, to stand behind the camera rather than in front of it.

For a New Yorker, the obvious place to start was the Clarence White School. White, an early member of the Photo-Secession, had taught photography since the 1910s. Although he first taught a soft-focus aesthetic, his students were now learning the modernist idiom. Some, like Paul Outerbridge and Ralph Steiner, "acquired a formal rigor and technical brilliance that served their ideas well," a historian writes, "while others learned only a handsome stylishness." Instructors at the school stressed design. The choice of subject, one's feelings about it, or what larger purpose the exercise might serve, were not important. How to fill the picture space mattered more than what went into it, an approach suited to the dynamics of advertising.

By 1929, one former student had already acquired a reputation. Like Elizabeth, Margaret Bourke-White, who was her age, learned a reverence for both machines and photography from her father, a printing-press designer. Bourke-White had also gone to college to study science. After refining her photographic technique at the White School, she chose the new medium as the means to realize her ambitions: "I want to become famous and I want to become wealthy," she wrote in 1927. Her timing was excellent. Bourke-White's images of Henry Ford's factories, Cleveland's steel mills, and Niagara Falls' generators expressed Ford's (and the decade's) view of machinery as the new messiah. "Her personal passion," Bourke-White's biographer notes, "ran in perfect synchrony with the nation's interests."

Elizabeth went about learning what she wanted to know in her own way. Lacking the disciplined habits that may result from an advanced degree or professional training, she picked up her knowledge as she went along. To her apprenticeship in theater lighting and design, she added the imagery of the consumer culture that embraced her. White's students approached images as design; Elizabeth saw them as shifting scenes in the theater of her mind—to be held and framed by means of the camera. But to earn her living as a professional photographer, she would need training.

The issue was indirectly addressed in *Vanity Fair* when the magazine ran a tongue-in-cheek "Modern Art Questionnaire" by the young critic Alfred Barr. His questions might seem dated, Barr wrote, because they included "no spellbinders such as, Name four important artist-photographers whose names begin with St—." The correct answer to this spellbinder, Steichen, Stieglitz, Steiner, and Strand, formed a roll call of photographers working in the "recent manner," but included no women. In the twenties, one apprenticed oneself to an established professional or attended his school (whether or not his name began with St—).

Steichen told Elizabeth about the inventive, well-paid photographer whose work reflected art's affair with the machine: the futuristically named Man Ray. A New Yorker, he had invented the rayograph (a photographic image made without a camera) before going to France in 1921. Since 1925, when he covered the Art Deco exhibition for *Vogue,* his fashion work had appeared in Nast's magazines, along with his portraits of French aristocrats. The *Little Review* had published some of his most abstract images; others in the 1927 Machine-Age Exposition had enthralled art students and mystified critics. Elizabeth could introduce herself to him as a prospective student provided she could get back to Paris—an idea that had, for some time, obsessed her.

New York's excitements were no longer satisfying. She had won fame as a model, consorted with the smart set, and had more love affairs than Lorelei Lee (or perhaps as many as Louise Brooks). Having recently seen Medgyès on his visit to New York, she wanted to return to the life he had shown her in Paris. Steichen promised to write Man Ray on her behalf; Condé Nast planned to introduce her to George Hoyningen-Huene, the head of photography at French *Vogue;* a fashion designer gave her a job illustrating vintage patterns in Florence, where she would spend the month of June. Tanja, also at loose ends, decided to accompany her on the *Comte de Grasse,* which was due to sail on May 10, two weeks after Elizabeth's twenty-second birthday.

Elizabeth's compliant lovers flipped a coin to decide who would see her off. With the Millers, De Liagre, the victor, watched her ship sail down the Hudson in the morning sun while Argylle followed in his biplane, then swooped close to the sundeck to let loose a cascade of roses in Elizabeth's honor. She had come of age with the decade when New York became the world's most powerful city, yet she was turning her back on its cocksure mood of self-celebration.

Part Two
Miss Lee Miller

Lee and Man Ray, c. 1930, Paris (Man Ray)

Chapter 5

Montparnasse with Man Ray

(1929–30)

W hile it is tempting to think that Elizabeth became Lee while crossing the ocean, the psychic shifts that accompanied this name
change took place more gradually. She was still her parents' daughter; her "angel" self was still at odds with the "fiend" inside. One night at the
ship's bar she surprised Tanja by admitting "that the reason she liked me was
that I gave her a false feeling of respectability." Despite herself, she still cared
about other people's opinions.

By Poughkeepsie standards, Elizabeth lacked the "finish" that the Old
World could confer. She and Tanja were to spend the summer doing Europe
like the heroines of a Henry James novel—though they more nearly resembled
Anita Loos's flapper duo. From Paris they went to Florence with letters of
introduction to the fin-de-siècle expatriates in residence there. Their chaperone, an English art dealer, took them to tea at Bernard Berenson's villa, a coveted stop on the grand tour for connoisseurs. The famous critic impressed
Tanja but failed to interest Elizabeth.

Her job required her to spend hours in the city's museums drawing
Renaissance ornaments—cuffs, laces, belts, and buckles—as inspiration for
current New York fashions. The work was painstaking. It occurred to her that

she could make better copies by taking photographs, even though the light was bad and she had only a folding Kodak. Drawing on the Miller ingenuity to solve these problems, she satisfied her employer's needs while strengthening her resolve to abandon art. In June, after a short stay in Rome, Tanja went to Germany and Elizabeth returned to Paris to look up Man Ray. She could learn more from him than from the English art dealer and Berenson combined.

∞

Lee went back to France in 1929, she explained, "to enter photography by the back end." Until then, she had stood in front of the camera: she had been intensely looked at but not looked into—as if her being stopped at the surface of her skin. And it intrigued her that no two photographers made her look the same. Since she could seem romantic, flapperesque, or conventionally middle class, she hoped to explore this "mystery" by going around to the other side of the camera—to see how the photographer's vision affected the outcome.

Entering photography from the back end also meant changing its power dynamic, since male photographers usually looked at female models. By the end of the twenties, Margaret Bourke-White, Berenice Abbott, and Germaine Krull were reversing this scenario. Yet it is unlikely that Lee would have chosen a female mentor had she known one. Adept at establishing a rapport with men whose work she admired, she learned best in situations of intimacy.

To our ears, "entering photography from the back end" is a suggestive way to describe her decision: since Lee's childhood, the photographic apparatus, the experience of posing, and the darkroom itself were all charged for her with sexual meaning. Becoming a photographer would make it possible to explore much unfinished business. Lee often told the story of meeting Man Ray as a turning point in her life. In each version of this encounter, she is the protagonist—reversing the dynamics of her "discovery" by Condé Nast.

Once in Paris, she made her way to Montparnasse and, after knocking on the door of Man Ray's studio at 31 bis rue Campagne-Première, learned from the concierge that Monsieur Ray had left for the summer. Disconsolate, she crossed the Boulevard Raspail to the corner café, climbed the narrow iron staircase to the second floor, and sat down to sip Pernod with the owner.

Suddenly Man Ray appeared before her. "He kind of rose up through the floor at the top of the circular staircase," she recalled. "He looked like a bull, with an extraordinary torso and very dark eyebrows and dark hair. I told him boldly that I was his new student. He said he didn't take students, and anyway he was leaving Paris for his holiday. I said, I know, I'm going with you—and I did." Another version of their first meeting underscores her boldness: "I asked him to take me on as a pupil. He said he never accepted pupils, but I guess he fell for me. We lived together for three years and I learned a lot about photography."

Becoming Lee Miller and entering photography occur simultaneously in "My Man Ray," the most extended version of this pivotal tale. When the café owner introduces them, she declares without hesitation, "My name is Lee Miller and I'm your new student." This version continues: "He said he was leaving for Biarritz the next day, and I said, 'So am I.' I never looked back." Ironically, the meeting that sealed her identity also led to her becoming, as the French said, "Madame Man Ray."

In the twenties, Man's reputation spread throughout Europe. To be "done" by him meant that you were someone. His portraits of writers, artists, and socialites, many of them published in *Vogue,* allowed him to lead a life of luxury. He wore custom-made suits, drove a sports car, and spent his holidays with the wealthy patrons who financed his experimental movies, which had, until recently, featured the previous Madame Man Ray, the high-spirited Kiki de Montparnasse. Kiki had left Man the year before, but he described their breakup as his decision. "Having terminated a love affair," he remarked, "I felt ready for new adventures."

Going to Biarritz for the summer with his young American "student" was the start of an adventure for both. Given Lee's attraction to older men, the age difference—nearly seventeen years—worked to Man's advantage; while she was a head taller, his energy was compelling. "If he took your hand or touched you, you felt almost a magnetic heat," she recalled; his hands, "square and even workmanlike," were soft. Moreover, Man had style. He sported white flannels and loose Breton shirts during the summer and wore a beret long before his compatriots adopted this headgear as a symbol of insouciance. The most striking thing about Man was his economy of motion. "He never seems to hurry," Lee explained, "but he always gets there."

It is easy to imagine how Lee affected Man. Everything about her—deep-set blue eyes, graceful long neck, lean, supple shape—was full of promise. She was the incarnation of that provocative French figure, the *garçonne*—an independent young woman who plans to enjoy her freedom. The term came from Victor Margueritte's best-selling novel of the 1920s, *La garçonne,* whose heroine's emancipated ways were read as a protest against bourgeois standards. The bob, or *"coiffure à l'allure garçonne,"* had become a postwar focus of cultural anxiety about the destabilization of gender roles. To the French, Lee looked like the sort of hoyden whose willfulness threatened the fabric of society. Man was used to women living alone or with lovers, but until Lee, none had gone so far as to model themselves on the *garçonne.* Lee's seductive manner made her all the more alluring.

At first, in deference to her new mentor, she went along with his plans. He took her to visit Rose and Arthur Wheeler, the American couple with whom he spent part of each summer. They had become friends in Paris when Rose sat for her portrait. After seeing Man's experimental movies, Arthur had insisted that Man devote himself to the cinema and offered both financial backing and the use of his estate in the Basque country, near Biarritz.

Lee and Man drove south through the countryside in his stylish Voisin sports car. Before coming to Paris in 1921, he had not dreamed of owning an automobile, but after becoming a success, he took up fast cars and dancing, another of "a series of accomplishments," he wrote, "which had seemed beyond me." Yet Man was not the sporty type, Lee recalled: "He liked to fiddle around in the water at the beach if the weather was good, but, as he said, he swam like a typewriter." Nor was her mentor moved by nature. The clichés of art—sunsets, panoramas, flowers—bored him, unless the flowers could be photographed as designs or evocations of the female sex. "I do not photograph nature," he observed. "I photograph my fantasy."

Man's snapshots of Lee on the road show a reserved young woman in a long linen jumper, white blouse, and beret—the counterpart of his darker one—posing demurely on the way to Biarritz. Another set shows her looking mischievous, as if about to escape from the car and take off into the country-side. Perhaps she already sensed that she would often go her own way.

During the long drive together, she would have disarmed Man's reserve with questions about his life in New York. If they told each other about their families, the class differences would have been obvious. His father was a tailor from Kiev who had made his way to the United States in steerage; his mother a blue-eyed beauty who stitched elegant clothes for her children but could be harsh and overbearing. He had shortened his name from Emmanuel to Man at twenty-one, at about the time the family changed Radnitsky to Ray—when anti-Jewish sentiment in the United States made this a practical decision. Signing his first artwork as Man Ray, he had, in effect, reinvented himself, as she would do by becoming Lee Miller.

On the journey south, it would have been clear to Man that his companion was nothing like Kiki, whose languid forms suggest the ideals of the nineteenth century. One of Man's best-known photographs, *Violon d'Ingres*, shows a naked Kiki wearing a turban and, superimposed on her back, the curlicue "f" holes of a violin. His title for this image, a witty tribute to Ingres's odalisques, is a pun on the French phrase for an artist's hobby (for Ingres, his violin; for Man Ray, Kiki). Man's many portraits of Lee, which also celebrate her body as an instrument of pleasure, do so instead in the vocabulary of modernism— perhaps because they hold the muted awareness of his new muse as a *garçonne* with a style, and a mind, of her own.

Lee at Man Ray's studio, 31 bis rue Campagne-Première (Man Ray)

Soon after their return from Biarritz, Lee informed Theodore that she was staying in Paris to study photography. Since Tanja would return for a month in September, she took rooms for them in a hotel on the Boulevard Montparnasse, a few minutes' walk from Man's studio and, in the opposite direction, from the expatriate cafés at the Vavin crossroads, the hub of Montparnasse.

Man's Art Nouveau building, a neighborhood landmark, dates from 1911, when this area replaced Montmartre as the city's artistic center. As the Boulevard Raspail was extended to the south, speculators built hundreds of live-in studios, of which Man's was one of the most desirable. The same frieze of ochre ceramic tiles still adorns its façade; the Art Nouveau muses framing the doorway seem to usher visitors inside. In 1929, a plaque with Man's name identified his ground-floor studio, which combined a large, well-lit salon with a small bedroom and an even smaller darkroom on the balcony. Man's oils and photographs hung on the walls; his objects—chess pieces, wooden cubes, pyramids, and artists' mannequins—decorated the furniture like so many little worlds assembled by their creator.

Each day Lee walked around the corner to the rue Campagne-Première, a block-long monument to modern art. She passed Chez Rosalie, where, before the war, Modigliani had traded drawings for meals. Man's friend Mina Loy, a poet and painter who supported herself by designing Art Deco lamps, had lived in a studio at number 17 (where Rilke also resided), then, more recently, at number 11. Americans often stayed two steps from Man's at the Hotel Istria (where, according to legend, Hemingway's Brett Ashley and Jake Barnes pursued their frustrated love). Louis Aragon lived next door at 31 with his companion, the Russian novelist Elsa Triolet, who eked out a living by stringing bead necklaces.

The neighbor whose work had the greatest impact on Man's was the photographer Eugène Atget, who, until his death in 1927, arose at dawn to record aspects of old Paris. Man had bought a number of Atget's images and offered to print his work on stable paper, but Atget said that he was too set in his ways for modern techniques. Yet in Man's view, the old man's images were Surrealist in spirit. (Man showed Atget's photographs to Breton, who ran one on the cover of La Révolution surréaliste, the movement's polemical magazine.) Atget's influence was palpable in Man's images of Paris and, indirectly, in the Surrealists' view of its crooked streets as a veiled map of the psyche.

Although Man kept his distance from the Surrealists' political squabbles, he was, in Breton's view, the one photographer who expressed the movement's vision. It was gospel among the Surrealists that reality could be transformed by freeing repressed libidinal energies. To illustrate his beliefs, Breton used Man's photographs in La Révolution surréaliste and his 1928 novel Nadja, which tracks the narrator's affair with a woman encountered in a Paris street. (Nadja goes mad at the end of the novel, but her disappearance is of no concern to the narrator, since their affair has deepened his process of self-discovery.) Man's erotic portraits of women seemed to confirm the Surrealists' hope that through sexual ecstasy the creative imagination would be unleashed.

As part of the group's ongoing research into sexuality, Breton asked the Surrealists to name the "essential" encounters of their lives and say whether these had been "fortuitous" or "necessary." Man replied enigmatically, "Any encounter I rejected was fortuitous; any I accepted and continued was necessary." After his return from Biarritz, he fell deeply in love with Lee. In the early stages of their affair, they hardly left the studio. Lovemaking alternated with picture-taking. For the first time, perhaps, Lee felt the intoxication of a love that takes itself as the center of existence, and Man, the implications of an encounter that would become more than necessary.

Decades later, Lee looked back on this time with detachment. What mattered were the details of her apprenticeship with Man. To the biographer, what she did not say is just as interesting. Her recollections, while hinting at the tangled interweave of personal and aesthetic matters, downplay her role in the transformation of their rapport into a partnership whose intimacy can be detected in the photographic record of their years together.

Man often said that photography was not an art but a way to paint with light. In the same way, technique was just a means to an end, that of isolating a subject in its particular aura. Most of the time, he would rather paint than photograph, but portraiture and advertising paid the rent. Lee offered to print for him so he could return to his easel. But first, he had to teach her his approach to the art that wasn't one, whose first principles, he said, were calm and control.

Man had everything in place before a sitter arrived. During a session, he gave simple directions, worked quickly, and photographed from a distance (ten to twelve feet), knowing that he would crop the negatives and enlarge the results. This procedure, which limited interactions with subjects, suited both his temperament and his aesthetic. Man's portraits were formal, in keeping with period expectations of a dignified likeness. "He dislikes the 'candid camera' attitude in portraiture," Lee explained. Yet his images, whether of people or of objects, were all expressions of "his personal mood."

This mood, a blend of reserve, inventiveness, and practicality, was as much a function of his working methods as a reflection of his engagement with the avant-garde. Man hoped "to extend the field of this newest of mediums to the limits of artistic expression," he explained. While in his opinion, photography was a matter of "light and chemistry," it also created "a new element of social contact." For those who had eyes to see, the distance between photographer and sitter was minimal: "As far as desires go, there is really not such a great gulf between the one who creates and the one who appreciates."

Man also liked to say that equipment mattered less than the person who pushed the button. Any camera would do. Man and Lee often photographed outside with their viewfinders. Although some photographers dismissed these small cameras as toys, their advantages included simplicity, low cost, and a final product that approximated what one saw through the finder, which was held at eye level. When indoors, Man often used a Graflex or a small studio camera with glass plates, although by 1930 this technology was on the way out. While plate cameras were cumbersome (one focused the lens by moving it on a track), their large negatives, which could be retouched, made them appropriate for portraiture.

Man taught Lee to work with his half-plate camera; its plates, which measured four by five inches, "had to be unpacked very carefully and loaded into the chassis," she recalled. When it came time to print, she went up the narrow staircase to the darkroom. Although it "wasn't as big as a bathroom rug," Man arranged his equipment as neatly as his objects: he was "absolutely meticulous." He showed her how to insert the glass plates into their holders, dip them into the basin, then rinse them once they had been fixed. He taught her to use the enlarger under mercury light and, when printing on his favorite eggshell paper, to retouch with a "Jenner," a triangular blade that scratched out wrinkles. The work, as painstaking as her stint as a copyist in Florence, was more gratifying: "You have something in your hand when you're finished— every 15 seconds you've made something."

Man shared all of his secrets with Lee. By the end of their first year together, she recalled, "he had taught me to do fashion pictures, he'd taught me to do portraits, he taught me the whole technique of what he did." He used colored backgrounds, white, gray, or silver, "which gave off different colors and reflected whatever was in the room or wherever you walked," she went on. "One of the things he taught me so carefully was how to photograph silver objects, because where you think a silver object is very bright it actually isn't, it's just reflecting what's in the room." Man obtained a brilliant light by putting a low-voltage bulb into a higher-voltage circuit—an early version of the photoflood. His true medium was light. Using it to model the sitter's face as a painter used a brush, he obtained "that very fine, delicate drawing that's so Renaissance-looking."

Lee also acted as Man's receptionist. She welcomed sitters—a cross-section of the French and expatriate art worlds, and the trendsetters known as le Tout-Paris—on whom she often made an indelible impression. The American composer George Antheil remembered her as "a sylphlike creature . . . a decor by herself." A visiting *Vogue* editor thought her "a vision so lovely" that one forgot the purpose of one's visit. But to the novelist Henri-Pierre Roché, Man's new companion was "pretty, perverse . . . and somewhat lacking in the bust." (About this time, a glass manufacturer with a different opinion designed a champagne glass modeled after her shapely breast.) To Cecil Beaton, whose sexual imagination made her into a nubile youth, Lee resembled, rather, "a sunkissed goat boy from the Appian Way." "Only sculpture could approximate the beauty of her curling lips, long languid pale eyes and column neck," he said.

Lee dressed becomingly in velvet trousers and jersey tops that set off her long neck and shining bob. In 1930, when the *garçonne* look came to dominate fashion, its mannish lines brought out her androgynous side. "Her athletic fig-ure made the simplest thing seem elegant," recalled Jacqueline Barsotti (later Goddard), who modeled for Man and who, despite some ambivalence about Lee, befriended her. Women who could wear the new style gained confidence, Jacqueline thought: "The men of our circles were astonished by the change in us." Lee had no qualms about reaping the advantages of her looks, she added. And while Jacqueline had mixed feelings about her new friend's self-centeredness, she envied her ability to get what she wanted.

Before Lee talked her way into his life, Man had had several assistants who, like her, developed, printed, and retouched photographs according to his specifications. Man had hired the sculptor Berenice Abbott because she knew nothing about photography; after three years with him, she opened her Paris studio, and they became friendly rivals—even photographing the same people: James Joyce, Jean Cocteau, and Peggy Guggenheim. By the time Lee arrived, Abbott had gone back to New York to document the city in the spirit of Atget, whose negatives she bought to preserve and take home as inspiration.

Man's next assistant, Jacques-André Boiffard, a Surrealist poet, had taken up photography after abandoning his medical studies. He photographed some of the Paris street scenes in Breton's *Nadja,* and often dropped by Man's studio when Lee was there. Bill Brandt, Man's other assistant at the time, worked with him until 1930, when he settled in England. Like Abbott, Boiffard, and, eventually, Lee, Brandt turned from studio work to documentary studies and photojournalism.

An indoor person by nature, Man relaxed by going out with friends. "He took me to wonderful restaurants with people who knew all about food and wines, and lunches that lasted from 1 to 7," Lee recalled. In the evening, they strolled down the Boulevard Montparnasse to dine at the Trianon or drink at the Jockey, "where you'd find James Joyce, Hemingway and all those people with their coteries around them." Other nights they joined the group at Le Boeuf sur le Toit, Jean Cocteau's jazz club near the Faubourg St. Honoré, or, once the Boeuf lost its cachet, Le Grand Ecart in Montmartre—a "narrower and smaller and more snobbish" place, Lee said, where one had to dress well to get in. Since Man was proud of having learned to dance, they practiced the latest steps at Bricktop's, the American-style nightclub whose unflappable owner crooned Cole Porter songs between glasses of Rémy Martin.

Man's pleasure in escorting Lee to all the spots where formerly he had taken Kiki was not lost on their friends. They went to cabarets to hear Kiki sing and often saw her at the Coupole, where she reigned over the habitués gathered in the narrow bar. Lee was delighted to meet the woman who had inspired the Broadway play, but "when [Kiki] realized that I had moved in with Man, she was a little piqued," she recalled. "She used to eye me and I used to eye her and finally I met her and we got along fine because I admired her very much." While the Surrealists treated Lee as Kiki's replacement, it was clear to friends that she was nothing like her predecessor.

Some said that Man had "created" Kiki by designing bizarre makeup and painting it on her—even shaving off her eyebrows and replacing them with new ones at odd angles. Lee needed no embellishment, nor would she submit to being redesigned. Paradoxically, Lee's belief in herself boosted Man's ego. While he still looked morose on occasion, he seemed more alive with her beside him. Kiki's friends were fascinated by Lee's self-absorption—a large

*Lee
modeling
Patou
gown
(Hoyningen-
Huene)*

part of her seductive aura, they thought. Watching Lee trade shamelessly on her beauty, they felt sorry for Man. "He loved her without restriction," Jacqueline Barsotti Goddard explained. "For the first and last time in his life, Man had to surrender. To have this fascinating, intelligent woman as his mistress was fatal."

To others in Montparnasse, they were opposites. People stared at them not only because of the differences in age and height but because Lee's radiance contrasted with Man's reserve. Yet they were complementary. Both were snappy dressers and liked to craft their images for their own amusement. On the Boulevard Montparnasse one day an acquaintance noticed a striking couple linked to each other by a golden chain. "The woman was taller than the man and strode along in spite of being tethered," she observed. As they drew closer, she recognized "the well-known photographer and his new assistant—he more attached to her than she to him."

On October 23, 1929, news of the Wall Street crash hit Paris. Within a few days, foreigners dependent on remittances began to decamp. Jewelers on the rue de la Paix, antique dealers, and art gallery owners saw their clientele vanish. Tourists stopped boasting about the superiority of the dollar. But unlike Tanja, who went back to New York, Lee saw no reason to leave Paris.

In the meantime, Man worried about the future. Fewer sitters came for portraits; Arthur Wheeler could not sponsor more cinematic experiments. Man's anxiety deepened as the Depression spread to France and his New York supporters turned their backs on avant-gardism. The art critic Henry McBride, one of his early advocates, observed tartly, "If an American artist must live in Paris for his soul's good, that's his affair, but in doing so he automatically becomes French and must gain French support rather than live, parasitically, upon funds from home."

To augment her own funds, Lee went to Paris *Vogue:* Michel de Brunhoff, the editor, welcomed her as Steichen's model and Condé Nast's protégée. It may have seemed ironic that the October issue, appearing just before the crash, illustrated the new fashion "consecrating the triumph of muscular young woman" with three shots of Lee in streamlined tweed and jersey ensembles—as if she epitomized what the magazine called the "aristocracy of elegance." For the rest of the year, French *Vogue* ("Frogue" to its staffers) existed in a parallel universe. The crash went unmentioned, luxury thrived, and occasions for its display—garden parties, costume balls, competitions of expensive automobiles—were chronicled in its pages.

The photographer in charge of Frogue's studio, which sent the U.S. and U.K. editions their fashion pages, was George Hoyningen-Huene, a temperamental Estonian baron. His father had been chief equerry to the tsar; his mother, the child of an American ambassador to Russia. After the revolution, the family fled to France. Man had taught Huene the rudiments of photography; together they produced a portfolio of Paris beauties for an American department store. Huene admired Man but revered Steichen. Like his idol, Huene wanted fashion to represent women "in their normal surroundings, pausing for a moment during their daily activities." Although he was known to terrify models, he showed Lee respect as Steichen's friend and Man's lover— and soon for her own sake.

Huene's portraits of Lee emphasize the relaxed stylishness that typifies his vision of the modern woman. In one, she turns to reveal the marcelled coiffure and jeweled evening gown that provide the photo's raison d'être, while her pose—arm resting on a fur draped over her chair—shows off her back and shoulders. In a variant, seated on one of the classical pedestals that Huene used as props, she wears an almost backless Lanvin dress called "Baghdad" and displays her "good profile." Huene sensed that Lee's contradictions made her more versatile than other models. She could look virginal in a white evening dress, her figure framed by calla lilies on a low table, or vamp unseen admirers in a black satin robe. For the first time, the magazine listed "Miss Lee Miller" in the photo credits, as if she were a celebrity.

Lee's apprenticeship with Huene began in 1930, she recalled, when she and a young German art student named Horst Bohrmann (later known only as Horst) "joined the *Vogue* studio to be [Huene's] slaves." Their workplace resembled a stage set. Models posed on platforms lit by brilliant lights that threatened to melt their makeup. Assistants wheeled the large studio cameras into position, raised and lowered them on their wooden frames, then turned a wheel to move the lens in or out. During the time it took for the elements of the picture to come together, the photographer entertained the sitter. Compared with working with Man, Lee observed, "that was an entirely different kind of photography." The baron's slaves absorbed their mentor's advice while struggling with the cameras and readjusting the tungsten lights, since light meters did not yet exist.

As Horst and Lee became Huene's collaborators, a triangular relationship developed among them. Three blue-eyed blonds who were vain of their appearance, they could have been siblings—with Huene in the role of older brother and, soon, protector where Horst was concerned. Their intimacy is reflected in Huene's studies of Horst's athletic torso and his "Hellenic" poses—an allusion to same-sex love. However Lee felt about Horst—there is a hint of a rivalry between them—Huene saw his assistants as counterparts. The same age and physical type, they complemented each other.

Huene's beachwear series for Frogue became the vehicle for his feelings about them. These striking scenes, which resemble snaps of a summer holiday for members of the leisure class, are marked by a redistribution of sexual energies. In one, Lee slouches in what must be the first pair of high-fashion overalls. In another, she lounges in a deck chair placed in front of a striped canvas cabana: the composition emphasizes her jawline, short hair, and apparently boyish chest. In yet another from this session, she gazes at a male companion shot from behind, the better to show his muscles; a companion portrait of Horst's torso accentuates the phallic vertical of the pole clasped in his muscular arms.

Swimwear by Izod, the best of this series and a hallmark of modernist photography, shows an athletic couple seated, judging by their garb, on a diving board. As we seem to gaze past them to the sea, the two figures all but merge into a single form. They share a pair of legs, the woman's; the verticals of their necks and trunks, their cropped coiffures and contrasting costumes form an androgynous whole. Like much of Huene's work, the image reflects the thirties' turn to Neoclassicism, but there is a Surrealist note. Huene photographed his sporty pair on the roof of the *Vogue* building; seated on a stack of boxes, they were gazing not at the sea but at the parapet above the Champs-Elysées. While studies of Huene's work identify the man as Horst, the woman is unnamed, but to those who know Lee's neck, torso, and place in Huene's imagination as Horst's "twin," she is instantly recognizable. *Friends,* as this portrait of Huene's favorites is also called, combines the seductive allure of androgyny with the desire for an elsewhere.

Horst, a shy man with limited English, began modeling himself on his patron. In time, the baron's self-assurance would rub off on his lover, who gradually took charge when Huene gave him assignments. "It used to intrigue me," Horst wrote, "to have power over my lovely sitters, to realize that they were reluctantly entrusting me with the task of rendering a likeness that would encourage a wavering faith in their own looks." One day he persuaded Lee to pose for him. The portrait captured her soft side. Holding a sprig of lily of the valley, she looks more like a romantic heroine than a *garçonne*. But when Horst showed her the print, Lee pronounced it "a howl." After looking up the word in the dictionary, Horst concluded that she was making fun of him. He decided not to repeat the experiment. "With strong-willed girls," he wrote, "you let them do it, you don't suggest."

Lee moved easily from the family atmosphere of Frogue to the café life of Montparnasse, where she was accepted, if not welcomed, as Man's lover. Few understood the intensity of their relationship. After working side by side with Man for a year, she had become necessary to him. Their bond, based in part on her absorption of his approach, transcended words. It was sometimes hard to say who took which image, Lee recalled. Photographs attributed to him might have been taken by her: their work overlapped. He set the scene and pushed the button; she took the image through the stages of development, retouching, and printing. The final product reflected their collaboration.

Man's portraits of Lee reveal the intimate dialogue that may occur between artist and muse. "What can be more binding amongst beings than the discovery of a common desire?" he asked in his 1934 collection, *Photographs by Man Ray.* Its many "autobiographical images" (including portraits of Lee) were not experiments, he wrote, but the residue of experience, "seized in moments of visual detachment during periods of emotional contact." Man's gift, Breton wrote in an accompanying essay, was to capture female beauty at the point "where it reaches its full power: so sure of itself as to appear to ignore itself!" His portraits of Lee depict what he saw as their common desire. His job was to capture the power of her beauty; hers, to seem to ignore herself.

Like a true portraitist, he began with her head. "The head of a woman is her complete physical portrait," Man wrote. "The more daring poets who have seen in a woman's eyes her sex, have realized that the head contains more orifices than does all the rest of the body; so many added invitations for poetic, that is, sensual exploration." He explored Lee's head from every angle, showing her full-face and staring at the camera, her uncertainty masked by her makeup; veiled by a wavy pattern of stripes that likens her to a wild animal (*Leebra*); childlike in sleep, with one finger at her lips (*La Dormeuse*); three-quarter face, both profiles, and each of her features as fragments. One of his favorite images shows her touching a manicured hand to her mouth as if inviting further intimacy.

While Lee's poses reveal a complicity of the kind she exhibited when sitting for her father, it is difficult to detect in them *her* sense of her relations with Man. Enacting his dream of a compliant femininity, she may have gained a measure of power. Perhaps she also sensed in these photographs projections of Man's feelings about the fluctuating dynamics of their rapport.

In his enlargement of her lips, half closed in a smile, it is easy to see another metaphor for the woman's sex. This image would haunt him, Man wrote, until he completed the large painting of red lips afloat in a blue sky entitled *Observatory Time—the Lovers,* which he used as the background for a series of photographs in the 1930s. "The lips because of their scale, no doubt, suggested two closely joined bodies. Quite Freudian," he added coyly. Lee's lips became his shorthand for the image of "two bodies fitting together in perfect harmony," he wrote, yet "when these lips break into a smile, they disclose the menacing barrier of the teeth." Beyond the dream of shared ecstasy lay its other face, the female sex as specter of castration.

The portrait of a loved one was not "just an image at which one smiles but also an oracle one questions," Breton observed. In Man's images of women, he continued, "we [men] are given to see the most recent avatar of the Sphinx." Lee as Sphinx may seem far-fetched, but it was through the Surrealists' "Freudian" readings of myth that they saw the real women to whom they turned for inspiration. Man took two "oracular" portraits of Lee's face seen upside down, one with her eyes closed, the other with them open. In the second, the image is cropped to emphasize the inversion (chin on top, hair below). The uncanny angle of vision and positioning create Medusa-like images as disturbing as Magritte's contemporary canvas, *Le Viol* (Rape), where the woman's naked torso replaces her features.

Like his fellow Surrealists, Man devised images of women's bodies to subvert the long tradition of the nude as raw material of art. One of his early photographs of Lee assimilates her to sculpture. Her forearms disappear into the diagonals formed as they bend behind her head; her torso, draped below the navel, suggests a modern Venus de Milo to whom the head and partial use of the arms have been restored. Lee also posed nude from the waist up for a series of shots taken as she gazed out a window, where, in turn, a mesh curtain, iron grillwork, and dappled reflections cast patterns on her torso. Man kept the series for himself, releasing only the variant that shows Lee's torso minus her head—the image cropped at the neck and pubic region. Paradoxically, when this variant is compared with the original, his symbolic beheading enhances her determination. The pose seems forceful, as if *she* is in charge.

In the Surrealist imagination, seemingly fixed categories like "male" and "female" were reversible. ("I wish I could change my sex as often as I change my shirt," Breton is said to have remarked.) Yet enactments of this reversal provoked anxiety, which was part of their allure. Man also took several photographs of Lee's neck and upper torso and entitled them, suggestively, *Anatomies.* In them, she takes an extreme backward bend. Because her head is obscured, the tense, columnar shape of her neck suggests an erect penis. (A variant of this image, cropped just below the clavicle, focuses even more tightly on her throat.) It is easy to see *Anatomies* as an ambivalent appropriation of the female form, or as an anxious allusion to the power of the "weaker" sex.

Another image of Lee's neck, shot from below, included her profile. Displeased with the negative, Man threw it in the trash. Lee printed it anyway and claimed it as *her* work. They quarreled over her appropriation; she left the studio and returned to find *her* image on the wall with red ink streaming from the throat. Man had slashed it with a razor. That he continued to resent her insubordination is evident from his *Le Logis de l'Artiste,* painted the following year. The contested image of Lee's neck, again slashed with scarlet, dominates the neat arrangement of objects in the artist's studio. Antony Penrose comments: "The reduction of Lee's head to an object and its inclusion in this visual context reveal even more perhaps than Man Ray intended."

One of the things it revealed was Man's difficulty with Lee's need for independence. He wanted her to be his *chose* (his thing)—like Kiki, Jacqueline observed. Gradually, Man came to understand that Lee's compliance was a pose, or a series of them. He liked to photograph her asleep, when she offered no resistance. In one such image, shot from above, she lies fully dressed and spread-eagled on a dark coverlet, which contrasts sharply with her white trousers rolled to the knee. The position and angle direct the eye to the veiled V of her crotch, as if her long legs had involuntarily opened to allow a better look.

Man also played with the shape of her legs in an amusing series taken with three female midgets who were in Paris with a vaudeville show. In one, a tiny harem dancer stands between Lee's legs; in another, a pair of twins in bathing suits admire her as she balances above them. The composition juxtaposes the midgets' limbs with her much longer ones, but cuts them off at the thigh— another V shape pointing to what, this time, is absent rather than veiled. Although fragmentation is a commonplace of Surrealist art, one may suppose that by shooting Lee this way, Man felt that he was breaking her into pieces, the better to hold on to her.

Man's focus on Lee part by part may be seen as the visual equivalent of the Renaissance poet's praise for his mistress feature by feature. But it can also be understood as the recourse of an artist whose resentment of his beloved's power expresses itself in symbolic violence. The sadistic charge of these images is hard to ignore, especially given the Surrealists' worship of the Marquis de Sade and Man's enthusiasm for this banned author. In an image suggesting a Sadeian source, Lee poses like a supplicant, one leg folded beneath her, the other stretched out on the floor. Her head tilts back; her hand touches her throat like a sacrificial victim. Man called this nude *Suicide* and gave it to her as a present.

La Prière, one of his best-known photographs from this time, is even more disquieting. Inspired by Sade's predilection for sodomy, it shows a nude bent forward on her knees, her feet beneath her buttocks and her hands cupped to shield her anus. Man's ambiguous title, *Prayer,* hints that she offers what is hidden as an orifice for exploration. As in much of Man's erotica, the image plays with ideas of cruelty and worship while raising questions about whose desire is on display—the subject's or the artist's. It is impossible to identify the sitter (kneeler?) since only her extremities and posterior are visible. However, given Lee's desire to shock, the date of the photograph (1930), and Man's gift of it to her, it is likely that she also posed for this daring "portrait," which uses the woman's body to stage fantasies of domination and submission, along with their entanglement in the sexual imagination.

Some photographs, Edward Weston's biographer writes, reveal "not the personality of the sitter; and not the personality of the photographer." They affect us, rather, by showing "an invisible, indefinable interaction of the two." Man's portraits of Lee are often of this kind. In their case, as in Weston's portraits of his sexual partners, "what we see, what we respond to, is the dialogue between subject and artist, unspoken, unspeakable." In actuality, however, this dialogue was one-sided. Man took hundreds of portraits of Lee. Only three of him by her survive.

Man sometimes made up the difference by speaking both parts. In a staged self-portrait, he stands next to a bed in a terry-cloth robe that seems about to fall open. Behind him is a small portrait of Lee looking down while the light of a tanning lamp called a Sunray—Man's stand-in—plays over her hair, breast, and thigh. Man's expression is melancholy; he seems to be pleading. The composition invites his lover to resume their intimacy but makes her part of the décor, her image subservient to the swirling Art Deco pattern on the wall behind him. Man's strategy vis-à-vis his muse, containment and miniaturization, bespeaks desperation more than it does dialogue.

"You are so young and beautiful and free," Man wrote Lee during a separation, "and I hate myself for trying to cramp that in you which I admire most, and find so rare in women." "My affection can stand an awful lot," he continued, "more than I can myself." He admired her insistence on doing things her way and wanted to defend himself against the charge that he was cramping her style.

Since the start of their affair, he admonished in another letter, "I promoted every possible occasion that might be to your advantage or pleasure, even where there was danger of losing you." She had grown tired of his "intensity," he worried. But was it intensity, or "sustained enthusiasm, whether in work, play, or love-making, or rather all three inseparably joined." Man could not voice his fear that Lee held more cards than he did. Despite his reputation, he was short, unattractive, and, socially speaking, her inferior. His success as an avant-gardist had erased neither his desire for respect nor his need to control the woman he loved, even while admiring in her that which caused him pain: her independence.

Against his inclination, Man encouraged Lee to find her own path. He sent her to work for firms that wanted a Man Ray but would accept the work of Madame. Among the more bizarre assignments he gave her was a stint as a photographer at the Sorbonne medical school, a job that appealed to her love of the macabre. One day Lee walked from the Left Bank operating theater to Frogue headquarters carrying a breast on a dinner plate, covered by a cloth. Having retrieved it from a mastectomy with the intention of taking a picture, she placed a knife and fork on either side, then added salt and pepper shakers to this morbid still life, a true *nature morte*. Her bravado shocked Frogue editor de Brunhoff and scandalized Horst. What Man made of her dark humor—a reply in Surrealist terms to his obsessive focus on her body?—is not recorded.

Despite her provocative lapse in taste, de Brunhoff encouraged Lee to work as a photographer. Soon she was taking Huene's place in the studio on minor assignments. New York *Vogue* published her Steichenesque shots of luxury items arranged like miniature still lifes. To set off Chanel's new perfumes, she arranged their glass bottles with several modernist props: African masks, bits of classical architecture, a chessboard that might have come from Man's studio. In the most original of this group, a silhouetted hand reaches toward the flacons of Patou's perfume bar, whose essences let the owner concoct her own scent. The caption for Lee's shot of Elizabeth Arden's new perfume—"l'Elan d'Elizabeth, which blends sweet and spicy"—may have seemed like another "howl." One can imagine her pride when images of Patou gowns such as she had modeled ran in the magazine above the credit "Lee Miller, Paris."

Frogue provided relief from the intensity of life with Man. De Brunhoff, a portly, talkative tease whose brother created the *Babar* series, was also a trained actor. His dramatic flair convulsed his collaborators, especially when he did one-man renditions of silent movies—acting all the parts while quivering uncontrollably to indicate the flickers. De Brunhoff was "a brilliant mime," a friend recalled; "he could act a feature as well as draw it; and over his squat little body he would cunningly twist the lapel of his ill-fitting jacket to indicate the subtlest new line." De Brunhoff considered Lee a kindred spirit, whose sense of the ridiculous matched his own.

One could say that Lee's feel for the incongruities of daily life made her a Surrealist, though she never joined the movement and no doubt laughed in private at Breton's pomposity. Too pragmatically American to adopt his view of photography as a path into the unconscious, she nonetheless sympathized with the Surrealists' wish to shock society by whatever means possible. Even as an apprentice, she had an eye for unsettling moments and used the camera's framing capacity to capture and re-present them. Her knowledge of art, drama, and lighting came together in the unstudied Surrealism of her early Paris images—a mature body of work for a young photographer. Having trained with the masters—Steichen, Huene, Man Ray—she had absorbed their authority along with their "personalities."

By 1930, when Man had abandoned his flirtation with Paris as a subject, other photographers—André Kertesz, Germaine Krull, Ilse Bing, Brassaï—were documenting its street life in the spirit of their common precursor, Atget. Like them, Lee walked around the city looking for scenes that spoke of their own accord. Working out of doors with a simple viewfinder gave her the freedom to capture the unexpected. In some of her earliest images, odd angles accentuate the humor implicit in the scene. In one, a canted vision marks her delight at spotting four small rats seated side by side with their tails draped over their narrow perch. In another "found" image, three painted carousel cows eye the camera as they rise, fall, and spin by: her composition leads the eye past these tethered creatures to a patch of sky—the beyond to which they will never escape.

The urban landscape yielded many surprises. In a tilted image of a man standing near a swatch of asphalt, the bottom of his legs and his shoes (all that is seen of him) seem to be endangered by the encroaching substance. Lee's handling of light and texture—dull fabric, shiny leather, hard pavement, viscous asphalt—turns an ordinary street scene into a quirky view of the shrinking interval between human and nonhuman. Another arresting image called *Exploding Hand*—one of a series of hands standing in for faces—illustrates Breton's idea of "convulsive beauty." As a woman reaches toward a glass door marked by a tracery of scratches, her hand seems to explode just before its manicured fingers grasp the knob; the tilt of the door, a natural frame inside the picture, heightens the drama. Having mastered the camera's framing capacity, Lee used it—less programmatically than some official Surrealists— to enhance the strangeness in the everyday.

Other images from this period play with presence and absence. In one, the idea of something missing is implied by a silhouetted hand reaching toward an almost abstract pattern of grillwork. In another, of birds in cages, the alternation of the cages' bell-shaped wires and the spaces between them suggests ideas of escape. An implicit irony or dark humor—one of her persistent notes—emerges when we see that the birds are shot against patterned grillwork that imitates their natural habitat, the forest, in its leafy curves. Similarly, a pair of wooden shoes found on a patch of earth imply the marginality of their absent owner. In an image that harks back to Atget, Lee photographed the entrance to Guerlain's headquarters on the oblique, as if looking askance at the luxury trade to focus instead on the trees reflected in the plate-glass window. With each of these shots, familiar scenes and objects are made new by re-presenting them at odd angles.

Given Lee's apprenticeship in the arts of vision, her approach to photography as "a mechanical refinement of the art of perspective" is not surprising. She had studied perspective, lighting, and composition with the best; she knew how to compose the image in her mind's eye, turn the lens in relation to the scene, and let the play among shapes speak for itself. Her sense of subjects positioned relationally in space aligns her with other modernists for whom "one of photography's fascinations has been to propose psychological connections between forms and figures in space." The gaps between the shapes defined by the varieties of grillwork in her Paris photographs, for instance, attest to her feel for spatiality—both the shifting dynamics of inside and outside, and the gaps between figures in relationship.

One wonders how Man responded to Lee's outdoor shots, found as she

Lee solarized, c. 1930 (Man Ray)

strolled around Paris in search of surprises. She may have reflected on the difference between working outside and in the studio's controlled atmosphere while printing Man's portraits, including the many studies of her own person. Perhaps the relative absence of the human figure in her early work (hands and feet stand in for bodies) was not accidental. Photographing the nonpersonal, the other-than-human, would have offered relief from Man's use of her as his material, just as controlling the distance, angle, and composition may have reversed feelings of complicity she experienced as his subject at a time when she was struggling to establish herself.

Their discovery of a mysterious technique in some ways illustrates their symbiotic, yet conflicted, relationship. While printing one day in the tiny darkroom, Lee turned on the light, forgetting that twelve negatives—nude studies of a sensational blond singer named Suzy Solidor—hung in the developing tank. Fearing that the work was ruined, she turned off the light and called Man, who barely curbed his anger. Since it was impossible to redo the session, Mlle. Solidor having left Paris, they plunged the negatives into the developer to see what would happen.

The result, a partial reversal of the blacks and whites, was startling. A delicate line detached Suzy's torso from the rest of the image. "The unexposed parts of the negative, which had been the black background, had been exposed by this sharp light," Lee recalled, "and they had developed, and come right up to the edge of the white, nude body." It was the first example of what she and Man would call "solarization"—a tribute to the charms of Mlle. Solidor (whose name means "sun giver") and a code name for their discovery. In the controlled experiments that followed, they exposed negatives for different lengths of time "so that you wouldn't lose too much of the goings-on in the shadow," Lee said, "or have the hair come out all despondent and gray . . . or melting." In time, they worked out how much overexposure was needed and learned to use "this quality of melting to enhance or give volume to the images." Yet solarization remained chiefly a matter of chance.

Once one gave up the idea of control, knowing that each solarization would turn out differently could be seen as an advantage. "You wanted to get different effects," Lee explained, and the approach suited some subjects more than others. In Man's 1930 portrait of Duchamp, one of a series of solarized portraits of artists, the fine line chiseling his friend's profile alludes to Duchamp's skill as a draftsman. "But somebody else's profile who was just as good-looking might have been completely coarsened by the technique," Lee remarked. Solarization worked according to its own laws. And despite Man's gradual mastery of it, material reality kept reasserting itself in the form of accidents, some more pleasing than others.

The female body could be approached afresh from this perspective. The subtle "goings-on" in the shadows, the "melting" quality enhancing its volumes, gave the nude greater dimensionality, and the silvery aura emanating from the body externalized its inner life. One day Lee and Man photographed a naked model as if she were asleep in midair, then solarized the result. The print's floating quality became emblematic to the Surrealists, who courted such states of being. Man's title, *Primat de la matière sur la pensée,* gives primacy to matter over thought—perhaps an ironic gesture since the solarized line surrounds and contains the naked body. It was the sort of joke that develops in intimacy. Decades later, Lee wondered which of them should take credit for the image. "I don't know if I did it but that doesn't matter," she remarked. "We were almost the same person when we were working."

In the next few years, as Man used solarization to turn bodies into dream anatomies, Lee remained his favorite subject. The technique stood for her presence in his life. His inclusion of her solarized profile in his autobiography, *Self Portrait,* connects her to the rebirth of creative energy he experienced in the 1930s, when solarization was hailed as an invention that elevated photography to fine art. In this famous image, her "good" profile is delineated by a black line that softens as it moves out from her body, paradoxically suggesting both the emanation of her energy and its containment. "In either case," notes a critic, "her body and the solarization process join forces here with the result that Miller's flesh becomes essential to the rhetoric of Man Ray's invention."

If her body was essential to his creative vision, Lee's lips remained an emblem of her power. Greatly magnified and on their own in another solarization, they pursued him, Man wrote, "like a dream remembered." The image held still other meanings: lovers entwined, but also the engorged genital lips. One wonders to what extent Lee, whose sexual repartee was often vulgar, accepted Man's view of her—whether she saw such images as erotic puns or as the latest version of familiar desires. (Or both?) Her solarized portrait of Man shaving wittily compares his sudsy profile with her own, and in the process, dissolves the pose's allusions to high art: the head turned as in Renaissance portraiture of notables. Here the noted photographer is trying to remove the traces of masculinity, her portrait suggests—pulling his (invisible) leg in a good-natured manner.

The enlargement of detail expanded the possibilities of photography, Man believed, by loosening the medium's ties to realism. What he did not say was that it also allowed him to explore his obsessions. *Photographs by Man Ray,* his 1934 retrospective in book form, includes a solarized image of calla lilies, one of several taken while living with Lee. The lilies' formal beauty is enhanced by the artificial light and the process of solarization: isolated on a pale background, the lilies resemble so many white, nude bodies. It does not take much imagination to see in the form of the pistil emerging from the flower another sexual metaphor, nor is the French word for *lily* (*lys,* to an American ear pronounced like *Lee's*) coincidental. Like the image of her lips, Man's lilies spoke covertly of his desire—of the fusion of energies he simultaneously feared and yearned for.

What Lee made of this photo one can only guess. Horst's portrait of her holding a sprig of lily of the valley had made her laugh. Man's allusions to her in the calla lily series may have given her pause. Much later, she recalled that in the process of solarization, "the background and the image couldn't heal together. . . . The new exposure could not marry with the old one." Metaphors often say more than is intended. Photographic development resembled psychological growth, but in neither had the healing taken place that was needed for "marriage," or wholeness.

Lee as "la femme surréaliste," *1930 (Man Ray)*

Chapter 6

La Femme Surréaliste

(1930–32)

L ee began the decade by moving to a duplex that was larger and more luxurious than Man's. He may have hoped that with this new arrangement, their bond would deepen. He had respected her wishes by helping her find her studio, and since it was just a few minutes from the rue Campagne-Première, they could go on living and working together. The move was commented upon at the Coupole once they were seen walking back and forth between Man's studio, their daytime headquarters, and Lee's, where they spent nights together.

Her building still stands opposite the Montparnasse cemetery on the rue Schoelcher, a street lined with artists' studios whose façades range from curvilinear Art Nouveau to the streamlined Art Deco of her own, at the corner of the rue Victor Considérant. Coming from Man's, they went past the concierge's loge into the courtyard, where a white parterre and cobalt-blue tiled fountains create the geometric look of the period, before taking the tiny elevator to Lee's duplex. Together, they hung one wall with gramophone discs set like bright lozenges against the diagonals of the wallpaper and others with silver panels to reflect light. They set Man's handmade lamps on pedestals, turned a carpenter's bench into a table, and hung spectrum curtains. As a finishing touch, Man placed a hanging based on a Cocteau sketch behind the low, spacious bed. The look was "moderne" with a difference—"he liked the effect of the shimmering light and the changing as you moved about the room," she recalled.

How did Lee respond to having a place of her own, albeit one that had been found, decorated, and perhaps leased by her lover? (The record does not say whether Theodore paid the rent, or Man, or whether Lee earned enough to cover expenses.) "You should have seen my studio in Paris," she told a reporter, adding that she had decorated it herself.

Lee's architectural studies from this period focus on her building's spare geometry. Almost constructivist in their emphasis on form, they convey her feeling for the play of fullness and void, interior and exterior. In one, a canted view from an upper story plunges us down into the tiled courtyard while at the same time patterns made by the parterre, the quoins at the building's corners, and the shadows thrown onto the balcony complicate our orientation. Depth is simultaneously suggested and denied; perspective is diminished by the diagonal lines leaning outward in opposite directions. It is hard to say where we are.

A companion image looking out one of Lee's windows seems more conventional. Pattern does not flatten space as dramatically; the angle of vision seems straightforward. Yet the gaze is blocked by the background: the opposite wall and another window, itself impenetrable. What looks like a familiar device—a window used as an internal frame—contains a reverie on what can and can't be seen through such an opening, where the ironwork separating the small panes inside the frame segment the composition.

The most atmospheric of these formal studies, a shadowy image of a walkway topped by the alternating darks and lights of an ironwork railing, similarly complicates the contest between surface and space that is the hallmark of modernist photography. The eye, disoriented by the deep shadows, darts about in search of an exit, but is unsure which way leads out. The brooding quality and the railing's delicate tracery recall Atget, as if she had absorbed his aesthetic into her new perspective.

Not all of Lee's Paris photographs are unsettling. An image of rattan chairs plays their interwoven darks and lights against the shadows they cast on the pavement; in another, the Eiffel Tower becomes an overlap of metallic circles and spokes. These early photographs surprise the viewer with familiar shapes seen out of context or from odd angles—as if for the first time.

∽

Lee's spirits improved once she moved to her studio, Jacqueline Barsotti observed. She often strolled down the Boulevard Raspail to the Coupole and made her way to the bar, where Kiki's group clustered in the musky atmo-

sphere of American cigarettes, turpentine, and perfume. But despite her overtures, the group did not warm to her. Kiki's friends crowded together on the
banquette to dissect the latest exhibitions and love affairs, but when Lee
walked in, conversation ceased. While the usual response to a new arrival was
to squeeze together more tightly, they never made room for her. Lee did not
grasp the codes of bohemia, nor did it occur to her to buy drinks for all—
although (they thought) she could afford to do so. "What was hers was hers
alone," Jacqueline observed much later.

Kiki's circle resented Lee's "American" qualities, but Jacqueline—herself
something of a *"femme moderne"*—found them fascinating. A statuesque
beauty with a mane of blond hair, Jacqueline had modeled for her father
before being discovered by Montparnasse. Foujita and Kisling had painted her
portrait; Man photographed her with her hair streaming out behind her like a
blaze of light. She was considered a *lionne*—a woman who sets the style—
despite her chaste home life. A regular at Jules Pascin's costume parties, where
guests disported in states of undress, Jacqueline lived with her mother. Man
flirted with her during sessions, but behaved respectfully: the reputation of a
jeune fille had to be maintained—even in bohemia.

Jacqueline's status changed after she fell in love with a painter, and Kiki's
circle adopted her. As a member of this closely knit group, she criticized Lee's
arrivisme while studying her modus operandi. Lee made use of her beauty,
Jacqueline thought. "A phenomenon, even in Montparnasse," she asked for
and was given the clothes she modeled, the photographs she sat for, the recognition she craved. Calling on Lee one day in her studio, Jacqueline found her
filing her nails. When she admired her manicure kit, a large box with a hundred colors, Lee did not offer to share her bounty; Jacqueline felt that she was
too self-centered to think of pleasing a friend. Pondering Lee's success years
later, she added, "Everyone had to please her, but she was never pleased with
herself."

Lee found her closest friend in the social circles to which, in Jacqueline's
view, she had always aspired. Tatiana Iacovleva, a Russian émigrée known as
Tata, resembled Lee both physically and temperamentally. A tall blonde who
"strode into a room like a tribal war goddess," Tata was the daughter of St.
Petersburg intellectuals who claimed descent from Genghis Khan. Her force
of character made others take her at her own valuation. Shortly after her arrival
in Paris in 1925, she began posing for hosiery ads that showed off her long legs,
then modeling for *Vogue* under Huene's direction and declaiming Russian
verse with Elsa Triolet, Man's neighbor. Tata soon acquired legendary status
among the émigrés as Mayakovsky's muse. The Russian poet had fallen in love
with her during a trip to France and tried to take her back to Russia. Tata's
refusal to leave, some said, had been the cause of his suicide.

Like Lee, Tata caused a stir when she entered a room. A tale went round

Paris about the night when, finding herself across a crowded bistro from her friends, she walked the length of the room on the tabletops to join them. It was the sort of thing that Lee did, and admired in someone brazen enough to carry it off. Soon people pointed to Lee and Tata as the two most beautiful women in Paris. Though one wonders how each coped with the other's need to be the center of attention, they became friends. What Tata wanted was a title—a goal she achieved by marrying Bertrand du Plessix, the son of a French viscount. What Lee wanted was less clear. It involved not marriage but recognition by the overlapping worlds of art, fashion, and privilege she shared with her counterpart, the Russian "phenomenon."

In this sense, Frogue had more to offer than the Coupole. Huene's friend Solange d'Ayen, the fashion editor, brought to the magazine her prestige as the duchesse de Noailles. The duchesse handled temperamental couturiers and socially prominent models with the same courtesy. When Huene blew up at Horst in photographic sessions she took the young man to a café to sip champagne and discuss German poetry. Staffers said that she spent her life trying to make people forget her title.

In these years, the bolder members of the French aristocracy mixed with artists and writers. The new social rites—costume balls, experimental films, artistic soirées—thrown by this privileged group were regularly reported in Frogue, whose photographers were welcome at such events provided they dressed properly. Huene was at ease everywhere. After learning the Black Bottom from Bricktop, he taught it to his circle, who then rushed to see the lighting Huene designed to set off the red and black decor of Bricktop's new club. It became the fashion for young French aristocrats to meet there, at Le Boeuf sur le Toit, when Kiki was singing, or to create their own versions of the amusements found in such places.

It is easy to see why *le gratin révolté* (the rebellious upper crust) liked to rub shoulders with the avant-garde—Man Ray, Cocteau, Schiaparelli, Chanel, the dancer Serge Lifar, and the illustrator Christian Bérard. They were the stars of a new universe. While prestige and pleasure motivated this group's enthusiasm for private spectacles, some adhered to the old idea of patronage. The alliance between visionary artists and progressive members of society produced entertainments whose brilliance was made more poignant by their brevity, since each performance lasted just one night. And if some members of the aristocracy had doubts about their appropriateness in depressed times, for most, occasions for the display of wit and imagination were their own raison d'être. Hosts vied with one another in devising themes. Guests were to dress as Louis XV's courtiers or, for the Bal Proust, as characters in the book that dissected their class. They might be told to come as someone famous—politicians, writers, one another—or "as you were" when the hostess's limousine arrived at the door.

Man's entrée into French society had come through his success as a photographer. The Count de Beaumont, one of his first patrons, invited him to photograph his guests and said to wear a dinner jacket so that he would not look "professional." This evening led to invitations from the Comtesse Greffulhe, one of Proust's models, and the vicomte and vicomtesse de Noailles, Charles and Marie-Laure. (At Marie-Laure's futurist ball, Man photographed her sharkskin gown while guests in silver spacesuits glared at his outfit: a clothes bag with holes for his limbs and a cap topped by a propeller.)

Unlike Huene, whose background paralleled theirs, Man was never comfortable with these wealthy eccentrics. For Marie-Laure's 1929 Bal des Matières, guests were to devise clothes made of materials like cardboard, straw, raffia, or cellophane. The writer Maurice Sachs arrived in a suit of pebbles (uncomfortable when he sat down), the publisher Paul Morand wore Gallimard book jackets, Huene's friend Nimet Eloui Bey, a Circassian beauty, dazzled everyone in a robe made of triangular pieces of mirror, which *Vogue* featured the month before Lee made her début in its pages.

In June 1930, three years after Condé Nast introduced Lee to café society, Man introduced her to high society at the most beautiful soirée held that year—the best costume-ball season, all agreed, since before the war. The 1930 balls were "frequent, fast, and mostly foreign," Janet Flanner wrote in *The New Yorker,* and for this reason, represented "the true spirit of their time." Of these, the most ethereal was the Bal Blanc, hosted by Anna-Letizia Pecci-Blunt, the niece of Pope Leo XIII. The Pecci-Blunts asked their guests to wear white, to match the décor. Man was enlisted to do the lighting and film show, with Lee as his assistant.

The ball took place in the formal gardens of the Pecci-Blunt residence. Since everything was white—including the dance floor constructed on a platform over the pool and the outdoor stage—Man decided to use the scene as a backdrop on which to project images, including some hand-colored film by the French cinematographer Meliès, which he had found at the Paris Flea Market. He and Lee practiced throwing random frames on a sheet, and a few days before the ball set up a 35-millimeter projector in a room overlooking the garden. Taking care to appear more soigné, Man wore tennis whites and helped Lee select her outfit, a tennis dress and shorts by Mme. Vionnet, who often lent her clothes as a means of free advertising.

The evening was magical. Imagine a spacious garden lit by hundreds of lanterns and filled with pale, graceful figures gliding on the surface of a white platform. Upon this scene Man and Lee threw images, first the hand-tinted Meliès scenes, then a sequence in black and white. The effect on the white costumes was "absolutely stunning," Lee recalled, but it shocked some of the participants, on whose limbs "rude letters" suddenly appeared. "You'd reach up and grab an 'e' or an 'i,'" she added, while people tried to decipher the messages from on high.

Guessing the identities beneath the disguises was less difficult than read-

ing the moving script. Arthur Rubenstein was recognizable as an oriental
prince, the Baroness Rothschild and friends as the Empress Eugénie and her
court. The most memorable costumes appeared later, when five guests resembling statues appeared. This mock-classical *tableau vivant* grouped Marie-
Laure, the Prince and Princess Faucigny-Lucinge, Princess Nathalie Paley,
and the couturier Lucien Lelong in white masks and wigs devised by Cocteau
and Bérard. Their entrance was deemed a success, especially when the group
plunged into darkness as the lights went out.

But from Man's perspective, the evening was a disappointment. Lee spent
most of the time on the dance floor. "I was pleased with her success, but
annoyed at the same time," he recalled, "not because of the added work, but
out of jealousy." Man's account is more telling than he knew. "As the night progressed," he continued, "I saw less and less of her, fumbled with my material
and could not keep track of my supply of film holders. I finally ceased taking
pictures, went down to the buffet for a drink, and withdrew from the party.
Lee turned up now and then between dances to tell me what a wonderful time
she was having; all the men were so sweet to her." It annoyed him to watch her
début, made, in a way, at his expense.

Man had another reason to be jealous that spring, when Lee agreed to act in
Cocteau's new project, a film to be called *La Vie d'un Poète*. One night at the

Enrique Rivero helps Jean Cocteau paint eyes on Lee's lids for The Blood of a Poet.

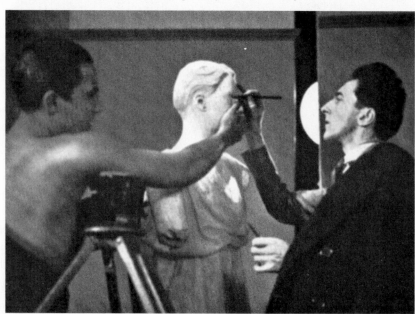

Lee in The Blood of a Poet

Boeuf sur le Toit, the poet stopped at their table and asked if they knew anyone who wanted to take a screen test. Having toyed with the idea since childhood, Lee said that *she* did. Man disapproved (the Surrealists condemned
Cocteau's politics along with his ingratiating ways), but thought it best not to
oppose her. Her test went well. She had the look Cocteau wanted for the
Muse—as if she had just stepped out of the Grecian tableau at the Bal Blanc.

Moving pictures were as much in vogue as costume balls among the aristocracy, who were then agog about the presence in Paris of Louise Brooks. It
didn't matter whether the films they sponsored were commercial. As in the
weeks of preparation for a ball, the important thing was to work closely with
artists like Cocteau or Man Ray. Charles de Noailles, whose ballroom housed
a private theater, had lured Man back to filmmaking in 1928, when he photographed the viscount's guests performing mysterious rites at his home in
Provence. (The film, *Les Mystères du Chateau de Dés,* combines Mallarmean
ideas of chance with shots of gymnasts in striped swimsuits.) But despite de
Noailles's enthusiasm, Man declined his offer to back another film. In 1930,
the viscount embarked on two different projects, the first with Luis Buñuel,
the second, a "talkie," with Cocteau. Regret over his decision to forgo filmmaking may have tinged Man's fury at Lee: she would be working closely with

the Surrealists' bête noir at a pastime that he, Man, had abandoned in order to spend more time with her.

Lee went ahead with her plans nonetheless. Each day at the film studio brought surprises. The mattresses lining the walls to keep out sound were full of bedbugs, which fell onto the set and bit the actors. The crystal chandelier, an important part of the decor, arrived in three thousand pieces and had to be assembled by hand. The script changed daily to accommodate the accidents of production. Enrique Rivero, the Brazilian who played the poet, had a scar on his back ("He'd been shot by his mistress's husband," Lee explained), which Cocteau covered with one of his trademark stars. When Féral Benga, the black dancer who played the angel, twisted his ankle, Cocteau declared him a limping angel. The director "liked it better that way," she added, "but people have read all kinds of things into it." Cocteau believed in working with chance: when the cleaners began sweeping up the studio, he told the cameraman to film the last scene through the dusty light.

Cocteau's talent for improvisation was less obvious in relations with the crew. "Elegant, shrill, and dedicated, [he] knew exactly what he wanted," Lee recalled. "He electrified everyone who had anything to do with the film." Few understood what it was about, however, except that the images showed where poems came from. In the first scene, the poet stands at an easel and draws a face, whose mouth starts to speak, then takes up residence in his hand. After a charged autoerotic moment—he uses the lips to caress his torso—the poet transfers the mouth to the plaster statue that comes to life as his muse, Lee's part. Like the Venus de Milo, she lacks arms yet sends him on a voyage through a mirror and into the hotel of "dramatic follies," where he observes a series of nighmarish scenes before returning to his room to smash the statue. The muse reappears as a woman in evening clothes at a card game played before a group of well-born spectators. In the final scene, she reverts to her former state and glides away while the poet's stand-in bleeds to death on the floor.

Whatever ambivalence Lee may have felt about the sinister side of her role she kept to herself. She had more to say about its discomforts: "My 'armor' . . . didn't fit very well: they plastered the joints with butter and flour that turned rancid and stank." To make her garments cling to her body, she was covered with a pomade that cooked under the lights. Cocteau painted dark eyes on her lids to turn her face into a mask and made her walk with her eyes closed, to give her performance a trancelike feeling.

The Blood of a Poet, Cocteau's definitive title, is a classic often seen in film courses. To us, it is an evocative period piece, an example of creative cinema on the theme of artistic identity. To Cocteau's peers, the film was either a revelation or a clever appropriation of avant-garde motifs. "It was the remarkable *Sang d'un Poète* that showed me that cinema could exist in Europe," Charlie

Chaplin told Cocteau. To de Noailles, the title of the last section, "The Profanation of the Host," struck an irreligious note, especially since Cocteau had edited the film to show him and his friends applauding the death of the boy on the floor beside the card players. Cocteau reshot these scenes at the viscount's insistence.

To the Surrealists, the film remained a scandal, though for different reasons. From their perspective, Cocteau had used Surrealist motifs—chance, dream states, the descent to the unconscious—in a pale imitation of their efforts to subvert society. Man had particular reason to take offense—had he not painted false eyes on Kiki's lids four years earlier in his *Emak Bakia*? Worse yet, Lee had gone along with Cocteau's use of her as *his* material. From Man's perspective, her "armored" torso belonged to him. "You don't lend out your mistress, do you?" he remarked on another occasion.

For Lee, the decision to dispose of her talents as she pleased was liberating, as if she too had gone through a looking glass to a place where all the elements of art flowed together. She had not betrayed Man in lending herself to Cocteau's vision. Rather, she had taken part in something that transcended the merely personal. "In a state of grace," she wrote years later, "we participated in the making of a poem."

∞

Man was annoyed with Lee for yet another reason. About the same time that she began work on *The Blood of a Poet,* she was collaborating with him on a project that was half erotic play, half home movie. This film, to which he gave the title *Self Portrait,* remained in Man's possession until his death. Its themes—identity, improvisation, the relations between artist and muse—resemble Cocteau's, yet are treated quite differently, except that both artists assumed their right to the muse figure as their material.

In this context, Man's anger at Lee's disloyalty is understandable. Their relationship was the most important of his life. Too reserved to entrust to words the feelings she aroused in him, he expressed them instead in the dreamlike sequences of his private cinema, where the female's dual role as stimulus to the imagination and the means of its expression links a heightened sexual charge to artistic innovation.

Before meeting Lee, Man had made Kiki's sexuality a central element in his scenarios. Light reflected from a window in *Le retour à la raison* (1923) caressed a headless torso—Kiki's—with shadowy stripes; the sequence of sleeping beauties in *Emak Bakia* (1926) ended with Kiki's eyes opening to show the second pair on her lids. In *L'Etoile de mer* (1928), inspired by Robert Desnos's poem on an artist's meeting with a *mystérieuse,* she played the mysterious woman: Man's fears about Kiki's role in his life—she left him after the film's completion—are reversed in the hero's dismissal of the woman. Yet anxiety about the female sex pervades *L'Etoile de mer* in the recurrent image of a starfish, whose predatory ways evoke that queasy male myth, the vagina dentata. Man said that he had abandoned film in 1929 because with the advent of sound, it needed serious backing. What he did not say was that Kiki's desertion removed the impetus from his engagement with the medium.

About that time, Man's feelings found expression in fantasies from which much may be gleaned. In 1928 Breton invited the Surrealists to a series of discussions entitled *"Recherches sur la sexualité"* (research into sexuality). The participants (mostly male) pondered such things as female orgasm and whether it mattered (Breton said it didn't), the number of orgasms achieved in a session (counts varied from two to twenty-seven), masturbation, impotence, and the relations between sex and love. Man joined Breton, Aragon, Boiffard, and the writers Benjamin Péret, Jacques Prévert, and Raymond Queneau at the second session, where voyeurism, homosexuality, fetishism, and sadomasochism were addressed. He kept quiet until Breton asked the group which sexual positions they preferred. Man said that he had no preferences, but added in an afterthought, "What intrigues me most is fellation of the man by the woman, because that's the thing that has happened to me most rarely."

Man said little until the group began recounting their sexual memories. He confessed that as an adolescent he had tried to penetrate "a little girl of ten" to whom he had promised a picture book "if she would show me her sex." The attempt failed when she complained that he was hurting her. His younger brother, who accompanied him, was more successful; the girl preferred him to Man. For those who knew how to listen, he had said enough. The conjoining of sex and pictures, of intercourse, pain, and failure, and of the wish for the thing that most intrigued him would be replayed in the private language of his objects, photographs, paintings, and cinema.

The following year, Man collaborated with Péret and Aragon on a pornographic book entitled *1929*, to which he contributed four images—one for each season—of a couple making love. Péret, a militant anticlerical, began the year with a poem in praise of "little girls who lift their skirts / and diddle themselves in the bushes." He extolled each sex's genitalia and the minor perversions before ending with an orgiastic vision of Parisians, animate and inanimate, engaged in rampant fucking—the baker's wife replaces him with a baguette while the Eiffel Tower buggers the Trocadéro. Since the speaker presented himself as a well-endowed cocksman, Man's photo for Spring shows a male torso positioned on top, the better to display his equipment.

Visually, things heat up in the second half of the year. Inaugurating Summer, Aragon's fairy tale for adults invokes full autonomy for *"la belle et la bite"* ("beauty and the prick"). These sexual parts come together in every possible location—"in a confessional at the Church of Saint Augustine . . . / before the eyes of a boarding school for young ladies . . . ," and in the full-scale orgy that ensues, where multiple couples enjoy fellatio in a profane version of the sacrament. This Bosch-like fantasy is introduced by Man's image for Autumn, a startling close-up of the woman's heavily rouged mouth performing the thing that, for Man, happened most rarely.

That autumn 1929 was printed in Brussels, then seized at the border in December due to its pornographic, anticlerical, and generally antisocial nature. The image for Winter depicts the darker aspect of taboo sex, buggery of the woman. The couple cannot be identified, but given the dates, it is possible that Lee posed for these pictures, which were taken in mid-1929—soon after the start of her liaison with Man. If this is the case, his obsessive interest in her rouged lips takes on yet another layer of meaning.

Lee *is* recognizable in *Self Portrait,* Man's erotic home movie begun about the same time and destined, presumably, for an audience of two. The fragment's alternative title, *Ce qui manque à nous tous (What We All Lack),* hints that what "we" all wish for is the activity featured in Man's image for the Autumn section of *1929.* After setting the scene in his studio, Man filmed Lee lounging naked in bed—blowing bubbles through a long-stemmed pipe. Next, he passed the camera to her, put the pipe in his mouth, and began blowing smoke into the bubbles, which swell and explode. Visibly excited, he exposes himself to her, and to the camera. In another sequence, they trade the camera back and forth in an erotic peekaboo. Man spies on Lee as she removes the covering from a large object, Brancusi's *Princesse X*—a sculpture known for provoking rude comments, since despite its title it resembles an erect penis. Following Man's directions (or improvising?), Lee caresses the sculpture and smiles, baring her teeth.

A few years later, Man gave solid form to this suggestive image—a ceramic pipe with bubble attached—to which he also gave the title *Ce qui manque à nous tous.* Although he often exhibited this object, he never mentioned its earlier, cinematic version, or his collaboration on it with Lee. Like her red lips afloat in *Observatory Time,* the pipe symbolized an aspect of their relationship—in this case, her sexual daring. His collaborator in more ways than one, she too enjoyed indecent images and lewd language. Man would have learned from Kiki, and Lee from him perhaps, the slang meaning of *pipe* and the infinitive, *piper—fellatio,* or, to put it vulgarly, a blow job. The most telling thing about Man's cinematic self-portrait is not that it stages the woman's reverence for the penis but that she appears to share his fantasy.

Despite Man's declaration that one did not lend out one's mistress, he was not averse to enlisting Lee in the staging of other people's fantasies. He introduced her to an American named William Seabrook, then enjoying some notoriety in the press. Seabrook's interest in the exotic—he had described what purported to be experiences of voodoo and cannibalism—extended to unusual sexual practices. He appointed Man his agent in dealings with the Surrealists, who hoped to publish photos of his African masks, and suggested costumes for the models in their photographic sessions. These included high heels, a black leather mask for the head, and a priest's outfit concealing "a wasp-waist hourglass corset finished either in some glittering fabric that looks like polished steel, or in black leather-like material to match the mask." After locating these items, Man took a series of shots to suit Seabrook's taste for pictures of the women he hired as sex slaves—with the resigned acceptance of his wife, Marjorie Worthington.

Seabrook was so pleased with Man's grasp of his fantasies that he asked him to design a high silver collar for Marjorie. Man outdid himself. The collar, hinged so that the wearer had to keep her chin up and studded with silver knobs, looked more like a choke collar than a piece of jewelry. Man photographed both Marjorie and Lee wearing the collar—Marjorie looking like an angry schoolmistress, Lee positioned below Seabrook with her eyes closed. At one level it was playacting, but at another, Seabrook's penchant for keeping women in chains made Man feel awkward, especially when he took Lee with him to babysit for one of them in the Seabrooks' hotel. The young woman, naked except for her loincloth, was to eat on the floor, Seabrook explained. Room service would bring whatever they wanted.

When dinner came they freed her, invited her to dine with them, and listened to her tales of kinky clients. Lee told Man that she knew about such things, having met a man who liked to whip women. "It was nothing new for her," Man recalled. "Nor for me either. I had whipped women a couple of times, but not from perverse motives." While Man recognized Seabrook's penchant for fetishism, he may not have understood his own.

Man's images of women bound, constrained, and missing their heads or other body parts bespeak his motives nonetheless. One of these was the exercise of power over his models. One day he asked Lee to pose for him with a new prop, an orthopedic mesh cast designed to immobilize the arm and shoulder. Knowing his habit of cropping negatives, Lee undressed to the waist, put her arm in the metal cast, and glared at Man. He had her pose for other pictures with the cast placed over her head like a mesh veil, to soften her expression. This series shows none of the quality of touch that informs his best portraits. Rather than intimacy, it registers the discord implied by the prop: another piece of metal jewelry, or armor, that restrains while protecting.

Like other men excited by the idea of lesbianism, Man had long been intrigued by scenarios with several women. Soon after his arrival in Paris, when a meeting with the couturier Paul Poiret led to a visit to the mannequins' quarters, he watched "beautiful girls with every shade of hair from blonde to black, moving about nonchalantly in their scanty chemises." Man longed to photograph them but they seemed "cool, almost forbidding." A few weeks later, he talked a model into bringing a friend to pose with her—explaining that he wished "to make some compositions for myself that had a little more variety." The women understood perfectly. "At my suggestion," he went on, "they took some intimate poses with arms around each other, making for rather complicated anatomical designs."

He may have been thinking of such designs when shooting another home movie at Lee's studio a few years later. He called it *Two Women*—hinting at a lesbian theme through his use of Gertrude Stein's title for her word painting of close female relationships. But unlike Stein's portrait, Man Ray's *Two Women* is pornographic. The women strike the kind of intimate poses thought to titillate a male audience. One stimulates a dildo, recalling Lee's caress of the Brancusi sculpture in *Self Portrait*; in another sequence, the women smile knowingly while taking positions for oral sex.

It is likely that Lee helped Man during the filming of *Two Women*, since the action takes place on the bed where she and he slept together. About this time, Man also photographed her mouth to heavily lipsticked mouth with another woman. It may have been exciting to capture such scenes from the other side of the camera. Perhaps she enjoyed seeing through masculine eyes.

Man's interest in female intimacy would also have been piqued when Tanja returned to Paris in 1930 to live with Lee—an arrangement that meant living with him as well. Tanja found work as a model and had her hair cut short, a coiffure that set off the gowns she wore on the runway and borrowed from the couturiers. Man would have been stimulated by the sight of these beautiful girls moving about the studio in their chemises. They posed for him dressed and coiffed alike. At one session, each wore the same satin gown with her hair parted in the middle and eyes heavily shadowed—like two priestesses of an obscure cult, two *belles dames sans merci*. Man left this portrait of Tanja unretouched, but traced lines across Lee's forehead, nose, and chin, as if defining his control over her features. A more informal study of the two young women dwells on their closeness—posed with their torsos spoon-fashion and hair sleeked back, they face the camera like complementary visions of the *garçonne* whose ambiguous allure inspired Man's fantasies.

Tanja had brought news from home. The Depression had dampened everyone's spirits, yet some were thriving despite the economy. Alfred De Liagre was making his mark on Broadway. Margaret Bourke-White, who had become famous overnight with her industrial photographs for the new glossy, *Fortune*, was having an affair with De Liagre's father. Condé Nast had lost much of his fortune in the crash, but found happiness with his young wife and their baby; Neysa McMein, having married, now spent less time riding elephants and more in her Long Island retreat.

Lee's parents, still comfortable despite the crash, were preoccupied with their health. In accordance with the diet advocated in Dr. William Hay's *Health via Food,* they ate only certain foods at each meal. They also made regular trips to Dr. Hay's sanatorium in the Poconos and underwent colonic irrigations in the hope of increased vigor. Florence recommended the diet to Lee even though she was unlikely to follow it in France, and sent her a copy of *Health via Food*—which told readers to avoid wine and worry.

Lee's brothers were following their respective paths. John, based in New Jersey, was an aviator at Teterboro Airport, where Lindbergh kept his plane; he often helped him bring it out of the hangar. (John would soon make the first cross-country flight in an autogiro, a precursor of the helicopter.) While still at school, Erik had helped his brother rebuild a wrecked plane formerly owned by a flying circus—a pastime that interested him more than his studies. At twenty, Erik planned to start as a freshman at Antioch, despite John's opinion of the college, but before settling down, to enjoy a visit to his sister—a gift from Theodore.

On his way over that summer, Erik fell in love with a lively brunette named Frances Rowley, known as Mafy, who planned to join him in Paris after her European tour. Toward the end of July, Lee and Man drove to meet Erik at Le Havre in Man's car; the oak-framed Warsaw sedan made as great an impression on the exuberant young man as his first French meal. Although Man decamped to the rue Campagne-Première while Erik stayed with Lee, Erik understood that they were lovers.

Like his sister, Erik was more interested in photography than in art. He was thrilled when Man demonstrated his recent inventions, a primitive tripod that was raised and lowered with a crank, and an improved version of his photoflood prototype—controlled with a rheostat to avoid burnout and arranged in banks to turn at different angles, which cast multiple shadows, like overlapping waves. Watching Lee develop Man's negatives or replace him on assignments, he saw that his sister had become a highly competent professional.

One day she took Erik to lunch with Huene, to his eyes the epitome of sophistication. When they ordered champagne, Erik was surprised to see the baron cut a piece of cheese into cubes and drop them one by one into the glass, to banish the bubbles—apparently without harming the champagne. They went back to the *Vogue* studio, where Huene photographed Erik, then brother and sister in a relaxed double portrait. Mafy met Man and Lee when she arrived in Paris. He seemed rather old and serious for a woman of twenty-three, she thought, but said nothing at the time.

Man and Lee often went their own way socially. Her friends from New York visited when in Paris. Henry Rowell, one of the Yale men, passed through in September on his way to an archeological dig. When Tanja met him at the door wearing red silk pajamas, she made such an impression that Rowell spent the

Paris, New York, Egypt

Solarized Portrait. Paris, 1930

Exploding Hand. Paris, c. 1930

A Strange Encounter. Paris, c. 1930

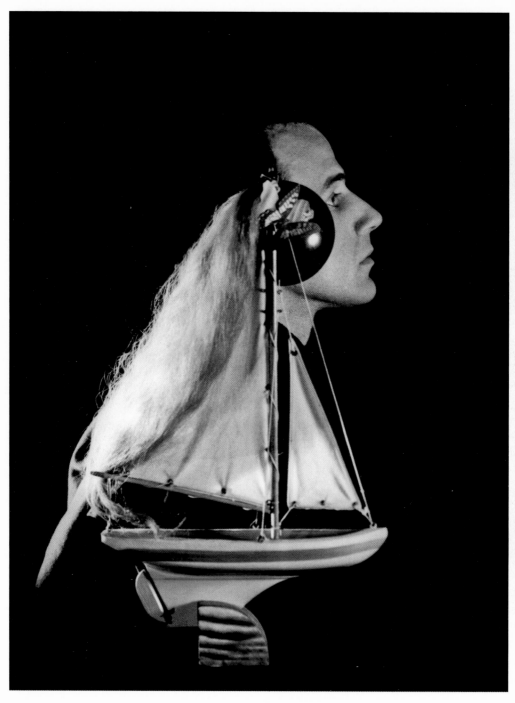

Joseph Cornell. New York, 1933

From the Top of the Great Pyramid. Giza, Egypt, c. 1938

Bus in street. Egypt, 1937

Mafy Miller. Cairo, c. 1937

Portrait of Space. Near Siwa, Egypt, 1937

rest of his time with her; they
planned to marry after his return
from Syria. That autumn, Huene
introduced Tanja to the Russian
émigrés, who were pleased to act
as escorts for an engaged model.
Tanja went out with Tatiana Iacovleva's friend, the decorator Zizi
Svirsky—a concert pianist whose
nerves kept him from playing in
public. Svirsky in turn introduced
her to Aziz Eloui Bey, an Egyptian
aristocrat with an eye for spirited
women. His wife, Nimet, the languid beauty who sometimes posed
for Huene, had caught movie
fever. (Nimet obtained a screen
test with Ernst Lubitsch, but having calmed her nerves with a number of drinks, ended her film
career before it began.) Tanja visited the couple at their villa, and
one evening, brought Aziz to
Montparnasse to meet Lee—who
asked after he left what Tanja saw in him.

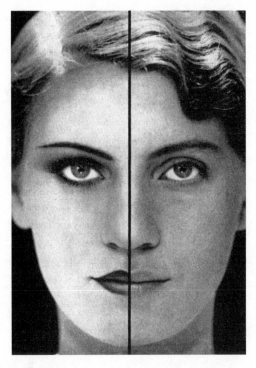

Lee with and without makeup (Hoyningen-Huene)

That autumn, while Lee worked on the final scenes of Cocteau's film and
did occasional fashion shoots, Tanja began modeling for Frogue. Her piquant
looks suited the new fashions. (The caption beneath her image in the November issue notes her "youthful charm" in a Chanel gown.) Huene photographed
Lee and Tanja together for a feature on the art of makeup. "Every woman can
be the artisan of her own beauty," it began. To illustrate this claim, Huene shot
each of them with half her face made up and half untouched—the fair and
dark versions of "refined womanhood." In October, de Brunhoff ran a feature
on Cocteau's film, with photos of the poet painting false eyes on Lee's lids and
of the controversial last scene. He selected a photograph of Lee for the editorial page, as if she typified his ideal, "the difficult art" of elegance.

A woman who is photographed often may look with detachment on
images of the female form. In reaction to her years of modeling and Man's
obsession with her person, Lee took few self-portraits. One day in her studio
she draped a dark scarf around her neck to contrast with her light blouse and
the darker background. After setting the shutter release, she sat opposite the
camera, looked to the side and, at ease, took her picture. This reflective self-

portrait must have pleased her: she signed it in French, "Lee Miller *par* Lee Miller"—not, for once, by someone else.

Given her close collaboration with Man and his continuing influence, it is instructive to compare Man's portraits of Tanja with Lee's during the time of their ménage à trois. In one, Man shot a tight close-up of the young woman with her hair flowing back from her head and solarized the negative, making her one more in a series of solarized women. Lee took a different approach. She enveloped her friend in a large swath of fabric, arranged the lighting to deepen the shadows, and took the picture of her head and torso from below. The result shows a woman lost in thought, troubled, perhaps, by her dark reflection.

Lee asked Tanja to sit for her again. The pose she had in mind was unusual—quite possibly an idea devised with Man, since Lee's sketches for the pose were found among her papers. Tanja was to stand behind a chest of drawers on which were placed a volume and a bell jar. Only her head would be visible. After putting her chin on the book, Tanja closed her eyes and waited while Lee photographed her behind the bell jar. The pose made her uncomfortable; the result, more so. Her head seems to float in the glass container like a specimen, something captured on an expedition. In another shot from the same session, the eerie quality is enhanced by the blindfold placed around her eyes: the woman can be seen but cannot return the gaze. Her encased head, which has Sadeian overtones, became another in the series of images—like Lee's lips—to which Man would return and make his own.

In the meantime, Man met regularly with the Surrealists, whose complicated schisms were fracturing the movement. That year, Breton purged twelve of his apostles for failing to toe the party line. While Man kept his distance, he supported Breton's attempt to align Surrealism with the Communist International in his new magazine, *Le Surréalisme au service de la révolution*—a mixture of "paranoia criticism" by Salvador Dalí, anticlerical and antisocial poems by Aragon, Eluard, and Péret, images of women (hysterical or ecstatic) from postcards and movie stills, homages to such diverse writers as Lewis Carroll and the Marquis de Sade, and Man's latest photographs.

The inaugural issue, appearing in July 1930, featured Breton's declaration of solidarity with Moscow. His second contribution, a Surrealist fable entitled "Once upon a (Future) Time," seemed to contradict the first: it pledged the movement's fealty to the imagination, in his view a vast mental palace where visions arise to "lead the world forward." Breton imagined this palace as a chateau outside Paris where men could come and go at all hours and where *jeunes filles* who had "distinguished themselves in some scandal . . . or by the strangeness of their spirit or beauty" were invited to live, although sexual activity was forbidden. Like so many storage batteries, these girls were the raw material for creativity. To illustrate the fable, Breton ran Man's photo of Lee's head in the orthopedic cast above a caption identifying her as one of the *jeunes filles*. The image implies her acquiescence in the role of stimulus to the male imagination—at a time when the idea of her "belonging" to Man heightened the tensions between them.

The magazine's October issue, an homage to Sade, would have fanned the flames of their disagreement. It included a letter by the marquis, essays on his work, and passages from Sade that, to the Surrealists, proved his stature as the seer of absolute freedom. Breton ran the photo of Tanja under glass as illustrative material, with the title *Hommage à D. A. F. de Sade* and the credit to Man. In this hyperexcited context, the photograph took on meanings that go beyond Surrealist fantasies about women's complicity in their own subordination. It hints at the woman's imprisonment, but also her decapitation: so much for females who tried to use their heads. Lee noted years later that her images sometimes appeared under Man's name. Whatever the nature of their collaboration, this use of Tanja's image made the point that it was meant to depict. Beautiful girls, however distinguished, were so much material for masculine fantasy.

In September, when the Sade issue of Breton's magazine was being put together, Man was still angry with Lee about her work with Cocteau, who was then completing *The Blood of a Poet*. It would have been some comfort when the movie was shelved after becoming entangled with the scandal that erupted over *L'Age d'or*, the de Noailles's other film project. This subversive classic provoked riots at its first showing—an outcome foreseen by Breton, who prepared inflammatory program notes and decorated the lobby with art by Dalí, Arp, Ernst, and Man. But the response was more than he bargained for. Right-wing gangs, the "Patriots' League" and the "Anti-Jewish Youth Group," came to the screening armed with crowbars. After they threw ink at the screen, attacked the audience, and slashed the art, the conservative press denounced the film as the work of Jews and Bolsheviks. Within a few days, it was banned. De Noailles faced excommunication due to the film's sacrilegious nature and had to resign from his club. *The Blood of a Poet* would not be shown for two years, until outrage over *L'Age d'or* died down.

The Surrealists soon published a tract in the film's defense, to which Man gave his signature. It warned about the consequences of compliance with right-wing tactics: "Is not the use of provocation to legitimize an intervention by the police a sign of fascistization [sic]," the authors asked; the film's suppression in the name of family, religion, and country had as its aim "the destruction of all those forces against the coming war." Lee understood the reasons for Man's concern: as an avant-gardist, a foreigner, and a Jew, he was a target. But there is no trace of her involvement in the "affaire" over *L'Age d'or*. Her mind was on other things.

In December, as the scandal was reaching its height, Theodore telephoned to say that he was in Sweden and asked Lee to join him. They had not seen each other for a year and a half. Lee arrived in Stockholm on December 17 when (Theodore's diary notes) the thermometer registered minus three degrees centigrade. They spent the day at the Grand Hotel, then arranged for him to move to a room adjoining hers. His diary records dinners with business associates, evenings at the opera, and a party where thirty guests were invited "on account of Elizabeth." There are also entries about photo sessions. Judging by the images from this time, Lee slipped into her familiar role. In one of Theodore's nude studies, she is again the nymph and her father the observer, gazing down at her as she sits, or poses, in the gleaming bathtub. What Sweden meant to her at this point is not known, nor can much be said about their relations except that she looks at ease in Theodore's photos.

After celebrating the new year, they traveled to Hamburg, where (Theodore wrote) they shared room 231 at the Atlantic Hotel. Back in Paris they dined with Tanja; Theodore arranged to have Lee's teeth recapped, bought her a taffeta gown at Mainbocher's, and returned with her for fittings. A few days later, Man returned from Cannes, where he had been organizing a show of his work. The two men reached an understanding, no doubt because each respected the other's scientific bent. Man invited Theodore to use his studio, where they took each other's portraits. Theodore persuaded Tanja to pose; he joined Lee and Man in a photographic session with two hired models ("Selena, a blond Italian and Rita, a brunette Russian," he noted). Within a short time he, Lee, and Man were taking their odd triangular relations for granted.

Theodore relished the opportunity to do as many nude studies as he could schedule. During his two weeks in Paris he had more sessions with Tanja, several with Lee nude or in her Mainbocher, and one with Natasha, Man's new assistant. He also liked scenes of the kind that Man favored, with two or three women. On January 20, after several nudes of "Te Te, Tanja, and Tytia" (a model) cavorting on Lee's bed, he shot one of Lee and Tytia in a position that stops just short of lesbian sex. (He also photographed Lee and Tanja in pajamas having breakfast in bed, and Lee's Martiniquaise maid, Caroline, in her uniform.) Nearly sixty, Theodore was so much at home in bohemia that he accompanied Lee to Kiki's latest performance, had lunch with Tristan Tzara, and enjoyed a reunion with Medgyès.

One wonders what went through Man's head as he watched Lee and her father. It was obvious that they were close; her trust in him was implicit. In Theodore's nude studies of Lee in her bedroom, even the most contorted poses—she arches back over the bed or lies with her legs up the wall, pubic region exposed—did not cause her difficulty. Man made the best of things by turning their intimacy into a series of portraits in which Lee's feelings for Theodore are enacted in her pose. She sits on his lap with her arms around his neck, nestles on his shoulder, gazes tenderly at him, and rests her head on his as if she felt utterly safe. Allowing Man to see her this way may have answered any questions: it implied that there was nothing to hide.

Man's portraits of their relationship also show the generous side of his nature. He may have been moved to witness the softening of her features as Lee sat with her father. Perhaps, accepting that he would never be as close to her as he wished, he took comfort in the thought that he had the regard of the man who held the central place in her affections—whose position he occupied in some respects as her mentor and support. One can imagine the welter of emotions on January 22, 1931, when Tanja, Man, and Lee drove to St. Lazare station with Theodore to put him on the boat train to Cherbourg.

The winter of 1931 marked a turning point for both women. In February, Tanja married Henry Rowell at the American Cathedral of Paris, with Lee as her attendant and a Yale classmate of Rowell's as best man. While Tanja's departure for the United States left a vacuum, Lee saw no reason to leave. Her photographic career was taking off: sitters now came to *her* for their portraits, and she was about to start work at Elstree Studios, the British branch of Paramount Pictures, a position that would mean frequent trips to London over the next six months.

Having absorbed as much as she could on Cocteau's set, she felt ready to go round the other side of the camera in *Stamboul,* a drama set in the Middle East. The first version, based on a French novel, had been filmed at the Joinville studios outside Paris. Paramount planned an English version with the director, Dimitri Buchowetski, a Russian who made the switch from silents to talkies that year with this tale of love in exotic places. (The plot justified the Turkish locale by having the heroine, a German countess, fall for a French officer on a trip to Istanbul; when her husband tries to catch the lovers, the officer kills him to protect the countess.) The film crew was as international as the plot. Margot Grahame, the countess, was a pouty siren known as "the Aluminum Blonde"—Britain's answer to Jean Harlow. The most intriguing cast member was Abraham Sofaer, the Burmese actor who played Mehmid Pasha, the potentate. After *Stamboul,* Sofaer would play more Turks, Arabs, Jews, and Indians in his long career; offscreen, he behaved like an old-school-tie gentleman.

Lee worked closely with the director, filming backgrounds, stand-ins, and images to be edited into the movie later. She also took publicity shots of the principals. Her portraits for *The Bioscope,* a film revue, show the Aluminum Blonde looking reflective and Mehmid Pasha in uniform. Although *Stamboul* in no way resembled Cocteau's celluloid poem, it had a charm of its own. "I love extravagant and gorgeous 'historicals'—melodramas, ambiguity, inaccuracy and all," Lee wrote, "as long as the heroes are close-up close and the background has panoramic splendour." Such films were lovable for their "strident nonsense."

Wanting to have her cake and eat it too, Lee relied on Man for long-distance emotional and professional support. In response to her first letter from London he answered technical questions, then told her about his dinner the previous night, by the Seine. "I haven't been so romantic since my teens," he wrote, "with the moon shining on pale green row-boats moored to the shore, I got away from the crowd for ten minutes and walked with you arm in arm along the edge of water." He "adored" her for writing to him so soon. "How big and empty the bed is," he continued. "I throw my arms and legs in every direction."

Man rushed to renew his passport after Lee asked him to visit. But on replaying their phone conversation, he grew suspicious. Was the "old pal" she mentioned casually keeping her company? Was she telling half-truths about this man's date of departure? She must tell the truth "down to the slightest detail"—even if it would hurt. "Bringing everything out in the open is the one real test of endurance," Man went on. This strategy—accepting Lee's affairs (real or imagined) as long as he knew about them—would come to seem like a desperate move, but for the time being, he promised, he would "try to be everything you want me to be toward you, because I realize it is the only way to keep you."

Lee returned to Paris when her schedule permitted. In some ways nothing had changed, except that Man was worried about finances. His Cannes exhibition had not been a success, the Depression had cut into business, and although he had several propositions, nothing was definite. The one bright spot had been a visit from the New York art dealer Julien Levy. Levy had married Mina Loy's daughter, Joella, in 1927 and with her help started the first American gallery to feature avant-garde photography. He was taking some of Man's images to New York for upcoming shows, including one on Surrealism, but Man would not see much in the way of returns until the following year. In the meantime, it was hard for him to accept the change in relations with Lee. "I've had only one fear all these last months," he told her, "that your wanderings might be dulling your emotion for me, while mine has been growing."

On her return to England, Man told her that he would let her "go through with your job in peace." But his deeper wish, to hold on tight, put him in an untenable position. More than his letters, Man's erotic images of Lee from this period express his desire to end the "dissipation of forces" her independence caused him. He could hold on to her in art if not in life. That spring, a commission let him give shape to his feelings for Lee while improving his finances. The Compagnie Parisienne de Distribution d'Electricité, a municipal utility, hired him to produce an illustrated brochure about electricity—a limited edition for their best customers. Man could treat the theme however he wished as long as his images extolled electric power. A short poetic text by the writer Pierre Bost would accompany his photographs.

During one of Lee's breaks from filming, Man enlisted her in the project as muse and as second-in-command—perhaps to show that they were still a team. But while Lee was his partner, she was also the raw material for his images. He planned to treat electricity as a strong but invisible current—like erotic energy, though more easily tamed. For the first image, *Electricité,* Man photographed Lee in a Venus de Milo pose. After cropping from neck to pubes, he made a second, enlarged image to put beneath the first, photographed them together, then drew undulating white lines across her torso— the *rayons,* or rays, emanating from their source. The pun would have been obvious, as would Bost's allusions to Electricity as a "dangerous Goddess," but also a "Beast" whose power is captured in Man's photographs, if not in his life. Another in the series, *Salle de Bain,* superimposes a white line connected to a cylinder on Lee's headless torso; the image shows the lady of the house at her toilette—tamed, yet radiating the energy that makes her so alluring.

The brochure, also called *Electricité,* was a collaboration in which "curious things happened," Lee recalled. "I think the use of a nude—that was me— was a little tough for the officials," she explained. "We were pretty shaken because we went and took a beautiful picture one night of the Place de la Concorde (I borrowed someone's roof to do it from) and discovered the whole thing was lit by gas! There was no end to th[e] complications."

The complications Lee did not discuss included her attraction to other men. Tanja's friend Zizi Svirsky invited her to his parties, where Russian émigrés mingled with artists, models, celebrities, and aristocrats. Zizi had been in love with Tatiana Iacovleva. After her marriage, he transferred his attentions to Lee and courted her with the promise of introductions to important people. Resorting again to half-truths, she took Man to one of Zizi's soirées as if it were just another party. Quick to sense the current between them, Man went on the attack. Zizi was too old, he argued (ten years older than he was), and though he had "enormous experience [and] marvelous Russian brains," he was interested neither in her work "nor in any new developments." (The irony of having as a rival a man of "enormous experience" whose name meant "penis" in French slang would not have been lost on Man, whose references to his own name and diminutive stature run throughout his oeuvre.)

Zizi's motivation was "selfishly human" compared with his own, he continued. "You started off on a different career with me," Man told her, "and now all the simplicity of it has been ruined." Barely able to contain himself, he asked:

> Would you like to know how my attitude compares with his? I have loved you terrifically [sic], jealously; it has reduced every other passion in me, and to compensate, I have tried to justify this love by giving you every chance in my power to bring out everything interesting in you. The more you seemed capable the more my love was justified, and the less I regret-ted any lost effort on my part. . . . I have tried to make you a complement to myself, but these distractions have made you waver, lose confidence in yourself, and so you want to go by yourself to reassure yourself. But you are merely getting yourself under someone else's control.

A powerful man's companion may find it hard to accept the idea of herself as his complement. At twenty-four and forty, Lee and Man were in different stages of life. Loath to remain in his shadow, she was unwilling to accept a relationship unless it indulged her wishes. While Man was planning their return to New York as a photographic team, Lee worked to establish herself as a portraitist. Sitters were now knocking at her door. She had "a run of roy-alty"—the Maharanee of Cooch-Behar, the Ranee of Mandi, the Duchess of Alba—then the literary set, actors, and socialites. She was not about to waste this opportunity.

During one of her trips to London, Man wrote in despair that they would have to separate—unless she gave him her preference and stopped worrying about "the material problem." "We have already managed together for a long enough period," he went on. "It hasn't been so bad if you are willing to adapt yourself to our limits. . . . I ask nothing better in the future than to pool every-thing with you." If she meant to continue in movies, he pleaded in another letter, "you must arrange to do work for Joinville if possible in the future, and you must arrange to live as my wife, married or not. I cannot see you in any other way."

That Lee could not see herself this way must have been obvious on her return in August, when she spent most of her time at work. Distinguished Americans in Paris came to have their portraits done: the New York publisher Donald Friede, the actress Claire Luce, who posed with her Siamese cats, and Charlie Chaplin, who lay down on the floor after posing beneath a large Art Nouveau chandelier that, in her striking image of him, seems to spring from his head. Given Lee's taste for an energetic sexual life, she may have joined him on the floor after taking his picture. Both of them enjoyed the session. Thinking about it years later she burst out laughing: "Charlie said he had never had such a good time in his life as he had with what he called my *surréaliste* photography," she recalled.

In December Lee joined Chaplin and his friends at Saint Moritz, the most fashionable ski resort in Europe. Each year *Vogue* devoted several pages to the celebrities who went there to recover from their social lives. For those who were not content to ski, skate, sled, or toboggan, a more relaxed version of Paris nightlife could be pursued in the jazz clubs and restaurants at the top of the vertiginous ski runs. Stars like Gloria Swanson and Gary Cooper vacationed there, the Prince of Wales was seen on the slopes, the ski instructors were ingratiating. Intrigue and romance flourished. Through Huene (who was on assignment in Saint Moritz), Lee became reacquinted with Aziz Eloui Bey and his wife, Nimet—who prided herself on her friendships with Rainer Maria Rilke and, more recently, Chaplin. The actor's stunts kept their group in stitches. Having just completed *City Lights,* he ate dinner as if he were blind, wrapped Nimet's head in a table napkin and proceeded to extract an imaginary tooth (a sugar lump) from her mouth, then posed for Huene before a snowy replica of his alter ego, the Little Tramp.

Had members of the group known what was happening, they would have been surprised to learn that Eloui Bey was falling in love with Lee, who found that she could, after all, see something in this cultivated Egyptian. Nimet— whom *Vogue* interviewed that year about her beauty regime—spent mornings accentuating her eyes with kohl and making her hair gleam, the better to resemble her heroine, Garbo. Lee photographed Nimet as *"la belle Circassienne";* coolly beautiful in her turban, pearls, and velvet robe, she stares at the camera, unaware that the woman behind it is her rival. Lee's affair with Aziz would destabilize his marriage and her relations with Man—whose request for the truth, down to the slightest detail, she failed to honor. Perhaps she felt that under the circumstances, it would have been disastrous to bring everything into the open.

The Millers, Thanksgiving 1932. Standing: Erik and John; seated: Florence,
Theodore, and Lee (Theodore Miller)

Chapter 7
The Lee Miller Studio in Manhattan

(1932–34)

T he new year marked the end of Lee's apprenticeship. But while it seemed that she *could* make her way as a photographer, the overlapping social and artistic worlds from which she drew support were closing in on her. Her private life was a tangle of conflicting alliances. Her liaison with Aziz called for discretion; more than a few half-truths were required to keep the peace with Man while she moved back and forth among the émigré set, the Frogue family, and the influential Americans abroad wanting to be "done" by Lee Miller.

Representatives from all of these worlds converged at the Théâtre du Vieux-Colombier on January 20, 1932, for the long-delayed première of *The Blood of a Poet*. While a cross-section of fashionable Paris—including the writers Julien Green, André Gide, and Jacques Maritain; Serge Lifar; and Cocteau's bartender from Le Boeuf sur le Toit—were in attendance, Breton's decision to boycott the evening put Man in an awkward position, since he was close to Breton but Lee was officially his mistress.

Tensions ran high as Cocteau, his hair artistically disheveled, made his way to the stage. His aim, he stammered, had been to capture creativity on celluloid. Following the example of Hollywood (Cocteau pronounced it

"Olioude"), he had used tricks to create what they were about to see. One such trick, he said with a nod to Lee, required his leading lady to close her eyes and walk as if blind: "This unreal way of walking," he explained, "adds to the unreality of her character." Moments later, Cocteau turned again to "Mademoiselle Miller," whose acting was "admirable." Indeed, while all his actors were admirable, he had chosen them not for their looks, "but for their moral attitude, since in a movie, the faces are huge and the eyes reveal all." As Cocteau summed up the muse's effect on the poet—"the statue comes to life, takes revenge, and involves him in ghastly adventures"—Lee may have wondered how much her own eyes revealed.

While Cocteau's film was dividing the Paris art world, another work appropriating Lee's vision was on display in New York in Julien Levy's new exhibit, "*Surréalisme*"—"a bewildering and splintering sense of conglomerate nonsense," according to the *New York Times*. Levy's choice of paintings, photographs, and collages by such artists as Ernst, Dalí, Picasso, Cocteau, Atget, Boiffard, and Man Ray provoked dismay in the gallerygoers, but the "objects" included in this controversial show (by Man, Marcel Duchamp, and Joseph Cornell) puzzled them even more. Man's *Boule de Neige,* the most disquieting of the lot, was a glass paperweight in which a cut-out image of Lee's eye, much enlarged, floated, then disappeared in a flurry of snowflakes when the ball was shaken. *The Blood of a Poet* had enhanced her "unreality" by making her walk with her eyes closed, but *Boule de Neige* removed that which a photographer needs even more than her camera. "Perhaps the 'eye' of Lee Miller was the photographer's eye," Man's biographer writes; "by separating it from her body, Man Ray was reclaiming authority over her sovereignty as an artist."

To New Yorkers, works like *Boule de Neige* produced the psychic "splintering" said to result from Freudian raids on the unconscious. To Parisians, Surrealism was an assault on the body politic. In the uneasy climate of the early 1930s, as France succumbed to economic depression and antirepublican groups espoused fascist tactics, even the nonaligned could not ignore the growing hostility to foreigners, Jews, and Communists. Man followed these developments closely. "It is some time now that the crisis has hit me," he told his sister. "I make it a point never to complain as everyone else around here does plenty," he went on. But his spirits were low, especially after Arthur Wheeler's death in a car crash.

While Man pondered the idea of returning to New York with Lee as his partner, she had other things on her mind. Her romance with Aziz, who spent half the year in Paris and the other half in Cairo, offered a way out of the impasse in which she found herself. Unlike Man, her new lover did not try to control her. Aziz was supportive and broad-minded. He was also good-looking and spoke English fluently, having studied engineering in Liverpool. His father, a well-known ophthalmologist, had run the Cairo Board of Health; his mother's father had been the Egyptian commander of expeditionary forces. He and Nimet lived together while maintaining a de facto separation, made possible by their not having children. And since Nimet's well-being required baths in Vichy water, walks in the Bois de Boulogne, and naps before soirées (as well as facials, manicures, and pedicures), she may not have noticed the change in her husband's spirits after their return from Saint Moritz. When friends mentioned her reputation as one of the world's great beauties, Aziz often replied, "She should be; she spends all her time painting her face."

Much can be gleaned about Aziz's feelings for Lee from his letters, which combine a lover's passion with a parent's tenderness. Nearly twenty years older than she, Aziz accepted her contradictions—the vulnerability beneath the surface, the need for a secure base from which to stray. Temperamentally, she was Nimet's opposite. While his wife held court on a chaise longue, Lee dashed all over Paris on assignments. Nimet ate one meal a day to control her weight; Lee enjoyed life's pleasures. Aziz may have supposed that she would bear him the heir he lacked. It is not known when he told Nimet of his wish for a divorce. Judging by the tales of suicide threats passed down in their circles, she probably made attempts on her life.

By spring, when Aziz returned to Cairo, he and Lee were in love. Man was furious: all Montparnasse seemed to know that she had left him. According to Julien Levy, who arrived in April on a gallery scouting trip, Man, already "half-dead with sorrow and jealousy," had gone on a liquid diet to purify himself but was said to be packing a gun—with which "in default of the Egyptian, [he] was threatening any other rivals." Since meeting Lee the year before, the young art dealer had wanted to know her better: "Her spirit was bright," he wrote, as were "her mind, her photographic art, and her shining blond hair."

Earlier that year, Julien had included Lee's work in his Modern European Photographers show, along with images by Man, Kertesz, Ilse Bing, Florence Henri, and Moholy-Nagy. As a group, their work challenged the belief in American art circles that photography was an art suited to realistic depictions of the industrial age but little else. Unexpectedly, the *New York Times* praised both Man's solarized portrait of Lee and Lee's shot of a woman's manicured hand grasping the curls at the back of her head; in the critic's opinion, these images transcended the purely "virtuoso" nature of the exhibition. Another critic described Man's profile of Lee as if she were his material, then added that she had, nonetheless, contributed "two of the most striking pictures in the show, the Greek statue with its dramatic spotlight effect and the study of a pink-nailed hand embedded in curly blonde hair." However matters stood between them, Man and Lee were linked by their work and their relations with Julien.

Just before sailing, Julien lent prints by both photographers to the Brooklyn Museum's spring show, International Photographers. This comprehensive

summary of contemporary camera work included both European experimentation (photograms, images turned upside down, and negative prints by such
artists as Henri, Moholy-Nagy, and Maurice Tabard); American industrial
studies by Abbott, Bourke-White, and Walker Evans; fashion shots by Steichen, Huene, and Beaton; and work by Tina Modotti and Imogen Cunningham. That month, as Lee turned twenty-five, New York seemed to beckon.
Thanks to Julien, the way was being paved for her return.

Julien had hoped to shock New Yorkers into accepting modernist photography with Man's first American one-man show in April. The exhibition produced some tart coverage by *Time,* which called it an assortment of "nuts and
nudes" (the "nuts" included portraits of Lee, Brancusi, Picasso, and Nancy
Cunard). *Time*'s critic pooh-poohed Man's Paris reputation, called him "a
kinky-haired photographer" whose real name was "Emmanuel something," and
judged his work "not quite worth all the furor that friends have raised." As if
these slurs were not enough, he made innuendos about Man's relations with
Lee: "Also exhibited were assorted sections of his favorite model, Miss Lee
Miller, known as 'Lee-girl' to her intimates, widely celebrated as the possessor
of the most beautiful navel in Paris."

Lee was outraged. It might have been amusing to make her return to
America piecemeal—first her eye, then "assorted sections," and now, her
navel. But at this point, as her own work was becoming known, *Time* had
exposed her to ridicule. It was one thing to see one's midsection displayed in
Montparnasse and quite another to have it mentioned by unknown persons

Julien Levy, c. 1930

claiming to know about her private life. "Lee suddenly became very proper about her navel," Erik Miller recalled.

Man, more distressed for Lee than for himself, insisted on the need for an apology. Lee's reputation was safe because she came from a good family, he told Julien, but the unwanted publicity *could* damage her career. At the same time, Theodore went into action. He cabled Lee, consulted a lawyer, and sued for libel. By May, Joella, representing the gallery, and Theodore, representing the family, were at war with *Time*. The magazine agreed to run Theodore's response to the "offensive and quite untruthful reference" in their review and extended to "Miss Lee Miller, and her family, an apology for the inconvenience caused by the erroneous publication." The apology did not mention the financial settlement. "It was a chance to make some money," Erik noted though he could not recall the amount. "Lee was very happy."

It was also a chance to get out from under Man's shadow. That spring, as cables from Julien, Theodore, and Lee flew back and forth across the Atlantic, it was clear that her dealer was taking more than a professional interest. Julien, who was Lee's age, was mesmerized by the "bold, bright aura" surounding her. Lee was the kind of woman about whom "one would hope to sing '*Auprès de ma blonde . . . ,*' " he mused, the ellipsis suggesting what he had in mind.

On his second day in Paris, Julien spotted Lee on the Boulevard Raspail. They made a date to meet later at the Jockey Club. "It promised to be a most pleasant evening if I could charm her," he recalled. "And so it proved," the passage concludes. In May, while coping with Man's wrath and the *Time* brouhaha, Lee began an affair with Julien. Honored to be shown "the Paris that all artists and very few tourists then knew," Julien savored their evenings together, which often included drinks at the Café Flore (where she sipped *menthe à l'eau*), dinner at an out-of-the-way bistro, followed by more drinks at the Jockey, the Boeuf sur le Toit, and, in the early morning, Zelli's in Montmartre.

During the day, Lee went with Julien on buying trips and introduced him to artists. When they called on the illustrator André Dignemont, a surreal music emanating from his antique music boxes greeted them. Their host brought out his collection of old photographs—Nadars and Atgets—and choice examples of nineteenth-century pornography. After Julien filled three suitcases with his purchases, Dignemont gave him a bonus: a volume attributed to Pierre Louys, whose erotic vocabulary included "various *argots* and incredible improvisations" hitherto unknown to the young New Yorker. Years later, Julien boasted in private about trying some of the improvisations with Lee.

Julien's published memoir fails to say how he handled matters with Man, what Man knew of his relations with Lee, how the situation affected their business dealings, or whether he said anything to Joella. Perhaps he too professed the Surrealist disdain of monogamy, or simply behaved like other men when their wives are across the ocean. And although Mina Loy might have been expected to upbraid him on Joella's behalf, his mother-in-law (with whom he stayed when in Paris) condoned his affair with Lee—reasoning that he had married young and, consequently, needed to sow some wild oats.

Over the course of the summer, Lee and Julien socialized with Mina, Lee took her portrait for Mina's upcoming show at Julien's gallery, and Julien—following in Man's footsteps—made home movies of both women. Mina, whose rivalry with Joella and affection for Julien would undermine their marriage, saw Lee as a surrogate daughter—a female artist of the younger generation and as such the antithesis of Joella, whose managerial skills made it possible for Julien to play at being a Surrealist but did not extend to creative work of her own. Characteristically, Lee took the complex bond between Julien and his youthful mother-in-law as lightly as she took their own relations, while counting on him to support her career.

Julien, excited to find himself in such racy company, took care to keep Lee amused. He had an artistic temperament and, from a European perspective, unlimited resources. (That he had recently come into the trust fund that underwrote his gallery was not lost on Lee's circle.) That summer, while shooting a series of cinematic portraits, he was a stimulating companion. After filming Mina at the Flea Market and capturing Lee's aura in a Cocteauesque sequence, he also filmed Ernst, Brancusi, and Léger in their studios. At the same time, he was looking to buy experimental movies like *The Blood of a Poet*, which he hoped to show at his gallery in homage to Cocteau and to the muse who inspired both men, though for different reasons.

When Julien learned that the still banned *L'Age d'or* would be screened at a small cinema in Vincennes, he invited Lee and Mina to the clandestine showing. "The surreptitious presentation added excitement to the performance," Julien wrote. Some of the right-wing extremists who had attacked the film two years earlier began brawls as soon as the projection started, shouting slogans like "down with the Surrealists" and "shit on the Sorbonne." Surprised to see that art could generate a furor, Julien decided to buy *L'Age d'or* as well. Seeing this scandalous film with the two women he most admired enhanced his sense that he was taking part in epoch-marking events, that avant-garde art "might be considered a moving factor in immediate politics."

Julien's Paris holiday, a heady blend of illicit love, banned art, and political passion, ended in September, when he sailed for New York. Along with his purchases—paintings, movies, flea-market finds, and erotica—Julien took a group of Lee's photographs. He planned to give her a one-woman show and place her work in other venues. One imagines that he encouraged Lee to join him in New York now that she had the settlement from *Time* and two prospective partners: Cliff Smith, Claire Luce's husband and heir to the Western Union fortune, and Christian Holmes, a Wall Street broker, had volunteered to finance her studio. Given her recent success as a celebrity portraitist, New Yorkers would seek her out; Dr. Mehmed Agha, the new art director of *Vogue,* was interested in her work.

But Lee was undecided. There was her understanding with Aziz, although it was on hold (from her perspective) while he was in Egypt. Arrangements had been made for her participation, with Man, in two European exhibitions that fall. (As planned, their photographs were shown at the Brussels Exhibition of Photography, with images by Germaine Krull, Moholy-Nagy, and Atget; this selection then traveled to Ghent for an exhibit organized by the Circle of Socialist Studies.) And she was about to make her debut in a new Surrealist magazine, *Le Phare de Neuilly*—probably due to Man's connections. To an observer of the photographic scene, her work had his imprimatur. It had developed under his aegis, in tandem with his own.

By September, it must have been clear to Lee that her mentor saw her as a threat. The violence implicit in the many works of art that cut her in pieces became explicit in another of Man's objects on the theme of vision. Some years before they met, Man had attached an image of an eye to a metronome; he called the work *Object to Be Destroyed*. During the summer of 1932, after her affairs with Aziz and Julien, Man replaced the image with Lee's eye, cut from one of his portraits, and gave the work a new title: *Object of Destruction*. As if warning her, he published a drawing of the object with instructions for its use: "Cut out the eye from the portrait of one who has been loved but is seen no more. Attach the eye to the pendulum of a metronome and regulate the weight to suit the tempo desired. Keep going to the limit of endurance. With a hammer well aimed, try to destroy the whole at a single blow."

Man reached the limits of endurance in October, when Lee booked her passage to New York on the *Ile de France*. Drawing her face in his notebook, he outlined her eyes and mouth, covered the page with her name—"Elizabeth Elizabeth Elizabeth Elizabeth Lee Elizabeth"—then printed on the reverse, "Accounts never balance one never pays enough etc. etc. Love Man." In case she missed the point, he folded the page around a second cutout of her eye— on the back of which he wrote in red:

POSTSCRIPT: OCT. II, 1932

With an eye always in reserve
Material indestructible. . . .
Forever being put away
Taken for a ride. . . .
Put on the spot. . . .
The racket must go on—
I am always in reserve.

Man dated this adieu the day of Lee's departure. After posting it, he walked to the Dôme in a downpour. Perhaps intending to prove that he no longer held himself "in reserve," he sat down beside Jacqueline Barsotti. "He seemed to have shrunk and not know where he was going," she recalled. When he hit the table with a gun and moaned, "I wish I were dead," she knew that he was desperate. Jacqueline took him outside; they walked round the Montparnasse cemetery in the rain for a last look at Lee's studio, then went back to Man's. Her account of what followed is worth quoting in full:

> He got out a pistol, a rope and other objects and started to arrange them for the now famous photograph of him in utter despair. In order to set the photograph up he asked me to pose in his place so that he could focus. Then we switched positions and he sat there with the gun pointing at his head and the rope round his neck. I was terrified because I had no idea if the gun was loaded or if he was actually going to shoot himself. Anything could have been possible, he was so distraught and I, myself, was upset. Anyway I took the picture and looking back on it, I felt it summed up the moment. He was utterly destroyed by her leaving him. He had lots of women but she was the one he wanted most. That might have had something to do with the fact that he couldn't have her.

Lee arrived in New York on October 17, 1932, to find reporters awaiting her. Looking pensive in a dark beret and fur coat, she smiled sweetly for the *World Telegram,* whose reporter called her the most photogenic of the "cargo of celebrities" on board. To a journalist who spoke of her early success as "one of the most photographed girls in Manhattan," she quipped that she would "rather take a picture than be one." Photography, she added, gave her "the joy I wanted from my work." The medium matched "the tempo and the spirit of today"—and, she implied, her idea of herself.

Erik and Florence greeted her at the pier; Theodore was away on business. They had arranged for her to stay in a Park Avenue hotel while she looked for a working and living space. In November, she rented a double studio at 8 East Forty-eighth Street, and with Erik, who was to be her assistant, drew up plans for a darkroom equipped with cypress sinks big enough for large format (8-by-10-inch) plates and, for the studio, remote-controlled lights rather than the cumbersome equipment in general use. Erik built everything to measure while Lee reactivated her contacts.

Being a celebrity had advantages, one of which was free publicity. Lee's appearance in the November *Vogue* reminded readers of her fame as an icon of elegance. Her sequined Lanvin dress, the copy gushed, was "smartest worn as

Miss Lee Miller wears it in the photograph, without a single ornament." The following month, in an interview with a journalist from the *Evening Post,* Lee explained that she wished "to settle down in her native land and photograph the American great . . . because everyone here is so good looking." Europe had its beauties, she continued, but American bone structure was "much better." The journalist wagered that her sitters would learn to be as *photogénique* as Miss Miller and said that her portraits could be seen at the Levy Gallery's current show—along with work by Abbott, Genthe, Huene, Steichen, Steiglitz, and Man Ray. Lee's reflective self-portrait ("Lee Miller *par* Lee Miller") illustrated the interview.

Lee also ran ads promoting her studio as the American branch of "the Man Ray school of photography." In a highly qualified account of her apprenticeship, she explained, "What you mostly do is absorb the personality of the man you are working with. The personality of the photographer, his approach, is really more important than his technical genius." While Lee had no qualms about dropping Man's name, he was outraged by her opportunism. Although averse to legal action, he told his sister that he would soon take steps to disconnect his name "from all these publicity-hunters."

Lee's name stayed in the news while she and Erik prepared the studio. Julien did his best to advance her career by linking it to his own. The nature of their friendship changed once Lee began socializing with both Levys and acting as the gallery's unofficial publicist. In November, she photographed Joella and Julien installing Max Ernst's exhibit for *Town & Country* and shot several portraits of Joella. One wonders what ran through the two women's minds during these sessions. "I really liked her," Joella said much later, then added, "She never really meant to hurt the other woman."

Lee also renewed her friendship with Tanja Rowell, who was working for Anton Bruehl, a pioneer color photographer. Tanja was amused to watch Lee's reputation soar once her studio opened in November. Prospective sitters spoke with awe of her talent, and how difficult it was to get an appointment. Lee booked one sitting a day, she told a reporter, since each session took several hours. Clients were served lunch and invited to relax; to avoid "an audience complex" or a "gallery smile," friends were not welcome. "It takes time to do a good portrait," Lee went on. "I must talk to the sitter, find out what idea of himself or herself he had in mind."

Moreover, male and female sitters behaved differently: "Young men never know whether they want to look like a pugilist or Clark Gable. . . . Older men often want you to catch the twinkle in their eyes, a certain angle of their profiles or their 'Mussolini jaw' that some woman has told him she loves." Men were more self-conscious than women, she observed, "because women are used to being looked at." As a profession, photography suited her sex. "Women are quicker and more adaptable than men," she believed. "I think they have an intuition that helps them understand personalities. . . . And a good photo-graph, of course, is just that, to catch a person not when he is unaware of it but when he is his most natural self."

Yet sitters who cared more for their public image than their natural selves—socialites, theater people, and professional beauties—sought her out because of her reputation. Clients came through the Levy gallery, Condé Nast, and her backers. Soon she was photographing New York's artistic elite: the publisher Donald Friede, literary critic Lewis Galantière, museum director Chick Austin, and actors and actresses of the day, such as Claire Luce, Selena Royale, Lilian Harvey, and Gertrude Lawrence. Her command of lighting in their portraits recalls that of Steichen or Huene: these theatrical shots repro-duced well in magazines like *Vogue,* which preferred high gloss to naturalness. Lee's portraits from the early 1930s demonstrate her professionalism and her sense that despite the Depression she might make her way by following in her mentors' footsteps.

But judging by Lee's photographs of friends, she felt more relaxed with noncelebrities. When Tanja posed for a bridal shop ad, Lee softened the light-ing to enhance her friend's thoughtful gaze at the other woman in the picture, a seamstress adjusting the waves of tulle at her feet. Two portraits of Tanja in a dark evening gown bring out her sensuous side through the deployment of the subtle gradations from white to black. Tanja's friend Dorothy Hill asked Lee to take her wedding portrait: the result, a solarized likeness of this stunning brunette, evokes her character in a composition recalling some of Lee's mod-eling stints with Man. For another portrait that harks back to Lee's past, she draped a dark cloth around the neck of her friend Mary Taylor. This striking composition, *Floating Head,* treats her sitter as a masklike visage and a mane of hair. Photographing these women allowed Lee to rethink her time as a model, to recall what she had felt on the other side of the camera.

About this time, she occupied both positions for an unusual self-portrait—for a fashion article on hairbands. Due to its commercial nature, this image does not reveal the self, but uses it by aestheticizing her person. Artfully coiffed, made up, and dressed in a dark velvet gown with elaborate ruching, Lee photographed herself in profile, facing a chair whose pale upholstery con-trasts with her garments and sets off the light on the shot's raison d'être, the hairband. More deliberately stylish and cooler than *Lee Miller* par *Lee Miller,* the image displays her command of the medium.

Not surprisingly, portraits free of economic pressures show a greater emo-tional range. Lee's friendship with Joseph Cornell, which dates from this time, moved each artist to depict the other. Julien, who was Cornell's dealer, may have mentioned the eccentric collagist to Lee during their affair in Paris, when he was combing the Flea Market for the antique boxes he brought back to encourage Cornell's homegrown Surrealism. After his return to New York,

Julien surely told Cornell, who admired women from a distance, of his relationship with Lee. Cornell began squirreling away scraps of information about Lee, starting with Huene's photograph of her in the October *Vogue*. While it is amusing to think of Julien introducing the shy Cornell to his former lover, their friendship shows his talent for bringing together like-minded people.

Cornell's shyness around women did not keep him from expressing his feelings for them. Lee complied with his request for stills of her as Cocteau's muse and answered his questions about *The Blood of a Poet*. One can imagine what the starstruck Cornell saw in his beautiful new friend. Three years older than Lee, the dreamy young man had grown up in Nyack, on the Hudson, and, like her, taken part in amateur theatricals. Enchanted by the bric-a-brac of popular culture, he saw Surrealism as an innocent magic. Cornell was no doubt awed by Lee's acquaintance with Ernst, whose collages had inspired him, and pleased by her interest in his own early creations, which expressed his emotional yearning.

Perhaps Cornell, too, saw Lee as a muse—the feminine side of his persona. One day he brought his latest creations to her studio to be photographed for his one-man show at Julien's gallery. It is difficult to know how she felt as she focused on his glass bell series, which shelter small objects—a mannequin's hand, a doll's head, a metronome recalling Man's *Object* (minus the eye)—and whether she saw Man's shots of Tanja's head under the bell jar as a dark precedent for Cornell's naïve counterpart.

Cornell also sat for a group of portraits that reveal this unlikely pair's artistic sympathy. One of his first objects, a toy boat topped with a butterfly and a mane of floating hair, was both a self-portrait—"a synthesis of voyager and ship, male and female, brought together in Cornell's ambiguous guise"—and an emblem of his guileless response to Surrealism. As if he had set sail in his imagination, Lee posed Cornell with the ship and turned his profile so that the blond mane cascading from the mast becomes his own. Cornell's exhibit ran at Julien's through December, with a group of etchings by Picasso. (Relegated to the back room, his objects were dismissed by the press as "toys for adults.")

On December 30, after taking down the Cornells, Joella and Julien hung Lee's photographs and sent out the announcement for her one-woman show. Stylishly printed on maroon paper, it contained an endorsement by Frank Crowninshield. Lee had left America four years before, he began, "a girl in her earliest twenties. She has now returned . . . an accomplished artist." Commending her apprenticeship "with the artistic radicals of France, the Surréalistes, and their photographic leader, Man Ray, as well as her gift for seeing artistic possibilities in all sorts of subjects, he felt sure that in Lee's new studio, she would "go on exercising her sensitive and rounded talent in an art in which she has shown herself naturally and peculiarly adept."

Judging by the announcement, which lacks a checklist, Lee's show included

most of her work from Paris—street scenes, architectural studies, still lifes—
and a number of portraits. Her celebrity status was underscored by the recent
publication of her portrait of Claire Luce in *Vanity Fair,* just as her friend began
her starring role on Broadway as Fred Astaire's partner in *The Gay Divorce.* The
publicity for Lee's show was carefully planned. In an interview published the day
of the opening, she again mentioned her apprenticeship with Man. But that was
in the past, she told the reporter, who noted, "She can do the same mysterious
stunts herself now, getting a third dimension by 'solarization,' spoofing pebbles
that they are Alps, and presenting people as 'cold' or 'warm' all by manipulating
her lights and lenses." Indeed, many of her shots were seen first in her imagination, then "assembled," as one would a painting. Julien told the crowd of well-
wishers at the opening that "the new light on the horizon of photography is Miss
Lee Miller." (Joella voiced her reservations in private: "We just opened the Lee
Miller show. . . . We don't think her photos are very good but they make a surprisingly good show.")

Fortunately for Lee, the critics agreed with Julien. Edward Jewell
remarked in the *New York Times* on her ingenuity: unlike other experimental-
ists, "her photographic work," he wrote, was "free from disconcerting tricks of
overstatement, evasion and palimpsest." Though influenced by Surrealism,
about which he had doubts, Miss Miller was more interested in "compositions
featuring highly contrasted light and dark masses." It was to her credit that
given this feel for abstraction, she did not try "to conceal a healthy affection in
subject matter as such—an affection that many modern artists have pretended
was unworthy of them." Among her portraits, he praised those of Gene Tun-
ney, Claire Luce, Charlie Chaplin, Selena Royale, and Man Ray.

"Lovely Lee Miller has opened a studio in New York," *Creative Arts*
gushed. "That seems the natural way to speak of her," the review continues, "as
for three years she kept many folk in Paris arguing as to whether she or Greta
[Garbo] was the more fascinating. She was generally considered more beautiful, but a proof of her ability as an *actrice* is to be found in Jean Cocteau's film."
Mixing admiration of her person and her celebrity subjects, it concludes, "The
number of famous people whom she has 'done' is extremely large and includes
all of the nobility of India who have been in Europe in the last few years." Surprisingly, few images sold. Julien kept most of them for his own collection.

Before the exhibit's close on January 25, 1933, Julien put four of Lee's portraits in Bergdorf Goodman's Exhibit of New York Beauty. Although the show
was chiefly a tribute to the store's most attractive customers, one reviewer
noted, it was nonetheless distinguished by Lee's presence among "the sixty
most." Julien claimed to take the event seriously. The camera alone could
identify beauty, he wrote in the announcement: "a relatively impersonal
judge . . . [it] offers an interpretation, so that you shall see yourself as others
see you." Lee could be seen as *Vogue* photographer André Durst saw her, but

also as she saw herself in her elegant subjects—Eden Gray, Renée Hubbel, Mrs. Donald Friede, and the ubiquitous Claire Luce. They were in good company. Portraits by Genthe, Steichen, Edward Weston, Toni Frissell (a contemporary of Lee's who worked for *Vogue*), Cecil Beaton, Horst, and Man also adorned the walls at the department store.

The Millers, a little disappointed at seeing so little of Lee since her return, came to New York on January 13 to see her one-woman show and the Bergdorf exhibit; typically, Theodore's reaction to her success is not recorded in his diary. Lee no doubt attended Julien's next opening, on January 28, for Mina Loy's Cocteauesque paintings. She also posed for an elaborate fashion sequence taken by her loyal assistant, Erik, who, seeing her fatigue, noted that it was due "to not taking care of herself."

Toward the end of the month, Theodore proposed a plan combining a restorative holiday and time with his daughter. On February 5, they drove to the Pocono Mountains for an eight-day "cure" at the Hay-Ven sanatorium. Like others obsessed by diet (in a time of bread lines and soup kitchens), the Millers had tried several regimens that held out the promise of enhanced health. New food fads kept sweeping the country. The Hollywood Eighteen-Day Diet emphasized grapefruit. "Two-food" diets promised fast weight loss through the consumption of paired foods: depending on the plan, pineapple and lamb chops, baked potato and buttermilk, raw tomatoes and boiled eggs, or, for the diehards, coffee and doughnuts.

Lee's parents still followed the philosophy of natural living detailed in Dr. Hay's *Health via Food*. This diet, variants of which are still popular, advocates "compatible food combinations": starches and proteins are not eaten together; fruits and vegetables may accompany either of these but only in accordance with Dr. Hay's directions; caffeine is eliminated from the diet. The Millers also drank Pluto Water, a "physic" in a distinctive green bottle that helped dieters cleanse themselves during the daylong fasts that were part of the regimen. One wonders what Theodore told Lee about its more challenging features, "hi-colonic irrigations" and the avoidance of sex unless its aim was procreation— advice she may have considered after several of her love affairs resulted in pregnancy, terminated by abortion. (The problem with "a too free indulgence in the sex life," Hay wrote, was not so much venereal disease as "the physical deterioration that is the direct result.")

Those who followed his diet, Dr. Hay claimed, would "get well and stay well through the detoxication and through inner cleanliness of the body." The food at Hay-Ven could not have been less like French cuisine. Spirits were forbidden; sugar, salt, and pepper were not recommended; one was not to eat when tired or "when nerve stresses may interfere with digestion." The record does not say whether Lee felt invigorated by her stay. Theodore's diary notes that they had adjoining rooms and makes no mention of photographic sessions. Perhaps that expression of their intimacy became a thing of the past. On her return to New York, Lee resumed her hectic pace—paying no further heed to Dr. Hay's recommendations.

∞

Within months of her return to New York, Tanja recalled, Lee was "THE photographer to be photographed by." Although the luxury trade was feeling the effects of the Depression, advertising agencies commissioned shots of perfumes and cosmetics, Saks Fifth Avenue and Helena Rubenstein hired her to publicize their wares, and Condé Nast featured her work. Lee became so well known that Macy's commissioned her to choose, then photograph, the new "Macy twins" (the store used twins as models). Old friends like Nickolas Muray sent assignments when work was slow; new ones, like Dr. Walter Clark, Eastman Kodak's head of research, explained the complex procedures of color photography before the advent of Kodachrome.

Lee refused to compromise even when times were hard. Having hired a lively young woman named Jackie Knight as her business manager and an unflappable black maid named Georgia Belaire, whose cooking pleased clients, backers, and friends alike, she kept them on salary even when uncertain she could pay the rent. Erik ran the darkroom and did most of the developing. "Lee could be intolerably lazy when she wanted," he noted, "but when the chips were down, she just would not quit."

Erik emerged from the darkroom at all hours to get her opinion of prints. "Lee was very insistent on getting the highest quality," he recalled: "She would grab hold of any that were even slightly defective and tear the corners off." Working together, they intensified dark areas with the warmth of their breath or fingers during development. Since Lee knew enough chemistry to fortify the solutions then available, "the resulting brew sometimes became quite deadly," Erik continued. They coughed and choked over the developing tanks; his nails turned brown. Years later, he still marveled at her eye for composition, "the way she could pick out what was wrong with a print, maybe something that had completely escaped my notice."

Lee's commercial work from this time is marked by precision, but also by its reserve—as if this sort of work held little interest. Sometimes she found creative ways around routine assignments: her decision to solarize the gleaming lid of a grand piano—essentially a high-class ad—lets one "hear" the silent music. For a shot of Elizabeth Arden perfumes, Lee aligned her subjects diagonally on a mirrored base, in whose depths the glass bottles, like self-obsessed starlets, seem to see their reflections.

Lee decided to use color, a complex three-step process requiring three separation negatives, in a more prestigious, and expensive, perfume ad. She and Erik surrounded the flacons with gardenias and, as their petals drooped, "ended up rushing the gardenias straight from the refrigerator, spraying them and then gently placing them on the mirror," Erik recalled, to keep them from moving during the time it took to complete the exposures. "We would hit the lights, make the first exposure, then bing, bing, change the film and filter for the second and third time." Despite these difficulties, the photograph was "very, very successful." Challenges of this kind brought out the best in Lee by providing antidotes to routine and boredom.

Lee's rise to fame coincided with that of her fashion mentors, Huene, Horst, and Beaton. These highly paid celebrities had a symbiotic relationship with the new media—magazines, advertising, public relations—that required a constant supply of high-quality images. While in their orbit, Lee had little contact with the practitioners of a new kind of lyrical realism, Berenice Abbott and Walker Evans, who by the 1930s were photographing New York in the manner of Atget. (Evans praised the Frenchman's "understanding of the street, trained observation of it, special feeling for patina, eye for revealing detail, over all of which is thrown a poetry which is not 'the poetry of the street' or 'the poetry of Paris,' but the projection of Atget's person.") Rather than follow Atget's lead, Lee avoided such projections, since commercial work had to convey the values of its audience.

Artistically, she had reached an impasse. Without meaning to do so, perhaps, she had abandoned the experimentation of her Paris years. And in any case, despite Julien's efforts, Surrealist-influenced photography did not go over well in the changed economic climate, when American photographers were moving toward a local focus. Invidious distinctions between native and foreign perspectives were not unusual. Of the Brooklyn Museum's 1932 Modern European Photography exhibit, a critic wrote that while the American school was "realistic, objective, and reverently attached to its native place," European artists "concerned with explorations of the medium's expressive range" often produced images that were "disconcerting and arbitrary"—not what the country needed during a depression.

It is not surprising that in this context, Lee's New York images lack the passion of her Paris work. Since commercial photography did not excite her, she put her energy into her social life—joining the guests at Condé Nast's, renewing ties with Crowninshield and the *Vogue* staffers, and forging new ones with Dr. Agha, Edna Chase, and Henrietta Malkiel, a writer who had worked at German *Vogue* (which failed before acquiring a nickname, like Frogue or Brogue, the British edition). Lee was now on equal footing with Genthe, Muray, and Steichen, and a peer of Bourke-White and Toni Frissell, with whom she shared a preference for informal fashion pictures resembling snapshots.

Lee also socialized with theater people—Gertrude Lawrence, Ira Gershwin, Lewis Galantière and his writing partner, John Houseman. Actors, directors, critics, and members of fashionable New York gathered after hours at her studio to play poker and enjoy Georgia's cooking. Erik watched Georgia baby Lee, letting her stay in bed when she was tired or when business was slow; to his dismay, the late-night poker games turned into all-nighters. By May, they were again doing well, he noted, but Lee was "ill or tired most of the time"—a fatigue he attributed not to work, but to bootleg booze and irregular hours.

John Houseman became a regular at the ongoing poker game—drawn, he wrote, "less by passion for gambling than by an unrequited lust for my hostess." He saved enough money to take her dancing one night in Central Park, to no avail. Still lusting and "bitterly jealous," Houseman watched Lee flirt with her admirers. He had a low opinion of the one who became her constant companion, a literary agent named John Rodell. (In Lee's portrait of Rodell, he looks like an elegant Humphrey Bogart, his face shadowed by a slouchy hat and his gloved hand dangling a cigarette.) Lee became "ugly, fat & bad tempered" while with Rodell, Joella told Mina with a touch of satisfaction. Although Lee spent a few weekends in Poughkeepsie with him, she was too busy to go home for her twenty-sixth birthday.

In May, Julien screened *The Blood of a Poet* at the New York Film Society, which he ran like a club. Committed to finding a New York audience for experimental film after seeing *L'Age d'or* with Lee, he had enrolled an enthusiastic group of backers (Crowninshield, Dos Passos, Sherwood Anderson, George Gershwin, and Nelson Rockefeller, among others) after his return from Paris. The film society had already shown *Ballet Mécanique* and *L'Age d'or*, along with Disney cartoons and Harold Lloyd silents. On May 17, 1933, the cognoscenti gathered in the society's rooms on East Fifty-seventh Street to watch *The Blood of a Poet*, preceded by Robert Benchley's *Sex Life of a Polyp*. To change the mood after this intriguingly titled short, Julien discoursed about Cocteau. For the Frenchman, film was another experimental medium, he said, and *Blood* "the visual transcription of a poem." The film had the right kind of artiness for connoisseurs. Lee was "extremely good, playing with . . . rapt intensity," a reviewer wrote. Houseman, mesmerized by her lips' migration onto the poet's torso, continued to dream about her sex life.

In June, the Millers became involved in wedding plans for their sons. After Catherine Sague, the daughter of a former Poughkeepsie mayor, accepted John's proposal, they were married beneath a floral pergola on the Millers' lawn. The newspaper noted the presence of "Lee Miller of New York City, widely known art photographer." Erik and Mafy waited for Lee's return from a vacation in Maine with Rodell to solemnize their vows in August; then, after a trip to Niagara Falls, Erik went back to work with his sister on a group of theatrical portraits—the kind of work that came her way now that she was the most stylish photographer in town.

∞

Lee's gift for remaining on good terms with ex-lovers, unsuccessful suitors, and assorted admirers resulted in her being involved in the most exciting event of the 1933–34 drama season. Through her old beau De Liagre and new friends like Houseman, the theater world adopted her. That she was a sought-after participant in avant-garde ventures became all the more apparent that autumn, when *The Blood of a Poet* began a two-month run at the Fifth Avenue Playhouse. Lee's photographs decorated the foyer; according to the program, the muse-turned-artist had been the source of inspiration for "Monsieur Cocteau."

The film became a topic of conversation at Kirk and Constance Askew's "at homes"—where one met the trendsetters who supported Julien's film society, the Museum of Modern Art, and the couple's new project, the world premiere of the Virgil Thomson–Gertrude Stein opera, *Four Saints in Three Acts.* Each Sunday at five some of the most innovative New Yorkers gathered in the Askews' drawing room to drink, flirt, and make contacts. After joining the regulars there, Lee met or remet such people as Thomson, Aaron Copland, Carl Van Vechten, Henry McBride, Lincoln Kirstein, Agnes de Mille, George Balanchine, Joella, Julien, and the Levy gallery artists—Dalí, Tchelitchew, Campigli, and the two Bermans, Leonid and Eugene. Everyone knew that their hosts were aligned with old money that could be called on in a good cause, provided it was also amusing.

When Thomson sailed to New York from Paris in October, he meant to capitalize on Gertrude Stein's unexpected fame in the United States after the recent publication of her *Autobiography of Alice B. Toklas.* Intending to mount *Four Saints* that winter, he persuaded Houseman to direct. Houseman's European manners, he insisted, made up for his lack of experience. The Wadsworth Athenaeum in Hartford would provide the venue; an Askew-backed group called the Friends and Enemies of Modern Music offered a budget of $10,000. Within a short time, Houseman engaged Florine Stettheimer to design the sets, Frederick Ashton to choreograph, and Lee to be official photographer. Since Thomson believed that American blacks would embody the opera's spirituality, Houseman also engaged the best singers and dancers in Harlem. This production is now part of theater history. In the winter of 1933, however, it was not obvious that an idiosyncratic modern opera would be taken seriously, let alone draw crowds. To the press, Stein was a joke—the mama of Dada, a literary Cubist, or, as the *Boston Globe* put it, "the high priestess of the cult of unintelligibility."

The press also seized on the novelty of an opera performed by Negroes. Thomson, who was not immune to the prejudices of his time, told Stein that

Four Saints in Three Acts *(White Studios)*

he wanted black singers because of their rhythm and style but did not intend to produce "a nigger show." Rather, he hoped to achieve the opera's note of "solemnity and grandeur" with an ensemble of dark bodies. (If necessary, he added, they could be painted white, to reflect the transparent light demanded by Stettheimer.) In the 1930s, black actors *were* seen on Broadway, but as mammies, minstrels, pickaninnies, or prostitutes. In Stein's opera, they would sing the kind of music reserved for white performers and play roles that went beyond clichés about "Negro life."

Thomson and Houseman found their singers through Eva Jessye, a classically trained teacher and choir director. Jessye, who had worked in Hollywood on King Vidor's *Hallelujah,* called *Four Saints* a breakthrough "because up to that time the only opportunities involved things like 'Swanee River,' or 'That's Why Darkies Are Born,' or 'Old Black Joe.'" With this opera, she explained, they were "on fresh ground." Shocked by the poverty in Harlem, Houseman took the unusual step of paying the cast for rehearsals, at a time when discriminatory hiring meant that black performers regularly earned less than whites.

Rehearsals began in December at St. Philip's Episcopal Church, on 137th Street. One cold day toward the end of the year, Lee went to Harlem to take photographs. After arranging her cameras in the warm, stuffy basement, she posed the cast—eighteen principals, twenty choristers, and six dancers—one by one. Eva Jessye faced the camera with the same self-assurance she showed in dealings with Thomson's attempts to authenticate her singers' diction (she explained that she had been a black person longer than he had). Similarly, Lee's portrait of Bruce Howard, the woman who played Saint Teresa II, brought out her force of character. Head shots of Edward Matthews (Saint Ignatius) and Embry Bonner (Saint Chavez) reveal the men's softer side, in the same way that her photographs of Houseman, Thomson, and Ashton suggest their creative vision. As a group, Lee's portraits are empathetic. The participants are seen not as professionals preparing public selves but as friends engaged in an unusual venture.

Four Saints opened on February 8 in subzero weather. The biting cold did not keep art-world movers and shakers from descending on Hartford "by Rolls Royce, by airplane, by Pullman compartment," the *Herald Tribune* quipped, "or for all we know, by specially designed Cartier pogo-sticks." (The New Haven Railroad added special parlor cars for the less adventurous.) It is not known whether Lee joined the stylish crowd that night but her work was present in the much-admired program—now a collector's item—which featured her portraits of the company.

It is likely that Lee attended *Four Saints'* New York opening on February 20, when Houseman took the opera to Broadway. In the audience that night were her old friends Neysa McMein, Dorothy Parker, Henry McBride, and other arbiters of café society. *Four Saints* became the hit of the season. Through its run of sixty performances—the longest for any American opera— guests at cocktail parties debated Stein's libretto, people waved the program at one another in the street, and George Gershwin found inspiration in the opera for *Porgy and Bess,* produced the following year with Jessye as choral director. By Easter, Gimbel's was displaying spring fashions as "4 suits in 2 acts," and Stein's enigmatic phrase "pigeons on the grass alas" had entered the American vernacular. Constance Askew spoke for her circle when she recalled, "It *does* stand for the best part of our lives."

One wonders whether Lee's work on *Four Saints* prompted *Vanity Fair* to name her as one of the seven "most distinguished living photographers" in May. (The list also included Huene, Beaton, Muray, and Genthe.) To the magazine's request for "pictures of the girls whom they consider the most beautiful they have ever photographed," Lee sent her image of Renée Oakman, a blonde of the Jean Harlow type whose features suggest a more reserved version of herself. Beaton chose his portrait of the well-dressed Mrs. Harrison Williams, and Huene a close-up of Nathalie Paley, of the Paris *bal masqué* crowd. "Thus do tastes differ," *Vanity Fair* mused, "and thus is the world saved from dullness." Bourke-White's shots of the new NBC radio tower, which ran a few pages before this feature, may have given Lee pause. While her portraits were said to be distinguished, judging by their restraint, her heart was not in them.

Toward the end of the month, Lee surprised her family and friends by turning her back on the stylish life in which she had become a fixture. After hearing from Aziz, who was on his way to New York on behalf of the Egyptian Railway, she closed her studio and went to a "fat farm" (Hay-Ven?). "She disappeared for a week," Houseman recalled, "and returned having lost about fifteen pounds, radiantly beautiful; she went out and bought or got someone to give her a few glorious dresses so that by the time he arrived, she was in prime condition."

A few days after Aziz's arrival in June, Lee took him to Poughkeepsie for the weekend. Theodore showed him around DeLaval, where he studied the separators, especially those used to purify oil; one engineer to another, they discussed ways to irrigate the Egyptian desert. Aziz celebrated Theodore's sixty-second birthday by presenting him a box of the best cigars. In July, when they returned to Poughkeepsie, Lee and Aziz went driving and swimming with Theodore but said nothing of their relations. Her parents accepted him as they had Rodell and other friends. It must have come as a shock when Lee asked Florence's opinion of Aziz. After hearing him deemed acceptable, she told her mother, "That's good—because I married him."

The wedding had taken place in Manhattan on July 19, in a civil ceremony with an official who warned Lee about marrying a foreigner who was also "black" (she became so angry that their paperwork was expedited). Later that day, they were also wed according to Muslim law at the Egyptian consulate. According to the marriage contract, Aziz could have up to four wives, divorce Lee when he pleased, and refuse to let her leave the house without permission. Contrary to custom, the bride had no dowry. Perhaps none of this mattered.

Of Lee's many friends, few made her husband's acquaintance. After she introduced him to the Levys, Joella told Mina that Aziz "although not distinguished is really very nice and much better than Man Ray," and added that Lee would "give up photography to go to Egypt." To some, the age difference was telling: Aziz was forty-three, and Lee, twenty-seven. But for most of her friends, Houseman recalled, Aziz was "a sort of mystery figure, out of the Arabian Nights, this man who was coming to claim her, and he did, and she vanished."

Lee's vanishing left several people in the lurch, including Erik. Although he and Mafy had closed their apartment for the summer and moved to her family's, he was out of work unless the studio could reopen in the fall. No doubt Lee also waited to tell the family her news because she felt guilty about deserting her brother. Casting about for a solution, Lee had Jackie Knight cable Man "to ask if he wanted to avail himself of her organization." When Man did not reply, she turned to Julien, who said to tell Duchamp of this opportunity for Man to return to New York. "The year seems propitious," Jackie wrote; Man's book had been well received; Lee would be glad to turn over "her many and profitable accounts." "My acquaintance with the field leads me to believe that he could command the best of the photographic business at the highest prices," the letter continues—in a shameless attempt to keep the "organization" going. But Man, who had long since ceased to hold himself in reserve for Lee, cabled by return, PULL YOUR OWN CHESTNUTS OUT OF THE FIRE.

A large party, including friends, family, and the Egyptian consul, came to the Italian Line pier on September 1, to see Lee sail in state on the *Conte di Savoia*. "Lee Miller a Bride," the *New York Times* announced a few days later. The article, probably dictated by the Millers, notes that the happy couple would live in Cairo and Saint Moritz. It also gives a highly selective account of Lee's life thus far: "Mme. Eloui Bey, whose father is works manager of the DeLaval Separator Company here, has been a commercial photographer in New York."

Part Three
Madame Eloui Bey

Lee and Aziz Eloui Bey, Cairo, c. 1935

Chapter 8

Egypt

(1934–37)

Lee embarked on marriage as if it were a holiday. Aziz had booked her on the *Esperia,* one of the Mediterranean's most luxurious steamships. At Genoa, passengers from the Paris-Rome Express, for whom the trip was an occasion to display their wardrobes, came on board in high spirits. For the next four days, as they cruised the Mediterranean, ladies exchanged their morning clothes for tea gowns, then, at night, robes suitable for dining at the Ritz. Lee had ample time to ponder her decision. She was now the wife of the generous man who would meet her in Alexandria. The struggle to maintain her studio was behind her; Aziz would take charge.

By 1934, Lee's modus operandi—spurts of activity followed by periods of exhaustion—had become self-defeating. She often regretted her lack of education, despite having learned more with Medgyès, Flanagan, and her teachers at the Art Students League than most did at college, and despite her professional training with the masters.

Her impulsive decision to leave New York also expressed her discontent with glossy magazines. In the 1930s, American photography was enmeshed in the country's ideals, its love of speed, machinery, and consumerism. More than before, ads featuring celebrities encouraged ordinary people to identify with their privileges; modernist techniques put to commercial uses urged them to accept the truths of the surface; Steichen was still turning out images that reflected the materialism of the day. This was "photography off its track," Walker Evans wrote, an aesthetic of "technical impressiveness and spiritual non-existence." Feeling the limits of this approach, Lee abruptly turned her back on the premise that what mattered was the sheen of metal and the glow of skin tones.

Before Egypt, she had lived on the surface of things—as if her childhood traumas had never happened. Aziz told the Millers that his fondest wish was to "bring peace to her heart." "I would like to impress upon you not to worry for her," he wrote in the first of the many letters that tell the story of their marriage from his perspective. As his wife, Lee would find the serenity that had thus far escaped her. If she did not like Cairo, he would arrange a transfer to London. "We have no secrets one for the other & we will get along in this difficult life quite well & despite our much troubled souls," he concluded.

Judging by the course of their life together, Lee kept more than a few secrets, and Aziz never fully grasped the nature of her trouble. Perhaps she did not understand it herself.

∞

Lee saw Egypt for the first time as her ship neared Alexandria. Ships approach the coast through billowing waves of color, the blue wash of the Mediterranean turning green, purple, or turquoise as the wind sends it crashing against the fortress at the harbor's entrance. The Bride of the Sea, the local name for Alexandria, is a place haunted by ghosts—Antony and Cleopatra, the great library, the ancient lighthouse of Pharos. In the 1930s, Alex (as it was called by expatriates) was popular with the Egyptian royal family, the upper class, and resident foreigners, who fled the heat of Cairo for their villas along the corniche. After Aziz guided Lee through customs and past the throngs of beggars, her holiday began with a rest at his beach house before the long drive south to Cairo.

Travelers new to Egypt need time to adjust to the landscape. It would take months before Lee picked up her camera and focused on the interplay of unfamiliar shapes and colors. At first, as she gazed out the window of Aziz's car, it may have seemed that there was little to see. When the sun came out, she would have noticed the silvery irrigation canals flickering across the alluvial plains, the clover and wheat bristling with red poppies, the fields where children in pink and yellow toiled with their blue-shirted fathers and mothers in head scarves—the fellahin, or Egyptian peasants. Perhaps she noted, too, how compositions appeared of their own accord in the villages—a minaret's spire forming a contrast to the low mass of peasant huts, or, in the distance, sandhills turning ochre, gray, and mauve toward sundown.

The delta depended on irrigation from the Nile, which had been flooding since August. By September, the floods had turned low-lying plains into an Egyptian Venice. Aziz surely explained that in winter, when the water receded, the fellahin would again wield their ancient implements—the *shaduf,* a bar attached to a bucket that swiveled and dipped into the Nile, and the *sakia,* a waterwheel turned by blindfolded oxen plodding in circles. But now, as the floods threatened the railway tracks, the problem was too much water rather than not enough.

Aziz had just held a meeting with his superiors at the Ministry of Railways. They were now obliged to confront a situation "which makes them look as if they had something to do," he wrote the Millers. (Government jobs offered educated Egyptians prestige and political influence: they were seen as sinecures.) It distressed him "to see this valuable water wasted into the Mediterranean," he went on, since with modern technology, it might be diverted to the desert for large-scale reforestation—which would change the climate and "make Egypt a more pleasant country." Having invested in the local branch of Portland Cement, he gave Lee the bulk of his shares as a wedding gift and earnest of his belief in the future.

Europeanized members of the elite like Aziz looked to technology as the means to bring Egypt into the twentieth century. But while the Nile might eventually be tamed with a series of dams, the fellahin were another matter. Nationalists and foreigners agreed that they had changed hardly at all since the pharaohs. These stalwart peasants were the guardians of traditional values, "the sinews of national strength," as Lee's *Baedeker* put it—their character "a product of the soil itself."

The myth of the eternal peasant was a source of both pride and concern among the Egyptian elite, in part because they relied upon the millions of peasants at the base of the social structure for their own comfort. (Labor was incredibly cheap; middle-class households had complements of servants.) The Wafd Party, a group of progressive nationalists, had for years focused on the "social question"—the huge gap in standards of living. Yet most fellahin would not have imagined their lot differently. Foreigners, especially those from the United States, often concluded that Egypt was a land of the past rather than part of the modern world.

Lee's first impressions of her new home and its contradictions have not survived. She may have been too disoriented by the heat, the flies, and the difficulty of travel to concern herself with the peasants as Aziz and she drove past their sodden fields. One wonders whether she took in the slow-moving traffic on the embankments, whether she noticed the women with water jars on their heads or bearing loaves of bread. Later, she would see in the fellahin photographic subjects combining the strange with the familiar. For now, she approached her new life as Aziz's bride.

∞

Baedeker's Egypt began by cautioning foreigners against "intercourse with Orientals." ("The average Oriental," the guidebook warned, "regards the European traveller as a Croesus, and sometimes too as a madman—so unintelligible to him are the objects and pleasures of travelling.") Travelers like Lee were unlikely to meet Egyptians other than servants and the Europeanized elite, who had, for generations, been attuned to such pleasures; but while their degrees and titles were listed in *Le Mondain Egyptien,* the Who's Who of Egypt, no guide to the expatriate colony existed. If one had been written, the author would have had to describe the many national and religious groups that made up the large foreign community.

To the entrenched British residents, Egypt was an outpost of the Empire—like India but closer to home. The British had established a protectorate in 1914 after decades of occupation; Egypt remained a de facto dependency. The British high commissioner, Sir Miles Lampson, was a favorite with King Fuad, but his impressive bearing (Sir Miles was six feet six) had not endeared him to the Wafd Party, whose campaign for nationhood would soon inspire widespread social discontent. Just as Sir Miles oversaw the administration of Egypt, British managers supervised their local counterparts, a situation that underlay Aziz's reservations about the British. (He nonetheless maintained membership in the Gezira Sporting Club, where members watched British military parades while sipping gin and tonic.)

Despite, or because of, his years in England, Aziz was a Francophile. To belong to the French-speaking elite, a contemporary wrote, "was to think of Cairo as home, but to believe that Paris was the navel of the world." In French-speaking Cairo, Lee's Paris years enhanced her glamour. And since members of the Francophone community, which included Greeks, Copts (Egyptian Christians), and Christian Arabs, spoke with a variety of accents, her Yankee twang was of no importance. Speaking French marked one as an educated person. The language of the courts, banks, and cotton houses, it was also the lingua franca in department stores, hotels, brothels, and among the well-to-do—Muslims, Copts, and Jews alike.

Within a short time of her arrival in Cairo, Lee's efforts to adjust were complicated by the hazards of life there, among them a plague of mosquitoes and the collapse of the sewer system—both consequences of the floods. Fearing for her health, Aziz took her back to Alexandria. They lounged in their beach cabin, played bridge, and visited the nightclubs, often with the Wissa family, prominent Copts with cotton plantations up the Nile, or with members of King Fuad's entourage. Lee became friendly with vivacious Gertie Wissa, a champion bridge player a few years younger than she, and met the king's chamberlain, Ahmed Hassanein Bey, a distinguished explorer. One can imagine the Oxford-educated Hassanein stirring her imagination with tales of his treks across the Libyan desert, and of the intrigues surrounding his post as tutor to Fuad's heir, Prince Farouk.

Lee looks relaxed in a snapshot taken about this time; one hand rests on Aziz's hand as she strokes his knee with the other. "Lee is happy," he wrote the Millers, then added, "It is not easy to settle down smoothly considering her much troubled soul" (a recurrent phrase in his correspondence). She might not be able to tolerate the discomforts endemic to Egypt—dust, flies, mosquitoes (nets over the bed were the only protection), and typhoid injections. But worse than these, the lack of stimulation made her restless. "Her brain must work to occupy Lee's time," Aziz went on. "When she is rested from the strenuous life of New York, she will be much better."

After their return to Cairo, Lee met more of Aziz's friends, whose wives took turns inviting her to their homes. She became an object of curiosity. As a foreigner and a non-Muslim, she was not required to follow the code that confined the women to their quarters, the *haramlek*. European women were known to be less inhibited than local ones, who had their reputations to think of (as well as their health, since syphilis was widespread). Cairenes gossiped about the few foreigners married to Egyptians: Vicki Sadik, a Jewish beauty said to have been the mistress of Iraq's King Feisal; the ex-barmaid Katie Osman Pasha, the wife of an influential Wafd leader; and Madame Abboud Pasha, a Scot married to one of the richest men in Egypt. Since marriage was normally a business enterprise, the alliance of clans rather than of individuals, Aziz's marriage to Lee was seen as a rich man's caprice.

Unlike Aziz, most men of his class kept their female relatives in *haramleks*. "None of their wives had seen a man since they were twelve years old—except for their fathers, brothers, and husbands," Lee recalled. "The harem wives would spend their time behind the grillwork on balconies playing brilliant bridge and poker and watching the men's parties in the room below where I, of course, as a foreigner would be allowed." Yet despite their isolation, these women knew "more of what was going on behind the bushes and in the shadows. . . . I became their Scheherezade, telling them stories which were as fantastic to them as the Arabian Nights were to me," she continued, "what it was like to work for a living, to be with men all the time, to travel with them." Their questions made her reflect on freedoms she had taken for granted.

Soon after her arrival, she and Aziz drove to Assyut, a Coptic market town in Upper Egypt, to stay with the Wissas. "We had a marvelous time except for an attack of mosquitoes, which made Lee very miserable," and the drive, Aziz wrote, which "nearly ruined our beautiful friendship." When not battling mosquitoes, they watched the river traffic—feluccas loaded with scrap iron and vegetables, paddleboats taking tourists to Aswan, river barges carrying fellahin and their goats from one bank to another. Perhaps they stopped to admire the local pottery, the silver and gold scarves made by the Copts and the dam across the Nile. Aziz would have explained Assyut's importance at the crossroads of caravan trails leading west to the desert and south to the Sudan.

They spent the next few days at the Wissas' estate at Beni Korra, where Gertie's brother Victor ran the family cotton business. The Wissas' fortunes had grown with the success of Egypt's prime export, the long-staple cotton prized around the world. Writing to Theodore after the trip, Aziz reported that Lee had played bridge with Gertie rather than inspect the mills and that both of them had enjoyed the Wissas' largesse. "We ate so much that we must have gained at least a pound," he added.

The photographic record shows that at Beni Korra, Lee began trying to know Egypt by photographing it—a process that would include reframing the scenes she had gazed at through Theodore's stereoscope. Some of these Egyptian images show her desire to comprehend her husband's country. Others reflect on her vantage point: her position as an independent woman is implied in their odd perspectives and hints of stasis or escape.

Lee roused herself from her bridge game to visit the Wissas' mills on at least one occasion, when she photographed piles of cotton sacks whose contents seem about to burst out of their containers. A latent sexual energy, here leavened by a teasing humor that associates woman and nature, informs what may be her first Egyptian landscape. As stand-ins, or cover-ups, for feminine anatomy (the sacks resemble breasts with pointy nipples), these suggestive shapes point toward their ethereal counterparts, the cottony clouds above them in the sky. A companion image, *Cotton Struggling to Escape from Sacks to Become Clouds,* conveys the same sense of restlessness along with an idiosyncratic perspective on Egypt's national crop.

Toward the end of 1934, Aziz was still thinking about leaving Egypt. Although the details are not known, it is likely that during her first year of marriage, Lee suffered a miscarriage, an event that colored their life together from then on. Though it was too soon "to decide whether Lee will definitely like to stay here," he told the Millers some time later, she was "happy & will be even better in the future." There was "nothing to worry about," he continued—reassuring himself as well as her parents.

∽

Over the next two years, Lee pieced together Cairo's social geography. At first, she and Aziz rented an apartment while the mansion he had shared with Nimet was being renovated. The Villa al Beit, which would be Lee's new home, was in Dokki, a residential section on the west bank of the Nile across from fashionable Zamalek, and near the Gezira Club. Like Heliopolis, to the northwest, and Maadi, to the south, these areas had been developed for Cairenes wanting to escape the dust and donkeys of old Cairo. English residents clustered in Zamalek's comfortable villas, shaded by scarlet flame trees and mauve jacarandas. Americans generally preferred the tidy garden villas of Maadi.

Although houses in these areas often copied the "Modern Style" buildings of Paris, their interiors warred with their façades. "With this new pretentious architecture," a Cairene wrote, "came a plague of cabinetmakers and agents for reproduction antique furniture from Paris, London, and Milan, all vying with each other to fill spacious halls with imitation Hepplewhite, Sheraton and Scottish Baronial." The prevalence of French copies prompted jokes about a local style called "Louis Farouk." Aziz's compatriots were "diseased by French bad taste," he told the Millers. Because Lee disliked the Villa al Beit's dark wood paneling and old-fashioned armoires (which had suited Nimet), Aziz planned extensive repairs, including American closets to replace the "ugly wardrobes" and the refitting of the top floor as Lee's studio.

While renovations dragged on, Aziz and Lee lived with his brother Kemal, the director of the Egyptian National Airlines. Scions of one of the Turko-Circassian families that had run the country for centuries, the Elouis were local aristocracy. Their father, Dr. Mohammed Eloui, had supervised the Cairo Board of Health, run the Egyptian National University during the Great War, and been the personal physician to King Fuad's sister. (A street named for him still exists near the Cairo Bourse.) Nicknamed the God of the Blind, Dr. Eloui made it his practice to visit villages where peasant children were losing their eyesight; he persuaded them to use the ointment he brought by calling it magic. While Aziz's father had been close to the royal family, he also maintained good relations with the Wafd Party.

Little is known about Aziz's politics. He belonged to the Mohammed Aly Club (which recalled the atmosphere of London's St. James's Club), but was also close to political figures like George Antonius, a Cambridge graduate who became a spokesman for the Arab cause. Like Aziz, Antonius bridged several worlds. When Lee met him, Antonius was in the process of writing *The Arab Awakening*. His wife, Katy, was the daughter of Dr. Fares Nimr, the publisher of a leading Arabic newspaper. Lee also met Katy's sister, Amy, a painter who had studied in Europe before her marriage to Walter Smart, the British diplomat known as "Smartie." While these worldly couples met regularly at the Smarts' house in Zamalek, Lee did not warm to Amy, whose taste seemed too obvious (her rooms displayed her fine china, Persian rugs, and English novels, all covered with gold or silver paper).

Intellectuals like the Nimrs and their spouses were the exception in Lee's circle. The frivolous set with whom she often socialized were members of the Greek-Levantine elite that lived on inherited wealth or the proceeds of their cotton works. They wore French clothes, shopped at Vuitton and Christofle, and vacationed in Europe. When at home, they preferred tennis and gambling to serious pursuits. Women of Lee's cohort, the "black satin and pearls" set, spent their days shopping, gossiping, and seeking out new arrivals who could bring excitement to their lives. Lee soon absorbed the thirst for novelty that afflicted Cairenes in winter, when the city became a stop on the Grand Tour.

For newcomers to Cairo, French *Vogue* explained the expatriate's typical day: "Before lunch, one drinks cocktails at Shepheard's, where you will meet travellers coming from Syria, India, and the East." (Lunch was to be taken at the hotel grill.) Shepheard's, founded in 1841, had begun as the Middle East

Rosezell Rowland, Baron Jean Empain, and Dianne Rowland in Cairo

headquarters for Cook's tours. From its shaded terrace the cognoscenti watched the hubbub on Ibrahim Pasha Street; inside, the Moorish Hall offered refuge from the heat. Habitués, lounging on antimacassared chairs, sipped Pimm's cups or tangoed across the ballroom, whose lotus pillars, it was said, were inspired by Karnak.

Shepheard's was not to everyone's taste. Its decor was "Eighteenth Dynasty Edwardian," a visitor quipped; another thought that it looked like the British Museum. But if you wanted to find someone, one of Lee's friends explained, "you'd call Shepheard's and ask the operator, who would say, she's playing bridge at so and so's." (Men headed for the hotel's Long Bar—where Joe, the Swiss barman, heard but did not repeat their secrets.)

Groppi's, an Art Deco café near the department stores, bookshops, and galleries, offered an alternative to Shepheard's. In the late afternoon, the black-satin-and-pearls set gathered beneath the glow of the pâte de verre lights or under the umbrellas in the café's garden. Waiters in white galabias and red sashes glided from table to table with trolleys of decorated cakes. Affairs of state and of the heart were dissected while patrons savored Groppi's chocolates or, for the weight-conscious (weight was increasingly a concern of Lee's), their sugar-coated almonds.

During the winter season, the same women displayed their pearls at the Royal Opera House (where harem wives hid in screened boxes) or at the Comédie Française, whose repertory company purveyed Racine and Molière to the Francophiles. Jazz lovers congregated at the Café de Paris; cinema buffs watched movies in English or French with Greek, Arabic, and Italian translations on the side. The well-to-do drank champagne at charity balls; the most attractive newcomers were invited to dine with the immensely rich Baron Jean Empain, who was said to own Cairo's tram and electric networks, half the Belgian Congo, and all of Heliopolis.

Cairenes speculated about what went on in the baron's residence, the Palais Hindou, which resembled a surreal Angkor Wat. Baron Jean, a cross between a playboy, a showman, and a debauché, was known to surround himself with comely young women, most of them foreign. People said that guests ate from gold plates while footmen stood behind them, that dinner ended when the baron blew ear-splitting blasts on his French horn, and that alcohol flowed before, during, and after these repasts.

Lee joined the festivities at the Palais Hindou the following winter, when Rosezell Rowland, a young American dancer known as Goldie, became the baron's favorite. (Goldie's nickname came from her dance routine, an elegant striptease in which she appeared nude except for a few veils and the gold paint covering her body—a performance that had caught the baron's eye when he saw her onstage in London.) During Lee's first Egyptian winter, her social calendar was restricted to invitations by members of le Tout-Cairo. Although she

had not yet formed close friendships, "everybody Lee meets likes her," Aziz
told the Millers. Renovations at the Villa al Beit would be done early in 1935,
he hoped, when they would start repaying their invitations now that he was
being considered as undersecretary of state.

In the meantime, Aziz engaged household help—some fifteen servants,
including a personal maid for Lee, a Yugoslav woman named Elda. Lee's passion for cooking in later life, she explained, began when their Italian-trained
cook refused her access to the kitchen. (He had adopted as his culinary bible
the French cookbook *Ali-Bab,* chiefly due to the title.) Lee took pleasure in
the local food—the round flatbread, charcoal-grilled lamb, mint and yogurt
sauce, okra and melokhia (the leafy green that makes Egyptians homesick),
and sweets made of apricots or scented with rosewater. Their cook's dishes—
the antidote to Dr. Hay's diet, in which food groups could not mingle—
were an alchemy of tastes. "I was delighted," Lee recalled, "by the wonderful
Near Eastern dishes he prepared, such things as cheese and cucumber
salad . . . and meat balls with cinnamon and cumin."

Like other foreigners, Lee learned enough "kitchen Arabic" to get along.
Unlike most, she began the study of the language at the American University
of Cairo. (The AUC attracted mostly Greek, Jewish, and Levantine students;
Muslims enrolled at the National University.) The university, which held
classes near Aziz's ministry, had the advantage of requiring her presence in
town; she enrolled in chemistry as well, to gain control of the solutions used in
photographic processing.

By the end of June 1935, when the temperature registered one hundred in
the shade, Lee and Aziz agreed that they needed a change. While Alexandria
was twenty degrees cooler, the prospect of life there was not appealing. "Both
Lee & myself feel we should be perched on a mountain for at least 6 weeks,"
he told her parents, even though she had "stood the test of a summer with
great courage." To please her, he was planning a flight to Palestine with Kemal,
who hoped, with Aziz, to create an association between the countries' transportation systems, as part of the government's plan to increase foreign revenues.

In July, they flew to Jerusalem and spent the day before going on to Cyprus
to fulfill Lee's desire to see the crusaders' castles, and to swim, Aziz wrote,
"where Richard Coeur de Lion got a headache from thinking whether he could
break his habit & take a bath." Traveling in the footsteps of these childhood
heroes motivated her to take more photographs, framing the perspectives they
had seen through the castles' doors and windows. "I . . . got sort of inspired,"
she told Erik, "and did about ten swell ones."

A week later they drove to Alexandria, put the car on board, and sailed to
Europe, where they would spend the next two months, starting in Saint
Moritz. Once settled at the Villa Nimet, Lee developed back pains—"a show

of sensitiveness considering the sudden change of weather," Aziz thought. Aspirin made the pains disappear, but after joining him for her first game of golf, Lee told her parents, in one of her few surviving letters to them from this period, that she felt "very stiff, lame & old" (she was twenty-eight). She and Aziz played bezique, cooked, and walked vigorously uphill, but were so dispirited by the outlook of the summer residents and the shopkeeper mentality of the Swiss that Aziz decided to sell the villa.

In September, they visited Basel and Berlin, then spent a month in London, where Aziz bought a British car. On their return to Cairo in November, Aziz learned that someone in the upper echelons had taken advantage of his absence to have him demoted—in order to make his post available for a relative. When he tried to resign, his superior talked him into staying on. "The atmosphere is charged with electricity," he wrote.

Following Italy's annexation of Ethiopia in 1936, the political atmosphere was also full of tension. Although Egypt's support of Britain was initially popular, it was soon undermined by Italian propaganda. Students disillusioned with the country's leaders took to the streets by the thousands; when soldiers killed several of them, the government resigned. "Only the presence of a large British army on account of the coming war prevented a revolution," Aziz told the Millers. Yet he had little to say for the occupiers: "They failed shamefully when they wanted to take advantage of their actual increased power." Aziz felt so strongly anti-British that he planned to sell his new car in protest.

The political instability disturbed Lee chiefly during AUC's closure in December. One day she was trapped in a crowd of demonstrators; flirting with their captive as the police surrounded them, the students led her through a narrow passage to safety. "You can be perfectly quiet about her," Aziz told her parents. Apart from such disturbances, Lee was "fit and happy," he reassured them. "She looks healthy & feels devilish," and when not in riots was "becoming a chemist." Now that she had a license, she drove the car to town—though her command of it gave him "the jitters"—a term he picked up from Lee, for whom it meant the periods of nervous agitation that had assailed her since childhood.

∞

While Lee had, for the time being, found ways of occupying herself, Erik had been unemployed since the closing of her New York studio. He and Mafy had been living with the Millers in Poughkeepsie, where Erik set up a darkroom for the rare assignments that came his way. "It was a good thing I didn't have to support myself on that kind of income," he recalled, "or I would have starved to death." It had broken his heart, Aziz told the Millers, to have caused Erik's difficulties: "I will try & find something for him," he promised, "maybe in the cement factory or [as] agent for an air cooling firm." Creating a job for Lee's brother in Cairo would assuage Aziz's guilt and provide her with company. Aziz studied the situation, but with the change in his own prospects was unsure how to use his influence.

Lee still hoped that Erik and Mafy would join them. In a letter probably written in 1935, she explained that the cost of living was low: "An apartment in the middle of the town costs about 5 pounds and a servant about 3 pounds. Food is much cheaper than in America, and the foreign colony is so enormous that any number of congenial friends should be available. Mine for instance are all gambling. Aziz's are all sport. It never rains—so there is permanently tennis, golf—swimming—sailing—squash and even cricket—god help us!— as well as duck shooting—snipe in winter—fishing in Suez and desert expeditions to make. The language is no problem because no foreigner ever learns more Arabic than the first ten days and English is spoken generally." (By then she had abandoned Arabic in favor of "rotten detective stories.")

Wondering whether Erik was still keen on photography, she added that she had gotten over her temporary "loathing" for the art, completed a roll of film, and found a printer. "I'm taking an interest again," she continued, now that a Kodak representative had come to Cairo to set up a Kodachrome plant. She had recently driven him to a nearby village to take photographs, she continued, but the trip was marred by an accident: "Unfortunately I ran over a man or something—you see if you hit anyone here in the country, you are expected to beat it—in fact the Consulates always say HIT AND RUN—and report afterwards—so it spoiled the trip and Aziz won't let me go again unless I have a sort of guide with me—but the pictures are swell."

Aziz's jitters had been premonitory. By the next summer, his nerves were frayed after trading his old job for two new ones. He was now chief technical adviser to the National Bank of Egypt and codirector, with Kemal, of Carrier air conditioning. For the bank, he devised projects to stimulate the economy—a marble-and-granite works, a power station, a button factory, and a plan to air-condition local hotels and cinemas. Demonstrating the Miller ingenuity, Lee came up with a plan for a glass factory, since all the materials were available. Unexpectedly becoming "an ace in business," Aziz told the Millers, Lee had prepared studies for the project and talked friends at AUC into writing technical reports.

What was more, due to Aziz's efforts to promote air-conditioning by installing it at home, Lee was no longer miserable during the summer: it was now so cool that friends came to the villa every day to play poker. After two years in Cairo, he wrote, she had put on weight (which pleased him) and developed "an Egyptian complex, which means being a spectator." As the most convincing publicist for his plan to install Carrier equipment in the Parliament and other government buildings, she was, he added, "having the time of her life."

Both Lee and Aziz felt that the time was right for Erik to train with Carrier in the United States and come to Cairo in 1937. "We have had you in our minds ever since we came here," Lee told him, "and although there have been several jobs that you could have done fine—they none of them had a future like this one." Erik's lack of credentials was no obstacle provided he took the course, which Aziz would finance.

Their letters say little about local politics. In 1936, after the death of King Fuad, the Wafd Party returned to power and negotiated the Anglo-Egyptian Treaty, ending Britain's occupation of Egypt and granting support for the country's admission to the League of Nations. But many felt that Britain had gained more than Egypt had. British forces would continue to supervise local troops and the Suez Canal; Egypt would provide military aid in the event of a European war—which seemed likely, given the German occupation of the Rhine and the civil war in Spain. While the government called the Anglo-Egyptian Treaty a triumph of national honor, most Egyptians felt that the British had too much power.

Seeing the world from her new Middle Eastern perspective, Lee also worried about the instability among the Arabs of Palestine. "I get so bitter when I even think of it," she told her parents, "all the money my good Jewish friends have sunk into it—and how wrong they were. You only have to take a good look at the blasted place to be completely floored as to why everyone from the time of Moses has been screaming for that rotten country." That autumn, she spent two months in bed "sulking and just too damn tired to bother with anyone," and in November she underwent a course of glandular treatments in Jerusalem with a specialist, despite her opinion of Palestine.

Feeling sufficiently refreshed to prepare for the arrival of Erik and Mafy, she asked for items that could not be found in Egypt, "a great deal of popcorn" and a popper, Golden Bantam corn seed, buttermilk tablets, Cape Cod lighters for the fireplace, and her raccoon coat for European winters. Aziz had them purchase a Chevrolet sedan in his name, fill its trunk with shotgun shells, and put the car in the hold. (This illegal cargo, Erik recalled, caused them as much distress as the rough winter crossing.)

After their arrival in Alex on March 4, 1937, Aziz shepherded Erik, Mafy, and the Chevrolet through customs by the traditional means: drinking many cups of coffee with the customs official and paying a bribe. Intrigued by this lesson in local business practice, Erik fell in love with Egypt. "I loved the dryness and the smells," he said, "the pungent odour of the smoke from cattle dung and cooking and mules and donkeys and camels." The two-lane road south seemed well engineered, though it was disconcerting to learn from Aziz that the British had built it to speed up the delivery of troops in case of an Italian invasion. Arriving at last in Dokki, he was deeply moved by the sight of Lee, "with her blond hair and her blue eyes and her arms tight around us, crying and carrying on and then all of a sudden very calm." The Villa al Beit expressed Aziz's position, Erik thought, as did the presence of servants "all over the place."

In a few days, Aziz took Erik to the ultramodern Carrier office and introduced him to the staff: a group of American-trained engineers; their supervisor, a Scot who had installed cooling systems in South African diamond mines; and the Egyptian foreman. After a short time, he and Mafy moved to their own apartment, taking with them their favorite servant at the Villa al Beit, a man named Mohammed, who became their cook, factotum, guide, and, in time, their friend.

Their compatriots, most of whom were with Standard Oil, were "impossible," in Mafy's opinion. They lived outside Cairo in Maadi (where they had their own country clubs), and "might as well have been in Kansas." The American University, which Lee had by then abandoned, was slightly more cosmopolitan, but the American Mission, a blend of Presbyterians, Baptists, and Evangelicals, was of no interest. While Mafy investigated the expatriate scene, Erik worked six days a week with Carrier, whose first assignment was to install air-conditioning in the House of Parliament in time for King Farouk's inauguration.

Left to her own devices, Mafy became Lee's partner in escapades, the foil in whom she saw her own predicament mirrored. Lee's photographs of her sister-in-law's encounters with Egypt bring out her impish spirit as well as her piquant good looks. A cinematic sequence of street scenes and close-ups of Mafy and a friend in the Khan el-Khalili bazaar show her first at the arched entrance to the maze of carpet merchants and trinket vendors, then inside an antique shop gazing at the display while the friend looks up at her from below. Lee's composition positions Mafy as a woman reflecting on her foreignness: shot through the plate-glass window, it frames an arresting moment of self-knowledge.

Residents loved to gossip about "the American girls," as Lee and Mafy were called, whose undefined social status allowed them to defy local custom. One day after an afternoon of shopping, rather than resort to Groppi's they made their way to a bar where they behaved like men in their clubs. Despite his anger at Lee's behavior, Aziz knew better than to interfere. ("He tried to be possessive with her," Mafy explained, "but it didn't work.") Emboldened, Lee and Mafy invaded the Long Bar at Shepheard's. By local standards, they were loose women, but excuses were made for them as Americans, and as Aziz's protégées.

Desert picnic, Lee sitting in the center, Egypt, 1938

Like Lee and Mafy, the women in Baron Empain's circle were among the most liberated in Egypt, though some said that they formed a European harem. The baron surrounded himself with beautiful women because their jealousy of one another made them behave, he insisted, but he had the sense to see in Goldie a mistress who accepted him as he was. Lee, Mafy, and Erik often dined at the Palais Hindou, where the festivities sometimes lasted through the night. In the early morning, guests were called to breakfast and urged by their host to shake off their hangovers with a ride in the desert.

Goldie survived better than most because she did not drink, took easily to riding, and did her best to learn Arabic. These years were, she recalled, an education, but one that had little to do with real life. Members of the black-satin-and-pearls set gloated over the details of the rival pregnancies in the Palais Hindou. When Goldie and another of the baron's companions became pregnant at the same time, he promised to wed the one who bore him a son.

Lee's conduct made her almost as notorious as the baron's lovers, yet she could not help being indiscreet, Gertie Wissa thought. It was no use trying to change her, she observed years later: "I took her as she was; she behaved like a man." Gertie recalled her dismay when Lee declared, "If I need to pee, I pee in the road; if I have a letch for someone, I hop into bed with him." She added, "This was natural to Lee. She had no morals." Nor did she have any use for the prevailing sexual hypocrisy.

Despite the sultriness of life in Cairo, sex outside marriage was unthinkable for Muslim women, though some of their husbands visited the brothels on the rue Clot Bey. Few risked their position by having affairs. While they indulged themselves in other ways (eating sweets, playing cards, gossiping), a shared sexual timidity kept women from venturing outside the *haramlek*. This fear, along with the mentality of bourgeois Cairo—where neighbors noted whose car was parked outside whose abode—created an atmosphere almost as claustrophobic as Poughkeepsie's.

In the spring of 1937, Lee organized the first of what would become her preferred means of escape, expeditions into the desert. Her plan, to visit the Coptic monasteries of Saint Antonius and Saint Paul, near the Red Sea, required careful preparation. After engaging a guide and a Sudanese soldier whose vehicle was equipped with a sun compass, she talked four carloads of friends into joining her. They were to bring supplies; Lee would provide drinks. Late in the day, as the guide went on to check the road while the group set up camp, Lee brought out a large thermos—which proved to be full of martinis. Everyone laughed, but hours of drinking alcohol made them so thirsty that they downed the guide's water supplies when he reappeared that evening.

Within a short time, Lee was planning desert expeditions with the skill of a military tactician. Treks to distant sites became the antidote to boredom, and taking photographs of them, a way to evoke and transcend her "Egyptian complex." As she moved from spectatorship to knowledge of the country—capturing it, piece by piece, with her camera—photography allowed her to say how she felt as an expatriate and reawakened her eye for incongruities.

She began by photographing sites of the kind that she had seen through her father's stereoscope viewer—the bazaars, pharaonic monuments, and ruins that for most Westerners typified Egypt. Along with such scenes, often taken from odd angles, she also photographed people at work—not as ethnographic subjects but as people like herself. In time, her camera became a means of transport, a way to escape from elite Cairo. Many of her images from this time seem to lack a human presence. Yet if one looks closely, an emotive quality may be implied in the framing, or in the details that shape meaning and show the acuteness of the eye that saw in the desert vast dimensions of shape and light.

Sand Track, taken on a trip to the Red Sea, is perhaps the first of Lee's Egyptian photographs in which space becomes tangible. The image is composed of wavy lines in the sand, not paths that one might follow but tracks made by the wind. There is no horizon, and in a sense, no frame—these patterns, the photograph implies, continue beyond its borders. The sense of unbounded space is further dynamized by the erotics of the image. *Sand Track* makes a subtle link between creative energy and the oddly lush landscape—here seen not as empty but as a plenitude to which she would escape with chosen lovers and friends.

If *Sand Track* conveys Lee's deepening response to the desert, an architectural study entitled *Stairway, Cairo* hints at the impasse from which she longed to escape. In this melancholy shot of a stairway leading nowhere (the picture edge edits out hopes of arrival), diagonal lines focus the eye on details that suggest confinement. Beyond the stairs a window crisscrossed with metal bars is obscured by a large black cloth. The inhabitants cannot look out, nor can we see in. This composition stages a "no exit."

Seeking a broader perspective on her life in Egypt, Lee went to the top of one of its most famous monuments, the Great Pyramid at Giza. Early one morning, she climbed its craggy footholds step by step with her equipment to take the bold shot that is one of her best-known images—one in which her presence is felt like an invisible signature. While the Great Pyramid is unseen, its mass is implied in the huge triangular shadow cast over nearby fields to the Western Desert, as if the monument points the way toward some new destination. With this theatrical photograph, she met her jitters head-on and defied them.

Nusch and Paul Eluard, Roland Penrose, Man Ray, and Ady Fidelin, Mougins, 1937
(Lee Miller)

Chapter 9

Surrealist Encampments

(Summer 1937)

Lee began planning her escape in May. For the next four months it would be too hot for desert treks; the prospect of another summer at home, playing cards while the air conditioner hummed, was not inviting. Aziz agreed to her spending the summer in France and with his usual generosity underwrote the trip. Her maid, Elda, would keep Lee company until he could join her there later. The two women sailed to Marseilles, took the train to Paris, and checked into the Hôtel Prince de Galles.

One of the first people Lee contacted was Julien Levy, who asked her to join him at a fancy dress ball that night. After unpacking, she changed into a dark blue evening gown—it was too late to devise a costume—and set off to the party. At first, she watched from the sidelines. The guests seemed to have stepped out of a Surrealist painting. Max Ernst, disguised as a bandit, had dyed his hair bright blue; Man Ray, whom she had not seen for five years, was equally eccentric. The women had gone in for displays of pulchritude. One was draped in ivy; others wore little more than scarves and bangles. Lee's elegance set her apart.

Ernst had brought with him Roland Penrose, a wealthy English artist and collector who was sloughing off his Quaker upbringing in the company of the

Surrealists. Like Ernst, Penrose came as a colorful bandit. His hair was green, his right hand blue, and his pants the colors of the rainbow—a costume that made him feel awkward, until, catching sight of Lee, he felt instead as if he had been hit by lightning.

The groundwork for this *coup de foudre* had been laid by the Englishman's awareness of Lee as muse: she had been the model for Man's most erotic images (Penrose had seen her lips in *Observatory Time* the year before in London), as well as Cocteau's statue and Julien's lover. Others at the party also found her entrancing. Georges Bataille and Michel Leiris agreed that they had never seen a more beautiful woman; Man embraced her as if the bitterness between them were forgotten. Lee stood before Penrose like Surrealist royalty. Delighted when she warmed to him despite "the abysmal contrast between her elegance and my own slumlike horror," the Englishman recalled, he persuaded Ernst to invite her to dinner.

The following night at Ernst's, Lee talked about Egypt, drank liberally, and flirted with Penrose. She awoke the next morning in his bed. For the next two weeks, they were inseparable; Lee returned to her hotel only to change her clothes. It is likely, given Penrose's worship of Picasso (whose work he collected), that they went to the Palais de Chaillot to see the artist's monumental *Guernica*, painted after Germans in Franco's employ bombed the Spanish town. While they delighted in seeing mutual friends, much of their time was spent alone. On his return to London at the end of the month, Roland wrote, "I have slept and woken at last from a dream—shall I ever dream again anything so marvellous?"

Included in his letter was an invitation to join him and some friends in Cornwall for July. Lee accepted immediately. She crossed the Channel with Man and Ady Fidelin, his Martiniquaise lover; Roland drove them to his brother's farmhouse, Lambe Creek, where they were joined by Paul and Nusch Eluard, the English artist Eileen Agar and her companion Joseph Bard, Max Ernst and the young artist Leonora Carrington, the Belgian painter E. L. T. Mesens, and later Henry Moore and his wife, Irina. Guests were urged to shed their inhibitions along with their clothes. "It was a delightful Surrealist house party," Agar wrote, "with Roland taking the lead, ready to turn the slightest encounter into an orgy. I remember going off to watch Lee taking a bubble-bath, but there was not quite enough room in the tub for all of us."

Roland's house party was also a celebration of the newly formed British branch of Surrealism. The year before, he, the critic Herbert Read, and the poet David Gascoyne, who at twenty had published a *Short Study of Surrealism,* conspired to launch the movement in England by rounding up recruits, including Paul Nash and Henry Moore, for an exhibition at the New Burlington Galleries that June. Breton, Eluard, and Man chose works to be sent from Europe; Penrose, Nash, and Read scoured London for British exemplars. On their visit to Agar's studio, which resembled a mermaid's grotto, they adopted her at first sight. "One day I was an artist exploring highly personal combinations of form and content," she recalled, "and the next I was calmly informed that I was a Surrealist!"

The exhibition—some four hundred drawings, paintings, sculptures, and objects (including Man's *Observatory Time* and Agar's fishnet bath curtains)—caused a sensation when it opened on June 11. "A nation which has produced such superrealists as William Blake and Lewis Carroll is to the manner born," Read declared. During its three-week run, T. S. Eliot stopped to stare at Meret Oppenheim's fur-lined teacup, Augustus John left the hall when Eluard called the Marquis de Sade a martyr for freedom, and a nearly suffocated Salvador Dalí had to be freed from his diving helmet, part of the suit he donned to speak on the depths of the unconscious. The critics' dismissal of the works only strengthened the group's resolve. That autumn, Penrose traveled to Barcelona in support of the Republicans, and the next spring, shortly before meeting Lee, he showed his paintings in the Surrealist section of an international anti-Franco exhibition.

By the summer, he and his friends were ready to celebrate the year's accomplishments—their recognition as the artistic vanguard and their invigorated love lives. The woods surrounding Lambe Creek let in the sun while ensuring privacy; the nearby tidal creek inspired nude bathing. Looking at the snapshots Roland took that summer as Lambe Creek's impresario (which he arranged in albums like still versions of home movies), one feels the group's mutual delight—including their love of al fresco romps and erotic poses. In one group of snaps, Max Ernst, dripping with seaweed, emerges from the creek as the Old Man of the Sea to fondle the breasts of his mermaid, Leonora; in others, Lee greets Roland from their bedroom window, revealing her form without allegorical justification. In still others, she sprawls seductively across the laps of Ady and Nusch while her lover moves in for a close-up.

Lee's jitters all but disappeared in the company of these unconventional friends, whose relaxed sensuality also helped Roland forget his Quaker past. For the time being, while reassuring Aziz with vague letters about her trip, she could live as if she were on her own. Like Lee, the other women at Lambe Creek were full of mischief. One day Ady, Nusch, Leonora, and Lee, all stylishly dressed, sat for Roland's group portrait with their eyes closed (but holding demitasse cups) in a satire on ladylike behavior. Women Surrealists, Agar wrote, dressed "with panache." "Our concern with appearance was not a result of pandering to masculine demands," she continued, "but rather a common attitude to life. Juxtaposition by us of a Schiaparelli dress with outrageous behavior or conversation simply carried the beliefs of Surrealism into public existence." What Agar did not say was that it also excited their partners.

From our perspective, their antics may not seem revolutionary, but at the time, the group's indulgence in shared fantasies felt like Surrealism in action. Sex, it was understood, nourished the imagination; it was obvious that the currents among them proved Breton's credo—that the lifting of inhibitions meant freedom for all. It would be hard to overstate the group's delight in playing at life rather than having to take it seriously, at a time when war seemed imminent. Eluard, having canceled plans to attend the International Writers' Conference in Spain to join Roland, said he preferred friendship to politics—in the company of those who (like Agar) saw Surrealism as a movement "bent on opening hilarious new avenues to free thought."

Agar also noted that despite Surrealism's liberatory stance, women did not enjoy equal status. A Surrealist's partner "was expected to behave as the great man's muse," she wrote, "not to have an active creative existence." And when it came to sexual freedom, men took the lead. Nusch did not object when her husband offered her to those he admired, a gesture he called an *hommage.* Eileen—for whom the poet was "a fountain of joy and faith in life"—converted to his cult of erotic freedom when they took the lead in what would became generalized partner-swapping. Her partner did not object, she recalled, "because he was himself enjoying a liaison with Nusch."

The group also encouraged exhibitionism, especially in women. In this context, Lee's penchant for unveiling her bosom may have seemed like an emancipatory gesture (as if she were Delacroix's Liberty leading the people), as well as confirmation of her fame as the woman with the most beautiful breasts in Paris. Breton thought of women as *"femmes-enfants,"* childlike repositories of sensuality or magnetic conductors whose sexual energy opened the dreamworld of desire. Reflecting on this fantasy years later, Leonora Carrington remarked that Surrealist women functioned like "talking dogs—we adored the master and did tricks for him."

In the group mythology, Leonora, then a twenty-year-old with wild black hair, personified the *femme-enfant,* and Lee the full-blooded female muse whose erotic freedom inspires creativity. Roland had, until their meeting, a limited knowledge of heterosexual passion. His first affair had been with a man; his marriage in 1925 to the French poet Valentine Boué had remained unconsummated due to her unusual anatomy, which prevented penetration. Roland rejoiced in Lee's air of barely contained recklessness. "You have given me something new, something so potent," he told her with the gratitude of one who doubts his amatory abilities, then finds that he is more than satisfactory. They amused themselves by painting a bare-breasted ship's figurehead—one of the sirens Roland called "cuties"; he began a series of works on the theme of a sailboat filled with wavy blond hair—in which friends saw his pleasure in sharing his fantasies with a cooperative muse. ("The blond season is favourable to my caresses / Your blond hair opens to me the boat of your body," Eluard wrote in "The Last Letter to Roland Penrose.")

Lee's "blond season" also fascinated Eileen Agar, who watched her closely. Lee was "a remarkable woman, completely unsentimental and sometimes ruthless," she believed, yet at the same time *l'élan vital* personified. The photographs and collages Lee and Eileen made of each other in 1937 reveal the ways in which each woman saw herself in the other. Lee took her most striking portrait of Eileen on a trip to Brighton, when both women brought their cameras: she caught Eileen's shadow silhouetted against a curved pillar in the Brighton Pavilion at the precise moment when the Rolleiflex hanging from her neck made it seem that she was pregnant with her apparatus.

About this time, Lee also posed Eileen next to one of her "poetic objects," an antique figure of a household god that she had painted and adorned. As if illustrating her views on the equal importance of dress and art, Lee's photograph makes the artist's patterned blouse part of the composition. Another of Lee's photographs of her friend, facing the camera, appears in a collage portrait of Agar as creative artist. Neither woman played the *femme-enfant,* nor did they go along with the double standard. "The men were expected to be very free sexually," Agar wrote, "but when a woman like Lee Miller adopted the same attitude, the hypocritical upset was tremendous."

Reading Lee's letters to Aziz, one learns that she took pains not to upset him. When she told him that she had gone to Cornwall to be with friends, he replied that she was like "a thoroughbred who has been kept in stables too long." In the dark about the nature of the exercise she was taking, Aziz agreed to her request for more money and asked her to join him for a holiday in Alex at the end of August. "Amuse yourself my darling but not too much," he continued. "Cairo is pretty boring as you can imagine, which makes me support the idea that you should be away for your own sake even though it makes me feel lonesome and dejected to be without you."

He would be without her for the next two months. Before the party at Lambe Creek broke up, the key couples (Roland and Lee, Paul and Nusch, Man and Ady, Eileen and Joseph) agreed to reconvene in Mougins, the Provençal village where Picasso was spending the summer with Dora Maar. Lee and Roland went first to Brussels to meet the Belgian Surrealists Magritte and Delvaux, then drove south down along the Rhône to the Riviera, stopping on the way at Hauterives, whose postmaster, Monsieur Cheval, had built a naïve structure he called le Palais Idéal. His Ideal Palace testified, the Surrealists claimed, to the instinctual creativity in free spirits.

In mid-August, the group converged on Picasso's summer quarters, l'Hôtel Vaste Horizon. The view from their rooms looked past the vineyards below the village to the rooftops of Cannes and, in the distance, the Mediterranean. Life there was even more pleasurable than in Cornwall. Mornings were spent sunbathing, swimming, and doing gymnastics at the Plage de la Garoupe, near Antibes, or at Juan les Pins. At noon, the group repaired to the hotel's vine-covered terrace to wash down the robust Provençal cuisine with local wines. Each meal was a celebration. The photographers—Man, Lee, Roland, Eileen, and Dora—took turns capturing one another on film, as if their intimacy were a kind of artistic collaboration. Picasso, in his role as *"le Maître"* (the Master), urged the party to work after lunch. Those who were less disciplined, or driven, retired to their rooms to rest and make love.

As at Lambe Creek, the air crackled with erotic energy. "I think if love comes your way you should accept it," Agar mused. After ending her fling with Eluard, she decided that theirs was a companionship of minds and befriended Nusch, "a delightful being who could never be permanently tamed." Lee photographed the poet with his arm wrapped protectively around Nusch against a background of ruins; in Roland's portrait of the couple, the poet, in a suit and tie, caresses his ecstatic wife, whose blouse is unbuttoned to reveal her torso. Nusch was the daughter of a circus performer, a past that endeared her to the Surrealists. In their act together, she was chained up first by her father, then by members of the audience, after which she freed herself—"a career," Agar wrote, "which was to prepare her well for later life with Eluard."

That summer, Roland, whose fantasies included similar scenarios, persuaded Lee to let him tie her up during lovemaking. He practiced bondage, he believed, because he had been plucked from his mother's breast and given to a wet nurse: "RP suffered," he wrote (as if he were someone else), "from an obsessive desire to make sure, so he thought, that the object of his desire would never escape him. . . . He longed to make sure of his girl . . . possess her in an imperative manner which would not offend her." Valentine had felt "honoured" when tied to a pine tree during his courtship of her but became angry "because the resin stuck to her tender skin." While Roland's memoir does not say whether Lee, too, felt honored by the manner in which he possessed her, their charged rapport gave birth to an intense artistic partnership.

Outsiders rarely have access to pacts made in the privacy of the boudoir—even when, as at l'Hôtel Vaste Horizon, friends stage them for one another in games and artworks. Like Lee, each woman worked out a different accommodation to her lover's desire. The many works of art showing these women's "submissiveness" assume their complicity, since the point of view is usually that of their male companions, but rarely hint at a particular woman's decision to play the *femme-enfant*, or femme fatale, in the unfolding scenario of sexual relations.

Having secured his object of desire (Lee was in love with him and he with her), Roland felt free to enjoy others. Judging by his photos of Ady Fidelin, which vibrate with sensuality, her relations with Man enhanced her appeal as the only dark-skinned woman in the group. Man and Roland took turns photographing each other with Ady on a boat, she swam nude for Roland's camera (in one shot, posing in the arms of her naked admirer), and let him photograph her as a water sprite in a remote coastal inlet. Their enjoyment of these romps did not change Ady's rapport with the other women. Together, she, Lee, and Nusch pose like fashion models for Roland (then perform a bump and grind), an exuberant Lee brandishes an octopus speared on a fishing trip, and Eileen dances on a rooftop after a party, her breasts visible beneath her diaphanous gown.

The best-known photographs from this golden summer record the *déjeuner sur l'herbe* attended by Man, Ady, Paul, Nusch, Roland, and Lee. The picnic's sylvan setting gives a sense of plenitude, as do their expressions, but it is the women's dress—or undress—that creates the racy mood. While the men are clothed, the women are topless, as if sexual abandon were contagious. In two images by Roland, a rakish Lee ignores the camera's focus on her torso. In Lee's voluptuous and narratively complex shot of the group, Paul embraces Nusch as she bends backward, Man looks slyly at Lee while Ady grins, and Roland has "the appearance of a liberated Englishman freed from the burdens of his puritan past." Lee's photographs celebrate the group's elective affinities while documenting her own role as catalyst.

In addition to the emotional bonds among the couples, the glue that held them together was their Picasso worship. Eluard often said "that he was happy to be alive in the 20th century if only to have met Picasso," while for Agar, the Spaniard was "le Peintre Soleil . . . his thoughts and moods somehow setting the ruling temperature." Unlike Eluard, he was not flirtatious yet he dominated both sexes through his powerful presence. Penrose, too, was struck by Picasso's "small, neat, well-built physique." "His well-bronzed skin," he wrote, "his agile controlled movement, his athletic figure and small shapely hands and feet seemed to belong to the Mediterranean scene as though he were the reincarnation of the hero of an ancient myth."

The artist wore his authority as if by divine right, but as group ringleader, he amused himself with games that were playfully transgressive. One day he told the group to exchange identities. He became Don José Picasso, Eileen's partner became Pablo Bard to match her Dora Agar, Man answered to Roland Ray—a revealing choice under the circumstances. One wonders whether Roland reciprocated by becoming Man Penrose, and how Lee, Ady, and Nusch handled the situation. It is unfortunate that their thoughts about the game went unrecorded.

Picasso also appreciated playfulness in others. He complimented Agar on her collages of flotsam and invited her to see his marine treasures—pebbles, shards, and shells—which he often made into jewelry for the women he loved. Dora wore a heavy African bracelet on which he had carved his emblematic minotaur cavorting with a group of maenads, and Nusch, a bone shard engraved for her. Gifts of this kind were marks of his affection.

Since Picasso's many portraits of Nusch mingle tenderness with reserve, there has been speculation about their rapport. Decades later, friends were still unsure what they felt for each other. At the time, their relations were complicated by Eluard's offer to lend Picasso his wife to express his love for both of them. The artist later told Françoise Gilot that his tryst with Nusch was merely "a gesture of friendship." "I only did it to make him happy," he added, yet later insisted that theirs was not a carnal affair. While it is impossible to know what happened, Eluard's gesture seems like an oblique avowal of homosexual desire—a tense subject among the Surrealists, for whom love between men was taboo, yet a recurrent urge that found expression in the exchange, real or fantasized, of their women.

It is clear from the portraits Picasso painted in Mougins that he was aware of this undercurrent. In contrast to the monochrome violence of *Guernica,* he chose acid yellows, greens, and pinks for a set of paintings of his friends as "Arlésiennes," the women of Arles whose picturesque dress had inspired van Gogh. Having already used their headdress as an intriguing shape in his Cubist period, Picasso returned to the theme in these fantastic portraits, based on the artist's idea of his subjects rather than on actual likenesses.

He began with Eluard. When he produced his portrait of the poet at lunch, members of the group were shocked: he was shown with large breasts, giving suck to a cat. "One could distinguish in the strong features and sparkling eyes a certain resemblance to the profile of Eluard," Penrose recalled, "but it was disconcerting to see his head surmounted by an Arlesian bonnet and that the poet had changed sex." Evoking the summer of 1937 years later, Penrose called the Eluard portrait a "joke," another instance of "the triumph of nonsense" that made Mougins so exciting. At the time, the likeness was troubling, the art historian William Rubin surmises, because it was "not only a transvestite but a transsexual image"—moreover, one that implies Picasso's sense of the poet as "a repressed homosexual, employing his wife as a means of entering vicariously into a sexual relationship."

Following Eluard's lead, Penrose told the Maître that he was welcome to enjoy Lee's favors. "Just as Eluard had made his wife, Nusch, available to Picasso, Penrose offered up . . . Lee Miller to the artist," writes John Richardson, Picasso's biographer. Surrealist women were, in a sense, interchangeable, to be traded as tokens of affection among men whose feelings for each other could not be expressed otherwise.

What Picasso made of Lee's charms may be deduced from his six portraits of her as an Arlésienne—one who is joyfully, unproblematically female. He began this series the day after painting Eluard. Lee's torso, naked from the waist up, appears against a gay pink background. Roland's description transmits his pleasure in this "astonishing likeness," which vibrates with sensuality: "Lee appeared in profile, her face a brilliant yellow like the sun with no modeling. Two smiling eyes and a green mouth were placed on the same side of

*Picasso portrait of Lee
Miller as an Arlésienne,
1937*

the face and her breasts seemed like the sails of ships filled with a joyous
breeze."

Picasso used the same loose brushwork and playful colors for the next five
portraits. In the best of these, a playful tribute from one artist to another, Lee's
torso is pink, her face and breasts a deep sky blue. But what distinguishes this
version from the others more than its coloring is the presence of her lower
body, including a vagina that resembles an eye—a witty detail in the portrait of
a photographer. Lee said years later, "You do not sit for Picasso, he just brought
it to me one day having painted it from memory." That day, in his mind's eye,
she had looked back at him from her source of energy—which opened and
closed like the lens of a camera.

Lee's role as Picasso's muse made her even more precious to Roland. She
was an *inspiratrice d'oeuvres,* he told her later, in a letter. During their euphoric
weeks at Mougins, he began a series of works inspired by her, the most original
of which are collaged arrangements of postcards forming patterns of color with
strong personal associations. Lee's solar presence is evoked in one of these,
Soleil de Mougins, which Roland began one morning when she was still in bed.
(She roused herself to photograph him fitting the pieces together on the floor.)

In another, *Real Woman,* a cut-out of Lee's body emphasizing the roundness of her breasts recalls Man's images of her light-dappled torso—perhaps an allusion to her place in her former lover's imagination. Lee would have gotten the joke in the name of the technique Roland chose for this image—*frottage,* from the French *frotter,* to rub: Roland claimed her form as his own by outlining it on a paper he placed on a wooden surface, then rubbing with a pencil in the artistic equivalent of lovemaking. "The work and the title point to a new and very different relationship in Penrose's life from the one he had had with Valentine Boué," a critic notes. "Valentine was fey, introspective and intellectual. Lee, on the other hand, was sensual and voluptuous—a 'real woman.'"

Picasso often said that his art was his diary. Roland's postcards, born in the creative rush of his affair with Lee, chronicle their rapport and assume her role in his discovery of the medium, which he would make his own. At the same time, his excitement sparked hers. Lee photographed Roland fitting pieces together into bright blocks of color; they drove along the Riviera to find cards with stimulating themes; he sought her advice about form, background, and composition.

During this time, Lee also made several accomplished collages, including one of Mougins, which she gave to Roland, and a montaged photo portrait of Agar that is her *hommage* to another woman artist. Lee placed her Brighton shot of Eileen pregnant with her camera (an image that made Picasso laugh) against a mottled background, then set an enlarged white cut-out of the artist's profile from the same image opposite its darker twin. The composition shows both sides of Agar floating above a bird's-eye view of the Riviera, as if she were surveying their artistic playground.

These collages surely amused the group at l'Hôtel Vaste Horizon, who understood their connotations. Before the war, when Braque and Picasso first played with collage, the word—which comes from *coller,* to paste or glue—had carried a meaning that reinforced their works' visual shock; in slang *collage* means an illicit love affair, one in which the lovers are "pasted" together. With Lee as catalyst, Roland had reinvented the form in the racy atmosphere of the group's affinities, using it to imply their delight in dalliance.

Breton, always adept at summing up character, called Roland a Surrealist *dans l'amitié* (in friendship) and Eileen a Surrealist *à l'accent ludique* (with a playful touch). One might use his terms to evoke this joyful summer, when the group's shared unleashing of desire produced a sense of mutual liberation. To be part of a group whose creative energies spilled into one another's lives at a time of impending social disaster would have been irresistible, and ties formed under such pressure, all the more binding. Appropriately, these affinities became tangible in combinations of disparate materials—objects, costumes, portraits, collages—that evoke the gleefulness with which people and materials came together when unconstrained by convention.

For Lee, the summer of 1937 was also the antidote to Cairo—where such "goings-on" (her term for risqué gestures) were unthinkable, even in the crowd around Baron Empain. Summing up their rapturous holiday in a draft of her memoir, *A Look at My Life* (1988), Eileen Agar thought it inevitable "to confuse the delights of being young with the place and the time one was young in; the south of France that summer, Surrealism on the horizon, Stravinsky in the air, and Freud under the bed." "The world was small then," she continued, "the freedom of the intellectuals and the pleasure loving twenties and early thirties were the privilege of those few with avant-garde ideas. . . . In spite of the increasing Teutonic fury," her memoir concludes, "we could still bathe and ignore it, bask in the sun, eat and have a merry heart."

Lee on sand-skiing expedition, 1938 (Mary Anita Loos)

Chapter 10

The Egyptian Complex

(1937–39)

The merriment ceased in mid-September, when Picasso returned to Paris and the others set off in different directions. Lee and Roland spent some days in the capital before her long-delayed return to Cairo. As tokens of his love, Roland gave her several etchings by Picasso, his own *Soleil de Mougins* (the collage she had inspired), books on Surrealism, and an antique necklace. They hoped to be together the next summer, but agreed that it would be foolish to forgo other loves. En route to Marseilles, Lee composed a note to Roland:

> *It's cold in the train—I'm alone with the noise*
> *—and my tears, unlike your chains*
> *—bind me—*
> *it was true—it is true*
> *—I'm leaving—I love you*
> *and I'll return.*

On board the *Mohamed Ali el-Kebir,* she began what would become a long correspondence with her lover, emphasizing their bond in sensual and painterly language. Shipboard life, she wrote, brought back all she disliked about Cairo: "the heat—the bad food—the mutual suspicion & hostility." Swimming, drinking, and sunbathing naked did not calm her sense of disjointedness. The different parts of her life resembled "a water soaked jig-saw puzzle, drunken bits that don't match in shape or design." And while she was trying to rearrange them, she went on, "I get nervous and jerk at them & wonder if I ever was meant to fit together."

During their separation, Roland was to tell her everything. "Cuties [will] fall in love with you," she wrote, "now that you find it's so easy, as with me." ("Cutie" was the right term for a bedmate, she teased, "tho I find Q.T. better, as it means in Yankee slang 'on the sly.'") In a letter to Man inviting him to Cairo she wrote that she had never felt "so miserable leaving or going anywhere—It seemed that all the people in the world that I love were together."

To neither did she mention one exception to the awfulness of shipboard life: a fresh-faced English officer named Wingate Charlton. Having noticed her before they set sail, Charlton was thrilled when she sat down at his table. They spent the crossing in the bars and at the prow, watching dolphins. Lee became fond of the young man, who may have reminded her of Roland. She was the most beautiful woman he had ever seen, he recalled, and "frightfully jolly . . . a bit raucous at times but there was always tremendous fun with her."

Aziz met their ship in Alex on October 12. The next day, they began an expedition across the Western Desert to Siwa with Henry Hopkinson, a British diplomat, and his wife, Alice. At Marsa Matruh, where they stopped for the night, the coastal town's reputation as a trysting spot for Antony and Cleopatra put Lee in mind of her amours. She noted "five shades of blue as the water changed depth," she told Roland, "and when I was in it the surface reflected the palest and tenderest of pinks—the sky all dappled and Belgian Magritte." After peering through the curved glass bars of the lighthouse's prismatic lens, she noticed some of them lying shattered on the ground. One wonders if she saw in this image the hope of fitting together the parts of her life like compositions glimpsed through her viewfinder.

Marsa's other attractions included Cleopatra's Bath, a rock formation with three rooms hollowed out by the sea. In one, Lee discovered "a sort of sunken pool tub which fills and empties with high and low water in which she used to sit all day long during the heat of the summer." A modern Cleopatra like herself could watch "infinite variations of blue and curious wave[s] and sand worn rocks, all of which have an even more weird surface, as if they had been heavily painted in violet gray, which is now dripping and melting." From this point on, Lee's letters dwell on the painterly aspect of her treks as if by this means she could continue her collaboration with Roland while taking possession of Egypt in a new medium, the written word.

The next day, the party crossed a landscape of eroded hills and sand seas. (Until 1932, when the road to Siwa was finished, this remote oasis had been unreachable except by camel.) Approaching Siwa at sunset, they made out the ruins of a fortress—"skyscraper towers built of mud, disguising themselves to look like the upjutting rocks all around," she told Roland. "In the distance the rocks look like savage thatched huts—with the hard surface thrusting out over the worn soft rock below." The oasis seemed like a mirage. Lee awoke the next day to the sounds of the Siyaha fantasia, a celebration of male friendship whose trancelike rituals, she went on, "brought me to life." As a foreign woman (or honorary man) she was allowed to watch the circles of dancing Siwans, Arabs, and Bedouins. When a local man jumped up to join a veiled belly dancer who appeared unexpectedly, "they outdid in sexual suggestion anything I've seen," she continued, though both were "covered in mountains of clothing."

But when she tried to photograph the Siwan women in their veils, they ran away "spitting and cursing, and making signs against the evil eye." While the women, who married young, could speak only to male relations, the men, she was told, were "all pederasts and even tho some of them marry . . . keep a boy on the ground floor and the woman on the top floor." The government had just banned same-sex unions to "stop the goings on"—the sexual escapades that sparked her libido and Roland's.

Near the end of October, she and Aziz went to the Red Sea to fish with the Hopkinsons: "rather a flop," she told Roland, "not especially from the fact that I caught no fish—but the combination of people." She feigned outrage when Henry declared his love and practiced forbearance with Aziz, who was sulking—perhaps because they were not sleeping together. "You can imagine what my nerves and temper are like," she continued. Although Aziz was irritable, she was trying "to be patient and unquarrelsome because he has so often been like an angel with me." Nonetheless, she suffered from "the jitters," as well as "an upset sex life."

What was worse, she distrusted her own emotions. "When I got married after fifteen years of fiddling around I really did it for better or for worse—I really thot that at last I was going to settle down and be consistently attached to someone—With that little idea blown to hell by the summer, and you, it makes me cynically suspicious of any attachment I might make,—of my love for you—of living with you and being always with you—my 'always' don't seem to mean much, do they. And yet I love you so much that I'm in a sort of ecstasy of agony most of the time." Her condition was that of "the flagellant saints or hysterically repressed nuns who make a mystic marriage." "I'm like a condemned person in a cell," she went on, "full of self pity, misery and sexual excitement."

Despite the tensions among them, Lee, Aziz, and the Hopkinsons set out again in November to the Wadi Rish Rash ibex preserve, an oasis surrounded by bloodred cliffs. "It was like being in the bottom of God's bathtub," she told Roland, but while the site was spectacular, she longed to be in Cornwall "or some place green with you." The only trips she did not describe in detail were those taken with Wingate Charlton—to the Sinai, the Suez Canal, and the Coptic monasteries at Wadi Natrun, known to expats as the Troon. They packed picnic lunches and, occasionally, gear for the night; the young officer introduced Lee to medieval romances, which he read aloud in their tent. During the day, he accompanied her as she photographed the rounded buildings from arresting angles. In one shot of the ancient retreat, the sensuality denied inside its walls is evoked in the breastlike curves of the roof.

Lee's jitters returned in Cairo when Aziz asked about her restlessness. "I do so want to seem well and happy after my long vacation," she told Roland, "so as to give a precedent of its being a good thing for me . . . but I'm afraid that I'm making a sorry job of it." While busy with golf, cocktails, and dinner parties, she felt "quite devoid of any inspiration." Drafting letters in their private language—a salty mix of innuendo, vanguardism, and left politics—and doing things that recalled their time together were her only forms of comfort. "Either I like doing things because they have some remote . . . relation to you," she wrote, "or I hate everything because it has no contact, or inside thought of you."

Becoming the local spokeswoman for modern art gave her another way to nourish "inside thoughts" of Roland. The right frames for the artworks he had given her, which to her eyes both concealed and revealed their relationship, became a preoccupation. Roland's *Holy Ghost* (her name for one of his watercolors) would be framed in two pieces of glass with a black border, she wrote, "so that if one day you make me a companion piece it can go on the back, and become reversible"—like a mirror image of their love. "Your two beautiful montages," she went on, would have "the simplest and narrowest of black frames—so that they have no interference" (a state she desired for herself). Her Picasso etchings were being framed in Republican red, to shock her "Fascist friends"—the English officers and diplomats who were pro-Franco.

One wonders what Aziz made of Lee's plan to hang Roland's collages opposite her bed, whether their placement on either side of the door suggested dreams of escape. ("The light is perfect on them and they are brilliant like jewels under the glass," she told Roland.) With her mind on "inside thoughts," Lee also equipped her camera with a remote shutter release to send him shots of herself in her studio, gazing at the typewriter on which she wrote to him and at objects that he alone would recognize—a pair of diving glasses, books by Ernst, and other items from their shared life. "I particularly wanted you to see my permanent state of disorder," she wrote. "This is my own little air-conditioned sitting room." With a remote, she added, "I can take as many pictures of myself as I want for you, only I expect you to do the same," as if by this means they could post themselves to each other.

Roland replied that she already shared his house in Hampstead through the artistry of Picasso, whose portrait of her (one of the six from Mougins) he had recently bought on a trip to Paris. He too was hunting for the right frame with which to secure Lee's image and wanted her permission to hang her portrait in a Surrealist show at Cambridge, after which he would send it to her. "You should mark it Portrait of Mme. X," she answered. "I've always wanted to be the mysterious and beautiful lady in a picture."

That autumn, Lee's portrait presided over Roland's hearth, "fill[ing] my room with your adorable presence," he told her. "It is so gay, contains all Mougins, all the summer, the sea and your laugh." Lee was everywhere present in his new collection, which included twelve Picassos from his Cubist period and a number of works by Miró and de Chirico, all purchased that year. He explained their location and effect. Picasso's *L'Arlésienne* and his *Young Lady with Mandolin* dominated the living room; Lee's Mougins collage hung on the mantelpiece with Man's portrait of her sun-dappled torso, his gift to Roland. "I wish that I were to see the house all stuffed with treasures, overflowing with all the new pictures, and overflowing with me too," she wrote, adding in an afterthought, "I'm so bored here! I think that I am slowly going mad."

Lee tried whatever Cairo offered in the way of distractions. She would go to the Hopkinsons' circus party as "the tattooed woman," she teased, "provided I can find someone to paint me in amusing designs." Others would be bearded ladies, lion tamers, strong men, trapeze artists, and animals with their trainers. "If I were a man," she continued, "I'd go as an orderly with a dust pan and a broom, to follow the animals around—and I'd love to annoy everyone with some live snakes as a serpent charmer or let loose a lot of white rats."

Roland was excited by the idea of Lee tattooed. "You will look marvellously beautiful all written over with fishes, dragons, lions, sailors and hearts," he wrote, adding, "Why aren't I there to draw them!" "I imagine you nearly naked," he went on, "bricks painted all up your legs, moss growing on the tops of these towers, a serene blue sky for your body with two cotton white clouds as your breasts, two black pigeons as your hands and the sun itself as your face." Since he knew that she wouldn't actually appear this way, Roland painted this vision of Lee, called it *Night and Day,* and after sending Picasso's portrait of her to Cairo, replaced it with his own.

Roland longed for her "physically," he explained, but also "in lots of other ways. Your way of seeing things when we are out together is a thing I miss all the time." He wished that she could collaborate with him on his next venture, a show of Surrealist objects at the London Gallery, and sought her advice about the ready-made "cutie" he planned to exhibit, using a shopwindow dummy's head adorned with a blond wig and hung upside down. Unsure what to put in her open neck, he saw several possibilities but felt that Lee would "as usual have a much brighter idea."

By return mail, Lee suggested a glass lens arranged to magnify several objects, "flat brass gearwheels all toothed together like a complicated time bomb . . . a wax model of an ear drum or a hand and arm reaching up from inside the head—with a bleeding sacred silver heart such as they leave at Lourdes." Roland adapted her first idea by putting six small glass funnels filled with tacks, shells, and seeds in the neck of his construction, which he called *Dew Machine.* Later that year, he included the inverted head of a woman whose waves merge with the ocean in his canvas *Seeing Is Believing,* another work linking his new muse to the truths glimpsed in dreams.

By dint of these exchanges, their imaginations remained in sync. Lee proposed a contribution to the show of objects provided he could make it for her: "It is a very beautiful wax hand, like in manicurists' windows standing up from the wrist, vertically, and on it I'd like a bracelet made of false teeth mounted in particularly false pink colored gums." He might also paint the fingernails with false eyes (shades of Man) or "have fur tipped fingers" (shades of Meret Oppenheim).

Roland rushed to carry out Lee's instructions. "I shall choose a hand as nearly like yours as possible," he wrote, "and decorate it with teeth as nearly like mine." They might call this suggestive object *Le Baiser (The Kiss).* After purchasing a wooden hand (wax ones were unavailable), he painted it "with great care inspired by your hands which I can still see with some accuracy." For the teeth, he had located a dental technicians' workshop where two old men in white coats manufactured "the most rosy pearly false jaws I've ever seen."

Lee's object was finished in time for the opening, at midnight on November 24. It appeared beside Roland's *Dew Machine,* a piece by Eileen Agar, and one by Ernst—all labeled "objects for everyday use." The show caused more of a stir than Roland had anticipated. The critics were unsure whether to call the objects arty Christmas presents, bad dreams, or Surrealist leg-pulling. Lee was in good company, albeit vicariously.

Unable to keep her love affair a secret, Lee told Mafy, who was sympathetic. A month later, she confided in another young American who had the distinction of being Anita Loos's niece. Mary Anita Loos, a sprightly Californian, would soon follow in her aunt's footsteps as a screenwriter; in 1937, she was making her grand tour before settling down in Los Angeles. When the attractive brunette was introduced to Lee by their mutual friend Charles MacArthur, of the Algonquin Hotel Round Table set, it was as if Lorelei Lee's confidante Dorothy had unexpectedly turned up in Cairo.

Mary Anita, a Stanford graduate and an amateur archeologist, was not about to succumb to the Egyptian complex. As they drove around Cairo visiting the mosques and museums, Mary Anita told Lee about the American Southwest, where she often went on digs. The subject piqued Lee's imagination. With Mary Anita, she discovered the fascination of Egypt's past: "I walk around for hours on end, even went to the Pyramids, the Sphinx, the Museum and the mosques," she told Roland. She was at last "finding amusing things to do." In December, these included a duck hunt on a private oasis, a trip to Luxor (where she stayed with Abboud Pasha and his wife), and a fantasia (a mock combat on horseback) at night in the desert.

Lee enlisted Mary Anita in one of her most amusing activities that winter: skiing on sand dunes. Convinced that *Vogue* would push the sport as the latest fad, Lee organized the party. Mary Anita would model; Robin Fedden, a writer friend, would write the article; and Lee would take photographs. Carrying their skis, camera, and tripod, they climbed the dunes barefoot—hard work because the sand avalanched almost as fast as they could climb. Robin, in his pith helmet, positioned himself a little way below. Mary Anita stripped to her two-piece floral bathing suit, skied for a few seconds, and fell on her duff. All three roared with laughter until Lee and Robin shouted at Mary Anita to get up. An asp was lurking near her foot. "Skiing in Egypt lasted twenty minutes," she recalled, "the shortest potential sports event in history." Before returning to Cairo, Mary Anita photographed Lee sitting on a dune, her Rolleiflex around her neck and a ski beside her—a portrait of the photographer on location.

In Cairo, their amusements included rounds of cocktails at Shepheard's, where Mary Anita studied Lee's set—"a thoughtless group," she concluded, "who had inherited money but not recently enough to enjoy the novelty of it." They drank Pimm's cups while watching the magicians in long robes who pulled canaries out of their ears to entertain the tourists. The more politically aware debated the impending war in Europe, whether, as the British thought, a victorious Franco might be made to end his pact with Hitler to side with them, and whether the Italian presence in Libya threatened Egypt. Mary Anita, who had watched Hitler and Mussolini drive through Munich that autumn, told them about the papier-mâché milkmaids that lined the streets there, like a Hollywood film set.

When she visited the Villa al Beit with Lee, Mary Anita could not help noticing that despite Aziz's kindness, "Lee would do anything to get away." She also saw that Aziz and Lee were not well suited. Gentle and hospitable, he adored her but was often moody and prone to worry, especially about Lee. He was, Mary Anita thought, a product of the old school, while Lee "was a free spirit and made it plain to all." "Her blonde beauty blazed among the elegant women of Cairo," she went on, "but unlike them, she was a live wire." Since Mary Anita was another, Lee talked to her about Roland, explaining that she missed him but meant to console herself with others.

After two years of marriage, Lee flouted as many conventions as she could manage. Surrealism was a guaranteed shocker in Cairo. Some friends had gone so far as to read the books she lent them about the movement, but "they still don't believe it's true," she told Roland. When an English acquaintance exclaimed over newspaper accounts of "a so-called art exhibition" of Surrealist objects at the London Gallery, Lee replied that she had contributed one of them. "You should have seen her face," she crowed, as if she had scored a point.

The long-awaited arrival of her Picasso portrait offered the chance to unsettle le Tout-Cairo at a combined unveiling and cocktail party. Thirty of her friends assembled before the canvas, which Lee had covered with a large piece of velvet. When she removed the cover, there was a shocked silence. After she insisted that it *did* look like her, Gertie Wissa replied, "Yes, it has a roving eye." Some mystified guests thought that Lee had shown it "as a deliberate insult," she told Roland, "and were convinced that it was all tongue in cheek . . . you see I am in Exile."

While her friends muttered that any child could paint that way, Lee planned her revenge. Two days later she produced art supplies, then invited her dinner guests to have a try. The party became a Surrealist soirée: "two boys who knew what we were doing after dinner arrived in Surrealist costumes— which included gas masks—pisspots full of flowers etc.," she told Roland. "I had my mouth painted in green make-up and my nails their usual blue green— everyone got very tight and painted beautiful pictures, except that they were all very realistic and very dirty minded."

While shocking the bourgeoisie let off some of the pressures bottled up inside, Lee also nourished private thoughts of rebellion. She aired her sexual fantasies in letters notable for their frankness after Roland began writing about the "cuties" replacing her in his bed. She had been celibate since her return from France, but in December, developed "a letch for a boy who can't be had, because there is neither opportunity nor place in the construction of our respective lives." (The "boy" was Henry Hopkinson, whose declarations of love finally produced a response.) "I hoped that I could transfer my troubles to a desire for someone else," she went on, "but even that is out, so I practice hydraulics [masturbation] from time to time and try to remember."

In addition to "hydraulics," she was reading an English version of the Marquis de Sade's *Justine,* which she had begun in Paris with Man. At that time, she recalled, she had been impressed by "a great deal of intimate goings-on" that seemed to be lacking in the English edition; she asked Roland to check the original. By reading Sade together they could meet in their imaginations if not in the flesh.

In the meantime, Lee took stock of her situation. She was often sad, she wrote, "altho I spend all my time in a wild burst of gaiety . . . then suffering from fits of depression, or just tiredness, or reaction until I'm suicidal and then cured of that by resting and sulking." She knew what was wrong: "I want to make love. I suppose that being in love makes love-making more interesting, even with someone else." And despite Surrealist dogma, she had "pangs of jealousy" about Roland's amours—"not because you are making love with other people, but because I can't also."

A trip to the Red Sea coast with Aziz and Henry brought relief. The Sinai mountains, like a "Max Ernst painting in Turner's colors," set the scene, and Henry's acute stomach cramps provided the opportunity. Though "plastered on rum," Lee drove him to the French hospital in Suez, where the doctor ordered him to stay in bed. "We had been looking for a bed for months and finally to find it filled with fevers, opiates and worry," she wrote, "but we did anyway, and made love to the accompaniment of two green hot water bottles and summonses to the telephone for all the long distance calls I had put in for Cairo to his wife and doctor. It was like a French comedy." At the same time, she could not stop thinking of Roland, "and the luck we had—to be independent, unattached, and certain of each other."

On Christmas morning, despite a bad hangover, Lee convinced Aziz of her need for "a certain fixed holiday every year as a bachelor." He gave her his blessing but said that she must visit her parents next summer and teased that if she married someone else, he would insist on being her lover. "Further than that I have never gotten even in an approach or thought of my own on the problem," she confessed. "All I know is that I couldn't possibly leave him—or hurt him, or open him to any sort of humiliation." As an afterthought, she mentioned his Christmas present to her, a beautiful gray Packard that she would have to drive carefully since, unlike her, "it's not allowed to go fast."

January brought a bad case of the jitters and a new malady, insomnia, both linked, Lee thought, to "those depressing Egyptian gray days when the world seems to have ended, and one senses the preoccupation of this country with death." Her mood was dark. The usual distractions—drink, desert trips, "French comedy"—were to no avail. "[Egypt] is just tombs, ruins, and embalmed bodies," she told Roland, "generations of people, dead people doing exactly the same thing, in the same way." She was becoming like everyone else: "The only thing that seems alive is the hope that I can get out of it."

Lee's gloom was not unusual among expatriates. "Many people find exile in Egypt difficult out of all proportion to the trials which at first appear to be tangibly involved," Robin Fedden wrote. The climate unhinged Europeans due to the lack of seasons "and the recurring stimuli they offer," he continued, but also because the landscape was "boneless and unarticulated"—except for the desert. The realization that Egyptian fields "are not soil but bone-mould and excrement" was known to produce "claustrophobic panic." Only Egyptologists or Muslims could appreciate the country. The isolation of the expatriate was deepened, he thought, by the "nightmarish unreality" of Cairo, where "the

Lee snake charming, 1938
(Guy Taylor)

black satin and pearls are complementary to rags and tatters"—the situation he described as "Levantine unreality."

Lee struggled with this unreality, she told Roland, by "spend[ing] a great deal of time doing extremely silly things." During another stay at Abboud Pasha's she behaved like "a Wild Western Novel Heroine." Although "neither a jockey or a rodeo girl," she insisted on riding a bad-tempered horse called Renown, who bucked, bit, frothed at the mouth, fell to the ground with her in the saddle, and was shot by the groom: "Evidently I'd driven him crazy."

For her next adventure, she became "the Sister of all the Serpents." In preparation, she took lessons from a snake charmer who made her promise that she would never harm a reptile, then draped her with vipers and cobras. "I have a perfect passion for snakes," she told Roland. They were "clean like jewels." The vipers had "wonderful eyes" but wiggled; "the cobras are gentle and come when you call." Once she had finished snake charming, she arranged to have the Aswan train stop for her to board, as if she were "the visiting queen of what not," then drank and "played love games" with a Viennese passenger before visiting the temple of Horus. "It was an exciting and satisfying adventure," she told Roland. "[M]aybe you're right, and I'm just another girl looking for trouble."

Roland paid no attention to the self-doubt that punctuated Lee's accounts of her adventures. "Your letters read like the most incredible news, real thriller[s] with all the colour and incidents required, snakes, mad horses, lovers in train-de-luxe, temples and champagne," he replied. He felt "small and gray by comparison." The only thing he looked forward to was a trip to Paris for the International Exhibit of Surrealism at the Galerie Beaux-Arts in January. Yet even there he would miss Lee. The organizers wanted to show Picasso's portrait of her, but it was too late. He had sent it to Cairo. "I'm sorry that your radiant face shouldn't be in the centre of it," he wrote, "that you should not illuminate the whole affair with your presence."

Lee's presence was felt in Paris just the same. Her torso, as depicted in Roland's *Real Woman,* hung behind one of the satin-lined double beds in the main room, her lips floated above the gallery in Man's *Observatory Time,* and for those who knew, their past together was evoked in his mannequin with soap bubbles, one of the fifteen window dummies revamped by the contributors to exemplify the Eternal Feminine. She also figured in the catalogue, an *Abridged Dictionary of Surrealism,* in which Man's shot of her in the orthopedic cast illustrated the section entitled *"Femme Surréaliste."* "Why the devil aren't you here?" Roland asked. At dinner with Picasso, Dora Maar, and the Eluards, everyone spoke of her: "Picasso asked after you a lot and wanted to know when you are coming back."

Lee replied that she had nearly run away to join him but after a stormy talk with Aziz decided to leave "peaceably" in the spring. In the meantime, she had taken up camel riding. "My current ambition is to have my own racing camel—do it up very fine in my own colors and ride it around wearing a galabiya." It was fortunate that Roland had filled her requests for various items, more Surrealist books and magazines, and the Tampax she would need in the desert—"on account of what you can't ride a camel and wear a Kotex." Despite her jaunty tone, Lee was depressed. "Are you forgetting how difficult and discontented I always am," she asked. "I think that a double life is what I was meant to live," she continued, "dividing my heart up into little bits. I've spent so much of my life having it torn—between this and that—between one or one hundred men—and still loving them all." What was more, she had been drinking too much: "I could easily and with pleasure become an alcoholic."

Since Roland heard from her irregularly in the new year, he surmised that Lee, like the rest of Cairo, must be "busy bedding your little queen" (English newspapers that winter featured the plans for King Farouk's marriage) and wondered whether she was "getting any fun out of it." Lee's letters from the spring of 1938 mention neither the royal wedding nor other sources of fun. They also fail to mention Giles Vandeleur, a captain in the Scots Guards with whom she began an affair after the departure of the Hopkinsons for Athens. She also went to Heliopolis to see Rosezell Rowland, who had recently returned as the new Baronne Empain. During her absence in Budapest, jokes had gone around Cairo about the Baron *"en panne"* (in trouble); true to his word, he married Rosezell after the birth of their son in November. But the goings-on at the Palais Hindou had ceased to be amusing. Lee's mind was on thoughts of escape.

Having persuaded Aziz to let her take a spring vacation in Greece, she hoped that Roland would join her. After telegraphing him about her plans, Lee sailed to Athens with Gertie Wissa, who was disturbed to learn that Vandeleur would accompany them. The other passengers could not help noting his visits to Lee's cabin since, accidentally or on purpose, she left the door open. Her behavior was scandalous, Gertie recalled, and worse when they reached Athens, where she came to a party in the nude. She continued her fling with Giles, who shared her penchant for practical jokes: they cabled Gertie in Greek characters that encoded four-letter words for those who knew English. Lee was nonetheless "hard hit" when a letter from Roland explained that he could not join her due to obligations in London. "By virtue of writing to you," she replied, "I'm in a state & will go practice hydraulics."

On her return to Cairo, Lee met Bernard Burrows, a handsome young diplomat who began work that year at the British embassy. Burrows, a product of Eton and Oxford, was interested in art, archeology, and letters as well as politics. He found Cairo society superficial and disdained the Empains' "totally empty way of life." While Lee struck him as very American, her beauty and mischievous humor were alluring. "With her looks and background she was of course sensational in that milieu," he recalled. "Her behaviour was often seen as excentric, but others too did as they pleased." She cared for Aziz in her way, he added, "did not always misbehave and was careful about her affairs"— except on foreign soil. And while Lee fretted about the narrowness of life in Cairo, "she did what she could to accommodate herself."

Unlike Burrows, Lee took little interest in the political scene. Throughout 1938, as Franco and Mussolini consolidated their power in Europe, Egypt's strategic position preoccupied her British "protectors." The Italians were reconnoitering in the desert from their base in Libya; Cairo was said to be full of spies (including Laszlo Almasy, the double agent whose expeditions inspired *The English Patient*). Lee went on desert treks for her own reasons, Burrows felt. These trips were her way to escape constraints by focusing on logistics— getting the expedition fitted out and organized. In this way she was her father's daughter, he added. It was technique, whether travel-related or photographic, that held her attention. She made up for her lack of education with sheer daring: on a trip to the Red Sea, she stripped off her clothes and swam naked despite the presence of sharks.

As a classically trained scholar, Burrows may not have fully grasped Lee's attraction to the desert, her sense that out there the past had fallen away. Some are terrified by the desert's emptiness. For those for whom the desert mirrors back the self, its vastness may be exhilarating. For Lee, the desert became the place where she could see more clearly who she was—and see herself seeing. From time to time, she abandoned the "extremely silly things" that amused her and went to the desert for refreshment—one might even say, for spiritual renewal, though the word *spiritual* was not part of her vocabulary. In its reaches, she glimpsed a place beyond technique, where the pieces of her life momentarily came together.

Lee's best-known Egyptian image, *Portrait of Space,* stages this kind of seeing as a moment of transcendence. The viewer, positioned inside a desert shelter, looks through the torn opening of a fly-screen door to the high plains on the horizon. Because this chance opening functions like an eye—or the aperture of a camera—a feeling of spaciousness opens in the body as one peers into the distance. Here the lucidity of her composition captures a split-second insight into another way of being. Although some of Lee's Egyptian photographs portray her response to the country while exploiting modernism's concern with the medium, in *Portrait of Space* she touched another dimension, joining the ranks of the few photographers, who, a critic writes, "understand this correspondence between outer and inner state, read the world as if it were an allegory and pass through it as if they were pilgrims on a journey, looking for signs."

Roland begged Lee to choose their reunion site. "I look to your arrival as the signal for a change," he wrote. Once she made up her mind, "we will be off to Iceland, Paris, Mexico, Dutch East Indies or wherever you like." The plan she presented to Aziz seemed plausible. In June she would sail to Athens with Arabella, her Packard, to tour the Aegean, then explore mainland Greece and Bulgaria with friends. She did not say that Roland was the only friend joining her, nor that she was packing a camp bed, blankets, and other essentials for the Eastern European equivalent of a desert trek. In the meantime, she told Roland to bring a driver's license, "some infra-red film, lots of hormones, and good humor."

Roland had many reasons to be happy. In June, on his way through Paris to meet Lee in Greece, he visited the Eluards. At Paul's urging, he bought the poet's art collection—including forty Ernsts, six de Chiricos, Picasso's portrait of Nusch, and work by Klee, Arp, Chagall, Dalí, and Man Ray. (The inclusion in the lot of Man's painting of Lee with her throat cut, *Logis de l'Artiste,* may have seemed like a sign, although an ambiguous one.) Thinking back on that moment, Roland mused, "Sometimes, almost never, an invitation arrives to explore distant countries with a girl with whom one is in love and, should this happen, one would be an obstinate fool to refuse."

Soon after their reunion they sailed to Mykonos, whose voluptuous goddess figures had long fascinated Roland, then, on a boat filled with honey, grain, and nuts, to Delos—where the huge stone phallus at the sanctuary of Dionysus hinted that chthonic powers still ruled the land. Judging by the photographs in *The Road Is Wider Than Long,* the "image diary" Roland kept of their trip (and later published), these ancient sites were inspiring. The image of biomorphic rocks on page 1 evokes the release of pent-up energies; the accompanying lines note with awe the harmony of landscape and emotion. To Roland, their trip was a journey through a "world become fertile," and they themselves, "Lovers who escape, who are free to separate / free to re-unite leave their tongues / plaited together hidden in the dry grass / folded in peasant made cloth / embalmed in the green memories of desire."

Nonetheless, they could not help feeling "the menace of approaching doom" as Hitler strengthened his alliance with Mussolini over the summer. Of their next stop, the oracle at Delphi, Roland wrote forebodingly, "Vapours escape from the rocks / writing tomorrow's news in the sky." They gleaned scraps of information on the drive to Bucharest. In Prague, the Czechs were temporizing with the Nazis; in Bulgaria, rearmament had begun. In Bucharest, they met Hari Brauner, the musicologist brother of the Surrealist Victor Brauner, who invited them to hear Maritza Lataretu, a Gypsy singer, and to join his recording sessions of folk celebrations in the Carpathian Mountains. Lee bought an embroidered costume to move among the peasant women; unlike the Siwans, they let her take photographs and, through Brauner, talked about their lives.

Some years later Lee described this leg of the trip with the recall of an anthropologist. "Magic to bring on rain or to fertilise the bride or the fields [is] traditional," she wrote:

> In the gypsy rites to produce rainfall, a boy and a girl are dressed in leaves arranged like Hawaiian skirts. They prance around singing a primitive prayer ditty while the adults throw buckets of water over them. The peasants' ritual harks back to a ceremony as ancient as the oldest of Greek literature. The pure children (under the age of 10) fashion a moist clay doll in relief on a board. Gentians make blue eyes, and a scarlet petal the mouth. The sex is well defined. The offering is trimmed with blossom, laden with fruits and carried by child pall-bearers to the nearest remaining water on the parched plains. Bearing lit candles and suitable prayers

the sacrifice, symbolic of one of themselves, is placed on the water where it floats away to death by drowning.

She photographed these scenes and others—the children in leaf skirts, a dead child, crosses carved in trees in a cemetery—to record their journey, but also to document folkways about to vanish.

In September, after Roland's return to London, Lee volunteered as driver and photographer on Brauner's recording expeditions. They spent several weeks attending Gypsy weddings and exorcisms and, at night, fending off the fleas that lurked in the peasants' featherbeds. "We drank quantities of hard liquor and gallons of Lapte Batute buttermilk," Lee recalled. "We made documentary photographs of all the frescoes painted on the outside of the ravishing steep-steepled churches of the Budkovina province, and accepted for [Hari's] institute the under-glass ikons which the churches might not destroy but were discarding in favour of chromos, oleos and plaster statues of saints *en grande serie* from mail order catalogues."

She was having an adventure a day, she told Roland, with "angry peasants, murderous cart drivers, armed bandits, etc.," not to mention a valley where a gas mine burned night and day, driving the peasants mad. "It's been going on for a year now and I think it is the most exciting thing I've ever seen," she added: daily life "on the brink of hell." Despite the outcome of the Munich conference, which gave the Sudetenland to Hitler, and the prospect of war in the Balkans, Lee felt oddly calm—even after foreigners were told to leave and she was declared missing. Reluctantly, she sailed to Egypt at the end of September.

Soon after her return, Lee told Aziz that she had had an affair with Roland in 1937, and that they remained close although unsure about the future. "He doesn't want to divorce me unless he is sure that I'm going to be happy," she told Roland. "I told him that I'd had enough of marriage for the moment and didn't want to marry you until I had at least sufficient adjustment to make up my mind." Her mutually contradictory plans included living with him in London, spending the winter in Switzerland with Aziz, and returning to the United States in case of war. In the meantime, she said that she would spend some weeks in Syria but did not name her traveling companion, Bernard Burrows. Judging by Lee's letters to Bernard, her confusion deepened with each new plan. Immersing herself in lists of travel gear (snake serum, flea powder, ointments for the eyes and stomach) did little to calm the jitters that, increasingly, beset her.

Lee met Bernard in Beirut at the end of October, then traveled with him through Transjordan and Syria, photographing all the way. At some point, Robin Fedden joined them to start work on a travel book. A letter to Roland omits any mention of Bernard but gives their itinerary—Palmyra, Baalbeck,

Jerash, Kerak, Sergiopolis, the Tigris and Euphrates, Homs, Hama, Aleppo, Damascus, and Antioch—and says that she took "some quite startling pictures" out in "all the great empty spaces." (Fedden's *Syria,* published in 1956, reproduces Lee's shots of Palmyra, Lebanon's mountain, a weaver, and two intimate portraits of Bedouin women, one on a camel and the others in their encampment—people like her, or her as she wished to be.)

Alone in Beirut, Lee took stock of her situation in a letter to Aziz. Having gone through "as many changes of scenery & weather here as there are kinds of religions & races of people," she had to conclude that "all of them [were] vaguely disappointing because of my own state of mind." "There is no further way of escaping some sort of plan, no way of pretending there isn't a problem & worst of all I am such a coward that I'd rather solve it from a distance. [It] ought to be much easier from here for me to say & know about coming back or about going any place else . . . it's too 'shymaking' to talk about it face to face." Wanting Aziz to initiate the break, she supposed that the solution was divorce: "I feel that you want most of all to be excused from further trouble for & about me & of course to feel absolved & in all good conscience free of responsibility & preoccupation with me. But either from tender-heartedness or misplaced faith in my possible reform[,] you are blinding yourself to my worthlessness as your wife."

As for herself, she did not know what she wanted, "unless it is to 'have my cake, and eat it too.' " Yet she *had* gained insight. "I want to have the utopian combination of security and freedom," she wrote, "and emotionally I need to be completely absorbed in some work or in a man I love." Given these desires, she would have to decide for herself. "I think the first is to take or make freedom, which will give me the opportunity to become concentrated again & just hope that some sort of security follows & even if it doesn't the struggle will keep me awake and alive." She would come home to discuss "yours, or my or our plans, for the future" if he wished. Otherwise she would go to Europe or America. While waiting to hear from him, she would keep on traveling.

From Palmyra, Lee wrote to Mary Anita of her interest in archeology and asked whether they might tour the Southwest together if and when she returned to the United States. Taking or making freedom was one thing; contemplating ruins while imagining oneself a refugee was another. Lee's Palmyra photographs are well composed archeological studies. At the same time, their desolate architecture—colonnaded temples eroded by sand, once-impregnable towers open to the winds—evoke a malaise. One feels almost viscerally the contradictions of this moment in her striking image of a blocked doorway: an impasse, a no exit, a dead end (the rounded shape above the lintel suggests a head, or an eye, for the door as body).

In January 1939, Roland asked for a decision. "All I want is to have everything taken out of my hands," she replied, "to wake up one morning and find myself already launched in my life with you." Ironically, while not up to fitting the pieces of her life together, she was dividing her time between jigsaw puzzles and losing herself in travel books about places she had visited or longed to see written by women explorers (including the work of Freya Stark and Alexandra David-Neel's *With Mystics and Magicians in Tibet*).

New acquaintances offered some distraction. George Henein, an Egyptian poet who had met Roland in Paris, took an interest in her. He hoped to start a magazine along the lines of the American left-wing review *The Masses*, with the aim of uniting Marxism and Surrealism in an Egyptian context. "Our gang of misfits are starting a semi surrealist magazine next month," she told Roland. She would help them despite her doubts—in between expeditions, parties, and card games. In the meantime, she asked Roland to help her choose a costume for Amy Smart's next event: guests were to come as their latest dream or nightmare. Veering between defiance and depression, Lee was energized by Kemal Eloui's sudden denunciation of modern art—after which she moved all her paintings to her studio in protest.

While Lee's social life was not uninteresting, she told Roland, her sex life was nonexistent. "In a fit of longing for you yesterday morning I played hydraulic games with myself," she wrote. "It's neither the first nor the last time." The effect of this letter was immediate. By return, Roland announced his departure for Egypt to document peasant dances with a friend who needed him as her photographer. Lee replied that she was thrilled by the news and his arrangements, which would "give me endless opportunities to be with you if you want me to be." But it was too late for her to change her plan to start a weeklong desert trip on January 30, the day of his arrival. Morever, she wanted to play it safe: "Aziz knows that I had a love affair with you," she wrote, "and I told him it was over and we were just friends." Canceling the trip "would look too suspicious," she went on, "and spoil any plans we have here."

Lee set out at dawn with Bernard Burrows, Amy Smart, Gertie Wissa, and a couple named Pereira to tour the oases of the Western Desert—known as the desert of all deserts because of its treacherous dune fields, which had swallowed whole armies. She was now following in the footsteps of Ahmed Hassanein, whose *Lost Oases* surely went along as their guide, at a time when the political situation made desert travel even more hazardous. (In 1939, when Laszlo Almasy was mapping the Western Desert for the British-run Survey Department, the Italians were on maneuvers there. It was not unreasonable to think that war might break out soon.)

Their trip went well despite the general anxiety. At Bahariya, a lush collection of villages known for their wine, they were received by the sheik, who plied them with sweets. Driving from oasis to oasis, they found much to admire. At Farafra and Dakhla, the Bedouins' mud-brick houses and luxuriant crops—dates, olives, figs, and oranges—formed patterns of color against the jagged pink escarpments. More than anything, it was the desert that held Lee's attention, the volcanic mountains of the Black Desert, the chalk statues carved by the wind—hawks, camels, sphinxes—in the White Desert, a Surrealist's dream. As seasoned travelers, they would have camped in the desert to see these shapes turn gold, then purple at sunset.

Lee was anxious to complete the trip. The last leg took them to El Kharga, a stopping place on the ancient forty-day caravan route from the Sudan, then to the Wissas' house near Assyut. Unable to wait any longer, Roland went to Assyut to surprise her. He brought as gifts the first edition of *The Road Is Wider Than Long* (inscribed "to Lee, who caught me in her cup of gold") and a pair of handcuffs made of gold from Cartier's ("pieces of sentimental jewelry," he believed, were "the symbolic equivalent of an orgasm"). One must imagine their reunion as "friends," and the discretion needed to bring it off.

On their return to Cairo, Lee introduced Aziz and Roland, who realized that they were already acquainted, Roland having visited the Villa al Beit in 1925, when Nimet was in residence. While it would have been reassuring to see that the two men liked and respected each other, it may also have seemed that one protector was handing her over to another. Yet in part of herself, this was what Lee wanted.

She was now free to travel with Roland provided they went in a group. As the political situation worsened, the authorities placed restrictions on travel by foreigners; it took Aziz's influence in high places to obtain the necessary permits. They set off for Siwa on March 12 with Mafy and George Hoyningen-Huene, who had come to Egypt to take photographs for a book on the classical past. The local sheiks welcomed them and showed their enthusiasm when, despite the rules for Siwan women, Lee and Mafy bathed topless in the hot springs. An active sex life rekindled Lee's love of mischief. Photographing the nearby rock formations with Roland, Lee saw them with a Surrealist's eye—as in *Cock Rock,* where a boulder stands at attention like an erect penis.

By the end of the trip, she had made up her mind to join Roland; he begged her to come to London, now that war seemed imminent. However, while Erik had also decided that he and Mafy would return to the United States, Lee was still unsure about leaving Aziz. Driving back to Cairo with Mafy (Roland had gone on to Alexandria with George), the two women "discussed our futures and our ficklenesses in a way only possible in the dark," Lee wrote, "not looking at each other, but fascinated by the diminishing lines of the road." At Marsa Matruh, they encountered a long convoy of army trucks, which Lee passed one at a time with her hands glued to the steering wheel. "It was like being very sick drunk in a nightmare," she told Roland. Although the Egyptian War Office had begun canceling permits for civilian travel, the next weekend Lee took Mafy and Erik to the Red Sea, to make up for not seeing much of them of late.

In April, as the couple packed their belongings, Lee came up with a plan. Since her brother and sister-in-law would be spending time in London on the way home, Roland should persuade Mafy to stay on. Lee could then set up housekeeping with her after Erik's departure. "My plans are maturing," she continued. "Everything will be smooth if there isn't a war." But she had to proceed with caution, having already gotten into trouble by going on another trip with Bernard. (She did not say that Bernard had fallen in love with her even though he knew about her relations with Roland.) Lee and Mafy had been "the last white women to visit Siwa," she wrote: "Anyone putting foot in the Western desert gets six months prison." What was more, Georges Henein was now under surveillance. "Don't send me any books with communistic leanings," she added. The War Office looked with suspicion on socialist and fascist tracts alike.

Lee should settle things at her own pace, Roland counseled from London, "but through all your plans don't forget that you *are* coming to me." Aziz had been "quite extraordinarily charming to me," he added. "I appreciate him very much but I love you." By May Roland was desperate for a decision. "If it's war scares that make you hesitate," he wrote, "all I can say is that here everyone is so used to them that they are beginning to treat them as weather forecasts, never to be relied on. . . . So don't let wild rumours upset you unduly—not that they ever would."

In a letter written about this time, Lee announced that she had booked passage to England on the *Otranto,* a "swell" ship sailing on June 2, with stops in Naples, Villefranche, and Toulon. Yet despite this decision, she felt too jittery to sort through her photographs. She would "bring the whole lot to London in a suitcase." Roland should find her a furnished flat, "as I might not be able to stay with you unless Mafy is there—altho also I might anyway." She would leave their summer plans to him.

Under the impression that Lee was taking a bachelor holiday, Aziz took her to Port Said and kissed her goodbye. On board the *Otranto* Lee avoided the "British bourgeoisie" and spent her time reading inspirational volumes: Vita Sackville-West's *St. Joan of Arc* and Negley Farson's *Way of a Transgressor.* "I'm not writing you more intimately of my thots & intentions," she told Roland from Naples. But in her "sick muddle of indecision," one thing was clear. "I'm never returning to Egypt," she wrote, "unless the ultimate in disasters & dejection overcomes me. . . . I'm glad that finally I'm coming back to you."

Part Four

Lee Miller, War Correspondent

Lee outside British Vogue studio in London, c. 1943

Chapter 11

London in the Blitz

(1939–44)

In a journal begun on her way from Egypt to England, Lee described her
state as "uneasy & nervous." Despite Aziz's generosity, she was unsure how
to live once she made up her mind to leave him for good, or what to do in
the event of war. Her finances were "ugly," she told Roland in a letter from
Toulon, "so unless I go back . . . to the family or husband etc. or someone
keeps me or I get a job it looks very depressing."

Lee was also corresponding with Bernard Burrows. Dismayed to learn that
he had reached Cairo one hour after her departure, Bernard declared his love,
admitting that until then, he had been "too timorous & undecided to press any
alternative." He would soon move to London to join the Federal Union, a
scheme for an anti-fascist alliance launched by the American journalist
Clarence Streit. "Would the idea of doing something like that bore you to distraction?" he asked. "I rather fancy it's too much of a generalization. My benevolent instincts are strong for the mass of people, weak for individuals—yours I
think the other way round."

"Altho these nice idealistic societies have to try & try again," Lee replied,
the "gangsters [Hitler and Mussolini] have several years more practice." Moreover, she was "not very convinced about Federal U" and had no faith in an

alliance led by "Perfide Albion," whose record in Palestine, Spain, and Czechoslovakia aroused her scorn. Bernard risked being a "champion of lost causes" if he moved to England for her sake. "I don't want you to do anything 'all for love' as I won't marry you," she wrote, "I won't live with you and I can't be depended on for anything."

∞

After a week of pondering the future while sunbathing, Lee arrived at Southampton—where Roland waited impatiently. One can imagine the joy of their reunion, although its full celebration was delayed until that night at Roland's house in Hampstead. A more conventional woman might have found it odd that his other houseguest was Man Ray. Apparently untroubled by the situation, Lee took up residence at 21 Downshire Hill, Mafy having followed Erik back to the United States.

The next day, Roland took her to the West End, London's center of modern art since the establishment there of the Cork Street "triumvirate": the London Gallery, the Mayor Gallery, and Guggenheim Jeune. It was another homecoming. At the London Gallery, run by E. L. T. Mesens and backed by Roland, she saw Picasso's portraits of Dora and Nusch, both from Roland's collection. At the Mayor Gallery, where his own work was displayed, she met new images of herself, reinvented in her lover's imagination. His 1937 *Night and Day,* which had replaced Picasso's portrait of Lee on his mantelpiece, foregrounds her role as muse. Two birds replace her hands, her creative powers; three funnels drain water into the ground beneath her, evoking her lover's sense of loss after their first summer together.

In contrast to *Night and Day*'s allegory of longing, Roland's two most recent paintings were overtly erotic. *Bien Visé* poses Lee's naked torso beside a chain and against a bullet-pocked wall; her arms, in the pose taken by prisoners of war, frame the landscape that replaces her head. Sadeian "goings-on" are implied by the chain and the figure's resemblance to the victims of firing squads; the low-slung garment over her pudenda is a visual echo of the girdle Lee wore in Man's headless image of her at a window. As in much Surrealist art, the composition's frontality makes the female subject complicit in seeming to offer herself to an implied male viewer.

A companion painting, *Octavia,* a critic writes, exhibits "morbid undertones." Here, the Sadeian themes underpinning *Bien Visé* take shape in the spikes protruding from the inverted figure—the woman's neck and shoulders, the long arms on which she balances, and the braids that become chains, anchoring her to the ground. *Octavia* disturbs the viewer "due to the ambivalence of the woman's arms, which can also be seen as a man's legs, the head then taking on a sexual meaning linked to the phallic spikes on the crenellated body." While Lee's journal does not mention Roland's fantasies, these paintings hint at his feelings about the cost of relations with her, and with women in general.

Roland had written to Lee about the American heiress Peggy Guggenheim—one of his bedmates in 1938. The founder of Guggenheim Jeune, she hoped to start a U.K. museum of modern art: as such, she was also Roland's colleague, one of London's small band of modernist pioneers. Their affair, in his view, had been "rather indifferent." Roland made up for his lack of passion with charm, Peggy recalled some years later, but he had a notable eccentricity: "when he slept with women he tied up their wrists with anything that was handy. . . . It was extremely uncomfortable to spend the night this way, but if you spent it with Penrose it was the only way."

It was also true that the only way to start a museum of modern art in London was with Roland's support. Peggy and Herbert Read had tried to enlist him in her project, but that spring, Roland, Paul Nash, Henry Moore, and most of the British Surrealists were making plans for a museum of their own—since Peggy's fortune gave her a power that provoked the London art world's distrust. One can imagine Lee's mixed feelings about her compatriot, who, having urged Roland to go to Egypt in pursuit of Lee, liked to take credit for their reunion. On June 22, unaware that local movers and shakers were mobilizing against her, Peggy threw a closing-night party at her gallery. A huge crowd came to see Gisele Freund's portraits—among them Joyce, Breton, and T. S. Eliot—and to help themselves to drinks at the well-stocked bar. Within a few weeks, Peggy abandoned her plan for a museum and went to France despite the mounting political tensions.

By June, when Lee arrived, Hitler had annexed much of Czechoslovakia, forged his "Pact of Steel" with Mussolini, and forced nonaggression treaties on Estonia, Latvia, and Denmark. In July, a peace effort by an Anglo-French mission to Moscow failed to enlist the Soviet Union in opposition to Germany. One could hardly overestimate the sense of dread felt by all those (avant-gardists included) who saw the coming war as a threat to civilization—despite their critique of its values. Paradoxically, Lee felt "vastly amused," she told Bernard. "They've got the world war fixed for the week of July 25th"; friends were planning to hole up "in country cottages, or on lordly well-provisioned estates." Thinking that she would join him later, Aziz suggested a month in Saint Moritz, adding that on their return home, he would rent an apartment which Lee could decorate without interference from Kemal.

Toward the end of July, Lee and Roland set off to see Picasso in Antibes; she told Aziz to write her there care of general delivery. On the way, they stayed with Max Ernst and Leonora Carrington in their farmhouse in St. Martin d'Ardèche. Max had sculpted fabulous birds and fish on the exterior walls; Leonora had decorated the interior with creatures from her private bestiary. In this magical space, the couple painted each other's portraits, Leonora wrote a book entitled *The House of Fear,* and with kindred souls (Leonor Fini was visiting when Lee arrived) lived as if untouched by the world. Lee photographed the couple, their house, and what was perhaps the last Surrealist picnic, at which Man and Ady joined them. Leonora's title proved to be prescient. Soon after Lee's departure, the authorities took Max to a camp for aliens, and Leonora suffered a nervous breakdown.

In Antibes, where troops were guarding the port, Picasso joked that the war was a plot to keep him from working. A man of disciplined habits, he swam every day and, in the evening, met with friends and his nephews, Fin and Javier Vilató, who had escaped from Spain after the defeat of the Republicans. "Their irrepressible high spirits helped temporarily to disperse the increasing gloom," Roland recalled. (Fin demonstrated an innate Surrealism by shaving his legs in horizontal patterns.) Lee's photographs—the group at the beach, the Maître holding a tame monkey—document a vanishing way of life.

On August 21, after the Germans announced a nonaggression pact with Russia, foreigners rushed to get visas and plan their escape routes. On September 1, when Hitler invaded Poland, Roland and Lee drove north to Saint-Malo, where they caught the last boat to England. They reached London on September 3 in time to hear the first air-raid sirens and watch the silver gray barrage balloons rise in the sky. The western powers had declared war on Germany. At Roland's house, Lee found a letter from the American Embassy telling her to take the next available ship home. She tore it up, events having decided what she had been unable to decide for herself. On September 5, she cabled Theodore: "staying Roland love Lee Eloui." The next day she informed Aziz that she would be waging her war from London.

∞

One kind of waiting had ended, another had begun—the period known as "the phony war." As they waited for the Blitzkrieg to begin, reserved Londoners talked to one another in public places, and war preparation—gas masks, blackouts, bomb shelters, evacuations—became a way of life. Then, the period from September 1939 to April 1940 was called the "Bore War," the "funny war," or, as wits said after months of anticipation, the "Sitzkrieg."

Throughout September, refugees from the Continent turned up in London. Eileen Agar invited Roland, Lee, and Herbert Read to the last of the Surrealist banquets, in honor of Walter Gropius, Marcel Breuer, and Moholy-Nagy, who were passing through on their way to the United States. Eileen decorated her Ping-Pong table with Surrealist objects—the strangest being the centerpiece, "a pedal-operated fretsaw hung with fruit and flowers"—and cooked oddly colored dishes, including pink potatoes. "The complexion of the dinner party was rather more abstract," she recalled, "but our guests took it all in their stride."

By October, Londoners were taking the increasingly surreal aspects of the Sitzkrieg in their stride. They covered windows with brown paper strips, installed "Anderson" shelters (named for the minister of home security) in the garden, if they had one, and, if not, prepared for the Blitz with government-issue earplugs. Signs saying TO THE TRENCHES showed the way to dugouts in Hyde Park. By November, when fog blanketed the city, flashlights were scarce; cigarettes gave a welcome source of light. People collided with one another; pedestrians found their way home by means of the white lines painted on the curbs and gateposts.

Fashion adapted to this state of affairs. For the first time, women went to work in slacks, with gas masks dangling from their necks. "Siren suits"—hooded coveralls, for nights in the shelters—made their appearance in Bond Street shops along with uniforms for the women's auxiliary forces—the Wrens (Women's Royal Naval Service), ATS (Auxiliary Territorial Service), Waafs (Women's Auxiliary Air Force), and the women of the Fire Service. ("The smartest seems to be the dark blue and scarlet of the fire service, faintly recalling a musical-comedy Zouave," *The New Yorker* noted.)

Lee found herself in a strange position. She had chosen to stay in England but as an alien could not join the thousands of Englishwomen enlisting in the auxiliary forces. Nor was she the type to stay at home and knit. "Learn to cook," U.K. *Vogue* urged readers who, like Lee, were at leisure. "Sew or knit something, preferably not too complicated. This is not to put your dressmaker out of work but to give you something to do." Not a good candidate for these activities (Roland's housekeeper kept order at Downshire Hill), Lee was at loose ends. Brogue's photographic studio did not require her services. Perhaps for this reason, she kept writing to Bernard and Aziz, who both hoped that she would return to Cairo soon, or when the war was over.

In the meantime, Roland joined the ARP (Air Raid Protective Corps) while Lee prepared for "siege, starvation, invasion." "I figured that if it were coming to . . . a diet of potatoes, field mice and snails," she told Erik, "I might as well make them taste nice, so the only hoarding I did was truffles—pimentoes—spices and all things nice," including tins of corn and clam chowder from Fortnum and Mason's, where she also bought a display basket full of dried seasonings. Roland installed an air-raid shelter, painted pink and blue, in the garden, with a Barbara Hepworth sculpture near the entrance. Like the rest of London, they listened to the radio at night (broadcasts by Lord Haw-Haw, the Nazis' English-speaking propagandist, were popular). By winter, nightspots were again packed with Londoners trying to cope with their discontent—the war of nerves having become "a war of yawns."

In December, the Royal Academy asked a number of painters, including Roland, to contribute to their "United Artists" exhibition—an unprecedented effort by this conservative bastion to boost morale. Due to the language ("sex," "flesh," "arse") with which he annotated one of his canvases, the committee asked him to replace it with something less vulgar. Roland followed Lee's nose-thumbing suggestion. "What I did," he wrote, "was . . . get a card in deaf and dumb sign language from which I chose a four-letter word S-H-I-T, and painted a row of hands saying this." The committee hung this work opposite a portrait of King George, where it remained until a deaf and dumb cleaner "started hooting with laughter, and gave away what it said."

The winter of 1939, the coldest in forty-five years, gave few opportunities for laughs. The Thames froze, pipes burst, snow fell until March. Not normally one to put up with hardships, Lee shivered with the rest of England. When several Brogue photographers left on war work, Lee joined the staff after Harry Yoxall, the managing editor, wangled a work permit for her. Condé Nast cabled his delight that her INTELLIGENCE FUNDAMENTAL GOOD TASTE SENSITIVENESS [AND] ART VALUES were again being mobilized on behalf of the magazine, but wanted to wait before naming her head of the studio. KNOWING MILLER INTELLIGENCE INDUSTRY FEEL MUST HAVE PATIENCE ARRANGE LONG PERIOD EXPERIMENTATION, the New York office's art director counseled.

For one of her first assignments, Lee posed a model wearing a leopard-trimmed suit in front of the map of Europe and beside an array of helmets, boots, and satchels—as if she were about to trade civilian garb for military gear. That winter, as paper rationing went into effect, the staff struggled to make their trimmed-down issues relevant. Debates about which shade of lipstick complemented khaki and endorsements of Harrod's luminous headgear were accompanied by "must" lists for the wartime élégante. These included a gas mask bag resembling a camera case, a white umbrella, and another item to enhance visibility: "not a life preserver but a nerve preserver in the guise of a white waterproof dickey, with tape shoulder straps and side ties."

For Lee, employment was itself a nerve preserver. Throughout 1940, while photographing haute couture, celebrities, dress patterns, and bargains, she befriended members of the staff—with the exception of her bête noire, Cecil Beaton. Lee grew fond of Sylvia Redding, the studio head; Roland Haupt, an Anglo-Indian printer whom she taught photography; and Doreen Impey, whom she took to taste wine nearby in Soho's Italian restaurants, apparently unconcerned that after these lunches, they returned to work "a little less efficient."

In time, Lee also formed a close working relationship with Audrey Withers, the Oxford-educated socialist who was Brogue's editor. Withers struck the note for the magazine in wartime: "Women's first duty is to practise the arts of peace," she wrote, "so that, in happier times, they will not have fallen into disuse." A woman of integrity and taste, she had the foresight to look beyond the ephemeral aspects of fashion while putting them to good use under the circumstances. Government officials sought her support on matters affecting civilian life; as the war progressed, she maintained that women's new roles were both a matter of style and a major social issue.

Brogue's offices on New Bond Street became Lee's second home. After work she often met Roland at the Barcelona Restaurant, a Surrealist haunt. Their Soho dinners, Eileen Agar thought, were good for morale, "for English artists are notoriously self-contained. . . . Some meetings were stormy, some merely cloudy, all lively and tempered by Spanish wine." On April 11, 1940, three days after the Germans invaded Norway, Mesens called a meeting. The Sitzkrieg had come to an end. Winston Chur-

Lee's portrait of Audrey Withers, her editor at U.K. Vogue

chill's call to action had roused the country. Surrealists must stand up for their principles, Mesens argued—by which he meant refusing to support, show with, or write for non-Surrealist institutions. Despite some resistance, the group was stirred to action.

In May, as the Germans swept through the Low Countries and the British narrowly escaped from Dunkirk, Mesens organized an exhibition entitled *Surrealism Today*. In the current context, Lee's photographs from St. Martin d'Ardèche, before Ernst's internment and Carrington's breakdown, testified to the fragility of the creative spirit. The exhibition opened on June 13, the day the Nazis marched on Paris. Its window display, an armchair upholstered as a Negro mammy and a bed whose rumpled sheets were pierced by a dagger, provoked some critics to deplore the group's taste, while the *Studio* asked "whether the surrealists did not instinctively sense whither the European society in which they lived was tending, and whether their movement was not, in fact, a criticism of that society."

At the same time, the Surrealist-inspired *London Bulletin* published an issue on the theme of war. Because "the enemies of desire and hope have risen in violence," page 1 declared, artists were obliged to combat Nazism "wherever it appears." Contributions included poems by Breton, Eluard, Mesens, and Péret, work by Agar, Moore, Penrose, Tanguy, and Delvaux, and two of Lee's most striking photographs: *Portrait of Space* and *The Native* (aka *Cock Rock*).

Although she was not an official Surrealist, these images were "an integral part of the movement," in the view of art historian Michel Remy. Moreover, the dilemma of the group as a whole—its self-perception as "an open movement, never fully *satisfied* with itself"—echoed her own.

Soon London would offer scenes such as card-carrying Surrealists could not have imagined. After the fall of France, Britain carried the full weight of the war against Hitler. Brochures entitled "If the Invader Comes" arrived in the mail. By July, weeping families crowded the stations as the authorities began sending children to Canada and the United States. Lee persuaded the Millers to take two young refugees, who sailed on the first ship. "You did so well," she told her parents, "in just removing them from here that I don't think anything that happens to them after is of much importance."

The Nazis' night raids on London began on August 22 and increased in fury until September 2, when seven hundred German planes bombarded the city. People went to their shelters at the sound of the sirens; there was little panic. In his "This Is London" broadcasts to the United States, Edward R. Murrow praised the courageous "little people" in the hard-hit working-class districts, who dug live bombs out of their gardens and chatted through pane-less windows after the explosions. "About an hour after the 'all-clear' had sounded people were sitting in deck chairs on their lawns, reading the Sunday papers. . . . There was no bravado, no loud voices, only a quiet acceptance of the situation."

From the heights of Hampstead, Roland and Lee watched the fireworks—searchlights piercing the night sky, antiaircraft beams tracking bomber squadrons, fiery clouds rising from the East End and the docks. Even at that distance, Roland recalled, fear "could seize a person and make him crawl like an animal." He felt calmer with Lee, who, he wrote, "innocently enjoyed the stimulus provided by danger."

Fear was less likely to take hold of those who kept busy. The War Artists' Committee, under Kenneth Clark, commissioned artworks from thirty artists, but no Surrealists were included. For the next few years, when British art favored morale-boosting tableaux, Roland's circle felt doubly isolated, since they were also cut off from Paris. One way to continue avant-garde pursuits was to adapt them to defense, an activity that engaged Roland from 1940 on, when he began teaching camouflage to the Home Guard. The following year, he organized the Industrial Camouflage Research Unit and published a book on the art of concealment, *Home Guard Manual of Camouflage*. (The manual, which treats of "deception, misdirection, and bluff," would have pleased Picasso, who claimed that the Cubists had invented camouflage in time for World War I.)

About the same time, Lee's first published prose, "I Worked with Man Ray," appeared in *Lilliput,* a review that featured photography. Although it had been drafted on the boat from Egypt to England, when published two years later, the piece seemed to celebrate the creative spirit that England was fighting to defend. (Man's iconic solarized profile of Lee was featured in the illustrations.) After detailing her modernist pedigree, the contributor's note concluded: "Has a wandering spirit, pre-war liked to go wherever opportunity offered. . . . Came to England when war was declared, says she wouldn't be anywhere else."

A photo-essay in *Picture Post,* Britain's counterpart to *Life,* showed Lee at work on a fashion shoot resembling the production of a play, "for which actors, producer, stage hands must all be experts." As producer, Lee is shown contemplating the set she designed to signal glamour, showing the pose to her model, and experimenting with the lights. "Why all this fuss about a photograph," the journalist asks rhetorically, "when the country is fighting for its life?" Lee's meticulous care was necessary "because now standards are more important than ever," the article concludes, because fashion "maintains Britain's position as the world's greatest exporter of fabrics," or, to put it bluntly, "fashion pays for planes and supplies."

Another way for artists to participate in the war effort was by documenting the Blitz. Cecil Beaton went to photograph St. Giles' Church, in the City, after one of the first German raids. "I marvelled at the freaks of air raid damage and the unfathomable laws of blast," he observed. "Scattered cherubs' wings and stone roses were strewn about—whole memorial plaques of carved marble had been blown across the width of the church and lay undamaged. The entire frontage of the deserted business premises opposite was wrecked. . . . Yet the lamp-post was standing erect with no pane of its lantern broken."

To a Surrealist, the laws of blast were not so much unfathomable as liberating. By wrecking some targets and sparing others, the bombs created wonders in the midst of chaos—as if Magritte or Dalí had remade the landscape. Lee was in her element. By day, odd juxtapositions in the wreckage spoke to her; at night the tension of air raids energized her. There was no reason to be bored with such strangely beautiful sights occurring daily: silver barrage balloons gleaming in the sunset, the stars visible in the dark sky, London spread out like an enormous stage in the moonlight.

One night, an unfamiliar noise awakened her. When she pulled back the blackout curtain, a mysterious substance filled the room—part of a barrage balloon that had landed on the house. It took all night to corral the balloon's silvery mass and hand it out through the front door. Coming across another grounded balloon in a park one day, Lee photographed the huge shape as if it were a giant egg—the offspring of two geese unexpectedly posing in front of it. The title, *Eggceptional Achievement,* is characteristic of her quirky response to life in the Blitz. From the first, Roland noted, "her eye for a surrealist mixture of humor and horror was wide open."

Lee captured some of the firestorms' most startling effects on the way to and from work. One day she photographed a smashed typewriter balanced on the remains of a pedestal: the image, *Remington Silent,* speaks mutely of loss and damage. A companion piece, *Piano by Broadwood,* shows a piano crushed by debris—an eloquent testimony at a time when wailing sirens and droning dive-bombers composed London's nightly music. One of her most poignant images of a fallen culture shows the shattered dome of University College reflected in a pool formed by the rain that has cascaded through the roof. On a lighter note, a wooden board promoting a newspaper proclaims LONDONS NO NIGHT RAID, ONE NIGHT OF LOVE.

Although Lee had felt "like a soft-shelled crab" at the start of the Blitz, she told her parents, like most Londoners, she grew a thick skin in the "three months of solid hell at night" that followed. Brogue's offices were hit by incendiary bombs, yet "it became a matter of pride that work went on. The studio never missed a day, bombed once and fired twice—working with the neighbouring buildings still smouldering—the horrid smell of wet charred wood— the stink of cordite—the fire hoses still up the staircases and we had to wade barefoot to get in." Staffers took prints at home at night when they had "the sacred combination of gas, electricity and water." Lee also took her models home. In one shot, two of them pose in front of the pink and blue shelter wearing protective eye shields, as if masked for a macabre costume party.

Artistically, Lee came into her own in these months, hitting the disquieting note of glamour mixed with dread that, in many of her best images, reflect on each other. Impressed with her feel for the laws of blast, Audrey featured Lee's pictures of Brogue's headquarters—the shattered roof, the staff at work in rooms full of broken glass, the studio in the wine cellar—in the November issue, which also ran her shots for an article entitled "Still Smart Despite All Difficulties."

Lee's spectacular images also caught the attention of Ed Murrow's friend Ernestine Carter, an American married to an Englishman in the Ministry of Information. "We saw eye to eye on the oddities and awesome beauty, as well as the horrors of the Blitz," Carter recalled. They began work on a book based on Lee's photographs, a project "conceived (and given a paper allocation) as a propaganda effort aimed at the U.S.A." Their project could not have been more timely. To continue the fight against Hitler, Churchill needed Roosevelt's support at a time when the United States was strongly isolationist. Their book would complement Murrow's broadcasts and perhaps help shift the tide in favor of intervention.

After each raid, Lee photographed the most arresting sights amid the debris—the Burlington Arcade's transformation into a Piranesi, the angels of St. James' Church raising their trumpets to the sky, once proud Knightsbridge homes joined by a bridge of sighs above their missing stories. While such shots reveal the city stripped bare, they also find humor in the wreckage. Store dum-

War Years

Nonconformist Chapel. London, 1940

U.S. Army nurses billet. Oxford, 1943

Ordnance Wrens. England, 1944

Liberation scene, children celebrating. Paris, 1944

U.S. infantry advancing. Alsace, 1945

Alfred Freyburg, the Bürgermeister of Leipzig, with his wife and daughter. Town Hall, Leipzig, 1945

Freed prisoners scavenging the rubbish dump. Dachau, 1945

Dead SS prison guard floating in canal. Dachau, 1945

mies take to the streets naked except for their top hats; the sign pointing the way to an establishment called Fifth Avenue reads, THE AMERICAN DRESS SHOP CARRIES ON! Lee's Blitz scenes plunge the viewer into a city turned theater of war. They show the new ways of understanding forced on its people.

Ernestine quickly compiled a book whose title, *Grim Glory: Pictures of Britain Under Fire,* echoed Churchill's description of England's spirit in 1940, a mix of "grim" and "gay." The publisher, in congratulating its authors, referred to them as Americans "whom matrimony and *Vogue* respectively have impelled to share with other Londoners their ordeal by fire." As for the images, they testified "to a quality which it is easy to admire but very difficult to analyse." The book was dedicated to Winston Churchill—"the embodiment and the inspiration of that indomitable spirit of the common people."

What could not be said in print was that for some the devastation unleashed on London was also energizing. It depended on one's point of view. One day, Lee found a damaged statue of a classical figure asleep in the ruins, a metal bar across her neck and a brick on her breast. She focused close-up and took the shot on the diagonal: the canted perspective heightens the drama of the statue's downfall. In the context of *Grim Glory,* where the image was featured, this female icon represents a civilization brought low. At the same time, Lee's sardonic title, *Revenge on Culture,* hints at personal themes. An emblem of femininity whose profile resembles her own has been overthrown, yet set free by destructive energies within the culture that first placed her on a pedestal.

Non-Conformist Chapel, another striking shot from *Grim Glory,* may not immediately appear to be a companion image to *Revenge on Culture.* This theatrical photograph of debris falling out the door of a Protestant church plays with the formal and thematic evocations of blockage figured in Lee's earlier photos of impassible doorways. Here, a congregation of stones leaves the chapel in a rush—an eccentric spirituality emptying out from its home, a body turning itself inside out. While such images faithfully record the laws of blast, Lee's compositions also seem to express personal issues: ideas of stasis and release, a sense of the blockage, or liberation, of body and soul.

At times, talk of Britain's indomitable will seemed like so much propaganda. Lee's letters from the early days of the Blitz had been "hopelessly false," she told her parents later, "the reflection of a very temporary mood of fright, bravado, indifference, anger or as often as not just plain drunk and sentimental." By November 1940, she felt tough enough to join Ernestine and a group of American journalists at the BBC for a Thanksgiving Day broadcast to the United States. They had twenty minutes to write about life in the Blitz, "just like at school," Carter recalled. To their surprise, the person in charge chose

Carter and Lee for the program, since their essays were "the only ones that didn't start with 'through shot and shell and bursting bombs this correspondent made his way here.'"

Toward the end of 1940, the Germans let up on the bombing. "We've been having the most extraordinary lull in the blitz since before Xmas," Lee told the Millers. "It's given us all a chance to catch up on being human a bit—instead of just hanging on to the edge of the precipice." Friends who could not get home at night or were bombed out of their homes stayed with Lee and Roland, playing cards, doing crossword puzzles, and drinking. Guests came and went constantly. "It was an agreeably relaxed household," one of them wrote. "There was no demur should two luncheon guests decide to take an afternoon nap in their double bed." In their circle of friends—artists, writers, journalists, and politicians—it was the way to be human rather than just hang on.

One of the first to take up residence was Valentine Penrose, who was stranded in London. Uneasy about contacting Roland after their divorce, Valentine made a date with him at the nearby pub—where she got into conversation with Lee without knowing who she was. After Roland found the two women chatting amiably, Lee invited Valentine to live with them. "Downshire Hill," a poem written in 1941, voices the "great fear" Valentine felt in her attic room during bombardments, but also her admiration for "the lovely woman" who "does what must be done" and keeps "her taste for life"—a tribute from one brave woman to another.

"We eat fine, but it's a career to manage it," Lee told Erik. "We have a field day with the cheese rations," she continued. "Everyone brings theirs along and we have a big toasted cheese and beer party." Rationing was introduced gradually (bacon, sugar, and butter, then meat, tea, and fats, and, in 1941, eggs and milk). The Ministry of Food urged housewives to cook grains and vegetables. Dinner might consist of lentil sausages, mock goose (a gratin of potatoes and apples), and victory sponge (potato pudding with carrots). A soup for air raids could be made from root vegetables, the ministry explained: "A hot drink works wonders in times of shock." On less stressful days, one could top vegetables with mashed potatoes—the infamous Woolton pie, named for the minister of food, went through many variations, the best being the one served at the Savoy Hotel. In 1941, Lee began a nonstarch diet on the advice of her doctor, who said that her system had been poisoned by the national mainstay, wholemeal bread. (She told Erik that she longed for the United States, where she hoped to "eat a lot of butter" after the war.)

In December 1941, when unmarried women were called for military service, the housekeeper announced that she was leaving to work in a munitions plant. "Xmas won't be much of a party as leave is impossible to co-incide," Lee told her parents. "Someone has promised me a goose—a bird, not a rude poke—and I've wangled a pudding—tho no brandy to burn on it, yet. . . . I'll have to cook it myself." "It seems pretty silly to go on working on a frivolous paper like Vogue," she continued, "tho it may be good for the country's morale it's hell on mine."

Since the outbreak of war, fashion magazines had maintained that keeping up appearances helped morale. In 1941, when clothes rationing came into effect, Brogue faced a new challenge: to support limitations on the use of fabrics (given the need for uniforms) while convincing readers that they could still dress well. "If the new order is to be one of sackcloth and ashes, we think some women will wear theirs with a difference," Edna Woolman Chase, U.S. *Vogue*'s editor, declared. In the same spirit, Audrey Withers asked Lee to take pictures for a series of articles on the new Utility designs, factory clothes "with a tough chic of their own." Such styles, the October editorial claimed, illustrated "our belief that fashion is *of* its period, not superimposed upon it."

By the end of the year, the tailored look prevailed. To compensate, women wore their hair long, à la Veronica Lake—a style that proved hazardous to those employed in factories. In response to the minister of labor's plea to ban long tresses, Withers ordered features on hair-concealing hats and the short coiffures said to be chic in Paris. Lee's photographs—turbans, draped cloches, sleek hairdos—helped launch the movement toward smaller, neater heads. "Within a few months . . . accidents had disappeared from our workshops," Harry Yoxall recalled with pride.

For Lee's next assignment, Withers sent her and staff writer Lesley Blanch to Greenwich, to photograph the women of the Royal Naval Service. Blanch assured readers that the Wrens took care to look "pretty and feminine"; Lee's shots of these competent women on the bridge of their ship, tracking planes and conferring with their male counterparts, stress their seriousness while confirming the widespread belief that of all the auxiliaries' uniforms, the Wrens' (two well-cut suits in navy, a matching coat, and stockings) was the most becoming.

December, already an eventful time due to female conscription, became even more tense with the loss of two of England's biggest ships in the Pacific— an incident that had greater impact in the United Kingdom than the news of the Japanese attack at Pearl Harbor. (Some were heard to say that it "served the Yanks right" for having refused to join Britain.) And while the American journalists who gathered at the Savoy were jubilant over Roosevelt's declaration of war, most people took the news calmly. "For me," Lee told her parents, "the declaration of war is a sort of anticlimax . . . as I've felt so much in it from the beginning."

Increasingly, she sought out other Americans who had been "in it" from the start. Since autumn, a lively group of Time-Life journalists had been reporting on the war from their base on Dean Street. At a dinner party in December, Lee met the group's catalyst, David Scherman, a wisecracking New Yorker who, at twenty-five, had already established himself as one of *Life*'s most inventive photographers. He drove her home; she invited him in for drinks. Overwhelmed by the Picassos on the walls, and even more so by his hostess—whose work he knew from *Vogue* and *Grim Glory*—Scherman became a regular at Downshire Hill soirées.

By February 1942, Lee was thinking about sharing a flat with Scherman and two friends from Time-Life, since Roland was often away and people thought that the Germans would invade Britain by spring. After discussing the plan with Roland, Scherman instead joined their household, where his education in art, food, wine, and Surrealism began. It is easy to see what Davie (Lee's nickname for this intense young man) saw in his hostess, who was nine years his senior. Educated at Dartmouth, a puritan stronghold, he considered Downshire Hill a crash course in the kind of sophisticated living he had only read about in *The New Yorker*. And while his colleagues enjoyed London on their American salaries, Lee's guests outdid them in worldliness—especially where sex was concerned. It amazed him to learn that in his new family, open relationships were the norm. Soon Dave was sleeping with Lee when Roland went on assignment. "It was a ménage à trois," he explained, "but Roland was in the army, so it soon became a ménage à deux."

Their ménage functioned well, due to the mutual respect between Dave and "Rollers," the young man's name for Roland. "I was very fond of Dave and admired him greatly," Roland said, though he recalled his pique on coming home to find their friend's pajamas under his pillow. The trio's intimacy is palpable in a contemporary photograph, Dave and Roland each in uniform on either side of a barefoot Lee. For a time, Dave's absorption in Lee blinded him

David Scherman photographing, c. 1942, (David E. Scherman)

to the situation, in which he was, in a sense, being exploited, while Roland was pleased that Lee had company. She would be less likely to stray, and Dave would look after her during the bombing.

It is also easy to surmise Lee's feelings for Dave, in whom she gained a brother, a mentor, and a friend, as well as a rapt though inexperienced lover. Judging by his portraits of Lee in her nightgown, gazing at her image in a mirror, the seductive older woman seemed like a goddess. While her poses recall those she struck for Theodore and, later, for Man, the power was now on her side. Yet as well as being Dave's lover, she was also a friend with a sense of humor like his own. "There was no chi-chi about Lee," Scherman recalled, "no nonsense, but great fun." (Lee called him her pal—the substitute for the faithful playmate she had had in Erik.)

In exchange for Lee's lessons in the pleasures of life, her compatriot taught her his approach to photojournalism as a story—"pictorialism with a meaning." Scherman had learned his métier from *Life* photographers Margaret Bourke-White and Alfred Eisenstaedt. While he endorsed the "exact instant" approach to photography, as in Robert Capa's famous shots of the Spanish Civil War, he also believed that if one missed the instant, one might convey its meaning by reframing the shot, or, better yet, faking it. "You invent a good picture," he explained, often some time after the fact.

The idea of staging a complex image or a narrative sequence appealed to Lee's sense of the theatrical. Between fashion assignments, she helped Dave "invent" pictures for *Life*—a "photo-dramatization" of a novel about love in wartime, grimy chimney sweeps posed to dramatize the shortage of soap, scantily clad dancers auctioning lemons to demonstrate the rigors of rationing. This sort of "one-page quickie," Dave told his brother Bill, was designed to be a *Life* picture of the week. For the lemon auction, he and Lee "cooked it up, painted sign, bought fish-bowl for raffle, etc. . . . This sort of fakery I have no conscience about." Most recently, with Lee as lighting expert, he had shot Piccadilly Circus at night from atop a tall building.

Lee also traveled with Dave on two assignments in the country, "England in the Spring" (it rained every day) and "The Horrors of Wartime England"— often climbing up church towers for the best vantage points. (In a shot taken from the balcony of a burned-out Bristol theater, a tiny Lee curtsies onstage, beneath the remains of a safety curtain.) That autumn, Dave did a feature essay on the Home Guard's capture of a mock French village, staged with Roland's help. They amused themselves by calling the village brothel "Chez les Nudistes" and writing in French script on a wall the names Picasso, Miró, Matisse, and Utrillo, as if French villages naturally honored artists.

As Dave's pal, Lee joined the hard-drinking Time-Life crowd—photo editor John Morris, reporters Mary Welsh, Charles Wertenbaker, and Lael Tucker, photographers Robert Capa, Eliot Elisofon, and Bob Landry. When not at the

Savoy bar, the group met at their Soho headquarters, the White Tower, whose Greek proprietor served unobtainable items like fresh corn and wrote the scores of their ongoing gin rummy game on the wall. Through this network of high-powered journalists, Lee met other American women engaged in war work.

Lee spent the day with Margaret Bourke-White, the first female photographer accredited to the U.S. Army Air Forces, after she came to London to photograph Churchill, then flew to a secret U.S. airbase to name one of the long-range B-17s that were about to start the offensive against Germany. Lee showed her chatting with army personnel, taking pictures of the bomber crew, next to the engine christened "Peggy," her nickname, and beside "her" bomber, the "Flying Flitgun." Bourke-White posed as one colleague for another. One can imagine their conversation during the shoot. Both women liked the Rolleiflex's square format; Bourke-White was annoyed that despite her fame, the air force would not allow her to fly missions.

Lee also photographed the equally glamorous Martha Gellhorn, a reporter for *Collier's* and the wife of Ernest Hemingway—who caused a stir in London when he took up residence at the Dorchester to report on the war. In a composition reflecting Lee's sense of the gap between public image and private persona, Gellhorn, her back turned, stares at the camera from her dressing-table mirror. Within a short time, Gellhorn ended her marriage to Hemingway. The Time-Life crowd were not surprised, since they had been watching Hemingway's flirtation with Mary Welsh, who had set her cap for him, at the White Tower.

Welsh's memoir, *How It Was,* depicts the charged atmosphere in their circle. "Bob Capa came to photograph the war," she wrote, "and one could . . . hear the upswing in female heartbeats around the office." When Lee appeared, Welsh continued, "her crusty, cool intelligence, smoothed down the office airwaves, but not the heartbeats." Lee's ménage à trois was not the only triangular relationship in the group. While Dave was living at Downshire Hill, he befriended Cynthia Ledsham, an English researcher at *Time,* and later courted her. Ledsham, a friend of Lee's despite her hold on Dave, recalled "the atmosphere changing when she walked in, because of her joie de vivre. It's funny how someone so self-absorbed can buck up others," she added, "even while she got them to do just what she wanted."

At the same time, "Wert" Wertenbaker, *Time's* foreign editor, began an affair with Lael Tucker, who worked under his direction—as did her husband. Sex in wartime carried "the demand to be casual," Wert wrote, since no one knew if he would be alive the next day. The war "made the English promiscuous," he believed, but kept "the deepest emotions for itself." Going to bed with someone could be intensely private but also "an irresistible expression of the forces around them . . . a gathering together of primitive passions and noble aspirations for the final orgasm of war."

Given their backgrounds, it is not surprising that the men at Time-Life took their female partners for granted. Although women worked as auxiliaries, they were unlikely to bear the hardships of military service. And while journalists like Lee and Lael were exceptions, the men considered reports from "the distaff side" (Scherman's words) less important than their own dispatches. What Lee thought of this attitude is implied in her portrait of Lael, whose mischievous smile hints at their complicity.

As the American "invasion" of Britain stepped up, Lee watched her friends at Time-Life become U.S. Army correspondents, a status that smoothed the way toward more exciting stories while also opening the doors of the well-stocked PXs—the source of cigarettes, Scotch, and other coveted goods. "The two phenomena, no-Kleenex-in-the-midst-of-plenty and the threat of being left out of the biggest story of the decade, almost drove poor Lee mad," Scherman recalled, "until I suggested that she too, a perfectly bona fide Yank from Poughkeepsie, apply for accreditation."

Though accurate, this explanation underestimates Lee's desire to see action as a photographer. Looking back on this period, one appreciates Audrey Withers's different sense of women's capabilities. She could see beyond reports of the hostilities to the social transformations taking place at home, which became the magazine's new focus. With her backing, "Mrs. Lee Miller Eloui" earned accreditation as U.K. *Vogue*'s correspondent on December 30, 1942. Unlike Scherman, Withers saw nothing odd in Lee's visit to Saville Row to order her uniform, since this was what all smart women did on receiving commissions.

"Now I wear a soldier suit on account of what I'm war correspondent for the Conde Nast press," Lee told the Millers. "You ought to see me all done up and very serious like in olive drab and flat heeled shoes," she teased, disinclined to admit that she *could* be serious. A month later, Lee posed in her new gear with five other writers—Mary Welsh, Dixie Tighe, Kathleen Harriman, Helen Kirkpatrick, and Tania Long—each wearing the triangular green WAR CORRESPONDENT badge on her jacket. The first official portrait of women journalists in the European theater, it implied that their presence there, contrary to popular opinion, mattered far more than their tailored uniforms and flat-heeled shoes.

As all realms of society mobilized in the war effort, fashion became serious business. Government officials sought Withers's support before launching the Utility clothes scheme, a system of rationing to save fabric; Brogue did its best to convince readers that austerity need not mean dowdiness. To this end, Audrey assigned Lee to photograph the tailored styles designed for the star of a film about a Wren in love with a Russian, and for the women diplomats

U.S. women war correspondents, 1943. Left to right: Mary Welsh, Dixie Tighe, Kathleen Harriman, Helen Kirkpatrick, Lee Miller, and Tania Long

posted to the British Embassy in Moscow (Russia having been England's ally since 1941). The illustrations for this article, "These Clothes Are News," bear a generic resemblance to Davie's "photo-dramatizations" but draw on Lee's long knowledge of staging and her sense that the women were as newsworthy as their outfits.

Throughout 1943, Brogue documented changes in British women's lives. Perusing these issues, one discovers Lee's commitment to being "in it" by chronicling the social upheavals wrought by the war, the first in which millions of women took part. Before she was accredited as a war correspondent, her assignments on women in the military were mainly domestic in emphasis. After accreditation, they treated the war as an opportunity for women, demonstrating her respect for the auxiliaries while giving her the chance to step into their shoes—in her imagination.

For the May issue, Lee photographed members of the Women's Land Army, a large-scale experiment that took women of different classes to be farm laborers: they drove tractors, thatched roofs, and reshaped hedges, activities that piqued her own interest in machinery and crafts. Among their few compensations for this backbreaking labor, the "land girls" received an ample wardrobe, including breeches, dungarees, and gum boots—indispensable for mucky farmyards. Lee's dissatisfaction with the layout and captions accompanying her photos dates from this period, when the studio staff assembled articles without realizing that she had shot a story.

Lee's first piece of photojournalism, "American Army Nurses Photographed and Described by Lee Miller," appeared in the same issue. Evoking the presence in Britain of these "blue-uniformed young girls with silver officers' bars on their shoulders," she outlined their training in hospital units designed to be airlifted abroad. "The Presbyterian Hospital of New York," she wrote, "has taken over the Churchill Hospital in Oxford which was a gift of America to England. . . . There the patients range from G.I. Joe, who got out too far on the big apple tree, to a lad back from too close attention in bombing the Continent; but mostly men suffering from frostbite of high altitudes, exposure in open boats, and wounds of just plain heroism."

Her illustrations show the nurses performing physical therapy, prepping for surgery, and eating "American food" in the mess hall. "They are not forbidden, but not encouraged, to marry," she observed thoughtfully. "They may not serve in the same unit as their husbands nor stay in the Service . . . if they start a baby." Reading between the lines one senses her empathy—for the GI who fell from the tree, the men with frostbite, women who "start a baby." From this point on, while recording the changes in her subjects' lives, her images imply her presence, as if she registered their experiences while peering through her lens. (In some shots, clothes substitute for their wearers, as in a playful image of nurses' panties framing the view from the window of their billet while a starched white uniform stands guard beside them.)

Lee occasionally took up her old position on the other side of the camera. One summer day when Roland was on leave, he decided to test an ointment recommended by a cosmetic firm to camouflage members of the Home Guard. The experiment, conducted in a friend's garden, began as the latest variant on Lee's role as Surrealist muse. She stripped and covered herself with the ointment, a thick green paste. "My theory," Roland wrote, "was that if it could hide such eye-catching attractions as hers from the invading Hun, smaller and less seductive areas of skin would stand an even better chance of becoming invisible." Dave photographed the group, Lee painted green, Roland in his shorts, and their friends taking tea on the lawn—a parody of English life in wartime.

The following year, for a photo-essay on a stylish revue inspired by the career of Cecil Beaton, Dave staged a mischievous Beaton-at-work photo with Lee as Beaton's model: she reclined languidly on a couch while Beaton focused on her from his perch high above on a mantelpiece. Judging by her wary look, her opinion of him had not changed. One guesses that she went along with the gag for Dave's sake, and as a joke for those who knew about the lack of sympathy between the celebrity photographer and his skeptical subject.

Increasingly, Lee collaborated with Dave. Their partnership gave her practice in shooting a narrative sequence and confirmed her sense of métier. Though she relied on him for technical support, they collaborated as equals. Her photos sometimes appeared under his name; several of his were attributed to Lee. (Exchanging cameras or using each other's images was not unusual. When under pressure to submit pictures as fast as possible, photographers often pooled their work, helping themselves to the most suitable images.) In another *Life* "photo-dramatization" of a London beauty contest, Lee told the Millers, "some of the pix are mine, done on a co-operative job and fun with Davie." To show his gratitude, Dave told his brother to deposit his U.S. funds in a New York bank for himself and Lee, since "if I croak or if she goes to her home in America she would need some dough."

While neither would have used such a term, one could call them soul mates. Both were driven and practical. Like Lee, Dave had to be immersed in whatever he was doing. They had an unspoken pact to take things lightly. He liked to talk tough, as if they were characters in a Damon Runyon story. Both loved words like *hooligan, rubberneck,* and *boondoggle,* which made them laugh. As photographers, Scherman explained, "we were looking for odd juxtapositions—like Lee's title, *Grim Glory.*" Lee had "something unusual in a woman," he went on, "the soul of a tinker." She loved the technical side of their craft and shared his dislike of those who called it art. As Yanks, they reveled in popular culture, the wit of Irving Berlin and Cole Porter, and wartime humor. (Since the simultaneous appearance in Britain of Utility clothes and GIs, a joke had been circulating about Utility knickers: "One yank & they're off.") Their partnership relied on an ironic stance toward things others took seriously.

Given Brogue's mission to support the war effort, there was little room in its pages for irony. The subhead for "Night Life Now," a June 1943 article, reads in bold: "Lee Miller photographs, Lesley Blanch reports the after-dark drama of the work of the Women's Services." The piece gave Lee the chance to put light and shadow to narrative use. With Dave, she went to an ATS (Auxiliary Territorial Service) defense site at Hendon, north of London, to photograph the all-female regiment that lit up the night sky with searchlight beams. Arriving in the midst of operations, she posed two of them silhouetted against the searchlight. The shot, a kind of reverse solarization, creates a halo around the women who work to illuminate the dark. (One of them, Nina Hamilton, recalls coming under enemy fire as soon as the photo was done.)

With this striking chiaroscuro image, Audrey ran Lee's shots of Wrens maintaining boats, Waafs bedding down barrage balloons, ATS gunners, and the full ATS crew against the diagonal streak of their searchlight. Style no longer mattered, Blanch wrote, now that night life was a matter of "scrubbing, polishing and perfecting each apparently insignificant cog in this vast war machine of ours."

On her next assignment, Lee spent two weeks in Scotland at an undisclosed location where the Wrens were honing their skills—from navigation, Morse code, ship maintenance, and "a certain amount of engineering, or mechanics," to repairing submarines that called into their station from the North Atlantic. Shadowing them at their labors, she photographed each aspect of their work, from the physically demanding, like climbing down rope ladders in thirty seconds, to the highly technical, servicing depth charges and regulating torpedoes. To get shots of Wrens racing down a ladder, crossing a boom, and clambering to a boat, she "nearly drowned," she told her parents, "or at least got damn wet stepping back to get a wider angle," another of her "Perils of Pauline style situations." She could not tell them about security measures, nor explain that some of her Wrens photos were being held by the censors.

In the same letter, she mentioned Dave's forthcoming books, two collections of photos due out in the United States in 1944. Building on a photo-essay for *Life* the year before, he had assembled his images of famous sites (King Arthur's castle, Charles Dickens's house, Canterbury Cathedral) under the title *Literary England.* "Davie says it's my idea," Lee told them. "It was the kind of book I wanted to read and see for a long time." His other volume, *First of the Many,* combined reportage and propaganda on behalf of the U.S. Eighth Air Force, whose bombers had been making strategic raids on Germany for the past year.

Watching Dave prepare these manuscripts inspired Lee to do a book of her own on the Wrens, using the "censored" pictures and the many shots not published in Brogue. As its title, *Wrens in Camera,* implies, it shows the women in private, but also at work—through the lens of one whose solidarity with them is apparent. Starting with a profile of their commandant, the Duchess of Kent, *Wrens in Camera* shows the women working as signalers, boarding officers, meteorological experts, cooks, and mechanics—mastering the kinds of techniques that piqued Lee's interest. She photographed them welding, servicing planes, testing radio equipment, and casting gears in the glowing furnace of a submarine depot—another chiaroscuro image of women in touch with pure energy. The book fulfills its function as a morale booster while honoring, by formal means, its subjects' engagement with power.

The time was right, Audrey felt, to show war artists at work. Lee's shots of Henry Moore sketching in a dimly lit tube shelter during the Blitz, Paul Nash seeking inspiration in a salvage dump, and Stanley Spencer, in the shipyards, illustrated an article on a new film called *Out of Chaos* that was intended to show the impact of chaos on the creative spirit. The artists agreed that "war turned them from abstract and surrealistic tendencies towards a more personal expression of their mind's eye"; the film, *Vogue* hoped, would "draw painter and public towards a closer understanding." Of the group, Lee's shot of Moore guarding his sleeping subjects while he draws conveys her empathy with the artist and the huddled bodies seeking repose.

That spring, Lee convinced Audrey to let her photograph and write about

Ed Murrow, whose comments were being cabled back to London for their authoritative overview. "You in the United States know why because you hear him," Lee told her compatriots in the version of their interview published in U.S. *Vogue.* "A radio prophet is a man without face in his own country," she said. Few knew that he was "literally tall, dark, and handsome."

After describing Murrow's accidental entry into broadcasting and the cramped office from which he electrified listeners, Lee explained his "seat of the pants" approach—as dazzling as that of any fighter pilot. "[Murrow] wing-talks with his right hand, pointing, circling his forefinger and putting in commas with steep left banks and right chandels [sic]," she wrote. "All the verbal 'hamminess' that some newscasters have is sublimated by Ed in these inaudible calisthenics. There are no crescendos, diminuendos, largos, or pizzicatos marked in on his script. There is no more writing on his page than meets the ear."

Lee's account of her friend "honestly writing what he honestly wanted to say" expresses her own ideal for prose. Murrow was her model, but when it came time to photograph him, she took charge. He was to sit at his desk and type, as if working on a story. "Lee says there is a difference between theory and practice," he wrote. "When Lee comes to take pictures she also straightens out the wiring."

In a note to Audrey accompanying the final draft of her article, Lee worried that the wiring still showed, that her idea—to write about a writer—had been a mistake. "I've spent fifteen or so years of my life learning how to take a picture, that thing that is worth ten thousand words," she fretted, "and here I am cutting my own throat." Writers were not, as she had thought, *"démodé."* She had been naïve to think that she could master the "technique" of prose. But unlike Lee, who lacked confidence in her writing, Audrey was bowled over. The article showed "how the acutely observant eye of the photographer was transformed into the words of a reporting journalist."

From February to April 1944, the time of the Little Blitz, Lee persevered with routine assignments—society portraits, film stars, celebrities' grooming secrets—while also photographing women in the news and learning new trends in color photography. The year before, using Kodachrome film sent from the United States by Bill Scherman, she had "cornered the color racket for Vogue," Dave told his brother, with full color pages in each issue. The June 1944 issue ran a color shot of hers on the cover. Although conventional in terms of composition, it showed Lee's mastery of the process, much of it acquired that winter through her friendship with the Russian photographer Planskoi, whose expertise and supplies she exploited while he was in England.

With the rest of London, she dealt with the return of German planes bearing bigger, more destructive bombs. Once again queues formed outside tube stations, people slept in shelters, nights were pierced by ear-splitting raids and defensive gunfire. It was "a bit dreamlike to hear broken glass being shovelled out of the gutters," *The New Yorker* noted, "to see a display of fluttering rayon stockings in a shattered shop window being guarded by enough policemen to make a Hope Diamond feel reasonably safe"—a scene one wishes Lee had photographed. At the same time, the rumble of military traffic produced talk of a brighter future, especially when the tide turned against the Germans and in favor of the Russians on the eastern front. In March, Roland left for Italy, where the Allies were fighting their way north, to study camouflage techniques for use in the European invasion, whose date was a matter of speculation now that General Eisenhower had taken command of SHAEF (Supreme Head-quarters Allied Expeditionary Force), based in England.

While the buildup of troops and supplies made it clear that the Allies were organizing a second front, the authorities took pains to keep its location secret. Londoners stopped betting on invasion dates, pretending to themselves that "this is just another spring, instead of the spring everybody has been waiting for since Dunkirk." With all of southern England become a military camp, the Time-Life staff lobbied New York headquarters for resources to cover the campaign. John Morris, *Life*'s head of photography, mobilized his own troops, including Capa, George Rodger, Ralph Morse, David "Chim" Seymour, and Scherman. *Life*'s cult of the "photographer-hero" was at its height; staffers' nerves were on edge despite the pretense of normality.

Lee's letter to her parents on May 29, 1944, mentions her "second-front nerves—which is affecting everyone—me particularly." After thanking them for their packages containing precious items like Kleenex, she asked for more food (canned corn, lima beans, Nescafé, "swell chocolates with soft insides"), and gave news of Aziz, whom her friend Henry Hopkinson had seen recently in Cairo. Aziz was "desperately ill," Lee wrote, "but I have no way of going there." Turning over in her mind the "shoulds," she wrote, "I ought to go—from human and moral obligation—and I ought to stay as my work would then be completely thrown away. So I dilly-dally around and am too cowardly even to find out whether there might be transport."

In the next sentence dilly-dallying gives way to insight. "All the reasons for which I left in the beginning come into play again—and the five years of making a new life would be thrown away. Not that Roland wouldn't understand but that selfishly I don't want to lose the grasp I have on work at the moment—I couldn't pick up another chance, and work is what I need for the rest of my life."

Lee in customized U.S. Army helmet, Normandy, 1944

Chapter 12

Covering the War in France

(1944–45)

On June 6, 1944, D-day, the Allies invaded Normandy. After photographing the onslaught from a U.S. Navy ship, Dave returned to London twenty-four hours later to find Lee preparing her own invasion.
This was the work she wanted. She did not intend to miss her chance.

Nearly sixty years later, it is hard to imagine the constraints under which
women journalists operated, even as they were becoming glamorous figures in
popular culture. *Life* publicized the exploits of Bourke-White, who posed like
a film star in her flight gear after gaining permission to fly with the air force.
Hollywood churned out movies about "girl photographers"—romances in
which the heroine's calling placed her at odds with the promptings of her
heart. But newsworthy female journalists knew that they were unlikely to see
combat. SHAEF protocol did not allow them to travel alone or visit press
camps in a theater of operations. Nor were they assigned jeeps and drivers. As
if they too belonged to an auxiliary corps, they were to stay behind the lines
with the nurses. On D-day, Lee and her women colleagues were told that they
must remain in England and file their stories from the invasion bases in the
south.

During the next weeks, Lee suffered through several rounds of vaccinations and, with the rest of London, coped with the new German missiles—the pilotless V-1s known as robots, doodlebugs, or buzz bombs. People ducked for cover at the sound of the V-1, which resembled the drone of a badly maintained motorcycle. Since it was hard to tell the start of a raid from its conclusion, nerves soon frayed from the sirens' constant wail. The weather—cold wind and driving rain—added to the strain. Lee coped by drinking the gin that came in the mail from Roland. "[It] saved my sanity," she told him on August 2. "See if you can do a deal for further supplies."

In July, SHAEF ruled that women journalists could report on the battle for France as it unfolded rather than return to London after each trip. Mary Welsh went on an official tour to cover the Medical Corps; on her return to the Dorchester, she related her experience to Hemingway, who was preparing to leave for France as *Collier's* war correspondent, Gellhorn having flown to Italy to cover the fighting. Iris Carpenter resented being assigned to an Allied hospital, but found that ambulances could be exciting when bombs fell all around her, shattering her eardrum. It was useful to have the backing of a major newspaper, a general, or both: Helen Kirkpatrick, the London bureau chief for the *Chicago Daily News,* convinced Ike to send her to France.

While it was not clear that Brogue needed a war correspondent, Audrey Withers tried to make each issue topical. "It was all very well encouraging ourselves with the conventional patter about keeping up morale," she recalled, "but magazines—unlike books—are essentially about the here and now. And this was wartime." Toward the end of July, as the Allies struggled to take the German strongholds along the Normandy coast, she sent Lee to report on the American nurses' postinvasion duties.

Lee's sense of the trip's strangeness pervades her published account: "As we flew into sight of France I swallowed hard on what were trying to be tears, and remembered a movie actress kissing a handful of earth. My self-conscious analysis was forgotten in greedily studying the soft, gray-skied panorama of nearly a thousand square miles of France—of freed France. . . . Cherbourg was a misty bend far to the right, and ahead three planes were returning from dropping the bombs which made towering columns of smoke. That was the front."

The sensuous particularity of this first paragraph would characterize her dispatches, along with her ability to focus the story with her photographer's eye. She regularly saw what others missed. "When you think that every situation she covered was completely outside her previous experience," Audrey reflected, "it makes the sheer professionalism of her text even more remarkable." In some ways Lee was winging it, inspired by Ed Murrow's seat-of-the-pants approach. Yet the many drafts in her archive attest to the care she took to get the story right. Reading these different versions, one is struck by her ability to go to the heart of the matter.

After landing, Lee took quick, painterly notes while her convoy drove to the 44th Evacuation Hospital, near Omaha Beach, and later, to a hospital near the front. France looked familiar—"the trees were the same with little pantaloons like eagles, and the walled farms, the austere Norman architecture." Yet it was also full of strange juxtapositions. Strands of barbed wire "looped into each other like filigree." A skull and crossbones on a board in a hedge barred the way to fields of poppies, daisies, and land mines. Signs at crossroads bearing American code names—Missouri Charlie, Mahogany Red, Java Blue—stood beside those of Norman villages.

Camera around her neck and notebook in hand, she toured the tents where the wounded awaited treatment. Following the same pattern as in photo shoots, she surveyed the scene from a distance, then moved in for close-ups: "In the shock ward they are limp and flat under brown blankets, some with plasma flasks dripping drops of life into an outstretched splintered arm, another sufficiently recovered to smoke or chat to see if he's real. A doctor and nurse are busy on the next with oxygen and plasma. The rest are sleeping or staring at the dark brown canvas—patient, waiting and gathering strength for multiple operations on unorthodox wounds."

Lee zeroed in on one of the most unorthodox: a man whose entire body was swathed in bandages, with slits for his eyes, nose, and mouth. "A bad burns case asked me to take his picture as he wanted to see how funny he looked," she wrote. Complying uneasily with his request ("It was pretty grim and I didn't focus good"), she showed the man as a grinning white mask. The "grimness" of the case is betrayed in the shot's blurred focus—a trace of the shock she felt in this first encounter with a badly damaged body.

Moments later, a surgical patient watched her take his picture. "In the chiaroscuro of khaki and white I was reminded of Hieronymus Bosch's painting 'The Carrying of the Cross,' " she wrote. "I didn't know that he was already asleep with sodium pentothal when they started on his other arm. I had turned away for fear my face would betray to him what I had seen." That day, she learned that one could photograph horror, but at a cost.

Arriving at a field hospital closer to the front, she focused instead on technique, the use of "the magic life-savers"—sulfa drugs, penicillin, and blood transfusions. Yet even then, individual cases suggested larger themes. Others felt the need to record the mayhem, she noted: "Without looking up from his snipping a surgeon asked me to write down for him what exposure he should use if he wanted to take a detailed picture of an operation in that contrast of white towels, concentrated light and deep shadows." The next day, watching a doctor "with a Raphael-like face" treat a badly wounded man, Lee saw the scene in her mind's eye as an archetype of compassion.

Her response to suffering often troubled her. She sympathized with the hardworking American nurses whom she photographed off-duty. But trying to sleep that night in a tent recently vacated by enemy staff, she recalled, "I entangled myself with distaste in the blankets of the German nurses"—an intimacy that disturbed her as much as the gunfire. Then, watching German and American doctors work side by side, she wrote, "I stiffened every time I saw a German, and . . . resented my heart softening involuntarily toward German wounded."

On the road to the collection station, where cases were assigned to treatment, she spotted many odd sights—behind the Utah Beach hospital, "roly-poly balloons with cross-lacing on their stomachs like old-fashioned corsets," children in pinafores and soldiers' caps directing traffic, "fields with whole, transplanted trees sharpened into spikes against our landings"—some of which she captured on film. But the bulk of her images from this first trip show the most urgent cases, the "dirty, disheveled, stricken figures" and those who cared for them.

Before returning to London, Lee posed for her own portrait. In it, she stands with her hand at heart level, just below her war correspondent badge, and wears a metal helmet borrowed from Don Sykes, the army photographer who took the picture. (His customized headgear had a striped visor that had been cut away so he could wear it to shoot movies. "Sykes had painted on the stripes for fun," she noted.) Though Lee's expression belies thoughts of "fun," U.S. *Vogue* ran this portrait in her "U.S.A. Tent Hospital in France" on September 15, along with her shots of medics at work, the bad burn case, and the trees with pantaloons. A helmeted Lee also appeared in ads announcing, "VOGUE has its own reporter with the United States Army in France"—as if the portrait's mix of decorum and eccentricity conveyed her unique perspective.

This story also appeared in the September Brogue as "Unarmed Warriors." Publishing Lee's reportage was "the most exciting journalistic experience of my war," Audrey declared, and a source of pride for the entire staff: "We were the last people one could conceive having this type of article, it seemed so incongruous in our pages of glossy fashion." Lee's article not only thrust the magazine into the here and now; it showed that high gloss and seriousness were not antithetical.

∞

Throughout the summer, V-1s bombarded London. Reports of a crisis in Germany after a failed attempt on Hitler's life filtered back, but there was little optimism about the war's ending soon. In August, Lee wangled an assignment in Brittany—to cover the U.S. Army's efforts to maintain order in Saint-Malo after its liberation from the Germans, another behind-the-lines job. She crossed the Channel on an LST, one of the large landing ships that had been ferrying troops to France since D-day. During the trip, she beat the captain at poker and talked with the crew about their adventures. Her own began when the LST ran aground at Omaha Beach and a sailor carried her ashore.

On her way to Brittany, Lee saw the devastation at Isigny, Carentan, and Sainte-Mère-Eglise. She reached Saint-Malo on August 13 to learn that, contrary to intelligence reports, the town had not been secured. The 83rd Infantry Division of the Third Army had arrived there a few days earlier to find minefields, antitank devices, and rows of steel gates meant to block their advance. The Germans, under Colonel Von Aulock, still held the heavily fortified citadel at the top of the bay, where they commanded positions around the port. In old Saint-Malo, the infantrymen who came in after the tanks were battling house to house with German snipers.

The head of the division's Civil Affairs unit (CA) took Lee to a hospital where U.S. medics were spicing their C rations with German herbs, then to their post at the once chic Hôtel des Ambassadeurs. "The wicker furniture tried to look gay and brave under the burden of machine guns and handgrenades," Lee noted. "Instead of a chattering crowd of brightly-dressed aperitif-drinkers, there were a few tired soldiers." From a window facing the port, Lee shot views of the old city, the citadel, and the Grand Bey fortress. Amused to find a pair of GIs artillery spotting from a bed in the honeymoon suite, she took their picture—an action shot in which the cold gleam of their guns contrasts with the decorative curves of the window rail.

For the next five days, while the Americans attacked the enemy's positions, Lee had Saint-Malo to herself. "I had the clothes I was standing in, a couple of dozen films, and an eiderdown blanket roll," she wrote. "I was the only photographer for miles around and I now owned a private war." After crowds of panicky French prisoners left the citadel during a truce, she helped the CA keep order: "Kept busy interpreting, consoling and calming people—I forgot mostly to take pictures." She watched mangy pets escaping, women taking morphine for hysteria, "a tottering old couple with no shoes, an indignant dame in black taffeta . . . a pair of pixie twins, exactly like the little imps at the bottom of the Sistine Madonna"—whom she photographed picnicking in the midst of chaos.

That night, Lee slept well despite the bedbugs. In the morning, she washed in her helmet and ate K rations. Nothing in this life resembled her old one. The urgency of the tasks at hand drew on her gift for meeting events as they arose; the excitement of combat fired her imagination. Screening female civilians for the CA, she talked to a female collaborator who begged for protection against the patriots who were punishing women like herself by shaving their heads. Another collaborator posed for Lee with her children. They stared at her with "big sullen eyes. . . . They were neither timid nor tough," she wrote, "and I felt like vomiting." There was no way to observe with detachment.

To report the facts, the number of bombs deployed and targets damaged, she needed to get close to the action. Major John Speedie, the 329th Regiment's handsome commander, took her on a tour of observation posts. In one, the sun streamed through the floor-length windows, making it hard for her not to be seen by the Germans (who were only nine hundred yards away), "especially with such shiny things as binoculars." At another post, in the Hôtel Victoria, she lay on the floor to watch the artillery, her binoculars in the shadows. The GIs were pleased to see her, she thought, "mostly because I was an American woman, partly because I was a journalist and they wanted to be in the papers."

That evening, Lee moved to a nearby CA office with a phone connection to military command. "They are cooking up the final assault on the citadel," she scribbled in a note to Roland. "I'm going down to an OP inside the bomblines—to watch and take pictures,—naturally I'm a bit nervous as it'll be 200 pounders from the air—ours—I know nothing will happen to me as I know our life is going on together—for ever—I'm not being mystic, I just know—and love you." Lee's account of the assault brims with the sort of details that animate her photographs. A company files past, "ready to go into action, grenades hanging on their lapels like Cartier clips." The next section conveys her excitement as the planes arrive:

> We heard them swelling the air like I've heard them vibrating over England on some such mission. This time they were bringing their bombs to the crouching stone work 700 yards away. They were on time—bombs away—a sickly death rattle as they straightened themselves out and plunged into the citadel—deadly hit—for a moment I could see where and how—then it was swallowed up in smoke.

Lee photographed this explosion not knowing that she had captured the Americans' first use of napalm. (Most of her shots were confiscated by the censors.) In one, in which the gaze passes through an inner frame formed by the curtain and railing, theme and composition merge. The contrast between the patterned foreground and the explosion catches the release of energy at the decisive moment.

Lee followed the GIs' ascent to the fort as if she were one of them. "I projected myself into their struggle," she wrote, "my arms and legs aching and cramped. The first man scrambled over the sharp edge, went along a bit, and turned back to give a hand in hauling up the others. . . . It was awesome and marrow freezing." But Von Aulock wouldn't surrender. At headquarters, "everyone was sullen, silent, and aching," including her. Before Saint-Malo, she had been a partisan observer. Now she was experiencing the war viscerally.

Later that day, when taking cover during a burst of gunfire, Lee stepped into one of the town's underground vaults, which by then "stank with death and sour misery." What follows gives a precise sense of war's horror: "I sheltered in a Kraut dugout, squatting under the ramparts. My heel ground into a dead, detached hand, and I cursed the Germans for the sordid ugly destruction they had conjured up in this once beautiful town. . . . I picked up the hand and hurled it across the street and ran back the way I'd come, bruising my feet and crashing in the unsteady piles of stone and slipping in blood. Christ, it was awful."

The GIs who rushed up a moment later were a benison. They joked and laughed with her, "asking me to talk American." Lee's spirits revived when they unearthed supplies in a nearby wine cellar ("bin after bin of sauterne, vouvray, magnums of champagne, Bordeaux, Burgundy"). She chose sweet wine for the soldiers, then joined Major Speedie and the officers at the hotel: "He opened a bottle of champage, aiming the cork at a helmet about as accurately as the bombers had done on the fort, and we drank from crystal glasses which I had polished on a bedspread." From this point on, the personal and public sides of war would be intertwined in her dispatches.

Dave Scherman turned up in Saint-Malo on August 17. After covering the battle from nearby, he wanted to see the results. Some of the most unexpected were the changes in Lee. She looked like "an unmade, unwashed bed" in her olive drabs and boots, he recalled. He photographed her seated on rubble while displaying her good profile, and beside a steel pillbox, while two soldiers from the 83rd peer at their tired, squinting mascot. Dave and Lee made plans to pool their shots, sending some of hers to John Morris and his shots of her to Audrey Withers.

When they reached the Hôtel de l'Univers, the best vantage point for the next assault, white flags appeared. Von Aulock had surrendered. They rushed to see the Germans emerge from their stronghold. The first to appear, a tall, erect man wearing gray gloves, a camouflage coat, and a monocle, was Von Aulock. As Lee ran to take his picture, he hid his face and cursed—he could not bear to have his defeat witnessed by a woman. "I kept scrambling on in front, turning around to take another shot of him," she wrote. It was a small victory, but an ambiguous one. She empathized with the man in spite of herself: he "seemed awfully thin under his clothes."

As Lee moved closer to the Germans with another group of GIs, those who looked carefully were amazed to find a woman among the cameramen. "She looked tired; she was covered with dust and dirt but she kept on taking pictures," one soldier recalled. (In Lee's shot of this scene, a German smiles at her, and the GIs watch without hostility, pleased that the battle is over.) When she saw Von Aulock later, his dignity restored after a change into uniform, she photographed him again from a respectful distance.

Her own dignity was deflated a few days later when SHAEF exiled her to Rennes after the news reached headquarters that she had been in the combat zone. (A memorandum dated August 20 recommends that henceforth "No female correspondent be permitted to enter forward area under any circumstances.") Lee moved into the Hôtel Nemours, U.S. press headquarters, where Dave joined her. She spent the week "in the doghouse for having scooped my battle," she told Audrey. "I'm mad about the 83rd Division," she went on. Her application to be attached to them had been turned down, but soon, she added, "I plan to rejoin them."

In the meantime, Lee bathed, slept, and caught up with colleagues. (Catherine Coyne of the *Boston Herald* followed her nose to Lee's room to find her rubbing cologne on her flea bites.) While Lee wrote up her private war, Dave wrote Audrey to ask whether *Life* could publish her historic shots of Saint-Malo: "Lee was the only reporter, and only photographer, let alone the only dame, who stayed through the siege with the infantry outfit that finally took the Port. She was exposed to small arms, machinegun, mortar, and artillery fire, as well as our own bombing," he bragged, "more than any girl journalist." He promised to keep her in the room until she finished the story—an improvement on the Normandy one, he thought, since it was "100% more exciting, and about 200% closer to the front line, in fact slightly ahead of it." What he did not say was that it was also ahead of most reportage in its courage and its quirky precision.

That week, Paris rose up against the Germans and on August 25 celebrated its liberation by the Free French and the Americans—though partisans and snipers were still battling in the streets. The women at the Nemours waited for SHAEF to issue travel orders. "It is very bitter to me to go to Paris now that I have a taste for gun powder," Lee wrote Audrey on August 26. "There they are already wearing swell uniforms like London—and I have only battle dress." (She asked for her new uniform, at her tailor's.) "I've just sat on my tail here in Rennes writing," she continued. But the day had not been a dead loss. She came across some female collaborators with shaved heads who stared as she ran ahead to take their photographs. "In that I was leading the parade," she explained, "the population thought a *femme soldat* had captured them." "I won't be the first woman journalist in Paris," she added, "but I'll be the first dame photographer, I think, unless someone parachutes in."

When Lee arrived, the capital was in the throes of a three-day celebration. "Paris had gone mad," she wrote. "The long, graceful, dignified avenues were crowded with flags and filled with screaming, cheering, pretty people. Girls, bicycles, kisses and wine, and around the corner sniping, a bursting grenade and a burning tank. The bullet holes in the windows were like jewels, the barbed wire in the boulevards a new decoration." She photographed GIs flirting with Parisiennes, children in torched vehicles, sandbags at Notre Dame, barbed wire around the Place de la Concorde, and women cycling in the full skirts they wore to defy the Germans' fabric rationing. One vibrant shot returns the gaze of the models waving from the windows of Maison Paquin; its diagonal pattern of lights and darks heightens their shared sense of joy.

Lee reported to the Hôtel Scribe. The elegant old hotel near the Opéra—until a few days before, the Nazis' press bureau—had been requisitioned for the Allied journalists converging on Paris. Making her way past the bedrolls in the lobby, she went to room 412, on the fourth floor. Dave joined her next door. Over the next year and a half, he watched Lee's room turn into "a cross between a garage sale and a used car lot." The chambermaid did not appear to mind. She took it for granted that Lee, her *petit lapin,* and "Monsieur David" were lovers. The door between their rooms remained open.

The Scribe staff adjusted to their new guests. The cable setups and broadcast studios were still functioning, daily briefings outlined recent events, the press bar in the basement served K rations, coffee, and champagne. Lee set to work. AFTER TREMENDOUS THREE DAY WELCOME AND HAND WAVING, EVERY ONE EXHAUSTED, she cabled U.S. *Vogue.* TOWN LOOKED LIKE BALLROOM MORNING AFTER, FOUNTAIN BASINS STREWN WITH CIGARETTE BUTTS, BUT NONETHELESS BEAUTIFUL. A medium requiring compression, the cable spurred her to paint the scenes imprinted on her mind's eye: IN ONE STREET FLAG WAVING AND KISSING; NEXT STREET, DUEL SNIPER VERSUS PARTISAN. . . . CIVILIANS TOOK WHOLE THING AS TERRIFIC PARTY WITH LIFE OR DEATH STAKES LIKE BACCARAT GAME.

Life was topsy-turvy. Most of Paris lacked water, gas, and electricity; only the Scribe had power and heat. Everyone walked, cycled, or took the Métro when it was running (there were no buses); Lee wangled rides in official vehicles through Herb Saal, the Scribe's dispatcher. Outside official circles and the black market, gasoline was unavailable. Paris was quiet, except for the jingle of bicycle bells and the clip-clop of wooden clogs, the only footgear available since the disappearance of shoe leather. "Everyone's feet hurt due to the ill fittingness of the sabots," Lee told Audrey. "No one . . . can kneel, on account of bruises and skinned knees from bicycle accidents. Everyone has neuralgia from wet hair, and if they had any tea, coffee, soap and tobacco they'd think heaven was here. So would I," she added.

Despite the confusion, life at the Scribe was an ongoing party. Lee hung out in the bar with the Time-Life crew—John Morris, Ralph Morse, Capa, and "Wert" and Lael Wertenbaker, now married—where they were often joined by Irwin Shaw and William Saroyan, who were making a film for the U.S. Signal

*Photographers and friends at Michel de Brunhoff's after the liberation of Paris.
Seated at lower right: Lee Miller, de Brunhoff. First row, from left: unknown
woman, Cynthia Ledsham, Robert Capa, Lucien Vogel, David "Chim" Seymour,
unknown man, Henri Cartier-Bresson. Second row: John Morris (behind Capra),
Charles Wertenbaker (raising glass)*

Corps. Others who came to drink champagne with them included Ed Murrow,
William Shirer, and Hemingway, who made forays from the room at the Ritz he
shared with Mary Welsh. The press bar became such a hot spot that *Life* published a caricature of its denizens, including Dave with his camera around his
neck and Lee in uniform.

Links between French and American journalists were also forged there.
Henri Cartier-Bresson introduced Morris to members of the Resistance group
Photo Presse Libération, who provided shots of the first wild days for *Life*.
When Lee realized that she had lost some of her film, Michel de Brunhoff
arranged for both *Vogues* to receive images from Photo Presse, as well as shots
of his own: de Gaulle's triumphal march down the Champs-Elysées, patriots
firing at German snipers, a Resistance fighter who resembled a Picasso. While
the substitute photos made up for Lee's loss, she felt "sick with rage and ill
with jealousy," she told Audrey, "to have been the only woman photographer
and then to muck it." And without directives from London, which were slow to
arrive, she didn't know what approach to take.

Reunions with old friends soothed her. De Brunhoff gave Lee an affectionate welcome; Solange d'Ayen, who looked like a wraith, embraced her. They told her the outlines of life at Frogue. He had suspended publication rather than work under the Nazis and used his office as a mail drop for the Resistance; tragically, a few days before the liberation of Paris, the Gestapo murdered his only son. Solange had herself been in prison; her husband was in a German concentration camp. Lee arranged transport for Solange to her chateau, which had just been vacated by the Nazis. "S. seemed very pleased to have me as an escort," Lee wrote, and was herself pleased to again be taken for a *femme-soldat.*

"This is the first allied soldier I have seen, and it's you!" Picasso exclaimed when she entered his studio. Lee was so changed that he wanted to paint a new portrait of her. With Dora Maar, they celebrated their reunion at a nearby bistro, which produced a chicken, wine, and brandy. Picasso asked whether the English artists had kept painting despite the bombs and chortled at the idea of Roland working on camouflage. Lee's shots of the three of them show their joy at finding one another, and their friendship, alive. "From the point of view of art in Paris," she wrote, "the most valuable contribution has been the fact that Picasso stayed here under the occupation as an inspiration to others." He had used what came to hand—vegetable juices as paint, corners of the tablecloth as paper. On a return visit, Lee ate a tomato from the plant that had been "his favorite model." "It was a bit moldy," she teased, "but I liked the idea of eating a work of art."

The Eluards had not fared as well. Seeing Lee's uniform, Paul flinched when she caught up with him, but Nusch grinned with pleasure when she walked in the door of the apartment where they were hiding. She was still beautiful, but had suffered so much under the Occupation that there was little left of her. The couple had moved eight times in the past six months to avoid the Gestapo: they were on the wanted list because of Paul's work with the clandestine publishing house Editions de Minuit. Lee photographed them in front of Picasso's *Night Fishing at Antibes,* the canvas he had been working on when they were last together. On another visit, Cartier-Bresson snapped a picture of Lee sitting on Paul's lap and smiling at Nusch, which captures their joy in one another's company.

It was reassuring to learn that some wounds had healed during the war. Picasso, Eluard, Aragon, and Cocteau had set aside their quarrels to work together in secret on books, films, and other projects. Cocteau was no longer the group's bête noire, although his contacts with the Germans had caused suspicion. Lee visited the poet in the apartment he shared with Jean Marais, the star of his new film, *Beauty and the Beast.* Cocteau seemed "younger than I thought possible," she told Audrey, "less nervous and not mournful or whining which was so much his style when I left Paris." She photographed him standing beside the wall on which he had written the names of the artists he admired, and then with Frogue artist Christian (Bébé) Bérard, who picked her up in his arms. Later, Lee went to the Coupole in uniform—"very large, padded all over," an acquaintance recalled. When she took off her helmet, the group saw that this was "the girl they'd known a decade before: she became the symbol of freedom, the Statue of Liberty walking into the Coupole."

After checking up on friends, Lee wanted to learn how others had fared. It was moving to meet the family of the playwright Tristan Bernard. French Jews, they had survived with the help of friends who obtained his release, because of his age, from Drancy, the Nazi camp near Paris. Throughout the war, they had had to wear the yellow star: it was "six pointed satinette," Lee informed Audrey, "overprinted in black ink. Not only must it be worn at all times, but they had even to give [ration] tickets for it." Mme. Bernard prepared a wartime meal for Lee: potato pancakes that were half cooked because the gas ran out, salad without dressing, a dessert of raw grain. Lee covered her recurrent gagging by claiming to have a hangover but realized that her "indisposition" was, in the main, emotional. Her angle, she decided, would be to recount the Occupation's effect on creativity by interviewing artists, writers, actors, and designers.

From this perspective, her next assignment—the rebirth of haute couture—could be the way to show that fashion, too, had been "part of the passive and active resistance." For the past four years, while English women conserved fabric, the Parisiennes defied the occupiers by dressing extravagantly. This was especially true of their headgear. In August, women still sported hats resembling cream puffs. At the millinery shows, Lee photographed models in foot-high chapeaux—soft helmets, flowerpots, and one that combined cabbage roses with sables. (For fun, she put her army cap on top of a mannequin's head and took a shot that testifies to her presence among the hatboxes.) Hats were "coming back to sanity," she told Audrey, but like the Parisians, they were "still gay and a little mad."

What was true of millinery also applied to clothing. It was chic to dress more moderately, yet "an unsuppressible exuberance still express[ed] itself in folderols." Lucien Lelong (whose clothes Lee had modeled in the thirties) brought her up-to-date in meetings to plan *Vogue*'s coverage of the new season. As president of the Syndicat de la Couture, Lelong had stood up to the German officials who planned to transfer the industry to Berlin. Arguing that *la mode* depended on the French spirit and a large group of skilled workers, he had managed to keep it in Paris. But a tight system of rationing had been imposed. That January, the Germans had closed Grès and Balenciaga for exceeding their fabric quotas; in July, they threatened to put an end to haute couture—which was saved at the last minute by the liberation.

Lee grew bored with waiting around while the fashion houses prepared their October openings. Audrey's praise of her Saint-Malo reportage ("good girl great adventure wonderful story") sharpened her desire to follow the action—provided SHAEF would renew her permit. In the meantime, Paris made her impatient: "I want to go to the wars again," she told Audrey, "before the collections tie me down."

In mid-September, Lee caught a ride to the Loire district, where the 83rd Division had gone after Saint-Malo. Arriving in time to watch them round up over ten thousand Germans, she recorded their surrender outside Orléans—a ritual arranged by Lieutenant Colonel John Speedie (who had recently been promoted) to suit enemy protocol. Lee photographed columns of German soldiers trudging in battle gear toward the field where they were to pass review. "They were armed but impotent," she wrote, and wary due to the presence of the newly formed French Army, which was eager for revenge. She and the Signal Corps were the only witnesses: "I am getting to be the surrender girl," she joked.

After promising Speedie copies of her Saint-Malo pictures, Lee went to Orléans—"scene of the triumph of Jeanne d'Arc," she recalled (visualizing the deeds of her heroine in silent movies?). It was a shambles: "Old ruins and new associate together; the statue of Jeanne d'Arc is askew on its pedestal." She photographed the damaged Beaugency bridge, which had been hit by both the Germans and the Allies, and a row of heavily laden prisoners clambering up the steps beneath it. The shot's perspective literalizes her position of superiority and underscores their "impotence." (Taking advantage of their plight, she liberated a pair of field glasses from a German officer.)

In the next few days, as she hitchhiked around the country, Lee began to feel that "life had somehow adjusted itself. The earth and the vegetation had healed the war wounds." In villages just freed from the Germans, people asked travelers to formalize their liberation. "Someone has to receive the champagne, the speech, the keys of the city," Lee told Audrey. "Sometimes it was me—for no reason except that it is a ceremony, and no other business of the municipality can function until that duty is done."

Returning to Paris with her taste for gunpowder satisfied, she looked up Helen Kirkpatrick, who invited Lee to share her apartment. On September 28, as Dave, Catherine Coyne, and Lee gathered in her room for drinks, a telegram arrived from Roland. He would soon be in Paris. Lee stripped off her clothes, Coyne recalled, "and said, 'I'm going to have a good clean bath for this!'" She was not the only one struck by Lee's aplomb. The night before, when John Morris came to room 412 for a drink, he found Dave in bed, reading. When John ran into Lee the next day, he wrote, "she again invited me up for a drink. There, reading in the same bed, was Roland Penrose."

Later that day, Lee and Roland went to Picasso's studio for a reunion, during which she took a formal group portrait: the Maître, the Eluards, Aragon and Elsa Triolet, with herself and Roland in uniform. They posed solemnly, aware of the moment's historic aspect. The night was full of joy and tears, Roland recalled: "They were all in tremendously high spirits, their enthusiasm hid at first glance the signs of strain they had been through. . . . My surprise was that any should have survived."

It is easy to understand Roland's response to Lee's new life. His role as "a home-bound instructor," he wrote, "gave me a sense of inferiority when I compared my own efforts to the immensely daring exploits of Lee." What was more, Dave's presence at the Scribe had changed the balance of relations. The young American spent more time in her bed than Roland did. And throughout his brief visit, Lee was organizing *Vogue*'s fashion coverage, which meant hitchhiking all over town for illustrations, harassing others for their reports, and arranging to send photographs. She felt torn between doing her own "reportages," she told Audrey, and meeting *Vogue*'s needs, which made her "schitzophrenic [sic]." Dave complained to his brother that Lee was exhausted from "trying to be the up and coming girl war photographer, reopening Paris office and generally knocking herself out."

The long-awaited openings began on October 1. Parisians saw the revival of haute couture as a labor of love since there were no foreign buyers. "They regard it in the nature of an art exhibition," Lee noted. "The whole thing has been done in good faith," she continued, "just as they gave the last resources of their larders to the liberators. Each dressmaker wanted to express some sort of *joie*." Joy was evident in the details. Sashes set off hips, armholes accentuated bosoms, and basques flaring out behind slim suits emphasized wasp waists. Jersey knits, ersatz wool blended with angora, and velvets stitched with sequins cheered the spirit as well as the body.

Lee took several models to pose outside, at the Chamber of Deputies, the Ministry of Justice, and the Place Vendôme, where bullet holes pocked Van Cleef's windows. One model strides past a flag-bedecked building in Schiaparelli's black "wool" coat, her hair tucked into a matching turban—wet heads still needed protection after hours at the coiffeur's. Another, wearing a nipped-waist "woolen" dress by Paquin, essays a dance step at the Place de la Concorde; another leans on her bicycle to set off Schiaparelli's fur culottes, fur-crowned helmet, and fur-lined windbreaker. Lee also photographed inside the couture houses. A shot of Paquin models relaxing on the floor between shows, she wrote, "reminded me of the between party scene in Gone with the Wind."

Lee's reportage is detailed and informed. For a fashion insider like her, the language of couture—its tucks, pleats, and bias cuts—held no mysteries. Yet it is the acuity of her cultural analysis that stands out as one reads her fashion writing, especially its levelheaded response to the charge of frivolity made against the industry. While she agreed that "seductive clothing has little to do with the starving bodies behind the scenes," she pointed out that it had "a lot to do with the starving souls." For the past four years, the situations of England and France had been different. The English had mobilized from top to bottom: "one hoped that a percentage of what one saved would reach the war . . . whereas here they were afraid it might. . . . Whatever they saved, it wouldn't help their own people."

On the last day of the shows, a telegram came from Audrey: EDNA CRITICAL SNAPSHOT FASHION REPORTAGE AND ESPECIALLY CHEAP MANNEQUINS URGES MORE ELEGANCE. Assuming that Lee's pictures were not typical of haute couture, Chase asked whether more WELLBRED WOMEN might be persuaded to model. Lee's reply was understated. "I find Edna very unfair," she told Audrey. "These snap shots have been taken under the most difficult and depressing conditions, in the twenty minutes a model was willing to give of her lunch hour most of which was being taken up with further fittings for unfinished dresses or after five o'clock in rooms with no electricity. . . . Any suggestion that *dames du monde* could and should have been used is strictly out of this world. Edna should be told that . . . there is a war on."

Increasingly, Lee tried to grasp the war's impact on civilians—the story that as a longtime expatriate she was qualified to tell. The French were now looking to the British system of rationing, she explained: "They realize that there are going to be several millions of political deportees, war prisoners and refugees from the battle areas to clothe properly, to feed, to rehabilitate. These millions will be detraquee [disoriented] to a much greater extent than any returning British prisoners." Through the autumn and winter, she alternated between stories about celebrities and reports on the political scene. "I want more than anything," she told Audrey, "to be able to follow the war to the finish over here, and more important, to watch the reconstruction or whatever of Europe."

But *Vogue* needed news of celebrities. In September, Lee supplied both editions with shots of Marlene Dietrich in a satin evening gown, Fred Astaire signing autographs for Folies Bergères dancers, and Maurice Chevalier being charming—after Aragon, who brought her to the press conference, said that the singer had not been pro-German, as some claimed, but had helped the Resistance. Now Audrey wanted her to assemble a scrapbook of cultural luminaries. Again playing impresario, she wrote captions for shots obtained from colleagues: Aristide Maillol had just died, Pierre Bonnard and Henri Matisse had gone on painting in the south of France, Albert Camus—who had edited the clandestine newspaper *Combat*—would soon make a name for himself. With these portraits, Lee sent her own of Bébé Bérard on his studio floor, Tristan Bernard representing the French theater, and Eluard admiring a Picasso with Communist Party leader Marcel Cachin. Lee squeezed in a visit to the Maître's exhibit at the Salon d'Automne, where policemen protected his work from its admirers. Paris still lacked the necessities, but cultural life was reviving, and with it the city's spirit.

∞

In October, Lee jumped at the chance to go to Luxembourg. The Allies, hoping for a quick end to the war, had tried in vain to cross the Rhine the month before in an assault on the Siegfried line, the three-hundred-mile-long fortification that ran along the old Maginot line. Since then, there had been protracted fighting in the forests south of Aachen, in Lorraine, and in the Vosges Mountains. On October 18, Eisenhower ordered the next phase of the campaign to break the German defenses with combined operations from Arnhem in the north to Basel in the south. Luxembourg, halfway between these two points, had been partly freed by the Allies, but its border with Germany was not secure.

Lee knew little about her destination: "The Duchy of Luxembourg, traditionally tidy and neat," she wrote, marking time, "peaceful and neutral as the Ruritania of musical comedy." The first part of the long article that resulted from this trip recounts Luxembourg's recent past: the population's response to the Germans' embrace of them as Aryans, their efforts, postliberation, to resume normal life, and the U.S. Army's attempts to help with the transition by herding cattle, harvesting crops, and escorting grandmothers through the rubble.

Lee's prose came alive as she recalled an unexpected reunion: "A jeep hove in sight. I recognized the numbers. In a few seconds I was in the street peering at the mud-splashed identification marks of all the cars and trucks which passed. I found one I knew and stuck my hand out. . . . It was Doc Berger and the chaplain of the 329th, 83rd Division. I was home again. Colonel Crabhill said, 'We consider you've been AWOL since Beaugency.' The Sergeant said, 'Lady, every time you turn up something's bound to happen.' "

Things began happening a few days later. Lee made her way to the 329th's post above Echternach, on the border. With Lieutenant Colonel Speedie, she walked through the forest overlooking the valley below, and eastward to Germany: "The Siegfried Line was just landscape to the unaided eye. Through the glasses I could see luscious flat lawns like putting greens. They were the fire areas between the black mushrooms which were gun emplacements—a tank trap accompanied by a gun was at a crossroads and on the horizon was a village which they said was housing two divisions of retreated Huns." A shift in narrative voice shows her emotional reintegration. When a German came in sight, Lee wrote, "I hoped we'd shoot him. . . . We could have slugged him with a machine gun but that would have given away a new position we were saving for tomorrow."

At dawn the next day, Lee slogged through the mud with Colonel Crabhill while he showed her the plans for actions along the front. Heavy mist hindered picture taking that day ("my cameras wouldn't be able to see any better than I," she wrote), but the gunfire was loud: "the whole valley echoed with the boom, bark, tattoo and cough of different styles and sizes of weapons." They patrolled the surrounding area in a jeep with a mounted machine gun, looking for civilians "who didn't match the landscape, as they could easily be and often were disguised Krauts."

Disappointed not to find any, Lee noted examples of the GIs' language. Since D-day, "to liberate" had acquired new meanings. One could "liberate" a bottle of wine by knocking down the price, or "liberate" a girl by eluding her chaperone. Being the only woman made things lively: "I keep my ear cocked to be told: 'It beats the . . . out of me, Mac,' followed by an apologetic 'oops, sorry, I mean Ma'am.' " Lee was proud of her rapport with the soldiers: "Some Tank-Destroyer men said they'd been talking and thought it was very good to have me around, as they minded their four-letter language. Thinking of some of the refinements of my own vocabulary I was deeply touched by their concern, which was reciprocal—I'd reformed for their sake."

At her billet in town with a veterinary surgeon, Lee learned to churn butter and make cream cheese with his wife; in the evening, they sat by the stove, drinking the local fruit brandies. Now and then German buzz bombs rattled past in retaliation for the 329th's attacks on the border towns. During the day, Lee photographed refugees praying, GIs herding pigs, and a woman known as the Blonde Bombshell, who turned up everywhere in her role as the CA's multilingual interpreter. Lee admired the Bombshell's ability to make villagers obey orders: "I don't know what she was saying, but it was violent and bitter; and she made it stick."

On the way back to Paris, Lee drove past "fields of purple cabbages like porcelain funeral flowers, long rows of biggish pink radishes for cows to eat, gold and scarlet autumn trees and factories cuddling into earth." Thinking of the homesick GIs who had pointed out this land's resemblance to the eastern states, she named them like a litany—Carolina, Virginia, New York, Maine, New Hampshire—and ended her Luxembourg piece with an admission: "Even I was homesick."

Since Helen Kirkpatrick's apartment was no longer available, Lee decided to stay at the Scribe for the duration. By winter, room 412 overflowed with guns, camera equipment, crates of cognac, and items looted on assignments; on the balcony, jerry cans of gasoline awaited the offer of a vehicle to take her on her next adventure. Dave photographed Lee's atmosphere: her Baby Hermes typewriter surrounded by half-filled glasses, a bottle of cognac, knickknacks, and ashtrays. This creative disorder was insufficient by itself. Lee also relied on Dave in his roles as taskmaster, lover, and friend, which he performed by turns during her all-night writing sessions.

It did not occur to either that Lee had become a journalist under unusual circumstances. While her knack for description and analysis are evident in her correspondence, she had picked up what she knew about writing as a sideline. In France, she worked without editorial feedback. Long delays between submission and publication meant that she had no idea whether her work was suitable until the magazine, having appeared months later, made its way to Paris after further delay. As if this were not enough, she heard from few readers other than Audrey.

Prone to feelings of abandonment (her "persecution complex"), Lee told Audrey that she found herself "coming to full, unnecessary stops in work because you never comment." After the Luxembourg trip, she wondered how to proceed. Although she kept detailed accounts of all she felt and saw, writing was torture: "Every word I write is as difficult as tears wrung from stone." She felt depressed, suicidal, or, less dramatically, in need of a new career.

One imagines that these difficulties were on her mind when she interviewed Colette. It had been hard to get an appointment. The celebrated writer, nearly seventy-two, was bedridden and very deaf. One approached her, as one did Cocteau, her neighbor at the Palais Royal, with the reverence due to *monstres sacrés*. When Lee arrived in uniform, Colette was amused to find Cocteau's statue become a soldier. From the depths of her fur-covered bed, she illustrated the story of her life with the books and photographs she asked Lee to fetch as she spoke: "I was an extension of her body and she stretched her hand on my arm to reach an envelope of pictures high on a shelf," Lee wrote. "Colette, the siren, the *gamine,* the lady of fashion, the diplomat's wife, the mother, the author."

The note of admiration for a woman who had led so many lives is apparent in Lee's reflections on the author. Approaching her profession as a craft, Lee asked what sort of implements she used. Different pens for different purposes, came the reply; hard ones for "digging," soft ones for first drafts. And what sort of paper? Blue sheets for drafts, their pages "scratched out, rewritten, rescratched and arrowed," Lee noted. "When the bright blue page will bear no more torture, she copies it over with larger spaces between, and starts the scraping and polishing again." Lee felt despondent on learning that even after fifty years, "a brilliant professional writer . . . suffers the same anguish for every paragraph."

Colette's husband, Maurice Goudeket, was the antidote to her anguish. Seventeen years younger than his famous wife, he spoiled her. Lee photographed the couple quarreling about his behavior during the liberation. After slipping into the Tuileries to watch the fighting, he had hid for two days in a shelter until it was safe to come up. "It was a favorite scene they like replaying," Lee observed; "her pointed elfin face was fifty years younger." The couple's rapport is palpable in her portraits. The nattily dressed Goudeket sits at Colette's side while she glances at him flirtatiously; he smiles as she touches a favorite pen to her mouth.

Moved by her visit, Lee left something of herself in the apartment. Colette was working on a tapestry: "I did a few stitches in the piece, like wielding a crowbar, and wrote my name along the side while Colette leafed through an old botany book from the case behind her to show me the watercolors and engravings she had taken for patterns. . . . Her fingers are so 'green' that the pictures came alive." Lee's portraits of Colette convey her zestiness in old age, and her own delight in their entente. "It was fun to tease her by talking very low," she wrote, "to get the flash of defiance and pique which daggered at us . . . greedy for everything that went on." She might have been speaking of herself.

Soon after their interview, Lee flew to Brussels. The city "was now more British than London," she wrote. Everything was done to feed, house, and entertain U.K. forces on leave. Following what was, by now, her journalistic formula, Lee told the history of the Belgian Resistance, discussed the fate of Belgian art treasures, and interviewed friends—Magritte (having abandoned Surrealism, he was painting "like a streaky Renoir") and Delvaux (his wartime skeletons had been replaced by warmer subjects). For British readers, she spent time with Hardy Amies, the London designer who was a liaison officer to the Belgians. She would have liked to write a piece on the British women's services, she told Audrey: "The Army of occupation is going to include a lot of dames." "I like the town in a way I never thought possible," she went on. "It's still bourgeois, polite, and reticent," virtues one would not associate with Lee under more normal circumstances.

About this time, Audrey asked Lee to describe the process of liberation. "This is a very difficult piece," she replied. "If I could find faith in the performance of liberation I might be able to whip something into a shape which would curl a streamer and wave a flag." Making shapes with words was harder than framing images in her lens. While Lee's eye for detail was acute, she had less feeling for verbal structure. Moreover, the relation of particular details to overall shape—an issue for all writers—was not obvious. Yet, she believed, truth resided in the details. "I'll try to put it all together for you into some sort of visual piece," she went on. Some of her colleagues were addressing Europe's future: "I, myself, prefer describing the physical damage of destroyed towns and injured people to facing the shattered morale."

At night, after copious amounts of morale-boosting cognac, Lee sat down to write. "The pattern of liberation is not decorative," she began. Along with "the gay squiggles of wine and song," there were "disappointed hopes, and bro-

Lee in jeep with model, Paris, 1945 (David E. Scherman)

ken promises." After four years of simply surviving, "there is grogginess like after a siesta, a 'sleeping-beauty' lethargy. The prince has broken into the cob-webbed castle and planted his awakening kiss. Everyone gets up, prepares a banquet, dances a minuet and lives happily ever after."

The next paragraph focuses on daily life to make a larger point, about matters dismissed as collateral damage:

> The story does, but shouldn't end there. Who polished the verdigrised saucepans? Who replaced the rusted well chain? Were the shelves dusted? The cupboards clean? . . . Did they start their quarrels and gossip where they left off? Did they ask what the neighbours had been saying about them all this time? Had the milkman left rows and rows of bottles on the sill? Had the tradesmen tried to collect their bills? Were there fresh lettuces and eggs in the larder? Maybe the prince solved all these problems and brought all these things too, or was liberation enough?

For Lee, the answer was no, it was not enough to heal Europe's shattered morale—or, one suspects, her own. The specter of Europe in pieces served, obscurely, as an emblem of her fragmentation, the scattered parts of her private jigsaw puzzle.

∞

When not engaged in "stone-wringing" (as she called her writing process), Lee liked to play word games. American soldiers knew only two "decent" French phrases, she told Audrey: " 'C'est la guerre' for T.S. and AH! OUI! (pronounced AWI), for pauses, exclamations, and as a variant on 'oh yeah?' " Residents of the Scribe had their own patois—the bilingual puns invented by Lee's friend Herb Saal. To amuse journalists waiting in the transport queue, he told the adventures of his imaginary friends, the boxers Jake Coote (*j'écoute*) and Nicky Taypar (*ne quittez pas*). "The winner of their forthcoming contest will fight the winner of the bout between two characters known as Sammy Tegal (*ça m'est égal*) and Harry Kovair (*haricots vert*)," Lee explained. "These mugs are always having girl trouble, and the quarrels between Jenny Saipa (*je ne sais pas*) and Elsa Mackie (*elle se maquille*) are usually caused by jealousy of the lovely Countess Mary de Billancourt (*Mairie de Billancourt*), who really only loves a certain party—Jerry Veyandré (*je reviendrai*)." To flesh out the dramatis personae, Lee invented a Scribe war staff—General Nuisance, Colonel O'Truth, Major Calamity—and some foreign correspondents: Lowering, of the *Evening Standard,* and Hitching, *Post.*

Friends (real ones) were another distraction. Lee fretted to Audrey about the long-deferred visit of Harry Yoxall, Brogue's managing editor. It was the coldest December in memory; nonmilitary billets were unobtainable: "The number of people sleeping on the floors of 'old residents' exceeds the 'stay-where-you-dine' sleepers in London during the Blitz." Yoxall arrived bearing twenty pounds of coffee and with a billet at the Ritz, both of which made him popular: "When the hotel had hot water," he recalled, "I could give a bath to a woman from the office, or to phrase it better, I could provide her with facilities for taking a bath." *Vogue* staffers worked in hats and coats; they slept in their clothes. "Whereas in England we had . . . all the necessities but no luxuries, in France they had all the luxuries but no necessities," he said. "There was plenty of *foie gras* but no toast to put it on; plenty of champagne, but no milk."

Lee enjoyed the Scribe's champagne with Janet Flanner, who stayed at the hotel when in town. Having just returned from America to resume her correspondence for *The New Yorker,* Janet was "slightly scratchy in places," Lee told Audrey, but like herself, "violently francophile." They agreed on the reasons for misunderstandings between France and America. Both feared for the future now that the French were settling old scores in the guise of postwar reprisals. The winter was harsher than the previous four; morale was plummeting. Explaining the situation one day to Carmel Snow, who was touring Europe as editor of *Harper's Bazaar,* they defended the ability of the French to endure hardships, like the heavy snowfalls. Carmel managed "a couple of semi-cordial compliments" on Lee's work for the U.S. edition of *Vogue* while feigning ignorance of Brogue. After she left, Lee vented her anger by throwing snowballs at Janet—however scratchy, she had a sense of humor.

Lee's spirits revived at Christmas—a luxurious reunion with Roland at Downshire Hill, where Dave joined them and helped consume the four turkey dinners put on by their cook after efforts to obtain one bird by placing multiple orders produced an unexpected bounty. On Lee's return to Paris, she found the city snowbound and the population acting like urchins—"the flics [cops] have battles in the driveway of the Opera, distinguished SHAEF officers feel the ammo shortage when the snow on their balconies runs out." She amused herself with shots of snow-draped street fixtures—a Joan of Arc statue in a mantel of ermine, the ubiquitous Wallace drinking fountain nymphs under their white cupola, a snow-topped pissoir adorned with posters urging one to give blood, so many quasi-surreal transformations of the city. While this unusual weather held, the snow kept producing surprises—coiffing the statues in the Tuileries, etching patterns on café windows, cooling the champagne on her balcony.

About this time, Bérard enrolled her in a project intended to put the French fashion industry in a new light by showing the next season's styles in miniature stage sets, with wire dolls instead of live models. The most prominent artists in Paris would be involved in the exhibition, *Le Théâtre de la Mode.* Bérard was to direct; Kochno, Cocteau, and some young designers and decorators would participate; Lee would be their photographer.

But staying in Paris made her edgy. Toward the end of January, despite the frozen ground, massive snowdrifts, and bone-chilling winds, the Allies moved to close the holes in the Siegfried line—the next step in the campaign to cross the Rhine. As the U.S. First and Third Armies pushed on in the Ardennes and the First French Army battled to expel the Germans from the Colmar region to the south, Lee went to Alsace.

Strasbourg was "frightening," she wrote; people were in hiding. The city had been liberated in November, but the Germans, encamped across the Rhine, threatened the population with their return: "They promised to collect ten heads for every Allied flag they found and to pass out other suitable punishments for people who had smiled in their absence." Lee took in the area's complicated history. Having been German soil since the Franco-Prussian War, it became French after the Great War and remained so until its annexation by Hitler in 1940. Some believed the Alsatians were German at heart. "They are like the children of divorced parents whose marriage was never a love-match," Lee wrote. "They are the children for whose custody the spectacular law-suits are conducted—these exhibitions which are selfish excuses for vengeance."

The French Army's liaison office in Strasbourg made arrangements for Lee to tour the area in a requisitioned jeep. Alain Dubourg, the young second lieutenant who accompanied her, was surprised that she planned to visit Struthof, a concentration camp in the mountains where the Nazis had kept thousands of slave laborers, often working them to death. At lunch in the village below this remote stronghold, Lee told Dubourg about her life in Paris with Man Ray, Cocteau, and Picasso. She was twice his age, but the young man was curious about her: "My sense was that she had been around."

It struck him as odd that she had heard of Struthof, the only camp of its kind in France. Since its liberation in November, it had housed hundreds of German civilians: only the gallows at the top of the hill reminded visitors of the recent past. The Allies would find more such places, Lee told Dubourg as she photographed the site. She mentioned one in Germany called Dachau, but had little knowledge of what went on there. On their visit she insisted on stopping for a bottle of Kummel, a caraway-flavored eau-de-vie. She said little during the long, cold ride. Dubourg found her "hard to decipher," especially when she said that having taken many perilous drives, she would return to Strasbourg on her own.

About this time, Lee joined a group of GIs who were liberating the contents of a distillery. Spying a Red Cross jerry can meant to hold sterilized water, she filled it with framboise (raspberry brandy) and painted the can khaki. From then on, she took this "gasoline can" wherever she went. At a time when gas was more precious than gold, people were not surprised by this precaution, but some were taken aback when they saw her drink from it. When the "gas" ran out, she filled the container with whatever came to hand, making unimaginable new cocktails and keeping herself in good spirits.

A few days later, following a French division through the frozen plains, Lee saw a crossroads sign pointing the way *"Vers l'ennemi."* While the Americans were synchronizing attacks on the fortified villages in the Colmar pocket, General de Lattre de Tassigny's Legionnaires trudged through the knee-deep drifts in their snow gear, providing Lee with several strongly marked chiaroscuro compositions. They bore no resemblance to the heroes of *Beau Geste* films, she wrote, but were hospitable. A group of them served her coffee in a sawed-down shell case, and after she photographed them cooking an al fresco stew, shared their bounty. "The hell with K-rations," she continued. "This is the way to live."

Compared to the light-fingered Legionnaires, Lee found the infantry "sullen." She sensed their fear as they watched the return of the wounded. "I'll never see acid-yellow and gray again like where shells burst near snow," she wrote, "without seeing also the pale, quivering faces of replacements, gray and yellow with apprehension. Their fumbling hands and furtive, short-sighted glances at the field they must cross. The snow which shrouds innocent lumps and softens savage craters covers alike the bodies of the enemy and of the other platoon which tried before." Death and snow were the great levelers.

The closing of the Colmar pocket, one of the bloodiest campaigns of the war, became the occasion for some of Lee's finest work thus far. She joined the U.S. command while they coordinated infantry, artillery, and engineers with French units for each day's battle. She photographed fortified villages where the GIs fought in hand-to-hand combat, extension bridges thrown across rivers to continue the advance, civilians putting out fires in their blazing towns. One of them, Neuf Brisach, she wrote, was taken after "a citizen with a candle led them through the mined moats, through bunkers and caves and secret passages into the impregnable town" while other infantrymen scaled the walls. She photographed an eerie scene in the ruins: a doll with its arms raised as if to surrender to the men sitting in what had been its home.

Picturesque Jebsheim, another fortified stronghold that was taken, lost, and retaken several times over the course of two days, reeked of death: "There were a great many German deaths in these streets," Lee noted, "and the stink of exploded shells was a taste in the mouth that matched the greenish coats and the strange faces of the newly dead for the Führer." That night, though she was "irreligious" by nature, Lee took comfort in the GIs' voices singing a hymn: "no one who has opened his heart to the sky in front of a fellow stranger, even though the words are not of his choosing or his meaning, can ever feel quite as alone again, quite as mistrusting as if he had not participated in this ritual."

She reached Colmar just after its liberation by de Lattre de Tassigny, who had been told that she was coming. As relations between the French and the Americans were shaky, de Lattre told his assistant, Edmonde Charles-Roux, to give "Lee quelque chose" free rein. Charles-Roux was astonished to learn that this important journalist was a woman, and even more surprised that she was the *"lionne"* of Paris in the thirties of whom she had heard so much from their mutual friends, Bérard, Kochno, and Cocteau—"the symbol of all that had been destroyed by the war, the Surrealists' blonde Venus. Now this living statue was among us," she said, "extraordinarily beautiful, against a background of ruins, in her strict khaki uniform."

As they toured the devastated region together, Charles-Roux took care to impress Lee with the role of women in the French Army. After meeting the *ambulancières,* the women ambulance drivers, Lee photographed them at their hospital while smoke billowed up from artillery fire in the background. They visited the civilian wounded lodged in gutted churches; a white-coiffed nun wept as Lee took her picture; others peered at her from their ruined sanctuary. They stopped for a moment in a field where evacuees huddled around smoking logs. In this "nightmare bivouac," Lee told Edmonde about the *Théâtre de la Mode* project and the roles of their mutual friends. "The circumstances as much as the setting of our conversation gave an almost surreal character to Lee's descriptions," Charles-Roux recalled.

By the end of their time together, the young woman (who would become a novelist, editor of French *Vogue,* and a member, then president, of the Académie Goncourt) was won over by her charge. "Lee was fearless, she had the soul of an adventurer," Charles-Roux remarked fifty years later—still amazed at her transformation into "a reporter of a kind we no longer have." Lee wrote as she lived, inventing her own brand of first-person journalism. "The muse of artistic Paris, the beauty among beauties," Charles-Roux reflected, "had become a writer."

Lee with Soviet soldier, Torgau, April 26, 1945 (David E. Scherman)

Chapter 13

Covering the War in Germany

(1945)

Frogue published an issue on the liberation while Lee was at the front. "One essential fact strikes those who are waging war," the editorial began, "which will strike its historians—women's contribution in all areas, social, medical, and military—their full participation in the immense effort that each nation is making." By thrusting women "into the terrifying spotlight where nothing stays hidden," it went on, the war had revealed their strengths. Lee Miller and Helen Kirkpatrick were singled out as exemplars— "great friends of France" whose work showed "an inspired understanding of our country."

It may have surprised Lee to learn that she was one of those journalists whose work mattered. That winter, her piece on Colette appeared in U.S. and U.K. *Vogues*, as did her reports on Luxembourg and Brussels. All were well received; the New York office gave her a bonus. Yet once back at the Scribe, her anguish about writing returned. Getting her through the process she called stone-wringing meant putting himself through an emotional meat grinder, Scherman recalled. In his role as writing coach, he kept her at her desk; as lover, he offered sex, comfort, and, when needed, more cognac; as partner, he wired funds to their U.S. bank account for the future. Their relationship kept him in thrall—but he could not imagine life without her.

The Allies began their drive toward Germany's heartland in mid-February. Lee and Dave wedged into the press room for Eisenhower's briefings on the engineering miracles needed to cross the Rhine—pontoon bridges topped with linked wheel tracks, oddly named duck and buffalo flotillas. Both longed to return to the front, but authorizations were not forthcoming. They talked of the work they would do after the war; Lee covered the spring fashions and wrote about Alsace while helping Dave with two photo-essays for *Life*. The first showed exhausted Allied soldiers on leave in the Grand Hotel, the second followed an army team investigating the black-market trade in U.S. supplies— soap, cigarettes, trucks, and gasoline. "What's wrong with this picture?" *Life* captioned his café scene, where the heads of embracing lovers are obscured by the cognac glass in the woman's hand—probably Lee's. (The answer: their black-market Chesterfields.)

For fun of a different sort, Lee wrote a piece on slang, with examples. To a GI, *with it* meant "elegant" or "hot stuff"; to army nurses, *weave* meant "promote" or "scrounge." "You can weave a person or a thing," she explained. "Perhaps you want a lift to Paris, so you 'weave' someone you know who is assigned to transport. Or you want a pal's extra coat or his second German helmet souvenir, so you 'weave' them. It has something to do with spinning a web." While it amused her to spin webs with words, such pastimes seemed like boondoggling compared with time at the front. After switching her accreditation to the air force when their press bureau arranged for male and female journalists to work under the same conditions, Lee awaited her orders.

Once authorized to travel, Lee drove to "Krautland" in mid-March. At Aachen, which had been bombed by the Allies the year before, she photographed the Gothic cathedral and some surreal sights: a Magritte-like wall peeled away to reveal the bricks below, a statue made by a GI with artificial limbs for legs and a teddy bear's face. Townspeople picked their way through the streets in furs and silk stockings. They were "arrogant and spoiled," Lee thought, "a prideless population who hoarded selfishly, cheated in food queues and had more money than objects to buy." Countless bodies lay beneath the rubble. When she climbed up some wreckage to take photographs, parts of it came loose and she fell to the ground: "The tightly packed earth surface opened, foul tomb smells swelled forth. Half-buried, putrefying flesh had turned over in its grave and clung to my hands, elbows, and bottom." The once proud city, she wrote with distaste, "smells and looks like a sepulchre."

From Aachen she went to Cologne, where she shared quarters with Janet Flanner, Marjorie "Dot" Avery, and Catherine Coyne. (They were joined later by Bourke-White and a young *Herald Tribune* reporter named Marguerite Higgins.) Unlike Aachen, Cologne had been flattened by three years of Allied bombing. Its population still lived like troglodytes. Emerging from their base-ments to meet their captors, they looked to Lee like so many worms, "well nourished on the stored and stolen fats of Normandy and Belgium." Their attempts to curry favor with journalists enraged her: "How dared they?" she raged. "Who did they think were my flesh and blood but the American pilots and infantrymen?" What kind of detachment could they find, she went on, "from what kind of escape zones in the unventilated alleys of their brains are they able to conjure up the idea that they are liberated instead of conquered people?"

Over the next few days, Lee interviewed many civilians. No one admitted to being a Nazi; no one claimed to have supported Hitler. "They were all party members because they would have lost their jobs otherwise, but no one ever believed in any of it," she wrote scathingly. "And the number of Germans who suddenly are confessing to Jewish relatives, and remembering how they spon-sored and saved the lives of accused Communists and Anti-Nazis, is growing to ludicrous proportions." They were unwilling, or unable, to tell the truth.

With a group of journalists at the Kingelputz Gestapo prison, Lee watched the survivors stumble into the courtyard and fall to the cobblestones. Some were too crazed for speech; others, like a tall Dutchman who shouted, "We must never forget!" still made sense. She photographed two emaciated young Belgians: a woman jailed for aiding RAF pilots and a Resistance fighter who had just buried his father in the prison's open grave. All bore the marks of their suffering. "It was good that a half dozen of us American journalists viewed them together," Janet Flanner wrote, "so that our eyewitness reports would be unanimous."

Some prisoners told Lee their stories: "Often the jailor would torture the suspect to unendurable pain, order him to be shot, and forget to sign the papers. The next day the same hideous routine would be replayed." The prison symbolized Nazism, she felt, and its acceptance by the population. "This went on in a great German city, where the inhabitants must have known and acqui-esced or at the very least suspected and ignored the activities of their lovers and spouses and sons."

At this point, Lee became viscerally anti-German. After leaving the prison, she told Audrey, she was beside herself. Moments later, when an old woman dropped her bag in the street, Lee bent to retrieve it, then stopped: "It hurt my stomach muscles to catch my gesture midair, but it hurt my feelings more to realise I had forgotten for an instant what I had just seen a thousand feet away." It felt "eerie" to be in Germany, "where the adrenalin, stimulated by hate, boils in the blood." She planned to analyze the German character, but felt "confused" by contradictory impulses—to see them as people like herself, to dismiss them as a nation of "schizophrenics." Until the Allies secured

Frankfurt and journalists received permission to follow, there was "nothing to write home about on Germans." What she could not say was that she was struggling with her own response—the adrenaline that fueled her outrage, the displaced anger at what had been done to her.

Taking pictures gave some relief. She photographed Cologne's cathedral not, as most did, from afar, contrasting its Gothic spires to the flattened city, but from inside its cavernous body. For this reason, the gaze is drawn into the soaring presbytery; one feels a sense of spaciousness, an attunement with the architecture. When this image is compared with Bourke-White's contemporary shot of GIs praying on the cathedral floor, Lee's focus on its ribcage of pillars suggests not a religious rite but a survival of the spirit. It is instructive to compare the two women's views of the same scenes. While Bourke-White's sometimes seem stagey (perhaps because they were taken for *Life*, but also because of her controlled aesthetic), Lee's convey a sense of intimacy. One seems to be inside such shots rather than standing at a distance.

Some of Lee's images of monuments embody both ruin and survival. A wrecked bridge across the Rhine projects the eye through its arches' metal tracery to the sky. In others, an ironic effect is created through the juxtaposition of contradictory elements. In Bonn, Beethoven's birthplace, she photographed the bombed-out music stores named for him around a devastated square, which was still being watched by a larger-than-life statue of the composer. Seen through her eyes, this site is an eerie tribute to the corpses in the air-raid shelter beneath this monument to civic pride. Seconds later, Lee found herself sharing a foxhole with two "home town boys" and their commanding officer. "I confirmed that Wappingers Falls and Poughkeepsie really do exist and that I spent all my American life exactly halfway between them."

After the Allies completed their Rhine crossings, the U.S. First Army extended the bridgehead at Remagen into Nazi territory; the Third Army pushed into Hesse to take Frankfurt on March 27. Lee, Helen, and Marguerite arrived a few days later to find fires raging and bodies in the streets. Dazed civilians came up from their hiding places; mobs of freed slave laborers raided their supplies; women carrying bouquets of lilac picked their way over corpses. Goethe's birthplace was "as messy and hollow as Cologne and Aachen," Lee told Audrey. While the town's façades had been wrecked by fire, carved statues framed cornices and doorways—"saints, heroes, bishops . . . calmly surveying a sea of dusty bricks."

In April, when the end of the war seemed imminent, it was still hard to find the front. The situation became hazardous. Troops lurched forward, unsure whether they had outrun the action or fallen behind. Cities raised white flags but no one came to accept their surrender. "The war has become so fluid," Lee went on, "that I can't keep up with my own ideas." She was using the Frankfurt press camp as her base for trips to nearby towns, but did not know what to emphasize: "I still haven't sorted out my impressions of German people enough to make a piece out of it."

Settled in Frankfurt, it would have been hard not to think of her Hessian ancestor, the Müller whose name she inherited in Anglicized form, and of her resemblance to the blond German *mädchen*. It was too disturbing to admit that she resembled the "schizophrenics" whose denial of the truth grated on her nerves. "I don't like Germany at all except it's too pretty to believe," she told Roland. "I'm getting a very bad character from grinding my teeth and snarling and constantly going around full of hate." Her anger revived as she toured the countryside: "I glare at their blossoms and plowed fields and unde-stroyed villages and work myself up into such a state that I have no human kindness in me when I talk to their victims."

When her knotted feelings became too painful, she thought of those she loved. At Lee's urging, Lieutenant Colonel Speedie had looked up Roland while on leave in London. He had written to say that she should spend the rest of her life with this fine English gentleman. Lee's letter to Roland ends with her teasing confession: "I guess I'll take his advice."

It was with mixed emotions that Lee recorded Frankfurt's smashed factories—where jet engines, rubber tires, and tanks had been built for the Nazis. In one warehouse, the GIs found a half-track in working order and drove it away: "After weeks of seeing nothing but charred walls and beaten up machinery," she told Audrey, "we all got [the] giggles." A tour of nearby Ludwigshaven offered equally strange sights. The ruined industrial center was "a nightmare of great vats tossed into odd positions by tanks of nitric acid leaking vapor to poison the already stinking air." Lee's photographs of steel compressors looking like huge spark plugs and liberated female laborers in babushkas convey almost palpably the devastation and, for the laborers occupying the factories, the unexpectedness of their freedom.

Heidelberg was intact, but the town's air of self-satisfaction enraged her. Escaped laborers camped in trolley cars; hungry refugees roamed the streets; the inhabitants grinned down at her from their windows. Returned German soldiers in civilian clothes strolled around "looking so cocky," she wrote on April 5, "and there is nothing to do about it." On a visit with a bourgeois family, she noted their up-to-date electrical equipment. "They live well," she contin-ued, "like everyone else in krautland." Here too the inhabitants insisted that they were not Nazis: "All these people claim entire ignorance of the treatment of slave labor—of deported Jews etc. They hide very neatly behind what we always say of them, that they were kept in ignorance by their press."

Lee returned to Frankfurt with quantities of film and a liberated generator—widespread looting having become a "legitimate" response to German abundance. While she could now work at night, she felt she could grasp the situation only in its particulars. A few days later, she joined a press trip to Bad Nauheim, where a refuge for the Nazi high command had been built below a camouflaged castle. What remained of its tunnels and catacombs after Allied bombings made good copy, she thought, even if the place gave her "the creeps": "For the next hundred years we're going to have Hitleriana like Napoleona." Hitler and his inner circle had houses nearby, with "magnificent tiled bathrooms, marvellous kitchen equipment." (A note of outrage about the Germans' access to electricity recurs in her letters.) Tracking the "master criminal" to his lair, did not, however, explain Nazism. "I'm taking a lot of kid pictures," she added. "They are the only ones for whom there is any hope, and also we might as well have a look at who we're going to fight twenty years from now."

While it is difficult to pinpoint Lee's travels from this point on, the outline is clear. "Things move very fast, as you may be noticing," a letter to Audrey in mid-April explains, "and Lee, here, is either moving when she wants to stay put, or planted when she has itchy feet. . . . Since I'm wearing the same trousers I wore when I left Paris six weeks ago—and my other shirt is lost, the only thing to do is to keep moving forward. However, I never finish a story at that rate—as you may have noticed."

Horrifying news reached the press camps about this time. South of Gotha, at a camp called Ohrdruf in the Thuringian Forest, Third Army soldiers found rotting bodies—inmates gunned down by the SS before they fled the site—and the bewildered survivors of the massacre. On April 12, Generals Eisenhower, Patton, and Bradley toured the camp, the first of its kind to be liberated in Germany. Eisenhower later observed, "I have never felt able to describe my emotional reactions when I first came face to face with indisputable evidence of Nazi brutality. . . . I have never at any other time experienced an equal sense of shock." (Patton, said to be tough as nails, threw up.) After inspecting Ohrdruf, Eisenhower cabled London and Washington to send journalists immediately, to counter claims that Nazi brutality stories were propaganda.

Those arriving at the camp over the next weeks learned that it was named for the nearby village where Bach had studied. Some noted the irony of the phrase above the gate, *Arbeit Macht Frei,* as many inmates died digging underground tunnels for secret munitions plants. Lee, too, felt an unparalleled sense of shock: she put down her camera. "I don't take pictures of these things usually," she told Audrey later, "as I know you won't use them. . . . I won't write about this now, just read the daily press and believe every word of it."

Articles on the successive discoveries of death camps—Nordhausen-Dora, Buchenwald, Bergen-Belsen, Dachau—appeared in U.S. and U.K. papers throughout April. The *Illustrated London News* showed a grim-faced Ike at Ohrdruf staring at bodies in the not yet familiar striped pajamas. The *Boston Globe*'s account of Belsen conveys the shock of unmediated vision: "I saw these dead," their reporter wrote. "I saw the living beside these dead. . . . I saw children walking about in this hell." Struggling to describe Nordhausen, where General Courtney Hodges made the residents bury the dead with their hands, Ann Stringer of United Press wrote, "You really had to grit your teeth to put what you'd seen into words." For most, language was inadequate.

In the same way, taking pictures of atrocities, in some ways simpler than writing about them, required a composure that few possessed. When asked how she could photograph such things, Bourke-White replied that she worked with a veil over her mind: "In photographing the murder camps, the protective veil was so tightly drawn that I hardly knew what I had taken until I saw prints of my own photographs. . . . I believe many correspondents worked in the same self-imposed stupor." Judging by Lee's images from the camps, she too worked in a stupor, but without a protective veil.

Lee reached Leipzig soon after its capture by the First Army on April 18. In the old city, women and children with spring bouquets cheered and waved at the troops, while around the corner, street battles continued. Over the next days, Lee photographed an enemy ambush at the town's Napoleon monument, a soldier playing his accordion, and some American POWs being housed in the apartment that was now the command post for Captain Charles MacDonald's Company G. She interviewed him at length because his recent experiences, she thought, showed "the consistent fashion in which comic adventures and opportunities for heroism presented themselves." The day before, when the chief of police tried to surrender the city to him, the captain had imprisoned the entire force for their own protection. Seeing MacDonald with the police, whose uniforms resembled their own, several enemy units surrendered, "causing a lot of trouble because there were not enough Americans to capture them."

MacDonald asked Lee to stay. "We were one of the few rifle companies in the US Army who could boast of having an American girl spend the night in its CP in such forward positions," he recalled. He liked her style and her American accent: it "sounded good in the strange surroundings." Lee enjoyed her time there but was troubled by the health of the POWs. They had been put on a starvation diet by the Germans, who hated Americans, she thought, "in a different and more intense way than other nationalities."

Lee's increasingly visceral hatred of the Germans found expression in the photographs she took at one of the strangest sites in Leipzig. Tales of mass suicides were circulating among the press corps. A factory director had invited a hundred guests to dinner; when the GIs took the city, he set off an explosion by pushing a button below the table. Top officials lay dead in Leipzig's town hall. Bourke-White rushed to document the suicides for *Life*. The city treasurer, his wife, and their daughter, in her Red Cross uniform, reclined on the heavy leather furniture of his comfortable office, their family papers arranged on the desk next to an empty bottle of poison. Bourke-White shot the scene from above, at a distance.

The treasurer and his family still lay on their deathbeds when Lee reached the site hours later. She photographed them not from above but on the same level, the macabre scene formed by the women in the background and the man in the foreground, his allegiance signaled by the portrait of Hitler opposite his desk. (Before taking this shot, Lee positioned the Führer's portrait, which is absent from Bourke-White's photograph.) Her close-ups of the dead women are more intimate. Standing on the Persian rug on which their own well-shod feet repose, she photographed the mother and daughter as if asleep, then moved close to the daughter, who seems to swoon luxuriously across the leather sofa, her mouth half open. She had "extraordinarily pretty teeth," Lee noted in her Leipzig captions.

What she did not say was that this blond Aryan beauty looks like a younger version of herself. Perhaps it was too disturbing to admit their resemblance. Perhaps her hatred allowed her to keep some psychic distance from the "Krauts." Yet the scene's unnerving intimacy betrays Lee's fascination with its blend of beauty and horror. Standing in her shoes, the viewer is drawn into the picture. Similarly, her photograph of a member of the treasurer's staff shows the dead man sprawled diagonally across the floor; his head and arm nearly slash across the frame separating subject and viewer.

Each shot in this sequence is informed by Lee's complicated feelings about her subjects. She could record violent death when the corpses were Nazis, but unlike Bourke-White, she could not keep her distance. More than Lee's dispatches, the photographic record suggests that she was aware of her tangled emotions—the mixture of outrage and empathy that mark these photographs. This disturbing blend is conveyed through her staging of highly scenic compositions that implicate the viewer, and the act of viewing, in their charged emotional spaces.

One little-known shot from the Leipzig sequence links the camera to deadlier weapons. In this image, the eye alights on a U.S. Army photographer taking an aggressive stance to "shoot" the dead man. By framing him as her (and our) stand-in, the composition connects the living across the bodies of the dead. It arouses the viewer's penchant for voyeurism, however uneasy.

∞

"Buchenwald is beyond all comprehension," one of the first reporters there observed: "You just can't understand it, even when you've seen it." Journalists and photographers toured the site in disbelief in the weeks after its liberation on April 11, when the inmates rose in revolt hours before Patton arrived to take charge. Helen Kirkpatrick and Marguerite Higgins went in the same day; Lee and Bourke-White arrived somewhat later.

Journalists were met by former inmates offering to show them the sights; consequently, their accounts follow a similar pattern. The first thing they noticed was the stench. Walking around the main camp they saw the charred corpses inside the crematorium; beside it lay stacks of bodies that had not been burned because the coal ran out. After their liberation, some survivors had taken revenge on the guards. Others remained there as prisoners in a strange role reversal. What struck those who had seen small camps like Ohrdruf was Buchenwald's scale. Fifty thousand inmates crammed into barracks meant to hold one-third that number had worked as slave laborers. As the population swelled, subsidiary camps proliferated around the original site—in the forest where Goethe used to compose poetry. In the infamous "Little Camp," Jews, Gypsies, and those too ill to work had been kept in subhuman conditions. "Their eyes were sunk so deep that they looked blind," a reporter wrote. "If they moved at all, it was with a crawling slowness that made them look like huge, lethargic spiders."

Bourke-White forced herself to record the camp's most shocking scenes: preserved organs, shrunken heads, tattooed skin used for lampshades. For many, her well-known photograph of skeletal survivors behind a barbed wire fence typifies Buchenwald. Under such conditions, she wrote, "using the camera was almost a relief. It interposed a slight barrier between myself and the horror in front of me."

Lee focused on some of the same scenes without this barrier. Her close-ups of corpses piled in a heap force the viewer to look each person in the eye, as if by this means the camera could deliver the dead from anonymity. Survivors are shown as agents rather than victims. They study the map of Europe or construct effigies of Hitler to stage mock executions for the "tourists"; those who are strong enough march in a funeral service or confront the piles of bodies as the spectators' stand-ins. In another sequence, Lee photographed five men contemplating a heap of bones and later cropped the shot to focus on the foreground; the composition formed by the men's striped trousers and the remains enlists the viewer's eye in a composition emphasizing survival.

"The ex-prisoners have found and recognized a certain number of their former torturers," she wrote. "If they catch them they give them a thorough working over and bring them back to the camp jail house." She photographed several "former torturers" as if condemning them with her camera. A highly constrained shot of two bloody-faced guards kneeling inside a tiny cell seems

to restage their beatings as an act of vengeance. Another, of a guard who had
hanged himself, transmits her pleasure at seeing the tables turned: "He was
taken out on a stretcher," she wrote, "stripped and thrown on a heap of bony
cadavers where he looked shockingly big, the well fed bastard."

Lee photographed the residents of nearby Weimar when Patton ordered
them to tour Buchenwald. Some fainted when they saw the camp; others
remained aloof. Since many had worked in factories with the inmates, the
issue of their responsibility is implicit in these shots. They were "not like the
rubberneckers of the blitz," she wrote. "They are not a funeral procession nor
are they holiday-makers." What were they? Lee continued to believe that Germany was a nation of schizophrenics.

In an intriguing reversal, Bourke-White's shots of these tours bridge her
usual barrier to show Germans weeping, while Lee's hold them at a distance.
One image underlines the indifference of a woman in a dirndl by foreground-
ing her escort, a black GI with a wary expression: "Even after the place was
ninety-five percent cleaned up," Lee noted, "soldiers who are used to battle
casualties lying in ditches for weeks are sick and miserable at what they see
here." Using both "tourists" and GIs as part of the composition, her images
restage the tour, eliciting the viewer's response by formal means. As in her
shots of the captured guards, she made quick decisions about distance, point
of view, and edges that mark these images as close-up and vengeful, or dis-
tanced and reflective.

Throughout the last weeks of April, massive columns of displaced persons
trudged through Germany as civilians fled the advancing Red Army and the
Allies prepared to link up with their Soviet counterparts—a meeting that
would signal the division of Germany. On April 25, having spotted a Russian
cavalryman on the bank of the Elbe, members of the U.S. First Army's 69th
Regiment crossed the river to greet his unit and radio news of their encounter
to headquarters. "I found it comic that the great symbolic joining of great
modern armies should be thus," Lee noted, "the Americans catching crabs in
rowboats across a swift river to meet Russians who operated horse-drawn
artillery."

The next day, racing to the scene in a jeep mounted with machine guns,
Lee watched the chaos along the road. Taking them for Russians, villagers hid
at their approach; others welcomed them as an advance party of the U.S.
occupation. She reached Torgau, the ruined town on the Elbe held by the
Soviets, at about the same time as her colleagues—Dot Avery, Iris Carpenter,
and Catherine Coyne—and the mob of reporters who turned the linkup into a
media event. Both sides took part in ritual exchanges—black bread and onions

Nuremberg, April 1945: GIs search for prisoners. (David E. Scherman)

for K rations, endless toasts to friendship with Soviet vodka and German wine; the men compared weapons and admired one another's insignia. Everyone cheered as the Russian women climbed into the Americans' tanks; some of them took Lee aside to compare the merits of their differently engineered underwear. "My entire ideological exchange with the Russians suffered a language impediment due to new methods of drinking Vodka," she observed.

When Scherman arrived later that day, few remained sober. The Russians sang raucously to entertain their guests, who returned the favor with renditions of "Birmingham Jail." Journalists joined the officers at an al fresco lunch under portraits of Stalin and Roosevelt hung from fruit trees. The Russians heaped the tables with ham, cheese, and sausages; the Americans contributed eggs and chocolate; they toasted one another all over again. "There was more food than any of the Americans present had ever seen on any table at any one time," Iris Carpenter noted, "and more liquor." The celebration ended when the participants fell asleep on the grass.

In Scherman's photos, Lee flirts with two Russian officers, holds hands with another who clearly enjoys the contact, and grins at the attractive Russian blonde who turns up in many of these shots. When not fraternizing with her new friends, Lee photographed Dave comparing cameras with his Soviet counterpart and, to commemorate the occasion, in front of signs pointing to Torgau with *Life* photographer Johnny Florea and another Russian (Scherman included this image in *Allies,* a book he coedited with a Russian colleague to mark this hopeful moment in U.S.-Soviet relations). "There was a terrible rat race of photographers," Lee wrote. In their efforts to scoop the story, "they were funnier than the main event."

From Torgau, Lee and Dave drove south into Bavaria in his Chevrolet, painted olive drab, following Patton's push to Munich. Stopping at Nuremberg, which had been leveled by the RAF, Lee's anti-German feeling abated: "This is the first German city or possession of any kind I feel sorry for having wrecked." A note of respect colors her account of conversations with the women there: "[They] cling to their ruins and personal possessions, preferring living in air-raid shelters to evacuation, and cook carp caught in local rivers over open fires." She talked with one who had "dirty ankles . . . [an] intellectual, speaking French, Italian, and English," for whom she felt an unexpected regard: the woman had worked in an underground factory as punishment for listening to the BBC. Unlike her shots of civilians elsewhere in Germany, Lee's snaps of these women do not judge them. They, too, are surviving the collapse of the Third Reich.

Lee and Dave caught up with Dick Pollard, a former *Life* photographer stationed at the Nuremberg press bureau. He gave them a tip: divisions of the Seventh Army were heading for Dachau, a village ten miles north of Munich, to free the inmates of the nearby work camp. They set off in pursuit.

∞

"How is it every time I arrive somewhere to cover a story you and Lee are just leaving?" Marguerite Higgins complained to Scherman. On April 29, she beat them to one of the last big stories of the war—under circumstances that still provoke controversy.

While Lee and Dave drove south toward Dachau, Higgins, journalist Peter Furst, and General Henning Linden of the 42nd Division raced there in their jeeps. Having heard rumors that major political figures—Léon Blum, Stalin's son, and the former Austrian chancellor—were held there, Linden hoped to rescue them, and Higgins to get the scoop. Once there, they learned that the 45th Division's 157th Infantry Regiment, under Lieutenant Colonel Felix Sparks, had already arrived by a different route. Sparks was trying to keep order, a task that was threatened when Higgins ran to the gate, nearly causing a riot.

To this day, each division disputes the other's claim to have freed Dachau, but both agree on the horrific scenes there.

"It was one of the most terrible and wonderful days of the war," Higgins wrote. "It was the first and the worst concentration camp in Germany." Built in 1933 to house Communists and others who opposed Hitler, Dachau became a hub through which slave workers were shipped in such horrendous conditions that many died before arrival at their ultimate destinations. In April, as trainloads of evacuees from camps near the Allied advance arrived in ever greater numbers, the extermination system—crematoria and mass graves—broke down. By the end of the month, Dachau was full of neatly stacked bodies, some of whose eyes were still blinking when the GIs appeared.

The long freight train parked on the railway line next to the camp that day held other horrors. On discovering the source of the stench that emanated from its open cars—thousands of bodies smeared with blood and excrement in the remains of their prison garb—many battle-hardened veterans wept. Others became angry. "It's haunted me . . . for 36 years," one recalled. "I mean, who are they? What's their name? What nationality are they? What is their religious faith? Why were they there?"

The sun shone the next day as Lee and Dave drove through the town of Dachau, where white sheets hung from the windows, and past the sumptuous villas along the railway to the camp. The train, still full of bodies, was surrounded by flies. Beside the track lay the corpses of those who had tried to escape. More than five thousand inmates of Buchenwald had been crammed into the transport earlier in the month. Only a few remained alive.

Lee documented the scene with deliberation. Closing in by stages and shooting from different angles, she photographed the train lengthwise from the siding, then (it appears from a shot in which two medics gaze in disbelief at a corpse) from a partly cleared car—an image that makes the viewer adopt a stance next to the dead man. Moving still closer to the bodies lying on rotten straw, she captured the sheer misery of "unaccommodated man": a naked corpse with boots on beside two empty tin bowls.

Her photos of the train are different from those taken by others that day in their consistent use of witnesses—medics and GIs—whose bodies register their shock and mediate our responses. In one masterful shot of two soldiers stepping up to a car full of corpses, their sturdy forms reframe the scene, shaping the mind's attempt to grasp the incomprehensible. (Scherman's image of the same scene lacks the elements of tension and balance due to the absence of this interior frame, since the second GI is missing.)

Looking at composed images of the unspeakable disturbs those for whom formalist composition and horrific content are at odds. While such viewers are right to be disturbed, their discomfort may result from concerns that did not hamper photojournalists at the time. Working at top speed and in chaotic conditions, Lee brought to her work a passion for justice and a mind's eye that saw arrangements of significant form even before they registered in her camera. After twenty years of experience in theater, film, and photography, she instinctively used the resources of the medium to draw the gaze into the picture—composition mobilized not for aesthetic reasons but as a momentary container for strong emotions.

What is even more disturbing to some is the thought that these images were taken by a woman. At the time, Lee's colleagues saw her as a professional who kept working under unspeakable conditions while experiencing, as they did, a jumble of emotions—rage, grief, disgust, and a queasy fascination. Jacques Hindermeyer, a French Army doctor sent by the Catholic Church to document the camp, was shocked to see a woman photographing the soldiers at the freight car. When bodies began tumbling out, he felt too ill to go on: "Lee took the pictures I could not take," he said decades later. As the only woman photographer at the camp, Scherman recalled, Lee was "in seventh heaven, shooting a scoop of tremendous magnitude. She never stopped to think about what she was seeing." But, he added, the shock went underground.

Inside the camp, Lee and Dave were mobbed by cheering survivors. Some were loading the dead onto carts for disposal. Others, too weak to leave their barracks, tried to smile at her from the three-tiered bunks where two or three lay together—another of her shots in which the tight photographic space enhances the scene's alarming intimacy. "In the few minutes it took me to take my pictures," she wrote, "two men were found dead, and were unceremoniously dragged out and thrown on the heap outside the block. Nobody seemed to mind except me." The rabbits at the prison farm were well fed, she noted with anger; the stables housed "fat-bottomed beasts which shocked the eye after so many emaciated humans."

The healthier survivors kissed the GIs, paraded them around on their shoulders, and waved the American flag with their own banners, stitched together in secret from scraps of fabric. Lee photographed some scavenging in the dump, others lining up for bread—anger, relief, and pleasure on seeing her apparent in their faces. After documenting Dutch inmates gathered in the square to mark their princess's birthday while their comrades raised their fists in victory from the top of a building, she put a new roll of film in her camera to capture their celebration. Ari Von Soest, a former inmate, recalls their shock at seeing a woman in uniform, and their gratitude when she asked to hear their stories: "She was the only one of the liberators who stayed with us; she went into the prison hospital where prisoners were sprayed with DDT; she joined our celebrations." The Dutch women asked Lee to sign her name on the commemorative cloth they were embroidering; it reads "Thank you for all you have done for the Dutch women."

The five hundred women laborers sent to Dachau during the evacuation of other camps were healthier than the men, but many had typhus and some had gone mad. In an effort to document the whole camp system, Lee photographed with equal objectivity the recently arrived prisoners who worked in the camp brothel to shorten their sentences, a distinguished Viennese doctor who also had a law degree, and the crazed Gypsy woman under her care. Dachau was a microcosm of the outside world. It reflected as in a distorted mirror the system it re-created.

Unexpectedly, Lee's shots of captured Dachau guards are not possessed by the anger that marks her similar photos from Buchenwald. Over a hundred SS had been killed by the soldiers and prisoners the day before she arrived: "The violence of Dachau had a way of implicating all, even the liberators," historian Robert Abzug observes. Perhaps that was enough in the way of retribution. Her job was to chronicle the suffering of the dead and the survival of the living. Her contact sheets include shots of captured guards disguised as prisoners, and several document a strange scene at the canal outside the camp— "a floating mess of SS, in their spotted camouflage suits and nail-studded boots," she wrote, "they slithered along in the current" while the soldiers tried to fish out their corpses.

Lee framed the scene at the canal from a distance before moving in for the close-up known as *German Guard, Dachau*—another image that meets reality on its own ground. The guard floats in his uniform, a strong diagonal mass in the dark water that will be his grave; his features blur as he starts to sink below the surface. This elegant composition provides objective testimony while using light, shadow, and reflections to hint that the guard's death, although justified, is somehow redemptive. Its mysterious beauty implies the issues— grief, responsibility, memory—that would haunt Lee long after the war was over.

A letter to Audrey after her tour of Dachau evokes the complex emotions that Lee felt there. "Dachau had everything you'll ever hear or close your ears to about a concentration camp," she wrote. "The great dusty spaces that had been trampled by so many thousands of condemned feet—feet which ached and shuffled and stamped away the cold and shifted to relieve the pain and finally became useless except to walk them to the death chamber. I fell on my knee once and the pain of tiny sharp stone on my knee cap was fierce; hundreds of Auslanders [foreigners] had fallen like that every day and night. If they could get up they could live, if they hadn't the strength, they were left to be hauled off to an unidentified end, just another unknown soldier." She and Dave left for Munich that afternoon, "gulping for air and for violence." The front would seem like "a mirage of cleanliness and humanity. . . . If Munich, the birthplace of this horror, was falling we'd like to help."

They arrived to learn that units of the 45th Division had taken the city. A doddering guide showed them Munich's Hitlerian shrines: the sites of the 1921 Beer Hall Putsch and the attempt on the Führer's life, the wrecked Hofbrau House, where Lee forced herself to taste the beer hauled up from the dank cellar.

Next they went to the house at 16 Prinzregentenplatz where Hitler had lived since the 1920s. In one of the war's macabre ironies, it was now the command post of 45th Division's 179th Regiment, whose CO told Lee and Dave to move in. "There were no signs that anyone more pretentious than merchants or retired clergy had lived there," she observed. "It lacked grace and charm, it lacked intimacy, but it was not grand." After buying the building in 1935, Hitler had made the ground floor into quarters for his guards, and the subbasement into a bomb shelter. His own apartment, on the second floor, included a private suite. Lee peered at his "mediocre" art collection, inspected cupboards full of china initialed A.H., and sat at the table where the German high command had plotted the Final Solution.

"Here was Hitler's real home," she continued. "Munich was his physical as well as spiritual home, and I started immediately to track down what went on here." The staff who remained in the building did not express remorse. "No Germans, unless they are underground resistance workers or concentration camp inmates, find that Hitler did anything wrong except to lose," she concluded. "I know that I will never understand them. I'm just like the soldiers here, who look at the beautiful countryside, use the super modern comforts of their buildings, and wonder why the Germans wanted anything more."

Among the modern comforts she and Dave tried that night, Hitler's bathroom was perhaps the most enjoyable, since neither had bathed in weeks. Before taking turns in the large tiled tub, they set the scene for the series of photos that mark the occasion. In the best of these, Lee's pensive, almost unreadable expression as she reaches to scrub her shoulder contrasts oddly with the objects around her, which look like props. On the rim of the bath, a photograph of Hitler surveys the scene; a classical statue of a woman stares back at him. Beneath this statue, Lee's crumpled uniform sits on a chair; her boots stand at attention on the soiled bathmat; a shower hose is looped behind her head. In this deliberately staged setting, her look suggests, it was impossible not to think of those who died in Dachau's "bathhouse": "the elected victims having shed their clothes walked in innocently. . . . Turning on the taps for the bath, they killed themselves."

News of Hitler's suicide came over the BBC at midnight. "We've all speculated where we'd be," she told Audrey in a letter describing this moment, "what city and friends we'd choose in the way of celebrations for the end of the war, or the death of Hitler. . . . We couldn't celebrate any more than we were already." Yet her expression, which acknowledges that Dachau will not wash off, is hardly jubilant. While the "machine-monster" was dead, "he'd never

Lee in Hitler's bathtub, Munich, 1945 (David E. Scherman)

really been alive for me until today." He seemed less unreal "and therefore more terrible" after touching what he had touched, rather like "an ape who embarrasses and humbles you with his gestures, mirroring yourself in caricature." "There but for the grace of God walk I," she added. This distorted mirror showed the potential monstrousness in all humans.

In perhaps the most telling irony in a photograph full of ironies, Lee saw herself in both Hitler and the statuette—which recalls her modeling career and role as muse for Man, Huene, and Cocteau. Having placed this miniature Venus, armed but cut off at the knees, opposite Hitler's portrait, she turns toward her counterpart, whose raised right arm echoes her own. This sly jab at cultural clichés about the eternal feminine is complicated by Lee's knowledge that as a blue-eyed blonde, she met Hitler's aesthetic standards—which concurred with the prewar period's return to classicism. This rapidly composed scene includes her recognition that she would have been considered an Aryan, one of the hated "Krauts."

Lee and Dave staged other photographs while in Munich. Some were serious: Lee, dressed but still pensive, posed next to a kitschy statuette on the Führer's desk; Dave in the Konigsplatz Mausoleum, whose strict Doric colums frame him while he photographs the tombs. Others were gags, like Dave's shot of a GI reading *Mein Kampf* on Hitler's bed. On May 1, Lee toured the apartment of Eva Braun, Hitler's mistress, in her attempt to grasp the heart of Nazism. Braun's small villa gave no clues: "Part of the china was modern peasant and part was white porcelain dotted with pale blue flowers. The furniture and decorations were strictly department store like everything in the Nazi regime." And her cosmetics—Elizabeth Arden—were the sort that anyone might buy. Lee took a nap "on Eva's bed," she told Audrey, as if she were on intimate terms with those she detested: "It was comfortable but . . . macabre, to doze on the pillow of a girl and man who were now dead, and to be glad they were dead."

Following another tip from Pollard, Lee and Dave raced to Salzburg, where units of the Seventh Army's 3rd Division were planning their assault on Berchtesgaden, Hitler's "Eagle's Nest." On the way, Dave liberated a Mercedes convertible from some GIs who ceded it in exchange for pictures of them posing with Lee for their local papers. With two soldiers and a driver, she and Dave wound their way up the steep mountain roads. They arrived at sunset, in time to photograph Hitler's house going up in flames, the SS having set fire to the Führer's residence before retreating into the forest.

Returning from the village below the next morning, they found the site full of soldiers and journalists, all happily looting. The champagne, whiskey, and cigars from Hitler's cellars disappeared immediately. "Everyone hunted for souvenirs of Life with Hitler," Lee wrote mockingly. "The main excitement was inside the mountain. Miles of library, dining rooms, cinema machinery, living rooms and kitchen space. . . . Cases of silver and linen with the eagle and swastika above the initials A.H. found their way into the pockets of the souvenir hunters." Dave chose a set of Shakespeare with Hitler's bookplate on each volume; Lee took an ornate silver tray engraved with his monogram. "It was like a very wild party," she observed, "with champagne corks whizzing over the flagpole, and the house falling down over our ears."

The Germans surrendered a week later, on May 8. Lee was typing her story in the Rosenheim press camp when a soldier said that the war was over. "Shit! That's blown my first paragraph," she exclaimed. Before sending her story to London, she cabled: I IMPLORE YOU TO BELIEVE THIS IS TRUE. Another wire states, NO QUESTION THAT GERMAN CIVILIANS KNEW WHAT WENT ON. RAILWAY SIDING INTO DACHAU CAMP RUNS PAST VILLAS, WITH TRAINS OF DEAD AND SEMI-DEAD DEPORTEES. I USUALLY DON'T TAKE PICTURES OF HORRORS. BUT DON'T THINK THAT EVERY TOWN AND EVERY AREA ISN'T RICH WITH THEM. I HOPE VOGUE WILL FEEL THAT IT CAN PUBLISH THESE PICTURES.

Lee's story, which appeared in the U.S. and U.K. victory issues in June, begins: "Germany is a beautiful landscape dotted with jewel-like villages, blotched with ruined cities, inhabited by schizophrenics." After describing fairy-tale vistas, hills crowned with castles, birches and willows along tranquil streams, she continued in the same vein: "The tiny towns are pastel plaster like a modern watercolor of a medieval memory. Little girls in white dresses and garlands promenade after their first communion. The children have stilts and marbles and tops and hoops, and they play with dolls. Mothers sew and sweep and bake, and farmers plough and harrow." The Germans, in other words, behave like real people. "But they aren't," the passage concludes. "They are the enemy."

In the U.S. version, entitled "Germans Are Like This," the New York studio ran three-quarter-page shots of the Torgau linkup and Dave's photo of Lee between two Russians. Her text followed, punctuated by sets of juxtaposed images—"German children, well-fed, healthy" next to "burned bones of starved prisoners"; "orderly villages, patterned, quiet" opposite "orderly furnaces to burn bodies"—then some of her most disturbing shots from the camps. "There are millions of witnesses," she wrote, "and no isolated freak cases." For readers who harbored doubts, *Vogue* ran Lee's cable below the headline in extra bold: BELIEVE IT.

U.K. *Vogue*'s victory issue ran a longer version of the article but only one photograph from the camps: the pile of corpses at Buchenwald. Reflecting on this decision decades later, Withers remarked, "The mood then was jubilation. It seemed unsuitable to focus on horrors." Instead, she featured one of Lee's shots from Frankfurt, the statue of Justice brandishing her sword and scales next to the cathedral. This image conveyed "the Christian and cultural heritage which the Nazis aimed to destroy," she wrote. "Now they are themselves destroyed. But statue and spire remain, symbols of justice and aspiration."

In this spirit, women's contribution had to be recognized. "Where do they go from here," Withers asked, "the Servicewomen and all the others . . . how long before a grateful nation (or anyhow, the men of the nation) forget what women accomplished when the country needed them? It is up to all women to see to it that there is no regression." In her view, *Vogue*'s war correspondent was one of those who pointed the way—a sentiment that could not have been farther from what Lee herself felt as she, Dave, and their colleagues tried to decide what came next.

Lee at trial of Marshal Pétain, Paris, August 1945 (David E. Scherman)

Chapter 14

Postwar

(1945–46)

By June 1945, most American journalists were on their way home. Once settled, Margaret Bourke-White wrote a book urging the United States to take on the role of postwar moral leader, Catherine Coyne returned to the *Boston Herald*, Helen Kirkpatrick became a traveling correspondent for the *New York Post*, Mary Welsh gave up her career to live with Hemingway in Cuba, and Janet Flanner continued her "Letter from Paris" for *The New Yorker*. They were among the fortunate. "A number of correspondents of both sexes joined the great postwar fraternity of the psychically displaced," a historian observes.

∞

Lee had no intention of leaving Europe. She and Dave could go on working as a team. They would cover the aftermath of the war in Eastern Europe, under the Soviets. But he was of two minds about the plan, which would keep him in thrall to her. He needed time to reflect.

Soon after their return to Paris, Lee drove Jemima, Dave's Chevrolet, through Germany to Denmark, "encased," she wrote, "in a wall of hate." She was tense with rage: "For several months I had held my eyes so rigid and my mouth so frozen that I could scarcely manage a smile. . . . I had to learn to relax, to go from war to peace." But at the Danish border, as she watched "arrogant German officers whisking around in super-charged cars," her anger flared, and on her trip north, columns of German soldiers plodding homeward "margined the panorama of peace [she] had expected." Their presence framed the edges of her vision.

Arriving in time to see the end of five years of German occupation, Lee took pleasure in documenting Denmark's denazification. One of her shots redresses the balance by formal means: laughing Danes massed on a bridge form the backdrop to a handover of power by German officials. There had been no collaborationist government as in France, she noted. Danish businesses had protected their own from conscription into forced labor. Women had mobilized at all levels: "The National Women's Council and the National Householding Organization doubled their energies in binding the women of the country together by extending their teaching facilities and establishing preserving, mending, and cooking classes. This not only encouraged food and clothes economy but legally broke the law forbidding crowds."

It was heartening to learn that the Danes had taken their Jewish compatriots to safety in Sweden, often by devious means: "Prominent citizens announced the death of a relative and kept hearses and flower wagons, complete with top-hatted pall bearers, wandering around the streets from house doors to cemeteries with the hunted people hidden under wreaths on the floor. Taxi drivers and pushcarters and dressmakers and barbers transformed and transported the Jews. Wedding parties took them to ports for lobster dinners, and fishermen and sailors buried them under their nets until they reached midstream, and a friendly Swedish pilot boat." Once in Sweden, many joined the Danish forces of liberation.

Copenhagen's euphoric mood lifted Lee's spirits. "The Danes are drunk on laughter and fun and freedom," she wrote—despite the lack of electricity and other essentials. The populace had retaken their city. The Tivoli amusement park had replaced its war-damaged pavilions with cardboard façades; joyriders pushed the roller-coaster cars uphill before careering down; couples strolled through the gardens; old people dozed in the sun. Lee climbed high above the crowds to photograph their celebration, a daring composition that spills over its borders. As far as the eye can see, citizens form "a conspiracy of gaiety"—with no margins.

The royal family had also served as a unifying force during the occupation. Stories circulated about the defiance of the current ruler, Christian X. When told by the Nazis that Jewish Danes would have to wear yellow stars, he insisted that he and his family would also wear them. Lee obtained an interview with the crown princess and her daughters, who played unaffectedly while she took their portraits. But however much she admired the courageous Danes, her own transition to peacetime remained on hold pending her return to England.

∞

Lee's homecoming was a public event. She was now a celebrated figure—the only female photojournalist to see combat, the one whose dispatches gave a visceral sense of the war. A British movie-news team wanted to film her return. The scene of her reunion with Roland at Downshire Hill required prior planning since he had to take leave from his post in Norwich. On the appointed day, they dressed in their uniforms. The crew filmed a smiling Lee being greeted by Roland, who kisses her, gives her a welcome-home gift, a kitten, and shows her some new paintings, a domestic scene suggesting the drift to peacetime.

Brogue welcomed her with a gala luncheon. "No correspondent has displayed a greater versatility," Harry Yoxall's postprandial speech began. "Who else has written equally well about G.I.s and Picasso?" he asked. "Who else can swing from the Siegfried line one week to the new hip line the next?" Praising her empathy and courage, he continued: "She has shown herself a good soldier, and my only regret . . . is that the British authorities are so slow and ungracious in recognizing how good a soldier a woman can be." Lee's articles embodied the "quintessence" of *Vogue* for the last five years, he maintained: "A picture of the world at war, an encouragement to our readers to play their part, with no flinching from the death and destruction; but with a realization that these are not all, that taste and beauty represent the permanent values, that a pretty and well-dressed woman (as we see indeed in the person of today's heroine) can serve the cause better than a slovenly virago." The guests then toasted their heroine—whose reflections on viragos were not recorded.

Audrey Withers gave a more realistic appraisal of Lee's state of mind. "She was reluctant to abandon the adventurous life in which she had found her true vocation," Withers recalled, "and sensed, rightly, that she would never again have the opportunities it had given her." They discussed ideas for new assignments in the United States. After learning that Lee would like to work in New York, Edna Chase replied, "We would be delighted to have her come home, at our expense, of course, whenever she wants to make us a visit." Lee filed an account of her expenses and pondered the idea of being "base[d] in America for the same kind of thing I've been doing here but for other countries."

Dave's sporadic residence at Downshire Hill that summer did not help relations between Lee and Roland, since by this time she was, in many ways, closer to Dave. They discussed joint projects for Brogue until Roland put an end to the plan by asking Sylvia Redding, the head of the photographic studio, to quash it. He worried about splits among the English Surrealists over whether to join the Communists, as Picasso had done, or to follow Breton's endorsement of Trotsky; struggling with his jealousy of Lee's success, he wondered whether he should return to painting. He wanted her to stay in London; she wanted to chronicle the war's aftermath, the dislocations of ordinary lives that needed to be set right.

In Dave's view, the much-delayed publication of *Wrens in Camera* in July confirmed the importance of Lee's work. Although she had all but forgotten the book, *Wrens* was attractive and timely, since it demonstrated that women *were* good soldiers. Dave hoped to sell a book of Lee's war pictures to a New York publisher: "She has written thousands of words of text and taken enough pix for 6, also is only dame who did," he told his brother. "I think it would be pretty good as her press suddenly became good in the US thanx to Vogue's handling." He might even publish the book himself: "She's a lazy bastard like me and would never do it."

About this time, Bernard Burrows wrote from Cairo to announce his engagement and to ask whether Robin Fedden might use some of Lee's shots in his book on Syria. "I found the pictures of our oasis trip the other day," Bernard continued, "& had quite a lump in the throat. . . . I wish I could see you. Come out here as official photographer for the Americans." Aziz, who had tried to keep in touch with Lee during the war and sent money whenever he could, also asked about her plans. He had been ill for the last two years and now felt his age. Having followed "the hiking thru the ravaged Europe of Lee Miller, the stranger," he hoped to settle their affairs—since they were still married and most of his holdings were in her name. Once again she was at a crossroads.

Coincidentally, Lee had come home in time for the elections that would determine England's future. Millions pondered the rival claims of the Conservatives and Labourites. It was disheartening to learn that Churchill had sunk to warning the country of the Gestapo tactics that would ensue if Labour implemented plans for nationalization. On July 26, after the Labour landslide, he resigned. In the meantime, the Potsdam conference partitioned Germany into four occupation zones and ratified Soviet spheres of influence, deepening the impression that the postwar world was one of shabby compromise. In August, after the United States bombed Hiroshima and Nagasaki, most in England reeled at the news of the slaughter committed by their allies.

In a climate of public alarm and private confusion, the conflict between Lee and Roland erupted in a violent quarrel. "I'm not Cinderella, I can't force my foot into the glass slipper," she told him. In mid-August, she left for Paris to join Dave, who had returned to the Scribe, after promising to keep Roland informed of her whereabouts.

Before leaving, Lee went up the hill to Hampstead Heath one clear night while a fair was in progress. The photograph she took high above London, of light squiggling across the landscape in a vivid release of power, recalls her panorama of Danish crowds celebrating the end of the war. Both record the present from the widest possible vantage point. But the Hampstead image hints that despite her intentions, it was too soon for peace, too difficult to relax for more than the seconds needed to take a picture of the world around her—and of the jagged energies inside.

∞

Lee reached Paris in time to attend the trial of Marshal Henri-Philippe Pétain, whose lack of remorse for his deeds as head of Vichy France left as great an impression as the guilty verdict. Daily life was still taxing. The "coffee" had the bitter taste of its chief ingredient, acorns; the Métro was running but so many stations were closed that one had to guess where to get off; the electricity came and went unreliably, leaving the unwary trapped in the city's small, shaky elevator cages. Although gasoline was scarce and the price of food had doubled since the year before, there were compensations. There was little traffic except for bicycles, and the air was balmy.

"I've spent a lethargic and useless week in Paris," Lee told Roland, "doing nothing just like London only less to drink. . . . We celebrated vj day several times before we finally gave up and decided we'd invented atomic bombs ourselves and dreamed up the jap surrender. The room and my affairs are a hopeless mess," she continued, "and I'm incapable of sorting them out." Their friends—the Eluards, Picasso and Dora—were away: "The whole town is closed down." She was organizing a solo trip to Austria, Hungary, and perhaps Russia, but doing so "with a great deal of dread and boredom." Dave was waiting around to see her off, after which he would return to New York.

By the time Lee set off for Austria in the third week of August, her methods of dealing with depression were mutually contradictory. She needed benzedrine followed by cups of bitter coffee to rouse herself in the morning, and rounds of drinks followed by sleeping pills to calm her nerves at night. Sporadic efforts to go on the wagon met with little success. Nonetheless, she had Jemima, official backing, and letters of introduction. ("This is to introduce Lee Miller, our famous war correspondent," a Frogue staffer told a friend in Budapest. "You will find her absolutely charming.")

She reached her first stop, Salzburg, at the height of the music festival normally held each summer in Mozart's birthplace—an event meant to mark the war's end, as the fashion shows had done after the liberation of Paris. But the Europe carved out at the Potsdam conference looked quite different than it had the year before. Austria was divided into four zones, under the jurisdiction of the occupying powers. The truckloads of soldiers—French, Russian, British, and American—pouring into Salzburg for the festival, Lee wrote, created "a babel of foreign voices." It had taken the skills of Barbara Lauwer, a former spy, to organize the event. The musicians, many of whom were Jewish, were coaxed out of hiding; the conductor, Reinhardt Baumgartner—who had spent the war in Switzerland—was retrieved at the border, and on arrival received a rousing welcome from the Russians invited there by U.S. General Mark Clark. Music brought potential enemies together; Mozart's harmonies bridged misunderstandings.

Lee became acquainted with a new dramatic form, opera, while in Salzburg, starting with *The Abduction from the Seraglio*. Mozart's theme of forgiveness was timely; the female leads befriended her when she took their pictures. Rosl Schwaiger, who stole the show as the soubrette Blondchen, took her to see director Max Reinhardt's bombed-out residence and sang for her in front of the derelict castle. On another occasion, when Maria Cebotari (Constanze in *The Abduction*) drove with Lee to a well-known inn, she began to thaw: "I'd always thought opera stars babied their voices and gargled at unsociable intervals, but she paid no attention to her flying hair and the whirling dust."

Later, Lee joined the crowds at the marionette theater, where singers hidden beneath the floorboards sang in English for the soldiers. Backstage she photographed the puppeteers looming over the set as they manipulated their miniature characters. In a comic opera about space travel, the little rocket that took the hero to Mars blasted across the tiny stage "with a bang and a shower of sparks, all too redolent of the V1s we were on the receiving end of last year," she wrote. Before reaching Mars, it landed on a planet with insectlike natives and squawking reptilian creatures whose ribs stuck out. "It's a comedy," she continued, "but I didn't laugh. The rocket is serious and the lizard beasts were like Dachau."

Salzburg proved to be a rehearsal for Vienna, where a fifth zone, under international control, deepened the confusion. On the way there through Russian-occupied territory, the mix-up of languages at checkpoints created a semantic babel. "The few road signs necessary for the limited traffic were painted white on infantry badge blue in cabalistic letters," she wrote, "candelabras, bedsteads and an assortment of our letters and numbers upside down or backwards like a witch's looking glass." The Russians waved red and yellow flags then saluted; the Americans wisecracked about her driving. The smartly uniformed bellboys at the Hotel Weisser Hahn, where she took a room, looked like members of the chorus.

Vienna was a cross between a comic opera and a puppet show, but one in which bureaucrats held the strings. Permits in quadruplicate were needed to move around the city, which kept two times: Viennese, for daily life, and military, based on the hour in Moscow. The press worked on local time but had to rise with the military. Soldiers who had Viennese girlfriends went to bed late and woke up early, "so they are losing weight and getting circles under their eyes," Lee wrote to Roland on September 30. There was a thriving black market. She photographed enterprising Russian soldiers fishing for carp in the ornamental pond at the Belvedere Gardens, and, like the other hotel guests, pocketed leftovers for friends. "Nothing ever happens to schedule," she complained, "and none of my reform acts ever works, such as being orderly, on time or respectful to my elders."

"Lonesome and not amused" by the omnipresent music, Lee felt too distracted to write. "Arpeggios give me the shudders," she said; waltzes annoyed her. "Now I do nothing but go to operas and concerts . . . and associate with coloratura sopranos." While Vienna's Opera House had been gutted, it made a dramatic setting for her photograph of Irmgard Seefried, captured in silhouette against the ruins while she sang an aria from *Madama Butterfly.* But at the performance (a reprised German-language version), Lee's mind kept returning to the war. Noting the resemblance between "Kraut" uniforms and those worn by the American sailors, she wondered which uniform Pinkerton wore. Soaring music and themes of doomed love failed to unlock her emotions.

Vienna depressed her because she saw in it a distorted image of her state of mind: "In a city suffering the psychic depression of the conquered and starving, the Viennese have kept their charming duality. *Gemütlich* as ever, they are drunk on music, light frothy music for empty stomachs." But in a city full of displaced persons and peasants bearing stacks of wood for fuel, music functioned like the old Roman games: "It keeps people's minds off their tightened belts and the failure of politics."

"This trip is working very slowly," she told Roland. "I'm not at all sure it's successful. . . . I seem to have lost my grip or enthusiasm or something with the end of the war. There no longer seems to be any urgency." Only individuals touched her. The great Nijinsky, whose mental deterioration had doomed him to a mercy death under the Nazis, miraculously survived with the help of his wife, Romola—also a dancer. On hearing Russian spoken by the soldiers, he had talked for the first time in years. "Shocked that the great Nijinskaya had no shoes," Lee told Audrey, they had "looted a red leather sofa from under the debris next door and cobbled her a pair of sandals." Lee brought the couple scraps from the hotel, apple strudel, a liver sandwich, and Nijinsky's favorite, white bread spread with peanut butter.

While most civilians suffered from malnutrition and related illnesses, the shortage of medical supplies was far more disturbing. Lee visited a hospital where children were dying for lack of drugs. "For an hour I watched a baby die," she told Audrey. "He was a skinny gladiator. He gasped and fought and struggled for life, and a doctor and a nun and I just stood there and watched. . . . This tiny baby fought for his only possession, life, as if it might be worth something." Her shots of this infant and the girl in the next bed are heartbreaking. There were millions of such cases, she noted in a passage that echoes reports from the camps: "There are a thousand here—I saw them." Memories of the dead and dying returned involuntarily. The dying baby was "dark blue when I first saw him," she wrote. "He was the dark dusty blue of these waltz-filled Vienna nights, the same color as the striped garb of the Dachau skeletons."

What could be done for the people of Austria, she asked herself: "We can liberate them and set them up as a going concern, but liberty and freedom and independence are not gifts; they are the reward of struggle and sacrifice." Moreover, it was impossible to forget that the Austrians had embraced Hitler. "This is a silly, fatuous town," she scrawled in her notebook. "It's not evil, wicked or tragic. Tragedy is the fate of the undeserving, not the earned justice of the wicked Nazis."

One of the few Viennese to win Lee's sympathy was the scrawny kitten she found in a gutter and named "Varum" (in English, "Why"). Tucked inside her uniform, he kept her company as she made the rounds of the occupying powers to obtain clearance for Moscow—where things might run more efficiently—or should this effort fail, Hungary and the Balkans. But even with Varum near her heart, hours with bureaucrats deepened her frustration. Her timing was wrong, people said. Winter was approaching; life under the Soviets was unstable. Lee persisted in her attempt, largely to persuade herself that she had not lost her grip.

Another letter to Roland drafted about this time begins, "Please, darling, I haven't forgotten you. It's part of my boondoggling habits and a piece of my current frustrations which I've tried many times to explain to you. Every day I'm expecting to find the solution, the key to the code. Every evening when I could take the time and certainly have the interest to write you I think that tomorrow I'll know the ultimate answer or my depression will have lifted." But the answer never came. "Now I'm suffering from a sort of verbal impotence," she continued. "When Europe was yet to be 'liberated,' . . . when I had thought and burned with ideas for years and suddenly found a peg on which to hang them, I found work and transport and transmission and courage. This is a new and disillusioning world. Peace in a world of crooks who have no honor, no integrity, and no shame is not what anyone fought for."

Lee's depression mirrored that of many displaced persons, she believed. "Really great groups of humans are suffering from the same shock symptoms caused by peace that I'm combatting," she said. "I don't in the least mean the boys going back home to find that they've become dependent upon benevolent maternal army, that they have outgrown their wives or become unsocially unfit or drunks or misanthropes. It's just an impatience with the sordid dirt which is being slung around compared with the comparative cleanliness and the real nobility of men in the lines, or men and women in lousy little jobs they thought were helping win the war, and the people who bought the bonds so that their disreputable government could continue after the war boom had been paid off, the families who are still on short rations so that a lot of grasping bastards with greedy gloating appetites should have enough schlag [whipped cream] on their coffee." She was sick of Vienna and its schlag-devouring residents: "A more disorganized, dissolute, dishonest population has never existed in the history books."

In late October, accompanied by an Austrian broadcaster, a Hungarian soldier, and Varum, Lee drove to Budapest. Their adventures made "good cinema," she told a friend in Vienna. On the road to Bruck, the checkpoint, they were chased by Russian guards who hauled out Lee's passengers and stuck a gun in her side. At headquarters, Lee charmed the commanding officer: "He thought it sporting of me to give a lift to two strangers," she went on, but warned her to be careful in Hungary—Hitler's most enthusiastic ally until earlier that year, when Budapest fell to the Russians after a long siege.

Lee's first impression of the capital was positive. The Danube shimmered "like a mirage"; Budapest rose from its banks "like a jewel studded icon." But the civilians' hotel, the Bristol, reeked of rat turds, and by the time she found a room at the officers' billet, Varum was missing. Retracing her steps, Lee found the kitten lying dead outside the Bristol, "arched like when he's pretending to be a warrior." She gave way to bitter tears—a delayed response to "weeks of frustration bursting on the doorstep of my objective as well as [to] the loss of my pet." Later, since her bed lacked sheets, she put the red Nazi flag she used as a scarf on her pillow, she said, "so that at least it'd be my own dirt, and the color came off on my nose and eyes, from crying."

Breakfast at the U.S. mess (butter, coffee, and six eggs) improved her mood. General Geoffrey Keyes, the military commander, made her feel welcome; an officer told her to move to the Sisters of Mercy convent, where some journalists were living at the pleasure of the abbess, Margit Schlachte—one of the many in Budapest who made known their dislike of the Russians. Despite their complaints, Lee preferred the Hungarians to the Austrians. One felt a bustle in the air. After moving to the convent, she dined nearby at the Park Club, headquarters for the Allied missions, and downed palinca, Hungarian apricot brandy, at the bar, where a U.S. colonel grumbled about journalists using their status to junket around Europe.

Surprised to find *Vogue*'s war correspondent living next door to them at the convent, *Life* photographer John Phillips and *Stars and Stripes* reporter Simon Bourgin welcomed Lee—as much for the legend surrounding her as for her fireplace, an asset as nights grew cold. (Their cells were far from monastic: the nuns provided palinca and foie gras in exchange for dollars.) Soon they formed a team of three, Lee in the role of sister to the two Americans. Phillips, a worldly expatriate who had begun his career as a society photographer in Nice, knew everyone; Bourgin, a fresh-faced young reporter from Minnesota, let Phillips arrange their appointments and map the terrain.

They were uniquely placed to watch the breakdown of Hungarian society, Phillips explained: it was taking place before their eyes. As for the future of Eastern Europe, he believed, it would be hard to get the Russians out of the areas they now occupied. Having known prewar Cairo, Phillips agreed that while life there had been pleasant for foreigners, most Egyptians wanted a German victory, to end British rule. They discussed politics into the night: Hungary's support of Hitler, the population's refusal to take responsibility for their defeat, the Russians' plans, which were, as yet, unknown, except that they backed the November elections, the first exercise of this kind in Hungary. "Lee was very aware of what was happening," Phillips recalled. "She had been to the college of life." One night she barged into their room with her bedroll and declared, "I'll be damned if I'm going to be excluded from this conversation because I'm a woman."

Panoramic shot of the Danube, a bombed bridge, and Pest taken while Lee and Simon Bourgin (the photographer) explored Buda together in October 1945

Remembering this time, Bourgin observed with a smile: "Lee and I almost lived together." Between appointments, they explored Buda, a romantic ruin across the river that was hard to reach since the siege, when the Germans blew up the bridges. Crossing the partially rebuilt Franz Joseph bridge was an adventure. One picked one's way past crowded trams, carts pulled by ancient nags, and homeless children who pilfered what they could in the confusion. After climbing the medieval streets to Castle Hill, Lee photographed the parapets of Fisherman's Bastion, an unlikely pastiche of Gothic and Romanesque built as a viewing platform over the fish market—where she framed Pest in the distance through the Bastion's doorways.

Street scenes in the more modern part of the city caught her eye for detail. She shot election posters pasted on the walls in decorative patterns, the outdoor market stocked "with abundant wonderful food at astronomical figures," she noted, and the geese she acquired and traded for a kilo of salt—but also the "freezing, starving returning deportees" and the few survivors of Hitler's last-ditch effort to eliminate Hungarian Jewry. "She hated the Fascists," Phillips recalled. "We were all anti-Nazi, but the strength of her hatred was unusual." He found it hard to fathom the depth of her anger.

Soon after her arrival, Lee met Robert Halmi, the son of a distinguished Hungarian photographer who was himself a cameraman. Halmi, who spoke good English, became her interpreter, assistant, and chess partner. "Our relationship was very basic," he recalled. He toted Lee's equipment, did setups, and translated at interviews. Soon he was also serving as her masseur, morning rubdowns being as necessary as the first shot of palinca to rouse her after the previous night's drinking. Lee was "absolutely fearless," Halmi went on: "she had a marvelous sense of humor." They became good friends, but the young man did not find her attractive. She drank too much and in her baggy army uniform looked "too masculine."

One day, Bourgin came into Lee's cell when Halmi was sitting astride her to massage her back. "Shake hands with Halmi," she told him. "He can get you anything you want." Once roused, Lee often joined Si and John at interviews or with Halmi's help photographed Budapest luminaries. Between engagements, she and Bourgin swam at the Gellert Hotel's Art Nouveau baths, where the guests strolled in their towels beneath the domed ceiling. The spa was maintained despite the hotel's extensive damage—proof of Budapest's taste for pleasure, Lee thought, like the nightclubs "flourish[ing] with champagne and girl acts, the latter being frequently padlocked as a reform wave strikes the government."

With her new friends, she spent evenings at the Park Club, which before the war had been the exclusive precinct of the Hungarian aristocracy. Former members were delighted to return as guests of Allied staff. She and Bourgin often took their well-connected English-speaking friends—Baroness Kati

Schell, who worked for Phillips, and Elizabeth Uhlman, the daughter of a Jewish baron and banker. The Park Club was "the mecca of all social Budapest," Lee explained for *Vogue* readers. It had excellent food, a famous Gypsy band, and the bar where "the Two Georges," musicians who had survived the camps, entertained while the waiters arranged sales of drugs or diamonds.

It became apparent to Lee that Halmi was not the only one who could get anything you wanted. Men in the street proffered cameras, binoculars, gold watches, and pistols; waiters had villas to rent or cases of champagne. "The American dollar is king," Bourgin began his report on Hungary for *Life*. "The dollar here can buy anything—all the luxuries and fineries that the rest of Europe only dreams about." With the collapse of the pengö following Hungary's despoliation by the Germans and the Russians, Americans were the new aristocracy. Working for Phillips at ten dollars a week, Kati Schell earned more than the foreign minister did in a month; a GI's monthly pay exceeded the prime minister's annual salary.

Kati explained the topsy-turvy social system to Lee and her friends. That spring, after the passage of the land-reform laws that ended the feudal system, the nobility had shown great resourcefulness. With whatever they could rescue from their estates—antiques, mink coats, the butler's gold buttons—they came to town to earn money. "The waitresses and nurse-maids trades union register of Budapest reads like the Almanach of Gotha," Lee noted. Baronesses worked as barmaids; a countess who was a famous horsewoman joined the team rebuilding the bridges. These women, she observed, had "learned courage and endurance and a long-term sense of values." Moreover, they knew "what good service should be like and weren't ashamed to give it."

Lee's ideas about the piece she wanted to write for *Vogue* seemed mutually contradictory. The political situation illustrated aspects of life in Eastern Europe under the Soviets, yet it was also peculiar to Hungary. The population's refusal to admit guilt for their pro-Nazi past enraged her, as did their treatment of the Jewish deportees who came home to learn that their neighbors had helped themselves to their property. "She had a strong streak of compassion for those caught on the wrong side," Bourgin recalled, "a political sense enlivened by an ethical feeling."

While Lee felt obliged to do a story on fashion, this was a joke, Halmi felt. Everyone but the aristocrats went around in rags. As in Paris, fashion showed the war's aftereffects: Lee photographed Kati Schell, a scarf round her head for warmth, at the Café Roszwurm in Buda and posed one of Halmi's friends in front of the Hungarian Parliament. She took a more original line by showing the nobility's efforts to turn hunting trips into a source of profit. "American and British officers (who have cars, travel permits and enough enthusiasm to batter against the rotten roads for a shot at a stag) transport the party," Lee explained. Since ammunition cost thousands of pengös, only the best shots were invited. The nobility were "cockeyed but courageous," Phillips recalled of these weekends. "Who else would have thought of hunting with the Allies in their jeeps?"

At the other end of the social ladder, the inhabitants of many villages still wore traditional dress. Toward the end of October, Lee and Halmi drove to Mezökövesd, "a living folkore museum," she told Audrey, where even Elsa Schiaparelli might pick up an idea. About fifty miles north of Budapest, the village had catered to tourists since the folk revival before the war. In October, after the harvest, the unmarried women paraded in their embroidered costumes to attract suitors; they married in white dresses decked with flowered streamers and headdresses of cascading white fringe.

The story combined fashion with anthropology. In contrast to their gorgeous clothes, the peasants "live primitively in crowded houses with permanently closed windows, stinking outhouses . . . and muddy manure sloshing streets," Lee wrote. (Oddly, they had "elegant baby carriages.") One old woman, "a sort of show piece," drew embroidery patterns for the women in the region. Stitching the blossoms for which she was famous, she made a proud subject in her dark clothes and headdress of pink pompoms. As Lee photographed her, a Russian barged in, shouting, *"Davai, davai"* ("come along," a phrase that often preceded demands for one's watch), then detained her for taking pictures without the proper papers.

Lee and Halmi were taken to Miskolc, the provincial capital, and placed under guard for two days. "I sat in austere rooms under a photo of Stalin, to be interviewed, scrutinised, and asked to wait by officers of various rank, amiability, and branch of service," Lee told Audrey. "Everybody was very polite and patient and I was given deli-

Women of Mezökövesd, where Lee was detained by the Russians, November 1945 (Simon Bourgin)

cious cigarettes." Although confined, she did not suffer. "I ate what I liked and was taken out walking or shopping when I was bored or sat in the cafe drinking palinca (I think it must be distilled paprika) and real coffee." She initiated the commanding officer into a variant of the Surrealist *corps exquis* by drawing imaginary monsters, section by section. But it was hard not to worry. "I couldn't think what I'd done wrong," she continued. "Was it enough for Siberia? Would my cameras be seized? Would I be exiled from Hungary?"

In the meantime, Lee and her captors toasted their respective governments and discussed "culture," for which the Russians showed respect. When she showed them copies of *Vogue,* they jeered, " 'Bourgeois,' pronounced 'boorjooey,' " which was "not a criticism of pink sheets and bed-lamps, crested silver, or heated motor cars but an implication that they were acquired by undemocratic means." The Russian colonel gave her new papers and sent her to tour the region, including the Tokaj vineyards and the fin-de-siècle spa of Lillafured. Her adventures made news in Budapest and soon, in the United States, when the New York papers published reports of her detention. (The Millers learned from the *New York Times* that she had been held by the Russians; since the invasion, her correspondence with them had been sporadic at best.)

Lee returned to the capital a few days before the elections. For weeks, she wrote, "Budapest had been seething with rumors about stronghanded methods and reprisals by the communists if the vote didn't swing to a left-wing majority." Yet on election day, November 4, "everyone voted exactly as they pleased"—resulting in a coalition government led by the Small Holder Party, which defended the landed peasantry while also attracting voters alarmed by the thought of a Soviet-style future. "The conservative elements of the country have [a] great interest in the failure of democracy," she continued. "Their publicized mistrust and dislike of the Soviet Union . . . results in the sabotage of sincere efforts on the part of modern minded people." While the Russians' plans for Eastern Europe are still a debated question, Lee thought that they should be given the benefit of the doubt.

Sister Margit Schlachte, who held the opposite view, found it increasingly difficult to accept Lee's modern-mindedness, even allowing for her nationality and profession. Halmi took her home at night when she was drunk and pleaded ignorance when she flouted the convent's rules—as if she were back at boarding school. Lee's presence was corrupting the nuns, Schlachte believed. She gave them silk stockings; a novice became hysterical on finding Halmi performing his morning massage while Lee lay naked in bed. "Schlachte told us, 'We don't do that,' " to which Halmi replied, "I'm sorry, I didn't know. I never lived in a convent."

One night, after Lee, John, and Si met some homeless refugees on their way to the convent, Lee gave them her cell and slept next door. In the morning, another sister berated them: "First we had the Nazis," she declared. "Now we have the Russians, but you people are the worst." They would have to leave; the convent could no longer tolerate such behavior. The trio moved to the Astoria, where the U.S. enlisted men's Hungarian girlfriends could stay until inspections at 4 a.m.

John and Lee remained at the Astoria after Si was posted to Belgrade. On December 22, she cabled Roland wistfully: WISH EYE WERE GOING TO HAVE AS MERRY A CHRISTMAS AS EYE HOPE FOR YOU STOP LOVE EVERYONE ESPECIALLY YOU STOP KISSES. She had, in a sense, become an eye—a courageous, highly esteemed professional. Unlike Bourke-White, Lee was "good company," Phillips explained: "Bourke-White just worked; Lee had a sense of humor." Although both knew what they wanted and went after it, they had "nothing in common." As for Beaton, Brogue's other "eye," John and Lee were in agreement. He was "a pure social climber," he recalled, "someone who would knife you in the back if it served his purpose."

John and Lee occasionally worked together on stories, such as the execution of Laszlo Bardossy, the premier during Hungary's alliance with the Nazis, who had been found guilty of war crimes. On January 10, they rose at dawn to document Bardossy's execution. Their photographs reflect their different perspectives. Leaning out of a window, Lee framed the scene as a theater of retribution: witnesses stand to the side as four soldiers take aim at the ex-premier, standing stiffly against a pile of sandbags. By contrast, Phillips's close-up of a priest kneeling over the body leaves the viewer in doubt. Few blamed Bardossy, he believed. His final words ("God save Hungary from these bandits!") were understood to refer to the Communists. That day, he recalled, "a pall of gloom descended on Budapest."

At Lee's hangout, the Café Floris, people said it was a disgrace to hang the premier like a criminal; they did not believe her when she said that he had been shot. "Next edition," she ironized, "he'd been shot and writhed in agony for forty minutes and neither his wife had been allowed to see him, nor absolution given. No women had been present and the press forbidden to take pictures. . . . Finally, one day I'd be walking down Bardossy Street to the executions of the present democratic leaders." The attitudes voiced in these remarks disgusted her: "I gave up, and left Hungary to its world of fable."

Taking stock the next day in a note to Audrey, Lee concluded that it had been "a mistake" to go to Eastern Europe. Her stubbornness, which had served her in the war, "turns out to be a bad peacetime habit," she continued, "and my bulldozing tactics tangle with the supple evasiveness which pervades this part of the world." In the current climate, she felt "as popular as a leper and as rational as a scattered jigsaw puzzle." Yet she wanted to keep on going. "I'd rather chew my finger nails right down to the elbow rather than retreat from here until I have something positive and convincing to say." At the moment, "the octopus of dishonesty" prevalent in Hungary had forced her into "numb sterility and appalling self-examination."

During these weeks, Lee received several kinds of disturbing news. Harry Yoxall cabled on January 7 that he and Edna Chase would no longer bear the expense of her stay in Europe. He urged her, RETURN LONDON SOONEST POSSIBLE VIEW PROCEEDING NEW YORK. On January 23, Audrey cabled that she had not received Lee's Hungarian coverage. AFRAID CIRCUM-STANCE RENDER IT IMPOSSIBLE, Audrey continued, MUST ASK YOU RETURN QUICKEST ROUTE LEAVING MID-FEBRUARY LATEST. About the same time, Dave cabled John Phillips to tell Lee to return to Downshire Hill, where another woman was installed in Roland's bed.

Lee put the cables aside. She was going to Romania with John in spite of everything—the news, the weather, the political situation. "Before leaving," Phillips recalled, "we invited three quarters of the expropriated Hungarians to the Park Club. With the inflation, we could pay two weeks later in dollars so it cost nothing." They watched their friends smash glasses, drink themselves silly, and behave "as if this were the old days," then took their leave just before the first Hungarian republic came into existence on February 1.

Lee's return to Romania began with a false start. After crossing the Great Plain's grasslands in a convoy—John and his driver, Giles Schulz, in their jeep, Lee in Jemima—they were rejected by the Russian border guards and sent back to Budapest to secure the correct papers. One Russian unit did not always recognize another's authority, Phillips recalled: "We had no idea which Red Army unit we were dealing with, and by the looks of things, the authorities in Budapest didn't either."

Despite this contretemps, the chain of command in Romania seemed clearer than in Hungary. In 1939, the Germans had turned the largely agrarian country into a satellite of the Third Reich. After King Carol's abdication in 1940, General Ion Antonescu had established the fascist dictatorship that lasted until August 1944, when the Russians invaded, and the country changed sides. For the past year, Prince Mihai (Michael), whom John knew from pre-war days, had ruled under Soviet protection.

After obtaining credentials signed in red, John and Lee plotted a new route. They crossed the border with a few hours' delay and drove through the waning winter light to Arad, where curious crowds, for whom foreigners other than Russians were a novelty, surrounded their cars. The French-speaker who translated for them booked the one hotel room available and took them to a restaurant whose decor retained traces of Arad's past as an outpost of the Austro-Hungarian Empire.

It was the start of a long, cold night of misunderstandings. They exchanged drinks with an inebriated Russian officer named Andrei, who told the band to play American tunes, including "It's a Long, Long Way to Tipperary." Later, after failing to persuade his new friends to stay up all night, Andrei banged on their door while they shivered in their beds—under the pretext that the translator, who was sleeping on the couch, had the wrong papers. "Lee, my driver, and I put on our shoes without a word," Phillips recalled: if Andrei took the translator, he would have to take all of them. The fuss ended when the chief of police arrived and found the man's papers to be in order. Andrei marched out in a snit; the chief sighed, "These Russians."

In the morning, they drove to Oradea, a center of imperial elegance that became a backwater when Hungary lost Transylvania after the Great War. To their surprise, a grinning Andrei invited them to his table in the hotel dining room, where he and some officers were downing Wiener schnitzel, pickles, chocolate cake, and quantities of beer and wine. "While it was hard to reconcile the way he had grimly stalked out of our lives only to re-enter it wreathed in smiles," Phillips wrote, "he looked genuinely pleased to be with us." After many rounds of tuica, Romanian plum brandy, Andrei said that he was "Russian SS"—part of the dreaded NKVD. He then sang lustily, did Cossack dances, and fell asleep outside the room that John and Lee were sharing. Later, on their return, they noticed his badly gashed forehead and disinfected his cuts with tuica before sending him away.

It snowed the next day on the drive through Transylvania, John and Lee in Jemima, and Schultz behind. "Through eyelids squeezed against the brilliance," Lee wrote, "I peered at the showy expanse of white plains and mountains topped by blue skies." The province had long been politically "ambiguous," she explained for *Vogue* readers. After each war, it ended up on a different side of the border (having been ceded to Hungary by the Nazis in 1940, the region had just been restored to Romania by the Russians). Under heavy snowdrifts, it was also "anonymous." There were no road signs—the Hungarian place-names having been taken down and the Romanian ones not yet put up: "I might have been in Russia, or Michigan, or Patagonia."

On the icy road to Sibiu, Lee visualized this mysterious town, where large eye-shaped windows nestled beneath the rooftops. "In 1938 I was very impressed by the peering prying eyes of the architecture," she wrote. "At this time this province was being proselytized by the bigger and better Germany crowd as well as by the Nem Nem Shoha gang of Hungary [revisionists who said 'no, no, never' to the transfer of Transylvania to Romania]. I was there as a simple tourist but under great suspicion by all." Steering Jemima along the slippery road, she thought of "the way the buildings peered just like the hidden microphones in Bucharest listened."

Suddenly, her car skidded off the road and onto a slope, where it came to a stop forty feet away. "I'm awfully sorry, John," Lee said calmly as Schulz rushed to their aid. By chance, soldiers from a Red Army unit that had been at the Torgau linkup drove up, asked their nationality, then shouted, "Yanks Goddamn sonavabich bastard okay!" After several failed attempts to dislodge Jemima, Lee, John, and Schulz drove to Sibiu in the jeep, then returned hours later to find that the car had been stripped by the bandits they had been warned about in Budapest.

The next day, on the road to Sinaia, a ski resort in the Carpathians, Schulz drove while Lee and John traded memories of prewar Romania. They hoped to see King Michael and the queen mother, whom John had met when photographing King Carol—an assignment that Carol saw as a chance to improve his image in America. (The king explained that as Queen Victoria's grandson, he had enlarged the royal residence to enhance its resemblance to Buckingham Palace.) While the current king had been unable to stop the deportation of Romanian Jews to Auschwitz, his recent coup d'état had realigned Romania with the Allies.

Michael and his mother, the former Helen of Greece, lived in a chalet but preferred to meet journalists in their official residence—which to Lee "looked like something Orson Welles might have chosen as the set for a Balkan mystery." Michael posed regally against the background of armor in his great hall. "A very satisfactory king he makes," Lee told Audrey, "an extremely astute clever cookie." He was respected by all: the peasants, the Russians, and the political parties. "In this moment of our side fostering all the wrong kings in the right countries," she continued, "it is curious to find that Mihai, with his coup d'état more or less on his own is the only outstanding post-war monarch." She approved of his hobbies—riding his jeep down the palace stairs, tinkering with machinery, taking photographs and printing them in his darkroom—though his contempt for the Rolleiflex (he had five Leicas) surprised her.

D-ra Lee Miller, corespondenta revistei „Vogue" în România

The queen mother, who joked about the "terrifying taste" of Romanian palaces, had

D. John Phillips, corespondentul magazinului „Life", la Bucuresti

Illustration for Poporul *(Bucharest) interview with Lee and John Phillips, February 9, 1946*

"great elegance and simple charm." Helen posed for Lee in a tailored frock and pearls against the swirling rococo stairway. "Even I recognized that the pearls were real," she told Audrey, "in spite of the fact that they . . . were worn in the simplest possible manner." It pleased her to bring Helen news of "what had happened to the various schlosses and castles various relatives of hers in Germany or Austria had been living in"—as if they shared a common past. Before leaving Sinaia, Lee photographed the graves of the American airmen who had died in raids on the Ploesti oil fields, their stark crosses in the foreground against the snow-covered mountains.

It was a short drive to Bucharest. The streets were full of oxcarts, barefoot peasants, and big American cars. After checking into the Athenée Palace, they learned that since the recognition by Britain and the United States of Romania's left-wing government, representatives from both countries were there making overtures to the state-owned oil company. In the new political climate, Lee and John were welcomed as the representatives of influential U.S. magazines. A reporter from the independent daily *Poporul* wrote about them as "guests" who had toured Romania before the war. During their interview, they reminisced about conditions in 1938. Lee, whose blue eyes and "beautiful hair, like freshly harvested corn," were much admired, the reporter wrote, waited patiently while John expressed his belief that a journalist was as much a combatant as a soldier—he needed "sang froid," but also "a sense of ambiguity . . . to participate not only with his heart but also with his mind."

On their travels, Lee listened to many observations of this kind. "Romania is a profession, not a nationality," John was fond of saying. Life in Bucharest was almost oriental, in that intrigue determined whom one could see or photograph. Lee still felt "rhapsodic" about the people, who were Latins: "The language was understandable, or at least readable," she explained. Moreover, the streets were a feast for the eyes: "Every shop had gay, primitive paintings by the door, of pork chops, sausages, hats, gloves, hammers, saws, and ploughs, whatever was stocked inside." And there were no shortages except for caviar. Nightlife had resumed. It was hard to distinguish the "nice" women from the professionals, since both dressed with equal flashiness. As in Budapest, she listened to Gypsy music while tossing tuica down her throat from a kind of bud vase, a custom dating to the time when riders knocked back the drink without dismounting—a trick she no doubt thought about trying.

While some aspects of peasant life were unchanged, the Gypsies who had wandered about Romania with their bears were nowhere to be seen. Before the war, the bears had danced for the villagers and walked up and down their spines to cure backaches. Eager to try ursine massage, Lee made inquiries. Her friend Hari Brauner, who had resumed his university post, explained the bears' fate. Under Antonescu, Gypsies had been forbidden to ply their trades, but after Michael's coup, they flocked to Bucharest. "Traffic was blocked by mobs of excited children and rheumatic oldsters surrounding the beribboned, flower-garlanded bears," Lee wrote in a draft for *Vogue*. But when typhus began to threaten public health, the government reinstated the ban on Gypsy travel. Lee waited while Hari asked his informants about venues for bear massage.

In the meantime, Brauner brought her up-to-date on their friend Maritza. Now a national figure whose records were often heard on the radio, she still wore peasant clothes and refused to be chic. Hari took Lee to photograph the singer in her element, a bistro where visitors followed the Gypsy code: "The guest never gives money to the singer," Lee wrote, "but places it in a piggy bank in the belly of the guitar." While Maritza cooed and chirped, the music unwound itself like a spring: "The minor half tones are almost oriental and the nostalgic or passionate verses gather a terrible intensity, sustained above the scrambling, scraping patterns of the orchestra. They say that once you drink from a certain well and listen to the music, you will return to Romania. I've done both and returned twice."

Lee dutifully reported on Romanian society. "Thinking you might want personalities," she told Audrey, she went to lunch with the wife of Romanian Oil's general manager to photograph the newly influential. Later, the minister of justice's spouse took her to a picturesque part of town where whole streets were covered with carpets, and street vendors bore their merchandise on their shoulders. The peasants interested her more than the society ladies: "All the most beautiful dames in town are either tarts or are living more or less scandalously with our officers." Maritza, on the other hand, was "authentic . . . a great friend of mine and a lovely woman."

Lee enlisted Maritza's help in her efforts to find a bear hotel, an inn with a courtyard where the animals slept curled up beside their masters. When Hari's informants provided the address of a bear hotel less than an hour away, Lee hired a taxi and with Hari "rumbled forth into a mysteriously foggy country on frighteningly bumpy roads, squashed through snow and ruts." The village had thatched roofs and unkempt gardens full of sunflowers. The one remaining bear had to be awakened. "Sleepy and sulky, she snapped at her keeper," Lee recalled. After a few growls, she stood on her hind legs to dance—a prelude to massage.

Before lying down on a carpet, Lee taught Hari to use her Rolleiflex so he could capture the event. "The bear knew her business," she wrote later. "She walked up and down my back on all fours as gently as if on eggs. Each big paw felt its way until it found an area which wouldn't squash in, and the weight was transferred from foot to foot with very little change of pressure. As the music started again, she raised up on her hind legs and shuffled up and down my back. It was crushing and exhilarating. All my muscles clenched and relaxed to keep from being flattened. Then she was led off, to return, facing the other direction. She sat her great, furry, warm bottom down on the nape of my neck, and with gentle shuffles, went from my neck to my knees and back again." Afterward Lee felt "marvelous . . . flexible and energetic. I discovered I could move my neck and shoulders in patterns I'd forgotten." The bear's owner reluctantly accepted payment, "the equivalent of a dollar and a half . . . all we had left with us at the end of a couple of months peregrinations."

One would hope that Lee was in this relaxed state when she read the missive from Roland that came near the end of her stay. He had heard from her once since August. Tired of loving someone who had become a "ghost," he was making a last attempt to reach her. "Our pact made from the whole bottom of my heart was one which gave you always your liberty," he

Lee being massaged by a bear, Romania, February 1946 (Lee Miller with Hari Brauner)

wrote. "Every hour spent with you was an hour of supreme happiness. Every hour without you was just too bad." But there had been too many of them lately, and no sign that the future would be different. "You asked me before leaving if I had some girl I loved as well as you," he continued. "Now I have. Someone you don't know, have never seen and who is here—real—no ghost." He would make his life with her unless Lee returned.

About the same time, Phillips recalled, officialdom caught up with him, in the form of an order from Allied headquarters to return to Vienna with his jeep and driver: "My task now was to make sure Lee got back to London." As long as she had Jemima, she had kept moving. But now, lacking transport and nearly broke, she had to admit that her plan to press on to Bulgaria seemed unlikely. They argued. John told her to go home to Roland: "That night Lee understood that Bucharest was the end of the line. Her war was finally over."

The next morning, Lee caught the train to Paris, then went to the Scribe.

She was exhausted. Her skin was covered with blotches; her hair was lank; her gums bled constantly. Living on her nerves for a year and a half had taken its toll. To *Life* staffer Rosemarie Redlich, who lived at the Scribe, "she looked very much the worse for wear." Redlich had been curious about the woman Dave Scherman had spoken of admiringly on his return to their New York office. While Lee had taught him about sex, he said, their affair was over: "He felt he had rescued her—but also himself—by sending her back to Roland."

On February 16, Lee ran into Roland, who had been celebrating his demobilization in Paris when he learned that she was on her way. He took her back to Downshire Hill, a burnt-out case. Not wanting to disrupt their long-standing relations, her rival, a blond art restorer named Gigi, moved out; Lee summoned the strength to make the commitment that Roland required. It was a compromise—and one that would include the continued presence in his life of Gigi, who was as charming and gentle as Lee was abrasive. (The niece of an art historian, Gigi shared Roland's values; unlike Lee, she drank, at most, a glass of sherry.) Lee accepted Roland's desire for another woman, she later wrote, "to prove that I loved you . . . the fact that your love for me was diluted and weakened was unimportant as long as you were happy."

One night he was massaging her feet, an experience that always gave her pleasure. "If only someone had massaged Hitler's feet like that there would have been no massacres," she murmured darkly. Despite Roland's efforts to reopen the London Gallery, the winter of 1946 was not a happy time in artistic circles. After seven years of mobilization, most felt demoralized and resented being told that they must choose between Russia and America. Food was still being rationed; shortages of staples increased in 1946 as supplies were redirected to the victims of the hostilities.

Lee's resumption of life at Downshire Hill was further complicated by the presence in London of Dave, who had returned from New York in January to do a photo-essay on Scotland Yard—but actually (he confessed to his brother Bill) to court an English researcher at Time-Life. He had taken a flat in St. James Place, near their office and far from Hampstead. But Lee's return was a major event. He felt responsible for her, he told Bill, because she was now "in bad odor with her office and home life." If she went to the United States, which seemed likely, he would write letters of introduction and lend her his car (not having been completely put off by the fate of Jemima). What he did not say was that Lee was interfering in his courtship, even though she was supposed to be patching things up with Roland. Reading between the lines, one senses Dave's abiding love for Lee, whose future he was trying to secure in spite of himself.

In March, as Lee alternated between rage and depression, Dave helped her with the *Vogue* article on Hungary; Timmie O'Brien, *Vogue's* managing editor, extracted a final draft by locking herself into Lee's bedroom one night with a bottle of whiskey. Lee told Audrey to use whatever parts she liked and promised to make her piece on Romania "non-scolding." Severely edited, both articles appeared in U.S. *Vogue* on May 15, an issue that also featured her advice for would-be photographers and a cover shot of a woman looking very much like Lee—photographed, ironically, by Cecil Beaton.

The issue, entitled "Travel and Camera, Charting Places and Clothes," sounded the note for postwar *élégantes*. "Now that everyone is camera-crazy," Lee wrote, the fashionable traveler's luggage should include two cameras (a Contax and a Rolleiflex), several lenses, a brush to remove dust, lens tissues, a photometer, and Scotch tape for accidents. Amateurs should remember to label exposed film, learn to say "Don't look at the camera" in the local tongue, and distract those who tried to interfere with "decoys and diversions." She warned of the medium's occupational hazards, ranging from "queasy stomach ulcers to mumbling jitters." (A stiff neck due to wearing too many gadgets on one's person could be dealt with by hiring "a small boy or a patient donkey.")

In the meantime, Dave lost patience with his Scotland Yard story and with London. He went to Paris on April 15 to start a book on literary France, but in his old room at the Scribe, gazing at Lee's jerry cans on the balcony, he wondered whether, as she had said, he was "a sucker." "I'm on my pratt," he told Bill, "no identity cards, no food tickets, no international touring club, no garage, no wife, no moustache, no expensive shops, no quaint little bistros in that little allee behind the Eglise de St-Simon-et-Ste-Eustache-de-chat-qui-puke." Lee was coming to Paris the following week to wind up her affairs. "Penrose almost gave her the run out," he continued, "but by herculean efforts I got her back in time, and after a touch and go month, maybe she's in the clear. . . . The best way to help patch things up is if they both go to America."

Lee felt sufficiently in the clear to celebrate her thirty-ninth birthday in Paris (Dave annotated his diary entry for April 23, "St. Lee's Day," though it was St. George's). They lunched with Michel de Brunhoff, saw Nusch Eluard, and parted on May 11, when Lee returned to London. Scherman's literary France project was taking shape with the help of Rosemarie Redlich: they had teamed up and would, in a few years' time, marry. The Scribe, Dave told his brother, was "very depressing, a few gnomes still hanging around from the war, nobody told 'em it's over." Lee, too, was finding the adjustment difficult. "She is having a tough time, largely through her own making," he reflected, "and sooner or later she is going to break all to pieces like a bum novel."

Part Five

Lady Penrose

Lee in Corsica, late 1940s

Chapter 15

Patching Things Up

(1946–50)

L ee and Roland flew to New York on May 19. The trip began well. Julien
Levy lent them his apartment. Since they had last been together, he
had divorced Joella, married the painter Muriel Streeter, and made the
gallery into a salon for the Surrealists exiled in New York during the war. The
Condé Nast staff celebrated Lee's homecoming. The American Museum of
Natural History asked for her help with an exhibition on France. Old friends,
amazed by her metamorphosis from muse to photojournalist, welcomed her as
a heroine.

After twelve years abroad, Lee was eager to see her parents. On the train to
Poughkeepsie with Roland, she pointed out the schools from which she had
been expelled as a prelude to his meeting with the Millers. Theodore made a
strong impression. Lee's father, Roland wrote, was "a highly skilled and inquis-
itive engineer" and a "benign atheist" whose educational theories had contributed to Lee's becoming "a menace to discipline." Theodore noted Lee's
efforts to improve her spirits by taking Roland for drives up the Hudson and,

unexpectedly, by cooking. While at home, she sorted through her photo-graphic equipment and the paintings stored at DeLaval during the war (including some of Roland's Picassos, Ernsts, and Mirós), which Vassar planned to exhibit before their return to London.

John Miller, his wife, Catherine, and their daughters, Patricia and Joanne, drove from their house in Long Island to greet Lee and Roland. Predictably, John and Lee quarreled. "She was not the same after the war," he recalled. "Her health had suffered and so had her looks," he continued, but more than her changed appearance, he noticed her irritability. During a visit to Bill Scherman, Lee felt so out of sorts that Bill wrote to ask Dave whether this was normal. "She is getting old and with it getting fat," Dave replied uncharitably, "and she won't face up to it." Gigi's presence in New York and Roland's trips to see her there would not have improved her temper. When in town together, Lee and Roland saw new friends like Alfred Barr and James Thrall Soby of the Museum of Modern Art, and Peggy Riley (later Rosamond Bernier), an ele-gant, vivacious writer who showed them around artistic Manhattan.

That summer, U.K. *Vogue* ran drawings of "those great war and post-war travellers, Lee Miller and Cecil Beaton." To the home office, she was a celebrity. Alexander Liberman, *Vogue*'s Russian émigré art director, had been thrilled by her accounts of the war: "She brought regular doses of reality, a commodity that had been lacking from *Vogue* until then." After persuading Edna Chase that Lee's coverage of the death camps had to be shown, Liber-man had chosen the images, done the layout, and run the headline, "Believe It." Lee's report on the linkup at the Elbe was equally impressive, he thought: "She was an adventurer and a Surrealist—going to the front was a Surrealist gesture." But she was also very American, he added: "She went religiously to Poughkeepsie to find her nourishment."

In New York, Lee photographed a number of celebrities—among them Damon Runyon, whose stories inspired the musical *Guys and Dolls;* Wilfredo Lam, a Cuban Surrealist painter; and her old friend Isamu Noguchi, who posed bare-chested among his sculptures. Despina Messinesi, Liberman's assistant, liked working with Lee because of her humor. "When you were pho-tographing luminaries," she recalled, "Lee got them to relax." Unlike Horst, Condé Nast's resident portraitist (who emerged from the camera's black hood with a scowl), Lee knew how to make her subjects laugh.

Her refusal to "dress" (in defiance of fashion, Lee wore trousers to work) shocked younger women at headquarters. Reflecting on Lee's career years later, photographer Frances McLaughlin-Gill remembered thinking that "she had everything—good looks, talent, and drive." "But Lee was a bit of a gypsy," she added, "which doesn't go with a career." She had made her way on her own, or with the help of male mentors, unlike the members of McLaughlin-Gill's generation, who were forming an association of women photographers.

Lee relied instead on members of the prewar *Vogue* family. Liberman had married Tatiana du Plessix after her husband's death in 1940. Since coming to the United States, Tata had been turning out whimsical hats for Manhattanites in her salon at Saks Fifth Avenue. "Tatiana had a past and Lee had a past," Liberman explained, "so they had a complicity about things that others didn't know" (including Lee's affair, in Paris, with Zizi Svirsky, who was often found playing the piano at the Libermans' apartment). Like Lee, Tata mocked bourgeois taste. "Diamonds are for suburbs," she liked to say. "Meenk is for football." But she too found it hard to understand Lee's disdain for fashion.

Between stays in Poughkeepsie, Lee and Roland looked up old friends. In 1941, with the help of the Emergency Rescue Committee (an organization backed in part by Peggy Guggenheim), Breton and his wife, Jacqueline Lamba, Victor Brauner, and others of their circle, including Max Ernst, had made their way to New York. After his release from internment, Max had gone to Lisbon, where Leonora Carrington was recovering from her breakdown in the company of a Mexican artist. He had joined the ménage consisting of Peggy, her ex-husband, Laurence Vail, and their two children, and Vail's four from his marriage to Kay Boyle—until plane seats were found for all. Max married Peggy in New York after the American declaration of war in 1941, when it seemed likely that he would be deported as an enemy alien.

Since then, Peggy's gallery, Art of This Century, had proved more successful than her marriage. Through Julien Levy, Max had met Dorothea Tanning, the high-spirited young artist whose canvases he selected for an all-women show there. The two fell in love. Soon Dorothea was attending parties in clothes decorated with snapshots of Max. Peggy vented her rage by dismissing her rival as someone who dressed in the worst possible taste—one of the many acid phrases in her memoir, *Out of This Century.*

Peggy's book, published in March 1946, had shocked members of the art world, who mostly took sides against its author, though some shunned Max and Dorothea (shortly after its publication, they moved to Arizona). When Lee and Roland arrived in May, people were still gossiping about Peggy's affairs and decoding her memoir's transparent disguises: "Florenz Dale" was Laurence Vail; "Ray Soil," Kay Boyle; "Beatrice," Leonora Carrington; and "Annacia Tinning," Dorothea Tanning. And while Roland ("Donald Wrenclose") did not object to Peggy's account of his taste for bondage, he *was* annoyed at being called a bad painter.

Lee and Roland planned to spend a week with Max and Dorothea on their way to Los Angeles to see Erik and Mafy, who had been there since 1941. They flew to Phoenix on July 23, then drove to Oak Creek Canyon, the artists' desert refuge near Sedona. "The surroundings were . . . like the most fantastic landscapes Max had painted," Roland noted, "as though he had designed the great red mountains and canyons himself." It was blisteringly hot. The house, which was still under construction, had no electricity or water; Dorothea cooked dinner outside on two stones.

For the next few days, they listened to Max chant exotic words like *sheetrock* and *two-by-four* while they coped with snakes, scorpions, centipedes, and the heat, which melted the tar on the roof. During a trip to the Grand Canyon, Lee was disappointed to see only "a large wet cloud filling it up to the brim," she told Bill Scherman, "so that it might quite easily have been a field full of sheep." On their return they watched the Hopis perform a rain dance and cooled off in the nearby creek. Lee recovered sufficiently to inspect the jagged desert shapes—Cathedral Rock and the suggestively named Cleopatra's Nipple.

On their last day, photographing nonstop, she used the building site to frame Surrealist interiors: Max and Dorothea through a just-completed window, the couple wiping dishes with Roland, Max cavorting in a Hopi mask. Other shots show group dips in Oak Creek, Max and his dog on a raft, Max sitting yogilike while hammering floorboards. Still others focus on the couple's highly self-referential art. Dorothea poses in front of a recent painting entitled *Maternity,* which shows a woman in a tattered gown holding a large, angry infant; in another shot, Max and Dorothea admire this canvas—a declaration, perhaps, of their decision to give birth to a life of shared inventiveness rather than have children.

For a composition that takes a more ironic view of their relations, Lee posed the couple in the rocky landscape—at the precise distance from each other that makes Max seem a giant and Dorothea a tiny figure shaking her fist at him. This wry image works on many levels. A comment on their respective status in the art world, it hints that even in a marriage of equals, the woman is diminished. "We cannot help . . . but read into this photograph a sense of protest," Jane Livingston notes. "At the very least, we glean from this image a feeling of feminine ambivalence in relation to a virile and creatively empowered man."

One would like to have been present while Lee and Dorothea discussed these matters. "A woman had to be a monster to be an artist," Dorothea mused years later, "and one who married another artist was branded—like a cow." (She also insisted that while there were many pitfalls for women artists, gender was not among them.) During her last day there, Lee staged two portraits on this theme, one of Max, the other of herself—both framed by an unfinished door. In one, Max stands bare-chested, gazing at the camera; in the other, an equally bare-chested Lee echoes his pose but presents her good profile. A portrait of the artist framed by his unfinished creation was a kind of joke, yet at the same time, Lee's composition sets herself up as equal to the "creatively empowered man" on whom she turned her gaze.

Lee and Roland landed in Los Angeles on August 17. Erik and Mafy did everything to make them feel welcome; the couple's affection buoyed Lee's spirits. Their fortunes had improved since 1941. Erik had found his calling as a photographer of airplanes at Lockheed; they had settled into the easygoing rhythms of California life. "Everyone goes around cherishing the idea that they're all slightly looney and behave in a surrealist manner which isn't the case at all," Lee told Bill Scherman.

Man Ray, who had lived nearby, on Vine Street, since 1940, shared Lee's view of the locals. Visitors to this busy part of town were surprised to discover the calm of Man's duplex, which was shaded by palm trees. While its upstairs balcony may have reminded Lee of the rue Campagne-Première, his new muse, a dark-haired dancer named Juliet Browner, in no way resembled Lee. A gentle, graceful young woman, she did whatever Man wanted. Yet the many photos of Juliet on the walls recalled those he had taken of Lee and, before her, Kiki—since female subjects were, in a way, interchangeable while their erotic energy inspired him.

Man called his new home "a beautiful prison" and often said that while New York was twenty years behind Paris where art was concerned, Los Angeles was twenty years behind New York. He missed Paris, especially the paintings, photographs, and objects he had left with Ady. Even more, he missed being known as an artist, having returned to an America where collectors sought out not *l'américain de Montparnasse* but the publicity-conscious Salvador Dalí. As a way of re-creating his private universe, Man was reconstructing some of his favorite works, which he planned to show under the title "Objects of My Affection." These objects included a small version of *Observatory Time*, the painting in which Lee's lips float in the Paris sky. One wonders what she made of this reduced image of their relationship.

Lee was also keen to see Mary Anita Loos, who by 1946 was a successful screenwriter whose friends included Paulette Goddard, Joan Crawford, and Cary Grant. When Lee introduced Roland and told Mary Anita about the Hopi dances they had witnessed, her friend noticed a sadness in her face. "She seemed worn down," Mary Anita recalled. "It seemed to me that she had been drained. The weight of what she had been through showed in her glance when we spoke about the future." Lee had changed, she added, "except for her strong character."

Vogue had commissioned Lee to photograph some of the celebrities who made Hollywood their home during the war. Her portrait of Igor Stravinsky focuses on the composer's muscular hands and pensive gaze. She took a series of informal shots at friends' houses, some on a visit to the Dada patron and poet Walter Arensberg, who showed her and Roland his collection of works by Duchamp. At Man's duplex, she photographed Juliet playing chess with Man, using one of the sleek Art Deco sets he designed as a source of income: in a variation on the theme of the muse, Juliet looks at her partner, invisible except for his hand, which is poised to take her pawn. Another shot, a double portrait of Man and Roland positioned at an angle to the oval mirror in which we see their profiles, parodies this classic pose, which Man had used for Lee's solarized profile.

Friends had arranged for Lee to visit a Francophile chef named M. F. K. Fisher, but their interview was canceled at the last minute when the producers of a radio show featuring visiting celebrities persuaded *Vogue*'s "real live lady war correspondent" to appear on the program. The interviewer, Ona Munson, the actress who played Rhett Butler's mistress in *Gone with the Wind,* met Lee and Roland in a Hollywood hotel. Munson's gushy tone dominates the interview. She began by saying that she hoped to interview Roland as well, since "two women need a man to balance the conversation." Promising to try "to sound like a fabulous character," Lee explained how she became Man's student, her "accidental" start as a writer, and her entry into war work. Minimizing her determination, she added, "I was very lucky."

When Munson asked how she had managed to photograph at the front, Lee replied coyly, "You can't blame a girl for that when she has a battle right in her lap!" The interview continued in this vein until Munson asked what Lee was doing in Hitler's bathtub. "I'd have to go back a bit," she began. Having long been fascinated by the Führer, she had gone to his house in Munich. "I took some pictures of the place and I also got a good night's sleep in Hitler's bed," she went on. "I even washed the dirt of Dachau off in his tub." *Vogue* had been right to print her atrocity pictures, Munson felt, because otherwise "most of us would think it had been a hideous nightmare." With unusual restraint, Lee replied, "Yes, here in America it does seem like that."

By mid-September, when she and Roland returned to New York, Lee knew that despite her love of the United States, she was too European to live there. They spent September seeing old and new friends. *Art News* sent a staffer to interview Roland about his collection. Having been brought up surrounded by Victoriana, he explained, he had formed a loathing for curios; he had been drawn through personal sympathy to the works that made up his collection. At the same time, his cordial relations with people like Barr and Soby of the Museum of Modern Art confirmed his desire to create its London equivalent, a strong modern collection that would build on his own.

Lee and Roland flew to London on September 30. Energized by his time in New York, Roland threw himself into the project that would take shape as the Institute of Contemporary Arts (ICA). Herbert Read, E. L. T. Mesens, and Douglas Cooper, an art historian and collector who, like Roland, idolized Picasso, formed the fledgling center's nucleus until Cooper turned against

Roland and resigned. (Roland was heard to say that having Cooper as his enemy, he needed no others.) With Lee's consent, he continued to see Gigi after her return to London.

That autumn, surprising news came from Los Angeles. On October 24, Max and Dorothea were married by a justice of the peace; Man and Juliet formalized their union on the same occasion. Their unlikely double wedding, which sent up the institution, was described as surreal in the Los Angeles papers. (Man took pictures of Dorothea, who painted Juliet as a bride; both couples had fun with their respective roles by playing dress-up, Max and Man in dresses, Juliet sporting a black mustache.) Unsure of what her own future held, Lee reported to Brogue.

The change in her attitude was clear to Lee's friends on the staff. Alex Kroll, then U.K. *Vogue*'s art director, believed that she was "bottled up" as a result of the war: "I felt a screen while talking to her," he explained. "I couldn't get through." Audrey was aware that Lee's assignments after her return failed to inspire her and wondered whether her talents might have been better employed with the photographic collective Magnum, then being set up by Cartier-Bresson and Capa, whose vision of photojournalism resembled her own. But for the next five years, Lee worked mainly as a *Vogue* photographer; the stories accompanying her images were often written by others.

That autumn, she spent three weeks in Ireland photographing Joyce's Dublin while rereading his work ("try reading Ulysses or Finnegan's [sic] Wake," she told her parents) and frequenting his favorite pubs. On her return, she photographed several "Bright Young Things," a new production of *Carmen*, middle-class children at the circus and working-class ones at a toy theater. In her shots of its miniature stage one senses a reduction of scope and imaginative response. In December, the news of Nusch Eluard's death deepened her sense of loss.

When Audrey arranged for Lee to go to Switzerland with *Vogue*'s newly appointed arts writer Rosamond (Peggy) Riley, she summoned up her enthusiasm. In the new year, they would travel to Saint Moritz, "scene of Aziz's and my romance," she told the Millers, then Berne, Lausanne, Zurich, and Geneva. Before leaving, Lee and Roland inspected the house across the street. "The owners were looking for a smaller house," she went on, "so we sold to each other." She looked forward to having a workroom where "all my camera junk and things I never pick up at all can just be locked in and Roland can't complain anymore that there is no place for breakfast because of my typewriters, or to sleep because of my negatives are spread out, or to bathe because I'm rinsing prints in the bathtub." What was more, she was negotiating her divorce from Aziz. Now that they had become "a little more amiable," he would either meet her in Berne or come to London to settle things.

Lee was to photograph the beautiful people at Saint Moritz, then take portraits of Swiss celebrities. Despina Messinesi, by then Paris correspondent for U.S. *Vogue,* would join her to write up the winter season and Rosamond would do the luminaries. While Lee's return to Saint Moritz was uneventful, she detested the place, she told Roland, especially the "international crooks and exiled royalty" at their hotel. Carrying out her assignment nonetheless, she photographed socialites on the slopes in the new fashion, stretch pants. Since their après-ski chitchat revolved around "how awful the people are this season," Lee was soon drinking too much. Her ski gear didn't fit; she wanted her combat boots—which were by now an extension of her self. On learning that Aziz's villa was to be sold at auction, she told Roland, "I miss you very much and wish I were home."

In the next weeks, Lee and Rosamond crisscrossed Switzerland to interview artists and intellectuals: Jean Arp, Hermann Hesse, Albert Skira, Arthur Honegger, Jean Piaget, and C. G. Jung. Between portrait sessions, she did what she could to amuse herself. "I could not have had a more entertaining, though drunken, companion," Rosamond recalled of their time together. Lee was curious about everything, a spontaneous, thoughtful, generous friend. But she had "lost her delicate beauty" and showed "a total disregard for her dress"—an attitude with which her friend was not sympathetic.

Together they visited a children's village near Lake Constance, where orphans lived in homes run by "parents" from their own countries. Lee photographed a French girl feeding her doll, whose hair bow matched her own. The children at the Polish house were well dressed but obviously disturbed. One boy, who had promised his dying mother to watch over his sister, had to be persuaded that the pediatrician would not harm her. Another drew pictures of Warsaw in flames: Lee photographed him in front of his war tableau, drawn on a blackboard in colored chalks. Of the blond Polish children whom the Nazis had deported to be raised as Aryans, Rosamond observed, "even their identities are lost. Many of them are too young to remember who they were before they were given new German names."

Lee was waiting to confirm an appointment with the Swiss president when she made an unexpected discovery. At the age of thirty-nine, she was pregnant. Feeling "rather peculiar about it," she wrote Roland a few days later:

> Darling, This is a hell of a romantic way to tell you that I'll shortly be knitting little clothes for a little man. . . . So far no resentment or anguish or mind changing or panic, only a mild astonishment that I'm so happy about it. I've had to tell Peggy [Rosamond], as otherwise she couldn't understand my insistence on returning so immediately to London when the job isn't really thru.

So much of their time was spent trying to keep track of Lee's tripod, she joked, that they feared the baby might have three legs. The letter concludes: "There is only one thing. MY WORK ROOM IS NOT GOING TO BE A NURSERY. How about your studio?"

When Lee returned to London in February, it was so cold that the pipes froze. Their supplies of coal and wood having run out, Lee and Roland burnt the base of a statue and two sets of bed legs to keep warm. "Just as I was eyeing some South Sea island sculpture in teak and mahogany, a neighbor lent us a sack of wood," she told the Millers. "Roland seems as impervious to the cold as he was to the heat in America," she went on. Oddly, this letter does not mention her pregnancy, but complains about having to sort negatives: "Every time I go on a story, I'm enthusiastic and bite off large hunks of stuff, and am mad with rage on return when I have to digest it all."

They moved to the new house, which had room for two studios and a nursery, at the end of February. While Roland wanted to legitimize his heir by marrying Lee once her divorce was final, some in their circle saw Lee's pregnancy as a last-ditch effort to hold on to him. In March, after summoning up the courage to tell her parents the news, Lee developed pleurisy, followed by pneumonia and a virus resembling the mumps. Nurses were hired after her confinement to bed—the warmest place to be, although not the best treatment for her back, which despite the bear massage had grown worse. "Due to all this illness I'm going to be all the more dependent on you for the things I'll need for the baby," she told the Millers.

"This baby business isn't all it's cracked up to be," Lee confessed soon after her fortieth birthday: "If anyone even ever mentions to me again how much I'm going to love it once I have it, I'm going to sock them in the nose." Roland was "angelic" when back pain made her miserable, but both were "depressed." As for the child's sex, it would have to be a boy, "so that it can use bad language becomingly, and I can play with engines and choo choo cars." She asked for knitting needles, wool for baby clothes, and fine white woolen fabric for nighties. While she had learned "to sew a fine seam" and would soon take up knitting, the lack of real work had reduced her to crossword puzzles: "It's very disappointing as it's the first time I've not been having work on my mind since 1939."

That spring, Aziz came to London to divorce Lee according to Muslim law. He and Valentine both stayed at Downshire Hill, forming an unusual but amicable household. Aziz entertained them with tales from *The Arabian Nights*; Roland, inspired by the acid colors of Picasso's portraits of Lee, depicted her as a goddess holding her globe-shaped belly, which shelters a rather reptilian fetus. Given a pregnant woman's prerogative, Lee made strange requests—an aquatic salamander called an axolotl (which may have inspired Roland's painting) and a family of hedgehogs, who were later set free on Hampstead Heath. After marrying Roland at the Hampstead Registry Office on May 3, Lee went back to bed.

Visitors were a distraction. In July, Jackie Braun, the former head of Lee's

Lee pregnant, 1947
(Alexander Liberman)

New York studio, came to stay. She took over the household and organized the layette. "You'd think it was her child," Lee told her parents; "she's so interested in it, much more than me." When Alex Liberman called at Downshire Hill, he photographed Lee resplendent in a green silk Chinese robe, though she felt that she "look[ed] and weigh[ed] about the same as a hippopotamus." The photographer Clifford Coffin, whom Audrey had recruited from New York when it seemed that Lee had disappeared in Eastern Europe, shot a series of portraits of her in the same gown. She took her former model's poses, profile, three-quarter turn, head shot; at the end of the session, he took a relaxed close-up that shows Lee's amusement with the process—or perhaps her sense that she was a different woman from the one who had sat for Steichen, Huene, and Horst.

Lee felt "apprehensive" about the baby, she told the Millers. Since child-birth at her age was considered risky, she planned to have a cesarean. "I think of all the worst things, such as it being a girl, or twins, or having six fingers, or birthmarks or being an idiot. The rest of the time I'm plain scared of the oper-

Portraits

Charlie Chaplin. Paris, 1930

Tanja Ramm. Paris, 1931

Eileen Agar. Brighton, 1937

Martha Gellhorn. London, 1943

Jean Cocteau. Palais Royal colonnade, Paris, 1944

Dorothea Tanning with her painting *Maternity*. Arizona, 1946

Pablo Picasso and Antony Penrose. Farley Farm, Sussex, 1950

Pablo Picasso. Villa La Californie, Cannes, 1958

ation, or tired and exhausted." Her parents outdid themselves with parcels of goods unobtainable in England: soap flakes, baby clothes, diapers, bed jackets, maternity smocks, dried milk, juices, and olive oil. Toward the end of the summer, Lee requested silk thread, name tapes, satin ribbon, and Fels Naptha for the layette, all required by the maternity clinic. Cesareans were performed at the last minute, she explained, "never just because of age and desire to have it that way." But taking into account her mental and physical state, her doctor had scheduled the operation for September 9. "So now I sleep much better," her letter concludes, "as I've got everything arranged."

In the last weeks of pregnancy Lee tried to take charge by making still more lists: for hospital, makeup, gin, cigarettes, playing cards, pen and paper, a typewriter and table, ear plugs, nail scissors, and knitting (her list specifies "pink"). In a semihumorous *Vogue* piece published the following year, she counseled expectant readers to create an "island of safety" around themselves while awaiting the event. It was wise to have things that made one comfortable—smart bed jackets, bras with hooks in the front, cosmetics that held up under bright lights, a radio, crossword puzzles, books that were neither long nor taxing, and "a written list with addresses and numbers of everyone who should be told the glad tidings."

Lee felt less jaunty than this account suggests. The night before the surgery, she wrote to Florence: "Dearest Mother, Tomorrow morning, almost without waking, I'll be a mother also. More than forty years ago you must have been waiting in somewhat the same way, curious, apprehensive and elated." Had Florence hoped that her baby would some day "understand all you did and dreamed?" Had she been disappointed "when a noisy stupid little brute appeared . . . who was insistent, demanding, uncooperative and ignorant after you'd felt such friendship and tolerance for many months?" Lee's fears became more obvious with each question: "Did you worry whether I'd be a monster? . . . Did you know you'd love me?" She wished Florence was there to tell her.

Early the next morning, she wrote instructions for Roland in the event of her death. Her finances were for his or Junior's use. Her cameras should go to Erik or else "someone with real talent," Cartier-Bresson or Berenice Abbott. Junior must not become a Germanophile, she warned, "or I'll come back to haunt him." Comparing childbirth with other times when she had awoken to realize that she was fully committed—plane flights, dawn attacks, marriage— she wrote, "and now a baby. This is like being a dumb beast, knowing something is happening, automatically house hunting and 'nesting,' but not quite realising the import of it."

The rest of Lee's dawn confession must be quoted at length: "I keep saying to everyone, 'I didn't waste a minute, all my life—I had a wonderful time,' but I know, myself, now, that if I had it over again I'd be even more free with my ideas, with my body and my affection. Above all, I'd try to find some way of breaking down, through the silence which imposes itself on me in matters of sentiment. I'd have let you, Roland, know how much and how passionately and how tenderly I love you. Next week, if I'm here, I'll probably be as off-hand again as in the past, or, at least, seem to. Does it puzzle you? You know that I love you, don't you?"

It had been impossible to tell him this the year before, when she returned from Romania "inarticulate with shock." She hoped that her decisions to accept his relations with Gigi and, now, to have the baby were proof of her love. In recent months, she had felt relaxed—"without a trace of the old urge to be out and . . . embarking on adventures." But while childbirth *was* an adventure, the sound of the nurse's trolley as it approached resembled "the swish and rattle of doom."

Junior proved to be a healthy boy. During the operation, Roland waited at home with Eluard, who was recovering from a triangular love affair that he had hoped could reconcile him to the loss of Nusch. After seeing his son for the first time Roland told the Millers, "He is so ugly, snout like a pig, hands like a bruiser and the toughest looks ever known." A name had not yet been chosen: "Lee insists on Butch Roland Penrose. I say no but a compromise on the lines of Anthony seems preferable." The baby was being bottle-fed. Lee, who was still being stitched together, had not yet experienced "the joys of motherhood."

In good Surrealist style, Eluard commemorated the birth with a poem: *"La beauté de Lee aujourd'hui / Anthony / C'est du soleil sur ton lit."* In rhyming *Lee* and *lit,* Eluard no doubt intended a compliment that is lost in translation. Yet the gist is clear: Lee's new beauty, in the form of Anthony, shines like the sun on her bed. Named Anthony William Roland Penrose (he would later drop the "h" to become Antony), Butch and his mother went home after a week in the hospital.

∞

Lee's letters to her parents over the next year and a half, as she coped with motherhood, unreliable help, and continued rationing, show her reliance on their willingness to come to her aid. After her return to Downshire Hill, Lee's highly strung maternity nurse looked after the baby for a month, then returned to the clinic. Her replacement handled the situation briskly, but on her days off, she left Anthony in such a state that he screamed and vomited—whereupon Lee, too, became so distraught, she told the Millers, "that I'd get my old stomach spasms too and start shooting my cookies, and life was hell."

This state of affairs lasted until November, with the arrival of a calm, elderly nurse named Mollie Woodward. Nanny Woodward was set in her ways, which struck Lee as old-fashioned: infants required one nursery for daytime and another for the night, with room for the nanny; they were to be fed on schedule and toilet trained as soon as possible. But she was willing to consider Lee's theories (one nursery, where the baby slept alone, feeding on demand, no toilet training for a year). Even more important, she did not object to her employers' unconventional household.

At two months, Butch had become "awfully cute," Lee told her parents. He giggled, followed his parents with his eyes, and gazed at a blue butterfly mounted under glass and at Roland's red necktie. (He might be a lepidopterist with communist leanings, she joked.) By December, he was smiling, cooing, and waving his limbs "like a real baby," she wrote, "and knows who Nanny is, and sometimes recognizes me or Roland as being at least familiar masses of flesh or color and noise." Since she was giving him a goldfish bowl for Christmas, she asked Theodore for the castle that had been in his fish tank since her childhood.

About this time, Audrey asked *Vogue*'s photographers to contribute one image that conjured up Christmas for the December issue. Lee took a portrait of Anthony, yawning beneath a tinsel-bedecked party hat. Her caption reads, "Gay tinsel and a brand new baby is my formula for a Merry Christmas this year. Maybe by the time he finds there isn't any Santa Claus this not so shiny world won't need one as badly as it does now." The portrait, which ran between Clifford Coffin's version of an English pantomime and John Deakin's shot of a diamond-encrusted Mae West, produced quantities of "fan mail," Lee told her parents, from acquaintances for whom it took the place of a birth announcement. "Poor little buggar, working for his living already," she teased. "Imagine your first pay check when you're six weeks old."

Before returning to Brogue in January, Lee had to solve the problem of disappearing supplies, which had plagued them since the arrival of their new housekeeper, who seemed to be feeding her adolescent son better than she was her employers. When the woman said that the work was too much for her, Lee fired her. "Of course that leaves me high and dry," she told her parents: she would have to do all the cooking during the Christmas holidays, when Rosamond and an American antique dealer would be their guests. "But I'd rather do it than see her sour face around any longer," Lee added, before requesting the culinary items—hickory-smoked salt, onion powder, grated cheese, ham, chocolates—that would help her through the holidays.

Unexpectedly, two Polish refugees, a mother and daughter, turned up the day that the thieving housekeeper departed. Since they didn't speak English, Lee used her own form of sign language—a method of communication whose humor was compounded by their dismay on being asked to cook shellfish, which they had never seen, and mushrooms, which, they believed, would poison the household, a fate they enacted in pantomime.

A large part of each letter home requested items unobtainable in Britain.

Given the postwar lack of staples like sugar, flour, and powdered milk, and the low standard of daily fare (Lee deplored the English tendency to boil vegetables into submission), her interest in cookery became a passion. Making an apple pie while waiting for the Poles was amusing except that having tippled while baking, she became "slightly tight," she told her parents. Cooking was a way to make the best of the situation while providing family and friends with good food in a time of culinary famine, but it was also an occupation that kept her in the moment, occupying her hands and mind in somewhat the way that photography had done, though in very different circumstances.

Lee hoped to use her furlough to shed the weight she had gained and strengthen her back. But despite attempts to limit her intake (except for alcohol), her clothes did not fit. And the treatment prescribed by her doctor—"agonizing girdles all strutted with steel bones"—protected her spine but poked "into every other part of my anatomy." These girdles did little for her libido, which had been low since childbirth. Since sexual relations no longer gave her pleasure, one assumes that Roland's feelings for other women—Gigi having ended their affair—were freely expressed. For those who had known Lee during the war, it would have been startling to visit the household over which she reigned in apparent tranquillity. "Am getting so fascinated by Butch," she told her parents, "that I'm considering not going back to work right away. As you say this will only happen once and I don't want to miss it."

After Christmas, catered in large part by the Millers' care packages, Lee began acting as Roland's secretary. He was "getting the dream idea of his life going," she told them: it was "a sort of thing like the Museum of Modern Art." After addressing several thousand invitations to the opening, she felt like the poor little match girl, she went on, or one of the children in stories "who addressed envelopes for thruppence a hundred with rheumatic hands, sitting in cold garrets." Rewarding herself after the completion of her task, Lee baked a pumpkin pie using ingredients sent by her parents: brown sugar, molasses, evaporated milk, and canned pumpkin. "I'll see that we drink a toast to you when we eat it," she joked.

The inaugural exhibit of the Institute of Contemporary Arts, "Forty Years of Modern Art," opened on February 10, 1948, in the basement of the Academy Cinema, on Oxford Street. Consisting of paintings and sculptures from private collections, including Roland's, it featured works by Picasso, Braque, Matisse, Dalí, de Chirico, and Magritte, as well as Lucian Freud, John Craxton, and Eduardo Paolozzi—who were included to encourage British artists. The show attracted attention to Roland's venture, but also resentment among those who felt that he had left the avant-garde and gone establishment. He should be asked to resign, Geoffrey Grigson wrote, "on the grounds that his position as a minor painter, buttressed by wealth and indeed by taste, and his sincere energy in furthering the ICA, does not outweigh his pursuit of compromise which is making the ICA ridiculous to those very artists it should help."

Unperturbed by criticism, Roland helped find a home for the ICA on Fitzroy Street. Ewan Phillips of the Courtauld Institute was chosen as the director; he was soon joined by a spirited young woman named Julie Lawson, whose organizational skills and languages were invaluable in the running of the institute. While Lee no longer had to address envelopes, she often lent her energy and talent to the furthering of the ICA: planning receptions, taking photographs, writing reviews, and inviting the artists and their spouses to stay in Hampstead. It was an ambiguous role, one that meant taking second place while sometimes feeling as if she were being paid thruppence a hundred—though she was rarely heard to complain.

There were other compensations. With Nanny Woodward in charge of Anthony and the Poles running the household, Lee and Roland could resume their travels. Ten years after their summer encampment at Lambe Creek, they stayed there again under calmer circumstances with Roland's brother Beacus. In the summer of 1948 they went to Venice for the Biennale, which Lee was to cover for *Vogue*—her first assignment in over a year. The Biennale's national pavilions had shown primarily academic art before the war. That summer, the presence in Venice for the first time of works by the masters of modern art and the outstanding postwar Italian artists was generating a buzz among the Serenissima's visitors.

Making the round of the British exhibits, Lee noted the contrast between their muted hues and the dazzle outside. Turner's canvases looked "almost Cubist in the subtlety of their colour after the bombardment of brilliance which makes up the Venetian scene," she wrote. In the same way, the contours of Henry Moore's sculptures were "reassuring" after hours in the sun. Like his statues, Moore was a familiar presence: "stocky, un-Latin, serious, and simple," he used his hands to communicate with his Italian counterparts and sipped Americanos (vermouth and soda) at the Piazza San Marco, where Lee took his portrait.

Of the five Italian artists whom she photographed beside their creations, Lee preferred those whose work showed a light heart, progressive leanings, or both. Renato Guttuso, "a vast, untidy, and charming Roman" whose scathingly anti-German drawings impressed her, blended abstraction with social themes, she noted, in the manner of Picasso's *Guernica*. Similarly, the Venetian Giuseppe Santomaso adapted modernist abstraction to scenes of daily life, "which assumed a sharper meaning during the terrible years of the war." Pleased to see that the art world had rediscovered the Metaphysicals—de Chirico, Morandi, Carrà—after a long period of neglect, she also admired Marino Marini's equestrian statues, which combined "the mysterious aura of Chinese dynasty art and the vitality of modern good humour."

While Roland may have had mixed feelings about seeing Peggy Guggenheim, Lee enjoyed their visit to her pavilion, the hit of the Biennale. Having moved her collection to Venice, Peggy intended to give it a permanent home after acquiring a suitable palazzo. "Her selection of 136 paintings, sculptures, and objects makes a historical survey of the trends of modern art from Dadaism through Cubism, Abstraction, and Surrealism," Lee observed in her *Vogue* article. What was more, seen together, Peggy's Ernsts, Picassos, and Brancusis "point[ed] up the significance of each artist in relation to the others." They took part in the general excitement—which was so contagious that an eminent Italian critic had been seen playing with Peggy's Calder mobile. Lee photographed Peggy with her Lhasa Apsos, "who flip-flopped around the exhibition looking extraordinarily like the dogs of the Renaissance Venetians," she concluded, "making her spectacular show look very much at home."

After Lee's review ran in both the U.S. and U.K. editions, the Condé Nast office drew up a new contract for "Lee Miller Penrose . . . hereinafter called Lee Miller." She was to write and take photographs for eight features per year. The company would supply film, equipment, and an assistant; when work took her outside London, they would pay expenses. She was to receive fixed remuneration (fifty pounds for short articles, seventy-five for longer ones). Although others could not use her photographs without Condé Nast's consent, the contract allowed an important exception. The Magnum Agency and its clients could publish her work, "but it shall not bear Miller's credit line." At this point, Lee hoped to reactivate her connections with Capa, whose reports on the USSR she had been reading. (Recommending them to her parents earlier that year, she explained, "I gave up reading anything about Russia or the Russians unless I personally knew and respected the author.")

Presumably she discussed these matters with Theodore when he and Florence came to England that summer. They brought suitcases full of toys for their grandson (now called Tony), household supplies, and foodstuffs, including a once-frozen roast beef that survived the trip to London. Florence was glad to find that conditions were not as dire as she had thought them from Lee's letters; when petrol became more readily available, they visited Ely, Cambridge, Stonehenge, and Truro, where they stayed with Beacus before driving to Land's End. In September, they helped organize Tony's first birthday party, a picnic on the lawn. On October 6, Theodore met the staff at Brogue and later, Lee's physician, Dr. Goldman, who told him about "neuroses brought on partly by the war," without recommending treatment. During their four-month stay, Theodore inspected power plants, bridges, and factories, shopped with Lee for gadgets, and made himself useful by repairing faucets, window sashes, and doorlocks. Before leaving at the end of October, he told Roland, "Florence and I have considered everything very carefully, and we want you to know that this is all not half as bad as we expected."

After their departure, Roland assembled the next ICA exhibit, provocatively titled "40,000 Years of Modern Art." Its purpose, to show modern masterpieces next to the ethnographic works that had in some way inspired them, seemed shocking at a time when many dismissed non-Western art. But to the young British artists in revolt against the social and aesthetic values that dominated the art world, the exhibit's nonhierarchical display broke down deep-seated distinctions between high and low, civilized and primitive, timeless and contemporary.

Welcoming any approach that turned authority on its head, Lee wrote a sprightly review. "In the time of our grandmothers," she began, "all primitive art was regarded as an ugly, beastly and sinful manifestation of idol worship." Taking *Vogue* readers on a vicarious stroll through the hall, she noted the "confrontations" created by the placement of a Henry Moore statue next to a prehistoric Venus, an elongated Modigliani beside a similarly shaped spirit carving from Gabon, Ibibio masks next to Picasso's *Demoiselles d'Avignon*. "Some of the confrontations are so gently allusive and subtle that they are to be sensed, not seen," she explained—like the affinity between the Ivory Coast carvings and Cubism. This exhibit would open visitors' eyes in the same way that ethnographic objects had "opened the new wider horizon to the artist."

When the show closed in January, Roland and Lee turned their attention to another of his dreams, life as a gentleman farmer. It made sense to have a country place where Tony could grow up in traditional surroundings; after the war, the price of rural property was low. Harry Yoxall informed them of a farm for sale in East Sussex, in the wonderfully named hamlet of Muddles Green, part of the parish of Chiddingly. It had the advantage of being near Lewes, which had good rail service to London, and Newhaven, where one could take the ferry to France. On the day they went to inspect, they could see only the house, which was large and well-proportioned. Farley Farm was blanketed by fog. Undeterred, Roland bought the property for £22,500—including the house, two hundred acres, three cottages, two barns, several sheds, and a malt house.

On their next visit, the sun shone brightly. Gazing toward the South Downs and the Channel, Roland spied the outlines of a prehistoric form cut into the turf to mark the solstice, the Long Man of Wilmington. The house's alignment with this spirit guardian, he later wrote, "gave Farley Farm a position in harmony with the sun, the moon and the stars in the heavens." The Long Man was an omen full of promise for the next phase of their life.

While Lee initially shared his enthusiasm, after months of struggling with the lack of creature comforts, especially heat, and the logistics of running two houses, she was heard to protest, "Fuck living in the country." In March, on Tony's first visit to the farm, the house was so cold that he, too, complained. Doors slammed, beams creaked, gale winds whistled through the cracks in the windows. The lack of carpets and curtains let in the Sussex mists; repairs were out of the question due to postwar shortages. Everyone huddled around the large Raeburn stove while Lee cooked for herself, Roland, Tony, and their guests.

Ironically, while attempting to make the farm habitable, Lee was writing a piece entitled "Bachelor Entertaining," in which she disclosed the secrets of London hosts whose kitchens resembled ship's cabins. Her friend Fred Bartlett of the U.S. Foreign Service ("and therefore nomadic," she observed in an aside) regularly performed "a magician's act of making a salad dressing in plain view of the audience to distract attention." John Tillotson, a publisher, did not allow anyone in the kitchen. (His rules for entertaining included practicing new dishes on oneself and noting preparation times in the margins of cookbooks.) An acquaintance with one gas burner cooked ahead and kept meals hot in insulated containers; a scientist friend steamed asparagus in a beaker and fried eggs on his Bunsen burner. One senses that Lee imagined herself cooking under similar circumstances.

"Here is a partial diary of the past few months," she told the Millers. "Go every Friday to country, taking all food and clothes and leftovers, where I cook and entertain a minimum of four guests beside ourselves . . . garden and weed like mad, try to make curtains and things and come back to London on Monday bringing all leftovers and family and dirty clothes. Work all week until Friday, do marketing for food to take back to country and run for trains and god knows what." The Poles having departed, she did all the cooking while also shooting fashions for *Vogue* and *Picture Post,* the U.K. counterpart to *Life.*

That spring, Lee went to Sicily for a *Vogue* feature on "travelling at ease" with BOAC. On the way to the airport, she suddenly felt "all sorts of panic about leaving you & Tony," she confessed to Roland. Before leaving she had been unable to tell him "how much I love you & how terribly happy I've been this last year, so much that I'm scared that it'll have a horrible pay off"—as if sorrow would inevitably replace happiness.

Despite Lee's ambivalence about the assignment, a ten-page spread of her photographs (chosen from the hundreds on her contact sheets) documented the *Vogue* team's flight from wintry England. Included in the group is one of Lee's most evocative images from this time: a stylish traveler shot in profile, her coat a circle in the wind, her hand shading her eyes as she gazes, and directs our gaze, toward the silvery airplane wing behind her. (This image compares oddly with Lee's 1942 shots of Bourke-White kneeling in front of "her" bomber.) But once in Sicily, photographing the models sunbathing in shorts or legs covered by cinch-waisted skirts gave her no time to follow their example.

"Travelling at Ease" ran in the May 1949 issue, which also included shots of people in the news—Cecil Beaton's triple portrait of Edith, Sacheverell, and Osbert Sitwell, and Lee's photograph of a pensive Roland in front of one of his paintings. "Roland Penrose holds an exhibition at the London Gallery," the copy ran. "He is a collector and authority on the Surrealist School as well as a painter, and is married to Vogue photographer Lee Miller." Soon after Roland's opening, Lee's back pain became worse, and the new cook gave notice on learning that they planned to spend the summer in the country.

Running two homes was "too much for me," she told her parents. "With my job to do as well it's sort of a handful." Consequently they were renting a two-bedroom apartment on Hornton Street, in Kensington—"no stairs [and] central heating"—and putting the Hampstead house up for sale. With summer approaching, she hoped to make quantities of jam with the fruit at the farm, provided the Millers could send enough sugar. She and Roland would also spend a few weeks in France, at Rosamond's Paris apartment, then at l'Hôtel Vaste Horizon in Mougins, where they would revisit the scene of prewar frolics with Picasso.

Lee's letters ignore, as she tried to do at this time, the contradictory nature of her double commitment: to her career, on the one hand, and to Roland's bucolic vision, on the other. Attempting to save energy by turning the farm into a subject or a setting, she put their adventures in a humorous light. "Our first summer on the farm was a camping foray in a practically empty house," she recalled in a *Vogue* piece on getting weekend guests to work, à la Tom Sawyer. "We never stopped laughing and learning while dealing with crumbly brick floors, ice-less larder techniques and the construction of pelmets."

To her parents she confided the realities of country life. During one of the worst gales in history, they had to move the stove away from the rain pouring down the kitchen chimney. There was still no heating; to go to the bathroom, one went halfway down the stairs, across the landing, and up the other side, "usually slipping and falling on your coccyx." In the winter, she had linoleum installed in the nursery and the staircase carpeted, for warmth. Each improvement seemed like a victory.

Other assignments mirrored the pattern of her week. "Travel light," counsels a *Picture Post* article on trips to the country commissioned by her friend Timmie O'Brien. Lee posed her models in town attire at the local station, feeding cattle in the barnyard, and in front of the Chiddingly post office and general store—an important source of supplies, and gossip, on weekends. Photographing models engaged in pastimes for which she had neither the time nor the interest, she produced a number of uninspired fashion shots but few features. In April 1949, the *Vogue* staffer who was reviewing Lee's work informed Audrey that she did not think that they could get eight illustrated features a year from Lee and suggested alterations to her contract. Always diplomatic, Audrey encouraged Lee to go on holiday: "I know very well that you find writing a strain and that you need to be feeling fresh and rested to do it."

By summer, Lee's exhaustion was apparent to all. Brogue colleagues found her unapproachable, as if the war and its aftermath had created a wall around her. She drank to excess, burst into tirades, and complained of depression to Dr. Goldman. "There is nothing wrong with you," he is said to have replied, "and we cannot keep the world permanently at war just to provide you with entertainment." This unsympathetic response expresses the doctor's—and the period's—failure to grasp the condition now known as post-traumatic stress disorder, which afflicted Lee as it did many combat photographers and journalists. But even those of her intimates who sensed what fed her sadness felt unable to help. She embraced the role of hostess as if she had chosen it deliberately, but her depressions proved otherwise.

Tony, on the other hand, was "enchanting." He talked "a mile a minute," she told her parents, and was "remarkably logical and mechanical," having demonstrated the Miller ingenuity in his mastery of locks, keys, and bottles. What was more, he took after Lee in his awareness of shadows, which to his way of thinking defined the presence or absence of light: "He shows you the sun," she explained, "by showing you where it isn't, like under a chair, or from his hand on the wall." A letter written toward the end of 1949 pronounces him "wonderful," requests finger paints for Christmas ("I think it comes in jars and I know it isn't dangerous to eat"), and boasts of her talent at turning sweet cream into butter: "This week I made almost a pound, which is four times our weekly ration."

Over the next few years, as Lee alternated between activities like butter making and photography, it became clear that she had lost what interest she once had in fashion. Features about eight different ways to tie a scarf or the return of the fitted coat were not inspiring. Dutifully, she photographed luminaries—T. S. Eliot, Claire Bloom, and, an assignment that must have given her pleasure, Max and Dorothea, who were in London for a retrospective of his work at the ICA and her stint designing sets for Covent Garden. (Lee posed the couple with Dorothea in the foreground and Max behind her—a more formal double portrait than those taken in Sedona.) Increasingly, Audrey turned to Lee as *Vogue*'s culinary expert, publishing her Christmas menus and original recipes, like Muddles Green Green Chicken, a savory concoction whose hue came from the herbs in the garden. "Lee took to cooking with all the passion and professionalism she had brought to her reporting," Audrey reflected before adding, "But still, it was not her life."

"Photography had been a passion for Lee," Roland wrote dismayingly in the section of his autobiography, *Scrap Book,* entitled "Lee the Hostess." "But after the war, photography became less important in Lee's life and instead she became absorbed in another art, cooking, which gave great pleasure not only to her gourmet friends but also to the flow of weekend visitors. She was by nature more at home in the flat in Kensington than in the country, but on arriving at the farm her consolation was to make straight for the kitchen."

Other consolations—drink, rages, bouts of tears—are not mentioned, nor are his own: the love affairs, casual and serious, to which he turned increasingly while Lee found solace in the kitchen. Nor does his memoir refer to his interference in her work, which, despite the grief it caused, had occupied her for the past fifteen years. Roland believed that it was time for her to stop. After many stormy episodes when Lee became miserable because she could not meet deadlines, he begged Audrey, "I implore you, please do not ask Lee to write again. The suffering it causes her and those around her is unbearable."

Reluctantly, Audrey accepted the idea that her star photojournalist's life did not inspire her. "Lee came into her own during the war," she explained. "It had an extraordinary effect on her. Afterwards, nothing came up to it. She was not meant to be married, have children, or live in the country. She thought she wanted security but when she had it, she wasn't happy. She couldn't write."

Lee and Roland, London, c. 1946; in background is Roland's portrait of Lee,
Night and Day (*Roland Haupt*)

Chapter 16

A Double Life

(1950–61)

In May 1950, Audrey and Lee met to discuss her contract. She had fulfilled her quota of fashion shots but failed to produce the illustrated features that were her unique contribution. When Audrey suggested that Lee shift to freelance status, Lee reminisced about her long association with *Vogue,* then agreed.

Audrey's distress at the loosening of their ties is evident in a letter summing up this conversation: "I hope you will remember how very sincere I was in telling you of my unbounded admiration for your features, and my conviction that they have made a great impression on our readers. I asked you if you ever felt like writing articles, or doing illustrated features, that you would let me know, and give us, if possible, the first refusal. As you say, you are a very long standing member of the Vogue family, and have a great gift for seeing and handling subjects from the Vogue point of view. If ever the mood comes on you again, I hope we can know about it."

∞

The people Roland employed to restore Farley Farm gradually became Lee's alternative family. Realizing that he needed help, Roland hired a sage villager

known as Grandpa White along with his grandson-in-law, Fred Baker, who
brought his brother to help with the cows. Determined to grow their own produce, Lee studied books on horticulture before directing Fred to turn a nearby
field into a vegetable garden. "My first encounter with this extended family,"
Antony Penrose recalls, "was through Fred, who arrived with unerring timing
at half-past seven every morning to bring fuel for the Raeburn, and deposit two
quart bottles of fresh milk on the kitchen table." The following year, Roland
hired Peter Braden to modernize the dairy operations, a job that sometimes
brought him into conflict with Lee. (When Braden had the Ayrshire cows
dehorned, Lee shouted, "I wish I could pull all your teeth out, then you would
know how these poor animals feel.")

The requirements of the holiday season got the better of her sympathy for
barnyard creatures. Just before Christmas, Lee spent "a most exciting Friday"
learning to slaughter a pig, she told her parents—"saw it up, cure it, salt it for
bacon, do the brawn sausages & everything." Plum pudding from Fortnum and
Mason saw her through Christmas Day; a new cook arrived in time to help
prepare for visits by the village carol singers and the local children on Boxing
Day—festivities that Roland enjoyed as Chiddingly's unofficial squire. Since
they also had six houseguests, she went on, "I was worked to the bone." (Both
Lee and the cook retired to the kitchen in tears.)

One senses Lee's mixed feelings about country life from photographs of
their first years at the farm. Affection is evident in her shots of Grandpa White
and Fred Baker transplanting seedlings and a portrait of the Ayrshires making
their way to pasture. A striking view through an upstairs window frame all the
way to the Downs is more enigmatic. The image brings to mind *Portrait of
Space,* but in this later gesture toward a far-off vanishing point, the shot is
taken from within the interior that, increasingly, bounded Lee's horizons.

In the meantime, Roland remade Farley's in accord with his vision. He
filled its rooms with French provincial antiques, arranged Henry Moore sculptures on the lawn, carved images on tree trunks, and placed Iris, the bare-
breasted ship's figurehead he had brought from Cornwall, beside the front
door (according to legend, she had defended herself against charges of
immorality by unveiling her charms). Next, he filled the dining room fireplace
with an elaborate mural of cosmic harmony in which the sun, moon, and plan-
ets align themselves while voluptuously shaped female cornucopias offer their
bounty—an invocation of nature as well as a premonition of the farm's opportunities for "goings-on."

At first, the farm's female population consisted of the various nannies who
looked after Tony, guests like Timmie O'Brien and, starting in 1950, Valentine
Penrose, who wintered there and became, in Tony's view, their resident witch.
Soon Lee's friends began turning up as weekend guests. On their return from
Egypt, Bernard Burrows brought his wife to meet Lee and Roland; Ernestine
and John Carter, Timmie and Terry O'Brien, and Robin Fedden spent the

Christmas holidays there; Max and Dorothea came at Easter and again during the summer; John Craxton and John Golding, both painters, became regulars. Farley's was the place where the different parts of Lee's life converged, and weekends there were a continuation of the openings and soirées that took place in London once the ICA moved to a permanent home on Dover Street in April 1950.

Roland's new project "opened with a bang & good press," Lee told her parents. That spring, T. S. Eliot inaugurated an exhibition on James Joyce, and the group staged a performance of Picasso's play, *Desire Caught by the Tail,* with Dylan Thomas as the Stage Manager. (When one of the two main characters, the Tart, requested tea after telling her lover, "I am all naked and I am dying of thirst," Lee and others in the audience imagined more potent remedies.) She was busy all week helping Roland with "branch activities like lectures on the history of modern art, meetings between the critics, the public & the artists," she continued. Her latest task, archival research for the ICA film series (which included Charlie Chaplin silents), was so demanding that in the future, she planned to "just leave them to it."

As Audrey hoped, the writing mood came on Lee again once the ICA was up and running, and life at the farm more settled. In November, a surprise visit from Picasso, on his way to a Communist Party peace congress in Sheffield, moved her to pick up her camera, and later to unpack her typewriter. Roland met the Maître at Victoria Station and whisked him off to Farley Farm. "We practically had to go into hiding," Lee told her parents, "as all of social climbing and curious London was & is still ringing us."

Picasso found much to admire in Chiddingly. His enthusiasms included "Ayrshire cows, open log fires, a whiskey and soda night-cap, hot water bottles, cooked breakfasts and tea," Lee noted in a tribute written the following year. "He could scarcely know that besides modern pictures, an English farmhouse doesn't have rows of French sabots inside the back door, garlands of garlic, and furniture which lived its first hundred years in Gascony. But a tinned plum pudding on my menu, holly wreathed and flaming was indeed English, *very* English." Amused to learn that Picasso had been an Anglophile since reading of Lady Hester Stanhope's adventures among the Bedouins, and that he had hoped to meet such a woman, she continued, "We speculated on the result if he'd become an 'English' painter instead of 'French.'"

Picasso had joined the French Communists soon after the liberation of Paris, chiefly because Eluard was a member. He was now their star recruit, having attended the Party's 1948 Congress of Intellectuals for Peace, given large sums to charity under their auspices, and lent his work for use in a recent youth festival. "Desperately conscious that wars had never ceased in his lifetime," Lee explained, he came to England in the hope that the peace congress would curtail future conflicts.

When the anti-Communist Labour government thwarted the peace con-

gress by refusing to admit most of the foreign delegates, Picasso returned to
Farley Farm. Lee's weekend guests having eaten everything in the larder, she
scoured Brighton for supplies while Pablo shopped for souvenirs—postcards
of the Pavilion, a toy double-decker bus, schoolboy caps for himself and his
son Claude, one of his children with his new companion, Françoise Gilot.
Throughout the Maître's stay, Lee recalled, "our three-year-old son Tony was in
ecstasy." Picasso took him in his arms, spoke with him in a language of their
own, and roughhoused on the floor. Soon Tony was wearing a beret, dipping
his bread in the sauce, and in general behaving "just like Picasso."

The farm also fell under his spell. "The winter jasmine came in flower,"
Lee remembered, "the hateful stinging nettles disguised themselves with frills
of hoar frost, even a great heap of trash and broken tiles produced a lovely
form." Picasso, Roland wrote, "had the effect of charging one's emotional batteries." One senses Roland's deference in Lee's photograph of the two men in
Roland's studio: Pablo stands in the foreground with Roland slightly behind, in
his shadow. By contrast, her shot of the artist with Tony on his lap shows their
mutual affection. Roland commemorated Pablo's visit with photographs of
him, Lee, and Tony admiring their bull and Iris, the ship's figurehead, as if
charging the batteries of animate and inanimate alike.

From 1950 on, Roland and Lee made numerous trips to see Picasso in
France. With Tony, they spent a week in Paris in 1951 to choose pictures for the
ICA's Picasso retrospective that autumn. His studio on the quai des Grands
Augustins resembled an ongoing salon; visitors included Jacques Prévert and
Tristan Tzara, filmmakers, critics, artists, writers, and Picasso's nephews, who
entertained while Roland and Pablo worked their way through his limitless
material. Although Roland knew Picasso's work "like a disciple," Lee wrote,
"he was amazed at the treasures." Intrigued by the objects—a bat's skeleton,
shells, pebbles, and snapshots—that collected themselves around him, she
observed, "Even my own used flash bulbs are still in the corner by the stairs
where I left them Liberation week."

One can imagine Lee's thoughts on this occasion, when the contrast
between her life as a *femme-soldat* and her new role as Roland's helpmeet
could not have been more striking. Her photographs of Pablo seated among his
paintings show their ease together as well as her glee on finding traces of herself preserved in his studio. When Picasso visited them in London, a trick of
the light streaming through the windows brought further revelations. As it
threw reflections of paintings onto the windows, superimposing them on
the world outside, a dancer swung from a tree; a collage replaced a window-
pane. From this perspective, Lee wrote, "street lamps and the road-menders'
red lanterns twinkled like Baedecker stars against masterpieces"—another
instance of Picasso's magic.

In June 1951, Lee, Roland, and Tony traveled to Saint-Tropez in time for

Paul Eluard's wedding to Dominique Laure, his new companion; Picasso and Françoise Gilot came from Vallauris to serve as witnesses. After the ceremony, the Maître invited the group to an al fresco lunch and drew their pictures while Lee took photographs. Her shots recall those taken at their prewar *déjeuner sur l'herbe* at Mougins, but without their emotional abandon. Tony, stimulated by the chocolate biscuits fed him by Françoise, roughhoused with Pablo until the painter, tired of his biting, gave him a nip and exclaimed, "That's the first Englishman I've ever bit!" Eluard confided to Roland that after Nusch's death, he had felt unable to go on, but with Dominique at his side, he had restored his spirits during a visit to the USSR.

"Picasso, Drawings and Watercolours Since 1893" opened at the ICA on October 11, 1951, two weeks before the artist's seventieth birthday. "If Picasso is ever going to be a Grand Old Man he'd better start now," Lee wrote in a review for *Vogue*. The works shown ranged from a drawing done at the age of twelve to a "Bacchanale" executed while the French battled the Germans during the liberation of Paris. As she walked readers through the exhibit, an elegiac tone colored Lee's review: "There are contemplative lovers watching over sleeping partners . . . beauties like Fernande Olivier, Picasso's first girl friend, and Nusch, fragile, lovely Nusch who died—she was the wife of his great friend, the poet Paul Eluard." (Soon Lee and Roland would also mourn Eluard, who suffered a fatal heart attack the following November.)

That same year, a young woman named Patsy Murray came to Farley Farm for two weeks after the departure of Tony's latest nanny. Unlike the others, she stayed on, bringing calm and predictability to the little boy's life. Patsy became the heart of the extended family. (Years later, Roland recognized her centrality in their lives: "If it was not for Patsy," he said, "I would have never been able to keep Farley Farm.") Having been brought up in a communal household headed by a philosopher and philanthropist named Josiah Oldfield (a friend of Gandhi's), Patsy was unshockable. When her mother joined her as housekeeper, Antony Penrose recalls, "Farleys stopped being a transit camp for itinerant nannies and took on an air of permanence."

After Roland and Lee began leaving the little boy there during the week, Patsy became, in effect, his mother—a development that created complicated emotions for both women. Friends noted a touch of rivalry in their relations, especially as Tony grew older. Finding herself supplanted in her son's affections, Lee nonetheless relied on Patsy and turned to her in times of crisis, whether culinary or emotional. Roland, who took the situation for granted, appreciated Patsy's care for their son. Since he had been brought up by nannies himself, turning his son over to a woman of Patsy's abilities seemed normal, even desirable, since Lee claimed not to like children.

Despite the establishment of a settled routine, the writing mood came on her rarely. Audrey tried to give Lee assignments that were appropriate to

Vogue's renewed emphasis on feminine subjects, like cookery. "A great deal of the hash slung around by me would seem banal to an American no matter how exotic it appears in Muddles Green," Lee explained when asked for her culinary approach. She liked dishes that could be made in advance, with her own produce. Americans hated tripe but loved Yorkshire pudding, watercress sandwiches, and trifle, she said. "If we have overseas guests, I try to give them one of their national dishes but unfortunately the best need meat." Since rationing was still in effect, it took work to find the ingredients for steak and kidney pie. But the "rare and noble" roast of farm-raised pork or veal, Roland's favorite, was "not to be monkeyed around with."

In response to Audrey's request for recipes "from international hostesses," Lee provided a Sunday lunch menu consisting of Muddles Green Green Chicken and English Trifle. In autumn 1952, she put together a plan for the Christmas holidays that warned readers, "Remember, this time, Christmas is thirteen meals long; exasperating, as well as exhausting slavery unless the emergencies are given as much consideration as the scheduled events." (Her recipes included a Betty-Crockeresque "master mix," from which one could make scones, waffles, and dumplings; she recommended hangover cures like fruit salts and vitamin B_1.) Since Lee's contributions were sporadic at best, Audrey hired another cookery expert, Elizabeth David, whose monthly food columns entertained *Vogue* readers even when they could not find the ingredients for her recipes.

Roland made use of Lee's talents the following year to conceptualize and hang an exhibit that showed in its own way that the ICA was keeping up with the eclecticism of the organization's younger members, Reyner Banham, Tony del Renzio, Colin St. John Wilson, William Turnbull, and Richard Hamilton, who called themselves the Independents. Titled "The Wonder and Horror of the Human Head," it grouped a mixed-media collection of heads from widely different times and places. Roland, who wrote with difficulty and may have been dyslexic, nonetheless produced a scholarly catalogue. Dedicated "To my Wife, without whose help this essay could not have been written," it drew heavily on Lee's editorial skills and long-standing interest in phrenology.

To have a say in her own right, Lee sent *Vogue* a lively review of the show, which—read between the lines—offers advice for former head-turning beauties struggling with the knowledge that they had lost their looks. "The next time you find yourself hunched and miserable, threading your way through masses of other hunched and miserable creatures on some wretched quest," she advised, "bluff yourself and them by bouncing along with a large smile." Women whose charms had faded might also consider the transformations wrought by plastic surgeons, or, like their Egyptian sisters, dress as they pleased. Beauty was a matter of particular times, she continued: "If we can't be 'beauties' in our own period, let's forget it and have fun." Yet it was true that "the free choice of a new head, with a new face; flashing carefree teeth; completely different and manageable hair" was as tempting as the thought of "escaping from oneself." Lee's sense of herself as one who managed by bluffing is evident in a sentence omitted from the final draft: "Humility, which is not one of the greatest attributes of the human, is quite a different thing when applied as a whip."

A few months later, Lee brandished a whip of her own in her last illustrated piece for *Vogue*. This tongue-in-cheek guide for weekend guests dismisses the conventional approach of the 1950s ("team-work on the part of husband and wife to make it seem that a bevy of pixies flits around doing the . . . chores") in favor of something like a Soviet workers' camp, whose motto would be "Joy Through Work." (One wonders if readers caught the echo of *"Arbeit Macht Frei."*) Her farm's assembly-line approach to meals, Lee wrote, offered companionship, discussions of art, politics, romance, and murder trials, and for those in need, occupational therapy. Moreover, it allowed her to enjoy "all the fun of being devious," assigning repetitive tasks to those who liked to be "free from the neck up," more demanding ones to "those who prefer to have their minds on the job." Having nearly completed her first five-year plan, Lee was planning the next one. She hoped to start a vineyard, to keep her friends, and herself, in drink.

Lee's Stalinesque tactics were illustrated with a series of staged photographs. Roland and Tony are shown clipping the grass; Henry Moore embracing his *Mother and Child*; Saul Steinberg battling a garden hose that threatens to turn into one of his drawings; Rosamond Bernier, Timmie O'Brien, and Cynthia Thompson (formerly Ledsham) shelling peas; John and Ernestine Carter filling worm holes in the furniture; H. D. Molesworth, keeper of sculpture at the Victoria and Albert, mending the chairs; and Alfred Barr feeding the pigs. (In a spoof on their labors in Sedona, Lee posed Dorothea as a master electrician and Max as a gardener planting borders of corn.) Despite her pleasure in orchestrating this story, Lee procrastinated, drank, and took out her distress on the household when she could not complete it on time—at which point Roland persuaded Audrey not to ask Lee for work. When Lee found out, she was furious.

The story, featured in *Vogue's* July 1953 issue, recalls the layout and style of Dave Scherman's photo-essays for *Life* with an important difference: the strongly domestic emphasis of the 1950s. Above the title, "Working Guests," the magazine ran Lee's haunting shot from her upstairs window to the Downs, a hint that these were now the limits of her vision. In the final image, Lee naps on the sofa while the guests toil, a send-up of her role as slave driver. "She was not suited to country life," Audrey reflected, "but it became a point of pride not to complain about the choices she made when she married Roland."

∞

At the same time that "Working Guests" marked the end of Lee's career, another event with ominous implications took place as if with Eluard's posthumous blessing. Before his marriage to Dominique, he had formed a liaison with a tall, radiant blonde named Diane Deriaz, whose many charms included a stint as a *trapéziste,* a circus tightrope walker. The young woman's specialty act—hanging from a rope by her heels—displayed her courage, and her toned body, to advantage. Although sufficiently excited by Diane to tag along on her circus tour, Eluard came to feel that she was too self-centered to replace Nusch. He introduced her to others in Surrealist circles, including Picasso. ("Eluard's love of women was generous and enveloping rather than promiscuous," Roland opined.)

In 1953, Diane appeared at the ICA and introduced herself to Roland as *"la trapéziste de Paul Eluard."* That July, they met again in Saint-Tropez, where Roland and Lee were staying with Dominique Eluard and her other guests, Man Ray and Juliet. The group often swam at Golfe-Juan, then dined with Picasso at his favorite restaurant. On one of these occasions, Diane recalled with satisfaction, Cocteau joined them but failed to recognize Lee. "She had been one of the most beautiful women in the world," the young woman wrote in her memoir, "[and] what was more, madly original, which made her all the more seductive. Unfortunately, she drank. She was a total alcoholic, which, little by little, destroyed her beauty." In Roland's photograph of the group at lunch, Diane smiles at the camera over Lee's shoulder.

Despite a severe case of shingles, a nerve disease, Lee invited Diane to stay with her and Roland in London that autumn to devote herself to fencing, another of her pastimes. The young woman moved into their Hornton Street apartment, foil in hand. She enjoyed ICA parties and weekends at Chiddingly but was shocked by Lee's drinking, especially when asked to bring her hostess a whiskey in her bath. (She also disapproved of Lee's habit of going braless, then peeling off her top in warm weather.) After Lee made inquiries about Diane's sexual life, the young woman realized that her new friends had plans for her: she was to be Roland's lover.

In the seduction scene recounted in her memoir, Diane defended herself so strenuously against his overtures that he fell in love with her—the only woman in his life to gain the upper hand and wield the whip with which he had sought to strike her. Lee then found herself in a ménage à trois that worked to her disadvantage—"the young beauty triumphed over the older woman," Diane reflected. Lee's affection turned to hatred, she thought: "Having tried to involve me in the perverse Surrealist game in which one lends one's partner to another, she had lost, and in her despair, held a grudge."

Roland announced that he wanted a divorce. Lee could return to the United States with Tony or leave him with Patsy. The crisis, temporarily defused after Diane's return to Paris, was still smoldering when she returned to Chiddingly at Christmas. Everyone's nerves were on edge. Housebound by the weather, the other guests—Max, Dorothea, Dominique, Valentine, and the O'Briens—dealt with the situation by playacting, making costumes from acid-colored felt, and parading around the house in their creations. Valentine read their horoscopes; the group scribbled New Year's greetings on a card to Picasso. When the emotional tension became unbearable, Lee took to her bed.

Valentine's "adoption" of her compatriot compensated for Lee's dislike, Diane believed: "We looked deep into each other's eyes. She said to Roland, 'Diane is beautiful. I like her very much.' " On Christmas Eve, after gesturing theatrically throughout dinner, Diane fell to the floor in a swoon. Valentine said that she was pretending, but Roland was too infatuated to see through her ruse. He became even more determined to marry her, and Lee, to banish Diane from the farm. Neither understood that the young woman, who valued her independence, did not want to cause a breach. "I ended up saying to Roland," she wrote, "I will never marry you and we will never be anything but friends."

For the next six months, after Diane's banishment, Roland made many trips to Paris to see her. His subjugation to the *trapéziste* was no less disturbing to Lee than if they had been lovers—even after Diane asserted her autonomy by becoming a flight attendant for Air France, which allowed her to indulge in another of her passions, foreign travel. Roland's infatuation let up sufficiently by June for him to go to Venice with Lee for the 1954 Biennale, where Max and Dorothea joined them. From Venice, they went to Vallauris to see Picasso and meet his new lover, Jacqueline Roque, who had moved in soon after Françoise Gilot's departure—yet another demonstration of the volatile nature of sexual relations.

One can only speculate about Lee's frame of mind as she boarded the SS *Olympia* at the end of July to attend her parents' fiftieth wedding anniversary. Their marriage had not been a model of fidelity, yet they had stayed together. Her brother John, his wife, Catherine, and their daughter, Joanne, met Lee on her arrival in New York on August 4 and took her to Vassar Hospital, where Florence was being treated for cancer. Her mother came home on August 9 and two days later felt strong enough for the party at John's house, where Lee photographed the extended family and the wedding cake that symbolized her parents' union. The next day they learned that the cancer had spread to Florence's liver and lungs. She returned to the hospital, underwent an operation, but died on September 11. Lee inspected the family plot and oversaw the burial preparations the next day, when Theodore left the room because, he confessed in his diary, he was "too emotional."

All that month, Lee looked after her father, who could not sleep. On September 22, they dealt with their grief by characteristic means: Theodore fasted and did a Pluto water purge, Lee made a batch of red-pepper marmalade. They watched a Hollywood romance, *Valley of the Kings,* whose Egyptian settings earned Lee's approval—the plot, in which an amateur archeologist (Eleanor Parker) explores Upper Egypt with a handsome guide (Robert Taylor), may have stirred up memories. She had some of Florence's clothes altered for herself, organized her mother's estate, and saw old friends, including Jackie Knight and Bert Martinson, who had studied photography with her in New York. Theodore's diary entry for November 8, when Dave Scherman drove to Poughkeepsie to see her, calls him "a pupil and old friend of Lee's now on Life"—suggesting that he remained in the dark about their relationship. She and Dave sorted through her photographic equipment; he took some of it home in memory of their partnership.

Lee renewed her local ties with visits to Agnes Rindge, the head of Vassar's art department, and began a new friendship, with John's liberal-minded daughter Patricia, a Vassar student who was keen on English literature, religion, and philosophy. Trish, who had the striking good looks of the Miller family, may have reminded her aunt of herself when young; Lee ordered copies of her textbooks with the idea of keeping up with her. Trish was fascinated by her aunt's "deep whiskey voice and free spirit" and impressed that Lee always spoke her mind, a bold move in a family prone to secrets. When Lee lamented her lack of schooling, Trish replied that her whole life had been an education, but she had the impression that Lee felt herself wanting.

Lee gave her approval to Trish's engagement to her beau because of his unconventional ideas, Theodore noted, but above all because he was Jewish. She counseled her niece about sex and explained how to cope with its consequences, especially cystitis (one should urinate after intercourse, she said calmly). There were two kinds of bodies, she explained, the straight up and down, or Nordic, sort, which as Millers they possessed, and the more curvacious Mediterranean type.

One night at a party where alcohol was unavailable, Lee badgered the hosts into opening the liquor cabinet, drank until she was tight, and danced with abandon—despite the fact that she wasn't wearing underpants. Lee was "unembarrassable," Trish said admiringly. "She spent her life trying for honesty; she was against hypocrisy and keeping things hidden." Yet during her visit, Lee mentioned neither her unhappiness nor Roland's infatuation with Diane—although she did ask her niece how she stayed calm under provocation.

Lee sailed on the *Queen Elizabeth* on November 27, to be at home for the holidays. Roland had missed her, but he was immersed in his new project, a biography of Picasso commissioned by the British publisher Victor Gollancz—

with which she could help him, since he doubted his ability to research and compose a lengthy manuscript. "They found they loved and needed each other, although they still found it hard to get on together," Antony Penrose recalls. "Their relationship settled into a fragile balance that alternated between affection and incomprehending strife. Lee accepted that Diane was part of Roland's life, but he was more discreet."

However much their son was protected from these events, it is hard not to ponder their effects on him. As a child, he found it difficult to accept change. Patsy did what she could to help him bear his parents' absences and Lee's mood swings. What bothered him most was her volatility. The little boy, who had inherited the Miller ingenuity, was happiest when learning the intricacies of the farm machinery. Like his mother, he loved taking things apart and putting them back together. In 1955, when he turned eight, Tony was sent to boarding school. Lee's American voice and manners intrigued his classmates during her visits, which made it clear to her son that she was nothing like more "proper" mothers. Whatever "the done thing" was, Lee didn't do it; what she did do was often embarrassing or alarming. (One weekend, when Audrey Withers showed Tony her house present, a pair of doves for Farley's dovecote, he begged her to hide them since Lee might put them in her freezer, one of the first in England.)

While other children adored Lee's subversive humor and practical jokes (she gave Tony fake puddles of vomit and papier-mâché dog turds as gifts), he found it hard to live with a mother who didn't care how she looked, what she said, or how her views affected others. It was bad enough that she wore scruffy trousers when other women did their best to incarnate the ultrafeminine New Look. What was worse, she sometimes appeared in public with a pink net toilet seat cover on her head, her preferred headgear in the kitchen, she explained, because it protected her hair from grease. "My chums thought she was the most enchanting and exciting person," Antony Penrose recalls. On visits, they saw Lee's flashing wit, far-ranging knowledge, and exuberance. Her angry outbursts were reserved for her son, whom she often dismissed as stupid. "I don't know what I represented to her," Penrose observes. "I may have reflected her own self-loathing."

Open warfare broke out by the time Tony was ten. "Please ask Patsy to meet me from the school train because if Mummy comes I am not sure if I will recognize her," he remarked, with an unerring sense of how to wound her. For the next two decades, he would alternate between being "deeply embattled with or icily indifferent to her," a pattern that in some ways replicated Lee's behavior with those she loved. One day when Theodore was at the farm on an extended visit, Patsy noted the strong family resemblance among the three generations of Millers. They shared not only their Germanic (or Nordic) genes but also their insistence on having things their own way. "Lee had a lot of her father in her," she said; Tony, despite his unease with his mother, had a lot of Lee.

Given their embattled relations, the inclusion of Lee's photograph of Tony in Steichen's enormously successful 1955 Museum of Modern Art exhibition, "The Family of Man," may have seemed ironic. The result of her mentor's three-year search for the most evocative images of common human experience, it concluded with photographs of children that, in Steichen's view, affirmed life by transcending cultural differences. (The show would tour the USSR at a time of increasing tensions.) Displayed with similar images of children from France, England, Morocco, and Soweto in the concluding part of the exhibit, Lee's shot showed an overalled Tony gazing beyond the frame and, in the foreground, a tabby cat facing the camera. When the catalogue became a best seller, this tranquil image replaced Lee's scenes from the death camps in the public's mind.

During the mid-fifties, as Roland's star rose and Lee's declined, her deviousness expressed itself in subversive gestures not always grasped by others. While Roland coped with the Independents group—their proto-pop aesthetic incorporated the shapes and colors of postwar culture into forms ranging from collage to installations—he remained the mainstay of the ICA, often propping up its shaky finances by selling his paintings.

The 1955 season featured an Independents-sponsored exhibit called "Man, Machine and Motion," with talks by Reyner Banham on topics like the iconography of the automobile. The younger artists, Paolozzi, del Renzio, and Banham, gathered in the ICA bar, "usually decorated by Lee's presence," Colin Wilson recalled. "Mostly she drank," he said, since she had little interest in the debates between the old guard, for whom Surrealism was the defining moment of modern art, and the Young Turks like him. "Yet she was open-minded, in fact bloody-minded, enough to support us," he observed, at a time when Roland found it hard to move beyond Surrealism—a vision that, to the Young Turks, was "claustrophobic and kinky, especially where sex was concerned."

Partly in response to divisions within London art circles, Roland turned increasingly to his biography of Picasso. He decided to tour parts of Spain associated with the artist's youth. Having published books of her own, Lee agreed to help—at what personal cost one can only speculate. Even then, it would have been hard not to see Roland's new project as competitive and harder still to grasp Lee's decision to polish her secretarial skills so that she could serve as his scribe—a plan she contemplated but did not execute once he said that he wanted her to document the trip with her camera.

Lee, Bill Copley, Max Ernst, Dorothea Tanning, and Man Ray in Paris (Man Ray)

They traveled to Málaga, Picasso's birthplace, in the spring of 1955. Lee photographed, as they toured the port's Moorish citadels, Picasso's first art school, and the family home on the tree-lined Plaza de la Merced. In Barcelona, they visited the Quatre Gats café, the fin de siècle anarchist locale where a cosmopolitan group of artists and intellectuals had befriended the painter, and the rundown areas where beggars and prostitutes were still in evidence. "The company of Lee and her ability to record so much with professional skill was invaluable," Roland wrote. "All this helped me to gain an idea of the atmosphere that had, some fifty years before, produced the paintings of the Blue Period." Lee had little to say about the trip, except to tell Picasso that she had seen her first bullfight. "It was better than I had imagined," she wrote. She witnessed the event "with enthusiasm."

Lee returned to England in July in time to greet her father, who had come for three months, while Roland stayed in Paris. Although Theodore enjoyed the British Museum, at eighty-three, he found Farley Farm more restful, despite the late dinner hour (Tony had tea at 5 p.m. and disappeared, he noted). He helped Lee pick peas and freeze them, accompanied her to performances at the nearby Glyndebourne opera festival, and took walks with weekend guests (that summer he met Audrey and her husband, the O'Briens, the Burrows, the Thompsons, art critic John Russell, Lady Vera Barry, and others with titles, which impressed him). After Roland's return, they took excursions to Lewes, Brighton, and the Channel beaches. On one occasion, when Lee and her father repaired to the pub in Chiddingly, the regulars tried not to stare. After Theodore became ill from eating Lee's green-pepper jam, he cured himself with a purge in time for Tony's birthday party.

Following Theodore's departure in October, Roland accepted a position with the British Council, the government's cultural organization, as its fine arts officer in France, in part because Roland and Lee's friends—Man and Juliet, Max and Dorothea, Miró, Braque, and Giacometti—had returned to Paris, in part because residence there would facilitate the completion of his book on Picasso. Starting in 1956, he would spend six months there each year, lecturing, organizing exhibitions, and promoting the work of British artists. Lee, who supported the plan, was "an essential asset," Roland wrote—as his hostess. Audrey took a different view. "One might think that, for Lee, that would be like going home," she reflected later, "but Paris, for her, was the city she had known in earlier days, when she was a free spirit—not a member of the Establishment; and when she represented nothing but herself."

For the next three years, Lee's life was shaped by Roland's status as a member of the establishment. He attended openings, wrote exhibition catalogues, traveled to Venice, Lisbon, Brazil, the United States, and Mexico on lecture tours, and took part in the effervescent life of the Paris art world, where he made new acquaintances—the writer Henri-Pierre Roché, painters Roberto Matta, Ossip Zadkine, and Yves Klein, and Princesse Jeanne-Marie de Broglie, of the Cordier Gallery. In addition to their longtime friends on the Left Bank (Man and Juliet had a studio on the rue Férou, near the Luxembourg Gardens), he was drawn to the elegant bohemians who gathered at the vicomtesse de Noailles's palatial Right Bank town house. Marie-Laure and Charles de Noailles had lived apart since the 1930s. The vicomte spent most of his time on the Côte d'Azur indulging his passion for horticulture. His wife, who possessed her own fortune, encouraged the eccentricities of those who frequented her salon—both to shock the aristocrats who had snubbed the couple since the L'Age d'or scandal and to perpetuate the idea that Surrealism was still outrageous.

One way to carry on in the old style was to revive the costume ball, where guests could act out their fantasies. At Marie-Laure's sumptuous bals déguisés, one might see Jacques Fath as a bear, Schiaparelli as a goat, the American ambassador David Bruce as a waiter in a dive, or Man Ray as a caricature of himself in a handmade mask. On February 14, 1956, Lee and Roland joined the vicomtesse's more than three hundred guests at a ball in honor of art and literature. Marie-Laure stood at the top of her grand stairway as they were ushered in by the servants. Resplendent in white satin and black velvet, she was impersonating Délie, the muse of poet Maurice Scève. Roland did not recall Lee's costume but wrote that he came as the clock "that disturbed at a crucial moment the father of Tristram Shandy in his pleasure with his wife." One wonders what thoughts went through Lee's head that night, whether she thought of the ball where she and Roland had met in 1937 under such different circumstances.

"The erotic enticements of Parisian nights were still there," he recalled of this time. Roland saw Diane when she returned from trips, and other women when she was traveling. It was her hold on him that hurt Lee the most, a friend observed: "She couldn't digest Diane; she stuck in her throat." Nor did Lee follow the example of Marie-Laure by surrounding herself with admirers, mostly homosexual, who offered the stimulus of unobtainable love. (Conversation at the vicomtesse's table contrasted oddly with the surroundings. While she talked of buggery and dildoes, liveried servants stood discreetly behind the guests' chairs.) Women sometimes felt uncomfortable at Marie-Laure's, since she preferred the company of the male artists who enjoyed her patronage while reassuring her that she was not *démodée,* a concern of hers in middle age.

In the 1930s, when Lee and Marie-Laure first met, the vicomtesse was considered a *jolie laide* (an ugly woman who contrives to be chic). By the 1950s, both had gained weight and let themselves go, in the view of their friends from before the war. But unlike Lee, Marie-Laure coped with aging by befriending people who sparked her creativity. She had published a novel, experimented with lithography, collage, and most recently, neo-Surrealist oils—often featuring her cat—that hung in galleries with the work of Man Ray, Leonor Fini, and her latest lover, the painter Oscar Domínguez. But when Marie-Laure urged Lee to make a fresh start with photography, she was disappointed by her reply: that part of her life was over.

While Roland maintained a hectic schedule, Lee did little but cook, drink, and attend cocktail parties, often with her close friends Ninette and Peter Lyon—also intimates of Marie-Laure. Peter saw her through "some tough times" when Roland worked for the British Council, he recalled, "especially when he was with Diane or some other woman." Ninette, a painter and writer, inspired Lee to take cooking seriously, while her husband became Lee's confidant, chauffeur, and companion in her search for an apartment with a modern kitchen.

On such occasions, which included stops for drinks, Peter talked with Lee about her unhappiness, and his own: Ninette was having an affair with Roland, to which Lee turned a blind eye. One day when Ninette inquired about the letters NA on Lee's dressing table mirror, Lee replied, "It means Never Answer—and it is to remind me that I am expected to carry on without protest." Her defiance came out nonetheless in provocative jokes and pranks or at costume parties, where she might appear as Marcel Duchamp's gender-bending version of the *Mona Lisa.*

In 1957, Lee found an apartment with a satisfactory kitchen in the Place Dauphine, the eighteenth-century square on the Ile de la Cité, which became their home for the rest of their stay in Paris. Roland gave her a six-month

*Lee dressed for a
costume party as
Marcel Duchamp's
version of the
Mona Lisa, 1955
(Dorothea
Tanning)*

course at the Cordon Bleu cooking school as a fiftieth birthday present, cookery having become chic in their circle. Marie-Laure, whose chef habitually
served elegant dishes like lobster à l'armoricaine and figs in cream, was
charmed to dine at a country kitchen where Schiaparelli boiled spaghetti while
the hostess roasted chickens in the hearth. (The reverse snobbery of simple
cuisine had not yet reached more conventional circles, where the thought of

doing without one's staff was unthinkable.) Lee found the Cordon Bleu school unhygienic (if a fish "flew out of the chef's hand," she said, "he would simply pick it up and slam it back into the pan"), but she learned the essentials— browning, simmering, skimming, straining, and sieving—in their time-honored order: the techniques of French cuisine as a self-contained system.

During these years, when Elizabeth David was introducing French provin- cial cuisine to the English and Julia Child was mastering the art of French cooking, Ninette Lyon was also writing cookbooks, several of which were translated into English. Unlike these other women, Lee would not become a professional chef, yet her extravagant dinners, which required days of prepara- tion, became legendary among their friends. The alchemy of the kitchen fired her imagination. While cooking, she could protect her autonomy by practicing an art that nonetheless enhanced Roland's status, though some of those who enjoyed it took her contribution for granted.

"Lee is still making remarkable dishes," Roland told Picasso in a letter announcing his visit to Cannes that autumn to check details for the Maître's biography. Starting in 1954, he made several trips a year to see Picasso, often with Lee. Her photographs make up a visual record of their relations, which were complicated by the presence on the scene of the collector Douglas Cooper: Cooper maintained that he, not Roland, was the English Picasso expert. Cooper's companion John Richardson, whose multivolume biography of the artist would one day expand on Roland's, sees Picasso as "a past master at dividing and ruling": "He would keep Roland . . . waiting for days at a time in Cannes, saying that he was busy with Douglas. Next time, Douglas would be reduced to begging Jacqueline to arrange an audience with the master. Whoever was the victim of these teases would usually be rewarded with a drawing."

While Roland was deferential, Lee teased Pablo with the intimacy of a for- mer lover, Richardson recalled: "Roland, as Boswell, was always saying, yes sir, no sir; Lee did as she pleased." On these occasions, she took what constitutes an album of relaxed domestic portraits—Picasso with wives, lovers, and chil- dren; Picasso with Tony, Roland, and Patsy on visits to Cannes. Toward the middle of the decade, by which time he had become a global star surrounded by acolytes, her images of him focus on the exuberance that remained the basis of his creativity. A series taken at Picasso's pottery in Vallauris during a visit by his estranged friend Georges Braque catches the Maître at play—kiss- ing the cheek of the ceramic infant he has just made for his *Woman with a Baby Carriage;* giving Braque a peace offering, a pottery dove. On another occasion, Picasso and his friend Sabartès don masks for her, and Sabartès cra- dles a nymph in his lap.

Picasso's ease with Lee is also evident in her images of the artist in the company of those whose vision complemented his own. Soon after his participation in *The Testament of Orpheus,* Cocteau's latest film, Lee photographed Pablo in conversation with the poet—an occasion that may have prompted her to rethink her prewar relations with both men, and her decision to take second place to Roland. In an image of Picasso with Jaqueline at their new home, La Californie, the couple's relative positions imply their emotional dynamic. Seated in a low chair, he stares at the camera while placing his hand on her knee; she turns edgily in the foreground, aware that despite his distance she is his support.

But it is in Lee's images of Picasso alone that their relations are most palpable. One particularly moving close-up all but erases the distance between them: Picasso gazes at his former muse as if recalling the history of their affections—an unusually intimate portrait at a time when, increasingly, he held himself in reserve. In another, a surreal double exposure, the two are literally superimposed on each other. As Pablo displays a drawing of a man looking at a nude model, Lee's white dress shadows the painter's face, and her sandal-shod feet appear at the place of his heart—an accident that mirrors their easygoing rapport.

In 1956, Roland organized an ICA exhibit called "Picasso Himself," including portraits of the artist by his friends—among them Beaton, Capa, Doisneau, Man, and Lee, some of whose shots were also used in Roland's catalogue *Portrait of Picasso.* Her portraits may be distinguished from those of other photographers by their focus on Picasso's gaze. Of a series taken in Picasso's studios a critic writes, "In these narrow and often heavily decorated spaces spirit is, as it were, put under pressure and forced into assertion—hence the power and urgency of those staring eyes. It is this prevailing condition in Picasso's art which is acknowledged by Lee Miller. . . . At one level they are documentary pictures, informative as to the look of this or that studio, but at another level they embody the artist's own way of working and show Picasso appearing in his own pictures, as though in a collaborative venture halfway between portraiture and self-portraiture." At the time, few noticed their collaborative nature, since her growing body of images of Picasso were not shown together.

Roland's biography, *Picasso: His Life and Work,* published in 1958, listed Lee among the artist's models and used one of her photographs. Soon after its publication, Roland accepted the invitation of the official U.K. funding body, the Arts Council, to curate a retrospective of the artist's work at the Tate Gallery in 1960, to which he devoted himself for the next two years. With the help of Joanna Drew, the exhibition organizer, he wrote the catalogue and cajoled collectors around the world to lend work from each of the artist's periods. In the lead-up to the opening, the ICA publicized the Picasso Party, its fund-raising gala at the Tate, by announcing that the guest of honor would be the Duke of Edinburgh, whose presence would compensate for the absence of Picasso.

During this time, Lee was seen chiefly as Roland's adjunct. With Audrey's retirement from *Vogue* in 1960, she had no outlet for stories should the writing mood return, of which she was doubtful. Nonetheless, having acquitted herself well on British television on the occasion of a show of Picasso's drawings, Lee was persuaded to compose a piece for the Picasso Party souvenir brochure. "Only Lee's family knew the agonies that were suffered in assembling those 500 beautifully crafted words," her son wrote of this effort. "The long nights hunched over the typewriter, 80 or 100 cigarettes a day and prodigious amounts of whiskey, the procrastination to build up the pressure against the deadline and the blackest weeping despair. Everyone associated with Lee breathed a sigh of relief when she announced she would never write again."

Reading Lee's "Picasso Himself," one would not suspect how much it had cost her. Lee began by evoking the artist's presence: "His flashing black eyes have fascinated everyone who has even only seen Picasso but those who meet him feel thrown into an exciting new equilibrium by the personality of this small, warm, friendly man." The piece combines intimate recollections with perceptive remarks on his attitude toward his work—while revealing much about her own. Picasso made sculpture from "lost and founds," she wrote, "a juggling feat which needs luck, observation and wit." Refusing to take his work seriously, he referred to it in "a gay and flippant way." To evoke Picasso's gleefulness, she described his wardrobe of false noses, beards, hats, and costumes. Finally, to explain his absence, she said that he could not be bothered. "He's too busy making new things to pay homage to the old," she wrote. "He's never been his own *aficionado.*"

Lee also gave an interview to a *Daily Mail* reporter for whom both Picasso and modern art were incomprehensible. After mentioning the titled guests expected at the ICA gala, the insurance costs, and Roland's devotion to the artist ("I feel it is good just to be alive at the same time as a man like Picasso," he remarked, echoing Eluard), the reporter described her visit to Lee's apartment and her struggle to see the resemblance between the artist's 1937 portrait and its subject. Lee told her to relax and "feel" the painting. "Can't you see it's like me," she went on provocatively; "it's got my grin." The reporter noted that Lee loved Picasso because, she said, "you never knew how he would react." Like her, he hated "people breathing down his neck."

On the night of July 5, 1960, a huge crowd, many in satin and diamonds, downed sangria on the lawn of the Tate under a pink and white marquee before mounting a specially constructed staircase and filing past banks of flowers to take their places at table, where they washed down paella with quantities of Spanish rioja. While the guests craned their necks to catch glimpses of Princess Margarita of Yugoslavia, the Marchioness of Dufferin and Ava, and the Princesse de Broglie, the organizers kept watch over the guest of honor.

Despite some concern, Prince Philip had been seated next to Lee, who might have been tempted to misbehave by drinking too much rioja. They were relieved to see her and the prince enjoying each other's company. Perhaps for that reason, she curbed her outrageousness.

Some of the younger members of their circle were disappointed by her failure to express in public what they were saying in private. The writer George Melly lambasted Roland for using the Duke of Edinburgh as a drawing card: "Honestly, I find the whole concept an insult to a great painter. What are you after? A title? A ticket to the Royal Enclosure?" The event was, he said, an "opportunistic little marriage of art and the establishment."

Roland's unease with his success is evident in his account of taking the royals around the exhibition. "I was required to act as a guide who would pilot round the Tate, first Prince Philip at the opening and later the Queen herself," he wrote: on a separate visit some weeks after the gala, Her Majesty responded sympathetically to the artist's Blue Period subjects and demonstrated "that she could laugh at Picasso's jokes and enter into the many phases of his work with wholehearted spontaneous enjoyment. It was an unforgettable experience for me to visit an exhibition of this importance in the rare company of one who showed such genuine pleasure."

Lee was not invited on the occasion of Queen Elizabeth's tour. Despite her good behavior at the gala, no one knew when her subversive side might get the better of her, or how she might respond to the marriage of art and the establishment. Nor does the biographical record include her reaction to the news, the following January, that Roland had been named a Commander of the British Empire. "It's because of you," he told Picasso, adding that they need not worry, since the empire was a thing of the past. As for himself, he did not require honors; he was happy being known as "the Picasso man."

Lee lost enough weight to look almost girlish in the evening gown she wore to the ICA's next big party, for Ernst's 1961 retrospective. The gala was "the largest of its kind at the Tate since the memorable Picasso exhibition last year," the *Tatler* gushed. The magazine, which featured the doings of the social elite, published pictures of ICA stalwarts—Julie Lawson, Victor Gollancz, and Dorothy Morland, along with Peter Ustinov and a beaming Max. Tellingly, the caption beneath the shot of Dorothea and Lee subsumes the women under their married names—"Mrs. Max Ernst with Mrs. Roland Penrose, whose husband organized the exhibition."

Much of her time, Lee wrote her brother John from London, was spent "mouldering in my schizophrenic life between the farm and here"—though she had recently gone to Paris to see Picasso, who was ill, and revisit the paintings that she and Roland had loaned to an exhibition there, including Pablo's *Weeping Woman,* just before the French police nabbed the thief who tried to cut it out of its frame. Since then, the farm garden had been overflowing with peas, beans, raspberries, and strawberries, which she preserved for the winter; consequently, she had not had time to find an electric typewriter to replace her Hermes. "But when all this double life I'm leading calms down," Lee promised, "I'll study the situation seriously"—to what end one can only imagine, the writing mood having abandoned her.

Foreground: Lee, Patsy Murray, Julie Lawson, Bettina McNulty; background: James Beard and Katie Laughton, in chair. Farley Farm, 1966 (Henry McNulty)

Chapter 17

A Second Fame

(1961–71)

L ee's past was overshadowed by Roland's present," a friend observed on recalling their circle in the 1960s. She rarely mentioned her former life. In the climate of England's recovery—the time of "Swinging London"—her reticence seemed to suit the general need to forget the past and celebrate the present.

Because Lee rarely spoke of the war, her entourage thought that this chapter of her life was closed. Few knew that it had gone underground, to resurface late at night when she could not sleep, or when drinking with a female guest or relation—a younger version of herself. You must be careful, she warned them, you could get in over your head. During the day, the war seemed to have receded into the background. Yet its unfinished business never left her.

Despite the changing cast of characters at the farm, Lee's weekends were much alike. To cater lunches, teas, and dinners for twelve or more required advance planning—designing meals that could be made ahead and relying extensively on Patsy. Still, most of her time was spent at the stove. Guests who wandered into the kitchen midmorning might find her breakfasting on fresh tomatoes and mozzarella while the more conventional ate kippers and toast. Those who stayed were given educational tasks, like fluting mushrooms; if talented, they were welcomed as sous-chefs. "I want to get some cooking out of you," she often told John Golding, who was invited to improvise with the exotic ingredients—Jamaican hibiscus or Egyptian saffron—he brought her from trips. "She was funny about cooking," he recalled; "she pottered around the kitchen laughing and swearing. Food amused her."

It also allowed her to be devious. Middle Eastern spices discomfited those who preferred plain English food. One night an eggplant dish was so hot that it caused Roland to leave the table. On occasion, guests who said that they did not eat such and such found themselves enjoying dishes in which the offending item was concealed. After the critic Cyril Connolly joined Roland in disparaging the American taste for marshmallows and Coca-Cola, Lee made a "bombe surprise" for dessert. "When they'd eaten every last mouthful," she recalled, "I was pleased to announce that they had just eaten my patriotic invention: marshmallow-cola ice cream."

Lee's "defiant" cooking (a friend's term for this subversive practice) was not incompatible with a more complimentary version of the art—her way of paying homage to people she liked. Lee invented meatless versions of dishes to suit Patsy's vegetarian diet, and with the help of Patsy's Polish friend Stan Peters, she perfected a sauerkraut stew called *bigos,* which improved on reheating. For Princess Jeanne-Marie de Broglie, whose ancestors also came from Poland, she prepared a complicated sauce from the southern part of the country after researching its cuisine. The princess wondered at Lee's immersion in cookery: "it was as if she had never lived in France, as if all she had done had never happened." One night, after the guests had downed more than the usual number of the stiff drinks Roland habitually poured, he stormed into the kitchen to ask when dinner would be served. Lee was preparing a blue fish in honor of a Miró painting, he explained on his return. "She had set her mind on the idea," the princess noted. "We just had to wait."

While some of Roland's friends took Lee for granted, she intrigued those who, knowing her past, did not understand how she had become the woman at the stove. The guests in Roland's orbit usually spent the weekend conversing with one another and following him around the farm. But for John Craxton, Lee was "the lure . . . an icon who represented the pre-war era, a time of utter freedom." Guests who were curious about her, like him, repaired to the kitchen—"a heavenly place always full of open bottles of booze and a potent cider anyone could swig at," he recalled. "She was an old soul," he continued, "a breath of fresh air in a country where people tended, even *tried* to conform; she collected all those who were deraciné, like herself."

When cooking with friends like Craxton, Lee was "in a world of her own, yet totally in the present," a visitor noted, "since cooking is a pastime that makes one pay attention." It was also an excuse to indulge in her love of gadgets. Lee amused the guests who watched her clean spinach in the washing machine or cook a chicken by inserting six silver spoons, covering the bird with water and letting it boil, then turning off the heat after six minutes, to let the hot spoons finish the process. She devised alternative recipes—like the low-calorie mayonnaise concocted with Craxton's help, using carageen moss instead of olive oil. Other tricks included washing strawberries in sherry, using leftover salad in meatloaf, and shaping ground beef and onion into a no-dough pizza "crust." There seemed to be no end to her inventiveness, nor to her appetite for research in her collection of two thousand cookbooks—which threatened to take over the house until Roland built a special room for them.

There, late at night, when everyone else was asleep, she sometimes talked about the past with younger friends who knew of her prewar fame but loved her for herself. Roz Jacobs, a starry-eyed New Yorker who had fallen in love with Paris on a buying trip for Macy's, met Lee and Roland there in 1955. Visiting Farley's at Lee's invitation, she learned that her impression of the couple as "sedate Brits" was unfounded. Lee embraced her as a member of the family—one who was, moreover, American. She asked Roz questions about herself and said when her opinions were naïve. "She was usually correct, so I didn't mind," Roz recalled. "I was pleased and flattered to be her friend."

During one of Roz's buying trips, which often included stays at Farley's, she sat up with Lee. The alcohol and the lateness of the hour loosened her tongue. "Lee saw herself as one of the boys," Roz said. "Drink was no big deal, sex was no big deal. She had wanted, and assumed, the same rights they had." But when she recounted her war exploits, she did not mention the camps. "She talked about being held by the Russians and matching them drink for drink, of her illness after the war, when her looks went, but never complained. She took joy in the moment."

Priscilla Morgan, a theatrical agent, met Lee in Paris through their mutual friend René Bouché, a *Vogue* artist who lived in a penthouse at the Hotel Crillon. The young woman arrived at Farley's to find Lee drinking martinis while preparing lunch. Intrigued by her accent, Priscilla asked where Lee came from. They nearly "fell into her martini," she recalled, when Lee said Poughkeepsie, which was also her hometown. "It was the basis of our friendship; we had both escaped. Later, when I asked my mother if she knew of Lee, she said, 'Everyone in Poughkeepsie knew of Lee Miller.'" But when Priscilla brought up Lee's work for *Vogue*, Lee became evasive: "She had used up that part of her life. Lee was a hugely creative person who wasn't fulfilling her potential." A passion for cooking, whether complimentary or defiant, was not a way of life her new friend understood.

Similarly, few grasped the reasons behind Lee's equally defiant non-walking. Roland's taste for country life included excursions in all weathers. While guests who wanted to walk off gourmet meals tramped across the fields in their Wellingtons, Lee cooked, napped, or curled up on the floor with her cookbooks. She purred when Craxton massaged her back, then slept off the aftereffects of early tippling. "She put her nose outside only to pick herbs in the garden," he recalled. One day when Audrey Withers returned from a walk to the nearby copse with a bouquet of bluebells, Lee confessed that she had never gone that far. Her rare excursions to the local pub, the Six Bells, were made in the car, often frightening her passengers as well as pedestrians on the short, winding road from Muddles Green to Chiddingly. Claiming to detest walks helped protect her realm, where Roland's eminence availed him not at all.

In the early 1960s, while completing her Cordon Bleu training at the school's London branch, Lee met several food professionals, including Henry McNulty, a wine and spirits expert, and his wife, Bettina, the *House and Garden* editor who became her cooking companion, co-conspirator, and best friend. Bettina's playfulness matched her own. Bettina and Henry, who represented the French Champagne and Cognac Federation in London, shared Lee's high-spirited, self-debunking American humor. The couple became regulars at the farm as part of Lee's orbit, which grew to include their friend James Beard and others who liked talking about food as much as preparing and eating it. (When Bettina invited Beard, Elizabeth David, and Robert Carrier to dinner with Lee and Roland, Beard concluded that the Penroses were "the maddest people in the world.")

Cooking was "pure therapy," Lee told Bettina, "and it's fun to work in a group like a sewing bee." She had "drifted into cooking," Bettina reflected later, for therapeutic reasons, but also to avoid the need for a career. She felt obliged to put her wartime experiences behind her, to the point of imposing self-censorship on the subject. Cooking was also artistic and practical. It allowed Lee to share the products of her imagination while stimulating conversation, "to guarantee a constantly renewing supply of this intoxicating elixir." But in her culinary endeavors, as in everything else, she required freedom. Lee thrived in the company of those who, like herself, "considered freedom an unalienable right and gave the same freedom to others." "A genuine original," Bettina wrote, she "abhorred manacles, whether political, social or domestic."

Like Lee, Bettina lacked a college education, but her curiosity and wit more than made up for it. She regaled Lee with tales of her years with Henry in France, sampling ten kinds of oysters with Jim Beard and picnicking with him and Alice Toklas; Lee told Bettina the story of her life. "I couldn't live without her," Bettina went on. "As well as planning menus, shopping, and cooking, we spent lots of time gossiping and giggling, talking about my travels

for *House and Garden,* which she enjoyed vicariously. We did things that people like ourselves didn't do then, like watching soap operas." They read English
history on their own terms, seeing the kings and queens (as portrayed in popular novels) as if they too inhabited a soap opera—a "Grand Guignol" view of
the past that made Mary, Queen of Scots, and Lord Darnley "the focus of a
lively conversation almost as if they were currently making newspaper head-
lines."

The two friends also planned trips with culinary themes. On a tapas crawl
through Spain in the early sixties, they deliberately ate only those small dishes
that, served together, subverted the formal Cordon Bleu tradition of many
courses each in the proper order (Lee's favorites included tapas made of mushrooms called nightingales, others of baby octopus and of "little sole the size of
my big toe"). Treating a stop-off in Tarragona as a pilgrimage, she brought
sprigs of tarragon to pay her respects, and in Barcelona, jotted notes about the
tapas dinner they planned to serve on their return to London. It would mean
trips to Jacksons of Piccadilly for green peppercorns, sesame oil, and tape-
nade; a long list of spices for seviche, celeriac, pine nuts, canned figs, and
other items that were then hard to find.

Culinary trips helped Lee cope with the bitter cold of English winters.
Over the years, Bettina recalled, she made herself comfortable by stocking her
kitchen with ingredients and equipment, like the saffron and paella pans
brought from Spain, and loading her freezer with homemade staples such as
pesto from her basil harvest, tarragon-flavored oil, and snowballs—"in case a
zany guest wanted to throw one in June." By the late sixties, the larder became
"a combination of gourmet shop and country store."

In 1963, Lee "jumped at the chance" to join an ICA trip to Lebanon and
Egypt, Bettina remembered, chiefly to see Aziz. The two women spent several
days in Beirut, visiting archeological sites and sampling the Lebanese equivalent of tapas: olives, pickled turnips, hummus, tabouleh, baba ghanoush, and
cumin-flavored boulettes. Lee went to find Aziz soon after reaching Cairo.
Having lost most of his holdings under nationalization, he was living in strait-
ened circumstances with their housekeeper, Elda, whom he had married. Aziz
seemed old and tired, Bettina thought, yet despite his reverses of fortune, "as
charming and elegant as Lee had said." Sitting around his gleaming mahogany
table, they reminisced in a language of their own; Lee decided to stay on after
the ICA tour to see more of him.

With the group, Bettina and Lee cruised up the Nile for the next week,
visiting places she had known before the war—Karnak, Luxor, Edfu, Abu Sim-
bel, and Aswan. On their return, she organized one last expedition: to Wadi
Natrun, where thirty years earlier, she had photographed the suggestively
curved roofs of the Coptic churches with Wingate Charlton. When a black-
robed monk invited the women inside the monastery, they took note of a huge

dry bread loaf in a trough that had to sustain the inhabitants all week—a striking contrast to the freshly prepared meal they enjoyed in the shade of their jeep after the tour. This time, rather than the martinis she had brought on an earlier trek, Lee provided an infusion of hibiscus flowers called karkade to wash down their meal of flat bread, hummus, tomatoes, boiled eggs, and Egyptian brown beans. For Bettina, their picnic in the desert ranked as the most exotic experience of its kind, while for Lee, it recalled more flamboyant times, when such meals were preludes to nights with a lover.

After Bettina's departure, Lee spent more time with Aziz. One wonders in what frame of mind she took the cure at Helwan-les-Bains, a European-style spa near Cairo whose waters were said to help rheumatism. On her return to London, the two friends began planning a reunion dinner, based, Bettina explained, on "our own idea of what Egyptian food should be." As with English history, they did it their way, inventing more fanciful dishes than actually existed. The menu featured savory bulgur wheat; Golden Chicken "for pharaonic cachet" (the chicken was stuffed with a rich farce and covered with gold leaf); Walnut Lamb, a concession to English taste spiced with garlic, coriander, and anchovies; and for the finale, Persian Carpet, a sensual composition on a silver tray spread with orange segments and rose petals, then strewn with candied roses, orange peel, and rosewater—in Bettina's view, a treat inspired by the romance of their trip.

The Egyptian dinner became the model for banquets based on their ideas of piquant taste and relaxed conviviality. Trips to the nearby Glyndebourne Festival provided the occasion for more picnics while reviving Lee's fascination with opera. On warm summer days, she served lunch outside. It might consist of cold borscht, fish mousse, seviche, crudités from the garden, and her own version of gooseberry fool, with whipped cream rather than egg whites. Sometimes, while Lee, Patsy, and Bettina worked all day on feasts including dishes from lands whose natives would never sit down together, members of the family "grumbled," Bettina recalled; they preferred English cookery.

Lee reverted to plainer fare when Theodore came to visit. During his three-month stay in 1963, he spent most of his time at the farm. On Tony's return from boarding school, the old man worked with his grandson in a woodworking shop set up in a trailer—where Tony displayed the Miller ingenuity by manufacturing tools of his own design. Theodore did minor repairs and visited nearby sights, including an abandoned British Railways steam train, with Lee. While suffering from a bad case of shingles, a recurrent ailment, she prepared a festive meal for Tony's sixteenth birthday and baked a cake decorated with sixteen grasshoppers—a tribute to his talent as a jack-of-all-trades. Before leaving in October, Theodore gave Roland his Swedish razors in trust for Tony, provided he learned to shave with both hands. "It's a great convenience instead

Theodore and Lee in Venice, 1961

of the contortions required with only one," Theodore noted in his diary, satisfied that his grandson would use these prized possessions when he came
of age.

One wonders what he made of the tensions in the household at this time,
when Lee's alcohol-induced panic attacks and bouts of self-pity were alienating many of her friends and family. Already in her cups at dinner, she would
upbraid Roland for recounting the same stories, then repeat some of her own,
or tell Tony that he was boring. Roland's hurt expressed itself in remoteness
(he was again thinking of divorce); the coldness between Lee and Tony that
had become entrenched in his early adolescence, when he took pains to avoid
her, erupted in wounding remarks on both sides. "We hated each other," her
son recalled, "and did it with such attention to the fine points that it became
an art form. We constantly lurked in ambush and never missed a chance to

assassinate each other's emotions." Their hostility was often enacted before friends, the uneasy audience for these humiliating battles.

Trips abroad became another of Lee's means of coping with the sadness caused by her estrangement from those who were closest to her. In 1961, she and John Craxton toured the USSR with a small group organized by the ICA. In a huge hostel "miles from anywhere," Craxton recalled, "Lee broke down like a child in floods of tears. I was surprised that a tough girl from Pough-keepsie needed reassurance and company. It was immensely touching." He was also touched by her taste for the unfashionable when she fell in love with the "Cecil B. deMille–like" prints of medieval Russian battles—"it was typical that Lee, who lived in a house full of surrealist and cubist masterworks, was no doctrinaire slave to fashion."

In July, Lee and Julie Lawson flew to Rome to travel with Theodore in Italy. "Still magnetic," Julie recalled, Lee attracted people, including the policeman who put her in a cab when her feet became swollen after a per-formance of *Aïda,* and the Venetians who helped her push the wheelchair to which, increasingly, Theodore resorted, over the cobblestones. (When they went to Peggy Guggenheim's palazzo for drinks, Lee danced until 2 a.m.; Peggy lent them her gondola.) Throughout the trip, Julie noted the tenderness between Lee and Theodore. "It was a great love," she said, "nothing peculiar." Theodore spent the next three months in London and at Farley's.

In autumn 1964, after another trip to Venice for the Biennale, Lee and Roland flew to the United States. On her own in Poughkeepsie, she showed greater interest in her father's new discovery, the TV dinner, than in her brother John's arrest earlier that year in Manhattan for cross-dressing (his case was defended by the American Civil Liberties Union). Lee spent five weeks with Theodore, taking care of him after cataract surgery, seeing friends like Minnow, eating more TV dinners, and baking cookies for Dave and Rosemarie Scherman, who drove up to see her. She returned to England in time for Christmas.

In the new year, Ninette Lyon came from Paris on an assignment from *Vogue,* to interview Lee as a former-celebrity-turned-avid-cook. Lee's culinary interests had begun on desert treks, she explained, when she learned to doctor canned food with spices. (Water was not required to wash dishes, since sand would do—a tip few readers would have put into practice.) She became a seri-ous cook during the war, she went on, because French cuisine reminded her of friends. Since her time at the Cordon Bleu, she loved talking with chefs—"the really enormous ones" (like James Beard). Her favorite dish was *truite au Chambertin;* her first original creation, Muddles Green Green Chicken, resulted from efforts to re-create the Belgian classic *waterzooi,* whose ingredi-ents—celery, parsley, and leeks—Lee had included in such quantities that they became the basis for the new dish's rich green sauce. The article gave her recipe for this fortunate accident, as well as for the chicken in sesame seeds she had served Miró after his recent retrospective at the Tate.

On reading Ninette's profile, those who knew its subject were astonished by the photograph of Lee looking tidy in a white apron—standing behind Roland's shadowy profile, which occupies two-thirds of the picture. Almost unrecognizable, she was wearing a wig and had had her front teeth replaced to close the gap between them. Although few ever heard her lament the loss of her looks—to which former admirers often alluded—it was clear to close friends that it mattered, especially when contemplating a return appearance in the magazine that had launched her career forty years earlier.

About this time, during one of Roland's trips abroad, Lee decided to take her own advice for fading beauties: a complete face-lift at the hands of Lady Claydon, a well-known plastic surgeon. "She was hellbent on having it done," Roz Jacobs recalled. "When I visited her in hospital, she said, 'Look at my chin!'" The operation removed the bags under her eyes and gave her face greater tautness; Lee regained some of her confidence. Her health improved and she felt happy, she told friends. But on Roland's return, she had to deal with his anger about the surgery, and his practice of seeking satisfaction elsewhere.

Theodore arrived in August 1965 for another three-month visit. At ninety-three, he was often confined to a wheelchair, which did not keep him from teasing and fondling the women who took care of him. "He was a dirty old man," Patsy said affectionately, "but harmless." (Her duties included bathing him once a week, when he stood naked before her to be dried.) Theodore also took a fancy to Anne-Laure Lyon, Ninette's eleven-year-old daughter, who stayed at the farm when not at her English boarding school. She walked him to the mailbox each day; he treated her with respect.

Moved by the girl's friendship with her father, Lee took Anne-Laure into her confidence. "Suddenly this scary adult, who drank to excess, became my friend," Anne-Laure recalled. When she got into trouble at school, Lee lied on her behalf. "She aided and abetted me," the young woman thought, "because she too had been a trouble-maker." In her teens, Anne-Laure sat up late with Lee and listened to her talk about her life. When she came to the subject of the camps, she broke down. Risk takers like themselves, Lee sobbed, sometimes rushed into situations unprepared. When she brought out her photos from Dachau to show what she meant, Anne-Laure could not grasp what she saw but felt nauseated. Lee went on sobbing. "She cried from loneliness as well as drink," her friend reflected, "from never really sharing that experience with anyone."

Although Lee was rarely alone, few understood her solitude, or her reactions to village society. It hurt that locals rarely invited her to their homes, that some

villagers' perceptions of Roland as an eccentric lord of the manor were reinforced on visits to Farley's. Lee's "ingrained sociability," Roland wrote, "allowed
her to run her household as a family, abolishing for ever the last remnants of
my punctilious and puritanical upbringing." By this, he appears to have meant
that in addition to their many guests, she included the farm staff, the neighbors, and local shopkeepers at events like the end-of-the-year bell-ringers'
party, when, for an evening, her innately democratic spirit dissipated other
people's class consciousness.

Christmas itself was reserved for the family, including Patsy and her
daughter, Georgina, Valentine, and the McNultys—who had become part of
it. The 1965 holidays were especially memorable for Bettina's five-year-old
daughter, Claudia. Arriving on Christmas Eve, she and her parents entered the
house by the old kitchen, renamed Aladdin's Cave. A giant tree reached the
ceiling; mistletoe and holly covered the walls. "Roland, in his surrealist holly-
king role," Henry McNulty wrote, "directed volunteer guests to hang, stick,
and nail box upon box of tinsel, stars, eggs, silver balls, strings of lights and spi-
rals of flashing silver paper into strategic positions until the sparkle and movement in the Cave was dazzling." The *bigos* that Stan and Lee had been stirring
all afternoon was served at dinner. Breakfast the next day was "do-it-yourself,"
lunch a smorgasbord of herring, patés, salads, fruit, and cheese, "washed down
with champagne," after which presents were distributed. Those who felt up to
it walked with Roland, then returned to await dinner by the fire.

Combining invention with tradition, Lee might stuff the turkey with green
rice or make vegetable purées—carrots and parsnips or potatoes and turnips.
"I have to serve plum pudding," she complained, "but I refuse to eat the stuff,
so I have lemon sorbet as well"; she colored the brandy sauce blue, "to get
away from that relentless red and green of Christmas." The candied fruits that
arrived as presents became the basis for "Nesselrodish things"—desserts using
these sticky sweets as found ingredients. At the combined bell-ringers and
farmworkers party, a traditional buffet was served—sandwiches, sausage rolls,
deviled eggs, and cake, with gin punch.

Roland was at his most genial on such occasions. He wrote the Christmas
pantomime, featuring the children in papier-mâché hats that made them into
mice, cows, or rabbits. When Claudia began to doubt the existence of Santa
Claus, he took her outside to watch Santa's sleigh (shooting stars crossing the
night sky). During the 1965 holidays, when Valentine dreamed of seeing a
ghost who resembled a Victorian child, Lee and Bettina dressed Claudia in
old-fashioned clothes and sent her to bring Valentine down for tea. "Startled,
then charmed," Henry recalled, she regarded apparitions as part of the season's magic.

On New Year's Day 1966, the festivities were capped by Roland's acceptance of the knighthood conferred on him by Queen Elizabeth in recognition

of his service. He had not renounced the tenets of Surrealism, as his decision implied, but would now be known as Sir-Realist, he teased, making light of the honor. The joke amused friends but failed to appease younger critics, who for the next few months regularly denounced him as a traitor to the avant-garde.

Lee had mixed feelings about Roland's elevation. She roared with laughter on reading a telegram from their friend Bill Copley that read SIR

Bettina and Lee in Stavanger, Norway, January 22, 1966

ROLAND, WHO WAS THAT LADY I SAW YOU WITH LAST NIGHT? Later, at the Ritz, she had herself paged to hear her title (Lady Penrose) and told friends to call her "Lady Lee," which was technically incorrect but matched "Sir Roland." For the next few months, telephone callers were surprised to hear her answer "Lady Penrose here" in her deep-throated American voice. "Hope you were gleeful about Roland becoming Sir R.," she wrote Roz. "Doesn't that sound like King Arthur's henchmen?" she went on. "That makes me Lady P. so I can look after the Round Table."

That January, Lee received honors of a different kind. Having decided a few months earlier to enter the Norwegian government's tourist board's contest for the best *smørbrød*—open-faced sandwiches—she practiced at home, concocting these small snacks for weeks. On the day of the contest, entries were presented anonymously to the judges, who decided, on tasting them, to give Lee first, second, and third prize. (First prize, a trip for two to Norway, was awarded for her Penroses—poached mushrooms stuffed with paté, herbs, and cheese, then set on buttered bread.) "I don't believe in drinking without eating," she told a reporter, though she might have put it the other way round. "A selection of interesting *smørbrød* make marvellous snacks at a party," she went on, though lately, her husband had "been complaining about being a little tired of open sandwiches." In Norway, she hoped to meet artists and "ordinary" people, visit a herring plant, and cook with the chef in a hotel kitchen.

Since Roland did not fancy more *smørbrød*, Lee took Bettina as her companion. They arrived in Stavanger on January 21 to find a photographer await-

ing them. Their tour became a media event. The newspapers published articles on the activities of "sandwich queen Lady Lee Miller Penrose," with
recipes and notices of her war work. At Oslo, their next stop, the shapes of
statues outlined by the snow were "like a coincidence of nature," Lee told a
reporter (perhaps thinking of her Paris-in-the-snow photos); residents vied to
have the two friends to dinner. At Geilo, a ski resort, Lee worked in the hotel
kitchen, making trays of Jansen's Temptation, a potato, onion, and herring
gratin, while downing aquavit with the chef. She and Bettina reached Bergen,
their luggage weighted with tinned fish, in time for a reception in their honor.
To a reporter who marveled at the thought of "an English Lady" winning a
Scandinavian contest, Lee explained that she was American—"one of the
brave," the reporter wrote, then noted that Lee had "fallen in love with Norwegian herrings," the vast variety of pickled and marinated fish that preceded
each meal.

After their return to London in February, Lee and Bettina produced an
eleven-course Scandinavian feast that featured herring, Jansen's Temptation,
and, for the less adventurous, Swedish meatballs. The trip fueled Lee's
appetite for culinary research. When family members asked why she compul-
sively clipped recipes and kept smuggling cookbooks into the farm, she replied
that cooking was her work. Friends like Bettina and Jim Beard knew that it had
become her modus vivendi.

That summer, when Beard was testing recipes for a cookbook, he often
spent weekends at Farley's with Lee and Bettina, concocting the informal
meals they all enjoyed, picnics being occasions for relaxed eating and Glyndebourne the preferred destination. Lee photographed Jim holding a just-caught
three-foot-long fish—the cover shot he chose for a new edition of *The James
Beard Cookbook*. Though not a professional, she participated as an equal in
the small world of cooking experts at a time before nouvelle cuisine, Bettina
observed, "when chefs were not yet like hairdressers and designers; only
Escoffier and Carême were famous, but everyone knew each other."

Lee's culinary reputation having grown since she became the sandwich
queen, the writer Shirley Conran interviewed her for an article, "Cook Hostess
in Action, Sandwiches *à l'américaine*." Lee's war reports, "though terse and
tough," Conran wrote, "bore a feminine touch"; while she had "the growly
voice and slightly toothy smile" of her compatriot Humphrey Bogart, she was
"efficient and sharp as a razor blade." Conran watched Lee's assembly-line
preparation of the open-faced sandwiches she served at informal suppers,
after a filling soup and before "a whopping rich dessert." Her approach was the
opposite of haute cuisine—which, Lee quipped, "has to be bloody haute to
make me gasp." Despite her title and Cordon Bleu training, Lee's attitude,
Conran implied, was American, the outcome of a democratic spirit. One thing
annoyed her: "people pinching my cooking wine. If I find that bottle has disap-

peared," Lee said, "I march into the sitting-room and replace it with a bottle of the best [Roland] has in the sideboard."

Lee also met Jim Beard's friend Chuck Williams, with whom she discussed recipes and ingredients. Williams, who came to Europe every year to purchase supplies for Williams-Sonoma, his San Francisco cookware store, was friendly with Rosemary Hume, of the London Cordon Bleu, and Elizabeth David, whose accounts of French, Mediterranean, and Italian cooking would inspire chefs on both sides of the Atlantic. In the company of these experts, Lee thought that she too might write a cookbook. But as she clipped, annotated, and filed recipes, the project grew to unmanageable proportions. In the same way that she couldn't be bothered to organize her photographic archive, she left the clippings in their boxes.

Lee's dislike for projects requiring long-term organization did not keep her from excelling in another kind of work: entering, and often winning, competitions staged by businesses to promote their products. When combing through magazines for recipes, she also clipped ads for slogan contests of the twenty-five-words-or-less variety still current in the 1960s. Theodore gave advice about how to install the electric range she won during his visit to the farm in 1967, when family members who had dismissed this new pastime had to recognize Lee's knack for snappy phrases. But apart from Bettina, few saw that she enjoyed the writing for its own sake, or that these contests stirred her delight in being devious by pursuing activities that to most seemed trivial, or worse—lowbrow.

Lee's pride in her winnings made sense to Theodore, whose American optimism she had, in many ways, inherited. At ninety-five, he was keenly interested in his grandson's future, noting with approval that after abandoning his studies in mechanical engineering, Tony, then twenty, was working as a farm student in East Anglia, a prerequisite for attending the Royal Agricultural College at Cirencester. Though arthritic, Theodore inspected the farm machinery and worked on an old project of his—the projection of images. His July 1967 diary records his idea for "a method of suspending a screen for projected pictures from a ceiling by means of an elongated or any shaped balloon which could be inflated by compressed gas." (It is not known whether the invention was tested.) While the villagers considered the inmates of Farley Farm people of dubious morals, they made an exception for Theodore, whom they saw as an emissary from another world. (The story went round about his shocking the nuns at the hospital where he stayed during an illness. On awakening from a coma, he proclaimed, "I want you to know that God does not exist!")

In the opinion of Chiddingly, then a parochial, "upright" village, the others at Farley's were artistic, foreign, or both—neither term being complimentary. Although English, Patsy was depraved because she didn't wear shoes; Valentine ("that Frenchwoman") wandered the country lanes to no apparent purpose except to steal cuttings from gardens; a heathen figure with bare breasts and painted toenails (Iris) stood at the kitchen door. Roland achieved respect on being knighted, but his having two wives in residence remained suspicious. As for the current Mrs. Penrose, she was American, and what was worse, she served strange dishes at ungodly hours.

There were exceptions to the general disapproval. Jane Brymer, whose family lived in the cottage across the road, loved Farley's for the same reason that Chiddingly remained aloof: because nothing was done according to local standards. Jane was ten when invited there to play with Claudia McNulty. They turned the Henry Moore statue on the lawn into a den, swung on the garden gate, and did pretend-cooking with Patsy. At lunch, the child's first meal at someone else's home, Jane enjoyed the taste of unfamiliar foods (like olives), the high spirits and laughter, and being told to call her hosts Lee and Roland, which felt like "a grown-up privilege." Though the villagers said that Farley's was not a "proper household," it was one where the little girl felt at home.

"Lee was the house and the house was Lee," Jane Brymer recalled years later. Her presence or absence was "palpable." In the kitchen she was always in motion, smoking and gesturing nonstop. One day Lee took Jane into her sitting room to chat. "She wanted to communicate with someone who was not judgmental," Jane thought, "and she made me feel that what I had to say was important." Lee emphasized the need for an isolated child like herself to read, go out in the world, follow her desires. At other times, she spoke to her as if she were an adult. Noting Jane's interest in their paintings, Roland took her round the collection. Lee gave her a book on art history and, without knowing it, the sense that Surrealism was "a natural reaction to life."

As a young girl, Claudia McNulty took the creative ferment at Farley's for granted and saw Lee simply as her mother's friend. As she grew older, she wondered why Lee was fond of her. While she and her mother were both independent spirits, Claudia felt too well behaved, especially when Lee recounted her adventures on railroad trains or in the desert. "She was a figure out of a story-book," the young woman reflected later, yet she had treated her like a daughter. During the 1960s, when Lee wounded Tony with acerbic remarks and he retaliated with boorish behavior, her affections were transferred to Anne-Laure, Claudia, Jane, and Patsy's daughter, Georgina—the girls in her entourage whom she tried to protect and embolden.

"I think she felt trapped in the country," Claudia went on. "Later, when I was reading Flaubert, I remember thinking that there was a bit of Emma Bovary about her, such an energetic person in this environment, even if there was a tremendous mix of people at Farley's." Claudia noticed Lee's feeling for the underdog, her refusal to say "snobbish things" about social inferiors, and realized that she "had a dark side." When Lee talked about the war, the teenager was shocked to learn that she had bathed in Hitler's bathtub—the story was "disturbing" as Lee told it. "She was someone who had wanted to do good," Claudia said. "When I was sixteen, she let me know that she would help should I become pregnant and not want to tell my mother. I was touched . . . that she wanted to be in a position of importance in my life."

In 1966, when Lee's niece Marnie, the daughter of Erik and Mafy, came to England with a friend after high school graduation, she decided that Lee was her own Auntie Mame. "I had been expecting to meet a lady," she recalled, "not someone who used coarse language and treated us like peers." During this "eye opener" of a visit, Marnie saw that like her mother, who drank in secret, Lee was an alcoholic. Yet her aunt's drinking did not keep her from "dashing off at the drop of a hat." And while she was not the motherly type, she loved frivolous escapades with the girls—taking them around London, to Carnaby Street and Mary Quant's to shop for clothes.

Later that summer, Marnie saw Lee again in Venice, where her aunt wanted to see a writer friend who had been imprisoned during the war for smuggling Jews out of Germany. Marnie and Lee were in St. Mark's Square when one of its many pigeons deposited a slimy white trail on Lee's hair—an event that gave both of them hysterics. "There is nothing I can do," Lee gasped between giggles. (When her hair dried, she combed it and went to her rendezvous.) If Lee had a touch of Madame Bovary when in Chiddingly, it vanished in places like Venice and New York; travel with kindred souls had the effect of a natural high.

∞

Lee's trips over the next few years took her to the United States to see family members and to old haunts like the south of France. She followed Theodore home shortly after his departure in 1967. In October, she divided her time between New York (Roland joined her to lecture at the Museum of Modern Art) and Poughkeepsie, where she helped her father sort through his possessions. In November, she met Erik, Mafy, and Marnie in Chicago, then flew to San Francisco, where she had dinner with Chuck Williams and discussed her ideas for a Lee Miller cookbook, a project that still fired her imagination. She returned to Poughkeepsie in time to celebrate Thanksgiving with Theodore, John, Joanne, Trish, and their families. Having turned sixty that spring, she felt the need to be with her kin.

Lee's annual visits to New York, where she often stayed with Roz Jacobs, Priscilla Morgan, or Rosamond Bernier, did not always bring out the best in her. At social events, some old friends avoided her because she drank heavily and became sentimental. "At her age," Priscilla noted, "Lee could have been an older beauty, but like most drinkers, she gave into it, which made her look worse. She had lived too freely; she hadn't protected herself." Rosamond lent

Lee in St. Petersburg, Florida, October 1969

Roland and Lee her apartment during one of their visits even though Lee was "epically untidy." While her affection for her friends did not waver, she was distressed by the chaos she found after their departure. Nor could she understand Lee's disregard for her appearance: "She made no effort to please, though she knew that Roland was sensitive to feminine beauty." The consensus in the art world, where appearances counted, was that Lee went too far in her disdain for convention and her desire to shock people, themselves included.

In 1969, Lee learned of Tanja Ramm's whereabouts when her daughter, Margit Rowell, ran into Roland in Paris. On a trip to New York that autumn, Lee and Roland visited Tanja and her husband, a professor at Johns Hopkins. From then on, the Rowells stayed with them when in England; Lee and Tanja took holidays together on the Riviera to make up for lost time. Moving in academic circles had not changed Tanja. When Margit showed her mother Man Ray's photograph of Lee's headless torso, she remarked, "You never forget the tits of the girl you room with"—though she professed a certain vagueness about Theodore's nudes of herself. The renewal of their relations brought Lee the comfort of being with a friend who had known her in her heyday but did not mind that she was no longer a beauty.

It also gave her another surrogate daughter in Margit, a curator and art historian. When Margit met Lee for the first time at the Rowells' fortieth anniversary party, "we became intimate immediately," the young woman recalled. From then on, they saw each other whenever Lee was in New York. Dressed in the white turban she often wore to hide her hair, Lee was still "very beautiful and very up front," Margit said. "She had lost neither her innocence nor her enthusiasm for life."

During Lee's 1969 visit to the United States, she spent much of her time with her father, then ninety-seven. Feisty but frail, he had decided after a stroke earlier that year not to risk transatlantic travel. His diary entry for September 25 notes in his arthritic hand the arrival in Poughkeepsie of "Lee, Lady Penrose"—as if it were a state visit. (The next entry relates the sweetly risqué story he told her: "Young man being introduced to a girl in a very revealing costume said I am very pleased to see you & I shall look forward to seeing more of you in the days to come.")

In October, Lee and Roland went to Florida as the guests of Nelson Poynter, publisher of the *St. Petersburg Times,* and his wife, Henrietta Malkiel, Lee's friend from New York theater circles. The *Times* reporter sent to interview Roland, who was to lecture on Picasso, emphasized his knighthood while noting that since the 1920s, he had "lived in the vanguard of art." Whatever direction painting might take with the advent of computer technology and "concept art," these developments would not replace oils, Roland believed, since "a painting can seize a moment . . . and carry this moment of time with it"—a philosophy illustrated in the accompanying photograph, which showed Lee and Roland rapt in contemplation of an abstract sculpture.

A portrait of a reflective Lee with her Hasselblad accompanied the *Times* interview with her the next day. A backward look at her life, it attributes her experiences as "a top model, an actress, an Egyptian, a world-renowned photographer-correspondent and an author" to her discovery of Paris at eighteen, when she escaped from the chaperone who had taught her French. In this account, everything flowed from that fortunate accident. Noting Lee's nostalgic tone when recalling her time with Medgyès, Man Ray, and Cocteau, and in Egypt, the interviewer asked her about the courage it took to be a photojournalist. Or was it luck, Lee replied, "a matter of getting out on a damn limb and sawing it off behind you." Although her current passion was gastronomy, she disliked most domestic pursuits, like flower arranging. "I'm no good with my hands," Lee teased, "though I am good with a screwdriver—taking a camera apart. But sewing on a button? I could scream!"

After spending November in Poughkeepsie, Lee returned to London in early December, in time to accompany Roland to an Arts Council dinner at 10 Downing Street, where she behaved herself in accordance with her status as Lady Penrose. Increasingly, Lee accompanied Roland on the lecture tours to which he turned in his disenchantment with the ICA, where younger members saw him "as an old fuddy-duddy," someone who, despite his avant-gardist past, was now "firmly in the establishment's camp." By the late sixties, when happenings had supplanted the modernist retrospectives Roland favored, he felt out of touch with the organization he had founded. At the same time, the ICA's move to an imposing classical building on the Mall in 1968 required massive infusions of cash as well as the continued support of the Arts Council, which looked with disfavor on the provocative exhibits being mounted as the latest in revolutionary art.

What was worse, in Roland's view, were the new director's associates—"an unruly clique, a 'mafia,' which began to defy and then openly to sabotage the instructions of the ICA Council." A break occurred following an event sparked by the new crowd's love of mischief. Invited by the "mafia" to stage a happening, an American performance artist named Rosalie filled the ICA auditorium with foam rubber tubes, took off her clothes, and invited the spectators, some of whom were on drugs, to join her. Lee disapproved of the event, which piqued the interest of the police and angered the Arts Council.

Another event linking art to notoriety further undermined Roland's sense of himself. In 1969, while Lee, Roland, and Tony, then in his first year at the Royal Agricultural College, were in Chiddingly, thieves broke into their London flat, ripped twenty-five of their paintings from their frames, and made off with them. Scotland Yard put its art squad on the case; Interpol was alerted; Roland went on BBC-TV in an appeal for information. The detective in charge of the case identified the thieves but not the location of the paintings—which turned up months later when some London workmen found what they took to be "an old pile of rubbish." Dusty but mostly undamaged, the priceless paintings were returned to Roland, who wept on seeing them. From then on, his son writes, "we lived among burglar alarms and security systems. The casual accessibility that Roland gave others to both the collection and his life was ended."

Roland made an exception when a vivacious young Israeli he met that year captured his fancy. Daniella Kochavi had made her way in London as a foreigner, and a Jew, with difficulty. Her outgoing nature, warmth, and dark beauty captivated Roland; her enthusiasm for modern art—she was then editing a film on Picasso—revived his sense of his importance in a lovely woman's eyes. Roland was enchanted with his young mistress. That he was seventy and she was twenty-two did not matter (except to friends who thought the affair silly). He told Daniella that sexual relations with Lee had ceased after Tony's birth, and that she agreed to his knowing other women. Since Daniella made Roland happy without posing a threat, Lee made her feel welcome at the farm.

Soon she began telling the young woman about her adventures at her age, treating Daniella like another surrogate daughter—who had the peculiarity of loving Roland. One evening when they were alone together, Lee asked Daniella what she saw in him. He had shown her the things that enhanced life, she explained—art, nature, good food (thanks to Lee), wine, and conversation—and made her feel comfortable in the company of the critics, artists, and writers who formed their circle. Lee and Roland were her English family.

"I adored Roland," Daniella remarked years later. "It was a Svengali-like relationship. He formed my taste, and Farley Farm showed me how to live." What he and Lee had created—the evening conversations, the flowers on the table, the mural over the fireplace, the Picasso in the kitchen—inspired and nurtured her. "You seem to be the initial source of . . . my pleasures and preoccupations," she wrote Roland on his seventy-fifth birthday, "so how could I not love you with all my heart and think that you are the most wonderful person." Basking in the young woman's affection, Roland took her to Paris (where she met Diane) and, later, on a cruise to Sardinia.

Roland asked Lee, rather than Daniella, to visit Picasso at his isolated villa, Notre-Dame-de-Vie, whose location on a hill near Mougins brought back memories of long-ago summers. Although Lee rarely bothered to travel with her camera, she always brought it on trips to see le Maître. In June 1970, as part of the Avignon summer festival, his drawings and paintings filled several rooms in the Palais des Papes. Lee photographed the majestic palace and took al fresco shots of Picasso with friends and patrons, showing some of her zest for odd perspectives by shooting the group from above while they inspected a Gobelins tapestry based on his *Women at Their Toilette*. Tired of admirers and depressed about his work, Picasso canceled their next appointment, but two days later greeted Lee and Roland "with his usual equanimity and affection."

By December Lee was "in a tizzy," she told her father, who was then ninety-nine. After the usual holiday festivities, she flew to New York on January 3, 1971, to join him on a cruise to the West Indies. She hoped to see friends like Tanja, she went on, "but mostly to relax on the most perfect family holiday possible—can't think of a better way to see a lot of you, & I can rub sunburn oil on your bald pate, & you can scratch my mosquito bites." The cruise would take them to Dominica, Jamaica, and Puerto Rico—another return to the past, in that their trip there in 1923 had been the actual start of Lee's adventures, at a time when Florence Miller saw her and her father as the resident troublemakers.

Nearly fifty years later, Lee's letter implies, she still felt like a runaway, but one who has acquired a position in the world. The passenger list for their ship, the MS *Gripsholm*, signaled the presence on board of Lady Penrose from Poughkeepsie—the most concise account of her career thus far.

Lee and Roland, Arles, 1976 (Marc Riboud)

Chapter 18

Retrospectives

(1971–77)

Theodore Miller died on May 5, 1971, two weeks after Lee's sixty-fourth birthday and a month before his centenary—an event he had hoped to celebrate with the family until pain undermined his will to live. Lee was left alone with her grief. Her father had loved her unconditionally, albeit too intimately, and she had returned his love. On June 3, his birthday, she cabled John Miller: THINKING OF DAD.

∞

Nineteen seventy-one was a year of thinking back to earlier times. Having been superseded by the war, Surrealism was now being claimed as an inspiration for the social upheavals of the late sixties. The movement's outlook was not restricted to particular times, its apologists said; "surrealism" would persist after "Surrealism" (the official phase having ended with Breton's death). This view of the movement—as something like a religion—revived that year in London art circles with Eileen Agar's retrospective at the Commonwealth Institute and an exhibit, "Britain's Contribution to Surrealism," that emphasized Roland's role in the movement he had started.

Since the publication of Roland's book on Miró the previous year, he was again in demand as a speaker. Lee accompanied him on lecture tours to Ontario, Hartford, and New York, where they attended the opening of the Guggenheim Museum's Miró retrospective curated by Margit Rowell. About this time, Lee dined tête-à-tête with Man Ray, whose life Roland planned to write next, in time for the retrospective he was organizing for Man's eighty-fourth birthday, in 1974. Mutual friends remarked on the closeness between Man and Lee, an abiding love born of their artistic collaboration and inti-macy—though Man remarked one day to Roz Jacobs, without a touch of irony, that Lee no longer excited him.

When not traveling, Lee brought together those she loved at the farm, where she entertained on a reduced scale. Though members of her extended family—the O'Briens, the Lawsons, the McNultys, Anne-Laure—came on weekends and holidays, the revels of earlier days had all but ceased, except for occasions like Anne-Laure's sixteenth birthday, an informal coming-out party at which Tony served as the disc jockey and Lee flirted with the young men, as if reliving her flapper days. New acquaintances also turned up—whenever she met people for whom she felt an affinity, she invited them to Farley's.

Lyn and Ed Kienholz met Lee and Roland in London when the ICA exhib-ited Ed's Surrealist-inspired assemblages. Lee took to Lyn, whose zest for life matched her own. The spirited young woman shared Lee's love of food and gadgets; when they sat up late drinking whiskey together, Lee encouraged her to explore her interests. Soon Lyn was sending her culinary supplies from Los Angeles: Cut-Rite wax paper (the English brand smelled odd) and, when Lee acquired a microwave oven, one of the first in England, recipes for her new "toy" and a Geiger counter to check radiation leaks. Lee asked about Lyn's basil crop and gave news of her own, sent recipes for butters made with herbs from the garden, and emboldened her friend after her divorce. She could do whatever she wanted, Lee insisted. She could live well on her own; she must follow her passions for food, art, and design. (Years later, Lyn reflected that Lee had not always taken her own advice.)

Following Tony's graduation from the Royal Agricultural College in 1970, Roland and he discussed plans for the future, his own and that of the farm, whose manager was not yet ready to retire. At Roland's suggestion, Tony decided to travel before settling down at Burgh Hill, the nearby dairy farm Roland had bought recently. In 1971, with a Penrose cousin and Robert Braden, the son of Farley's manager, he began what would become a three-year trek around the world in a specially fitted Land Rover named Que Sera. Valen-tine, then in residence at Farley's, read the expedition's tarot cards, which pre-dicted their safe return, and Roland marked their travels on a map of the world.

For the first time in many years, Lee and Roland did not spend Christmas at the farm. Lee's tolerance for what she called "this bloody English weather" being low at the best of times, they went instead to the Canary Islands—"all volcanos, dragontrees, rainstorms & rainbows," she told Lyn. She hoped that they would travel to Spain together soon, to sample recipes.

Bettina's long-standing plan to write about Lee for *House and Garden* came to fruition in the summer of 1972. The staff photographer arrived at Farley's when the vegetable garden was full of peas, beans, and artichokes, and the freshly mown lawn ready for croquet. Lee and Bettina set the table outside for an informal lunch—cold borscht, salads, fish mousse, rice salad, and her signature dish, the prize-winning Penroses—all enhanced with edible blossoms from the garden and displayed in bright, amusingly shaped dishes. Lee, neatly attired but less glamorous than in Ninette's *Vogue* piece, was photographed preparing dessert in the old kitchen, itself gussied up for the article, "How to Make an Art of the Happy Weekend."

Subtitled "The Personal Strategy and Beautiful Food of Lee Penrose," the full-color spread was a retrospective look at an approach developed over the last two decades, during which Lee had learned to amuse herself by entertaining friends. This "compulsive cook," Bettina wrote, retained the speed and flexibility of her years as a war photographer. She enjoyed rethinking her *plan de bataille* when extra guests arrived; she loved time-saving devices and ingredients made in advance—roux, clarified butter, toasted filberts. Before giving Lee's recipes, Bettina explained her strategy. Dishes must be easy to serve (no joints of meat), right for the guests (including vegetarians), and, if possible, surprising (summer pudding made in season, then frozen, to serve in winter). "I like one-implement desserts, simple things that keep the conversation going," Lee explained while the photographer snapped pictures of her at work on the pudding.

By the time the *House and Garden* piece appeared in 1973, the weekends depicted in its glossy pages no longer occurred as often as before. Family members objected that lunch at Farley's was never so elaborate, but Lee was delighted. The article "makes us look luxurious," she told Margit, and alerted friends to pick up copies. Now that she was becoming known as a cook, others requested interviews.

For a *Vogue* piece, "The Most Unusual Recipes You Have Ever Seen," Arthur Gold and Robert Fizdale featured Lee's "Surrealist surprises." Lee had invented culinary Surrealism, they wrote, by putting familiar ingredients in odd contexts. Her Mack Sennett cream pies were both cinematic and Dadaesque, she explained—"delicious to eat and fun to throw." Her food paintings (veal scallops encased in gold foil valentines, relish-stuffed lychees beside cherry tomatoes full of dark green mayonnaise) were "as amusing to look at as they are delightful to eat." Interspersed between recipes, they gave the highlights of Lee's past in art and photography, her marriages, and life as a cook. Her love of contests ("Dada high camp," in their opinion) illustrated particularly well her "you-know-this-is-all-in-fun" spirit. The piece ended nostalgically with Tony's favorite, "Antonio's Sweet-Sweet" (a hazelnut meringue filled with apricot brandy cream), and Lee's tale of besting Cyril Connolly with her marshmallow-cola ice cream.

Henry McNulty's "Christmas at Muddles Green," published in *House and Garden*, struck an equally nostalgic note. "Christmas can be a gastronomic desert," Henry wrote, "bound and gagged as it is by tradition." But due to Lee's role as "mastermind, magician, [and] chef-gastronome," this had never been the case at Farley's. "Lee's Christmases are a memorable mix of personal nonconformity with custom," he continued. After describing the meals, rituals, and surprises of a typical holiday season, he ended with Claudia's recollections of Christmases past: "It was huge tree presents, being taught to ride a bike, loudness, fun—but Christmas really only began at lunchtime."

Each of these backward looks emphasized a different facet of Lee's culinary career. Together, they validated her postwar years from her current vantage point. About this time, Roland was also trying to depict the past in his book on Man Ray. Informative about its subject's work but reserved about his character, the book's attitude toward Man's relationship with Lee is puzzling, even though it is dedicated to her. She appears briefly as Man's "provocative assistant," the model for the lips in *Observatory Time* and the nude in *Electricité*, in which, Roland wrote, "sex and industry were subtly united"—the awkward use of the passive voice indicating some discomfort. While these well-known images are included in the book, Man's use of Lee's eye in *Object to Be Destroyed* is not mentioned. (After quoting his directions to destroy the eye of "one who has been loved but is not seen any more," Roland wrote that they "hide an inner rage.") The book notes Lee's "inadvertent" part in the discovery of solarization, but treats her as one of Man's muses—especially in the section where her profile and Juliet Man Ray's head, both solarized, are on adjoining pages.

In December 1974, Lee and Roland flew to New York for the opening of "Man Ray, Inventor, Painter, Poet," the New York Cultural Center's retrospective curated by Mario Amaya at which these iconic images of Lee were on display. One wonders what she made of Man's portraits of herself, whole and in pieces, as she toured the exhibition, which also included *Ce qui manque à nous tous*, the suggestive pipe and soap bubble assemblage that encoded the erotic charge of their relations. He had declined to come for the show, but mutual friends—Bill and Noma Copley, and Roz and Mel Jacobs, who lent works from their collections—reminisced with her about Man. Lee was, Bill Copley wrote, "his favorite of all models." Her presence in his life "marked his return to painting" with *Observatory Time*—a work "having a warmth and a naive erotic implication that was embarrassing even to some of the Surrealists."

Soon after the opening, their rapport was again evoked (for those in the know) at a Cultural Center party thrown as a re-creation of the Pecci-Blunts' 1929 Bal Blanc, at which Lee's admirers had sent Man into a jealous fit. John Loring, Amaya's assistant, asked Lee to help him cook an all-white dinner for the guests, one hundred celebrities and supporters of the arts. She accepted with glee. That afternoon, as they cooked and drank martinis, Lee was "ebullient," he recalled: "She had the presence of a woman who has always known she was beautiful." Starting with the first course, *brandade de morue,* they were soon "up to our ears in cream, olive oil, and codfish," Loring continued. Lee tasted the dish, then cried out, "More garlic! More olive oil! More martinis!" They took care to spice each of the courses—veal with cauliflower, rice, and endives, and vanilla ice cream with lychees. Lillian Gish pronounced theirs "the first acceptable meal" she had eaten, but Lee and John concluded that "food of one color made them uneasy."

When the retrospective came to the ICA the following spring, Man and Juliet flew to London for the opening, which featured a Man Ray–inspired installation instead of an all-white dinner. Feeling his age (almost eighty-five), Man accepted the wheelchair Lee hired for him and the attendant who wheeled him through the crowds in the long gallery. Meeting Lee by chance in the installation room, where large transparent plastic tubes lay on the floor in snaky patterns, he got up from his chair and crawled into one end of a tube while Lee crept into the other. They met in the middle and backed out laughing. Each day, Lee visited Man at his hotel. They sat side by side on the bed and didn't always talk, Man's assistant recalled: "There was great tenderness between them. Juliet seemed like a stranger when Lee was there; she seemed like his wife."

Lee's bond with Man was very much on her mind when Mario Amaya talked to her about their relationship. Amaya had acquired a certain notoriety in 1968, when a deranged Valerie Solanas shot him and nearly killed Andy Warhol. Since then, he had remade his reputation as an energetic art-world figure and a writer on subjects ranging from Art Nouveau to the fringe subcultures he frequented when in London. Charming and witty, he made Lee laugh. She agreed to a series of interviews with him, the first of which, "My Man Ray," appeared in 1975. Lee's "intense personal and working relationship" with the artist was one episode "in a colorful and varied career," Amaya wrote in the introduction, but one that had marked both artists' lives—as shown in "the two most interesting images that Man Ray ever created," the lips of *Observatory Time* and the eye of *Object to Be Destroyed.* The lips were "one of his fantasies," Lee said obliquely, the eye "something like a wax statue to poke needles into."

Amaya asked Lee to discuss her work with Man, to tell how, "besides learning all of his techniques, she accidentally invented one of the most important of them . . . 'Solarisation.' " Describing her work as his printer, she acknowledged making "the initial mess" that led to their discovery, the image "that started this whole sequence off." (The sensuous feel of their work together is palpable in her metaphors: the black line coming "right up to the edge of the white, nude body"; the new exposure being unable to "marry with the old.") But it was Man who learned to control her discovery, she explained, "and make it come out exactly the way he wanted it to." During the interview, Lee did not discuss her own work as a photographer. What mattered was her long friendship with Man—that despite his stubbornness and her bullying, they fell "into each other's arms" each time they met.

Lee spent the summer of 1975 in "an orgy of freezing things," she told Lyn Kienholz. In her role as purveyor, Lyn brought her a new cookbook for her microwave, Freezettes to preserve produce, and cherry tomatoes in cardboard containers. By September, Lee had "not quite recovered from overdoing it in the heat," she wrote, but was still enamored of the microwave: "I'm very bold now and try anything"—her latest creation, a ham loaf made from leftovers in twelve minutes. By Lyn's next visit, "all those damn beans and zucchini will be over their season. No picking, no blanching, no packaging, labelling etc."

Meanwhile, her gadgets were living a life of their own. "My 'Toys' have been breeding," she told Lyn in another letter. "The oven and the Cuisinart got together I think and made me a Crock Pot, which I either haven't got the hang of, or had meat which hadn't been hanged as it took 18 hours to make a pot roast, and since I'm just recovering from acute muscular rheumatism and fever, my arm won't yet rotate easily enough for me to use my electric pancake maker, so I'm saving it for next week. Every week a new Toy, I hope!"

Her other news concerned Tony, who had come home from his trip around the world with Suzanna Harbord, the young ballet dancer he had met on his travels and married in New Zealand. Once the couple returned to England, having made their way through the Americas and Canada, Lee and Roland embraced Suzanne, who did all she could to effect the gradual rapprochement between Lee and Tony that took place over the next few years. "She would invite Lee to our home as often as possible," Antony Penrose writes. "Slowly we came to understand each other. We would never have a usual mother-son relationship, but we found that like many enemies who become friends we had a lot in common." Lee's drinking was under control; New York publishers were considering her cookbook proposal; Tony was, in his own way, by making films, pursuing the career she had abandoned.

Still other changes had occurred while Tony was away. Roland's differences with the ICA management had intensified. By 1976 there was "a bloody battle raging," Julie Lawson told Lyn. The new director ruled "with an iron fist & a teeny weeny mind." Roland, she said, "*can* get angry & outraged but cannot *fight!*" By then, Julie was doing most of the work on the exhibitions Roland proposed, including a 1976 Ernst retrospective. The director's henchmen took advantage of the rift to sabotage their work for the show in petty acts of vengeance: removing Roland's office furniture and smearing the gallery walls with purple paint. That November, he resigned. "I no longer recognise in the present situation," he wrote, "the fundamental aspirations or the enthusiasm which have during the last thirty years caused me so willingly to give to the ICA all I could afford in time and money."

Roland was also grieving the loss of close friends. Picasso's death had been devas-

Lee with two hats, Arles, 1976 (Marc Riboud)

tating. "The news on the morning of Sunday 8 April 1973 that he had died at first seemed incredible," he wrote, "another of those diabolical jokes he delighted in inflicting on friends." Since then, Roland had been embroiled in the controversy surrounding the gift of Picasso's work to France in lieu of taxes—an onerous, and depressing, obligation.

Max Ernst's death on April 1, 1976, deepened the gloom. Lee invited Dorothea to Farley's in June. They found temporary solace at Glyndebourne in performances of *Così fan tutte* and *The Marriage of Figaro,* then returned to Paris together because Dorothea could not bear to be alone. "We never left the house it was so hot—played scrabble in our nightdresses for a solid week," she told her old friend Jackie Braun, although she made an exception to see Man, who received visitors on his sickbed; she later went to represent him at the Rencontres d'Arles photo festival. "The show was much appreciated by the 500 photographers present (and 2000 cameras)," she told Julien Levy, though, oddly, she failed to bring her own.

Other old friends were feeling their age. Julien sent sections of his memoirs for Lee to critique. What he wrote about her was "near enough," she replied, though she didn't recall their Paris trysts as he described them. "BUT," she continued, "I don't like you saying that Man Ray hit the bottle. . . . Man was never a boozer, even in his moments of drama he wouldn't have been drinking away his sorrow." Saying so would distress him. Since he was "very fragile, can't get out and about at all without considerable pain," she hoped that Julien would eliminate the hurtful passage. (He did.)

In the meantime, David Travis of the Art Institute of Chicago mailed Lee a questionnaire about her photographic career, in order to document the thirty-six Lee Millers Julien had donated to the institute and to catalogue his collection. Since Travis was also trying to reconstruct the photographic milieu in Paris in the 1930s, he hoped to learn more about her work. Lee replied that most of it had disappeared—"lost in New York, thrown away by the Germans in Paris, bombed & buried in the London Blitz," and recently "scrapped by Condé Nast." It was simpler, at this point, to dispatch her career as if the damage had been done by others than to sort through the trunks full of negatives stored in the attic—about which she maintained a kind of amnesia.

Despite Lee's reluctance to revive the past, filling out a questionnaire for Travis reawakened her sense of having had a career. She listed her one-woman show at Julien's gallery, New York studio contracts, *Vogue* articles, *Grim Glory* and *Wrens in Camera,* as well as her film career with Cocteau and at Elstree Studios. On the strength of this information, Travis wrote a biographical notice for the catalogue, which Lee corrected. Mario Amaya "wants to do a biography with and of me," she wrote on October 9, and a French art historian hoped to exhibit her work. "I've been delayed, by a variety of things, mostly inertia," she went on. "I haven't yet managed to take off on the project of digging around and thinking of the past."

Lee left for Paris the next day, to be with Man. Although he was usually in too much pain to see people, Lee found him in good humor. Sitting beside him, she asked questions on Travis's behalf about old acquaintances—his assistant Boiffard, who "knew nothing about photography & said so" when hired, Germaine Krull, Berenice Abbott, and Eugène Atget, whose work Man had tried to print on stable paper only to hear him express distrust of "this modern stuff." Despite his weakness, she told Travis, Man "was in a good mood & for once, didn't mind talking about the old days." This was the last time she saw him. On November 18, Juliet phoned Lee and Roland to say that Man had died in his studio, where he had spent most of the last year wrapped in blankets, contemplating the effects of age.

Suffering with depression following the loss of Pablo, Max, and Man, Roland found solace with Daniella. Lee bored him, he told a close friend. Increasingly, she sat by herself in her downstairs room, listening to music, sorting her correspondence, and revisiting her cookbooks. While her passion for cooking remained, classical music became another "personal strategy." She cooked with the radio blaring until a new toy, one of the first Walkman devices to reach England, allowed her to listen in isolation. When the cassette player first arrived, she took it everywhere, startling Londoners who saw her walking around in headphones, humming to the inaudible tunes that filled her ears. Her favorites included Mozart and Beethoven; like her cookbooks, tapes of their compositions piled up everywhere.

In the mid-seventies, when Lee threw herself into her new passion, she attended concerts with a music-loving friend in London and listened to Antony Hopkins's music programs on the BBC, which she often recorded to hear over again. Many in their circle were astonished by her new interest. "There was something absolutist about her," a friend reflected. "With music, she was there, but not there, as if enchanted. For some, music is a kind of inner voyage." Although Lee professed a hatred of religion, especially its traditional forms, her feeling for music may have opened the door to a dimension akin to the spiritual—the vastness she had glimpsed through her lens in *Portrait of Space* and, later, across the reaches of the South Downs.

Visits by Miller relatives buoyed her spirits. Erik, Mafy, their daughter, Marnie, and her husband, Victor Ceporius, all came to England in 1975. When British immigration threatened to expel Victor, who lacked the correct passport, Lee phoned the head of the department to say that Lady Penrose would storm the gates if they did not let him in. That August, her niece Trish also stayed at the farm. She helped Lee with meals and made a blackberry pie. And they discussed one of their favorite topics, sex. Lee said that it was a privilege to initiate a younger man—thinking, perhaps, of Dave Scherman. She comforted Trish, who was going through a divorce. "Lee was tender-hearted and sympathetic," she recalled later. "Her bravado was a façade to deal with bullies and patriarchs, the Miller men and people like them."

By 1976, Lee was seeing few people. A local writer came to lunch to taste her new creation, elderberry-flower ice cream. He noted that she was not the sort of cook "of whom Swiss punctuality could be expected, but there were always endless Camparis and soda to pass the time." Nancy Hall-Duncan, a curator at the International Museum of Photography in Rochester, New York, wrote to ask permission to show Lee's work in an exhibit of fashion photography, but when she arrived at Farley's to choose images, Lee could find only one of her wartime shots for *Vogue*. Most of the time "she sat alone and desolate," Julie Lawson recalled with sadness. "You wouldn't dare ask what was wrong. She was unhappy, but she didn't want you to know."

The one bright note was Suzanna's pregnancy. Lee would be a grandmother by spring, she told friends proudly; she bought her daughter-in-law resplendent maternity clothes and basked in their mutual affection. In the meantime, her own health had worsened. "I've been almost continuously away or ill," she told David Travis. While she was "trying to put order in and around the edges of the mountain" of her papers, she did not feel up to it. "I've scarcely recovered from the last horrible year with Man Ray, Max Ernst & so many others dying," she continued. "That nasty Indian Goddess Kali & the Chinese Dragon year really wreaked havoc. I'm beginning to believe in them."

∞

The new year brought little relief from her rheumatism, recurrent pneumonia, and a new ailment, a deep, persistent cough. "This is the last winter I'm going to spend in this filthy climate," she wrote Lyn, "so find me a civilized cabin in Calif. for next winter, near a nice market as I *have* to cook & want to learn all sorts of Mexican dishes." Having recently returned from Iran, where he was filming a documentary, Tony was exhilarated about future film projects and "even more exciting," he told Erik and Mafy, "the new sport of watching Suzanna grow bigger and bigger every day." Lee had "medical problems" for which she had been checked, he added. "It seems that there is a non malignant fungus growing on her lung—father claims it's a load of mushrooms." By mid-March, Lee was responding to treatment—"back on the party/dinner/etc circuit with all usual stamina"—while Roland spent every other week in Paris, "buzzing around with usual high energy."

About this time, Lee spent several days with Tanja Rowell, who had come to London on a theater tour. They had last been together in 1974, when Lee went to stay with her in Baltimore and spent all night reminiscing about their long friendship. On their last evening in London, Lee told Tanja that she had just been diagnosed with cancer but did not want to discuss it. (Lee also told Bettina and said that she was growing her own cannabis.) Writing to Lyn in April to thank her for more tomato seeds (which she "rushed into the ground"), Lee mentioned only the "medical high-jinks" about her sinus allergy—traceable, she thought, to dairy products. She still hoped to go to the United States and could "hardly wait" for Lyn's next visit.

On April 25, two days after Lee's seventieth birthday, Suzanna gave birth to a healthy girl, Ami Valentine—whose arrival in the world gladdened Lee's heart despite her official disdain for children. "Suzanna is radiant as a mother," she told Lyn, then gave her another shopping list: Mazola oil, refrigerator deodorizers, a cookbook called *The Taste of America*. Lee enjoyed a brief remission in May, when she found the energy to accompany Roland to Paris. He was to deliver a slide lecture on Man Ray at the American Center; they could stay nearby at the Lyons' apartment and she could see Dorothea, Juliet, and other dear friends.

On May 16, Lee and I met by chance. I went into the center's lecture room at the rue du Dragon and sat down beside a woman who was noticeable because she was badly dressed by Parisian standards. Yet she seemed familiar, especially her profile—since I was immersed in research on Paris in the 1920s for a life of Mina Loy and had been studying Man Ray's portraits of women. "Are you Lee Miller?" I asked, to my surprise. Not the least disconcerted, she said that she was. We began talking. Our conversation continued after the lecture, when she asked me to join Roland and their friends at the Café de Flore, and the next day at the Lyons' apartment, where we sat side by side on the bed. What prompted me to write about Mina, she asked. What drew me to her?

My reply about the boldness of Mina's wish to live as a modern woman amused her. Mina was her mother's age, Lee said, but she hadn't thought of her as the previous generation. Age didn't matter, she went on. At seventy, she was now taking an interest in childbirth. Just before coming to Paris, she had held her first grandchild in her arms. Did I have children, she wanted to know. When I replied that my daughter was not quite three and learning French, she asked what it was like to have a girl. Then she looked me in the eye and said calmly, "I'm dying, you know; I have terminal cancer." I said, "I hope not; we've only just met." She asked me to come to Farley Farm, then changed the subject.

We talked about names, Mina's and her own. She had chosen Lee, she explained, because it was androgynous—an asset at a time when women artists were not taken seriously. It had been difficult to make her way as a photographer after being a model, all the more so while she was with Man. As for the Surrealists, she laughed, if you played it their way, you could have a good time, especially with Picasso. The war was another matter. She had done some work of which she was proud, "but," she confessed, "I got in over my head. I could never get the stench of Dachau out of my nostrils." Hoping to get to England by the end of the summer, I promised to send her Mina's childbirth poem, "Parturition," and noted the directions to Chiddingly.

"We are so looking forward to seeing you," Lee wrote to Lyn a week later. "Roland and I've just spent a week in Paris, where the weather was foul, but the friends were fine." She did not mention the seriousness of her condition, only "the compost heap" in her lungs and her allergy to dairy products. She had started using kosher margarine, which was tasteless: "The cows moo and glare at me as if I were a traitor. . . . The hell with them," she said; "they're ugly." As spirited as ever, she wrote that she was having "great games" adapting menus to her dairy-less diet. "Perhaps they're mistaken," she went on, "and it's wheat that is doing the damage, which is unfortunate, on account of whiskey, mm. Everyone awaits you."

Lyn did not get to England in time for more nocturnal whiskies. By June, Lee was confined to her bed. Roland watched over her day and night. As her appetite waned, Patsy cooked her favorite meals, saw to her every wish, and

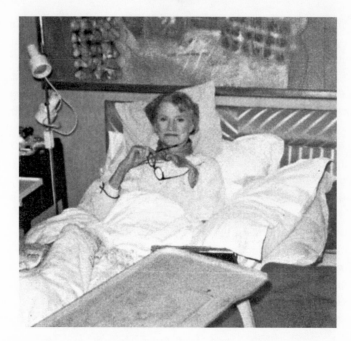

Lee after bedside picnic, July 20, 1977 (Bruce Bolton)

did her utmost to make her comfortable. Suzanna visited often with Ami, who was said to resemble Lee at that age. Tony returned from another filming trip in time for a long, intimate talk with his mother, the first in which she was able to reveal her love and concern for him; she asked him to take care to nurture Suzanna's creative spirit. Meanwhile, a team of nurses administered morphine for the pain. "She was wonderful," Patsy said. "She didn't complain. The nurses loved her, especially her wisecracks."

Lee faced dying as she had everything else, head-on and with courage—often phoning friends to come down from London for a last drink. "She had guts," John Golding reflected years later. Golding went to the farm in mid-July to be with her despite Roland's warning that she was sometimes incoherent. She summoned the energy to cook with him. They watched a nature program while he massaged her feet. "I'm only going to do this once and I want to concentrate on it," she said, "but all I can think about is the next fucking pill!"

When Peter Lyon came to Farley's, he and Roland carried Lee down the stairs in a chair and set her outside in the sun, to enjoy the garden. Bruce Bolton, a cooking friend from New York, arrived a few days later. On July 20, they had drinks and a bedside picnic. He took pictures of Lee, her hair combed, lipstick neatly applied, a scarf tied jauntily round her neck that matched the blue of her eyes. She smiled lovingly at her visitor—having gone beyond the need to pose. On July 21, Lee died at dawn, in Roland's arms.

∞

The next day, the *Times* announced the death of "Lady Lee Miller, beloved wife of Sir Roland Penrose." The *New York Times* obituary reduced her life to its essentials: "Lady Penrose Was Noted for Photos of the Blitz." The *Los Angeles Times* noted, "Model-Photographer Succumbs." Following the memorial service, the Agnus Dei from Bach's Mass in B Minor was played at top volume, in accord with Roland's wish that "it should resound." Two weeks later, on the night of the full moon, the family scattered Lee's ashes around the places she had loved—her herb garden, Henry Moore's *Mother and Child,* the lawn outside the parlor. Roland said almost inaudibly, "We must put some beneath the ash tree, for the joke of it," and burst into tears. "We walked back across the top lawn and he flung the last of the ashes widely," Antony Penrose recalls. " 'I want her to be HERE—ALL AROUND HERE,' he said with deep anguish in his voice."

Roland's massive grief surprised everyone. Of this time, he wrote, "Death had ploughed its furrow in my bed and was now to sit at my table. . . . Its dark presence in Lee's absence was overshadowing." Lee was mourned, and remembered with love by all who knew her. "What a remarkable personality," Bruce Bolton wrote to the Jacobses. "I wish she had written more of her life. . . . What was that book she was working on—I never got it straight whether it was a book on food or on her adventurous life."

By chance, a last interview with Lee appeared a few months later in the *Sunday Times.* Entitled "That Special Face," it paid tribute to her as "one of the first and the loveliest faces to acquire a name"—the prototype of the model "whose look is exactly right for its time." Eerily, its pages showed a radiant Lee in the deck chair where Huene had placed her for a fashion shoot, along with Man's backlit shot of her on the bed in her Paris studio, the light dappling her naked torso.

Years before, Man had given this portrait to Roland, as if to say "Take her, she's yours." It had been on their bedroom wall since then, but (he realized on seeing it in the *Times*) had lately gone missing. Its disappearance, and reappearance, seemed like a posthumous gesture. Lee had given it to the writer knowing that she would be dead when their interview was published, but also knowing, one suspects, that sooner or later, her adventurous life would be told, her photographs rediscovered, and her name—the one she chose with such deliberation—synonymous with a wholehearted way of seeing, and being in, the world.

Afterword

M an Ray always used to say that one of the things Lee did best was make work for other people," Antony Penrose reflected some years later. "In her own mischievous way, that is what she did for me."

Lee's posthumous mischief, or legacy, came to light soon after her death, when Suzanna Penrose discovered the more than sixty thousand photographs and negatives Lee had left in cardboard boxes and trunks in Farley Farm's attic. Slowly, she and Antony catalogued her "lost" archive and sorted through some twenty thousand pieces of memorabilia she had also stuffed haphazardly into containers—documents, journals, cameras, love letters, Nazi souvenirs—while comparing the many drafts of her articles with the published versions.

Growing up, Antony Penrose had known little of Lee's past. When visitors like Man Ray or Max Ernst mentioned her accomplishments, he recalled, "the etiquette was to be condescending. Since the woman I saw before me was incapable of darning a sock, that view suited me." Now, poring over her images and touching the bric-a-brac of her life, Penrose felt that he had been "cheated out of knowing someone exceptional." Not long after Lee's death, Roland had suggested to him the idea of a book about her. Suddenly, the materials for one had appeared, and a publisher, Thames and Hudson, expressed interest. Penrose began the voyage of discovery that would result in his pathbreaking biography, *The Lives of Lee Miller.*

The year after Lee's death, Valentine Penrose also died at the farm, deepening Roland's grief. He and Daniella Kochavi parted company about the time that Diane Deriaz came back into his life. They traveled together, and with Diane's encouragement, Roland returned to the postcard collage form that he had begun in Mougins with Lee. A retrospective of his work was held in Barcelona before coming to the ICA in 1980: "The grand old man who introduced Surrealism to the British in 1936 has finally been given a show to commemorate his 80th birthday," the *Evening Standard* wrote, echoing Lee's article on the exhibition there for Picasso's seventieth. Roland's "image diary" of his travels with Lee, *The Road Is Wider Than Long,* was reprinted that year, and his autobiography, *Scrap Book,* was published in 1981, with many images of, and by, her. He died at the farm on April 23, 1984—Lee's birthday—before their son could complete the book he had encouraged him to write.

In the meantime, Antony and Suzanna Penrose established the Lee Miller Archive at Farley Farm to make her images, papers, and memorabilia available to researchers, and, with the help of Carole Callow, the archive's curator and printer, to bring her work before an increasingly fascinated public. On a research trip to the United States, he learned from Lee's brothers about her childhood traumas and their aftermath, events she had never mentioned to Roland or to him. "Can you imagine living with a person, being married to a person, and not knowing that she'd been raped at the age of seven?" he asked an interviewer. "She kept that kind of thing in water tight compartments; nobody knew." By the time *The Lives of Lee Miller* was drafted, he had revised his sense of her: "I passed through the old enmities and understood how misunderstood Lee had been."

In these years, Penrose spent as much time as possible with Dave Scherman, who was also mulling over his relations with Lee and their significance for his later life. His close collaboration with Penrose—Scherman gave him the title for *Lives* and wrote the foreword for *Lee Miller's War,* Penrose's 1992 edition of her *Vogue* dispatches—helped both come to terms with Lee's contradictions. "A consummate artist and a consummate clown; at once an upstate New York hick and a cosmopolitan grande dame; a cold, soignée fashion model and a hoyden," she was, Scherman believed, "prodigious," or rather, her lives were. "She was the nearest thing I knew to a mid-20th century renaissance woman," he explained. "In the less grandiose but perhaps more appropriate pop culture patois of her native land," he went on, "she was a *mensch.*"

By the time Scherman's reminiscences appeared in print, shows of her work had begun their travels. "Lee Miller: An Exhibition of Photographs, 1929–1964," organized by Lyn Kienholz and curated by Jane Livingston, toured the United States in 1989–90, providing my first close-up look at her poignant, unflinching images; "Lee Miller's War" hung at the ICA in 1992 before touring

Britain and Europe. Since then, her work has been on display around the world in exhibitions on Surrealism, Picasso, art by women, fashion photography, war photography, and images from the death camps, and in the numerous shows circulated by the Lee Miller Archive.

Two recent exhibitions emphasized different aspects of her extraordinary range. "The Surrealist and the Photographer: Roland Penrose and Lee Miller," at the Scottish National Gallery of Modern Art in 2001, showed her images to maximum advantage, in comparison with which her husband's accomplishment seemed muted. "Surrealist Muse," at the Getty Museum in 2003, placed her work in the context of her creative exchanges with Man Ray and Roland Penrose, revisiting hotly debated questions about Lee Miller as a muse who is herself an artist.

Despite such attempts to evoke her gift for meeting, and capturing, her life's decisive moments, a museum is not the only venue in which to conjure Lee Miller's élan. A recent critical study, Richard Calvocoressi's *Lee Miller: Portraits from a Life,* has brought new perspectives. Two novels inspired by her have also appeared. Marc Lambron's *L'Oeil du silence* presents her as a woman who refuses to be entrapped by her legend; Robert Irwin's *Exquisite Corpse* explores the code of mad love through the narrator's pursuit of a woman whose panache recalls that of Lee Miller (herself a character in the book).

Lee's ways of being, and working, were highly theatrical, even cinematic. Because she looked for "the flash of poetry" she admired in the cinema, many of her own images seem like movie stills. Her life and work have inspired filmmakers: a recent documentary about Man Ray uses snippets from his home movies to convey Lee's seductiveness but, also, her participation in their filming; three documentaries have been made about her, most recently, the BBC's *Lee Miller: A Quirky Way of Seeing* (whose title echoes a remark by Scherman).

Building on the work of my predecessors, this biography tries to see through Lee Miller's eyes. Carole Callow writes that while printing from Lee's war negatives, especially those shot in the camps, she "had to detach [her]self from their content." Yet through this experience, she also felt "privileged to be a witness to many forgotten and hidden images, resonating with passion and energy, bursting to be released and acknowledged in their own right."

Similarly, this portrait of Lee, composed with an eye for the grain and texture of her life, acknowledges her passions in their own right. Writing it has been my way of keeping the promise I made to her, to stay in touch. It has felt like a privilege to resonate with the brave joy of this defiant spirit, who, like her friend Dorothea Tanning, sometimes felt that it was "monstrous" for a woman to devote herself to what she loved—but could not keep from trying.

Appendix

A Lee Miller Dinner for Eight

This menu has been assembled from recipes published in *Vogue* and *House and Garden*, and others found in Bettina McNulty's notes for a Lee Miller cookbook. It seemed appropriate to start with Lee's prize-winning *smørbrød* recipe and end with her "bombe surprise"—two of the unlikely culinary creations with which she delighted friends and startled food writers.

Penroses

16 very fresh, closed mushrooms, about 2 1/2
 inches in diameter
olive oil
salt and pepper
Madeira or Marsala
mousse de foie gras or other delicately
 flavored liver paté
paprika
16 slices white toast
1 bunch watercress
thin strips or zests of carrot, for garnish

Remove the stems from mushrooms by cutting carefully: do not pull them out, as the mushrooms will collapse in cooking. To retain juiciness, sauté open side down first, then outside down. Add salt, pepper, and Madeira or Marsala to taste, and cook until tender. Cool.

Pipe or fill caps with a spiral of pale, pinkish mousse de foie gras or other paté; sprinkle paprika into the grooves.

Butter and carpet bread with watercress; arrange mushroom roses on top; sprinkle with a few strands of raw carrot. Serve two per person.

Goldfish

> *1 whole codfish weighing 5 or 6 pounds,*
> * including head*
> *4 1/2 pounds carrots, coarsely grated*
> *1 1/2 pounds onions, sliced*
> *8 ounces sherry, half to season inside of fish,*
> * half to sprinkle on fish*
> *juice of 1 lemon*
> *3 ounces butter*
> *3 tablespoons olive oil*
> *salt and pepper*

Put carrots through an electric or hand rotary-disk grater with large holes. Slice onions to approximately the same size. Sauté the vegetables in butter and oil until tender. Season with salt and pepper. Preheat oven to 350 degrees.

Season the fish inside and out with salt and pepper and 4 ounces sherry. Butter a pan to fit fish (if pan is too wide for the fish, lay foil, grease it, and pull up the sides to make a narrow foil pan).

Place some of the carrot-onion mixture on the foil. Place the fish on top and mound the rest of the mixture over the entire fish. Pour remaining 4 ounces sherry over the fish and sprinkle with lemon juice. Bake about 45 minutes, being careful not to burn the top; cover loosely with foil if necessary.

If you wish to expose the cod's head, after cooking push back some of the carrots, or garnish it with chopped parsley or watercress on the platter.

Sesame Chicken for Miró

> *4 1/2 pounds broiling chickens*
> *1/2 cup sesame seeds*
> *1 cup dry bread crumbs*
> *1/4 pound butter*
> *salt and pepper*

Cut the chickens in quarters, removing the carcass bones from the breasts. Remove the skin.

Heat the sesame seeds in small amounts in an ungreased skillet. When they explode, remove to a bowl. When all are done, add bread crumbs to bowl. Season with salt and pepper.

Melt the butter and dip the chicken in the butter, then roll in the sesame-seed-and-bread-crumb mixture. Place in a roasting pan to fit, dot with butter or pour the remaining melted butter over it. Bake in a preheated 350 degree oven for 35 minutes or until crisp and golden, or broil under a hot flame for 10 minutes on each side.

Lee served this dish to the artist accompanied by corn on the cob, guacamole, and rice salad. "I wanted to amuse him by giving him dishes unknown in Spain," she recalled.

Burghul

1 cup finely chopped celery
1 cup finely chopped onion
5 tablespoons butter, divided
3 cups bulgur wheat
1 handful finely chopped parsley plus more
  for garnish
salt and pepper
grated rind of 1 lemon
juice of 1/2 lemon
6 1/2 cups fluid, half tomato juice, half water
chopped fried almonds or pine nuts

In a large skillet, sauté celery and onions in 2 tablespoons butter until limp. Add 3 more tablespoons butter and bulgur, parsley, salt and pepper, and lemon rind and juice. Add liquid, bring to almost a boil and simmer about 30 minutes. The liquid should be absorbed and the grains separate, well cooked but not mushy or sticky.

Sprinkle with chopped almonds or pine nuts and bake uncovered at 275 degrees for about 10 minutes to brown. Garnish with more chopped parsley.

Celery Purée

1 pound, 3 ounce can celery hearts
2 tablespoons parsley
1/4 cup chopped onion
3 to 4 tablespoons powdered potatoes
5 tablespoons butter

In a blender, purée celery hearts with their juice, parsley, and onion. Heat mixture in a saucepan. Add powdered potatoes, stir until excess liquid is absorbed, then add butter. Heat until fluffy and serve.

Salad of Bibb Lettuce
with Nasturtium Blossoms or Fresh Garden Herbs

Crusty French Bread

Marshmallow-Cola Ice Cream

24 marshmallows
1 can Coca-Cola (12 ounces)
juice of 1 lemon
pinch of salt
2 tablespoons rum
1 cup heavy cream

Dissolve marshmallows in half the Coca-Cola over low heat. Add remaining cola, lemon juice, and salt. Whip together; freeze in ice-cube tray.

When frozen but still mushy, remove, add rum and cream, and whip again. Refreeze until solid, whipping once again after half an hour for a smooth ice cream—a "flag-waving rebuttal to British critics of American cuisine" (Bettina McNulty).

Notes

Lee Miller's papers—personal documents, notebooks, drafts of articles, *Vogue* service letters, and photo caption sheets—are held in the Lee Miller Archives, which also holds her correspondence with members of the Miller family, Man Ray, Aziz Eloui Bey, Roland Penrose, Bernard Burrows, David Scherman, and other close friends and associates. All archival material referenced in the notes comes from this generous source unless otherwise noted. Lee Miller correspondence in other collections is indicated by the names of the recipients.

Published works for which full references appear in the bibliography are referred to by the author's name in the notes or, for frequently cited sources, initials. When more than one work by an author has been cited, the short title is also given. Correspondence and unpublished works are referred to by the author's name, or initials in the case of frequent citations. All translations are my own.

Archives and private collections are abbreviated as follows:

AIC	Art Institute of Chicago
BMcNC	Bettina McNulty Collection
CBC	Carolyn Burke Collection
DSE	David E. Scherman Estate
GRI	Getty Research Institute. Man Ray papers
JMC	John Miller Collection. Theodore Miller diaries, correspondence
LKC	Lyn Kienholz Collection
LMA	Lee Miller Archives
MNP	Musée National Picasso, Picasso archives
RJC	Roz Jacobs Collection
SNGMA	Scottish National Gallery of Modern Art. Roland Penrose Collection
UKCNA	UK Condé Nast Archives. Audrey Withers papers

Frequently cited names are abbreviated as follows:

AEB	Aziz Eloui Bey
AP	Antony Penrose
AW	Audrey Withers
BMcN	Bettina McNulty
DS	David Scherman
EA	Eileen Agar
EM	Erik Miller
FM	Florence Miller
JBG	Jacqueline Barsotti Goddard
JL	Julien Levy
JM	John Miller
JP	John Phillips
LM	Lee Miller
MHF	Miriam "Minnow" Hicks Feierabend
MM	Mafy Miller
MR	Man Ray
PM	Patsy Murray
PMT	Patricia "Trish" Miller Taylor
PP	Pablo Picasso
RP	Roland Penrose
TM	Theodore Miller
TR	Tanja Ramm Rowell
WS	William "Bill" Scherman

Introduction

xii an American free spirit: Phillips, *Free Spirit in a Troubled World,* p. 401.

xii Who else has written: Harry Yoxall, unpublished talk, 1945.

xiv don't match in shape: LM to RP, Oct. 11, 1937.

xiv I feel about as popular: LM to AW, n.d. [Jan. 11, 1946].

xiv for therapeutic reasons: BMcN to the author, Jan. 20, 2002.

1. A Poughkeepsie Girlhood

6 driven by a dynamo: Platt, p. 234.

7 the orderly progress: William B. Rhoads, "Poughkeepsie's Architectural Styles," in *Dutchess County Historical Society Year Book,* vol. 72 (1987), p. 28.

7 the better for: Rhoads, p. 29.

13 a thrill-packed reel: LM, "What They See in Cinema," p. 46.

15 take things so natural: Astrid Kajerdt to FM, n.d. [1914].

16 as though she: Herman, *Trauma and Recovery,* p. 43. This response, known as constriction, produces a state of detached calm as a response to inescapable pain and may trigger other forms of dissociation that comprise the syndrome known as post-traumatic stress disorder, which afflicts survivors of sexual and combat violence alike.

16 the most sacred: Ulman, p. 117.

16 a breaking and entering: Maya Angelou, *I Know Why the Caged Bird Sings* (New York: Bantam, 1997), p. 78.

17 It changed: JM interview with the author, May 29, 1996.

17 Gonorrhea was: Prince A. Morrow, *Eugenics and Racial Poisons* (New York: Society of Sanitary and Moral Prophylaxis, 1912), pp. 12–13.

17 The flower: Dr. Abraham Wolbarst, cited in Brandt, p. 15.

17 Before sulfa drugs: E. T. Burke, *Treatment of Venereal Disease in General Practice* (London: Faber & Gwyer, 1927), pp. 121–23. The mysterious final sentence states that "in every female case detoxicated vaccines should be given."

18 damaged goods: The 1913 Broadway production of Eugene Brieux's *Damaged Goods* dramatized the social consequences of venereal disease through the story of a syphilitic who brings suffering on his wife, their child, and the wet nurse. The play became controversial because it treated VD openly, a consequence hailed by some and lamented by others. See Brandt, pp. 47–51.

18 *September Morn*: After Anthony Comstock, of the Anti-Vice Society, denounced *September Morn,* songs were written about the painting, versions appeared in the form of dolls, statues, and cane heads, sailors had the nude tattooed on their chests, and some seven million copies were sold at a dollar apiece.

19 He was the only: EM interview with the author, Dec. 13, 1992.

2. Never Jam Today

21 something to hand down: LM, 1926 notebook (misdated 1927).

22 Elizabeth had tantrums: TM diary, Jan. 21, 1918, JMC.

23 Bring your vacation home: Quotations from Kodak ads are from Strasser, pp. 102–5. On the Kodak girl, see West, passim.

23 the true stereoscopic effect: TM diary, Mar. 2, 1916, JMC. Information in this paragraph from EM interview with the author, Dec. 13, 1992.

24 That one, she: Miss Freer cited by PMT in interview with the author, Feb. 8, 1997.

24 At dinner the family: On Henry George, see Geiger. G. B. Shaw, who adhered to the social reform movement while under the influence of George, discusses Georgism in his *Intelligent Woman's Guide to Socialism and Capitalism.*

26 Dishevelled girls staggered: Unless otherwise indicated, all quotations in this and the next twelve paragraphs are from LM, "What They See in Cinema."

26 portended a change: *Poughkeepsie Eagle News,* Dec. 11, 1917.

27 as full of life: *Poughkeepsie Eagle News,* Dec. 7 and Dec. 8, 1917.

28 You will never hear: *Photoplay,* June 1921, p. 47.

28 were full of naked: MHF interview with the author, Nov. 3, 1999.

29 "A Song" and "Chinese Shawls": Both poems are in LM's 1926 notebook but were written c. 1922.

29 "Distributing Letters": dated Jan. 26, 1922, and signed Betty Miller.

30 vulgarity of some: *Poughkeepsie Star,* Jan. 23, 1919.

31 the King who suffered: TM to LM, May 2, 1922.

31 but being rather disturbers: TM to "My dear Sister," Oct. 26, 1923.

32 Elizabeth had misbehaved: TM diary, May 29, 1924, JMC.

32 where a great dent: TM diary, July 1, 1924, JMC.

33 It is at these ages: Brill, p. 164.

34 filled with the sorrowful: Marion McKay, "Plus Fours and Books" [n.d.], Lindmark file, Adriance Memorial Library.

34 sitting on a million: MHF interview with the author, Nov. 23, 1999.

34 Elizabeth made: Information from *Poughkeepsie Evening Star and Enterprise,* May 10, 1923, p. 8.

36 I do not want: Zelda Fitzgerald, "Eulogy on the Flapper," *Metropolitan Magazine,* June 1922, reprinted in Bruccoli, p. 78.

37 the accent [had] shifted: F. Scott Fitzgerald, cited in Frederick Smith, "Fitzgerald, Flappers and Fame," *Shadowland,* Jan. 1921, n.p., reprinted in Bruccoli, p. 79.

37 She refused: Zelda Fitzgerald, "Eulogy on the Flapper," in Bruccoli, p. 78.

37 An artist in: This and quotations in next paragraph from Zelda Fitzgerald, "What Became of Our Flappers and Sheiks?" *McCall's,* Oct. 1925, p. 30.

3. Circulating Around

39 merely applying: Zelda Fitzgerald, "Eulogy on the Flapper," in Bruccoli, p. 78.

40 It took my chaperones: LM quoted in Gold and Fizdale, p. 161.

40 I loved everything: LM quoted in Keenan, p. 63.

40 One look at Paris: LM quoted in Nancy Osgood, "Accident Was Road to Adventure," *St. Petersburg Times,* Oct. 5, 1969.

41 but it didn't matter: Ibid.

41 If you will roll: Frank Crowninshield, quoted in Flanagan, p. 276. For information on Medgyès in the next paragraphs, see Flanagan, pp. 275–78.

41 as gay, as sad: Medgyès, quoted in Flanagan, p. 278.

42 Like marionettes: Flanagan, p. 276.

42 Every once in a while: LM, 1926 notebook.

42 an appetite in which: Flanagan, p. 273.

43 all the various: LM, 1926 notebook.

43 Her teacher was "Maestro": Information from LM, 1926 diary, Mar. 8 and 21 entries.

44 Moreover, in 1926: Chafe, pp. 103–4. Information in the following paragraphs from Chafe, passim.

44 to play a part: Mary McCarthy quoted in Carol Brightman, *Writing Dangerously: Mary McCarthy and Her World* (New York: Clarkson Potter, 1992), p. 65.

45 more interested in Medgyès: LM, 1926 diary, the source of quotations in this and the next five paragraphs.

47 In one of these: LM, 1926 notebook.

47 inhibitions, repressions: LM's 1926 diary is the source of quotations from LM in the rest of this section. The diary includes references to a number of theatrical productions staged in the spring of 1926.

48 Hedda's attempts to control: Brooks Atkinson, "The Play," *New York Times,* Feb. 21, 1926, sec. 7, p. 1.

48 a mystery play: John Mason Brown, cited in *The Encyclopedia of the New York Stage, 1920–1930* (Westport, Conn.: Greenwood Press, 1985), p. 312.

49 You who read this: LM, 1926 notebook, the source of all LM quotations in subsequent paragraphs.

50 There were large quantities: *New York Times,* July 1, 1924, cited in Paris, p. 67.

51 mooching around: Louise Brooks, quoted in ibid., p. 64.

51 finding debutantes a threat: Louise Brooks, quoted in ibid., p. 68.

4. Being in Vogue

55 This ravishing young woman: Livingston, p. 27.

56 I was so: TR to AP, June 9, 1984.

56 that all the paintings: LM, quoted in Amaya, p. 55.

56 circulating around: Ruth Seinfel, "Every One Can Pose," *New York Evening Post*, Oct. 24, 1932, p. 10.

57 both an escort service: Seebohm, p. 156.

57 the intangible quality: Ibid., p. 181.

57 the crowding of Fifth Avenue: *Vogue* [1927], as cited in Seebohm, pp. 279–80.

57 Women don't faint: Seebohm, p. 162.

59 He managed to give: Helen Lawrenson, managing editor of *Vanity Fair*, cited in Johnston, p. 201.

59 Big, rugged and bony: Marguerite Tazelaar interview with Steichen, "Portrait of a Pioneer," in *Amateur Movie Makers* 2 (1927), cited in Johnston, pp. 128–29.

59 satisfying and effective: Johnston, p. 128.

60 In one, she turns: *Vogue*, Aug. 15, 1928.

60 It was Steichen: LM, quoted in Amaya, p. 59.

60 Lee also observed: LM, quoted in Osgood, "Accident Was Road to Adventure."

60 take a man's view: "Flapping Not Repented Of," *New York Times*, July 16, 1922, as cited in Douglas, p. 247.

60 A modern woman: Dorothy Bromley, "Feminist—New Style," *Harper's*, Oct. 1927, as cited in Showalter, p. 16.

60 I wish I had: Both writers are cited in Douglas, p. 247.

61 which sets the pace: As cited in Watson, p. 175.

61 We went to many: TR to AP, June 9, 1984.

61 a harmless old goat: MHF interview with the author, Feb. 9, 2000

61 the man-who-knows: Watson, p. 176.

61 at the mere sight: Crowninshield, quoted in Seebohm, p. 104.

62 opening a new movie house: Alexander Woollcott, quoted in "Neysa McMein," *Current Biography 1941* (New York: H. W. Wilson, 1941), p. 548.

62 we all started: MHF interview with the author, Feb. 9, 2000

64 Lindbergh was the most: Lindbergh's stardom was confirmed with the appearance of the latest dance craze, the Lindy Hop, which was named in his honor.

64 It was vital: In this and the next paragraph, Jane Heap and Fernand Leger quoted in *The Little Review Anthology* (New York: Hermitage, 1953), pp. 341–44.

64 The moving picture: as cited in Goldberg, *Bourke-White: A Retrospective*, p. 12.

64 Photographs mingle romance: Professional Photographers of America, cited in Lemagny and Rouillé, p. 160.

65 I looked like an angel: LM, quoted in Keenan, p. 63.

66 WASP vision: Fox, p. 101.

66 At tea, two women: The advertisement is reproduced in Fox, p. 143.

67 Theodore was always: TR to AP, June 9, 1984.

68 If you didn't do it: MHF interview with the author, Feb. 7, 268

68 acquired a formal rigor: Hambourg, p. 33.

68 I want to become: Bourke-White, cited in Goldberg, *Margaret Bourke-White*, p. 77.

68 Her personal passion: Goldberg, *Bourke-White: A Retrospective*, p. 8.

69 The issue was indirectly: Alfred Barr, *Vanity Fair*, Aug. 1927, as cited in Hambourg, p. 41.

69 With the Millers: Elizabeth learned much later that Argylle died in a plane crash that day, while teaching a novice to fly.

5. Montparnasse with Man Ray

73 that the reason: TR to AP, June 9, 1984.

74 to enter photography: LM, quoted in Osgood, "Accident Was Road to Adventure."

74 Since she could seem: LM, quoted in "She Found Art Too Long and Full of Melancholy," Dec. 30, 1932, clipping.

74 He kind of rose up: Brigid Keenan, *The Woman We Wanted to Look Like* (London: MacMillan, 1977), p. 136, as cited in AP, *Lives,* p. 22.

74 I asked him: LM, quoted in Gold and Fizdale, p. 186.

75 My name is Lee Miller: LM, quoted in Amaya, p. 59.

75 Having terminated: MR, *Self Portrait,* p. 291.

75 If he took: LM, quoted in Amaya, p. 58.

75 The term came: *La garçonne's* publication in 1922 caused a scandal. Its heroine worked, drove a car, tried alcohol, drugs, and lesbianism, and supported progressive causes. The novel sold extremely well and by the end of the twenties had launched a new fashion.

76 a series of accomplishments: MR, *Self Portrait,* p. 198.

76 He liked to fiddle: LM, quoted in Amaya, p. 58.

76 I do not photograph: MR, cited in Schwarz, p. 228.

76 His title for this image: To French speakers, the title of Man's photograph also suggests the possibility of violence (*violon/violent*) and madness (*dingue,* crazy).

78 Any encounter I rejected: MR, *Minotaure,* nos. 3/4, p. 114.

79 He dislikes the "candid camera": LM, "I Worked with Man Ray," p. 316.

79 to extend the field: MR, "Man Ray: On Photography," *Commercial Art and Industry,* Feb. 1935, p. 66.

79 had to be unpacked: LM quotations in this and the following paragraphs are from Amaya, pp. 55, 58, 54.

80 a sylphlike creature: George Antheil and Madge Garland, as quoted in Baldwin, pp. 157, 156.

80 pretty, perverse: Henri-Pierre Roché, "Journal Intime," Feb. 9, 1930, LMA.

80 a sunkissed goat boy: Cecil Beaton in *Vogue,* c. 1960, as cited in AP, *Lives,* p. 29.

80 Her athletic figure: JBG interview with the author, Aug. 24, 1997.

81 He took me: LM quotations in this and the following paragraphs are from Amaya, p. 60.

83 He loved her: JBG, unpublished memoir.

83 The woman was taller: Pony Simon interview with the author, Feb. 7, 1998.

83 If an American artist: McBride, p. 293.

83 consecrating the triumph: French *Vogue,* Oct. 1929, pp. 76, 78.

84 in their normal surroundings: George Hoyningen-Huene, unpublished memoirs, as cited in Ewing, p. 98.

84 joined the *Vogue* studio: LM, quoted in Amaya, p. 59.

85 It used to intrigue me: Horst, *Photographs of a Decade* (New York: Augustin, n.d.), p. 9.

85 With strong-willed girls: Horst, cited in Lawford, p. 60.

86 What can be more binding: MR, "The Age of Light," *Photographs by Man Ray,* n.p.

86 where it reaches: André Breton, "The Visages of Woman," in MR, *Photographs by Man Ray,* p. 42.

86 The head of a woman: MR, "Inventory of a Woman's Head," in MR, *Self Portrait,* p. 393.

86 This image would haunt him: MR, *Self Portrait,* pp. 255, 393.

86 just an image: Breton, "Visages of Women," p. 42; his essay follows the image of Lee with her hand on her mouth.

87 The uncanny angle: Breton used a related Magritte painting on the cover of his 1934 *Qu'est-ce Que le Surréalisme?,* as if the enigma of the female sex-as-face offered a mocking answer to the question posed in the title.

87 The reduction of Lee's head: AP, *Lives,* p. 32. The image of Lee's neck continued to haunt Man. *The Necklace,* his 1965 collage made from a tightly cropped print of *Anatomies,* attaches a string arranged in overlapping coils around the base of the same powerful throat.

88 not the personality: Ben Maddow, *Edward Weston* (New York: Aperture, 1973), p. 55.

89 Man's strategy vis-à-vis: While Man's self-portrait could be seen to mock the genre, it wants to have it both ways—making fun of his supplicant position while also indulging in it.

89 You are so young: Undated MR correspondence in this and the next paragraph, LMA.

90 To set off Chanel's: *Vogue,* Dec. 8, 1930, and Sept. 15, 1930.

90 a brilliant mime: Yoxall, p. 87.

91 a mechanical refinement: Eugenia Janis, in Sullivan, p. 11.

91 one of photography's fascinations: Janis, in Sullivan, p. 17.

93 The unexposed parts: LM quotations in this and the next paragraph are from Amaya, pp. 56, 57; additional information from Baldwin, p. 158.

94 I don't know: LM as cited in *Atelier Man Ray,* p. 56.

94 In either case: Lyford, p. 233.

94 like a dream remembered: MR, *Self Portrait,* p. 255.

6. *La Femme Surréaliste*

98 he liked the effect: LM, quoted in Amaya, p. 58.

98 You should have seen: LM, "She Found Art Too Long," Dec. 30, 1932, clipping.

99 What was hers: JBG interview with the author, Aug. 25, 1997, the source of quotations in this and the next two paragraphs.

99 strode into a room: Francine du Plessix Gray, "Growing Up Fashionable," *New Yorker,* May 8, 1995, p. 54.

101 frequent, fast: Flanner, *Paris Was Yesterday,* p. 67.

101 absolutely stunning: LM, quoted in Amaya, p. 59.

102 I was pleased: MR, *Self Portrait,* p. 170.

103 The film, *Les Mystères:* The cast included Man Ray and Boiffard as men traveling to a destination chosen by a throw of the dice. The cubelike forms of the de Noailles' "chateau" (designed by Mallet-Stevens) made Man think of dice—hence the title.

104 He'd been shot: LM quotations in this and the following two paragraphs are from Steegmuller, pp. 408–9.

104 It was the remarkable: Chaplin, cited in Touzot, p. 336.

105 You don't lend out: Man Ray, quoted in Jan-Christopher Horak, ed., *Lovers of Cinema.* (Madison: University of Wisconsin Press, 1995), p. 127.

105 In a state of grace: LM, "What They See in the Cinema," p. 98.

106 What intrigues me: MR, in Pierre, p. 29.

106 a little girl: MR, in Pierre, p. 33.

106 little girls who lift: quotations in this and the following paragraph, Péret, Aragon, Man Ray, *1929* (Paris: Alyscamps Press, 1996 [trans. of 1929 edition]).

107 The couple cannot: The couple are identified as Man and Kiki by Klüver and Martin, p. 184; this seems unlikely, as Kiki left him early in 1929.

108 a wasp-waist hour-glass: William Seabrook to MR, cited in Baldwin, p. 166.

108 It was nothing: MR, *Self Portrait,* p. 193.

108 beautiful girls with every shade: MR, *Self Portrait,* pp. 123, 132.

109 He called it *Two Women:* Stein's "Two Women" was published in Paris, in Robert McAlmon's *Contact Collection of Contemporary Writers* (1925).

110 He was thrilled: Information in this and the following paragraph from EM and FM interview with the author, Mar. 16, 1996.

111 Every woman can be: French *Vogue,* Feb. 1931, pp. 72–73.

111 the difficult art: French *Vogue,* May 1931, p. 23.

113 To illustrate the fable: André Breton, "Il y aura une fois," *Le Surréalisme au service de la révolution* 1 (1930), pp. 2–4. Breton's 1938 *Dictionnaire abrégé du Surréalisme* uses this image of Lee as an example of *"la femme surréaliste."*

113 Is not the use: "L'affaire de l'age d'or," cited in Lewis, p. 94.

114 Lee arrived in Stockholm: Information in this and the next four paragraphs, TM diaries, Dec. 1930, Jan. 1931, JMC.

115 Having absorbed as much: *Stamboul Quest,* a World War I drama filmed in 1934, starred Myrna Loy as an American spy, capitalizing on the vogue for espionage plots crossed with love stories.

116 I love extravagant: LM portraits in *The Bioscope,* July 1, 1931, p. 19; LM, "What They See in Cinema."

116 I haven't been: This and other quotations from MR letters undated for the rest of the chapter, LMA.

117 curious things happened: LM, quoted in Amaya, pp. 56–57. It is possible that MR changed his mind about using Lee's image in *Electricité.* Comparing the nudes in the brochure with other shots by him of a different model, art historian Stephanie Spray Jandl concludes that he may have had photo sessions with this woman as well before selecting the images in *Electricité* (private communication, Mar. 13, 2001).

118 Charlie said he had: LM, quoted in Seinfel, "Everyone Can Pose."

7. The Lee Miller Studio in Manhattan

121 Tensions ran high: This account derives from Jean Cocteau, *Le Sang d'un poète,* in Touzot, p. 331.

122 a bewildering and splintering: *"Surréalisme"* ran from Jan. 9 to Jan. 29, 1932. The *New York Times* critic deemed it "one of the most entertaining exhibitions of the season" (Jan. 13, 1932, p. 27).

122 Perhaps the "eye": Baldwin, p. 169.

122 It is some time: MR to Elsie Ray Siegler, Feb. 12, 1932, Man Ray Papers, Getty Research Institute.

123 She should be: AEB, quoted in AP, *Lives,* pp. 39–40.

123 Judging by the tales: Although it was thought that Nimet committed suicide, she recovered sufficiently to sublet Djuna Barnes's Paris apartment in 1933, and after her divorce, to marry Prince Nicholas Metchersky. Nimet died on Aug. 4, 1943. See Jaloux.

123 half-dead with sorrow: Levy, *Portrait,* pp. 121–22.

123 Unexpectedly, the *New York Times:* "On View in New York," *New York Times,* Feb. 28, 1932, p. 11.

123 Another critic described: K.G.S. [Katherine Grant Sterne], "European Photography on View," *New York Times,* Feb. 25, 1932, p. 19. The show ran from February 20 to March 11; the Millers came to New York on March 8 to see Lee's photographs.

124 *Time's* critic pooh-poohed: "Rayograms," *Time,* Apr. 18, 1932. *Time* ran Lee's portrait of Man as an illustration.

125 Lee suddenly became: EM quotations in this and the following paragraph are from "Tea at Trumps" radio tape, Mar. 1989, LMA.

125 The magazine agreed: "To Miss Lee Miller," *Time,* Aug. 1, 1932.

125 Julien, who was Lee's age: JL quotations and information in this and the following paragraphs are from Levy, *Portrait,* p. 151, passim.

127 And she was about: The first issue of *Le Phare de Neuilly,* with illustrations by Man and Nadar, appeared in February 1933, with Lee's photograph of a lizard in a lilac tree on p. 3.

127 Cut out the eye: *This Quarter* (Sept. 1932), p. 55.

127 Elizabeth, Elizabeth: MR to LM, LMA.

128 He seemed to have shrunk: JBG interview with the author, Aug. 25, 1997.

128 Looking pensive: "Cargo of Celebrities That Was Brought Here by the Ile de France," *New York World Telegram,* Oct. 18, 1932, p. 3; LM, quoted by Julia Blanshard in "Other Faces Are Her Fortune," *Poughkeepsie Evening Star,* Nov. 1, 1932, clipping.

128 Her sequinned Lanvin dress: U.S. *Vogue,* Nov. 1932, clipping.

129 to settle down: LM quotations in this and following paragraph are from Seinfel, "Every One Can Pose."

129 from all these publicity-hunters: MR to Elsie Ray Siegler, GRI.

129 I really liked her: Joella Levy Bayer interview with the author, Oct. 2, 1991.

129 an audience complex: LM quotations in this and the next paragraph are from Blanshard, "Other Faces Are Her Fortune."

131 a synthesis of voyager: Dickran Tashjian, *Joseph Cornell: Gifts of Desire* (Miami Beach, Fla.: Grassfield, 1992), p. 48.

131 Lee had left America: Frank Crowninshield, "Lee Miller, Exhibition of Photographs," LMA. This was her only solo show in her lifetime.

132 Her celebrity status: LM's portrait of Luce appeared in *Vanity Fair,* Dec. 1932, p. 47. Lee and the popular blond actress resembled each other. The similarities in their backgrounds—Luce came from upstate New York, studied dance with the Denishawn School, and performed in Ziegfeld's *Revue* in 1926—would have amused them. Claire Luce is *not* the writer Clare Boothe Luce, who married Henry Luce, of *Fortune.*

132 She can do: LM, "She Found Art Too Long and Full of Melancholy," Dec. 30, 1932.

132 the new light: JL is quoted in the *New York Times* art section, Jan. 1, 1933, p. 8.

132 We just opened: Joella Levy to Mina Loy, Jan. 3, 1933, CBC. Lee's portrait of Mina was included in the show.

132 her photographic work: E. A. Jewell, "Two One-Man Shows," *New York Times,* Dec. 31, 1932, p. 18.

132 Lovely Lee Miller: William Gutman, "News and Gossip," *Creative Art,* Jan. 1933, p. 76.

132 the sixty most: "News and Gossip," *Creative Art,* Feb. 1933, p. 87.

132 a relatively impersonal judge: JL, "The Bergdorf Goodman Exhibit of New York Beauty," CBC.

133 to not taking care: EM diary, May 9, 1933.

133 Lee's parents still followed: Hay's philosophy is explained in his *Health via Food,* pp. 87–88, 289.

133 when nerve stresses: Hay-Ven "Compatible Food Combinations" card, CBC.

134 THE photographer: TR to AP, June 9, 1984.

134 Lee could be: EM, quoted in AP, *Lives,* p. 55.

134 Lee was very insistent: EM, quoted in AP, *Lives,* p. 45.

135 ended up rushing: EM, quoted in AP, *Lives,* p. 55. EM explained to the author the help Lee received in her early work with color from Dr. Walter "Nobby" Clark, director of research for Eastman Kodak, whose interests included color photography, specialized instruments like sensitometers, and aerial photography.

135 understanding of the street: Walker Evans, quoted in Hambourg, p. 49.

135 Of the Brooklyn Museum's: Katherine Grant Sterne, "American vs. European Photography," *Parnassus,* Mar. 1932, pp. 16–20 (as paraphrased in Hambourg, p. 54).

136 ill or tired: EM diary, May 9, 1933.

136 less by passion: Houseman, p. 96.

136 ugly, fat, & bad tempered: Joella Levy to Mina Loy [summer 1934], CBC.

136 For the Frenchman: JL, Film Society Program #5; Howard Barnes, quoted in "Praise Is Paid to Miss Miller," *Poughkeepsie Evening Star,* Dec. 5, 1933; John Houseman, NPR "Morning Edition" tape, Mar. 2, 1989, LMA.

136 Lee Miller of New York City: "Catherine North Sague Bride of John H. Miller," *Poughkeepsie Eagle News,* June 19, 1933, p. 4.

137 Lee's photographs: program quoted by Phil Rhynders, letter to the editor, *Poughkeepsie Evening Star,* Dec. 7, 1933.

137 the high priestess: *Boston Globe,* quoted in Eugene Gaddis, *Magician of the Modern* (New York: Knopf, 2000), p. 233.

138 a nigger show: Virgil Thomson, quoted in Watson, p. 213. My account of this production is indebted to Watson.

138 because up to that time: Eva Jessye, quoted in Watson, p. 245.

139 The participants are seen: Ironically, when the black actors asked Lee to lighten their skin tones, she experimented with a red filter that gave the desired effect. (AP to the author, private communication.)

139 by Rolls Royce, by airplane: Lucius Beebe, quoted in Watson, p. 265.

139 It *does* stand: Constance Askew, quoted in Watson, p. 6.

139 Thus do tastes differ: *Vanity Fair,* May 1934, p. 52.

140 She disappeared: John Houseman, NPR "Morning Edition" tape, Mar. 2, 1989.

140 although not distinguished: Joella Levy to Mina Loy [summer 1934], CBC; John Houseman, NPR "Morning Edition" tape.

140 To ask if he wanted: Jackie Knight to Marcel Duchamp [c. summer 1934]; MR cable to LM, cited in AP, *Lives,* p. 56.

141 The article, probably dictated: "Lee Miller a Bride," *New York Times,* Sept. 6, 1934, clipping.

8. Egypt

146 photography off its track: Walker Evans, "The Reappearance of Photography," *Hound and Horn,* Oct.–Dec. 1931; reprinted in Alan Trachtenberg, ed., *Classic Essays in Photography* (New Haven: Leete's Island Books, 1980), p. 186.

146 bring peace to her heart: AEB to FM and TM, Aug. 26, 1934.

147 which makes them look: Ibid.

147 the sinews: Baedeker, p. xxxvi.

148 The average Oriental: Ibid., p. xix.

148 was to think of Cairo: Magdi Wahba, "Cairo Memories," in Derek Hopwood, ed., *Studies in Arab History* (Oxford, U.K.: Macmillan, 1990), p. 107.

149 One can imagine: Ahmed Hassanein, a much-decorated fellow of the geographic societies of France, Britain, and the United States (and also of Bedouin descent), made the first major expedition to the interior of the Libyan desert in 1923. His account of this trip, *The Lost Oases* (1925), was the standard guide to the region.

149 Lee is happy: AEB to FM and TM, n.d. [winter 1934].

149 None of their wives: LM, quoted in Gold and Fizdale, p. 186.

149 We had a marvelous time: this and the next four paragraphs are from AEB to FM and TM, n.d. [winter 1934]

151 With this new pretentious: Wahba, "Cairo Memories," pp. 103–4.

151 diseased by French: AEB to FM and TM, n.d. [winter 1934].

152 Before lunch: "En Route vers les Pyramides," French *Vogue*, Nov. 1929, p. 56.

153 Eighteenth Dynasty Edwardian: Cooper, p. 37.

153 you'd call Shepheard's: Mary Anita Loos interview with the author, July 6, 1999.

154 everybody Lee meets: AEB to FM and TM, n.d. [winter 1934].

154 I was delighted: LM, quoted in Gold and Fizdale, p. 186.

154 Both Lee and myself: AEB to FM and TM, July 7, 1935.

154 I . . . got sort of: LM to EM, n.d. [1935]; AP, *Lives*, p. 65.

154 a show of sensitiveness: AEB to FM to TM, Aug. 8 [1935].

155 The atmosphere is charged: Quotations from this and following two paragraphs are from AEB to FM and TM, Dec. 30, 1935.

155 It was a good thing: EM interview with the author, Dec. 13, 1992.

155 I will try: AEB to EM and TM, n.d. [autumn 1934].

156 An apartment: LM to EM, n.d. [1935]; AP, *Lives*, p. 65.

156 an ace in business: AEB to FM and TM, July 7, 1936.

157 We have had you: LM to EM, n.d. [1936].

157 I get so bitter: This and the next paragraph, LM to FM and TM, n.d. [winter 1936]; AP, *Lives*, pp. 65–66.

157 I loved the dryness: EM interview with the author, Dec. 13, 1992.

158 Their compatriots, most: This and the following two paragraphs, MM interview with the author, Dec. 13, 1992.

158 Goldie survived: Baronne Empain interview with the author, Feb. 2, 2002.

160 I took her as she was: Gertie Wissa interview with the author, May 20, 1996.

160 In the spring of 1937: This trip is described in AP, *Lives*, pp. 71–72.

9. Surrealist Encampments

164 His hair was green: RP quotations in this and the next paragraph, R. Penrose, *Scrap Book*, p. 104. Breton's *L'Amour fou*, published earlier that year, hailed "mad love" as a revolutionary force, one generally lived outside of marriage.

164 I have slept: RP to LM, June 25, 1937.

164 It was a delightful: Agar, p. 133.

165 One day I was: Ibid., p. 115.

165 A nation which: Herbert Read, "Introduction," *The International Surrealist Exhibition* catalogue (London: New Burlington Galleries, 1936), n.p.

165 Women Surrealists: Agar, p. 120.

166 bent on opening: Agar, quoted in Simpson, p. 26.

166 was expected to behave: Agar, p. 120.

166 a fountain of joy: Ibid., pp. 132–33. Roland commemorated their affair in a witty profile shot of the couple joined and separated by a phallic megalith.

166 talking dogs: Leonora Carrington interview with the author, Dec. 28, 1999.

166 You have given me: RP to LM, Oct. 10, 1937.

166 The blond season: Eluard, quoted in AP, *Roland Penrose*, p. 78.

167 a remarkable woman: Agar, quoted in Chadwick, p. 56.

167 the men were expected: Agar, p. 121.

167 a thoroughbred who: AEB to LM [July 1937], quoted in AP, *Lives*, p. 75.

168 I think if love: Agar, pp. 133, 132.

168 RP suffered: RP, quoted in AP, *Roland Penrose*, p. 29.

169 the appearance of: AP, *Roland Penrose*, p. 80.

169 that he was happy: RP, *Flashart* 112 (May 1983), p. 31; Agar, pp. 135, 138.

169 small, neat, well-built: RP, *Picasso*, p. 312.

170 a gesture of friendship: Gilot, p. 137.

170 One could distinguish: RP, *Flashart* 112, p. 34.

170 Evoking the summer: Ibid.

170 At the time: Rubin, "Reflections on Picasso and Portraiture," in Rubin, pp. 78, 86.

170 Just as Eluard: Richardson, p. 25. AP writes, "The subjects of Picasso's best female portraits tend to be the women he slept with, and Lee was no exception." (*Roland Penrose*,
p. 80).

170 Roland's description: RP, *Scrap Book,* p. 109.

171 You do not sit: LM, quoted in *Daily Telegraph,* July 29, 1968, clipping.

172 The work and: Keith Hartley, "Roland Penrose: Private Passions for the Public Good,"
The Surrealist and the Photographer, p. 19. It did not occur to the Surrealists that intellect and sensuality could be found in the same woman.

173 to confuse the delights: Agar, quoted in Chadwick, p. 56.

10. The Egyptian Complex

175 It's cold: LM to RP, Oct. 5, 1937.

176 the heat—the bad food: LM to RP, Oct. 11, 1937.

176 so miserable leaving: LM to MR, n.d.

176 She was the most: Wingate Charlton interview with the author, Jan. 21, 2001.

176 five shades of blue: quotations in this and the next three paragraphs, LM to RP, Oct.
15, 1937.

177 rather a flop: quotations in this and the next paragraph, LM to RP, n.d. [Oct. 27, 1937].

178 It was like being: LM to RP, Nov. 8, 1937.

178 I do so want: LM to RP, Oct. 22, 1937.

178 so that if one day: LM to RP, Oct. 28, 1937.

178 The light is perfect: Quotations in this and the next paragraph, LM to RP, Nov. 9, 1937.

179 fill[ing] my room: RP to LM, Oct. 25, 1937.

179 I wish that I: LM to RP, Nov. 9, 1937.

179 the tattooed woman: LM to RP, Oct. 28, 1937.

179 You will look: RP to LM, Nov. 14, 1937.

179 Roland longed for her: RP to LM, Oct. 22, 1937.

180 flat brass gearwheels: Quotations in this and the next paragraph, LM to RP, Nov. 9,
1937.

180 I shall choose: RP to LM, Nov. 14, 1937.

180 with great care: RP to LM, Nov. 21, 1937.

180 I walk around: LM to RP, n.d. [Dec. 1937].

181 Skiing in Egypt: Quotations in this and the next two paragraphs, Mary Anita Loos
interview with the author, July 6, 1999.

181 they still don't believe: LM to RP, Dec. 23, 1937.

182 The long-awaited arrival: Gertie Wissa interview with the author, May 20, 1996.

182 as a deliberate insult: Quotations in this and the next paragraph, LM to RP, Mar. 9, 1938.

182 a letch: Quotations in this and the next paragraph, LM to RP, Dec. 23, 1937.

182 altho I spend: Quotations in this and the next two paragraphs, LM to RP, Dec. 25, 1937.

183 those depressing Egyptian gray days: LM to RP, Jan. 7, 1938.

183 Many people find: Robin Fedden, "An Anatomy of Exile," *Personal Landscape* (London:
Editions Poetry, 1945), pp. 7–11.

184 spend[ing] a great deal: Quotations in this and the next paragraph, LM to RP, Jan. 7, 1938.

185 Your letters read: RP to LM, Jan. 11, 1938.

185 Why the devil: RP to LM, Jan. 18, 1938.

185 peaceably: LM to RP, Mar. 9, 1938.

185 busy bedding: RP to LM, Jan. 18, 1938.

186 Her behavior: Gertie Wissa interview with the author, May 20, 1996.

186 hard hit: LM to RP, n.d., in reply to RP's letter of Apr. 2, 1938.

186 He found Cairo society: Information in this and the next two paragraphs, Sir Bernard Burrows interview with the author, Sept. 3, 1997.

187 understand this correspondence: Michael Lesy, *Bearing Witness* [n.p.], as quoted in Paul Hendrikson, *Looking for the Light* (New York: Knopf, 1992), p. 95. *Portrait of Space* is said to have inspired Magritte's canvas *Le Baiser.*

187 I look to your arrival: RP to LM, Apr. 18, 1938.

187 some infra-red film: LM to RP, June 18, 1938.

188 Sometimes, almost never: RP, *The Road Is Wider,* n.p., is the source of quotations in the next two paragraphs.

188 magic to bring on: LM quotations in this and the next paragraph are from "Romania," unpublished manuscript, quoted in AP, *Lives,* p. 87.

189 angry peasants: Quotations in this and the next paragraph, LM to RP, Oct. 15, 1938.

190 some quite startling pictures: LM to RP, Jan. 6, 1939.

190 as many changes of scenery: Quotations in this and the next paragraph, LM to AEB, Nov. 17, 1938.

190 All I want: LM to RP, Jan. 6, 1939.

191 Our gang of misfits: LM to RP, Jan. 23, 1939.

191 In a fit of longing: LM to RP, Jan. 6, 1939.

191 give me endless opportunities: LM to RP, Jan. 23, 1939.

192 He brought as gifts: Lee's copy of *The Road Is Wider* was full of innuendos, including a note stating that the memoir was "bound in gold handcuffs with 69 original inventions by the author." RP on pieces of sentimental jewelry: *Scrap Book,* p. 118.

192 discussed our futures: LM to RP, Mar. 23, 1939.

193 My plans are maturing: LM to RP, n.d. [Apr. 1939].

193 but through all your plans: RP to LM, Mar. 19, 1939.

193 If it's war scares: RP to LM, May 1, 1939.

193 a "swell" ship: LM to RP, n.d. [May 1939].

193 British bourgeoisie: LM to RP, June 7, 1939. That Lee failed to tell Aziz of her decision to leave him at this point is clear from his letters to her for the rest of 1939, which anticipate her return. On June 6 he asked her to join him in Saint Moritz for August; on September 4 and 6 he discussed his plan to rent them an apartment in Cairo that she could decorate as she liked; on September 20 he wrote, "you will have to postpone your arrival for a while, that is if you have decided to come right away."

11. London in the Blitz

197 uneasy & nervous: LM 1939 notebook.

197 Her finances: LM to RP, n.d. [June 1939]. Aziz continued to send money.

197 too timorous & undecided: Bernard Burrows to LM, June 2, 1939.

197 Altho these nice: LM draft of letter to Bernard Burrows, LM 1939 notebook.

198 *Bien Visé* poses: *Bien Visé*'s English title, *Good Shooting,* would be better translated

Well Aimed (*viser* means to fix in the line of sight). To an English-speaker (for whom *visé* sounds like *vissé*), it hints that the woman has been "well screwed down."

198 A companion painting: Remy, p. 185. AP calls *Octavia* an expression of Roland Penrose's struggle "to resolve whether to allow himself to be ruled by his intellect or his hormones" (*Roland Penrose*, p. 96).

199 rather indifferent: RP to LM, Oct. 25, 1938.

199 Roland made up: Guggenheim, p. 160.

199 Within a few weeks: Peggy's abortion influenced her decision at this time, see Remy, pp. 164–66, and Jacqueline Wald, *Peggy, the Wayward Guggenheim* (New York: Dutton, 1986), pp. 175–82.

199 vastly amused: LM to Bernard Burrows, June 27, 1939.

200 Their irrepressible high spirits: RP, *Picasso*, p. 323.

200 a pedal-operated fretsaw: Agar, pp. 145–46.

201 The smartest seems: Panter-Downes, p. 10.

201 Learn to cook: As cited in McDowell, p. 45.

201 siege, starvation, invasion: LM to EM and MM, Aug. 25, 1942.

201 a war of yawns: Panter-Downes, p. 15.

202 What I did: RP, quoted in AP, *Roland Penrose*, p. 99; cf. RP, *Scrap Book*, p. 126.

202 INTELLIGENCE: Condé Nast to LM, as quoted in AP, *Lives*, p. 98.

202 KNOWING: Dr. Agha to Betty Penrose, Mar. 1, 1940.

202 not a life preserver: As cited in wall note, Imperial War Museum, London.

202 a little less: Doreen Impey to AP, Jan. 18, 2001.

202 Women's first duty: AW, quoted by Drusilla Beyfus in obituary, *Guardian*, Oct. 31, 2001.

203 Their Soho dinners: Agar, p. 146.

203 whether the surrealists: T. McGreevy, "London's Liveliest Show," *The Studio* 120 (Oct. 1940), p. 137, as cited in Remy, p. 211.

203 the enemies of desire: Quoted in Remy, p. 212. The *London Bulletin* was edited by Mesens and Penrose.

204 an integral part: Remy, p. 171.

204 You did so well: LM to FM and TM, n.d. [1940].

204 "This Is London": Murrow, p. 145.

204 could seize a person: RP, *Scrap Book*, pp. 127–28.

205 Has a wandering spirit: "The Contributors to This Issue," *Lilliput*, vol. 9, no. 4 (Oct. 1941), p. 332.

205 A photo-essay: Anne Scott-James, "The Taking of a Fashion Magazine Photograph," *Picture Post*, Oct. 26, 1940, pp. 22–25.

205 I marvelled at: Beaton, p. 37. The War Office hired Beaton as an official photographer soon after the raids began; by 1941 he was with the Royal Air Force.

205 her eye for: RP, *Scrap Book*, p. 128. Murrow thought that the balloons resembled "queer animals with grace and beauty" (*This Is London*, p. 232).

206 like a soft-shelled crab: LM to FM and TM, n.d. [Dec. 1940].

206 We saw eye to eye: Carter, *With Tongue in Chic*, p. 36.

207 "grim" and "gay": As reported in Murrow, p. 215.

207 The embodiment: Carter, *Grim Glory*, Preface; Publisher's Note [n.p.], published in the United States as *Bloody but Unbowed: Pictures of Britain Under Fire*. Murrow calls the images "honest pictures—routine scenes to those of us who have reported Britain's ordeal by fire and high explosive" (Preface).

207 hopelessly false: LM to FM and TM in this and the next paragraph, n.d. [Dec. 1940].

207 they had twenty minutes: Carter, *With Tongue in Chic*, p. 64.

208 It was an agreeably: Barbara Skelton, *Tears Before Bedtime* (London: Hamish Hamilton, 1987), p. 26.

208 We eat fine: LM to EM, Aug. 25, 1942.

208 Xmas won't be: LM to FM and TM, Dec. 14, 1941.

209 If the new order: Chase, p. 291.

209 with a touch chic: "They Have Been Here Before," U.K. *Vogue*, Oct. 1941, p. 33.

209 Within a few months: Yoxall, p. 153.

209 For Lee's next assignment: Lesley Blanch, "W.RN.S. on the Job," U.K. *Vogue*, Nov. 1941, p. 92.

209 For me: LM to FM and TM, Dec. 14, 1941.

210 It was a ménage: DS interview with the author, May 28, 1996.

210 I was very fond: Cited in AP, *Roland Penrose*, p. 103.

211 There was no chi-chi: DS interview with the author, May 28, 1996.

211 pictorialism with a meaning: DS quotations in this paragraph are from Loengard, p. 113.

211 one-page quickie: DS to WS, Oct. 17, 1943, DSE.

211 Lee also traveled: "This Above All," *Life*, Jan. 26, 1942, pp. 68–77; "The Horrors," *Life*, July 20, 1942, pp. 53–57; "Death in the Village," *Life*, Nov. 2, 1942, pp. 108–10.

212 Bob Capa came: Welsh, p. 89.

212 the atmosphere changing: Cynthia Ledsham Thompson interview with the author, Sept. 5, 1999.

212 the demand to be casual: Wertenbaker, pp. 245, 244. After becoming pregnant, Lael divorced her husband and married Wertenbaker.

213 The two phenomena: DS, in AP, *Lee Miller's War* (henceforth cited as *LMW*), p. 9.

213 Now I wear: LM to FM and TM, May 3, 1943.

215 Lee's first piece: LM, "American Army Nurses Photographed and Described by Lee Miller," U.K. *Vogue*, May 1943, pp. 54–55, 88. A passage on p. 88, on the nurses' love of literary pilgrimages, reads as if the author were British: "They are brought up on 'English Literature'; but as they did not play pirates in Penzance or go to church in a cathedral, as we did, the geography of literature and history remain unreal"—a possible concession to the British readership?

215 My theory: RP, *Scrap Book*, p. 130.

215 The following year: "Speaking of Pictures," *Life*, Apr. 19, 1943, p. 13.

215 Increasingly, Lee collaborated: Information in this and the following paragraph from DS interview with the author, May 28, 1996.

216 some of the pix are mine: LM to FM and TM, Jan. 23, 1944.

216 if I croak: DS to WS, Feb. 23, 1944, DSE.

216 scrubbing, polishing and perfecting: "Night Life Now," U.K. *Vogue*, June 1943, p. 29.

217 nearly drowned: Quotations in this and the next paragraph, LM to FM and TM, Jan. 23, 1944.

217 war turned them: U.K. *Vogue*, Feb. 1944, p. 39.

218 You in the United States: LM, "This Is London . . . Ed Murrow Ready," U.S. *Vogue*, Aug. 1, 1944, p. 96.

218 Lee says there is: Edward R. Murrow, quoted in AP, *Lives*, p. 114.

218 I've spent fifteen or so years: LM to AW, quoted in AP, *Lives*, p. 116.

218 how the acutely observant: AW, Institute of Contemporary Arts lecture, 1992.

218 cornered the color racket: DS to WS, Oct. 9, 1943, DSE.

219 a bit dreamlike: Panter-Downes, p. 313.

219 this is just: Ibid., p. 320.

12. Covering the War in France

221 On D-day: There were exceptions. Martha Gellhorn crossed the Channel as a stow-away, joined a group of stretcher bearers, and filed a piece about the wounded but was confined to quarters on her return. Ruth Cowan and Iris Carpenter went to France several weeks later but were not allowed to cover the slow progress of the Allies against German strongholds along the coast. My account is indebted to Sorel.

222 It was all very well: Withers, *Lifespan*, p. 53.

222 As we flew: Quotations from LM in this and the next eight paragraphs from AP, *Lee Miller's War* (henceforth cited as *LMW*), pp. 15–26. Lee arrived in France when the battle of Cherbourg was still raging.

222 When you think: Withers, *Lifespan*, p. 92.

224 Sykes had painted: "Normandy Nurses" photo caption no. 88 reads: "Lee Miller wearing special helmet borrowed from U.S. Army Photographer Don Sykes."

224 VOGUE has its own: *New York Herald Tribune*, Sept. 11, 1944, n.p. The ad continues: "On D-Day plus 5, Lee Miller VOGUE writer-photographer, crossed the channel in the wake of the AEF. Her stirring article, *U.S.A. Tent Hospital in France*, appears in the current issue of VOGUE. In terse prose and unforgettable pictures, VOGUE shows the efficiency of the American Medical Corps, the devotion of American nurses under fire. Here is a straight-forward account of on-the-spot-surgery . . . field hospitals at the front . . . air evacuation of the wounded."

224 the most exciting: AW, quoted in AP, *Lives*, p. 118.

225 The wicker furniture: LM quotations in this and next nine paragraphs from AP, *Lives*, pp. 32–65.

227 an unmade, unwashed bed: DS, "Foreword," AP, *LMW*, p. 10.

227 She looked tired: Author interview with Raymond Perrussel, May 21, 2001. "We were happy the battle was over," Perrussel recalled, "and they were happy to be alive." He is the tallest of the GIs observing the Germans' departure.

228 in the doghouse: LM to AW, censor date Aug. 29, 1944, AP, *LMW*, p. 65.

228 Lee was the only: DS to AW, Aug. 23, 1944.

228 It is very bitter: LM to AW, dated Aug. 26–27, AP, *Lives*, p. 65; photo p. 64.

228 Paris had gone mad: LM, AP, *LMW*, p. 67. The date of Miller's arrival in Paris is not known. Given that the women journalists in Rennes were allowed to go there only after it was secured from the Germans, she probably arrived on August 27th.

229 a cross between: DS, "Foreword," AP, *LMW*, p. 11.

229 After tremendous three day: U.S. *Vogue*, Oct. 15, 1944, p. 148.

229 Everyone's feet hurt: LM to AW, service letter, (mis)dated August 18 [1944].

230 The press bar: This drawing is included in David E. Sherman, ed., *Life Goes to War* (Boston: Little, Brown, 1977), pp. 250–51.

230 sick with rage: LM to AW, service message, n.d.

231 From the point of view: LM, AP, *LMW*, p. 73.

231 younger that I thought: Ibid., p. 77.

232 very large, padded: John Houseman, quoting Joan Courtney, his wife, "Tea at Trumps" radio broadcast, Los Angeles, 1989, held at LMA.

232 six pointed satinette: LM to AW, service message, Oct. 12, 1944; see also AP, *LMW*, pp. 79–80.

232 part of the passive: Quotations in this and the next paragraph are from LM to AW, Oct. 13, 1944.

233 I want to go: LM to AW, Sept. 8, 1944.

233 They were armed: LM quotations in this and the next two paragraphs are from AP, *LMW,* pp. 87–91.

233 On Sept. 28: Catherine Coyne, as cited in Sorel, p. 226.

233 The night before: Morris, p. 89.

234 They were all: RP, *Scrap Book,* p. 104.

234 a home-bound instructor: RP, *Scrap Book,* p. 132.

234 She felt torn: LM to AW, n.d.

234 trying to be: DS to WS, Oct. 22 [1944], DSE.

234 They regard it: LM to AW, service message, Oct. 10, 1944.

234 reminded me of: LM to AW, service message, Oct. 4, 1944.

235 seductive clothing has: LM to AW, service message, Oct. 10, 1944.

235 I find Edna: LM, AP, *LMW,* pp. 83–84.

235 They realize that: LM to AW, service message, Oct. 12, 1944.

235 I want more: LM, AP, *LMW,* p. 93, censor date Dec. 7, 1944.

236 The Duchy of Luxembourg: LM quotations in this and the next six paragraphs are from AP, *LMW,* pp. 114–30.

238 coming to full: LM to AW, Dec. 7, 1944, AP, *LMW,* p. 92.

238 I was an extension: LM account of her interview with Colette is in AP, *LMW,* pp. 105–9.

239 was now more British: LM to AW, service letter, Nov. 30, 1944; see LM, "Brussels," U.S. *Vogue,* Mar. 1, 1945, pp. 132–35, 162, 164. "Brussels" is not included in AP, *LMW.*

239 This is very difficult: LM to AW, service letter, Dec. 4, 1944, and LM quotations in the next two paragraphs, AP, *LMW,* pp. 110–13.

241 American soldiers knew: LM to AW, service letter, Dec. 7, 1944.

241 To amuse journalists: LM to AW, service letter, n.d.; see U.S. *Vogue,* Apr. 1, 1945, pp. 102, 131.

241 the number of people: LM to AW, service letter, n.d. "Older residents" were those who had hotel rooms for some time, often since the liberation of Paris.

241 When the hotel: Yoxall, pp. 188–89.

241 slightly scratchy in places: LM quotations in this and the next paragraph from LM to AW, service message, n.d.

242 Strasbourg was "frightening": LM, AP, *LMW,* p. 150.

243 My sense was that: Quotations in this and the next paragraph, Dr. Alain Dubourg interview with the author, May 25, 2001.

243 Since its liberation: The camp at Natzweiler-Struthof was built in 1941 by German prisoners who were made to carry the materials up the mountains on their backs. Thousands died as a consequence of conditions there, which included medical experimentation. In September 1944, the prisoners (Poles, Russians, Dutch, French, and Norwegians) were transferred to Dachau.

243 About this time: LM told the tale of her "gasoline can" to Henry McNulty, whose version appears in "High Spirits from White Alcohols," *House and Garden,* Apr. 1970, p. 182.

243 A few days later: Information and LM quotations in this and the next three paragraphs, AP, *LMW,* pp. 135–45.

244 "Lee quelque chose": Information and quotations in this and the next two paragraphs, Edmonde Charles-Roux interview with the author, Mar. 3, 1998.

13. Covering the War in Germany

247 One essential fact: G.B., "Nous n'avions pas d'uniforme," French *Vogue,* Jan. 1945, p. 41. This issue includes Lee's shots of Dietrich, Astaire, Colette, Paul Eluard, Bérard, and the Wrens.

248 What's wrong with: "Paris Black Market Robs U.S. Army," *Life,* Mar. 26, 1945, p. 29.

248 You can weave: LM, "G.I. Lingo in Europe," U.S. *Vogue,* Apr. 1, 1945, p. 131.

248 arrogant and spoiled: LM, "I See Germany," U.S. *Vogue,* June 1945, p. 193; AP, *LMW,* p. 169.

249 well nourished on: LM quotations in this and the next paragraph are from U.S. *Vogue,* June 1945, p. 193; AP, *LMW,* p. 166.

249 It was good: Flanner, *Janet Flanner's World,* p. 95.

249 Often the jailor: LM, "Germans Are Like This," U.S. *Vogue,* June 1945, p. 102; AP, *LMW,* p. 166.

249 It hurt my stomach: LM to AW, service letter, n.d. [late Mar. 1945].

250 When this image: Bourke-White's image of Cologne cathedral ran in *Life,* Apr. 23, 1945, p. 31.

250 I confirmed that: LM to AW, undeveloped German film, photo captions, n.d.

250 as messy and hollow: LM quotations in this and the next paragraph, LM to AW, Apr. 5, 1945.

251 I don't like Germany: LM to RP, n.d. [c. Apr. 10, 1945].

251 After weeks: LM quotations in this and the next paragraph, LM to AW, Apr. 5, 1945.

252 the creeps: LM to AW, Apr. 9, 1945. Lee caught up with Dave Scherman about this time; his shots of Bad Nauheim appeared in *Life* on Apr. 30, 1945.

252 Things move very fast: LM to AW [mid-Apr. 1945], quoted in AP, *LMW,* p. 159.

252 I have never felt: Dwight D. Eisenhower, *Crusade in Europe* (Garden City, N.Y.: Doubleday, 1948), pp. 408–9.

252 I don't take pictures: LM, Jena photo captions, Apr. 25, 1945, p. 4.

253 I saw these dead: William Frye, "Thousands Tortured to Death in Camp at Belsen," *Boston Globe,* Apr. 21, 1945, pp. 1, 3, as cited in Zelizer, p. 67.

253 You really had: Ann Stringer, as cited in Sorel, p. 351.

253 In photographing the murder camps: Bourke-White, *Portrait of Myself,* pp. 259–60.

253 the consistent fashion: LM to AW, n.d. [c. Apr. 20, 1945].

253 We were one: Charles B. MacDonald, *Company Commander* (Short Hills, N.J.: Burford Books, 1947), pp. 258–59.

253 in a different: LM to AW [c. Apr. 20, 1945]; AP, *LMW,* p. 178.

255 Buchenwald is beyond: Percy Knauth, cited in Abzug, p. 45.

255 Their eyes were sunk: As cited in Abzug, p. 56.

255 using the camera: Bourke-White, *Portrait of Myself,* p. 259.

255 The ex-prisoners have found: LM quotations in this and the next two paragraphs are from LM, Buchenwald photo captions [c. Apr. 21, 1945].

256 I found it comic: LM quotations in this and the next paragraph are from LM, Torgau ms.; AP, *LMW,* p. 155.

257 There was more food: Iris Carpenter, cited in Sorel, p. 345.

258 There was a terrible: LM, Torgau ms.; AP, *LMW,* p. 155.

258 This is the first: LM, AP, *LMW,* p. 181.

258 How is it: Higgins quoted by DS in interview with the author, May 28, 1996.

259 It was one: Marguerite Higgins, cited in May, *Witness to War,* p. 91.

259 It's haunted me: Henry Dejarnette, cited in Abzug, p. 92.

259 Lee documented the scene: There is still uncertainty about which of the "death" trains taking inmates from Buchenwald to Dachau LM photographed: the first left on April 7, 1945, and arrived on April 28; the second left on April 9 and arrived on April 27. See Bertrand, pp. 49–69. My account relies on this authoritative source and my interview with Bertrand, Feb. 25, 1998.

260 Lee took the pictures: Jacques Hindermeyer interview with the author, Feb. 20, 1998; DS interview with the author, May 28, 1996.

260 In the few minutes: LM, AP, *LMW,* p. 182.

260 She was the only one: Ari Von Soest interview with the author, May 30, 2001.

261 The violence of Dachau: Abzug, p. 93.

261 a floating mess: LM, AP, *LMW,* p. 182.

261 Dachau had everything: LM to AW, AP, *LMW,* pp. 188–89.

262 There were no signs: Quotations in this and the next paragraph, LM, AP, *LMW,* pp. 191–93.

262 the elected victims: LM, AP, *LMW,* p. 182.

262 We've all speculated: LM to AW, n.d. [c. May 3, 1945]; AP, *LMW,* p. 188.

263 Part of the china: LM, AP, *LMW,* pp. 198–99.

264 Everyone hunted for souvenirs: LM, AP, *LMW,* p. 200.

264 Shit! That's blown: LM quoted in AP, *Lives,* p. 144; LM cables to AW, n.d. Cf. LM, "Germany—The War That Is Won," U.K. *Vogue,* June 1945, pp. 40–43, 84, 86, 89.

265 In the U.S. version: LM, "Germans Are Like This," U.S. *Vogue,* June 1, 1945, pp. 102–8, 192–93.

265 The mood then: AW interview with the author, May 5, 1996.

265 the Christian and cultural: AW quotations in this and the next paragraph are from U.K. *Vogue,* June 1945, pp. 45, 84.

14. Postwar

267 A number of correspondents: Sorel, p. 390.

267 Soon after their return: LM quotations in this and her next three paragraphs are from LM, "Denmark," U.S. *Vogue,* pp. 138–41.

269 No correspondent has displayed: Harry Yoxall, unpublished speech [July 1945].

269 She was reluctant: AW interview with the author, Oct. 6, 1997.

269 We would be delighted: Edna Chase quoted by AW, July 25, 1945, UKCNA.

269 base[d] in America: LM to AEB, n.d. [1945].

270 She has written: DS to WS, July 7 [1945].

270 I found the pictures: BB to LM, June 28, [1945].

270 the hiking through: AEB to LM, n.d. [1945].

270 I'm not Cinderella: LM, as quoted in AP, *Lives,* p. 147.

271 I've spent a lethargic: LM to RP, n.d. [late Aug. 1945].

271 This is to introduce: Bettina Wilson to "Mendy," Aug. 17, 1945.

272 a babel of foreign voices: LM quotations in this and the next two paragraphs are from LM, unpublished ms. on Salzburg, some of which is quoted in AP, *Lives,* p. 151.

272 The few road signs: LM, unpublished cable ms.; quoted in AP, *Lives,* p. 152.

273 so they are losing: LM quotations in this and the next paragraph are from LM to RP, Sept. 30, 1945.

273 In a city of suffering: LM, "Report from Vienna," U.K. *Vogue,* Nov. 1945, p. 40.

273 It keeps people's minds: LM, unpublished notes for Vienna ms.

273 This trip is working: LM to RP, Sept. 30, 1945.

273 Shocked that the great: LM quotations in this and the next paragraph, *Lives,* pp. 152–54. Unpublished cable draft, partially printed in AP, *Lives,* pp. 152–54.

274 We can liberate: LM Vienna notebook, partially printed in AP, *Lives,* p. 153.

274 Please, darling: Quotations in this and the next paragraph are from LM to RP, n.d., partially printed in AP, *Lives,* pp. 147–48.

275 Their adventures made: Quotations in this and the next paragraph are from LM to "Ralph," Oct. 25, 1945.

276 Lee was very aware: JP interview with the author, June 14, 1994; this is the source of all JP quotations unless otherwise noted.

277 Lee and I: Simon Bougin interview with the author, May 28, 2279; this is the source of all Bourgin quotations unless otherwise noted.

277 with abundant wonderful food: LM photo captions for Hungary.

277 Our relationship was: Robert Halmi quoted in letter from Simon Bourgin to AP, Apr. 8, 1994.

277 Shake hands with Halmi: Simon Bourgin to the author, May 26, 1999.

277 flourish[ing] with champagne: LM unpublished ms. on Hungary. Unless otherwise indicated, all LM quotations about Hungary are from this ms.

278 The American dollar: Simon Bourgin, "Inflation in Hungary," *Life*, 1946, clipping, p. 13.

278 The waitresses and nurse-maids: LM, "Hungary," U.K. *Vogue*, Apr. 1946, p. 92. Information and quotations from LM in this and the next seven paragraphs from "Hungary," original manuscript partially published in U.K. *Vogue*, pp. 52–55, 90, 92, 95–96; and in U.S. *Vogue*, Apr. 15, 1946, pp. 164–65, 197–98.

280 In the meantime: "Russians Hold U.S. Woman Reporter," *New York Times,* clipping; "Miller's Daughter Released After Detention by Russians," *New Paltz New Yorker,* Nov. 10, 1945.

280 Schlacht told us: Robert Halmi, quoted in a letter from Simon Bourgin to AP, Apr. 8, 1994.

281 First we had: JP, *Free Spirit*, p. 402.

281 Taking stock: LM to AW, undated [Jan. 11, 1946].

282 About this time: JP, *Free Spirit,* p. 413.

282 We had no idea: JP, *Free Spirit,* p. 407.

283 Lee, my driver, and I: JP quotations in this and the next paragraph are from *Odd World,* p. 211.

283 Through eyelids squeezed: LM, original ms. of "Romania," U.K. *Vogue,* May 1946, pp. 64–67, 98–100; U.S. *Vogue,* pp. 166–67, 208–9; AP, *Lives,* pp. 168–70.

283 In 1938 I was: LM, Romanian photo captions.

284 I'm awfully sorry: JP interview with the author, June 14, 1996.

284 looked like something: This and the next paragraph are from LM, Romanian photo captions.

285 beautiful hair: "Cu Jon Phillips Si Lee Milelr" [sic], *Poporul,* Feb. 9, 1946, p. 1.

285 On their travels: LM, original ms. of "Romania"; AP, *Lives,* p. 168.

286 The guest never gives: U.S. *Vogue,* May 15, 1946, p. 209.

286 Thinking you might: LM, Romanian photo captions.

286 rumbled forth: LM quotations in this and the next paragraph are from original ms. of "Romania"; AP, *Lives,* pp. 171–72.

287 Tired of loving someone: RP to LM, Jan. 15, 1946.

287 my task now: JP, *Free Spirit,* p. 413.

288 she looked very much: Rosemarie Redlich Scherman interview with the author, Sept. 26, 1999.

288 to prove that I: LM notebook, Sept. 9, 1947.

288 If only someone: LM cited in AP, *Lives,* p. 176.

288 in bad odor: DS to WS, Mar. 8, [1946], DSE.

289 Now that everyone: LM, "Travel and Camera," U.S. *Vogue,* May 15, 1946, pp. 123, 199, 200, 205.

289 I'm on my pratt: DS to WS, Apr. 20, [1946], DSE.

289 very depressing: Ibid.

289 She is having: DS to WS, July 27, [1946], DSE.

15. Patching Things Up

293 a highly skilled: RP, *Scrap Book,* p. 140.

294 She was not the same: JM interview with the author, May 29, 1996.

294 She is getting old: DS to WS, July 27, [1946], DSE.

294 those great war: U.K. *Vogue,* Aug. 1946, p. 29.

294 She brought regular doses: Alexander Liberman to the author, June 14, 1996; also the source of subsequent Liberman quotations.

294 When you were: Despina Messinesi, interview with the author, Feb. 22, 1998.

294 she had everything: Frances McLaughlin-Gill, interview with the author, Apr. 29, 1998.

295 Diamonds are for: Tatiana Liberman, quoted by Francine du Plessix Gray in interview with the author, Jan. 24, 1997. See also Gray, "Growing Up Fashionable," *New Yorker,* May 8, 1995, pp. 54–65.

295 The surroundings were: RP, *Scrap Book,* p. 140.

296 a large wet cloud: LM to WS, n.d. [July 1946].

296 We cannot help: Livingston, p. 96.

296 A woman had to be: Dorothea Tanning interview with the author, Feb. 20, 1997.

297 Everyone goes around: LM to WS, July 1946, a letter asking about DS's work for *Life.*

297 Man called his: Baldwin, p. 240.

297 She seemed worn down: Mary Anita Loos, interview with the author, July 6, 1999.

298 real live lady: Quotations in this and the next paragraph from LM and RP taped interview with Ona Munson, "In Town Tonight," Aug. 1946. When Munson asked Penrose whether he went "battling around Europe like our real live lady war correspondent," he said that his war experiences had been "dull in comparison."

298 Having been brought up: RP interviewed in "The Age of Picasso," *Art News,* Nov. 1946, p. 31.

299 bottled up: Alex Kroll interview with the author, Sept. 1, 1997.

299 try reading Ulysses: LM to FM and TM, Dec. 12, 1946.

299 In the new year: Ibid.

300 international crooks: LM to RP, n.d. [Jan. 1947].

300 I could not have: Rosamond Bernier interview with the author, Feb. 20, 1997.

300 even their identities: Rosamond Riley, "Children's Village in Switzerland," U.S. *Vogue,* Apr. 1947, p. 173. Lee's photographs illustrate the story, which also appeared in the U.K. Oct. issue, with fewer illustrations.

300 rather peculiar about it: LM to RP, n.d. [Jan. 1947].

301 Just as I: LM to FM and TM, Feb. 6, 1947.

301 Due to all this: Ibid.

301 This baby business: LM to FM and TM, May 2, 1947.

302 You'd think it was: This and the next paragraph, LM to FM and TM, July 31, 1947.

303 In a semihumorous *Vogue* piece: LM, "The High Bed," U.K. *Vogue,* Apr. 1948, pp. 83, 111, 112.

303 Dearest Mother: LM to FM, Sept. 8, 1947.

303 Early the next morning: This and the next two paragraphs, LM, London Clinic notebook, Sept. 9, 1947.

304 He is so ugly: RP to FM and TM, Sept. 11, 1947.

304 that I'd get: LM to FM and TM, Nov. 24, 1947.

305 awfully cute: Ibid.

305 like a real baby: LM to FM and TM, Dec. 11, 1947.

305 Lee took a portrait: "Vogue Photographers Interpret Christmas," U.K. *Vogue*, Dec. 1, 1947, p. 58.

305 The portrait, which ran: Quotations from LM to FM and TM in this and the next paragraph, Dec. 11, 1947.

306 slightly tight: LM to FM and TM, Dec. 18, 1947.

306 And the treatment prescribed: LM to FM and TM, Nov. 24, 1947.

306 Am getting so fascinated: LM to FM and TM, Dec. 18, 1947.

306 getting the dream idea: LM to FM and TM, Jan. 29, 1948.

306 He should be asked: Geoffrey Grigson, quoted in AP, *Roland Penrose*, p. 130.

307 almost Cubist: quotations in this and the next two paragraphs, LM, "The Venice Biennale Art Exposition," U.S. *Vogue*, Nov. 1, 1948, pp. 190, 191, 193, 195.

308 After Lee's review ran: Contract between LM and Condé Nast dated Nov. 15, 1948, UKCNA.

308 I gave up reading: LM to FM and TM, Jan. 29, 1948.

308 They brought suitcases full: TM 1948 diary; TM as quoted in AP, *Lives*, p. 186.

309 In the time: LM, "40,311 Years of Modern Art," U.K. *Vogue*, Jan. 1949, pp. 65–69, 82–83.

309 gave Farley farm: RP, *Scrap Book*, p. 163. For more about Farley Farm, see AP, *Home of the Surrealists*, on which my account relies.

310 "Bachelor Entertaining": U.K. *Vogue*, Mar. 1949, pp. 68–69, 114–16.

310 Here is a partial diary: LM to FM and TM, May 31, 1949.

310 all sorts of panic: LM to RP, n.d. [spring 1949].

311 Running two homes: LM to FM and TM, May 3, [1949].

311 Our first summer: LM, "Working Guests," U.K. *Vogue*, July 1953, p. 90.

311 To her parents: LM to Millers, n.d. [1949].

311 In April 1949: U.K. *Vogue* interoffice memo, Miss Hill to Miss Withers, Apr. 12, 1949; AW to LM, June 30, 1949, UKCNA.

311 There is nothing wrong: Dr. Carl H. Goldman, quoted in AP, *Lives*, p. 188.

312 Tony, on the other hand: LM to FM and TM, n.d. [1949].

312 A letter written: LM to FM and TM, n.d. [1949].

312 Lee took to cooking: AW, ICA talk, 1992.

312 Photography had been: RP, *Scrap Book*, p. 186.

313 I implore you: RP, quoted in AP, *Lives*, p. 193.

313 Lee came into her own: AW interview with the author, May 5, 1996.

16. A Double Life

315 I hope you will: AW to LM, June 2, 1950, UKCNA.

316 My first encounter: AP, *The Home of the Surrealists*, p. 68.

316 Just before Christmas: LM to FM and TM, n.d. [c. Feb. 1951].

317 Roland's new project: LM to FM and TM, n.d. [c. Feb. 1951].

317 We practically had to go: LM to FM and TM, n.d. [c. Feb. 1951].

317 Ayrshire cows, open log fires: Quotations in this and the next two paragraphs from LM, "Picasso," U.K. *Vogue*, Nov. 1951, pp. 113, 160, 165.

318 The winter jasmine: LM draft for *Picasso Himself*, 1956 ICA exhibition catalogue, cited in AP, *Home of the Surrealists*, p. 71.

318 had the effect: RP, *Scrap Book*, p. 208.

318 like a disciple: Quotations in this and the next paragraph from LM, "Picasso," p. 160.

319 Tony, stimulated by: This paragraph and next from LM, "Picasso," p. 113.

319 If it was not: RP, cited in AP, *Roland Penrose*, p. 145.

319 Farleys stopped being: AP, *Home of the Surrealists*, p. 77.

320 A great deal: LM to AW, n.d. [1953], BMcNC.

320 In autumn 1952: LM, "Plan for a Thirteen-Meal Christmas," U.K. *Vogue*, Dec. 1952, pp. 85, 114, 116.

320 To my Wife: RP, *Wonder and Horror of the Human Head* (London: Lund Humphries, 1953), p. 6.

320 The next time you: LM, "The Human Head," U.K. *Vogue*, Apr. 1953, pp. 146, 168, 170.

321 Humility, which is not: LM, draft for "The Human Head," quoted in AP, *Home of the Surrealists*, p. 82.

321 This tongue-in-cheek guide: "Working Guests," U.K. *Vogue*, July 1953, pp. 54–57, 90, 92.

321 She was not suited: AW interview with the author, June 14, 1996.

322 Eluard's love of women: RP, *Scrap Book*, p. 161.

322 She had been one: Quotations in this and the next four paragraphs, Deriaz, pp. 151–53, 237, 240.

323 too emotional: TM 1954 diary, Sept. 11 entry.

324 Trish was fascinated: PMT quotations in this and the next two paragraphs from PMT interview with the author, Apr. 26, 1998.

325 They found they loved: AP, *Roland Penrose*, p. 148.

325 One weekend, when Audrey: AW, ICA talk, 1992.

325 My chums thought: AP, "How I Learned to Love My Surrealist Mother," *You*, Aug. 19, 2001, p. 39.

325 Please ask Patsy: AP, *Lives*, p. 196.

325 deeply embattled with: AP, "My Mother, Me, and Hitler's Bathtub," *Mail on Sunday*, Mar. 14, 1999, p. 33.

325 Lee had a lot: PM interview with the author, May 10, 1996.

326 usually decorated by: Colin St. John Wilson interview with the author, May 20, 1996.

327 The company of Lee: RP, *Scrap Book*, p. 215.

327 It was better: RP and LM postcard to Picasso from Barcelona, June 21, 1955, MNP.

328 an essential asset: RP, *Scrap Book*, p. 230.

328 One might think that: AW, ICA talk, 1992.

328 Roland did not recall: RP, *Scrap Book*, p. 231.

329 The erotic enticements: Ibid., p. 230.

329 She couldn't digest: Quotations in this and the next two paragraphs, Peter Lyon interview with the author, Feb. 24, 1998.

329 It means Never: LM, quoted in AP, *Lives*, p. 196.

331 flew out of: LM, quoted in Gold and Fizdale, p. 187.

331 Lee is still making: RP to Picasso, Sept. 26, 1957, MNP.

331 a past master: Richardson, p. 234.

331 Roland, as Boswell: John Richardson interview with the author, July 28, 1999.

332 In these narrow: Jeffrey, n.p.

333 Only Lee's family: AP, *Lee Miller in Sussex*, p. 11.

333 His flashing black eyes: LM, "Picasso Himself," in *Picasso* (ICA Picasso Party brochure, July 5, 1960).

333 After mentioning the titled guests: Olga Franklin, "They've Even Insured Pablo for Ten Million," *Daily Mail*, July 1, 1960, p. 10.

334 Honestly, I find: George Melly to RP, June 23, 1960, cited in AP, *Roland Penrose,* p. 153.

334 I was required: RP, *Scrap Book,* p. 249.

334 It's because of you: RP to Picasso, Jan. 4, 1961, MNP.

334 the largest of its kind: "Party for a Painter," *The Tatler,* Sept. 20, 1961, pp. 596–97.

334 Much of her time: LM to JM, July 4, [1961].

17. A Second Fame

337 Lee's past was: Joanna Drew interview with the author, Sept. 30, 1999.

338 She was funny: John Golding interview with the author, May 20, 1996.

338 When they'd eaten: LM, quoted in Gold and Fizdale, p. 187.

338 it was as if: Princess Jeanne-Marie de Broglie interview with the author, May 29, 2001.

338 the lure . . . an icon: John Craxton interview with the author, Oct. 4, 1999.

338 a heavenly place: John Craxton interview with the author, June 26, 2000

338 in a world: Princess Jeanne-Marie de Broglie interview with the author, May 29, 2001.

339 She was usually correct: Roz Jacobs in this and the next paragraph, interview with the author, June 14, 1996.

339 Intrigued by her accent: Priscilla Morgan interview with the author, June 11, 1996.

340 the maddest people: James Beard, *Love and Kisses and a Halo of Truffles* (New York: Arcade, 1996), p. 331.

340 pure therapy: [BMcN], "How to Make an Art of the Happy Weekend," *House and Garden,* June 1973, p. 87.

340 drifted into cooking: BMcN, "Notes for LM Cookbook," unpublished, BMcNC.

340 I couldn't live: BMcN interview with the author, Aug. 8, 1997.

341 the focus of a lively: BMcN, "Notes for LM Cookbook."

341 little sole the size: LM to BMcN, n.d.

341 Over the years: Information and quotations in this and the next four paragraphs, BMcN interview with the author, Jan. 20, 2001, unless otherwise indicated.

341 in case a zany: [BMcN], "How to Make an Art of the Happy Weekend," pp. 66, 87.

342 It's a great convenience: TM diary, Sept. 26, 1963.

343 We hated each other: AP, "The Enigma of Lee Miller."

344 In a huge hostel: John Craxton interview with the author, June 26, 2000

344 still magnetic: Julie Lawson interview with the author, Jan. 21, 2002.

344 Lee's culinary interests: Ninette Lyon, "Lee and Roland Penrose: A Second Fame."

345 She was hellbent: Roz Jacobs interview with the author, June 14, 1996.

345 He was a dirty: PM interview with the author, June 12, 1996.

345 Suddenly this scary adult: Anne-Laure Lyon interview with the author, June 1, 1999.

346 ingrained sociability: RP, *Scrap Book,* p. 189.

346 The 1965 holidays: Quotations and information in this and the next two paragraphs from Henry McNulty, "A Christmas at Muddles Green," U.K. *House and Garden,* Dec. 1975, pp. 102, 106.

347 Lee had mixed feelings: Information from Roz Jacobs; LM to Roz and Mel Jacobs, Jan. 12, 1966.

347 I don't believe: LM quoted in "The Reindeer Meats Ball Lost the Battle of the Roes & the Roses," *Kensington Post,* Nov. 7, 1965, clipping.

348 The newspapers published: "To glade engelske damer til Stavanger i går," Jan. 22, 1966, *Stavanger Morgenavis,* p. 3.

348 To a reporter: "Bergensk slutt på historien om et smørbrød," n.d. [Jan. 1966], clipping.

348 when chefs were not: BMcN interview with the author, Jan. 20, 2002.

348 Lee's war reports: Shirley Conran, "Cook Hostess in Action, Sandwiches à l'améri-caine," n.d. [1966], clipping.

350 Jane enjoyed the taste: Quotations in this and the next paragraph, Jane Brymer inter-view with the author and AP, Jan. 23, 2002.

350 She was a figure: CMcN interview with the author, Oct. 2, 1999.

351 I had been expecting: Quotations in this and the next paragraph, Marnie Miller Cepo-rius interview with the author, Mar. 14, 1996.

351 At her age: Priscilla Morgan interview with the author, June 11, 1996.

352 epically untidy: Rosamond Bernier interview with the author, Feb. 20, 1997.

352 In 1969, Lee learned: Information and quotations in this and the next paragraph from Margit Rowell interview with the author, Feb 12, 1997. When Lee talked about Roland's girlfriends, she said that she had agreed to be accepting, but that there was one—"la trapéziste"—whom she could not stomach.

353 The *Times* reporter: Charles Benbow, "In Vanguard of Art," *St. Petersburg Times,* Oct. 5, 1969, clipping.

353 a top model: LM, quoted in Osgood, "Accident Was Road to Adventure," *St. Petersburg Times,* Oct. 6, 1969, clipping.

353 as an old fuddy-duddy: AP, *Home of the Surrealists,* p. 127.

353 What was worse: RP, *Scrap Book,* p. 263.

354 Another event linking art: AP, *Roland Penrose,* p. 160. The thieves were caught and jailed; Picasso repaired the painting they damaged, *Negro Dancer,* when they cut out his signature to send as a ransom note—but he did so only after telling Roland that there was no need for him to sign it again, since each brushstroke was his signature.

354 I adored Roland: Daniella Kochavi interview with the author, Oct. 1, 1999.

354 You seem to be: Daniella Kochavi to RP [Oct. 1975], RP correspondence, SNGMA.

355 With his usual: RP, *Scrap Book,* p. 247, illustrated by Lee's photo of the group inspect-ing the tapestry. Other shots from that day appear in the 1971 revised edition of RP's *Portrait of Picasso.*

355 By December Lee: LM to TM, Dec. 15, 1970, JMC.

18. Retrospectives

359 Lee's tolerance: LM to Lyn Kienholz, n.d., LKC.

359 Subtitled "The Personal Strategy": [BMcN], "How to Make an Art of the Happy Week-end," p. 87.

359 makes us look: LM to Margit Rowell, n.d. [c. May 1973].

359 Lee had invented: Gold and Fizdale, pp. 160–61, 186–87.

360 Christmas can be: Henry McNulty, "A Christmas at Muddles Green," *House and Gar-den,* Dec. 1975, pp. 102, 106, 107.

360 She appears briefly: RP, *Man Ray,* pp. 95, 99, 109.

360 his favorite of all: William Copley, "Man Ray: The Dada of Us All," *Man Ray, Inventor, Painter, Poet* (catalogue), New York Cultural Center, Dec. 19, 1974–Mar. 2, 1975; ICA, Apr. 11–June 1, 1975.

361 That afternoon, as they: John Loring interview with the author, Apr. 30, 1998.

361 They sat side by side: Lucien Treillard interview with the author, Oct. 8, 1999.

361 Amaya asked Lee: Amaya, pp. 55, 56, 57.

362 Lee spent the summer: Information and quotations in this and the next two para-graphs, LM letters to Lyn Kienholz, n.d. [c. 1975–76], LKC.

362 She would invite: AP, *Home of the Surrealists,* p. 131.

362 By 1976 there was: Julie Lawson to Lyn Kienholz, Jan. 25, 1976, LKC.

363 I no longer recognise: RP letter of resignation, Nov. 1, 1976, SNGMA.

363 The news on the morning: RP, *Picasso,* p. 479.

363 We never left: LM to Jackie Braun, June 28, 1976.

363 The show was much: This quotation and those in the next paragraph, LM to JL, n.d. [Aug. 1976].

364 lost in New York: LM to David Travis, June 28, 1976, AIC.

364 wants to do: LM to David Travis, Oct. 9, 1976, AIC.

364 Sitting beside him: LM to David Travis, n.d. [late Oct. 1976], AIC.

365 There was something: Jeanne-Marie de Broglie interview with the author, May 29, 2001.

365 Lee was tender-hearted: PMT interview with the author, Apr. 27, 1998.

365 of whom Swiss punctuality: *Wheeler's Review,* 1978, clipping.

365 she sat alone: Julie Lawson interview with the author, Sept. 29, 1999.

366 I've been almost: LM to David Travis, n.d. [Jan. 1977], AIC.

366 This is the last: LM to Lyn Kienholz, Mar. 14, 1977, LKC.

366 Having recently returned: AP to EM and MM, Mar. 16, 1977.

366 Writing to Lyn: LM to Lyn Kienholz, Apr. 17, 1977.

366 Suzanna is radiant: LM to Lyn Kienholz, May 25, 1977.

367 Are you Lee Miller?: Quotations and information in this and the next two paragraphs, LM interview with the author, May 16–17, 1977.

367 We are so looking: LM to Lyn Kienholz, May 25, 1977, LKC.

368 She was wonderful: PM interview with the author, May 13, 1996.

368 She had guts: John Golding interview with the author, May 29, 1996.

369 The next day: LM obituaries (clippings); RP note about funeral service, n.d.; AP to the author, Aug. 28, 2003.

369 Death had ploughed: RP, *Scrap Book,* p. 205.

369 What a remarkable: Bruce Bolton to Roz and Mel Jacobs, Aug. 2, 1977, RJC.

369 By chance, a last: Keenan, p. 63.

Afterword

371 Man Ray always: AP, quoted in "Mother in Her Own Images," *The Times,* Jan. 17, 1986, p. 11.

371 the etiquette was: AP, quoted in "My Mother, Me, and Hitler's Bath," *Mail on Sunday,* Mar. 14, 1999, clipping.

372 The grand old man: Carine Maurice, *Evening Standard,* Aug. 29, 1980, as cited in AP, *Roland Penrose,* p. 167.

372 Can you imagine: AP, NPR *Morning Edition* tape.

372 I passed through: AP, *Roland Penrose,* p. 169.

372 A consummate artist: DS, "Foreword," *LMW,* p. 13.

373 Her life and work: Documentaries include Mel Stuart, *Man Ray: Prophet of the Avant-Garde* (1999); AP, *The Lives of Lee Miller* (1986); Sylvain Roumette, *Lee Miller: Through the Looking Glass* (1995); and Sarah Aspinall/BBC, *Lee Miller: A Quirky Way of Seeing* (2001).

373 had to detach: Carole Callow, "Through the Eyes of Lee Miller," *The Surrealist and the Photographer,* pp. 135–36.

Bibliography

Abzug, Robert. *Inside the Vicious Heart*. New York: Oxford University Press, 1985.

Ades, Dawn. *Dada and Surrealism Reviewed*. London: Arts Council of Great Britain, 1978.

Agar, Eileen. *A Look at My Life*. London: Methuen, 1988.

Al-Sayyid Marsot, Afaf Lutfi. *A Short History of Modern Egypt*. Cambridge: Cambridge University Press, 1985.

Amaya, Mario. "My Man Ray" (interview with Lee Miller). *Art in America*, May–June 1975.

Angelou, Maya. *I Know Why the Caged Bird Sings*. New York: Bantam, 1997.

Anon. [Bettina McNulty]. "How to Make the Art of a Happy Weekend." *House & Garden*, June 1973.

Atelier Man Ray, Abbot Boiffard Brandt Miller, 1920–1935. Paris: Centre Georges Pompidou/Philippe Sers, 1982.

Aury, Bernard. *La Délivrance de Paris, 1924 Août 1944*. Paris: Arthaud, 1945.

Baedeker, Karl, ed. *Egypt*. Leipzig: Karl Baedeker, 1902.

Baldassari, Anne. *Picasso and Photography: The Dark Mirror*. Paris: Flammarion, 1997.

Baldwin, Neil. *Man Ray: American Artist*. New York: Clarkson Potter, 1988.

Ballard, Bettina. *In My Fashion*. New York: David McKay, 1960.

Baraka, Magda. *The Egyptian Upper Class Between Revolutions, 1919–1952*. Reading, U.K.: Ithaca Press, 1998.

Barker, Charles Albro. *Henry George*. New York: Oxford University Press, 1955.

Beaton, Cecil. *The Years Between: Diaries, 1934–1944*. New York: Holt, Rinehart and Winston, 1965.

Bertrand, François. *Notre Devoir de Mémoire, Convoi de Buchenwald à Dachau de 7 au 28 avril 1945*. Pau, France: Editions Héracles, 1997.

Blanshard, Julia. "Other Faces Are Her Fortune." *Poughkeepsie Evening Star*, November 1932.

Bourke-White, Margaret. *Dear Fatherland, Rest Quietly*. New York: Simon and Schuster, 1946.

———. *Portrait of Myself*. New York: Simon and Schuster, 1963.

Brandt, Allan M. *No Magic Bullet.* New York: Oxford University Press, 1987.

Breasted, James Henry. *Egypt Through the Stereoscope.* New York: Underwood and Underwood, 1905.

Brill, A. A. *Basic Principles of Psychoanalysis.* Garden City, N.Y.: Garden City Books, 1949.

Brittain, Vera. *England's Hour.* New York: Macmillan, 1941.

British Surrealism Fifty Years On (catalogue). London: Mayor Gallery, 1986.

Bruccoli, Matthew, ed. *The Romantic Egoists.* New York: Scribner's, 1974.

Burke, Carolyn. "Framing a Life." *The Surrealist and the Photographer.*

———. "Lee Miller in Hitler's Bathtub." *Heat* 12 (1999).

Burke, E.T. *Treatment of Venereal Disease in General Practice.* London: Faber & Gwyer, 1927.

Butcher, E. L. *Things Seen in Egypt.* London: Seeley, Service & Co., 1922.

Calder, Angus. *The People's War.* New York: Pantheon, 1969.

Callahan, Sean. *Margaret Bourke-White, Photographer.* Boston: Little, Brown, 1998.

Calvocoressi, Richard. *Lee Miller: Portraits from a Life.* London: Thames and Hudson, 2002.

Card, James. *Seductive Cinema: The Art of Silent Film.* New York: Knopf, 1994.

Carey, Gary. *Anita Loos: A Biography.* New York: Knopf, 1988.

Carter, Ernestine, ed. *Grim Glory: Pictures of Britain Under Fire.* London: Lund Humphries/Scribners, 1941.

———. *With Tongue in Chic.* London: Michael Joseph, 1974.

Caws, Mary Ann, Rudolf E. Keunzli, and Gwen Raaberg, eds. *Surrealism and Women.* Cambridge, Mass.: MIT Press, 1991.

Chadwick, Whitney. *Women Artists and the Surrealist Movement.* New York: Thames & Hudson, 1991.

Chafe, William Henry. *The American Woman.* New York: Oxford University Press, 1972.

Chase, Edna W. *Always in Vogue.* London: Victor Gollancz, 1954.

Chéroux, Clément, ed. *Mémoire des camps.* Paris: Marval, 2001.

Clarke, Graham, ed. *The Portrait in Photography.* London: Reaktion Books, 1992.

Cooper, Artemis. *Cairo in the War.* London: Hamilton, 1989.

Cord, Steven B. *Henry George: Dreamer or Realist?* Philadelphia: University of Pennsylvania, 1965.

Deriaz, Diane. *La Tête à l'envers.* Paris: Albin Michel, 1988.

Deutsch, Helen, and Stella Hanau. *The Provincetown.* New York: Russell & Russell, 1959.

Douglas, Ann. *Terrible Honesty: Mongrel Manhattan in the 1920s.* New York: Farrar, Straus, and Giroux, 1995.

Edwards, Julia. *Women of the World: The Great Foreign Correspondents.* Boston: Houghton Mifflin, 1988.

Eileen Agar (catalogue). Edinburgh: Scottish National Gallery of Modern Art, 1999.

Ewing, William A. *Eye for Elegance: George Hoyningen-Huene.* New York: International Center of Photography and Congreve Publishing Co., 1980.

———. *The Photographic Art of Hoyningen-Huene.* London: Thames & Hudson, 1986.

Fedden, Robin. *The Land of Egypt.* London: B. T. Batsford, 1939.

———. *Personal Landscape.* London: PL Editions, 1945.

———. *Syria: An Historical Appreciation.* London: R. Hale, 1946.

Flanagan, Hallie. *Shifting Scenes.* New York: Coward-McCann, 1928.

Flanner, Janet. *Janet Flanner's World.* New York: Harcourt Brace, 1979.

———. *Paris Was Yesterday.* New York: Viking, 1972.

Foresta, Merry, ed. *Perpetual Motif: The Art of Man Ray.* New York: Abbeville, 1989.

Fox, Stephen. *The Mirror Makers: A History of American Advertising and its Creators.* New York: William Morrow, 1984.

Frizot, Michel, ed. *A New History of Photography*. Cologne: Könemann, 1998.

Geiger, George Raymond. *The Philosophy of Henry George*. New York: Macmillan, 1933.

Gellhorn, Martha. *The Face of War*. New York: Atlantic Monthly Press, 1988.

Gilot, Françoise. *Life with Picasso*. New York: McGraw-Hill, 1964.

Gold, Arthur, and Robert Fizdale. "The Most Unusual Recipes You Have Ever Seen." U.S. *Vogue*, April 1974.

Goldberg, Vicki. *Bourke-White: A Retrospective*. E. Hartford, Conn.: United Technologies Corporation, 1988.

———. *Margaret Bourke-White*. New York: Harper & Row, 1986.

Guggenheim, Peggy. *Out of This Century*. Garden City, N.Y.: Anchor, 1980.

Hale, Nathan G., Jr. *Freud and the Americans: The Beginnings of Psychoanalysis in the United States, 1876–1917*. New York: Oxford University Press, 1971.

———. *The Rise and Crisis of Psychoanalysis in the United States: Freud and the Americans, 1917–1985*. New York: Oxford University Press, 1995.

Hambourg, Maria Morris. *The New Vision: Photography Between the World Wars*. New York: Metropolitan Museum of Art, 1989.

Harrison, Tom. *Living Through the Blitz*. New York: Schocken Books, 1976.

Hay, William. *Health via Food*. Aurora, N.Y.: Sun-Diet Foundation, 1929.

Herman, Judith Lewis. *Father-Daughter Incest*. Cambridge: Harvard University Press, 1981.

———. *Trauma and Recovery*. New York: Basic Books, 1992.

Hewison, Robert. *Under Siege: Literary Life in London, 1939–45*. London: Weidenfeld and Nicolson, 1977.

Houseman, John. *Run-Through: A Memoir*. New York: Simon and Schuster, 1972.

Hubert, Renée Riese. *Magnifying Mirrors: Women, Surrealism, and Partnership*. Lincoln: University of Nebraska Press, 1994.

Jaloux, Edmond, ed. *Rainer Maria Rilke, His Last Friendship: Unpublished Letters to Mrs. Eloui Bey*. New York: Philosophical Library, 1952.

Jeffrey, Ian. "Picasso's Gaze," *Lee Miller and Picasso* (catalogue). London: The Photographers' Gallery, 1984.

Johnston, Patricia A. *Real Fantasies: Edward Steichen's Advertising Photography*. Berkeley: University of California Press, 1997.

Keenan, Brigid. "That Special Face." *Sunday Times Magazine*, November 6, 1977.

Kirkpatrick, Helen. *Under the British Umbrella*. New York: Scribner's, 1939.

Kluver, Billy, and Julie Martin. *Kiki's Paris: Artists and Lovers, 1900–1930*. New York: Abrams, 1989.

Krauss, Rosalind, and Jane Livingston. *L'amour fou: Photography & Surrealism*. New York: Abbeville Press, 1985.

Lawford, Valentine. *Horst: His Work and His World*. New York: Knopf, 1984.

Lemagny, Jean-Claude, and André Rouillé, eds. *A History of Photography*. Cambridge, UK: Cambridge University Press, 1997.

Levy, Julien. *Portrait of an Art Gallery*. New York: Putnam, 1977.

———. *Surrealism*. New York: Black Sun Press, 1936.

Lewis, Helena. *The Politics of Surrealism*. New York: Paragon House, 1988.

Life Goes to War: A Picture History of World War II. Boston: Little, Brown, 1977.

Livingston, Jane. *Lee Miller: Photographer*. New York: California International Arts Foundation, 1989.

Loengard, John. *Life Photographers: What They Saw*. Boston: Little, Brown, 1998.

Lyford, Amy. "Lee Miller's Photographic Impersonations, 1930–1945." *History of Photography*, vol. 18 (1994).

Lyon, Ninette. "Lee and Roland Penrose: A Second Fame." U.S. *Vogue*, April 1965.

Malcolm, Janet. *Diana & Nikon.* New York: Aperture, 1997.

Marcuse, Harold. *Legacies of Dachau.* New York: Cambridge University Press, 2001.

May, Antoinette. *Witness to War: A Biography of Marguerite Higgins.* New York: Beaufort Books, 1983.

McBride, Henry. *The Flow of Art.* New York: Atheneum, 1975.

McDowell, Colin. *Forties Fashion.* London: Bloomsbury, 1997.

McNulty, Bettina. "Notes for Lee Miller Cookbook." Unpublished manuscript.

McNulty, Henry. "A Christmas at Muddles Green." U.K. *House and Garden,* December 1975.

Messenger, Charles. *The Chronological Atlas of World War Two.* New York: Macmillan, 1989.

Miller, Lee. Taped interview with Ona Munsen. "In Town Tonight." Los Angeles, August 1946.

———. "I Worked with Man Ray." *Liliput,* October 1941.

———. "What They See in Cinema." U.K. *Vogue,* August 1956.

———. *Wrens in Camera.* London: Hollis and Carter, 1945.

Morris, John G. *Get the Picture.* New York: Random House, 1998.

Morrow, Prince A. *Eugenics and Racial Poisons.* New York: The Society of Sanitary and Moral Prophylaxis, 1912.

Murrow, Edward R. *This Is London.* New York: Schocken, 1985.

Niven, Penelope. *Steichen: A Biography.* New York: Clarkson Potter, 1997.

Panter-Downes, Mollie. *London War Notes, 1939–1945.* New York: Farrar, Straus, and Giroux, 1971.

Paris, Barry. *Louise Brooks.* New York: Knopf, 1989.

Patten, Marguerite. *The Victory Cookbook.* London: Hamlyn, 1995.

Penrose, Antony. "The Enigma of Lee Miller." *A Propos Lee Miller.* Frankfurt: Verlag Neue Kritik, 1995.

———. *The Home of the Surrealists.* London: Frances Lincoln, 2001.

———. *Lee Miller in Sussex* (catalogue). Gardner Centre Galleries, May 1984.

———. *Lee Miller's War.* Boston: Bulfinch Press, 1992.

———. *The Lives of Lee Miller.* London: Thames and Hudson, 1985.

———. *Roland Penrose: The Friendly Surrealist.* London: Prestel, 2001.

Penrose, Roland. *Man Ray.* Boston: New York Graphic Society, 1975.

———. *Picasso.* Revised ed. Los Angeles: University of California Press, 1981.

———. *Picasso: His Life and Work.* 3rd ed. London: Granada, 1981.

———. *The Road Is Wider Than Long.* London: London Gallery, 1939.

———. *Scrap Book, 1900–1981.* London: Thames and Hudson, 1981.

Phillips, John. *Free Spirit in a Troubled World.* Zurich: Scalo, 1997.

———. *Odd World.* New York: Simon and Schuster, 1959.

Pierre, Jose, ed. *Investigating Sex: Surrealist Research, 1928–1932.* London: Verso, 1992.

Platt, Edmund. *History of Poughkeepsie, 1683–1905.* Poughkeepsie, N.Y.: Platt and Platt, 1905.

Prose, Francine. *The Lives of the Muses.* New York: Harper Collins, 2002.

Ray, Man. *Self Portrait.* Boston: Little, Brown, 1963.

———. *Photographs by Man Ray.* New York: Dover, 1979.

Remy, Michel. *Surrealism in Britain.* Aldershot, U.K.: Ashgate, 1999.

Rhoads, William B. "Poughkeepsie's Architectural Styles, 1835–1940." *Dutchess County Historical Society Year Book,* vol. 72, 1987.

Richardson, John. *The Sorcerer's Apprentice.* New York: Knopf, 1999.

Robbins, Ian, ed. *The Independent Group: Postwar Britain and the Aesthetics of Plenty.* Cambridge, Mass.: MIT Press, 1990.

Rodger, George. *The Blitz.* New York: Penguin, 1990.

Rubin, William, ed. *Picasso and Portraiture.* New York: Museum of Modern Art, 1996.

Sarlos, Robert K. *Jig Cook and the Provincetown Players.* Amherst: University of Massachusetts Press, 1982.

Schaffner, Ingrid, and Lisa Jacobs. *Julien Levy: Portrait of an Art Gallery* (catalogue). Cambridge, Mass.: MIT Press, 1998.

Schwarz, Arturo. *Man Ray: The Rigour of Imagination.* London: Thames and Hudson, 1977.

Seebohm, Caroline. *The Man Who Was Vogue.* New York: Viking, 1982.

Simpson, Ann. *Eileen Agar, 1899–1991* (catalogue). Edinburgh: Scottish National Gallery of Modern Art, 1999.

Showalter, Elaine, ed. *These Modern Women: Autobiographical Essays from the Twenties.* Old Westbury, N.Y.: Feminist Press, 1978.

Sontag, Susan. *On Photography.* New York: Farrar, Straus, and Giroux, 1997.

Sorel, Nancy Caldwell. *The Women Who Wrote the War.* New York: Arcade, 1999.

Stavrianos, L. S. *The Balkans Since 1453.* New York: Rinehart, 1959.

Strasser, Susan. *Satisfaction Guaranteed: The Making of the American Mass Market.* New York: Pantheon, 1989.

Steegmuller, Francis. *Cocteau.* Boston: Little, Brown, 1970.

Sullivan, Constance, ed. *Women Photographers.* New York: Abrams, 1990.

The Surrealist and the Photographer: Roland Penrose and Lee Miller (catalogue). Edinburgh: National Galleries of Scotland, 2001.

Tanning, Dorothea. *Birthday.* San Francisco: Lapis Press, 1986.

Toussaint, Yvon. *Les Barons Empain.* Paris: Fayard, 1996.

Touzot, Jean. *Jean Cocteau.* Paris: La Manufacture, 1989.

Train, Susan, ed. *Théâtre de la Mode.* New York: Rizzoli, 1991.

Ulman, R. B. *The Shattered Self: A Psychoanalytic Study of Trauma.* Hillsdale, N.J.: The Analytic Press, 1988.

Vatikiotis, P. J. *The Modern History of Egypt.* London: Weidenfeld and Nicolson, 1969.

Voss, Frederick S. *Reporting the War: The Journalistic Coverage of World War II.* Washington, D.C.: Smithsonian Institution Press, 1994.

Wahba, Magdi. "Cairo Memories," in Derek Hopwood, ed., *Studies in Arab History.* Oxford: Macmillan Press, 1990.

Watson, Steven. *Prepare for Saints.* New York: Random House, 1998.

Weber, Eugen. *The Hollow Years: France in the 1930s.* New York: Norton, 1994.

Welsh, Mary. *How It Was.* New York: Knopf, 1976.

Wertenbaker, Charles. *The Death of Kings.* New York: Random House, 1954.

West, Nancy Martha. *Kodak and the Lens of Nostalgia.* Charlottesville, Va.: University of Virginia Press, 2000.

Wineapple, Brenda. *Genêt: A Biography of Janet Flanner.* New York: Ticknor & Fields, 1989.

Withers, Audrey. *Lifespan.* London: Peter Owen, 1994.

———. Unpublished lecture. Institute of Contemporary Arts. London, 1992.

Yoxall, H. W. *A Fashion of Life.* London: Heinemann, 1966.

Zelizer, Barbie. *Remembering to Forget.* Chicago: University of Chicago, 1998.

Zox-Weaver, Annalisa. "When the War Was in *Vogue:* Lee Miller's War Reports." *Women's Studies,* vol. 32 (2003).

Acknowledgments

I have been fortunate to meet many remarkable people during the seven years it took to complete this biography, which would not have been written without their support. It is a pleasure to begin by acknowledging my profound indebtedness to Antony Penrose, Director of the Lee Miller Archives, who not only gave me full access to the work and materials of Lee Miller and Roland Penrose and introductions to their friends but generously read, reread, and commented upon my book, which builds on his invaluable studies of his mother's life and dissemination of her work through the Archives. I am also deeply grateful to the Archives staff, especially Carole Callow, Curator and Fine Printer, and Arabella Hayes, Registrar, for assistance of all kinds; to Roz Penrose for her warm hospitality; and to Patsy Murray for delicious meals and clear-eyed recollections of the Farley Farm household.

I can never fully express my profound thanks to Lee's family: John Miller, who helped me visualize the Poughkeepsie of his childhood and lent me his father's diaries, the late Erik Miller, the late Mafy Miller, Marnie and Victor Ceporius, Joanne Miller, and Patricia Miller Taylor, without whose generous hospitality and collaboration I could not have documented Lee's early years. Members of her extended family also contributed precious insights. David Scherman granted me an illuminating interview toward the end of his life, when he was still mulling over his relationship with Lee; Bettina McNulty filled out the picture of Lee's later years with anecdotes, recipes, and her unique perspective as Lee's closest friend.

I also take pleasure in thanking all those whose insights, introductions, references, and refuges made it possible for me to write this book. In Great Britain: Mary Banham, Jane Brymer, the late Sir Bernard Burrows, Phil Cairney, Wingate Charlton, John Craxton, Joanna Drew, Madge Garland, David Gascoyne, Sir John Golding, the late Jacqueline Goddard, Richard Hamilton, Eric Harbord, Sir David Hare, Tom Hawkyard, Doreen Impey, Dawn Jackson, the late Audrey Withers Kennett, Alex Kroll, Julie Lawson, Sarah Macdonald, Mollie Matthews, James Mayor, Claudia McNulty, James Mellor, Patricia Mitchell, Robin Muir, the late Timmie O'Brien, Jane Peyton, Miranda Preston, Lady Spender, Daniella Kochavi Stark, John and Cynthia Thompson, William Turnbull, Patricia Warner, Colin Wilson, and the late Gertrude Wissa.

In France: the late Hélène Azenor, Mihaela Bacou, Marie Balmary, Naomi Barry, Edwige Belorgey, Georges Bernier, François Bertrand, Pierre-Yves Butzbach, Catherine Chaine, Edmonde Charles-Roux, Georgiana Colville, the late Henri Cartier-Bresson, Diane Deriaz, Alain Dubourg, Princesse Jeanne-Marie de Broglie, Emmanuelle de l'Ecotais, Baron Edouard Empain, Baronne Jean Empain, Xavier Gary, Catherine Gonnard, Annick Gratton, Danielle Haase-Dubosc, Marilyn Hacker, Jacques Hindermeyer, Diane Johnson, Sylvain Labbé, Gentry Lane, James Lord, Gérard Messadié, Bernard Minoret, John G. Morris, Jean-Claude Moscovisi, Richard Overstreet, Raymond Perrussel, Marc Riboud, Sylvain Roumette, Jacques Serrier, Robert Solé, Edmonde Treillard, the late Lucien Treillard, Yvon Toussaint, Susan Train, and Arie von Soest.

In the United States, Canada, and Mexico: the late Richard Avedon, Timothy Baum, the late Joella Bayer, Susan Bedford, Gretchen Berg, Rosamond Bernier, Simon Bourgin, John Burnham, Leonora Carrington, the late Josephine Carson, Whitney Chadwick, Bill Cleveland, Noma Copley, Carolyn Crumpton, Betty Daniels, Mary Dearborn, Dan Dougherty, Warren Dunn, Jesse Effron, Donka Farkas, Miriam Feierabend, Harry Finley, David Friend, Francine du Plessix Gray, Robert Halmi, Nina Hamilton, Mike Harris, Shirley Hazard, Hedwig Herschop, Lisa Jacobs, Roz Jacobs, Stephanie Spray Jandle, Peter Kenez, Lyn Kienholz, Hans P. Kraus Jr., William Leiberman, Maya Lev, the late Julien Levy, Tom Levey-Galleguillos, Joel Leivick, Alexander Liberman, Mary Anita Loos, John Loring, Anne-Laure Lyon, M. C. Marden, Hank Massie, Frances McLaughlin, Despina Messinesi, Kats Miho, Sandra Mock, Priscilla Morgan, Weston Naef, Eugenia Parry, Marilyn Pearl, the late Oreste Pucciani, Nan Rosenthal, John Richardson, Tom Riordan, Jim Robinson, Ned Rorem, Naomi Rosenblum, Margit Rowell, Betty Jane Rowland, Naomi Sawelson, Ingrid Schaffner, John Scherman, the late Rosemarie Redlich Scherman, Tony Scherman, Pony Simon, Mel Stuart, Elizabeth Pathy Salett, Lee Eitingen Thompson, Dorothea Tanning, Marcia Taylor, Kim Vandervoort, Jeff Wales, Steven Watson, Charles Williams, and Annalisa Zox-Weaver.

In Australia: Carol and Tony Berg, Pam Brown, Rowanna Couch, Anne Deveson, Juno Gemes, Helen Greenwood, Margaret Harris, Robyn Johnston, Robert McFarlane, Drusilla Modjeska, Paul Patton, Tony Richardson, Gary Rogers, Erica Seccombe, and Jane Zemiro.

I have also been fortunate to have invaluable help with research and manuscript preparation from Jane Arons, Maria di Chiara, Renée Divine, Judy Foreman, Sylvia Gale, Natalia Lusty, and Rachel Servi, who will recognize their contributions in these pages. I am more grateful than I can say to my webmaster, Stephen Pollard, whose wizardry with images made it possible to imagine and prepare a book that would honor its subject's eye as well as her iconic beauty.

The staffs of the University of California, Santa Cruz library and the Santa Cruz Public Library went out of their way to find what I needed. To them I owe a profound debt of gratitude, as well as to the following institutions and people: Adriance Memorial Library: Myra Morales; Art Institute of Chicago: David Travis; Bardavon Opera House Archives: Annon Adams; Center for Creative Photography: Nancy Lutz; Condé Nast, London: Robin Muir; Condé Nast, New York: Stan Friedman, Charles D. Scheips Jr.; Condé Nast, Paris: Caroline Berton, Michelle Zaquin; Getty Research Institute: Susan M. Allen, Beverly Faison; Musée National Picasso: Anne Baldassari, Sylvie Fresnault, Laurence Madeline; National Museum of American Art: Merry Foresta, Linda Hartigan; Oakwood School: Kathy Meyer; Scottish National Gallery of Modern Art: Richard Calvocoressi, Jane Furness, Alice O'Connor, Ann Simpson; Tate Gallery: Sarah Fox-Pitt, Adrian Glew; Vassar College: Nancy MacKechnie, James Mundy, Dean M. Rogers.

The Florence Gould Foundation provided generous aid when I most needed it. Periods of residence at the Research Institute for Humanities and Social Sciences, University of Sydney, and the Columbia University Institute for Scholars in Paris afforded precious writing time, research support, and the chance to try out portions of this book with sympathetic audiences. I am grateful to the Division of the Humanities at the University of California, Santa Cruz for assistance of all kinds.

I would also like to thank my agents, Anne, Georges, and Valerie Borchardt, for their practical and moral support, and to express my deep appreciation for everyone I worked with at Knopf: Bob Gottlieb, for his sense of humor, tunafish sandwiches, and unparalleled editorial skills; Diana Tejerina, for gently unruffling me through all the phases of production; Iris Weinstein, for grasping the story through the photographs; Jon Fine, for sound advice; and the other exceptional people who worked on this book.

My deepest debt is to Poppy Burke, Terry Burke, and Valda Hertzberg, who made it possible, nourishing me, reading for me, sustaining me with their love and patience.

Index

Page numbers in *italics* indicate photographs.

Photo Credits

All photographs in the inserts are by Lee Miller.

Grateful acknowledgment is made to the following:

Harry N. Abrams: A Strange Encounter, by Lee Miller, from *Women Photographers,* edited by Constance Sullivan, appears courtesy of Harry N. Abrams (insert 1, page 3).

Artists Rights Society: Portrait de Lee Miller en Arlésienne, by Pablo Picasso, private collection, © 2005 Estate of Pablo Picasso / Artists Rights Society (ARS), New York (page 171). Photograph by Man Ray appears courtesy of Juliet Man Ray, © 2005 Man Ray Trust / Artists Rights Society (ARS), NY / ADAGP, Paris (page 77). Photograph by Man Ray appears courtesy of Dorothea Tanning, © 2005 Man Ray Trust / Artists Rights Society (ARS), NY / ADAGP, Paris (page 327). Photographs by Man Ray appear courtesy of Telimage, © 2005 Man Ray Trust / Artists Rights Society (ARS), NY / ADAGP, Paris (pages 72, 92, 96).

Beinecke Rare Books and Manuscripts Library: Photograph by White Studios appears courtesy of Yale University Collection of American Literature, Beinecke Rare Books and Manuscripts Library (page 138).

Simon Bourgin: Photographs by Simon Bourgin appear courtesy of Simon Bourgin (pages 276, 279).

Condé Nast: Photographs of Lee Miller in *Vogue* appear courtesy of Publications Condé Nast (pages 82, 102, 103, 111). Photograph of Audrey Withers from *Vogue* appears courtesy of Lee Miller/*Vogue* © The Condé Nast Publications Ltd. (page 203).

George Eastman House: Photograph by unknown appears courtesy of George Eastman House (page 23).

Harry Finley: Advertisement from *Delineator* appears courtesy of Harry Finley (page 67).

A Note About the Author

Carolyn Burke met Lee Miller while conducting research for *Becoming Modern: The Life of Mina Loy.* Burke has taught at Princeton and the University of California at Santa Cruz and at Davis; at the universities of Western Sydney and New South Wales in Australia; and at the Sorbonne and the University of Lille in France. Her many articles and translations from the French have appeared in *Art in America, The New Yorker, Heat, Sulfur,* and *Critical Inquiry.* Born in Australia, she now lives in Santa Cruz, California.

A Note on the Type

This book was set in Fairfield, a typeface designed by the distinguished American artist and engraver Rudolph Ruzicka (1883–1978).
In its structure Fairfield displays the sober and sane qualities of the
master craftsman whose talents were dedicated to clarity. Ruzicka was
born in Bohemia and came to America in 1894. He designed and
illustrated many books, and was the creator of a considerable
list of individual prints in a variety of techniques.

Composed by North Market Street Graphics,
Lancaster, Pennsylvania

Printed and bound by Berryville Graphics,
Berryville, Virginia

Designed by Iris Weinstein

Wandering Paysanos

Ricardo D. Salvatore

Wandering Paysanos

STATE ORDER AND SUBALTERN EXPERIENCE

IN BUENOS AIRES DURING THE ROSAS ERA

DUKE UNIVERSITY PRESS   DURHAM AND LONDON   2003

© 2003 Duke University Press

All rights reserved

Printed in the United States

of America on acid-free paper ∞

Designed by C. H. Westmoreland

Typeset in Quadraat

by Keystone Typesetting, Inc.

Frontis art: Raimundo Monvoisin,

Gaucho federal—Buenos Aires,

oil on canvas, 1842.

Reproduced from B. del Carril,

Monumenta Iconográphica (1964).

Library of Congress Cataloging-

in-Publication Data appear on

the last printed page of

this book.

To my parents, Marica and Chili,

and to Laura

Contents

Acknowledgments

Various institutions and many people contributed to make this book possible. I started this project back in 1988–1989, during a year's residence fellowship at the Institute of Advanced Studies at Princeton. The Institute's seminars made me aware of the complexities of the interpretation of "social texts." There, I began to read *estancia* and criminal records from a new perspective, focusing on power relationships, the positionality of subjects, and the meaning of messages. During this time, I benefited enormously from conversations with Albert Hirschmann, Lynn Hunt, Clifford Geertz, Greg Denning, Joan W. Scott, Gavin Wright, Mary Steedly, and Margaret Weir. New intersections between anthropology and history, together with poststructuralist modes of interpretation, greatly influenced the formulation of the questions I wanted to pose concerning the history of postindependence Buenos Aires province.

In 1992–1993, thanks to an Advanced Research Grant from the Social Science Research Council, I was able to spend two years investigating archives in Buenos Aires and La Plata. Librarians and archivists at the Archivo General de la Nación, the Academia Nacional de Historia, the Archivo Histórico de la Provincia de Buenos Aires, the Instituto Ravignani, and the Instituto Di Tella helped me find my way through a maze of materials that would later constitute the textual corpus of my investigation. Later, while trying to translate the first ideas onto paper, a grant from the University of Buenos Aires allowed me to spend a year of productive interaction with Argentine colleagues. I recall with pleasure the discussions that ensued after seminars at the Instituto Ravignani and at the universities of Tandil, Luján, Mar del Plata, and Córdoba. I thank all those who made comments and suggestions, too many to mention by name.

In 1993–1994 a year's residence at the Agrarian Studies Program at Yale University gave me the opportunity to draft a substantial part of the manuscript. The reader will easily recognize the influence of James C. Scott's works in this book. Jim's seminars were filled with a warm, convivial, and intellectually exciting atmosphere. This was a place where, despite unending winter storms, I felt at home. The commentaries of my colleagues and friends Akhil Gupta, Prabhu Mohapatra, Stacy Pigg, Catherine LeGrand,

David Nugent, and Robert Baldwin enhanced my comprehension of the dynamics of peasant societies and cultures. By then, I was in contact with scholars working in the United States from a subalternist perspective. Walter Mignolo and José Rabasa asked me to contribute to a collective volume the group was preparing. Through them, I came to know other scholars whose work has greatly influenced my perspective of history and interpretation, among them John Beverley, Patricia Seed, Sara Castro-Klarén, and Ileana Rodríguez.

In 1998, a Mellon Visiting Professorship at Yale University allowed me to write the final chapters of the manuscript. During that semester, Stuart Schwartz and Gilbert Joseph provided me with an excellent work environment to complete this task. I thank the librarians of Mudd and Sterling libraries for their assistance. My thanks extend to the Universidad Torcuato Di Tella (to its former rector, Gerardo Della Paolera, and former vice rector, José María Ghío) for a generous leave to complete the manuscript. Also, I thank my colleagues at Di Tella (Klaus Gallo, Guido Pincione, Ezequiel Gallo, Fernando Rocchi, and Roberto Gargarella) for their valuable commentary.

Over the years, Carlos Mayo, Eduardo Saguier, Carlos Forment, Noemí Goldman, and Alejandra Irigoin (among others) contributed bibliographical references, advice about archival repositories, and relevant ideas to improve my analysis. Other scholars have commented on earlier drafts of materials later included in this book. In Argentina, the list includes Enrique Tandeter, José Carlos Chiaramonte, Nora Domínguez, Cristina Iglesia, Carlos Cansanello, Jorge Myers, Ricardo Cicerchia, Samuel Amaral, Martha Becchis, Marta Goldberg, Silvia Palomeque, Jorge Gelman, and Raúl Fradkin. In the United States, seminars at Stony Brook, NYU, Minnesota, SMU, the New School, Yale, and Harvard, among others gave me the chance to try out my ideas in front of receptive audiences. Scholars have been generous with their time and advice. Among them, I would like to thank especially Michael Gimenez, Tulio Halperín Donghi, William Roseberry, Emilia Viotti da Costa, Barbara Wainstein, Jeremy Adelman, Daniel James, Brooke Larson, John Coatsworth, Eric Van Young, and John French.

Other debts go further back in time, to the years I worked on my dissertation at the University of Texas. I want to mention two of my professors. Jonathan C. Brown guided me onto the path of the historical profession and showed me the complexities of the Buenos Aires countryside in the postindependence period. Harry Cleaver directed me onto the terrain of social theory and taught me to pose important questions. My concerns for the dynamics of social conflict and meanings of archival documents stem from their teachings.

Over the years, various edited collections diverted my attention from the writing of this manuscript. In the end, however, these enterprises proved valuable for affirming certain concepts, discussing methodological concerns, and getting better acquainted with the fields of social, political, and cultural history in Latin America. To my coeditors and friends Noemí Goldman, Carlos Aguirre, Gilbert Joseph, and Catherine LeGrand I owe back tons of encouragement and kind affection. Finally, my gratitude to the editors of Duke University Press, to Valerie Millholland, Rebecca Johns-Danes, and Miriam Angress in particular, for their patience and craftsmanship.

Tables and Illustrations

Introduction

Between 1829 and 1852, under the leadership of Juan Manuel de Rosas, the province of Buenos Aires underwent a peculiar experiment in republicanism, one characterized by strong centralization of authority, factionalist politics, populist gestures, and an unmitigated cult of personality. The period witnessed an unprecedented mobilization for war of the rural population, the consolidation of stereotypical political identities (*unitarios* and *federales*), and an increasing intrusion of the state into the lives of ordinary folks. Persuaded that the laws had to govern social interactions, Governor Rosas emphasized the enforcement of existing legal statutes, making the return to tranquility and order in the countryside a major objective of his administration. This was also a period of economic growth based on the export of livestock goods (hides, tallow, wool, jerked beef). Naturally, this export bonanza produced an impact on the internal circulation of commodities and on labor markets. A fourfold increase in the value of exports, combined with a significant increase in population and a substantial expansion of land appropriation, provided the context for an intensified demand for labor power that, in turn, reinforced preexisting patterns of internal migration.

These forces—military mobilization, federalist politics, the juridification of social relations, and expanding markets—increased the spatial and occupational mobility of rural folks and put them in close proximity to state judicial and military authorities. A reorganized provincial state, with a strong centralized authority (particularly after 1835) and an enhanced capacity for legal enforcement at the local level, took upon itself the tasks of registering, classifying, training for military duty, and disciplining the rural (male) population. The strengthened provincial state tried to impose order on the rural subaltern and to prepare reluctant peasant-citizens for war against the unitarios. This produced frequent disciplinary encounters between state authorities and migratory workers, ex-soldiers, and "delinquents," encounters that enriched the state's knowledge of this rural Other, collectively called the "country peon class" (*la clase de peón de campo*).

In this book I offer an interpretive reconstruction of this "class"—its experience, sensibilities, opinions, claims—through a double interrogation.[1] On the one hand, I interrogate the order instrumented by state authorities in its economic, legal, political, and military dimensions. On the other hand, I try to recuperate the fragmented utterances of subaltern subjects, endeavoring to comprehend their possibilities for defiance and resistance to this particular state project. Instead of reifying and homogenizing the two extremes of a dominant-subordinate relationship, I seek to deconstruct the various, overlapping layers of the state's order, while reconstructing the fragmented and diverse voices and positions of the subaltern. Examining the multiple intersections of this complex power relationship, I present an alternative understanding of the postindependence period, one that takes into account the interactions between the state and the rural subalterns in the construction of the nation's history.

My interrogation concentrates on the relations between the provincial state and its rural folks, or *paysanos*. It traces the multiple manifestations of this conflictive relationship in a particular social, political, and cultural context: the postindependence transition.[2] Traditionally considered an aberration or long delay in the history of nation-state formation, the post-1820 period (including the Rosas administration experience) represented a formative, crucial epoch for rural folks. The extension of the vote to male rural inhabitants incorporated the countryside as an important balancing force in the politics of the province. The reorganization of the militias, which endowed neighbor-residents with new rights and obligations, created increasing tension between them and the transient population (rural laborers, in particular). As the criminal justice system stretched its arms to rural areas, its rhetoric and example reached the most distant frontier towns. Justices of the peace became central figures in the lives of rural communities, preaching their gospel of order, legality, and federalism. Still, the postindependent transition continued to be marred by conflict, instability, and insecurity. Civil wars continued to consume the lives and erode the resources of many paysanos. Males were forcefully drafted into the army or pressed to join the militias, and proprietors small and large were forced to surrender horses, cattle, and provisions to a militarized state.

The study focuses on the experience of some subaltern subjects. Peons and peasants drafted into the armies and militias of the Federation and ex-soldiers (deserters) seeking reinsertion into rural communities occupy a central position in this historical narrative. Only occasionally does the study touch on poor women, peddlers, and domestic servants. The emphasis on male peons and poor peasants was dictated by the availability of sources and, ultimately, by the nature of the state during the Rosas government. Military and judicial authorities supplied the "ethnographies" that allow us to "hear" and "see" these subaltern subjects. With the utmost zeal and regularity, the provincial state interrogated the rural poor for purposes of identification and classification. Immersed in a struggle to impose disciplinary order (legal, economic, political, and military), the state built an impressive archive of information on subaltern subjects. This archive contributed to delineate the contours of an alterity (the peon or peasant soldier) or "class" (the "country peon class") that has remained relatively unexplored by historians.

Some limitations of the study should be posed from the outset. This book does not examine in depth other important forms of subaltern experience. Lower-class women, Afro-Argentines, indigenous peoples, and children appear here and there in the narration but without the profound interrogation these social actors deserve. This study concentrates on male "wandering paysanos." By necessity, my reconstruction of the lives of peons and peasants concentrates on the space illuminated by the gaze of the state, that is, on policing, military recruitment, judicial processes, and market regulation. Hence, issues of coercion, patriotism, work, and rights overshadow other aspects of peasants' and peons' experience, such as religious beliefs, family relations, interpersonal interactions, and leisure activities.

Official Transcript and Subaltern "Voices"

The study is based on my reading of multiple sources: military and judicial records, Rosas's official correspondence, political poetry and narratives, and secondary materials. Among these documents, none are more revealing than the *filiaciones* and *clasificaciones*, personal files on prisoners and recruits filled out by state authorities. A source of valuable statistical information, these documents also register the multiple voices of the subaltern. Usually, the first part contains information about the subject under interrogation: name, place of birth, parents, age, marital status, literacy, occupation, and equestrian skills. Next follows a visual appraisal of the subject, supplying additional information on clothing, general appearance, and skin color.[3] After this, we find a series of open questions about the prisoner's military past or employment record.

This second part of the questionnaire opens up a space for the narration of individual experience.[4] Here we find peons and peasants (and other subaltern subjects) telling their military or judicial inquisitors about the occasion on which they joined the army or the militias, about their participation on the battlefield, about their "perambulations" through the province searching for jobs, about their dramas of family separation, or about abuses of power committed by state authorities. The "stories" contained in these interrogations were crucial for recovering fragments of subaltern experience, discourse, and mentality.[5] These fragments were valuable for understanding peons' and peasants' reactions to the state's notions of social and legal order, economic normalcy, and patriotic duty. Through these subaltern narratives I was able to imagine the roads and itineraries peons and peasants traversed to find jobs, escape from police persecution, or find solace after a long military campaign.

Undoubtedly, finding subaltern narratives inside the official transcript was a surprise at first. Here were peons and peasants reporting in front of the authorities—on occasion, at great personal risk—various misfortunes and injustices. They were revealing hidden aspects of power relations during the process of state and nation formation. As important, these stories illuminated previously unknown dimensions of paysanos' experience with labor markets: freedom of movement, bargaining practices, nonwage compensation, and more. State power and labor markets, it seemed, had shaped the world of poor peasants and laborers. Later, a closer reading of judicial and military documents led me to discover the subtleties of subaltern politics and the paramount importance of the legal system. Subaltern voices pointed me toward the existence of a common territory of experience, one marked by fluid labor markets, the violence of war, mass recruitment, and "swift justice."

Immediately, the problem of agency arose. The voices recorded in those files (filiaciones) presented a subjectivity or agency that was difficult to characterize in terms of class. Many of the interrogated subjects worked as peons; others were small-scale livestock owners, farmers, or skilled workers. Though state authorities tried to group them as members of a class, they saw themselves as individual paysanos fallen into the grid of a coercive regime of governance. Most of them were well informed about political and military affairs. Many claimed to be federalists though their enthusiasm for the Federalist Cause varied. The most salient element they had in common was their spatial and occupational mobility. Itinerancy and movement characterized the lives of many of these peons and peasants. Many perambulated through different partidos (districts) and rural towns searching for a livelihood or seeking a safer place of residence. Others, displaced from their town by the civil wars, wandered through the territory searching for family members, co-provincianos, or previous employers.

How to characterize these subaltern narratives and the voices that emerged from them? What is the nature of the subjectivity they insinuate? In Domination and the Arts of Resistance, James Scott (1990) distinguishes four main theaters for the communicative exchange between dominant and subordinate classes: (1) the "public transcript," where the true voices of the subordinates appear repressed and the language of self-interested deference prevails; (2) the "hidden transcript," where subordinates build an oppositional culture based on inversion and defiance; (3) an intermediate terrain, where, with the help of disguise and anonymity, subordinates can make public, in subtle and ambivalent ways, some of their views on domination and exploitation; and (4) those situations that collapse existing divisions between public and hidden transcripts, leading generally to greater repression or to rebellion.

Most of the stories and voices I found belonged to a theater that fit uncomfortably in any of these characterizations (some of them, to be sure, appeared to be located in terrain 3). They were subaltern utterances transcribed into the official transcript. They pertained to a particular conversation and power relationship: the interaction between state authorities and laborers and peasants. The voice that emerged from this interaction both conformed to and confronted authority. While trying to accommodate to the image of the "good federalist," peons and peasants expressed—for the record—their lamentations and demands about the state and the fatherland. Rather than being submissive, these agents "talked back" to state authorities. The stories themselves contain traces of the "hidden" transcript: subaltern disguise, gossip, false documents, and irony make their way into the narration of events as fragments of a counterdiscourse about the fatherland.

Voices of "lamentation and defiance"—as Josefina Ludmer 1988 calls them—appear in texts in which paysanos' patriotism and federalist sympathies are questioned by the state. Hence, our speakers (peon and peasant soldiers) place themselves into the territory of service, patriotism, and rights. This location relates to the particular postindependent transition, a time when factionalist conflicts around the formation of the nation-state put in doubt the initial universality granted to these principles of equality, fraternity, and freedom. As a consequence, subaltern groups found themselves contending over the concrete meaning of these abstract rights. In multiple ways, they tried to reclaim the social and political rights promised by the postindependence leadership: good treatment, paid labor, freedom of mobility, and the rights associated with residency. Not surprisingly, peons' and peasants' lamentations and demands related to quite modern constructs: wage contracts, republicanism, independent bodies, and citizenship.[6]

Unknowingly, in trying to impose Rosas's vision of order, judicial and military authorities found themselves immersed in a conversation about the republic and the place it occupied in the lives of poor rural folks. At a time when the state's project of order began to clash with paysanos' notions of self, place, and rights, subaltern voices were enunciated and systematically recorded. Clearly, the state intended to classify the rural population for purposes related to military recruitment and social control, but the communication established was a two-way street. In search of pardons, transfers, or dismissals, peon and peasant soldiers addressed the authorities of the state, openly voicing their discontent about some important aspects of state and social power. Such daring acts—using the military and judicial platforms of the state to present claims—appear now as a remarkable eruption of the "hidden transcript" into the public sphere.

The Subaltern(ist) Perspective

Since the mid-1980s, the Indian subaltern studies group has produced an important renovation of cultural and social history, critically incorporating the contributions of Gramsci, the British Marxist historians, Foucault, Derrida, and others. The group tried to redress the absence of subaltern agency in the history of the formation of the modern Indian nation and, simultaneously, attempted to problematize the "archive" and the "perspective" that constituted the foundations of existing historiography.[7] They started by recognizing that subalterns always constructed their subject positions in relation to dominant figures (classes, castes, male figures, and colonizers) and within certain "idioms" of subordination pervaded by tradition, religiosity, and patriarchy. They argued that subalterns did not constitute a unitary or homogeneous subject, except in the gaze of the dominant, who reduced them to the condition of "masses" endowed with certain attributes and predispositions. They acknowledged also that the subaltern's past was not fully recoverable for, in spite of the abundance of its textual presence in the discourse of the dominant, the "evidence" that historians had to interpret was always fragmentary, multilayered, and opaque.

As noted by Ranajit Guha and his colleagues, both imperial and nationalist history had relegated peasants and industrial workers to the role of victims or followers of the makers of history, the colonial and Indian elites. "Rescuing" those subalterns required laborious deconstructive work, for subaltern identity and consciousness were buried in a deep layer of registers and representations that were not power-neutral. Hence, the challenge was double; on the one hand, to understand the diverse strands of discourse that constituted and legitimated relations of domination/

subordination; on the other hand, to use the reconstructed voice of the subaltern to carve up a new critical location in history, a "subalternist perspective."[8] Because all "evidence" about the subaltern had been produced in the context of D/S relations, the only possible alternative to elite history was a fragmented, multifaceted, and nonlinear history.

Though the work of Indian subalternists recognized important intellectual debts to the British Marxist historians, their project was different in at least two ways.[9] First, it was less teleological, in the sense that it did not expect to find the formation of a "working class" as a culturally autonomous and homogeneous entity. Not class formation, but the changing conditions of "subalternity" (referring to all relations of domination, not only class) was the object of study. Second, their project was more aware of the problems of representation, rejecting the notion of texts as simple "reflections" of reality.[10] Accepting the dialogical and disciplinary nature of the discourse of the dominant, subalternists subjected to criticism the very notion of "working-class" agency. Workers organized and struggled against capitalists and colonial authorities, guided by conceptions derived from the mixture of Indian and British idioms of domination. The concept of a counterhegemonic, autonomous working-class culture seemed to be at odds with the nature of discursive and power relations.

This study acknowledges certain affinities, in methodology and perspective, with the project of subaltern history.[11] It shares a similar preoccupation for deconstructing the discourse of the dominant and for repositioning into history the voices and recollections of subaltern agents. While recognizing the enormous distance that separates the respective postcolonial situations of India and Argentina, my analysis problematizes the presence of rural subalterns in various types of representations: judicial reports, recruits' files, people's petitions, and literary and historical reconstructions of the Rosas period. I probe the utility of the concept of subalternity for reconstructing the activities and mentalities of populations subjected to both textual and disciplinary domination. I suggest that the resistance, negotiation, or acquiescence of these groups needs to be examined in relation to dominant narratives, alterities created by elites and government, and local, institutional practices of power.[12]

Peons and peasants of postindependence Buenos Aires province lived in a world organized by dominant signifiers and institutions: federalism, the law (and the Restorer of Laws), the military (the fatherland), the market. At crucial moments in their lives, they stood in a subordinate position vis-à-vis military commanders, justices of the peace, employers, and the political leadership. Deconstructing the languages and mechanisms of domination embodied in these signifiers and institutions has helped me understand the fragments left by subalterns in the official transcript. While the voices of subalterns buried in the judicial and military archives presented a new perspective regarding the events of postindependence, the texts themselves were the products of a disciplinary interaction between dominant and subaltern. This book attempts to recover peons' and peasants' opinions, recollections, and stories, without divorcing them from the dominant/subaltern relations in which they were inserted.

Subaltern(ist) history deals mostly with fragments: small groups (often forgotten and abused) within society; fragments of evidence scattered throughout the landscape of representation; particularistic, located understandings (see Pandey 1992). This perspective acknowledges the great difficulties of reconstructing subalterns' actions, viewpoints, and language, due not only to the lack of transparency of most texts at the disposal of the historian, but also to the overlapping of subject positions from which events are narrated (see Amin 1995). To an extent, all subaltern history is the analysis of lack and excess: lack of recognition by elite history of the roles played by subalterns in the making of nations, markets, political regimes, and cultures; excess of elite negative portrayals of the subaltern—as children, uncivilized, violent, indolent, ignorant.

My work of reconstruction has found similar obstacles: only fragments of evidence about subaltern experience, scattered here and there, and excessive characterizations aimed at disciplining, moralizing, or simply censuring subalterns' ascribed behavior, sentiments, and beliefs. The rural masses were alternatively taken as objects of criticism and victimization, but not as historical agents.[13] Layers of literary and historical writings contributed to consolidate this refusal of agency and lack of recognition. Hence, writing the history of subaltern subjects required disarming powerful constructions about the Argentine past. Notions of cattle ranching feudalism and caudillismo, characterizations of Rosas's government as a regime of fear and illegality, and images of *gauchos* as rebels living outside of market society had to be reexamined before any new appraisal could be made about peons' and peasants' experiences.

To the subalternist historian, postindependence Buenos Aires province presents a double challenge, for it involves searching for subaltern action and identity in a context saturated by two contradictory tendencies: political modernization and the extension of the disciplinary state.[14] Peons and peasants reacted to a special sort of modernity, one based on the dramatic expansion of citizenship, the abolition of colonial legal and social privileges, the military mobilization of the peasantry, and extension of the jurisdiction of the judicial system into the countryside.[15] The extension of the franchise to the rural population with almost no qualifications and the simultaneous militarization of rural towns restructured the nature of politics and made the subaltern important for the governing elites. If political modernization empowered the rural subaltern, the extension of state disciplinary institutions (in particular, the judiciary and the military) subjected poor paysanos to more frequent encounters with "the authority" and gave them greater visibility in the official record.

Through textual and disciplinary interventions, the state structured the experience of the subaltern. The provincial state used military garrisons, militia units, and justice houses as sites for the deployment of a strong disciplinary pedagogy.[16] Under Rosas's leadership, these institutions interpellated the subaltern as a reluctant patriot, as a potential criminal, and (secondarily) as a possible "vagrant." This interpellation defined the terms and circumstances in which the subaltern entered into the official record. In a historical conjuncture characterized by the tension between the promise of rights and the reality of coercive recruitment, disciplinary institutions constructed the "peon class." That is, they engendered the "classifications," the accusations, the credentials, and the rules of conduct that defined peons and peasants' positions of subalternity.

It was in relation to these definitions and conditions that rural folks struggled, maneuvered, and complained. My task was to search into the state's archive for traces of these interactions, characterizations, indictments, and reactions. In this regard, the archives of regiments, justices of the peace, and prisons proved crucial to the double task of deconstructing the discourse of the dominant and rescuing subaltern actions and mentality. In these textual sites I encountered the collision between the promise of new republican rights and the language of authority of the state (legal order, moralization of customs, military duty). In these institutional records I found the most interesting traces of an unstable and conflictive interaction between state order and subaltern experience.

Myths about Coercion, Class, and Politics

Though Argentine historiography is rich and diverse, a few motifs, repeated over time, have served to organize the historical reconstructions of the Rosas period.[17] Three constructs, in particular, have survived the challenges of different waves of revisionism, interpretation, and ideological reappropriation: (1) the thesis of cattle ranching feudalism and dependent peonage; (2) the view of Rosas as representative or leader of the cattle ranching class; and (3) the ambivalent relationship (of rigor and emulation, of seduction and punishment) between Rosas and the lower classes.[18]

These constructs remained central to the explanation of the Rosas era, not because of the preponderance of evidence, but mainly because they served to locate the subaltern in a particular, convenient site: a subordinate, contradictory, almost impossible location, devoid of agency.

Among these motifs, none has been more enduring than the image of a dependent peonage trapped on cattle ranches at the mercy of powerful cattle ranchers. The association of cattle ranching feudalism (*feudalismo ganadero*) with the Rosas's regime has been a common denominator of different strands of historiography. First enunciated by the unitario leaders as an indictment against the hated Tyranny, the rumor that Rosas gave refuge to and tolerated on his ranches all sorts of common criminals soon became central to the historical understanding of the period. To the liberal émigrés Rosas's toleration denoted the barbaric, illegal nature of his regime; historians elevated this politically charged accusation into a founding metaphor: the idea of a "feudal past" centered on the dominant cattle ranch.

At the beginning of the century, José Ingenieros, the most influential positivist thinker of his generation, argued that vagrancy laws had pushed the rural poor into servitude, contributing to the consolidation of a seignorial "*hacendado* class."[19] Although there are some obvious differences between temporarily hiring fugitives and creating labor servitude, Ingenieros preferred to ignore them. The notion of feudal-like servitude was key to understanding the backward state of culture and society in nineteenth-century Argentina. In light of this metaphor, Ingenieros interpreted Rosismo as a return to the past, a restoration of tradition, custom, religion, and social hierarchy.[20]

After Ingenieros, other well-established historians replicated the motif of seignorial authority and power. Manuel Gálvez, Ricardo Levene, and Enrique de Gandía, among others, presented the cattle ranch as a personal fief where landowners exercised unbounded territorial power.[21] Later, the image of a strong but benevolent patron was recovered by nationalist and *dependentista* historians and put at the service of a different historical narrative. José M. Rosa (1962, 113), for instance, imagined peons and landowners reciting the rosary together and fighting side by side against common criminals and unitarios. Andrés Carretero (1972, 45) went even further, arguing that landowners became the substitutes for laborers' unknown fathers. Like the master of a southern plantation, the ranch owner consented to marriages, provided health care for the peons' families, and served as godfather of many of their children.

From the left, historians such as Gaston Gori, Milcíades Peña, and Ricardo Rodríguez Molas reinforced the other side of the same story: state coercion had driven peasants into peonage. Rejecting the view that ranchers were benevolent employers, these historians described a *gaucho* class and culture victimized by the postindependent state.[22] Recent reincarnations of this perspective can be found in the work of John Lynch (1981) and Richard Slatta (1983). Both revisited the question of state coercion and ranchers' paternalism to reinforce the traditional narrative of victimization. According to Lynch, vagrancy, the draft, and passport laws drove the free-spirited inhabitants of the pampas into a situation of peonage or wage servitude.[23] Powerful landowners offered deserters and draft dodgers permanent employment on their ranches in exchange for protection from press gangs, military officers, and justices of the peace. This, argues Lynch, attached peons to the cattle ranch in ways that resembled European servitude.[24] Slatta resorted to the same trope of state entrapment to explain the "disappearance" of gauchos and frontier culture under the forces of modernization. The gauchos finally lost their freedom when the state and the rancher class (with the help of wire fencing and railroads) were able to fragment the gauchos' space, drastically reduce their mobility, and criminalize their customary activities.[25]

A second motif, also persistent in the literature, states that Rosas represented or expressed the interests of the emerging cattle-ranching or rancher class. It was with a mandate from this class that the governor intensified the enforcement of existing vagrancy laws to augment the "supply" of laborers at a time of soaring exports of livestock products. It was for the benefit of this class that Rosas distributed land and maintained low levels of taxation on rural property and livestock exports.[26] Renditions of this thesis vary, ranging from accusations of cronyism and class-biased policies to Marxist notions of class representation. Vicente F. López, a liberal historian, believed that ranchers followed Rosas's leadership in the improvement of agriculture and livestock raising, later transforming this admiration into political support (in Trias 1970, 28). Ingenieros put the argument in stronger terms. Since 1817 Rosas, Terrero, and a few other estancieros and owners of meat-salting plants had formed a solid coalition (a "trust") that predated public finances and extracted privileges from the state.[27]

Soon, the view of Rosas as representative of a class overshadowed the more traditional (liberal) narrative that presented Rosas as a tyrant who followed his own instincts and ambitions. In the work of Jacinto Oddone (1967) and others, Rosas had produced the "landowning class" (through the distribution of public lands) and also represented the interests of this class in government. Scholars debated whether Rosista federalism represented a political, organizational position or only the interests of Buenos

Aires cattle ranchers. They took for granted that this "class" existed and had a definite "class project."[28] It appeared self-evident to historians (Levene among them) that the great cattle rancher (Rosas) would enact policies that favored other members of his "class."

A third powerful motif permeating the historical representations of the period referred to the contradictory relationship between Rosas and the urban and rural masses. Rosas's popularity among the subalterns puzzled historians. In a political regime generally regarded as a ruthless dictatorship, this popularity was problematic and called for explanation. The formula chosen to solve the puzzle was a Janus-faced Rosas: on one side was the Rosas who seduced the plebe, with his egalitarian dress, inflamed rhetoric, equestrian skills, and paternalistic gestures; on the other side was Rosas the disciplinarian, who tried to reform the conduct of the poor with the rigor of military service, prisons, and corporal punishment. This construct, perfected at the height of the "positivist moment," was consistent with the idea of a "savage democracy," a notion molded by liberal historiography.

The genealogy of this interpretive synthesis is itself interesting. Countering the federalist press, unitario publicists presented the regime as a "tyranny," in which the authority of a single man had abolished all the institutions and liberties proper to a republic.[29] These writers rejected federalists' claims that the Argentine Confederation was a republic governed by laws, arguing instead that Rosas's power was sustained only by terror. It was all coercion: coercion against the poor peasant drafted unwillingly into the army and coercion against the landowner whose properties were confiscated.[30] Later, historians returned to the period of "anarchy" to find keys to interpret the nature of Rosismo. Bartolomé Mitre (1947) pioneered this path of interpretation, suggesting that out of the social and political turbulence of 1820 emerged a "savage democracy" based on notions of political fragmentation, guerrilla warfare, and spontaneous (instinctive) leadership.[31] In the end, it was the backwardness of the rural masses and the collapse of social and political authority that gave way to this peculiar form of government.

The positivist generation revisited the question of Rosas's popularity (already established by the work of Saldías and Bilbao) and found new answers. Resorting to contemporary studies in mass psychology, J. M. Ramos Mejía (1907, 1932; see also Ayarragaray 1904) presented Rosas as a neurotic with the capacity, due to his very excesses, to exert an enormous appeal on the rural masses. In a specular relationship, the masses' immaturity and desires translated and accumulated into the power of the dictator, stimulating the permanence in power of a man with all kinds of psychoses. As De Gandía (1946) explained later, the key to understanding Rosas's popularity consisted in picturing his politics as a performance in flattering and deception. With promises of equality and false love and disguised as a gaucho, Rosas conquered the imagination of the semi-savage plebe; they were hallucinated by his speech and performance.[32] The interpretive circle was thus complete. Rosas not only was the "social product" of the barbarism of the pampas (as Sarmiento would have it), he was also the man who could manage and direct the energy of the masses. At the same time, he was the Seducer and the Disciplinarian.[33]

Recent studies of cattle ranches and rural life have rendered obsolete the vision of cattle ranching feudalism. This scholarship has shown that, since the late colonial period, cattle ranches were profit-seeking enterprises employing wage laborers to produce cattle, hides, and tallow for local and overseas markets.[34] Temporary employment was the norm, seasonal variations were marked, and labor shortages were chronic.[35] The previous image of powerful great landlords has been reduced to a more humble dimension, while a variety of local studies have confirmed the economic importance of small-scale livestock-raisers (*criadores*) and farmers (*labradores*), first indicated by J. C. Brown in 1979.[36] Similarly, the thesis of a dependent peonage is rapidly crumbling as more evidence accumulates on the migratory patterns of rural workers and the high labor turnover on estancias and in other workplaces.[37]

This book joins the criticism against the conventional wisdom, showing how peons dealt, quite assertively, with a multiplicity of small-scale and medium landholders rather than with great hacendados. Peons cherished these short-term contracts because they allowed for greater mobility, an important asset at a time of acute confrontation with the state over the issue of military service. They were not confined in any way to the "domain" of the great cattle ranch; labor markets worked on the basis of economic stimuli, and in spite of state coercion.

The alleged collusion of interests between Rosas and the rancher class also needs important revisions, not only because this thesis collapses important differences, but because it ignores political and ideological fractures that were evident to contemporaries.[38] Far from creating a collusive situation, the politico-ideological articulations of the time (unitarios versus federales) tended to divide landowners along party lines. Those who were not committed to the Federalist Cause had to withdraw into private life or emigrate. New studies also show that Rosas's land policies did not have the impact originally assumed.[39] Clearly, there were points of contact and mutually beneficial exchanges between the autocratic state and the ranching economy of Buenos Aires, but there were also tensions, conflicting goals, and different visions of the social and political order. Particularly on the question of military service, the interests of both actors, state and ranchers, were in conflict.[40]

Rosas's relationship with the urban and rural plebe is perhaps the most problematic of the three constructs. Recent work has called into question the traditional notion of *caudillismo* as applied to the Rosas regime and has revalorized the importance of republicanism as its constitutive discourse (Goldman and Salvatore 1998; Myers 1995). Yet no attempt has been made to deconstruct the disciplinarian/seducer duality that is at the core of much of the historiography of the Rosas period. Implicit in this duality is a great deal of textual violence against the subaltern. The Rosista plebe appears characterized as a primeval, organic mass, reacting to the "stimulation" radiated from a charismatic leader. Mitre's notion of a "savage democracy," which blamed the masses for the advent of Rosismo, still finds resonance in recent historiography.[41] Rosas's followers continue to be portrayed as attracted by "natural" forces they could not control.[42] The three motifs or constructs are problematic, for they locate the subaltern in a situation of triple subordination. At the level of production, they appear as victims of a system of entrapment that places them in a situation of high coercion (dependent peonage). In society and culture, they appear as a "mass" ready to destroy any attempt to construct republican institutions and a civilized social order. In the political sphere, they appear dominated by the forces of their own impulses, supporting and stimulating the excesses of a dictatorial regime. In actuality, subalterns have been "trapped" by history into an impossible (inescapable) situation. Located in a primitive, almost natural state, they have not been allowed to become true agents of history.

To undo the work of this elitist historiography, it is not sufficient to demonstrate the entrepreneurial sagacity of ranchers or to posit the diversity of productive situations and strategies in the Buenos Aires countryside. It is necessary to reposition in history major participants in the construction of the postindependence transition: the soldiers who fought the civil wars; the peons who labored the land, tended the cattle, and provisioned the city; the resident-neighbors who supported the Federalist Cause. This book presents a critique of traditional interpretations of Rosismo and the postindependent transition by interrogating these social actors. I believe poor paysanos' work practices, sufferings, language, beliefs, and memory belong to the history of the formation of the Argentine nation.

Dimensions of Subaltern Experience

This book explores four dimensions of subaltern experience: labor and commodity markets, the law, the military, and politics. These dimensions should be considered "fields of power," semibounded spaces endowed with particular sets of rules where dominant and subaltern faced each other in a more or less regular fashion.[43] Each field of power presents a different combination of coercion and persuasion (distinct repertoires of disciplinary power), hence occupying different locations in the continuum between domination and hegemony.[44] Each domain confronted subalterns with a different predicament: freedom of contract and mobility, the need to persecute delinquents and extend the governing of laws, the duty of federalists to defend their threatened fatherland, and the demonology of unitarios as the ultimate enemy of the republic. These predicaments were bound to affect the language and self-perception of peons and peasants. The polarities and motifs embedded in these affirmations colored subalterns' narratives of experience.

In each of these domains, rituals and rules defined the relative position of dominant and subaltern and regulated their interactions. Military codes, Rosas's circulars about "classification" and crime control, the design of patriotic festivities and federalist propaganda, branding laws, and regulation of cattle markets all imposed rules of conduct on social actors. In proximity to these nodes of power, subalterns had to either learn the rules of the game or face the consequences, Paysanos had to be aware of the need for passports when traveling, needed to respond to the community's call for militia drill, could not afford to ignore the prohibition against carrying knives in taverns and at festivities. A new lexicon of property was written on the skins of animals (branding) and on the back of oxcarts. The demands of the fatherland were transparent in officers' admonitions every time a recruit registered for service. Not surprisingly, Buenos Aires province appeared to the subaltern to be an assortment of regulations emanating from different sources of authority.[45]

Rural laborers and peasants drew lessons from their passage or involvement with each of these four disciplinary domains. Many peons and peasants, willingly or not, became involved in the civil wars as federalist soldiers. The experience of war was central to their sensibilities, expressions, and knowledge. From the federalist campaigns or from service at frontier garrisons, soldiers came back with an experience in bargaining and a clear territorial perception of the fatherland. Their awareness of the political, their demands concerning economic justice, and the array of arguments used to contest the "authority" of power holders show traces of the experience of military life. The law also informed the way subalterns conceived of their place in the new federalist republic. The intensified enforcement of penal legislation confronted subalterns with a regulating power that distributed, systematically, harsh penalties in swift fashion. Migratory workers and itinerant peons were bound to meet the agents of the law (justices of the peace or their police assistants [*tenientes alcaldes*]) in their perambulations. The law, as a didactic of customs and a reality of police surveillance, was closer to the lives of paysanos. From these encounters with legal authority subalterns derived a clearer knowledge of judicial practices, a language about legal equality and rights, and the realization of the importance of acquiring the status of neighbor-citizen.

Federalist politics pervaded everyday life. Frequent elections, patriotic festivities, and political rituals confronted subalterns with a symbolically laden reality, heightening their awareness of national and international politics. Paysanos could not afford to be apolitical; they had to show their allegiance to federalism in their appearance, contributions, and military service. Politics was both repressive and empowering. The compulsion to adopt federalist sympathies—or, at least, a federalist appearance—put many paysanos under a permanent cloud of suspicion. On the other hand, federalism provided subalterns with a new interpretation of the Epic of the Fatherland and a position from which to address authority: federalist patriotism. Transposed to military quarters, this knowledge and language became important instruments for bargaining, organizing collective or individual protests, and strategically deciding when to abandon military life.

In the economic terrain, the Rosas era meant an affirmation of property rights to cattle, a greater degree of competition in cattle markets, and a dramatic expansion in the demand for rural laborers. Markets for labor and goods flourished, despite the coercion of vagrancy laws and the trade disruptions caused by foreign blockades. The influence of markets was pervasive in shaping peons' and peasants' experiences. Searching for jobs on horseback, demanding "rights" to income, selling illegally obtained hides, purchasing clothes and other necessities, arguing against market regulations, peons and peasants became engaged with market mechanisms and ideology. They took advantage of a labor-scarce economy undergoing an export bonanza to advance certain basic demands in pay, treatment, and mobility.

Distinct combinations of coercion and persuasion meant that room for maneuvering and the tactics used by subalterns varied from one institutional space to the other. A prisoner at Santos Lugares had little chance to escape, refuse to answer, or defy the inquisitors. Paradoxically, it was this situation of extreme powerlessness that produced the more interesting fragments of subaltern criticism of the state, the war, and the conditions of military life. His movement limited, the prisoner invested his chances for improvement in "voice." The proximity of subalterns to the center of power (Rosas's military headquarters) made their criticism more poignant. Expecting the protection of the Restorer of the Laws, imprisoned paysanos recounted the injustices and humiliations suffered at the hands of justices of the peace and local policemen.

In the terrain of politics, the messages of Rosismo left little room for noncommitted individuals. Unanimismo implied that all citizens had to be federalists; hence, many ex-soldiers and prisoners strove to narrate credible stories about their loyalty to the Federalist Cause. Outside of federalist subject positions, there was no possibility of addressing the dominant. Yet arrested peons and poor peasants showed little compliance with the mandated emblems, much less, in fact, than mid- and large-scale proprietors. Itinerant peons blended into the festivities of federalism, but it was the middling paysanos who organized these demonstrations. The federalist allegiance of the peon soldier was based on active duty (service). Having rendered these services, ex-soldiers and militias used them as a platform from which to enunciate concrete economic and social grievances. The practice of petitioning to the governor became quite common among subordinate groups.

In the military, the situation was different. Acting as a group or individually, soldiers directly negotiated with their commanders and officers the conditions of service and the benefits owed them by the state. Military quarters were sites of continuous renegotiation of authority, in which the threat of mass desertion and rebellion was always present. This was truly a situation of domination without hegemony.[46] In fact, the fragile and contingent nature of discipline in frontier regiments was a source of constant preoccupation for the regime. The state's pedagogy about obedience and duty found little resonance in the recollections of soldiers; their loyalty to the flag appears conditioned to economic benefits and the respect of individual rights.

In the legal terrain, the degree of hegemony was greater than within the military. As the makers of "tranquility" and "order" in the countryside, justices of the peace received a great deal of cooperation from resident neighbors. The latter contributed their labor to the patrols, acted as witnesses in the instruction of criminal cases, and in their declarations and petitions expressed their belief in the possibility of attaining "justice." Nonresidents looked at the law somewhat differently; to them, the law inspired both fear and contempt.[47] The little that transpired into the public transcript shows a more cautious, ironic position vis-à-vis "justice." Very rarely, nonresidents openly and directly confronted the authority invested in law enforcers. In general, they waited until presented with a higher authority to denounce corrupt practices by justices of the peace and military chiefs.

The market was the least coercive of the four fields of power. Workers' mobility in and out of employment prevented the formation of a dependent peonage or any other form of enduring personal servitude. Contemporary travelers saw product markets saturated by subalterns' presence. Itinerant workers and peasants were full participants in market sociability and market culture. Their dealings with ranchers and other employers were freer and more equal than their relationships with justices of the peace, military officers, or the governor. Little has survived of peons' and peasants' opinions of merchants and other elite figures that is not infected with federalist ideology. In at least one instance (the cattle market at Buenos Aires, 1834), subalterns were able to organize a show of force, sprinkled with a rhetoric of radical liberalism. Although this was a rare case of open protest against market regulations, the *peones-vendedores*, enjoying a situation of extreme freedom of contract, resisted the imposition of controls in both labor and product markets.

Micro- and Macronarratives (Text and Context)

Micronarratives of experience (stories), particularly if fragmentary and subaltern, relate to the grand narrative of the nation (history) in complex, interdependent ways.[48] History enfolds and cuts across stories just as context envelops and interpenetrates a given literary text. National-mythical time intrudes and limits the narration of experiential time. But, at moments, the richness of individual narration overpowers with detail and diversity the linearity and homogeneity of history.[49] This book locates its narrative at the intersection between stories and history. This relationship presented perhaps the most important methodological challenge to this study. How do the recollections of paysanos relate to the history of the nation? How did the events of politics and war affect the way peons and peasants conceived their own place and time? Can fragmented and incomplete stories reveal something new about postindependence history? Can they interpellate history?[50]

The grand historical narrative of the postindependence transition provides the time reference, the location, and, sometimes, the tone of soldiers' and peons' individual narrations. Interrogated about their past contributions to the Federal Cause, veterans felt compelled to anchor their narration to a given military campaign. Naturally, as subalterns tried to establish a subjectivity or identity under suspicion (the loyal federalist soldier), they replicated some lines of the grand history of federalism. Political events such as the federalist "restorations" served to connect their individual experience with that of the Confederation. But they did so by bringing us back to the territory of lived experience, to battles of small significance, to events of heroism not recorded in our history texts, to interactions between soldiers and officers not included in military reports.

Though produced in the context of interrogatory proceedings (involving unequal power relations), these stories bring to light a hidden dimension of the history of the nation. Soldiers' stories displace the problematic of civil war and patriotism to a terrain of contested rights, unfulfilled promises, and injustices committed by state authorities. They bring into the picture the contentious nature of military discipline and the personal costs of war. In addition, these stories disrupt and destabilize the metanarrative of federalism, the rise to prominence of J. M. de Rosas and his various accomplishments, placing at the same level the requirements of the fatherland and the personal interests of the subaltern narrator (family, residence, employment, and liberties).

Ex-soldiers were not aware of campaign strategy, the strength of federalist forces, or the support federalism enjoyed in each province. Therefore, they tended to recount military campaigns as if moved by external forces; their recollections were sequences of movements over the territory, victories and losses, gatherings and dispersions. Precisely because they had a limited vision of war strategy, their stories appear fragmentary, sketchy, and incomplete. On the other hand, their stories are quite focused and detailed on particular aspects of a battle or maneuver. They supplement the metanarrative of the civil wars with a subtext that points toward other realities, toward alternative understandings of duty and fatherland. More poignant, they stress a presence obscured by the historiography. Veterans' war recollections recuperate this participation of common folks in the making of the Confederation's history.

Can these "stories" interpellate postindependence history? I believe they can. Not in the sense of providing an alternative, popular version of elite history, for subaltern stories are only fragments of individual experience, not the narration of a collective agency over a period of time. Their "time" rarely corresponds to chronological time, for they are the residues of memory, a fragile register of events. Lapses and silences outnumber the detail of names, places, and movements contained in these narrations. Nevertheless, the individual stories told by soldiers, peons, and peasants to the authorities helped me unpack the established historical knowledge about the Rosas period and question its validity. Their chief work has been to displace the terrain and the problematic under investigation.[51] These narratives focus on aspects overlooked by historians: the separation of families, bodily wounds and disease, humiliation and punishment.

The stories themselves present us with an organized past, a hierarchy of problems as processed by personal memory. Peons and peasants attributed different weight to the components of the postcolonial transition (socioeconomic, political, and cultural). First and foremost, this was lived as a time of civil wars. Factional, political conflict dominated all types of social interactions and permeated most forms of cultural representation. This entailed an across-the-board military mobilization of male inhabitants and, more noticeably, the division of political opinions and sympathies into two irreconcilable camps. Second, this was a time of the consolidation of "order." Buenos Aires province witnessed a gradual "arrangement of the countryside," thanks to intensified legal enforcement and surveillance at the local level, and a remarkable predictability in punishment at the center of power.

Factional conflict, militarization, and the restoration of a legal order had a definite impact on the lives of rural subalterns. The drama of the civil wars was fundamental to soldiers and their families. The periodic drills of the militias and the celebration of federalist victories interrupted the tranquil existence of rural communities. Male peons and peasants spent a good part of their adult life providing service, either in the militias or in the regular army. Similarly, the expansion of state surveillance over the rural population multiplied the instances in which wandering peons confronted (face-to-face) legal and police authorities. Job seekers lacking proper documents became a special target of interrogation, for they were suspected of being deserters or fugitive delinquents. Many of the arrested joined the ranks of the provincial army, so that in the end army service became the quintessential punishment for crimes or misdemeanors.

A political transition mediated by a civil war was at the center of subaltern stories. The capitalist, market transition produced fewer reactions (at least in the official transcript) than the questions of politics, state coercion, and the events of the civil war. The export bonanza and its increasing demand for rural laborers was implicit in peons' easy entry into and exit from the labor market. But subalterns did not provide more than passing references to these short-term employments. The formation of a great hacendado class or the question of land acquisition and appropriation was not given any space in these renditions of memory.

Subaltern stories addressed mainly the military, legal, and political aspects of the postcolonial transition. At stake was their position as patriots in a nation threatened by dissolution. In this regard, paysanos responded to the interpellation of republican federalism and its great narrative of the fatherland. This by itself constrained the limits of argument. The inability to escape or avoid this interpellation was only one aspect of their subalternity. Peons' and peasants' notions about politics, the legal order, and the military were shaped by their own experience, read in the light of the state's rhetoric and pedagogy. In addition, interrogations captured fragments of these subjects' experience as workers. The state, in its obsession to classify the rural population into class categories for recruitment purposes, gathered some information about peons' and peasants' occupational trajectories.[52]

It is in this context or "transition narrative" that the multiplicity of subaltern stories should be understood. This book examines an important question raised by postcolonial studies, the question of the involvement of subaltern subjects in the formation of nation-states. Here, the history of the dominant, the official history of Rosista federalism, seems to have left strong marks in the historical memory of the subaltern. To many of those interrogated in the 1840s, the history of the nation started in 1828, as if the Epic of Independence had been washed away from memory and its values replaced by more powerful signifiers. But subaltern understandings of this "new era" differed substantially from the official one. Peons and peasants interpreted the political and military aspects of this transition in terms of an unwritten contract between the state and the rural masses. This contract established that the state would use the labor of free men for war and in exchange would recognize and protect their civil and political rights. Implicit in this contract was the recognition of a contingent form of patriotism, one that recognized the free nature of the rural subaltern, circumscribing the discretionary powers of the state to the unusual circumstances of war. Subaltern voices constantly interpellate this imaginary contract, demanding from state authorities the recognition and enforcement of these rights.

Classification and Social Difference

Though I started with the idea of constructing a collective biography of a "class of workers," the voices and narratives found in the archives boycotted that project.[53] Most of the stories projected an individual rather than a collective subject.[54] The different trajectories of deserters, migratory workers, and peasants and peons turned into soldiers had in common only the movement—the "perambulations" and "wanderings"—and the encounters with authorities. Furthermore, the problem of false names and invented identities prevented me from linking the data (seeking to reconstruct kinship, community, or other associations) in any meaningful way. As rural subalterns changed subject positions in the course of the narratives (turning, for instance, from peons to soldiers, then to deserters, and then to small cattle raisers), treating them as fixed socioeconomic categories would not do justice to their stories.

It then became clear to me that the malleability of class was a general feature of the period. The postindependence state had abolished the old colonial taxonomies of race and status, leaving to civil society the task of redefining the new boundaries of class as "distinction." Furthermore, the dynamics of the labor market, military service, factional politics, and the legal process made all class positions unstable. At the top, a rancher or a merchant could, from night to day, descend into poverty by simply being characterized as a unitario. At the bottom, peons could quite easily amass the initial capital to become owners of a driving team or of a small oxcart business. But it was not just a problem of vertical social mobility. There was something in the culturally embedded notion of class that made it different from our conventional (Marxist) understandings of the term. An example will serve to clear this point.

In May 1837, from the public jail, Miguel Anso wrote a letter to Governor Rosas asking for his freedom. He tried to persuade the governor that his arrest had been a mistake, that he was neither a vagrant nor a draft dodger. He presented himself as "an honest and industrious man," who belonged to "a well-known and well-regarded family in the country." While implying that his family was part of the *clase decente*, he made transparently clear that he was not ashamed of manual labor. In fact, for a while, he had tried to find employment as a rural peon, after his various businesses in the capital failed. Anso did not consider this something that diminished his social standing. He took "the peon class" as a sort of temporary condition or station in life, not a permanent attachment or a way of life. "In that class," he recollected, he had made a trip to Tandil, driving cattle for rancher Don Miguel López. To him, class was like a piece of clothing, something a person could put on and take off according to the function he was performing.

The fluidity of Anso's understanding of class contrasts sharply with the rigor with which the state tried to impose its own taxonomy of class on the rural male population.[55] The state's notion of class constituted an act of force, a procrustean allocation of people into fixed social categories. The "country peon class" was clearly a categorical order imposed from above on unwilling subjects. Under the gaze of state disciplinarians, class rankings resulted from acts of classification, the ordering of rural subjects according to their appearance and skills. This notion of *class* was inextricably linked to state practices of surveillance that gave visibility to the rural poor.[56] It was to this concept of *class* that subalterns responded.

The multiple vignettes contained in criminal and military files (*clasificaciones*) convinced me that rural laborers did not want to belong to this class. Rather than pride, the term "the peon class" evoked, like the word *gaucho*, an indictment of social inferiority. Standing in a subaltern position vis-à-vis the interrogators, these workers, peasants, and soldiers could do little to boycott the classificatory enterprise of the Rosista state. But they refused to accept the state categories as their own. When they had the chance, they explained to the authorities that they were "country folks" (*gente de campo*) or, more frequently, that they were able to perform "country tasks" (*tareas de campo*). Among themselves, they preferred to use the term "paysanos," a word that denoted peasant origin and comradeship among equals and was associated with notions of residence and citizenship. The term "paysano" indicated belonging to a rural community or town but did not entail social inferiority.

In a period of civil war and factional politics, class differentiation among large landowners, small-scale farmers and cattle raisers, and landless workers operated quietly, generating little resonance in the political and social sphere. But the rural communities produced other sources of internal differentiation. The distinction between *residents* (neighbors) and *transients* (usually itinerant peons) was a crucial marker of social difference. Second only to the polarity of unitarios/federales, this distinction functioned as the nearest substitute for the European notion of class. The resident or "neighbor" confronted the itinerant worker as a social superior, looking down on him as a reluctant patriot and a potential criminal. Itinerant workers tried by all means to become residents, for this entailed acquiring the rights of citizens and becoming accepted members of a rural community.[57] Then there was the array of differences exacerbated by factional politics: the distinction between country folks (*gente de campo*) and urbanites (*gente de pueblo*); the tensions between the Federalist plebes and the upper-class *cagetillas* (European-dressed urbanites), usually merchants, professionals, and artists.

During the period 1820–1860, due to reasons beyond their control, wandering peons and peasants immersed themselves in a transforming experience: the civil wars. Hence, their recollections referred necessarily to that experience. State order and federalism were the main reasons they went to war, the beginning and cause of their sufferings. Consequently, it was to the keepers of the federalist fatherland that they addressed their grievances and lamentations. Peons and peasants of Buenos Aires confronted not a class but a disciplinary system, in its legal, military, and political incarnations. It is this confrontation and its ambivalent results that this book addresses.

CHAPTER I

The Ways of the Market

The export bonanza of the postindependence period affected subaltern groups in significant ways. Due to the rise in employment opportunities, state expenditures, and availability of consumer goods, subaltern groups (in particular, itinerant peons, artisans, and peasants) began to relate to markets more frequently and intensely than before.[1] The gradual liberalization of the economy, combined with better enforcement of property rights, brought forth a rapid incorporation of subaltern groups as consumers and producers. Yet, subalterns' economic transactions have remained elusive to historians. A rhetoric of otherness that stresses the noneconomic proclivities of subalterns and a historical narrative that presents the economy as a field dominated by a few cattle ranchers and merchants have obscured our comprehension of subalterns' engagement with market society. Literary and historical representations have placed the peasant, the laborer, and the artisan outside the realm of markets (and within the fields of coercion and nature). They have been posed as either victims of economic modernization and state building or the carriers of natural propensities that conspire against productive labor and economic progress.[2] Tied to powerful ranchers by fear of recruitment, immobilized by debt peonage and passport laws, bypassed or cheated in the distribution of new state lands, peons and peasants have been constructed as passive subjects rather than participants in the making of Rio de la Plata's market society and culture.

In this chapter, I attempt to restore subaltern experience to the history of the postindependence economy. That is, I inquire about the presence of subalterns in the marketplace, about their reactions to government market regulations, about the dissemination of market rationale and economic ideology. The restitution of subalterns as participants in the formation of a market society must start with a reconsideration of the nature of postindependence market culture and society. During this period, the market economy was a much more porous and open social space than we are accustomed to think. In Buenos Aires and surrounding towns, markets for basic goods (such as cattle and grain) became more competitive. In the main marketplaces of the city, quite visible subalterns offered elite observers the vision of a disorderly, plebeian sociability. Advertisements show the lack of demarcation between "high" and "low" taste in matters of consumption. Factional politics gave subalterns opportunities to become producers or merchants, while the provincial state granted veterans, poor women and working *provincianos* certain protection against the risk of absolute poverty. Market spectacles displaying the logic of bidding and competition (public auctions and raffles) engaged subalterns as either viewers or participants.

What was the place of subalterns in the marketplaces of the postindependence period? Were they victims of impersonal forces beyond their control? What possibilities and new forms of engagement resulted from government regulation of markets? How did federalist politics affect the economic opportunities opened to subalterns? To answer these questions we must take a long journey. The narration moves from a description of colorful produce markets to the discussion of "popular liberalism." First, I describe the economy that subalterns faced: the sites of transactions; the movement of goods, people, and animals; the information involved; and the density of interactions. Next, I discuss "market spectacles," public rituals displaying and valorizing price competition, acquisitiveness, and other positivities associated with markets. Next, I locate subaltern economic interventions within the political realities of the period, focusing in particular on public policies regarding market transactions, consumption, and property rights. Finally, I examine the conflicting perspectives of capitalists and peons concerning the regulation of the *abasto de carne* (meat provision) to the city.

This chapter focuses on three dimensions of markets: (1) as sites of social interaction and spectacle; (2) as spaces for government regulation and state welfare policies; and (3) as a discursive configuration or "ideology." In each of these dimensions, fragments of subaltern experience and discourse help us to reconsider the nature of the postindependence economy, as well as the participation of subalterns in the building of a market society in Buenos Aires province.

Marketplaces, Consumption, and Spectacle

At one level, the market is a space for social interaction. It is a terrain of practice on which actors seek to complete economic transactions (sales and purchases) and, in so doing, engage in other types of exchanges: sharing political information, initiating or consolidating social relationships, and participating in recreational activities. On a different level, the market is a spectacle where audiences witness how prices are fixed and assets change hands. In this sense, the market presents itself as a composite of signs about the diffusion of commodity relations and, simultaneously, as a set of performances about market competition.

During the period 1820–1860, marketplaces were depicted as sites of lively sociability, saturated with subaltern culture. As producers and consumers, subalterns were key participants and spectators in these marketplaces. Their consumption was so important to the city's economy that regulating meat and grain markets constituted a crucial task of government. The intensity of market interactions disseminated an economic rationale among subalterns. By the 1830s and 1840s, subalterns seem to have embraced market culture with few reservations or objections. Fragments of evidence show them captivated by the availability of cheap imports and a greater variety of goods, immersed in the intense sociability of marketplaces, and fascinated with the possibility of acquiring goods by lottery.

Sites of Social Interaction

The city of Buenos Aires, the center of attraction for both foreigners and internal migrants, had been a commercial entrepôt since the late colonial period (Brown 1976; 1979, chaps. 1–2). After the revolution, stimulated by the expansion of the export economy, its thriving marketplaces became sites of animated social interaction. At the square in front of the Fortaleza people could find retailers of meat, vegetables, fish, and articles of local manufacture (Richelet 1928, 12). The Recova surrounding the plaza hosted the shops of artisans as well as the retail and wholesale outlets of foreign merchants. At key points of the city, three *mercados* (south, central, and north) equipped with slaughtering facilities supplied the city with meat, wheat, and other farm produce.[3] In addition, a vast number of *pulperías* (reaching six hundred by mid-century) provided the daily necessities of the population: beverages, bread, flour, salt, tinder, charcoal, and a variety of other items (see Mayo 1997c).

Travelers saw city markets stocked with all sorts of fresh provisions. In 1852 Sir Woodbine Parish claimed that "few markets in the world [were] more plentiful and cheaply supplied than that of Buenos Ayres" (121). To Colonel Anthony King (1846, 324), poultry, fish, game, beef, and other products were abundant and cheap in Buenos Aires, in contrast to similar markets in Europe. Although there was less variety in vegetables in the city, travelers concluded that the River Plate was a land of easy living, a territory propitious for indolent behavior.[4]

1. The Oxcart Market. *Mercados* (the arrival points of oxcart troops) were sites of intense social interaction. In this painting, federalist soldiers (in scarlet uniforms and caps) socialize with migrants just arrived from the interior provinces (wearing striped ponchos). Some of the participants share *asado* and *mate*, others listen to a singer-orator (*payador*). On the right, a trader is selling a saddle. At the center of the scene, a *provinciano* dictates a letter to a *pueblero* scribe. Carlos Morel, El mercado de carretas en la Plaza Monserrat—Buenos Aires, oil on canvas, ca. 1840. Reproduced from B. del Carril, *Monumenta Iconográphica* (1964).

In addition to the colorful produce markets, travelers often pointed out the variety and generalized acceptance of European commodities among the "natives" (textiles in particular), a positive development they credited to the liberalization of trade brought about by independence. Even Campbell Scarlett (ca. 1836), who saw Buenos Aires as lacking the excitement and civility of European cities, found stores well supplied with European commodities (1957, 41). In European and North American narratives of South America, plentiful marketplaces condensed the expectations for economic and social progress associated with the abolition of colonial commercial restrictions (see Salvatore 1996d).

From 1850 onward, travelers noticed the presence of foreigners dominating the import-export business and the wholesale and retail trades (Arrieta 1944, 101). Their shops added touches of European refinement and civility to a market space saturated with the presence of mixed-race, vociferous, and untidy subalterns. Travelers recognized that the elite had its own spaces for socializing—the tertulias and cafés—but they were captivated by the vitality and picturesque quality of marketplaces, the sites for the social interaction of subaltern subjects. It was difficult for travelers who visited the city during the administrations of Rivadavia, Dorrego, Balcarce, and Rosas to associate marketplaces with luxury, elegance, and good manners. For the markets they saw, whether taverns, cattle markets, or cloth shops, were still infused with popular tastes and sociability.[5] Colorful markets also stood for racial and social confusion. The main market scene (the plaza) captured in Vidal's lithographs prior to 1820, showed the interaction of multiple characters: Indian traders, shawl-covered ladies, black servants, mestizo peons, friars, clergymen, and military officers. The power of this visual message, reproduced in various narratives, served to present the marketplace as a confusingly active and democratic space.

But the noisy and disorderly presence of racialized subalterns added a preoccupying feature to marketplaces. Haigh celebrated and, at the same time, bemoaned the activity and noise he found at the market at Plaza de la Victoria, for here the wheels of commerce, activated by European mercantile capital, had the distinctive mark of the subaltern: "Numerous carts of a horrible form, with squealing wheels of enormous circumference—though not all round—, with no type of adornment, driven by mestizos de indio, almost as brutal as the animals they drive, blacks and mulattos, Indian porters loaded with bundles and boxes of merchandize, or with talegos of strong currency (pesos fuertes)" (qtd. in Baudizzone 1941, 75). These racialized subalterns shared the market space in an animated interaction. This was the sign of an undifferentiated, almost anarchic public space. Contemporary narratives leave no doubt about the importance of black labor to the economic life of the city. All the porters were black, commented Brabazon (1981). Many African workers worked independently; others, still in bondage, sold pastries or cigarettes on street corners (17–18).

On the outskirts of the city, public cattle markets and slaughtering plants appeared as the territory of the plebe, spaces impregnated with reproachable sociability, manners, and language. Open disgust was the common reaction. Various visitors shared Charles Mansfield's impression (1852) that the stench of rotten meat coming from the slaughterhouses enveloped the whole city, impregnating its air with a constant source of pestilence (in

Arrieta 1944, 37). The invasion of this unclean and barbarous culture was nowhere more explicit than in the distribution of beef: from dirty oxcarts racially mixed *peones-vendedores* (peon-sellers) sold large chunks of meat covered with dried blood and dirt (in Baudizzone 1941, 74).

A series of scenes of production, appropriation, and consumption configured the territory of a "popular economy." The familiar scene of black washerwomen banging their clothes against the rocks of the riverbank presents us with one aspect of poor families' subsistence strategies. Similarly, the repeated narration of black women picking up tripe and bones among the waste of the slaughterhouse speaks of common forms of direct appropriation among the subaltern classes (see, e.g., Hinchliff 1863, 73). All the materiality of commodities points to the centrality of the native laborer in this popular economy. The partridges that travelers saw piled up in the plaza, the otter skins (*nutria*) and the ostrich feathers peddled in taverns, and the inexpensive and fresh fish they praised were produced by independent fishermen, poachers, and hunters who belonged to a culture and people that travelers characterized as *gaucho*. The movement of big wheeled oxcarts, the frenetic and brutal scenes of the slaughterhouse, and the stench produced by rotting meat, boiling grease, and tanning leather were markers of workers' activities. They showed the necessary connection between export production and plebeian (peon/paysano) culture. Peons, poachers, sellers, drivers, and porters enjoyed great visibility in travel narratives because they were essential for generating the prosperity of the export sector. Evidence drawn from judicial and police sources helps to extend to rural areas this panoramic view of subaltern economic interventions. We find here women selling *empanadas* (meat pies) during the branding season, bread peddlers competing with established bakeries, and traveling *pulperos* installing their stands near the peons' tents or *ranchos* (thatched huts). Despite Rosas's repeated prohibitions, peasants continued to hunt otters, ostriches, viscachas, and other small animals and send them to the market. Several individual stories assert the entrepreneurial drive of subalterns in an expanding economy.[6] This fragmentary evidence points to the market as a privileged site of working-class reproduction.

Despite the dramatic political and social transformations of the postindependence period, marketplaces continued to act as centers of interaction and communication among subalterns from different origins and conditions.[7] The Rosas era brought greater regulation to these spaces, a certain degree of spatial differentiation, and an enormous expansion of its volume of trade. Cattle markets in particular benefited from the demise of the old monopoly system, and new regulations and better enforcement brought greater security to cattle traders and consumers. In the consumption of cloth there were small but significant changes. Since the mid-1840s, as the presence of immigrant retailers and customers grew, market scenes varied somewhat in the direction of greater differentiation and variety. The downtown commercial area became more European, as mixed-raced subalterns were displaced to peripheral cattle and produce markets in the south and north of the city.[8] But the political culture of Rosismo, with its emphasis on similar dress and its critique of European fashion, helped to delay this process and to cushion its impact.

Market Dissemination

A cursory look at Buenos Aires newspapers at the time of Rosas's first administration presents us with the image of an active commercial society, not yet closed to the interventions of subaltern subjects. By 1829, the *Gaceta Mercantil* featured, alongside notices of the arrivals of foreign vessels and the opening of public auctions, a series of advertisements indicative of the economic transactions of artisans, clerks, servants, and peasants. Through these ads we can infer that the boundaries demarcating elite from plebeian culture—the lines dividing the tastes of the "gente decente" from that of the working classes—were not yet set. Black maids competing with the ladies of the house in elegance and fashion, peasants trying on the new boots imported from Europe, federalist soldiers proudly wearing their red jackets made of British cloth speak of the blurring of the frontiers of distinction and appearance that once regulated social interaction.

With penetrating insight, Halperin Donghi (1982) suggested long ago that the tremendous increase in textile imports of the early 1820s was chiefly due to "popular consumption." The insatiable appetite of the lower classes for British textiles fed the first "consumer boom" of the post-independence era. Auctions offered imported textiles in a variety that would impress contemporary observers. The list of items for sale shows that merchants were catering to a public with few resources and also to the elite. The lists included the *zarazas* (printed chintz) with which the slave clothes were made, the *bramantes* (Brabant linen) for making the peasants' and peons' drawers (or leggings), the *paño estrella* (a type of cotton cloth) of which soldiers' uniforms were made, as well as the fabrics of privilege: satins, tafetans, and cashmeres. Auctions offering *artículos de pulpería* presented a great variety of goods: "soles from Tucumán," "ladies' shoes," "sperm candles," "Brazilian coffee," "tobacco from Virginia," "fireworks from India," "bottled oil," "French rapé," "wines from Bourdeaux or Madeira," "English trousers and coats," "firearms, spices, hats, and embroidery."[9]

The 1830s and 1840s also saw a revival of domestic consumption. Chiefly because of the weight of popular consumption and the undifferentiated nature of consumer desire, imported goods failed to displace domestic production. Flour from San Juan, shoes and cigars manufactured in Buenos Aires, and ponchos and jergas (woolen saddle blankets) from Córdoba survived the competition of imports. Locally produced boots, clothes, and hats found a sustained demand among growing segments of the population. The abundance of leather stimulated local entrepreneurs to make boots and shoes. To benefit from the prestige enjoyed by North American boots and shoes, the American Factory announced that its local production imitated North American patterns and styles and that its operatives had been trained in the United States.[10] Both country and city people were attracted to the new products, but the process of incorporation was slow. In the aftermath of the Anglo-French blockade, country folk were still experimenting with the new leather boots, which were quite uncomfortable. Paysanos used their *botas de potro* (smooth moccasins) on an everyday basis, reserving leather boots for special occasions (they carried their new leather boots tied to their saddles; Brabazon 1981, 93).

Local production of clothes—simple workshops cutting shirts, trousers, skirts, blouses, and jackets—found outlets in downtown stores. Hatmakers found an abundant and sustained market demand; to compete with foreign imports, they established local outlets where they could sell directly to the public (Mariluz Urquijo 1968). By the 1830s and 1840s, ponchos and jergas manufactured in the northern provinces (Córdoba, Santiago del Estero) still controlled an important share of the market in Buenos Aires, though sales had been in decline since the 1820s (Garavaglia and Wentzel 1989). Items collected by poachers and hunters (ostrich feathers, "tiger" pelts, game meat, armadillos, and other skins) kept reaching the market, indicating the resilience of earlier forms of direct appropriation, now reactivated by the export bonanza.

Clearly, the abundance of food noticed by foreign travelers and the "native" or "popular" character of marketplaces were related to the persistence of domestic production, direct appropriation, and popular (rural) tastes. William MacCann, a keen observer of customs, noticed that around 1848–1850 ranchers were still divided about their allegiance to European or local products. While some ranchers lived with the same simplicity as gauchos (almost no furniture in their homes, a meat-only diet, and riding gear hanging from the walls), others more connected with city life and foreigners had just begun to adopt European consumption habits. Among the new incorporations were furniture, fruits and vegetables, imported wine, and other "luxuries" (1969/1853, 118). MacCann's inability to identify ranchers by their personal appearance, diet, or belongings speaks of the undifferentiated character of consumption at the time of the Rosas government. In part, this was the result of the uniformity of appearance demanded by federalist ideology but, more important, it reveals the hybridity of country styles in a period of market transition.

Advertisements indicate the lack of specialization in mercantile activities. Firms engaged in retail and wholesale indistinctly. Auctioneers offered all sorts of imports, from furniture to farm tools, from china to cheap textiles, from flour to books. The market was a place of convergence and proximity. The products of farming and domestic industry (watermelons, sweet potatoes, maize, preserves, flour, and ponchos) coexisted side by side with imported goods (Spanish oil and wine, British textiles, North American flour and shoes). Ads for horns, hides, and horsehair were placed next to offers of ornamental shell combs (peinetas), black soap, candles, and firewood. The lack of market segmentation also produced the apparent leveling of economic actors. Those (presumably wealthier) selling houses or slaves commanded the same space in the newspaper as those advertising their crafts (shoemakers, tailors, silversmiths) or seeking employment (cooks, clerks, amas de leche [wet nurse]). Over time, new products expanded the dimensions of the market without significantly changing its nature. By 1836 Gowland Co. offered a greater variety of imported goods in its traditional auctions, particularly in the lines of hardware, perfumery, and food. Book merchants and publishers found a new demand; practical books of advice on household management, cookbooks, commercial guides, and handbooks of "rural industry" shared the lists with catechisms and almanacs. By 1847–1849, more sophisticated and expensive articles entered the market, among them iron sheets, steam engines, steel cylinders, shearing scissors, leather fungicides, lathes for shoemaking, and rail cars for meat-salting plants.[11] More frequently than before, city newspapers carried ads for houses for rent or sale, and even money and credit became commodities appropriate for advertising.

Labor itself became an advertised commodity during this period. An export economy in expansion increased opportunities of employment, making labor arrangements more flexible. Advertisements demanding brickmakers, tailor apprentices, journeymen shoemakers, washerwomen, amas de leche, servants, and cooks give us an approximation of the diversity of the labor market.[12] As a novelty, in the 1830s workers themselves began to advertise their services. With the decline of slavery, the market for slaves dwindled significantly; by the late 1840s newspapers ceased to carry ads offering slaves for sale.[13] Market fluctuations made commercial and financial information more necessary. By 1836, statistics about the variations of the exchange and of metallic coins could be purchased for 4 pesos.[14] In cattle markets too, there was a great deal more information about supplies and prices. Almost on a weekly basis, the *Gaceta Mercantil* published information about the heads of cattle entering the various markets, the names of drovers (*conductores*), and the districts from which the cattle were dispatched. If density of economic information marks the maturity of a market, then the cattle markets of Buenos Aires were, by midcentury, quite developed.

Some of the transactions implied in the ads refer to interactions among subalterns. The owner of a used oxcart wants to barter it for some bulls. Small farmers carry a few sacks of maize to the market. Oxcart entrepreneurs search for honest and hard-working foremen and drivers. Poor masters hire out their slaves in the expectation of making additional income. Ads convey a sense of openness and diversity in the marketplace. Small houses advertised as "fit for *casas de trato*" (brothel and tavern) and *atahonas* (domestic flourmills) created tangible opportunities for economic improvement for those with "short capital."

All these are signs of an economy still quite open to the interventions of people with very limited resources, a porous economy in which the lines demarcating proper and improper, or high and low, were not clearly established. The possibilities for subalterns to enter the market appear ample: only a few economic activities seem to be denied to them on account of their poor appearance, pastoral skills, and limited social connections. Within this territory of diffuse boundaries—the "economy"—one can distinguish some special sites for the interventions of subaltern subjects: the slaughterhouses, the cattle markets, the wool and tanning plants near Boca, the meat-salting plants south of the city, and the regiments.

Bargaining Spectacles

Auctions were a normal, everyday occurrence in the life of the city.[15] They provided retailers opportunities for cutting costs and enticed consumers to find bargains, compare the new products, and socialize. Announced in newspaper ads, on signs in the streets, or by word of mouth, these auctions attracted potential buyers as well as onlookers. All the ads included the customary formula: "They will be sold to the best bidder." This method of sale entailed a learning experience for the lower classes. Subalterns had the chance to see the market fixing prices in an animated and vociferous exchange. These auctions differed from the system of credit sales (*habilitaciones*) established by the British in one crucial respect: they required purchasers to pay on delivery. Under the system of habilitaciones, commodities were almost forced on retailers (who had little say on the price of goods) with the incentive of credit. Public auctions did not offer credit. Under the system of auctions, market conditions (the conjunction of buyers and sellers) determined prices. For a people accustomed to the rigidities and absurdly high prices of the Spanish commercial system, this method must have seemed like a market revolution.

The government contributed its share of bidding spectacles. In part to defuse criticism about corruption and favoritism, the government left to the market the allocation of public contracts. A variety of public works (bridge building, street paving, dock repair) and government provisions (the supply of horse feed for the police department, of stones for street pavement, of uniforms and weapons for the army) were contracted out through public auctions. Through these auctions the government expected to maximize its revenue while providing a public service.

The public lottery, one of the most profitable ventures, was allocated through competitive bidding. Days before, the *pregonero* (town crier) announced (shouted) the auction, walking around police headquarters. On the day of the auction, the chief of police (*Victorica*) and the public notary stood in front of the gates of the Police Department, waiting for the bids (the auction closed at 7 P.M.). Individuals presented their written proposals, specifying the annual or monthly rate they were willing to pay. The offers were opened and read aloud to the public. Occasionally, the call was postponed several times to increase the number of bidders, but, in the end, the highest bidder was awarded the contract.[16] The winner and his offer were publicized through the newspaper, becoming an issue of public commentary.

The same type of spectacle resulted from the periodic auction of cattle, hides, wool, and other products confiscated for some violation of property regulations. Through these auctions, Rosas expected that people would learn the importance of conducting their economic transactions through legal channels and with proper documentation. These public sales made evident that property illegally obtained or transacted could be easily lost. Beyond this pedagogy of property, these spectacles served to legitimate competition as an honorable and honest endeavor. The police posted signs (*carteles*) in various public sites announcing the auction and, on the scheduled date, received the offers (in writing) and read them aloud.[17] Auction organizers had only one rule to follow: accept the highest price offered.

The way these contracts were allocated had an important impact among the public. The ritual of open bidding accustomed the public to the ebb and flow of prices, informed them of the cost of public services, and increased their trust in government procedures. Auctions produced the impression that markets could work in an orderly fashion if supervised by authorities who guaranteed the transparency of transactions. To be sure, the poor could only look at these spectacles, not participate in the bidding. The lottery contract was beyond the possibilities of common folks, the bids running as high as 31,000 pesos annually (in 1837). But the game established by the public lottery—selling promises of luck at a small price—could be easily replicated on a reduced scale. Soon, the game filtered down to the population at large.

Eager to earn easy money or to dispose of valuable items, ordinary folks adapted the mechanism of the public lottery to their private ends. In 1850 the police were inundated with requests for permits to hold raffles (rifas). Ordinary folks were apparently using market mechanisms to dispose of their valuable assets in a profitable, though risky, fashion. Through private lotteries, people sold items large and small (from a ship worth $10,500 to a knife with a silver inscription valued at $900), goods useful for production (oxcarts, spurs, harnesses), as well as items of distinction (jewels).[18] Sellers of lottery tickets included silversmiths, ship owners, sailors, fishermen, oxcart owners, foremen of driving teams, and widows. In fact, anyone with some cartons, ink, and a feather pen could improvise a raffle.[19] When the price of the object was sufficiently high, the raffle was advertised in the newspaper. Alternatively, signs were posted in the most public places of the city.[20]

The mechanism was simple. Don Pedro Incigaray, for example, decided to sell a new cart (carro) by public lottery. He printed 260 tickets of 10 pesos each and went to the police to have them approved. Genoveva Pérez put a pair of silk reins with golden pins in the lottery, dividing the value of this "jewel" ($2,200) into 440 tickets at 5 pesos each. Private lotteries combined the joy of gambling with the mechanism of public auctions.[21] Because the dice customarily decided the lucky number, this procedure entailed a form of collective gambling. To satisfy the curiosity of suspicious purchasers, the person selling the lottery had to throw the dice in public until one of the tickets was favored with the greatest number. This activity could take hours, on occasion more than a day.[22]

The lottery of the poor, raffles were an expeditious way of raising money in an economy with a credit crunch. Cabinetmakers used this method to sell their seasonal production and silversmiths used it to dispose of unsold jewels, as did clothing shops, grocery stores, bakeries, and sellers of lace.[23]

To artisans and small shopkeepers the private lottery was a means of by-passing the credit shortage, an alternative to installment payments but without the risk of collection. The same mechanism could be used to purchase a house and as a means of collecting public revenues. For the purchasers of tickets, the raffles were means of trespassing class boundaries; if luck went his way, a poor day–laborer or clerk could become a small entrepreneur. The expectation of acquiring with little money properties of large value motivated people to purchase the tickets. How could a foreman pass up the opportunity of getting ten oxcarts with twenty horses and all the accessories for only 20 pesos?

The importance of gambling among subaltern groups cannot be over-stated. Gambling with cards, in particular, was a widespread pastime that the state tried unsuccessfully to eradicate with fines, arrests, and, in some cases, forced military service.[24] Many contemporary observers presented the addiction to gambling as an intrinsic attribute of gauchos. But, instead of an activity inimical to the work ethic, gambling reflected a desire for personal improvement. With a stroke of good luck, a worker could turn rapidly into a tavern owner, a farmer, or the owner of a driving team.

Public auctions, lotteries, and raffles disseminated among subalterns the notion that, under certain circumstances and with a dose of good luck, poor folks could claim a piece of social wealth. This expectation can help us understand the enthusiasm with which subalterns participated in the public auctions of 1840 and 1841 resulting from the confiscation of unitarios' assets.[25] The auctions generally included a variety of personal items, large and small. The list of one of these auctions, carried out in Cañuelas in December 1840, displayed furniture, kitchen utensils, farm tools, books, linen, clothing, medicines, and sewing articles.[26] People of modest means were able to enter these auctions, obtaining at bargain prices goods they could never have enjoyed otherwise. "Unitario goods," Ramos Mejía (1907) points out, became synonymous with good bargains.

The State and the Popular Economy

The Rosas administration brought more order to markets, regulating transportation, transactions, and certain property rights. These policies had an expansive effect on economic activity, particularly in the livestock industry. Cattle and sheep owners, secure in their property rights, expanded their operations in both magnitude and frequency. In addition, through its war expenditure and its contracts for services, the government provided greater economic opportunities for subalterns. The seizure of unitario property, in particular, provided subalterns a way to appropriate resources without much work. Finally, the civil war generated particular rights regulating food that, actualized by veterans' wives, mothers, and daughters, sustained a system of welfare provisions formidable for this time period.

Ordering Markets, Regulating Property

The marketing of cattle, an important moment in the reproduction of the wandering working class, became subject to state regulation during this period. To protect consumers and producers, the state imposed stringent controls on the distribution and transport of cattle, hides, and other by-products. Better-enforced property rights added a burden of paperwork to economic activities such as cattle droving, meat-salting plants, and slaughtering corrals. The control of *guías* (cattle-transit vouchers), cattle brands, and municipal taxes turned into a normal component of the operation of cattle markets. These controls established a degree of predictability among buyers and sellers, making transactions more transparent and reducing, to a certain extent, the circulation of stolen hides and cattle.

During 1829–1831, justices of the peace, in cooperation with corral chiefs, began to exercise routine controls to determine the origins and rightful ownership of all cattle introduced into local markets.[27] An essential piece of this process was the verification of *guías*, vouchers containing information about cattle transported, owners, consignors, brands, and drovers. Those who issued these vouchers (usually the seller) had the document signed by the local police chief or justice of the peace.[28] If the number of animals entering the market was discordant with the number registered in the voucher or if there was a brand not consigned in the document, the authorities had the power to confiscate the lot, sell it at public auction, and arrest the drover. Even the lack of proper seals could bring trouble with the law, converting a normal sale into a nightmare of bureaucratic proceedings.

The control of brands aimed at preventing the illicit traffic in hides, the most lucrative product of the livestock industry. This implied additional controls. Oxcarts carrying hides into the city were detained and scrutinized by personnel of the *corrales de abasto* (cattle markets), tanneries were subjected to unexpected inspections, and even the meat-salting workshops were not exempt from occasional searches. Impounded cattle and hides resulting from these inspections were sent to the police deposit.[29] The enactment of a Reglamento de Corrales de Abasto in 1834 made controls even more rigorous. A justice of corrals and a team of peons were permanently assigned to control all cattle entering the market; at their booths (casillas) they stood vigilant, guarding property rights. To guarantee the honor and solvency of market operators, cattle dealers and drovers were required to obtain a license and to deposit a bail bond with the police.

The regulatory wave extended to other stages of the circuit, to other products and other activities. The justices of corrals also controlled the introduction of sheep, horses, mules, sheepskins, horsehair, horns, and other livestock products. Retail trade and manufactures were also subject to greater regulation. Pulperías had to register and pay a license fee (patente), as did general stores, flourmills, and meat-salting plants. Even the pulperías volantes, the itinerant shops of small-scale retailers, had to obtain a license to operate. The scope of state supervision was imposing. Between 1845 and 1847 the police carried out a general registration of all wheeled vehicles, obliging owners to place a numbered license plate on their oxcarts and carriages.[30] This registration, though strongly resisted, implied that every stevedore at the port, every porter of wool or hides, every oxcart driver had to get authorization from the police or the justice of the peace. The state drive for a general registration of property led to some exaggerations: the authorities demanded that rural families register (and pay taxes for) all of their dogs.[31]

On the consumer side there were also important changes. The production and retail distribution of bread, regulated since colonial times, came under strict supervision. Early in the first Rosas government (1830), bakeries had to send monthly reports to the government with detailed information on daily production. This was part of an effort to assure consumers a minimum of quality for the amount they paid for the bread. As the price was fixed, it was the government's responsibility to ensure that the weight of each piece be in accordance with regulations. Heavy fines were imposed on those who violated this ordinance.[32] In 1834, an ordinance compelled all bread peddlers (repartidores) to register with the Police Department, depositing a bail bond of 250 pesos.[33] Something similar occurred with the distribution of meat. At cattle markets (corrales), the change toward sales by weight (and not on arbitrio), registration of all suppliers, and the effective payment of the corresponding taxes (derechos de corrales) made transactions more fluid and reliable. Maximum prices were set for cattle destined for consumption, as during the Rivadavia administration; a commission appointed by the government fixed this price every term.[34] In rural towns also, contracts for the provision of meat continued to establish a fixed price. Only meat supplies to military garrisons, admittedly an important proportion of the market, were deregulated: commanders had to bargain for prices with cattle ranchers and were urged to pay the prices current in the location.[35]

While enjoying greater commercial freedom than during colonial times, producers and distributors of meat and bread, two staples of the local diet, felt the pressure of a more imposing regulatory state. By 1847, the abasto was a more ordered market than in the 1830s, mainly due to the fact that the powers who regulated transactions (the justices of corrals) had accustomed operators, through the rigor of fines, to accept basic rules about weighing, cutting, and deliveries. Lower risks associated with the transportation, slaughtering, and sale of cattle products permitted an expansion of transactions that, in turn, benefited workers and consumers. The same could be said about the market for bread. Regulations permitted that, in spite of the ebb and flow in the supply of flour (affected by variations in local harvests and by foreign blockades), consumers were supplied with this basic commodity at affordable prices.[36]

What effects did these regulations have on subalterns? As consumers, they benefited from a system that maintained the price of meat and bread at a time of significant inflation.[37] Controls on the weight of meat and bread prevented the reduction in quality that is generally associated with systems of regulated prices. The better enforcement of branding statutes confronted subalterns with a whole new experience. Property in cattle, sheep, or horses now had its own language of expression: a collection of signs or drawings identifying a piece of movable capital with its owner. The new semiology of capital demanded from peasants and peons an acute understanding of the new system of signs. Otherwise, they could be liable for severe penalties. Now the subaltern had to face a more efficient system of identification of cattle ownership, one that required reading messages of property on the skins of animals.

The proliferation of brands added confusion to the individualization of property rights. In a criminal case in which Doña Ceferina Castro accused a neighbor of stealing her cattle (in Tapalquén in 1850), the judge found it difficult to identify and adjudicate ownership. On their patrón's orders, two peons and a foreman had separated, killed, and skinned 1,916 head of cattle. When the justice of the peace went to verify the evidence, he found among the hides (two oxcarts full of them) 105 different brands.[38] How could neighbors and the authorities identify property rights among such a profusion of signs? The peons testified that they used drawings (dibujos) provided by the employer to recognize the brands belonging to the ranch.

Drawings on paper or on wood assisted the process of diffusion of the marks of property among neighbors and peons, but it is clear that the excess of these signs created a great deal of confusion, reducing the readability of property at the level of practice.[39]

Market Competition

Since the meat crisis of 1817–1818, Rosas had argued for the need to deregulate cattle markets. In a well-known document written in 1818, he warned the director supremo that big ranchers, who were at the same time suppliers (*abastecedores*), had the capacity to influence the market in ways that were detrimental to consumers, small cattle raisers, and traders (in Montoya 1956, 52). Rosas was in favor of deregulating the sales to meat-salting plants (export sector) while imposing controls that would ensure the city's consumption.[40] In 1836, after years of contention regarding the best way to regulate the cattle markets of the city, Rosas found a compromise. For the export sector (meat-salting plants), he let the forces of competition do their work. For the city's meat supply, he continued with regulated prices and consumption quotas. (The 1836 decree established a minimum supply to the city before operators could sell cattle to the meat-salting plants). But, instead of granting the supply of the city to a monopolist, Rosas allowed many cattle dealers and ranchers to participate in this market. The sales in the export market were unregulated and so was the price, usually higher than that paid by consumers. A commission appointed by the governor would fix the price of the cattle destined for consumption, taking into account the profitability of the cattle dealers (or suppliers). As a result, consumers received a subsidy and the guarantee of sufficient supplies, while the export sector could benefit from the free play of supply and demand. As we shall see, this view, favoring a combination of free market and consumer protection, was shared by workers of this trade.

Contrary to the assertions of Ingenieros and other scholars, state regulation of cattle markets did not translate into monopsonistic power (Ingenieros's "trust *saladeril*"). Rather, putting market transactions under a system of rules meant an improvement for all cattle producers, large and small. True, the availability of credit and capital for the purchase of cattle was not evenly distributed. But the dispersion of suppliers, the existence of different types of purchasers, and the need to subcontract the transport of cattle to independent cattle drovers made the concentration of decisions either at the supply or the demand side almost impossible. The state regulated the price of meat, but left to the market the fixing of the price of cattle at the corrals, a price that fluctuated with the changing demands of the meat-salting plants and the changing supplies of cattle dealers.

Information published by La Gaceta makes evident that the provision of this market was very competitive. In a single day (February 27, 1847) fifty-seven different drovers (capataces, commissionists, or owners of troops) entered the Southern Cattle Market (Tablada del Sud), each bringing herds bought from fifteen to twenty different producers of the southern and central districts. That is to say, about nine hundred to one thousand cattle raisers supplied the city on a given day (selling on average ten cows or oxen each). Suppliers came from afar. Of the 19,073 head of cattle that entered the market on that day, 81 percent came from the districts south of the Salado River (mainly from Vecino, Ajó, Tuyú, Mar Chiquita, and Azul), lands of relatively recent settlement.[41] This, however, had little bearing on the alleged concentration of the cattle market. For in the south, as much as in the north, small cattle raisers outnumbered the big ranchers.

The small size of the average transaction—fewer than ten head of cattle—contradicts the argument that a few large landowners dominated the market. With regard to cattle transactions at the ranch, it is more likely that the intermediary (a drover, a city trader, or a foreman working for a meat-salting establishment) had greater bargaining power than the seller (the big rancher or the small cattle raiser). Big ranchers who had the financial resources to buy their neighbors' cattle and the manpower to send herds to Buenos Aires could conceivably pocket a profit from the price difference. But the limit to these extra profits was set by the price secured in Buenos Aires.[42] Once at their destination, the cattle commanded a higher or lower price according to the daily demands of meat-salting plants and cattle merchants. Here conditions were different from those on the ranch, as the purchasers for the meat-salting plants bought volumes three to four times greater than those demanded by butchers and other local distributors.[43] Big producers (sending herds of three hundred to five hundred cows each time) found it more profitable to sell to meat-salting plants than to cattle dealers. But this did not constitute a symptom of monopolistic power. The number of purchasers remained sufficiently large to preclude the collusion of certain groups within the market. Different operators visited this market to buy their daily provisions: butchers, street sellers, tavern-keepers, hotel clerks, and, of course, the agents of the various slaughtering and meat-salting plants. The "meat-salting combine" ("interés saladeril"), as J. Ingenieros would call it, was in reality divided into many agents.

The Rosas administration had a significant impact on the economic inter-ventions of peons and peasants, opening opportunities and, at the same time, adding restrictions. The "popular economy," the space carved out of the economic system by the transactions of subalterns, was affected in various ways by the ideology and policies of Rosas. First, there was the *egalitarian ethos*. Rosas tried to instill in the population certain habits and attitudes that eroded class differences. This authorized subalterns to feel proud about the way they dressed and lived and stimulated a degree of animosity toward the possessions of the rich. Second, the government tried to defend the economic opportunities and property rights of soldiers who had participated in the defense of the fatherland. By conditioning the outcome of the economic game to questions of service and patriotism, Rosas imposed a critical limit on the individual accumulation of capital. Third, Rosas's confiscations of unitario property increased the oppor-tunities of subalterns. To the extent that confiscated ranches became pub-lic property, their resources were open to a sort of common use among poor neighbors, families of federales, and, of course, the army. Fourth, government expenditures in defense translated into important stimuli to the local economy. Suppliers of cattle and horses, military equipment, weapons, and construction materials saw their sales and profit margins enhanced by the war economy. At least part of this increased purchasing power filtered down to the lower classes.

Throughout the civil war, Rosas tried to keep a balance of opportunities between soldiers and nonsoldiers. In March 1841, when many federalist soldiers were outside of the province, marching with the Vanguard army, Rosas ordered justices of the peace to temporarily suspend the separation of cattle herds (*parar rodeo*) and the branding of calves in order to protect veterans' property. In the absence of veterans, unscrupulous neighbors could easily appropriate their cattle simply by branding strays and calves. The question, as the governor understood it, was one of distributive jus-tice: "It is not fair that while some ranchers are in the army or in related commissions and others cannot attend their ranches, those who can, do it at the expense [*en perjuicio*] of the others."[44] It was also important to convey the right message to communities who had long supported the war effort; on their return, soldiers should expect to find that their family and prop-erty had been preserved and protected—not pillaged—by the federalist community.

The neighbors insisted, though, that their herds were mixed with those of the absent soldiers and that normal seasonal activities such as branding and castration could no longer be postponed. In June, the government, aware of the necessity to stimulate food production, allowed cattle raisers to brand the calves and to castrate the bulls—on the condition "of not harming in the least those who cannot do it, being in the Vanguard armies, or in the General Quarters of Santos Lugares de Rosas . . . or in any of the divisions they belong to."[45] To make this condition effective, Rosas ordered veterans' relatives to participate in the roundups, while the justices supervised the whole operation.

Powerful reasons of state informed the governor's consideration for soldiers' property. The news of an unfair redistribution of property at home might put additional strain on military discipline in the garrisons, giving soldiers an additional reason for deserting. The protection of soldiers' property was also consistent with the rhetoric of federalism, a predicament that emphasized the cooperation among neighbors (vecinos) for the conclusion of the civil war. If the state rewarded soldiers for military victories, it also had to guarantee their property during military campaigns. Pressure from below also informed this public policy. In April 1841 Agustín Reinoso, a corporal of the Second Infantry Regiment on campaign, submitted to his superiors a letter received by one of his soldiers, Mariano Flores, a peasant who had left his family and farm in Villa Luján. The soldier's brother, back in Luján, had sent the letter. It informed Mariano that neighbors, with the consent of the local justice of the peace, were slaughtering his cattle and advised him to lodge a complaint as soon as possible: "DesPues de saludardo Paso amanifestarle a U. Como el Pardo Juan Galarce adado Principio oy se a desgaretado una Baca de Las Sullas y echo el Reclamo llo al Jues y cemeacontestado qe el adado orde y llo Le Einformado Como qe Elganado Es sullo Bajo de ESta ynteligencia y qe U. Esta Encervicio Puede acer algun Reclamo al Gefe Para que no Lescigan Perjuicio asus animales Pues U. save qeno tenemos En qe andar ni quidar ni coral Par Encerar Porqe Lo Salvajes Celo qemaron."[46] ("After greeting you, I proceed to inform you how the pardo Juan Galarce has started [the slaughter] . . . has stricken down and slaughtered one of your cows. Having made the complaint myself to the Justice, it was said to me that he had given the order, and I have informed [him] that the cattle is yours. Knowing this and [in view of the circumstance] that you are in service, you can place a complaint to the Chief in order to stop the injury to your animals, because you know that we do not have [horses] to ride nor to give, nor corral to enclose [the cattle] because the Savages had burned it.")

The letter underscores the existence of communications between the war front and the soldiers' communities, the importance of movable property for the peasant economy, and the cooperation of family members in the preservation of property rights. The letter also tells us something about the politics of the subaltern. Although the complaints by Mariano's brother back in Luján did not achieve very much, the letter itself reached the highest authority in the land. The corporal presented it to his superiors, with the expectation that he might get *una ordencita* for the justice of the peace in Luján, preventing any further destruction of the cattle. The letter was read by Major Millán, who in turn mailed it to Rosas.

For the subaltern, politics was a site of comfort and a trap. The dramatic transfers of property resulting from war and political confiscation created spaces in which subalterns could exercise some traditional rights (direct appropriation) and enhance their access to economic resources. According to Ramos Mejía (1907), the urban plebe, the ill-mannered rural town dweller (*guarango*), and the itinerant gaucho took advantage of these opportunities by taking possession of these properties and using their resources during the time they were under government control. Émigré literature dealt extensively with these property seizures, which they considered the Dictator's way to pay for the favors of *mazorqueros* (members of the secret police, Mazorca). While it is clear that federalist functionaries got the best of the public auctions in the city, in the countryside the policy of direct occupation and pillage made subalterns participants in this confiscated wealth. In December 1839 a group of soldiers led by a lieutenant and a sergeant (not following any superior order) assaulted the ranch of unitario Eustaquio Díaz Vélez. They entered the house and took everything they considered necessities: clothes, money, cigars, soap, sugar, flour, bread, riding equipment, and farm tools. Then they distributed the spoils among the participants. After the event, the soldiers attested that the invitation to steal came from the lieutenant, though they were happy to participate in expropriating the enemy's wealth.[47] Other soldiers waited outside the ranch, declining to participate in the action. The lieutenant and his soldiers acted as if they were provisioning themselves to continue the campaign.[48]

More often, however, the army took possession of the confiscated properties, setting up horse or cattle feed lots (*invernadas*) or other productive activities geared to military provisioning. Neighboring peasants, considering these ranches and farms common property, took firewood, fruit, hides, and occasionally cattle or horses for their own use. In the city political opportunities presented other forms of seizure. Federales would move to a house owned by a unitario and occupy it, then petition the government for a reduction or waiver of the rent.[49] It is clear that this kind of interaction promoted clientelistic ties, but it was also a means by which subalterns could have access to subsidized rent at a time of inflation.[50] Another way to access property was to participate in the auctions of confiscated property. These auctions offered at reduced prices furniture, clothing, and house utensils that were commonly out of the reach of lower-income families. In some cases, the articles on sale could serve as the basis for a new economic activity: horses, oxen, boats, sheep skins, or carts could be the working capital a subaltern needed to abandon his or her condition of casual laborer or servant.[51] The message conveyed in these auctions was unequivocal: like the attacks against men of frock coat, they were an invitation to subvert the inviolability of property rights. They marked a denial of property based on political difference, making the assets of unitarios accessible to "good federalists."

If political affinities granted subalterns some economic benefits, the war economy itself was a source of great economic opportunity. "The true industry of the Tyranny," wrote Ramos Mejía, "was the war budget" (qtd. in Franco 1946, 201). Through budget allocations, large portions of custom revenues transformed into effective demand for the domestic economy. The army purchased a variety of goods (cattle, horses, meat, bread, sugar, hides, alfalfa, saddles, harnesses, uniforms, weapons, bricks, etc.) whose production had an expansive effect on the economy. Part of the stimulus went to support foreign imports (particularly the textiles for making uniforms); still, an important demand was placed on the internal market. A diversity of producers, from the bottom (tailors and seamstresses, brick kiln workers, peons of tanneries, cattle drovers) to the top (cattle merchants, import-export traders, ranchers), participated in the expansion of the defense budget.

Women, Veterans, and Welfare

Rosas's consideration toward veterans stimulated new subaltern claims on the economic resources of the state. After 1841, a bargaining process involving women, local justices, military commanders, and the governor engendered a novel system of poor relief centered on the distribution of meat to veterans' families. Different in substance and scope from the system established during colonial times, this system produced a notable improvement in the conditions of livelihood and nutrition of the rural poor (see Salvatore 1998b). This was, undoubtedly, part of the state's response to the panic of 1840 prompted by the invasion of Lavalle. Also, a dose of patriotic paternalism was implicit in these transfers. But, as we shall see, more was at stake than politicomilitary strategy and state paternalism.

The war presented soldiers' households (now headed mostly by women) with a thorny problem: how to keep the farms and ranches in production while the men were away. Unable to tend cattle or harvest wheat with a much-reduced family labor force, the women would soon face serious shortages of food. To solve this problem, the state developed a system of poor relief that, though informal, helped to alleviate the penury of veterans' families. Justices of the peace in cooperation with local military commanders were to distribute meat among local families whose sons and husbands were fighting in the federalist army or had died defending the federalist colors. The cattle were to be taken from the neighbors. In addition to meat rations, veterans' families received "vice" rations (*yerba mate*—Paraguayan tea—tobacco, and sugar) and, occasionally, money. The funds for these transfers came from the sale of hides and tallow produced by the garrisons' slaughter.

The recipients of such welfare benefits were the so-called *familias de federales*, a somewhat ample category that included most of the women, children, and elders of humble condition in each rural town. As the justice of Lobos explained in March 1841, initially the vices were distributed among the people helping the *juzgado* and those tending the horses at the "invernadas" (mostly militiamen). But soon, he found himself handing out sugar, tobacco, and yerba mate to "poor families who had no means to purchase" these goods. Later, as the army started to provide vices regularly to militiamen, revenues from the sale of hides accumulated, leaving substantial savings. The justice then started to distribute subsidies among "some honest and indigent families according to their condition." Special targets were the wives and widows of federalist soldiers; these women, reasoned the justice, were unable to harvest their crops because the war had taken the farms' most productive hands. He assigned these women 30 pesos if their husbands or sons were in the campaign and 50 pesos if their husbands or sons had died in combat.[52]

As the civil war lingered for another decade, the system of poor relief developed accidentally in 1841 became a permanent feature in rural communities. With time, money subsidies were reduced or eliminated, but meat rations continued to be delivered with remarkable regularity. The simplicity of the system made it easy for women to gain access to food. After the daily slaughter, poor women approached the justice of the peace's office and asked for their meat rations; a cross on a piece of paper was all that was required to receive their rations. Over time, these expenditures became part of the normal operating cost of military garrisons. In 1845, the commander of Fuerte Federación (San Nicolás), trying to explain why his garrison was consuming so many head of cattle, listed 459 persons as part of his *fuerza consumidora* (as opposed to his military force).

The Ways of the Market 47

Included in this list were the officers and their families (8 women and 18 children); the troops and their families (53 women and 150 children); and the *pobladores* (53 men, 77 women, and 100 children). The last were, apparently, poor members of the town and its surroundings who depended for their subsistence on the provisions from the garrison.[53] Considering that Fuerte Federación had by this time under one thousand inhabitants, the army was feeding more than half of the population of the town.

By 1848–1851 these practices of state patronage, no doubt a response to the great fear caused by Lavalle's invasion, had grown into a system of poor relief that cemented the relations between rural communities and the state. Twice a month, the justices of the peace distributed meat among soldiers' families, "purchasing" cattle from the neighbors and seizing cattle with unknown brands.[54] The beneficiaries of food subsidies, initially limited to the soldiers of each garrison and their families, with time extended to include poor families in general.[55] Direct controls by the governor of the allocation of revenues made the system more reliable and predictable. The state provision of meat rations produced an unintended effect: empowering women as sole "provider" for their family. Without doubt, women were the chief beneficiaries of this system. Of the 82 persons listed by the justice of Villa Luján in December 1842 as recipients of meat rations, all were close relatives of soldiers: 30 were mothers, 47 were wives, 3 were daughters, and 2 were elderly fathers. Apparently, these women consistently claimed their meat rations, for almost the same list of names appeared in different accounts throughout the period 1842–1845.[56] The state, trying to comply with its part in the unwritten pact with the soldiers, ended up creating a new clientele for state provisions: poor women.

Clearly, the food subsidies were consistent with the state's interest in maintaining support for the Federalist Cause among the poorest segments of the rural population. To this extent, these benefits belonged to the web of patronage knit by Governor Rosas in relation to indigenous peoples, peasants, peons, and Afro-Argentines. But we should not overlook the active role of women in constructing this set of state obligations. Poor women, with their constant petitions to commanders and justices of the peace, made these welfare benefits more regular and predictable; in fact, they converted them into something close to an entitlement. Rights to food needed to be actualized by bargaining practices similar to those employed by soldiers in the regiments. In April 1841, Rosas received a group of women who had come from Cañuelas to ask for the government's assistance and understanding. Rebuffed by the justice of Cañuelas, they went directly to the highest authority in the land to get what they wanted. Rosas's secretary at Santos Lugares captures the episode in a letter: "Yesterday, a woman showed up at this garrison, saying that she had four sons in the Vanguard Corps (*Ejército de Vanguardia*) and that she had a family of small children (*familia menuda*) as her burden and also three of her children's sons, and two other women who had their husbands and sons in the Vanguard Corps, who had come also to present themselves to Your Excellency in order to communicate that they do not have means of subsistence and that, like them, there are many other families of [soldiers] who had marched [to the war] that had come to the justice of peace at Cañuelas to see if they were given the meat, for all of them belong to the district of Cañuelas, and they received as an answer that [the justice of peace] had no order from Your Excellency to do this. Because of this, they have come [here] in order to present themselves to Your Excellency and to supplicate Him to order this assistance [*auxilio*] be given to them."[57] Rosas responded to this request by ordering the justice of Cañuelas to distribute among these women (and other daughters, wives, and mothers of veterans) all the meat that was necessary, taking it from the ranches confiscated from the unitarios. He also ordered that the hides from these cattle be sold and the proceeds be distributed among veterans' families. It is clear from this episode that poor women were influential in actualizing the delivery of food subsidies.[58]

Women's constant petitions to local authorities helped to sustain and expand this provisional system of poor relief. At Quilmes, women of the "meritorious federalists" who were already receiving meat rations, demanded the distribution of firewood when they saw that the justice of peace had stockpiled lots of it for supplying the army during the coming winter. The insistent supplications (based on the argument that they, as women, could gather only thistle for firewood and not hard wood) finally paid off, the justice being obliged to allocate part of the army firewood for local distribution.[59] Rather than asking for an illusory pension, payment of which could be suspended according to the situation of the treasury, rural women petitioned for items that were essential to the reproduction of their families: meat and firewood. Perhaps they were actualizing, under the new conditions of civil war, older rights over the commons customarily exercised by settlers (*pobladores*) and squatters (*agregados*). Not being citizens, women's claims were based on their husbands', fathers', or sons' contributions to defending the federalist fatherland. This made their rights contingent on developments beyond their control. Nevertheless, there is evidence that women's appeals to the state for food rations continued after Rosas's fall.[60]

In combination with other factors, the informal relief system created during the Rosas period has a significant impact on average levels of nutrition. At a time when the state was liberalizing the market for cattle and meat, the existence of these new types of "entitlements" allowed poor families in the countryside to maintain their level of meat consumption—in spite of the ups and downs in the price of beef. The government's decision to preserve the property of soldiers while on campaign also worked in this direction. The creation of an informal, proto-welfare system of food distribution may help to explain the remarkable improvement in nutrition noticed in height statistics during this period (see Salvatore 1998b). As a result, the market, transformed by the exercise of rights to food (based on a war pact between peasants and the state), had a more positive impact on the rural poor than would have been so otherwise.

Subaltern Perspectives on Markets

Ideology is an important dimension of market society. Through readings, discussions, and practical experience, economic actors gather a sense of the benefits and costs of participating in market settings. To the extent that they can articulate these sensations and practical lessons into a set of dispositions, opinions, and ideas, they contribute to the formation of an "economic ideology." Rather than a set of principles, I prefer to see economic ideology as a discursive space uniting distinct propositions about the functioning of markets. Subaltern subjects contribute to this discursive space with their own perspectives.

The discovery of an extraordinary set of documents relating to the 1834 regulation of the Public Provision (*Mercado de Abasto*) allows us to read the "implicit understandings" about the market of a particular set of subalterns: the so-called peon-sellers (*peones-vendedores*). That year, this group of peons entered into conflict with cattle owners and dealers over the nature of the regulation envisioned for the cattle market. Both groups made evident in writing their ideas and opinions about freedom of contract, the wage system, and state regulation. The peon-sellers exhibited a definite preference for the free mobility of labor and the contractual fixing of wages and were suspicious of state regulations. Though this form of popular liberalism cannot be easily extrapolated to other subaltern groups, this case reveals attitudes, perceptions, and verbalizations that are consistent with other traits discussed in other parts of this book: mobility, acquisitiveness, right to income, and risk-taking behavior. This source reveals also the disputed nature of property and control—indeed, the tenuous hold of capitalists—in the marketplace of the most important wealth-generating activity of the epoch.

An Unsettled Market

In January 1834 a group of abastecedores—traders in cattle supplying the city—asked the government to intervene in the cattle market. The southern corrals were, in their opinion, a site dominated by peons, a place without rules. Petitioners complained that the peon-sellers were unlawfully using their capital, slaughtering cattle and selling meat without their consent, retaining sales revenues, appropriating part of the meat and grease, and damaging the hides.[61] What concerned proprietors most was the lack of subjection of peons to any "master," a situation they attributed to the absence of regulations. Going for the best bidder, peons changed bosses with ease, showing no loyalty to their employers. Though cattle dealers owned the oxcarts, the stands, and the cattle, the peon-sellers seemed in control of the processes of production and realization.

This was the time of the Restoration of the Laws (only three months had passed since the events of October 1833), a time cattle suppliers considered ripe for restoring order to the operation of cattle markets, a space saturated with subaltern pretensions, insubordination, and waste. Enacting and enforcing new bylaws in the Public Provision would be a test case for the new power of the *restauradores* and their ideology of order. In this political climate, cattle dealers found no difficulty interesting government in the regulation of the meat market.[62] Within a month, a commission appointed by the government (which included prominent federalist military chiefs and members of the Mazorca) drafted new bylaws for the operation of the corrales.[63] The new bylaws were examined by a commission of cattlemen and various government agencies and rapidly enacted. In August 1834 they went into effect.

Cattle capitalists and government officials expected that, from then on, the Public Provision would become a regulated space. The new bylaws contemplated an enhanced control of transactions, the registration of peons, the arbitration of disputes between employers and workers, and the weighing on sight of all meat slaughtered and sold.[64] The market would operate at fixed hours (from 10 A.M. to 3 P.M.) and all participants would be required to register. A justice of corrals and four assistants would control the documentation presented by drovers and sellers and would supervise the slaughtering. Order seemed to have finally arrived at this enclave of subaltern disorder.

2. Work at the Abasto Corrals. The corrals for the city's supplies (*abasto*) are here presented as an extension of rural life. Peons are performing the same tasks as on a cattle ranch. *Corrales de Abasto*, lithograph, ca. 1838, from Gregorio Ibarra, *Trajes y costumbres de la Provincia de Buenos Aires* (1839).

The new bylaws (*Reglamento de Corrales*) are a class document. Each of its clauses describes a moment of workers' power and attempts to disarm it. Two aspects of the labor process preoccupied employers: how to control cattle products and how to recover the money invested. The bylaws made clear that every piece of meat had to be weighed and accounted for. Peons were made responsible for delivering to their employers the grease and tallow of each animal, were forbidden from taking the meat left near the bones, and were no longer allowed to cut hides to make their own boots. The judge of corrals had to prevent people from picking up the guts after the slaughter; even the leftovers of a day's sale had to be weighed and registered. Order—for cattle traders—meant maximizing the appropriation of cattle products. Retaking control over money revenues was also important. Payments had to be made on the spot (at the corral) to the owner of the cattle. The cattle dealers were to receive the revenues from retail sales within three days following the slaughter. Peons who kept the money longer than that were fined, and recidivists were punished with terms of service in the army. Leaving employers without having paid all debts became a felony. And, to complete their financial attachment, peons had to make a $200 security deposit with their employer.

This overall assault on workers' traditional appropriation, this attempt to reduce "waste" to a minimum, was no different in spirit from the instructions Rosas (1968) gave his *mayordomos* about productivity on the ranches. The implicit logic was the same: to subject peons to the wage relationship, owners needed first to reduce the opportunities open to peons for earning nonwage income. But here, unlike the situation on private ranches, the state mediated the relationship between peons and employers. A judge in the field supervised the legality of each transaction, both sales and hirings, and enforced the letter of contracts. In addition, cattle merchants needed to regain control over the labor market. Hence, they included clauses in the new bylaws that amounted to an almost total regulation of labor contracts. Once a month, the judge had to fix the daily wage for slaughtering, imposing heavy fines on those cattle owners who paid higher rates. This, the proprietors thought, would prevent cutthroat competition for laborers and, hence, avoid significant rises in wages. The bylaws also contemplated a fixed rate of *vendaje* (2.5 reales per head) as the unique compensation for the labor of selling. Peons' previous manipulation of prices, deliveries, and monetary revenues, too costly to cattle traders, was replaced by a standardized monetary payment.

Resisting Regulation

On December 3, 1834, a group of peon-sellers petitioned the government for a suspension in the enforcement of the bylaws recently approved. They considered the measure an attempt by a group of wealthy proprietors to reduce competition in the marketplace. The peons protested against the possibility of a meat market cornered by a few producers and of a regulated labor market, defending a broad conception of market freedom. A month before, the peons had organized a collective action that effectively postponed the application of the bylaws for a short time. The new bylaws, peons knew, would significantly curtail their income and freedom. So they approached a person they trusted, Don Benavente, who had struggled with them during the *journeés* of October 1833. They asked him to attend a meeting where they would collectively denounce the attempts of cattle traders to enslave the market and deprive peons of their livelihood. The invitation, signed by thirty-nine peon-sellers (most of them illiterate) and three "dons," had the tone of a revolutionary manifesto: "Los Ciudadanos qe a continuación de ésta firman, suplicamos a Usted como Gefe más inmediato a nosotros y en particular considerando que es nuestro mejor amigo como lo ha demostrado en todas las épocas de la Restauración de las Leyes, Es que suplicamos a Ud se digne el asistir el lunes 24 del corriente a la Junta de los Corrales del Alto a defender nuestro derecho, y librarnos de la Red qe nos tienden para esclavisarnos y qe nos libre de caer bajo el yugo de un tribunal sin apelación a otro y querer hacer esclusivo el ramo del abasto sobre las ruinas de nuestras familias."[65] ("The Citizens who sign below, beg You as the most immediate Chief to us and, in particular considering that you are our best friend, as you have demonstrated in all moments of the Restoration of the Laws. We supplicate You to attend [a meeting] at the *Junta de Corrales del Alto* on Monday 24 of the current [month] in order to defend our rights and to free ourselves from the net [meaning "trap"] that they had thrown [upon us] to enslave us, and that [you help to] free us from falling under the yoke of a tribunal without appeal and [from those who want] to make the Public Provision (*Abasto*) an exclusive trade over the ruin of our families.") The invitation evokes the chains of slavery, the evils of monopoly, the rights conferred on citizens, and the legal rhetoric of Rosismo for an unlikely purpose: to defend the freedom of labor contracts and cattle trading in the Public Provision.

We do not know what happened during this meeting. The next trace of the peons' actions is the December 3 petition to government. Here again, peons used arguments that blended elements of political and economic liberalism. The owners, they argued, were acquiring (on account of their wealth) privileges that went beyond the rights of normal citizens. The cornering of the provision of meat by a few wealthy proprietors not only threatened the well-being of industrious citizens and their families, but also subjected the consumer to the tyranny of the few. Behind their reasoning was the argument, dear to political economists, that only free competition could avoid the greed of the few from dominating the many.[66] The peons' petition was the "outcry of a sizeable class" expecting the government's "fatherly consideration." Abasto peons addressed government with rhetorical ambivalence: claiming rights of citizens and expecting, at the same time, the protection given by monarchs to their subjects.

Peons presented the government with alternative by-laws more rooted in workers' customs and, at the same time, more liberal than the one designed by the cattle merchants. Though agreeing with the proposed registration of all meat suppliers, they rejected the imposition of barriers to enter the market. According to their own regulations, people's participation in the market would not be restricted by capital requirements: any person could bring cattle to the southern corrales and slaughter them without owning oxcarts or stands. Nor should any group have special privileges concerning the selling and buying of cattle.

Under these provisions, peons and capitalists would have equal access to the market, and peon-sellers would be able to maintain the unusual condition of being workers and sellers at the same time. In addition, peons wanted the freedom of contract to prevail in the wage-setting process. Unlike the owners' bylaws, which tried to regulate wages, peons demanded total liberty in labor contracts.[67] Article 2 (chapter 3) of the peons' by-laws was an anthem to free labor markets: "Será libre todo abastecedor ó amo de ganado el pagar lo qe fuere de su agrado al peón qe ocupa; pues es claro qe *convenidos Patrón y peón en el jornal qe debe dar el primero al segundo, no se perjudican, y el peón debe ser libre en servir al individuo qe le proporcione mayores ventajas*."

This is liberal ideology at its best: individuals contracting freely in the market produce outcomes that cannot be harmful to either of the contracting parties. An attentive reading of the article leaves no doubt that workers were stating a principle based on self-interest. Peons wanted to serve whoever paid them the highest wages. For them, the *freedom of labor* was understood as a lack of subjection to any particular master. In fact, in the next article of this alternative regulation, peons defended their right to change masters. Whoever paid for their labor was their legitimate employer as long as there was work to be done. No employer could expect any loyalty from a peon if he had no cattle ready to be slaughtered.

Why this defense of occasional, short-term contracts? By changing employers from one day to the next, peons could maximize their income, not only because they could earn better wages but also because of the many "perks" involved in the slaughtering. They could not afford to lose this nonwage income. Yes, buyers deserved a fair and visible weighing of the meat, but peons should be granted one *arroba* (11.5 kgs) for *destara* (a reduction in weight to account for the weight of the container) and the weight of the hook. Accustomed to keep part of the meat as payment for their labor, peons were not ready to abandon this income without a fight.

Their petition, as we shall see, did not prosper, perhaps due to the fact that Rosas himself felt more confident about imposing his own views about order. In the end, peons miscalculated their own political support in the changing political waters of federalism.

Restoring Order to the Market

After studying the workers' petition, the judges of corrals sided with the proprietors, rejecting the revisions demanded by the peons. According to the judges, workers pretended to be participants in the market without owning capital; this was inadmissible. In addition, the judges thought, peons were deceiving the public trust: they had registered as cattle dealers using as bond bailers people who could not assume any financial responsibility. Rather than cattle traders and meat distributors, the peon-sellers were vagrants who, to escape military service, had taken refuge in this business. Judges rejected also the free, individual negotiation of wages on the grounds that this would put capitalists at the mercy of the peons' threats of abandoning work.[68] Peons' freedom to choose employers was not to be touched, but it was necessary to put everything in writing: if peons wanted to serve a new patron, they had to ask for a written permit; this would give cattle owners the chance to collect outstanding debts. It was time to terminate the workers' practice of paying themselves *anticipos* (advances on wages) from the product of meat sales. Proprietors needed to regain control of the valorization process if the Public Provision was to transform into a true business.

The solution provided for a greater demarcation of property rights and for the enforcement of labor contracts without reducing the power of competition. The number of sellers in the market was not fixed, and this, by itself, could guarantee an ample degree of freedom in the labor market. With changing participants in the cattle market, it was quite difficult to maintain commitments about wages. Even if wages became more uniform, workers were able to retain their freedom to choose masters and to quit. Traditional sources of nonwage income, however, were lost; what was tolerated before as a customary practice became an illicit appropriation punished by law. Also gone was the possibility of peons assuming the role of capitalists, exercising rights over capital. In the order of markets, subalterns needed to act as such.

Popular Liberalism

The incident, though decided in favor of cattle merchants shows the existence of a "popular liberalism" among the working classes, an ideology that, under conditions of labor scarcity, served to support workers' material interests and the preservation of workers' traditional rights of use. Peons articulated the principle of equality under the law and the rights of citizens to be free from personal dependency and coercion for the preservation of market rights. Freedom of contracts until that point had served the peon-sellers well: high wages, extra pay for distribution, control over financial resources, forced bonuses taken from sale revenues. Hence, workers' defense of free labor and of the operation of competitive markets in cattle and meat was not against their best interests.

Was this attitude toward markets peculiar to this particular segment of the Buenos Aires proletariat? Apparently, it was not. A petition by a bread peddler shows important similarities in language and reasons for defending the freedom of trading. In December 1839 Pascual Aguilera was arrested near San José de Flores for selling bread of unusual size and weight. Two days after his arrest, he wrote to the chief of police asking for his freedom and defending his right "to earn a livelihood." He was a Buenos Aires resident who specialized in buying bread from the city's bakeries and reselling it to taverns and families in the countryside. As he explained, people asked him to bring a richer quality of bread, of a weight and size different from that required by government regulations. He was assured by customers that they would pay more (1 real for a bread of "tres cuartillos") for bread of great quality, and so he did. He arranged with his baker a new price scheme and went about selling the new bread among the paysanos. Soon, his innovation proved a market success—so much so, that he could barely cope with market demand.[69]

A subaltern with a horse, some connections among bakers, and a keen sense of market opportunity, Aguilera was upset when the police confiscated his bread for not corresponding to the official weight. In vain, he asked the police to inspect the other distributors and compare the quality of their bread with his. He was sure of "having committed no felony." He had provided what the customers wanted by honest labor. So he demanded the freedom to earn a livelihood ("the free use of my abilities to earn a living") without the obstacles of government regulation. The justice disagreed, upheld the confiscation, and ordered Aguilera to pay a fine.

During the Rosas period the state also tried to regulate the retail trade of rural towns. It mandated that all taverns obtain a state license, pay a tax, and be ready to support the armies of the federation with provisions when needed. To prevent the spread of trading in illicit goods (stolen hides, chiefly), Rosas prohibited the operation of *pulperías volante* (itinerant retailers). To bypass the prohibition against their business, itinerant peddlers got licenses from different district justices, a strategy that entailed great transaction costs. A petition from Don Mateo Quintela to Rosas in 1832 shows how difficult the justices made the business of these merchants. Quintela complained that the justice of Monsalvo had confiscated his merchandise, despite his being a resident of the town and having paid his license fee. His market, explained the merchant, was all over the district of Arroyo Grande, so he had taken a second license in this district. But the moment he came to tend his cattle back in Monsalvo, the justice arrested him on charges of running a pulpería volante (itinerant tavern business). Supplicant, the merchant appealed to Rosas to get his license renewed and his goods returned.[70]

The petition of the itinerant salesman did not embrace any particular economic ideology. But it is clear that he made efforts to bypass the red tape of government regulation, though less vociferously than the peon-sellers and in a more composed and quiet way than the entrepreneurial bread salesman. His commodities reveal the extent to which he was attuned to the market opportunities opened in rural areas. He carried in small quantities items such as woolen and linen pieces, sugar, cotton shirts, waistcoats, handkerchiefs, saddle blankets from Córdoba, bread, tobacco, cotton thread, ribbons (for making the federalist emblem), women's shoes and stockings, and knives. The market, it appears from this list, was based on peons' and peasants' demands. To satisfy this demand, traveling salesmen had to break the law, upholding with their practices the principles of free trade.

Conclusions

In a 1988 article Halperin Donghi suggested that Argentina was a "born-liberal" nation. Economic liberalism, with its dual defense of free commerce and industry and free labor, had been a moving force behind the revolutionary leadership, the Rivadavian experiment, and the constitutionalists and ruralists of the 1850s and 1860s. Judged by his commercial policies Rosas can also be considered part of this tradition.[71] But his relationship with economic actors was, at best, ambivalent. Rosas believed in the beneficial effects of entrepreneurship, competition, and market forces, to the extent that they did not conflict with his project of order. His government imposed strict controls over the traffic in commodities, more systematically enforced property rights on livestock, brought some order to the markets of beef and bread, and persecuted itinerant peddlers and smugglers.

In this chapter, I have shown the subaltern side of economic activities, attitudes, and impressions. I described the visibility of subaltern subjects and the lack of separation between plebeian and cultured tastes in the marketplace. I pondered how deeply the logic of the market had penetrated into the cognitive world of peons, peasants, itinerant peddlers, bakers, and butchers. I examined the connection between the popular engagement with raffles and lotteries and the risk-prone nature of market activities. Even when this review is not comprehensive, my attempted reconstruction of the economic dimension of the subaltern has borne fruit. The location of the subaltern in the market now appears a bit more intelligible.

During the Rosas government, the city of Buenos Aires was the theater for frequent spectacles of economic competition. British and American commercial houses sold their wares in public auctions, the Police Department contracted public services via competitive bidding, and justices of the peace used the same mechanism to dispose of goods confiscated from the unitarios. To subalterns these spectacles reaffirmed the legitimacy of the market as an impersonal, participatory, orderly institution. Public bidding familiarized them with the dynamics of the price system and put them in contact with a variety of commodities. Raffles and auctions of confiscated goods created expectations for the redistribution of wealth and brought subalterns into the game of (individual) economic improvement. Marketplaces, in spite of the transformations brought about by political polarization and war, remained sites permeated by lower-class sensibilities and interactions. They were places crucial for working-class sociability and reproduction, which failed to produce a class segmentation of commodities and tastes. Under a process of rapid commodification of social relations, the "economy" remained a territory porous to the interventions of subaltern groups.

The state's efforts to regulate markets were consonant with the general mission of Rosista federalism: to bring order to the tumultuous anarchy of the republic. Regulation coexisted with a greater degree of competition in key markets for working-class reproduction (meat and bread). The Rosista state made possible certain welfare benefits for veterans, women, and poor families whose impact on the nutrition and economic improvement of the rural poor we have only recently begun to understand. The new semiology of capital (the grammar of property inscribed on the hides of animals), the transformation of cattle markets into spaces of surveillance and judicial decisions, the farming out of government contracts, and the disposing of unitario property contributed to the long learning process by which subalterns discovered the ways of the market. That this learning process was riddled with contradictions must be clear by now. Subalterns resisted state regulations, took advantage of the expanding markets opened by the export bonanza, and—some of them, at least—fought against undue concentration of market power. In multiple ways, subalterns participated and therefore helped to shape the market culture of Buenos Aires. They carved out a space of rights in which the labor market could really function and where the logic of market competition did not necessarily translate into exclusion and malnutrition. The war gave reasons for women to demand from the state basic food rights, conferred on soldiers a claim to a more just distribution of property rights in the countryside, and presented black slaves with the chance to push forward their transformation into free wage workers.

The Ways of the Market   59

Were subalterns willing participants in a "born-liberal" nation? The contention of 1834 between capitalists and peons/sellers shows the extent to which a particular type of liberalism had permeated the consciousness of workers. Peon-sellers demanded a freer labor market—preferring, in fact, short-term, casual contracts—combined with minimal regulation in the buying and selling of cattle for consumption. The connections built by the peon-sellers between the preservation of custom and nonwage income and the freedom of mobility and contracts are a good reminder that in addition to the two basic principles of economic liberalism, there are other interpretations, other perspectives that constructed the location of subaltern experience. Popular liberalism seems a stage of workers' consciousness appropriate for this particular phase of the formation of agrarian capitalism in Buenos Aires province, a phase characterized by contestation and ambivalence in the spheres of property, regulation, production, and marketing.

CHAPTER 2

Cash Nexus and Conflict

This chapter locates the subaltern in the wage-labor relationship; that is, it interrogates the situation of workers as subjects of wage contracts and the difficulties and ambiguities implicit in the realization of these contracts. My concern focuses on the tension between formal and real subsumption (that is, between the sphere of labor contracts and the realm of the imposition of work) in an economy characterized by labor scarcity.[1] I discuss the diffusion and nature of the wage form in Buenos Aires province, highlight the importance of labor mobility as a crucial feature of labor markets, and present the microconfrontations within the sphere of production. By situating peons and laborers in relation to private and state employers, I locate subalternity in a context of conflict and negotiation. What is at stake is the degree of workers' subjection to employers under the particular conjuncture of postindependence: recurrent warfare, labor shortages, ill-defined property rights, and tensions between landowners and the autocratic government.[2]

The narration unfolds against the grain of various established preconceptions: first, the notion that the wage form was relatively undeveloped in the pampas and that crude forms of exploitation and unpaid labor prevailed over contractual wage relationships; second, the conception that paternalism and deference governed labor relations on private ranches and that the cattle ranch provided Rosas with a theory of governance; and third, that peons sought refuge in wage contracts because of the fear of military conscription. All these misconceptions have biased our comprehension of labor relations during this period, obfuscated the role of rural workers as economic agents, and underestimated their bargaining power vis-à-vis ranchers, farmers, and other employers.[3] This chapter seeks a new point of departure for the consideration of subalternity by highlighting the relevance of labor conflicts in the export economy.

In Buenos Aires province accommodation and contract characterized most labor relations. Resistance, however, cropped out here and there—on the ranch, in the slaughterhouse, in the tannery, among oxcart troops—showing the undefined nature of labor contracts and the difficulties employers faced in securing control over the labor process. Threats, insults, and, on occasion, violent interactions disturbed the peace of the work-place. Furthermore, under conditions of generalized labor shortages, la-borers were able to obtain wage increases, maintain meat rations, and preserve their most important bargaining tool: free mobility. My recon-struction of the collective experience of paysanos as laborers contradicts the notion of peons' passivity and helps us understand the lamentations of landowners about labor shortages, work abandonment, and the intrac-tability of rural laborers. Peons, the perfect embodiment of the notion of "abstract labor," appear here as agents endowed with an acute under-standing of the logic of labor markets and quite aware of their bargaining position in a labor-scarce economy.

The Diffusion of the Wage Form: The City

The commodification of labor, already quite developed by the end of the colonial period, reached a new plateau during postindependence. An un-precedented expansion of primary exports during 1815–1825 intensified the demand for rural labor, while the corresponding expansion of imports presented potential workers with desirable consumer goods at reduced prices. Army recruitment, of course, reduced the pool of potential laborers but, in return, familiarized young draftees with the discipline of wage labor: monthly pay, subordination to orders, and time regulation. In addi-tion, military experience gave workers some basic training in the struggle against state coercion. Generalized resistance to forced recruitment (levas) during the War with Brazil (1825–1827) was followed by a multiplicity of manifestations of popular rejection of military despotism and of a grow-ing demand for social equality.

During the early 1820s efforts were made to increase labor supply and improve labor discipline by penalizing job theft, vagrancy, drunkenness, and begging. The government believed that the toleration of these ac-tivities was a major obstacle to the expansion of the labor supply (Bagú 1966, 47). Together with this, the government tried to formalize labor contracts to make them more reliable. An 1821 decree prohibited em-ployers from accepting apprentices into their workshops unless they signed a proper labor obligation. Another decree in July 1823 made com-pulsory the use of written work contracts (contratas) when hiring a rural peon. Peons without contracts were threatened with forceful enlistment in the army (48–49). Committed to enforce this decree, the government printed thousands of these forms and distributed them throughout the countryside. Local justices of the peace or commissars were instructed to carry these forms to all the producers in their district and to persuade ranchers to formalize their labor contracts.[4]

Because the obligation to register labor contracts was costly to employers and promised small returns in terms of compliance with labor obligations, the formalization initiative never developed into a generalized social practice. In 1825 the justice of Ranchos complained that the "formality" ordered by the 1823 decree was not observed by the majority of ranchers.[5] Later, during the War with Brazil, the indiscriminate and forceful drafting of peons put ranchers on the defensive, making them more willing to occult peons from the government's gaze.[6] Formal enlistment papers (*papeletas de conchabo*), ranch administrators knew, would not protect peons during war. Generalized levas forced poor paysanos to abandon their fields and join the ranks of wandering laborers seeking short-term employment.

Written labor contracts reappeared during the first government of General Rosas, when the city police were instructed to keep registers of employers and their workers. Compliance with this instruction was disappointingly low. The resurgence of the civil war and the need to expand the federalist armies made control of recruitment papers more pressing. Consequently, employers began to "regularize" their peons by getting them enlistment papers instead of issuing or registering their work contracts. Most employers hired their peons through verbal agreement; as a result, the benefits expected from the formalization of labor contracts failed to materialize. Ranchers and farmers continued to complain about the frequency of work abandonment and the haughtiness of peons in the face of labor shortages.[7]

The rapid transformation of slavery into an almost contractual arrangement resulted in a further expansion of the salaried workforce (Brown 1979, 188; see also Salvatore 2000). Between 1836 and 1846 the prospects for slavery—and also the market for slaves—were radically altered. Increased government supervision of the work and treatment of *libertos*, the state's purchase of many slaves for the military, the decline in masters' prerogatives to apply corporal punishment, and the increase in the number of self-manumissions severely reduced the value and effectiveness of slavery as an institution of labor control. In addition, the increasing defiance of domestic slaves against the authority of masters stimulated slave owners to sell their bonded laborers. Others signed agreements for gradual emancipation that guaranteed a minimum of respect and work for a number of years.

Newspaper ads reflect this radical transformation. Masters offer slaves at reduced prices because they had manumission agreements, were too old

3. The Meat-Salting Workshop. A traditional activity, meat salting involved a number of specialized tasks concentrated in a single workplace. It was a sort of manufacturing activity, like tanning or wool cleaning. J. L. Palliere, *El saladero (Rep. Argentina)*, lithograph, ca. 1859–60. Reproduced from J. L. Palliere, *Escenas Americanas* (1864), plate 155.

to work, or showed little respect to their masters.[8] Tensions between masters and slaves over the issue of household discipline had intensified since independence. Judicial records confirm the augmented autonomy of bonded laborers. The slaves who appear in the records had become a problematic (recalcitrant and opinionated) labor force. They had control of their wages, held promises of freedom from their masters, demanded the right to choose their masters, and were not willing to perform degrading work.

By the 1840s, the peculiar institution had turned into a set of quasi-contractual obligations resembling the wage form. Because slaves were put for hire on the open market, their sale price reflected the present value of future wages minus an amount for subsistence that slaves kept for themselves. Already accustomed to seek employment on their own and to pay their masters a percentage of their wages, slaves started to act like waged proletarians. Indeed, they began to measure their labor time in terms of wages. When unjustly imprisoned slaves demanded their accusers compensate them for the time lost, they calculated the amount of wages they ceased to receive while in prison. By the late 1840s, slavery seemed to have run out of steam. One rarely finds advertisements offering slaves for sale. They seem to have suddenly disappeared from the market.

Apparently, by the early 1830s the wage form had already permeated the fabric of Buenos Aires society. In a social milieu lacking strong traditions of artisan guilds and apprenticeship, the experience with "salaried slavery" helped to disseminate the wage form. An extant police register of work contracts for the period 1829–1834 provides important insights into the penetration of wage relations in the city. Though incomplete, the *registro* carries information about wage contracts in bakeries, sawmills, farms, oxcart businesses, water suppliers (*aguateros*), candle factories, flour mills, brick kilns, and a variety of craft shops (carpentry, masonry, shoemaking, saddle making, hatmaking, etc.).[9] Salaried agreements prevailed in a variety of productive activities and workplaces: in agriculture, livestock raising, fishing, manufacturing, transportation, commerce, and domestic service (see Table 2.1). Most of the employers who registered their labor contracts with the police had one or two dependents.[10] Short-term agreements were the norm, reflecting the time horizon of employers and workers: 55 percent of registered workers had contracts for up to six months, 32 percent had contracts from six to twelve months, and only 2 percent held contracts for over a year. Most day contracts, of course, escaped registration.

Unlike societies dominated by craft traditions, where extensive and complex "price lists" reflect the fragmentation of skilled labor, in Buenos Aires the wage structure was quite simple. Here unskilled, casual, mobile labor prevailed over craft labor. Wages by time (month or day) outnumbered other forms of payment, such as piece rates. Piece rates were used in activities of difficult supervision, such as bread retailing and fishing, or as a sign of status, for instance, in hatmaking and shoemaking workshops, journeymen were paid by the piece but apprentices received monthly wages.

There were important variations in the price of labor, even within the categories of unskilled manual labor. Work paid by the day was significantly more expensive to the employer. Journeyman carpenters, masons, and lumber workers hired under this modality earned monthly wages ranging from 42 to 52.5 pesos, whereas rates for skilled workers were 20 to 30 pesos. Peons' wages ranged from 15 pesos (farm work) to 40 pesos a month (work in a brick kiln or in a flourmill), depending on the activity's value added and work intensity. Variations within a given category (ranch peons, or farm peons, or ox-cart peons) were quite important, indicating differentials paid for experience, productivity, good conduct, and loyalty.

TABLE 2.1 The Wage Hierarchy (1829–1834)

Work	Average Monthly Wage (in pesos)	Average Term of Contract (in months)	Work	Average Monthly Wage (in pesos)	Average Term of Contract (in months)
SKILLED WORKER			PEON		
Produce buyer	$60.0 (1)	2 (1)	Cattle tender	$36.7 (3)	8 (3)
Shell-comb factory	$55.0 (1)	12 (1)	All-work peon	$31.4 (11)	6 (9)
			Cattle drover	$30.0 (3)	6 (3)
Bread distributor	$50.0 (1)	n.a.	Vegetable farm	$30.0 (7)	4 (4)
			Carts	$30.0 (6)	5 (5)
Baker	$50.0 (1)	4 (1)	Lumber mill	$30.0 (1)	6 (5)
Harness maker	$50.0 (1)	6 (1)	Candle maker	$30.0 (1)	12 (2)
Printer	$45.0 (1)	36 (1)	House servant	$28.3 (3)	10 (3)
			Bakery	$26.2 (19)	6 (29)
FOREMAN			Milk man	$25.0 (2)	9 (2)
All-work foreman	$60.0 (1)	n.a.	Farm	$24.7 (9)	6 (9)
			Oxcart driver	$23.6 (32)	8 (30)
Cattle tending (feedlot)	$60.0 (1)	12 (1)	Ranch	$22.4 (17)	18 (14)
			Yerba mill	$22.0 (5)	3 (5)
Bakery	$53.1 (9)	6 (1)	Porter	$21.3 (12)	9 (11)
Porters troop	$50.0 (1)	6 (2)	Country peon	$21.2 (5)	11 (6)
Cattle droving	$50.0 (2)	6 (2)	Horse tender	$20.0 (3)	10 (3)
Water supply	$50.0 (1)	6 (1)	Carriage driver	$20.0 (1)	6 (1)
Cart troops	$50.0 (1)	n.a.	Shoemaker	$20.0 (2)	12 (4)
Ox-cart troops	$40.0 (2)	9 (2)			
Farm	$40.0 (2)	9 (1)	PEON	Daily Wage or Piece Rate	
Ranches	$28.3 (3)	9 (2)			
Horse keeper	$20.0 (1)	6 (1)	Carpenter	$2.25	
			Mason	$2.00	
PEON			Lumber mill	$2.00	
			Farm tilling	$2.00	
Brick kiln	$40.0 (1)	6 (1)	Hatmaker	$5/hat	
Flour mill	$40.0 (1)	6 (1)	Shoemaker	$10/dozen shoes	
Mule tender	$40.0 (1)	6 (1)	Fisherman	1 real/fish basket	

Source: "Cuaderno en donde se anotan los peones que se contratan que da principio en tres de Noviembre de 1829," Departamento de Policía, AGN X 31-9-5.
In parenthesis: number of observations.

Supervisory and organizational skills (*capataces*) commanded a high premium, paying from 62 percent (farm labor) to 135 percent (transportation labor) over the unskilled rate. Manufacturing labor, particularly the production of necessities (flour, bricks, bread, lumber, candles), was better paid than other types of work. The same could be said for occupations in which the capital at risk was relatively high, such as cattle driving and oxcart troops.

The rarity of apprenticeship contracts and the early dissolution of artisan guilds created occupations with no barriers to entry and, consequently, competitive conditions from the supply side.[11] To secure the future of their sons, mothers continued to place them under the care of craftsmen, but apprenticeship contracts were not enforced; the police did not prosecute, save for a few exceptions, runaway apprentices. Advanced penetration of the wage-form, short-term contracts, and ample differences in wages characterized the urban labor market. Short-term commitments afforded workers greater flexibility to move from one job to another. Employers in turn were able to renegotiate labor contracts according to demand conditions. In an environment characterized by ample labor mobility and high labor turnover, wage differentials according to skill, work intensity, or value added acted as effective incentives.

Absent from the police register were workplaces that constituted important centers of activity and social interaction during the Rosas period: the slaughterhouse and meat-salting plant, the government workshops, the police, and public works. Payroll lists from these institutional settings show them to be important employers of the wandering proletariat. Palermo de San Benito, the house of government since 1844, hosted a variety of workshops and facilities (carpentry, iron smithing, a hospital, a church, a cemetery) that, together with the farm, the fruit garden, the stable, and the slaughterhouse, commanded a significant labor force (Saldías 1968, 3:203). The slaughterhouse, in particular, was a place of intense activity. It employed a workforce larger and much more diversified than any cattle ranch; the number of peons fluctuated between 170 and 280 throughout 1845. This was perhaps the work site where the division of labor was most developed: over twenty categories of workers with tasks perfectly specified and coordinated.[12] In addition to high wages and credit, the Palermo slaughterhouse offered peons the possibility of spatial mobility; cattle drovers in particular were constantly moving in and out of the city.

The city also offered jobs in construction, transportation, cattle markets, and military supplies. The state itself was an important employer, demanding workers for the construction of bridges, country roads, street (stone) paving, river defense, and other urban improvements. Here also the wage form was the most effective mechanism for mobilizing labor. On occasion, the labor of convicts, police, and soldiers was used, but, if improvements were to be finished on time, additional laborers had to be hired on the market. The carpenters who worked in the construction of the Barracas pier earned according to their skill: masters, 4 pesos a day; journeymen, 2 pesos 4 reales a day; apprentices, 1 peso 2 reales a day.[13] Transportation was the territory of free (i.e., nonslave), occasional wage labor. The Parque de Artillería hired cart drivers (*carretilleros*) on a regular basis to transport ammunition, uniforms, lumber, and "vices." They charged by the trip, according to the distance and the load transported.[14]

Labor arrangements included supplementary sums for food and horses and, occasionally, the provision of clothes. Supplements and payments in kind reflected the flexibility of the wage form to accommodate different situations. Public occupations, in the army, the police, or municipal public works, set the pace. Workers at the Police Department or the cemetery earned, in addition to their salary, a sum for *rancho* (meals during the performance of the job). To cemetery peons this benefit represented 28 percent of their wages. Police watchmen received 29 pesos as salary and 10 additional pesos to pay for horse feed. Workers hired for public works (improving roads, repairing bridges, building hospitals) usually earned day wages plus a supply of yerba, rice, and *farinha* (manioc flour). On occasion, these laborers also received clothes taken from military stocks. In flourmills workers received part of their wages in hard money and part in *galleta* (ship biscuits).[15]

Short of full proletarianization—for workers in the 1840s rarely worked the whole year—the commodification of labor power was already quite developed in Rosas's Buenos Aires. The wage form was sufficiently widespread to act as a regulator of social relations. Periodical cash payments taught workers the self-discipline of the wage: to consume within one's budget. At the slaughterhouse of Palermo, peons were paid in groups or parties. At payday, each of these groups' foremen received a notebook with the payroll and paper money inside. After payment, the foreman of each party returned the notebooks with signs or crosses next to the peons' names and the money retained to cover the peons' debts.[16]

Wage relationships permeated popular culture, stimulating workers' participation in the market. In the 1840s, common people made occasional appearances in the newspapers, advertising their services as bricklayers, tailor apprentices, journeymen shoemakers, washerwomen, wet nurses, servants, or cooks. These ads reflected a plebeian perception of the possibilities opened by labor markets. To the white shoemaker or black washerwoman who advertised their services in La Gaceta Mercantil the labor market was a public "place" where they expected to meet prospective employers. Neither corporate regulation nor social stigma limited their expectations of good employment. These advertisements were exceptional; most workers used social connections and everyday conversation to get the information they needed to enter the labor market.

By the 1840s most labor services, from wet nurses to horse breakers, could be hired for a price. Labor had become "abstract labor," a malleable, comparable, and measurable commodity offered at the marketplace. Even though most wage contracts were verbal, the wage form was already the prevailing form of social interaction for production and services.[17] The presence of a strong state in constant need of soldiers charged this market with instability and uncertainty. But the casual or unstable nature of most labor contracts endowed this market with enough flexibility to respond to changing conditions of supply and demand. Furthermore, the relative absence of social stigma on manual labor and the almost total freedom from state or corporate regulations made the urban labor market one of the freest and most competitive.

Estancieros and Rural Labor

By the 1840s in rural areas too, the wage form was the prevailing relationship between proprietors and workers. Though we lack registers of work contracts for rural areas, scattered information taken from ranch records show that wage relationships were generalized, being complemented in labor-intensive activities (sheep raising and wheat farming) by various forms of sharecropping. In practice, the "logic of the wage"—attracting workers with economic incentives—had already displaced alternative methods of labor recruitment and retention. Despite isolated examples, ranchers were persuaded that the labor market was the most reliable mechanism to recruit needed peons. To a certain extent, the same was true with regard to small farmers, who combined permanent family labor with occasional or seasonal wage labor.

Having tried other alternatives unsuccessfully (i.e., protection contracts, coercion, indentured labor, slavery), ranchers came to accept the "cash nexus" as another feature of the institutional and social landscape of the pampas. The trial-and-error process that led to this conclusion can be followed in the case of Rosas's private ranches. After the attempt to retain Indians proved illusory and with the market for slaves dramatically reduced, Rosas brought in Spanish indentured laborers. They composed almost half the workforce of estancia San Martín in 1845. When their contracts expired, Spaniards tended to abandon the estate, leaving the administrator with the same unresolved problem (Salvatore 1991a, 264–265). Similarly, attempts to offer "protection contracts" to peasants escaping the levies proved impractical. As ranchers could not prevent military and judicial authorities from entering their estates and arresting peons, the value of such arrangements was limited.

Hence, attracting workers with economic incentives came to be perceived as the only workable mechanism. The advice given by landowner J. J. Anchorena to his administrator, J. M. Saavedra, in 1831 was transparently clear: "You must pay peons at least as much as neighboring hacendados pay if you expect to demand work from them and not to suffer from lack of peons."[18] Rosas too, well understood that, to attract good peons, it was necessary to offer competitive wages; thus, although known for the severity of his disciplinary methods, Rosas was also regarded as a rancher who paid high wages.[19] In 1832 he wrote to ranch administrator, J. Décima, "Flatter and encourage the peons in the way you think more convenient."[20] The flattering, of course, referred not to nice words but to rewards in money and in kind. South of the Salado River competition for laborers was intense. Two years earlier, Décima had written to Anchorena, "Landowners are desperate for peons and offer high wages"; they were paying 5 pesos a day at a time when the monthly rate was 40 pesos.[21] Though leading employers used the language of "custom" and "fair prices" to refer to their recruiting policies, in actuality they had accepted the logic of the market, paying for labor what the market demanded.[22]

The war with Brazil had accustomed ranchers to this way of reasoning. The scare produced by massive levies drastically reduced the supply of laborers, leaving ranchers with two alternatives: to hide peons from army recruiting parties or to offer additional economic incentives to retain workers. Some ranchers instructed their administrators in the best legal and political arguments to use against recruiting parties; others tried to protect their workers using different subterfuges.[23] But the levies proceeded unabated. As a result, peon wages rose and the price of recruiters— the foremen—went through the roof. In 1827 Deputy Obligado complained that foremen earned a salary comparable to the best urban jobs of the higher class (in Burgin 1946, 54). A report on wages paid at the Camarones ranch shows that between November 1826 and March 1827 foremen received wage increases on the order of 47 to 50 percent.[24] Though much of this increase was in compensation for inflation, the ranchers who survived the war with well-running estates learned that only economic incentives could buy them some degree of labor stability.

During the Pax Rosista, despite significant inflation, real wages increased 23 percent (nominal wages increased from 40 pesos a month in 1836 to 120 pesos a month in 1849; Slatta 1983, 36). These increases were the result of a bargaining process in which workers exerted pressure on landowners through their administrators. Of course, whether ranchers conceded to wage demands depended on the situation of the labor market and the specific labor needs of the ranch at a particular time. But the fact that some of them preferred wage increases to retain peons shows to what extent the logic of the wage was incorporated into the discourse and mentality of ranchers. Once he was persuaded that workers were discontent with their earnings, Rosas ordered his administrators to raise the wages of peons and foremen. Rancher Don Nicolás Anchorena knew well that, to get "the best men" to perform certain services, he had to offer them *sobresueldos* (additional pay).[25]

Seasonal and wartime labor shortages encumbered the process of hiring peons for livestock ranches. Those close to hiring decisions were quite aware of this problem. During the Entre Ríos campaign, mayordomo Ramírez from the Chacabuco ranch repeatedly complained to his patron about labor shortages. In March 1845, for instance, Ramírez made the ranch's ability to put new cattle stalls in production conditional on the hiring of new peons. The failure to find those needed hands, he explained, had already caused the postponement of necessary tasks at the ranch. To form cattle droves peons had to be diverted from their daily roundups; while this occurred there were no peons to tend the mares.[26] In May of the same year, Ramírez reported that his foremen were almost without peons. Workers had only taken contracts for two or three months and then had moved on to other locations or ranches.

The shortage of laborers reflected in ranchers' and administrators' correspondence referred to situations in which labor markets did not clear at the locality or firm level.[27] At a given wage rate, a group of ranchers and farmers were unable to get as many peons as needed or to secure work commitments for longer periods of time. Situations of localized labor scarcity were compatible with the seasonal or frictional inactivity of many potential laborers (to speak of "open unemployment" would be anachronistic).[28] Of course, labor shortages impacted producers differently. If, in a given rural district, a major rancher was able to recruit as many peons as necessary, this served as poor consolation to the small rancher or farmer who was unable to offer similar wage rates or other nonwage incentives.[29]

Nothing is more indicative of the seriousness of labor scarcity than the premium employers had to pay for labor hired on a daily basis. The daily rate premium over the equivalent monthly rate measured the true scarcity of labor in a locality. Indeed, the employment of day laborers for everyday ranch activities is indicative of the ranchers' failure to secure enough monthly peons. More than a problem of labor recruitment, this was a problem of work culture and class relations. Ranchers and the government failed to persuade the wandering proletariat of the need to be "subjected to wages" year-round. If employers wanted to reduce labor costs, they could mobilize family connections, search for monthly peons in neighboring towns, wait until some provincianos (migrants from the northern provinces) showed up, or simply apprentice local youths into ranch labor. But all this required time. In the short run employers had to hire peons by the day at a cost that was sometimes extraordinarily high (a ratio of 1 to 5 between the daily and the monthly rate was not unusual). The intractability of the problem of labor scarcity emerges clearly from the correspondence of Rosas's administrators. In 1849, four years after Rosas ordered his administrators to minimize expenditures for day laborers, the ranches were still dependent on this type of labor. Day laborers were hired for separating rodeos, driving cattle, and sheep shearing, but also for occasional tasks such as ditch digging, planting trees, and killing ants.[30]

Dealing with labor shortages—whether chronic, cyclical, or seasonal—was part of the experience of ranch managers in Buenos Aires province. It was a recurrent problem that confronted administrators and foremen with the reality of subalterns who acted as proprietors of a coveted commodity (labor force) and moved freely from one employment to the next. The problem was expensive for ranchers and farmers not only in terms of labor costs; shortages of labor also caused serious inefficiencies in production. With small crews it was difficult to make the daily roundups needed to keep control of the livestock.[31] Lack of peons caused delays in the castration of bulls, the branding of cattle, the separation of herds and the delivery of cattle to the market. In addition, labor shortages prevented a rapid response to natural disasters such as draughts and floods, when cattle had to be moved to minimize losses.

Cattle ranchers developed various strategies to cope with this problem. Small-scale producers resorted to family labor, hiring waged peons only during the branding and harvest season. Ranch administrators rode long distances seeking cattle tenders or horse breakers. Medium-size ranchers hesitated between hiring costly day laborers and getting help from neighbors for tasks such as roundups, sorting, gelding, and branding. Farmers cultivated good relations with families of northern migrants as a means to secure laborers for the harvest season. But, by and large, the best method to retain peons was to offer economic incentives. These incentives helped the cattle ranches continue supplying cattle, meat, tallow, and hides to the market.

4. The Branding. Branding was a cooperative activity, involving work crews from various ranches. Cooperation was key to separate yearlings belonging to different owners. Anon., *Hierra en una estancia—Buenos Aires*, lithograph, 1835. Reproduced from B. del Carril, *Monumenta Iconográphica* (1964).

Ranchers' ability to find solutions to the problem of labor scarcity depended on the relative size of their estates and on their relations with the center of political power. Clearly, Governor Rosas had an advantage over other ranchers in labor recruitment; he could use his official establishments in the city (the *matadero* in particular) to recruit peons and send them to the countryside.[32] Other ranchers were unable to do the same. It is also clear that justices and commissars, abusing their positions, intimidated some lower-class travelers into accepting jobs on their private ranches and farms; similarly, some military chiefs posted in frontier garrisons made soldiers perform work on their private establishments. But most ranchers and farmers did not have this extra-economic (coercive) advantage. The ownership of several estates gave great ranchers a competitive edge; at times of labor shortage, they could shift part of their workforce from one ranch to the other, concentrating workers where they were most needed. The same logic applied within a ranch; peons from various puestos—grazing lands or small settlements within the cattle ranch— would be called to assist in a given labor-intensive task.[33]

Small ranchers with no connections in the military or the judicial apparatus of the state found it difficult to fill their labor needs, particularly during times of branding, sorting, and gelding. In May 1844, back from the war, General Pacheco confronted the problem of labor scarcity on his own ranch. To complete the sorting and branding of cattle, he asked for his neighbors' help, a solution he reached reluctantly, for it entailed opening his stock to all sorts of abuses and losses. Moreover, this placed Pacheco in the situation of having to reciprocate in the future. The other alternative he could not afford: peons demanded $300 and up per month.[34] Resorting to the neighbors (including squatters and settlers) was unavoidable when it was necessary to separate cattle belonging to several owners. In cooperation, various neighbors could gather work teams of up to fifty hands. This help, however, had to be paid in yearlings, vices, and other provisions.

Labor shortages stimulated a few administrators to find methods of ranch management that would reduce labor requirements. Administrator Ramírez, for instance, experimented with the method of dividing the livestock into potreros (wood-fenced grounds). The method required less labor than the daily roundups, liberating the workforce for other necessary tasks.[35] Yet, it is well-known that most ranchers were reluctant to change their traditional methods, especially during times of declining export prices. At most, they were willing to shift the composition of production to a more diversified mix (cattle, sheep, horses, and grain), unloading part of the problem of labor recruitment on mediero (sharecropper) shepherds and tenant farmers. If anything, labor scarcity made ranchers intensely aware of the importance of economic incentives (wages) in mobilizing labor. Unable to secure laborers via extra-economic coercion, ranchers developed a variety of incentives designed to attract and retain them.

At the core of the problem of labor scarcity was the intense mobility of the workforce, a situation that generated high rates of labor turnover at ranches.[36] Peons abandoned employment with remarkable ease; they did not feel that a labor contract tied them to a particular locality or employer. At the time of his arrest in June 1845, Miguel Giménez carried in his belt a labor contract he had been unable to fulfill. In the contract, he had promised to work for his employer, Anastacio Villafañe, from May to December, performing farm labor; he was to receive 60 pesos a month.[37] Five weeks after signing the contract, Giménez was arrested in another province

(Santa Fe) on charges of horse theft. Apparently, he did not feel bound by the contract to remain at Guardia de Luján. With his small herd of horses, he moved constantly between Luján and Chacras de Chivilcoy, driving cattle. To him, a labor contract was not synonymous with immobility.

This type of behavior frustrated employers. Ranch administrator Ramírez, upset with the news that his peons quit after a minor criticism, complained, "These men think they are the arbiters of their own actions, paying no respect to those whom they are subjected to."[38] To the experienced ranch administrator, the excessive independence and arrogance of the lower classes was at the root of labor scarcity. Ramírez expressed his disappointment at subaltern conduct in the language of the old order: though tied or subjected (sujetados) to their employers by social hierarchy and work contracts, peons refused to acknowledge their subjection. While employers' complaints about the excessive independence of laborers can be traced back to the colonial period, ranchers in the 1830s and 1840s faced an intensified labor mobility as the result of institutional and cultural forces. Clearly, the political culture of postindependence had made peons and peasants more aware of their rights and freedoms—in particular, the right to earn a living and the freedom to travel. In addition, the experience of forced recruitment and the increasing regulation and surveillance of travelers had heightened workers' sensibility of restrictions imposed on those rights and freedoms.

Short-term contracts, intense labor mobility, and recurrent labor shortages were the main attributes of rural labor markets. Employers learned to operate within these constraints, trusting that economic incentives could bring them migratory workers, at least to compensate for those peons taken by military recruiters. To prolong the stay of provincianos, foremen pleaded with workers to remain until replacements were found. Wage dispersion was another feature of labor markets.[39] Asymmetries in cost structure prevented the equalization of wages across regions and establishments. Workers on the move found difficulty obtaining reliable information about wage differentials.[40] High transportation costs also conspired against wage equalization, reducing workers' incentives to migrate where labor demand was most acute. Labor markets were a mosaic of regional and local situations (connected through flows of information and people) that did not converge during this period into a single wage rate.

In a context of high labor mobility, one would expect a greater regional convergence of wage rates. But only some of the peasants and peons who perambulated through the landscape of the province were job seekers; the rest were escaping judicial prosecution or forced military recruitment. The latter group tended to seek employment in places where they expected less intense police activity, which did not necessarily coincide with areas of acute labor demand or high wages. To the extent that this hypothesis holds true, the skirmishes between the "peon class" and the state can be considered an important source of market imperfection. Workers had to compute the loss of family and social protection at the new locality as the opportunity cost of moving and the chances of getting arrested in another district. State coercion modified workers' basic calculations concerning space, income, and security.

Incentives and Penalties: Market Logic

Because of the centrality of recruiting and retaining peons for the profitability of livestock raising, ranches developed a complex system of incentives and penalties to regulate work. Among these incentives were monetary advances, payments in kind (including food), and the toleration of certain forms of direct appropriation and land intrusion. Rewards for seniority, night work, special skills, and supervisory work are evidence that ranchers were trying to efficiently allocate their limited labor resources. The prevalence of incentives over penalties and the undefined nature of work rules show the limits of private coercion in the context of labor scarcity and high labor mobility. More crucial, the complexity of economic incentives reasserts the importance of market-regulated behavior for both ranchers and peons.

Labor contracts usually involved various forms of payment. Ranches paid wages in paper money (with change in copper coins), unless peons insisted on receiving their wages in silver, a medium hard to obtain during inflationary times.[41] In addition to monetary wages, workers were offered other perquisites as incentives to work and remain. Payments in kind (food, clothes, saleable goods), credit, and rights of use of ranch resources complemented the wage, making the option to stay on the estate more attractive. As a supplement to their wages, ranch peons received a ration of vices, generally made up of yerba, tobacco, paper, and sugar. Less frequently, administrators included salt and soap in the periodical distribution of provisions. In the mid-1840s Brabazon (1981, 31) found that it was common for peons to receive a piece of soap, tobacco, two sheets of paper, two pounds of yerba, a pound of salt, and, occasionally, a pound of manioc flour. Meat rations were a tradition in Río de la Plata, reaching back to colonial times. When Juan Pablo Aguirre acquired a new ranch in Boca del Salado in 1827, his foreman asked him to send the beef ration because "this is the way peons are hired."[42] During the 1830s and 1840s, Rosas's ranch administrators distributed meat rations and "vices" (yerba and tobacco) among peons. On the estates confiscated from the unitarios (1840–1842) administrators had to deliver meat rations, for this was the prevailing custom.

While immersed in a cash economy, workers defended such nonmonetary income as a cushion against the variations in the value of money. Limited commercial outlets in the pampas and the ample variation in the prices of basic items such as yerba, tobacco, and sugar made these rations a necessary component of rural wages, and with the valorization of cattle, meat rations became all the more important. With the consent of their *capataces* (foremen), workers slaughtered cows when needed; in this way, periodical meat provisions were replaced by peons' direct appropriation. The same could be said of the practice of making boots from mare hides. In spite of landowners' efforts to discourage this practice, slaughtering mares for boots continued unabated. In the 1840s, with the employment of Scottish immigrants on sheep farms, new modalities in the payment of the labor force began to appear.[43] Itinerant work gangs were hired on a piece-rate basis to complete the shearing. In addition to their monetary wage, shepherds received sheepskins, grease, and the right to milk cows (Brabazon 1981, 53).

For workers, the possibility of expanding their purchasing power through credit was an important aspect of the labor contract. To attract peons, ranchers offered monetary advances (*anticipos*), which varied with the relative scarcity of labor. Evidence drawn from one of Rosas's ranches in 1838 shows that twenty of the twenty-three peons had received this type of incentive. On average, the wage advances amounted to a week's salary of 24 percent of monthly wages.[44] The practice of anticipos was also common in rural industry. At the Palermo Slaughterhouse advances of money were more frequent and more substantial than on private ranches; they were distributed among the peons who had proven most reliable to the establishment.[45] These advances responded to needs expressed by the workers.[46] To fight rising prices, peons demanded advances that, after a while, turned into a renewable source of credit.

The government payroll dramatizes the importance of monetary advances in employer-worker relations. Shortly before the fall of Rosas in February 1852, the Provincial Accountancy listed all the workers and employees at the Government House who had received money advances since November 1850.[47] Apparently, many workers were in debt to the government for sums that were far from trivial. Employees in debt were a great risk to the employer, for they could abandon their jobs and leave the treasury with large outstanding debts. Only the shortage of labor can

5. Patron-Peon Relations. An air of equality and harmony informs this representation of patron-peon relations. The better-dressed *capataz* (foreman) is looking up to the plain-dressed peon: two armed men treat each other as equals. An inversion of posture and gaze (the peon is above and looking down) is compensated for by the differences in clothes and riding apparel. Prilidiano Pueyrredón, *Capataz y peon de campo*, oil on canvas, 1864. Reproduced from B. del Carril, *El Gaucho* (1993).

explain the existence of these advances, granted before any work was performed and for sums larger than a monthly salary.

On the ranch the performance of workers depended on a combination of good treatment, incentives, and occasional warnings and penalties. Vast extensions of land without fences and reduced supervisory personnel conspired against enforcing too rigid disciplinary codes. Rather than a demonic force that eroded pastoral traditions, the wage system of the Buenos Aires countryside was a delicate equilibrium between incentives and penalties geared toward work performance. Wage differentials were crucial in this regard. They were used to separate night from day labor, to reward seniority and skill, and to value some rural tasks over others. In a situation of loose property rights and limited law enforcement, managers' efforts had to be specially rewarded. As Amaral (1998, especially chap. 9) reminds us, the productivity of a cattle ranch depended on good managerial decisions regarding stocking rates, horses, control of predators, and the ability to recruit workers. Hence, there were important differences between the wages of foremen and those of peons. In addition, foremen and *puesto* keepers were allowed to raise their own cattle on the premises. Workers with special skills, namely horse breakers, sheep shearers, tanners, and twisters of lassos, received significant wage differentials. In other trades, scarcity was the main reason to pay more; this was the case with good cooks, reliable house servants, and pathfinders.

Though ranches were organized around a simple, three-tiered hierarchy of wages (administrator, foremen, and peons), wage differentials and special rewards gave flexibility to the wage structure. Some activities were at a premium at private ranches, chiefly due to their importance in producing revenue. Special seasonal tasks, such as branding and gelding, demanded higher wages. On these occasions ranchers were prepared to pay by the day much higher rates than equivalent monthly wages. During the week, a day laborer working in the branding and gelding season could earn 75 percent more than a monthly peon working a full month.[48] On a ranch in Loberías in 1841 the ratio between equivalent daily wages and monthly wages was 5 to 1. Night work commanded higher wages because of the need to protect the livestock from intruders and rustlers.[49] In time, ranchers rewarded reliable workers with the position of foreman, a position that entailed greater responsibility and the possibility of becoming an independent (small) cattle raiser.[50] In other cases, job experience was rewarded with wage increases. Rosas, for example, paid his Spanish peons wages that were directly proportional to their age; their wages were raised at each peon's birthday. This was a reward for seniority.[51] On several occasions, Rosas tried other incentives: he gave a horse to every Spanish peon who had learned to tame broncos and was ready to grant a postponement of debts to those who wanted to stay.[52]

In the political economy of incentives and penalties, the toleration of direct appropriation played a crucial role. Allowing peons to keep the tallow of slaughtered animals, the meat around the bones, or damaged hides smoothed relations between foremen and peons. Not denouncing workers' occasional slaughter of stray cattle or sheep was a gesture that countered existing tensions at the workplace over the imposition of discipline. Permission to hunt on the estate's land (ostriches, otters, game, armadillos) brought workers additional sources of income as well as a break from the routines of the work day.

Disciplinary penalties applied against workers, such as fines or suspensions, were a rarity. Ranchers instead tried to penalize absenteeism. Since the early 1830s, Rosas gave instructions to his ranch administrators and foremen to control the work attendance and to discount all *fallas* (absences) at the time of payment.[53] Payroll records show that this order was strictly observed. As a result of the discounts for absenteeism, the twenty-five workers on Rincón del Rosario's payroll received on average $40 a month out of a nominal wage average of $45. (Peons apparently worked twenty-three or twenty-four days each month, that is, a six-day work week.)[54] This method of payment served to minimize ranch expenditures while accustoming workers to the rule of "a day worked, a day paid." Discounts for absences were limited to weekdays. When in 1846 Rosas wanted to extend the discount to weekends and festive days, administrator Schoó persuaded him that this was going too far.[55]

By the 1840s corporal punishment was no longer a legitimate or useful method for enhancing labor productivity or for producing obedience on the ranch. Though still pervasive in the literature, the argument that Rosas enforced a strict code of conduct on the ranches he administered (which included corporal punishment for minor violations) is far from established. Evidence of corporal punishment on Rosas's or Anchorena's ranches relates to the early 1830s; afterward, the records are silent on this issue (Carretero 1970, 19). Whenever punishment of peons was mentioned in the 1840s or 1850s, it was in the context of state jurisdiction, a symptom that the *imperio de las leyes* had made some progress at the expense of private justice.[56] Scholars working on estate inventories failed to locate traces of instruments of punishment and torture after 1840. Like slavery, corporal punishment rapidly dwindled as free peons managed to establish new standards of treatment on estates.

In the 1840s, Rosas's advice to his administrators, in contrast with the draconian and authoritarian policies suggested in his 1819 *Instrucciones para Mayordomos*, presents a model of ranch management more accommodating of workers' demands. We see him granting wage raises when repeatedly claimed by foremen, ordering the regular distribution of rations, making concessions for peons' families, and arranging wages according to seniority and skill. Although important pieces of advice remain the same—the need to closely police workers' activities, the importance of administrators' good behavior and respectability—policies relating to labor recruitment seem to have incorporated market logic. Wage differentials, monetary advances, credit, and other kinds of "flattering" were now part of a sensible style of ranch management. Although the results in terms of labor discipline and labor turnover were not ideal, the cattle ranch was no longer the insecure place Rosas had found in 1819–1820 near the Salado River.[57] It was now a social field of negotiation and conflict in which both employers and peons had incorporated, in their own ways, the information and dictates of the market and had learned to respond to it.

Unproductive Paternalism

Various authors have presented labor relations on the estancia as tempered by the paternalism of ranchers and the passivity of peons. An implication of this interpretation is that the permanence of peons on the estate was governed by noneconomic incentives. Loyalty to a patron is supposed to have replaced the workings of price signals to attract or repel peons to or from occupations and estates. Here, I examine a series of social conditions that severely limited the actual functioning of paternalist relations between employers and workers. I focus particularly on the extent to which peons themselves felt bound by paternalistic obligations to their employers, for the efficaciousness of social relations based on loyalty and deference depends ultimately on the subalterns' internalization of these obligations. The exercise of paternalism provided little assurance that peons would remain on the ranch. Labor mobility, unclear property rights, the expansion of the judicial apparatus, and the egalitarian ethos of federalism conspired against the construction of an effective paternalism in the field of production.

In the opinion of some historians, paternalism was nurtured by the fear produced in paysanos by recruiting gangs and passport laws (e.g., Lynch 1981, 107–8). This thesis (which I have called elsewhere the fear-protection thesis) is erroneous. Offering and maintaining protection agreements depended crucially on the possibility of exercising absolute property rights over a given domain. In an institutional environment characterized by fuzzy property boundaries (constant invasions and dispersal of cattle, minimal repression of cattle theft, and the virtual impossibility of controlling squatters), ranchers simply lacked such leverage. Restrictions to the full exercise of private property rights over land reduced in practice the power of great ranchers. Once tolerated, squatters invited other newcomers to settle on the land, adding confusion to property rights and generating an overstocking of cattle.[58] Shielding themselves behind customary rights and informal agreements with prior landowners, squatters refused to move, in some cases forcing proprietors to sell the land with the squatters included.[59]

Unable to enforce their property rights in land and cattle, ranchers had to accommodate peons' demands for the set of reciprocal, customary obligations that governed relations among "neighbors." In similar ways, they had to bargain with their peons over almost every aspect of the wage relationship. Having to search for jobs in an environment where travel was made difficult by the presence of a state avid for new recruits, peons could have benefited from some degree of proprietor's protection. This benefit, however, was something that few cattle ranchers could guarantee. In 1845 peon Toribio Barrionuevo, a cattle driver, complained bitterly against foreman Damaso Pacheco for unfulfilled promises of protection. Barrionuevo was working under the understanding that his employer would "fix him up" (arreglarlo) with the district authorities. As soon as he found out that these were empty promises, he decided to seek protection elsewhere. Another landowner introduced him to Justice Roque Baudrix, who gladly enlisted him in the district's militia and gave him a passport to travel.[60] Ultimately, Barrionuevo's protection had to be bargained for with state authorities.

Short-term employment also conspired against the formation of clientelistic ties. Consider the story of José Rosas, a black laborer from Córdoba. In May 1842 he was put in charge of a small farm confiscated from the unitarios. A few months later, he abandoned his duty and went to the land of new wheat farms, where he found a job with Mateo Palomeque, a casual job to be sure, for he stayed there only a few days, working on other farms as well. He then spent a month at the Villanueva ranch, property of the Anchorenas, and from there moved to Cañuelas, where Facundo Rosas gave him a job.[61] Due to his occupational mobility, José Rosas was unable to develop any sense of commitment and loyalty to his employers; he treated all his employers with respect, but not with deference. So ephemeral were work contracts that some peons, when interrogated by military or judicial authorities, could not remember their employer's name.

Disguised as marks of paternalism were various gestures and practices that were actually responses to labor scarcity or signs of hospitality and reciprocity among paysanos. Small cattle raisers and farmers in need of additional hands offered their laborers money advances, horses on loan, and free meat for their families. Ambrosio Coronel, a Lobos rancher, was a generous employer. He not only allowed his peon Gregorio Rea to visit his family in San Nicolás but also gave him five horses and a mare for the travel.[62] Similarly, the Guardia de Luján farmer who hired Pedro Chávez paid dearly to secure the peon's labor services; against the promise of future farm labor, he advanced Chávez over $620 to assist his family. The largesse of these employers could easily be mistaken for signs of paternalism; in fact, employers' generosity had much to do with the condition of labor markets. As the Guardia de Luján farmer soon discovered, a monetary advance guaranteed neither the quality of work nor the permanence of his peon in the neighborhood.[63]

After a season's work in the southern estancias (Mar Chiquita) and taking advantage of his new job as cattle driver, José María Olguín returned to see his old patron at Navarro, Don Cayetano Rocha. He had lost his previous passport and wanted Rocha to help him get a new one. Olguín had known Don Rocha since childhood (he grew up on a neighboring estate) and regarded him "as his father."[64] But the admiration and respect he felt for Don Rocha in no way compromised Olguín's freedom of movement. On the contrary, a good "father" was supposed to assist his "son" in securing the legal protection needed to avoid police arrest or other constraints to mobility. Olguín trusted that with the help of Don Rocha, he could get a passport to continue his travel to the south.

Underlying the relationships between employers and peons were some assumptions about the nature of society that contradicted the very concept of paternalism. Accustomed to bargain over wages and perquisites with employers who were neither powerful nor wealthy, peons were ill trained in the etiquette of deference. Even the concept of loyalty carried the mark of the postindependence egalitarian ethos. Sometimes, loyalty became synonymous with complicity among equals rather than a sign of hierarchy and social difference. Saturnino Maldonado, a peon employed at Pablo Giménez's ranch, had no trouble presenting his patron as a partner in crime. Both had freely slaughtered the neighbors' steers, and this, in Maldonado's opinion, placed patron and peon on the same level.[65] Sometimes, demonstrations of loyalty contributed in practice to the erosion of social hierarchy. To retake a stray steer from a neighbor's property, foreman Juan de Dios Troncoso insulted and beat rancher Don Toribio Ovejero in the presence of the latter's foreman.[66] Clearly, Troncoso was defending his employer's property with tenacity and determination, but he did so at the expense of respect for social hierarchy. His interpretation of loyalty erased every trace of social difference.

The justice system contributed to create the illusion of social equality. Peons serving as witnesses were able to accuse their own employers, subverting the everyday relation of subordination and dependence. In Navarro in 1838, José Benito Cabrera was cited to provide information about his patron, Romualdo Díaz. Whereas at the beginning of the interrogation

Cabrera remained evasive, as he gained confidence he provided substantial incriminating evidence against his employer.[67] As a result of his declarations, his patron was arrested on multiple charges and sent to jail. Apparently, the justice system was ready to take the word of a peon against his employer and to intrude into the private domain of the great rancher. Certainly, employers of different economic capacity combined fatherly attitudes with economic incentives in different ways. Farmers and small cattle raisers with reduced access to credit were pressed to offer more protection and toleration to their peons than were substantive landowners and merchants. In the context of an uneven competition for laborers, even false promises of protection seemed fair game. State authorities often accused small producers of tolerating intruders and criminals on their lands; as the justice system persecuted *abrigadores* (those who protected deserters and fugitives of the law) with unusual zeal, the risks assumed by small-scale producers who protected fugitives and deserters were high.

Paternalistic attitudes on the part of employers did nothing to alleviate the constraints posed by the labor market and the high mobility of laborers. Offers of protection against state persecution did not suffice, for the mobility of workers was predicated on culturally constructed notions of autonomy. Peons' and peasants' mobility was ultimately rooted in conceptions of independence and equality decanted from the experience of the revolutionary wars. In 1851 peon Juan de Dios Córdoba left good employment at the Palermo works to find a job in the wheat harvest of the Chivilcoy district. To the authorities his excuse sounded like an act of political rebellion: he felt free to leave the governor's estate because "he owed nothing to his patron" Rosas.[68] In 1844 Juan Gutiérrez abandoned his job at Rosas's *matadero* to search for a job in the salting plants or ranches beyond Puente Federación. Asked the motive for his desertion, his answer sounded equally irreverent: "He left the Quinta without permission determined to never return and with the intention of working wherever he chose to [*donde le pareciera*]."[69] This radical sense of personal independence contrasted with the ranchers' notion of "subjection." To peons, a job was called a *conchabo*, a word that denoted casual and occasional work engagements. But to landowners, peons were *sujetados* (tied or fastened) to their positions, implying that they had made a commitment to stay on the ranch. Curiously, even this notion was permeated by market principles, for it was the wage, a cash nexus, that secured and retained workers. It was not unusual among ranchers to talk of workers, foremen, and administrators as being "tied to their wages" (*sujetados a sus salarios*).

Conflicts at the Workplace

By and large, private workplaces, their work relations and conflicts, re-mained outside the gaze of police, justices, and officers, protected as it were by misinformation and lack of interest. Nonetheless, some conflicts at the workplace did reach the public transcript, either because they pro-duced violent outcomes or because the nature of the alleged felonies forced justices to substantiate sumarios (initial phase of a criminal case). Generally, it was the employers who denounced workers for work aban-donment, insubordination, sloppy work, or violence against foremen. Workers rarely appear in the records charging employers of unfair treat-ment; when they do, their voices are too fragmentary and mediated to infer anything about their "consciousness." Commonly, interactions between workers and employers occurred within the confines of the workplace (the ranch, the farm, the slaughterhouse). The issues that motivated those confrontations varied. Questions such as work abandonment, obedience, theft of produce, and the mistreatment of livestock preoccupied em-ployers. Workers in turn complained about the curtailment of acquired benefits: the possibility of residing with their families on the ranch, the punctual payment of wages, and respectful treatment from foremen. One suspects, however, that various other issues might have hindered the nor-malcy of work relations during this period. The prospect of leaving the ranch ("exit") prevented many from expressing their concerns ("voice") and, more important, from engaging in confrontations that could leave traces in the official records.[70]

First, peons' abandonment of work created a source of constant com-plaint from employers. By advancing money to new peons, ranchers as-sumed a great risk in case peons abandoned the ranch before the end of their contract. An account of the money advances granted to one peon, Macedonio Britos, from estancia Loma Verde (Azul) gives us an insight into the magnitude of this problem.[71] In less than a month, between November and December 1844, Britos received advances for a total of $313 in goods and silver, a sum that exceeded his monthly wages. The outlays included provisions of a horse, riding apparel, clothing, and debts con-tracted at the local tavern. In addition, the rancher trusted Britos with $320 in silver and $75 in goods to be delivered to a third party. When the peon ran away with the money, the ranch had to assume the loss.

The practice of cashing advances without delivering the corresponding work was too widespread to be ignored.[72] It involved workers in all types of activities: ranch peons, oxcart drivers, butchers at slaughterhouses, do-mestic servants. Few workers, however, were apprehended and punished for breach of labor contracts. (Justices paid work abandonment less attention than other pressing issues, such as apprehending deserters, murderers, or cattle rustlers.) We know about these incidents from workers who were arrested for other felonies or because they returned to the town of prior employment; in some cases, it is due to the visibility of their work.[73] The great majority, however, were never apprehended.

The exceptional cases captured by judicial records are telling. In 1844 José Barbosa, a cordobés peon employed in oxcart troops by a Dolores rancher, was arrested for not complying with a work contract. A month after signing the contract he got into a fight with his employer, insulted him, and left, taking the advanced wages with him. In 1846 Marcos Costilla, a tucumano oxcart driver, was arrested for work abandonment and unpaid debts. He had received 200 pesos in advance for a trip to the south but, instead of fulfilling his contract, he abandoned the oxcart and tried to return to Tucumán accompanied by his brother. The explanation he gave the police was similar to those of many deserters: he decided to abandon work after the foreman had reprimanded him.[74]

Deception in the compliance of work contracts warned employers about trusting new peons. And employers had reasons to be distrustful. Some peons made breaking contracts a lucrative business. Fermín Saavedra, a day laborer arrested in Lobos in 1840, managed to infuriate the local justice of the peace. We read in Saavedra's criminal file: "He has this justice office fed up with citations and tricks, overloaded with demands against him, because [he] takes work with everybody, to everybody he asks money, and to nobody he serves well, spending most of his time as an idler. He is truly an artful knave when it comes to service." This angry reaction reflected the frustration shared by ranchers and justices over their own lack of power to make peons comply with work promises. Almost the same charged language can be read in the 1840 report of the justice of Navarro about peon Nicolás Morales. The peon had "the habit of going about offering his services to different bosses from whom he takes money in advance and later leaves, because he is a troublemaker and swindler (embrollón), he usurps in this way money from employers."[75]

A second issue of contention was theft. Workers' direct appropriation of goods on the job was a constant preoccupation of employers. Rosas's almost obsessive insistence in his Instrucciones that foremen should police the workers day and night was not so far off the mark. A great deal of direct appropriation was tolerated by employers; the theft of cattle, horses, and hides was not. Foremen, administration, and small cattle raisers usually denounced these violations and wanted the justices to arrest and prosecute the offenders. Similarly, appropriations that entailed deceit or abuse transformed workers into delinquents not worthy of employer tolerance or protection. The question of theft reflected the ambiguity of labor contracts. Meat rations constituted one of the peons' customary rights, but the slaughtering of a cow without permission from the foreman or administrator subjected the worker to an accusation of theft. The same could be said about peons who killed and skinned mares for making their traditional *botas de potro*. In an unwritten system of concessions and gifts aimed at securing peons' loyalty and cooperation, it was the failure to inform the foreman or administrator that transformed a tolerated appropriation into a felony.[76]

The confidence employers rested in their peons, using them to collect money, make payments, and deliver cattle and horses, exposed ranchers to important losses. Peon Manuel Bravo, for example, sold six cows belonging to his employer, used the money to reclaim some pawned goods, and left.[77] More commonly, workers appropriated sheep and cow skins, items they could sell at the nearby tavern as if they were part of the ranch's sales. Peons who abandoned work usually took stolen horses with them. If they returned to the estate within a reasonable time, this appropriation could be considered a "loan" and their temporary absence forgotten; if not, horses constituted a form of compensation for wages in arrears or for past mistreatment.

In *barracas* (warehouses) and *saladeros* (meat-salting plants), where wealth was concentrated in a single space, the risk of losses due to workers' theft was greater. The valuable commodities in stock (hides, sheepskins, tallow, horsehair) and the existence of alternative (illegal) outlets made these establishments particularly vulnerable.[78] The same could be said of brick kilns, where peons could fail to report some loads, separate bricks for their own construction sites, or pocket the income from sales.[79] Oxcart transportation was subject to a great deal of theft. From otter skins to tobacco leaves, from manioc flour sacks to clothes, most loads suffered some degree of attrition during the trip. Similarly, in country stores the theft of money and clothes by attendants was quite common. A limited number of reported cases makes any generalization difficult, but it is clear that work-related theft constituted another arena of confrontation.

A third conflictive issue was discipline. Imposing obedience in workplaces was not an easy task. Many times peons refused to obey commands, talked back to their bosses, or carried out instructions in their own time and manner. Peons were particularly sensitive to the content, tone, and intensity of work orders. They resented verbal abuse—humiliating words, threats, and insults—as an unacceptable form of managerial authority. A simple command given in a mean tone or manner could lead to an exchange of insults between worker and employer and, if no restraint was exercised by either, result in a fight. When foreman Francisco Suárez, a ranch foreman from Quilmes, ordered black peon Gregorio to go out and round up the cattle, he did not anticipate that Gregorio would talk back to him, insult him, and chase him with a knife. According to the foreman's version of the events, the peon's aggressive reaction forced him to use his bolas in self-defense. Only after he struck Gregorio on the head did the latter calm down and return to work. A similar case was reported in Arrecifes in 1837, when a drunken peon assaulted his employer on the ranch. As narrated by Luis González, owner of Fontezuela, peon Angel Puebla had defied his order to start the daily roundup. To punish Puebla's daring behavior (*atrevimiento*), Don Luis got a sword and pistol and tried to intimidate the intractable peon. In this case, the peon responded in kind, wounding his boss. A summary proceeding conducted in Lobos in April 1838 presents us with the case of a peasant farmer who killed his peon over a question of work discipline. Farmer Guillermo Agüero had accused peon Manuel Mosquito of theft and fired him. The day the peon came back to "settle his account," a curious exchange developed: the farmer offered Mosquito beef if he stayed and helped with the slaughter. But as the employer began to admonish the peon for his sloppy work, Mosquito became furious. He had had enough of his boss's criticisms of his work. So, he took a log and began to beat him. Agüero responded, killing Mosquito with his knife. In this case, a peaceful exchange between worker and employer turned violent when "bad language" short-circuited the relationship.[80]

Why did apparently minor disputes about work performance and obedience result in violence?[81] Various factors contributed. Short-term labor contracts, rarely registered and almost never enforced, afforded workers the possibility of abandoning the job as soon as conditions turned unacceptable. The short social distance separating peons from employers also conspired against the imposition of work discipline; feeling mistreated by individuals they considered their social equals, peons tended to react openly and defiantly. Also important was the tendency to interpret work disputes as offenses to manliness and respectability. Peons' sensitivity to insults, improper orders, and criticism shows that, in addition to differences in the labor process, deeper sensibilities were at stake. In a context of unclear social hierarchies and high labor turnover, peons' demands for respect sometimes required asserting their maleness with a weapon in hand.

Disputes over work discipline took other forms as well. Violence directed against property—beating horses, maiming cattle, uprooting trees—was also part of the conflictive relations on the cattle ranch. Juan Silva, a foreman at one of Simon Pereyra's ranches, was fired for his bad manners: he had insulted his patron, uprooted the plants of the *huerta*, and left, carrying the plants with him. On other occasions workers wounded cows and bulls apparently for no reason. In 1846 mayordomo Schoo reported that slaughtered bulls showed large tumors and old wounds, which he attributed to the cruelty of oxcart drivers and farm laborers.[82] The meaning of this violence was not always transparent to employers. In general, they blamed the mistreatment of animals and plants on paysanos' insensitivity, brutality, or inexperience, bracketing out other possibilities.

Foot-dragging and slow work, forms of resistance typical of deferential societies, seem to have been rare in Buenos Aires. In these cases, complaints reflected their own expectations about workers' performance rather than objective evaluations of work rhythm. Remarkably, letters from administrators and foremen did not contain references to the proficiency of individual peons, in part because ranch management was geared to the control of group tasks (branding, roundups, gelding, building fences, etc.). There was no measure of individual productivity, no control of individual work time, and obviously no concern about raising work intensity.

Concerns over gambling and poaching were widespread, but, due to lack of cooperation, ranchers were unable to control these problems. Trying to halt workers' "bad habits" proved illusory in many instances. Administrators who tried to punish peons who played cards or hunted wild animals during work hours risked ridicule, for it was almost impossible to exercise surveillance over every tree or bush on the ranges. Employers' attempts to eliminate gambling during work hours were fraught with difficulties. On the ranch, gambling was tolerated much less than in meat-salting plants, where work was seasonally concentrated and work intensity was greater.

The presence of women on the ranch constituted a fourth conflictive issue. During this period, cattle ranchers began to question the wisdom of allowing peons to bring their spouse or lover with them. Women on the estancia, they argued, increased the incidence of fights among men, produced higher investment outlays (the building of thatched-roof huts), and could stimulate the usurpation of the rancher's land. Peons defended their right to bring their families to the ranch. Peon Crisóstomo González had been working for a year at Don Francisco Bosch's ranch in Loberia when his lover, María Paz, insisted that he take her to the ranch. Don Francisco's decision not to allow women on his estate precipitated the couple's separation.[83] Not all employers were as rigid in this regard. When deserter Manuel Gómez took his wife to Navarro, Don Miguel Peralta offered him employment and the possibility of building his dwelling next to the estate's house.[84] This type of tolerance was a double-edged sword, however: peons could later use it as an entitlement to live free on the estate's land.

Complaints raised by workers about the payment of wages were not common. In the 1820s, workers resorted to the courts as a complementary means of settling disputes. Understandably, this route was open only to workers whose past was "clean" and who did not fear an encounter with the justice system.[85] This incipient confidence in the courts to settle labor disputes seems to have eroded somewhat two decades later, for I found no similar cases during the Rosas period. Instead, peons defended their rightfully earned wages in direct confrontations with employers. The case of Agustín Pereyra, a slave who had to resort to violence to collect his wages, is a good example of this type of interaction. Early in 1837 Pereyra had been rented out to a neighbor from Arrecifes for "country tasks." After he finished this work, he approached his employer to claim his wages. His employer refused to pay. When Pereyra insisted, his boss began to strike him with a sword (palos), forcing Pereyra to use his knife in self-defense.[86]

The rarity of this type of wage dispute might indicate that workers were regularly paid for their work or that if this was not so, they "paid themselves" with goods of equivalent value taken from the workplace. The army's custom of paying regularly "sobre tabla y con dinero en mano" (on the table and with cash) might have contributed to the practice of paying peons and laborers at the end of each task or month. Employers, aware of the possibility of violent reactions from peons, usually paid as agreed. With regard to discounts, the other potentially conflictive issue, the records are silent. Either peons accepted the discounts registered by employers against their wages or they were unprepared to discuss them due to illiteracy or lack of sufficient information about prices.

Violent Interactions

Incidents of violent interactions in the workplace alert us against taking too seriously the two complementary motifs of peons' passivity and ranchers' paternalism. Resentments on the ranch occasionally resulted in individual confrontations between bosses and workers. In February 1840, Santiago González, a santiagueño peon who previously had been fired from D. Boscovino's ranch, came back to the establishment and challenged the foreman to a knife fight. Unwilling to face the angry peon, the foreman escaped, leaving the peon in temporary control of the house. In March

1843, rancher Francisco Laborda had his peon Santos Tolosa arrested; the peon had wounded his foreman in reaction to an apparently rough wake-up call. In January 1837, Chilean peon Pedro Barbosa was arrested in Navarro for the attempted murder of his employer. José Paulino González, arrested in San Nicolás in May 1838, succeeded in this enterprise, killing his employer while the latter slept.[87]

Was this violence related to discipline, wages, productivity, punishment, or other elements of the work relationship? Or were workers simply defending their honor and manhood from perceived humiliation from their bosses? Actually, both elements were operating. Peons interpreted their bosses' behavior in terms of standards of respectability and social equality established during postindependence; in this context, bad treatment was an affront to their masculine free selves and, at the same time, an assault to their conception of social equality. In most cases, the opacity of the records makes it difficult to interpret the motivation for workplace violence. In 1837, black peon José Avila Cochengo stabbed his foreman Alvino Suárez in front of the estanciero without uttering a word. We know that an argument between peon and foreman took place (as reported by other peons), but the source is silent about the nature of their "difference."[88] In cases where the connection between provocation and violence appears more transparent, workers seem to defend their social place (respect) against undue or rough discipline. When asked why he had attacked his boss with a whip, Inocencio Molina answered that the latter had reprimanded and beaten him for taking a piece of meat without permission. Molina responded to this aggression with the first weapon he had at hand. He was unwilling to tolerate either punishment or verbal abuse.[89]

In general, we can assume that most conflictive relations in the workplace were settled without resort to violence. Employers' pragmatic adaptation to the logic of the market meant that higher wages, monetary advances, gifts in clothes, and other incentives could be used to improve work performance. The whip and the stocks, now in disrepute and under greater control by state authorities, no longer rendered docile and productive workers; on the contrary, they could generate a level of resentment that later translated into direct violence.[90] The possibility that peons could challenge their bosses to a knife fight restrained employers from imposing a too rigid discipline in the workplace. Workers also had a vested interest in avoiding violence. Even when the abuse surpassed the peon's threshold of tolerance, it was less costly for the worker to leave the workplace than to engage in violent confrontations with his employer. Besides, there were multiple ways of countering mistreatment and deception: talking back, open complaints, property destruction, and petty larceny.

For these reasons, and also because of its unpredictable outcome, violence was reserved as a means of last resort. On occasion, worker-employer quarrels spilled over into the public sphere, assuming scandalous and violent forms. In such cases, the outcome could not be anticipated. The fight at the tavern produced a disturbing leveling among contenders, making the engagement extremely dangerous for both parties. Knife fights outside of the sphere of production were regularly explained as the result of alcohol, offended masculinity, bad manners, or the irritability of one of the parties. It is difficult in these circumstances to connect these public contentions with tensions in the workplace. When employers and peons resorted to the knife to settle their disputes, the imposition of work discipline, the payment of debts, or the return of stolen goods was already a lost cause. In a knife fight, honor and masculinity were the chief stakes, overshadowing all other concerns.

Conclusions: Workers, Self-Activity, and the Labor Market

This chapter throws doubt on the historical construction of a passive peon class dominated by paternalistic ranchers. Passing comments by peons and peasants during judicial interrogations provide us with fragments of evidence to reconstruct productive relations within the private economy. These enunciations tend to disarm the powerful and persistent construct of "peaceful cattle ranchers," a fiction founded on the suppression of social or class conflict. The fragmented voices of the subaltern reemerge to undermine the established historical consensus, presenting the imposition of paternalism and deference as a project ridden with obstacles. The perambulation of workers in a relatively large space prevented the formation of personal ties of dependence between patrons and peons. To the extent that workers defended their right to abandon work, there was little room for the development of ranchers' paternalism.

Ranches, farms, meat-salting plants, and cattle droves were not free from contestation from below. Disagreements between workers and employers developed around issues of debt, unfulfilled contracts, women, punishment, and undue treatment, disagreements that in some cases generated violent confrontations. Were these conflicts at the workplace *class confrontations*? Not quite: issues of respect and manhood were often mixed with economic demands; more often than not, complaints were put forth by individuals rather than by groups; and, most important, a collective identity and sense of injustice and exploitation *as workers* had not yet developed. The undefined content of labor contracts was often at the root of the tensions within the workplace. In Marxist terminology, these were confrontations over the question of "real subsumption" of labor, the actual extraction of labor from workers. Workers' unchecked mobility, their occasional disregard for work commitments, and their failure to accept the authority of foremen at all times produced intense animosity. Wages and benefits generated, by and large, less intense conflicts.

The confrontations we have encountered were mild and limited compared with peasant rebellions, revolts, and social revolutions. They were skirmishes on the edges of contractual agreements, tough forms of bargaining used to enforce common, unwritten understandings about obligations and rights not clearly defined in the work contracts. Given the ease with which peons abandoned their employment, it is not hard to understand why the state and its functionaries attracted a greater degree of hostility. Government abuses were more visible and arbitrary to paysanos than the commands given by foremen, the punishments ordered by hacendados or the insults uttered in the yard of a meat-salting workshop. Recruiting parties, requisition of horses and cattle, military drills, felons in the stocks, and executions—the multiple manifestations of the presence and power of the provincial state—formed part of the collective experience of rural communities. Humiliation and exploitation in the private productive sphere, on the other hand, were experienced individually and dealt with directly and on the spot—with voice, knife, or flight.

Which were the tactics used by subalterns to improve their condition? Resort to the courts and knife fights were probably two extremes on a continuum of actions by which workers defended their income and autonomy. In a context dominated by informal work agreements, work abandonment was perhaps the most effective weapon. Peons considered low wages and bad treatment sufficient reasons to quit an employment.[91] When voicing a complaint was not sufficient, they abandoned their employment. This alternative, of course, was made possible by the postindependence conditions of labor markets. The relentless attitude to change occupation or to move elsewhere could be maintained only in a labor-scarce economy.

What does this tell us about the subaltern's integration into market society and culture? (1) That wages and other economic incentives must have informed workers' decisions to migrate or move from one locality to the next. (Other factors such as military recruitment, police persecution, family connections, and the march of the civil wars also influenced their decisions.) (2) That wage bargaining in workplaces constituted an important dimension of subaltern activity. Wage bargaining is generally a contested process; the wages and conditions agreed on result from repeated petitions and elaborated arguments, reinforced by credible threats of job abandonment.

The records hint at this contested process. Foremen reminded ranch administrators that their peons were expecting a raise, hinting about the possible consequences of not attending to peons' complaints.[92] Because the valorization of capital was at stake, administrators often took these warnings very seriously.

Looked at through the lens of ranchers' instructions to administrators and of their practical incentive systems, peons appear as cunning economic agents. They seem to have bargained with employers about wages, rations, leaves, and other benefits.[93] They continued to seek protection from the powerful, to build reciprocity bonds with middling paysanos, and to resort to family connections at times of economic malaise. But their tactical movements and actions were guided also by market signals: the incentive system built on the ranch and the rumors gathered at taverns about the need for laborers in certain areas, localities, or ranches. The peon, after all, was an agent motivated by self-interest, a proprietor of a valuable commodity, a wanderer in search of income, work, and respect.

CHAPTER 3

Provincianos' Paths to Work

Provincianos or, more specifically, *arribeños* (upper or northern migrants) came from other provinces to work in Buenos Aires. Placed from the start in a subaltern position, that of being "transients," provincianos struggled to find their place in the booming economy of the province and in the political life of rural communities. Northern migrants faced special opportunities in the labor market but also important disadvantages in the legal terrain. They were at the same time welcomed as laborers and suspected as delinquents and potential deserters. Their double utility as workers and soldiers conditioned both their acceptance by local communities and their integration into the categorical slots defined by the new state order.

The tension between political incorporation and economic insertion made provincianos a particular object of state concern. Judicial and military authorities interrogated these migrants about their origins, destination, place of residence, and prior employment. Through these records, we can reconstruct the mental geography of migratory workers, focusing on the itineraries or pathways they followed in their search for jobs and personal safety. The activities of northern migrants as job seekers also bring to light an important dimension of subaltern experience: the economic and family motivations that guided their perambulations through the territory of the forming nation. Through sketchy passages and references made to their interrogators, we learn about the information provincianos had of the different regions of the province, about the spatial preferences of first-comers, about the importance of family in facilitating their journeys, and about their explicit search for jobs and relatives in Buenos Aires province.

The ambivalent position of these subalterns in relation to state authorities makes their itineraries and work experience all the more interesting. In this chapter, I reconstruct their job-seeking strategies, their attempts to integrate into the host local communities, their conceptions of family and nation. Like other peasants and peons, migrants were subject to state surveillance and classification. They suffered coercion, and yet they managed to sustain long-term strategies of economic survival. The civil war left crucial marks on their narratives and on their experiences of dispersed families and impoverished conditions at home. Thus, many ventured south trying to improve their economic condition and to reunite their broken families.

Welcome but Suspect: The State's Perspective

In 1832, in the aftermath of a bloody campaign against the unitarios in Córdoba and Santiago del Estero, federalist troops returned to Buenos Aires. The temporary peace brought back also the traditional migratory current from the northern provinces. Concerned with the increased presence of migrant workers in the district, Villa de Luján's police chief put to the consideration of General Rosas two related policy issues: first, how to deal with provinciano ex-soldiers who had remained in the district (partido) without known employment; second, how to treat those who had come from the interior with the declared purpose of working but had failed to enlist for military duty.[1] Did seasonal laborers deserve to be exempted from military conscription? Were demobilized soldiers from the upper provinces subject to vagrancy laws? The tension between military and economic uses of the migrant workforce preoccupied local state authorities.

In his reply, Rosas recommended treating the two kinds of migrants differently. For ex-soldiers turned into "vagrants," he recommended a lenient attitude: "For now, you may admonish them and exhort them to labor." A federalist veteran deserved respect, even if temporarily not engaged in any useful occupation. With time, they would become producers and, quite probably, permanent residents. With regard to seasonal migrants, he advised temporary legalization. The commissar was to extend work licenses to all who could prove they had come from the interior seeking employment. Northern labor migrants had to be considered a valuable economic resource but could not be given the status of residents or neighbors. At least, not yet. These permits, he added, should be extended only to the new arrivals, not to those who already lived in the district. How to proceed with those "in between"—those who were neither ex-soldiers nor recent migrants—Rosas did not specify.

The acceptance of provincianos into the province's workforce, Rosas acknowledged, would lead, sooner or later, to a process of social and political incorporation. This required close monitoring by the state. Though welcome as laborers, there were many questions as to whether northern migrants would become good citizens of Buenos Aires and, by extension, zealous guardians of the Federal Cause. Because of this, fine distinctions were required from the local authorities. Those who had rendered valuable service to the federal fatherland deserved full freedom to move and work as long as they were honest workers and neighbors. On the other hand, those migrants who, due to their transient condition, did not aspire to full rights of citizenship deserved only temporary work permits. They were to be treated as foreigners, as a mere labor force.

Six years later (1838), the issue of how to treat migratory laborers reappeared, this time in connection with the question of militia registration and service. The justice of Guardia de Luján asked Rosas's *edecán* (aide-de-camp) for instructions concerning the treatment of provincianos who came annually to the wheat harvest.[2] It was not clear to the justice if seasonal migrants should be expected to enroll immediately in the militias. Apparently, provincial migrants had been arriving earlier than expected (it was traditional for them to arrive in December, when the wheat harvest started) and, as temporary visitors, had petitioned for exceptions to the militia law. The governor considered the matter and ordered the justice to proceed on a case-by-case basis. Though trusting the justice's judgment, Rosas wanted him to distinguish between seasonal and permanent migrants. To assist him in these decisions, the governor instructed: "Take for instance, a peon who has just arrived from his country. If he is well-known [*conocido*] and understands clearly that he will remain only a few months as a transient [*transeúnte*], in this case he has enough with a work permit [the *papeleta de conchavo*] and with the justice's assurance that [the subject] is a well-known transient beyond suspicion. But, if he is an unknown man, then the justice should know what must be done according to the orders and circulars in force." That is, the migrant was to be detained and interrogated to determine his latest place of residence and occupation. "If [the subject] is well-known," Rosas continued, "or there are reasons to consider him honest, and he remains longer than usual without returning to his land, then *he should not be considered transient* [my emphasis]. In such a case, [he] should be enrolled in the militia and, if he disobeys, be sent to serve in the regular army."

Clearly, the Dictator wanted the justice to distinguish between migrants who came to the province looking for temporary work and migrants who came to stay. Only the latter would become citizens, once they enrolled in the militias. *Milicianos* were considered residents or *vecinos* and, as such, endowed with political rights and subject to military duties (see Cansanello 1995). The transient could not aspire to this condition; he was just a laborer, and therefore, his legality could be assured with a simple work permit. In this classificatory exercise, it was crucial to judge migrants according to their connections in the local community (*conocidos/descono-cidos*) and in terms of their conduct (*honrado/delincuente*) before allocating rights of residency. In both cases, it was the local community that contributed much of the opinion on which these distinctions were to be based.

Distinguishing transient from resident migrants was essential to the allocation of the rights (citizenship) and obligations (military service) among the newcomers. In addition, state authorities were interested in identifying migrants who might jeopardize the establishment of law and order in rural communities. The influx of migrants who remained in Buenos Aires province for longer periods of time created anxiety among political and judicial authorities. Hence, the government established clear rules of access to residence-citizenship: first, temporary work permits, then militia enrollment and practical citizenship. Serving a term in the regular army was the punishment reserved for those migrants who, staying in the province, failed to enlist in the militias. This two-step process of legal incorporation, tied to the basic transient/resident distinction, served also to provide for defense and justice at the local level without disrupting the functioning of the seasonal labor market, so necessary to the economic well-being of the province.

In November 1851, responding to Governor Urquiza's *pronunciamiento* (a document challenging Rosas's authority over the Confederation), Rosas called for the general enlistment of militias. To support the federalist cause (against the "Loco Traidor"), all districts had to produce a list of all men between 18 and 45 able to bear arms. Now (on the eve of Caseros) that military and political demands were pressing, the state desperately needed the services of provincianos. But, curiously, Governor Rosas was hesitant about enlisting recently arrived migrants. After decades of peasants' quiet resistance against compulsory enlistment, Rosas knew he could not always depend on the support of northern migrants. He could rely only on "true federalists." So, when he ordered the justice of Chivilcoy to deliver four hundred of these militiamen ready for combat, the governor was cautious: "You must endeavor, when possible, that, among the 400, those who are not sons of this province [Buenos Aires], show more than six years' residence in it. For example, a córdobes, santafesino, santiagueño, tucumano, mendocino, puntano, sanjuanino, etc. having more than six years of residence is preferable to one having only one, two, three, or four. Thus, the more years of residence they have in the province the more preferable they are for the purpose of military service."[3] What was the rationale for this policy? Did Rosas believe that long-term residents made better soldiers? Did he suspect that recent migrants would not respond to the call to arms?

Or was this a way to distinguish between migrant workers and migrant citizens?

Rosas's insistence on the necessity of recruiting long-term residents underscores a preoccupation not present in his 1838 instructions: the possibility that recent migrants would later desert the federalist army and join the enemy forces. Their illegal or immoral behavior was no longer at issue: what concerned the government was the political loyalty of provincianos, transformed over time into "practical citizens." In 1838, six months to a year was the line dividing a transient from a permanent migrant; this was the time needed by the community to judge the migrant's good behavior and cooperation. In 1851, this standard was no longer sufficient. Now, six years were needed to prove the migrant's commitment to the federal cause, that is, to full partisan citizenship. Apparently, the criterion had shifted from economic to political considerations, from a concern about labor resources to a preoccupation with residential empowerment and political loyalty.

Between 1838 and 1851 social and political conditions in the Buenos Aires countryside had changed. Now migrants constituted a large proportion of the population and their voices were more pressing in the life of local communities. In Chivilcoy, for instance, that enrollment list included 1,458 active and reserve militiamen. Many of them were provincianos, men who, responding to the invitation from the government of Buenos Aires, had taken residence in the town and become citizens.[4] They were no longer a mere labor force. In other rural towns, the same process took place. Taking advantage of a growing economy and an open polity, northern migrants had formed families and settled in Buenos Aires, becoming residents and militiamen. Empowered by the rights of citizens, they felt they could negotiate about further military service.

Rosas's advice in 1851 was a clear recognition that provincianos could act politically; they could support or undermine the defensive capabilities of the province. Newcomers, unapprenticed in the rhetoric and sentiments of Rosista federalism, could not understand the necessity of the impending war. Many of them were perhaps too young to have heard about the federalist "restorations" (popular movements to restore true federalists in government) or about the heroic battles of the federalist army in defense of the fatherland. Consequently, the defense of the province was better left to long-term residents, presumably good citizens and *buenos federales*.

Official policy toward migrants from other provinces betrays the tensions between private and public demands for rural laborers. Though the Rosista state tried to accommodate both demands, interfering as little as possible with seasonal and permanent labor migrations, at crucial times the subordination of private interests to political and military objectives was inevitable. During peacetime, authorities left transient migrants un-molested (if they were employed) and imposed militia service only on those who became residents. In time of war, the issue of residency acquired political importance. All permanent residents, whether native to the province or not, needed to contribute to the war effort. This was an obligation that accrued to migrants who, after long residence in the province, had acquired social and political rights similar to those of *porteños* (natives of Buenos Aires province). When the state needed to cash in its previous enfranchisement of provincianos, distinctions between short- and long-term residents became politically and strategically crucial.

A Common Labor Market

Early in the postindependence, when migrants from the upper provinces began to appear to be the solution to the chronic shortage of labor in the pampas, ranchers or their agents traveled to the inland provinces in search of laborers. Apparently, the new landed bosses offered the migrants wages and conditions of employment that compared favorably with those prevalent in the provinces.[5] The consolidation of an annual migratory flow from the northern provinces, particularly during periods of relative peace in Buenos Aires, presented ranchers and farmers with the possibility of substituting northern migrants for local, temporary, undependable peons. Thus, provincianos and porteños began to compete for employment, wandering from one district to another.

Did both groups compete on an equal basis in the local labor market? Or were internal migrants at a disadvantage with respect to native-born workers in terms of legal protection, the estimation of their employers, family assistance, and social connections? The question is important, for the labor market was the door through which northern migrants entered into the gradual process of social and political incorporation into the life of rural communities. If it can be demonstrated that provincianos were equally prepared as porteños to face labor market conditions, then there is less reason to think of northern migrants as a special sort of subaltern. If a common, nonsegmented labor market existed the perambulations of migrants in Buenos Aires province can be taken as representative of other itinerant workers who left fewer traces in the archives. Hence, following the spatial itineraries of northern migrants, we can begin to understand the process of sociopolitical incorporation of "outsiders" and, more

6. Oxcart Drivers. As depicted in this engraving, *provincianos* usually traveled as members of oxcart troops. They traveled with their families and carried with them all sorts of provisions, cooking utensils, and basic house furnishings. Carlos Morel, *Una hora antes de partir*, engraved by Gregorio Ibarra. Reproduced from F. Chávez, *Iconografía de Rosas y de la Federación* (1972).

crucially, the relationship between labor market mobility and the expansion of rural citizenship.

Evidence taken from criminal and military files (filiaciones) (N = 525) points to the existence of common attributes for both groups of workers. In the eyes of the military and the rural police, provinciano and porteño detainees looked quite similar. Most belonged to the lower strata of the rural population, those classified as "country people" or "country peons." With regard to employment opportunities, there seems to be no significant structural difference. Among those arrested, day laborers, peons, and people classified as doing rural labor constitute the majority, regardless of their origin (see Table 3.1). Differences in the employment attained by the two groups are minor: provincianos outnumbered porteños in jobs related to farming, crafts, and transportation. The reverse was true among ranchers, foremen, merchants, and workers lacking employment. These differences underscore the strengths and weaknesses of northern migrants in the Buenos Aires labor market. Better prepared in certain skills (crafts and farming), northern migrants were arrested more often for vagrancy (a code word for being unknown to the community) or for not carrying a passport when conducting animals or commodities to the market.

TABLE 3.1 Occupations of Natives from Other Provinces and
Natives of Buenos Aires Province (in percentages)

Occupations	Natives from other provinces	Natives of Buenos Aires province	Other	Total
Peasant farmers	5.2	2.8	8.0	4.3
Peons	37.0	38.0	16.0	36.2
Day laborers	15.0	14.0	20.0	15.0
Country workers	11.0	13.0	—	11.1
Foremen	0.8	2.8	—	1.7
Landowners	0.8	2.3	4.0	1.7
Transportation	15.0	6.6	16.0	11.1
Rural industry	3.4	2.8	8.0	3.4
Artisans	6.0	2.8	16.0	5.1
Commerce	4.3	6.1	—	4.9
Personal service	0.4	0.5	—	0.4
Military	0.4	2.3	4.0	1.5
Other	—	1.4	4.0	0.9
Unemployed	0.8	4.7	4.0	2.8
TOTAL	100.0	100.0	100.0	100.0
N	233	213	25	470

Source: Filiaciones (N=525)

With regard to their marital status, migrants were not different from local workers. Most of the arrested were single (73 percent), with little difference between provincianos (70 percent) and porteños (77 percent). Obviously, the nature of the sample (police arrests) contains a bias against married men. For reasons that are not difficult to imagine, the women and children who accompanied migrants and itinerant workers escaped the official transcript.[6] And, quite likely, state inquisitors considered a consensual marriage as no marriage at all. But labor demand itself contributed to the asymmetry shown in the data. Given ranchers' bias against married men, single men had a better chance in the labor market.

If age was important in determining the bargaining power of job seekers vis-à-vis employers, northern migrants were not among the weakest labor suppliers (see Table 3.2). Whereas 49 percent of the porteños arrested were under 25 years of age, only 34 percent of the provincianos arrested were in that age group. Above the age of 30, migrants from the interior outnumbered local workers in a ratio of 1.5 to 1 (41 percent versus 27 per-

Age (years)	Natives of Buenos Aires province	Natives from other provinces	Other	Total
Less than 15	5.0	0.8	—	2.7
15 to 19	13.4	10.8	3.6	11.4
20 to 24	30.6	22.9	28.6	26.4
25 to 29	23.5	24.9	14.3	23.3
30 to 34	7.6	16.5	10.7	11.8
35 to 44	15.1	16.9	17.9	15.8
45 and over	4.6	7.2	24.9	6.8
TOTAL	100.0	100.0	100.0	100.0
N	238	249	28	527

Source: Filiaciones (N=525)

cent).[7] It is unlikely that these age differences were the product of arrest policies. As Table 3.2 shows, the local police did not target any particular age group: they arrested with the same frequency youngsters 15 to 19 and more mature men age 30 to 34. To them, every delinquent or suspicious person was a potential soldier, regardless of age. Hence, other explanations seem more plausible. Apparently, provinciano families preferred to send their older male kin to work in Buenos Aires, keeping the women and the young to take care of the family farm back in Santiago, Córdoba, Tucumán, or San Luis.

Still, there were some minor differences. State inquisitors found northern migrants to be of a darker complexion than the natives of Buenos Aires. There were more trigueños—sun-burned mestizos—(55 percent vs. 41 percent) and aindiados—people with Indian features—(6 percent vs. 2 percent) among the provincianos and relatively more whites among the porteños (39 percent compared with 20 percent). The proportion of blacks and mulattos was similar (around 15 percent). Also, officers and justices perceived that a greater proportion of natives from Buenos Aires province looked like "town people" (14 percent compared with 3 percent among provincianos). There were also differences in reading skills, migrants from other provinces showing a slightly lower rate of literacy than porteños (12 percent vs. 18 percent).

These minor differences in color, literacy, and appearance, however, did not translate into differences of aptitude for military service. To the provincial state, both groups of men were equally valuable as potential soldiers.

Most (95 and 97 percent) were considered horsemen (*hombres de acaballo*) and classified as "good for cavalry" (73 percent) or for both cavalry and infantry (7 percent).[8] And, except for a minority of "town people," the rest were a homogeneous mass of peasants and peons, of similar dress and equestrian skills, who could be subsumed under the state category of *clase de peón de campo*.

Nor did these differences create conditions for discrimination in the labor market. Employers could have used the darker complexion and lower literacy of northern migrants to place them in a lower stratum of the labor hierarchy, but apparently this did not happen. The occupational structure of both groups of workers looks strikingly similar. In part, this was due to the special skills and work experience that northern migrants brought to the labor market. In addition, differences among both groups were minimized by the very nature of the Buenos Aires labor market. The chronic scarcity of laborers, the malleability of labor demand in terms of occupations and skills, and the persistent alternatives to wage labor tended to reduce discrimination among job seekers of different origins.

Arrest statistics highlight a particular segment of the workforce—the wandering proletariat—among whom differences in origin were inconsequential to employment. In their search for work, both groups (provincianos and porteños) were subject to the same pressures and incentives: a given composition of labor demand, leaning strongly toward farm laborers, cattle-ranching peons, and good-for-all-work day laborers; and a certain distribution of policing across the territory, determining the localities and occupations at greater risk of arrest. To be sure, some "resources" were not so equally distributed. Northern migrants had fewer initial social connections to establish themselves as farmers, foremen, or merchants, and they were more likely to engage in unskilled jobs related to transportation. But, in compensation, they were older on average and possessed greater skill in the artisan trades and longer work experience in agriculture.

Migrants' Spatial Preferences

Buenos Aires province was not a homogeneous territory. Different regions offered different opportunities of employment and levels of personal security. The northern coastal area (an area that included the farmlands of the districts of Pergamino, Arrecifes, Areco, and Zárate) offered migrants agricultural employment as well as rapid escape to the coasts of the Río de la Plata and the delta. The northwest-southeast corridor was the route taken by northern migrants on their journey to Buenos Aires. It traversed

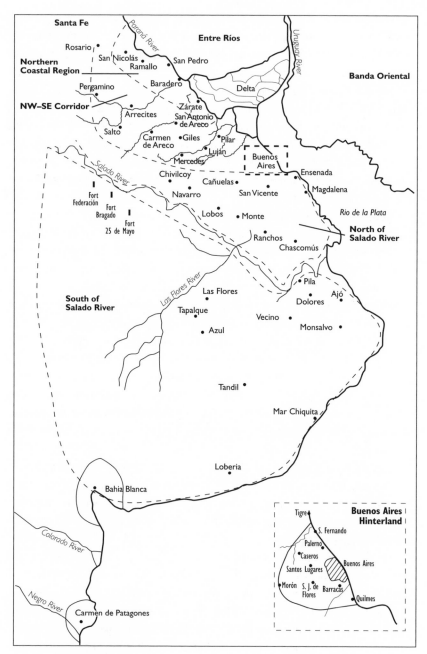

Santa Fe

Rosario

San Nicolás
Ramallo

Northern
Coastal Region

Pergamino

NW–SE Corridor

Arrecites

Salto

Carmen
de Areco

Chivilcoy

Entre Ríos

San Pedro

Baradero

Zárate
San Antonio
de Areco

Giles

Mercedes

Paraná River

Delta

Pilar
Luján

Navarro

Lobos

Fort
Federación

Fort
Bragado

Fort
25 de Mayo

South of
Salado River

Salado River

Cañuelas

San Vicente

Monte

Ranchos

Las Flores River

Las Flores

Tapalque

Azul

Vecino

Tandil

Mar Chiquita

Loberia

Bahia Blanca

Colorado River

Negro River

Carmen de Patagones

Banda Oriental

Uruguay River

Buenos
Aires

Ensenada

Magdalena

Rio de la Plata

North of
Salado River

Chascomús

Pila

Dolores

Ajó

Monsalvo

Buenos Aires
Hinterland

Tigre

S. Fernando

Palerno

Caseros

Santos Lugares

Morón

S. J. de
Flores

Barracas

Buenos Aires

Quilmes

Buenos Aires Province c. 1840

towns settled in the colonial period, with close-knit communities, better policing, and fairly segmented landholding: Rojas, Salto, Fortín de Areco, Giles, Villa Luján, and Guardia de Luján, among others. North of the Salado River was a region where cattle and sheep ranchers had settled since the 1820s. From west to east a string of recently established towns (Chivilcoy, Navarro, Lobos, Monte, Ranchos, and Chascomús) provided farm and ranch employment as well as points of provision and marketing for those traveling from Buenos Aires to the "New South." Finally, the region south of the Salado River was settled by cattle ranches, generally located in areas recently "conquered" and, consequently, not well protected from Indian attacks.

Both provincianos and porteños tended to concentrate in the areas of older settlement, in the regions of the northwest-southeast corridor, north of the Salado River, and the Buenos Aires hinterland. In these areas resided 53 percent of the detainees (see Table 3.3). Only 15 percent of the sample resided in the New South. Areas such as the northern coast and the frontier were the least preferred regions, receiving 8.7 percent and 1.2 percent of the sample. The ranking of spatial preferences differed among provincianos and porteños. Whereas both groups ranked Buenos Aires and the hinterland in first place, provincianos ranked second the region south of the Salado River, whereas porteños ranked this region fourth, after the northwest-southeast corridor and north of the Salado. That is, although both groups tended to prefer areas of older settlement, northern migrants were more willing to venture into the lands south of the Salado River.

Clearly, both groups avoided areas subject to attacks from Indian *malones* (invasions of towns or ranches) or littoral *caudillos*. This might indicate a common aversion (or precaution) of provincianos and porteños to areas with less legality and safety but which, labor being in scarce supply, provided better-paying jobs.

Due to their condition, northern migrants appear to be a more mobile group, less attached to a particular residence or district: 32 percent of provincianos (compared with 13 percent of porteños) showed no fixed address in the province. In addition, 8 percent still considered their native province as their permanent address. Their relative lack of attachment made migrants suspect to police and judicial authorities. Local authorities found the "informal" papers carried by northern migrants a motive for detention and interrogation. But against this suspicion operated the orders of the Dictator: not to disturb migrants if they were just looking for seasonal employment or if they had a relatively short term of residence in the province.

TABLE 3.3 Patterns of Residence: Natives from Other Provinces versus
Natives of Buenos Aires Province (in percentages)

Region	Natives from other provinces	Natives of Buenos Aires province	Other	Total
Northern coastal	4.6	3.1	—	8.7
NW–SE corridor	12.1	19.4	7.7	15.0
Buenos Aires hinterland	16.7	24.3	34.6	21.0
North of Salado River	11.7	23.4	15.4	17.0
South of Salado River	15.0	14.9	11.5	14.8
Frontier	0.4	1.8	3.8	1.2
Interior provinces	7.9	0.5	3.8	4.3
Without fixed address	31.7	12.6	23.1	23.0
TOTAL	100.0	100.0	100.0	100.0
N	240	222	26	488

Note: Northern coastal = Zárate, San Nicolás, San Pedro, Baradero; NW–SE corridor =
Pergamino, Arrecifes, Salto, S.A. de Areco, Fortín de Areco, S.A. de Giles, Gda. de
Luján, Luján, Pilar; Buenos Aires hinterland = Ciudad, San Fernando, Santos Lugares,
Morón, Palermo, S.J. de Flores, Barracas, San Isidro, Quilmes; North of Salado =
Navarro, Lobos, San Vicente, Cañuelas, Monte, Ranchos, Chascomús, Ensenada,
Magdalena, San Borombón, Matanza; South of Salado = Pila, Tordillo, Dolores, Vecino,
Monsalvo, Ajó, Tuyú, Mar Chiquita, Lobería, Tandil, Chapaleufú, Azul, Las Flores,
Mulitas, Bragado, Tapalquén; Frontier = Patagones, Bahía Blanca, Delta del Paraná
Source: Filiaciones (N=525)

In the absence of information about wage differentials, the evidence
presented here speaks against the segmentation of labor markets along
lines of origin. Both provincianos and porteños had similar profiles,
showed similar preferences regarding districts of residence, and had access to the same kinds of employment. If anything, the evidence shows
that migrants from the interior provinces were slightly better prepared to
bargain with employers; on average, they were older, more skillful, and
prepared to travel longer distances in search of better employment. In
compensation, porteños showed greater social connections at the local
level. But this advantage evaporated over time as northern migrants were
able to settle and make themselves part of the local society and polity. Also,
the greater mobility of migrants gave them a stronger bargaining position:
in their perambulations through the rural districts provincianos held open
the possibility of returning to their province of origin, and, for this reason,
employers had to treat them with care.

To employers, the mobility of provincianos was threatening, difficult to manage, and costly. In January 1847 Laureano Ramírez, foreman of Chacabuco, one of Rosas's ranches, wrote to his patron complaining of the shortage of ranch hands. In vain, he had tried to keep the herds within reach (*sugetarlas a rodeo*), using peons ordinarily engaged in other tasks. But this was not enough. New peons were needed if the ranch was to round up all the strays from the three puestos (work stations within the ranch). To complicate matters, northern migrants employed at the ranch were talking of returning to their provinces.[9] The approaching end of the wheat harvest anticipated this inevitable outcome. To accompany cousins, brothers, fathers, and sons on the journey back to Santiago or Córdoba, peons would soon abandon the ranch. How to stop this return migration was beyond the foreman's powers; it was like an unavoidable fact of life.

As Rosas's instructions make clear, the status of provincianos was ambiguous. While their participation in the labor market was welcome and protected by the Rosista state in consideration of the essential services they provided to the local economy, local authorities looked at them with suspicion. According to the reports provided by justices of the peace, in eleven of eighteen rural districts provincianos outnumbered porteños and foreigners among the arrestees (see Table 6.8 in chapter 6). The temporary nature of their engagements with the local communities and, more important, their ambiguous position between transient and resident made these subalterns the focus of state surveillance. But we should not confuse the economic and the politicomilitary personas of these subalterns. It was provincianos' lack of fulfillment of their military duties to the state that preoccupied authorities the most. Hence, the complex rules devised to distinguish when they ceased to be transients and became residents. As workers, they were treated the same as the native-born.

Porteños and provincianos were job seekers with a clear vision of the spatial dimension of labor markets. They concentrated their search for employment in areas of dense population and older colonization, where the chances of getting a job were greater. Many gravitated toward Buenos Aires and its hinterland, at least as part of a longer work itinerary. Southern districts, an area of vast ranches, a less visible state presence, and, hence, greater arbitrariness of the powerful, were less preferred as destinations. In this regard, both groups of workers coincided. Their perambulations in search of employment and residence/citizenship had to take into account the relative probability of getting a job and also questions of personal security, legality, and freedom. On balance, southern ranchers' offer of "refuge" to itinerant peons seemed less appealing.

Not So Traditional Migrants

Apparently, the migrants of the 1840s came predominantly from areas that had had direct participation in the civil wars: 46 percent of those arrested (with extant personal files or *filiaciones*) came from Santiago del Estero and another 29 percent came from Córdoba; the rest were native to Mendoza (7 percent), Tucumán (7 percent), Santa Fé (4 percent), San Juan (4 percent), Entre Ríos, San Luis, and Corrientes.[10] All of these areas had been sites of military confrontations since the early 1820s. As they passed through these provinces, the armies forcefully enlisted soldiers, transporting them to other provinces and, eventually, to Buenos Aires, where the headquarters of the federal army were located. The civil wars, it could be argued, disrupted the gender and age balance of peasant economies in the interior, shifting the burden of rural work to women, children, and older adult males.

Economic, military, and cultural factors influenced the decision to migrate to Buenos Aires. Whereas the civil wars provided the impetus for the relocation of the population in the 1820s and 1830s, later the expansion of commerce seems to have been more influential. The booming cattle ranching economy of Buenos Aires and its correlate, the recovery and expansion of traffic along old colonial roads, acted as magnets for potential migrants (Brown 1976, 1994; Assadourian 1983). After 1842, as the country went into a period of relative tranquility, northern migrants began to travel to the littoral by the thousands. Not by coincidence, 64 percent of our sample of northern migrants correspond to the period 1844–1846.[11] Besides peace and expanded job opportunities, the consolidation of labor migrations resulted from a process of communication embedded in culture. A set of stories of successful migrations (rumors, anecdotes, and hearsay) and the material evidence shown by returned migrants (new clothes, fabrics, and riding apparel, silver coins in the belt) contributed to feed the migratory flow.

To an extent, the migration of santiagueños, cordobeses, and puntanos was the continuation of practices known in the colonial period (see Farberman 1997; Garavaglia 1993; Mateo 1993b). During the late eighteenth century, laborers from Santiago, Córdoba, and San Luis made their way to the northwestern region of Buenos Aires province in search of work in the wheat harvest. This was apparently a short-term, seasonal migration.[12] In the first two decades of the nineteenth century, as the economic condition of the interior deteriorated in relation to Buenos Aires, santiagueños and cordobeses began to move in family groups, seeking more permanent settlements in the new cattle and farming frontier. During the Rosas era, this pattern was altered by the political and disciplinary practices of the state. Now provincianos had to consider modes of social and economic insertion that took into account the new political and military reality. Still, better-paid employment constituted the main stimulus to migrate and seasonal migrations were prominent, but as the assessment of the risks and opportunities involved in the process changed, so did paysanos' strategies to circumvent state policing. The presence of staged migrations, the direction of migrants toward areas of reduced police control, and the massive return of migrants during periods of intense recruitment speak of the adaptation of colonial migratory habits to the new conditions.

Seasonal migrations related to the wheat harvest were much less common by the 1840s than during the late colonial period. Information about the months the prisoners arrived in Buenos Aires province indicates that harvest months (December and January) represented only 13 percent (5 and 8 percent, respectively) of all arrivals. Greater or similar proportions of migrants came in June (17 percent), February (15 percent), May (13 percent), and September (10 percent). Separating the same data by season, we find that 28 percent arrived in Buenos Aires in summer, 27 percent in fall, 32 percent in winter, and 13 percent in spring.[13] Without rejecting the presence of seasonal labor migrations, this evidence points to the existence of other types of migration. Arrest statistics taken from *Partes de Novedades* confirm this finding. The largest number of migrants did not come to work in the harvest season. Provincianos expected to find employment in various lines of work; their migration had transformed into a more permanent movement accompanying the flows of commerce.

Complex strategies of survival guided the perambulations of northern migrants in the Buenos Aires countryside. Farm labor might have provided part of the income generated by a migrant, but it was not the only alternative. Consider the case of Juan Pablo Sánchez, a santiagueño arrested in Guardia de Luján in 1838.[14] He arrived in the province in August, moving immediately into the city, where he worked until it was time for the wheat harvest. In December he moved to the farm area surrounding Guardia de Luján; by March he was back in Santiago. A temporary worker, Sánchez did not consider it convenient to travel to Buenos Aires just for the harvest; he arrived four months earlier, staying longer in the city's hinterland than in the farm area. This was probably an indication of the relative income that could be derived from urban and rural employment. Provincianos kept coming to the farmlands, but their status was no longer clearly identifiable as that of temporary migrants.

Provincianos' stay in Buenos Aires before their arrest is not consistent with a pattern of seasonal migration. True, 51 percent of the arrested had been in the province for less than a year, but the rest had stayed longer: 17 percent between one and two years, 13 percent between three and five years, 8 percent between six and ten years, and 11 percent for ten years or more. In analyzing this evidence we should keep in mind that the rural police tended to arrest people little known to the towns, namely recent migrants (60 percent of the arrested had reached Buenos Aires between 1841 and 1845). Hence, it is likely that a much larger proportion of the town's population was made up of permanent migrants, people already incorporated into the social and political community. The growing disparity of economic opportunities between the interior and Buenos Aires and the relative tranquility of the latter favored the settlement of migrants there.

Implied in the provincianos' decision to migrate to Buenos Aires was the prospect of returning to their native province. The explanations contained in criminal records present an array of different possibilities and projects. Some considered their southern journey temporary. In September 1850, santiagueño Manuel Aguirre, having made up his mind to go to Buenos Aires "with the purpose of working," got a passport from the district judge of Salavina and departed. He reached Guardia de Luján, hired himself out as "peon for all work," and remained there until March. His journey closely resembled the traditional harvest migrations of colonial times. Another migrant from Santiago, Florencio Almarás, reached the farming district of Chivilcoy, worked there for two months driving oxcarts, then tried to return to Santiago and was arrested in Arrecifes in 1851. José Pio Miranda, a young santiagueño arrested in Quilmes in 1849, declared at the time of his detention that he had not enrolled in the local militias because he did not intend to stay long in the province. He just wanted to obtain salaried employment in the city, earn some money, and return to Santiago.[15]

For others, the decision to return was not assumed from the outset; how and when this decision was made depended on the circumstances faced in the adopted province. When economic success was interrupted by the threat of coercion, migrants returned to their native province. Santafesino Manuel Sánchez, for instance, decided to return to his province after he received news that he was to serve in the infantry of the Lobos militias, "a force to which he had always shown aversion." Sánchez's decision to return may not be typical, for he was well established in the town of Lobos. After two years of residence, he was enrolled in the local militia (in reserve service), and worked as the local butcher in addition to being a farmer. A similar economic success story undermined by the presence of the military state can be found in Avelino Luna's criminal file. In January 1845 Luna came to Buenos Aires to purchase cattle and, after finding paid work and favorable conditions to augment his capital, he decided to stay. He moved to Dolores, where he devoted himself to livestock raising and tried to become a neighbor, enrolling in the local militia. He resided there for fourteen months before deciding to return. The mistreatment of a corrupt commander (who put him and other provincianos to work in his private establishment) led Luna to desert and go back to his native Santiago.[16]

The decision to stay in Buenos Aires province also depended on relative success in the job search, amicable relations with the authorities, and stability in the family. Francisco Suárez was one of those provincianos who succeeded in integrating themselves into the host society.[17] A native of Santiago del Estero, he had come to Buenos Aires province in 1829 and remained there until his arrest in 1842. After thirteen years of residence Suárez had good reasons for not returning to Santiago. He had had a remarkably stable employment record and had acquired a certain degree of social recognition in the region. Between 1829 and 1833 he was employed as a foreman at Juan Olivera's ranch in Chascomús. From 1833 to 1842 he had worked in the same town, serving Captain Francisco Echagüe. Later, he moved to Quilmes to work as foreman for rancher Faustino Giménez. At the time of his arrest he was a ranch foreman, probably earning a share in the ranch's production.

At the height of the Rosas period the annual pilgrimage during the harvest season had turned into a multistage migration leading to settlement. Through repeated attempts, migrants came to learn the obstacles and benefits of the southern journey, gathering key information that facilitated their social and political insertion. They learned about the geography of different districts, about employment opportunities, about the personalities of the judicial and military authorities, and, most crucial, about ways to blend into the local communities. Social acquaintances made on earlier trips helped them improve their chances of success on the following journey.

When Andrés Montenegro was arrested in July 1845, he was leading a party of six workers back to the upper provinces.[18] According to his own account, he had come first to Buenos Aires in 1838 with the intent of purchasing cattle. On this occasion, he stayed with Pedro Maciel, a fellow countryman settled in Cañada Honda (Baradero). After three months, he returned to his native Córdoba accompanied by his brother and other companions. The second time he journeyed to Buenos Aires, in November 1843, he took shelter in the same place and house. This time, Maciel himself hired him (he earned monthly wages as well as day wages), so he stayed for a year and eight months, after which time he returned to Córdoba with five other compatriots. This migrant seems to have avoided arrest by returning to the same place and employer.

Domingo Noriega migrated from Córdoba to Buenos Aires on at least three occasions.[19] In his last deposition (1850), he explained that he had come to Buenos Aires when he was 8 years old (in 1829), accompanied by his older brother. For thirteen years he helped his brother in the oxcart business, until he was old enough to seek work on his own. At the age of 21 he entered Cándido Pizarro's meat-salting workshop near the city (at Quilmes). Three years later Noriega was caught gambling in the workplace, arrested, and put to work at the service of the city's police department. At the time, he was a *capataz de tropa* (foreman of cattle drivers) and had traveled back to the upper provinces. In January 1846 he escaped from the police and went back to his province. In 1847 he returned to Buenos Aires and went directly to La Matanza, where he met Juan Rosas (Pizarro's partner), who sent him to his ranch in Lobería. This time he was put in charge of the ranch, communicating occasionally with his patrons at Quilmes and Buenos Aires. Clearly, the connections Noriega had established on previous trips to the city paid off later, as he was trusted with the administration of a southern ranch.

Workers in transportation, oxcart and mule drivers, had greater opportunity to explore the Buenos Aires landscape before settling in a given town. Over repeated trips they could gather information about employment, wages, police vigilance, and other key aspects of rural life. Good information could lead to better employment or increase their chances of *avecinamiento* (the process of becoming a "neighbor"). Alejandro Funes, an oxcart driver from Córdoba arrested in 1844 on charges of theft, recounted his ascent from oxcart driver to sheep farmer (*aparcero*).[20] In 1842 he traveled to Buenos Aires in an oxcart troop belonging to a tucumano, worked in the city for six or seven months, and returned to Córdoba in another troop. Five months later he was again on the road, this time working for a mendocino's oxcart troop. In the winter of 1843 he arrived at Buenos Aires; this time he moved directly to Quilmes, where neighbor Estevez Correa gave him a job. After four months, his employer offered him a partnership in his sheep and dairy farm. By joining different troops, Funes found this opportunity to improve his livelihood.

Migration was multistage in yet another sense. Migrants carefully tested the territory of their adopted fatherland (*patria*) before they brought their families with them. This was part of their strategy of social insertion. To assure a good reception for their families, they made connections with ranchers, justices of the peace, and local policemen (*tenientes alcaldes*). Given the high degree of discretionary authority exercised by local authorities, migrants wanted to minimize the risk of family members being unjustly arrested. This might explain the frequency of repeated migrations as well as the relatively high average age of migrants.

Job Seeking, Itineraries, and Information

What triggered the decision to migrate to Buenos Aires? Was this an individual or a family decision? What role did market information play in these decisions? These are questions that, given the available evidence, cannot be given more than tentative answers. In his informative *Memoria descriptiva* (1889), Fazio equated santiagueños' migration to Buenos Aires with an inveterate custom: a tradition nourished by Santiago's lack of employment opportunities and the spirit of adventure in the natives of the province.[21] To Fazio, "push factors" were crucial. A limited amount of annual rainfall and the periodic overflow of the rivers created a type of agriculture that concentrated work to a few months, leaving peasants inactive during the rest of the year. Colonial and contemporary observers emphasized the influence of jobs and money in the decisions of migrants, that is, "pull factors." A colonial observer pointed to the attractions of wage labor in the littoral for a poor peasant society: santiagueños were driven by "the prestige associated with those who had seen other lands, of those who wore fabrics purchased in other provinces with the product of their own labor."[22] Travelers of the late 1820s (such as Beaumont and Purchappe), who witnessed the arrival of provincianos at the farms of northern Buenos Aires at the time of the wheat harvest, assumed this to be a strictly seasonal migration that ended in late January or February. If this was the case, migrants had enough time to collect the carob bean (*algarroba*) harvest on their return to Santiago.

More recently, researchers pointed out the existence of family migrations and related these to changes in the structure of families brought about by economic crises (see Garavaglia and Moreno 1993). Judith Farberman (1997), examining the Indian towns of late colonial Santiago del Estero, has suggested that a selectivity process was at play in the origin of migration, a process that ensured the survival of peasant families in Santiago.[23] Those peasants "poorer in relatives" and, therefore, less able to withstand the ups and downs of a low-productivity and unstable agriculture, had to migrate to complement their family's subsistence. Migrants, then, came from families with fewer women to produce textiles or to tend the family cattle. Gradually, migration disintegrated certain families so that those with the least number of kin were forced to migrate definitively.

From this perspective, migration resulted from collective decisions made at origin, decisions that centered round the question of the survival of peasant family units.

Criminal and military files do not help us much in separating push from pull factors (in fact, the stories contain very little about the conditions in the upper provinces) or in isolating the influence of economic incentives, family reasons, and custom. It is clear, though, that those who verbalized their reasons for traveling to Buenos Aires pointed to the need to find employment as the principal motivation.[24] More significant, many of them reported that they had traveled as salaried members of a troop of oxcarts (commonly, *boyeros*—peons who take care of bulls—or *picadores*—oxcart drivers). To them, the travel itself was a job. Those who failed to state in so many words the motivation of their trip made it clear by their subsequent actions that they had migrated south in search of paid work. Yet job seeking was not the only objective of these migrants; equally important was the need to find relatives or rebuild family relations disrupted by wars or earlier migrations. Thus, economic and family objectives were inseparable. The family was the context in which provincianos inscribed their search for income and, conversely, the labor market provided a way to reconstitute families. Mediating the formation of family or individual objectives were flows of information transmitted through rumor, stories, and impressions disseminated by earlier migrants.

Before taking the long journey southward, northern migrants had to gather information about future work prospects, the health of relatives, and the general political situation in Buenos Aires. For the *tropero* (oxcart troop owner) who took them south (and was about to risk his capital in draft animals and carts on a long and difficult journey), information about the road, the weather, and potential disruptions of the journey was essential.[25] Once arrived in Buenos Aires province, northern migrants had to decide where to go next. Again, this choice depended on information about the relative situation and opportunities of each county (safety, wages, employment, social connections). Both in the provinces of origin and in Buenos Aires, such information circulated among paysanos in markets and taverns, at horse races, and at other places of social interaction.

In Santiago, near the Dulce River, large numbers of oxcarts concentrated at the oxcart square as they arrived with commodities from Cuyo, Córdoba, or the littoral (see Fazio 1889, 240–245). Merchants, oxcart troops, and peons gathered there for days, some waiting for customers while others finalized provisions, repaired oxcarts, and hired peons for the next trip. Women and children joined their men folk and camped on the grounds near the square. Most were interested in hearing news coming from "southern lands" (*tierras de abajo*). The *fogones* (night fires) offered good opportunities for this purpose. On these occasions, peons inquired into the whereabouts of their kin, about economic opportunities in the southern lands, and about the tranquility or "altered state" of Buenos Aires.[26] Similarly, in Buenos Aires, those who required information had to frequent certain meeting places: the taverns, the cattle markets, or the oxcart square near the church of La Piedad. Those with previous experience in the migratory journey could bypass these visits to the city and go directly to localities where they knew *provincianos* would be welcome.

Generally, the route taken from the interior to Buenos Aires was decided by the *tropero*; peons had no say in this decision.[27] But once the troops reached their destination in Buenos Aires province, it was for the peons to decide where to go and search for work. They could remain in the farmlands of Luján, Chivilcoy, or Pergamino or travel further south to the territory of livestock raising. Alternatively, they could continue their journey to the city. Those who took the first choice must have found the farm districts safer than the cattle lands of the New South. Those who continued their march to the city must have considered the wage differentials there and the greater chances of getting transportation jobs. The job of drover (*acarreador*) for the city's cattle markets would most certainly give them the opportunity of traveling south to the most productive cattle lands. Others deviated south before reaching the city and went directly to the area north of the Salado River.

The *decisions* migrants made about their itineraries can be substantiated in the stories of oxcart drivers. Sometimes, the place of arrival was not of their choosing, as was the case with peons of oxcart troops dismissed by their employers at the end of the journey.[28] But once they were in the territory of Buenos Aires province, they had to calculate where to go to maximize their chances of getting paid employment.

Consider these two contrasting stories. Manuel Pavón came from Santiago in 1843 in a troop of oxcarts destined for Arrecifes. Having reached this town, he decided to continue to Buenos Aires city. His decision paid off. At Retiro, one of the city's markets, Pavón met a peon employed at the Quinta de Palermo who took him to see Governor Rosas. In this way, Pavón found his first job. Three weeks later, while at Palermo, he learned that Colonel Fabián Rosas needed shepherds for his sheep farm and decided to apply. In December 1848, santiagueño José Pio Miranda headed for Buenos Aires. Before reaching his destination, he abandoned the oxcart troop at Chivilcoy and went south to Tandil, where his uncle Juan de la Cruz lived. Apparently, he preferred the security afforded by family to the prospect of facing the city labor market on his own. After four months

TABLE 3.4 Migrants' Spatial Preferences (in percentages)

Region	Place of Arrest	Place of Residence	Place of Arrival	Place of First Job	Place of Second Job
Northern coastal	3.8	4.5	8.6	7.4	12.9
NW–SE corridor	22.8	21.6	22.2	19.8	24.2
Buenos Aires hinterland	35.4	27.3	40.7	33.1	30.6
North of Salado River	24.7	18.2	13.5	14.9	12.9
South coastal	1.9	18.2	11.1	16.5	4.8
South inland	11.4	10.2	3.7	8.3	14.6
TOTAL	100.0	100.0	100.0	100.0	100.0
N	158	73	83	121	62

Note: South coastal = Pila, Tordillo, Dolores, Vecino, Monsalvo, Ajó, Tuyú, Mar Chiquita, Lobería; South inland = Tandil, Chapaleufú, Azul, Las Flores, Mulitas, Bragado, Tapalquén
Source: Filiaciones (N=525)

working with his uncle in the cattle-driving business, Miranda was ready to face the city. He traveled with his uncle to Buenos Aires and offered his services as a cattle drover for one of the city's cattle markets.[29] The two stories illustrate two strategies of job hunting. Pavón visited the city as an intermediate step in his job search; Miranda went first to the country before facing the urban labor market. To find a job, Pavón appealed to the solidarity of provincianos and other peons and dared to reach the center of power, Rosas's house; Miranda, on the other hand, used family connections as a means to obtain information, work training, and a certain degree of protection.

Table 3.4 summarizes information about migrants' movements through the provincial territory. It shows that migrants had definite preferences about their first destination. Of eighty-three provincianos who reported the place of their arrival, 40 percent went directly to the city and its surroundings. Another 22 percent remained in towns of the northwest-southeast corridor (Pergamino, Arrecifes, Areco, Luján) before ever reaching Buenos Aires. Another 13 percent "deviated" south to seek work in the lands north of the Salado River; they went to small rural towns such as Navarro, Lobos, Monte, Ranchos, and Chascomús. Another 15 percent of the new arrivals went directly to the New South; of these, most went to the coastal districts (Dolores, Monsalvo, Ajó, Tuyú, Mar Chiquita), where policing was lax.

Before migrants could attain such stability in employment and social recognition they had to move around a lot. The mobility across districts and regions was remarkable. Individually, workers crossed regions quite often and, even more frequently, traveled between neighboring districts (*partidos*). Only 32 percent (of the eighty-three) remained in their place of arrival until their arrest; the majority moved to a different location or declared no fixed residence.[30] Of those who remembered the place of their first job (122), only 34 percent remained in the same locality at the time of their arrest. Not surprisingly, provincianos mentioned a variety of places and jobs as part of their recollection of job experiences.[31]

This perambulation through different towns and districts was part of a long-term process of trial and error by which provincianos chose their place of residence. Among the circumstances that influenced their location decision were the relative risk of the district in terms of state coercion and the availability of jobs. Buenos Aires and its hinterland was the first preference for settlement; it also ranked first in proportion of arrests. Evidently, migrants chose this center because it offered greater chances of finding employment, in spite of the risks posed by police and military recruiters.

That workers avoided places of intense policing is clear in the region I have called "south of Salado–Coast." This part of the south seems to have been favored because of its reduced state presence. The region was mentioned as a place of residence by 18 percent of the detainees, yet only 2 percent of the sample were arrested there. This was not the case in the "southern inland" region: here the state had a more visible presence and, therefore, workers were less willing to settle there. The region north of the Salado River, an area of recent development and devoted mostly to livestock raising and sheep farming, was also a risky region for compulsory drafts and other compulsory service. Workers who sought employment in this region because of its relative wealth and activity knew that the risk of being arrested was high.

Another dimension of migrants' preferences can be examined by contrasting place of arrival and place of residence. In this regard, the three first choices were identical: first, Buenos Aires and hinterland; second, northwest-southeast corridor; and third, north of the Salado River. But Buenos Aires and its surroundings were for many only a step to get work experience, social connections, and information in order to move elsewhere. Whereas 40 percent said they arrived first in Buenos Aires, only 27 percent named the city as their place of residence. The reverse happened in the areas north and south of the Salado River; clearly an area of rapid development characterized by the establishment of large cattle ranches, it attracted migrants. The New South, in particular, was preferred as an area of settlement (28 percent took residence there) rather than a place of first entry (15 percent arrived first to this area).

Migrants' mental geography of opportunities and dangers was clearly represented. Information about migrants' first and second jobs shows the stability of their preferences: the three most likely places to find employment were the same and ranked in the same order: first, the city, with its variety of job opportunities; second, the farmlands of the northwest-southeast corridor; third, the New South, a cattle ranching area. The political core of the support for Rosista federalism (the area north of the Salado River, with mixed sheep and cattle farms and strong militia units) stood out in the choices for first or second jobs.

Up to this point, I have focused on choices about itineraries, circumstances for returning, and the like made by individual migrants. This was not always the case. Some workers traveled in small groups united by common experience, regional sympathy, or kinship ties. When José Coronel (25) was arrested at Ranchos in July 1845, he was in the company of his brother Francisco (18) and three other provincianos, José León Aguirre (26), Ramón Aguirre (22), and Pascual Espejo (20). The Aguirres and the Coronels were santiagueños and probably cousins (the Aguirres' mother was Felipa Coronel); Espejo was born in Córdoba. Coming from different locations, they had joined at Arrecifes. The Coronels had been working at Baradero, the Aguirres had deserted from the Salto garrison, and Espejo came from a ranch in Pila.[32]

Traveling in groups provincianos could reduce the risk of the journey to the upper provinces. In July 1845 Andrés Montenegro and seven compatriots were arrested for traveling without proper documents. The party was composed of three Argüello brothers (Pablo, Lorenzo, and Abelardo), Apolinario Verón and his wife María Argüello (quite possibly a sister of the Argüello brothers), Benito Cabrera, and a girl named Camila Rivas. They were all from Córdoba and at least some of them were close relatives. They all had departed from Cañada Honda, a small hamlet in Baradero, where cordobés farmer Pedro Maciel had given them shelter. On their return journey, they rode to San José de Flores and from there to Quilmes. In these two towns they stayed overnight at the houses of acquaintances.[33]

Those who traveled southeast (the Aguirres and the Coronels) shared information and social connections to find employment. Those who traveled north (the Argüello brothers) shared common resources (friends to stay with, false documents, and provisions) to return to their provinces. In both cases, kinship and friendship constituted the basis of their informal communities. Almost circumstantially, they gathered at a certain intermediate point after riding in solitude or in smaller groups of kin. In both cases, fellow countrymen and relatives provided important assistance to the travelers: shelter, temporary work, and, quite likely, information to avoid police controls. The family appears in these stories in a state of flux, its members separated in their journeys southward and reunited in their journeys northward. Returning kin admitted other individuals to the group, usually peons who had worked on the same or a nearby ranch or farm. On the way back to their provinces, these informal groups carried with them information to pass on to their relatives and friends, who eagerly waited for them at the oxcart squares of Santiago, Córdoba, or San Luis.

Families Dispersed

The typical interior migrant was male, single, and young; this is reflected in the filiaciones, where 72 percent of the arrested provincianos declared themselves to be single, the overwhelming majority were male, and their average age at the time of migration was 23 (SD = 7.4).[34] For a peasant society in which children started to work at 12 or 14, this was a rather late age. Quite likely, the presence of repeated migrations tended to increase the average age of migrants. But it can also be argued that migrants' families in Córdoba, Santiago, San Luis, and elsewhere acted conservatively. They avoided sending to Buenos Aires men under 20, probably calculating that younger men could not command a sufficient wage to cover more than the expense of the trip. This assumption is consistent with Farberman's hypothesis, in the sense that peasant families tried to keep their younger members home for family labor.

At first glance, our source puts in doubt the status of the family in the process of migration. That 70 percent of migrants arrested were single males speaks against the existence of an important flow of migratory families. Moreover, even married men seem to travel without their immediate family; wives always appear to live elsewhere. There are reasons to think, however, that this picture is somewhat biased. In a society with a tradition of consensual marriage and scarce women, there are strong motives to keep women out of the official transcript (see Mayo 1985). The fact that men could be accused of kidnapping conspired against the open display of female partners. Also, male police, justices, and military officers coveted young women. Hence, more often than not, "wives" traveled with their male relatives rather than with their "husband." As Mateo (1993b) has indicated, the migration process itself produced new "marriages" along the road. In the transition to permanent residential status, single men married in one town and then moved to the next.

Looked at closely, families seem to be a basic substratum of migrants' experience. The story of provincianos' perambulations across the Buenos Aires countryside is also the story of families, of their separation and reunification, of their struggles for survival in the context of a militarized society and an expanded economy. Intertwined with economic motivations (finding a job, earning some cash, buying a new set of clothes or some horses) was the need to travel for family reasons, in particular, to search for or to visit relatives. Civil wars and the protracted crisis of the inland economies had disseminated provincianos' families into a wider space that included Buenos Aires, the littoral provinces, Santiago, and Córdoba. Hence, the location of kin was a common concern of migrants.

Resonance of these concerns can be found in many provincianos' accounts. Santiagueño Domingo Pacheco (28) came to Buenos Aires in 1844 looking for his brother Agustín, who was at the time residing in Azul. Day laborer Nicolás Montenegro (from the same origin) escorted his sister back to her husband, José María Acosta, employed on a ranch at Lobos. Six months after arriving from Santiago, farm worker Gregorio Rea temporarily left his job at Lobos to visit his brother-in-law in San Nicolás. Pedro Pablo Roldán, a cordobés (40) arrested in Lobos in 1845, told his inquisitor that he had come to Buenos Aires to look for his son. Though unimportant to the Rosista state, family was a crucial concern for migrants.

The search for relatives gave meaning to migrants' perambulations and itineraries. To an extent, the spacing out of family members across the territory of Buenos Aires—a result itself of earlier migrations—provided migrants with a degree of comfort and protection. By visiting relatives or fellow countrymen from their provinces along the way, migrants could expect relay horses, food, and clothing. This type of "resource pooling" facilitated migrants' travels through the new landscape. When Blas Ponce went to Buenos Aires to work, he left his wife in Santiago. His itinerary, however, was paved with family connections. He was arrested with three horses and a mare; when interrogated, he clarified: two of the horses belonged to a sister residing in Chascomús, one to a brother residing in Ensenada, and the mare he had brought from Santiago. In addition, relatives provided travelers with key information about the conditions of roads and pastures, the existence of paid jobs (*conchavos*), and the state of "politics" (war, conscription, and police repression).

The very separation of family members engendered an ampler sense of belonging, a different relationship to the space. Commonly, migrants had family members in different districts of Buenos Aires, either because they separated at some point in the journey to enhance the possibilities of finding employment, or because the migration had proceeded in various stages (father and older brothers first, then younger brothers, sons, and female kin). To migrants, the family represented a network of relationships expanding across a vast territory—much ampler than their local homeland (*patria chica*). Their migration promised to recreate those basic ties and, at the same time, contributed to the economic well-being of the family.[35]

The relationship between family and the labor market can now be made more explicit. To the extent that interior migrants had a chain of family members along the way, they were better able to confront the job search. They could withdraw their labor power for some time while receiving support from brothers, sisters, cousins, or uncles. They could resort to relatives for help with the legalization process (getting a passport, a work contract, or a militia certificate). They could command better information about wages, employment, and safety conditions in the region. In short, a family-rich migrant was better prepared to face the Buenos Aires labor market.[36] The stories contained in criminal and military records emphasize the role of family as an important resource in the perambulations of the poor.[37]

Migrants' information about the whereabouts of their relatives depicts most clearly this new territoriality of the family. Felipe Acuña, for example, knew quite well where the rest of his brothers were: all four had joined the federalist armies, now in campaigne at Banda Oriental (1847). Knowing the names of the commanders of these regiments, Felipe thought, might help him to locate his brothers. Manuel Tuli was informed that his brother Calixto was imprisoned in Santos Lugares, just as Pacheco was certain his brother Agustín was in Azul and Aguirre knew that his mother resided in Chascomús. This mental geography of the family, this knowledge about the spatial dispersion of kin, was complemented by valuations assessing the losses and gains attained by relatives in earlier trips. These valuations reinforced familiar distinctions of freedom and coercion, patriotism and undue service, wealth and poverty.

Quite likely, migrants' double search for employment and relatives changed their views about the "nation." What migrants told their inquisitors in Buenos Aires casts doubt on the traditional view that peasants from the interior remained attached to their "little fatherlands" (*patrias chicas*). It must have been difficult for Angel Córdoba to define precisely what his homeland was. Though he was born in Santiago and his wife and two children lived there, he considered Rosario (Santa Fé province) his place of residence. Having worked in this area for some time, he participated with the santafesinos in important federalist campaigns (first in Oribe's Ejercito de Vanguardia and later in the persecution of unitario leader Mascarilla). Was he a santiagueño or a santafesino? Consider also the situation of Roque Gorosito, a recruit born in Santiago, who had lived two years in Cerrillos (Santa Fé) with his family, and, at the time of his arrest, claimed to be a peasant farmer from Guardia de Luján (Buenos Aires). His displacement to Santa Fé (as he escaped prison at Santos Lugares) was itself the result of a previous migratory experience. Was he santafesino, santiagueño, or porteño? Both Córdoba and Gorosito had known other homelands (patrias), in addition to their birthplace, before entering Buenos Aires.

A Parallel Story

Criminal files, though an invaluable aid in my attempt to understand provincianos' perambulations through the Buenos Aires countryside, leave aside important dimensions of migrants' experience. Coercion or politics in the province of origin is rarely mentioned. Employment opportunities at home are never the subject of commentary. Also absent is information on gender relations. These records also fail to make any reference to the other key competitors in the labor market: the Irish workers who, following the famine of 1844–1845, came to the Buenos Aires countryside and found work on cattle ranches and sheep farms and in various other activities (see Korol and Sabato 1979).

The lack of discussion about the economic situation in the upper provinces is problematic, for it undermines the possibility of explaining the general economic and political context of internal migrations. In particular, we are unable to reexamine some basic "push factors" considered crucial by the historiography: the crisis of the peasant economies of the interior and the unemployment of craftspersons that followed the flood of imported textiles during postindependence. The fact that migrants failed to dwell on these issues should not be taken as proof of their unimportance, for the inquisitors at Santos Lugares or local justices simply did not pose these questions. Thus, any explanation of the migratory process based on wage differentials or the distinct political or disciplinary scenarios faced by migrants must depend on other types of information.

The narrative left by Irish immigrant John Brabazon (1981) can serve as a point of reference to evaluate provincianos' encounters with the labor market. Brabazon begins the narrative of his own perambulations through the pampas at almost the same time as many filiaciones: 1845–1848. On the face of it, the differences between this narrative and those of native paysanos appear striking. Brabazon's writing skills set him apart from native migrants: the fact that he can represent his own experience and address a broader audience through writing undermines the comparison, for, in this regard at least, the Irish immigrant is not speaking from a subaltern position. Provincianos instead speak from a coercive situation. Their stories had been extracted from them in a sketchy and selective manner by the authorities. They are poor; at the time of their arrest, a few horses and clothes are their only property. Brabazon, in contrast, presents his account from the outset as a success story, as something to be imitated by others. Starting from humble, almost degrading jobs at the Buenos Aires port, he rose to the condition of a small merchant dealing in hides and wool and sharing the property of a sheep farm.

Brabazon was a jack-of-all-trades or, as paysanos would say, *peón para todo trabajo*. Immediately after his arrival, he realized a basic fact about the Buenos Aires economy: to take advantage of the various economic opportunities a person needed to change occupations constantly. Hence, he strove to learn different useful trades (or to pretend he knew them). Over the three years he moved around in the Buenos Aires countryside (1845–1848) he tried no fewer than fifteen different trades or occupations. In the beginning, he accepted humbler jobs: tavern clerk, stable boy, meat-salting shop peon, carpenter's assistant. He started earning day wages but, as soon as he familiarized himself with the ways of the country, he began contracting services on a piece-rate basis. He bathed and sheared sheep, made ditches and river fences, cut grass, built thatched huts, made adobe bricks, built shelves for a rural tavern, made cheese and butter, and skinned sheep. At the peak of his career he was a sheep farmer, a merchant in *frutos del país* (hides, wool, furs), and a cultivator (maize, alfalfa, and potatoes).

None of our stories shows such diversity of occupations; at most, workers recollected five different jobs. The difference lies perhaps in the degree of detail with which Brabazon recounted his occupations: provincianos were less interested in the content of labor than in the fact of having had a conchavo (paid job). Many simply responded "country work" or "peon," without other specification. Provincianos did not mention the specific tasks involved in a job unless they involved some humiliation or impropriety and, in general, tended to omit those occupations performed without a boss or outside the wage relationship. Hunting weavers or ostriches, collecting horsehair, making boots from mares' hides, and other independent or illegal activities were often absent from the narratives unless presented by the inquisitor as a felony. While paysanos rarely mentioned sheep shearing and ditch digging, these were the two most common and remunerative occupations for Brabazon. Conversely, the Irishman never worked as a soldier or as a farm peon. Can this be taken as a sign of labor segmentation? If so, was this due to employers' preferences? Brabazon's account suggests that, in a labor market apparently open to all, employers preferred foreigners for certain occupations.

Brabazon's insistence on accumulating wealth through labor is remarkable. Like other paysanos, he tried to form his own herd of horses. He thought this was the poor man's road to riches. He stole horses from ranches confiscated from unitarios, got other horses as gifts from his patron, and tamed some broncos. This he learned from paysanos. At first, he did what any northern migrant would have done: he moved to the city and obtained employment at the meat-salting workshop. With what he was able to save, he returned to the countryside and bought some sheep; maybe a paysano would have invested in horses or cattle instead. Soon Brabazon discovered that sheep shearing and ditch digging produced instant cash. In an economy rapidly switching to sheep raising and with new lands under survey and demarcation, these two skills were in great demand. With the help of a young assistant he sold these services at inflated rates, recording the income earned in each job. Many native peasants and peons could not have done this; they were illiterate.

The accumulation of wealth guided the Irish immigrant's narrative.[38] For him, wandering produced "profits," a word alien to paysanos' vocabulary.[39] His will to accumulate and his predisposition to work, he posited, distinguished him from native workers, who gambled away their hard-earned cash and were not willing to take all job opportunities.[40] This was obviously a constructed difference. The stories of provincianos show their constant search for employment, the importance of wages, and their familial responsibilities. Rather than compulsive gamblers and indolent idealists, native workers were, like Brabazon, job seekers. Brabazon's road to wealth was paved by aid he received from other Irish immigrants and from the members of his own family. In fact, he resorted to kinship ties and regional connections, just as provincianos did. A friend of his brother's got him the first job; when traveling to the countryside, Scottish and English shepherds gave him shelter; his brother Thomas and three other Irish workers helped him finish a ditch. And, like provincial migrants, he built bonds of solidarity only with his compatriots. His sheep-shearing team was made up of two Irishmen, his brother-in-law Richard Nevels and Thomas Gaynor. His assistant in the ditch-digging business was also an Irishman, youngster Dan Dickinson.

Coercion is not absent from this narrative. Brabazon's first patron, Mr.

Gordon, threatened him with conscription in Rosas's army. Later, at the Araza ranch, he listened to the administrator reprimand a mulatto peon; the threat was similar. At one point, his experience coincided with those of many provincianos. At Chascomús, the police arrested him for not carrying proper documents; eight days later, a letter from his consul set him free. Native migrants could not use this leverage. After this incident, the police never interrupted his perambulations through the pampas. His business, on the other hand, suffered again from military coercion: he lost a good native peon to recruiters. Whereas in 1845 he found a majority of native workers (criollos) among the shearing teams, at the end of his narrative all he could see were English men and women. The reason? "All the native workers had been enlisted in the army" (Brabazon 1981, 16, 28, 42, 135–136, 149).

This particular account illuminates hidden aspects of the labor markets facing native migrants. The lesson Brabazon learned about the pampas could easily have been part of the common wisdom of paysanos: to change occupations frequently was to one's own benefit. Maybe northern migrants lacked some of Brabazon's entrepreneurial skills: his ability to buy and sell, to organize work teams, to recognize promising market opportunities. Probably, native migrants were less concerned with accumulating wealth than with locating their relatives or escaping the press gangs. Brabazon, by and large, did not have to deal with this type of coercion. In fact, his condition as a foreigner granted him greater freedom of movement. He had no clear-cut obligation to the federalist cause. Military obligations marked a big difference; in other aspects, such as mobility and opportunities, the account left by the Irish worker-writer shows greater similarity to the accounts of paysanos. In fact, we can read this narrative as "filling in the blanks" in the descriptions of work experience left by northern migrants. Perhaps native workers had to change occupations as frequently as Brabazon did but they told their interrogators only part of the story. To this extent, Brabazon's narrative confirms the high degree of mobility of workers in the Buenos Aires countryside.

Conclusions

Throughout the Rosas period, provincianos maintained an ambivalent position via-à-vis state power in Buenos Aires province. Welcomed to the province as laborers, their condition as potential citizens (but without complete "residence qualifications") made them a special concern for the powerful. To the local authorities in charge of policing the countryside, their mobility was unsettling, particularly if the travelers carried no documents and showed no evidence of service to the local justice offices. Their migratory movements made them visible and vulnerable to arrest. As many were not sure about their place of residence, they were suspected of desertion or vagrancy. On the other hand, the politics of Rosismo—a popular republicanism based on universal male suffrage—created opportunities for migrants to integrate into the social and political life of rural communities. As a result, santiagueños, cordobeses, santafesinos, and puntanos gradually settled in the host province, aspiring to become full citizens. (The notion of citizenship, we must keep in mind, was at this time rather ambiguous, combining notions from the repertoire of republicanism with those taken from the ancien régime.)[41] It is likely, then, that the Rosista experiment transformed the pattern of internal migration from seasonal farm labor migrants to settlement and assimilation.

Yet, despite promises of incorporation, migrants retained an ambivalent status in the political life of rural communities. The presence of "in-between migrants" (the 30 percent who had resided for more than one year but less than five years) preoccupied the authorities. Staying longer than seasonal migrants, they could not be protected as temporary laborers. Their mobility through different jobs and localities was taken as proof of their evasion of military service. Rosas's instructions to the justices reflected the shifts in state concerns about these migrants. In 1832 he saw them as temporary labor migrants whose activities could be "legalized" with a simple work contract. By 1851, these migrants had turned into "suspect citizens," political actors who could either support the federalist cause or side with the enemy. Apparently, the slow but persistent work of migrants—their perambulations through the rural districts, searching for a place of their own—proved effective. While newcomers were still considered "transients," many provincianos had already become "neighbors" or settled residents (domiciliados), a social situation that endowed them with practical citizenship. These migrants had traveled far—from being a mere economic resource to becoming political agents.

After reading these fragmented stories, one conclusion appears evident. We cannot easily separate the search for employment from the politics of incorporation. During the Rosas epoch, northern migrants found better opportunities for definite settlement in Buenos Aires province. Earlier seasonal journeys gradually gave way to more permanent or definitive migration. This situation caught the attention of state authorities, for provincianos, now endowed with the possibility of acquiring social and political rights, could challenge the basis of local power. The stories of individual migrants underscore the importance of social incorporation for political empowerment. By becoming locally known (*conocidos*) and by enrolling in the local militias, provincianos rapidly acquired the rights and obligations of those born in Buenos Aires province.[42] This leveling of differences must have acted as a powerful brake against discrimination in the labor market.

With regard to the effects migration produced on the local or regional consciousness of northern migrants, particularly those who became residents of Buenos Aires, we can only express doubt about the inherited wisdom. Traditionally, it has been assumed that the emergence of political segmentation into quasi-autonomous provinces after 1820 produced fragmentary territorial identities.[43] The natives (*naturales*) of one province learned to consider those born in other provinces "foreigners."[44] Modes of self-reference widely used by paysanos also pointed in the direction of a fragmented territorial identity. When asked about their homeland (patria), most people responded about the locality or the province in which they had been born. This traditional view needs some revision, for both the civil wars and the internal migrations produced forms of solidarity and social interactions that worked in the direction of redefining local allegiances. Provincianos and porteños wandered the same territory in search of employment, fought side by side in federalist battalions, and cooperated whenever possible to defend their rights against the authorities. Moreover, my sources do not present any incident or case in which the localism of the participants was the main issue. No provinciano seemed to be defending his local homeland as a question of honor. No porteño used his place of residence as a reason to sustain any pretension of social superiority. The high mobility of both groups and the possibility of insertion of provincianos in the social and political life of Buenos Aires province tended to erase local differences. The evidence—fragments of voices of subalterns uttered under interrogation—cannot solve the question of national versus provincial identities. But it is clear that, with regard to labor opportunities at least, provincianos and porteños had much in common.

CHAPTER 4

Class by Appearance

In this chapter, I propose that the "order of appearance" governing people's attitudes toward clothes, colors, and fashion was part of the communicative interaction between the state and the population and, at the same time, a product of struggles for distinction that stemmed from society itself. During the Rosas period, civil wars and the consolidation of a militarist state turned clothes into a field of acute contention. Dress was the territory chosen by the government to test the political allegiances of the governed. At the same time, dress was the instrument used by the state to "classify" the population fit for military service. Rosas's preoccupation with creating and controlling uniformity of appearance in his restored republic creates a small window through which we can glance at some other aspects of subaltern politics, tactics, and understandings.

Pierre Bourdieu has taught us to think of the social world as a multidimensional space where various forces of differentiation, corresponding to distinct forms of capital (economic, cultural, social, and symbolic), operate simultaneously (see Calhoum 1993, especially 69–70). Within this complex space, social groups and individuals struggle to gain wealth, power, social connections, and status as a means to reproduce and maintain a given set of social differences ("distinction"). The terrain of contestation is often the field of lifestyle, where agents project deep-rooted conceptions of the social order and their position and possibilities within it.[1] Everyday practices of consumption in the areas of food, culture, and presentation reveal a constant struggle for distinction. By eating, dressing, reading, or practicing sports, social agents reaffirm the "sense of place" that is essential to a class-divided social order.

Skirmishes for distinction help to construct the boundaries of class. Through practices of consumption, social groups define what is refined and what is vulgar, differentiate the necessary from the superfluous, and separate what is useful from what is proper. Block by block, social groups build up the fine walls that separate class perspectives and tastes. Where this is so, dress style, food preferences, house decor, manners of speech, and private possessions carry the imprints of the practical taxonomies that mediate the individual's apprehension of the social world.[2] Clothes in particular serve to assert a group's social identity in relation to other groups, sometimes reinforcing but often redefining existing differences in terms of income, occupation, and education. As such, clothes can be used to "read" the state of class differentiation in a given society.[3]

Though never simple, the reading of clothes acquires greater complexity when, in addition to class and group differentiation, other forces such as state coercion and factional politics compete for expression in the field of appearance. When the state contributes its own taxonomies to the organization of the social, people's appearances carry these marks. This was the case in Buenos Aires province during the Rosas era. During this period, clothes came to be laden with a multiplicity of meanings: political, cultural, and social. The federalist state, through a series of practices of classification, surveillance, and punishment, tried to distinguish sympathizers from opponents, soldiers from deserters, peons from small-scale producers. In these interactions clothes became privileged markers. To state authorities, clothes were key for visually classifying the rural population prior to their incarceration or conscription. In addition, clothes served the state as a measure of people's political adherence to federalism. As a result, a truly federalist order of appearance emerged and consolidated during this period, a visual regime governed by certain colors (scarlet red and navy blue), dress styles (paysano attire), and emblems (the federalist ribbon worn on vests, jackets, and hats).

Factional politics gave new meanings to clothes, meanings that went beyond the practices of class distinction. The protracted confrontation between unitarios and federales was encoded into different styles of dress and colors.[4] Scarlet red was the color representing federalism; light blue and green stood for unitarianism. The Federalist Party made compulsive the use of color emblems—scarlet ribbons on men's chest (*divisas*) and headgear (*cintillos*)—and favored the simple and austere attire of paysanos over the pretentious dress styles of fashionable urbanites. This simple, political distinction contrasted with the classificatory practices of the state, aimed at separating the "peon class" from the rest of the rural population. Thus, the "peasant look" was both a blessing and a curse, for it assumed the federalist sympathies of the wearer but put that person at risk of forceful arrest and conscription.

Competing normative conceptions about social difference and equality found expression in the language of clothes. Favoring the simplicity of paysano clothes, federalists presented their opponents as the new rich (generally merchants or tavern-owners), who had severed their ties to the people. Their change in attire—the shift from *chiripá* (rectangular cloth tied to the waist, reaching to the knees) and poncho to trouser, frock coat,

7. Gaucho Attire and Riding Apparel. After the fall of Rosas, the gaucho continued to dress in the traditional "country" style: *poncho, chiripá, calzoncillos,* and *bota de potro.* But now his clothing showed no sign of political identity. J. F. Herring, *El apero y las prendas gauchas,* oil on canvas, ca. 1858. Reproduced from B. del Carril, *Monumenta Iconográphica* (1964).

and tie—was emblematic of an illegitimate upward mobility, and this was interpreted as a sign of aristocratic pretension, foreign connections, and antipopulist politics.[5] To unitarios, on the other hand, clothes were symbols of class distinction that had to be rescued from the dangerous egalitarianism of the postindependence period. An individual who did not dress according to his or her social position or occupation faced "ridicule."[6] Unitarios identified those wearing jacket, poncho, and chiripá (paysano clothes) with the "rabble" inhabiting the outskirts of the city, people lacking in social distinction and good sentiments. From this rabble came, in the unitario legend, most of the dreadful *mazorqueros.*

Impregnated by politics, colors became important vehicles for the expression of political ideas. To federalists, scarlet red (punzó) symbolized the kind of "organic democracy" they so proudly proclaimed, the independence they had maintained in the face of foreign intervention, and the peace and prosperity of their cattle-rich province. To unitarios, light blue and white were the colors of unity and fatherland, the forgotten values of the May revolution they tried to recreate.[7] Unitarios rejected the imposition of red ribbons in hats and jackets as an act of tyrannical government and saw the federalist preference for scarlet as a return to the colonial past, if not as a sign of a dangerous Jacobinism. For both parties, personal appearance was expressive of a basic confrontation between two distinct models of political society. *Pueblero* clothes, favored by unitarios, rejected the rural-centered politics practiced by caudillos. Conversely, paysano clothes, favored by federales, denied legitimacy to enlightened aristocratic government, controlled by urbanites.

Both parties expected clothing style to translate their political models into the practice of everyday life. In the public sphere the social egalitarianism proclaimed by federalism would visually confront the individualism and freedom promised by the System of Unity. Unitarios' fashionable dress, quite distinct from the clothes of country folks, alluded to an ideal polity: a centralized republic guided by men of letters. Federales instead privileged a chromatic uniformity and paysano dress style as expressions of a political model based on social egalitarianism and the symbiosis between the Restorer and the rural masses. Dressing like paysanos, federalists kept a distance from the educated elite. Against the unanimity of opinion demanded by federalism, unitarios presented an ideal society tolerant of diversity, in opinions and colors, a society that allowed for a greater degree of social distinction.[8]

Regarding fashion, unitarios looked to Europe and the United States for models of appropriate personal conduct and appearance and were ready to adopt fashionable clothes. Adapting local dress to European fashions was looked on as a civilizing influence in culture and society. In addition, unitarios expected that the excitement of fashion would prepare the public to consume new political and social ideas.[9] Federales instead favored the traditional rural attire, modified only by items that underscored military valor and fraternity. (Frigian caps, gilded braids, scarlet waistcoats, and dark blue ponchos were symbols of people's contributions to the Federal Cause.) To federalists, fashionable urban clothes were for people of frail character, such as the merchant and the literati, always ready to abandon local traditions in favor of imported novelty. Fashion to them was the mark of decadence, of an effeminate and pretentious elite, now debunked by "the people."

Acts of Class-ification

Clothes helped the provincial state classify the rural population. In a social environment dominated by the leveling of appearances, the state found it necessary to demarcate differences among rural inhabitants to enforce its penal and draft policies. The purpose of such an operation was to separate out recruits for the army without creating much tension in the rural communities. Justices of the peace, police chiefs, and military commanders were entrusted with the task of separating poverty from riches, as perceived from appearances. To produce this classification, clothes were essential. Paysanos' social status and condition, it was believed, could be read in their clothes.

The description and registration of the clothes of paysanos was part of the surveillance apparatus that regulated the activities of the rural poor. We know about the clothes of country folk mainly because the provincial state made compulsory the observation and description of the appearance of all those arrested for alleged crimes or detained as potential recruits to the army. At the time of each arrest, officers and judges had to prepare a filiación or clasificación, a personal file containing information about the prisoner. Drafting these documents involved a long inquiry in which the personal appearance of the arrested was observed, evaluated, and recorded. Skin, hair, and eye color, height, scars, and other physical traits were recorded as a means to individualize each prisoner. The detainee's clothes, considered essential for categorizing prisoners in a prearranged hierarchy of social types, were also recorded.

Inquisitors were advised to provide an adequate description of the subject's clothing, including details about fabric, style, and type of footwear.[10] In addition, they had to observe the subject's compliance with the obligation to wear the federalist ribbons (divisa and cintillo), a sign of his political opinion. Besides the obvious value of these descriptions as aids to police identification and political control, filiaciones and clasificaciones embodied the idea that appearance could be used as a way of establishing class distinctions. Detailed observation and description turned each of these interrogations into a classifying activity. Bodies and clothes, once mapped into categories that combined attributes of property, urbanity, and occupation, served to delimit the boundaries of class. State practices of classification asserted the logic of this "safeguard": only those who looked like vagrants, thieves, and deserters (usually those wearing the clothes of poverty in the countryside) were good material for the army.

These class-ifying acts required inordinate observation skills. The inquisitor had to infer, just from the subject's appearance, the "class" to

8. Federalist Gaucho. What made this gaucho (or *paysano*) look "federalist"? Though his striped poncho had the right combination of colors (dark blue and red), it was the scarlet ribbon in his hat (*cintillo*) and the head adornment of his horse (*testera*, also scarlet) that made his political affiliation apparent. R. Monvoisin, *Gaucho federal—Buenos Aires*, oil on canvas, 1842. Reproduced from B. del Carril, *Monumenta Iconográphica* (1964).

which he belonged. He had to distinguish *puebleros* (town people) from paysanos, and among the latter to distinguish peons, peasant producers, merchants, and ranchers. Rosas, in particular, was interested in identifying the members of the itinerant working class of the pampas, those belonging to the "country peon class," for they were the prime target of military conscription. Separating country residents from upper-class urbanites, an all-important distinction in Rosas's disciplinary system, was relatively simple.[11] Yet Rosas demanded from military recruiters and country justices a more subtle distinction, one that reflected the relative wealth and political affiliation of rural detainees. This required a closer observation of fabrics, colors, and general appearance of prisoners' clothes. Ideally, the people who were members of the "peon class" would exhibit their condition in their appearance. In practice, due to differences among the inquisitors' ability to perceive class or to the leveling of appearances favored by the Federal Party, these distinctions were difficult to establish.

In the countryside, paysano attire was mandatory for everyone in commemorative celebrations, and the expression of adherence to the Federal Cause was better received when coming from people who were not ostentatious in their dress.[12] The iconography of the period confirms this view: ballroom scenes show all participants wearing the same type of clothes, without distinction. The same uniformity of dress can be found in scenes of work at the slaughterhouse and in leisure activities such as dances, cockfights, and barbecues.[13] Though federalism did not condemn wealth as such, the ideal federalist should not elevate himself, in words or appearance, over the rest of his paysanos. Those who did so risked being mistaken for unitarios. Affluent merchants and the educated sons of the urban upper class were the ones who often dressed differently from other paysanos; because of this, they were suspected of unitario sympathies.[14]

State criminal files tried to untangle this apparent homogeneity of dress, setting apart those paysanos who, by their itinerant habits, occupational skills, and perceptible lack of property, could be considered country peons (peones de campo).[15] This implied a closer look at the subject to detect finer distinctions. Differences in fabrics as well as adornments, together with other indicators, such as skin color, military experience, and prior relations with the law, helped to establish these distinctions. Properly implemented, these practices of observation, description, and selection could become the basis for two basic functions of the state: the administration of justice and defense.

In practice, the classificatory apparatus of Rosismo produced less clear results than expected. The authorities' concern for prisoners' patterns of residence and lifestyle permeated the actual taxonomy produced by the interrogations. Polarities such as civil/military, country/town, and laborer/ farmer dominated the system of classification. In a sample taken from arrested felons (n = 170), 44 percent were classified as "country peon," 23 percent as "country man," 15 percent as "horseriding man," over 11 percent as "town man," and 6 percent as "military." Expectedly, a vast majority of the arrested were viewed as country people, a "fact" that was made evident by their dress style and riding skills. But only some of them, those who wore poor clothes and had itinerant lifestyles, were classified as country peons. An important percentage fell into the ambiguous categories hombre de campo and hombre de a caballo, terms that implied rural origin but not necessarily poverty.

Clothes, the interrogators discovered, were an imperfect measure of class. Members of various occupations and social positions (peons and foremen, independent agricultural producers, and people without occupation) dressed in the country style. Servants, clerks, artisans, and soldiers—occupations that could hardly be considered belonging to different classes—preferred to dress in a combination of country and town clothes. Moreover, paysanos of all conditions tended to display pieces of uniform and military regalia as part of their quotidian look, complicating the process of classification.

The felonies for which the subjects were arrested (felonies often attributed rather than proven) mattered less than residential habits, occupation, and clothes, for inquisitors were more interested in demarcating the boundaries of class within the *paysanaje*. Who among the rural inhabitants should bear the burden of forced military service? This was the question Rosas expected his army of inquisitors to answer. At a time when military service became an almost universal form of punishment, it was not unusual for middling paysanos who had committed grave crimes to be arrested and sent to Santos Lugares together with poor country folks. But, by and large, state authorities had to select the young and poor of the countryside, particularly those who seemed to have no fixed occupation or no clear attachment to the cause of federalism. At the same time, they had to spare those men already engaged in productive activities or state service (commerce, ranch work, rural industry, police work), especially if they were committed federales.

In one aspect at least the classificatory apparatus of Rosismo was effective. It forced paysanos to mind the clothes they wore. In addition to displaying relative well-being or poverty, country folks knew, their clothes were used by the authorities as indicators of class, criminality, and potential service to the army. Appearance, they discovered, could mean the difference between forced recruitment and freedom. Those who looked like poor peasants or rural peons had a greater chance of being imprisoned and sent to the front.[16] Better-dressed middling paysanos and urbanites, on the other hand, could avoid the draft, especially if they contributed money, cattle, or horses to the Federal Cause. This awareness forced paysanos into innovative adaptations in their clothing, adaptations that involved various forms of disguise, cross-dressing, and dressing up.

Well-Dressed Militiamen, Poorly Dressed Prisoners

Differences between urbanites and rural people were highlighted by a sharp contrast in dress styles. Well-to-do urbanites wore trousers, waistcoats, and boots; peasants and the urban poor wore the typical *paysano* attire: poncho, chiripá, calzoncillo (drawers usually worn underneath the chiripá), and bota de potro (mare-skin footwear resembling socks). Despite federalist leaders' preference for more egalitarian attire, in actuality clothes separated the better-off *gente decente* (city gentry) from the rest of the populace. This difference is made evident when we compare the clothes of reserve militiamen with those of rural prisoners.

The clothes of 301 reserve militiamen registered on Rosas's orders in 1851 show the extent of elite practices of distinction. The urbanite militiamen, most of them exempted from active duty, wore quite expensive garments: 41 percent had *levitas* (frock coats), 29 percent *paletós* (overcoats), and 15 percent *fraque* (dress coats). Almost all of them had a waistcoat (95 percent) and tie (96 percent); those wearing jackets were a minority (7 percent); only one was reported wearing a poncho. All the militiamen had trousers; none wore chiripá. There were no barefoot among the militiamen: 65 percent wore boots, 17 percent shoes, and 18 percent high-laced shoes or *botines*. Fine fabrics and costly materials underlined reserve militiamen's claim to distinction. Trousers made of cashmere and brim (65 and 18 percent), frock coats made of woolen cloth (84 percent), paletós made of cashmere and merino woolens (40 and 30 percent), and waistcoats (*chalecos* or vests) made of silk and satin (52 and 33 percent) were the most common. But there were also "Pekin" and velvet waistcoats, lutestring (glossy silk) overcoats, and astrakhan frock coats. Wearing silk ties was the norm (83 percent wore them), though some preferred satin, Pekin, or muslin. Most militiamen wore boots and shoes made of patent leather (*charol*), and all of them wore hats made of felt.

Who were these men who dressed up for a civic-military registration? What was their social background? And what claims were they making through their appearance? They were young residents of the city, proportionately whiter than veteran soldiers (65 percent of them white, 34 percent trigueños or sun-burned mestizos) and with better-paying occupations. Those deriving their livelihood from salaries (i.e., employees rather than peons) were few, only 22 percent of the sample. Most were merchants and dealers earning profits (55 percent) or commissions (4 percent), professionals earning honoraria (9 percent), students, sons of wealthy families (8 percent), and renters (1 percent). If they had been summoned into

TABLE 4.1 Clothes and Occupational Categories (in percentages
of each occupational group)

Occupation	Leggings	Drawers	Trousers	Waistcoat
Artisans	50.0	40.0	50.0	50.0
Peasants	95.5	90.9	0.0	27.3
Peons (agriculture, livestock)	98.7	88.3	1.3	28.6
Semiskilled workers	100.0	91.6	0.0	25.0
Transport, commerce	81.3	75.0	15.6	15.6
Military	85.7	57.1	14.3	28.6
Owners, foremen	66.7	66.7	33.3	66.7
Domestic servants	0.0	0.0	100.0	0.0
Unemployed	100.0	100.0	0.0	0.0
Total with information	90.4	80.7	8.4	27.1

service, they would certainly be called the "merchants' battalion," as 69 percent were owners or clerks of mercantile establishments.[17]

The urban militiamen were literate: 93 percent of them knew how to read and write, a remarkable advantage in a society with few elementary schools and no mandatory education. On the other hand, many did not know how to ride a horse (15 percent) or rode very poorly (68 percent). Clothes, literacy, equestrian ability, and income source divided the social universe in two, separating reserve militiamen from rural people.[18] But clothes were their most evident claim to social distinction. As though enacting a script already written in federalist poetry, these urbanites were all signing up to claim an exemption to the call to arms: they were defending Money and Mammon over the Fatherland. Exhibiting themselves so flagrantly fashionably and elegantly dressed, they were taking a great risk: the populace would associate them with the hated unitarios and probably denounce them as unpatriotic. But the risk was worth taking: elegant and fashionable clothes could keep them out of military service.

At the opposite end of the order of appearance were the men who made up the province's regular army, normally itinerant peons, laborers, and landless peasants forcefully drafted by rural justices of the peace. A small sample (170 prisoners) drawn from the justices' quarterly reports allows us to examine their clothes at the moment of arrest and interrogation.[19] Poor paysanos' clothes were different from those of urban militias, not only in cost but also in style: 91 percent of the arrested wore chiripá in lieu

TABLE 4.1 (continued)

Poncho	Jacket	Boots	Shoes	Mare-skin Boot	Barefoot
50.0	80.0	0.0	40.0	10.0	20.0
63.6	40.9	0.0	0.0	59.1	31.8
77.9	47.4	9.1	1.3	44.2	39.0
50.0	50.0	0.0	0.0	53.8	30.8
56.3	53.1	21.9	6.2	25.0	43.8
28.6	42.9	28.6	0.0	0.0	57.1
0.0	100.0	33.3	66.7	0.0	0.0
0.0	100.0	0.0	100.0	0.0	0.0
100.0	0.0	0.0	0.0	0.0	100.0
63.9	50.3	10.2	8.4	38.0	37.3

Source: *Filiaciones* (N=235)

of trousers, 81 percent calzoncillos (linen or cotton underwear), 65 percent ponchos, and 52 percent *chaquetas* (jackets). Their footgear was also distinctive: they wore the traditional bota de potro (80 percent) or went barefoot. Few of the prisoners had trousers (8 percent), waistcoats (27 percent), and boots or shoes (19 percent), the clothing of town people. Undoubtedly, prisoners to be drafted into the federalist armies dressed like paysanos; the difference that separated them from town folks (puebleros) was apparent to any viewer.

Within this group of prisoners, minor variations in clothing reflected differences in occupation, status, and wealth. An ample majority of prisoners, those classified as peasants, rural peons, and semiskilled workers, had no boots, shoes, or trousers. It was usually owners, foremen, artisans, and clerks who wore these items (see Table 4.1). Though residents of the countryside by and large dressed as paysanos, landowners and foremen exhibited their relative well-being in their more expensive footwear and some wore trousers instead of chiripá. Army officers and domestic servants, due to occupational requirements, had also accustomed themselves to wearing trousers; trousers by themselves did not constitute a mark of distinction.

Other garments worn by peasants and town people alike served to indicate gradations of well-being rather than rural or urban origin. Waistcoats or vests, for example, were not uncommon among country people: 50 percent of artisans, 28 percent of peons, 27 percent of peasants, and 25 percent of semiskilled workers wore them. A typical federal garment, the waistcoat was the mark of distinction of a paysano, a sign of importance and elegance. With a good vest, a man looked more tidy and presentable. No rural folk, however, would wear a tie. Jackets, though more frequent among owners, foremen, servants, and artisans, were also common among other rural workers. The poncho, the garment most commonly associated with gaucho life, was so widespread among the arrested that it did not constitute a good indicator of difference among rural inhabitants. Country folk felt "naked" without their ponchos.

Did clothes function as an important marker separating social groups according to cultural competence and aspirations for social recognition? Clearly, class distinction played a role in the politically charged order of appearance of Rosista Buenos Aires. It was implicit in the claims for military exemption made by militiamen. Better clothes represented a demand for privilege in a society struggling to impose uniformity of colors and appearance. For the mercantile and professional classes, wealth corresponded to a higher degree of cultural competence and, consequently, required differential treatment from state officials. As they knew well, their frock coats, overcoats, paletós, and dress coats protected them from being confused with the urban rabble and, therefore, guarded them from forceful conscription into the regular army.

The differences in the clothes of militiamen and rural prisoners also expressed a wider cultural cleavage, that between town and countryside. Through their clothes, rural peons and peasants on one side, and urbanite merchants and clerks on the other were asserting membership in two distinct social and cultural milieus. These categories strongly inflected people's social and cultural identity. To country folks, wearing chiripá, calzoncillo, and poncho was in no way a sign of social or cultural inferiority. In a political environment that condemned the urbanite not only for his moral feebleness but also for his allegiance with the cause of the rebels, country folks had reason to feel proud of their origins. Whether out of habit or because they considered it right, paysanos refused to wear the clothes of urban "civilization." At most, they would add to their traditional attire garments that showed their affinity to federalism, their military involvement, or their relative well-being. But the majority remained impervious to the advance of fashion.

Both militiamen and prisoners carried in their clothes the marks of the politics of the period. Curiously, it was the members of the city gentry who disguised themselves politically to please the ruling regime. More than the peons and peasants, merchants and clerks submitted to military authorities by displaying the mandatory scarlet emblems. The red of their ribbons and vests must have contrasted against the white of their shirts and the black of their coats. Against the accepted representation of clothes, militiamen were asserting compatibility of social distinction with federalist sympathies. It was possible to be federalist and still wear expensive clothes. At least in the city, the territory of commerce, professions, and "culture," federal allegiances could be expressed in a socially distinct manner. Peons and peasants also, as we shall see, exhibited a color preference (federalist) in their attire. Beyond that, their clothes carried the affirmation of their belonging to a different civilization: the countryside. This was dangerous, for by wearing paysano clothes, a man was putting himself in the sight of state recruiters. Claiming no particular distinction or privilege, rural folks risked being classified as belonging to the "peon class" and, consequently, "fit for duty."

Skirmishes for Distinction

Distinctions between paysano and pueblero clothes were also meaningful to the inhabitants of Buenos Aires. To well-to-do city dwellers dressing up was one of the "rules of urbanity," the customs and habits that separated their lifestyle from those of peasants and the urban plebe.[20] Attaining distinction in personal appearance was considered part of the "civilizing process," the gradual refinement of taste and the taming of natural human passions (see Elías 1982). Social distinction had a spatial dimension. In the city, there were places where the upper classes were able to exhibit their "superiority" without risk and places where the habits and customs of the populace reigned supreme. The city provided protected environments for display of wealth and status: the theater, private tertulias, salons, public walks, and the cafés. These were spaces where established families exhibited their social credentials, the young could show their taste for European fashion, and the emerging business elite (merchants, professionals, clerks, and, in general, men of property) could meet. In these spaces, the established and the up-and-coming consolidated family and business connections.[21]

In the circumscribed social spaces of the gente decente, dressing up was part of moving up. Those who could not keep up with fashion were excluded from the social circles of the Republic of Letters and, hence, denied the possibility of social ascent. Clerks and young merchants aspiring to a better position in life tried to dress well. Expensive clothes, being the ticket into the best circles of urban society, created anxiety for those who strove for admission. José Aguirre, the son of a cordobés merchant, committed suicide in 1850 during his stay in Buenos Aires. He was deep in debt when he died, in part due to expenses for personal clothes. Aguirre had taken goods on credit from the tailor amounting to $1,245. The bill included a green dress coat, a pair of violet trousers, a pink waistcoat, a black cashmere overcoat, a tie, two white trousers, and gloves.[22] These were undoubtedly clothes of distinction, proper to a dandy. The clothes were found spread along the staircase of Aguirre's rented house, as if exposing one of the motivations of the suicide.

This case underscores the importance of clothes as a language of class in Rosas's Buenos Aires. Aguirre's attitude toward clothes, the same as those well-to-do urbanites who responded to Rosas's call in 1851, contrasts with the egalitarianism of appearance promoted by the regime. Wearing fashionable and expensive clothes, Aguirre expected to make a good impression in urbanite elite circles, separating his persona from the stigma of the crude and uncultured provinciano. Though he could have used other means to achieve this goal (family influence or landed property), he chose clothes. This was the city's idiom of distinction.

Outside of these protected and socially marked spaces, the risk of social contamination and undifferentiation was always present. As the story of E. Echeverría's El Matadero shows, a member of the elite risked verbal or physical abuse if he ventured outside of his social milieu. Fashionable and well-dressed urbanites were called cagetillas (soft-mannered, vain, and stylish) by the peons, drovers, and butchers of the city's outskirts. Conversely, manual workers who dressed above the requirements of their occupation and social position could expect the derisory treatment of compadritos (boaster). On the outskirts of the city as well as in the main squares, the spatial boundaries of class were not yet clearly demarcated. The constant movement of oxcarts, cattle, and peddlers of all sorts created social interactions between poor and rich; in these spaces the order of appearance remained ambiguous.[23]

Impervious to fashion and unaffected by upper-class pretensions, paysanos continued to wear chiripá, poncho, calzoncillos, and bota de potro.[24] Federalism, with its chromatic politics and festive uniformity, gave them the ideological support they needed.[25] Yet, in spite of the apparent uniformity in clothing style, subtle distinctions in paysanos' appearance reflected individual economic and social aspirations. Like urbanites, paysanos participated in a culture of consumption (product of the industrial revolution), a culture that Mukerji (1983) has called "textile materialism." This culture combined the social egalitarianism of the postindependence period with the increased availability and relative cheapness of imported fabrics. In the countryside, differences in clothing were less striking than

9. Dress Styles at a Card Game. At this card game, we see two soldiers dressed in their federalist (red) uniforms. One (center, looking to the left) wears a costly headkerchief. The card player on the left, clearly a civilian, wears a scarlet *chiripá* and his *poncho* is predominantly red. The other players do not conform to the federalist dress code. A small ribbon in their hats is the only mark of their political identity. Juan I. Camaña, *Soldados de Rosas jugando a los naipes*, oil on canvas, 1852. Courtesy of the Museo Histórico Nacional, Buenos Aires.

in the city (ranchers and peons wore similar types of clothing), but those that existed marked distinctions meaningful to paysanos. To a keen observer the relative well-being of paysanos could be read in their clothes: "luxury" and "necessity" were written in the quality of the fabrics and in the condition of the garments.

Among the arrested, 40 percent lacked footwear of any kind, 35 percent had no poncho, and 8 percent possessed no hat (the source does not indicate cases of people without a shirt). These were the "countrymen in need," people in a condition close to "nakedness," a term closely associated with poverty in rural Buenos Aires. At the other extreme were those (12 percent of the cases) who added adornments to their clothing to display well-being and individuality. Some wore gilded buttons on their jackets, silver coins on their suede *tiradores* (belts with pockets), or gold-colored braid (*galones* or *trensillas*) on their hats and jackets. Others had their *calzoncillos* (leggings) embroidered (*cribados*) or with flounces (*flecos*). A few (only three of the arrested) wore silk ties. Combined with silver adornments in riding gear, these items of "luxury" conveyed an air of affluence and independence that separated their users from poor paysanos.

In the traditional attire of paysanos there was room for distinction; fabrics themselves contributed to differentiation (see Table 4.2). Of course, those using the coarser and cheaper materials were the majority—ponchos made of woolen cloth, chiripás made of heavy and coarse friezes, cloth, or flannel, shirts of cotton *zarazas* (printed chintz) and *listados* (striped ginghams), cotton leggings, and cloth jackets. A few had more expensive Brabant linen (*bramante*) drawers and shirts. Outside of this group were those wearing the marks of *resguardo* (safeguard; i.e., clothes protected the wearer from police suspicion), trousers and waistcoats. Here fabrics like cashmere and brim for trousers and satin, velveteen and silk for waistcoats competed with woolens.[26]

Judicial authorities knew how to read differences in clothing. In 1829 peasant farmer Antonio de los Santos was charged with stealing clothes (trousers, waistcoats, ties, felt hats, etc.), fabrics, riding apparel, jewelry, and coins from a tavern in the city. The judge found the goods in Santos's possession and concluded that "no person without occupation could own all this": the clothes, fabrics, and valuables were more appropriate for a merchant than a peasant. Conversely, wearing poor clothes made a person suspect for illicit behavior. Juan Vázquez, an hacendado resident of Luján, was arrested in 1838 for the possession of hides and skins with other people's brands on them. Different brands were not unusual in Buenos Aires; what was suspicious was Vazquez's appearance. Having been filling up *biscacheras* (rodent holes) in the countryside, his clothes were muddy and his appearance miserable when the policeman arrived. Vázquez later tried to demonstrate that he was not what he appeared to be: he was a proprietor, an independent producer, and an honest citizen. But, because the order of the state was based on appearance, he was arrested.[27]

In a context where proper dress could mean the difference between prison and freedom, paysanos strove to establish distinctions in outlook. Finer fabrics and adornments (buttons, silver coins, embroidery) served to convey to their peers their individual economic achievements. Implicit in these practices of distinction was an attempt to separate themselves from devalued social positions or categories. For paysanos, it was important to belong to the class of militiamen and not to be mistaken for regular soldiers (*clase de soldado de línea*).[28] Similarly, black freemen dressed in ways

TABLE 4.2 Fabric of Arrestees' Clothes

	Number	Percentage		Number	Percentage
PONCHO			LEGGINGS		
Woolen cloth (paño)	61	92.5	Poncho	54	39.0
Bayeta (flannel)	3	4.5	Jerga (saddle blanket)	42	30.2
Other	2	3.0	Cloth (paño)	17	12.2
			Bayeta (flannel)	17	12.2
JACKETS			Other	9	6.5
Woolen cloth (paño)	56	76.7			
Bayeta (flannel)	14	19.2	DRAWERS		
Other	3	4.1	Lienzo or liencillo (linen cloth)	29	81.4
SHIRTS			Bramante (Bravant linen)	7	16.3
Zaraza or listado (chintz)	18	42.8	Bayeta (flannel)	1	2.3
Bramante (Bravant linen)	13	30.9			
Lienzo or liencillo (linen cloth)	9	19.2			
Other	2	4.4			

Source: Filiaciones

that separated them from the enslaved "servant class" (*clase de criado*), and soldiers with war experience aspired to the social respect granted veterans and wanted to avoid any association with deserters or draft dodgers.

In multiple skirmishes for distinction, paysanos used clothes to state something about themselves, their aspiring social identity, and their past. Separating themselves from slaves, regular soldiers, and deserters, paysanos were expressing in their clothes the claim to rights owed to free men, patriotic militiamen, and good federales. In a social milieu characterized by an imposing egalitarianism of appearance and by an unquestioned ascription to paysano attire, clothes served as vehicles for a continuous struggle for differentiation. But the meanings deployed were different from those of well-dressed urbanites. Here, a "decent appearance" showed paysanos' pride of well-earned income or past participation in heroic military campaigns.[29] These distinctions, gradually introduced into the day-to-day interactions of peasant communities, operated in social spaces not yet permeated by the state.

Uniforms and Ambivalence

Uniforms were an important element in the disciplinary grid of Rosismo. They helped to distinguish men-at-arms from civilians and signaled to the population, in the language of colors, the overriding concerns of a nation at war. With the provision of uniforms Rosas expected to gain contentment and obedience from soldiers and, thus, improve the chances for military victories. Victories in turn would stimulate the involvement of the population in the "holy cause" of federalism. A politically and militarily mobilized countryside, with an important proportion of its youth joining the federal armies, was the best guarantee against the return of the "devilish" unitarios.

The attention Rosas and his chief commanders gave the provision of uniforms was remarkable. Particularly at times of military campaigns, this issue commanded as much attention from military chiefs as the supply of horses.[30] Soldiers, considering uniforms part of their wages, demanded regular provision from their officers. To the provincial state, this was a costly proposition, for each soldier carried to the front two shirts, two drawers, a cap, a pair of trousers, a jacket, a pair of shoes, a poncho, a shirt made of flannel, a chiripá, and a neckerchief. In spite of high costs, Rosas thought it necessary to supply uniforms regularly as a way to keep the troops content and the battalions distinguishable. Uniforms were, after all, the identifying mark of a battalion; devoid of them, soldiers looked much like paysanos.[31]

In military units, uniforms served as marks of hierarchy. To each rank corresponded a given type of uniform and, hence, certain claims to authority and privileges. Rosas's regiments respected these basic principles with rigor. The uniforms of black, creole, and Indian soldiers were almost undistinguishable among themselves but significantly different from those of officers.[32] Uniforms also varied from one corps to the next. Scarlet jackets, blue trousers with red bands on the sides, scarlet Phrygian caps (*gorros de mango*), blue ponchos with red inside, chiripás of different grades of red, white drawers, and more made for a colorful and heterogeneous soldiery. Only scarlet red (punzó) prevailed in all of them, for this was the color of the Federation.[33]

Intended to mark a visible difference between soldiers and peasants, uniforms became in practice a malleable commodity and a sign of ambiguous meaning. The circulation of uniforms and military regalia among the peasantry made the identification of soldiers quite difficult. Contrasted with paysano attire, uniforms presented both similarities and differences. Red bands on blue caps and blue bands on red trousers were not common

10. Federalist Distinction (Col. Santa Coloma). This colonel of the federalist army wears the signs of federalism—
his horse has red adornments in head and tail, his jacket is
scarlet with a dark blue chest—as well as the marks of
"distinction." Notice the silverwork in his saddle and har-
ness, the embroidery of his *calzoncillos* and *chiripá*, his silver
spurs, and the shape of his hat. Felix Revol, *Retrato del
Coronel Martín Santa Coloma*, oil on canvas, 1847. Courtesy
of the Museo Histórico Nacional, Buenos Aires.

in paysano attire, yet many federal soldiers wore chiripá, poncho, and bota
de potro, typical peasant garments.[34] Scarlet jackets were proper for soldiers, but nothing prevented paysanos from wearing scarlet ponchos that
conveyed a somewhat similar appearance. Common folk knew quite well
what a Rosista uniform looked like. When in April 1831 Gregorio Casales
burned an effigy of Judas dressed in a federal uniform, most of the residents of Ranchos were able to testify that the dummy's clothes were,
unequivocally, the representation of a federalist military.[35] For us, not apprenticed into the complex symbolism of braids, buttons, jackets, bands,

and ribbons, the distinction between civilians and soldiers appears more problematic. Looking at representations of the period, we fail to recognize who is a military man and who is a paysano. The chromatic uniformity of Rosismo, with its preponderance of scarlet red (*rojo punzó*), confuses us.[36]

Paysanos' position in relation to federal uniforms was equally ambiguous. The few who still held out hope for a unitario victory saw federal uniforms as a symbol of oppression. The majority of rural inhabitants, however, felt ambivalent about the military and their clothes. Part of the reason for this ambivalence related to the army's recruitment methods, combining force with economic incentives. A person in a uniform could be either a delinquent forced into service or an honest paysano serving as a veteran soldier; the wearing of the uniform itself said little about the person's social identity and past, for once recruited, the prisoner and the militiaman, if they happened to serve in the same corps, wore identical uniforms. The ambivalence also derived from the ways peasants, laborers, and soldiers confronted the state on the issue of military service. On occasion, they rejected their uniforms and pretended to be paysanos; on other occasions, they wore their military uniforms with pride. Paysanos' arts of deception rendered ambiguous the symbolic value of uniforms.

The clothes of the arrested show a selective appropriation of uniforms into paysanos' attire. Though few of the arrested in our sample were wearing military uniforms, many had pieces of uniforms with them. Military caps, jackets, trousers, or ponchos complemented the typical garments of paysanos. Blue ponchos with red inside provided by the army were in common use among country folk, and so were the cone-like scarlet caps used by federal policemen and soldiers (*gorra de manga*). Some peasants attached gilded braids to their caps or hats, while others wore jackets and chiripás made from recycled fabrics taken from uniforms.

For those trying to escape the grip of the state, wearing a uniform presented a disadvantage. Sometimes the simple rumor that a prisoner had been seen in uniform was considered sufficient evidence of desertion. Hence deserters, to avoid detection, abandoned their uniforms and took on paysano clothes. When soldier Tomás Bravo deserted the Masons battalion in October 1849, his commander reported: "It is known that he has been in Zárate for some days disguised in paysano clothes, and that from there he has gone to the county [San Nicolás] where his mother Isadora Herrera lives." Young deserter José S. Vivas, who after his escape found work in a Quilmes tavern, was seen by the policeman in the act of hiding his uniform in a thistle field.[37] The word "disguise" in relation to the clothes of peasants corresponds quite well with the response of most persecuted persons: the attempt to hide by changing their outward appearance.

This need to change clothes after a desertion explains the relatively small proportion of uniformed men among the arrested (less than 5 percent, whereas 30 percent of the sample were deserters). Under the circumstances, getting rid of uniforms was a quite rational decision. Absconding with or selling one's uniform and taking paysano clothes was part of a disappearing act that required other "arts of deception." Frequently, deserters changed names to start a new life with a whole new identity. Some presented themselves to the authorities carrying false identity papers (passports, enlistment *papeletas*, and work contracts); others lied as a means to reduce the penalties associated with lack of prior military service.

On the other hand, uniforms represented a salable asset, a commodity that, once realized, could facilitate the survival of those escaping persecution. To contain this illegal traffic channeling state goods to private, working-class circuits, military authorities severely punished the sale and purchase of uniforms.[38] But the theft and sale of uniforms continued as long as there were customers avid for these clothes. To paysanos stolen uniforms were a cheaper alternative to purchased clothes. Peasants participated in this illegal traffic, buying uniforms and adapting them to civilian life: a pair of trousers could easily be transformed into a chiripá by cutting the sides and closing the front part.[39] Uniforms were also an important reservoir of value. Inventories of officers' possessions at the time of death indicate that uniforms, together with riding apparel, were their most important assets. One or two knitted ponchos, a pair of cloth jackets, a pair of pantaloons of the same material, three *zaraza* shirts, three pairs of drawers (*calzoncillos*), a pair of boots, and a liberty (or Phyrgian) cap amounted to $454, a sum inaccessible to common soldiers. While the better off could show their "savings" (gold or silver coins) on their belts and in the possession of a few horses, poor veterans kept their uniforms as a valuable possession to be converted to cash in time of need.[40]

While some deserters were discarding their uniforms and some soldiers were earning extra cash by selling theirs, others carried their military clothing into civilian life. Anacleto Gómez, a peon resident of Morón, continued dressing in military fashion two years after he was dismissed from the army. Civilians with braids on their hats or jackets or with military jackets or scarlet chiripás were often seen in taverns, along roads, and at festivities, making it difficult to identify a true soldier.[41] Why did paysanos adopt some items of the military attire? Surely, there were those who had no other clothes after their discharge, but it is also clear that such items acquired a symbolic value that facilitated social relations, particularly among men.

Wearing military garments and regalia garnered respect from the population and a convenient neglect from judicial authorities. A gilded braid, a medal, or an army poncho served as key marks for recognition among veterans. Pieces of uniforms recalled a personal history and evoked moments of common experience in military campaigns. In addition, uniforms gave veterans an opportunity for expressing their patriotism. Perhaps these signs allowed their bearers to avoid some unnecessary proofs of masculinity, thus reducing the risk of knife fights. In this symbolic economy, even the mustache (a privilege of federalist troops) constituted a sign of pride for some veterans. After the fall of Rosas, when the advantages of wearing federal uniforms were no longer evident, we still find some soldiers holding on, stubbornly, to their weapons and uniforms.[42]

Dressing like a military man or like a paysano was a tactical decision whose convenience depended on rural people's position vis-à-vis the powerful. Those on the run needed to trade their uniforms for paysano attire. Veterans who were already established in the towns, those who were socially recognized as good federalists, were able to blend their traditional paysano clothing with items of military use. For economic or symbolic reasons, peons and peasants acquired uniforms, recycled them, and used them as reservoirs of value. The traffic in uniforms, the mixing of styles, and the art of disguise gave the Buenos Aires countryside a confusing appearance. Beyond the preponderance of reds, everybody seemed to be in between: neither a soldier nor a civilian. To an extent, this confusion corresponded with the identity that peon soldiers wanted to display: they were federalists committed to the "Holy Cause" but with an ambivalent relationship to the state and its representatives.

The Politics of Colors

No resident of Buenos Aires during the Rosas administration could fail to notice the importance of colors in the social and political life of the province. Allegiance to federalism seemed to be reducible to a chromatic uniformity. It mandated the use of scarlet red emblems on an everyday basis and made scarlet the preferred color of federales. Anxious about its popularity in the countryside, the government tried to monitor as closely as possible the colors used by paysanos. Orders given to justices and police chiefs emphasized the need to enforce the ordinances on federalist emblems and colors. After 1836, the question of colors became an obsession for the regime. Rosas himself became preoccupied with the possibility of country folks changing the color of their clothes. A rumor, circulated widely in the countryside, stated that paysanos were dyeing their clothes light blue as a result of the devilish influence of unitarios.[43] Possibly, blue ponchos were turning light blue as a result of use, but Rosas preferred to believe in the political sagacity of his enemies.

Despite the coercive nature of the regime, compliance with Rosas's color regulations was less extensive than we tend to think. Even in the port city, a territory better controlled by Rosas's police, the wearing of federalist ribbons (divisas and cintillos) was not widespread. As late as 1839 General Pacheco thought that their use was not mandatory in the city, as so few wore them.[44] Many town dwellers carried their ribbons with them but did not wear them unless confronted by authorities. Others considered that a good scarlet vest was a proper substitute for the emblem. Those rich enough to afford a portrait or a daguerreotype had their ribbons added to the image, for they themselves rarely wore them (Cuarterolo 1995). In the provinces, the situation was worse. Though federalism was popular in the littoral, scarlet ribbons were much less visible there. If we are to trust the word of some of the arrested coming from the littoral, the scarcity of scarlet ribbons made compliance with the federalist code almost impossible. Some travelers from Corrientes and Entre Ríos put on their ribbons only after crossing the Buenos Aires border.

Something similar occurred in the countryside, despite constant assertions to the contrary of justices of the peace and military commanders. According to the evidence provided by statistics of arrests in the countryside, the compliance fell short of the governor's expectations. Only 27 percent of our sample complied with the requirement to carry both divisa (red ribbon on the chest) and cintillo (red ribbon around the hat): 16 percent wore only the cintillo, 9 percent only the divisa, and 47 percent wore none of the symbols of federalism. Viewed from a more optimistic perspective, we can say that 52 percent of the arrested had on their clothes some kind of federal emblem. This, however, was not reassuring news to the regime, which expected everybody to use these emblems.

A significant proportion of rural folks, on the other hand, dressed in federal colors (scarlet and navy blue): 52 percent of all chiripás were scarlet red, as were 59 percent of jackets and 95 percent of shirts. A full 67 percent of all ponchos were blue, some (17 percent) with red inside. Paysanos preferred white shirts (51 percent), though rose and purple were also common. For jackets, dark colors were the norm (black, blue, dark brown, and lead), red the exception. Light blue and green, the colors that represented opposition to the Federal Cause, were almost absent (see Table 4.3).

Apparently, indigo blue and scarlet red, the colors of federal uniforms

TABLE 4.3 Color of Arrestees' Clothes

	Number	Percentage		Number	Percentage
PONCHO			**LEGGINGS**		
Solid blue	27		Blue	14	
Blue with red inside	26	66.7	Blue with stripes	4	19.6
Blue with stripes	3		Striped various colors		15.2
Scarlet red	6	16.7	Other (white, almond,		13.0
Red with stripes	8		rose, coffee, purple,		
Striped various colors		8.3	green		
Other (almond, rose,		8.3			
lead, black)			**SHIRTS**		
			White	16	51.6
WAISTCOATS			Rose	8	25.7
Scarlet red	26	59.0	Purple	4	12.8
Blue	7	15.9	Other (blue, red)	3	9.6
Black	6	13.6			
Other (yellow, almond,	5	11.4	**JACKETS**		
lead, white)			Blue	29	41.4
			Dark brown	14	20.0
LEGGINGS			Scarlet red	10	14.3
Scarlet red	45		Black	10	14.3
Red with stripes	3	52.2	Lead or dark	5	7.1
			White	2	2.9

Source: Filiaciones (N = 235)

and emblems, were ubiquitous, implying that, however defiant of law and authority, arrested paysanos rarely challenged the chromatic symbolism of federalism. Why was this so? Undoubtedly, the supply of fabrics conditioned their "preference." Foreign merchants dealing with the Buenos Aires market understood well the art of selling under federalist hegemony. They knew that light blue and green fabrics were unsalable under the Rosas regime, and that fabrics of different tonalities of red had an expanding market (Chapman 1979). As they could do little to influence local politics and ideology, they took porteños' color preferences as a given and sent an inordinate proportion of scarlet and "claret red" fabrics to Buenos Aires. Other colors not demanded in Buenos Aires could find purchasers in Río de Janeiro, Lima, or other centers of distribution.[45] "Red, pink and scarlet ground print are now all the rage here," advised James Hodgson in 1838 to his partners in Manchester, "these being the popular or Federal

TABLE 4.4 Origin of Arrestees' Clothes

	Leggings		Poncho	
	Number	Percentage	Number	Percentage
BRITAIN	41	61.2	11	52.4
DOMESTIC	26	38.8	10	47.6
Córdoba	13		4	
Pampa Indians	8		3	
Santiago Estero	1		2	
Mendoza	1		—	
Arribeño	3		1	

Source: *Filiaciones*

Party colors, and what is more: to every appearance, as far as can be seen forwards, they are certain to remain so" (qtd. in Reber, 1972, 130).

Other suppliers, most notably those trading in Indian rugs and ponchos and in woolens and cottons manufactured in the northwest, also provided an assortment of red clothes (see Table 4.4). Despite reports describing country folks as clothed from head to foot in British manufactures, paysanos continued to purchase fabrics and clothes produced in the northern provinces or in Indian camps. British ponchos and chiripás (made of ponchos) constituted more than half of the clothes worn by those arrested.[46] On the other hand, the proportion of people wearing ponchos *pampa* (ponchos made by pampa Indians) or ponchos *arribeños* (ponchos made in northern provinces) was remarkably high considering the devastating competition by British fabrics.[47] These alternative suppliers (indigenous tribes and women weavers in the upper provinces) were less concerned with the chromatics of federalism. By necessity, they used red dyes in their products, but not the scarlet red preferred by Federalists.

The higher compliance with Federalist colors than with Federalist emblems may reflect the supply conditions encountered in the market for fabrics and clothes. But more was at stake than simple market preferences. Underneath the preponderance of scarlet red was the paysano tradition, developed in the midst of their confrontation with the state, of appropriating and recycling uniforms. And, quite significantly, paysanos' politics of ambivalence developed through the adaptation of uniforms to civilian use. Not surprisingly, justices of the peace and military inquisitors had trouble identifying deserters. It was not easy to distinguish when a red chiripá was part of the uniform, or whether the person wearing a military-like poncho (blue with red inside) had the right to use it. The "outward conformity" of paysanos to the chromatics of federalism had as much to do with their military experience—with their ongoing confrontation with state authorities over issues of recruitment, pay, and leave—as with their "preferences" for one political party.

Making a Good Impression

In February 1835, four men assaulted Jose M. Miranda's pulperia in Lobos.[48] The thieves—Toribio González, Lorenzo Ardiles, Simeón and Francisco Caravajal—arrived at the tavern at dusk, tied up the patrons, and took their booty. González took a silver stirrup, a whip with a silver handle, and other things for himself, while the rest put the load of ponchos and cloth (the chief part of the booty) into three large leather cases (*maletas*), which were later loaded onto the horses. In their escape, they rode together for a mile, after which they divided the clothes and rode off in separate directions.

From this point on, the narration (provided by the justice of Lobos) deals with the manner in which the different members of this group distributed their share of the booty among friends, bosses, and women. González and Ardiles escaped in the direction of Navarro, where they hid the booty in the bush (*entre la paja*). Carrying only some items with them, they then paid a visit to Manuela and Cruz, the daughters of farmer José de la Cruz Cabrera, and tried to buy their "favors" with gifts. González gave Cruz a length of zaraza (chintz) for a dress, a pair of shoes, a cotton handkerchief, and a pair of silk garters. Later that night, González went to Luján to see his ex-employer, D. Pedro Parra, and further distributed the rest of the clothes. He gave Parra a *vara* (about 2.8 feet) of red flannel, a pair of drawers, and a small knife, and regaled Parra's wife with a length of listado (striped gingham) for a dress and a cotton kerchief for a *rebozo* (head shawl). He left other items of clothing with Fructuosa Pérez, a woman residing in the neighborhood, and pawned some silver objects at Juan Lavalle's tavern for $30 cash. One of the ponchos went as a present to his brother.[49]

In the meantime, Ardiles paid a visit to his friend Juan A. Coll. As his friend was not home, he took from his luggage two lengths of printed chintz, a blanket, a dress, and some nice kerchiefs and offered them to Coll's wife, Jacinta Ballesteros, who later helped him escape from the police. Manuel Medina, his nephew, joined him at Coll's ranch and received as gifts a hat, some drawers, and a poncho. When Don Juan arrived,

Ardiles gave him a short sable and silver spurs, and then, to solidify their friendship (and also to confuse the police), they exchanged ponchos. Despite this precaution, Ardiles was arrested near Coll's ranch. Simeón Caravajal went to Montes, where he sought refuge at the house of an ex-employer, and then went back to Lobos to meet his brother and reclaim the booty. The two decided that Francisco should take the booty first to Buenos Aires and from there to San Nicolás. Their strategy, unlike that of Ardiles and González, consisted in selling most of the clothes in relatively distant markets. Apparently, Francisco was successful in this enterprise, but was arrested when he returned to Buenos Aires. Simeón was arrested shortly after the assault. The four men received a summary instruction and were sentenced to several years of service in the army.

The theft of clothes can introduce us into popular meanings of clothes that differ somewhat from the logic of distinction, political conformity, or draft resistance. In this story, clothes acquire different value and meaning. The thieves distributed the garments and fabrics as gifts to get the attention of women, as payment of favors granted to them by relatives, as a means to impress ex-employers, and as seals of enduring friendship. Like money, clothes served to cement social relations among paysanos. It is unclear which part of the booty the thieves cashed in for money (the illegally obtained commodities would probably have found a ready market in Buenos Aires and the surrounding farm areas), as most of the narration concentrates on the gifts. Friendship, family, and sex figure prominently in this story as the key motivations for distributing the booty. Also important are the relations between the thieves (peons) and their ex-employers (small-scale farmers and ranchers), making clear that in their confrontation with the justice system, class divisions were suspended.

The goods stolen and distributed were also meaningful. They were items coveted by women (chintz dresses, cotton kerchiefs, silk garters, and shoes) and men (riding apparel with silver adornments, ponchos, knives, drawers). They were objects of "necessity" (as they satisfied a basic need) but, at the same time, objects that conveyed distinction to their owner. Additionally, clothes and fabrics were goods easy to hide and sell. The thieves made an impressive effort to spread out the booty in as many locations and among as many people as possible to confuse the authorities. If the operation had gone as planned, their social investment would have paid great dividends. They would have favored many friends, relatives, bosses, and women who could help them later in time of need. Their strategy was one of generosity and delayed reciprocity.

Connections among the thieves are not wholly spelled out in the narration. We know, however, that the four were natives from Santiago del

11. Gaucho in Town Clothes. According to this contemporary engraving, peasants dressed up to go to town. This gaucho is wearing an elegant waistcoat, a bow tie, jacket, and trousers. To avoid suspicion, he wears the federalist ribbon on his jacket. Carlos Morel, *Gaucho en traje de pueblo—Buenos Aires*, lithograph, 1841. Reproduced from F. Chávez, *Iconografía de Rosas y de la Federación* (1970).

Estero and that at least two of them had met in the militias. Probably their friendship congealed in relation to the abuses of officers. They were all peons, moving from one place to another in search of jobs. Apparently, this experience gave them the knowledge of the territory they needed to plan their escape. Their chief protectors were their ex-employers, all small-scale producers. Pedro Parra had a small farm in Saladas, and Juan Coll worked an *estanzuela* (actually, a farm) on lands belonging to Don Felipe Rojas in Guardia de Luján. Women played a central role in this episode, acting as depositories of the goods stolen and beneficiaries of important gifts, and they helped the thieves escape the authorities.

A small window into the mentalities and sensibilities of peons, peasants, and poor women, this case reveals the existence of networks of solidarity among poor paysanos against state authorities and the justice system. The relations alluded to in this narration (family, friendship, and comradeship) speak of a different arrangement of power than the one envisioned in the state classifications. These networks of solidarity, though insufficient to support the notion of "class" as an autonomous construction from below, point to the existence of an alternative perspective or understanding of the order of appearances. We find here a subaltern, picaresque perspective, based on the negation of the absoluteness of property. From the thieves' viewpoint, the stolen goods can be used to make a good impression. Here clothes, instead of separating people, served to cement social relationships.

In a culture of delayed reciprocity and tolerated illegalities, the theft and distribution of clothes reaffirmed the importance of appearance among paysanos. Clothing gifts, this story seems to say, were an excellent means for consolidating friendship, love relationships, and patronage. Not altogether opposed to distinction, this type of solidarity from below, solidified by exchanges of clothes, signals a different structuring of experience, another layer of meaning separated from class-ification, the chromatics of federalism, and the power of uniforms. Immersed in the culture of "textile materialism," subaltern men and women are interested in accepting clothes, regardless of their illicit origins, in exchange for cooperation, food, or sex or as a token of friendship.

Conclusions: Class-ification, Distinction, and Resistance

In this chapter, I have presented various dimensions of a project of class predicated on the outward appearance of people, a project that stemmed simultaneously from the state and from civil society and that found, in its deployment and realization, multiple obstacles and contradictions. More directly related to the process of class formation were two sets of practices: skirmishes about clothes aimed at constituting social distinction and state policies of class-ification geared to the identification and separation of the "peon class." Both tried to connect appearances with class, but their aims and instruments were different. Class-ification used the order of appearance to separate recruits for the army, subordinating the making of class to the goals of the state. Distinction stemmed from the social fabric: from the pretensions of men of letters to social superiority, from the aspirations of paysanos for greater autonomy, well-being, and respect, from notions of rights derived from the experiences of peons and soldiers, from the tensions between uniformed men and civilians. Both state and civil society contributed to the formation of an order of appearance that had social, political, and cultural ingredients.

In the contrast between the clothes of urban reserve militias and those of prisoners we found some support for the idea that, under Rosismo, class distinctions were important and meaningful. Appearance divided urbanites and rural people and stimulated the need for differentiation among rural folks. The clothes of paysanos show some traces of subaltern distinction, the display of the little affluence and independence gained through wage labor. On their horses, on their belts, on their hats and clothes paysanos carried the signs of well-being that sustained their claims to citizenship and individual autonomy. In this regard, their unspoken values differed little from those of the educated elite: for both groups, *appearance* constituted the territory for the assertion of claims about social distinction and economic achievement.

Two other forces, the militarization of society and the colors of federalism, which disseminated uniforms, military regalia, and scarlet clothes among the population, were not so clearly related to the process of class formation. In fact, it could be argued that these forces generated conditions that conspired against the project of class division: symbolic ambiguity and chromatic uniformity. In the context of intensified ideological and political strife, social differences could be only modestly displayed. Politics imposed particular inflections on the order of appearance, interfering with and complicating the formation of class distinctions.

The ambivalence and contradiction of official discourse about appearance resulted in ambiguities for both dominant and subaltern. The contradictions among the different claims of the Rosista state must have been evident to contemporary observers. Quite often—in poems recited in taverns, in declarations by local justices, during patriotic festivities, or in official proclamations of federalist doctrine—country folks heard praises for the simplicity of paysano clothes and calls to wear the federal colors, all in uniformity. But recruiting practices contradicted this ideal. Whereas the ideology of federalism penalized the display of fashionable urban clothing, the military-judicial apparatus put a premium on the wearing of more expensive clothes by arresting those who looked like peons. This was indeed a confusing set of messages.[50]

Paysanos reacted to these contradictory and complex messages about what constituted proper dress. Through a variety of small acts of resistance and accommodation (which I prefer to call "skirmishes for distinction"), poor country folks defied the dress codes defined from above, adding ambiguity and confusion to separations based on social class. The state objective of separating a peon class was jeopardized by the multiple arts of deception through which paysanos made their appearance an ambivalent sign to decipher. Itinerant peons and laborers used the language of clothes to confuse state authorities. Dressing up they could pass for a middling cattle raiser, for a farmer, or for a ranch foreman and thus avoid recruitment. In this case, distinction was a matter of finer fabrics, medals or coins in their belts, waistcoats and jackets, embroidered drawers, and silver adornments on their horses. Ex-soldiers who exhibited pieces of military regalia on their clothes projected a distinction of a different kind; asserting that they had already paid their dues to federalism, they expected to remain unmolested by the authorities and respected by the rest of the community.

Cross-dressing and mimesis, the same tactics that made Rosas so popular among paysanos served the poor to alleviate their condition in a repressive society. Through dress, poor women, soldiers, peons and peasants, and indigenous peoples could advance their positions beyond those granted by their possessions, residence, legal status, and ethnicity. Disguise was a common strategy of deserters, potential draftees, and even unitarios.[51] Multiple instances of "social cross-dressing"—the ability to clothe oneself in a different social identity—are indicative of a generalized resistance to an arrangement of class based on appearance. Female servants imitating their mistress, Indians dressed as gauchos, peasants disguised as military men, soldiers in the clothes of country folks, unitarios passing for federales speak of the ambiguities and fluidity of a society so concerned with social, racial, and political definitions.

We have seen also how the political conflict colored the order of appearance, leaving a definite imprint on the clothes and lives of peasants and peons. Though less subordinate to state logic, paysanos' skirmishes for distinction had to work within a language provided by the state: the chromatics of federalism; its egalitarian postures; its understandings of fatherland, citizenship, and service; its criminal and recruitment policies. The appropriation (physical and symbolic) of clothes and uniforms by paysanos depended on a broad social and political context in which the state played a principal role. For it was the state, with its land, military, and judicial policy, that set the terms for the ordering of social life in the countryside.

The politics of federalism affected the way paysanos dressed as much as the practices of class-ification and distinction. Peons and peasants lived and struggled within this politically and socially loaded symbolic system. How did they accommodate their "consumer preferences" (i.e., their defined taste for textiles, shoes, and colors) to this system? My evidence suggests the limited extent to which paysanos complied with Rosas's regulations on federal emblems. This same evidence shows a definite preference for federal colors in their clothing. The latter might have resulted from the massive appropriation and recycling of uniforms, itself a moment in the confrontation between peon soldiers and authorities over the payment of military services. Or, it could be related to the increased availability of red cloth in the market.

On the political and ideological continuum, the dress of poor country folks was certainly biased on the side of federalism. They were not prepared to change their clothing style (*vestir a lo paisano*) to follow the vague idea of national union and the literate civilization proposed by unitarios. But this should not be interpreted as a sign of political conformity, for there is evidence that people did not conform in all respects with the order of appearance projected by the regime. Rather, I am inclined to think that paysanos selectively incorporated in their clothes the political symbolism of federalism while rejecting with their feet—as the stories of deserters and draft dodgers show—the authoritarian features of the federal state. Constantly harassed by military recruiters and justices of the peace, paysanos might have felt little inclination to legitimate, through their clothes and on a daily basis, the continuity of the regime. Hence, many defied the ordinance about the compulsory use of federalist emblems.

Within a grid of power relations that characterized life in the countryside, wealth, eloquence, and social connections, paysanos knew well enough, served to make a good impression. So did clothes, particularly when used as gifts. Among the rural poor (among northern migrants, small-scale cattle raisers and farmers, and women) clothes served to cement social relations. At the other extreme of the social scale, clothes acted as a filter that prevented outsiders from entering into the sociability of the city gentry (*gente decente*). Reciprocity and exclusion were two registers of the class use of clothes.

During the Rosas period, class-ification and distinction remained in balance, countering each other as markers of class. It was only later (after the fall of Rosas) that the signals provided by markets, social interaction, and state policy began to work in the same direction. In the 1850s and 1860s, no longer contained by the ideology of unanimismo—the unanimity of opinions—and the corresponding chromatics of federalism, clothing became an unambiguous marker of class. Distinction and fashion returned with a vengeance, as perceptively described by H. S. Ferns: "It even became a civil offence to appear in the parks of Buenos Aires without a jacket, collar and tie. Fashionable churches, fashionable theatres, fashionable tea-rooms, and fashionable clubs flourished to emphasize the pride of riches and positions" (qtd. in Calvert and Calvert 1989, 191).

CHAPTER 5

The Power of Laws

Despite ample disagreements among historians about the meaning and nature of Rosismo, most accounts of the period 1825–1852 coincide on one point: the Rosas regime lacked any credible system of justice.[1] Its self-proclaimed "restoration of laws" was mere propaganda. The corresponding title bestowed on the governor by the legislature, the Restorer of the Laws, seems a farcical misrepresentation of a regime of terror and arbitrariness.[2] Whatever their differences regarding the nature of Rosas's popularity, system of government, or policies, historians agree that the dictatorship could not truthfully claim to have restored the "imperium of laws." Powerful arguments support this view. The terror and confiscations leveled against unitarios, the concentration of all powers in the Dictator, the use of summary proceedings, the abuse of judicial discretion, all contradicted the notion of the "rule of law (even if understood in the restricted sense of a government bounded by rules)."[3] Contemporary observers conceded that Rosas was able to provide some political stability, creating the preconditions for a functioning legal order, but regarding the efficacy of the laws in regulating social behavior, they were silent.[4]

Rosista contemporary rhetoric, on the other hand, asserted that the laws had a central place in the construction of the postindependence federalist order and that Governor Rosas, having restored legitimate government and intensified the enforcement of existing laws, was able to reestablish people's belief in the legal order. When Rosas assumed the "sum of public power" on April 13, 1835, he promised to complete the enterprise of moralizing and ordering civil society, a campaign envisioned in 1820, when "anarchy" shook the foundations of the republic. His government, he stated, would sustain the cause of "religion, justice, humanity, and public order." Relentlessly he would persecute "the impious, the sacrilegious, the thief, the murderer and, above all, the traitor who had taken advantage of and mocked at our good faith."[5] Although the main target of the persecution was the unitario—an enemy of mythical proportions who embodied all the above attributes—the threat was intended also for the common criminal who, in the troubled political waters of the times, found impunity for his crimes.

"Restoring the laws," a commitment the people of Buenos Aires entrusted to Rosas in a landslide plebiscite, involved at least three major tasks: reestablishing a credible political authority, guaranteeing the rights enjoyed by the townships (pueblos) since the revolution, and bringing public order and tranquility to the countryside. The achievement of political order entailed recuperating the principle of obedience to authority, and this, in turn, demanded building the consensus necessary to consolidate the legitimacy of rule (Myers 1995, 74–77). But, as Rosas's promises and threats indicate, the program was much more ambitious, aiming at the reformation of the customs and values of inhabitants as they related to the legal order. The population needed to feel the power of laws and accept the institutions of justice.[6] The reconstitution of a peaceful republic, according to the federalists, required nothing less than rebuilding "public morality," a good rooted in the structure of feelings and the everyday practices of paysanos.

Restoring the Laws: The Law in Federalist Discourse

Before examining the law as a form of political engagement or popular pedagogy, we need to recognize the obvious: the restoration of laws was a discursive reality of ample dissemination and profound implications. The discourse of the law informed popular legends, public speech, political poetry, and official propaganda. The political project of federalism was unimaginable without this all-encompassing signifier, the Laws.

According to a contemporary popular legend, a beggar put in motion the Revolution of the Restorers (October 1833). Governor Balcarce's attempt to close and bring to trial the Rosista newspaper El Restaurador de las Leyes caused indignation among liberal-minded residents. The urban populace, in the mistaken belief that General Rosas had been arrested and convicted, soon began to gather in front of the courthouse. On the morning of October 11, facing a crowd that stood expectantly, a beggar started to shout "Viva el Restaurador de las Leyes!" He was immediately followed by a chorus of angry citizens who responded "Viva!" Showing solidarity with the imaginary prisoner, the crowd proclaimed, "His crime is our crime," and started to move against the police squad protecting the courthouse.[7] The voice of the beggar transformed a subterranean "general sentiment" into an open, collective protest for public rights and legality.

In this popular rendition, the crowd attacked the judiciary, seeking to reestablish the freedom of the press and, at the same time, trying to defend the Restorer of the Laws against a malicious and unrepresentative elite. The story deals with a quite modern concern: the emergence of public opinion and collective action in a context of democratic principles in peril. The legend destabilizes commonly accepted interpretations of Rosismo, pointing to the centrality of laws in the constitution of the moral community that supported Rosas. However ambivalently, this narration presents the subaltern as the force upholding the law (meaning both public liberties and the legal system), recuperating along the way the egalitarian, democratic ethos of the event. A radical inversion reaffirms the connection between popular government and the law. It is the beggar, a subaltern usually subjected to the repression of vagrancy laws, who reminds citizens of the value of a free press and legal order.

Official propaganda contributed significantly to the enterprise of placing the law at the center of the federalist imaginary. In 1842 the Chamber of Representatives published a small book that narrated the entangled lives of Rosas and the Confederation: *Rasgos de la vida pública de S.E. el Sr. Brigadier General D. Juan Manuel de Rosas.* Intended for a didactic purpose, the official biography presented the question of legality as paramount to the survival of the fatherland.[8] Not surprisingly, the account started in December 1828, when Lavalle's overthrow and later execution of Governor Dorrego put at risk the institutional continuity and unity of the republic. This original crime—to have assaulted and closed the Legislature, the "sanctuary" of the laws—unleashed a sequence of illegalities that eroded people's belief in the legal order. At this moment Rosas, the visionary citizen, spoke up and managed to unite the outraged citizens under the "banner of the laws." Together, militias and Rosas pledged before God not to return to their homes until they had "rebuilt the temple of laws."[9]

From that day on, the federalist narrative stated, the Confederation engaged in a prolonged and costly war against the "impious" and "anarchist" rebels. For thirteen years thousands of soldiers sacrificed their lives to the "saintly cause of the laws." By 1842 such sacrifices had borne fruit and the federalist victory was complete: the institutions of the republic had been recovered, the "temple of laws" reconstructed, popular sovereignty reinstated. Rosas had extirpated "the principle of social insubordination" and subjected people to authority. He had reestablished, in short, "*el imperio augusto de las leyes*" ("the magnificent reign of the laws") (*Rasgos de la vida pública* 1842, xxxv).

To a good federalist, this was a well-known story: the account of the fall and rebirth of the republic under the guidance of a visionary and virtuous Citizen. Biblical metaphors served to dramatize what was in essence a republican epic. The leading signifier, the law, represented the "temple" of representative government and also the "banner" that joined citizens' will in a common cause. Images of a desecrated "sanctuary" and of a community mobilized for a "holy war" were commensurate to the task to be accomplished: the elimination of the impious unitarios and the rebuilding of the legal order.[10] Though the narrative did not mention the judiciary, terms such as "the reign of laws" alluded directly to the power of a reconstituted state to make citizens abide by the law. The thing being "restored" was, in other words, the hegemonic power of laws: a republican power that produced compliance and belief.

The central place attributed to the law in the making of the federalist republic was complemented with a specific conception of justice, one that combined expediency and duress with respect for legal procedures. To Rosas, the restoration of laws conveyed the idea of "swift justice." Only a justice system able to rapidly arrest, indict, and sentence criminals would be able to demonstrate to the population the necessity and benefits of a legal order. Embedded in this ideal of justice were the duress of exemplary punishment and the predictability of regular, systematic, local enforcement. The law was a crucial component of the order imagined by federalists. Effective and exemplary, this justice was also democratic and egalitarian, conceived as the complement of a political system founded on universal (male) suffrage.

In an address to the Chamber of Representatives on February 2, 1850, Judge Baldomero García presented the restoration as the true origin of equality before the law in the republic. "General Rosas," stated judge García, "imposing with robust effort the observance of the law, equal for all, has for the first time made effective the word Republic among us" (qtd. in Myers 1995, 305–306). Before Rosas, political rights were a mockery because no public functionary dared to act against the city gentry. Under Rosas's leadership, people and authorities, the rich and the poor, commanded the same respect before the law. "With regard to rights, we are all equal," claimed García. This rather strong assertion from the president of the Superior Tribunal points to an overlooked dimension of the Rosas regime: the connection between law enforcement and political equality.[11]

In official rhetoric, restoring the laws alluded to the double task of civilizing the plebe into a legal culture and reestablishing legitimate political authority. With variations, echoes of this powerful discourse found their way into political poetry, theater, popular sayings, military proclamations, and other public manifestations. *Lanuzza o el Defensor de las Leyes*, a play performed on January 7, 1836 as a benefit for the captives rescued during the Campaign to the Desert, pondered the necessity of a system of laws for the preservation of a republic.[12] Military proclamations (addressed to federalist soldiers) explained in unambiguous terms the nature of the civil war: it was a response to the threat posed by unitarios to the institutional continuity of the republic. The federales, officers told soldiers, were only restituting the legitimate authorities and the rule of law.[13] Similarly, in contemporary political poetry the law became a new focus of attention, a powerful point of reference for evaluating the progress made since the revolution of independence.[14] The recollection in verse of a civic-military demonstration in favor of Rosas in September 1851 replicated the association of the federalist order with legal equality and the enforcement of laws.[15] Paysano Justo Calandria contrasted the past, a time of inequality, with the federalist present, a time when an unbiased justice ruled over the land. Poor and rich received the same treatment and crime found its punishment wherever it fell.[16] As the poet put it: "Today, crime is punished and virtue rewarded."

Enforcing the Laws

The credit attributed to Rosas for having restored the laws referred chiefly to the greater enforcement of existing laws and institutions, rather than to innovations implemented in these matters.[17] The laws Rosas enforced were those left by previous administrations, especially those enacted by Rivadavia and by the earlier revolutionary governments. In criminal cases in particular, ancient colonial laws were still in use (the Siete Partidas and the Novísima Compilación) as a result of the failure of postindependence governments to produce a modern penal code.[18] Rosas himself added very little to this impressive, and disarrayed, corpus of legislation. A similar continuity can be observed with regard to the institutions of justice. Rosas maintained the Superior Tribunal, the Appeals Court, and the four "first instance" courts (two for penal cases, two for civil cases) almost without change. Besides the expansion in the number of members of the Superior Tribunal (from five to seven) and the replacement on two occasions (1835 and 1838) of judges who were avowedly nonpartisan, the formal structure of the justice system remained unaltered.[19]

The most visible expansion of the judicial system was the increase in the number of justices of the peace, a situation that resulted from the remarkable growth of population and towns in the province. Between 1833 and 1845 the number of rural districts rose from thirty-two to forty-three and so did the number of justices, the new positions corresponding almost exclusively to the southern districts.[20] The increased cadre of law enforcers (at a minimum, each justice commanding a force of four policemen) extended the presence and visibility of the state in the countryside, facilitating the enterprise of restoring the laws.

Justices were given ample powers in matters of correctional justice, local administration, military logistics, and politico-ideological control. They had to monitor neighbors' compliance with religious and patriotic festivities, collect taxes and contributions, prevent the use of knives and card games at taverns, keep public registers, patrol the neighboring country in search of deserters, thieves, and fugitives, inspect travelers' identification papers, make arrests, and instruct the first phase of a criminal case. They proved indispensable in the logistics of the military force, administering the state's horse and cattle feedlots, enforcing the enlistment laws, sending *contingentes* of young recruits to the army, and facilitating the delivery of provisions for military garrisons (Salvatore 1994b). In addition, justices exercised an important degree of political control, keeping alert for any expressions of antifederalist sentiment.[21]

The human resources that justices could command did not keep pace with the expansion of their responsibilities. Commonly, a corporal and three policemen formed the force of a justice of the peace, complemented eventually with a fluctuating force made up of volunteers.[22] With such reduced manpower, the local justice needed the collaboration of the neighbors and militia commanders to complete its multiple tasks. This required from justices an intense work of persuasion, for the neighbor-citizens (the militiamen) were not legally obliged to cooperate on all occasions and for all types of services.

At the beginning of the regime, justices of the peace and military commanders fought constantly over questions of enlistment procedures and the collaboration of soldiers and militiamen in judicial procedures.[23] These jurisdictional disputes were rooted in two conflicting uses of paysanos' labor power: as auxiliaries of justice and as soldiers.

During times of military campaigns, soldiers temporarily assigned to the justices' offices were reassigned to military posts, causing resentment among the justices and local commissars. Similar tensions arose when militiamen were used as auxiliaries of the justices' offices. Military commanders and chiefs of militia units complained bitterly about this practice, claiming that as *citizens*, militiamen were exempted from this type of service. Justices strove to eliminate these "exemptions," which undermined the collective spirit of federalism and clogged the wheels of justice. With threats of resignation, denunciations, and court actions, justices endeavored to put an end to "military protection."[24]

In the early 1830s, a clearer delimitation of jurisdictions, together with

166 Wandering Paysanos

the centralization of judicial decisions in the executive, released some of these tensions, easing the way toward a juridification of social interactions.[25] Gradually, military courts had to relinquish their authority to hear cases involving military personnel, and military chiefs were persuaded to cooperate with local justices in matters of recruitment. In 1831, Rosas determined that justices could no longer place "vagrants" directly into military regiments; instead, they had to send all prisoners to Santos Lugares for further interrogation and sentencing.[26] Justices also lost their ability to conduct verbal trials; they could only instruct written summary proceedings as the initial part of a process.

As compensation for the loss of a key source of discretionary power, justices carved out a space of authority within the local communities. They became brokers of disputes among neighbors, local custodians of good customs and public order, representatives of the law and the Federalist Party, organizers of political and patriotic festivities. In part, their enhanced authority rested on ideological bases: the federalist patriotism that moved neighbors to cooperate with the administration of local justice. The ideology of federalism and the necessity of continuous contributions to the war effort united the local communities around their justices. The justices, in turn, maintained their promise to uphold the laws, an objective shared by local vecinos. Justices' efforts to defend private property, promote the work ethic, and maintain public order were consistent with paysanos' expectations of order, respectability, and wealth.

True, material interests played a role in stimulating the performance of justices. The possibility of establishing social and business connections while in office, rewards in land after the completion of their term, and other perquisites made the office attractive. But ideological affinities also proved a powerful incentive to the justices' work. Most candidates included in the triads presented for appointment were men of "medium fortune," that is, men of property who did not need the job to survive. More than just performing a job, some justices engaged in a crusade against lawbreakers. To them, upholding the laws became a form of expressing a political sentiment.[27] Juan Andrés Viqueredo, after receiving his commission as justice of San Nicolás in 1838, wrote Rosas a letter of appreciation. In it, he restated his pledge to the Federal Cause and expressed his desire to "sustain forever the good order, the Peace, and the tranquility that our province enjoys today." An orderly countryside was to Viqueredo an integral part of federalism; participating in the effort was for him a source of pride.[28]

In spite of the manpower difficulties and jurisdictional disputes, law enforcers in the countryside were persuaded that they were doing a good job in preserving this order. Every quarter, justices sent the governor a statement that read something like this: "These men [the alcaldes] and their tenientes (rural policemen) fulfill with exemplarity the tasks assigned to them, complying and making others comply with the Superior Decrees and orders imparted; vagrants and disturbers of the peace (mal entretenidos) are persecuted with tenacity; the use of knives and gambling are also problems of [our] first attention; and You will observe, by the prisoners sent and by the fines imposed, the exactitude and vigilance with which [we] have proceeded."[29]

To the justices, certain regulations were more important than others, the "pacification" and "good order" of their districts overshadowing other aspects of the administration of justice. Arrests and fines were to them the best indicators of legal enforcement. Having sent alleged lawbreakers to Rosas and having applied "corrections" (fines) to the authors of misdemeanors, justices expressed satisfaction for a job well done. When they claimed that their towns rigorously complied with the laws of the land, they were not exaggerating. They were translating into words what they observed at the local level: that there were in fact relatively few violations of a particular set of legal norms (those relating to property, vagrancy, card games, drinking, knife carrying, etc.). Or, put in other terms, that, with regard to the illegalities that interested the Restorer, policing and justice were producing acceptable outcomes.

A Swift and Procedural Justice

Right up to the beginning of Rosas's second government appellate courts had managed to counter the executive's claims for increased judicial prerogatives. The courts challenged the authority of the executive to make arrests and constantly reviewed sentences passed without formal procedures (Barreneche 1997, 295–296). After 1835 all this changed. Granted the "sum of public power," Rosas commanded an enhanced authority over the judiciary, intervening quite frequently in the resolution of criminal cases. Some cases, instructed at the level of sumario by the justices of the peace, were sent directly to Rosas for revision and sentencing. Others, instructed by first-instance judges, went to the governor with a drafted sentence for approval or disapproval. The result was an unprecedented centralization of judicial decisions.

This centralization was predicated on the need to speed up the machinery of justice so as to deliver an effective and visible justice. Rosas's commitment to swift justice was part of the promised ordering of the province's political and social life and, to that extent, enjoyed the highest priority. One of the ways the governor had of speeding up the administration of justice was to appoint special prosecutors for "grave and scandalous" crimes (Barba 1962b, 86). In the knowledge that a professional judge was supervising their procedures, local justices and commissars were stimulated to produce well-instructed indictments. On other occasions, the goal of delivering swift justice required bypassing certain procedures; this was particularly true about the way "vagrants," deserters, and thieves were treated. Once sent to Santos Lugares, prisoners had no right to legal representation or advice, their cases passing directly from indictment to sentence (no plenary proceedings).

By and large, however, the concentration of sentencing was compatible with the preservation of certain procedural rules. In fact, Rosas's control of the machinery of justice crucially depended on a ritualizing of judicial practices. As agents of the state machinery justices had to follow certain procedures: they had to interrogate the arrested, collect evidence, substantiate sumarios, have the testimonies reconfirmed, and send prisoners to Buenos Aires with their corresponding dossier. Rosas and his military secretaries reprimanded those who did not pay attention to these "formalities." Regularly, instructions about how to administer the oath to witnesses, or how to enunciate questions, or how to describe the accused reached the offices of the justices. This, together with the oversight of professional judges, helped to improve the substantiation of sumarios and, more generally, to disseminate legal know-how in country towns. In a murder case with no eyewitness, judge and camarista Baldomero García advised the justice of San Vicente on how to instruct the indictment. He was to proceed carefully, gathering "in a prolix and detailed fashion, all the antecedents, data, and circumstances that could serve as clues or as proofs to find the true author of the crime."[30] To reach that legal certainty, justices had to contrast the declarations of defendant and plaintiff (a procedure called careo), and, when answers resulted in contradictions, they had to repeat the interrogation.

Professional judges in Buenos Aires reminded local justices to administer the oath to witnesses before every interrogation and, on occasion, prepared the questions they had to read to witnesses.[31] Attention to detail in conducting a sumario sharpened when the justice was subject to some degree of expert supervision. When justices of the peace were left to their own conception of swift justice, the results were less prolix. They either failed to write a complete indictment or sent it without any trace of corroborating evidence.[32] Rather than ruled by arbitrariness and caprice, the judicial system of Rosismo was guided by procedural rules and sustained by documented acts (indictments, presentations, arraignments, allegations, and proofs). The Dictator considered this an important aspect of the enterprise of restoring the laws. In an 1846 civil dispute between a foreign artisan and a retired colonel, the governor restated his conception of justice as bound by procedural rules. The petitioner, he stated, was confused in raising the case, for a simple dispute between two parties did not constitute a judicial process. A true judicial process had to follow certain steps. Rosas wrote: "Without citation, substantiation, careo [the confrontation of delinquents or witnesses], or proof, there can be no trial."[33]

An accusation could only be cause for a criminal investigation if performed in front of witnesses and properly documented. In 1832, before the Navarro juzgado, neighbor José Sosa denounced the officer of a patrolling party for stealing clothes. Such a grave accusation prompted the justice to call two "honest and truthful neighbors [vecinos de providad y honradez]" to hear Sosa repeat the charges. In front of these witnesses, the accuser was asked to recount his version of the events and, after the end of his statement, was warned about the legal consequences of his accusation. Undisturbed, Sosa responded, "All will be proven [Todo será probado]," as if he knew the steps of the process and was prepared to perform his part.

Criminal investigations, when well conducted, entailed an intense and purposeful search for evidence. A murder investigation conducted by the justice of Salto in 1847 illustrates this point. After receiving a report that a woman (30) and her niece (13) had been killed at a league's distance from the town, the justice went to the site of the murder. Assisted by a party of neighbors, he examined the corpses and the terrain and collected evidence. He recorded that both victims were without their ponchos, and found two important pieces of evidence, a button and a fragment of ribbon, apparently ripped from one of the victims' ponchos. Then the justice interrogated neighbors, friends, and relatives of the victims and militiamen until general suspicions pointed to Sergeant Videla as the possible assailant. He then asked the military commander to detain the suspect and went seeking additional evidence. When the instruction was completed, the justice sent all the material evidence (the testimonies, the clothes, the buttons, the ribbon, the murder weapon, and the forensic report) to Rosas, together with a copy of the indictment and the felon secured by shackles.[34]

This case illustrates the investigative nature of the sumario process. Cases of murder that affected the tranquility of rural towns engaged neighbors and authorities in a search for truth. The labor invested by the justice in collecting evidence (both testimonial and material) was substantial and effective.[35] The neighbors, women as well as men, contributed valuable information to solve the case. Perhaps due to the brutality of the crime, even the local commander willingly collaborated with the investigation. The engagement of the local community in the substantiation of this case put many in contact with the terms and rules of the judiciary, even if only at the indictment level.

Two modes of justice coexisted, indeed overlapped during the Rosas period. One was expedient and effective, interested more in punishing the community's offense than in finding out the truth. The other was concerned with procedural rules and oriented to the investigation of the circumstances, motives, and responsibilities of a crime. "Swift" and "procedural" justice complemented each other, reflecting the ambivalent nature of governance during this period. The tension between decentralized enforcement and centralized judicial decisions consolidated over time. Rosas reduced the judicial discretion of justices in criminal matters, but significantly extended their powers in "correctional" cases (misdemeanors). For the latter offenses, justices had the possibility of applying a variety of penalties (flogging, public works, fines, etc.) without even reporting to the governor.[36] For more serious crimes, they had to attend to certain procedures that helped to legitimize in the eyes of paysanos the notion of equitable and effective justice.

Equality before the Law

The claim that the laws had been restored became more credible due to significant improvements in people's equal treatment under the law. These improvements were noticeable in at least three fundamental areas: the practical abolition of special privileges granted to the military, the reduction in the exercise of "private justice," and the control and penalizing of cases of nepotism.

Military Fueros

Though the law of July 5, 1823 had imposed severe limits to military fueros (privileges or exemptions) (Barreneche 1997, 301), in practice military courts were able to retain ample jurisdiction and discretion until the early 1830s, when a variety of circumstances conspired to reduce their importance and influence. Around 1829, complaints about the protection granted by military chiefs to their men started to pile up on the desks of Rosas's secretaries. Asked to share the burden of a prolonged war, paysanos began to demand reassurances that the felonies committed by military men against civilians would not go unpunished. This prompted the governor to consider ways of reducing the privileges of the military vis-à-vis civilian authorities. Rosas's legal advisors viewed the autonomy of military courts as a risk of unpredictable political consequences, but could not easily prevent the formation of military tribunals. So they recommended concentrating judicial decisions in the governor, making Rosas the "court" of first instance for sensitive criminal cases involving civilians and military personnel.

The attorney general and the comptroller general, under the close supervision of the governor, assigned cases involving civilians and military personnel to civilian courts, to military courts, or to mixed courts.[37] In cases in which juridical practice was inconclusive and there was an opportunity to display a dose of didactic punishment, Rosas's councilors passed all responsibility to him. Military courts concentrated on cases involving only military personnel and regulated by military bylaws: desertion, insubordination, conspiracy, and attempts of insurrection. Even in these cases, however, the governor reserved for himself the right to review the proceedings. In cases initiated by the military and put under his review, Rosas tended to apply the same rules as in civilian cases.[38] This situation was equivalent in practice to the abolition of military legal privileges. In other politically sensitive cases emanating from military indictments, the governor constituted mixed tribunals (made up of military and civilian judges) to avoid the suspicion that the military would protect their own. In the end, the concentration of sentencing power erased the boundaries separating military from civilian jurisdictions in ways that participants had not anticipated.[39]

Private Justice

In his memoirs, Lucio V. Mansilla left the unambiguous impression that, despite the rhetoric of the "reign of laws," the Rosista state was unable to penetrate the fortresses of "private justice": the patriarchal household and the cattle ranch. In his view, a situation close to servitude prevailed on the great ranches, and in the urban household the despotism of masters was unbounded. Ranchers and slave owners exercised their own justice (Mansilla 1994, 30–31). These assertions conflict with the evidence gathered from judicial archives.[40] Actually, the scope for private justice diminished substantially under the Rosas dictatorship. The governor's persecution of *abrigadores* (protectors of criminals and deserters) undermined the autonomy of the landed estate, making the presence of the law visible within the supposedly secluded space of the cattle ranch. And, though some masters continued "correcting" their slaves privately (or sending them to the public jail for "correction"), their right to inflict punishment began to be successfully challenged in the courts.

Aware that the discipline and strength of the army could erode if desertion got out of control, Rosas took special care in capturing and punishing deserters, persecuting with equal zeal those who gave refuge to them. The *abrigadores* were accomplices to a grave crime, one whose toleration threatened the very foundations of state power. For that reason, every time a possible crime-concealer (abrigador) emerged from the confession of a deserter, Rosas ordered a sumario to investigate who had provided assistance to the deserter and what were the reasons for such behavior.[41] Those who unknowingly gave protection to deserters were merely reprimanded, whereas those who could be held accountable were subject to severe penalties: prison terms and years of service in the army.

Summary investigations against *abrigadores* abound in police and judicial archives, indicating that the prosecution of this type of offender was a priority for the state. These investigations were very intrusive into the sociability of rural communities, for to prove this type of offense, justices gathered intelligence about paysanos' private social relations. Traditional gestures of hospitality among country folks became objects of suspicion.[42] Before giving lodging to a traveler or employment to a peon, peasants had to check the person's papers and inquire about his prior residence and employment. Faced with an intrusive state power, ranchers also learned to cooperate with local judicial and military authorities on matters of recruitment. Justices and local patrols customarily violated the boundaries of ranches and the prerogatives of ranchers when they needed to sequester and arrest a peon (see Salvatore 1991a).

The case of a conflict in 1843–1844 between the justice of the peace of Mar Chiquita Manuel Saavedra and Nicolás Anchorena's administrator illustrates to what extent the authority of justices penetrated private domains. A minor dispute turned into a violent confrontation when Justice Saavedra discovered that Anchorena's overseers and foremen were protecting deserters and common delinquents and openly defying his authority. The justice documented the violations, sent the information to Rosas, and tried to settle the dispute amicably. But when Rosas gave him instructions to proceed against the offenders, Saavedra entered Anchorena's ranch, arrested several peons and foremen, and warned everybody about the penalties awaiting crime-concealers (abrigadores).[43] Anchorena's response was to write to the governor, not claiming exemption to the laws (no good federalist would dare to do this), but complaining about the uncivilized manner with which Saavedra made the arrest.

The investigation of various cases of protection led Rosas to discover that some military commanders and justices of the peace were themselves providing refuge to deserters and fugitives in exchange for their labor.[44] Having private businesses to attend to, some of these authorities used their offices to secure labor. But Rosas and the inquisitors at Santos Lugares knew that repeated interrogations of felons would in the end reveal the names of those who violated the law, no matter how powerful. The persecution of crime-protectors enhanced the legitimacy of the Restorer of the Laws in the eyes of the rural poor. The peons who witnessed the police bursting into Anchorena's ranch must have gathered the impression that the law, when actually enforced, could produce some amazing results.

Nepotism and Influence Peddling

A long tradition of interpretation in Argentine history has presented the Rosas dictatorship as a case of flagrant nepotism.[45] These characterizations tend to exaggerate the dependence of the regime on nepotistic relationships, obscuring the fact that Rosas's popularity and votes depended to a large extent on his own efficacy in restoring legal order. By extending favored treatment to his relatives, Rosas risked alienating many of his supporters who believed, like Judge Baldomero García, that one of the merits of federalism consisted in judging poor and rich with the same rod.

In 1848, Felipe Escurra, one of Rosas's nephews, entered into conflict with the justice of Chivilcoy, Lázaro Molina.[46] Justice Molina, investigating the kidnapping of a young woman, had asked Escurra to send a peon for interrogation. Escurra refused, arguing that he had already reprimanded his assistant and that the justice had no authority to enter his ranch. Unperturbed, Molina sent the police squad and had Escurra arrested for obstructing justice. Once in prison and with the knowledge that his assets had been confiscated, Escurra sent a petition of mercy to the governor, his uncle, using his infant daughter as a messenger. Almost at the same time, his mother wrote to Manuelita (Rosas's daughter) asking for his freedom, as did his wife, who appealed directly to the governor. None of these petitions, however, produced results. Rosas conceded to the *desembargo* of Escurra's assets but he kept his nephew in prison for six additional months. After this time, Escurra was granted release due to his deteriorating health. Physically and emotionally exhausted, he had learned his lesson: his kinship with the governor did not protect him from the agents of the law.

Rosas's conduct greatly impressed Justice Molina, renewing his belief in the *Imperio de la ley*. In a letter to N. Terrero, Molina wrote: "Sr., the public, which had been scandalized by [Escurra's] words, is now convinced that His Excellency the Governor, his uncle, by the mere fact of having him in prison, as he had been until now, has corrected and corrects evil wherever and whomever the perpetrator is." To the justice, this was a lesson in equality before the law, an exemplary action that could generate a positive ripple effect on the governed. This lesson served after all to preserve federalism's most important capital: the people's belief in the ubiquity of the law. If the Escurra case was a "theater" it was so in the sense of providing a stage for the population to contemplate the meaning of the restoration of laws. It was a case of politics via example, a show that both government and governed knew how to read.

The Pedagogy of the Law

Restoring the authority of law as a regulator of social interactions— rebuilding "the walls of respect," as Rosas put it—required disseminating among the paysanos the prescriptions, prohibitions, and penalties contained in the laws. Paysanos had to know the texts and value of laws, understand the necessary connection between law abidance and republican government, and provide practical support to the restoration of order. In principle, the task appeared formidable, almost utopian. Addressed to a population mostly illiterate, with no other schooling than everyday experience, the teaching of the law required imagining new ways of communication and interaction. The justices of the peace (the teachers) had to turn all encounters with paysanos into lessons for inculcating the laws. The rural police stations, the calaboose, the public squares, the courtrooms in the city, the army barracks, all sites of public interaction looked promising in this regard.

The first requirement of this pedagogy was, of course, that the enforcers of the law themselves know the norms they were applying and understand the importance of compliance to them. For this purpose, Rosas commanded justices of the peace to collect laws, decrees, and circulars so that they could consult them, understand their meaning, and, more important, memorize their contents. Extant inventories of justice houses show that these rustic "offices" had trunks filled with useful manuals (usually copies of the *Manual de Policía* and the *Manual del Juzgado de Paz*), legal compilations (*Extrato de Leyes*), cadastral maps, population and cattle brand registers, and official communications classified by ministry or theme.[47] These "archives" were a concrete extension of the reach of the state into the rural towns.

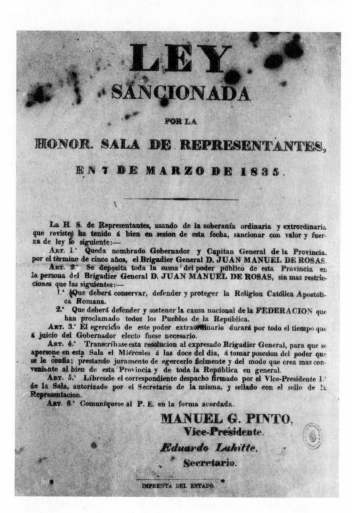

12. Publicizing the Laws. The law validating the election of Governor Rosas on March 7, 1835 was published in leaflets and posted in public places.

Besides collecting the laws, justices had to memorize them. At the end of each quarter, every justice of the peace had to report to the governor (as part of the Parte de Novedades) the faithful compliance of his town to each and every one of the "superior decrees." This implied copying one by one the multiple norms that they thought constituted the laws of the land. The act of writing these dispositions over and over—adding at the end, as a formal ritual, "all the above norms are being observed"—helped justices keep an active mental archive of the dispositions in force. To be sure, they copied only a short number of decrees and circulars concerning mostly local administration, good neighborly relations, and public order.

Keeping archives in the middle of the pampas and copying decrees at candlelight were practices that cannot be understood outside of the regime's obsession with the pedagogy of the law. Because justices could get too lenient with local residents or too lax in persecuting deserters and fugitives, Rosas felt the need—perhaps too often—to remind the justices about their duties. The messages, repeated in letters and circulars, emphasized the necessity to make all comply with the law, granting no exceptions. Rosas's insistence that justices learn the proper ways to interrogate suspects, draft arrest reports, issue passports, and make copies of delinquent records (filiaciones) was aimed at inculcating the value of the law, not only as an array of rules but also as a set of procedures to be followed. Rosas's aide-de-camps were obsessive about the completion of "formalities" and the reception of documentation. When a justice delayed the delivery of provisions to the state feedlots, when he did not comply with his quota of recruits for the army, or when he failed to send two copies of the filiación with each prisoner, reprimands were to be expected.[48] The admonitions (reconvenciones) became severe when justices overlooked any of their principal obligations: the identification, arrest, and interrogation of lawbreakers.[49] At once a reprimand, a threat, and a reminder, these admonitions were an integral part of the state's pedagogy of the law.

Once law enforcers were well apprenticed in the principles and practice of the law, it was necessary to pass on this learning to the population at large. Traditionally, commentators emphasized the governor's preference for exemplary punishment (whipping in particular) as the appropriate pedagogy for the ignorant and rebellious plebe.[50] This conception actually misplaces and distorts the meaning of Rosas's pedagogical predicament. For if corporal, exemplary punishment was an important component of this educational project, other forms of interactions—namely, interrogations, public readings, and proclamations—proved in the end more effective or, at least, more ubiquitous. Legal principles could be transmitted to the poor inhabitants of city and countryside by simply reading the regulations in the appropriate social spaces. Reading aloud the decrees, circulars, and resolutions in the rural taverns was an important means for inculcating the law in paysanos. Rosas constantly advised the justices of the peace to do this, sending them newspapers, decrees, circulars, and other documents to that effect.[51] The distribution of printed materials and the practice of reading aloud in public helped to bridge the gap between an illiterate citizenry and the government's need to inculcate news, laws, and republican principles.

Besides reading them in taverns, justices distributed copies of newspapers among the most representative neighbors of each town.[52] In 1841,

13. Reading Aloud at the Pulpería. The scene captures a common practice in country taverns. The tavern keeper reads the newspaper aloud to the illiterate audience. Although the engraving refers to the post-Caseros period (the tavern keeper is reading La Tribuna), the same was true during the Rosas administration. J. L. Palliere, La pulpería (campaña de Buenos Aires), lithograph, ca. 1859–60. Reproduced from L. Palliere, Escenas Americanas (1864), plate 114.

the justice of Ranchos acknowledged receipt of a package containing twenty issues of La Gaceta Mercantil; the issue featured Guizot's address to the French National Assembly concerning peace with the Argentine Confederation. The justice reported: "[We] have all read the news of the triumph of our federal arms [weapons]" and afterwards, "[We] have all demonstrated, expressing with our voices." The plural in the letter indicates the collective nature of reading, a way neighbors had of sharing news about politics, war, and social events.[53] Poor paysanos expected that literate neighbors and social superiors would keep them informed of news and laws.[54] In 1832 Matías Lima, a small farmer in charge of the army horses at Fort Areco, was accused of improperly using state property (a *patrio* horse) for private ends (moving wheat after the harvest). When asked if he was aware of the decree that prohibited the use of *caballos patrios* for private purposes, Lima responded that he did not know how to read, and that, consequently, he paid no attention to signposts. He put all the blame on Don Bartolo Saravi, his landlord, for sending him to gather the horses. "Don Bartolo Saravi, as a man of *instrucción leída* (with reading skills), should be the one to know about the prohibition," he insisted."[55] Lima trusted the literate would read the signposts and keep him informed about the law.

Paysanos also learned about the law through the traditional practice of posting signs, information, or edicts on poles. A means by which colonial authorities communicated orders to their subordinates, this practice was still in use during the Rosas period. Public executions, in particular, were advertised through *carteles* (signposts) posted in visible places in and around a town. In the same way laws concerning public property, branding, deserters, and a variety of other topics were communicated. The law had a presence in the form of signs even in the more distant sites of the frontier. In 1831, Doña Nicolasa Sáenz de Cortina, a widow resident in a rural area of Navarro, presented a petition to be excused from paying a fine. According to a recent decree she was supposed to deliver her *liberto* José Cortina to the military or to the justice of peace within twenty days of the publications of the decree. After paying a heavy, $400 fine, she protested: "It is very hard that a decree, even though published in all newspapers and communicated to justices of the peace and commissars of all the countryside . . . could reach so soon to the inhabitants in the midst of the countryside, in places isolated, solitary, and deserted. Even more difficult it is for [the decree] to be known by a poor widow, 'constituted' in loneliness and who, due to her sex, cannot leave her establishment to gather the news."[56] The widow's argument was not well taken by government officials in Buenos Aires. They claimed that the law of Freedmen Exchange (the *rescate de libertos*) was widely known, for the government had made extra efforts to publicize it. The justices and their officers traveled (on horseback) across their districts informing all ranches and households about this decree and, in fact, sequestering the unregistered freedmen. Interrogated again, the widow had to admit that the *teniente alcalde* (policeman assisting the justices) from her district had visited her ranch and informed her of the decree.

Day-to-day judicial and military practices served also as didactic experiments. In jails, militia encampments, and military forts, authorities used their encounters with subaltern subjects to teach them about the law. During the summary proceedings, justices recited important legal precepts, asked the accused and the witnesses whether they knew the law, or, more frequently, whether they knew why they were being arrested. The oath administered to all witnesses at the beginning of every interrogation added solemnity to these interactions. Criminal interrogation included questions that reminded paysanos of specific legal obligations: Were they enrolled in the militias? If not, did they serve in the regular army? Did they carry papers of identification or "safeguard"? Implicit in this type of interrogation was the attempt to make the arrested admit the authority of the law.

In military garrisons, it was common practice when registering new recruits to read a short paragraph warning them that desertion was punished with death and that claiming ignorance of this law would not exempt them from the punishment.[57] On occasion, the reading of this warning coincided with the oath taken by the new recruits. Formed in squads, recruits pledged their allegiance to the federation and promised to comply with its laws. In this way, in solemn ritual, the new soldiers were acquainted with this great and invisible power: *las leyes penales.* This phantom would surely return later: following established procedure, prosecutors interrogating deserters had to ask, "Have you been read the penal laws?"

The law had long arms, reaching populations in the most remote frontier areas. "Riding" on horseback, the laws could travel long and fast to the different towns that constituted the nuclei of civic life in the countryside. By means of signposts, newspapers read in taverns, oaths and legal warnings in military garrisons, and criminal interrogations, paysanos were informed of the renewed value of legal statutes and of the government's determination to enforce them.[58] As long as peasants and laborers were in touch with the social (verbal) circulation of news and official dispositions, illiteracy was no obstacle to their acquaintance with the ways of the law. First-time migrants from the interior might ignore the documents required by the Rosista state, but resident neighbors were well aware of the importance of carrying work and enlistment papers, passports, and permits to drive cattle.

The enactment of the law reached even the apparently closed world of cattle ranches. Rosas frequently reminded his administrators of the obligation to comply with laws and regulations. On one occasion, the governor reprimanded his administrator Dionisio Schoo for complaining about the just arrest of one of his peons.[59] The governor's warning not to expect any privileged treatment was addressed not only to his trusted administrator. At the ranch, Rosas knew, the letter would be commented on in the kitchen and around the *fogones* (fireside gatherings) and rumor would soon spread the news to the boundaries of the ranch, to the distant corners where squatters (agregados) and settlers (pobladores) lived. Each spin of the tale would enhance Rosas's fame as the Restorer of the Laws and diminish the authority of those who neglected the law.

Belief and Compliance: The Terrain of Hegemony

The hegemony of the law has several dimensions: the compliance to rules without the need for direct coercion, the degree to which individuals of different social conditions cooperate with the administration of justice, the willingness of citizens to denounce violations of the law, and the trust deposited by different social agents in the overall justice of the political order.

Belief

The expectations on the part of the public that, given the prevailing configuration of power, some sort of distributive or retributive justice could be attained constitutes an important dimension of hegemony. If, despite present injustices, people believe that in the future, at higher levels of authority there will be a reversal of past unfavorable decisions, then the legal order can be said to have attained a certain degree of credibility. During the Rosas era, this belief was quite widespread. Naturally, belief in the justice system was stronger among the custodians of the system: the justices of the peace. But there is evidence that the same belief motivated the actions of petitioners, small proprietors, widows and mothers of veterans, and occasionally wage earners.

Ideologically committed to a party that presented the restoration of laws as its own achievement, the justices defended the legality of the system, trying to conduct their actions within the sphere of legality and respectability. When in 1839 Justice Benito Sosa went to Guardia de Luján to attend a patriotic festivity, he became the object of the insults and aggression of Colonel Vicente González, a high-ranking military chief. Brandishing his sword, González told Sosa that "the justices of the peace were worth nothing," that he "had no respect for them," and that "they could do no harm to him."[60] Insulted and incapable of taking arms against the colonel (one of the main leaders of the Federalist Party), the justice sought reparation in the courts. To that object, he presented his resignation to Rosas; in this way, he said, he could make use of the warrantees that protected every citizen. Sosa believed in the possibility of achieving compensation in court for the excesses committed by a higher authority.

Expressions of belief in the overall justice of the institutional order were common among middling paysanos. In 1837 a peasant farmer from Luján, Juan Esteban Vázquez, was unfairly arrested and punished by an overzealous justice. Vázquez was whipped with a belt when he refused to confess that he was stealing cattle from neighbors. Arrested and sent to the

Cárcel Pública in Buenos Aires, his situation was later compromised by the accusation of a false witness. As his wife explained in the letter addressed to the government, her husband withstood the extralegal abuse (ultraje), thinking that General Rosas would later punish the justice "who had the obligation to respect the Laws and all the other guarantees that they afford."[61] As the indictment made clear, the farmer had the opportunity to resist the arrest, but he did not. He let justice follow its course, trusting that, at some point, Rosas would intervene and repair the injustice.

Also remarkable was the confidence expressed in the justice system by a foreman who, having tried to collect arrears wages, was physically assaulted and threatened with a gun by his employer. Instead of taking justice in his own hands, the foreman resorted to the justice of the peace. In the letter addressed to the justice, the foreman wrote: "I ask that [the accused] be punished according to law, because I do not consider myself safe if his felony remains unpunished." Similarly, when the master of a horserelay station at Fortín Areco wrote to Rosas complaining that the local justice had unduly drafted his postmen and physically abused his father, he expected the governor to punish the outrageous and illegal behavior.[62] Apparently, the sphere of justice provided a territory where disputes over abusive authority could be aired and possibly resolved.

Belief was also strong among the many subaltern signatories of petitions to the governor. Soldiers' mothers and wives constantly wrote to Rosas asking for the release of their sons and husbands taken by recruiting parties.[63] Using a submissive, almost suppliant tone, the petitioners made clear the unfair treatment received by their loved ones. The letters pointed out the industriousness, dedication to work, and patriotism of those arrested, adding at the end a phrase condensing the petitioner's expectation that Rosas would do justice: "Se hara justicia" ("Justice will be done"). Those women who invested energy and money in these presentations were convinced that they were not a futile exercise. They believed in the possibility of a reverse decision if additional evidence (i.e., character witnesses) were to be considered. In many instances, they were not disappointed.

Even in the enclosed space of a frontier garrison, where chiefs and officers commanded a great deal of disciplinary power, the hope that Rosas could repair injustices remained high. In November 1846, Sergeant Pedro Sánchez, a scribe at Fort Angentino (Bahía Blanca), sent Rosas two confidential reports denouncing a series of acts of corruption at the garrison.[64] Aware that the commander of the fort (against whom many of the accusations were directed) could read and confiscate the packages, Sergeant Sánchez took precautions: each report, containing over twenty manuscript pages, was disguised under the cover of the payroll list addressed to the inspector of arms. The denunciations were extremely grave—involving charges of theft, illicit use of state property, denial of rations, and mistreatment of soldiers, among others—and, consequently, great was the risk taken by the sergeant if the report was discovered before reaching its destination. Why did he assume such a risk? In the sergeant's understanding, the corruption had undermined the morale of the troops, causing resentment and lack of discipline. But Sánchez's moral indignation stemmed chiefly from the realization that the fort was an island of injustice. Here, criminals were protected, legal procedures went unobserved, and soldiers and other settlers lacked the minimal guarantees granted to citizens. Remarkably, Sánchez expected the governor to untangle this tight network of corruption and illegality.

Cooperation and Compliance

Another indicator of hegemony is the degree of cooperation that citizens offered law-enforcement agents in activities related to recruitment, criminal trials, and policing. This cooperation, unlike belief, seems to have varied with the social condition of the subject. The great ranchers of the southern districts showed less respect for the laws and less enthusiastic support for the justices than medium and small-scale cattle-raisers and farmers, arguably the main supporters of Rosismo. The citizens-in-arms, the militiamen, held ambivalent attitudes toward the justice system, being reluctant to contribute additional police or military duties but collaborating with some tasks of the justice office (such as the substantiation of sumarios). Finally, itinerant peons and laborers, with almost no protection from the local communities, obeyed the laws generally under compulsion.

To the justice of Mar Chiquita Mariano Saavedra, the south was still (in 1844) in a "state of despotism." The neighbors' lack of compliance with the demands from his office was rampant, compromising his ability to supply cattle to the army and security to the countryside. The most disobedient and uncooperative were the great ranchers, who lacked the patriotism and civility of poor livestock raisers. In spite of ten years of legal pedagogy, some landowners acted with an arrogance and presumptuousness improper to citizens. Nicolás Anchorena, for instance, considered the law a useful instrument in the moral education of the plebe, but dispensable if other means (such as paternalism) proved more effective. Accustomed to a world of patronage and private justice, Don Nicolás was unable to think in terms of modern legal procedures and penalties. Legal penalties were irrelevant to him; he would punish and pardon "his own" people. The great rancher still lived and functioned within an older conception of justice, one built over patriarchal powers, admonition, and mercy.[65]

On the other hand, there are abundant counterexamples of medium and small ranchers who cooperated with the justice system. They provided testimony, contributed information, joined patrols, helped to make arrests, and transported felons to the city. Without their help, the justices would have faced severe limitations in their day-to-day activities. In 1834, Don Joaquin Cárdenas, a cattle rancher from Monte, took his two African peons to present their enlistment papers to the military commander of Monte, as was required. After this was completed, the three drank together in a local tavern and returned, in separate ways, to the ranch. That night, in a confusing incident, one of the peons got killed. Suspecting that the surviving peon was the murderer, the rancher took him to the local justice.[66] The readiness to comply with the ordinances regarding enlistment and to present a murder suspect before the justice illustrates the extent to which this small rancher had accepted the power of law to regulate social relations.

According to the justices of the peace, the militias—subalterns with citizenship and property rights—were intractable when it came to providing military service. Protected by their own commanders, the militiamen openly disobeyed the commands of justices of the peace and local policemen (alcaldes). As the justice of Baradero reported in 1841, militias refused to assist the justice with their services. One militia, complained the justice of Ensenada in 1833, had the audacity to confront the police with arms.[67] In general, the militias were willing to cooperate with the justices when services were short and did not interfere with the conduct of private life and work. Their reluctance to serve, however, should not be taken as an indication of antilegal behavior, for militiamen were protected by legal exemptions. Their relative independence served to preserve the appearance of a working system of rights and exceptions, which ultimately enhanced the hegemony of Rosista federalism.

Itinerant peons and laborers, on the other hand, had a more reserved attitude toward judicial and police authorities. Repeatedly arrested on insubstantial charges, they learned to respect and fear the local justices. Aware that past desertions, the lack of documents, or the mere suspicion of resident paysanos would put them in trouble with the law, peons tried to avoid the justices. Their collaboration with the justices was, therefore, minimal. In many cases, the justices themselves subjected peons and laborers to forced labor, corporal punishment, and humiliation. In these instances, they only waited for the first opportunity to escape. But, as I discuss below, the politics of federalism provided them with opportunities to level, temporarily, the social distance separating them from the "men of justice."

Denunciation and Defiance: The Tones of Resistance

Resistance can take the form of open defiance to the authority of the law, though, more frequently, it appears as the denunciation of injustices committed by law enforcers and other authorities. Denunciation and defiance constitute two different tones of resistance, two modalities for expressing dissent with the functioning of a regime. A justice system lacking legitimacy produces less judicial litigation and fewer investigations than one in which people deposit some expectations for achieving justice. To this extent, denunciation is an expression of hegemony, but, at the same time, it constitutes a moment of resistance. Instances of denunciation of injustice can reveal aspects of subaltern subjects' reactions against state oppression. Similarly, though open defiance generally represents the complaint of a subaltern vis-à-vis a dominant power, the defiant voice may articulate modern or premodern grievances.

Denunciation

During the Rosas period, small livestock-raisers and farmers, the men who constituted the majority "opinion" in each rural town, tended to present their complaints to the justice of the peace, particularly when the abuse came from the military. Peons and other subalterns (and people who had doubts about the equanimity of the local justice) addressed their grievances to higher or extralocal authorities, expecting in turn that the latter would redress abuses committed at the local level.

In 1836, two neighbors from Dolores presented themselves to the justice of Monsalvo, complaining that the military *comisionados* (levying parties) had forcefully and illegally searched them and taken their men. One of the neighbors reported that the military took his foreman; the other (apparently a foreman) claimed that, although he had his papers in order, the commissioner tore them to pieces, saying they were invalid. Unable or unwilling to ignore the pressure from these residents, Justice Piedrabuena wrote to the governor requesting some control on the activities of levying commissions. "The Clamors of the Neighbors about the abuses [*tropelías*] committed by the said commissioners are many," he wrote.[68] To the justice, the rough behavior of levying parties compromised public tranquility and constituted an infringement of legality. The commissioners had no right to arrest people who had committed no violation of the law. As long as the peons and foremen carried their legal papers, they were supposed to travel free and unmolested. The order and tranquility of the countryside rested on this implicit agreement.

When military authorities tried to extract cheap or coerced labor from them, neighbors could go to the local justice and file a complaint. Militiaman Andrés Camacho did exactly that. When Commander Ozona wanted to force him to cut some adobe for the commander's house, Camacho refused, arguing that this was "private work" and that the commander had no authority to oblige him to do it. Later, he presented a complaint to the justice of Navarro, who proved supportive of his case. In Camacho's view, the justice constituted a positive containment against military despotism. Facing a common adversary, neighbors and the local justice were able to carve out a mutually beneficial space of justice. The question of service to justice officials, however, created tensions between justices and local ranchers. In 1836 attorney Julián González Salomón presented a petition to the Police Department to prevent the justice of the peace of Arrecifes from harassing the foreman of Don Linares's ranch. The justice's constant calls for service to an old citizen exempted by law from any active duty made this "injunction" necessary.[69]

The engagement of subalterns with the justice system was different. Subjected more frequently to the abuses of local justices, itinerant peons devised alternative means of interaction: they responded with silence or noncooperation, recruited the help of a social superior, or bargained with the authorities for a reduction of penalties. Though not totally devoid of a notion of rights, subalterns approached the local justices with greater caution and apprehension. In some cases, peons preferred to wait and voice their complaint before extralocal authorities. Patience and legal cunning could give the subaltern liberty or, at least, a proper judicial process. Luis Noriega, a peon resident of Tordillo, was arrested in 1846 on suspicion of assisting another paysano to slaughter a stolen cow. Though he denied the charge, the alcalde had him under arrest for three months without any evidence, in fact, without a proper indictment. During all this time Noriega refused to confess, waiting until his interrogation in Buenos Aires; only there was he willing to speak. When asked what charges were leveled against him, he claimed that the justice's accusations were invalid for he had never been interrogated under a proper sumario.[70]

Another tactic was to request the assistance of a wealthy or influential employer. In 1837 Manuel Riquelme, a farm peon from Arrecifes unfairly accused of stealing some meat, wrote to his employer, Don Juan Antonio

Linares, for help. Despite terrible orthography and syntax, the peon's letter clearly narrated a case of malicious prosecution. He told of the threats, torments, and humiliations suffered from a justice who would not believe the meat belonged to him. The letter is worth quoting in its entirety:

Apresido Patron; Hoi me allo preso en este destino mi delito todo asido por haberme hallado Carne en mi Casa la Cual la habia traido de su estancia Como di la razon al Juez y abiendo mandado indagar dio la my razon Da Felipa que ella me abia dado la Carne por tener horden de U y dicho Juez no toma Credito y me a dado martirios de Colgarme de una mano y me iba a Castigar en la Plaza y de temor de estos martirios me bisto obligado a Confesar que he carniado una res no habiendolo echo por este motivo se me ase el sumario por dos años a las tropas y en esta virtud suplico a U que aga las deligencias que le sean posibles aber si concige mi libertad que la Carne llo le aseguro que es de su estancia dice el Juez que no es su Estancia de tanto Fondo por darme la mantencion y esto es prebencion que atenido porque siendo llo un miliciano que no estado dado de baja del Regimiento me queria obligar que sirbiera en los sibicos y no pudiendo Conseguir esto me sentencio que no perdio las esperanzas de echarme a las tropas Conque ahora atenido el gusto de martirizarme y aserme servir a la Fuerza que erobado para aser el su gusto areglado a esto agame el Fabor dar los pasos que le sean posible afin de consegir mi libertad Soi de U su serbidor. Manuel Riguelme.

Dear Patron: Today I am in jail at this place. All due to the justice of peace finding meat in my house, which I brought from your estancia, as I said to the justice. Doña Felipa gave me the reason telling the justice that she gave me the meat after receiving orders from you. The said justice does not take credit (on my words) and has tortured me by making me hang from one hand and he was about to punish me in the square. For fear of this punishment I was forced to confess that I had slaughtered a calf when I had not. For this reason, they opened a sumario with (a possible penalty of) two years in army service. Because of this, I beg you to do whatever you can to obtain my freedom. The meat, I assure you, is from your ranch. The justice says that your ranch is not so big as to provide for my subsistance. He has prevention against me because I am still registered as a miliciano from the regiment and the justice wanted to force me to serve in the civic corps and, unable to attain this, he sentenced me and nurtured the hope of sending me to the troops. Now he has had the pleasure of torturing me and making me to serve against my will. He says I have stolen to make his pleasure. In view of this, please, take the steps necessary (and possible) to attain my freedom. I am your most (loyal) servant. Manuel Riquelme.

Linares, sympathizing with his peon's claim, wrote a short and sharp petition to the government. In it, he leveled a series of accusations against Justice Gregorio Ponce. The justice, Linares stated, had arrested his peon without more evidence than his own suspicion. The meat found in Riquelme's house, instead of "evidence" of pilfering, was payment for the peon's labor. "Moved by personal resentment," Ponce had tortured his peon (hanged him from one arm), then threatened him with floggings in public, and finally offered him a sentence of two years in the army if he did not confess. To Linares, a respected rancher and resident of Arrecifes, this was a case of absence of justice. The confession, taken under coercion, was illegal. The justice had refused to hear valid and relevant testimony. Riquelme was an industrious peon and a well-regarded man who did not deserve this kind of treatment. The illegality of the procedures required the substantiation of a new indictment.[71]

Linares's petition to Rosas was argumentative and respectful, but not deferential—it was, in fact, a demand for justice. In the same year (1837), a free African named Antonio del Valle wrote to the governor requesting his freedom from prison in exchange for service in the armed forces. As a result of a dispute about the ownership of a horse, Valle was assaulted with a *rebenque* (whip) and beaten until his eye bled. In a defensive move, he had wounded his attacker with a knife. The language of his petition was respectful, his words legitimating, not challenging, the justice system. (He called the police headquarters where he was arrested the "House of Justice.") Acknowledging that he had committed violence, he asked for Rosas's mercy. But Valle was not stepping back from something he considered an entitlement: his right to be considered equal to people of other races. "Exmo Sor yo sé que lo he herido libremente en una mano y que he echo muy mal; pero también advierto que dicho Señor *no debía valerse por ser blanco para irme a castigar como a su criado* por lo que acosado del castigo vusqué mi justa defensa" ("Your Excellency: I know that I have freely wounded you on one hand, and that I have done wrong; but it is also true that the said Señor should not have tried to punish me as his slave simply because he was white. I, harrassed by this [uncalled] punishment, sought to defend myself").[72] Rejecting corporal punishment as a humiliating treatment improper for a citizen, the African subaltern appealed to the right of legitimate self-defense. Instead of demanding justice, as in the former case, Valle was ready to make a deal with the authorities, exchanging his freedom for some years of service in the army. Unprepared to challenge police authorities (and probably unaware of the possibility of resorting to the *Defensor de Pobres*), he directed his denunciation to Rosas, the highest authority in the province. As credentials, he presented a personal history of service to the federation and a determination to again join the army in defense of the fatherland.

Denunciations revealed an expectation about justice. Justice seekers trusted that the mere denunciation of an illicit act would initiate the investigation that would lead to the punishment of those who had abused their authority. Only in exceptional cases did complainants follow up these denunciations with a court action.

The way denunciations were presented varied with the social position of plaintiffs and with the circumstance. Middling paysanos sought reparation from military injustices by resorting to local justices. Peons and ranchers denounced the arbitrary actions of justices before justices of other districts, military commanders, or the governor. The tactics of the powerful and subaltern were different. Whereas the rancher was able to hire legal representation and openly challenge the local authority, peons and deserters had to keep silent, waiting for the proper situation. Later, they would try to negotiate their way out, recalling the primordial contract of the fatherland. Those with influential connections tried to engage their social superiors.

Defiance

Legal authority is particularly fragile when not accompanied with a credible threat of coercion. The few women who defied authority during the Rosas period found, to their surprise, that judges were hesitant to use force with them. In 1841 Justice Manuel José Vila complained to Rosas's secretary Corvalán that his authority had been mocked. A key witness in an investigation he was conducting refused to testify, openly defying his authority. Doña Rosario Linares, summoned to appear before the justice, had sent him a note stating simply that "it was not proper for a señora to obey a justice of the peace."[73] Understandably, such a note infuriated the justice, who ventilated the case in the highest echelons of power.

Defiance of authority sometimes took the form of public exposure and humiliation of judges. In 1830, a reader called "The Lover of Order" sent a letter to La Gaceta Mercantil complaining against "the abuses of the judges against the laws." The letter, it was later discovered, came from a free African who was pursuing the liberation of his spouse, a slavewoman, through the courts. Published by the newspaper, the letter compromised the prestige of the judge, implying that the latter was delaying the resolution of the case (possibly to keep the money left by the plaintiff as a deposit) and siding with the slave owner. To save his reputation, the judge was compelled to reply through a different periodical.[74]

Though rare, there were cases in which subalterns used "papers of exception" to defy police and judicial authorities. This was the case of Juan Angel Ullúa, a deserter who, though wanted in two counties (San Vicente and Cañuelas) for various felonies, still was able to move freely by showing a paper of exception (a passport apparently signed by a high authority). Shielded by this paper (which turned out to be forged) and spreading rumors that he was under the protection of a superior authority, Ullúa was able to get out of jail, make threats to his captors, and ultimately assault the residence of a justice with impunity.[75] His claim to exception was clearly defiant, not only of the legal authorities but also of the principle of equality before the law.

Rather than showing open hostility, the resistance to authority of settled paysanos took the form of quiet disobedience. Commonly, subalterns found in the space of the regiment or the militia some degree of protection against judicial and police authorities. Using militia commanders to issue them resguardos (certificates of enlistment or passports), paysanos were able to bypass the power of the local justice. According to a report by the justice of Navarro in 1830, the local commanders had instructed his milicianos not to obey the civil authorities. As a consequence, many militiamen were in open defiance of the laws ["they did not want to obey the justice"] ("no han querido obedecer a la justicia").[76] Rarely, peons and deserters took justice into their own hands, challenging judicial authorities to arms. But this option was too costly; it closed off any further negotiation and made the assailant embrace the fate of a fugitive of justice. Those who committed armed assault against authorities had their criminal record circulated through different justice offices and were objects of special persecution.

The defiant voices of the subaltern point to a modality of resistance of greater intensity than denunciations. Women refusing to provide testimony in sumarios, deserters claiming to be above the law, Africans publicly challenging the moral authority of judges, and militiamen seeking the protection of their commanders constitute examples of attitudes of defiance eroding the credibility and legitimacy of the justice system. These instances illuminate the contested nature of authority in the period and the difficulties judicial and police authorities met in establishing hegemony. These cases also show the possibilities open to subalterns to delimit the space of legitimate coercion. These few moments of resistance—only dots in a vast mosaic of power relations—indicate the various practical ways by which subalterns resisted the authority of the justice system. Embarrassing a judge through slander in the press or threatening retribution to the police based on a superior's protection was not, to be sure, an option open to many subalterns. But they indicate a limit, a maximum of defiance that reveals the obstacles faced by the pedagogy of the law.

Subaltern Politics: Demanding Justice, Resisting Authority

Gauchesco literature has presented the relations between gauchos and the law as marked by distrust and ironic distance. Defiance and lamentation, the two principal modes by which gauchos address the question of legal authority, are complemented, in extreme cases of injustice, by escape to the Indian frontier (Ludmer 1988). In these sources, a closer engagement with the institutions and discourse of the law appears negated by the very injustices generated by the postindependence state and those who benefited from it. The strong belief in equality before the law evident in Hidalgo's *Diálogos patrióticos* (1822, 1825) turned into irony in Hernandez's *Martín Fierro* (1872), as if with the consolidation of republican institutions and the advent of capitalist ranches paysanos had drifted away from the law, to the point where they joined the "barbarism" prophesized in Sarmiento's *Facundo* (1845).

The evidence, fragments of the practices and words of peons, peasants, women, and African servants extracted from judicial and military archives, paints a more complex picture of the relationship between subalterns and the law. Subalterns' relations with the law depended on the circumstances, the right asserted, and the power confronted. By and large, the tactic of maintaining a cautious and respectful distance from law enforcers remained the norm among provincianos seeking employment on the province's ranches and farms and among deserters searching for a new home. But the intrusive nature of the Rosista state forced subalterns to try other means of engagement. Ironic remarks, claims of being above the law, refusal to cooperate with justices show a sense of alienation similar to that portrayed in gauchesco literature. But the promises of equality embedded in the official rhetoric encouraged subaltern subjects to denounce to the authorities cases of corruption, abuse of authority, lack of due process, and excessive punishment.

Like other social groups, peons and other subalterns related to judicial institutions with cooperation, defiance, denunciation, and belief. But their situation vis-à-vis the law differed from that of middling paysanos and great ranchers. Open defiance of judicial institutions often came from subalterns: women, Africans, peons, and deserters. Facing situations of malicious or illegal prosecution, they expressed their discontent with the justice system by challenging the legitimacy of law enforcers. They disobeyed summons from justices, refused to collaborate with the justice officers, accused some judges of corruption, and, on rare occasions, boasted of their exemption from the rule of law. To demand justice they resisted authority. In addition, subalterns contributed to the legitimacy of the justice system by denouncing situations of injustice every time they thought a higher authority could redress them. In this regard, they shared with middling paysanos a similar conception about government.

Defiance and direct denunciation, rather than cooperation and belief, were the chief modes of subaltern engagement with the justice system. Imprisoned rather than persuaded, peons and laborers tended to "collaborate" with the local justice only to the extent that this ensured their transition to residency and citizenship. Otherwise, their most common tactic was to run away, seek the protection of another high authority, and denounce abuses from afar. The trust invested in the institutional system ("belief") was greater among members of the Rosista administration, military personnel, and middling paysanos than among peons, Africans, and lower-class women.

In practice, the lamentations of gauchesco literature translated into denunciations of illegalities and injustices, some of them undertaken at great personal risk. These denunciations point to a particular way of demanding justice. Subaltern grievances, when made public, had to reach the figure subalterns considered in a position to redress all injustices: Governor Rosas. Underlying these requests for justice was a conception of politics and political authority that we may characterize as *republican paternalism*.[77] Under this conception, the governor was not only the warrantor of a legal order (the guardian of the "temple of laws"), he was the moral force who policed the purity of the administration and the equity of justice. Only he was entrusted with the ability to eradicate privilege, selfish interest, and illegal coercion. The idea of a Restorer of the Laws was carved deep in popular mentality, sometimes producing naïve expectations. For instance, women who had been deceived with false promises of marriage resorted to Rosas to expedite the resolution of their court cases. They expected the governor to put pressure on the judges and the other parties so that their fiancé complied with his promise.[78]

Beyond this populist interaction with the Dictator, direct appeals to higher authorities reflected subalterns' keen understanding of the actual workings of the justice system. Subalterns knew that, with regard to local justices, some degree of distrust and caution was justified. The self-serving attitude of some local justices and the relaxation of rules in favor of power holders could easily turn the "reign of laws" into fiefdoms of private justice. Appeals and denunciations reveal also the possibilities open to subalterns under the federalist system. In a highly polarized political climate peons and other subalterns found paths of action that minimized coercion. Enthusiastically embracing the Federalist Cause, subalterns could avoid the most repressive aspects of the justice system. They knew that the nature of the civil war (a *guerra santa*) and the politics of unanimism left little room for negotiating political identity: it was either federalism or death. Service, on the other hand, was negotiable. Providing service entailed the possibility of regaining citizenship and, hence, a voice in the political system. Rosas's insistence that soldiers be treated as individuals endowed with rights rather than as criminals made all the difference for subalterns.

Politics could grant subalterns positions of relative empowerment. In B. Echevarria's *Nuevo diálogo patriótico*, the protagonist, paysano Justo Calandria, was struck by fear when he first met the justice of the peace. He stood up, straightened his body (as a soldier would do in the presence of a superior), and immediately essayed an apology, as if protecting himself from incoming accusations.[79] The justice, as was his duty, inquired about Calandria's place of residence and reasons for stopping in town. The paysano answered both questions respectfully. Soon his initial caution and fear turned into familiarity and confidence when he learned that he was to participate in a federalist demonstration in the capital. He welcomed the chance of participating in such an event, moved by a combination of patriotism, curiosity, and convenience. Next, the justice told him that he had done nothing wrong. This made Calandria regain his self-confidence: no longer a suspect, he was now treated as a federalist comrade, as a citizen. Calandria's accommodating self, changing from humility to comradeship, reveals an understanding of the complexities of power relations under Rosismo. Devoid of politics, the Law could be a weapon turned against the powerless; inside of politics (and on the right side of it), the Law became a contested terrain in which it was still possible to demand justice.

The defiant attitude of subalterns in the face of arbitrary authority and their willingness to denounce injustices to the governor underscores the importance attributed by peons, lower-class women, and Africans to the enterprise of restoring the laws. To them, Rosas's promises in 1829, 1833, and 1835 represented a sort of pact that required constant actualization in practice. Appeals to the governor exemplify conceptions of legitimate authority and good government that combined postindependence ideals with colonial traditions of governance. The political experience gained by paysanos in the "restorations" combined with the tradition of *equidad* (distributive justice) left by colonial courts (Cutter 1995). By writing directly to the governor, petitioners reaffirmed the belief that Rosas was the guarantor of public and individual liberties and that the republic still held a place for those humble paysanos who had defended in battle the federalist colors.

This belief, contradicted so many times by the many injustices of judicial authorities, was maintained because it related to concrete gains made by subalterns since independence. The increased surveillance of peons' and peasants' activities and the state's pedagogy of law had shortened the distance between subalterns and the sphere of state justice. This no doubt engendered discontent and alienation. Arbitrary detentions, disproportionate penalties, and corruption nurtured their resentment and distrust toward the justice system. But, at the same time, the Dictator's institutions provided subalterns with a terrain to redress situations of injustice. More important, some of the benefits afforded by the increased enforcement of the laws (the reduction or elimination of privileges, less impunity for arbitrary corporal punishment, the hearing of complaints, and the right to petition) reaffirmed subalterns' beliefs in the overall justice of the political regime.

Arbitrary corporal punishment, one of the more noisily articulated grievances during the postindependence period, came under greater judicial control during Rosas's time. Similarly, various judicial cases challenged masters' authority to inflict corporal punishment on their slaves. The organization of local militias conferred on stable peons and foremen a legal persona, represented by the papeleta de enrolamiento (enlistment voucher), which protected them from undue arrest and prosecution. Lower-class women gained a credible voice in the substantiation of criminal indictments. This type of warrantee, though not always sustained, gave reasons to soldiers, peons, Africans, and lower-class women to continue supporting federalism.

Conclusions

The Rosas era was anything but a vacuum of legality. References to the "reign of laws" impregnated federalist rhetoric. The regime's pedagogical machine successfully disseminated among paysanos an elementary literacy in rights and obligations. A more systematic enforcement of the laws confronted paysanos regularly with the agents of the law and their predicament. The law—as official rhetoric, as pedagogy of costumes, as a reality of power—was hard to ignore. The increasing presence of the "documentary state" in the countryside (a state overtly concerned with documents and identification) and the "lessons" imparted by justices must have left clear imprints in the behavior and mentality of paysanos. The practices of the judicial system produced familiarity with legal procedures and this, in turn, generated awareness and engagement.

Under these conditions, the Laws acquired a greater persuasive power than historians have generally granted. The legal system constituted a necessary referent in the lives of peons and peasants: its predicament and mission structured possibilities for individual or collective action; its key symbolic value in Rosista federalism helped subalterns understand the meanings of the state and its order. To this extent, it is undeniable that the Laws played a crucial role in constructing the hegemony that supported Rosas's government. We cannot blame subalterns for the expectations they invested in the legal system. Widely publicized achievements of the regime—such as the abolition of military legal privileges, the persecution of crime-protectors, the restrictions on masters' powers to flog slaves, and the punishment of law offenders independent of family connections— made peasants and peons believe that the "restoration of laws" was not an empty phrase. But, precisely because the Laws gained such ascendancy in paysanos' lives and identities, they also became a source of subaltern resistance.

We can only speculate how subalterns experienced the Rosista Imperio de la ley, their admiration of the new legal archives in the pampas, the reaction caused by signposts announcing an execution, a new decree, or an incoming collection, the comments they made after collectively "reading" a newspaper in the tavern, the soldiers' assent or rejection of the rhetoric contained in the proclamations, the thoughts and feelings of prisoners after signing (with a cross) their "confessions." These are reactions, feelings, and utterances that will remain in the hidden transcript, their text blurred to both state authorities and historians (J. C. Scott 1990). The final subaltern verdict on Rosista justice is probably unrecoverable.

Nonetheless, we can suggest (on the basis of the evidence presented in this chapter) that the distance separating the subaltern from the justice system shortened during this period, that the apparently contradictory practices of defying authorities and seeking justice through denunciation implied a greater engagement of peons and laborers, Africans, and lower-class women with the judicial apparatus of Rosismo. Certainly, the degree of engagement of subalterns was less intense and more distant than that of those who constituted the core of the federalist political community. Middling paysanos responded with cooperation, belief, and occasionally, court action, reinforcing the image of communities united in their efforts to fight "criminals" and "anarchists." Acculturated into the practices of sumarios and criminal investigations, neighbors defended a notion of "procedural justice" over the effective and "swift justice" promoted by the state. To the subaltern, the logic of direct denunciation seemed more appropriate—to appeal to a higher authority—for redressing an injustice committed at the local level. Their occasional defiance of the justices' authority was clearly counterhegemonic.

Challenging authority in order to gain greater equality and individual rights was, of course, not an invention of the Rosas period. It was a postindependence tradition that emerged most clearly in the period 1815–1828, when urban militias, peasants, and military officers engaged in intense conflict over the definitions of personal autonomy, respectability, and social equality. What was new was the didactic of the law, the documentary presence of the state, and the small army of rural justices constantly reminding paysanos of their obligations and responsibilities. Apparently, by the 1830s and 1840s, the law had made some inroads into the mentality and conduct of poor paysanos. Seeing on the horizon the end of "military despotism," subalterns confronted the new powers on the land, the justices, and tried to set limits to their authority and prerogatives.

CHAPTER 6

The Making of Crime

England in the 1830s and 1840s produced, among other things, a heightened concern about crime and criminals. Important transformations in society (the replacement of men by machinery, women's greater visibility in the economy, the demise of apprenticeship, the unhealthy environment of factories, the crowded conditions of the new industrial towns) predisposed people to believe that passions were flowing beyond the limits imposed by morality and custom and that, consequently, England was experiencing an unprecedented wave of criminal activity. This consensus diagnosis generated a criminal policy centered on the notion of individual responsibility: if people could regain control over their own impulses, the crime craze would reduce itself to a manageable concern. Over the infrastructure of popular anxieties, publicists, novelists, and social reformers managed to build the idea of a "criminal class" separated from the "respectable classes."[1]

In contemporary Buenos Aires province, anarchy and civil war (rather than crime) were at the root of most social anxieties. The word anarchy evoked the peculiar political history of the nation after independence, projecting a longing for an idealized order lost circa 1820. That year the inflamed passions of the postrevolutionary leadership had pushed the country into political and social chaos. Images of crime were linked to memories of that anarchy. Federalists assumed that unitario leaders, having violated the institutions of the nation, had made permissible all types of illegalities among the populace. For their part, unitarios blamed the federalists for the establishment of an amoral dictatorship, one that sowed the seeds of evil among the lower classes. Diverse conceptions of disorder competed in the representation of postrevolutionary society. Upper-class city dwellers blamed wanderers, undisciplined youths, and immoral women for the degradation of customs and morals. To rural communities, disorder was a question of lack of patriotism and bad manners, traits they attributed to "transients." Crime per se was not the overriding concern. Accounts of crime in the printed media before 1852 are rare; novels and plays dealt with crime and punishment only as an allegory of political injustice. Murder, theft, rape, and other felonies not related to politics received much less attention.

In this chapter, I examine the role of small rural communities in the construction of criminality. Paradoxically, at a time dominated by the state's legal pedagogy, rural communities reinforced informal methods of social control. Rural towns (societies dominated by small property owners) produced a conception of crime that pitted local residents against "outsiders," in particular the itinerant or migratory laborer.[2] These same communities tolerated the traditional appropriation of cattle among neighbors. To analyze criminality, I use statistics drawn from local crime reports. The reconstruction and critical reading of arrest data provide valuable insights into the anxieties and tensions that characterized paysanos' everyday interactions. My goal is to present the subaltern in yet another constructed position, that of "delinquent," examining the way that construct was produced and the moral economy that facilitated this construction.[3]

Other Anxieties: Romantic Constructs

In England, sociological, literary, and ethnological inquiries into the worlds of the poor served to magnify public anxieties about crime. Novelists, factory inspectors, moral reformers, and amateur sociologists (Mayhew, Malthus, Chadwick, Dickens, and Carlyle, to name only a few) propagated the idea that society contained within itself a subterranean class of demoralized, impulsive, obscene, and brutal folks that nurtured criminal activity.[4] In Buenos Aires too, writers associated with the romantic movement configured the image of a violent and brutal working-class culture capable of the most aberrant crimes.[5] But their project was radically different from that of England's reformers. Romantic writers' approximation to the world of the poor was circumstantial and politically motivated. Rather than investigations into the worlds of labor and crime, their narratives constituted anatomies of the Dictatorship, supported by fictionalized encounters with peasants, urban laborers, and indigenous peoples. Their uncharitable descriptions of working-class life served to explain lower-class support for the hated dictator.[6]

Detachment, if not repulsion, marked the relationship between romantic writers and the subaltern. Sarmiento's (1974/1845) discourse on the gaucho was extemporaneous and distant. The story of Facundo was placed in the history of the revolution and in a province (La Rioja) that bore no resemblance to Buenos Aires. This displacement obeyed a political and historical necessity: understanding the country's thirty years of internal strife and political instability. Those who, unlike Sarmiento, located the caldron of political violence and savagery in the city showed no interest in working-class ethnographies. Romantic writers deployed images of lower-class brutality, ignorance, and backwardness as means to differentiate the future republican subject from the federalist masses. The killing of a bull at the slaughterhouse, the buffoon at Palermo, oxcarts full of human heads, house doors painted in light blue were all motifs emblematic of the excesses of the regime.[7]

Romantic writers located in nature (and in the social other produced by nature) most of the obstacles to the country's progress.[8] They attributed to "the desert" a crucial role in the shaping of popular mores and propensities. By itself, this operation could not produce a "crime problem," for a country built on a desert could never conjure up the type of anxieties provoked by factories, industrial slums, and pauperism. According to Sarmiento, the pampas produced a highly ritualized, violent sociability.[9] In the same taverns where paysanos met to get fresh news, talk of politics, and drink, gauchos frequently challenged each other to knife fights at the slightest provocation. Knife fights were traces of the democratic and individualistic heritage of the revolution. Other than this, there is little mention of the question of crime in *Facundo*. Common crimes, only one aspect of popular/natural customs and inclinations, were in actuality not the central issue. The true fear raised by the book was that of state terror. Incarnated in Rosas, Quiroga's soul could turn into a machine of perfect terror.

Romantic texts processed, in exuberant and militant ways, anxieties and fears of the urban upper classes. Esteban Echeverría's (1997) works deployed two prevalent fears of the gente decente: the gratuitous violence of the federalist plebe and the kidnapping of white women by pampa Indians. In *El matadero*, the slaughterhouse appears as a federalist enclave endowed with a peculiar sort of popular justice. With the same ease and brutality that the federalist rabble slaughtered a cow, it could end the life of a suspected unitario. All about this underclass was excessive: their loud and violent struggle for the animal's waste; the blood and mud that colored them and their environment; their swift and irrational throat cutting of people and beasts. The poem *La cautiva* blended the worst of stereotypes about Indian brutality, alcoholism, and cruelty to invigorate long-standing white fears of the dangers of an open frontier.[10] Blood-sucking and drunk Indians who violated the bodies of white women could destabilize and emasculate Christian society. In the desert and within the logic of total war, only male-like women (such as María) would stand up to defend the fortress of civilization.

José Mármol (1991/1851) presented readers with the greatest fear of all: the terror unleashed by the Dictator on the decent part of the population.

In *Amalia*, the whole city becomes a dangerous site: at night, in mid-1840, groups of killers sent by the Mazorca (Sociedad Popular Restauradora) roamed the city in search of their prey. In the story, five urbanites of the traditional elite plot against Rosas, are betrayed by a mazorquero passing for a friend, and subsequently suffer all the violence of federalist terror. A tragedy of a romantic love (between Eduardo and Amalia) serves as an excuse for exposing the culture of fear that caged the will and muzzled the voice of the city gentry. Though the novel indirectly indicted the lower classes for their complicity with the regime, the main criminal accusation was laid against the Federal Party leadership.

The absence of a discourse on common crime or a clear separation between "criminals" and "workers" is remarkable for intellectuals educated in law schools. This omission can be attributed only to the urgency of military and political confrontation: in civil war, there was no place for such subtleties. The social war between the urban gentry and the rabble was first and foremost a political struggle between unitarios and federales. It is not surprising, then, to find that the same sites operated as enclaves of lower-class brutality and places for the production of federalist sympathies. After 1852 various political and social commentators tried to recount the experience of dictatorship. L. V. Mansilla (1994/1852) devoted many pages of his memoirs to describe the excesses committed by both parties, the confusion of classes and races produced by political violence, and the fear that permeated everyday life.[11] His narrative reaffirmed the romantic axiom: *all crime stems from political origins.*

Miguel Estevez Saguí (1980), a lawyer with unitario sympathies who lived through the dictatorship, explained the demoralization of the city in similar terms. Criminality, he concluded, grew in the apprenticeship of political terror. The Dictator had transformed sons of "good families" and honest proletarians into criminals, forcing them to denounce and kill innocent citizens. The culture of fear blurred all moral limits, unleashing "vices and crime, disloyalty, distrust, hypocrisy, and lies" (25). In 1862 J. B. Alberdi revisited the question of anarchy to argue that the origin of national disunion was rooted in regional economic inequalities. The maldistribution of resources between Buenos Aires and the rest of the provinces had created unstable agreements and nurtured constant rebellions and warfare. This had devastating effects on the life of the republic, creating "war, nakedness, backwardness, all types of crimes and violence."[12] Although the cause of anarchy appears displaced onto a novel territory, we find here a repeated motif: crime results from the political failure to organize the nation.

Other Voices: Neighbors and the Quest for Order

Parallel to this discourse runs a long-standing predicament of the "disorderly state" of the countryside. From Azara to Rosas and beyond, spokesmen for the propertied classes complained about the existence of a "class" of vagrants and dangerous men who preyed on the property of honest farmers and ranchers. In this type of rhetoric, "disorder" was basically rooted in the structure of property rights and in peasant culture: confusing property boundaries nurtured a culture tolerant of illegal appropriation and idleness. Crime was embedded in the customs and traditions of peasants. Not surprisingly, the culprits were always those persons living on the frontier or at the margins of the cattle-ranching economy: squatters, settlers, itinerant peons, cattle rustlers, and so on.

For Pedro Andrés García (writing in 1810–1811), unsettled and fuzzy property rights were at the root of the problem of disorder in the countryside. The most important crime on the frontier was cattle theft: wandering cattle rustlers who sold their exploits to itinerant merchants; poor squatters who furtively appropriated cattle from the nearby ranches; and Indian tribes who recurrently raided towns and ranches in search of cattle and captives.[13] Due to the inhabitants' indifference, the prosecution of these crimes remained a practical impossibility. In addition, there was a problem of simulation. Passing as honest farmers or peasants numerous indigent families actually lived off stolen property. A few years later (1817), Rosas repeated García's findings: the frontier near Monte was a territory threatened by Indian raids and the predatory activities of a "multitude of vagrant and ill occupied men" who prayed on other people's property (qtd. in Montoya 1956, 41–42). Estancieros lived as if in a state of siege, afraid of losing their life and property. As "vagrants" were always in groups and very skilled in the use of arms, ranchers felt defenseless in their presence. The rude habits of these frontier inhabitants—the violent and festive way they hunted ostriches and game, otters and armadillos—and the lack of respect for law enforcers prevented the demarcation of property rights.

To Rosas and García, the excessive theft on the frontier related mainly to the customs of peasants and the failure of law enforcement. Theft was thus a problem of sociability and customs, compounded by the nomadic habits of frontier inhabitants. In their perspective, vagrancy and theft were connected: some settlers were harmful (i.e., thieves) because of their preference for leisure ("vagrancy"). What Rosas and García were indicting was a way of life.[14] Only the delimitation of property rights, the improvement of transportation, and the diffusion of agricultural knowledge could reverse this state of affairs.

Within the city, the political turmoil of the 1820s generated a sense of social insecurity among the urban gentry, toughening their views with regard to order and public morality. Illegitimate births, the excessive number of strangers in the streets, children who avoided school, and the disrespectful attitude of the lower classes gave porteños a sense that society was undergoing a period of moral decay.[15] Sensitive to these anxieties, the government of Rivadavia and Martín Rodríguez enacted a series of regulations destined to regain control of the public space: passport controls, prohibitions against card games, rounding up of vagrants, and the policing of street vendors, children, and public festivities. The end of the Rivadavian experiment added fuel to the fears of the city gentry. The presence of rural militias bordering the city in 1829 created rumors of pillage, killings, and depredation.[16] Rural militias created, in the opinion of the British Packet, a liberation of criminal propensities among the rural poor.[17]

Among rural communities also the 1820s were experienced as a time of disorder.[18] It was during this period when the tensions between farmers and cattle ranchers intensified. Ranchers' cattle damaging the wheat and maize fields, farmers dispersing or maiming ranchers' cattle, and recurrent disputes over brands, water rights, and trespassing characterized this decade. The peaceful sociability of small communities came under severe strain. From these disputes over property rights emerged a consensus about the need for greater law enforcement at the local level.

Also important was the incorporation of the countryside into the political system as a result of the electoral reform of 1821. The convergence between the new political rights and the traditions of local communities elevated the neighbor-citizen as a central figure in rural towns.[19] Local residence and service in the militias became the conditions of effective citizenship and, at the same time, the basis of social respectability. From this resulted a greater differentiation between settled men (domiciliados) and transients (transeúntes). Not eligible for the local militias and considered people "without fixed residence," transients were denied political rights. They became the convenient other. Their wandering habits and unknown social and work relations made them crime suspects.

After the invasion of Salto in 1820, the fear of Indian invasions or raids (malones) became a recurrent anxiety in the life of frontier communities. Rumors of upcoming "invasions" mobilized rural towns around their military and judicial authorities. Evidence of the fear generated by these raids was everywhere; for instance, frontier ranches had ditches specially designed to detain Indian invasions. News of tumults in the Indian encampments of Tapalquén and Chapaleufú spread waves of fear among the surrounding populations. Occasionally, individuals organized groups to rescue or purchase back Christian captives.

In the 1830s and 1840s, the increasing militarization and politicization of social life added new pressure to the life of rural communities.[20] The anxiety of forced drafts continued to divide local communities. Intensified rituals of patriotism, new schemes for political identification and differentiation, and new opportunities for social mobility generated additional venues of conflict. Local residents were forced to relate to the provincial state on a more frequent basis. They had to contribute horses and cattle to the army, collect money for military campaigns, investigate allegations of unitario conspiracies, and organize festivities to celebrate the victories of the federalist armies.[21]

Four sources of anxiety—property disputes, militarization, partisan politics, and Indian raids—constituted rural communities' notion of disorder. Building tensions related to property claims underscored the necessity of better law enforcement. The need to allocate the "military tribute" (the quota of men each town had to deliver to the army) among local residents contributed another source of tension. In the allocation of the "military tax," or draft, rural residents displaced their responsibility onto itinerant laborers or, more generally, onto those unknown to the community. Paradoxically, federalist politics generated fewer disagreements. Local communities selectively processed the orders from Buenos Aires: they tolerated the permanence of *unitarios pacíficos*, prosecuting only the most vociferous opponents of the regime (see Salvatore 1998a). Finally, the threat of Indian invasions united neighbors around the defense of rural towns and prompted them to demand stronger actions from the state.[22]

While neighbors of small rural communities shared some of the misgivings of Rosas and García about the harmful effect of vagrants and "predators" (chiefly settlers and squatters living off the ranches), they directed their accusations to the "unknown" (desconocidos). These were usually itinerant laborers seeking jobs or deserters seeking refuge. The term *desconocido* captures well the increasing anxieties of local residents over the predatory, immoral behavior of itinerant laborers and other "outsiders." Although the distinction between transients and neighbors did not congeal into a clear-cut notion of a "criminal class," resident neighbors used this convenient other to build their own notions of disorder and community.

Local (Unequal) Justice

Though immersed in the web of the Rosista power system and guided by its peculiar political principles, the local justices developed into a separate sphere of justice. Justices of the peace were given an ample degree of discretion in classifying offenses, applying penalties for correction, and granting mercy. They used this discretion to keep local communities in "good order." Their perspectives on order combined the repressive dimension of Rosas's legal pedagogy with a valorization of harmony in local social relations. Their actions, directed to the policing of families and morals, presented a different side of the justice imposed by the Dictator.

The justices' opportunities to exert discretional judgment were significantly greater in the terrain of correctional justice, a sphere more directly connected with the community's moral order. Misdemeanors were offenses that, though generating moral indignation in the community, could not be used as excuses for sending people to the military. Carrying knives, drunkenness, petty larceny, unpaid debts, brawls, insults in public, challenges to paternal authority, and wife beating constituted the usual range of illicit behavior sanctioned with "correction."[23] The penalties imposed on misdemeanors usually involved fines, jail terms, and community labor. They were stiff in relation to the offense but much lighter compared with the fate that awaited those accused of serious crimes: a small fine for carrying a knife or playing cards; one or two weeks in jail for fighting in a tavern or for wife beating; a few days in jail for drunkenness and public disturbance. In general, jail terms depended on the reparation of the damage: a man accused of eloping with a young woman was kept in detention until he decided to marry her; debtors remained in jail until they paid their debts. In cases where the harm to the community could be compensated in money, local justices assessed the fines according to the offender's wealth or the needs of the community.

Because these offenses altered local conceptions of harmony, neighbors expected the local justice to take strong action, admonishing and punishing offenders in ways that would correct bad behavior, repair the harm done, and restore tranquility. Correctional (local) justice aimed at the reparation of the damage and the repentance of the offender. Payment of a debt, compensation for stolen property, apologies for insults delivered while drunk or enraged, or the promise of stopping scandalous behavior generally put an end to the arrest.[24] Correction by arrest entailed public exposure (the hands or legs of the subject fastened in the stocks in view of the public) and, hence, the expectation that humiliation would change the bad habits of the offender. At other times, short terms of public work (repairing roads or building the local temple) served as visible evidence that the lawbreaker was mending his ways, paying back to the community in concrete ways.[25]

The repression of antisocial behavior underscores the importance of harmony and respect to local communities. Shouting on the streets, for example, was considered an affront to public morality, the same as threatening a defenseless person with a knife, insulting the honor of a woman, or calling a policeman names. Other controls within the orbit of local justice were more intrusive. Justices mediated in cases of marital conflicts to avoid public scandals and reestablish domestic harmony. They also intervened in cases of illicit unions, usually forcing the "kidnapper" (the eloper) to extend the woman's family a promise of marriage.[26] The importance of moral policing appears evident in the case of prostitution. Justices arrested prostitutes when their scandalous public behavior caused harm to others; prostitutes accused of enticing married men and "destroying" families were banished from the town.

These interventions are indicative of the meaning attributed to order at the local level, a notion that comprised the idea of peaceful interaction in both public and private spaces. Justices were expected to teach a moral lesson to wife beaters, scandalous women, and couples living out of wedlock.[27] Apparently, they also kept an eye on the public observance of religious festivities and sacred sites, for instance, keeping children out of the cemeteries and demanding that taverns remain closed during Catholic services. Most justices failed to report the violations of these ordinances to the governor; their intervention in these cases seems to have been preventive rather than punitive.

Working under the pressure of the local community and endowed with ample discretion, justices produced decisions that many times diverted from the postulate of equity. Though Rosas insisted on measuring all offenders with the same rod, local justices acted with greater leniency in cases in which the accused was a well-regarded member of the community. In 1837 the justice of San Nicolás arrested Bartolo Barrera for wounding a person in a knife fight over an unpaid debt; fourteen days later, he was set free and the episode was forgotten. The reason? The wounds did not seem serious and the accused was an "old neighbor" of the district and an "honorable man."[28] In June 1836 Serafin Acuña, a corporal of the Chascomus local partida, lightly wounded a black freeman. After ten days in jail, he was released. The justice in this case argued that Acuña had acted under the effects of alcohol, that he was unfit for service, and that he was a "neighbor."

Justices exercised ample discretion in deciding what was a serious crime and what was merely a contravention. This extended not only to cases of wounds, where harmony might have guided the decision, but also to sensitive enlistment violations or political incidents. In June 1837 José Montes (20) was arrested in Arrecifes for lacking enlistment papers. Instead of sending him to Buenos Aires, as was his duty, the local justice released him after two days in jail. Though Montes was considered a vagrant, he was given another chance mainly because he was a resident of Arrecifes. On March 7, 1840, Spaniard Antonio Martínez was arrested for wounding with a knife a local paysano who had reprimanded him for the incorrect color of his attire (light blue). Rather than initiating an indictment and charging the Spaniard with unitario sympathies, the justice set him free on the condition that he never return to the town.[29]

Montes's release and Martinez's banishment were not part of the mandated procedures. They were ad hoc decisions made in accordance with the unwritten norms of neighborhood, norms that established privileges for local residents simply on the assumption of their greater respectability and peaceful conduct. Neighborhood and membership among the productive classes were often synonymous. José Branizan, arrested in San Nicolás in 1832 for leaving the town without a passport, was almost immediately released on account of "being a neighbor and a blacksmith." Due to their profession, tailors, carpenters, and other artisans received greater consideration in cases regarding felonies or misdemeanors.[30]

The other side of the coin was harsher punishment for outsiders. Particularly in what was the most important local issue, the allocation of the town's contribution to the war effort, localism prevailed. Between May and June 1832 the justice of San Nicolás arrested and sent directly to the commander of Fort Federation ten individuals. Eight of them were men of working age coming from Santa Fé, Corrientes, Santiago del Estero, and Mendoza.[31] The other two were local residents. One of them was a 30-year-old man accused of stealing cattle from neighbors and selling them at the local market, a flagrant act of disloyalty to the town. The other was an 18-year-old boy with "unknown address," probably chosen as the town's contribution to the war effort. Apparently, the notion of "outsiders" included not only transients or recent arrivals but also migrants who after some time failed to make an honest living. Among the arrested men from Santa Fe were people with bad reputations: Fructuoso Silva and his son Juan de la Cruz, who lived in a thatched hut close to the town with no apparent (licit) source of income, and Bernabé Ramos, who, due to repeated complaints from neighbors, was regarded as an hombre vago (vagrant). The three were considered harmful to the community mainly because of the suspicion that they were living off other people's cattle.

Directly, by accusing a person, or indirectly, by spreading rumors about that person's behavior, neighbors played an important role in the enforcement of local justice. In fact, it could be argued that local communities had their own mental gallery of delinquents. Neighbors' memory served as an archive of information that could be retrieved every time a stranger came to town. The commonly used phrase "he has accumulated" (such and such felonies) referred chiefly to the association between individual delinquents and their past felonies. Information passed from one person to another helped neighbors label a person as a delinquent. Neighbors' memory of violent crimes was indeed remarkable. In March 1841 Santos Alarcón was arrested in San Antonio de Areco for carrying a false document. The neighbors identified him as the one who had murdered a local resident, Juan Francisco Peralta, eleven years before.[32]

One of the drawbacks of this system of justice was that suspicions often constituted the sole basis for an arrest. Rumors that a person had stolen a hat, had hosted deserters in his house, or had slaughtered a neighbor's cow ended up with the detention of that person until the suspicion was confirmed or denied. Only after the arrest did justices conduct informal interrogations, collect evidence, and try to verify the validity of documents and brands. If the evidence did not corroborate the accusation, justices proceeded to release the accused.[33] Thus, local justice was a form of unequal or biased justice. Heavily leaning toward the control of public morality and peaceful social interaction, this was a justice that granted local residents privileges not accorded transients or migrants. To an extent, this justice was communal, for it arrested people on the basis of neighbors' suspicion and character evaluation.

This discretionary justice coexisted with a more systematic, less lenient, and more effective form of administering punishment: the one commanded by the governor. Despite the exceptions granted on account of localism, justices had to send to Buenos Aires all those who defied the laws of property, skirted their obligations to defend the fatherland, or disturbed with violence the tranquility of the countryside. By and large, justices accomplished this commitment, producing a criminality that in many respects bore the imprint of state concerns and demands.

Crime: A Statistical Reconstruction

In a sense, the local Juzgados were the main centers for the production of crime and class during this period. In the absence of a local press, the justice's office–house functioned as a resonance box where the suspicions and gossip of neighbors found their outlet. Their classifying activities served to distinguish those members of the "peon class" from the rest of the population. Their prosecutions, whether originating in the neighbors or mandated by Rosas, criminalized the activities of the mobile part of this "class," resolving along the way the problematic question of how to distribute the "military tribute." A statistical reconstruction of rural crime in Buenos Aires province during the period 1831–1851 can help us understand the complex and multifaceted process of the production of crime.

This reconstruction is based on the *Partes de Novedades*, quarterly arrest reports sent by the justices of the peace to Rosas. In these reports, justices included cases of delinquents sent to the governor for a decision and, prior to 1836, those delivered to a nearby regiment.[34] Though the reports are incomplete, the available data (1,674 observations or arrests) could be taken as a representative sample of felons transported from the countryside to Buenos Aires. I estimate that these observations constitute between 23 and 37 percent of the total number of arrests during this period. Coverage for most counties appears sufficiently ample, ranging from 21 to 64 percent of the estimated number of felons. Only in Las Flores, Chivilcoy, and San Nicolás is the sample small, ranging from 2 to 5 percent (see Table 6.1).

The crimes reported in these sources are subject to some degree of underestimation. Perhaps the greatest bias was the justices' tendency not to report what they considered "crimes of correction," misdemeanors usually penalized with fines, a few days in jail, or a simple warning. Mainly because these crimes did not require sending the prisoner to Buenos Aires, most justices decided it was not necessary to report them. On occasion, they made this clear in their reports. In the Report corresponding to June–August 1839, the justice of San Nicolás wrote: "In the time that corresponds to the current four-month period, we have arrested 27 more individuals for causes that did not merit more than a reprimand . . . those have obtained their freedom after a few days."[35]

In addition, we know that the infamous *contingentes* (people arrested for the sole purpose of fulfilling military recruitment quotas) were only partially registered.[36] In a 1835 *Acuerdo* Rosas mandated that all justices of the peace send two or more men each month to the federalist army. How effectively did justices comply with this order is hard to estimate. In many instances, those sent as the district's periodical quota were boys age 14 to 18 drafted for the regiments' music bands. It was quite difficult to forcefully draft adult males on a periodical, regular basis. In my sources the number of prisoners taken to fulfill the justice's quota (usually registered as prisoners "sent by Superior Order") seems suspiciously small. At

TABLE 6.1 Sample Size and Estimated Number of Crimes, Buenos Aires Province (1831–1851)

Partido	Months w/records	Sample Size[1]	Estimated Number of Crimes[2]	Sample Ratio[3]
Lobos	116	214	482	0.44
Arrecifes	82	100	338	0.29
Areco	156	215	373	0.58
Azul	134	81	158	0.51
Tordillo	104	41	140	0.29
Monsalvo	44	39	246	0.16
Quilmes	86	132	439	0.30
Chascomús	154	104	253	0.41
Luján	108	241	699	0.34
Baradero	96	34	144	0.24
Cañuelas	108	41	135	0.30
Dolores	48	47	414	0.11
Ensenada	132	23	109	0.21
Ranchos	180	112	175	0.64
Las Flores	6	18	840	0.02
Chivilcoy	14	19	540	0.03
Navarro	100	155	504	0.31
San Nicolás	44	58	1,082	0.05
TOTAL	1,712	1,674	7,071	0.23

Source: "Partes de Novedades," AGN, sala X.
[1] Number of crimes reported; [2] Number of crimes reported/months with records times 252 months; [3] Sample size divided by estimated number of crimes

most, they represent 2 percent of total arrests. As in the case of misdemeanors, some justices understood that they did not have to include these arrests in their quarterly reports.

After correcting my estimates to allow for underreporting, we are still left with a number of felonies that seems modest for a countryside reputed for its violence and disorder. My estimated total (7,070), even when augmented by 40 percent to account for unreported misdemeanors and people arrested for the contingentes (9,900), amounts to fewer than 500 arrests per year in the whole province, that is, between one and two prisoners sent by each county each month. This exiguous figure seems insufficient to support Rosas's recruitment policies and evinces either a lenient enforcement of laws at the local level or a low rate of criminality. The low number of prisoners per month is consistent with the fact that, on many occasions, justices reported that a term had passed without any prisoners.[37] Reports with no new prisoners represented 9 percent of extant reports for Chascomús, 12 percent of the reports from Azul, 18 percent of those from Monsalvo, 21 percent of those from Areco, 31 percent of those from Baradero, and 34 percent of those from Ensenada.

Taken at the site of arrest (the small rural towns where the justices sat), my source represents better than other studies the incidence and nature of "rural criminality" or, from another perspective, the intensity of local law enforcement.[38] These statistics could be read as the attempt of an incipient state to produce information about the rural population. They reflect the labeling process by which crime was constructed and, at the same time, the informational demands of the provincial state. Indirectly and rather imperfectly, these statistics reveal also the multidimensional conflictivity of local communities. State imperatives, neighbors' prejudices, and social conflicts combined to produce the statistical portraits I present next.

Against Property, Against the State

The structure of crime of a given society reflects the dual pressure of police repression and crime incidence (see Gatrell and Hadden 1972). The information provided in Table 6.2 presents a structure dominated by two types of offenses: crimes against property (33 percent) and crimes against authority and the state (37 percent). The importance of theft and other property offenses is not surprising in a society undergoing a process of rapid economic expansion and a substantial redistribution of property rights. What is remarkable is the fact that the most important form of crime was directed against the authorities or the state.

I include under this general category (crimes against the state) a series of illegalities surrounding the obligation of males to provide military service to the provincial state: deserters, draft dodgers, neighbors who avoided military drills or provided "bad service" to local justices, and migratory workers traveling without identification. These crimes were directed not against property or particular persons but against the state. They represent a rejection by poor paysanos of their obligation to provide military or police service in the terms and time demanded by state authorities. To this extent, they constitute one aspect of peasants' and laborers' resistance against forced recruitment. Deserting a military unit and traveling without proper identification were the two most frequent violations covered under this category. Desertion was a breach of the implicit contract between paysanos and the state for the provision of military service.

TABLE 6.2 Crimes by Type, Buenos Aires Province (1831–1851)

Type of Crime	Number of Cases	Percentage
AGAINST PROPERTY	552	33.1
Theft	508	
Other	44	
AGAINST PERSONS/HONOR	216	12.9
Wounds and beatings	96	
Homicide and related	63	
Rape, kidnapping, etc.	33	
Insults	23	
Other	4	
AGAINST THE STATE	627	37.6
Desertion	285	
Draft dodgers and "bad service"	39	
Without documents	295	
Other	8	
AGAINST PUBLIC ORDER	225	13.5
Vagrancy	141	
Drunkenness	13	
Fights	22	
Gambling	1	
Carrying a knife	14	
Runaways	14	
Desconocido	13	
Other	7	
POLITICAL	17	1.0
Insurrection/conspiracy	2	
Unitarios	15	
OTHER	32	1.9
Orden superior	20	
Other	12	
TOTAL NUMBER OF CRIMES	1,669	100.0

Source: Database "Presos Remitidos," N=1674 from Jueces de Paz, "Partes de Novedades."

After a short term of service (ten months on average), a sizable portion of the men drafted into the army (about 25 percent) rejected the terms and conditions of their engagement and fled.[39] Later, under interrogation, deserters explained that conditions of life in the army (length of service, inadequate pay, bad treatment, unlawful private use of their services) were the chief motivation for their desertions (see chapter 9).

Traveling without identification and related offenses (forging passports, changing names) involved both resistance and accommodation. Clearly, there were paysanos who resented the increasing documentation of their movements as a requirement that conflicted with their independent way of life. For others, not carrying identification resulted from ignorance or fear. Unaware of this requirement or afraid of facing the police authorities to obtain a passport, many northern migrants were apprehended on their way to Buenos Aires without proper papers. Those who knew the consequences of traveling without a passport tried to get one, by legal or illegal means. Forging passports and *guías*, traveling under another person's name and stealing documents were quite common practices. Although many paysanos tried to accommodate state requirements, the multiplicity of papers they were supposed to carry and the justices' insistence on the formality of such documents turned many law-abiding peasants and laborers into delinquents.

This offense was only tangentially related to the question of labor control. In an overwhelming majority of cases, the arrests proceeded after the subject's failure to produce enlistment papers, travel passports, or temporary permits (for men-at-arms). The lack of employment papers (*papeleta de conchavo*) certainly complicated the situation of the accused but was not the main cause of arrest. Crimes against property were important, constituting 33 percent of the registered cases; among these, theft was prevalent. Of the cases with information, the theft of cattle and horses ranked first, at 70 percent of the sample. The theft of clothes, riding apparel, and merchandise followed in importance (16 percent of the cases), underscoring the thieves' need for goods easily exchangeable in the marketplace. Hides, the most valuable by-product of cattle raising, served the same purpose; consequently, it was preferred to wheat, fowl, pigs, or other types of agricultural produce. Cases involving the theft of money constituted only 6 percent of the sample.

Most thefts were committed by one or two individuals operating under the protection of night or in the absence of witnesses. The object stolen was often of small significance: one or two head of cattle, one horse, fewer than half a dozen hides, a few items of riding gear. The victims of these crimes were described as male (89 percent), neighbor (42 percent), employer or hacendado (21 percent), tavern-keeper or merchant (13 percent). Perpetrators were presented as people with no clear attachment to the community, such as temporary peons or newcomers, or as indigent residents living off their neighbors' property. The modalities of appropriation varied: of 279 cases, 15 skinned the animals to make *botas de potro* (mareskin "boots") or to sell the hides; 16 were found riding stolen horses; 39 sold stolen cattle or forged cattle brands; 50 slaughtered animals on the spot to consume the meat; and 154 had driven stolen cattle to the market.

On a first reading, these crimes could be taken as a reaction by poor paysanos to state regulations that criminalized the customary appropriation of free-roaming cattle. At a time when the state tried to consolidate property rights in cattle, the appropriation of horses and cattle, a tolerated behavior among neighbors, became a crime when committed by "outsiders." On a closer reading, however, more was at stake. Clearly, the desire to become a small property owner with other people's livestock (forming their own cattle or horse herds) coexisted with the urge to satisfy more immediate and basic needs (wearing boots, eating beef). There were apparently two types of thieves: the fugitive from justice who needed a horse, riding gear, or money to continue his journey, and the poor paysano (probably a recently settled laborer) who wanted to increase his capital at the expense of his neighbors. And this places us back in the tense relationship between the subaltern and the state.

Most delinquents were apparently passing by the town; the horses they rode and the bulls they drove served as evidence in their arrest. Most horse thieves fell into that condition as a requirement of travel, and a deserter had to procure a good horse and riding apparel to make a successful escape. Thus, many horse thieves were suspected of desertion and vice versa. Livestock theft cannot be extricated from peasant resistance against recruitment. Paysanos' illicit trade in cattle and horses made a mockery of the most visible signs of property. In defiance of state regulations cattle and horse thieves forged brands and transport papers. Those who were caught, due to the painstaking surveillance of brands carried out by justices and the community of neighbors, probably constituted only a fraction of a larger universe of poor people on the move.

It was customary for justices to accumulate charges on a felon to justify his remittal to Buenos Aires. Hence, a felon could be accused of robbery but also be suspected as a possible deserter or the kidnapper of a young woman. In Table 6.1 I have considered only one of these charges, the most important and concrete of them, placing as a second or third charge all other accusations. If we add all these charges (in this sample they amount to 2,432), almost the same distribution of crimes results: crimes against the state, 37 percent; crimes against property, 30 percent; crimes against public order, 16 percent; crimes against persons, 12 percent; political crimes, 1 percent. Rather than a statistical fiction, this particular representation of criminality presents us with an undeniable social fact: local communities and the state endeavored to eradicate the two great illegalities affecting the countryside, theft and desertion.

A Violent and Disorderly Countryside?

Arrest statistics do not correspond with the image of a violent countryside or with a state decidedly committed to the repression of crime. Felonies against persons were remarkably few, representing fewer than 13 percent of all arrests. Wounds and beatings were the most frequent felonies falling under this category, followed by homicide and related offenses; reported homicides were relatively few (47).[40] This could be interpreted in three ways: knife fights resulting in homicides took place far from the gaze of the authorities; the police devoted little effort to the instruction of these cases; or paysanos, as Sarmiento suggested, went to a duel only to mark the opponent's body or face, not to kill him.

We can imagine that many deaths went unreported in this society, but it is difficult to estimate the importance of these cases. On occasion, justices reported to Rosas that they found bodies on the outskirts of their town but were unable to locate the assassin.[41] It is possible that the violent death of people without much support within the community (acculturated Indians, free blacks, and migratory workers) passed unreported or was never investigated. Deaths resulting from knife fights, though important, did not represent the principal form of homicide or, at least, not among the reported cases. Cases of robbery aggravated with murder, treacherous murders committed against unarmed victims, and crimes of passion (involving women, husbands, and lovers) take us away from the stereotypical scene of the tavern knife fight.

The scenes and circumstances of these crimes were diverse. In the reported cases of homicide and wounding (numbering 130 in the sample), 87 percent of the victims were male, 83 percent of the perpetrators acted alone, and 82 percent of the attacks were committed with a knife. Guns were almost unknown; *rebenques*, *palos*, and *bolas* (whips, sticks, and lariats with ball-tipped ends) accounted for a small proportion of murders. Most homicides were committed in private homes, taverns, or the open countryside; murders on ranches or farms or in the street were much less frequent. Apparently, violence was largely an exchange among males, circumscribed to certain spaces of sociability. The victims of this violence cut across the social spectrum: 39 percent were labeled neighbors or militiamen, 33 percent peons or soldiers, 19 percent policemen, state officials, or employers, and the rest were women, children, and tavern keepers.

The few cases of rape reported indicate state authorities' preoccupation with punishing this type of crime. The state's interest in protecting rural women's honor obeyed the logic of war: it was necessary to extend soldiers the guarantee that "their" women would be protected while they were on campaign.[42] The indignation that energized these prosecutions came, however, from women, either the victim herself or her mother. Women fearlessly denounced this kind of offense to the authorities, even when the accused was an officer or the village priest. Kidnapping women, an aggression that served as a substitute for or complement to courtship, was also punished, sometimes very severely.[43] The fact that these types of offenses were prosecuted reveals something about the role of women in this productive war economy. Left to care for farms and households during military campaigns, women were essential in the lives of small communities and therefore deserved the protection of the state.

Crimes against public order (disturbing the peace, drunkenness, fights, gambling, carrying a knife, etc.) were less numerous than expected. Drunkenness and disturbing the peace, a major cause of police arrests in the decades following 1880, were rather rare in this period (see Blackwelder and Johnson 1982). This could mean that the claim of the regime to have restored the order of the countryside was accurate or, alternatively, that this type of offense was subject to a greater degree of underreporting. A combination of both circumstances is more than likely: paysanos' public culture provided methods of self-restraint, and better policing reduced the opportunities for violent interactions. Paysanos knew that the combination of bad language, gambling, and drink could lead to challenges that ended in mortal wounds, so they tried to avoid confrontations. As the justice of Cañuelas explained to Scottish worker William Walter, one took out the knife (*facón*) only if one could not defend oneself by other means—the knife was a weapon of last resort.[44] The police, lax about many other regulations, were particularly strict when it came to the collection of knives at taverns.

The police also controlled public expressions of anger. Insults themselves were a cause for arrest, mainly because they eroded respect and authority, two pillars of paysanos' sociability. Insults were considered the first step toward a knife fight. On occasion, they carried a definitely political connotation. Apparently the community had clear notions about when insults became intolerable and knew how to distinguish the drunkard's bad language from other types of verbal abuse. Certain members of the community with a perceived stronger claim to respectability (neighbors, ranchers, foremen, police, officers, and older people) were often the plaintiffs. Fights and insults reveal the complex conflictivity of rural towns: people expressed in the public space a series of tensions in family, work, and community. In the cases reported, we see peons fighting ranch administrators or foremen, militiamen defending their honor in front of regular army soldiers, paysanos facing the authorities, outsiders challenging locals. Usually, arguments about debts and work, political affiliation, authority/obedience, love, and male honor preceded these confrontations.

The most frequent offense among crimes against the public order, vagrancy, was more a moral condemnation than a felony. Justices used charges of vagrancy to underscore the negative valuation made by residents about newcomers whose morality and willingness to work were in doubt. Added to the criminal record, the term *vago* (vagrant) served as an aggravating circumstance to another crime when not as the justification for a socially motivated arrest. Indeed, the term vagrant (often accompanied by other descriptions, such as harmful, injurious, thief, or disorderly conduct) implied suspicion of robbery or, more generally, an indictment of the accused's independent and defiant way of life. An apprentice who escaped his master would be called a vagrant due to his unwillingness to accept submission (*por no querer sujetarse*). The charge of vagrancy was not simply a punishment for unemployment, as many historians have claimed (e.g., Díaz 1952; Gori 1951; Rodríguez Molas 1968; Garavaglia 1997a).

Very few were arrested on charges of being a unitario or expressing unitario ideas; I found 17 cases in a sample of 1,669. This should not surprise us; outspoken unitarios were a minority in rural towns (a minority associated generally with the commercial and propertied classes) and, after the repression of 1839–1840, disappeared from public scrutiny. Local residents had little trouble identifying this type of offender: unitarios felt no joy at federalist victories, spoke with sarcasm about Rosas and his family, made provocative statements about the future of the federation, refused to wear the federalist ribbon, and kept aloof from Catholic celebrations. Neighbors denounced to the authorities unitarios who expressed their political opinions in public, protecting those who were *pacíficos* (composed and reserved). Those who, during the time of Lavalle's invasion, had made visible efforts to support the cause of Unidad were negatively marked in the collective memory of the federalist community.

Rather than engage in a war against property owners or decimate themselves in the defense of honor, poor paysanos were involved in a quotidian confrontation with the state around the issue of military service. The state of Buenos Aires, preoccupied with manning its armies, had criminalized the customary activities of peasants and laborers (including the direct appropriation of cattle and horses) and punished law breakers with long terms in the army. The rural poor responded in kind, avoiding militia registration, shirking regular military service, and deserting the army when conditions became intolerable. To remain out of the reach of military recruiters and the rural police, poor paysanos put into practice multiple "arts of deception" (J. C. Scott 1990): forging passports, permits, and release papers; hiding their uniforms; changing names; seeking refuge among relatives and friends; keeping their past to themselves; changing jobs frequently.

The interrogations that led to the arrest of paysanos could not avoid the question of service. In fact, as many filiaciones show, questions concerning this matter generally outnumbered those directed at the circumstances and motivations of common crimes. Serving the Cause of the Federation was in the minds of all justices and, consequently, influenced the writing of crime reports and individual criminal records. Information about battles, commanders, and battalions of past federalist campaigns fattened these reports, revealing the concerns of law enforcers. Inquiring why certain paysanos, being of age, had not complied with their military obligations was the main puzzle that preoccupied Rosas and his military chiefs. As an essential practice in the mechanics of governance, local justices were instructed to ask a series of questions that revealed in part subalterns' experiences in the civil war.

The results of these interrogations were preoccupying to the authorities. In a period of recurrent wars and heightened patriotism, paysanos cooperated with the Cause of Federalism much less than expected. Although all males 18 and older had to enlist in the militias, many tried to avoid this obligation by moving from town to town. As a result, 71 percent of the arrested (the most mobile part of the province's peon class) said they had not complied with mandatory registration in the militias. Those who said they had were unable to prove it; only 6 percent of the arrested were able to produce enlistment papers at the time of their arrest. Those who were not registered militiamen could still be regular soldiers and fulfill their obligation to the federation. But few actually did. When asked whether they belonged to a regiment or army unit, fewer than 8 percent of the arrested said they did. Fewer still were those who could prove their military engagement, for under 3 percent carried passports with them and fewer than 5 percent were able to produce release papers (*licencias* or *bajas*).[45]

This left the impression among military recruiters and justices of the peace that poor paysanos, particularly those unfamiliar to neighbors, were always resisting the draft. This resistance appears all the more remarkable when we consider that rural communities did not mount a collective opposition to the draft after the unpopular war of 1825–1827. Unlike the French and Catalan peasant communities of the revolutionary and Napoleonic periods, which defied the central state from a position of autonomy and cooperative labor, the towns of rural Buenos Aires failed to organize against the intrusions of the "central" state (Cobb 1987; Forrest 1989; Brunet 1986). Under such circumstances, resisting the draft was often an individual enterprise assisted by friends and relatives, rarely a collective, townwide struggle.

Few among the arrested (37 percent) declared they had provided military service to the federation. Among this group, what constituted military service differed: 48 percent said they had had combat experience; 16 percent had joined an army unit or a militia or had served temporarily in frontier outposts or camp drills (*destacamentos* and *cantones*); (see Table 6.3). The rest reported service that the army classified as "passive": driving cattle to a regiment, tending horses at a military *caballada*, slaughtering cattle for soldiers' consumption, taking care of ranches confiscated from the unitarios, or helping the justice or the local police chief on occasional patrols. All these services appeared to military recruiters much less patriotic and demanding than defending the Federal Cause on the battlefield. Furthermore, none of these services exempted males from their obligation to enlist in the militias or the army. Consequently, recruiters insisted that arrested paysanos not showing proof of being in the militias or in the regular army be given a military assignment. Paysanos, on the other hand, wanted these "passive services" to count as military duty.

Those who had provided no service to the federation or had been only marginally involved in its defense could expect a punishment proportional to their "crime": years of service in the federal army.[46] To military recruiters, the worst crime was noncompliance with the obligation to serve the fatherland; consequently, the identification and arrest of deserters constituted a major objective of the justice system. This explains the degree of detail found in the depositions about deserters and common delinquents around the question of service. Those who wrote the reports made an effort to include something about the military record of each arrestee; thus, we possess information about paysanos' participation in different

TABLE 6.3 Type of Military Service Rendered by Prisoners

Type of Service	Number of Cases	Percentage
Joined an army corps	44	6.0
Joined military campaign	356	48.7
Joined local militia	27	3.7
Did destacamentos	50	6.8
Tended army's horses	55	7.5
Served police patrulla	26	3.5
Served the local justice	30	4.1
Served in own province	19	2.6
Participated in cattle drives	85	11.6
Carried mail	7	0.9
Participated in branding	7	0.9
Carried firewood	6	0.8
Slaughtered cattle	3	0.4
Served the postas	3	0.4
Tended state ranches	3	0.4
Other	9	1.2
TOTAL	730	100.0

Source: "Partes de Novedades," AGN, sala x.

campaigns and wars that otherwise would have passed unreported (see Table 6.4). The information itself is revealing of the state's interest in the question of service. The responses collected paint a dismal scenario for military authorities: only a third of the arrested were able to give some detail of their participation in the wars of the federación.

We should try to read the statistics in the context provided by the anxieties of the state. The question of service, being essential for the conduct of war, was the major preoccupation of the Rosas administration. Against this imperative, the defense of property and the moral management of rural communities took second place. As far as the central state was concerned, the interrogation of prisoners aimed at identifying deserters. Whether arrested for theft, fighting, or vagrancy, felons were requested to tell their "histories" to the justice of the peace. As the felon recounted his past, he dropped information about past campaigns and wars; this made him a suspect in draft dodging or desertion. Usually, having "dispersed" after a battle counted as desertion, regardless of the soldier's efforts to rejoin his battalion. During the interrogation, cases that started as crimes against property or persons could easily turn into crimes against the state.

TABLE 6.4 Military Campaigns in Which Arrestees Participated

Military Campaign	Number of Cases	Percentage
War of Brazil (1825–28)	19	3.4
First "Restoration" (1829)	157	28.3
Campaign to Córdoba (1830–31)	63	11.4
Second "Restoration" (1833)	49	8.8
Indian Campaign of 1833–34	41	7.4
Southern Rebellion (1839)	52	9.4
Invasion of 1840	57	10.3
Entre Ríos Campaign (1840–42)	38	6.8
Cuyo Campaign (1841)	14	2.5
Chasing Indians	20	3.6
Other	44	7.9
TOTAL	554	100.0

Source: Filiaciones (N=525)

Only if the arrested was a neighbor and a good federalist was his military experience taken for granted and the interrogation allowed to concentrate on his civil wrong-doings.

Manufacturing Difference: A Criminal Class?

To an extent, the Rosista judicial system was implicated in the production of social difference. Its practices of identification, description, and classification aimed at separating the so-called "country peon clan" from the rest of the peasantry (see chapter 4). People who worked as peons and laborers, wore chiripá and poncho, were unable to read and write, and possessed no more than a horse, a set of clothes, and rustic riding apparel were, by official definition, members of this "class." On their shoulders fell most of the burden of manning the federalist armies. Other members of rural society (hacendados, small livestock raisers, farmers, foremen, merchants, and artisans), though obliged to perform some type of service to the state, were generally exempted from active military duty; as vecinos (neighbors or residential citizens) they had to enroll in the local militias and render "passive services," occasional and limited duties in detachments, cantonments, or patrols.

Thus, a legal system predicated on the concept of social equality produced discrimination. The power of the law fell more heavily on those who shared the appearance of poor paysanos, had no fixed residence, and usually earned their living as peons or day laborers. The target of police surveillance and the object of neighbors' suspicions, the "peon class" was considered criminal only to the extent that it did not cooperate with the documentary and militaristic state, failed to respect the new arrangement of property rights, or offended local norms of sociability and civility. In practice, the identification and separation of people into socioeconomic classes was ridden with difficulties.

Regarding occupational status, social difference was ambiguous, to the extent that many rural residents reported to work in *faenas de campo*, a general category encompassing the work of small-scale cattle raisers and farmers as well as that of peons. (Few were given the chance to explain that they considered themselves *criadores* or *labradores*.) Wage labor was not a good indicator either. Nonproprietary residents such as squatters, tenants, and laborers all had to engage in occasional work on neighboring estates. Thus, the practical separation of a *peon class* had to rest on a difference that was simpler and easier to establish: the difference between local residents and outsiders. The questions regarding *papeletas*, the state requirement for identification, provided justices with an opportunity to examine the origins and social connections of travelers, facilitating the construction of this essential distinction.

Neighbors contributed to his production of difference. Those who were long-term residents of a rural town or district tended to see criminal propensities in the recently arrived and the traveler. Though welcome as wage laborers, migrants were perceived either as persons not tied to the locality by the responsibility of family or as immorals living in concubinage. Their drinking habits were unknown, hence the need to inquire how alcohol affected their behavior. Their autonomy, interpreted as a challenge to the tranquility and order of the province, made young men on the move key suspects for interrogation and arrest. The property of lower-class travelers, or at least the documents that acted as proof of ownership, were always under suspicion. Residents assumed that itinerant workers, particularly those who claimed to come from distance places, were escaping justice; hence, they looked for some sign in their attire that betrayed a prior engagement with the military and checked the brands on their horses to see if they had illegally obtained their transportation.

As noted, with the growth of rural towns and the subsequent consolidation of the justice and police apparatuses, there developed a distinction between vecinos (residents) and transeúntes (nonresidents) that profoundly affected the functioning of the justice system (Cansanello 1994). Whereas neighbors could be trusted to perform a multiplicity of small

The Making of Crime   221

TABLE 6.5 Mobility of the Arrestees

Arrested in	Born outside Their Country (in %)	Born outside Buenos Aires Province (in %)	Total Number of Arrested
Lobos	83.3	53.3	201
Arrecifes	83.9	67.7	99
Areco	72.8	42.0	212
Azul	89.4	46.9	32
Tordillo	100.0	42.9	35
Monsalvo-Mar Chiquita	100.0	65.2	23
Quilmes	84.1	51.7	118
Chascomus	89.8	54.2	96
Luján	76.3	55.5	238
Baradero	47.1	29.4	34
Cañuelas	93.0	30.0	40
Dolores	100.0	55.3	47
Ensenada	83.7	34.8	23
Ranchos	76.2	52.3	111
Las Flores	66.7	55.6	18
Chivilcoy	100.0	52.6	19
Navarro	100.0	39.1	115
San Nicolás	63.8	61.5	52
TOTAL	82.2	51.8	1,554

Source: Database (N=1674) from Justice of the Peace's "Partes de Novedades."

tasks required for the functioning of a well-ordered town (arrests, prosecutions, transportation and slaughtering of cattle, road repairs, mail, etc.), nonresidents were suspected of avoiding not only these services but also the more fundamental task of defending the federation. Outsiders, *desconocidos* (unknown people), and youngsters without parental supervision were made the first target of press gangs or levies precisely because older male residents found their manners and morals lacking with regard to the ideal of order in the federalist republic.

Consequently, it is not surprising to find that transients, most of them peons, were given a disproportionate share of the burden of active military service, whereas neighbors provided mostly "passive services." The data on prisoners reveal the bias of the judicial system against these itinerant workers and fugitives. It is true that migrants were an important part of the population of most towns to the south of the Salado River, yet migratory workers appear overrepresented in arrest statistics. And this was true also in older towns where one would expect a lower participation of outsiders (see Table 6.5). Over 82 percent of the arrested had been born outside of the district in which they were arrested. Considering that the proportion of those arrested for traveling without papers was much lower (17 percent), we cannot attribute this asymmetry to a question of travel control or of labor control. The proportion reached 100 percent in the case of counties of recent settlement to the north (Navarro, Chivilcoy) and south (Tordillo, Monsalvo, Dolores, Mar Chiquita) of the Salado River but was also high (over 70 or 80 percent) in older districts of the northwest-southeast corridor such as Arrecifes, Areco, and Quilmes. Nearly 52 percent of the arrested had been born outside of the province of Buenos Aires; most were provincianos coming from the northern provinces, but there were also Africans, Europeans, and migrants from neighboring countries.[47]

The occupations of the arrested cover the whole spectrum of economic activities in rural society (see Table 6.6). The largest group worked in agriculture, husbandry, and forestry (50 percent). Most were peons, though there were also farmers and cattle raisers (small-scale producers), ranch foremen and administrators and, occasionally, a great rancher. Then followed day laborers (18 percent), transport workers (8 percent, mostly oxcart drivers and cattle drovers), and people classified as unemployed (8 percent).[48] There were also soldiers, merchants, workers in rural industry (leatherwork and meat salting), and others. Totaling peons, skilled rural workers, other laborers, workers in rural industry, transport workers, and day laborers, we find that 70 percent of the arrested belonged to the "peon class."[49]

How does this compare with the breakdown of occupations for the population as a whole? Recent studies of rural towns such as Lobos and San Antonio de Areco found that, in the period 1815–1838, peasant farmers and shepherds outnumbered peons, laborers, and slaves by an ample margin (see Mateo 1993b; Garavaglia 1998, 10). The 1854 census of the campaña classified 19 percent of the population as ranchers and cattle raisers, 11 percent as farmers, 4 percent as workers in "manufacturing" trades, 7 percent as merchants and clerks, 1 percent as government employees, 9 percent as holding employment in personal services, and 39 percent as peons. The census of 1869 found a more substantial "middling sector." Ranchers, farmers, merchants, clerks, professionals, and government employees made up 24 percent of the population. Combined, the number of day laborers and peons reached 37.5 percent, a much lower proportion than in arrest statistics (Sábato and Romero 1992, 45, table IV).

Racially, the arrested constituted a mixed bag, leaning slightly toward

TABLE 6.6 Occupation of the Arrestees

Occupational Group	Number of Cases	Percentage
Artisans	29	3.2
Rural industry	23	2.5
Transportation	70	7.8
Commerce	20	2.2
Farming, husbandry	449	49.9
Estanciero/proprietor	24	2.7
Administrator/foreman	17	1.9
Labrador/criador	29	3.2
Peon	288	32.0
Skilled workers	48	5.3
Other country laborers	43	4.8
Armed forces	59	6.5
Other employment	6	0.7
Day laborers	166	18.5
Unemployed	77	8.5
TOTAL	899	100.0

Source: Database (N=1674) from Justice of the Peace's "Partes de Novedades."

the "colored" population, but not significantly different from the rural population at large: 40 percent of those arrested were *trigueños* (sunburned mestizos), 32 percent were white, 8 percent black, 9 percent mulatto, 5 percent with Indian features (*aindiado* or *achinado*), and 3 percent Indian.[50] The Buenos Aires justice system, though not racially blind—recruiters were asked to register the skin color of all soldiers—did not seem to discriminate in terms of race. A slightly greater proportion of trigueños (sun-burned mestizos) than in urban areas reflects the weight of the rural population among the arrested. The stigma against "people of color" remained probably as strong as in colonial times, but the freedoms and opportunities blacks, mulattos, and mestizos had gained since independence made the implementation of racial justice very difficult.[51]

The age distribution of the arrested was not significantly different from the population at large: 43 percent were younger than 24 and 78 percent younger than 34.[52] This means that 57 percent of the arrested were 25 or older. This age distribution might seem odd for a state preoccupied with producing young recruits for the army (and using the justice system for this purpose). But we know from other sources that the federalist army was not so discriminating in terms of age. The obligation to enlist in the militias and regiments involved all males between 18 and 45. Moreover, the system of extending service as a punishment for disciplinary violations tended to raise the average age of the corps. As Sarmiento (1950, 87–88) reported in his *Campaña en el Ejército Grande*, old soldiers constituted an important proportion of the Dictator's regiments.

Neither age nor race seems to have been the basis on which the justice system identified and separated the "class" that would man the federalist armies. Justices had instructions from Rosas to look at the appearance of subjects, identify which ones belonged to the "peon class," and annotate the details of the crime. Before that encounter, however, neighbors had constructed the criminal in their own terms, making transients and unknown men the main culprits in actual and imagined crimes. In so doing, they were carrying into practice a long-standing discourse that associated poor people on the move with robbery, vagrancy, and lack of patriotism. This type of criminalization—focusing on the most "nomadic" or mobile part of the population—was consistent with a particular definition of citizenship, that which equated permanent residency and property with political rights.

These statistical portraits provide insights into the provincial state's criminal policy. The profile of the delinquent shows that the Rosista justice system weighed heavier on the humblest portion of the rural population, more frequently arresting those who were day laborers and peons (the country peon class). Intent on pacifying, recruiting, and safeguarding property, the system more frequently arrested the members of this "class" than those of other social groups. The majority of the arrested were engaged in temporary and mobile wage occupations, whereas the "middling sector" (squatters, farmers, and small livestock raisers) constituted a minority.

Pax Rosista: Time and Spatial Dimensions

The consolidation of the Rosas regime produced important modifications in the structure of criminality. Crimes against the state more than doubled between 1830–1834 and 1843–1852, indicating the growing intensity of the conflict between paysanos and the state over questions of recruitment. On the other hand, crimes against property declined significantly, showing the increased efficacy of state controls over the slaughter, transportation, and distribution of cattle (see Table 6.7). The other dimension of Rosista "pacification," the control of public disturbance and vagrancy, was also a success according to this evidence: these offenses declined as a

TABLE 6.7 Crimes by Period and Type (in percentages)

Type of Crime	1830–1834	1835–1838	1839–1842	1843–1852
Against persons	12.7	14.3	11.1	12.8
Against the state	25.4	22.4	35.4	54.1
Against property	39.5	40.6	35.8	22.4
Against public order	19.7	21.0	10.5	6.0
Other	2.6	1.7	6.6	4.0
TOTAL	100.0	100.0	100.0	100.0
	(228)	(532)	(296)	(613)

Source: Database 'Presos remitidos' (N=1674) from Justice of the Peace's "Partes de Novedades."

proportion of total arrests.[53] The incidence of interpersonal violence, on the other hand, remained practically unchanged.

Judging by the decline in property crimes and public disturbances, we can infer that the Pax Rosista benefited mainly "middling" paysanos and ranchers, the propertied citizens of rural towns. This type of criminal policy, on the other hand, was costly for the wandering proletariat. Greater demands for military and judicial services in local communities translated into a more intense persecution of deserters, draft evaders, and itinerant laborers. Greater control of passports and other identification papers was only the outward sign of the heightened pressure of the state on the poorest part of the peasantry. From a different perspective, the rise in the proportion of crimes against the state could be read as a growing resistance to the imposition of the military tribute in the context of rapid economic growth.

Apparently, this particular order did not emerge as an outcome of the increased powers of the Dictator after 1835. The structure of crimes shows no significant change between 1830–1834 and 1835–1838. Instead, greater control of property crimes and a significant reduction in public disturbances were long-term developments that accompanied the general "pacification" of the countryside after the turbulent years of 1839–1842. It was in the period, 1843–1852, years characterized by an acceleration of export growth and a reduction in military confrontations, when the "ordering of the countryside" acquired a definitive meaning in terms of crime control.[54] Table 6.5 also sheds some light on the years of political terror and its meaning for the wandering proletariat. The path of criminal policy operated in two stages: first there was an increase in the prosecution of deserters, draft evaders, and itinerant laborers (between 1835–1838 and

1839–1842), and only later did the countryside experience a significant decline in theft and other crimes against property (1843–1852).

Concerning the spatial dimensions of the Pax Rosista, the evidence is not conclusive. Garavaglia and, before him, Halperin Donghi have suggested that in the south law enforcement was more lax either as a result of greater patrimonial control exercised by large ranchers, or as the natural consequence of a lower density of population, which facilitated the escape of lawbreakers.[55] Although this formulation (a north-south divide) is attractive for its simplicity, acknowledgment of the more complex social composition of rural towns, of the new political articulation of the countryside, and of the hegemonic power of law forces us to reconsider this piece of conventional wisdom.

First, state capacity, measured by the ability of justices, commissars, and military commissioners to control their territories, varied across the province, not only in relationship to population density but also in terms of the relative autonomy of local state authorities from the local grandees. Second, each district was construed as more or less risky for the fugitive, the deserter, and the traveler according to information spread through "tavern talk." This information was not reliable. (Some evidence suggests that some peons and deserters thought of the southern districts as a haven for fugitives, but this in itself does not constitute proof that this was so.) It is likely that state capability for surveillance and arrest did not coincide with socially constructed notions of dangerousness. Third, spatial diversity in criminal prosecution was affected by other factors: variables such as the strategies of deserters on their way to freedom, the contentious sociability of workers in suburban districts, and the greater vulnerability of farming communities to attacks against property should also be factored in.

Table 6.8 gives a fragmentary picture of regional differences in crime.[56] According to this information, districts of older colonization such as Areco, Arrecifes, and Luján showed fewer incidents of interpersonal violence than the districts immediately north of the Salado River (Lobos, Navarro, Ranchos, Chascomús), a region of most recent colonization, where most of the new cattle ranches were located. A greater proportion of crimes against persons appears in two contrasting environments: Quilmes, a district near Buenos Aires, the site of various meat-salting plants and numerous farms; and Fort Azul in the extreme south, a place of very large estates quite close to the Indian frontier.

This evidence is consistent with the view that areas more densely populated and of older colonization were better able to control interpersonal violence. These areas had better police capabilities and their more stable communities generated more efficient means of informal social control

TABLE 6.8 Type of Crime by Region (1831–1851)

Region	Against Persons	Against the State	Against Property	Against Public Order
NORTH INLAND				
Arrecifes	6.0	27.0	41.0	25.0
Areco	4.6	39.5	42.8	6.0
Luján	16.2	33.3	29.6	19.6
BUENOS AIRES				
Quilmes	19.8	44.3	22.9	12.2
NORTH/SALADO				
Lobos	11.2	46.5	31.0	10.3
Navarro	14.8	29.7	36.7	14.8
Ranchos	17.0	44.6	25.0	8.0
Chascomús	14.4	40.4	36.5	7.7
SOUTH				
Azul	19.0	29.1	44.3	1.2

Source: Database 'Presos Remitidos' (N=1674) from Justice of the Peace's "Partes de Novedades."

(more frequent neighbor-to-neighbor communication or more widely accepted codes of public behavior). But for other crimes, the distinctions are not so transparent. The northern districts of Areco and Arrecifes had a similarly high incidence of crimes against property as the district of Azul in the southern frontier. Azul shows one of the lowest percentages of crimes against the state. Was this due to the leniency of justices and to the protection offered by great ranchers? Or was it simply the reflection of the efficacy of special military commissioners in apprehending deserters? Alternatively, this result could be related to the circuits of working-class mobility, many peons finding work before reaching the far south. If Azul was a haven for deserters, what made Arrecifes and Navarro share this condition? Clearly, the relative population density or the date of settlement of a district cannot account for the observed variations in the structure of criminality, for the ranching areas near the Salado River present a greater proportion of crimes against the state than northern farming districts of colonial origins.

With regard to desertion and violations in the carrying of personal papers, one might assume that police capability and the commitment of justices to road controls produced the greatest numbers of arrests. To the extent that this capability depended in turn on the cooperation of neighbors and the relative distance (geographical and ideological) to Buenos Aires, we should expect some variation from town to town, rather than a clear north/south difference. Paradoxically, the greatest density of sociability in the farming communities of the north might help to explain the relative lower incidence of crimes against the state in these districts as compared with those on the (middle) ranching frontier. Networks of solidarity built by provincianos on the farms might have given them greater protection in the north than in the middle districts. But again, there is no reason to assume that these networks were uniformly distributed in space. Thus, the three-region scheme suggested by Brown (1979) cannot be easily translated into the mapping of crime.

Conclusions

Due to its detachment from subaltern subjects and its naturalistic reading of the social, romantic literature failed to construct enduring ethnographies of lower-class life and crime. The romantic indictment of Indian raids, the Mazorca, and the federalist plebe serve instead to articulate upper-class fears in a decidedly political direction. The romantics demarcated, it is true, spaces of danger—the slaughterhouse, the Indian frontier, city streets at night—but other than this, they contributed minimally to the making of crime. It was in other territories of textual production and power that the "delinquent" could be interpellated, assessed, and reconfirmed. As is now clear, the justice offices of small rural towns were these other territories. Here the prejudices of neighbors—expressed in a rich vocabulary that echoed the charges made by Azara, García, and Rosas against wandering gauderios (cattle rustlers), *perjudiciales* (harmful men), and vagos (vagrants)—converged with the penal policies of the state to produce a "class of delinquents" that was almost indistinguishable from the "peon class."

The dual nature of justice during the Rosas era generated a complex profile of arrests.[57] Central justice was conceived as a mechanism for recruiting soldiers. In a variety of ways, justices made common delinquents pay their tribute to Rosas's war machine. Locally, the justice system was built as a way of restoring the moral order imagined by the governor: respect for property and authority, compliance with the practices of Catholicism, political conformity with the federalist regime, and no public display of defiance of the values of family and work. Naturally, this dual system generated a dual criminality: people arrested for violations of their primordial obligation to defend the fatherland and people fined or arrested for misdemeanors concerning the public morality and tranquility of rural towns. In addition, there was the traditional prosecution of offenses against property, magnified in this period due to the state policy of clarifying and enforcing private property rights.

Reconstructed arrest statistics allow us to investigate the production of delinquency and to imagine the power space through which many poor paysanos circulated. The importance of crimes against property and the state authorizes a displacement of the analysis away from the question of vagrancy and the criminalization of custom. Our statistical findings force us to examine the production of crime in relation to the conflictive relations between peasants/laborers and the state over the question of military service. This important issue marked the criminal records of the period so clearly that to assimilate these offenses into one of the more traditional categories would entail a major error of judgment. Instead, crime statistics present a peasant society strained by the demands of a militaristic state.

The countryside that most poor paysanos inhabited was one not so overridden by interpersonal violence as we are accustomed to believe.[58] In fact, wounding and murder were rather rare and so were violations that affected public order and morality. A constellation of small towns concerned with constraining public expressions of violence—this was rural Buenos Aires during the Rosas period. As far as paysanos were concerned, these towns were already on the road to "civilization." On the other hand, the countryside was a contested terrain where large ranchers, middling paysanos, itinerant workers, and the state negotiated a series of contradictory demands. Among these diverse axes of conflict, one stood out: the differentiation and tensions between local residents and transients. This was a society that criminalized outsiders' direct appropriation of items necessary for transportation and food, despite its tolerance of similar offenses committed by neighbors.

Criminal portraits paint a rural society with unclear property boundaries and a profound sense of localism. To the extent that residency and political rights were intertwined, the tensions between locals and outsiders produced profound asymmetries not only in society's contribution to the war effort but also in relation to the achievement of justice. Local justice, though efficacious in the achievement of order, became synonymous with unfairness and discrimination. From the perspective of authorities, there were obligations to the fatherland and property rights to be enforced. Local communities tried to graduate the harshness of repression according to local labor needs and local social connections; the governor, however, insisted that all deserters, vagrants, robbers, and murderers be punished.

From below, the distinction between the two justices became blurred. Poor paysanos conflated in their survival strategies the defense of custom, resistance to authority, and accommodation to the documentary order of Rosismo. In their view, all crimes were related. Reading the fine print of the *Partes de Novedades,* I have to agree. Their acts of direct appropriation cannot be dissociated from their struggle against the state to avoid or lower their military obligations. The mobility of poor paysanos was key to their survival strategy. Whether they were escaping the police or searching for a job, peons and day laborers had to travel a lot. Itinerant rural workers or deserters needed food, means of payment, good horses, and a credible identity to continue on the move. This might explain why they slaughtered cows, stole hides, money, and horses, and forged documents as frequently as they did.

CHAPTER 7

The Experience of Punishment

In *Los Dramas del Terror*, a fictional account of the dictatorship, Eduardo Gutiérrez directs the reader's attention to a scene that captures all the brutality of the Rosas regime: the massacre of pampa Indian families in 1835.[1] That year, in a raid against the Cañuquil tribe, federalist soldiers captured 110 Indian men, women, and children and took them to the capital, where they were paraded through the streets carrying signs with the usual slogans against unitarios. Unsuspecting of what the Dictator had prepared for them, the prisoners were conducted from Retiro to the bull ring (today, San Martín plaza), where they stood in the center of the square listening in confusion to the screams and gestures of an excited crowd. Before they could understand what was happening, Colonel Maza's squadron opened fire on them, shooting indiscriminately. As many were still alive, the soldiers took their knives and proceeded to cut the throats of (*degollar*) all prisoners, adults and children. Next, they hung the beheaded bodies from poles and trees and retired to the taverns to drink, taking with them some human remains as mementos.

According to Gutiérrez, the objective of such senseless brutality was to instill fear among the unitarios. The bodies of indigenous peoples were only a vehicle for conveying a message of terror to the hated political enemy. The message was clear: "savage" unitarios should expect retribution similar to the ones carried out against "savage" pampas; their deaths will be swift, indiscriminate, and without mercy.[2] In Gutiérrez's narration, the power of simile and the theater of terror produce the effect anticipated by the state: fear, silence, and withdrawal. In the houses surrounding the square, people opened their windows to see what was happening and were shocked by the view: beheaded hanging bodies, soldiers carrying human remains in their belts, a curious crowd swarming around the cadavers. The unbounded violence of the federalist soldiers and the support they received from the crowd horrified observers. Those still having unitario sympathies were paralyzed, silenced by fear.

Gutiérrez was not alone in recasting the Rosas era as one of political terror. Much earlier, from exile, writers such as J. Rivera Indarte, D. F. Sarmiento, Florencio Varela, A. Lamas, and V. F. López had invested their talents in persuading the world that Buenos Aires was a city living in fear.[3]

To all of them the Rosas tyranny was synonymous with a regime of terror. As Victor Gálvez recalled in his memoirs, terror shaped the consciousness and behavior of the upper classes. The fear of being denounced by their servants or neighbors compelled the urban gentry to a self-imposed silence and retreat from social life (in Bajarlia 1969, 60). The liberals who constructed the provincial state after Caseros also presented the *Dictadura* as an era in which the language of terror dominated all communications and social interactions.[4] Around the turn of the century, positivist historians and interpreters (Ingenieros, Ayarragaray, Bunge, Ramos Mejía) revisited these themes—dictatorship and fear—fascinated with the psychological and racial dimensions of the problem.[5]

To an extent, the threat faced by unitarios was quite real. As Ascasubi's famous poem *La Refalosa* suggests, federalist politics entailed a promise of exterminating unitarios in such ruthless and cruel ways that an incapacitating fear would take hold of all their friends, relatives, and sympathizers. The Sociedad Popular Restauradora (SPR, or Mazorca) took upon itself the responsibility of putting this threat of "divine" punishment into effect.[6] In his *Tablas de Sangre*, a sort of quantitative and nominative inventory of federalist violence against the unitario cause, Rivera Indarte (1946) left a vivid picture of the crimes of the Mazorca during the events of October 1840 and April 1842. Then, at the height of antiunitario frenzy, groups of mazorqueros (members of the SPR) went about the city killing members of the urban gentry as presumed sympathizers with the Unidad. To Rivera Indarte, this was state-organized violence at its worst. He wrote about signals announcing the beginning of each massacre, about killers using handsaws to make the beheading more painful, about the rough music that accompanied each slaughter, about the orgiastic and religious flavor of the events.

These scenes, taken from personal memory and from testimonies presented at a public commission in Montevideo in July 1843, were corroborated later by Pedro C. Avila (1847), an ex-*mazorquero* who published in Lima a recollection of the 1840 and 1842 massacres. Presenting himself as a privileged observer who had participated in the murders, Avila added macabre details to Rivera Indarte's narrative. Lists of victims were distributed by the SPR to its members with precise instructions about when and where to conduct the murders. Reenacting a biblical episode, the mazorquero squads searched houses with doors painted in light blue or green and killed the inhabitants. The murder of male heads of household was often complemented by the looting of their property, the rape of their female relatives, and the smashing of all icons of the "Old Fatherland" (images of San Martin or Belgrano). Soon, the federalist crowds joined the

14. Mazorqueros Killing the Innocent. A scene of *mazorqueros* killing innocent children, sons or servants of *unitarios*, attempts to convey all the brutality of the regime. The legend reads: "Death to Unitarios!—said the assassins!" Anon. engraving, ca. 1857. Reproduced from M. M. Nieves, *Los mártires de Buenos Aires* (1861).

punitive raids, transforming the whole undertaking into a grotesque ritual of Rabelaisian proportions.[7]

In all these narratives, the main target of state terror was the unitarios, a group of intellectuals, professionals, merchants, and military upholding freedom in the midst of tyranny. As the victims of state terror, they considered themselves the natural inheritors of the country's revolutionary traditions and ideals. In their publications, the need to repossess a country unlawfully appropriated by the Tyrant always stemmed from a drama that recognized only two principal characters: Rosas and themselves. Other subjectivities were either erased or presented as instruments of the will of the Dictator. The federalist crowd, present in most of these accounts, was a site of barbarism rather than a historical agency (Svampa 1994; Shumway 1991). Central to the predicament of the émigrés was the notion that Rosismo had established "barbarism" (the crowd, blacks, poor women, and rural peons) at the core of public life, displacing the urban gentry from their rightful position of leadership. Without doubt, this view betrayed a racial and class position, one that denied the "lower sorts" and the "mixed races" any right and agency in the construction of the republic.

This interpretation had so profound an effect on Argentine historiography that it seems almost sacrilegious to suggest an alternative reading. To correct this account, we need first to state the obvious: unitarios were not the only targets of Rosas's pedagogy of terror. Peons, peasants, and soldiers were other recipients of state violence, a violence that, because of its ubiquity and persistence, could be assimilated to a form of terror. This violence was exercised in military garrisons, militia units, justice offices, police stations, jails, public squares, anywhere the wandering proletariat encountered the disciplinary powers of the provincial state. These other stages of terror have been neglected by a historiography not concerned with capturing the experience of state coercion in *all of its dimensions*. The punishment experienced by peons, peasants, and soldiers was, to be sure, a different type of state violence: disciplinary violence. It was a terror more systematic and continuous, predicated on the need to control the movements of a quite mobile and assertive workforce and to inculcate (federalist) patriotism in peasants and peons. In this *other terror*, death loomed as a threat for those who did not comply with their patriotic duties and for those who committed treacherous crimes. This was a conditional, disciplinary violence, oriented toward the formation of subservient, patriotic subjects.

Though less publicized than the violence against unitarios, the terror unleashed against the lower classes was quite visible and widespread. Any migratory peon traveling across the province could have seen a murderer hanging from the pole of a town square. Any resident of a small rural town passing through the local comisaría (police station) could have watched a felon subjected to the stocks. Any soldier who had stayed long enough in the army could have witnessed the execution of a deserter. Older neighbors could recall times when black servants were whipped in public for "correction." Systematic and pervasive, and quantitatively more extensive than the violence against unitarios, the violence against peons and peasants served to sustain the authority on which the provincial state rested.

In this chapter, I describe Rosas's machinery of pain as a means to map the territory where state authorities and subalterns met in a relationship of domination and spectacle. I am interested in the devices of confinement, torment, and terror used by the state, and the position and function of these devices within the larger political machine of Rosismo. Also part of the endeavor is a reading of the messages contained in different stages of suffering, a sort of ethnography of punishment aiming at a reconstruction of the experience of ordinary people in relation to the disciplinary institutions of the state. The experience and the spectacles of punishment, I suggest, profoundly marked the lives of subaltern subjects.

Rosas and the Machinery of Pain

The punishment Rosas, military commanders, and judges ordered as part of the normal, everyday administration of justice was systematic. It obeyed a logic that graduated the penalties according to the offense, exhibited in delimited spaces the powers of the provincial state, and disseminated lessons of morality among the poor population of city and country. Judged as excessive, brutal, and arbitrary by its political opponents, these punitive practices were actually quite predictable, their intensity proportionate to the transformations expected in the conduct of peasants, laborers, and soldiers. In fact, we can describe Rosas's punitive system as a calculated and graduated system of pain, which, applied to the bodies of the poor, promised to regenerate the social and political body of the nation.

The objective of this disciplinary machinery was to extirpate, by example and fear, the "cancers" left on the nation's social and political body by the years of "anarchy," a past in which the energies and promises of liberty were said to have degenerated into libertinism, social disorder, and political violence. The urgency of war had made it necessary to transform deserters, murderers, and vagrants into obedient citizen-soldiers ready to risk their lives in defense of the fatherland. To effect this transformation, Rosas conceived of the regiments, militia units, and justices of the peace as institutional spaces where it would be possible—by employing sufficient, systematic, and graduated coercion—to reestablish the respect for authority, property, and life lost during the 1820s. The militias could serve as "schools of civic and military instruction" for resident paysanos, aiding their transition into citizenship. And, in the absence of good prisons, army regiments would serve as centers for the punishment and regeneration of delinquents.

Rosas's disciplinary project, envisioned in the solitude of his frontier ranch in the early 1820s, never congealed into a blueprint, government plan, or penal code. But it is clear from Rosas's decisions in criminal cases that there was a systematic and consistent effort to apply punishment as a didactic tool vis-à-vis the poor population of city and countryside. Despite moments of negotiation and adaptation to local circumstances, the governor's penal policy shows a remarkable consistency. Due to judges' discretion in classifying crimes and to the absence of accepted jurisprudence, the penal legislation inherited from the colonial era rendered penalties uncertain, subject to great variation. Rosas's sentencing practices, in contrast, were quite predictable. Compared to the colonial past and even to the first two decades of independence, the spectrum of his sentences and the chances of negotiating commutations and pardons appear more limited (Socolow 1990; Szuchman 1988, chap. 2).

Exemplary punishment was central to the state's disciplinary project. The power of the Law and the importance of the Federalist Cause were the compelling signifiers sustaining the necessity of discipline and justifying the use of physical torture. This pedagogy operated through personal suffering—pain itself was supposed to produce the necessary restraint to unlawful behavior—and also through spectacle. The sight of a thief in the stocks, a soldier being flogged, or a murderer hanging from a pole was expected to produce fear among the spectators, usually poor paysanos. The didactic purpose of punishment was apparent. The lessons taught were dictated by the requirements of governance: peaceful and respectful conduct vis-à-vis neighbors and employers, obedience to state authorities, and a commitment to support the war effort.

Due to the lack of secure prisons, the most common penalty used by the governor against delinquents was military service. This form of deprivation of liberty was complemented by other torments. The instruments of punishment were not new: flogging to correct first offenders, disobedient soldiers, and runaway slaves; the stocks and the calaboose to treat hardened delinquents and "incorrigible" soldiers; and public executions, a penalty of last resort. Lashes, the stocks, and military confinement constituted the triad of Rosas's disciplinary pedagogy. Though not unbounded like the violence promised to unitarios, the exemplary punishment of the "lower sorts" was also based on the logic of terror.

Those who applied these penalties (judges, justices of the peace, military commanders, Rosas himself) shared a confidence in the transforming power of pain for both the punished and the observer. If sufficient doses of pain were inflicted, the conventional wisdom stated, soldiers would think twice before attempting desertion and peasants would refrain from committing crimes. The mechanics of this behavioral change were never made explicit, but it is possible that disciplinarians' belief in the reformatory powers of corporal punishment was based on a utilitarian calculation of pain and pleasure. Clearly, Rosas's sentencing practices obeyed a quantitative logic, one that balanced the physical pain of the condemned against the future utility of that individual as a soldier.[8] Obedience and patriotism were the main attributes that pain could inculcate.

There was some economy in this system of punishment. A limited number of exemplary punishments in each garrison or rural district could adequately convey disciplinary pedagogy to the many. The public visibility of punishment greatly increased the social productivity of pain, disseminating messages about the law and the fatherland among the various communities of spectators (paysanos, soldiers, militiamen, women, indigenous peoples, unitarios). Moreover, the very predictability of Rosas's sentences gave these messages enhanced credibility among paysanos. Contrasted with the unbounded violence and state terrorism directed against political opponents and indigenous peoples, Rosas's exemplary executions of deserters, murderers, and thieves appeared as austere, limited, and ritualized spectacles of power.

The main subject of this disciplinary experiment was the more mobile portion of the rural workforce, those classified as belonging to the country peon class. These were the men whom federalist armies sought to enlist and whom Rosas tried to discipline. They were the part of the population that, viewed from the heights of the state, needed to be instructed in the power of the law. Their mobility, their defiance of authority, their intense sociability and opinions, their staunch defense of social equality, their traditions of direct appropriation of sustenance were threatening to a provincial state committed to upholding property rights, military discipline, and social tranquility. In the official dramas of crime and punishment two villains were always present: the peon turned delinquent and the soldier turned deserter. The two constituted the other side of an "orderly countryside" and a "disciplined army" on which the power of the provincial state was based. The very sustainability of the Dictator's power and the Pax Rosista depended on a military force that was, by contemporary standards, formidable. Maintaining this force's capability required curbing, with dramatic efficiency, the incidence of desertion. At the local level, a tranquil countryside presupposed the identification and punishment of real or potential delinquents, separating them from the "good neighbors." Migratory workers, fatherless youngsters, and people unknown to the community constituted the population at risk of falling into crime. Both transitions (peon-to-delinquent and soldier-to-deserter), considered as threats to the social and political order, were dealt with by determination and duress.

On the surface, the Rosista regime of punishments resembles Foucault's (1979) "punitive city." This was an ideal system of measured and regulated coercion designed by moral reformers for the purpose of regenerating the criminals' souls while simultaneously displaying the power of the law among the republic's new citizens (104–131). In this model, cruel and aberrant forms of punishment give way to more "humane," regulated, and public penalties. Because the object was to produce both reformation and instruction, a penalty such as constructing public works satisfied both objectives. Convicts working on public roads could experience the redemptive power of hard labor, while those watching them could clearly identify the relationship between law and punishment (in the ideal model, prisoners would wear signs identifying their crimes). Variations in the intensity of suffering, proportional to the nature of the crime, ultimately reflected society's moral order, fixed into law.[9]

The Rosas administration, a republican government endowed with extraordinary powers, had to represent itself in a double fashion: as the source of all legitimate authority and as a government committed to the enforcement of the law. This was a regime committed to the pacification of the country and the moralization of its peasant majority, objectives that required staging public representations of state power: floggings, the stocks, executions. Corporal pain, however, was not the only solution envisioned. Particularly at the local level, where it was necessary to control the "excesses" of citizen-peasants, state authorities used more graduated penalties. Thus, the spectacle of the scaffold combined with other, more moderate, educational, and republican modalities of punishment: fines, sentencing to public works crews, and imprisonment. Army service (replacing long-term imprisonment) presented authorities with an effective way to combine the requirements of war with those of social discipline.

The double predicament of a state engaged in recurrent warfare and of local communities striving for the restoration of tranquility produced a duality in penal policy. In particular, the regime translated the traditional distinction between correctional and penal justice into two different spheres of discipline: correction of *faltas* (misdemeanors) at the local level, and punishment of *delitos* (felonies) at the center of state power. Local justice was concerned with settling minor disputes over property, controlling excessive drinking, scandalous public behavior, and gambling, and preserving the community's respect for religious sites and practices. Central justice was concerned with grave felonies such as murder, theft, and rape and with violations of the basic "contract" between paysanos and the state: draft evasion, desertion, and traveling without papers.[10]

Consistent with the division of labor, there were distinct practices of punishment. The governor preferred terms of army service to punish deserters and draft evaders; the justices utilized a combination of fines, public works, and whipping for violations of the public order. Uniting these two sides of punishment were ideological assumptions about the nature of an "ordered society." Good neighborly behavior and strict obedience to military rank constituted two modes of the same obsession with order in a republic threatened by anarchy and social disorder. In theory, these two modalities of social control could accommodate social and political differences in local towns. If the citizen-soldiers committed only misdemeanors and the nonresident peons (usually destined for the regular army) committed most of the felonies, the combination of local and central justice would be effective to curb social disorder.

Limited by the lack of modern prisons and compelled by the need to man the federalist armies, Rosas made military service the quintessential form of punishment.[11] Available information about the fate of the arrested underscores the state's use of the criminal system for recruitment purposes. From our sample of filiaciones (criminal and military files), we know the destination of 532 prisoners: 411 were sentenced to serve in the army or were directly assigned to a nearby regiment, 4 were sent to the police department, 5 were punished with an extension of service, 50 were freed, 55 were given a pardon, 2 were released from service, 3 were executed, and 2 were banished. As we can see, Rosas managed to drastically reduce the penal options for grave felonies in spite of the multiplicity of penalties prescribed in the colonial legislation. In fact, he practically eliminated the penalty of presidio (confinement to a prison), in use until the late 1820s, replacing it with military service.

Rigor and uniformity of sentencing were the marks of Rosas's penal policy. In the city, where first-instance courts retained a certain degree of autonomy, judges put most of the accused back on the street (Szuchman 1984). At Santos Lugares, however, prisoners sent by the justices were certain to be penalized with years of military service; very few indeed were released from service or freed.[12] When petitioning for pardons, deserters understood that the most they could get was a commutation of penalties, which translated into an extension of military service. The leniency of first-instance courts contrasts with the severity and consistency of the governor's sentences. In a murder case presented in June 1836, the public prosecutor asked for a penalty of five years in prison.[13] Rosas dismissed that suggestion and punished the accused with six years of service at Fort Independence. The southern fort offered more opportunities for hard labor and a type of learning not available at a penal colony: combat experience against Indians.

If delinquents constituted an important proportion of the federalist armies, then the very reproduction of military capacity depended on the production of delinquency. This might explain the undifferentiated pattern of sentences. But a second interpretation is possible: that the use of service terms to punish all sorts of felonies simply reflected the governor's belief in the regenerating power of military life. Critics of the regime liked to emphasize that the federalist armies transformed good citizens into delinquents by the mere fact of mixing volunteers with condemned felons. Rosas saw the process the other way around: regiments could teach delinquents lessons in patriotism and law-abiding conduct. In the absence of institutions of confinement, the army could serve as a prison, a place for the regeneration of bad patriots, vagrants, and other lawbreakers.

As in every disciplinary system, Rosas's machinery of pain had an extra-legal side. There were punishments not decided by the judicial process, which reflected the arbitrary power of local, bureaucratic authority. At both extremes of the disciplinary continuum (local and central) there was always some dose of surplus coercion: the forced labor imposed by some justices as part of their private business, the extensive periods of incarceration without sentencing that attended most involuntary visitors of Santos Lugares, and the excessive corporal punishment inflicted on soldiers by their officers. But as long as this suffering, this illegal coercion, was kept from public scrutiny, the machinery of pain could still claim that the arm of the law, though cruel, reached everyone with the same intensity of purpose. Insofar as the regime could show that it investigated the excesses committed in the application of legal coercion, claims about the illegitimacy of punishment in general could easily be dismissed.

Rosas's disciplinary machine relied on a combination of visibility and invisibility. The military prison at Santos Lugares was a site remote from most citizens at which the interrogation, imprisonment, and flogging of felons and soldiers took place without much public visibility. Detainees could spend months waiting for a resolution to their case without anyone noticing their suffering. Unitario prisoners kept at the Retiro camp thought of this "prison" as a place of no return, as a sort of internal banishment where prisoners were subject to all kinds of extralegal torments (see *Rasgos de la política de Rosas* 1911). At Santos Lugares and Retiro, the invisibility of punishment (typical, according to Foucault, of republican governments) corresponded with the need to centralize authority in the person of the governor. By contrast, much of the punishment dispensed by the justices of the peace was public, designed to impress public sensibilities and orient future behavior. In garrisons also, executions and floggings were organized as spectacles for the view of the soldiery.

The punishments envisioned by Rosas were consonant with a republican experiment. Various differences separated his machinery of pain from the violence unleashed by absolutist monarchies. First, there was the question of pardons. A government pursuing the restoration of laws had to limit the use of this instrument of justice; otherwise, criminals might surmise that the penalties were negotiable and that patronage reigned in lieu of the law. In a limited number of cases, when the accused had shown good conduct before desertion, Rosas was willing to reduce the sentence (from four to two years of additional service, and no lashes).[14] More frequently, however, his pardons consisted of mere commutations of sentences (from death to long periods of service). These commutations did not invalidate the rigidity of his penal policy. Second, although the pacification of the countryside demanded some degree of flexibility in the application of punishment at the local level, the sentences issued by the governor were characterized by their uniformity. First-time deserters, murderers in fights, and thieves could expect a fairly standard punishment: a fixed term of service in the army, complemented with floggings in proportion to the aggravating circumstances of the offense. Third, unlike the unbounded violence unleashed against unitarios and *indios enemigos* (Indian foes), the didactic violence the state directed against peons, peasants, and soldiers was ritualized, bounded, and, mostly, subject to law.

Prison Sites and Movements of Bodies

Taking inventory of prison sites during the Rosas era, one stumbles on the spatial dimension of punishment. In fact, by visualizing the movements of bodies across different institutions of detention, another crucial aspect of subaltern experience can be examined. In the capital, the Police Depository and the Public Jail, the two facilities of the central Police Department, handled the largest movement of prisoners. There, most prisoners were at the "disposition" of the governor, while some were under the care of one of the two professional judges.[15] These two facilities were complemented by jails or *crujías*, operating in the two largest military garrisons of the city, Retiro, closer to the river, and Santos Lugares to the north, the government and military headquarters after 1838. In addition, each local comisaría (police station) or *juzgado de paz* (justice office) had a room that served as a jail where prisoners were fastened to shackles installed in the floor.

The Police Depository served as a jail for the punishment of misdemeanors and also as a temporary detention center for felons to be transferred to Santos Lugares or waiting to be assigned to a judge.[16] Many of the prisoners entered the depository on charges of gambling, petty theft of their patrons, resisting an order, carrying a knife, or insulting a member of the city gentry. The Public Jail, on the other hand, was chiefly the site for the "correction" of female slaves, servants, and unruly women. Here the mulattoes and black women (presumably in bondage), who had defied the authority of the lady or master of the household or helped themselves to some goods or money, were kept and flogged on their master's orders. But the Public Jail also received men (apparently blacks) awaiting their military destinations, and occasionally a pampa Indian, a unitario, or a male slave. Also in the capital was the Night Watchmen Quarters that served as a jail for members of the same corps and for soldiers of various regiments. Among the arrested we find night watchmen who had wounded other men or caused public disturbances as well as soldiers arrested for traveling without a passport, stealing goods or horses, or engaging in brawls.[17]

Santos Lugares was the site of a large military unit, comprising various divisions of the army. At the same time, it functioned as a detention center where prisoners were questioned, sentenced, and dispatched to their final destinations. The various barracks containing prisoners, close to one another, were filled with unitarios, runaway slaves, and common delinquents. There is little doubt that prisoners of war, taken at San Cala, Quebracho, and Rodeo del Medio, were kept at Santos Lugares in fenced corrals and subject to periodic beatings and humiliations. We know that some of them were executed (January and February 1842; *Causa Criminal* 1864, 13–17). During periods of less political turbulence, most of the inmates of Santos Lugares were people who had been detained at the Police Department and, at Rosas's request, "released to the army." Until the justice system or the governor himself arrived at a decision with regard to their punishment, they remained in detention.

Santos Lugares, the feared center of Rosas's disciplinary archipelago, hosted all sorts of subaltern subjects besides the unitario prisoners. An 1840 list of the prisoners sent to this military camp included two French citizens (one of them a priest) arrested in San Fernando for complicity with the unitarios, two black slaves sent by Don Tomás Anchorena, two pampas Indians arrested near Navarro, a deserter, people who gave refuge to deserters, and several common delinquents.[18] Prisoners coming from north and south, east and west converged on this nerve center of political and military activity. To émigré critics, this prison camp contained within itself all the *chusma* or plebes that supported the regime (Indians, black women, and peon soldiers), either as prisoners or as free residents.

These detention sites had one element in common: the diversity of their inmates. Here, the white, upper-class unitarios shared the premises with pampas Indians, black slaves, mestizo deserters, and provinciano laborers caught by the system of control of roads and documents. The Public Jail (or Cárcel del Cabildo) was perhaps the most confusing for its mixture of inmates. At this facility, the unitario prisoners were able to hear, through the adobe walls, the screams of Africans being flogged and the conversations of deserters and thieves, all housed under the same roof. On occasion, this jail hosted a full-blood, unacculturated Indian (most of those who were taken as hostages for future peace negotiations resided in the

Chacarita) or a foreign sailor detained after a tavern brawl. The women housed in the Cabildo probably occupied a different wing. Their presence, nonetheless, must have been quite visible, as they were constantly entering and leaving the premises, being flogged, or being sent to the Women's Hospital.[19]

Local jails at the justice offices were simply adobe rooms used as places of temporary detention for felons who had to be sent to Buenos Aires for further interrogation. As a result, a felon rarely stayed at the local jail more than a few days or weeks. If we consider that on average each justice arrested two prisoners per month, it is easy to deduce that most of the time these jails were empty. There were exceptions, however. The justice of the peace of Azul, for instance, kept unitario Santiago Salto in jail from November 1839 until April 1841. Two other felons, Norberto Manzano and Tomas Aquino Ayala, spent eight years in the local jail, secured by shackles. Something similar happened to Gregorio Roldán, a militiaman belonging to the Tordillo district; he remained three years and eight months in shackles at the local juzgado.[20] Ayala, Manzano, and Roldán, all accused of murder, were perhaps victims of the discretionary justice that operated in areas too distant from Buenos Aires to be under the supervision of the governor.

These prisons, given their undifferentiated and premodern nature— none of them resembling anything close to a penitentiary—were not conceived as places of penitence and repentance. They served instead to facilitate a vast movement of bodies, those of the poor. Disciplinarians were unconcerned with the leveling of social and racial differences that occurred within the prisons, or with how inmates used their time, for they were there only temporarily. Their final destination was "outside," so to speak, in a place where they could defend the federalist fatherland.

Santos Lugares, Retiro, the Public Jail, the Police Depository, and the local jails constituted a connected system of detention and torture at the service of Rosas's project of moralizing the rural masses. Unitario prisoners eventually spent some time at one or several of these prison sites, but they were not the natural targets or subjects of Rosas's disciplinary machine. It was poor peasants and peons who more frequently filled the prisons in the Rosas era. It was they who circulated from one prison to another in a systematic and continuous fashion. Their itinerary was already prescribed: from local jails prisoners went to the Buenos Aires Police Department, then to Santos Lugares, and from there to the military garrison of their destination.

During this penitential itinerary, subalterns experienced a situation of subjection and powerlessness. Initially, they traveled secured by shackles.

Later, at the Jail or the Depository, they were confined in small, humid, and dark rooms divided by bars. At Santos Lugares they had their share of punishment, suffering long periods of confinement without sentencing (and without legal advice). But, gradually, as they were transformed from criminals into soldiers (after they received their destination), they regained part of their freedom of movement. Their actual sentence usually took place in a military battalion. The suffering they experienced along their disciplinary pilgrimage varied according to the circumstances faced by each felon; more so when they reached their battalion, for here it was the bargaining power of soldiers, the personality of commanding officers, and the vagaries of war that determined prisoners' fate. The prisons prepared the subaltern—softening his will, breaking his independence—for a different, subsequent training in obedience and patriotism.

Means of Containment and Torture

During the Rosas period, practical reasons determined the continued use of some traditional instruments of containment. At a time when detainees often escaped through holes carved in the adobe walls of jails, shackles (*grillos*) became a necessity for securing the arrested. Most prisoners, whether in the city or the rural towns, were kept in shackles until they were brought to the judge or presented before Rosas's inquisitors at Santos Lugares.[21] The sight of a felon being conducted on horseback with hands or feet fastened in irons must have been common on the roads of Buenos Aires province. Governor Rosas insisted that whenever justices transported a prisoner, they should not forget to "secure [him] with fetters [*barra de grillos*]" or to send the corresponding clasificación, in duplicate.[22] So widespread was this practice that the word *prisiones* was commonly used as a synonym for *grillos* (fetters or shackles), the former term signifying at the same time confinement and the instrument of containment.

To Sergeant Major Antonino Reyes, the superintendent at Santos Lugares, shackles and the stocks were normal, unavoidable requisites for the containment of detainees. Long after the fall of Rosas, Sergeant Major Reyes was asked about the fate of Antonio Romero, one of the peon soldiers kept there. Reyes responded that the felon "was put in shackles [*en prisiones*] without any other special punishment." His answer implied that, for him, to be "in shackles" was not a special form of punishment. Asked if Romero was put in the *cepo* for seventeen days, as the opposition claimed, Reyes responded "that he does not believe it possible this could happen, nor that Romero had the strength to resist such a punishment. . . .

That this individual was in such a way incorrigible that he was constantly in prison and, instead of punishing him with the lash [*azotes*] he was put in the Prevención. That when someone was put in the *cepo de cabeza*, he was put there for two hours, alternating this with the *cepo de pie*, for this is what was ordered when the felonies or offenses were serious."[23]

Casually, Reyes was giving away one of the rules governing the mechanics of punishment at Santos Lugares. The *cepo de cabeza* (head stocks), being quite painful—bending the spine, contracting the neck, channeling blood circulation to the feet—was more sparely used than other kinds of stocks. The arrested could better resist the *cepo de pie* (foot stocks), which gave some freedom of movement to the upper part of the body. Both types of torment applied only to "incorrigible" felons or recidivist offenders, those who were not easily broken or shamed by the lash. As Reyes made clear, jailers at Santos Lugares had instructions to alternate between the different kinds of stocks so as to avoid having prisoners faint, incurring irreparable damage to their body.

An instruction given by Rosas to his overseer Laureano Ramírez confirms the rules governing this device or technique. A peon of Ramírez's ranch caught in Palermo (at the slaughterhouse) was to be placed in the head stocks for three hours and then in the foot stocks for the rest of the day, including the night.[24] The treatment, Rosas indicated, should continue until the subject showed some signs of repentance; only then would the peon be allowed to return to the ranch and continue working. How would the officer applying the punishment recognize repentance in the face of the punished? Rosas did not explain. It was clear, nonetheless, that the governor believed that this instrument of torture had definite effects on the conduct of subjects, making their bodies more docile, their wills less assertive.

Both justices and military officers employed the *estaqueo*, a traditional and feared instrument of torture. The method was simple: the felon's body was placed immediately above the ground, each of his limbs tied by a leather strip to a stick planted on the ground; as the leather strips dried under the sun, the body stretched to the breaking point. Its effectiveness in projecting fear among onlookers was undoubtedly greater than that of the stocks or the shackles. In a few of the military sumarios opened to investigate alleged abuses by officers we find references to this torment. Pedro Figueroa, a Carabinier at Barrancosa, complained in 1839 that his lieutenant had him *estaquiado* for two hours just for wasting some ammunition. In another military indictment (Mulitas, 1838) Captain T. Cárdenas was accused of inflicting this torment on five soldiers for playing cards. Yet it is difficult to find traces of this device in judicial archives. Of the 525 criminal records of prisoners sent to Santos Lugares, none mentions having been subjected to it. The *estaqueo*, it seems, was used in peripheral military garrisons and rural justices or police stations but with less frequency than the stocks or the lash.

Two decades after instruments of torture had been legally banned in 1813, corporal punishment remained the preferred pedagogical tool among military and civilian disciplinarians of the wandering proletariat. This was particularly true of floggings, whose use did not indicate symptoms of decline. During the Rosas period this method of punishment became an efficient complement to terms of forced service in the military. It was used to mark the graveness of the offense: information taken from the *Partes de Novedades* indicates that there was a pattern to the use of floggings. Petty theft was punished with 25 lashes; cattle rustlers usually received short terms of service in the military, rarely any flogging; first-time deserters and draft dodgers received 100 lashes and, usually, four years of additional military service. Next came recidivist deserters, most of whom received 200 to 300 floggings in addition to a considerable extension of their terms of service (four to six years). In some cases, when the recidivist deserter was also an ex-slave, sentences were even harsher, reflecting the common view that those socialized under slavery better tolerated the punishment (and were less responsive to it). Crimes such as forging and selling passports merited 300 lashes (Ibañez Frocham 1938, 242 table). At the top of the ladder were murderers who, by the nature of their crimes or by their accumulated offenses, were considered incorrigible. They usually received the same corporal punishment but longer terms of service.[25]

The logic of these numbers is clear. Desertion was high up on the scale, close to treacherous murders, as a crime that, from the perspective of the state, deserved the greatest condemnation. Recidivist deserters could expect, in addition to an extension in service, a punishment sufficiently severe to make an imprint in their memories. Two hundred to three hundred strokes with the sword or whip produced excruciating pain and could lead to disability or, in some cases, death. This punishment far exceeded in intensity the punishment reserved for disobedient slaves and deceptive servants (usually given twenty-five to fifty lashes) and was, without doubt, greater than the penalties reserved for theft. Compared with the punishment that soldiers received during the wars of independence, the floggings during the Rosas period were several times more severe.[26]

Between independence and the Rosas period, there were important changes in the application and meaning of floggings. Certain humiliating public punishments, particularly those inflicted by slave owners and military officers, lost legitimacy and, presumably, became less frequent. Since the 1820s, people had challenged the authority of military officers to strike civilians in public. With the growth of the militias as nodal organizing points for the political life of rural towns, the military lost much of its power to "correct" civilians.[27] The flogging of slaves tended to decline in the 1840s as the number of slaves fell and the state constrained the powers of slaveholders (Goldberg 1976; Crespi 1995; Johnson 1995). As a result, floggings gradually retracted to enclosed spaces, away from public scrutiny. The army, the Public Jail, and the justices of the peace, in that order, became the institutions that generated the greatest complaints about floggings.

Limitations in the punitive power of slaveholders and military officers reflected not so much the strengthening of civil society as the consolidation of a centralized (provincial) state extending its surveillance, lessons, and reasons to the countryside. The enhanced power of the Dictator translated into a restriction of the punitive prerogatives of private owners and officers. Though on occasion the punishment inflicted on soldiers could result in death, officers had a limited and regulated authority to administer punishment.[28] In regiments, officers were granted, according to rank, the authority to administer floggings without any consultation; beyond these limits, the penalty would be considered an abuse of their rank and be subject to a superior's review. Cases of officers put on trial for abusive, excessive, or arbitrary punishments demonstrate the bounded nature of punitive power in the barracks. In 1838 Captain Trifón Cárdenas was put on trial in Fort Mulitas for having exceeded his authority with arbitrary punishments. He was accused of making two soldiers stand still for four to six hours, something a captain was not authorized to do.

The power to inflict pain was concentrated at the center of all political decisions: Santos Lugares. The governor and his secretaries commanded a disproportionate authority to punish compared with military officers and justices of the peace. True, justices occasionally went beyond their legitimate authority and used corporal punishment to enhance their own local power. When this happened, Rosas usually reprimanded them. In April 1841, the justice of Quilmes sent a young deserter, Martín Sánchez, to Santos Lugares. A letter accompanied the prisoner stating that, contrary to custom, the lad had already received three hundred lashes at the local level. Overstepping his authority, the Quilmes justice had ordered the flogging of the naked body of the arrested ("a culo limpio y bolas al aire") for his own entertainment ("por vía de diversión").[29] This additional, unnecessary, and extralegal violence was both intolerable and unproductive. Perhaps local members of the community, those who considered flogging good medicine for disobedient boys, supported the justice's action but, in the long run, this type of humiliating punishment was counterproductive.

More significant, this kind of punishment went beyond the justice's authority; he was authorized to impose fines, a few days of compulsory work, and a few days in the stocks, but not floggings. This was the governor's judicial prerogative.

What does this pattern of punishment say about the state's interests and nature? The state's concern for upholding property rights and controlling interpersonal violence was overridden by the preoccupation with curbing desertion, perhaps the most formidable threat to the stability of government. The extreme severity in the punishment of deserters, when contrasted with the lax and unsystematic persecution of peons abandoning their jobs, indicates clearly where the conflict was most intense. The repression of vagrancy, associated by historians with ranchers' dominance, was in fact a lesser priority to the state. The punitive system reflects also the emergence of the citizen as a privileged subject. Military officers lost their power to flog militiamen, who found a shield in their own militia commanders. Floggings became a debasing form of punishment applied chiefly to regular soldiers and criminals.

Also in Rosas's "punitive city," corporal punishment became mainly a mode of disciplining bodies into obedience and subordination, crucial ingredients for the construction of a (federalist) patriotic subject. The governor's belief in the pedagogical function of militias and regiments transformed corporal punishment (lashes, the stocks, estaqueos) into a complementary penalty for "tough cases." The proportionality between offenses and punishment, evident in Antonino Reyes's confessions and in the number of lashes added to *destinados*, speaks of the centralization of punitive power, of a "moralizing state" sending clear disciplinary messages to the lower classes. Contrasted with the terror unleashed against indigenous peoples and unitarios, the punishment of the wandering proletariat was bounded. To maintain his own power and his aura as the Restorer of the Laws, the governor restrained the punitive authority of military commanders, justices, and judges. Within the general and systematic policy of punishment there could be variations in the forms in which power was exercised locally, but these deviations were checked by constant surveillance from Santos Lugares.

The continued use of instruments of torture, most notably the stocks and flogging, was predicated on the belief that by inflicting sufficient pain on the body the subject would modify his behavior and avoid committing such wrongs in the future. Rather than arbitrary and capricious, the punishment imposed by the Rosista state was systematic and predictable. It was part of a didactic machinery designed to train docile and obedient bodies for the purpose of fighting a holy war. The torment produced by these devices was conducive to a double objective: breaking the will of the arrested and showing the consequences of criminal behavior to others. Rosas's system of punishment included a graduation of pain according to the gravity of offenses and a hierarchical distribution of punitive authority among the different parts of the state.

Spectacles of Death

Within the machinery of pain, the firing squad and the hanging pole constituted special instruments for impressing into the minds of the lower classes the need to observe the law. They were performances of state power geared to definite purposes. The governor used the death sentence against deserters, common murderers, rapists, kidnappers, thieves, and unitarios in a selective way, with the expressed intention of generating correction through fear (escarmiento).[30] The staging of public executions was a means of conveying authoritative messages to the lower classes, to those who manned the armed forces of the Confederation, and to the youngsters who were the future citizens of the republic.

Capital punishment was a penalty of last resort, applied in limited and exemplary fashion. Homicides that received the greatest public condemnation (by their aggravated circumstances or by the defenseless condition of the victim) were likely candidates for the death penalty. Another important proportion of death sentences involved recidivist army deserters. The governor usually sentenced first offenders to four or five years of army service, but, when the deserter repeated his crime or when a soldier tried to involve others in a group desertion, capital punishment was the prescribed sentence. Abduction and rape received the death sentence only if the felon had committed various other crimes. The same was true of theft and aggravated assault; these felonies were punished with terms of military service unless the accused had repeat offenses.[31]

General Rosas believed in the didactic utility of executions and was persuaded that no "civilized nation," if it was to maintain social order, could do away with this kind of punishment. After his fall, Rosas declared that "Not a single drop of blood [was shed] that cannot be considered within the sphere of the ordinary. . . . Ordering the shooting of this or other *fascineroso* [rascal or villain] is common in all parts of the world; and nobody notices this, nor is it possible for a society to live if it does not do so" (qtd. in Dellepiane 1956, 254). Pedro de Angelis, editor of *La Gaceta Mercantil*, defended Rosas's record on this matter. He argued that the numbers of public executions in European nations far exceeded those ordered by Gen-

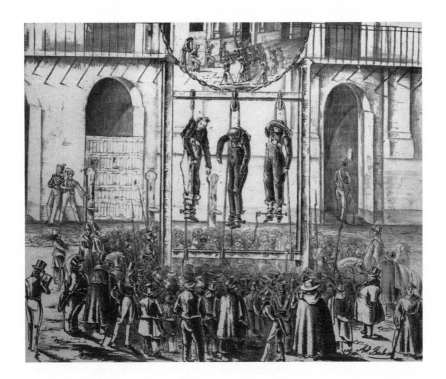

15. Public Execution. The engraving shows the executions of the assassins of General Facundo Quiroga, the Reynafé brothers, and Santos Perez. Andrea Bacle, lithograph (1836?). Courtesy of the Museo Histórico Nacional, Buenos Aires.

eral Rosas and that, given the threats the republic faced from external and internal enemies, the penal policies of the regime were quite restrained and conservative.[32]

The arguments used by Rosas and his publicist referred to executions ordered according to the rules of military and civilian courts, not to those on campaign ordained by federalist commanders (usually outside of Buenos Aires province). It is a well-established fact that the civil wars in the interior provinces generated an extraordinary level of violence, in which commanders of both parties (unitarios and federales) customarily ordered the *degüello* (throat cutting) of all prisoners.[33] These murders after battle, of course, followed no judicial procedure. Rosas's executions, in contrast, obeyed a different logic: *escarmentar* (exemplary punishment) was their objective. The fear generated by these spectacles of death aimed at the moral regeneration of the paysanos, those who constituted the public at executions.

How many executions were ordered during the Rosas period? Rivera Indarte (1946), in his *Tablas de Sangre*, attributes to Rosas 1,393 executions of people accused of sympathizing with the unitarios and estimates that another 1,600 soldiers were killed for desertion (the author does not clarify if they were federalist or unitario).[34] Most of the executions included in the first figure were actually ordered by the commanders of the Confederation (Oribe, Pacheco, Aldao, Maza, Echague) during war campaigns. They were not signed by Rosas and certainly did not emerge from any judicial process. The "political" executions reported by Rivera Indarte in his lists did not include working-class people. The figure given for deserters executed seems totally speculative; it is not corroborated by any nominal list (as was the case with the upper-class unitarios reportedly assassinated by the Mazorca).

Rosas's own trial, initiated in absentia in 1857, brought attention to the executions of soldiers and civilians. The fiscal alleged that Rosas had ordered the execution of 52 individuals with an indication of the crimes committed and had executed another 83 people without stated cause or motive. Among the former group, 24 (46 percent) were deserters, 9 were murderers, 8 were thieves, 3 were executed for political reasons, and the rest were accused of woundings, escape from prison, and other felonies. Though incomplete, this statistic confirms what I stated about the penal policy of Rosismo: setting aside the unitarios, deserters were the most likely target for the death penalty. Much more conservative than Rivera Indarte's estimate (the executions of unitarios had mysteriously dwindled from 1,400 to near 100), the 1857 inventory indicates that capital punishment was used in an exemplary, limited fashion.[35]

Apart from the unitarios, most of the civilians executed were peons, born in the interior provinces, illiterate, and poor. The soldiers sent to the firing squad were generally from the same social background. Here are some examples. Soldier José Pita, accused of planning a mass desertion, was executed in the fort of Patagones in 1838. The same year, José Paulino Villalón, a farm peon, found death before the firing squad; he was found guilty of murdering his young patroncito on a farm near San Nicolás. Sandalio Carrizo was executed in Lobos in November 1832 for kidnapping a "family girl" (niña de familia), assaulting an alcalde (policeman), and various accounts of theft. Soldier Francisco Iturrieta, a former cattle drover from San Juan residing in San Pedro, was sentenced to death, accused of deserting during combat. Domingo Correa, a peon of the Public Provision who had wounded a foreigner in 1844, was sentenced to death in 1851 for abandoning the police force after he had served his term.[36]

This type of state terror had a definite class dimension. The condemned belonged to the same social class, the one that Rosas wanted to fix through the judicial and military apparatuses of the state: the peon class.

They were all part of a mobile proletariat searching for work and community in Buenos Aires province. They were peons or poor peasants who had committed a crime in their perambulations through the landscape of the province, or soldiers (ex-peons or -peasants) who had deserted the federalist armies for a variety of reasons. Their executions responded to the imperative to reestablish order in the countryside and obedience in military quarters. Their violent crimes and their refusal to fight for the federation led them to the firing squad. On the other hand, no upper-class citizen was ever executed for these types of crimes (their punishment was generally less severe). The members of the urban gentry who filled the lists of the *Efemérides sangrientas* (1911) were all killed, tortured, and beaten for "crimes" related to their political allegiances and opinions.

The procedure followed in the execution of common criminals was fairly standard. In August 1845, General Rosas sentenced a couple from Santiago del Estero (Carmelo Rodríguez and Tomasina Ponce) to death for the crime of assault and murder. The prisoners were taken to the place where they had committed the murder, Guardia Luján, offered religious counsel, and then escorted to the public square. There a peculiar sexual division of labor took place: the man was shot by the firing squad while his female partner watched the procedure. She remained there until sunset, when the cadaver of her partner was taken down and buried. Tomasina Ponce's punishment consisted of watching her loved one die. In another execution conducted at San Nicolás in April 1838, the same procedure was used. While the principal murderer, José Paulino Villalón, was executed, his accomplice, the freedman Felix, was made to witness the execution and then punished with one hundred lashes.[37] Apparently, what was sufficient punishment for a woman was not for a young black servant; blacks were believed to be less impressionable and more resilient to punishment.

This was a variation of the "lottery," a method by which, if various men were sentenced to death, only one of them was actually executed; the rest were compelled to watch the execution, their death sentences exchanged for lighter penalties.[38] Underlying this procedure was the overriding need to make lawbreakers contemplate the consequences of their own actions. Undoubtedly, the executions were pedagogic spectacles destined for current or potential lawbreakers. Additionally, the lottery was animated by a desire to economize lives in a context of acute labor shortages. If the lesson of death could be learned with one casualty, the rest could be spared and recycled back into the war machine.

Visibility was a constitutive element of these rituals. Seeing the body of the condemned, the public would know that the crime committed had received retribution. This is why the executions took place, most of the time, in the same district where the crime was committed. Hung from a wooden pole, the bodies of the executed were exposed to public view from morning until sunset. If the prisoner arrived at the place of execution after midday, the justice was instructed to delay the proceedings until the next day. This was necessary to give the prisoner sufficient time for confession and repentance (two hours of *capilla*), and also to give local residents a chance to contemplate the body of the condemned.[39] As was officially expressed during the execution of the Reynafé brothers (Lynch 1981, 225) in 1837, the exposure of bodies was meant to discharge in part the *vindicta pública* (popular hostility and resentment).

In cases where the crime was considered an affront to both the fatherland and civil society, the state had to emphasize the dangerousness of the criminal with an additional demonstration of power. Deserter and murderer Manuel Butierres was sentenced to death and conducted to the town of Arrecifes in January 1838. He was put to death according to the established ritual: at night, after receiving religious counsel; execution by firing squad inside military quarters; and hanging his body in the town's public square. But a significant ingredient was added to the spectacle in this case: because he had raised his hand to shoot a peaceful civilian, his executioners were instructed to cut off his right arm before the body was exposed to the public. This detail made the state's message transparently clear.

Executions within the garrisons served the military to keep within bounds the constant scourge of desertion and to abort occasional attempts of insurrection or rebellion. Usually addressed to captive audiences unable to express themselves while in formation, these spectacles were calculated to remind soldiers of the sacred nature of their commitment to the fatherland. They were acts of visual and verbal communication used by the governor and the military hierarchy to establish the authority of the law, remark on the enormity of the crime committed, and reaffirm the importance of the Federal Cause.

Early on, in the Campaign of the Desert (1833–1834), Rosas's generals discovered the communicative potential of executions. In September 1833, soldier Gerónimo Martínez was executed in a military camp at Choele-Choel for wounding an officer. General Pacheco, in command of one of the two divisions of the campaign, took the opportunity to address the soldiery. In his proclamation he explained the army's need to punish cases of desertion severely, so they would not be repeated. He emphasized the need to complete the campaign against the "southern savages" and exalted the bravery of the soldier who had defended the wounded officer.

General Pacheco wanted soldiers to understand the multiple meanings of the spectacle. A successful conclusion of the war against the southern tribes required soldiers to comprehend that the "contract" they had signed with the army was binding, that military laws remained sovereign during the campaign, and that soldiers should expect punishment for their wrong-doings.[40]

By the beginning of Rosas's second government, military executions had developed into a well-established ritual. When deserters Prudencio Guerreros, Juan Francisco Medina, and Hilario Avellaneda were executed in the Mulitas garrison in January 1837, officers followed a ceremonious procedure. A team of officers, including the commander of the garrison, was designated to carry out the sentence. On the scheduled day, the condemned were taken to the execution site and placed at the center of the squadron. Then a *bando* was read reminding soldiers of the penalty the Military Ordinances prescribed for the crime of desertion. Next, the condemned knelt down to listen to the reading of their sentences (as do Catholics when the Scriptures are read). Only then was the squad ordered to shoot. Afterward, a notary wrote down all the proceedings in an *acta*, and the squadron was ordered to disassemble.[41]

The punishment offered a lesson, not only about the severity of the offense and the will of the state to repress it, but also about the celerity of justice under a dictatorship. The carabiniers had run away on December 14 from the fort of Mulitas and had been apprehended two days later at the Barrancosa camp. On the same day, December 16, the sumario was taken, and the next day Rosas issued the order of execution. On December 21, Minister García formed the execution commission, which scheduled the shooting for January 10. On that day, at 5:30 P.M., the execution was carried into effect. Only twenty-five days had passed since the time the deserters were arrested, and it is likely that, were it not for Christmas festivities, the execution would have been even more expedient. This was swift justice indeed.

Though circumscribed to a frontier garrison, the spectacle had a large audience. The two other carabineros pardoned by the lottery procedure, Mariano Ponce and José Antonio García, received two hundred lashes. They were advised "in the presence of the Squadron, the Artillery corps [*piquete*], and the Patrician Militia corps, that if they deserted again, they would be shot in the act of apprehension. "The whole garrison watched the execution. Larger regiments provided, of course, a wider audience for these spectacles of death. The execution of deserter Félix Oguendo, carried out on March 20, 1849 at Retiro square, featured the deployment of 991

men (832 troops, 52 horns and drums, and 52 officers). In square formation, the troops witnessed the shooting of the soldier and proceeded to
parade in front of the dead body as they retired to their quarters. Oguendo's cadaver was left hanging for the rest of the day, so that the nonmilitary public could contemplate the spectacle.[42]

Retiro, being at the same time the site of a military regiment and
a market for the concentration of oxcarts and cattle, was a gathering
place for many people. From there, like expanding waves, the news of
Oguendo's execution could disseminate into the countryside, carried by
oxcart drivers, cattle drovers, tramping peons, and traveling peddlers. But
this was an exception. More commonly, executions took place in the interior of army garrisons, all spectators being military except for a number of
relatives residing on the premises. On other occasions, the executions
were conducted on a private ranch, with still fewer viewers. The direct
visibility of these shootings was much more limited, but their impact
might have been greater. Executions conducted on ranches took the civil
war into the terrain of production, multiplying the awareness of the severity of military discipline and serving as warnings to peons, squatters, and
neighboring peasants.

War: That Other Terror

For the soldiers who followed the federalist flag through long campaigns
in the interior provinces, war must have been a journey into terror, not
only because of the rigors of tyrannical officers but also, and especially,
because of the way the war was conducted. Commanders had no means of
maintaining and controlling prisoners, so neither side took prisoners.
After each battle, soldiers were ordered to "knife" the prisoners so that the
unit could continue its march. Immersed in a holy war, each army endeavored to exterminate its adversary. Some federalist commanders, such as
Colonel Maza, rejoiced in these mass executions, persuaded that the defense of the Holy Cause required the extermination of the unitario "race."[43]

Rivera Indarte (1946, 68, 71–72) spared no words—or metaphors—to
describe the brutality of federalist commanders in the interior. The way
Felix Aldao ordered the death of publicist José M. Salinas from Mendoza
exceeded all imaginable cruelty: "After pulling his eyes out and cutting his
arms, they [the federalists] cut his tongue, opened his chest, and took his
heart out." The body was later left for the "public expectation" for a day.
Oribe's troops in Banda Oriental, according to Rivera Indarte, used to

castrate unitario prisoners before killing them. An insistently circulated motif in émigré texts (later presented as evidence at Rosas's trial) stated that federalist soldiers skinned their prisoners and used this material to make lassos, hobbles, and tobacco bags.

The policy of beheading the enemy was not a monopoly of federalists. Unitario commanders also committed acts of extreme brutality. In fact, the destruction and terror unleashed by the unitarios was equally memorable. For years, the bombardment of Paysandú in February 1847 stood as a symbol of unitario barbarism. The attack launched by Rivera, simultaneous to the bombardment, spread devastation among civilians. While the fires provoked by the bombardment consumed many residents' huts, unitario soldiers persecuted and killed survivors—children, women, and elderly included—on the street, in the hospital, and in private homes.[44] The impressions left by this episode on the memories of soldiers who lived through this attack must have been impossible to erase, as it was impossible for the émigrés to forget the violence of the Mazorca in the streets of Buenos Aires during the journeys of October 1840.

The exaggeration and political bias contained in Rivera Indarte's *Tablas de Sangre* should not obscure the fact that wars generated an enormous amount of unregulated violence. The response of the civilian population was, expectably, one of fear and retreat. Federalists in the interior provinces were terrified of approaching armies, even if they were of the same ideological persuasion. In a contemporary song sung in Tucumán, a federalist, afraid of the ravages of Oribe's forces, commends the protection of his town to the "shadows" of two dead leaders (Dorrego and Heredia) held as exemplars of moderation.[45] Another song, composed in Catamarca ca. 1841, describes the death of governor Cubas in graphic terms: "Al cuerpo del señor Cubas/La cabeza le cortaron/Y en la punta de una lanza/En la plaza la clavaron" ("To Mr. Cubas, they cut/the body and the head/and, at the point of a pike/in the square they planted it").[46] After the battle of Oncativo in February 1830, the people of Tucumán considered Quiroga a "second Attila" who had razed on his way the property and civil rights of four provinces.[47] In the face of such demonstrations of brutality, contemporary peasants in the interior provinces must have lived the civil wars as a period of terror.

Scenes of terror such as these could expand many times, replicated in stories, songs, and everyday conversation. Stories of beheadings, quarterings of cadavers on display, and mutilations became commonplaces in the interior. Newspapers contributed to disseminate the horror, publishing accounts of massacres, executions, and spectacles of violence.[48] Thus, the interior provinces came to represent the site of an unprecedented, unbounded violence. Lacking the finances to support strong armies, their governments had to surrender to the invading armies and withstand the pillage that followed each invasion or change of government. Buenos Aires province, on the other hand, aside from the excesses of October 1840 and April 1842, enjoyed the reputation of a place of greater tranquility. Not surprisingly, many peasants from the interior provinces, directly affected by the civil wars or simply responding to the fear and instability created by these conflicts, migrated to Buenos Aires province.

Regiments on campaign probably generated, at the time of combat, moments of excitement and release that certainly left marks on soldiers' lives. These moments would later be recounted in terms of glory, courage, comradeship, and patriotism. To this extent, the campaigns through the interior could have served as rites of passage to manhood or, perhaps, as builders of solidarity among soldiers of different origins. But regiments on campaign had a darker side. They were like moving prisons. Each unit kept soldiers within certain physical boundaries; beyond these limits, they could not move without a passport. In the camps, soldiers were subjected to the rigors of military discipline, receiving the treatment of prisoners; many of the soldiers were, in fact, condemned criminals, purging past felonies in the military.[49] The punishment they received was disproportionate to their offense, not only because their sentence extended in practice far beyond the original term but also because the war itself imposed heavy costs in terms of disability and disease.

Soldiers came back from the war with a new experience, and their bodies carried the marks of this experience. Many had scars on their faces and traces of bullets or lances in their skin. Some showed these marks in their interrogation to emphasize their contribution to the war effort. To others, the cost of the war was still greater: they came back mutilated and ill. Documents on the Invalids Corps allow us to look into the ailments and disabilities of veterans.

In November 1849, Rosas instructed military commanders to send the *inválidos* (disabled) to Buenos Aires to be medically inspected and dismissed. Among those were seventy-one veterans of the campaigns of Santa Fé, Entre Ríos, and Uruguay. Most had embarked at Paysandú and reached the port of Buenos Aires in December 1849. This group of soldiers was somewhat special: they had experienced one of the longest campaigns of the civil wars; most had spent the prior nine years on the front line (most had enlisted in 1840, others in 1842). They had fought the unitarios at Santa Fé and Entre Ríos, marched to the Banda Oriental (some had been at the long siege of Montevideo), and confronted the Anglo-French forces along the Paraná River. Among them were porteños, northern migrants, Africans (ex-slaves), and orientales (born in Banda Oriental).

Half of the group were old, in fact, too old to be on active duty. Older veterans had the ailments proper to their age: they could not hear well, some had lost part of their sight, others suffered from rheumatism, one had lost all his teeth. The rest were 25 to 45 years old. These men presented all sorts of symptoms of disease. Some had broken ribs, the result of falling from horses; many suffered from rheumatic pain, due to the *mojaduras* (wetting) they experienced while on campaign. The physician, Martiniano Martínez, who examined them annotated a long list of ailments: "does not contain urine," gout, "groin hernia," swollen arms, legs, or stomach, suppurating wounds, aneurism in the heart or in the abdomen, "blood vomit," asthma attacks, syphilis, "venereal rheumatism," "heart pains," various tumors, chronic dysentery. In addition, Raymundo Antonio, 28, had lost a leg; Felipe Atencio, 35, had returned with a broken foot; Santiago Monzón, 29, could not move his left hand.

These veterans were living evidence of the cost of the civil war, a cost laid disproportionately on the rural subaltern. Of the psychological impact of the war we can only speculate. Many had been separated from their families for years. Many had spent their youth in service of the Federalist Cause. The scars and marks on their bodies were sufficient proof of their manhood in a society that appreciated bravery and courage over any other attribute of masculinity. They were hardened by the war experience, but also deprived of precious assets (youth, loved ones). Some, having borne witness to torture, beheadings, and unbounded killings of adults, women, and children, returned from the civil war with their senses numbed to the horror of violence. For those who stayed six, eight, or more years under the flag, the army became a true prison, an institution that constrained their freedom of movement and their possibilities for self-realization.

Conclusions: Subaltern Reactions to Punishment

In September 1839, six deserters from the army camp at Barrancosa presented a complaint against Lieutenant Fernando Sánchez. Each soldier reported one or several instances of abuse of authority. Though the intensity of the coercion reported was not great (only one of them spent two hours *estaquiado*), soldiers presented these incidents as moments of great personal humiliation and injustice. In fact, at least four of them pointed at maltreatment as the main reason for their desertion. More than physical pain, it was the humiliating nature of the officer's punishment that upset the soldiers. The lieutenant had insulted them, slapped them, grabbed them by the hair, pushed them, struck them with a whip, and repeatedly threatened them with corporal punishment.

The humiliation these soldiers felt moved them to desert the Barrancosa encampment. The officer's insults—accusations of robbery or insinuations that they were unworthy of the uniform—had aggravated their resentment. In addition to physical abuse and insults, the lieutenant had made them shave their beards or mustaches. This action attacked their self-respect and manhood as well as their federalist patriotism (wearing a mustache was a privilege granted to good federalists). Combined, these small disciplinary actions amounted to an intolerable breach of the contract these soldiers had made with the fatherland—so much so that they were prepared to risk the consequences of group desertion and present their case to a superior authority.

The six deserters went to speak to their old commander, now commissioned to a garrison in Zárate. They traveled many kilometers, expecting that their old chief would understand their plight. And he did: Militia Commander Dionisio Sagasti, who took the "verbal narration" of these deserters and later ordered the corresponding investigation, helped them achieve some type of reparation. Lieutenant Sánchez was put in jail for a month and later transferred to a different regiment. The deserters themselves were recommended to Rosas for a commuted sentence.[50]

This case illustrates the other side of the disciplinary archipelago: subalterns' reaction to illegitimate and abusive punishment. Soldiers denounced those punishments they considered humiliating and unnecessary. Lieutenant Sánchez's actions seemed more like small acts of vendetta than disciplinary penalties. Soldiers' reaction to this treatment affirmed the notion of legitimate punishment, one proportional to the offense and contemplated in the military by-laws. To these subalterns, certain forms of punishment were tolerable; others, perhaps less violent, were not. Insults, slaps, forced shaving, and hair pulling were acts of improper behavior for an officer. Floggings and *estaqueos* went beyond the disciplinary prerogatives of a lieutenant.

The story of the Barrancosa soldiers fits well with that of many other deserters. Soldiers mentioned the "fear of punishment" as a major motivation for desertion (see chapter 9). They preferred the prospect of harsh penalties in the future (an extension of service or the capital penalty) to enduring humiliating and unjustified pain. The high incidence of desertion shows that the threat of execution was not enough to deter potential deserters. Within the barracks, soldiers tried to bargain with their superiors to improve their material conditions and to reduce the level of abuse and arbitrary punishment. They threatened their officers with collective desertion, moved to other garrisons when their grievances were not heard, spread rumors of impending attacks of enemy forces, and, in extreme cases, defied their superiors (see chapter 8).

Physical and verbal abuse was part of the extralegal or surplus coercion that awaited peons and peasants who entered a regiment. But the sub-alterns who inhabited these disciplinary spaces were not defenseless crea-tures at the mercy of their superiors. They knew how to react to the imposition of illegitimate punishment, they had a low tolerance for humil-iation, and they understood well the politics of patronage and legality of a republican era. Soldiers challenged superiors to put verbal accusations on paper; they tried to stop abusive punishment by resorting to superior ranks, and when confronted with unjustified suffering, they reacted vio-lently.[51] Their notions of unjust or excessive punishment were rooted in their understanding that a process of legalization was on the way, even in regiments, and that officers' claims about their power to punish could be challenged by denunciations to superiors.

With regard to floggings ordered directly by Rosas and applied generally at Santos Lugares, the sources are silent. Subalterns denounced the abuses committed by justices and other military authorities in frontier garrisons, but were unable (or did not dare) to criticize the central power. The same is true of subalterns' reactions to public executions.[52] Soldiers knew about the executions (when they were asked if they knew the penalty for deser-tion, they unambiguously said "the ultimate penalty") but did not openly talk about them. In their interrogations, they only tangentially mentioned executions; this was when their officers threatened them with the firing squad or when their own commanding officers were taken prisoner and executed.[53]

Also absent from soldiers' testimonies is the brutality of the civil war. The cruelty of unitario commanders and the verbal abuse they received from their own officers during campaigns were bracketed out from their declarations. Though the horror they experienced must have left perdu-rable psychic marks, nothing of this transpired into the public transcript. Soldiers erased these scenes of terror from their spoken, public memories, recounting only moments of personal bravery and patriotism. The war, on their return, acquired a positive value. They counted their wounds and scars as marks of their contributions to the making of a federalist fatherland—as if these wounds and scars were outside the system of punishment.

CHAPTER 8

Regiments: Negotiation and Protest

Having examined the situation and activities of poor peasants and peons with regard to the law and the market, I move now into the world of paysanos' military experience. Crucial to the Pax Rosista was the construction of a formidable and disciplined army able to preserve the territorial integrity of the province, to affirm the supremacy of Buenos Aires within the country, and to inculcate in the peasantry notions of subordination, obedience, and patriotism. Regular armies and militias constituted a central aspect of political control and social discipline during this period, influencing enormously the lives of subaltern subjects. Recurrent calls to arms, periodical military drills, and the involvement of rural communities in the victories and losses of the federalist armies kept the Buenos Aires countryside in a situation of almost permanent military mobilization.

Enacting a script envisioned by Rosas in 1820, militias and armies were to play a central role in the pacification and civilization of the countryside. Due to recurrent wars on multiple fronts, the federalist armies were forced to mobilize a large portion of the population into war; to do this, they had to blend militia corps with regular soldiers. This entailed the mixing of two systems of rights that, until then, had remained separated: those associated with citizen-soldiers and those pertaining to regular soldiers. For paysanos, joining the military meant either the expiation of crime or the expression of federalist patriotism. Hence the experience of soldiering was more than confinement and military discipline; it involved a learning experience in which subalterns of different origins found common ground for resisting arbitrary authority and excessive service.

This chapter investigates subaltern strategies and politics in relation to one of the pillars of state order: military discipline. Ideally, regiments and militias were sites for the production of obedient and patriotic subjects. The militarization of the countryside was itself a means to engender orderly communities. This vision of order, which placed the subaltern as malleable subject interpellated for his patriotism and his subordination, emerges clearly from a *memoria* Rosas wrote in 1820. In this document, Rosas spelled out the two most formidable threats confronting the cattle-ranching economy.[1] To him, recurrent Indian raids on cristiano towns and ranches and the uncultured manners and habits of gauchos constituted the major obstacles to the pacification and wealth of the countryside. To restore order, it was essential to extend the Indian frontier to the south (by peaceful or violent means) and to change the state of "utmost disorder and licentiousness" in which the rural poor lived.

Militarizing the countryside provided a solution to both problems. Sufficient frontier garrisons could check Indian invasions, bringing tranquility to ranches and rural towns, and compulsory military training could teach the itinerant poor to respect law, property, and country. Rosas was concerned with the erosion of social hierarchies and with the disrespect for private property that the revolution had produced (Ingenieros 1920, 2:159, 162; Arana 1954, 284). Managing a ranch in a frontier area, Rosas felt threatened by Indian raids and by the presence of vagabonds near his property. A multitude of "thieves, vagrants, highwaymen, and anonymous disturbers" infested the countryside, poaching on ranchers' lands, disbanding their herds, and threatening their lives. To tame these men, he suggested the creation of compulsory militias, to which all men in the countryside, young and old, would belong. The militias' chief objectives would be to defend ranches and populations from Indian attacks and to apprehend criminals and put them to work. In addition, the militias would serve to reshape the most negative aspects of gaucho culture by subjecting the itinerant, rural poor to a system of military discipline.[2]

This vision of order found multiple difficulties in its implementation. Although the project of militarizing the countryside took on a life of its own during the federalist wars, military discipline failed to accomplish the social and cultural transformation envisioned by Rosas. Instead of "schools of social discipline," military garrisons became sites of negotiation and protest, places saturated by subaltern politics, where "discipline" itself was the object of negotiation. In these bounded spaces, soldiers and officers continually negotiated pay, work, and leadership. Contestation within the barracks was related to the material conditions in which most soldiers lived: irregular pay and provisions, officers' mistreatment and despotism, long terms of service, and more. But the tone and modalities of soldiers' demands denounce the presence of popular ideologies and traditions, transformed by the war experience.

Soldiers' materialism combined with notions of respect and equality learned in the 1820s. Before the Rosas period, militiamen, using the language of equality and citizenship, had been able to defy and contain the arbitrary authority of military officers, excusing themselves from much combat service. This option was not open to regular soldiers. They could not use the law as a valid excuse for service; hence, their protest consisted mainly in desertion and other forms of noncompliance. The Rosas administration eroded this basic distinction, putting together militiamen and regular soldiers in the armies going to the war front. In addition, it was quite common for militiamen to turn into regular soldiers as a result of a disciplinary penalty. Thus, the federalist army became a leveler of social differences—convicted felons and neighbor-citizens united in the defense of the federation.

At the same time, regiments became schools of experience. Here, people of rural origins learned about injustice, ill treatment, "necessity," and abuse of authority. The arbitrariness and abuse of campaign service pushed soldiers to learn ways to negotiate with the authorities. Army barracks became "schools of protest" in which soldiers learned to express their grievances in a more direct fashion. Soldiers threatened officers with collective desertion, moved to other garrisons when their grievances were not heard, spread rumors about impending attacks of enemy forces, and, on rare occasions, defied their officers in front of the troops. Soldiers' subaltern condition—being by definition subject to subordination and obedience—served, paradoxically, as a means of empowerment. Subjected to common misfortunes, veterans and militiamen tried to alleviate their condition by acts of individual or collective protest.

Within regiments, the voices of subalterns acquired a menacing tone, for most of their petitions and negotiations implied the possibility of abandoning the ranks. Subalterns indicated to their commanding officers that their federalist patriotism (and commitment) was conditional upon the satisfaction of material needs. In the context of a civil war, soldiers' means of protest, what I call "bargaining by threat of desertion," appeared to the federalist leadership as acts of political conspiracy. Hence, the intelligence machinery of the state related these "conspiracies" to popular politics, a terrain in which rumor reigned supreme. Soldiers' negotiations and threats were often taken as political acts, for they presented, as a latent possibility, the reversal of the war situation and anticipated the fall of Rosista federalism.

Resistance on Two Fronts

The division of (male) rural society into two "classes"—residents and transients—projected itself onto the forms of serving the fatherland. On one side were the citizens-in-arms, the militiamen, who contributed their services to the state in the areas of defense, justice, and policing; they were just fulfilling their duties. On the other side were regular soldiers (*soldados de línea*), people who, out of necessity, chose the career of arms or, more frequently, felons sentenced to the military by the criminal justice system. On the latter fell the heaviest burden of active military service: the persecution of unitarios, the defense of the Confederation's coasts, the long campaigns to Banda Oriental, the littoral, and Cuyo, the constant vigilance on the two Indian frontiers. Residents enlisted in the militias, on the other hand, could more easily escape active duty or, at least, bargain their contribution to the defense of the province.

The distinction between militiamen (*milicianos*) and regular soldiers (*veteranos*) was established early in the postindependence period.[3] The Militia Law of 1823 made it obligatory for every man between 17 and 45 to enlist in the active infantry militia (20 to 45, in the case of the cavalry). They had limited responsibilities: two "assemblies" or reunions each year and a maximum period of six months of military duty. Those exempted from the active militias were automatically enlisted in the reserve or "passive" militias and, as a result, relieved from active duty. In addition, the law contemplated many causes for exemption: illness or physical defect, belonging to certain professions, owning property, or being the supporter of a family (Domínguez 1898, 1:358–361). The army, on the other hand, recruited "volunteers" (later called *enganchados*) and also contingentes or quotas of unwilling draftees. The Recruitment Law of 1823 charged the notable neighbors (propertied, married, and over 30) of each community with the responsibility of selecting these quotas (small groups of forced draftees) and sending them to the army. Presumably, the more respectable neighbors generally nominated the sons of the poor or transients they saw as "vagrants" to fulfill their community's obligation.[4]

The laws of 1823 established important differences that continued into the Rosas period. All those enlisted in the local militias acquired, by the sole act of enlistment, a set of civil rights. They were considered residents who could own property, vote in local elections, petition the authorities, or be appointed to local government. In contrast, regular soldiers were usually recruited through compulsion: the arrests of unsuspecting poor travelers on the road, the detention of those suspected of being deserters, and the forced draft of young drinkers, gamblers, or vagrants in the taverns. Though Rosas's troops also included contracted soldiers (enganchados), felons sentenced by the justice system constituted the core of the Dictator's regular forces. These soldiers entered the military devoid of rights.

By law, militiamen had to contribute to the preservation of order during peacetime and be prepared to bear arms in case of war. In practice, however, as the law did not specify all the conditions and situations in which these contributions were to be rendered, militiamen usually ended up performing "mechanical" or "passive" services. Arguing that active military duty interfered with their private interests (the management of farms, ranches, and other businesses), militiamen were able to avoid enlisting in military campaigns or *destacamentos*. In contrast, regular soldiers—in particular those who had reached Santos Lugares in shackles—had little room for argument and negotiation during recruitment. These "recruits" could expect only to minimize their penalty by telling a convincing story of their previous contributions to the Federalist Cause; they could not refuse service or argue about the basis of their "selection."

Thus, resistance against the military took two forms. Those with unclear social and local credentials (interior migrants, itinerant workers, or undocumented people), unable to articulate a language of rights, had to evade service by fleeing. Delinquents by suspicion, they were denied the possibility of negotiating their assignment or the nature of their services. Militiamen, on the other hand, were protected by their commander (usually a local notable) and by their rights as residents (citizens and neighbors). Through petitions, lack of cooperation, and influence peddling, they positioned themselves as part of a community struggling against "arbitrary authority," usually military commanders and local justices of the peace.

Once in the regiment of their destination, regular soldiers recovered their voice and were able to bargain for economic benefits and fair treatment. Within the barracks, soldiers were ruled by the codes of military discipline and by a contract that stipulated their salary, their term of service, and the equipment and benefits to be expected (food rations, horses, uniforms, and weapons). Consequently, those who wanted to denounce situations of material deprivation, injustice, and maltreatment had to phrase their claim in relation to this contract and to those disciplinary rules. By resorting to a superior, they could always bargain for the improvement of their situation. If this failed, they could raise the stakes of their protest, threatening authorities with rebellion and mass desertion.

The resistance of neighbors against arbitrary recruitment was predicated on a language of equality and liberty and was rooted in traditions of civic protest that stemmed from the wars of independence. These traditions formed in the context of the self-organization of rural towns to man the revolutionary armies. These interactions among neighbors for purposes of recruitment (and also to form the patrols required to maintain order in the rural towns) engendered the language of rights with which citizens could confront abuses of authority. Apparently, these traditions and language, formed in the late 1810s and 1820s, persisted into the Rosas period. In his early public addresses, Rosas himself legitimized these claims to equality and the rights of the "peoples," making them compatible with the demand for order and civility that stemmed out of the "convulsions" of the 1820s.

By contrast, the protest and negotiation of soldiers in the barracks borrowed from military traditions built around the actual experience of combat, institutional comradeship, and conflict. The practice of collective bargaining vis-à-vis the officers, the use of rumor to prepare the terrain for negotiation, and the ultimate resort to rebellion and mass desertion were part of a popular/military understanding of politics. Whereas militia politics emphasized the importance of the law in carving out a space for the autonomy of the citizen, soldiers favored the terrain of action—negotiation, intimidation, and revolt—to impose minimal rules of conduct on the officers corps. Though the same ideas (equality and liberty) nurtured both types of resistance, the meanings attributed to them by militiamen and regular soldiers were different. The struggles and utterances of militiamen tended to support order and legality; those of soldiers conspired against the stability of the regime: they fragmented the polity into a contractual institutional space where the rule of law was reduced to a minimum.

Winds of Equality

To understand the moral economy that sustained the claims of neighbors against military authorities, we must return for a moment to the late 1810s and early 1820s. Although Rosas used a conception of "equality in order" to legitimize his government, the construction and diffusion of this ideal dates back to early postindependence. The system of legality imagined by independence leaders promised to eliminate all legal and social privileges. Everyone was to be equal before the law. This promise was verbally conveyed by Castelli to the Indian towns of upper Peru in 1810, deployed at the 1813 ceremony that abolished instruments of torture and titles of nobility, and was written into the Artigas decree of 1815.

Initially promoted by the Jacobin liberals, the idea of the law as a leveling rod, as a destroyer of privilege, penetrated deep and wide into all spheres of life, particularly among the lower classes. Soldiers, after listening to hundreds of military proclamations on the subject, were well acquainted with this language. Bartolomé Hidalgo's poem *Diálogo patriótico interesante*, said to have circulated widely among soldiers and militiamen in the first decade of independence, states clearly this notion of equality. The law was for all; it made no distinction in color, property, birth, or regional origin.[5] This radical egalitarianism was later reenacted in various events having

16. Rosas's Militiamen. This illustration for a sonnet was composed in honor of the Red Patrician Militias, who in 1820 restored the legitimacy of government in the city. Anon., *Colorados del Regimiento V de Milicias Patricias*, colored lithograph, ca. 1822. Reproduced from Luis L. Houssay, El *caballo de guerra en la iconografía argentina* (1971).

great repercussions: the popular revolt of 1811, the reforms of 1813, the army rebellions of 1815, and the militias that rescued Buenos Aires in 1820.[6] In a variety of social spaces, a language learned in military quarters during the independence campaigns spread among artisans, neighbors, small proprietors, mulatto women, and peons. Tapping into this common resource, neighbors and civilian and military authorities came to discuss, during the agitated period of 1815–1824, the nature of social and political organization in their districts.

During these years, two different interpretations of equality developed. One conceived it as opposite to arbitrary authority, hence emphasizing the rule of law. The other, a more radical type of equality, aimed at eliminating all distinctions and privileges (racial, educational, economic) and demanded unquestioned patriotism from everyone. Neighbors tended to subscribe to the former interpretation and military officers and regular soldiers favored the latter. This conflict of interpretation no doubt echoed the transition from a period of military mobilization for a common enterprise (to preserve independence, threatened by a new Spanish invasion, 1819–1820) to a period of relative peace and administrative reform (1822–1825).

During this transition, the erosion of the colonial basis for authority and privilege put in question all claims to social distinction. From all fronts came voices demanding the end of privilege and a halt to the abusive exercise of authority. Those who felt entitled to command and prestige clashed against those who found that these claims violated the egalitarian basis of the new society. This produced numerous conflicts about the limits of military and civilian authority. Militia commanders defended neighbors against the abuses of military officers, justices and police chiefs asserted their authority vis-à-vis that of military commanders, and common soldiers and paysanos tried to put limits on the excesses of policemen, justices, and military officers. In 1820, neighbors denounced the military commander of Ranchos Policarpo Izquierdo for his abusive treatment of civilians. His intentions, as perceived by the neighbors, were to disarm the militias, pillage the town, and expropriate some neighbors (the "Europeans"). Two of Izquierdo's officers, Suasnávar and Funes, were accused of similar abuses. They had gathered the militia, urged them to reject the new commander appointed from Buenos Aires, and distributed new ranks among those present. They had threatened the neighbors with pillage and verbally abused the gente decente. Suasnávar was quoted as saying: "Sino han bisto montonera ahora la han de ver" and "Qué desentes ni desentes! pronto se hande acabar los desentes" ("If they have not seen a montonera [guerrilla warfare], now they will" and "Down with the decentes [upper crust]! Soon, there will be no decente left").[7]

As an assertion of their radical egalitarianism Suasnávar and Funes enlisted Dr. Joaquín Campana, an ex-secretary of the Directorio, as a common soldier, dragging him shirtless into the formation.[8] When Campana tried to protest this debasing act, they both shouted at him, "We are all one; we are all equal. Return to the formation." In the view of Campana, these rough military commanders were a threat to the security of the neighbors and their rights.[9] To the traditional local elite (decente) neighbors, there was a crucial difference between the militias and the military parties. The former could be trusted with the task of restoring order; the latter, made up of deserters and vagrants, could only spell disorder and pillage. The new military leaders allied to caudillos and Indians represented a different, threatening form of politics.

Similar incidents were reported in Chascomús, Pilar, and the outskirts of Buenos Aires. In Chascomús in 1819, commander of the militias Juan L.

Castro punished army Commissioner Pedro Funes for striking defenseless neighbors. Neighbors used their militia units to put limits to military absolutism. In 1824, the neighbors of Pilar, in an address to the judge of crime in Buenos Aires, denounced the local justice for abusing his authority and for protecting thieves. In this case, the local residents tried to limit the authority of the justice. In 1819 neighbors of Buenos Aires denounced militia Sergeant Gaspar Rodríguez for disturbing the peace and abuse of authority.[10] We see here a common complaint: the walls of respect behind which the neighbor/proprietors could live and prosper were being undermined by the corruption of civilian authorities and the brutality of military chiefs.

The same type of social war was being waged in the streets of Buenos Aires. Tension between militia and army officers reflected not only a conflict of jurisdiction, but also distinct understandings of equality. In December 1819, army Lieutenant Mariano Cabrera, moved by compassion and a sense of racial equality, risked his career by confronting authorities of equal or superior rank, two militia officers of the professional classes. He tried to defend a "colored" (chinito) militiaman, a 15-year-old carpenter, from arbitrary and humiliating punishment. In the incident, the lieutenant made evident that racial insults (the young militiaman was called "Ayba el lobo") were improper in a society of equals. But the militia officers did not consider the young black militiaman a social equal and were ready to assert, by force, their social superiority over a lieutenant of the regular army.[11]

Two years earlier (1817) another incident made it evident that the struggle for social equality entailed the rejection of corporal punishment as an officer's prerogative. Soldier Martín Herrera raised his hand against his superior, Corporal Ignacio Díaz, to defend his honor and to stop a disciplinary punishment in public. Unwilling to tolerate the beating, Herrera took out his sword and wounded Corporal Díaz. The exchanges of words during the fight showed that both contenders were in agreement about the substantial equality of men underneath their uniforms.[12] Military rank was a circumstantial distinction in a society of equal, free men.

Clearly, militiamen and veterans were struggling for different notions of equality. In the face of confusing and overlapping jurisdictions of judicial, military, and police authorities, neighbors tried to carve out a space for respect and security. Assembled in their militias, they resisted the intrusions of military and civil authorities. They saw in military officers the representatives of abusive power. On the other hand, common soldiers and veterans attempted to carry into practice the egalitarian promises of the republic, rejecting the marks of social difference central to the old colonial order: military legal privileges, racial distinctions, and the authority to punish subordinates. To them, the radical egalitarianism of some military officers resonated better than an illusory equality promised by law enforcers and politicians.

During the Rosas administration, as the privileges associated with the old regime declined, the institutional power of justices and military officers grew. Consequently, the conflict between civil and military authorities intensified. Cases of woundings and beatings resulting from quarrels between policemen and military officers or between militiamen and soldiers abound. At taverns and popular dances, army officers voiced their discontent against the militiamen who had gained respect without the experience of war. Justices and comisarios for their part, tried to disarm veterans or scale down their pretensions. Neighbors, assisted by their justices, contested the self-endowed right of military officers to punish neighbors without trial. Military commanders reciprocated by trying to obstruct the labor of justices, protecting soldiers who committed crimes or denying them as witnesses for the substantiation of cases.[13]

Resisting Recruitment, Avoiding Service

Compared to regular soldiers, militiamen had an easier time. During peacetime they had to attend "doctrinal exercises" every Sunday or every other week. When needed, they served two to four months at detachments in nearby forts. If they missed a military drill, they could justify their absence (regular soldiers who did that were invariably sent to the calaboose). Militiamen who worked in the local feedlots were replaced periodically (every one or two months). Some militiamen provided services eight to ten days a month, working the rest of the time on their own ranches or farms.[14] Their services to the local justices and military garrisons consisted of short-term assistance in the roundup, transportation and branding of army cattle, tending horses, or police patrols. In times of war, they were called on to take arms, but their enlistment, unlike that of most regular soldiers, was considered a voluntary contribution to the Federal Cause.

The service required from citizens deserved proper payment. During training, militiamen's labor was remunerated on a daily basis, receiving in addition food, vicios (tobacco and sugar), and firewood. At other times, their daily pay (prest) was similar to those paid to policemen and soldiers. Militiamen had to contribute their own horses and riding apparel to the war effort; this was a small price to pay for the honor and tranquility afforded by belonging to the force.[15] To be a regular soldier presupposed an inferior social condition; to be a member of the militias did not carry a social stigma. Because most male residents of the towns (property owners, peons, foremen, family workers, squatters, postboys, and ex-soldiers) made up the militias, the composition of these units was more diverse than in the regular forces, composed chiefly of members of the "peon class."[16]

Some of the militiamen were temporarily placed at ranches, farms, stables, and meat-salting plants belonging to justices, military chiefs, or other government officials.[17] When the work was connected with military provisioning, they had to accept these assignments without grumbling. This was the case in all the work related to the maintenance and care of ranches confiscated from the unitarios, generally administered by local justices, policemen, or military commanders. In other cases, when they worked for free for the private business of a civil or military chief, militiamen's complaints appeared loud and clear in the records.

The better treatment militiamen received vis-à-vis regular soldiers was predicated on their condition as citizens. Unlike soldiers, militiamen could vote in local elections; in fact, they were often required to do so.[18] The confusion between the two attributes of the militiamen (as soldier and as voter) was made clear at the time of enrollment: the lists of those fit for military service served later in the election process. Precisely because the militiamen considered themselves legal residents and citizens, they were ready to contribute to the Federalist Cause only to the extent that this contribution did not endanger their private ranches, farms, or mobile property. If this was the case, they tried to negotiate the terms of their engagement with the fatherland. Having said this, it is necessary to recognize that the Federal Cause, because of the recurrent civil wars, called militias to arms on repeated occasions, and, once incorporated into the regiments in campaign, their units blended with those of the regular army.

Resisting the draft took various forms. One was to claim legal exceptions to active service. Various exceptions were contemplated in the 1823 Militia Law. Those with physical disabilities, those supporting widowed mothers or aging fathers, students, state agents, teachers and professionals, foremen and overseers of ranches valued over $4,000, and foreigners could expect to be registered in the "passive" militia.[19] These exceptions created an avalanche of petitions to the governor. Parents asked for exceptions for their sons; ranchers and merchants demanded the same in relation to their peons and clerks. Young men tried to avoid service by claiming to have a debilitating disease or a disability; very few, however, were exempted on these grounds. Those with enough resources (merchants and ranchers) could appoint a *personero* (paid substitute) and relieve themselves from the burden of military duty.

A second form of resistance consisted simply of refusing service to the local justice or the police chief.[20] The justice of Navarro complained bitterly in 1831 about the resistance of militiamen to serve. He had asked the chief of the militias to send a sergeant and five men to help General Quiroga with his travel. After three days of waiting, only three men showed up; by that time, the justice complained, they were no longer needed. In February 1833 the justice of Ensenada reported that the local militiamen, "persuaded by their officers or by their own advice that they must neither serve nor obey civilian authorities," refused to provide any help in the roundup of horses needed by the army. Some of them even took arms against the justice. A similar argument was given to the justice of Baradero when he requested the help of local militiamen: they refused to help on the grounds that they were already serving under the local military commander.[21]

In 1843, Mariano Saavedra, justice of Mar Chiquita, found the attitude of militiamen intolerable. He had appointed four peons of a ranch at Arroyo Grande to perform various services for the state: branding the cattle confiscated from the unitarios' estates, gathering and slaughtering the cattle needed for the garrison's consumption, carrying official mail, and other minor tasks. But none of them wanted to actually perform these tasks, arguing that they had orders from their employer, "Se me ha negado todo el servicio correspondiente al estado" ("They had refused [to perform] any service corresponding to the state"), the justice complained. Juan Crisóstomo Escobar, a merchant of Ajó, used an even more daring argument. Summoned as a drover of army cattle he refused, stating that he had sold his *población* (livestock, huts, and other investments) and was moving to the district of Pila. He was leaving, he said, to avoid the harassment of the local justice.[22]

Those without proper documents or good social connections in the locality—the case of many recent migrants from the interior provinces— could not negotiate their services to the Federal Cause. Their only option was to flee, returning to their own province or seeking temporary refuge in another district. This option was quite risky for, if arrested, northern migrants exchanged their situation as temporary resident for that of a fugitive of justice.

In November 1845, near Tapalqué, the police arrested a group of nine "Indians and Christians" traveling north with false passports.[23] Among them was Manuel Carrizo, a tailor from Santiago, who had arrived in the province nine months earlier seeking work. In the south, he had worked as a ranch peon without ever enlisting in the local militias. On two occasions, when asked by the authorities, he had contributed his labor driving cattle for the army, but when he heard the news of a general call to arms for the campaign to Entre Ríos, he decided to leave. He hid in the hills for a while, then joined three other fellows from Santiago and headed for the farmlands of Chivilcoy. There, they obtained false passports and started the long march toward Santiago. On the road, they were joined by four other natives of Santiago, also escaping the draft. With determination and a dose of skill in the arts of deception, they thought they could reach their native provinces.

Militiamen facing an impending war campaign were also tempted to escape. But, by doing so, they relinquished their rights as neighbors and their slowly accumulated social capital. Years after the events, militiamen recounted how, after hearing about a general call to arms, they hid in the *pajonales* (tall grassland), on the ranch of a relative, or on the outskirts of the city. By and large, these were individual decisions, supported by relatives or friends, never by the whole community. These decisions transformed them into outlaws or made them suspects in the support of unitarios.[24] After hiding, militiamen, just like deserters, needed to search for a new residence and find ways to become accepted by the new host community.[25] Because of this, many preferred to stay and face the consequences of military conscription.

A general mobilization equalized the condition of militiamen and soldiers, reducing the possibilities for negotiation. Militiamen who did not respond to the call to arms were as good as deserters in the regular armies. During peacetime, however, militiamen had greater room to maneuver. They could refuse passive or mechanical service and not be prosecuted. The arguments used by residents for refusing auxiliary duty are indicative of their social power. The need to attend to their "private affairs" was often used by small livestock raisers and farmers as an excuse for withholding help from the local police or JP. It was understood that, during peacetime, private economic interests took precedence over the needs of government. A poem written by a santiagueño peasant clearly expresses this feeling.[26] In the poem, a poor man asks the government to call him only when his services are needed for the defense of the fatherland; otherwise, he "will not serve." Having only his labor to sustain himself and his family, he cannot waste time *de consigna* (as watchman) in an army garrison; he has to work. The peasant wants to give proof of his patriotism in combat and not in the drudgery of "mechanic" service.

A second type of argument—that they were already serving their militia commanders—was validated by the existence of conflicting claims over militiamen's services. As long as the boundaries between different juris-dictions remained unclear, militiamen could use this ambiguity to avoid communal service or military drills. To justices, militia commanders (usu-ally army officers) were protecting their men from compliance with their obligations as citizens. But few dared to confront them. The justice of Monsalvo was cautious in using the service of militiamen, for, he believed, any requisition from them could trigger a conflict with the local com-mander, something he preferred to avoid.[27]

Conversely, when the requisition of men seemed the result of an arbi-trary or capricious decision by a military commander, local communities defended their young men. In these cases, the justice of the peace acted as a representative of the neighbors, demanding that the central state repri-mand the excesses of military recruiters. Neighbors expressed particular resentment about the *comisionados* sent by Rosas to apprehend deserters. These commissioners did not care to report to the local authorities and arrested people indiscriminately, regardless of their local standing and their documents of identity.[28] To avoid further conflict with local military authorities, justices resorted directly to the governor when presenting the complaints of the neighborhood.

Occasionally, neighbors exercised informal verbal pressure on local au-thorities to secure the release of their sons. In 1837, the justice of Ba-radero, Juan Magallanes, overwhelmed by the lamentations of weeping women whose husbands and sons had been taken by a military commis-sioner, sent Rosas a risky letter. He said the men were taken by violence while working at Simón Pereyra's ranch. They were all *hombres de bien y trabajadores*, family providers, and militiamen who deserved better treat-ment. Rosas wrote back, obviously upset. He said the commissioner had acted within the limits of the law, using no unnecessary violence. The drafted men were working outside their counties, carrying no identifica-tion or passport; the justice should have arrested them when they entered his jurisdiction. In spite of his negative reaction, Rosas let the men walk free. Did he heed the pressure of the local community? Or did he simply consent to the rights invoked?[29]

Parents of draftees, with their constant and numerous petitions to gov-ernment, kept the authority of recruiters in check. Widows with one sup-porting son could demand his exemption from service; many actually did. This was the case of Carmen de Borches, who, in September 1834, asked for the release of her son, Esteban Dobal, a youngster from a poor neigh-borhood (Monserrat) press-ganged and "destined" for three years to the army.[30] She contended that her son was not a vagrant, as the police claimed, but a journeyman mason who provided with his wages sustenance for the whole family. Doña Borches stated clearly that her petition was founded in the law that granted these exemptions. The minister of government, after checking the information with the chief of police, the local justice, and the priest, had to agree: the police had made a mistake.

That year (1834) the ministry of government was swamped with petitions from mothers demanding the release of their sons. María de la Cruz Velázquez, for example, asked for the freedom of her son Toribio Guerreros (a forage supplier), arrested for vagrancy. She "implored" the governor "for the enforcement of the laws that protected honest and working men." Her son, she said, was not a vagrant and had not committed any crime. In a similar situation was Cisnona Quiroga, a woman from Flores whose son, Gregorio Andrade, had been arrested for vagrancy and assigned to the Escolta Battalion. Working as a cart driver, the boy was his mother's only support. To prove this, Dona Quiroga submitted a certificate of conduct extended by a militia captain. With equal intensity Nicolasa Machuca endeavored to get the release of her son Hilario Maya, arrested for his association with a delinquent. Doña Machuca rejected the idea that her son was a delinquent and urged authorities to check his employment condition. After his boss confirmed that the boy was employed in a bakery, Hilario was immediately freed.[31]

Little seems to have changed during Rosas's second government. Parents and neighbors continued to complain about arbitrary arrests and drafts. As before, official labels imposed on the young recruits were contested and legal exemptions vigorously defended. Without putting in doubt youngsters' need to serve the Federal Cause, parents strove to show that law was on their side, that their sons were honest workers deserving of government protection. Petitions were invariably addressed to Governor Rosas. He was the ultimate authority and, as such, the only person who could revise decisions made by justices, police chiefs, or military commanders. But as the civil wars demanded greater numbers of recruits, the governor became more reluctant to grant exceptions. Militiamen, after all, needed lessons in obedience and patriotism, the same as regular soldiers.

A Common Fate

Once in the barracks militiamen and soldiers shared a common fate. Here, military discipline replaced the law, arbitrary authority and corporal punishment took the place of neighbors' amicable relations, and the social differences seemed to be temporarily suspended. In time of war, as militia

17. Life in the Regiment: A Card Game. In regiments, there were moments of leisure time in which soldiers and officers shared a card game. This engraving emphasizes comradeship, harmony, and equality. Officers (two on the right) and soldiers (two on the left) wear the same marks of distinction: gold belts, lace drawers, and silver spurs. *Vivac*, after Favier, colored lithograph, 1844. Reproduced from B. del Carril, *Monumenta Iconográphica* (1964).

units were incorporated into a regiment of the regular army, the basic distinction between citizens-in-arms and forced recruits became irrelevant. From the perspective of the state, soldiers were either delinquents whose sentences had been converted into a paid contract or men who had joined the federalist armies out of commitment to the Federal Cause. On campaign, this difference too became elusive. All were reduced to the common fate of soldiers defending the federalist colors.

Perhaps this was the most important mistake of the Rosas administration: to undo in the practice of war what rural communities had painfully built over decades, the difference between militiaman and regular soldier. It was quite common for a militiaman to end up as a regular soldier, in the same way that it was common for a veteran once dismissed to enter the local militias. The army functioned as a site of punishment, even for milicianos. In 1849 militiaman Juan Constantino escaped his quarters by jumping over the walls. Because it was his second desertion, Commander Casto Cáseres had him arrested, secured by irons, and sentenced to serve four years in the Restaurador Battalion as a regular soldier.[32] That is, by deserting twice, Constantino lost his condition of militiaman and, consequently, his rights as a citizen.

This change of roles produced a radical leveling of unexpected consequences for the state. By uniting people of different social backgrounds and claims of citizenship, the army generated a social space quite different from that intended by the governor—a space in which protest and negotiation often complemented obedience and subordination. Indeed, it could be argued that the regiments on campaign acted as levelers of social differences, not only with regard to the difference between militiamen and regular soldiers, but also concerning important distinctions about regional origin and race. It was in the regiments that provincianos learned to cooperate with porteños, suspending their differences in order to negotiate with their superiors. It was in the regiments, that black men blended with soldiers of other racial backgrounds, for Rosas disbanded "colored" battalions and distributed free blacks throughout the different regiments. Regiments were a substitute for the prison system that, curiously, promised to treat its "inmates" as wage laborers, giving them pay, clothes, and a document of freedom (baja) once they reached their term. In 1832, the Subinspector de Campaña Elías Galván explained this apparent contradiction. Instead of allowing them to corrupt themselves in a prison, Rosas generously gave felons the chance to serve the fatherland. When entering the army, they made a contract in which they promised to defend the fatherland, to act honestly, and never to desert. In exchange for this, the state promised them wages, uniforms, and their release at the end of their term.[33] In this way, punishment turned into a contractual relationship. This left the door open for a variety of subaltern interpretations and interventions. Some soldiers considered that certain deficiencies in the documents that validated this "contract" (the filiación) were sufficient reason for their dismissal; others took the delays in the delivery of food and uniforms as a motive for abandoning the ranks. If the state failed to fulfill its part of the agreement, soldiers did not feel obligated to continue serving.

With their everyday actions, soldiers transformed this disciplinary space into a territory of negotiation. Gradually, there was a transition between coercion and contract. Soldiers forced officers to comply with this contract. Officers had to see that rations were distributed evenly, that payments were made on time, that uniforms were replaced periodically, that the terms of soldiers' destination and release were respected. On occasion, soldiers tried to renegotiate the terms of the original contract; in particular, they tried to minimize the amount of disciplinary punishment and attain some respect from their superiors. Arbitrary and humiliating treatment was considered intolerable. Though the terms and conditions of the negotiation varied, it is clear that the federalist armies maintained readiness for combat because they combined incentives with penalties and were ready to attend to the most urgent claims of soldiers.

The need for new recruits in a labor-scarce economy forced the military to offer economic incentives. Despite the fact that many of the regular soldiers had been sentenced, at the end of their term they were offered sums of money to reenlist.[34] At times of intense recruitment, the governor sent envoys to the provinces to enlist paid soldiers (*enganchados*). Rosas and other leaders of the time understood that, by itself, patriotism was not strong enough to maintain a well-disciplined military force. In a letter to Balcarce, Rosas explained how the militiamen who had so bravely saved the city from political anarchy soon disbanded and took jobs here and there. In fact, most of his own peons were gone. To form new militias it was crucial to offer economic incentives. Rosas wrote, "The inducement of interest should not be lacking when honor is not sufficient incentive."[35] Aside from the income they received for military drills, militiamen once enlisted for a campaign received the payment of soldiers. And, quite naturally, they lost the protection of their own commanders and were subject to the same rigid discipline applied to regular soldiers.

By design or by adaptation, regiments became sites of economic negotiation. How else to explain the multiple incentives granted to soldiers? The bonuses in money (*socorros*) paid during campaigns (in some cases, proportional to seniority); the distribution of hides among the soldiery after the slaughter; the ration of sugar and tobacco conveniently increased during situations of impending invasion; the government concern that soldiers receive their pay "in hand"; the officers' practice of granting "work permits" when rations or paychecks were delayed—all these incentives were the practical results of a continuous bargaining process that took place within military garrisons, between officers and soldiers.

Bargaining by Desertion

In March 1845, Colonel Vicente González read a report filed by a high-ranking officer, Major José Morales, about an act of intolerable insubordination: in front of the troops soldier Pascual Escalante had defied his officer's orders. The report read: "This soldier, belonging to the Dismissed squadron, to the first company under the command of Captain Antonio Sosa, having [this chief] ordered that all companies be arranged by height, this soldier should have moved to the third company but, questioned about his name *he refused to pronounce it* [my emphasis] and, questioned again, he answered : "Why should I say it? for little it will last [que para qué lo había de decir, que poco había de durar]."[36]

After another lieutenant inquired about his name with similar negative result, Major Morales himself went to observe this act of insubordination. There, in front of the troops, was a soldier refusing to pronounce his name, a soldier who, in addition, was hinting at a possible desertion (i.e., changing his name). Major Morales asked him the same question and the soldier responded as before. Escalante was then put in the calaboose. A few days later, as the fort faced an imminent attack by Indians, he was set free and ordered to prepare for combat. He obeyed, and once mounted on his horse and about to march, he commented, "Now they will see! These officers given to strike their men, [they] who gain honors at the expense of the soldiers and only on these occasions remember us."

Escalante's lamentation and threat were justified. At the time, Urquiza's forces were confronting Rivera's army in the Estado Oriental; a few soldiers left in the littoral were supposed to defend the frontier from Indian attacks. Intensified work, in Escalante's view, demanded at least a quota of good treatment and recognition. Officers instead were taking credit for the soldiers' bravery while treating them to the same old didactic of beatings. Escalante's defiant voice, though unable to right the wrong, served to redirect the prestige of combat to those who deserved it and, at the same time, to remind officers that they depended on the soldiery and should treat them better. If they did not. . . . The soldiers who listened to Escalante's comments probably completed the sentence in whispers.

Within the barracks such acts of open individual defiance were rare. More commonly, soldiers showed their dissatisfaction about treatment and payment through a variety of nonverbal actions: tardiness, disobedience, drunkenness, and slow work. Away from the officers' gaze, they might proffer insults, utter threats, and conspire, but in the presence of officers they had to obey and be quiet. Some engaged in physical confrontation with officers, but only in the taverns, where their aggressions could be attributed to excessive drinking, or where corporals, sergeants, and soldiers assumed momentarily the condition of free and equal men. Occasionally, soldiers would answer orders ironically or pretend not to understand the command.

These actions and attitudes were the means of a passive resistance that resulted in the gradual erosion of discipline, a problem that every c.o. had to confront. These actions were seen by commanders as manifestations of a natural inclination of peasants and rural laborers to resist all forms of authority. Like Escalante's veiled threats and ironic commentary, these were the weapons of a war of attrition waged against the imposition of arbitrary punishment and the uneven distribution of economic benefits. Terms like *indisciplinados* (undisciplined), *incorregibles* (incorrigible), and *desobedientes* (disobedient) were used to convey the difficulties of instilling discipline in "naturally" rebellious men and, at the same time, the innocuous nature of their resistance. Yet commanders knew that these quotidian acts of disobedience could lead to open rebellion or mass desertions if not checked in time.

To be sure, soldiers were constantly probing the limits of tolerance and paternalism of their superiors, personally asking for leaves, socorros (financial aid), and uniforms. They were, indeed, continuously renegotiating their contract with the nation. But once their individual grievances were rejected or unattended to, they were left with few options but to desert. Soldiers unhappy with the treatment they received found that individually, their demands could be easily dismissed.[37] How to proceed when officers were oblivious to the demands of soldiers? How to assert demands for respect when corporal punishment and bad language were accepted as natural elements of "military discipline" by the officers corps? How to impress on them the urgency to consider soldiers' "nudity" or undue work? In these cases, soldiers had to act collectively, threatening officers with mass abandonment of the garrison.

Army garrisons, imagined by Rosas as sites of reformation of criminals, became the stage of a bargaining process between officers and soldiers over issues of pay, uniforms, rations, and leaves. Groups involving soldiers, corporals, and sergeants carried out these negotiations. Methods of informal representation—a group of soldiers delegating authority to a sergeant or corporal—and some degree of extortion seem to have characterized these interactions. As the threat implicit in all these negotiations was mass desertion it would not be inappropriate to call these actions *bargaining by threat of desertion*.[38] This type of collective protest reaffirmed a contractual view of soldiering and, at the same time, invoked a type of popular politics based on deliberation, rumor, and group pressure.

A few cases will help to illustrate the nature of these interactions. One of them was reported to the inquisitor at Santos Lugares in 1843. After the battles that defeated Mascarilla, a group of soldiers headed by four sergeants struck (or walked out) against the captain of the San Pedro garrison demanding salaries, clothing, and "vices." Unsatisfied with the officer's response, they deserted en masse. Sixty men marched south with the intention of presenting themselves to Colonel Vicente González. Before they arrived, another chief, Colonel Martín Santa Coloma, came and persuaded them to stay in his unit. He promised the men clothing and to speak in their favor to Governor Rosas. Most soldiers accepted the deal and stayed.[39] Walking out was, apparently, an effective mechanism of negotiation.

Discontent could be expressed through other means. Inside their garrisons, soldiers tried various ways to make their demands heard by their commanding officers. Verbalizing their grievances in front of the troops, sending threatening letters, or circulating rumors that a mass desertion was in the making, soldiers could get the attention of officialdom. Few of these interactions between soldiers and officers reached the official transcript. The cases I found refer to frontier regiments, peripheral sites far away from Rosas's headquarters that were, nonetheless, of paramount importance for the Confederation's defense. In these cases, soldiers negotiated work conditions and payment, maintaining the possibility of a mass desertion.

In late January 1839 the commander of Fort Patagones, the southernmost garrison of the Confederation, found an anonymous letter addressed to him in his room.[40] According to its author, soldier Juan Collante, the letter was a sort of lampoon advising (or warning) the *señor coronel* that he should try "to pay the people within two days or otherwise face the consequences." Disguised as a friend, the anonymous writer warned the colonel of an impending attack to his person (*que no se descuidase*). Suspecting that the letter threatened something more than his physical integrity, the colonel ordered an investigation. The proceedings uncovered a desertion plan involving at least eight soldiers and two junior officers.

From the statements contributed during the investigation, part of this conspiracy can be reconstructed. Two soldiers, Juan Santos Villagra and Juan Allende, had induced soldier Juan Collante to write the threatening letter. Soldier José Antonio González had spread the word of the coming desertion, inviting other soldiers to join. Soldier Páez, for example, recounted how González approached him on his way to cut firewood and hinted about the plan. Sergeant Dupré, González, and Iturres (one of the most veteran soldiers) had conversed about the plan in the nearby tavern.[41] At this meeting González had promised to take soldiers back to their native land and to give them all that was needed for the trip. To obtain the cash needed to facilitate their escape, Sergeant Dupré agreed to sell some clothes. Under pressure, González provided other details of the plan. The group was to meet in the granary, take weapons and riding apparel, lasso horses in the country, and ride in the direction of Buenos Aires. On the way, they would stop at a rural tavern to get some civilian clothes. The timing of the desertion was to coincide with the expected "French invasion." Those who had met at the tavern also discussed the possibility of liberating the prisoners at the calaboose and of joining sixty deserters said to be camping near Tres Arroyos.

The plan was threatening to the authorities for various reasons: it involved junior officers conspiring with common soldiers; the conspiracy pointed to the existence of spaces out of the control of the officers corps (the woods surrounding the fort and the tavern) where conspiracies could develop; it showed the awareness soldiers had of political events (the possibility of French invasion and the existence of bands of deserters) and their foresight in planning resources (cash, weapons, horses, and disguises). Soldiers, in fact, had been able to combine oral and written forms of communication to organize support and threaten the fort authorities. Consequently, the military court issued stiff sentences to those implicated. The four soldiers accused of sedition and mutinous behavior—Collante, Villagra, González, and Allende—were executed by firing squad in front of the whole company on the morning of February 2, 1839. Iturres and Pueblas, charged with attempted desertion, were sentenced to an extension of service. The rest received only "correctional" penalties.

The episode illustrates the difficulties of collective bargaining in a highly sensitive and politically charged atmosphere. A collective negotiation about the payment of wages could end in a military tribunal and its promoters in front of the firing squad. The suspicion of treason—the possibility that deserters might join the enemy forces—that was associated with any group desertion compounded officers' anxieties. In the context of a civil war, soldiers' challenges to authority could become politically explosive. The medium chosen to communicate the soldiers' concerns, the threatening letter, served as a proof of the "conspiracy" and implied an inversion of the traditional division separating officers (literate) and soldiers (illiterate).

A different method of bargaining was essayed at Fort Independencia (Tandil) in October 1837. Soldiers Hilario Mena and Pedro Carrasco and Sergeant Fulgencio Iturres were accused of mutiny.[42] (Earlier that morning, Sergeant Iturres had announced to the fort's commander that the forces were dissatisfied with the work they were doing and saddened by the lack of payment, and that they planned to speak out in the formation.) From Iturres's own testimony, we know that, while cutting grass, a few soldiers discussed the anomaly of performing "private work" and the need to be compensated for it, and agreed to present their claim to the officers as soon as they returned to the fort. From then on, the process of negotiation followed certain steps. Iturres first presented their concerns to Major Francisco Palao; the work they were doing, he told him, was to the benefit of a private person and not the state; consequently, they expected to be paid for it.[43] Without a satisfactory answer from the major, they decided to go public, presenting their claim to their peers.

Once the troop was in formation, the commander demanded that whoever had something to complain about should step forward. Only Carrasco, Mena, and Sergeant Iturres did. Iturres, representing the group, said "that they did not want to cut *juncos* [rush] near the new port any longer for this was private work, and not state work." The commander then explained to the troops that the work aimed at building ranchos (thatched-roof huts) for the militiamen who took care of the horses. Their protest, he insisted, was wrong-headed. After this, Sergeant Iturres took the stage, repeated the men's refusal to work and, turning to the troops, urged them to speak out: "Have you never seen a major in front of you before? He is a man like the rest of us." Iturres's attempt to counteract the fear of the soldiers by leveling the commander's authority did not work: the rest of the soldiers stayed put.

Why the strategy did not work is difficult to say. Perhaps Iturres's rhetoric was not persuasive to the rest of the soldiers; the rumor circulated that Iturres wanted to stir trouble to murder an officer who had taken "his" woman. Perhaps the soldiers' fear of confronting authority was too great, or the major's argument had clarified the confusion between private and state labor. Clearly, Iturres and the two soldiers had not gathered a critical number of votes in their favor before making public their protest. Other soldiers confessed not to have understood the nature of Iturres's complaints. Soldier Hilario Mena, one of the mutineers, viewed their failure as a wrong choice of medium: the sergeant should have put his complaint in writing rather than speaking out in the formation.

Another type of negotiation, one that involved a better bargaining position on the part of soldiers, occurred outside of the barracks. "Dispersed" soldiers or deserters bargained their reincorporation into service with civilian or military chiefs. Often, these groups sought a pardon together with some economic benefits. In practice, they were choosing their own commanders and imposing certain conditions for their continued support to the war effort. The authorities were always ready to hear their cases, particularly if the deserters or *dispersos* constituted a large group.

The account of Francisco Iturrieta, a cattle drover from San Juan arrested in Villa Luján in 1845, illustrates the bargaining power of *dispersos* (soldiers dispersed after combat, temporarily separated from their units).[44] Having returned to San Pedro after serving for three months on the coast of the Paraná River, Iturrieta witnessed an act of collective negotiation between a group of dispersed soldiers (like himself) and the justice of the locality,

Benito Veraco. Fifty dispersed soldiers belonging to different companies under General Mansilla assembled in San Pedro and collectively asked the justice of the peace for passports to travel to Rosas's headquarters. The justice unable to comply with the request, promised *vicios* and rations instead and asked the soldiers to wait until he received orders on the matter. Soon, an officer sent by General Mansilla arrived and ordered the men to return to their companies. The justice communicated this to the soldiers (gathered in the militia quarters) and, to his surprise, "all in a single voice [*todos a una voz*]" rejected the order. They demanded from the justice their weapons, kept in custody since their arrival. Two days later, the men received news that other dispersed soldiers camping in the surroundings of San Pedro had also defied the order to return, so they continued their march south, probably with the expectation of negotiating with another chief, if not the governor himself.

Another story tells of a negotiation between a justice and a large group of deserters living in the forested areas of the Paraná delta. Juan Romero was a soldier who had had enough of war and maltreatment.[45] He had fought first for the unitarios, then joined General Oribe's army in Banda Oriental, then deserted, lived in the islands for a while, and then worked cutting trees in the neighborhood of San Pedro. Next, he had moved back to the forested islands to avoid General Mansilla's massive recruitment efforts. He was assured that he would be punished for avoiding service, so he decided not to return. He lived in the islands until, in 1845, he heard about Rosas's decree pardoning deserters who volunteered back into the army.

Romero sent a woman to confirm the news in San Pedro and to begin negotiations with the local justice. Through his female negotiator he let the justice know that during his long stay in the islands, he had assembled a group of sixty-five men, all deserters or fugitives from justice, and that they were ready to join the army if certain conditions were met. The justice was to speak with General Mansilla and ask *indultos* for all his men. He had to demand for Romero the rank of captain and the command over his island comrades. The deal struck, Romero came to San Pedro, escorted by four of his men, and was ready to take his next assignment: spotting enemy ships along the Paraná River.

What can we make of these episodes? We see groups of soldiers, represented by sergeants or corporals, collectively addressing their officers on questions of salary, clothing, and rations. From the inside, they had few options to express their grievances: they could speak out in front of the formation, send a veiled threat to the commanding officer, or organize a collective desertion. Military garrisons had their "back stages," places where soldiers could talk about injustice and the ways to redress it. Once outside of their garrisons, soldiers' bargaining power increased. They could strike a deal with a commander they trusted or continue their perambulation through the countryside (or hiding in the delta) until the time was ripe for a successful negotiation.

These negotiations and conspiracies force us to rethink the possibilities and power of the subaltern. The reason these actions ever reached the public transcript relates to the trouble they caused those in charge of the design and execution of military campaigns. This type of collective action—more than the ironic commentary of a veteran—reasserted the contractual basis of military service. Regardless of the mechanism by which soldiers had been recruited (voluntary or sentenced), they could renegotiate their agreements over time. Moreover, once they were outside and acted as a collective, soldiers' decisions acquired political transcendence. They could negotiate the continuity of their contribution to the war effort and, if their claims were not satisfied, move on to another battalion, pitting one commander against the other for material gains and responsible leadership.

About the efficaciousness of this type of bargaining little can be said. As the story of soldier Escalante demonstrates, individual defiance did not alleviate the situation of soldiers; it only made officers aware of the constant possibility of desertion. Collective protests were more successful, but only under certain circumstances. Clearly, those already on the move had stronger bargaining power than those confined to the barracks. In this regard, soldiers were no different from itinerant peons. Quite likely, these cases capture only instances of a trial-and-error process by which soldiers probed the limits of authority within the army. As soldiers moved from one garrison to the next, from voluntary service to compulsory and humiliating work, their experience might have helped them perfect the mechanisms of bargaining and protest.

These conspiracies and group negotiations, because they presupposed collective choices made outside of ideology, were quite menacing to the federal system. If the soldiers' support and patriotism depended on material benefits, the whole edifice of the Saintly Federal Cause could fall due to a momentary lack of funds or a maldistribution of wages and provisions. Soldiers could, as a matter of fact, find better terms among the unitarios. Generally, individual rebelliousness was not considered politically dangerous, for soldiers would not dare to openly criticize porteño federalism and its leader. It was only when soldiers' defiance and irony hinted at the possibility of mutiny or mass desertion that comments like that of Escalante attracted the attention of commanders.[46] The line dividing noncooperation and open defiance was thin; individual dissatisfaction could turn into collective protest in a moment. Because of this, military chiefs were always on the lookout for conspiracies of mutinies and mass desertions. They knew that both belonged to a type of politics that was uncontrollable, a politics rooted in subaltern experience that blended secrecy, mass desertion, and bargaining.

The Power of Rumors

At a time of very limited diffusion of the printed press, rumor was a dangerous political weapon. It disseminated with great rapidity, exaggerated the magnitude of political or military events, and could easily turn around public opinion (about a policy, a candidate, or a faction).[47] Understandably, the authorities paid close attention to rumors as both a measure of forthcoming events and a threat to the stability of the Federal Cause. An apparently innocuous remark could become uncontrollable if spread sufficiently throughout the social fabric. Hence, it was essential for the stability of Rosas's government to constantly test the state of opinion of the country by collecting and investigating political rumor.

In March 1831, for example, Rosas ordered the justice of Guardia de Luján, Julián Solveyra, to investigate retired Captain Gregorio Iramaían. Solveyra collected various rumors in town and sent them back to Rosas. The rumors confirmed Rosas's suspicions. Some said Iramaían had sent military equipment to Santiago del Estero; others asserted that he had been persuading santiagueños not to enlist in the federal army or in the militias; others pointed out that Iramaían's wife had been spreading false news that federal Governor Ibarra had been assassinated. But perhaps the most damaging "evidence" against Iramaían was the rumor that he had expressed his political opinion in public—an opinion that, in the eyes of many neighbors, belonged to the repertoire of the hated unitarios.[48]

In 1838 justice Roque Baudrix discovered a conspiracy in Monsalvo headed by military officers and local proprietors. To investigate the extent and scope of dissatisfaction with the government Baudrix sent an envoy (an alcalde) to Quequén Grande and the surroundings of Sierra de la Tinta "to find out if there were rumors."[49] This envoy used the cooperation of local ranchers to inform the government about "any news" in their districts. Keeping the rumors on the side of government—as a means to identify and unmask political adversaries—was essential to the stability of the regime.

After 1839, the regime resorted more systematically to terror and expropriation to eliminate and discredit the opposition. The scrutiny of political opinion became stricter; justices of the peace reported any public expression that smacked of opposition. Losing in the military front and unable to express views in public, unitario sympathizers found more subtle ways of conveying their dissatisfaction. One of these was political humor. In private, everyday conversations or in local taverns, jokes with a political bite circulated, giving people greater room for evaluating the state of the republic. Some of these jokes with an obvious oppositional stand were captured on the record and their tellers arrested.

Neighbor D. Antonio Delgado was arrested in Fortín de Areco in 1839 for "speaking badly" of the government. Among the evidence contributed by other neighbors was the following joke, told at the local tavern: "That after her death, Doña Encarnación [Rosas's mother] had gone up to Heaven and had said that this was not her place, for everything was light blue [the unitarios' color]. From there she went down to Purgatory and said that this too was not her place, for there were too many 'black backs' [lomos negros; Rosas's opponents in the city]. From there she went to Hell and found herself in the company of late General Facundo Quiroga and late Governor Manuel Dorrego. She said that this was her place, for all were federales and they were all red."[50]

This apparently innocuous joke was explosive. It presented politics in the moral planes constructed by Christian doctrine—a frame of reference immediately accessible to paysanos—and reversed the meaning of the chromatic imagery of federalism, associating light blue with Heaven and red with Hell. For telling this joke Delgado was imprisoned. The evidence against him was all hearsay, for, as the justice of the peace acknowledged, he was unable to report who gave him the information ("these have been voices he heard"). The justice was only sure of the report of alcalde Quintanilla, who heard Delgado say that "the goods that His Excellency had promised had turned into thorns, for he had betrayed the offerings he made about the tranquility of the province and about the circulation of metallic [currency]."

In a culture dominated by oral forms of transmission of information, rumor, hearsay, jokes, and gossip were the very stuff of politics. Spreading rumors was clearly a political act. Unitarios made ample use of this weapon, disseminating "news" destined to create fear among the population and confusion among the federalist commanders. In February 1840, the justice of Lobos informed Buenos Aires that an "immensity of deserters" had left the garrison of Dolores and were assaulting the neighbors' persons and property. According to this "news," the commander of the Third Regiment advised neighbors to gather weapons and horses and organize in self-defense. Rosas, in possession of better intelligence, explained to the justice of Lobos that the desertions had been few and that the exaggerations of their numbers and their supposed depredations were all fabrications of the unitarios.[51]

The use of political rumor was not new; what surprised state agents was that poor paysanos were acting in this manner. Deserters, poor peasants, Indians, and ex-slaves were contributing "voices" to the confusing whispers about the state of the fatherland. In March 1845 Angel Córdoba, an exemplary soldier with long service to the cause, was put in the calaboose and whipped for spreading tendentious rumors. He "spread voices" that near San Pedro a party belonging to Governor Echagüe's escort passed by and said that they were on their way to the Chaco to join unitario Mascarilla. He added that many of General Echagüe's people were joining Mascarilla, and for that reason, all men were being taken forcefully to Santa Fé. This was dangerous talk, for if many soldiers at the camp believed this to be true, their confidence in the hegemony of the Federal Cause could wane, doing serious damage to the corps' morale. Four months later, a menacing rumor reached the southern frontier of Tapalqué, where Catriel and his "friendly Indians" were settled. A Spanish-speaking Indian by the name of José Catrié was spreading "alarming voices" that Mascarilla had already entered into the city of Santa Fé with three thousand men and was killing everyone (*tocando a degüello*). He said also that Baigorria's forces were ready to join him.[52] Catrié was a federal soldier who had deserted from the Salto garrison in response to his captain's cruel treatment. He said he had heard the news from other deserters who had assaulted him on the road.

Even more threatening to the political stability of the frontier was the rumor, spread in the midst of the unitario uprising in the south, that Rosas had died. The rumor became important when many allied *caciques* began to reconsider their allegiance to the Federal Cause. Wary of the political implications of this rumor, the commander of Fort Independencia sent a translator (*lenguarás*) to "make the Indians understand the error in which they had been placed by those who had led them to believe that our Illustrious Restorer was dead, and other absurdities of this kind."[53] Lieutenant Romero's concern was justified. Convinced that Rosas was dead, the Indians settled in Tapalqué had already taken arms, and most of the Indian soldiers at Independencia were abandoning the fort. Weeks after the southern revolt was quelled (November 1839), envoys from Rosas were still trying to persuade Indian chiefs that the governor was alive and that they should return to their military posts.

Controlling the news about the victories or defeats of the federal armies was of paramount importance to the Rosista state. Fernando Guzmán was arrested in Arrecifes in February 1844 for spreading false news that the forces of unitario Rivera had defeated the Federalist Vanguard Division. Tomás Bustamante, a policeman at Buenos Aires, was arrested a month earlier for publicly contradicting an officer when the latter informed his subordinates about the recent victories of the Confederate Army. Tendentious or premonitory, news about the other enemy, the Indians, also required close supervision. Though justices and military commanders customarily reported every bit of news about forthcoming Indian invasions, their reports often conveyed their concerns about the accuracy of this news. Alarming "voices" about Indian attacks were, after all, a common tactic used by unitarios to create panic among the population. Still clear in the memories of many federalists was the Indian uprising of 1836 at Bahía Blanca, initiated by false news disseminated by unitarios.[54]

Rumor was a double-edged sword. It could threaten the powerful as well as the subaltern. Military authorities could use it to prevent desertions and maintain discipline in the ranks.[55] But rumor could also be used against the powerful, creating suspicion about their political loyalties and services. José Ignacio Gómez, an alcalde and cattle raiser from Chapaleufú with proven service to the Federal Party, was thrown into trouble when he fell prey to a rumor. The news circulated that one hundred men had gathered in the Sierra de Paulino with the intention of murdering rancher Daniel Arana. To alert his superiors, Gómez sent notices to various district justices. Later, it was discovered that such a plan never existed, but the rumor itself served to destroy Gómez's credibility. Rumors could also be used to create an imaginary shield around a person otherwise devoid of influence. Prisoner Juan Angel Ullúa, for instance, found it to his advantage to spread news that he was soon to be freed, that a "character of great influence was coming to town to exempt him." Although the justice of the peace of Cañuelas knew this to be a lie (he had examined Ullúa's paper of exception and found it to be forged), the rumor itself brought fear to the policeman who arrested him and later moved the justice of San Vicente to free the prisoner.[56]

The type of rumor spread by soldiers, peasants, and Indians conveyed less a political opinion (as was the case with the rumors spread by unitarios) than a general concern for the stability of the fatherland and for the injustices created by those who conducted war. In several instances, rumor was a form of getting back at the authorities for abuses committed against soldiers and peons. Soldiers angry at bad treatment, lack of pay, or corruption of officers were the most likely to spread rumors about impending Indian invasions, battles lost by federales, or unitario military prowess.

Curiously, those accused of spreading rumors had generally rendered long and important service to the Federal Cause. The target and scope of their complaints (usually the military institution or the justices of the peace) were more limited and, because of this, lacked the messianic or religious tones found in unitario rumors and jokes.

Rumors were an important weapon of the powerless to voice their discontent. Lower-class rumor referred to impending military invasions, to the casualties inflicted by the enemy forces, and to the power of soldiers in influencing the result of campaigns. Countering an official rhetoric that was always triumphant and, at times, eschatological, rumors reestablished the possibility of reversal in the war. If certain chiefs could gather sufficient support (from santafesinos, Indians, or discouraged federales), the enemy could win. Also significant was the role of rumor in asserting the cruelty of the war; the fact that both armies executed prisoners, decapitated peasants, and raped women all across the land was often made explicit through rumor. If many parts of the political body of the nation were still assaulted by fear, it was because the promises of tranquility made to them by the federalist leadership remained unfulfilled. More important, rumors circulated the politically explosive notion that soldiers, if they decided to do so, could shift the course of war simply by voting with their feet against an unpopular military chief.

Conclusions: Political Acts

Rosas's secretaries at Santos Lugares accumulated volumes of politically threatening information coming from the state's periphery. But they were unable to use it efficiently chiefly because it was difficult to separate truth from fabrication. The social proximity between officers and soldiers permeated military garrisons with a popular understanding of politics that was destabilizing to the regime. The means used by paysanos to circulate relevant political information (rumor, hearsay, jokes) filtered into military garrisons, feeding soldiers' ways of resisting arbitrary punishment and material deprivation (conspiracy to rebel, threat of desertion). To the dismay of local authorities engaged in minute control of people's opinions, jokes, hearsay, and rumors continued to defy the regime's hegemony, creating doubts about its powers, popularity, and sanctity.

Soldiers' understanding of politics linked peasants' contributions to the Federalist Cause to the maintenance of certain basic rights. It subordinated military leadership to popular opinion and turned military garrisons into fields of negotiation and deliberation. Military commanders found important fissures in discipline. They discovered that whipping, the calaboose, and strong language did not deter soldiers from demanding rations, "vices," wages, and good treatment. Nor did exemplary executions serve to contain the massive problem of desertions. A popular material culture and the promises of the rights of the postrevolutionary leadership countered the urgencies of the holy war and the cause of federalism.

Insofar as rumors generated in the interior of military garrisons spread to the sphere of rural sociability (taverns, horse races, roundups, and festivities), Rosas's disciplinary project had little chance of success. As long as soldiers' stories circulated among paysanos, the realities of war and the experience of resistance could not be easily suppressed. Soldiers would continue to evaluate their officers' actions, not in terms of patriotic duty, but in relation to the notions of equality, respect, personal independence, and well-being that constituted the moral world of paysanos. Based on these same notions, the men who populated the towns and hamlets of the province continued to resist the intrusions of military power in their lives. Refusing service, deserting, spreading rumors that questioned the official rhetoric about the war, and making public the inequalities of recruitment and the sacrifice of the poor, they left open the venues for the circulation of an alternative (popular) public opinion.

The threat of this sort of popular politics to the stability of the regime was quite real. Not in vain, the agents of the regime kept measuring the state of public opinion: collecting rumors, drawing up lists of supporters and noncommitted, looking for unitario expressions in the clothes of peasants and on the walls of country stores. If not controlled, rumors could open the space for noncooperative or adversarial positions. Soldiers could change sides and influential neighbors could refuse their appointments and turn their militias against the state. Insurrections in frontier garrisons and lack of cooperation among rural militiamen constituted an ever-present possibility.

Before the forces of the Grand Army (Ejército Grande) could assemble and start the final offensive against the Rosista army in January 1852, the town of Rosario began to show signs of a political reversal that anticipated the fall of Rosas. According to Pedro Gómez, a sergeant in the forces of General Echagüe, at the end of December 1851, Rosario was experiencing a commotion of singular proportions.[57] Months earlier, rumors circulated that Urquiza was coming and that Rosario would support the rebel instead of defending Rosas. Seamstresses and ranchers alike talked of the impending war. Though General Echagüe sent officers with troops to calm the excitement and counter the rumors, the militias began to disobey their officers and organize independently. When Gómez entered the town on the morning of December 25: "Nobody was able to explain to him what was happening. He heard the sounds of the drums, and he saw the *cívicos* running in different directions until all came to the Square and, with them, the Commander General's escort. At this point, a smith who came from Commander Fernandez's camp entered the Square with a sword in his hand (half of the urban militias were there, the rest were three blocks away) and shouted, among the *cívicos*: *Patria, Libertad, Muera el Tirano y Viva Urquiza!* [Fatherland, Liberty, Death to the Tyrant and Life to Urquiza]. To which all responded *Viva!*"

Quietly, Gómez escaped and hid on the outskirts of the town until he could reach Pavón the next day. There he heard news that the rebel cívicos (urban militias) had elected a new officers corps and deposed the old authorities, including the major and the commander general. Governor Echagüe was considered a trickster (*pícaro*) who still supported Rosas, while the city militias wanted to "be by themselves and not to join or depend on anybody."

What made this insurrection possible? Rumor. A rumor spread through kitchens, stores, taverns, and militia quarters that a new military leader, Urquiza, had defied the power of the Restorer and was marching down to depose him. But also the decision, rhetorical skills, and outrage of common people. In a moment, the old notions of fatherland and liberty had turned against Rosas. Suddenly, the Restorer of the Laws had turned into a Tyrant in the *Vivas* of the crowd. The Rosario uprising was not a ranchers' conspiracy, as the Southern Rebellion (1839) had been. This was an insurrection lead by militiamen, the citizens in arms, against the abuses of a military leadership. The bold decision of Rosario's militias was preceded by a string of abuses committed by General Echagüe against the civilian population.[58]

Already in 1843–1845 the soldiers of garrisons near the delta (near San Pedro and Camp Pavón) had "voted out" some generals and joined more humane and cooperative commanders. Since then, subalterns had been whispering about the possibility of an alternative political leadership. Their collective protests together with the rumors circulated among the towns' artisans and peons created the context in which the reversal of February 1852 was possible. When the Grand Army (the forces led by Urquizo) entered the field of Caseros, they found very little resistance from the federalist battalions. According to Rottjer (1937, 32), these battalions did not really engage in frontal combat. Several squadrons, those that did not rebel and kill their chiefs, either disbanded or surrendered in passive formation. Federalist soldiers showed the invading forces their clean rifles as proof that they had not fired. Perhaps, as several historians have suggested, it was Rosas's own soldiers who made the political decision not to defend the Dictator in 1852. Perhaps this was a cumulative result of years of bargaining inside the garrisons, a learning process that turned soldiers' economic grievances into political acts.

CHAPTER 9

Deserters' Reasons

Les alvierto solamente
y esto a ninguno lo asombre,
pues muchas veces el hombre
tiene que hacer de ese modo:
convinieron entre todos
en mudar alli de nombre.

I'll merely say,
and let no one be surprised by this,
for often a man has to act thus:
it was agreed by all
that they should change their names,
then and there.

—José Hernández, *Martín Fierro*,
translated by Henry A. Holmes

In their face-to-face encounters with recruiters, justices of the peace, and military commanders at Santos Lugares, prisoners were asked to justify their desertion. Knowing why they felt entitled or motivated to leave the ranks was of extreme importance to military chiefs, to the governor, and to the future of the Federal Cause, dependent almost entirely on the continuity of the war effort. Deserters too had a vested interest in explaining their behavior. If they could show that, despite their best wishes to serve the Federal Cause, they were forced by circumstance to abandon their battalions, their punishment might be reduced. But their stories were not only a reflection of what authorities wanted to hear. Beyond the explanations lay *reasons*: arguments rooted in common understandings about appropriate and reasonable behavior; appeals for comprehension of and benevolence toward the needs, expectations, and frustrations of common folks. These reasons consisted of a combination of defiance and lament that expressed the position and perspective (I do not dare to call it "consciousness") of these quite assertive political-economic-social agents.[1]

Deserters' stories open the door for an analysis of the moral economy of the rural poor.[2] Their preoccupations with needs, family relations, military service, undue punishment, violence, and political commitment take us into a terrain relatively unexplored in Argentine historiography: the question of subalterns' voices and resistance. Their arguments speak of the possibility of the powerless to construct meaningful subjectivities vis-à-vis the powerful. Their "confessions" were necessarily confined to a bounded colloquial space: the unequal conversation between the authority and the delinquent-soldier. Yet, they provide us with clippings and profiles of subalterns' experience and consciousness. Deserters' reasons articulate a moral discourse about the state that calls into question the equality and respect promised by an imagined primordial contract and, at the same time, constructs subject positions that underscore the social, cultural, and political tensions and differences masked by that contract.

In this chapter, I trace the contours, motifs, and organizing principles of deserters' stories as means to uncover aspects of these subjects that have remained hidden, obscured, or subsumed under the weight of literary and folkloric representations of the gaucho-soldier. Deserters' concern for family, their search for a place in the community of vecinos (neighbors), their quite political demands on the military establishment, and their economic interventions appear as the most important of these aspects. To unravel the relationship between subaltern language and experience, I follow a straight trajectory. First, I examine deserters' reasons for abandoning service. Next, I discuss the itineraries followed by deserters in their search for jobs, safety, and community. Then, I analyze their strategies for social and political reinsertion and conclude with a reflection on the tone, scope, and directionality of deserters' voices.

Explaining Desertion: Four Idioms

A simple tabulation of deserters' answers helps us begin to appreciate the significance and hierarchy of their explanations (see Table 9.1). The reasons given by deserters tend to concentrate in four areas: punishment, needs, family, and disease.[3] The fear of punishment or the actual suffering of whipping, shackles, or imprisonment prompted the greatest proportion of deserters. Explanations concerning needs—the lack of adequate rations, clothing, or money—combined with those related to soldiers' desire to earn a living. Next are motivations related to family and locality of origin, and then claims related to soldiers' health. Other reasons, not unconnected to these four, refer to the conflictive relations between

TABLE 9.1 Reasons for Desertion

Reasons Given	Number of Cases	Percentage
Return to family	19	17.8
Return to province	8	
Fear of punishment[1]	17	21.0
Punishment/ill treatment[2]	15	
Needs and lack of clothes[3]	18	
Refused license/leave	5	19.0
To escape forced/unpaid labor	6	
To recover from illness	16	17.8
Did not return after a leave	11	
Refused to serve an officer or regiment	7	6.6
Disputes w/comrades and officers	3	
Invitation of comrades	4	4.6
Offered a job or protection	3	
To avoid combat	7	4.6
To escape a "disgrace"[4]	3	2.0
Other	10	6.6
TOTAL	152	100.0

Notes: [1]After losses of military equipment and other violations of military rules
[2]Corporal punishment, imprisonment, insults
[3]Including the need to find a job
[4]Knife fights causing wounds or death
Source: Filiaciones (N=525)

officers and soldiers in the barracks, to the lure of the outside world (jobs and protectors), and to the influence of gambling and group pressure in soldiers' lives.[4]

These "reasons" were more than tactical choices within the rhetorical repertoire of the rural poor.[5] At one level, these groupings of reasons operated as *motivations* generating certain types of behavior. At another level, they served as *explanations* of perceived violations of social norms; implied in this is a subaltern reading or interpretation of political affairs. At yet another level, they were *articulations* of a particular language, one that located deserters' discontent within the discourse of the fatherland and the promises of the republic. Four idioms constituted this discourse: those of punishment, the family, mutilated bodies, and needs/paid labor. Each called into question one aspect of rural workers' relation with the state: military discipline, the unequal distribution of military service, the impact of war on families, and the peculiar situation of draftees in relation to the labor market. These idioms related to notions of equality, freedom, and fraternity that circulated freely among the lower classes during postindependence. They present us with a subaltern interpretation of military experience, an interpretation that constantly evokes the unwritten contract between peasants and the postrevolutionary state.

Fear of Punishment

Punishment or the anticipation of punishment ranks first among deserters' reasons to leave the army. This was the result of widespread use of corporal punishment within the barracks as a means of instilling obedience and the expression of soldiers' rejection of this form of mistreatment. Corporal punishment was considered a debasing act, more properly adapted to the disciplining of slaves and children. Free men deserved better treatment, particularly those who were called to serve the fatherland at the cost of great personal sacrifice. Thus, deserters' complaints against punishment reflected the self-perception of soldiers as free citizens of the republic. Faced with disciplinary practices proper to the colonial past and armed with the egalitarian language of postindependence politics, soldiers engaged in a relentless struggle for respect and equal treatment.

The expectation of the calaboose, shackles, or floggings after committing a violation of military rules prompted soldiers to desert. This was the case of Andrés Arnold, who sought the protection of his father after wounding a comrade in a knife fight. Luis Roberto also chose to escape when confronted with the possibility of punishment, after having lost his poncho, part of his uniform. José Diaz, a young soldier in the city's music band, decided to desert rather than arrive late for a practice. He wandered through the outskirts of the city for a week, for he feared *ser correccionado* (being punished). Domingo Moyano gave a similar explanation after his arrest. Having lost his uniform and afraid of the punishment that awaited him, he rode to Pilar to ask a relative for money to replace his lost uniform.[6] Soldiers' explanations of why they deserted show the success and also the failure of the didactic of punishment. The fear generated by corporal punishment, instead of internalizing obedience and appropriate norms of conduct, led men to abandon their regiments. Certainly, not all "correction" (disciplinary punishment) led to desertion. But it is clear that soldiers had a threshold of tolerance beyond which they were ready to abandon their unit and face the consequences. This threshold was related to the rank of the officer carrying out the disciplinary "correction," the nature of the punishment (humiliating or inappropriate), and its excessive or repetitive use.

Those who experienced punishment felt that they had had enough of mistreatment. José Antonio Da Silva, a Brazilian mulatto serving the federal army at Arroyo de la China, fled to Santa Fé after receiving too many palos (strokes made with the sword) from his sergeant. Repetitive or excessive corporal punishment prompted soldiers to desert, particularly if they had already rendered good service to the federalist army. Such was the case of militiaman Martín Garay, who left the Chascomus jail the night before the day he was scheduled to suffer three hundred strokes for a previous evasion of service. After long service to the Federal Party, veteran Garay expected to be treated with more respect. He had participated in the restoration of 1828–1829, had then joined the militias of his district, had responded to the call to arms again in 1839 at the time of the southern rebellion, and in 1845 had served another five months in the militias.[7]

Others reacted more violently to punishment if they felt mistreated by a person with insufficient military experience. In 1848 a young officer, the commander's son, ordered soldier José Patricio Romero to pull water from the well. He obeyed without complaint. Then the young officer protested his sluggishness and, without warning, began to flog him. Romero, "unable to suffer such a punishment," picked up a rock and threw it at his young boss, wounding him in the head. After this, he fled to avoid further punishment.[8]

Rather than correcting deserters, the use of calaboose, flogging, and the stocks produced more resentment and, consequently, additional desertions down the road. The same could be said about the maximum punishment for a deserter: execution. The spectacle of the firing squad and of hanging bodies left vivid impressions among soldiers. Still, soldiers continued to flee the army at rates that would be alarming to any commanding officer.

Underlying these responses to ill treatment was a shared notion about the disproportion between crime and punishment. Due to the lack of a military code prescribing penalties according to the nature of the offense, military officers held great discretionary power to administer discipline. Soldiers contested these prerogatives, distinguishing between legitimate, correctional punishment and illegitimate, humiliating punishment. As I argued in chapter 8, there were not only thresholds of tolerance to abuse from their superiors but definite protocols to follow to redress the unfair treatment. If soldiers opted for desertion after rather minor violations (the loss of a uniform or an unforeseen delay returning to quarters), it was because they considered the penalty that awaited them (some form of corporal punishment) disproportionate to their faults.

Equally important, soldiers' discourse about the fear of punishment was sustained by a belief in the inviolability of the bodies of citizens, a product of the postindependence predicament about equality and freedom. Strong reactions to punishment reflected the limits to social interaction and institutional discipline imposed by this discourse. Images of broken chains, instruments of torture being burned in public bonfires, and the theatrical liberation of slaves had construed the republic as a site of independent and autonomous bodies, not subject to state intervention. Corporal punishment flew in the face of this concept of liberty and was, for that reason, unacceptable. Those who were liable for corporal punishment were persons who, because of their personal dependence, could not be considered citizens.

This could be clearly seen in the case of insults. Willing to accept reasonable orders, soldiers were not prepared to tolerate insults. Their explanations and actions underscore the belief that even under the flag, free men deserved respect. Various narratives tell us of the importance of bad language and insults in the decision to escape service. Juan Romero, after six months of service with Colonel Gómez and "finding himself continuously insulted and referred to as Savage Unitario, saw himself forced to desert." Previous participation in the unitario army had put him in a vulnerable position, the target of verbal attacks of comrades and officers. Other insults used to debase soldiers employed references to race, natural indolence, and cowardice. The case of Andrés Payllaquén, an Indian soldier (indio chileno) who deserted in response to the bad language employed by an officer when referring to his fellow Indians, is perhaps symptomatic of the racial tensions underscoring the relations between officers and soldiers.[9]

Family Matters

Seen from above, the family assumes a key role in the reproduction of the social order. It appears as a space for instilling notions of authority, work, respectability, and "civilized" behavior (see Danzelot 1979). The discourse of nation building and patriotism blends quite well with this patriarchal notion of the family. It is within family units that sons learn to love the fatherland and develop a disposition to defend it from foreign or domestic aggressors. Deserters' voices present us with a quite different perspective. In their narratives, the family appears as a refuge against the state, a pool of resources to draw from in times of need, and a unity of affections put in jeopardy by recurrent war campaigns. Subalterns conceived the family as a set of obligations and affections that kept soldiers connected to their kinfolk and to their native land, despite the separations imposed by war and coercive military service. Almost casually, with the naturalness of a common concern, deserters spoke of their families to their military or judicial interlocutors. They spoke of families separated by migration and civil wars, of their efforts to locate relatives, and of their concerns for the material well-being of parents and children, siblings and cousins. In their reasons for desertion it is possible to read a critique of the effects of war on families, as well as a perspective on family relations that stresses responsibility and cooperation over authority.

The forced separation from their families looms large among deserters' motivations to abandon the barracks. Long campaigns in the interior provinces, months or years of service in frontier garrisons, and long prison terms separated son from parents, husband from wife and children. Civil wars, more than internal migrations, created a diaspora of family members throughout the national landscape. When Nicanor Torres, arrested in Las Flores in 1844, thought of his family he could clearly see it dispersed across a wide space. He had seven brothers serving the nation in different battalions, most of them at the front, while his mother and sister were living in San Vicente. Under these unfavorable circumstances, soldiers strove to maintain family connections. Examples of soldiers who deserted the ranks to reunite with their families abound.[10]

José Diaz, a soldier with ample combat experience, including the suppression of the 1839 revolt and various campaigns against the Ranquel Indians, deserted his post "only because of the desire to see his mother in Buenos Aires." Francisco Coria, who had escaped the army twice, first in the campaign of La Rioja and later from the prison of Santos Lugares, declared after his arrest that his intention on both occasions had been to "reach his home and see his family" in Guardia del Monte. After a long military campaign in the interior provinces (Córdoba, La Rioja, Tucumán, Catamarca, and San Juan), Genaro Alvarez deserted the federal army because, as he stated, he "wished to return to his homeland [Buenos Aires] and to his family." Pantaleón Ibarra (or Navarro) had been serving the army on the Uruguayan front for four years when he decided to leave his battalion to "see his family," at the time living in Navarro.[11]

Those who had lost track of their close relatives engaged in a search that was often risky and time-consuming. In 1843 Francisco Trivino, a mendocino recently arrived from a long campaign in the western provinces, received news that his father was working in the farm lands (chacras) of Morón. He set out to look for him, risking arrest for not carrying a passport. Then, as he heard his father had moved to Lobos, he rode in that direction. Vicente Pérez, an 18-year-old tailor from Santiago, went to Buenos Aires in 1845 searching for his older brother. Fortunately, he found his brother ready to return to Santiago and with enough resources to clothe him. As they returned in an oxcart troop, Vicente was arrested for traveling without documents. On occasion, the search for family members involved a pilgrimage through different military garrisons. Some deserters declared that they had abandoned their battalion with the aim of joining brothers, cousins, or uncles enlisted in other battalions. At the new destination, they expected to extract a transfer from their superiors that would reunite them with their relatives.[12]

For some, home served as a pool of resources to which young recruits could resort in case of need. Family-provided "vices" and clothes complemented the provisions distributed by the army, making life in quarters more tolerable. Nemecio Coronel went back to his home in Ranchos, seeking tobacco, sugar, and yerba, unavailable in his garrison. Calixto Aguilera, in charge of the army's *invernada* (winter pasture) at San Antonio de Areco, traveled to his grandmother's home to replace his worn-out clothes. Both in the militias and in the army, it was common to grant temporary leaves to visit families and gather provisions and "vices."[13] These transfers of goods imposed a new burden on military commanders, who had to grant soldiers periodic leaves or face the possibility of desertion.

At the same time, the family required contributions from their members to survive times of war and scarcity. The informal system of poor relief established by the army was, apparently, not always effective.[14] Hence, deserters tried to provide for their family's needs, even at great personal risk. In January 1846 José Bustamante, a soldier of the Vigilantes Battalion, left the city with the intention of "carrying beef to his family from cattle [he] might encounter in the countryside." The sustenance of aging parents was always a pressing concern of soldiers. At the time of Lavalle's invasion (1840), Estanislao Cufré voluntarily joined the federal army. Already on campaign, after reaching Cañada de la Cruz, his brother Captain Juan Francisco Cufré ordered him to return home and take care of the family. He did so, stubbornly refusing afterward to serve in the local feedlot.[15]

When other members of the family were already serving in the military, paysanos resisted further contributions to the state. Cirilo Medina, who deserted from the army's *caballada* (horse stable) at Ranchos, explained that his family had already contributed four men to the war effort: his father and two brothers were serving Colonel Laprida and another brother had died in the battle of Quebracho.[16] The survival of the family imposed a limit to the demands of the state.

In their resistance against forced military service, family networks provided an invaluable resource. This was so for Apolinario Gómez, who took refuge in his sister's house in San Nicolás after his escape from the navy. It was so for Manuel Gómez, who resorted to his wife's aunt in Luján for shelter and temporary protection. When Juan Pedro Rocha escaped the Lanceros Battalion, where he was tending horses, he first went to his parents' house in Quilmes. Then, facing persecution, he moved to a neighbor's house a few miles down the road. He stayed there for eight days and then went to visit his aunt in Monte. From this new home, he could move back and forth from the city to the "outside" while earning good money working as a cattle drover.[17] Thus, families facilitated soldiers' perambulations through the landscape of the pampas.

Families might also have functioned as a reservoir of experience to interpret subalterns' obligations to the state. When Pedro Santa Ana (19) deserted from his service to Colonel Fabian Rosas, he had various motives for complaint. One was that his service was being used for private purposes; the colonel had him cultivating his own land for free. Another derived from his family experience: his father had deserted the army many years before, forcing the family to move to Buenos Aires; to feed Pedro and his sister, his mother entered into the service of a porteño family, probably as a maid. The same military regime that had caused such suffering in his family was now trying to extract unpaid labor from young Pedro. He deserted, just as his father had.[18]

The Logic of Necessity

Complaints about the army's neglect in providing adequate food, clothing, and money to its soldiers represented another set of reasons for desertion. These complaints emphasize the economic nature of the contract between soldiers and the state. This was a salutary reminder to state officials, who instead stressed patriotic duty, political allegiance to the Federal Cause, and the disciplining of the rural poor. Soldiering was, after all, an economic contract mediated by exchanges of services for money, provisions, clothing, and other benefits. When that basic contract was violated, soldiers felt free to pursue other avenues for subsistence. Desertion for reasons of "necessity" expressed soldiers' demand for adequate recognition and remuneration of their services to the fatherland. Underscoring their expressions was a staunch defense of the right to paid work.

Paysanos' code word for poverty was "nakedness" (desnudez). Old and ragged clothes made peasants and laborers look poor; new and colorful ponchos and chiripaes, expensive rastras (belts adorned with coins) and aperos (riding gear) served to exhibit relative or momentary affluence. To soldiers, worn-out uniforms or the lack of jackets and ponchillos (finely made ponchos) spoke of the army's neglect of its brave men. Their poverty or nudity reflected an intolerable breach of contract on the part of the state.[19] Repeatedly, deserters referred to their nakedness as a main reason for leaving the barracks.

According to deserter Elias Duarte, nakedness was the only reason for his desertion: he planned to get new clothes outside and return to his military duty. To Juan Pío Leguizamón, an ex-slave serving in the militias at Fort Mulitas, the army's distribution of a batch of clothes every three years and a salary of 10 pesos every month were insufficient for a decent living. He was unable to clothe himself according to the contemporary standards of decency. So he fled to the farms of Luján to work temporarily and earn enough to buy a set of new clothes. The words of José Benigno Villagra, a deserter from the Patricios Battalion, articulate with unusual clarity the connection between freedom to work and the rejection of institutional poverty: "About a month ago, he deserted because he was very naked and his chief was unwilling to grant him permission to go to work. So he crossed to the other side of the Barracas bridge and worked in the meat-salting workshops, confiding in absolutely nobody about his desertion." Villagra's argument stresses the understanding, common to other narratives, that if the army could not provide for its soldiers, they had the right to earn their living elsewhere. Or, put another way, when the service to the fatherland pushed soldiers into poverty, it was time to leave. Bonifacio Martínez's explanation resembles Villagra's: "This individual explains that he had no other motivation for committing this fault than his desire to work in order to remedy his [urgent] needs. [He was] unable to get his Chief to grant him a leave for this purpose. He promises Your Excellency that if his crime is pardoned, a crime he committed under the impulse of the necessity and poverty he was in, he will not incur [again] the same felony."[20] In his appeal for mercy, Martínez evidenced a bipolar categorical universe: he placed freedom and paid work on one side, and poverty, need, and coercion on the other.

Soldiers' materialism was even more acute when they sensed that resources within the army were not equally distributed. Raymundo Ramallo clearly expressed his sense of outrage in his narrative. Before deserting, he had slaughtered seven steers from the army's herd and sold them to a nearby tavern keeper. He confessed that he deserted "induced by necessity and the shortage of money, and disgusted at the same time, for in the five years he had been serving in his division he had received nothing in addition to the salary provided by the state. When he knows too well that in all other divisions in actual service in the countryside, soldiers receive besides their salary, periodically, a hide or its value in money as compen-

18. Federalist Soldier in the Provinces. In the provinces, suggests Rugendas, a soldier preserves few marks of his federalism. This soldier's shirt was probably scarlet when new; it is now pink. His *chiripá* is light blue, a color prohibited to a good federal. Only his cap is unambiguously federalist: scarlet and in the shape of a liberty cap. Juan M. Rugendas, *Soldado de frente—San Luis*, watercolor, 1838. Reproduced from B. del Carril, *Monumenta Iconográphica* (1964).

sation. To this date he had received neither one nor the other. He believes he is the only one to whom this compensation, to which he is entitled, is not distributed. His other comrades receive this [compensation] every three or four months."

Living near subsistence, soldiers demanded every additional resource or remuneration they could get. A hide on the market represented as much as a month's salary for a soldier. This helps us understand Ramallo's daring and insistent protest for his missing "compensation." A 64-year-old veteran of many campaigns, he felt cheated by the army; thirty years of service were being paid in discriminatory practices and neglect. Less articulate speakers could only resort to the argument of necessity as nudity, underplaying the complexity of the wage form (salary, bonuses, aids in cash, provisions, and uniforms) on which the contract between soldiers and the state was based.

Appeals to the logic of necessity were also used to criticize other types of inequalities, among them the use of unpaid, involuntary labor and the corruption of officers. In 1845, Gerónimo Rodríguez, a militiaman from Cañuelas who had helped the army in different ancillary tasks, refused to work without pay for the local justice of the peace. Considering this a private service, he abandoned the locality and went to work as foreman of a cattle ranch. Months later, under interrogation, he presented his decision as one guided by necessity: "He was very poor," he said to his captors. Similarly, Fermín Colares, a deserter from the frontier garrison of Mulitas, used the argument of nakedness to show another common injustice. He deserted, he confided to the justice of San Nicolás, "because they had him naked and working as a *quintero* [orchard worker], never allowing him to handle a rifle." To him, this was not military labor.[21]

Complaints about corruption complemented the arguments on poverty. In an 1845 investigation in which several soldiers and subaltern officers were involved in selling stolen hides and tallow to the local tavern, soldiers denounced the corrupt practices of their superiors. In addition to profiting from the sale of hides, involving soldiers in their scheme, officers used various individuals to represent the deserters and the absentees at payday, so as to pocket their salaries. Juan Ferreyra, one of the soldiers accused of selling state-owned hides, justified his action in this way: "If he committed this crime, it was on account of the extreme poverty he was in, and because he knew that his *alférez* (second lieutenant) Martínez used to do the same, selling unbranded hides [state property]."[22] Ferreyra was a veteran soldier with thirty years of service and a medal of honor pendant around his neck. This entitled him to voice his complaints about the hypocrisy of his superiors.

Disease and Mutilation

Soldiers' complaints about their ailments and diseases provide valuable insights into the world of popular health. Disease was a consistent argument for soldiers to avoid service. Their most common disabilities included lack of mobility of arms or legs, reduced vision, and various impairments of the spine. These were usually the result of combat wounds or falls from horses. But military campaigns left other marks on soldiers' bodies. To the army physician soldiers invoked a variety of symptoms of unidentified diseases, among them: aneurysms; tumors, palpitations or heart pain, rheumatic pain, respiratory problems, and, more rarely, epilepsy (a general term for nervous afflictions). Groin itching and other symptoms of venereal disease were also common.

Paradoxically, combat experience incapacitated soldiers for many types of civilian work but failed to exempt them from further military service. Contrary to their expectations, army physician Dr. Martínez systematically denied soldiers' allegations to be true or sufficient reasons to prevent them from performing military duties. His refusal to consider soldiers' pains and mutilations as anything but theatrical postures must have shocked veterans. Their quite evident sacrifices for the defense of the fatherland (lost arms and fingers, scars, crippled legs, respiratory problems, etc.) were made invisible by an act of "classification."[23] In spite of their disabilities and diseases, they were declared "fit for service."

Deserters' complaints about their disabilities and infirmities addressed a problem hidden from official or elite discourse: the effects of war on the actual bodies of citizens and the disregard shown by the state toward its aging soldiers. Old soldiers narrated with pride their combat experience, stressing the moments and localities where they were wounded or mutilated, only to add, a few sentences later, how they still carried with them recurrent pain or permanent disabilities. The federal army, infamous for retaining soldiers beyond their fighting age, was not prepared to hear this subtle criticism.[24] Generals expected unlimited patriotism; everybody, young and old, healthy or not, had to be ready to give his life to defend the federation. For this reason, the tone of deserters' explanations was subdued. To avoid being considered unpatriotic, veterans added phrases or adjectives ("honoring bullet wounds") that left no doubt of their commitment to federalism and the war effort.

Deserters' stories make clear that the army did not provide adequate medical attention. Battles in the interior provinces generated a continuous supply of mutilated or disabled bodies, but there were no nearby hospitals to treat the wounded or ill. During campaigns, as the army could not wait for the ill or wounded, soldiers stayed at improvised "camp hospitals" or private homes with the idea of joining their battalions when they recovered. Failure to locate their battalion and to present themselves to their former commander converted them into deserters. Often, to recover from respiratory diseases or ill-treated wounds, soldiers resorted to their families, to local healers, or to the solidarity of strangers. It was not unusual for soldiers in the middle of a military campaign to return to their home or to that of a close relative "to recover" from wounds and illnesses. Usually, they were granted permission to do this. Many, however, failed to return at the expiration of their leave.[25] In these cases, desertion was more an imposition of their bodies than a conscious decision. To distinguish themselves from the lot of the unpatriotic, those who had received wounds or contracted diseases and, as a result, lost contact with their battalion stressed the fact that they were *dispersos*, not deserters. Occasionally, veterans mentioned the unmentionable: that not all wounds were caused by the enemy. Arms and legs blown away by the federalist army's own artillery and the loss of eyes in exercises were common occurrences during campaigns, as is evident from the claims of disabled veterans.[26] Other mutilations and wounds resulted from the violent interactions between soldiers and sergeants and corporals.

Other Reasons

Though corporal punishment, family, necessity, and disease made up an important proportion of reasons to desert, other motives articulated in the *filiaciones* are also significant, for they reveal aspects of soldiers' moral economy: the system of norms, the boundaries of tolerance, the perspectives that governed soldiers' responses to military power. One such reason was the rejection of unpaid or private service.

The case of Ramon Rivero, a 40-year-old veteran from Santiago, exemplifies this type of resistance. He had answered the call to service on several occasions. He had made *destacamentos* (commissions) to Ensenada and Chascomus and, after moving to Azul, had helped in roundups, police patrols, and other tasks. During the prior ten years since he migrated, he had been enrolled as *miliciano* in the local squadron of Carabineros. But in 1845 he deserted because his major tried to force him to work without pay on his private land. Pedro Santa Ana's experience was similar. Arrested by a *teniente alcalde* (assistant to the alcalde) near Quilmes, he was put under the orders of Commander Fabian Rosas, who used him to till his private farm. Santa Ana did not consider this to be a service to the Federal Cause; for him, this was a private and illegitimate use of his labor power. Unwilling to stomach this, he deserted.[27]

Soldiers' refusal to provide services outside of their military obligations and their insistent demand that their work be paid deserves special attention. First, this attitude helped to prevent the generalization of forced labor to other spheres: if the military could not impose forced labor, nobody could. Second, deserters' statements reinforced a principle that slaves had fought for long before: the right to wages. The assertion of this principle, under the pressure of an increasingly coercive state, was not a minor achievement.[28] Third, in a context of confusing boundaries between the private and the public, where government authorities tried incessantly to privatize resources for their own benefit, the clarity with which soldiers defined and criticized this private use of service is remarkable.

Certainly, the belief that services were owed to the nation (the federation) and not to particular individuals was itself a spinoff of the new, postindependence discourse about the "nation." This abstract imagined community was based on a foundational contract between the citizens-at-arms and the revolutionary state, a contract for the provision of military services that had a double purpose: to gain independence and the "freedom of the people." Misuse of the soldiery constituted an all too evident violation of this foundational principle. In addition, soldiers' critique of private service reflected a widespread position of postindependence workers: the rejection of unpaid labor, grounded in turn on the spread of market relations. Thus, desertions to escape situations of unpaid and involuntary labor belonged to a larger discursive field that included at its center rural workers' struggles for equality, paid work, and representative government.

Conflicts with officers, peer pressure, and gambling debts appear in several of the deserters' stories. Though soldiers strove to maintain a distant relationship with their officers, disputes over authority, work, or money were common. In some cases, they escalated into open strife. The motivating factors of these disputes ranged from rather innocuous interactions, such as card games, to contestations about the very nature of military authority.[29] Lucas Ferreyra's desertion is a case in point. He abandoned the army's feedlot where he was serving because he did not want to obey arbitrary orders. He was assigned to break horses, a task he was not prepared for; when he refused, he was flogged. In 1845 soldier Bruno Perez got very angry with his sergeant. He was working at an army feedlot when his sergeant, quite drunk, cut him with a knife without any apparent reason. Perez complained to his commanding officer about this abuse of authority and, because the latter "did not do justice, siding instead with the sergeant," he deserted.[30] This desertion exposes one of the boundaries of tolerance referred to earlier: wounds inflicted as part of a machista power game were neither legitimate nor tolerable.

Gambling debts brought about many disputes among the ranks. Sergeant Norberto Sayago, for instance, left the army in Santa Fe after a long military career on account of a gambling debt. Some left their battalions enticed by other soldiers and, on occasion, by their corporals or sergeants. Gerónimo Zalazar, for example, confessed to justice of the peace Jurado that he deserted "because he saw that so many others were deserting."[31] Another important "pull factor" motivating desertions was the rumor that circulated inside army garrisons that there were "protectors" out there eager to give refuge to deserters. Renowned military and political figures were mentioned among these benefactors. The list included Anchorena, Rosas y Belgrano, Mascarilla, all the way down to ranch administrators.[32] Guided by these rumors, some deserters sought the protection of certain authorities to deliver them from the unfair treatment received in their regiments. Unwilling to tolerate more military drills and the mistreatment of their chief, Valerio Leguizamón and his comrade, Ramón Andrade, escaped in the direction of Azul. They had heard that other deserters found there the protection of Pedro Rosas y Belgrano. They assumed that with the help of this notable figure (Rosas's nephew), they would easily get a transfer to a different destination.[33] The idea of a safe haven in the south where deserters could find a livelihood without fearing arrest was a myth, but it served as a way to attract many deserters to the burgeoning economy there.

Itineraries, Mobility, and Jobs

The itineraries that deserters followed in their search for security and subsistence give us some clues about the spatial "preferences" of subalterns. Few deserters (6 percent) stayed in the same area where their regiments were located (see Table 9.2). Reasons of personal safety, related to the state's circulation of information about deserters among neighboring counties, made deserters travel long distances. On the other hand, few ventured to return to their native province or tried their luck in the littoral (7 percent). At these destinations, deserters could find job opportunities or the comfort of family, but faced greater risks of falling into coercive situations.[34] Against the predictions of gauchesco literature, no deserter in my sample moved to the Indian frontier. The best strategy was to move within Buenos Aires province, seeking the safest economic opportunities. In the end, due to the distribution of employment opportunities and the risk of police surveillance, deserters perambulated through the same circuits as northern migrants.

Deserters' order of preference was, first, the city and its hinterland (Barracas, Quilmes, S. J. Flores, Palermo, etc.); second came the area north of the Salado River; the third was shared by the northwest-southeast corridor and the area south of the Salado River (the so-called New South). For deserters looking for jobs, these areas looked more promising or safer

TABLE 9.2 Destination of Deserters

Destination	Number of Cases	Percentage
Interior provinces	13	7.3
Northern coastal	14	7.9
NW–SE corridor	31	17.4
Buenos Aires hinterland	41	23.0
North of Salado River	35	19.7
South of Salado River	31	17.4
Same area as desertion	11	6.2
No information	2	1.1
TOTAL	178	100.0

Notes: Northern coastal = Zárate, San Nicolás, San Pedro, Baradero; NW–SE corridor = Pergamino, Arrecifes, Salto, S.A. de Areco, Fortín de Areco, S.A. de Giles, Gda. de Luján, Luján, Pilar; Buenos Aires hinterland = Cuidad, San Fernando, Santos Lugares, Morón, Palermo, S.J. de Flores, Barracas, San Isidro, Quilmes; North of Salado = Navarro, Lobos, San Vicente, Cañuelas, Monte, Ranchos, Chascomús, Ensenada, Magdalena, San Borombón, Matanza; South of Salado = Pila, Tordillo, Dolores, Vecino, Monsalvo, Ajó, Tuyú, Mar Chiquita, Lobería, Tandil, Chapaleufú, Azul, Tapalquén
Source: Filiaciones (N=525)

than the northwest territory or the interior provinces. Deserters' itineraries do not support the simplistic view of a unidirectional migration to the New South. Rather, these itineraries point to a more "circular" conception of their movements, more in consonance with the uneven distribution of jobs and policing in the provincial landscape. Moreover, deserters' preferences validate the notion of the littoral and the interior provinces as an "outside" riskier to human life and lacking in citizen rights. The northwest territory was a "contact zone" between the orderly Buenos Aires and the unsettled littoral. Deserters who went there probably expected to migrate to the littoral in a second stage.

Buenos Aires was the commercial entrepôt of the Confederation but also the site of government and military power. Despite the concentration of repressive forces, the city provided greater possibilities of employment in meat-salting and tanning workshops, slaughterhouses, and cattle markets. The incessant movement of oxcarts and cattle in and out of the city created socially active spaces where newcomers could find employment and, at the same time, a certain degree of anonymity. Other deserters came to the city with a different purpose: to petition Rosas for a pardon or to ask for a transfer to a different regiment.

More popular than the New South was the area immediately to the north of the Salado River, where cattle and sheep ranchers had settled since the 1820s. In this area, deserters could expect farm and ranch employment as well as points of provision for travel to Buenos Aires or the New South. Navarro, Lobos, Monte, Ranchos, and Chascomús were the main rural towns here. This area was crucial to the support of federalism; from here came the militias (headed by Rosas) that restored order to the city in 1820. The New South (to the south of the Salado River), an area of large cattle ranches and presumably less policing was third in the preference of deserters. It shared this place with the northwest-southeast corridor, a rosary of towns of older settlement (Pergamino, Salto, Areco, Arrecifes), which constituted the best-known road to the upper provinces; here, deserters could find close-knit communities, better policing, and fairly segmented landholding.

The expansion of the export economy was felt both in coastal and inland areas, in farming as well as ranching zones, in the new as well as the old frontier. For deserters looking for jobs, all these areas looked promising. Quite likely, the spatial distribution of family and friends, rumors about the district (its "authorities"), and knowledge about the region's geography must have conditioned the choice of initial destination. But the key to survival for fugitives from justice consisted in securing a job that ensured invisibility from state agents. For that purpose, task or day labor and short-term employment were ideally suited. A branding, digging, or harvesting job was done before employers could inquire into the character and background of itinerant peons.

Deserters were job seekers in need of protection. Finding abrigo (refuge/shelter) was not an easy task. Deserters needed connections to gather provisions, horses, and a new set of clothing. Many resorted to their families; in fact, family employment (working on a relative's land) was a common tactic. Deserters divided their search for refuge into the need for shelter, provided by relatives, and the need for a job, supplied by local patrons and authorities. Of the 178 cases selected, 72 (40 percent) indicated the jobs they entered since their desertion. Of these, 27 mentioned two successive occupations and 11 mentioned three. In total, they mentioned 110 jobs. A summary of these reports can be seen in Table 9.3. Ranch peons, farm laborers, peons at meat-salting plants, and day laborers were, expectedly, the most frequent occupations. Jobs in transportation (oxcart drivers, cattle drovers, porters), though less frequent, were also significant. Few mentioned occupations in the city's slaughterhouses or the country's sheep farms. More common was to find employment with local judicial authorities or to pursue some type of independent activity, such as tavern keeper, grass and timber cutter, or horse breaker.

TABLE 9.3 Deserters' Occupation

Occupation	Number of Cases	Percentage
Farming	10	9.1
Ranching	32	29.1
Transportation	15	13.6
Commerce and administration	3	2.7
Rural industry	10	9.1
All-purpose labor (peons)	28	25.5
Other	12	10.9
TOTAL	110	100.0

Source: Filiaciones (N=525)

In their journeys through different districts deserters entered into contact with distinct groups of employers. Ranchers did not have the monopoly on employment. Farmers, *quinteros* (orchard growers), cattle drovers and beef merchants, owners of meat-salting plants, and individual residents also demanded their labor. Deserters' relationship with these employers was, at best, temporary. From the cases that provided information about the duration of employment (62), it is apparent that a very high labor mobility was involved: 51 percent worked less than three months, and 72 percent worked less than six months. Of course, the short duration of employment was conditioned by the possibility of capture (50 percent of deserters were arrested or recaptured within three months of their escape). But, considering that 15 percent of deserters were at large for more than two years, there is sufficient grounds to believe that they did not allocate all their time to work.

Mobility and a certain degree of anonymity were crucial in this job search. So was family. Relatives could aid deserters' search for jobs while maintaining the secrecy or ambiguity needed to avoid police detection.[35] That is why Mateo Aguilar, after deserting, headed for the cattle ranch where his father worked as a ditch-digger, and why Anacleto Quiroga, a deserter from the music band at Guardia de Luján, went to his brother-in-law's farm, and why Vicente Veron, having deserted in the Córdoba countryside, sought employment with his cousin in Navarro.[36]

Those who sought comfort in family and local connections discovered that the arms of the law extended deep into the countryside. The secrecy about a desertion could be maintained only at the cost of putting relatives and friends in jeopardy. Cosme Blanco, a young deserter, chose the help of his father to reenter his native community, Cañuelas. Both father and son went to see their neighbor, Don Eusebio Acosta, well known in the county and with the reputation of being a good federalist, and asked for a job. Acosta, not knowing that Cosme had deserted, gave him employment. In the end, however, the scheme failed. Cosme and his father were arrested, and so was the "protector," Don Acosta.[37]

Tactics of Reinsertion

To ensure membership in the town's social and political life, deserters needed a new identity. This required them to find a position in the network of local social relations and to relocate themselves vis-à-vis civil and military authorities. Only new identities could turn deserters from *desconocidos* (unknown) into *conocidos* (known) and from transients into neighbors. I call this double process of social and political relocation *avecinamiento* (neighboring), for it was the washing away of the ex-deserters' debt with the state and the acceptance by other neighbors of the ex-deserters' rights of residence that made them members of the local communities.

At the local level, disguise and false representation were useful tools for acquiring a new social identity; secrecy about the past was a must. A new name represented the possibility of a new beginning. Of the 178 deserters selected from the set of military and criminal files, 36 (20 percent) said that they kept their desertion a secret from employers as well as families and neighbors; 27 (15 percent) confessed to changing their name; and 9 (5 percent) were arrested carrying false documents.[38] These falsifications should be considered a fraction of a much vaster set of illegalities, for my figures do not include those deserters skillful enough to avoid detection and arrest.

The first act of disguise was to drop the uniform and adopt civilian clothes. Evidence of this transformation is rare or indirect, as many of these acts took place beyond the gaze of the authorities. We know of José Santos Vivas's change of clothes because he was caught in the act of hiding his jacket and military cap in a *cardo* (thistle). We can infer that others left their uniforms in the open countryside thanks to reports such as that of Antonio Domínguez, foreman of a state-owned ranch in Areco. He found a scarlet vest with the federal ribbon on it lying on the ground. Occasionally, a young deserter would recount how he was offered employment as an oxcart driver after he dropped his uniform.[39] Afraid to add another felony to the list, most deserters fail to mention what they did with their uniforms, but the fact that most were wearing paysano attire at the time of arrest indicates that such was a general practice. The road to a new identity started with the assumption of a civilian appearance.

Strategies of reduced visibility afforded some protection to those still on the move. As several deserters' accounts make clear, separating shelter from work was one way to avoid encounters with the rural police.[40] Lorenzo Pérez, for example, a deserter from the Dolores garrison, used his uncle's house in Montes Grandes (Mar Chiquita) as his temporary residence every time he went to work in the ranches near the coast. His various employers knew little about Perez's place of residence and, consequently, could tell little about him to the rural police. Others avoided detection by the police patrol by spending the night in the open, near a relative's land, or in less comfortable hiding places.[41] Riding to work during the day and returning at night to safer and familiar places kept some deserters out of the reach of the police.

To achieve *avecinamiento* (becoming a neighbor), it was advisable to make oneself well-known to other residents. This implied some degree of exposure to neighbors and potential employers. The extant *sumarios* of those who gave shelter or work to deserters are quite precise on this point. Several employers declared that they had provided deserters with a place to stay or with temporary employment because they were well-known. Sharecropper Juan de la Rosa López, who employed deserter Pedro Morales for twenty days, declared that he had known Morales since his childhood and, for this reason, did not imagine he could be in trouble with the law. Rancher Pedro Colman said something similar: when he employed deserter José Sisterna as a peon, he was not unknown to him; he had previously met him, though casually, in the town of Navarro. Gertrudis Marchant, a widow in charge of a ranch in Lobos, declared that deserter Peñalva, who had worked for her during the days of branding in exchange for healing services she provided him, was quite well-known. She knew that he belonged to the town's feedlot and that it was normal for its soldiers to go out and work in the local brandings.[42]

Rural norms of hospitality established that a head of household would allow a stranger to stay for one or two nights. Beyond that, strangers needed to prove their "legality" by disarming the host's natural distrust. Fortunato Peralta used a very effective line: he persuaded farmer Pedro Díaz to give him shelter by stating that he was on his way to Camarones Chico, one of the Anchorenas' ranches. Peralta's reference to a powerful cattle rancher, friend of the government, did the trick. In fact, deserters exploited this notion of "legality by association" by invoking the names of well-known ranchers, government officials, and military commanders. If they could convey the impression that they were part of the workforce of these personalities, other ranchers and farmers would give them a job without asking questions.[43] Saturnino Gómez was a master of this art. His statements got several of Rosas's subordinates in trouble. According to him, he went to work on one of Rosas's ranches due to a protection offer by Pascual Peredo. Mayordomo Peredo rejected this claim, stating that he had never met Gómez. Foreman Benancio Obaendo, also implicated by Gómez, said he provided Gómez with shelter because he had worked as peon for another of his patron's ranches, Encarnación. The foreman of this estancia, Soldariega, had hired Gómez for three months in the belief that he was sent from Azul by mayordomo Pedro Fuentes. In the end, nobody knew exactly where Gómez came from, but all assumed that he came recommended by people who deserved Rosas's confidence.[44]

Stretching the truth could prolong a deserter's perambulations in the countryside or help him keep a good job. Perhaps few were as ingenious or resourceful as Juan Garay. He made his coworkers at the meat-salting plant, his patron, and the justice of San Vicente believe that Doña Manuelita, Rosas's daughter, had pardoned him in celebration of a federal military victory in the north. Other peons at the meat-salting plant, accustomed to this kind of gesture from Manuelita, thought he was telling the truth ("We all believed him," declared peon Manuel Gamboa). A year after he escaped from town as a common delinquent, Juan Ullúa came back to San Vicente to take revenge on his persecutors and reestablish his honor. This time he brought a *resguardo* (safe pass), a paper supposedly granted by a higher authority that protected him from being molested by local officials. He showed this paper everywhere he went, bragging about his "privilege." The document was actually forged, but it proved quite effective in protecting Ullúa.[45]

But the most daring lie—or, at least, one with far-reaching implications—consisted in changing one's name. In this way, the whole past of a deserter could be recreated. This disguise brought confusion to the authorities and granted the deserter a protective mask. In 1845, the justice of the peace of San Nicolás wrote on the margin of Juan José Flores's filiación: "This individual is a deserter without doubt, but he is such a liar [*embustero*] that he has changed names on three occasions." Arrested for desertion in August 1842, he presented himself as Juan José Flores. Three years later he began to work for the justice of San Nicolás using the name Justo Morales. In 1846 he was arrested in Quilmes; this time the military record carried the name of Ramón Acevedo. On each occasion, this deserter created new names for his parents as well. At first, he said he was the son of Rosendo Flores and Petrona Baldia; later, he changed their names to Rosendo and Juana Morales and then to Luciano Flores and

Juana Rosa. His *patria* or origin was also a variable matter. First, he claimed to be a native of Banda Oriental; to the military inquirer at Santos Lugares he presented himself as a man from Misiones; to the justice of San Nicolás he was a *criollo* (native) from Pergamino, until he confessed to being from Entre Ríos.[46] The account of his first desertion was also transformed several times. In all accounts, he stressed his participation in the campaign to Entre Ríos and Corrientes, mentioning the names of famous battles and making his interlocutor aware of the wounds he received in these battles. But the circumstances of his desertion kept changing. In his first narration (1842) he said he had been a prisoner of the unitario forces, so that his desertion looked like a patriotic act. In his second interrogation (1845), he confessed that he and two comrades simply "dispersed" after combat, later asking different commanders for passes to return to Buenos Aires. A third rendition of this episode states that he and his comrades deserted from Guardia de Salto and moved to Arrecifes, where they tried to make a living by working in the farmlands. Each variation of the story represented a different claim against the state. In the first was the lament that he had contributed enough to the defense of the fatherland, that he no longer needed to prove his patriotism. In the second was a veiled challenge to the authority of the state: a group of deserters were able to negotiate their reincorporation with high military chiefs. In the third, desertion was an assertion of his individual right to work, to earn a livelihood. Quite clearly, the persona that this ex-soldier was trying to construct started from a strong base: claims of citizenship, patriotism, economic/social equality, and bargaining power. The name mattered little. Flores (or Morales or Acevedo) presented himself as a soldier, a citizen, and a worker.[47]

This story anticipates the second stage in the process of becoming a neighbor, a set of activities that, for lack of a better term, I call legalization. Deserters who established their claims to a new identity or who became well-known among neighbors and employers chose to legalize their new status. They could do this through various means: joining the local militias (a choice they called *arreglarse*), obtaining a work contract (or contrata), or, more expediently, petitioning for a pardon (or *indulto*). The three strategies underscored the same desire to rejoin the community of neighbors as full political, economic, and social actors.

Enlisting in the local militias entailed a passage from military to civilian status, a sort of normalization by which ex-soldiers returned to the sphere of citizenship, law, and rights. Although at times the distinction between the terms "soldier" and "militiaman" becomes confused, for rural inhabitants it was quite clear that militiamen belonged to the sphere of civilian life and soldiers belonged to the military sphere.[48] A militiaman was liable to be called to arms less frequently than a soldier and often could enjoy the social and political status of a vecino (neighbor). It should not surprise us, then, to find that deserters, disguised as paysanos, joined the local militias under a new identity.

Rosas was quite surprised at this discovery. In 1845 Captain Mariano Soto warned him of the concentration of deserters in the very ranks of a frontier garrison, Fort 25 de Mayo (Mulitas). Furious, Rosas ordered a list of all deserters who, disguised as paysanos, had entered the Fort since 1841. The inquiry produced twenty-four deserters enrolled as militiamen and earning wages as such. The commander of the Fort, J. M. Plaza, tried to excuse himself from this irregularity. These were volunteers who, obviously, did not state at enrollment time that they had been deserters.[49] One of these volunteers was Narciso Casas. He had escaped from Santos Lugares after remaining three months in prison. Next, he spent two years working in the districts of Arrecifes and Areco, until he made the decision to enlist at Fort Mulitas. He cut his ties to his native Lobos (his mother had moved to Navarro), and relatively confident in the new territory, legalized his new condition as a Mulitas resident and paysano.[50]

The gradual conversion from deserter into militiaman with claims to vecindad (residents' rights) involved repeated encounters with the most visible local authority: the justice of the peace. Nicolás Bustos's story is illustrative of this gradual transition. He deserted twice from the army, the first time as a soldier, the second as a militiaman in service. He had entered the military by compulsion, arrested by the Quilmes justice of the peace for not carrying a passport. After his desertion from Santos Lugares, he headed to Lobería, where he found a job at R. Galindez's ranch. After some time, he moved to San Isidro where, as a paysano, he served the local justice by carrying firewood for the army. He then moved back to Lobería and tried to become a neighbor. After four months helping the justice of the peace in mule breaking and cattle roundups, he enrolled in the local militia and was sent to a detachment in Dolores.[51]

A second route to legalization was getting a work contract. This proved a riskier tactic. In Tucumán, Gregorio Carpio had deserted the federal troops and joined the local militias. He remained there for four years. In his native province he worked in a fairly circumscribed area, after legalizing his situation with the local commander. Back in Buenos Aires province, he worked at various ranches in the district of Lobos, before he presented himself to the justice and applied for an employment voucher. The judge inquired about his past and had him arrested.[52] In his long journey after desertion, Carpio experimented with two strategies of reinsertion. In Tucumán, he chose to enlist in the local militias as the most expedient way to carve out his own space in local society. Whereas the first method served him well, the second proved disastrous. To enlist with a local militia commander less interested in knowing about the recruits' past, Carpio must have concluded, was a wiser strategy.

The process of becoming a neighbor required more than a simple arrangement with the authorities. This was often the last stage of a complex process involving strategies of limited visibility, family connections, and the construction of an alternative identity. This last component assumed not only the adoption of a new name but also the building of a new set of relations; these helped a paysano become something more than an outsider. The fascinating story of Inocencio Monsalvo, a war veteran who settled in Quilmes, allows us to see the delicate edifice of this protective network. He managed to remain at large for five years after he deserted the army in Entre Ríos. In Buenos Aires province he worked for two years on a ranch in Lobería and then moved to Quilmes, where he began the process of claiming neighborhood (avecinarse). He changed his name to Inocencio Ramallo and moved to the house of a local policeman, Bonifacio Ferreyra, married to Monsalvo's sister-in-law. His house was next to the police assistant's with whom he became acquainted. In time, he befriended the sergeant in charge of the local patrol, adding insurance to his claims of legality. His respectability also stemmed from his new job; having gathered a small herd of horses, he started his own cattle-driving business, combining this income with occasional partridge hunting. His prolonged absences from town, given his occupation, did not raise any suspicion. For three years his desertion passed unnoticed; as he recalled, not even his partridge-hunting friends knew about his desertion.[53] Using relations based on kinship, friendship, and local connections, Monsalvo had managed to construct a whole new social identity.

Deserters could also appeal directly to the benevolence of the governor for a pardon. No doubt this was a courageous move, for it necessitated confessing a crime to a civil or military authority and asking for his mediation to approach the governor or, more frequently, for a passport to travel to Palermo. In spite of the risks involved, twenty-three of our deserters asked for either a mediation or a pardon. Those who responded to government decrees calling for a blanket amnesty had an easier time, for they could trust that military commanders and justices were informed about this transaction.[54] More commonly, however, deserters risked being mistreated by several authorities and spent some time in jail before they could see Rosas.

To avoid these complications, deserters resorted to various resources. For example, the parents of a young deserter would appeal to Rosas for a pardon, particularly in proximity to some patriotic or political festivity. On other occasions deserters obtained the mediation of the captain of the militias or the justice to appeal to the governor. Others declared openly that they had been looking for some "recommendation" (a letter, a passport) before presenting themselves to the authorities. Aware that military and civil authorities would listen only to those carrying identification, they asked for a passport before soliciting a pardon. To make the decision to present themselves, deserters consulted with their families and close friends.[55] Too much was at stake in this type of decision to be left to one person's opinion.

More rarely, some deserters put their petitions in writing. Juan José Etchegaray wrote such a petition in 1846. Presenting himself as a *ciudadano federal* (federal citizen), Etchegaray tried to persuade Rosas of his condition of a *provinciano* unfairly arrested and drafted into the army. At a time when the "unjust and odious Anglo-French intervention" had heightened suspicion in the countryside, he lost his documents while traveling from Dolores to Buenos Aires. Though he considered his imprisonment unjustified (he was, after all, a foreman and had resided less than a year in the province, hence exempted from service), he appealed to Rosas's benevolence to free him from his suffering. His family in San Juan, already impoverished by their contributions to the Federal Cause, could not survive his incarceration.[56]

The arts of deception described in deserters' stories contributed to the construction of new social personas. These recreated identities entered the social milieu of rural towns and, indirectly, the political sphere of the Rosista republic. False representations, disguise, and new names marked the distant, ironic position of ex-soldiers vis-à-vis the justice system created in the postindependence era, but also the affirmation of their belonging to the body politic of the republic and of their desire to return to their communities.

Deserters' complex tactics for reinsertion, a process I have called *avecinamiento*, speak of this desire to "come back" and of the difficulties they encountered in carrying this project to fruition. Deserters' decision to change their name—the completion of the process leading to the construction of a new identity—can now be reinterpreted from the vantage point of the subaltern. At the end of the second book of *Martín Fierro*, the protagonist, his sons, and a friend made a pact of secrecy and decided to change their names before departing in four different directions.[57] With new names, they could now shed a past of illegality and defiance and adopt new identities more appropriate for the new Argentina molded by law, progress, and property. Our deserters tell a different story. Changing names was not a prelude to reformation or to marginality; it was, rather, a means for escaping persecution and, at the same time, the precondition for regaining the economic and political rights of citizens. *Avecinamiento* helped to engender new social and political identities, positions from which these wandering subalterns who paid their military dues to the state could reclaim their place in the construction of postindependence society.

Conclusions: Lamentation and Defiance

Having presented the contours of deserters' discourse and their strategies of social and political reinsertion, it is time to return to the question of subalterns' voices, positionality, and tactics. Let us start with the nature of deserters' voices. Faced with the inquisitors at Santos Lugares, deserters had to justify their desertion, even if at times this entailed contradicting state reasons or denouncing military and civilian authorities. In the expectation of a pardon, they tried to justify their illegality and, at the same time, reestablish their political connection with the fatherland and its keepers. For this purpose, they had to articulate persuasive stories connecting their individual experience with that of the federation. While explaining an act punishable by death, deserters tried to insert, between the lines, their particular view of the state and its policies.

Deserters' voices were not like rumors behind the backs of the powerful. They were voices aimed at state authorities. They were acts of denunciation and petition, inscribed in the official record, intended to reach the highest echelons of power. Deserters knew their confessions would, sooner or later, reach Governor Rosas. Necessarily, their stories contained traces of deference and defiance. Their speech bowed to the legitimate powers and, at the same time, demanded that the authorities redress concrete situations of injustice. In this regard, the performance of conformity and respect acted as a necessary prologue to the denunciations and lamentations that followed. Their stories reminded the state of its promise to sustain the "rights of the people," while reenacting the peon soldiers' continued commitment to the Federal Cause.

Unable to hide in the anonymity of rumor, gossip, or folktales, deserters used first-person narrations. Their explanations and reasons were necessarily personal: a chain of war-related events punctuated by key battles, responses to the call to arms, acts of personal heroism, and bodily losses (see chapter 10). In them, deserters reinscribed into the public transcript what Rosas and the military establishment preferred to ignore: the real costs of civil war and the inequities of the republic. More than excuses, the reasons of deserters contained phrases of lamentation and defiance that in retrospect seem quite risky, especially when uttered within a prison.

Deserters' complaints against the state and the fatherland, though still grounded in peasant traditions and tactics, related to quite modern processes: wage contracts, independent bodies, and the rights of citizenship. Their claims assumed earlier promises, made by the postindependence leadership, about social and political rights. The rhetoric of equality, freedom, and fraternity seems to have reached deep into the political understandings of the rural poor. Deserters articulated these ideals to produce concrete demands against the Rosista state. In their confessions, they demanded good treatment, sufficient food, payment for labor, freedom of mobility, and the possibility of reuniting with their families. While paying allegiance to the ideal federalist republic, paysanos contested the practice of abusive punishment, family separation, unnecessary material deprivation, and the corruption of the powerful.

They were able to wage this war of meanings because of two favorable circumstances: the situation of labor scarcity and the high mobility of the rural population. The armies needed increasing numbers of soldiers and ranchers required growing numbers of peons. Neither could keep soldiers and peons indefinitely. This brings us to the question of the positionality of these subalterns. Paysanos were able to ride long distances in search of paid labor, respect, and personal freedom. This differentiated them from peasants and laborers of other peasant societies with limited spatial mobility (slaves, serfs, and lower-caste members). Desertion itself was a means of negotiation. It was the mobility of deserters that gave subalterns the opportunity to speak in front of a higher (or different) state authority. Unlike other subalterns (runaway slaves, for instance), deserters returned, seeking amnesty, regiment transfer, or dismissal. They came back to voice their discontent.

If they were lucky and could clear their debts to the fatherland, deserters settled in small rural towns and created new lives as resident-citizens. In these cases, they called themselves to silence. Minimal visibility was to their advantage. Deserters' arts of disguise served a political motivation: the reinsertion into the body politic of the republic by means of a job, a new social identity, and a new name. The set of practices aimed toward this end complemented their explanations about the reasons for deserting. Deserters' search for new identities through forged documents, the protection of relatives, and a previous testing of the region reproduced the rhetorical resources used in their confessions. In acts and words they defended their spatial mobility, their dignity as individuals and citizens, and their right to paid labor. They denounced acts of corruption and mistreatment by talking (voice) and fleeing (exit).

The tone of the stories extracted from deserters' narratives—of defiance and lamentation—is similar to that employed by gauchesco literature. As Josefina Ludmer (1988, especially chap. 2) has argued, this genre embodies a discourse (or treatise) about the fatherland. The negotiation at the center of the genre between the oral and the written, between gaucho speakers and literary narrators, represents the tensions that marked the formation of the postindependence state. The set of alliances within the text, its polemical and multivocal space, and the peculiar double tone of the poems allude inescapably to the politicization of subaltern subjects (mostly soldiers and citizens) brought about by the independence wars. Both the defiance of the soldier-singer and the lament of the literate patriot speak of the modern project of nation building and its obstacles (the fatherland divided, theft and corruption at the top, criminal law creating social difference).

The reasons of deserters are fragments of a discourse about the fatherland, enunciated from a subaltern perspective. Deserters' complaints about illegitimate and abusive punishment situated officers and soldiers in the terrain of "duties" and "rights" proclaimed by the republic and its laws, a terrain in which personal independence and mobility were taken as a given. Yet subalterns complicated this discourse, adding new angles and pointing out new problems. In the face of a power structure that minimized the value of human life, deserters reminded military inquisitors of the human cost of frequent wars. Veterans insisted on customary rights to income and food, and consistently put the promise of social equality under examination. In their perspective, military service was a contractual relationship with payment for services and rules of conduct. It was a contract that had clear thresholds of tolerance. Outside these limits were unnecessary punishment and bodily losses, broken families, officers' private use of their labor, and inexplicable delays in pay.

Clearly, the reasons of deserters reinterpreted the claims of the fatherland over its citizens, reassessing the original contract between peasants and the postindependence state. Contrasted with the discourse of gauchesco poetry, deserters' narratives present important differences. Deserters never challenged the ideological repertoire of federalism. Associations of the Rosas government with tyranny, terror, and sadistic violence, proper to gauchesco unitario poems (Ascasubi's *Paulino Lucero*, for instance), are absent in these stories. Also missing is the critique of rural culture, better represented in Sarmiento's construct of the degrading effects of the desert. More significant, deserters' personal narratives point to practices and goals that escape the frame of gauchesco literature. I refer in particular to deserters' calculated tactics of reinsertion: disguise, *conocimiento*, and legalization.

Through a series of acts of deception and disguise as well as direct appeals to state authorities, ex-soldiers strove to construe new social and political identities. Unlike the verses quoted from *La Vuelta de Martín Fierro*, deserters' arts of deception had a political motivation. Rather than a prelude to reformation or marginality, changing one's name was the precondition for regaining the economic and political rights of citizens. Deserters' arts of deception led to avecinamiento (becoming neighbors), the reinsertion into community and politics. Their enunciations and actions engendered new identities, positions from which paysanos who had paid their military dues to the state were able to speak of their experiences.

In this chapter I examined a small sample of voices in the public transcript: the explanations or reasons given by deserters. Beyond these interrogations and the stories they produce lies a vast, unexplored territory: that of popular opinion. It was surely present in the conversations at horse races, cock fights, and patriotic or religious festivities. It was the motivation of occasional fights at rural taverns; it was the commentary of peons gathered in the ranch's kitchen; it was the theme of discussion at the public squares where cattle drovers and oxcart drivers met. Unfortunately, many of these subaltern voices remain inaccessible to us. We have recovered only a small portion of this universe of subaltern opinion: the narratives through which peon soldiers speak to the state, providing reasons for defying a fundamental law of the land. These narratives speak of defiance in a double sense. They refer to desertions, perhaps the most important form of resistance against the state, and they refer to subaltern interventions into the official record. Such daring acts were moments in which popular political culture erupted into the open, official transcript.

CHAPTER 10

Memories of War

"¡Qué Mayo el de entonces! ¡Qué glorias aquellas!
¡Pasaron! ¡Pasaron! . . . Ni memoria de ellas
Consiente el tirano que el mando robó."
. . . "¡Ay! sella tu labio antiguo guerrero,
Y no hables ahora, si ansioso extranjero,
La gloria de Mayo pregunta ¿Cuál es?"

"What May we lived then! What Glorious days were!
"They passed away! They passed away!" . . . Not even their memory
Consents the tyrant who took away our government
Oh! Seal your lips, ancient warrior
And do not speak now, if an anxious foreigner
Asks you 'What is the Glory of May' "

—Juan Cruz Varela, 1838

Like other events generating great emotional and physical strain, wars usually produce vivid recollections from the participants. War veterans tend to recount events with a multiplicity of details, as if their minds revisited the site of combat at the time of the narration.[1] Recollections prompted by interrogation, however, lose much of their vividness and detail. As respondents try to answer questions, they simplify the events, avoid unnecessary details, and, out of fear or respect, direct their narration toward fields of minimal conflict. The oral nature of the narration imposes additional limitations on these recollections. Without the ordering power of writing, the act of recovering memories becomes difficult to organize, as mental images place events and characters of different chronology and significance on the same plane. *Dispositio*, the ex post facto arrangement of events that gives a written narrative its overall coherence and meaning, works differently in oral recollections. Mnemonic devices are privileged over historical accuracy or literary verbosity.

Understandably, paysanos' stories did not have the embellishments of other narrative genres. When recounting their participation in the federal campaigns to a superior officer or to a justice of the peace, veterans conveyed only a sketchy sequence of events, punctuated by names of battles, commanding officers, and regions traversed along the march.[2] But their stories lacked neither plot (the structuring operation underlying every narration) nor intensity.[3] A basic story line leading the character-narrator through a succession of military engagements organized every narration. Military files reveal the pride felt by most soldiers as they joined their first campaign, as well as the severe stress that the civil wars caused on soldiers' bodies and predispositions.

Narrated under duress, these stories need to be interpreted with caution. The accounts respond to the inquisitor's main interest, namely, to know the whereabouts of veterans during key moments in the history of the federation. Because of this, these "memoirs" present an air of conformity that may prove deceptive. Trying to prove their federalism, soldiers narrated their involvement in the federalist campaigns without directly challenging the aims of the war or the official characterization of unitarios. Underneath this language of conformity, however, were veiled complaints against the federalist leadership. In their accounts, veterans inserted details of their personal history that did not pertain to the federation's history. Deviating from the authorized line of argument, they expressed personal opinions, accused functionaries of corruption, or gave unrequested details about family relations, work, or the injustice of military life.

Soldiers' oral "memoirs" can help us decipher the ways they experienced and later recalled their own participation in the civil wars. Attention to narrative structure and to selectivity of memory can allow us to read, beyond the question-answer framework, the underlying tensions created by military campaigns as well as the transformations of identity engendered by the war experience. What peon soldiers remembered and what they forgot about the civil wars furnish us with clues about the process of memory construction among subaltern subjects. At stake is the tension between personal stories and the history of the fatherland, a tension able to generate insights into the position of subalterns vis-à-vis the civil war.

In this chapter, I am interested in the ways paysanos recollected their experiences in the civil war. In particular, I seek to understand the replacement in veterans' memories of one epic of war (independence) with another (the federal campaigns). This replacement is key to characterizing the patriotism of peon soldiers during the Rosas era. The erasure of memories of the Old Fatherland entailed a peculiar selectivity in the way veterans represented war experiences, for they showed a remarkable memory with regard to commanding officers and battles of federalist campaigns. This chapter interrogates war experience as it was perceived by peon soldiers. It focuses on the ambivalence of feelings produced by military campaigns, on the sense of territoriality soldiers gained while "riding across the fatherland," and on the negotiated or conditional nature of soldiers' commitment to the Federal Cause.

A Disappearing Epic: The Wars of Independence

In 1826, a group of officers who had participated in the independence wars petitioned the authorities to be reincorporated into the military and given commissions in the war against the Brazilian Empire. Others, unfit for active service, asked for financial relief. In their petitions officers underlined their commitment to the fatherland and called attention to the sufferings endured during the wars of independence. From a situation of privilege, these officers recounted their involvement with the fatherland as a story of deception and false promises. Having committed the best years of their youth to fighting for their country's independence, they expected a return in economic security and social respect. In actuality, they had received neither.

One of the petitioners was Feliciano Chiclana, a member of the revolutionary junta and a high-ranking officer of the army in Peru, now, in 1826, reduced to inactivity and poverty.[4] As "a citizen" who had contributed to "plant the Tree of our Freedom," favoring at the Congress of Tucumán the decision to separate from Spain, he demanded recognition. Embittered, he reported that all he had received in payment for his political and military services were *boletos* (promissory notes), which he was forced to sell at 70 to 75 percent of their value. Denied his half salary and without his remittances from Peru, he had sold most of his possessions to sustain his family. The language of Chiclana's petition reflects the disillusion of this group of officers with the fate of the republic in the turbulent 1820s, a period in which the nation seemed to have forgotten its "true heroes."

Veterans of independence were confronting injustice and lack of recognition. Against the high ideals and glories of the past, the petitioners presented the harsh realities of the present: insufficient income and muchreduced social prestige. When Sergeant Major Juan Argüero returned to the capital after the end of the war in Peru, he found his wife and children "reduced to indigence." During the eight years he remained in Peru, his family had received no assistance from the Argentine army. Back in Buenos Aires, he was facing eviction for unpaid rent. Julián Corbera, excaptain of artillery, complained that after twenty-seven years of service to the new republic, he was forced to abandon his military career due to the violent turmoil of 1820. As a result of "anarchy," he had lost his "privileges" and income.[5]

Astonished by the ease with which the citizenry had forgotten the Independence Epic and its heroes, ex-officers reminded authorities of the "true history" of the nation. In their view, the history of Argentina was marked by two epoch-making events: the May Revolution (1810) and the Year of Anarchy (1820). The former was recalled as the starting point of a prolonged war that required great sacrifices to sustain grand ideals: the triumph of liberty over tyranny. The latter was remembered as a time of fall, a dramatic moment in which political disunity led to military demobilization and, consequently, to the loss of status and impoverishment of the "makers of Independence."[6] To the members of this military *patriciado*, the wars of independence demanded both emotional investment and material deprivation. Hence, they assumed that the republic owed them monetary recompense or commissions on account of their patriotic renunciation of privilege and comfort.[7]

To assert the veracity of their presentations, these ex-officers submitted certificates of commission or letters signed by superiors emphasizing the length of their service to the fatherland and the sacrifices endured. Captain Antonio Segovia expected to be compensated for having participated in three major campaigns (Banda Oriental, Paraguay, and Peru) and for having spent seven years in prison in Lima after the defeats of Vilcapugio and Ayohuma. Captain Justo Barbosa believed it was "his right" to be commissioned in one of the new regiments, given the fact that he had received nine wounds during the wars of independence. Celestino Balmaceda, a sergeant during San Martín's campaign to Chile, said that, motivated "by hatred of tyranny and love of [his] fatherland's emancipation," he had rejected all comforts and defied the education he received from his Spanish parents to join the revolutionary army.[8]

Although some of the petitioners alluded to their military expertise and past good behavior, most framed their grievances in the language of social distinction of the colonial past. Having imagined themselves members of a creole patriciado, they found their current poverty socially demeaning. Not so long ago, in 1810, Captain Segovia recalled, his father had used personal influence to secure his admission in the Patricios Battalion, using as proof of respectability a certificate of *limpieza de sangre* (racial purity). Victor Güiraldes added to his military record the fact that he was the "son of a good family" and enjoyed a "good education." Don Manuel Castro, a sergeant major during the campaign to Chile (who retired in Buenos Aires earning half salary), petitioned for a full salary to be able to live "with the decency that corresponded to [his] class." Don Francisco Castelli demanded a commission as the son of a military officer who wanted to "distinguish himself" in the career of arms.[9]

Good family, education, and class were code words for claiming the privilege granted under the old regime to people of a certain condition and race.[10] Arguments of this type, already less than persuasive in the 1820s, became irrelevant and politically incorrect in the 1830s and 1840s. The social egalitarianism of Rosista federalism provided little room for this rhetoric of privilege. On the contrary, Rosistas believed that the old patrician elite had turned against their own ideals, siding with the foreign and domestic enemies of the republic. In 1832, Juan Fernández, an officer of the independence wars, wrote four letters to Rosas to solicit a commission. Fernández's letters were rejected or unanswered. The suspicion of his association with the unitarios was enough to erase all his contributions to the independence effort.[11] It no longer mattered that he had fought "in defense of America's Freedom" and "against the Spanish tyrants."

The poverty and incomprehension faced by these ex-officers reflected a dramatic shift in collective memory. The glories of independence, though still evoked in public festivities, had lost much of their original meaning. The war with Brazil created new enemies ("the Portuguese"), brought new figures onto the Altar of the Fatherland (Admiral Brown and General Alvear), and reduced the scope of the imagined national community (from "Americans" to "Argentines"). The assassination of General Dorrego in 1828 caused a new break with the past. In the new political and social environment there developed a collective aphasia about the origins of the nation. The urgency of civil war, the "holy war" between unitarios and federales, overshadowed all prior military glories, including the recent war with Brazil. A new leader, Rosas, and a new generation of generals—Pacheco, Santa Coloma, Echagüe, Aldao—appeared as the new "saviors" of the republic. As a result, people gradually forgot the epoch-making events of the wars of independence. By the 1830s and 1840s the time of revolutionary patriotism had evaporated from public memory. The era when enemies were called *gachupines* (a derogatory term for Spaniards residing in America) and *americanos* were united in the struggle for independence seemed to have vanished.

Forgetting the Old Patria

Rosista symbolism contributed to this reconstitution of historical memory. The break with the past constituted a major political necessity of Rosismo.[12] Official documents, iconography, and propaganda entailed a new narrative of the history of the nation, emphasizing rebirth and re-generation. Almanacs reminded people that the Confederation had actu-alized the "political regeneration" of the republic (see, e.g., *Almanaque Federal* 1848). Rosas's official biography, *Rasgos de la vida pública* (1842), and the profusion of images printed by the state's press marked the period 1828–1830 as a major divide in the history of the nation. The assassination of Dorrego and the unitario assault against legitimate government had placed the republic in great danger, triggering a reaction that saved the republic under a new federalist pact.

The official letterhead conveyed this displacement of the origins of the nation, presenting the current era as the true consolidation of indepen-dence. Every year had to be dated in relation to three points of departure: 1810, *Libertad;* 1816, *Independencia;* and 1830, *Confederación.* Thus, 1845 was the thirty-sixth year of Liberty, the thirtieth year of Independence, and the sixteenth year of the Confederation. The last pointed to the rebirth of the nation under federalist leadership. At this time, the nation overcame the threat of dissolution by anarchy and foreign intrusion. To Rosista publi-cists, the new federalist "order" sharply contrasted with 1820 (the Year of Anarchy) and the series of "convulsions" that followed. The defense of the independence and stability of the republic against all odds was central to the Epic of the Federation.

The new era, the Confederation, was to be celebrated as a separate epic, with its own heroes, victories, and days of commemoration. The federalist republic, according to Rosas's version of history, had undergone three major political "restorations": one in 1820, another in 1829, and the third in 1833. In addition, the federalists had endured one "rebellion" (1839), one "invasion" (1840), and a series of attacks by European powers. Fol-lowing each of these climactic events were long marches or campaigns in which the federal armies had repeatedly defeated the unitario forces.

Aided by a discontinuity already installed in popular memory, Rosas's publicists managed to superimpose a contemporary epic (the federalist wars) over an old and forgotten one (the wars of independence).[13] Federal-ist campaigns were presented as affirmations of nationhood; with each federalist victory the nation appeared to better withstand the forces of disunity and segregation. This naturally displaced the memory of indepen-dence and its heroes into a second plane. Gradually, the names of the great liberators (San Martín, Belgrano, Güemes, Rondeau, Pueyrredón) disap-peared from public discussion and the Independence Epic became a dis-tant and blurred memory. New federal heroes now guarded the Altar of the Fatherland (Pacheco, Echagüe, Quiroga, Aldao, Ortiz de Rosas, etc.), their names displayed in public ceremonies as saviors of the nation.

Did this shift in official history translate into popular or subaltern memory? The new epic reached soldiers and paysanos through various means: playing cards illustrating key events of the federation; poems to commemorate federalist victories; and *santos-y-señas*, passwords used by night watchmen in the army. These passwords spelled out for soldiers the meaning of the federalist epic. Phrases such as "Unitarios Stained History," "Order the Pillar of Laws," "Republic Without Freedom Comedy," "Anarchy Scourge Federalists," and "Justice Armed Triumphant" presented the federalist republic as a community threatened by anarchists and traitors and saved by the Restorer. Those who exchanged these passwords must have felt they were living in a crucial moment of the nation's history, a new era of national rebirth and regeneration.

Judged by the narratives of ex-soldiers arrested during the 1840s, the wars of independence had ceased to be an epoch-changing event. Of the 525 filiaciones gathered for this study, only two mentioned General San Martín, one named General Belgrano, and none uttered the names of Rondeau, Pueyrredón, Güemes, or Artigas. Correspondingly, there were only a few mentions of the principal battles of the war of independence; three of the veterans recalled the war "against the Portuguese" (1825–1828) and one mentioned "Alvear's revolution" (1815). Curiously, the most dramatic and prolonged epic of war associated with the birth of the nation seems to have waned from popular memory.

The relative absence of references to the independence wars, a prolonged period of suffering and anguish that tore families apart and inspired so much popular enthusiasm and poetry, is intriguing. Raymundo Ramallo, a 64-year-old veteran who claimed to have served his fatherland for thirty years, had nothing to report about the independence wars. All he remembered when he was arrested in 1844 were his contributions to the federal cause since 1828. He recalled his participation in the combat of Puente de Marquez, his role in the 1833 "restoration" helping to gather the militias of two districts, his joining of Colonel Aguilera's battalion in 1839 to persecute dispersed enemies, and his last five years of service in the Azul division. Not a word about his prior military experience.[14]

José Antonio Villasante, a Paraguayan veteran age 60 with ample service to the Federal Cause (including the Campaign to the Desert), reported two wounds in his left leg: one he got during the *guerra del inglés* (the British invasions of 1806–1807) and the other during the war with Brazil (1825–1828). What happened in between? Did he manage to escape the recruiting parties during the wars of independence? The military record does not say. Consider also the case of Rafael Rojas, an old veteran (he was 49 when interrogated at the Palermo headquarters in 1849) who had been forcefully drafted in 1816 to fight in the campaigns of independence. He gave no details about this experience; all he said was that he had served for six years and afterward returned and stayed in the city of Buenos Aires until 1825, when he was drafted again to fight "the Portuguese."[15]

Others casually mentioned their participation in the war of independence as a prolegomenon to their social and economic insertion in the life of Buenos Aires. Agustín Delgado, after serving under General Belgrano in upper Peru, returned to Buenos Aires province and found a livelihood in the southern town of Dolores. He worked in a tavern, did "desk service" for the local justice, and was put in charge of the local militia. His federal sympathies helped him to secure a position in Dolores. In 1833 he joined the "second restoration" under direct orders of Rosas and later became a member of the Sociedad Popular Restauradora. Returning to Dolores with a captain's salary, he remained unmolested until the events of 1839 and 1840, when he again volunteered his services to the Federal Cause, first capturing a famous unitario and later guarding Rosas's house.[16]

Why did veterans forget or not speak of the wars of independence? True, many were too young to remember that period, but this is not a sufficient explanation, for 134 of the 541 respondents were old enough to have known or fought in the independence wars. The insistence of military and judicial inquisitors on key moments in the history of the Confederation could have biased their answers. This factor, however, cannot completely explain their reluctance to speak of independence, for the questionnaire included a military history, starting with first enlistment. The need to avoid self-incrimination must also have played a role, for the more a veteran talked about his participation in past wars, the greater was his chance of being accused of desertion. But again, the verbosity of peon soldiers runs against this argument; veterans narrated their experiences in the federal wars quite extensively.

Contrasted with the silence about the events of independence, veterans' understanding of the events that followed the assassination of Dorrego was quite substantive. It is hard not to be impressed by the information soldiers possessed about the political and military history of the federation. Antonio Cabrera, a peon from Morón arrested in Guardia de Luján in 1844 for wounding two neighbors, knew quite well the basic outline of this history. He remembered 1828 as the year "of the mutiny headed by Lavalle." He associated 1833 with the year of "the popular movement to overthrow the 'refractory' government of savage unitario Balcarce." Still fresh in his memory was 1839, the year of "the Southern Rebellion in Dolores and Monsalvo." And 1840, as everybody knew, was the year of "the invasion of Lavalle."[17]

Cabrera was not an exception. Pascual Escalante, a day laborer from Tucumán settled in Lobos, referred to the unitario rebellion of 1828 in these terms: "when the Savage Unitario Lavalle rebelled against the legal authorities of Buenos Aires province." His recollection of the 1833–1834 campaign was also politically informed: "when the Illustrious Restorer Marched to the Glorious Campaign of the Desert against the Savage Indians." Tavern keeper Mariano Torquemada recalled "the treason of Unitario Maza" as well as "when the unitario Lavalle rose in rebellion." Francisco Medina, referring to his participation in the 1833 campaign, said the campaign aimed at "restoring the laws."[18] They were all well aware of the principal landmarks in the history of the federation. At the same time, they remembered close to nothing about the Epic of Independence.

Were these formulaic constructions memorized in order to be recited in front of authorities? Did federal veterans truly understand the meaning of the terms they used? What was the role of scribes in translating the lexicon used by veterans? Were these "for-the-record" statements countered by a "backstage" talk on the history and politics of the civil wars? To answer these questions we need to pay attention to the narratives of war themselves—to their structure and content. We must interrogate the mnemonic devices used by subalterns to tell war stories. And, as important, we must examine the relationship between war memories and cultural forms common to the experience of peon soldiers.

A Remarkable Memory

Scholars investigating the construction and transmission of memory in nonliterate cultures have noted the importance of mnemonic devices, narrative structure, and social environment.[19] Through folktales, poetry, and theater peasant societies circulate and preserve a given set of stories in ways that differ from literate cultures. The unavailability of written versions allow ample malleability of verbally transmitted poems, plays, and stories, forcing narrators/performers to improvise ways in which a given story can fit into a given frame or structure (a metric stanza, for example). To achieve this difficult balance—to preserve the basic structure and meaning of a story within a context of improvisation in performance and selective recollection—narrators rely on a set of signposts: names of things, simple phrases, or standard ways of describing a character or a scene. These are markers that help the narrator or poet jump from one unit of meaning to the other without losing direction (see Fentress and Wickham 1992, 41–86).

In a context marked by verbal communication certain sounds, concepts, and scenes turn into the key aids of memory.[20] The ability to remember is assisted by the very structure of the narration (the signposts marking the cadence and rhythm of an oral poem, for example). This explains why orally preserved stories tend to show a remarkable degree of stability. In folktales, for example, great variations in narrative detail (characters, situations, and developments) combine with a similar basic structure (see Darnton 1984, 17–68). Oral recollections of individual stories partake of this characteristic: a diversity of stories are told within the framework of a given narrative structure, an ordering marked by a set of signposts that organize and give coherence to the narration.

Historians of popular songs and poems have noticed that, in Spanish America, numbers have been used as signposts for remembering key concepts in the Catholic religion. Numbering biblical episodes or religious mysteries, people could structure their knowledge of the faith without the aid of catechisms. Songs collected in nineteenth-century Argentina confirm the relevance of these numeric *versos acumulativos* as aids to popular memory.[21] Organized in this fashion (pairing numbers with mysteries), the stories of the apostles, of Mary's pregnancy, of Moses' tables of the Law, of the evangelists, of Christ's wounds could be easily retrieved and renarrated, perhaps in ways that dazzled Catholic priests.[22] In a poem-song entitled *Yo Soy un Pobre Soldado*, a veteran of the independence wars uses this numeric logic to deploy his knowledge and interpretation of the Catholic creed—except that he uses as a catechism a pack of playing cards (*naipes*). The ace, he says, reminds him of the "Only True God"; the 2 makes him see Christ among two thieves; the 3 evokes the Trinity; the Jack represents Christ entering Jerusalem, and so on (Becco 1960, 128).

If religious memory was encoded in numbers, commanders' names, geographic sites, and dates of famous battles facilitated the recollection of military events. Like folktales and orally transmitted poetry, the narrations of combat contained in the filiaciones present a certain regularity in their structure. A set of signposts seems to guide the recollections. In relation to names of commanding officers, places, and battles, narrators displayed a remarkable memory. Let us examine, for instance, the recollection made by Bonifacio Martínez, a black peon soldier from Santa Fé, of his various military commissions:

[He says] that in the year 28 when the military mutiny of December 1st headed by Savage Unitario assassin Lavalle he rendered no services because he was working as a *peón enlazador* [lasso thrower] in the Miserere Corrals. That in year 33 when the popular movement to defeat the refractory government of

Savage Unitario Balcarce, he was engaged in the Campaign to Colorado with His Excellency, and after its conclusion he received half release and medal, both of which he lost. That afterwards he went to join the Constitution's Guards sent by His Excellency under the command of Captain Don Eugenio Esquiros. That in the year 39 when the Southern Insurrection of Dolores and Monsalvo headed by the Savage Unitarios they were camping at Juncal, in Dolores district, under the command of Sr. Colonel Don Martiniano Rodrí-guez. From there they went out chasing Savage Unitario Baldéz under the orders of Sgt. Major Don Miguel Reynoso and, that, not having been able to reach them, they returned to the division stationed at Juncal. That from there they went to Chapaleufú where, he says, he remained until the death of the above mentioned Colonel Martiniano Rodríguez, marching thereafter to Azul under the command of Sr. Colonel D. Juan Aguilera.

The account, though simple and framed by the questions posed, is histor-ically accurate: it refers to actual events that occurred in the chronology in which they are narrated and to people and places that were well-known to any officer acquainted with the civil wars.[23] If Martínez intended to show the authorities his commitment to the Federal Cause, this was probably the right amount and quality of information to be conveyed. He gave the names of four federal commanders, three unitario chiefs, seven geograph-ical sites, and one battalion, placing this information within a narrative structure punctuated by references to major events in the history of the federation.

Narrating this short story required a dose of political awareness, atten-tion to detail, and a whole lot of memory, yet the degree of historical accuracy and detail found in Martínez's account was replicated in thou-sands of narratives, as veterans tried to explain their long and complicated relationship with the military affairs of the fatherland. Most interroga-tions, we should remember, took place in the 1840s and dealt with events that had occurred fifteen to twenty years before. Collectively, these narra-tions contributed a wealth of information. The list of commanders, bat-tles, and sites named by veterans in their accounts is commensurate to that found in a detailed historical tract about the civil wars.[24] How did soldiers manage to preserve and retrieve from memory the elements needed for a successful reconstruction of their war experiences?

Written documents did not help much. Their *bajas*, *pases*, or *licencias*, used over and over to certify identity and compliance with military duties, did not survive the passage of time.[25] Medals with inscriptions of dates of battles could assist recollection but were rare, for they became tradeable objects. To retrieve information from memory paysanos could not trust written sources; they had to rely on other devices. The construction of war

19 a, b, and c.
Commemorating
Federalist Events.
The instruments of a
political pedagogy,
these leaflets were
intended to help people
remember certain key
federalist events.
Allegorical leaflets, collected
in *La Rosa de Marzo* (1843).

1830.

VEINTE Y CINCO DE ENERO.

*La Honorable Junta de Representantes, teniendo en con-
sideracion los relevantes servicios rendidos á la
Provincia por el benemérito Ciudadano* D. JUAN
MANUEL DE ROSAS, *lo declara* RESTAURA-
DOR DE LAS LEYES E INSTITUCIONES DE LA
PROVINCIA DE BUENOS AIRES, *y le confiere el
grado de Brigadier General.*

(a)

1833.

ONCE DE OCTUBRE.

La Provincia entera, alarmada con los extravios de un
Gobierno que se desvió de la Ley, traicionando
la Santa Causa de la Confederacion Argentina,
invocando el nombre sagrado de NUESTRO ILUS-
TRE RESTAURADOR DE LAS LEYES, que se halla-
ba entonces en el desierto, recobró sus sagrados
derechos. La HEROINA de la Confederacion,
digna Esposa de NUESTRO AMADO RESTAURA-
DOR, la SRA. DA. ENCARNACION EZCURRA DE
ROSAS, manifestó en esta ocasion toda la gran-
deza de su alma heróica. Simpatizando con el
Pueblo, y tomando una parte activa en defensa
de las Leyes holladas, dirigió con una politica
previsora los elementos que se pusieron en ac-
cion para restablecer el órden legal. La Provincia toda, llorando sobre el sepulcro de esta Ilustre Matrona, le ha demostrado su amor y reco-
nocimiento.

(b)

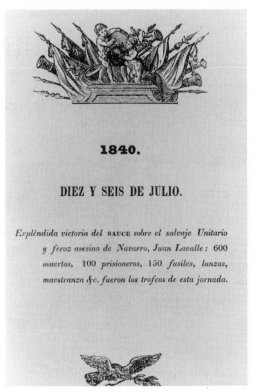

1840.

DIEZ Y SEIS DE JULIO.

Espléndida victoria del SAUCE *sobre el salvaje Unitario*
y feroz asesino de Navarro, Juan Lavalle : 600
muertos, 100 *prisioneros,* 150 *fusiles, lanzas,*
maestranza &c. fueron los trofeos de esta jornada.

(c)

memories by veterans, I suggest, followed certain signposts: first, the fragmentation of time according to the major threats experienced by the federalist fatherland; and second, the naming of battles and officers as a way of locating one's experience within the history of the civil wars. In addition, the insulting of unitarios gave a tone to the narrative, constructing the narrator as a devout and compliant federalist soldier.

Fragmenting Time

Soldiers' historical reconstructions tended to concentrate on years such as 1828–1829, 1833, 1839, and 1840. At each of these moments the nation had been threatened by the devilish unitarios, forcing the good federales to arm themselves to defend the fatherland. By fragmenting time into spans marked by climactic events, *gestas patrióticas*, soldiers could place their own stories within the chronological order of the official history of the Confederation.[26] These events acted as the signposts and aided the reconstruction of memory (no different from the breaks in rhythm and cadence that guide the reconstruction of a popular tale or an oral epic).

Prompted by a question, Antonio Cabrera tried to relate his personal history to that of the federation. What was he doing in each of the crucial moments of his fatherland? In 1828, he joined the forces of Commander Francisco Sosa after the "action" of Navarro. In 1833, he did detachments in Tandil as a militiaman of the Third Regiment. In 1839, Cabrera recalled, he was in Tapalqué on the orders of Colonel Granada when the rebellion broke out, so he marched with his regiment to repress the rebels. In 1840, he joined Colonel Vicente González's battalion and was assigned to an army feedlot commanded by second lieutenant Martínez.

In these fragments of narration we see three operations at work: the use of the major *gestas* of federalism as aids to memory; the display of political knowledge about the history of the nation; and the matching of personal story and national history. Over time, Cabrera had learned to identify important changes in his life with key moments in the federation's history. This he had to remember; periods in between these climactic moments, on the other hand, could be left unclear, forgotten, or silenced. Associating changes in jobs, migration to or from the provinces, periods of illness, and so on with "restorations," "rebellions" and "invasions," veterans located themselves within a particular federalist achievement.[27] This demanded an understanding of what 1828, 1833, 1839, and 1840 meant for federalism.[28] Otherwise, veterans would not have recalled so precisely their particular whereabouts during these epic events. If the year 1828 was not associated in their memories with words like Dorrego, *decembristas* (December rebels), mutineers, treason, and Lavalle, it would have been very difficult for them to remember their particular place and activities in that moment.

The majority of the soldiers interrogated ordered their war memories according to these few climactic events, and the questions posed by interrogators maneuvered the narratives in that direction.[29] Those who followed a different periodization awakened suspicion on the part of the inquisitors. More important, the subdivision of the federalist epic into campaigns or great moments served the purposes of narration, making the task of recollection easier. Veterans such as Cabrera showed a remarkable memory for places and names precisely because they were able to organize the past around a few meaningful moments.

Veterans framed their memories in a secular time, a time defined in relation to the politics of the state, not in relation to the history of salvation. As Christians, soldiers were accustomed to a multiple arrangement of time. Liturgical calendars measured time in relation to different and multiple origins called *épocas memorables*. These included both biblical moments (such as the creation of the world, the universal deluge, or Christ's incarnation) and political events (such as the revolution of 1810, independence, 1816, and the beginning of Confederation in 1830).[30] These liturgical calendars, popular during the Rosas period, contained no indication of the events of 1829, 1833, 1839, or 1840. Thus, the fragmentation of time within the federation age (1828–1852) must have proceeded, not from religious practices or understandings, but from cultural artifacts and practices closer to the experience of soldiers.

Communicative interactions between peon soldiers and the state assisted the retrieval of war memories and facilitated paysanos' fragmentation of time. In particular, patriotic festivities, military formations, discussions at taverns and horse races constituted special occasions on which subalterns could remember patriotic deeds and construct or restore their patriotic personas.[31]

The history of the federation was activated on every social occasion. Veterans must have seen news of these events posted in the streets, must have heard about them through proclamations read by public officers or newspaper articles read by the tavern-keeper, or through tavern gossip. In local celebrations of military victories or in the patriotic festivities, the key dates of federalism were constantly relived. Peons recited in taverns, adventure tales recounted by returning soldiers, and the rumors about politics in the city enhanced their signification. Even in the privacy of a game of cards, peasants were reminded of the principal dates and events that had made the history of the Confederation.[32] In a social environment saturated by politics, it was difficult not to know about the crucial military battles, commanders, and dates that made federalism what it was.

Remembering Names

For a veteran under interrogation, remembering names of battles and military commanders was important. It served to impress inquisitors with his commitment to the Federal Cause. Oxcart driver Norberto Sosa from Tucumán was able to recall his participation in the battle of Viscacheras, during Lavalle's invasion (1840), and also his contribution to the Campaign to the Desert in 1833–1834. Seven and twelve years after the events he gave the complete names of his commanders. Though his appearance was that of a poor paysano and he was initially suspected of being a deserter, his account was considered credible. The same can be said of Sandalio Fuentes, a 20-year-old porteño from Pergamino who, despite his age, was able to persuade the military officer conducting the interrogation

TABLE 10.1 Federal Authorities Named in Soldiers' Accounts

GOVERNOR	COLONEL
Juan Bautista Bustos	Ventura Miñana
Marcos Figueroa	Nicolás Granada
Felipe Ibarra	Pablo Reynoso
Pascual Echagüe	Juan Aguilera
	Martiniano Rodríguez
GENERAL	Valerio Sánchez
Félix Aldao	
Juan Fdo. Quiroga	COLONEL
Gregorio Paz	Vicente Gonzáles
Alejandro Heredia	Pedro Ramos
Pablo Aleman	Marcos Rincón
Manuel Oribe	Hilario Lagos
Angel Pacheco	Pablo Muñoz
Prudencio O. de Rozas	
Lucio V. Mansilla	COMMANDER
Estanislao López	Norberto Zabalía
	Pedro Lorea
EDECAN	Francisco Sosa
(Rosas's private secretary)	Juan B. Navarrete
Manuel Corvalán	Mariano Barrales
Antonino Reyes	Francisco Ibarra
Juan J. Hernández	
	CAPTAIN
LIEUT. COLONEL	Fco. del Castillo
Manuel Mestre	Nicolás Núñez
José María de la Plaza	Nicolás Quinteros
Baldomero Lamela	Pablo Solveira
	Vicente Zabala
MAJOR	Lorenzo Galeano
Mariano González	Rosendo Parejas
Miguel Reynoso	Juan Francisco Cufré
COLONEL	SGT. MAJOR
José J. Arana	José María Ordoñez
Benito Maure	Carmelo García
Camilo Yleno	Marcos Rubio

Source: various *filiaciones*

of his participation in the last campaign. To accomplish this, he mentioned the battles of Pago Largo, Paso de Ceferino, Caagancha, and Don Cristóbal and the name of his commanding officer.[33]

Many years after their engagement, veterans were able to recall the complete name and rank of their commanding officer and build a credible story of their war experience. Their recollection of the war was thus tied to the campaigns of a given commander and battalion. Soldiers' memories in this regard were remarkable, so much so that, listing the names taken from these narratives, one could potentially reconstruct the chief structure of the federal army (see Table 10.1, which contains only some of the military and political leaders mentioned by soldiers). Not surprisingly, soldiers more frequently mentioned their nearest commanding officer. The name associated the soldier with a given regiment or battalion and, by extension, with a set of possible military campaigns. Soldiers recalled their chiefs without much praise; they said they had "followed" a given chief, or that they had "fought in" his company and sometimes that they had "served under" him. In the same narrative, we read that they ran away from the battalion, that they asked for a transfer, that they were constantly questioning orders or negotiating the conditions of service. Association with a given chief, rather than a proof of clientelism and servitude, served as a mnemonic device ordering the memories of narrators.

Also interesting is the "familiarity" veterans had with important political and military authorities (governors, brigadiers, generals, Rosas's aides-de-camp). Some claimed to have seen General Rosas or to have received papers signed by him; many said they had personally dealt with Antonino Reyes, General Pacheco, Governor Echagüe, or President Oribe. This proximity to the leadership, no matter how ephemeral, gave their narrations a special air of verisimilitude. Mentioning a higher authority also served as a way to legitimize soldiers' accusations of corruption or abuse of authority; knowing and naming the authorities was crucial for their survival and well-being.

No less impressive was soldiers' recollection of names of battles, large and small. The information presented in Table 10.2 is taken from veterans' accounts; included are major battles such as San Cala, Quebracho Herrado, Pago Largo, Vuelta de Obligado, and Rodeo del Medio and also lesser known skirmishes or *guerrillas* barely discussed in history textbooks. Names such as Vista Larga, San Pedrito, La Ramada, Monte de San Bernardo, and Paso de Ceferino belong to the latter category. Not part of the shared history of federalism—they were not celebrated in the towns and hardly ever mentioned by the generals—these skirmishes pertained to the restricted world of soldiers' personal experiences. Being a rare witness to

TABLE 10.2 Battles Named in Soldiers' Accounts

Quebracho Herrado	Chascomús	Monte Grande
Colastiné	San Pedro	Las Canas
Mte. de San Bernardo	Caaguazú	Don Cristóbal
Sauce Grande	Fraile Muerto	San Cala
Martín García	Vuelta de Obligado	Arroyo del Medio
Rodeo del Medio	Cañada de la Paja	Costa Brava
Paysandú	Catamarca	Arroyo Grande
Diamante	Pago Largo	Puente de Marquez
Durazno	Ituzaingó	Punta del Agua
Las Viscacheras	Navarro	La Tablada
Ramada	El Tala	Paso de Ceferino
Caagancha	Palmitas	Valle Amargo
Vista Larga	Manantiales	Campos de Alvarez
San Pedrito		

Source: various *filiaciones*

these events, a veteran felt entitled to name these combats according to the place (*paraje*) in which they were fought.

How did veterans manage to remember their commanding officers and the names of battles years after the campaigns? One possibility is that the intensity of war experiences created such an attachment to the past that remembrance came naturally. After all, these campaigns constituted rites of passage into manhood, produced moments of true comradeship, and, to some, represented their first incursions into the interior. A second possibility, more closely related to our current understanding of memory formation, is that the social environment (the "expressions" of federalism in the city and in the countryside) constantly reactivated the memory of the civil wars. Talking about, listening to, and commemorating military campaigns converted memory into a common asset or possession.

Of the variety of social practices that served to activate war memories, I want to examine one: epic/military poems.[34] Sitting around the *fogones* (bonfires), soldiers recited poems composed to narrate the events of each campaign. These poems served to communicate to soldiers the importance of these events. Designed to fix in soldiers' memories a given battle, the poems repeated the date and name of the combat, praising the exploits of a given commander.[35] One of these poems, recited by soldiers under General Pacheco during the Cuyo Campaign (1841), clearly shows this mnemonic and pedagogical function (in Quesada 1975, 114–115). In an unambiguous fashion, the poem reasserts the purpose of the campaign: to exterminate the unitarios.[36] Part of the refrain reads: "Let Lavalle die a thousand times/Let LaMadrid die a thousand times." In addition, the poem names the chiefs who were leading federales to victory (Pacheco, Costa, Flores, Sosa, Lasala, Granada, Rincón, Ramos, Domínguez, García), embracing all under the title *bravos guerreros de Rosas*.[37] The poem also praises two major recent victories of the federal army, Quebracho (Herrado) and San Cala, projecting the expectation of more victories in the future.

Naming commanders and battles was a central device for constructing war memories. Apparently, this way of ordering memory stemmed from the wars of independence. In his *Cielitos Patrióticos*, Bartolomé Hidalgo assumes that paysano audiences can easily evoke the Independence Epic with reference to a rosary of battles and generals. In a "dialogue" (a conversation in the form of poem) situated in 1820, narrator Jacinto Chano reviews the events of independence simply by naming a parallel sequence of generals and battles: Posadas/Las Piedras; Tristán/(Salta-Tucumán); Muesas/Cerrito; Marcó/Chacabuco; Osorio/Maipo; Quimper y O'Relly/ (Lima).[38] In this case dates are missing; the battles, mentioned in chronological order, are the true organizations of time. Perhaps the battles not mentioned—Salta, Tucumán, Lima—were too well-known to the audience to require naming. The names of Spanish generals, on the other hand, required additional characterization. A few attributes (Posadas "el mentao," Tristán "triste," Marcó "flojo y sanguinario") accompany the last names to assist recollection.

Naming the Enemy

Whereas soldiers knew the complete names of a host of federal officers, their knowledge of unitario chiefs was more limited. Unitario names (referred to only by last name and a host of adjectives) used in the accounts included those of Lavalle, Rico, Valdéz, Mascarilla, Paz, LaMadrid, Salas, Brizuela, Cullen, Acha, and Maza y Vilela. Besides conveying the narrator's awareness of the rebel leadership, naming the enemy served as a way to communicate their understanding of federalist war policies. Because war objectives often were limited to the defeat and assassination of a given unitario chief, knowing the name of the enemy implied understanding of the politics of war.

Popular imagination associated the names of Rivera, Balcarce, Lavalle, and Mascarilla with the main insurrections and invasions led by unitarios. Correspondingly, these were the names most frequently mentioned in soldiers' narrations. Other important leaders, such as LaMadrid, Acha,

"Manco" Paz, and Chacho, received less attention. Leaders such as Rico, Vilela, Valdéz, Cullen, and Maza, despite the official propaganda, were only occasionally referred to in soldiers' accounts of war experience. In part, this was related to the official demonology created around the four major characters. Rivera, Balcarce, Lavalle, and Mascarilla were the names that paysanos could see and hear in burning effigies, in cockades and proclamations.[39]

Invariably, veterans placed a derogatory adjective next to the name of a unitario commander, for narrators presenting themselves as loyal federales gained credibility when they insulted the unitarios. The insults showed soldiers' familiarity with the lexicon of federalism. The preferred list of insults included the terms savages (*salvajes*), mutinied (*amotinados*) or insurrectionists (*sublevados*), traitor, assassin, filthy (*inmundo*), arsonist (*incendiario*), denaturalized (*desnaturalizado*), and, sometimes, thieves and wanderers (*errantes*). A collection of unitarios was referred to as a horde (*horda*), a gang (*gavilla*), or rabble (*turba*), all terms evoking disorganized units made up of thieves, vagabonds, and rebels. Some unitario chiefs were known by nicknames (LaMadrid as "Pilón," Rivera as "Pardejón," and Paz as "Manco") related to sexual potency, race, and physical disadvantage.[40] Illegitimately obtained, the ranks of unitario chiefs never preceded their name, only derogatory adjectives.

Ramón Cejas, a small cattle raiser from Chascomús, called the unitarios "a horde of savages" and Lavalle a "Savage denaturalized unitario." Julían Mercado, when referring to the Southern Rebellion, recounted that the federal army gave "exemplary punishment [*escarmentaron*] to the filthy, Savage Unitarios." Peon Juan José Flores called Juan Lavalle "Savage Assassin" and referred to his Uruguayan ally as the "Pardejón Rivera," an unambiguous racial slur. Adding more adjectives to the name of the enemy consolidated one's position as a devout federalist. In his declaration, Facundo Cantero, a paysano from Santa Fé, used four adjectives—*Salvaje, Traidor, Unitario, Pelafustán*—to refer to Mascarilla.[41] In the official phraseology of federalism there were hundreds of names to call the enemy. This repertoire of insults included words such as impious, enemies of religion, vile masons, anarchists, assassins, traitors, slaves to the French, disguised enemies, and bad sons (see Ramos Mejía 1907, 1:265). The peon soldiers who recounted their war experiences did not use most of these insults; they felt more at ease with libels associated with uncleanness, savagery, and the unnatural (many of them rooted in the Christian tradition) than with accusations of masonry, anarchism, or service to foreign governments. Also, the idea that unitarios were somehow related to the devil seemed far-fetched to veterans. The word *errantes* referred directly to itinerants or vagabonds and indirectly to Jews; in this sense, the unitarios' condition of being unclean and denaturalized tied in well with the definition of a religious Other. On the other hand, words like mutinied, rebellious, or arsonists directed the anger to a more historically precise time: December 1, 1828.

To an extent, there was a homology between the official rhetoric and the language used by soldiers to refer to unitarios.[42] Soldiers' understanding of the enemy replicated the official notion of a gang of renegade savages fighting against legally constituted authorities. Veterans' insults stressed the original treason committed by unitarios and their childish and "unnatural" rebelliousness. The treachery of Lavalle topped the list of infamies. Referring to the invasion of 1840, Anacleto Galván, a peon from Guardia de Luján, said: "when the Savage Unitario Lavalle dared to step on the soil of this province his filthy and loathsome foot [inmunda y asquerosa planta)."[43] Lavalle was the enemy par excellence: traitor, daring, and unclean. Mascarilla, a unitario leader who had first belonged to the Federal Party, was bitterly criticized for his treachery and referred to with adjectives such as traidor (traitor) and pelafustán (idler and wasted).

The moral outrage evident in these expressions took some time in forming. Soldiers' conceptual divide between federales = defenders of legal government and unitarios = rebels and traitors stemmed from social practice. There were many instances in which this political division was voiced and apprehended. In the passwords designed by Rosas and used during the night watch, soldiers learned about the meaning of the Federal Cause and the treachery of the enemy. In celebrations of federalist victories paysanos were invited to shout Vivas for federales and Mueras to unitarios. With their voices they separated the names of the republic's heroes from those of its traitors. Peasants and peons saw the effigies of unitarios burn during patriotic festivities; in these events even children could recognize that red was good (friend) and light blue was bad (enemy). Political papers read aloud in taverns (such as El Gaucho, El Torito de los Muchachos, and El Negro) provided the lexicon that made the unitario a completely devilish foe. Perhaps subalterns memorized some of this poetry. All of these message-producing practices built the archive from which soldiers could draw to identify the enemy. Ultimately, these were the sources peon soldiers used to retrieve fragments of the past and reconstruct war memories.

Participation in the federal campaigns left soldiers with a few tangible mementos: medals, uniforms, and release papers. Some soldiers carried these mementos close to their body. Juan Ferreyra, a 47-year-old peasant farmer from San Vicente with almost thirty years of military service, had a medal hanging from his neck while responding to the interrogation. As a militia soldier of the Sixth Regiment, he was wearing a military uniform and had the federalist emblems (*divisa* and *cintillo*). The medal, he said, was awarded to him during his last battle, in 1840 (his arrest was in March 1845).[44] Other ex-soldiers used military *galones* (braids), *gorras* (hats), and other pieces of uniform to distinguish themselves from paysanos without war experience. Such items, together with their release papers, were "proofs" of identity to the new documentary state and, at the same time, emblems of the pride felt by soldiers for having participated in the defense of the federation.

Another means to convey pride was to emphasize heroism in the face of danger. Heroism on the battlefield and relentless commitment to the Federal Cause were the stuff of many soldiers' accounts. Nicasio Mendoza recalled with pride that, when General Paz rebelled in 1830, he enlisted as a volunteer with Colonel Benito Maure "in defense of the sacred rights of the Saintly Federal Cause." He suffered imprisonment at the hands of the unitarios because of his refusal to serve them. Released, he reported again for combat (this time to Governor J. B. Bustos in San Luis) and "had the glory of fighting the unitarios in the action of La Tablada." He fell prisoner for a second time and escaped. After some time at large in Mendoza, he reported again for action to General Quiroga and fought against the forces of Videla Castillo in Mendoza. He then chased the unitarios to Tucumán and participated in the battle of Ciudadela, where he received bullets in both legs. And so the story continues, full of action, scenes of bravery, prisons, and bodily losses.[45]

Together with insulting the enemy and stressing the qualities of federal troops, the narration of scenes of heroism formed part of a political language destined to assert one's unambiguous commitment to federalism. Subalterns could not address federalist authorities in a different way. Such was the language used by santiagueño veteran Blas Ponce when he said that he had served his country during "the shameful flight of Savage Unitario Juan Lavalle and his horde," or Antonio Peralta's statement that he had "the glory" of being among those who "knifed" Unitario Valdéz, or the emphasis of various veterans that they had persecuted the unitarios until their "total defeat."[46] Bravery at the service of the federation, veterans expected, would erase any doubts about their "federal opinion." Also, scenes of heroism helped to silence other moments, the periods in between, when soldiers were pursuing their own interests rather than those of the federal fatherland.

Heroism played against the narrator when desertion followed a heroic deed. In November 1845, Francisco Iturrieta, a drover from San Juan, was found among the soldiers dispensed after the battle of Vuelta de Obligado. To impress Justice Juan Aparicio, Iturrieta recounted the events of Obligado in high-sounding terms: "That he served as artillery man in the Restaurador Battery, and that he fought in the heroic and glorious defense which took place against the Anglo-French pirates last 20th of November. That, when the sun came down that day, when there was no bullet left to shoot, he went out riding with his Wife, who showed up on a Horse in the midst of danger, among the bullets, the wounded, and the corpses. Leaving that field of honor, they went to San Pedro, reaching there the next day, and presented themselves to the justice of the peace."[47] His and his wife's heroism was a pretext to a story that, in actuality, led to his desertion. In fact, Iturrieta was later executed by order of General Mansilla when it became clear that he and others had left the battalion and refused to return. His abandonment of the "field of honor," justified by the lack of ammunition and the adverse results of the first day, convinced neither the local justice nor the inquisitor at Santos Lugares. The same combination of heroism and escape can be found in Pedro Salomón's story. Salomón, a young peon, was a veteran of the Entre Ríos campaign with a long and proven combat experience. He had fought under the command of General Servando Gómez at Pago Largo, Caagancha, Don Cristóbal, Sauce Grande, Diamante, and Caaguazú. He was particularly proud of an act of boldness that saved the life of President Oribe. After that act of heroism, however, Salomón had used a permit granted by General Gómez to stay out of combat for almost two years.[48]

Suffering frequently accompanied heroic deeds. This was the other side of war memories, recounted with caution, as if establishing the basis for future complaints or requests of discharge. Fermín Lares said he had "the body full of wounds" as a result of the war against Brazil. Eugenio Flores, serving under Admiral Brown, had been wounded during the naval battle of Costa Brava, and as a result spent nineteen days in the military hospital at Bajada del Paraná and later in the General Men's Hospital at Buenos Aires. Facundo Cantero recalled that during the fight against Mascarilla he was shot three times in the right arm and that the wounds failed to heal.

20. Fierce Combat (Civil War). The ferocity of the civil wars is evident in this contemporary watercolor. On the right, a federalist soldier is beheading a *unitario* foe. Though fighting with spears, unitarios wear upper-class hats. Juan Carlos Morel, *Combate de caballería en la época de Rosas*, watercolor, 1830. Reproduced from Luis L. Houssay, El *caballo de guerra en la iconografía argentina* (1971).

José Ignacio Saagarra, a porteño soldier serving in Oribe's escort in Entre Ríos and Uruguay, said he was forced to abandon the war due to a bullet he received when chasing Lavalle near Santiago del Estero.[49]

Contradicting the official rhetoric asserting that General Rosas had definitely conquered and stabilized the frontier, soldiers gave testimony of the continuity of the war against indigenous peoples. They recalled the fight against Indian foes as moments of utmost violence.[50] José Díaz had a collection of wounds from his days of fighting the Indians. In an attack against the Ranqueles he had received various spear blows in his left arm

348 Wandering Paysanos

and wrist. In another attack against the Borogas his right arm and side were wounded. The wounds in his left arm had penetrated the bone and his fingers were paralyzed. Manuel Candiota, an ex-soldier retired to an island in San Nicolás, had a bad leg resulting from a lance blow he received during the Campaign of the Desert, twelve years earlier. José Manuel Correa, a young militiaman of Fort Mayo, was lame and one-handed as a result of twenty-three spear wounds the Indians inflicted on him. Undoubtedly, these campaigns left vivid impressions on soldiers' memories. Pedro Jerez remembered quite well the names of the Indian enemy: he had fought against cacique Alon in the Pueblos Chicos, against cacique Chiqueta in the Cortaderas, and against the Indians of Baigorria at Pueblos Grandes.[51]

Fighting with Indians was a liminal experience for soldiers, not only because of the frontier location of these encounters but also because of the ferocity of the combat. The wounds reminded veterans how fiercely Indian warriors had defended their family and property, and the soldiers were proud to have survived these encounters. Eulogio Zamudio said he had participated in the "Glorious Campaign to the Desert," where "innumerable tribes of enemy Indians were defeated." Others even rejoiced in the killings. Such was the case of Eugenio Molina, a veteran of the Dragones Escolta Battalion who had fought Indians in southern Córdoba. They had marched toward Río Quinto chasing a band of three hundred "Indian thieves" and, after reaching them, "knifed them all." We find the same pride in Juan Crisóstomo Alvarez's story. In August 1829, a party of fifty men launched a surprise attack against Indian toldos (tents or tepees) at Tapalqué. In this punitive expedition, Alvarez was able to "kill a few," to "take some families," and to rescue some captives, receiving as a reward a commission as second lieutenant.[52]

Pride and pain constituted the two registers of combat experience. Both served to place soldiers' individual war experiences within the larger history of the federalist fatherland. The stories of combat on the Indian frontier emerged naturally from soldiers' recollections, though Rosas and the leaders of federalism preferred to consider this as a secondary, less important war. Veterans presented this other violence as a plus in their records, as another dimension of their federalist loyalty.[53] In a quieter voice, they separated themselves from the other Savages—the "savages from the desert"—and claimed to belong to the side of "civilization."

Riding across the Fatherland

The Argentine civil wars provided provincianos and porteños an opportunity to ride across the fatherland, a "pilgrimage" that produced important transformations in the conceptual world of paysanos.[54] War experience created the conditions for the emergence of an enlarged horizon of perception. Military peregrinations helped paysanos to develop a wider (quasi-national) sense of territoriality and to get acquainted with a new political identity: federalism. As peon soldiers moved around the territory of the nation, they faced authorities who urged them to define their identity in broader terms than those they had used so far (their localities). Outside of their native provinces, migrants were no longer atamisqueños or riocuartenses but santiagueños and cordobeses asked to serve an even larger and more abstract entity: the Argentine Confederation. True, veterans continued to associate the term patria (homeland) with their locality of origin, but in addition, they learned the meaning of that larger imagined community called federación.[55]

This categorical displacement, from the local to the provincial to the national, prompted by necessities of the state, had its correlate in the experience of paysanos. Veterans' perambulations across the national territory were experiences that, reconstructed later, could assist veterans in reinserting themselves in the small communities of Buenos Aires province. The campaigns acted as rites of passage in which paysanos acquired a sense of the national space, an acquaintance with military authorities and military life, and some measure of their own bargaining strength. This accumulated experience, as many depositions show, helped paysanos to articulate a double sense of identity (soldier and job seeker) that, in the end, made possible their claims to the rights of free workers and citizens.

Almost invariably, veterans' war recollections go from military campaigns to a search for civilian identity. Gradually, as the narration progresses, the emphasis turns from helping the fatherland fight its enemies to regaining the attributes of paysano respectability: a job, a town of residence, a name, and a good reputation. After returning from their military pilgrimage, soldiers wanted to be counted as workers and citizens. The campaigns themselves appear as an empowering experience, a time when veterans discovered a sense of balance between the sacrifices demanded by the federation and their own individual well-being. The narrative of return is punctuated by the need to have a source of income and a social identity in civil society. This balance is inscribed in the very structure of the narrative, in the distinction between the leaving and the return. This clear duality and transition underscores veterans' search for personal freedom and economic well-being once the debts to the fatherland have been abundantly paid.

Genaro Alvarez was a soldier committed to the Federal Cause. Working as a butcher in the city's corrals, Alvarez was arrested in 1833 for wearing light blue pants (a political offense) and assigned to serve in the Libertad Battalion. In 1840 he had his first combat experience, as the forces of Lavalle disembarked in the province. His battalion chased Lavalle through the interior provinces. At Coronda (Entre Ríos), a dispute with an officer prompted him to commit his first desertion. But he did not abandon the war; an appeal to General Oribe placed him at the service of a different commander (Colonel Granada) and back into the fight against the unitarios. He proudly remembered the victory at Quebracho and chasing enemy forces to Tío (Córdoba). Called by his old commander, Colonel Maza, he returned to Buenos Aires province and marched again against the unitarios. This time he journeyed through Córdoba, La Rioja, Tucumán, and Catamarca, participating in various famous battles (San Cala, Valle Amargo, etc.). Before long, he committed his second desertion. In the north, he offered his services to the governor of Catamarca with the view of obtaining a passport to return to his corps and began to work in his personal escort. As these papers were not forthcoming, he and two other soldiers deserted (his third desertion) and were later arrested. After three months in prison, Alvarez joined General Valboa's forces near Belén (Catamarca) and returned to action. After the dispersal of Valboa's forces, he joined General Nasario Benavídez and chased "Chacho" across La Rioja and Tucumán, defeating the rest of the unitario army at Puerta de la Cordillera, in the western confines of the Confederation.[56]

Here Alvarez's narrative reaches a point of reversal. With two spear wounds in his shoulder, he decided that it was time to return home. He stayed ill in San Juan for a while, longing "to return to his homeland and his family." After this, he obtained a passport to travel to Buenos Aires and started his journey back. Not fully recovered from his wounds, he had to stay in Cabeza de Tigre (Córdoba) for two months. Then, finally, he headed back to Buenos Aires province. He rode directly to one of Nicolás Anchorena's ranches, where he worked for two weeks. From this point onward, the journey acquires a different tone, and so does the narrator: Alvarez is now a worker seeking a job. The space of his perambulations is the Buenos Aires labor market, and so his journey proceeds from one temporary employment to the next. After leaving Anchorena's ranch, he found a job as a cattle drover, then went to Quilmes, and there got employment in a meat-salting workshop. Soon afterward, he abandoned this employment and moved to Chivilcoy to work on a farm. Four months later, the rural police arrested him for lack of papers.

Before reaching Buenos Aires, Alvarez had already decided to abandon his commitment to the Federal Cause. In fact, he did all he could to distance himself from the gaze of the state. A heavy rain had destroyed his papers and this forced him to travel without an identity. In Buenos Aires he found the anonymity he wanted at the very site of Rosas's military might, on the city's outskirts, working for a salting plant. After that he moved to Chivilcoy, where he thought of blending into the neighborhood under a new identity. When arrested, he did not bother to show deference. In his view, he had paid a great service to his fatherland and expected some recognition for this. In the interrogation, he stated his desire to continue his service with the condition that he be placed in a cavalry division; due to his multiple wounds, he said, he was unable to perform any foot service.

Several points stand out in this narrative. First, this soldier gained first-hand knowledge of the nation's geography and politics. During the twelve years covered by his account (1833–1845), he joined the federal armies on various occasions, following them across the country. He visited no fewer than five provinces of the interior, from Entre Ríos in the east to La Rioja and San Juan in the west. Territory plays a key role in this narrative, for the return to civilian status starts at the confines of the national territory, near the Andes.[57] His journeys across the fatherland following the federal armies had given him valuable experience; along his odyssey, he dealt directly with the powerful, offering them his services, asking for passports and transfers, and collecting knowledge about the names and places that constituted the political geography of the federation. Back in Buenos Aires at 25, and with three charges of desertion against him, he bargained with military authorities the conditions of his reincorporation.

Second, the narrative is divided into two parts: a first part in which he shows unrelenting commitment to the Federal Cause, and a second, where he decides to abandon fighting and reenter civilian life. In this second part, the narrator has ceased to be a soldier: he is a job seeker. Job opportunities and safe environments now guide his journey. Having ridden across the interior provinces, he now travels within the territory of Buenos Aires province. His body, wounded and weak, is no longer available for combat, only for production—and only at good wages. Though the federation still claims him as a deserter, he acts and speaks as a free worker.

Let us take another narration of war experience. Gregorio Carpio, a day laborer from Morón, age 33, had involuntarily joined the Dragones Squadron in 1839, when he was destined to the service. His first assignment was to join the campaign in Entre Ríos headed by General Echagüe. From this campaign, Carpio recalls his participation in several battles: Caagancha in Uruguay, Don Cristóbal and Sauce Grande in Entre Ríos. Later, he moved to Santa Fé, where the army initiated the persecution of General Lavalle across the interior provinces. He recalls the battles of Quebracho Herrado (Córdoba) and Monte Grande (Tucumán). In Tucumán, he remained in the city after his battalion restarted its southward march. Obviously disengaging from the regular army, he signed up with local militias as a sergeant and was able to participate in the battle of Manantiales against the forces of Chacho.[58]

He stayed almost four years in Tucumán (from 1841 to mid-1845) before initiating his return. He had already gained civilian status (as a militiaman) before entering the second part of his narration. From Tucumán he "descended" to Buenos Aires in a troop of oxcarts and soon moved to the district of Lobos, where he found employment with rancher Don Manuel Caminos. For five months he resided at Lobos, undetected by the police or the army. Later, he moved within the district in search of temporary employment until one of his bosses sent him to get an employment voucher and the justice had him arrested for abandonment of service back in 1841. He was sent, as customary, to Santos Lugares.

As in the previous case, Carpio's narration can be divided into two parts: first, a period of military wanderings following different chiefs; second, a period of labor itinerancy initiated by desertion or dispersal from the army. A porteño from Morón, Carpio was uprooted twice; he was first forced to reside in the northern province of Tucumán and was later compelled to seek a new type of living in Lobos, a town south of the Salado River. When interrogated, he recalled his passage from soldier to job seeker as a natural "dispersal" after the "end" of a campaign. In fact, when his regiment marched to Buenos Aires after the defeat of Chacho, Carpio *decided* to stay in Tucumán. His duties paid to the fatherland, he had to start looking for a job.

Félix Montenegro, an older cordobés soldier residing in Buenos Aires province, found the civil war in Mendoza. A migrant working in Lobos, in 1837 he decided to return to his native Córdoba to settle family affairs after his father died. From Córdoba, he got a passport to travel to Mendoza, where he enlisted in the militias. During Aldao's campaign to Cuyo, Montenegro joined the actions against unitario General Brizuela. He distinctly recalled his participation in the battle of Punta del Agua in La Rioja, an occasion on which he was wounded in the wrist. Chasing the unitarios, he went to Los Sauces first and to Chilecito later. Ill, he stayed there while the rest of the army marched to San Juan. Once recovered, he went to Córdoba and, once again, enlisted in the militias. He remained for two years at Córdoba, until his colonel gave him permission to return to Buenos Aires. On the journey back south, he passed through Rosario, where he worked as a tailor for three months. From there he returned to Buenos Aires, first trying his luck in San Nicolás and later moving to Fortín de Areco.[59]

Like other northern migrants Montenegro was accustomed to traveling, but the civil wars added more steps to his pilgrimage across the Confederation. His stays at Mendoza, La Rioja, San Juan, and Santa Fé were probably not anticipated as part of the normal migratory experience of cordobés peons. Having lived in six different provinces, he had acquired something close to a "national experience." His journey across the provinces started and ended as a civilian; in between he had become engaged in the civil wars. Though he tried to avoid the army, his recurrent enlistments in the local militias put him back on the front line. When he finally reached Buenos Aires province, he avoided going to the capital (moving directly from San Nicolás to Fortín de Areco) to minimize the risk of being drafted into the regular army.

In all three accounts, the civil wars significantly expanded the geographic horizons of the narrators, pushing them into journeys across the "national" territory that they would not have undertaken otherwise. These pilgrimages enhanced soldiers' political understanding and increased their bargaining strength. Perhaps these marches across the federation transformed their sensibilities and loyalties from local to national, from provincianos to federales. It is clear that these long journeys left vivid impressions on the veterans. The experiences allowed them to amass firsthand knowledge about the customs of other natives from the interior provinces, about labor market conditions in the interior, and about the degree of freedom enjoyed by each of the provinces. But, unfortunately, much of this knowledge went unrecorded. What is left for us to read is the strategic placing of the subaltern within the narrative of the federation. What we see is a collection of names, places, and events pertaining to different military campaigns connected together and used to justify soldiers' personal engagement with the Federal Cause. We read stories about marches across the national territory of the Confederation and about combats against the fatherland's enemies (unitarios, French, indigenous peoples). These stories represent the subalterns' enactment of an old contract between the revolutionary state and the peasantry. At first, the location chosen by the subaltern was that of heroism and loyalty, but after so many scenes of combat and long marches, the patriotic subject transforms itself into something different. Sooner or later, soldiers turned into deserters and deserters turned into job seekers.

In the end, soldiers' perambulations through the national territory turned into a search for personal freedom. In the narrative, this search assumes the form of a *return home*. This is revealed by the structure of the narration, which repeatedly divides the story into two parts. This break, present in almost all narratives of veterans, represents the conversion from soldier to citizen-worker hinted at in their reasons for desertion. Bargaining with military chiefs, frequent transfers, scattering of battalions, and the escapes speak of the ever-present tension between two social identities and claims: those of soldiers forced into service and those of citizens who voluntarily choose whom to serve and how.

Conclusion

Like Natalie Zemon Davis (1987) marveling at the "literary" or fictional qualities of pardon tales in sixteenth-century France, I was surprised by the complexity and style of war memories narrated by veterans under interrogation. Like good pieces of fiction, the stories contained in filiaciones had moments of climax as well as movement and progression and directionality. Aimed, like pardon tales, at self-dispensation—that is, to counter the suspicion of having paid little or no service to the Federal Cause—their plot was punctuated by acts of bravery, repeated reporting to combat, and frequent "expressions" of federalism. As aids to memory as well as an attempt to gain credibility, narrators mentioned names of federal commanders, battles, and places, locating them strategically in a narration that led toward a common finale: the return to civil society after years of relentless fighting.

The structure of the narrative, determined to a large extent by the interrogation, privileged an ordering of time divided by federalist feats (insurrections, restorations, invasions, key military victories). The soldiers followed these stepping stones, making their individual stories merge with the official history of the federation. Concentrating their moral outrage against a few enemy chiefs, adding insults to the names of unitarios, and repeating key terms borrowed from the official rhetoric of Rosista federalism, veterans produced "memories" that apparently replicated, in tone and directionality, the official Epic of the Federation. By asserting the official frame of memory, soldiers' stories displaced the glories of independence to a distant and unspeakable past.

The common narration contained in filiaciones, on the other hand, departed in many ways from what authorities expected. It was not just a reproduction or adaptation of the triumphal narrative of Rosismo, for soldiers, having dissipated all doubts of their federalist credentials, told stories that aimed at the reconstruction of their civilian status as workers and citizens. In fact, of the two parts in which the narratives were divided, only the first presented the narrator as an enthusiastic patriot and warrior. The "return" part of their accounts brought home the issue of the federation's debts to its most devout and suffering sons, the federalist soldiers. In this second moment the personal and the official stories parted ways, creating awkward tensions within the narration. Soldiers' recollections took stock of the sacrifices and sufferings endured for the fatherland and contrasted them with the benefits attained in terms of rights and individual well-being. This comparison, evident in many of the stories examined in this chapter, directly evoked the implicit contract between the postrevolutionary state and the peasantry for the preservation of Federation, Independence, and Equality.

Soldiers returned from the campaigns with ambivalent feelings. Pride and pain constituted the contradictory pillars on which veterans structured their war stories. The narration of heroic actions, many times exaggerated in intensity and effects, placed federalist soldiers as essential makers of the history of that imagined community called the Argentine Confederation. The suffering was visible on their bodies and prominent in their stories. In retrospect, it puzzles us to find veterans referring to "a glorious bullet wound," as if federalist patriotism had so permeated their language that it had become impossible for them to separate national glory from individual pain. But, on another level, soldiers' suffering appeared as a lamentation. Like the officers of the independence wars, they presented their disabilities and diseases as debts of the nation. Wounds also appeared as a revelation. The wounds received during the Indian campaigns made manifest the other war that the state wanted to relegate into the past—as an achievement of the "Memorable Expedition to the Desert."

The civil wars entailed a perambulation through the national territory that gave soldiers a new sense of community and a whole set of experiences in bargaining with the powerful. These rides across the fatherland facilitated a practical understanding of what the federation meant in spatial and political terms. Surely, they found this "nation" fragmented into various territories with their own militias and predatory chiefs. But they knew that by articulating the lingua franca of federalism they could better endure the unexpected circumstances of their journeys into the interior. During these perambulations they accumulated a powerful asset: knowledge about the state of the fatherland and its recent history, a sort of practical, experiential knowledge that included a capacity to name battles, campaign chiefs, and major strategic movements by the federalist armies.

Later, this type of proto-national experience empowered them to articulate, in the face of Rosas's most powerful agents, a series of complaints against the state.

Recollections of war also point to a puzzling fact: the capacity of the official rhetoric to displace the memory of independence in favor of a more recent and less revolutionary gesta, the war against unitarios. Though there were powerful reasons for soldiers to forget the Independence Epic—and to reject, in a more egalitarian climate, the demands of the aging officialdom of those times—this silence is intriguing. It leaves us with many unanswered questions: Was the memory of the previous period actually prohibited by the Dictator, as the unitario poem of the epigraph claims? Or was the silencing of the Independence Epic a result of soldiers' self-restraint in the face of a regime that promised more stability, participation, and social equality? Did federal veterans agree with the official notion that federalism was the true expression of the ideals of May 1810? In what sense were federal heroes superior to those who had fought to separate the country from Spain?

While many of these questions remain open, soldiers' war recollections suggests that the pedagogical apparatus of the Rosista state was more successful than that of the independence leadership in popularizing a given historical memory. This was due in part to the efficacy of official propaganda. Commemorative playing cards, lithographic images of heroes, placards with patriotic legends displayed at public ceremonies, and other representations carried to the rural masses a new knowledge of the nation and its dangers. But the propagation of federalist patriotism was also due to cultural forms embedded in the sociability of barracks and towns: the epic poems of battles recited around the *fogones* (gatherings at the fireside), the passwords (*santos-y-señas*) used by soldiers on night watch, or the patriotic compositions (*diálogos*) circulating the details of a federalist celebration. Together with the dating of recent history (the times of Liberty, Independence, and Confederation), the symbolic apparatus of Rosismo managed to inscribe onto the collective memory some key signifiers lending coherence to the moral history of the federal fatherland.

Rosista propaganda stressed the importance of *remembering* as a way of *being federal*. The conflict between unitarios and federales was also a combat about historical memory. "Good federalists" were encouraged to remember the crucial events of the Confederation; that is, they were to place experience within a particular fragment of time and be able to narrate events in that framework. Soldiering was a privileged site for the development of this type of historical memory. In a federalist poem (diálogo) composed to describe the popular celebration of September 28, 1851, two

21. Santos-y-señas. Night watchmen had to remember the passwords (*santos-y-señas*) created by Rosas. These three-word phrases encapsulated crucial elements of federalist ideology. Contemporary broadsides. Courtesy of the Museo Histórico Saavedra, Buenos Aires.

federalist paysanos, Perico Bienteveo and Justo Calandria, recall the federalist epic: "Acuérdese camarada,/De la infame rebelión/De Lavalle el salvajón/Y su salvaje manada" ("Remember comrade/Of the infamous rebellion/Of Lavalle, the great savage/And of his savage droves"), says Justo, recalling Rosas's restoration of the laws immediately after the assassination of Dorrego and his 1833–1834 campaign against the Indians. To remember, Justo resorts to memory aids that could have been learned only in the barracks—the *santos-y-señas*:

Me acuerdo bien de aquel santo	I remember well a *santo* [password]
Que no me olvido en mi vida,	That I will not forget in my life
Red-Unitaria-Tendida	Unitarian—Network—Spread
Que a todos nos causa espanto.	That frightens all of us
Otros nos largó de gusto	Other *santos* he gladly threw upon us,
En seguida y por completo.	Without delay and completely.
Mire si sabe el sugeto:	Look how much this person knows
Dios-Federales-Es Justo.	God—Federalists—Is Just
	(Chávez 1975, 47–49)

Later in the poem, Justo confesses that he is getting old and is losing his memory, but that passwords (*santos*), conveniently memorized, help him to recall the main events of the fatherland: "Yo sabía cinco o sais/Pero en memoria soy lerdo,/Velay este que me acuerdo/Es La Unión-Remedio-Al País" ("I knew five or six/But I am slow in memory/Pay attention to this, that I remember/The Union is—Remedy—to the Country"). And, a few verses later: "Fíjese como me fio/en los santos que he mentao/Y verá como ha pasao/Conforme el rubio lo dijo" ("See how I trust/upon the *santos* I mention/And you shall see that it happened/Just like the blond said" [the "blond" is Rosas]). History, according to Justo, tends to fit into the story lines suggested by the mnemonic triads called santos. The device was efficient, for with only three words a veteran like the author (Bernardo Echevarría) was able to retrieve the meaning of a whole historical period.

In this chapter I have sought to show the ways in which subalterns constructed their memories of the civil war and the extent to which these orally delivered "memoirs" revealed soldiers' experience and identity. Regarding the question of experience, it seems clear that military campaigns expanded peon soldiers' knowledge of the state and the nation. The federal campaigns in the north, center, west, and east of the territory of the Confederation gave soldiers an expanded horizon and a greater awareness of national politics. Concerning the question of identity, war narratives underscore the transformation from soldier to job seeker (and later to neighbor), plotted as a journey of adventure and return. Going/returning, engaging/disengaging, fighting/searching for a job represented the two parts of an identity in transition molded by the experience of war. This narrative structure served to convey a double discourse about soldier's experience: on the one hand, the narration of "sacrifices" established soldiers' patriotism and commitment to the Federal Cause; on the other hand, their suffering entitled them to demand a place in the community of producers and citizens envisaged by federalists. At the end of their long pilgrimage through the territory of the nation veterans wanted to return to the "condition of militiamen," to the "paysano class"; they no longer wanted to be subjected to the fate of delinquents, wanderers, and peons. In a subdued and subtle way, they were contesting the class and juridical imperatives designed by the state.

CHAPTER II

Rituals of Federalism

We deal in this chapter with a different dimension of the intersection between state order and subaltern experience: political rituals. This is generally a terrain overflowing with symbols and messages about the nation and its prospects.[1] Political rituals also display a certain model of governance. According to Clifford Geertz, state rituals convey a set of messages relating to the sovereign's power and to rules governing social interaction. In rituals, the state performs society's obsession with status and hierarchy and, in so doing, displays an explanation of what power is and how it works, a sort of self-reflexive state semiotics.[2] This chapter examines the politico-ideological dimensions of the Rosista order, focusing on the regime's most important political rituals. Rather than concentrating on the repressive, farcical, or paternalistic aspects of the regime, I seek to understand the nature of Rosismo by looking at one of its chief forms of self-representation: federalist festivities. These festivities present valuable insights into the crucial relationship between Rosas and the governed: the rural masses and the proprietor-neighbors.

Historians of the period, while puzzled about the popularity of Rosismo, have failed to seriously examine the architecture and semiotics of political rituals.[3] Hence, their readings of the relationship between the state and the rural masses have been limited and biased. Many have presented Rosismo simply as a dictatorial regime that terrorized its opponents and eliminated freedom of expression. Some have seen the emergence of Rosismo as a product of the barbarism of the countryside (Sarmiento), as the reflection of a peculiar subaltern culture, grotesque and violent, located on the outskirts of the city (Echeverría), or as the result of the political infantilism of the plebe (Ramos Mejía). Others have presented Rosismo as a peculiar Hobbesian compromise between frightened property owners and the state (Lynch, Ibarguren, Ansaldi),[4] repeating Sarmiento's assertion that Rosas extrapolated to the political arena a form of organizing social relations within the cattle ranches.[5] My reading of federalist festivities presents the basis for a different understanding of the communicative exchange between Rosas and the governed—a revision that calls for a reconsideration of the nature of the imagined political community (the federation) and the role of its constitutive subjects.

The Anxieties of a Threatened Republic

The French Revolution produced an assortment of representations destined to impress on the vision and understanding of its participants the concept of a nation and its foundational principles (Ozouf 1988; Baczko 1991, 39–46; Agulhon 1981; Weber 1976, chap. 21). Intended as part of the pedagogic experiment of the revolution, a diversity of festivals attracted the enthusiastic efforts of designers, propagandists, and activists. For a moment, the building of a new nation became equated with the production of images that could represent such an entity. To produce the feeling of union, fraternity, and nationhood, festival organizers trusted in the simultaneity of the ceremonies, the pilgrimage of delegates, and the spatial arrangement of the culmination ceremony in Paris (the Festival of the Federation; Ozouf 1988, 33–60). These efforts resulted in an impressive array of motifs and artifacts, among them, different designs for the Champs-des-Mars, blueprints for the mountain dedicated to the cult of the Supreme Being, different statues of Liberty, and an assortment of pyramids, aerostatic globes, liberty trees, Roman chariots, Greek columns, and Chinese pavilions.

If the birth of a modern nation entails such a display of creativity, creating the illusion of the persistence of "the nation" in the face of civil wars and political fragmentation requires a double dose of ingenuity. The task of reassembling different images and rites into a coherent set of ideological messages is indeed a difficult one. Festival organizers must take as a given what is not yet established (the nation), while rallying support for the continuity of a war that divides "the nation" and makes evident the fictional nature of the collective of reference. If, in addition, the model of governance and the ideology projected from the center of power appear as a compromise between a revolutionary past and a stable and more ordered present, then the representation must produce an ideological continuity as well: a hybrid, ambiguous, and polysemous display of symbols to which both the seekers of order and the seekers of liberty can relate. The urgencies of a civil war contribute additional representational dilemmas. As a force that obviously disrupts tranquility and generates tensions about the allocation of its human and monetary costs, civil war must be presented as a temporary anomaly in the process of nation building.

The *fiestas federales*, a set of ritual practices common in Buenos Aires province during the administration of Juan Manuel de Rosas (1829–1852), tried to create this illusion. Rosismo presented in these festivities a comprehensive view of the achievements since the revolution of independence, the nature of the confrontation between unitarios and federales, and the relationship between Rosas and the people. These festivities can be seen as part of a communicative exchange between the government and its constituency. In front of vast audiences, urban and rural, the fiestas enacted the ideological continuity between Rosismo and the radicalism of the postindependence period, transformed the meaning of the ideals of the revolution of independence, and appealed to religious and festive motifs for understanding the connection between government and the governed. Reestablishing the revolutionary credentials of a new system of governance—the extraordinary powers of the executive, the new administration of justice, the coexistence of a regular army with compulsory militias, the documenting of people's movements, the registration of property, and so on—demanded the repeated use of patriotic and military festivities.

The festivals of federalism in Buenos Aires province combined a certain theatrical display or self-representation of the state with a republican invitation for citizens to congregate and serve the federation. In this chapter I examine the semiotic politics embedded in these communicative exchanges to problematize available understandings of the social basis of the Rosista state. The continuity of republican ritual practices and symbols urges us to reconsider inherited notions about the ideological foundations of the regime. Embedded in these public rituals is a different relationship between the governor and the rural and urban masses, one that accommodates the notion of hegemony through mobilization within the discursive space of republicanism. Examining federalist festivities and ceremonies also helps us to reflect on the degree to which Rosista federalism took root in popular culture and how it blended with its ideological precedent, revolutionary radicalism. At stake is the location of the subaltern in the new representations of the nation: his visibility in the political sphere, the limits to his political expressions, the recognition of his contributions to the war effort.

To the extent that Rosista federalism managed to retain and resignify the rhetoric of the revolution of independence, the support of poor paysanos (country folks) appears less problematic and puzzling. The semiotics of Rosista federalism replicated expressions and values embedded in popular culture, forms of acting politically based on a combination of republicanism and Catholicism. This homology, though not a proof of shared understandings between Rosas and "the people," points to the existence of an effective communication between the two. Moreover, the organization and practice of the fiestas indicates that an important part (or at least a vociferous part) of the resident paysanos, including women, supported the regime. Others (indigenous peoples, transients, and common soldiers) were excluded or given less prominent roles in the festivities. The political rituals of federalism point to the exclusions and differences of this peculiar imagined community, the Confederation.

Federalist Festivities, or, the Continuity of the Republic

The federation, a "nation" recurrently at war and insecure in its borders and identity, had a boundless appetite for public rituals. Easter Sunday, the arrival of a foreign envoy, the celebration of Governor Rosas's birthday, victories of the federalist armies were all good occasions for remembering the recent history of the federation and for reconstituting the bonds that held together the federalist political community. From north to south, small rural towns organized and participated in these celebrations as their collective way of expressing adherence to the Federalist Cause.

Judas Burning

In February 1845, in anticipation of the Easter festivities, Rosas ordered the Artillery Garrison to make eight cloth effigies of Judas to be displayed in the most visible and frequented sites of the city.[6] The effigies, representing two well-known leaders of the unitario party, Rivera and Paz, were laden with political symbolism. The Judases were dressed in unitario colors (light blue) and wore narrow U-shaped sideburns that continued into the beard (French style).[7] In case observers were unclear about the political identity of the effigies, each Judas had a big light blue ribbon (*divisa*) on its jacket with the inscription: "Life to the Savage Unitarios! Death to the Defenders of American Freedom!" This was an inversion of the federal motto that reasserted key elements of federal ideology. The Judases' hands carried additional messages: "In the right hand the purse with the money for which Judas sold our Redeemer Jesus," an invitation to associate unitarios with the mercantile class, with money and avarice, with the treason that brings suffering; in the left hand, the four Judases that represented Rivera carried a placard with the following inscription: "I am the Savage Unitario *pardejón* Rivera, filthy deserter of the Saintly Cause of the American Continent's Freedom, enemy of God and of men; I escaped [December] the first, on the 6th I threw away my sword and my uniform, I threw away the papers that reveal all my ferocity, the enormity of my crime: I seek my tomb: I roar, blaspheme, tremble, throb, sigh, and die."

In these effigies, the symbiosis between the political and the religious imaginary was evident. Using a metaphor as old as Christianity, Rosas presented American Freedom as a good threatened by an ancestral treason. Judas, in his unitario incarnation, has sold the republic (independence) to foreign powers; his treason (dropping the sword and the uniform) revealed his true identity: not just a political opponent but the Devil himself. Once he is stripped of his military garments and journalistic propaganda, his true nature comes into the light: as if possessed, he emits animal sounds and curses, but then weakens, loses energy, and dies. The Devil, having taken possession of the body (of the republic), is destined to die, exorcised by the moral force of federalism.

The burning of Judas, programmed in careful sequence during Easter Saturday and Sunday, reenacted the endless battle between Good and Evil in its concrete manifestation: the war between federales and unitarios. Celebrating the revelation and death of the Devil, federalists paid tribute to the vitality and "sanctity" of federalism, the cause of the defense of independence. Those who watched these ceremonies, Rosas expected, would interpret politics in a religious, transcendental way. The people's merriment about the resurrection of Jesus would be transformed into republican joy: the celebration of the continuity of independence. The burning of Judas announced not only the death of the unitario demon and the unmasking of its local representatives (the merchants, the uppity urbanites, the artists) but the very renewal of the republic's soul.

The symbiosis between the political and the sacred also had a didactic purpose: to recognize and name the enemy, to put proper faces and names to the devil that threatened to destroy the independence and tranquility of the townships of the Argentine Confederation. French traveler A. Moure found that these Judases were used across the Confederation as a means to identify the enemy: "I have seen [the people] burning as Judas General Flores, president of the Republic of Ecuador, General Santa Cruz, General Paz, Generals Lavalle and Rivadavia of Buenos Aires, and Generals Rivera and Pacheco of Montevideo. . . . Would [the readers] believe that in this period, Louis Phillipe I the King of France, Victoria the Queen of England, Mrs. Deffaudis, Thiers, Guizot and many others had been burned as Judas? In the long list we might offer [our readers] one would recognize all the distinguished characters of the moment" (1957, 57). What Moure observed was a peculiar communicative interaction between the government and the people aimed at clarifying the positions, actors, and nature of the civil war. In the changing circumstances of the war, when new alliances and desertions were common, the Judases reaffirmed, made clear, who the enemy was. Through this ritual international politics could reach the masses deep in the interior of the Confederation.

What better opportunity than Easter, with its evocation of treason, suffering, death, and rebirth, to activate the memory of the people and remind them of the main obstacles facing the republic? Easter, a festive Catholic tradition, was now used to represent the treason of unitarios, to name the fatherland's enemies, to renew the people's confidence in the final defeat of the unitario. Underscoring these representations and communicative interactions was the conception of the Confederation as a moral, organic republic. Rosas's inaugural address of 1835, for example, promised a relentless persecution to "the impious, the sacrilegious, the thief, the murderer, and above all to the treacherous who had the audacity to take advantage of our good faith."[8] This moral crusade was consonant with a Manichaean representation of society and politics, evident in official correspondence, in the proclamations commanders read to their soldiers, in the poems published by the federalist press, in the sermons the priests delivered from the pulpit, in the placards hanging from Judas's hands.

Correspondingly, the language of federalist politics was undeniably religious. The enemies were the embodiment of Evil. The Federal Cause was a holy one. José M. Ramos Mejía (1907, 1:217–218) argued that Rosismo tried to turn politics into a feeling and replaced, in language and in practice, the federal for the Catholic. This transfer of sacrality, however, served the construction of a modern state, not the revival of Catholicism.[9] Rosas merely borrowed from religion a vocabulary and a form of representation that was conducive to sustain the political practices of a republic. His political use of the myths, lexicon, and liturgy of popular Catholicism facilitated the communication of ideas and policies at odds with the notion of a democratic republic. Behind this rhetoric was a powerful reason of state: the need to legitimate the use of state violence against a part of the citizenry. Portraying the civil war as a transcendental confrontation between Good and Evil and the unitarios as traitors and demons, Rosas expected to erase the claims to citizenship of his adversaries and, in this way, advance the notion of an ideal harmonious republic united behind its leader.

Patriotic Festivities

In 1832, the justice of the peace of San Nicolás gave this report about the way his town celebrated the festivities of May 25:

> They began with a general and complete illumination the night before, and at dawn, [with] a salvo of artillery and rifles, which continued on the 25th with a solemn chanted mass with Te Deum in thanks for the day of our political regeneration, with the music band playing, with drums, and three rifle salvos

executed by the citizens' civic companies in their best uniform in front of the authorities and all the neighborhood; great acclamations for our political liberty, for the constituted authorities of the Province, and finally for the permanence in government of Mister Don Juan Manuel de Rosas, followed the salvos; then followed the game of bulls tied in the square, in which the *paisanaje* amused itself during the three days, and, in the evening of the 25th a famous ball . . . which was supplied with a great variety of liquors and candy for the pleasure of all the neighbors without distinction; the attendance was extraordinary, a real success, more than fifty youngsters in their best dresses attended, order prevailed. The following two days, besides the bull games, there was music dedicated to authorities and public; on the last day a company of young men on horseback, dressed as gauchos and masked men, all with their federal badges, danced in the streets to the music, and ended up playing the game of *sortija*; at the end, the public gave *vivas* to the provincial authorities and, in particular, to the current Governor; the night of that day there was another public ball and various private ones in town, which concluded with the same acclamations.[10]

Unlike the Easter festivity, here we find a predominantly civic ritual in which the state and its relationship to the citizenry are portrayed in an egalitarian, modern fashion. This is a citizens festivity where social distinctions are minimized, where authorities meet the neighbors, the civic corpus par excellence, to celebrate independence. The major actors are the government and the people, the public that praises the authorities and is in turn treated by them (the ritual exchange included music and food). The *paisanaje*—the part of the neighbor community that appears more "rural"— wears two types of clothes: militia uniforms and colorful, carnivalesque costumes. They assume the condition of citizens in a quite evident fashion: shooting their rifles, shouting *vivas*, occupying the public space of the square, and participating in the games and dances. The festivities are a blend of Rabelaisian ingredients (the public meals, the balls, the libations, the disguises, the different forms of entertainment) and republican ones (the acclamations to political freedom, the parades of militiamen, the federal badges, the flags, the salvos).[11] The religious part of the ritual (the mass) is here integrated into the patriotic celebration.

The merging of the popular-festive with the civic-patriotic points to a different representation of the political, to a sort of festive social contract. Rosismo blended both elements and allocated them well-defined boundaries. The lighted houses, the dances, the salvos, and the colorful uniforms evoke the Enlightenment/revolutionary project, the concept of awakening and activating an inert population for a war of liberation. The festive part indicates the affirmation of the rights gained since the revolution. Dressing as gauchos or sharing drinks and meals "without distinction," paysanos celebrate the equality granted by the new order. Now the celebration of the fatherland puts at the center main elements of popular culture: the different games, dances, feasts, and competitions that transform paysanos into actors of the festivities. What is commemorated here are modern phenomena: the regeneration of political liberty, social equality, and the union between the governor and his people.[12] These are the principles of May cloaked in the order and the tranquility of Rosismo and expressed in a context of greater popular participation.

In 1842 Ranchos celebrated May 25 with similar enthusiasm and similar rituals as San Nicolás and many other small and mid-size towns of the Buenos Aires countryside.[13] The same lights, artillery volleys, masses, music bands, bull games, dances of masked men and paysanos dressed as gauchos, the same formation of militias in red uniforms, the same acclamations to the representatives of the state for preserving the republic's independence. But by this time, new elements had been added to the ritual. On the morning of the 25th, after the salvos and the anthem, the justice of the peace, the main civil authorities, and "many soldiers" walked the few streets of the town chanting patriotic songs. This is the first innovation: a parade of chanting citizens and soldiers. At noon a smaller group took Rosas's portrait from the justice house and carried it to the church, where the local priest celebrated a mass. This is the second novelty: the portrait entering the church. In the afternoon, people played the game of sortija and enjoyed the masquerades (comparsas); in the evening, a great number of people gathered to watch the fireworks and the burning of two effigies: "one, dressed in light blue, represented a woman; the other, [a man] in military attire with short jacket of the same color and a horrendous aspect, was known by the name of Mascarilla." As the two effigies burned, the fireworks ignited, generating "shouts of universal joy." This is the third novelty: the Judas traditionally associated with the Easter festivity has been adopted as part of the celebration of independence.[14] On the 26th, after the mass, there was a "popular walk" (paseo): "Two long rows of citizens, many of them with a flag in their hands, opened the way; the masquerade troupes dressed a la Turca marched after them in couples: preceded by many ladies waving little flags, the Portrait of His Excellency was carried by two principal ladies who alternated sides; two distinguished Federalists, wearing crimson bands and red tufts on their hats and swords in their hands, made up the guard of honor. During the march, persons of both sexes chanted federal songs, accompanied by the band, with the most expressive jubilation shooting, from time to time, a cannon ball." Here we find two additional novelties: men disguised as

22. Patriotic Festivity (May 25, 1844). Patriotic festivities during the Rosas period served to display federalist military might. The square is surrounded by soldiers (infantry and cavalry in double line). Inside the square the public enjoys the game of *cucaña*. But nobody penetrates the space surrounding the May pyramid. Albérico Isola, *25 de Mayo de 1841*, colored litho-graph, 1844. Reproduced from B. del Carril, *Monumenta Iconográphica* (1964).

Turks with "a graceful turban with its half moon and red plumage" re-enact a traditional theme, the dance of Moors and Christians, an assertion of the triumph of religion over the infidels; and women are incorporated into the political community.

The various changes in the ritual between 1832 and 1842 correlate with the transformation in the nature of the Rosista regime, increasingly au-thoritarian, xenophobic, and boastful after having survived the southern insurrection, the French blockade, and the invasion of 1840. Apparently, the celebration of the independence of the republic had turned into a cult of personality with a greater dose of rituals borrowed from relations and colonial festivities, all curiously presented with the pomp of a military march. Now the main expression of patriotism takes the form of a proces-sion in which women participate more actively than before and in which the military parade blends with the carnivalesque. With politics approx-imating worship, women appear more secure in expressing their federal-ism. Paysanos dressed as Turks join the Rosista procession anticipating the triumph of the holy cause. The portrait of Rosas now acts as a synthe-sis of the Federal Cause, evoking the defensive union of townships in a holy war against the unitarios and their foreign allies.

Homage to the Governor

Patriotic festivities invoked expressions of a cult of the Dictator that reached paroxysm during the events of November 1839 (the southern insurrection) and August 1841 (the attempt on Rosas's life). The festivities that celebrated the federal victory over the southern insurrectionists was, according to Ramos Mejía (1907, 1:253), the spark that ignited the fire of the cult of Rosas. Decorated houses, cannon volleys, processions with the portrait, poems written for the occasion, and a commemorative carriage pulled by members of the Sociedad Popular Restauradora (SPR) created the impression of the beginning of an era of "unanimism," infusing terror in the political opponents of the regime.[15] In 1841, when a conspiracy to assassinate Rosas failed, the celebrations spread throughout the territory of the province.

One of the towns that celebrated the Dictator's miraculous survival of the assassination attempt was Dolores, a frontier town 200 km south of Buenos Aires. The festivities, as described by the town's justice of the peace, involved an impressive mobilization of men: five hundred soldiers from the cavalry division of the Fifth Regiment and eighty militiamen.[16] The participation of neighbors and country folks was also important. Led by a commission of four, the neighbors took care in decorating the square. At the center, the neighbors built a large pyramid (8 meters high and 5 meters wide) made of wooden frames and cloth and illuminated from inside. On top of the pyramid they raised a federal flag and, on each of the stairs, placed other flags and placards with poems to the Dictator. Twenty-four columns with flags and candle lanterns (*candilejas*) and eight shorter square pilasters (*pilastras*), also illuminated from inside, surrounded the pyramid. Outside, surrounding the square, were twenty illuminated pilas-ters on pedestals painted in red and white. In front of the square and adjacent to the saloon the neighbors situated the two-column pedestal that supported Rosas's portrait and a flag; a group of militiamen was assigned to guard both symbols.

Games were not absent from the design. At both ends of the street were two arches destined for the game of *sortija*, also decorated with flags,

23. Public Entertainment at the Fiestas Mayas. At this public gathering to celebrate May 1810, the public participates in a variety of games. On the left, people watch as a youngster attempts to climb the "slippery pole" (*palo enjabonado*). The arrangement is traditional: twelve pillars (with as many flags) surround the pyramid. An aerostatic balloon rises into the air (quite like in the festivities of the French Revolution), symbolizing expectation of progress. C. E. Pellegrini, *Fiestas Mayas—Buenos Aires*, colored lithograph, 1841. Reproduced from B. del Carril, *Monumenta Iconográphica* (1964).

lanterns, and small roses. Within the square "in various interstitial spaces a *rompecabezas* [a waxed pole for climbing], and a swing [*columpio*] were set up" for the delight of the youth. In addition, a troupe of men masquerading as bulls and monkeys or dressed in fashionable but baggy outfits (*figurones*) managed to make the public applaud and laugh. Disguise, mockery, equestrian competitions, and the audacity of the young defined a festive, playful space located next to the altar of the federalist fatherland.

The physical layout of the square of Dolores closely resembled the design of the Plaza de la Victoria for the celebration of May 25. Almost identical pyramids, columns, and pilasters were built annually in Buenos Aires since the mid-1820s to commemorate the revolution. Expense accounts for the 1828 festivities show that eighty-four columns, friezes, and cornices were built for the occasion, besides decorating the pyramid.[17] A program describing the preparatory works and the layout of the square presents a pyramid surrounded by a string of lighted columns and the whole square circled by another string of lighted columns. Inside the square and diagonally opposed were the rompecabezas or *cucaña* (greased pole) and, in the principal street, the arches for the game of *sortija*.[18] Apparently, this design remained basically untouched until the end of the Rosas era. (A painting by A. Isola, *Plaza de la Victoria 25 de Mayo de 1841*, shows almost the exact layout and decorations.)

The replica of this May revolution design for federalist festivities involves two types of displacements: one temporal (this was August, not May or July), the other spatial. Far from the center of power, Dolores celebrated a patriotic festivity with a blueprint identical to Buenos Aires'. This shows that the political model embodied in that design was replicable even in mid-size and small towns. The images of the federalist fatherland and its guiding figure could circulate in iconic form across the territory of the Confederation. Undoubtedly, the political incorporation of the countryside had extended the bounds of the imagined political community. The appropriation of the model of the *fiestas mayas* for other purposes—in this case, celebrating Rosas's survival—entails an additional association: that between the person of His Excellency and the preservation of independence.

What was the political model implicated in this argument? Are we in the presence of a new form of governance? The design of the Dolores festival points to a mixed regime of representation, a system of governance that, despite its authoritarian features (unanimity, exclusion, and terror), still claims a continuity with the republicanism of May. To the pyramid representing the altar of the fatherland and the promises of the Enlightenment, the Federalist neighbors added Rosas's portrait and the federalist procession—one a sign of the new devotion, the other a means of exorcising the evil unitario from the body politic. Yet the unanimous, organic federation is still a republic, a government representing popular sovereignty. Rosas's portrait remained separate from the pyramid, facing it, as if guarding the altar of the fatherland and the principles associated with it.

The arrangement of the square at Dolores validates this interpretation. The scene is overflowing with patriotic references: there are at least thirty-three flags and seventy-six banners (*banderolas*) in the square. Rosas's portrait and the pyramid also hoist large flags. The inscriptions over the steps of the pyramid allocate prestige equally between Rosas and the military hierarchy said to have preserved the unity and independence of the Confederation. The verses pay tribute to the Dictator's generosity, patriotism, and wise policies and, at the same time, exalt the heroism of the generals victorious at Quebracho and San Cala.[19] The symmetry of the whole design evokes the order of this peculiar republic, an order based on the disciplinarian interaction between the governor and the people and dependent on paternalistic gestures and reassurances of rights on the part of the former. The regime's different modes of interaction with "the people" (the body of federalist neighbors), a combination of coercion and consent, order and amusement, find expression in the *fiestas*. This explains the merging of the popular-festive with the military-patriotic in the federalist festivals. At a time of perceived national danger, the presence of games suggests the state's need to emphasize the other side of patriotic sacrifice. Besides the evocation of military victories and praises to the Dictator, the public space contains the carnivalesque, festive expressions of "the people," the true heirs of the May revolution.

The Cult of Heroes

In May 1839 the residents of Arrecifes, a town 180 km to the northwest of Buenos Aires, commemorated the federalist victories of Pago Largo, Altos de Córdoba, and Yungay with four days of festivities.[20] These victories anticipated the end of wars waged on multiple fronts: Pago Largo marked the victory of the federal troops in Corrientes, Altos de Córdoba was another chase of unitarios through the interior provinces, and Yungay put an end to the Bolivian war. With 1,800 pesos produced by a public subscription, the neighbors were able to finance several balls, a mass, a public barbecue (*asado con cuero*), an orchestra, and a game of *sortija*.[21] Unlike the festivities at Dolores (1841), here the budget was allocated mainly to public entertainment. The occasion merited no decoration of the public square and almost no political speeches. The only harangue was heard at the church, where the local priest exhorted his federal parishioners to unite in defense of the holy cause and to thank Providence for the victories federalists had won.

People of diverse social standing—"the principal hacendados of the district," "a great number of neighbors," and "the public"—joined the different festive events to renew, with their presence and expressions, their vows to the Federal Cause. Eating and drinking in abundance was an important part of these festivities; it was, in fact, a form of politics. Every so often, someone interrupted the feast and proposed toasts to the cause in the form of *Vivas* to federal generals and leaders and *Mueras* to the enemy; the public responded with the same. This ritual, replicated over and over, united the military victories of the federal armies with the other achievements of the regime—"order, abundance, and happiness"—closer to the heart (and the stomach) of small-scale producers.

In 1840, seven years after the "second restoration" (a popular uprising in defense of true federalism and against the government of Balcarce), the town of Areco commemorated that event with similar rituals: houses lit up for several nights, meetings at the justice office, marches with bands along the streets, fireworks, shouting of *vivas*, burning of Judases and light blue cards, a procession with portrait, a *sortija* game, and a barbecue open to everybody. The extemporaneous festivity was probably a means to unify the population behind the Federal Party in the event of an invasion by *unitario* forces. Organized in the devotional-patriotic mold but with less formality than the May festivities, the celebration took place in a climate of mandated social equality. "The meeting was purely federal, without etiquette," commented the justice of the peace, proud that all neighbors, the poor and the rich, abided by the instruction to dress *a lo paysano*. This leveling of appearances reminded the neighbors of one of the principles of the May revolution: equality under the law. Under the Rosas regime, this equality was predicated on war, that is, on a division of political society into two irreconcilable parties, two religions. In the square, while the adults burned light blue cards to scare the *unitario* sympathizers in town, the children played war: one group (the "federales") chasing, arresting, and whipping the other group (the "unitarios").[22]

Victory elicited festive celebrations from the neighbors (in Arrecifes), while the anticipation of an enemy attack brought back the military parades and the processions (in Areco). What these celebrations had in common is that they served to communicate, in a quite visible manner, the ebb and flow of the civil war. The town's residents could not ignore the noisy celebrations; usually, the festivities involved salvos with cannons and rifles, fireworks exploding, the clanging of bells, and groups of neighbors shouting on the streets or singing to the beat of military marches.[23] In a context of widespread illiteracy, these events contributed to spread news about the war that connected common folks to the affairs of the nation. Indirectly, these festivities aided the ordering of collective memory around military and state events (victories, treaties, campaigns, popular uprisings, etc.). Like the episodes of Judas burning, festivities of military victories and common defense in the face of impending attacks contributed to people's political literacy and understanding of international relations.

War, a common experience for people living in the Rosas period, recurred in other local events as well. The visit of an allied general or of diplomatic representatives kept neighbors informed (and often worried) about the evolution of the federation and its shifting alliances and conflicts. Governor Estanislao Lopez's visit to Areco in 1837, for example, merited the following ritual: salutations by a local worthy (*benemérito*) citizen, a welcome speech by the captain of the militias, a ride through streets specially decorated for the occasion, the infantry in formation presenting arms, cannon salvos, and a group of neighbors accompanying the visitor on horseback to the next town.[24] Similar protocol was offered the next year to a military envoy from England. The town selected twenty-five neighbor militiamen, the "most judicious and of better presence," all dressed in red, to accompany the visitor from Areco to Villa Luján.[25] In this way, the neighbor-citizens could participate in the events of the nation without being on the war-front.

In fact, life in the Buenos Aires countryside was significantly transformed by the civil war, despite the fact that most of the fighting took place outside the territory of the province. The Sunday exercises of the militias, the celebrations of victories, the periodic recruitment drives, and the need to collect and send horses or cattle to nearby regiments maintained connections with the affairs of war. The church played an important role in spreading news about the civil war and in organizing support for the Federal Cause. To commemorate the victory of the federal army over the insurrection of Dolores and Monsalvo, the neighbors of Ranchos, led by the local priest, organized a procession around the image of the virgin of Pilar, a procession that ended with *vivas* to the federation.[26] Church and state, neighbors and authorities united, built the collective memory of the federation: its victories, betrayals, and alliances.

Thus, through the self-organization of neighbors or the instructions and protocols emanating from Buenos Aires, the countryside developed ritualized forms of honoring the heroes of the fatherland. This cult included the figure of Rosas in a double position: as the leader and as the Hero of the Desert. On the altar of the fatherland there was a hierarchy. First came generals such as Pacheco, Echagüe, LaMadrid, and Quiroga, who had commanded major victorious campaigns for the federal forces; next came generals whose fame was limited to a certain region (Prudencio Ortiz de Rosas, Vicente Gonzáles, among others); and then came the local authorities and captains of militias who contributed to the logistics of the war. Governor Rosas did not belong in this military pyramid. He was more of a political hero; his rank as Captain General of the federalist armies was never the object of a festivity.

A proclamation read by the justice of the peace of San Nicolás after the federal victories of 1831 gives us insight into the nature of Rosas's leadership or, put in other words, of his relationship to the fatherland.[27] Rosas, the document explains, has become the hero of Buenos Aires simply by staying on his ranch and not becoming involved in city rumors and factional politics.[28] Then the proclamation praises Rosas for arranging, in coordination with General Estanislao López (from the neighboring province of Entre Ríos), "the salvation of the republic"—an allusion to both the military actions they commanded and the agreements they reached. His political skills had "given the townships back their liberty"; his master plan was to rescue the republic from the "tyrants" and to reinstitute the federal system. Rosas and López are positioned here at the top of the republican altar; they are the Heroes of the Argentine Republic. But their work is the construction of the political apparatus of the Confederation (the pact of 1831) and the pacification of their respective provinces, not the conduct of war.

Thus, Rosas's heroism differed from that of the military hierarchy. He was the hero of a political and moral confrontation of enormous proportions: the conflict between the forces of Order and the forces of Anarchy. It was his negotiating skills, his tenacity in the pursuit of order, and his strategic retreat from the public space that was celebrated. This was the basis for his claim to undisputed rule. Implicit in this subject position was the attribute of protector or guarantor of rights. In this construction, his regime of governance was based on popular support and republican principles. The declaration ends with a summons to "the citizens of all classes" to demonstrate the recognition Rosas deserves for having recovered "the liberties of the people" by organizing illuminations, marches, and various forms of entertainment. The federal festivities would reenact this republican compromise: citizens would celebrate in public the federal republic and their support of the governor in a festive, civic, and religious manner.

Continuity and Change in the Fiestas Federales

We can identify at least three models of political representation in the festivals: the colonial, the revolutionary, and the federalist. In different degrees, these express the sacralization of politics—the collapsing of religion and state politics—but the function of each is quite different. In the colonial model popular festivity appears tied to a deferential cult of the Crown as the champion of the values of Catholicism. The festival merely reproduces an ideal conception of a moral society fragmented into castes and strata; its function is merely expressive. The colonial procession enacts both the subjects' religious fervor and their corporate subordination to the center. The revolutionary model attempts to educate the masses about the meaning of independence, positing a relationship of resemblance between national and individual liberty; its theater is didactic. Whereas the colonial model celebrates key moments in the calendar of royalty and church as a concession to the festive spirit of the locality—replicating, therefore, a paternalistic mode of governance—the revolutionary festival attempts a pedagogy of ideals (Independence, Liberty, Equality, Fraternity) destined to change popular understandings. The federalist model enacts a Manichaean politics in which the "sane" part of the republic is engaged in a holy war with foreign and domestic foes; its function is interpretive. In a context of greater popular participation and experience with modern rights, the festival reasserts a conceptual continuity of republican ideals and resignifies the legacy of independence. Its sacred moments serve to redirect the energy of popular morality toward a new enemy: the upper-class unitarios.

Colonial festivals combined the traditional dance of Moors and Christians with bullfights, masquerades, fireworks, equestrian competitions, and baroque theater.[29] Corpus Christi in particular served to deploy popular representations of biblical themes. Figures of dragons (tarascas), giants, big-heads (cabezones), and masked men alluded to the different incarnations of evil in a socially diverse polity (Duarte 1987). The procession organized this diversity by reestablishing a hierarchical order: first marched the viceroy, the bishop, and the judges; next the local authorities (majors and regidores); next the religious orders and the distinguished neighbors; only then came the trades, each representing a particular drama or allegorical piece (Carvajal y Robles 1950). Occasionally, the other colonial subjects, Indians and blacks, were allowed to participate in the procession. The placards, hangings, and paintings decorating the streets as well as the praises (loas) recited for the occasion alluded to the divinity of the King's rule and its paternalistic model of governance. The Crown permitted the enjoyment of its people within a framework that combined reverential disposition with mockery and role inversion.

Revolutionary leaders accustomed the people of Buenos Aires to festivities characterized by expensive decorations, artillery volleys, and illuminations, true spectacles of the birth of a nation.[30] The government took this occasion to celebrate liberty and paternalistic elite rule, granting freedom to a few "meritorious" slaves and distributing subsidies among widows, invalids, and needy artisans. In these celebrations the people acted as spectators, contemplating in wonder the aerostatic balloon, the theatrical representations, the fireworks, the illuminated pyramid, the music band. Their active role in the square was circumscribed to games such as cucañas, the rompecabezas, and the sortija. The relationship between government and people was educational. An enlightened government related to its people by teaching them the principles of freedom and popular sovereignty. The presence of military troops was limited. Numerous schoolchildren (as many as seven hundred participated in the events, marching with flags to the square, forming around the pyramid, and chanting the national anthem (Saénz 1969).

Federalist festivals preserved some of the icons introduced by revolutionary designers: the pyramid, the columns, the flags, the illuminations; others, they abandoned. In the Rosista ceremonies, formations of militiamen and soldiers replaced those of schoolchildren. Removing schoolchildren from the patriotic festive space (children represented the future of the young nation) underscored the abandonment of the civic-pedagogic model in favor of "new" forms of representing the political: the devotional, the festive, the military. Also absent were Inca motifs, used repeatedly by the revolutionary leadership. The ordered procession of the enlightened *notables* gave way to the more inclusive procession of federalist neighbors, a more participatory and, at the same time, more threatening ritual. The relationship between this new political subject and the government, now fixed in the portrait, assumed that the people understood and participated in politics.[31]

One element of continuity between the colonial and the Rosas period was the dance of Moors and Christians. A tradition brought from Spain during the sixteenth century, these dances commemorated the Spanish *Reconquista* from the Moors (see Warman 1972; Guastavino Gallent 1969; *Relación de las fiestas* 1830). During the celebration of Corpus Christi, two bands of colorfully dressed combatants (one in Moorish attire, the other in Spanish chivalry garments) would simulate a confrontation using canes, wooden swords, and shields. Usually the Moors would steal a chalice or a sacred image or storm a wooden castle, triggering the war of reconquest. Obviously, the Spaniards would have the final victory, the Moors relinquishing their conquest and accepting conversion. The dance enacted a common theme in Spanish medieval and early modern culture: the unity of the forces of God against the infidels (represented respectively by the cross and the half-moon). On American soil, the dance suffered a series of transformations that reflected the new dramatic experience of the *Conquista*.[32]

Postindependence patriotic celebrations avoided this motif in the attempt to separate civic from religious festivities. Only later, in the second part of the Rosas period, do we see the reemergence of this ancient dance, now at the service of a different representation: a republican nation threatened by internal and external foes. Paysanos dressed as Moors would enact a Manichaean vision of the republic in a festivity destined to unite efforts

378 Wandering Paysanos

behind a war of extermination against the unitarios. The dance of Moors and Christians was, in this sense, an appropriate drama for representing the federalist wars, except that who was on the winning side was no longer evident. Federalists were surely on the side persecuting the "infidels," but they were also there to prevent a *reconquista* by imperialist powers.

During postindependence, the creole leadership tried to educate its audience about the meaning of independence by means of morality plays centered on the indigenous character of America and the plight of indigenous peoples. In these dramas, Indian chiefs would break their shackles and lead the pueblo to independence; in the end, they would all pay tribute to Civil Liberty.[33] These motifs disappeared in the Rosas period, replaced by other forms of entertainment, among them the parade of *gauchos beduinos* or *enmascarados*. The theatrical and pedagogic was replaced by the burlesque and participatory, resembling colonial modes of representation. Indian dramas gave way to a highly ritualized procession that united the church, the justice system, and the public square. Devoid of the didactic, enlightened flavor of early republican festivals, Rosista festivals no longer celebrated Liberty in its double dimension (personal and national liberation). Instead of placards saluting the conquest of civil liberty, we find placards with names of generals and military victories. In part, this change at the level of representation incorporated the new requirements of politics, now transformed from an elite concern into a popular demand. The dramatic expansion of the Buenos Aires electorate after the 1821 franchise gave new meaning to the figure of the paysano-citizen, now in charge of saving the threatened republic (see Ternavasio 1995).

A parallel contrast may be established in relation to the festivals of the federation during the French Revolution.[34] Thousands of similar festivities celebrated across the country led to fraternization between neighboring communities. The pilgrimage of delegates to Paris helped to actualize the concept of federation. A multitude of *federés* marching in military order entered the Champs-des-Mars to deliver the civil oath and join in a massive communal meal. An open sacred space, the amphitheater anticipated the boundless joy of people celebrating liberty. Few monuments interrupted the view: the mountain, the liberty tree, the obelisk, pyramids, all pointing toward the heavens, where an aerostatic balloon concentrated the attention of viewers (Ozouf 1988, 33–60). The pedagogy of such a combination of horizontal vastness and elevation of sight was clear: the federation ushered in a new period of brotherhood. Through their ritual activities, the delegates were creating a new political entity.[35] In Paris, the concept of union or federation overshadowed that of equality. The design privileged a new hierarchy: in the inner circle surrounding the altar of the fatherland were the soldiers; around them was a circle of notables; and around them were the people, mere spectators of the festival (58–60). Thus, the festivals enacted two major exclusions: that of the people, transformed into spectators of a military parade, and that of the aristocracy, displaced out of the spectacle by design.

Federalist festivities showed little concern with simultaneity. The emphasis was placed instead on the shaping of a collective memory around episodes of war and key moments in the history of the federation.[36] With few exceptions, the celebrations took place in the local community without a pilgrimage or peregrination to a center of power; instead, Rosas's portrait, a tangible representation of the center of this political system, went to each town. Furthermore, rural towns tried to replicate, at least during the patriotic festivals, the model of the city. The spatial design of these festivals (particularly the May festivals) also points to a different conception of political society. Instead of an open space flooded with militia delegates we see a space with clearly defined boundaries for expression. The altar of the fatherland is guarded by the local uniformed militias (armed neighbors). "The people" occupy the festive space in the interstices of the square or as spectators on the side of the streets. Surrounding them is the regular army, which constrains the possibilities of expression of "the people."[37]

The bazaar-like quality of the French festivals related to the novelty of the concepts represented. The profusion of mismatched icons found in the French festivals contrasts with the simplicity of the fiestas federales, where a few elements (pyramids, columns, arches, flags) are sufficient to evoke the past. The Rosista republic was from the start conceived as a preexisting reality. Taken as a given, the federation was something to be defended from external and internal enemies, a moral force recurrently in need of regeneration. Hence, the rituals appropriate for a new beginning and the images to help people envision the nation (the liberty tree or the representation of the Supreme Being) were absent. One other absence is also noticeable: the near invisibility of notable property owners.

The festival preserves a three-pronged division of space: the sacred, the patriotic, and the festive. Within the square, the focal point granted to the pyramid emphasized the solidity of the republic and the desire to immortalize its heroes.[38] The status produced by the ceremony, as in the ceremonies at Champs-des-Mars, accrued to the military hierarchy. With regard to the pyramid, the portrait occupies a side position, not a central one, underscoring the role of Rosas as a custodian of independence. During the day masquerades and games and at the night balls there was little intrusion of the state; the portrait remained inside the church while people danced and feasted. This particular representation of the republic underscores the nature of Rosas's rule. As the head of a republic predicated on the order produced by the justice system and the war waged by the military, Rosas still needed the support of neighbors. Hence, reenacting their support through a procession was not a superfluous exercise. The actors of this procession were the members of the new political community, the federalist neighbors, some of them dressed as federales or militiamen and carrying or accompanying the portrait, others disguised as Moors, figurones, or animals—all *acting politically*.

The Popular Reception of Federalism

Political rituals are also exercises in communication between state authorities and the people. Rather than extraordinary events disconnected from the structure of everyday life, they contain forms of expression and meanings that emanate from the latter. They express—not without tension—the confluence between top-down representations of the state and popular ways of understanding the political.[39] Because of this, the very texts of these communicative exchanges provide clues for understanding subaltern politics. Understood as communicative exchanges, the discourse of political rituals could be measured against other forms of communication. Speeches by military leaders and priests, in particular, contain in their very structure and rhetoric significant similarities to the "language" of the federalist festivals. Addressed to popular audiences gathered in public spaces different from those of the *fiestas* (the pulpit, the military garrison), they emphasize the symbiosis between the two conceptions of the republic—one civic-political, the other popular-religious.[40]

Catholic priests contributed to spread this association between politics and religion, persuading their parishioners that the federation meant peace in their homes and good luck in their labors. More important, they told parishioners that the lessons of federalism were not against Christian teachings. Some even argued that the federation had brought an end to the droughts, producing abundant rain, green pastures, and general prosperity (Ramos Mejía 1907, 1:262–264). This association must have resonated well with the small-scale producers of the pampas, whose material well-being (the reproduction of cattle, the wheat harvest) was tied to the vagaries of weather as much as to the conscription and requisition activities of the state. Priests also contributed to spread the powerful religious metaphors that helped to explicate the role of Rosas (and of Encarnación, his wife) in sustaining the republic.

The sermon delivered by the priest of the Quilmes parish in a mass given in celebration of Rosas's survival of the attempt against his life is symptomatic of this rhetorical articulation.[41] The Savior, explained the priest, despite all the multiple inequities and humiliations, suffered in silence until the moment he saw the *desacatos* (insubordination) in the temple: "Reassuming his ancient name of God of Revenge, he took the whip in his sacred hands and expelled from there those *inicuos* [sic] that profaned it [the temple]." If we replace the unitarios for the Pharisees, Rosas for the Savior, and the republic for the temple, the logic of this interpretation of the biblical episode becomes clear: the legitimization of the holy war against the unitarios as a means of regenerating the republic. In the same sermon, the priest dedicated the chapel to the Virgin of Rosario, the patron of the army. Only the Virgin, he stressed, can give security; because of her role as Mother, only She can protect independence. The Savior– Vengeful God and the nourishing Virgin-Mother were the foundations of the purity and abundance of the federated republic.[42]

Military harangues addressed to the soldiery provide a second communicative interaction we should pay attention to. In 1833, as commander in chief of the Campaign to the Desert, Rosas explained to the soldiers through various *ordenes del día* read aloud by their commanding officers matters of high politics: the meaning of federalism; the province's need for a constitution; and the conduct of "civilized war" (a war without excesses, robberies, and insubordination):

> Federation is in effect the illustrious Union which gives life to the *pueblos* and forms of all them a happy family. . . . It is [also] the sepulchre of the tyrants. The Heavens! Eternal Justice has favored, federals, our Holy cause! The day we yearned for is coming, the day of our Provincial Federative Constitution. And we should hope that all provinces will sanction theirs under the same form, and then they shall all start working on the foundations of the great National Federative Charter; that, when the passions have calmed, our legislators, guided by the lights of these provincial codes, the lessons of the past, and the concepts [produced] by experience, will sanction and will present to us the masterpiece of our future life.[43]

Remarkably, Rosas felt the need to explain to common soldiers the central debates about the need and opportunity for drafting a national constitution, hence about the relationship between legislators and soldiers and the future of the republic. To do so, he cast the Confederation in a language familiar to the audience. In his address, the Confederation appears as a great family brought about by the will of the people, as a moral organism sanctioned by divine justice, as a house that admits no tyrants, as a system of rights to be encoded into a constitution. Popular sovereignty, God, family, and the legal order—all constituted the federalist republic.

A second way of assessing the reception of federalism among the subaltern classes entails studying the practices at the festivals in relation to the set of actions that defined what was a legitimate political expression. The correspondence among the ways of political expression, within and outside the fiestas, constitutes further confirmation of the mundane character of these displays of federalist support. Outside of the festive space, in everyday life, federalism accepted different expressions of adherence, sympathy, or support for the Cause. These expressions referred to the way people dressed, talked, or provided goods and services to the defense of federalism. Politics was closer to the world of quotidian experience and, hence, involved the subaltern more directly than in literate societies. The adherence could vary from lukewarm to hot, from quiet to enthusiastic. Most people, especially if they were resident-neighbors, were subject to less intense demands of political conformity. It was enough to dress as a federal, not to openly defy the Federalist Cause, and to contribute occasionally with goods and minor services (see Salvatore 1998a).

There were four ways of being a federal. An obvious form was to verbally express one's federalism in public places and without compulsion. Those who acted this way were called *federales de opinión*. This form of commitment was subject to the community's judgment. A more prescriptive form consisted in rendering services to the Federal Cause, chiefly military duty but also ancillary services to the judiciary and the police. Those who expressed their federalism in this way were called *federales de servicio*. Only state authorities, through interrogations, could certify that a given person had contributed service to the Cause. Citizens with resources could express their commitment to federalism by contributing money or goods (cattle, horses, and foodstuffs) to the war effort. These were called *federales de bienes* or, more pejoratively, *federales de bolsillo*, implying that they "purchased" rather than gained or proved their federalist allegiance. Finally, people were expected to dress as Federalists in accordance with the prescribed attire; all members of the federalist community had to be *federales de apariencia*.[44]

The various forms of expressing one's federalist sympathies created tensions within the federalist community, the "federalists of service" accusing the "federalists of purse" of not being sufficiently committed to the defense of federalism, and, clearly, merchants and great landowners were suspected of not supporting the Cause with the same enthusiasm as small-scale farmers and livestock raisers did. More important, the diverse forms of political expression fragmented the notion of citizenship into at least three classes in relation to the question of military service: those who paid no service at all (reserve militiamen); those who were called occasionally, but only when the fatherland was in great danger (the active militiamen); and those who, without having the right to vote, were drafted for war service (the regular soldier).

These distinct forms of expressing adherence to the principles of federalism (and to Rosas) were present in the federalist festivities. To organize the fiestas neighbors had to resort to public subscriptions, a practice generally used to show support of the Dictator's decisions in matters of foreign and military policy. The *vivas* shouted during processions and feasts together with the uniformity of dress contributed to the illusion of federalist unanimismo (uniform political opinion). Neither form of expression was confined to the ritual space of the fiestas. Paysanos' toasts to federalism were a common practice at taverns and dances. Soldiers also responded with *vivas* to the proclamations read before battle or to the reports of a successful negotiation with officers. Travelers noted landowners' preference for simpler paysano dress. Similarly, the unwritten social pact by which citizens should arm in defense of the nation was reenacted in the federalist festivals; neighbors put on their militiamen's attire to guard the altar of the fatherland and soldiers of nearby regiments were summoned to guard the square. The federalist republic, the festivals indicated, accepted different expressions of federalism (voices of support, contributions, military service, and wearing federal insignias and clothes), none apparently superior to the other and all of them already integrated into the structure of everyday life.

Further understanding of the meaning of the federal festivals for the "people" (federal neighbors and the rest) can be derived from the interactions that took place at the festivals themselves. The very location of the festive space within the wider sacred space of the republic, I have argued, represents the particular symbiosis, typical of Rosista republicanism, of popular-festive elements with the military parade and the quasi-religious procession. This particular arrangement or design partly derived from the revolutionary festivals of the period 1811–1828 acknowledged the dependence of government on the consent of the electorate, except now more as a celebration of a reciprocity between authorities and "the people" than as a form of revolutionary didactic.

Obviously, the life of the republic was not all politics. Consequently, the festivals also celebrate the equestrian abilities of paysanos, the acrobatic skills of youngsters, and the preference of the public for dancing and gambling. In relation to this other sphere of life, the state appeared to be a passive and patient observer. Clearly, this gesture was the reverse of everyday life, in which justices attempted to control every aspect of paysanos' leisure time (card games, horse races, poaching) and tried to instill rules of good conduct among reluctant youngsters and tavern goers. Whether paysanos rejoiced in the temporary permissiveness of the state without raising the question of Rosas's strict order must remain an open question. The justices who reported these festivities always took care to emphasize that even in the festive spaces (the dances, the barbecues, the public games) "order prevailed."

In relation to the neighbors who organized and participated in these festivals, their voices and actions leave no doubt of their devotion to the Federal Cause and its leader. Their participation in the processions, Judas burning, portrait carrying, and *vivas* were consistent with other indicators of popular support for the regime.[45] In relation to the spectators, some of them might not have been resident neighbors of the town or federales; the festivals themselves give no indication about their presence or actions. We cannot infer from the mere observation of the ceremonies whether they (the subaltern, the peons, the provincianos) conceived the republic as both a religious crusade against the unitarios and a system of rights predicated on the continuity of the revolution.

The role of disguise in the fiestas is also difficult to interpret from the point of view of the participants. Federalist festivities provided special moments to interpret politics in the burlesque mode. Here, political adversaries acquired the shape of demons, animals, and pretentiously dressed figures. These disguises, one could argue, followed the official semiotics of federalism. They expressed in an obvious manner the blind obstinacy of unitarios, their savage behavior, their devilish intentions, and the divine sanction ordained for their treason. Yet, some elements escape the simplicity of this correspondence between display and reception. What to make, for example, of the troupes of paysanos dressed as Turks? On a first reading they seem to be a replica of the colonial parades of Moors and Christians, indicating both the holy nature of the war and the association of unitarios with pagans. But other interpretations are also possible. The Bedouin gauchos might represent the aspirations of many paysanos for independence, spatial mobility, equestrian abilities, and luxuriant dress. Here the Turks seem to have a favorable potrayal; instead of being defeated by other riders dressed as Spaniards, they participate in the parade without engaging in any confrontation. In fact, Moors were seen at the time as the embodiment of rebelliousness and independence. Rosas, explaining the cause of the southern insurrection (1839), stated that without a close supervision from an agent of the law, men were like *Moros sin Señor* and, for that reason, easy prey to the agitation of unitarios.[46] The gauchos who disguised themselves as Moors might have been celebrating their independence from old masters, a situation not unrelated to the rights guaranteed by the new republic.[47]

Another reading of this representation emphasizes the identification of paysanos with Arab peoples, also defending their territory from foreign imperialistic aggression. Here the figure of Abed el-Kader and his defense of Oran (Algiers) against the French forces of Mariscal Clauzel (1835–1841) must have constituted a powerful mirror for paysanos. Accustomed to hear rumors about the war *contra el francés* and familiar with the names of Louis Phillipe, Guizot, and other French statesmen (they had seen them burned as Judases), paysanos might have empathized with the brave Algerian.[48] Although no direct evidence exists on the diffusion through the Buenos Aires countryside of stories about Arab resistance to French colonial adventures, there is evidence of the rapid and massive response to the Chamber of Representatives' decision to resist the 1838 French ultimatum. In Fuerte Federación (Bahía Blanca) the reception of that decision moved neighbors to organize celebrations similar to the ones described earlier: "As soon as this town's vecindario knew about the decision (*pronunciamiento*) by the Chamber of Representatives, whose members met and let the whole world know that it is not opulence that humiliates justice but a Divine power that protects innocence, the electric flame of patriotism burst and, as if all were organs of a common center, with a unanimity of feeling, all my compatriots, moved by the same ideas, resolved to organize a subscription [big] enough to demonstrate the jubilation that such an outstanding event provoked."[49] After the funds were collected, the citizens put on their uniforms, gathered in the *comandancia* and took Rosas's portrait for a walk around the town to the sound of music. Then they moved the portrait into the church, where they participated in a Te Deum. At the end of the mass "the citizens took the symbol of [their] happiness" (the portrait) and returned it to the regiment. There, tables laden with liquor and beef barbecue (*vacas asadas con cueros*) waited for the participants. They ate and drank, shouting *vivas*. In the evening they went back to the square and played sortija. The fiesta ended with a dance in the army's headquarters. Those who did not join the procession showed their support by placing *santos* (icons of saints) along the way. Reactive nationalism? Neighbors of this remote outpost seemed to be informed of Rosas's policies concerning national defense, and they seemed to reaffirm and support in their own political language (with public barbecues, subscriptions, and saints) the decisions of government.

Fiestas and Social Difference

Tensions between the model of governance projected from the center and the perceptions and understandings of paysanos become evident when we consider the question of social equality. Contrasting with the idea of an organic republic raised in holy war against a common enemy, the practices of the Rosista state created some divisions among rural society and unevenly allocated the costs and rewards of the civil war. The criminal justice system punished with forced military service every type of crime of the country poor (those who were classified as country peons). To them accrued most of the services of the regular army and few of the benefits of the military campaigns. The provincial state allocated new lands gained from the Indians to a relatively small number of proprietors, who also purchased the bonuses in land distributed by the regime among military officers. The festivities, organized as a celebration of the ideals of independence, obscured these tensions, emphasizing instead the egalitarian aspects of the regime.

Federalist festivals, predicated on the unanimity of an organic republic, were designed to produce feelings of cohesion and equality among the members of the federalist community. The mandated style of clothing that countered the trends of urban fashion, the balls and barbecues at which the rich blended with the poor, and the processions without a clear class or racial stratification—and with the significant participation of women— appeared to suspend existing social differences. In particular, certain moments of the fiestas provided opportunities for lower-class subjects to challenge claims of the urban gentry to social distinction (clothing, literature, and sexuality).[50] The very representation of the hated unitarios was an exercise in social leveling. Masquerade companies, blending colonial motifs with federalist propaganda, portrayed unitarios as *figurones* (well dressed but ridiculous upper-class urbanites), demons, Judases, and monkeys. In the space of federalist festivities, the politics of the enemy was rendered ridiculous and ineffective, though the enemy itself was presented as devilish and treacherous.

The *figurones* made spectators accomplices in a criticism of city style and fashionable attire. Those who wore frocks and trousers placed themselves outside of the federalist community, which preferred country dress. Invariably, the fiestas recreated the association, frequent in the federalist press, between the swanky and pretentious *cagetillas* and the unitarios. Mockery at the ridiculous and pretentious social figure entailed a criticism of the very concept of social "distinction."[51] The spectators applauded and laughed; at the ball, in a fairly egalitarian environment where everybody dressed a lo paysano (even the great ranchers), mockery gave way to communal eating, drinking, and expressions of support for the Federal Cause.[52] The ideological message of equality, central to the self-understanding of federalists, was carried into social practice, at least temporarily.

The city festivities honoring Rosas's victory over the southern conspiracy exhibited two other forms of social leveling less influenced by the state. After the cart that conducted Rosas's portrait reached the chapel of Pilar, a crowd made of both plebe and neighbors gathered to pronounce interminable acclamations and toasts to Rosas. Next followed recitations of poems by generals, justices, and common folks. Ramos Mejía found in these recitations a fundamental reversal of the literate/illiterate social division. Poetry, usually the territory of the enlightened upper crust, had been appropriated (and debased, according to Ramos Mejía) by the lower classes: "The sonnet metrics [lira] of 'La Cautiva' have fallen into the hands of cattle-tenders [puesteros] and beef-sellers [abastecedores], like those precious objects of art that a soldier, after the looting, destines to a domestic use."[53] In this text, subalterns are directly implicated in the subversion of "natural" social distinctions.

Not only poetry was up for grabs in the egalitarian atmosphere of Rosismo. Lower-class subjects took dancing as the occasion to shorten social distances. Black and mulatto women and men dancing the media caña (a dance performed by lower classes) in the streets showed little reverence for social distinctions. "Even the most upper-crust [encopetada] lady was treated to the federal turn [vueltita federal; a dance step] by any mulatillo [young mulatto] who, inflated by the customary grace of his democratic insolence, asked for her" (Ramos Mejía 1907, 1:258). White ladies dancing with mulatto servants pushed to the limits the egalitarian rhetoric of the regime, threatening the urban gentry with loss of control over women's sexuality. These close encounters do not appear in the reports of the justices, who probably censured any mention of improper sexual conduct or racial difference, but in the reconstruction of a historian.

Federalist festivals were also exercises in social exclusion. The Rosista republic was not celebrated equally by all. The concept of "neighborhood" (vecindario) considered for the organization and performance of federal rites rarely included the transient population (the wandering proletariat in search of jobs usually suspected and arrested by the rural police). In disguise or with a different identity, they might have been present at the fiestas of the fatherland, but the state itself had denied them the condition of equal participant.[54] The other conspicuous absence in the festivities was the Indian, either as enemy or as ally.[55] By depicting and mocking a single adversary, the Moorish unitarios, the federal citizens erased from public memory the participation of indigenous peoples in the reconquest of Buenos Aires (1806–1807) and in the independence wars (1810–1824). The provincial state now at war against Pampa Indians could not present indigenous America as a foundational metaphor of the republic.

The unequal allocation of military service caused resentment among the rural population. Resident neighbors with enough resources were able to pay their contributions to the republic in money, goods, or "passive services," whereas the nonresidents, usually laborers traveling for work-related reasons, were engaged in active military service for longer terms, often without their consent.[56] The difference between militiamen and soldiers was apparent even in the fiestas. Militiamen, specially dressed for the occasion (many decorated their horse with a red plume to match their hat, occupied a central position in the festivities. Regular soldiers, whose uniform and horse were provided by the state and whose presence in the square was not voluntary, had a minor and less pleasurable role in the festival; they stood guarding the square for long hours. The federalist republic honored the military hierarchy, placing the names of generals close to the pyramid (the altar of the fatherland). To the soldiers who defended the federation on the battlefield, the republic acknowledged nothing.

Conclusions

In this chapter, I have argued for an interpretation of the fiestas federales as an exercise in communication between the Rosista state and its popular base of support. With a focus on four episodes of ritual activity related to state power, I have examined what we might call the semiotic politics of the Rosista state and pondered its resonance in popular culture. Three generalizations can be derived from the evidence presented: the sacralization of political language, the continuity of the republican imaginary, and the complexity, polysemy, and ambiguity of the symbols deployed at the federalist festivities.

The resort to a language and imagery heavily influenced by Catholicism facilitated the construction of the imagined political community and its tensions. A demonology of political opponents fit well with the idea of an organic moral polity, now divided and threatened by the forces of Evil. The federation was a large family of brothers united in a holy war against its enemies; the unitarios constituted the most salient target of federal contempt because they threatened from within the ordained unity of the nation.[57] The sanctity of the claims of the Federal Party—the maintenance of independence and the rights of peoples and townships—validated the need for unanimous support of the Federal Cause, displacing arguments in favor of individual liberties and political dissent. The idea of a holy war could also serve to communicate the dramatic implications of an alliance between the unitarios and foreign powers (the French, the British) at a time of increasing imperialist pressures.

Rosas's ability to present federalism as a continuity of the ideological project of *Mayo* (and himself as the defender of the legacy of independence) was predicated on a resemanticization of the vocabulary of the porteño Jacobins.[58] The concept of liberty, construed during the French Revolution in opposition to monarchical tyranny and feudal dependence, was assimilated into the concept of independence, the liberty of *americanos* from Spanish tyranny. To Rosas, the preservation of liberty meant the maintenance of independence, not the liberation of men from any existing social bondage (though Rosas did much to disarm the institution of slavery). Rosista federalism also resignified the term equality. Under the new terminology, equality meant two things: equality of citizens under the law, in particular the right of all citizens to petition government, and uniformity of dress and expression among the different social classes.[59] The idea of fraternity—a community of individuals joining in brotherhood under the inspiration of common principles—was translated into the idea of federation, a loose term signifying the union or pact among the different towns and provinces of a given territory.

Rosista republicanism incorporated an assortment of disparate conceptions to define the pillars of the nation: the legal order imagined by enlightened and utilitarian philosophers, the concentration of power in the hands of the executive to conduct the affairs of government; and the demand for unanimous support from the citizenry. The contradictions among these organizing principles were apparent. Extraordinary powers in the hand of the executive violated the principle of independence of the judiciary, a basic condition for guaranteeing the legitimacy of a justice system predicated on statutory law. Similarly, the demand for unanimous expression from the electorate violated the principle of representation. What was expected from the citizenry was not the election of representatives who could carry their private demands into the public sphere but a passive consent to policies assumed to be unanimously desired.

With an assortment of symbols the *fiestas federales* articulated the various strands of Rosas's model of governance. The republic, initially conceived as the space of deliberation of virtuous citizens representing the people's will, was replaced by a more radical, yet more conservative ideal community: more radical because it purported to carry into practice the egalitarianism preached by the porteño Jacobins; more conservative because it subordinated the preservation of liberty to the pursuit of order (an order that enshrined the state and its representatives and recognized no political dissent). The symbols deployed in these celebrations advanced a set of definitions about the state, the fatherland, and the political community that contained elements of continuity and elements of rupture. Contrasted with the colonial festivities celebrating royalty, the federalist festivities lacked the hierarchical order of a highly stratified society. Compared with the revolutionary festivals, the fiestas federales showed no fear in representing a new collective organism: the nation. They had to represent instead a threatened republic assuming the preexistence of "the nation."

The episodes of political ritual examined here show a transition from a didactic of freedom and sovereignty to a communal celebration of the continuity of the republic. With minor exceptions, the design of postindependence festivals was maintained intact in the federalist festivities, adding to the protocol few but important innovations: the vociferous procession, the portrait, the paysanos dressed as Turks, the federalist woman, the burning of unitario Judases. These incorporations should not be read as a nostalgic retreat into the colonial past but as part of the resemanticization of the revolutionary discourse under the new conditions created by civil war, foreign power blockades, and people's assertion of the rights promised to them by the postindependence leadership.

The federal republic imagined by Rosas and his followers left much to be defined. The territorial boundaries to which the terms fatherland and nation referred were quite flexible. They allude at times to the territory the leaders of independence tried to convert into a nation, at other times to the province of Buenos Aires, and on yet other occasions to the individual attachment that people had to their native land (their *patrias chicas*). The terms confederation and federation also had ambivalent meanings. Seen as a political entity, the federation referred to a loosely defined territoriality, to a political pact among different provinces that varied over time in membership and actual control of territory.[60] This might explain why, in his address to the soldiers, Rosas tried to separate the "model" of a federation from the actual Confederation. Viewed as an ideological force, the "federation" was a "cause" and as such expandable and contractible with the fluctuations of political and military processes.

Rosista federalism provided space for the articulation of an imaginary of nation without its corresponding territorial space. Loose concepts of federation, nation, and federalism served to advance the ideal of a moral republic (the *Santa Federación*) which was compatible with a porteño or a provinciano identity. To the extent that this imaginary avoided territorial claims and emphasized the preservation of people's rights (another ambiguity collapsing individual, community, and "national" notions of rights), followers of federalism could assume the Cause without renouncing their local and provincial affiliations and sympathies.

To a large extent, the reception of federalism (the doctrine, the Cause, the imagined republic) by the "people" was facilitated by the profusion of images and statements containing similar messages. The model of governance deployed at the fiestas found its confirmation in sermons, military proclamations, and other communicative interactions between government and its constituency. Moreover, the model of interaction privileged by the fiestas (contributions, verbal expressions, service, and dressing up) replicated a way of acting politically that seemed to be general among paysanos. The participation of neighbors (resident paysanos) speaks also of the adherence of small-scale producers to the cause of federalism. What did they see in the regime? Probably what the regime projected: a republic threatened by a small group of "anarchists," the promise of the preservation of property, order, and legality, and state protection vis-à-vis the large ranchers and the city merchants. Federalist festivities left few doubts of the relative minor role the rancher class played in the construction of the imagined federal republic. Estancieros had no special place in the fiestas; they participated like everybody else in the balls, barbecues, and games, dressed in chiripá and poncho.

This interpretive exercise does not fully answer the question about the reception of federalist political semiotics in popular culture.[61] Nevertheless, my reading points to a more complex and reciprocal relationship between government and people during the Rosas period than that contributed by the model of caudillismo.[62] The alertness of paysanos to events of national and international politics, their role in the construction of a historical memory of the federation, and their ways of expressing political allegiance can no longer be discounted as part of the fanatic religiosity of the lower classes. The Rosista regime does not seem to be the result of a devilish transformation of a Rousseauian ideal civil society into a Hobbesian state, molded by the collective hand of hacendados. As the federalist festivities made clear, the Rosista regime was based in part on the consent and support of the neighbors, most of them small-scale producers with a definitive political identity. Rosista republicanism projected a model of governance that contained both the civility of peasant communities and the brutalities of a protracted war, judged essential for the continuity of the republic as well as the moral strength of those communities.

On the other hand, the fiestas committed to reinforcing the unanimity of opinions and the equality of appearances, did not leave room for enacting the other rifts in the community: that between neighbors and transients and between Christians and Indians. Already of tragic consequence for indigenous peoples and for poor itinerant creole laborers, these divisions and tensions found little confirmation in the rituals of the republic. Landless paysanos now dressed in military uniforms were forced to contribute service to the nation in a way that contradicted the promises of equality and freedom made to them by the republic. They stood at the patriotic festivals, guarding from outside the joy of others, awaiting the opportunity to desert. Pampa Indians fared worse; when they contributed as allies to combat the unitarios they were invited to participate in the republic as subordinate, captive tribal states, but if they defended their autonomy from the civil war or resisted forceful relocation and humiliating dependency from the provincial state they faced extermination. The invitation of the republic was fatal for them, and not only in the iconographic sense (see Salvatore 1996b). In contrast, rural women seemed to have gained a space within the festivals of the federation, a visibility that, without challenging their traditional roles as vehicles of religion and mothers of soldiers, presented them as political actors.

The revolutionary festivals in France, Ozouf (1988) reminds us, were not a spontaneous expression of the people but an effort to control it, the representation of a collective need to bring the revolution to a close (Baker 1981). The Rosista republic attempted equally to find a form of governance that would put an end to the political and social "anarchy" of the 1820s. Ironically, the tranquility of the countryside and some of the rights proclaimed in the postindependence period were made compatible only in a system that presented the nation as an organic community fighting a holy war. But most ironic is the fact that Buenos Aires paysanos came to reinterpret an old colonial dance and, disguised as Moors, expressed both their support for the Rosista state and its defiance of the French invaders. The French nation whose revolutionary icons the federales had borrowed was now (1838–1840, 1845–1847) an ordered and repressive entity, overflowing with imperial ambitions. Its military and naval power appeared closer now to the experience of paysanos. It could be seen blockading the port of Buenos Aires, pillaging the coasts of the Paraná River, and aiding the forces of Rivera—the Uruguayan General Rivera, whom paysanos had learned to associate with the enemy and had seen many times burned in effigy.

CHAPTER 12

Subalterns and Progress

The decade that followed Caseros (1852–1862) brought significant changes in the lives of peons and paysanos. The freeing of restrictions on commercial activity (river transportation, in particular) gave new impetus to the export economy and to domestic trade. An unprecedented inflow of European immigrants served to alleviate shortages of labor and reduced the government's dependence on native soldiers. Innovations in government institutions (the municipalities and the reform in the justice system) added new depth to the changes. Railroads emerged as an emblem of progress, promising to restructure relations between city and countryside and to definitely conquer new territory for "civilization." According to most publicists, the decade was experienced as a postdictatorial, democratizing period. Whether the topic was criminality, the family, or politics, writers always referred back to Rosas's *Tiranía* to express their expectations for change and to mark their distance from that proximate past.

This chapter assesses the achievements of the post-Caseros period in relation to the experience of peons and peasants. I examine issues of coercion, civil and political rights, and economic and social benefits in connection with a new form of governance ("Progress") that changed the state "legibility" of subaltern experience.[1] The main argument underlying this chapter is that the change in the form of governance reduced the visibility of the "peon class," changing the nature of their subalternity. To the extent that rural subalterns lost importance in politics, their voices vanished from the official record. Their presence, consequently, became more elusive to the historian, while at the same time more "representable" for literary writers. The closure of subaltern visibility should not be taken as a real "disappearance" of agency, but as a displacement of positionality (and hence, as a transformation as a figure or object of discourse). From a more central political role during the time of federalist wars, wandering paysanos moved into a marginal, fixed category, available for a variety of representations, indictments, and interpretations.

Progress

"Progress" was an experiment in social engineering that promised to radically transform the society and politics of the pampas. Railroads, immigration, schools, and private property constituted its elementary parts. These institutional and technological innovations were conceived as central forces for the erosion of rural "barbarism," the end of "caudillo politics," and the modernization of the countryside (Botana 1984, 349; Szuchman 1990). At first, progress appeared more as a set of expectations and desires than as an actual constellation of forces creating institutions, technologies, and values. The anticipation of technical change (steamships, railroads, gas-illuminated cities, canals, and other technological marvels) brought excitement and confidence to the middle and upper classes. The railroad, in particular, played a crucial role in raising porteños' expectations. Construction plans of the Western Railroad moved publicists and politicians to foresee the demise of barbarism in its multiple incarnations.

Publicists reminded middle-class readers that economic and political renovation went together. The sensation of living in a postdictatorial age— a safer and more peaceful environment guaranteed by the new political "fusion"—stimulated new contracts and enterprises.[2] The resolution of internal political conflicts would give way to a period of peace and prosperity. No longer engaged in war, common folks would be able to devote their energies to the production of wealth. Also, the promise of greater security to property rights and of a reduction in monetary instability improved the prospects for economic growth.[3]

Elementary Parts

During the 1850s, progress was more spectacle and rhetoric than real. The general outlook of the city—except for gas streetlights, the new Colón theater, and the first stations of the Western Railroad—did not experience major changes.[4] Though the promotion of European immigration was central to the vision of social restructuring of the liberal leadership, the government allowed immigration to proceed spontaneously.[5] The railroad, heralded as the great emblem of modernization, had a modest impact on economic transactions. In 1857 the country possessed only seven miles of railroad tracks.[6] Until much later, oxcart troops continued to be the common means of transportation (Goodwin 1977). Advances in elementary education proved insufficient to secure the goal of turning peasants into citizens; with meager budgets and organizational problems, elementary schools remained a "luxury" for the few (in 1856 two thirds of

24. Caseros (February 3, 1852). The battle of Caseros ended the Rosas's regime. A coalition of forces defeated a less-than-enthusiastic federalist army. Carlos Penuti, *Batalla de Monte Caseros*, engraving, 1853. Reproduced from Luis L. Houssay, *El caballo de guerra en la iconografía argentina* (1971).

the pupils attending public schools came from middle-class origins).[7] Progress was also modest in matters of land policy. Without new public lands to redistribute, provincial authorities concentrated on undoing the policies of the past Tyranny.[8]

Two forces sustained the illusion of progress: immigration and the revival of commerce. After Caseros, the reduction in internal tariffs and the reopening of river navigation brought about a revival of domestic commerce. Vicente F. López reminded his critics that, thanks to the abolition of internal customs, the nation's domestic trade had been revitalized.[9] The economic renewal of the interior was surpassed by that of Buenos Aires, a province with substantial custom revenues and where the import-export trade concentrated. Enjoying greater security in property rights, investments flowed to agriculture and livestock raising (Halperin Donghi 1963; Brown 1994). A general improvement in the relations with Great Britain brought about an inflow of British subjects and capital.[10]

No sooner had peace returned to the province than immigrants started

396 Wandering Paysanos

to arrive in greater numbers. Italians concentrated in the river trades and the artisan crafts, constituting a lively working-class community at La Boca (Devoto 1989; Gradenigo 1987, 144–145). In the countryside, raising sheep became a favorite occupation of Irish, Scottish, and English immigrants (Ortiz 1974, 54–83). Contemporaneously, the Basque took over their occupations in the city, in meat-salting plants, brick kilns, and food distribution (Brabazon 1981, 112–114; Sábato 1989, chaps. 3, 5). According to contemporary narratives, the inflow of immigration turned the city into a Tower of Babel of languages, colors, and commerce. People of all nationalities and ethnic backgrounds walked along the streets, producing confusion and astonishment in visitors. "No city in the world," commented William MacCann, "can host such a dense collection of peoples" (qtd. in Trifilo 1959, 65). In the countryside, European immigrants had already started transforming the landscape. Two towns in particular, Chivilcoy and Bragado, spearheaded a process of economic and political modernization. Even the estancia was affected by the immigrant flow. The incorporation of immigrant peons and shearers brought significant changes to labor and social relations. While the technological modernization of ranching and agriculture lay in the future, the ranch became a space of multinational diversity. The sheep-raising ranch that Brabazon visited in 1862 hosted workers who spoke English, French, German, and Indian dialects, in addition to Spanish. At balls and barbecues musicians played the Argentine anthem, followed by the *Marseilleise* and the march to Garibaldi (Brabazon 1981, 186).

Integration and Displacement

Together with increased revenues, greater circulation of goods, and the inflow of European immigrants, the decade produced a profusion of optimistic images and texts about social integration. Seen from above and from a distance, paysanos appeared as full participants in the market economy, docilely contributing their labor to valorize the new lands, mixing peacefully with the newcomers, and adopting European consumption patterns. These idealized visions tended to reinforce the association between economic progress and democratization, as understood by the elite. Progress served to integrate rural and urban culture. The city, the center of "civilization," radiated optimism about the possibility of a social and cultural fusion. An overenthusiastic Sarmiento equated the city's Europeanization with the erosion of class divisions: the whirlpool of progress was dragging along the last traces of peasant society, transforming traditional customs and sensibilities.[11] The image of gauchos adopting European dress styles anticipated the possibility of a new society with less precise class boundaries.

The market itself was conceived as a powerful instrument of social integration and improvement. Increased commerce meant an expansion in farming and husbandry, greater numbers of travelers on the roads, and intensified social interaction. The relationship between progress and the reconstruction of community was the subject of many contemporary representations. Landscape painter Prilidiano Pueyrredón saw poor paysanos as full participants in the economic bonanza sweeping the Buenos Aires countryside. Un Alto en el Campo (1861) presented the road to San Isidro crowded with prosperous paysanos, men and women, young and old. In the painting nobody seems poor; even horses' riding apparel are colorful and new. Criss-crossed by roads and inundated with travelers, the countryside presents a thriving, hopeful outlook. Well-dressed and proud peasants engage in animated conversation as they stop for a rest near a pulpería. The whole scene evokes intense sociability, conviviality, and social equality.

Palliere's watercolor La Tienda (ca. 1860) also works with the idea of the integrative power of markets. Inside a fancy cloth store, a seller is attending to the requirements of a female customer, a lady wearing fashionable clothes and carrying a parasol, while a male paysano waits to be attended. The store sells fine fabrics, guitars, and other fashionable goods. The expansion of markets, the watercolor suggests, will sooner or later integrate the gaucho into "civilization." Earlier conceived as the emblem of the uncivilized and violent past, the paysano is now entering the house of fashion—voluntarily and as a customer. Cloaked as consumer desire, progress is an irresistible force.

In the aesthetic of progress, market integration engenders social harmony. Differentiation in clothes was a sign of the acceptance of social difference. In El Rodeo, a painting of 1861 depicting the gathering of cattle on a ranch, the country is a place of intense work and peaceful social interaction. The main social actors—the owner-administrator, the foreman, and the peon—are differently clothed as an indication that the confusion of the previous epoch has ended and that now each actor harmoniously accepts his social position. Through a profusion of colors and an emphasis on peaceful communication among the unequal, the picture celebrates the restoration of hierarchy on the ranch. The integration of subalterns into the enterprise of progress is even clearer in Palliere's lithography El Agrimensor. Here seven peons are assisting a land surveyor. All peons (except the one who is riding far afield trying to plant the measuring rod) are looking attentively to the expert, the agrimensor, dressed in

25. Surveying the Land. On horseback, three peons are holding measuring rods. Cooperation between expert and peon signals the acceptance of the rule of property among the "peon class." Now that political differences do not count (one of the peons is wearing a *gorra de manga*, a symbol of the past Rosista militia), harmony prevails on the ranch. J. L. Palliere, *El Agrimensor (Rep. Argentina)*, lithograph, ca. 1860. Reproduced from L. Palliere, *Escenas Americanas* (1864), plate 134.

city attire, and his theodolite. They are consciously participating in a crucial operation for economic progress: the measurement and appropriation of land.

These and other representations of the period upheld the vision of a socially integrated rural community adapting voluntarily to the transformations in the economy and society. In social spaces, marketplaces, and production sites, subalterns appear as guests at the banquet of progress. But complementing this invitation to integrate and share the benefits of progress stood a threat of displacement if paysanos did not readily adapt to the challenges of the new economy and polity. This alternative construction—presenting the gaucho as an irredeemable criminal, an innate barbarian, an accomplice to the past dictatorship—consolidated precisely during this decade. Native inhabitants (the inheritors of the past dictatorship and barbarism) become obstacles to progress. Not new (the field had already been prepared by the writings of the *románticos*), but certainly better articulated, this discourse acquired more poignancy and immediacy after 1852.

In 1866, celebrating the inauguration of the railway line to Chivilcoy, Minister Nicolás Avellaneda addressed a crowd of paysanos from the coach of the train. After the anthem was sung, he shared his particular version of the nation's history, a story of progress plagued with racial undertones. Originally, the "Indian" reigned supreme on the land, until cattle and gauchos gradually displaced him. With the same evolutionary logic, Avellaneda prophesied the displacement of gauchos by the new agents of civilization: immigrants and technology. Though in actuality neither Indians nor gauchos were gone, the speaker had them die a rhetorical death.[12] To Avellaneda, the amazing power of the new technology—the railroad—was about to produce a second conquest: the reappropriation of the prairies by civilization. The tone of his speech was prophetic: "Sirs . . . we are summoned here before the world to witness one of the biggest events in its history: *the disappearance of the desert in America*" (my emphasis). The railroad was the force behind this irreversible process: "The century's giant is the one called to solve the problem of the desert, invading it to its limits in order to suffocate barbarism with its iron arms" (in Birabent 1941, 98–102).

Textual disappearance went along with criminalization. In *Facundo* Sarmiento had presented only some types of gauchos as prone to illicit behavior (the *gaucho malo*), but characterizations produced in the 1850s and 1860s construed the gaucho as inherently incapable of accepting the law. According to the characterization provided by Valentin Alsina at the time of the drafting of the new Rural Code, the gaucho was a delinquent who could easily evade the law and the authorities due to his superior equestrian skills (in Moncaut 1977, 72). Gradually, creole paysanos became identified with gauchos and consequently vanished from the territory of progress. The future held promise only for those who accepted the new Pax Estanciera and the new market economy and its system of social differences. Those who dared to demand political and economic rights were immediately branded as *rosines* or mazorqueros.

To rural subalterns, the rhetoric of progress entailed both an invitation and a closure. They were invited to admire the marvels of the machine age, to share in the benefits of free commerce and political tranquility, and to enjoy the new civil liberties. But together with this invitation came a greater social differentiation that relegated poor paysanos to marginal positions in society and politics. Especially in rural areas, liberal reforms accentuated the division between respected neighbors and the itinerant working class. Rural peons, already considered the natural incarnation of barbarism, became in this period the living legacy of a dictatorial and violent past. The decade of progress translated into a sense of disillusion as soon as subalterns discovered that the urban elite had engineered a dramatic displacement of subjects and identities.

A New Form of Governance

Traditionally, the building of new political institutions, the promotion of free trade, and the establishment of a government of "public opinion" have been presented as the major achievements of this period. However, more than an era of free trade or democracy, the post-Caseros decade was a period of dramatic changes in state administration. The state that emerged after Caseros was quite different from that of the Rosas era, but not in the sense that the liberal apologists claimed. It was a state whose interaction with the governed population required statistics, land surveys, credit, agricultural extension, railroads, and schools. Agricultural production and markets became subjects of greater concern. It was, to be sure, a more decentralized state based on a more democratic notion of community, but one that persecuted the rural subaltern with equal or greater duress.

Taking progress to rural communities required decentralization of state decisions. As municipalities began gradually to replace the control exercised before by justices of the peace and military commanders, propertied neighbors gained greater participation in the management of local affairs. Transformations in the regular army and the militias proved of little substance. Initially, the reconstruction of the army meant a reduced demand for compulsory recruits, but now the state returned to coercive recruitment. The reconstruction of the system of justice brought about important implications for rural subalterns. The need to reestablish public order in a political and social context still burdened with the legacies of Rosismo resulted in an increase in public executions.

What emerged from the political "fusion" of 1854 was a new form of governance, one characterized by a combination of institutionalization and terror, personal rights and coercion, and the expansion of surveillance by subtle means. New instruments of state policy—statistics and agricultural improvement—changed the relationship between government and the population. Under this form of governance, peons and paysanos had reasons for enthusiasm and also for grief. The spectacle of the death penalty and the return of forced conscription tended to reinforce the situation of subalternity of poor paysanos. The control of the municipalities by wealthy neighbors kept the wandering working class distant from the promises of progress.

Municipalities and Statistics

The new style of governance was characterized by a more decentralized administration (through municipal councils) and the greater importance attributed to statistics. If the Rosista state had attempted to reconstruct the origins of a national history, the new liberal state was interested in keeping a record of progress. Provincial authorities wanted to document in a modern, scientific fashion the transformation underway in population and markets. In Buenos Aires, the new Statistical Department, created in 1853, began to collect data on the geographic and productive aspects of counties. Its surveys of agricultural producers, its meteorological observations, its measurements of distances and locations, its maps of rural towns, and its registers of births and deaths produced a wealth of new information.[13] The object of this statistical mapping was twofold: to publicize the province's potential to prospective immigrants and to provide reliable information to government.[14]

Statistics help governments gain a different view of the population.[15] Through statistics, populations are classified into types, their occupations registered, their family and civil status specified, the productivity of their land assessed. To this extent, statistics are a form of modern, comprehensive surveillance. The Buenos Aires government, by building a statistical apparatus, produced an important displacement in the state's gaze. Instead of local political sympathies or military supplies, justices of the peace found themselves reporting on water sources, soil fertility, agricultural practices, and the like.[16] The collection of information on rural production carried out by the local justices was no longer based on the notion of a "federalist community." Now, farmers, ranchers, and "industrialists" were interpellated in their condition as producers.

Municipal reform (1852–1855), perhaps the most important experiment in locally elected government, responded to the new conception of governance. The municipality was conceived as one big family of propertied men united by common interests, assets, and rights. In the city of Buenos Aires an elected municipal council assumed ample responsibilities in the areas of policing, public health, local contributions, street lights, cleaning, control of weights and measurements, and urban embellishment.[17] In addition, the new authorities had to conduct the registration and certification of births, marriages, deaths, elections, and so on and look after the welfare of orphans, apprentices, abandoned children, and domestic servants. In the countryside, municipalities became crucial instruments for building the edifice of progress.[18] The law of 1854 established a regime similar to that in the city: the local justice and four propertied neighbors constituted the municipal government; authorities were elected by popular vote and election results sent for approval to the provincial legislature. The depoliticization of rural districts was one of the goals of municipal reform. Rather than engage in the old factional politics, the new authorities had to concern themselves with the order, safety, and prosperity of their districts.

Municipal reform and the emergence of a statistical apparatus changed the nature of the relation between government and the population. The old warrior state based on the collective, patriotic compromise of citizen-soldiers gave way to a state committed to building the foundations of progress, that is, population growth, transportation, communications, free trade, and private property. The individual producer, represented locally by the municipal council, was the new locus of sovereignty. The state could now disengage itself from its prior inquisitorial role into the political affinities of paysanos. A wealth of new information about production and population came to replace the individual filiaciones of the Rosas period. Reports about new recruits and new prisoners continued to be filed but not with the same degree of detail and political information as in the previous regime. Thus, the voices of the subaltern gradually disappeared from police and recruitment records.

Archives reflect this transition. Instead of the defiant interventions of subalterns encountered in the filiaciones, we find after 1852 sketchy references to events involving subaltern subjects, insufficiently developed. Consider, for instance, a report issued by the justice of Pilar in 1856. A black man found without passport and asking for employment is sent to the justice of the peace, who, suspecting he is one of the dispersed soldiers from the last rebellion (General Flores's rebellion of 1856), orders his arrest.[19] The notice is brief, containing no description of the subject, much less any answer in quotation marks or any narration of the man's experience. The contrast between this casual reporting and the intense and detailed questioning to which peons and peasants were subjected during the Rosas period cannot be greater. Justices are no longer interested in gathering details about wandering peons and other lower-class subjects. Now aggregate data about the rural population are sufficient for the task of government.

More important, the new state is no longer concerned with imposing artificial class categories on the rural population. Peons have ceased to be members of a class identifiable by external appearance; they now constitute an occupational category. Similarly, the distinction between *hombre de campo* and *hombre de pueblo*, so crucial to the self-understanding of federalist communities, has disappeared from the official transcript. The justices, interested before in questions of military service and political opinion, now focus on such matters as civil status, illegitimate births, health and mortality, immigration, and literacy. Progress redefined the way the state looked at the rural poor, erasing class categories from the official language precisely at the moment when the economy and society were accentuating class divisions.

The Return of Forced Recruitment

The fall of Rosas created the expectation among paysanos that forced recruitment would soon disappear as an anachronistic trait of the past regime. Initially, in an attempt to reduce government expenditures and to free the labor force for productive activities, Urquiza reduced the size of the army.[20] Poor paysanos, anticipating an era of peace and demilitarization, returned from their hiding places. Seven months later, this expectation began to crumble. After the *enganche* failed to produce enough recruits, the government instructed commanders and justices to round up vagrants, suspicious fellows, and men of disorderly conduct to recompose the army.[21]

At the end of the siege of Buenos Aires, it looked as if the *enganche* (paid soldiery) system would soon replace the hated *levas* (forced drafts). Beginning in 1853, the government offered 1,000 pesos to those who wanted to enlist in the cavalry for two years. But as the budget destined for this purpose was limited, the army continued to depend on *destinados*, common delinquents sentenced by the courts, vagrants arrested by local authorities, and all those who failed to register in the local militias.[22] Paysanos who had erroneously anticipated a situation free from military and police persecution must have been very disappointed. In August 1852, faced with increasing difficulties in the recruitment process, military authorities suggested the creation of "commissions of neighbors" to identify and apprehend vagrants (in 1854 this task was taken over by municipal commissions).[23] As a result, respectable neighbors began to cooperate with the state in coercing vagrants into service.[24]

The National Guard, the citizens' militia proposed as the solution to the problem of forced recruitment, failed to consolidate as an alternative army.[25] When it became evident that the Guard could not defend the frontier, now threatened by renewed Indian invasions, the military command resorted to the regular army, with its old mixture of mercenaries and forced recruits. Municipal reform, considered an impediment to arbitrary arrest, produced nothing of the sort. The greater prerogatives of *munici-pales* failed to constrain the local influence and power of justices. Counter-ing the expectations of paysanos, justices recovered their old prerogative of arresting and sending people to the army or to public works. After 1855, the liberal leadership returned to the old practice of *contingentes* (fulfillment of a quota of unwilling draftees for the army), bringing additional burdens to justices. The quota was augmented to twenty or twenty-five forced draftees per county in 1856.[26] Understandably, military service continued to be regarded as a site of torture and punishment.

Spectacles of Death (Again)

The deployment of the project of progress brought about greater eco-nomic and social differentiation and, with it, the perception of increased personal insecurity. Considering that crime was on the rise, publicists demanded harsher penalties. Anxieties about crime made possible a re-fashioning of the criminal justice system. Newly appointed professional judges gained public notoriety and social respect as they began to empha-size adherence to procedural rules and promote the cause of judicial re-form. Magistrates, imbued with the new spirit of political reconciliation, contributed to the construction of the new governance. Responding to public opinion, they assumed the crucial responsibility of reviewing the abuses of the past regime and of ridding society of thieves and murderers.

Exemplary executions marked the commencement of the reconstituted criminal justice system. Between August and November 1853, a tribunal tried the political assassinations of 1840 and 1842. Of the nine felons accused of these crimes, five were sentenced to death; among them were key figures of the past dictatorship: Badía, Troncoso, and Cuitiño. During the trials, newspapers encouraged the public to engage in the proceed-ings, to contribute information and personal stories. When the trial was over, El Nacional published the complete sentence against the *mazorqueros*, presenting the judicial decision as crucial to the forging of a stronger political community. Los Debates celebrated the execution of mazorqueros as a popular, democratic achievement that marked the end of the era of Tyranny.[27] Soon after these executions, however, the judiciary tried to put an end to this revision of the recent past. Some judges refused to consider new cases about abuses committed during the Rosas era, and, in the few cases prosecuted, lenient sentences or total absolution was granted.[28] Judges justified these unexpected rulings by arguing that agents of the past regime, governed by fear, were not in control of their own actions.

The same judges, however, were not lenient in cases of murder or aggravated theft committed by ordinary folks. They treated these cases with uncommon severity. Between 1855 and 1864, forty people, most of them charged with aggravated murder, found death by public execution.[29] Generally, judges extended the death sentence when the crime was committed with some degree of premeditation and treachery. The brutality of these crimes reminded judges of the violence of the past dictatorship; these horrible crimes, they understood or interpreted, were an enactment of the barbarism left by an epoch of terror and violence. Ironically, the executions themselves barely differed from those of the Rosas era. After a priest delivered his sermon, the condemned was placed on a stool or bench (banquillo) and shot by firing squad. After the shooting, the body was hung from a pole or placed on an elevated wooden structure (patíbulo) and exposed to the public gaze.[30]

The pedagogy of exemplary punishment was addressed to peasants and peons. Authorities believed that the fear produced by these spectacles would suppress the natural aggression of the rural poor. To the liberal leadership capital punishment was a necessary instrument of political stabilization. The death of mazorqueros was a precondition for the functioning of liberal republican institutions. The executions of common murderers (which surpassed those of political criminals in a proportion close to 7 to 1) addressed the anxieties of the propertied classes (i.e., the perceived rise in interpersonal violence). Exemplary executions, liberals expected, could halt such violence. In addition, public executions served to remind citizens of the brutality and excesses of the past regime. They marked both the end of an epoch and the possibility of a new beginning. Public executions contributed to the construction of the rural poor as a subject endowed with an excess of aggression rooted in the experience of Rosismo.[31] They directed public attention to the double danger of a past always ready to reemerge (caudillo politics) and a culture still uncivilized and violent (rural culture).

Through these spectacles of death, the liberal state communicated to the population important lessons of governance. To liberal publicists, the death penalty was necessary, not only to curb the rise in criminality but also as a first step toward dismantling the Rosista legacy. A common argument, frequently used in the press, stated that rural subalterns were accustomed to violence; they worked with knives and blood all the time, slaughtering cattle, mares, and sheep for a livelihood. Having contributed to the Pax Rosista with their military service—killing unitarios and Indians with the same passion and brutality—violence was already part of their predisposition. Disarming this violent rural culture required a dose of exemplary state violence.

A New Democratic Ethos

The process of political institutionalization and liberalization of political expression that followed the revolution of September 11 permitted the emergence of new subjectivities but, at the same time, removed the peasant-citizen from the center of the political stage. The "free press" that reemerged after two decades of censorship construed the idea of a government based on "public opinion" (see Lettieri 1999). The expansion of the public sphere, marked by the increase in voluntary associations and new publications, created a sense of enhanced freedom of expression and association (see González Bernaldo 1992, vol. 1). In the cracks of a liberal order and middle-class "public opinion" new actors raised their voices to demand greater political participation, to challenge the legitimacy of police and judicial authorities, and to request new economic and political rights. Immigrants and rural producers—the new democratic subjects—carried into the public sphere contending versions of liberty and of a republican order. As a result, the new democratic ethos generated increased ethnic tensions and an open rift between rural and urban residents.

In the city, the growing rift between immigrant workers and native policemen brought about new tensions, resulting in public accusations of corruption and demands for justice. In the countryside, the Lagos rebellion, a popular reaction of paysanos to the centralism and isolationism of the Buenos Aires government, was emblematic of the challenges facing the new liberal administration. The resistance of middling paysanos to continue contributing *auxilios* to the state and the demands from immigrant farmers for land redistribution made evident the narrow limits of the notion of progress held by the city's elite. The emergence of new political interactions and forms of addressing authorities presented subalterns with new opportunities. But not for all. The new political subjects— middling paysanos, urban residents, immigrant *colonos*—backstage subjects who had constituted the center of state concerns during the Rosas era: peons and peasants.

New Economic and Political Rights

The consolidation of property rights in cattle, produce, and land brought about some changes in the economic rationality of paysanos. Whereas before, some goods were transferred to the state as patriotic contributions, now everything produced by ranches and farms had a monetary value. The government, ranchers thought, had to play according to market rules—as did everybody else.[32] Middling ranchers and farmers defended their property rights, breaking with a practice (supplying cattle to the army) that had been a defining characteristic of the past dictatorship. The passive resistance of producers forced the Ministry of War to order the purchase of meat rations on the open market. This solution was a good sign to ranchers and farmers, yet many remained distrustful. Some producers demanded immediate cash payment for deliveries; others simply preferred not to sell to the government.[33]

Distancing themselves from the state, ranchers and middling paysanos tried to carve out a space of economic autonomy. This was evident in the case of rural communities located far from Buenos Aires. Considering themselves unprotected by the military, these communities tried to conduct their own "Indian policy," reactivating the traffic in cattle (most of it illegally obtained) with seminomadic tribes. Confronting Buenos Aires policy recommendations, neighbors of southern towns formed "subscriptions" for the rescue of captives, traded gifts with belligerent tribes, and defended their right to "free trade" with Indians.[34] Southern ranchers' and merchants' refusal to obey the dictates of Indian policy, the reluctance of paysanos to contribute cattle and labor to local authorities, and the demands for payment for all government purchases represented symptoms of the new position gained and assumed by "producers" in the post-Caseros period. Emboldened by a discourse that emphasized the sacredness of private property, property owners interpellated the state as the bearer of economic progress.

During these years, the countryside also witnessed the emergence of land redistribution claims. Chivilcoy, a community of immigrant farmers, was the first town that forced the government to grant preemptive rights. In 1854 its residents petitioned the government for the annulment of all the *enfiteutas'* (long-term tenants') rights to the land they tilled.[35] They accused their landlords of preventing them from occupying and populating the land. Long-term tenants' "monopoly" on the land, they argued, hindered the potential economic progress and civilization of the region. Presenting themselves as pioneers of progress, the immigrants of Chivilcoy construed the old landowners as a "feudal" class, endowed with privileges that were incongruent with a country open to immigration and offering opportunities for self-improvement. In the end, the small settlers (colonos) of Chivilcoy obtained an important concession from the state: a decree of November 4, 1854 freed the land from previous concessions and burdens, making them rightful possessors of the land. In October 1857, colonists (or settlers) were able to purchase their plots at moderate prices.

After the Lagos rebellion, paysanos strove to expand their political influence on different fronts. In San Fernando, taking advantage of the organization of the National Guard, neighbors requested the right to "elect" their own military authorities.[36] Ninety-three residents signed the petition. This daring proposition emerged from the participatory environment of the Lagos rebellion. In various rural towns the neighbors had recently conducted elections to nominate representatives to the provincial assembly.[37] Requests for electing their own military authorities and the defiant elections of the representatives to the Constitutional Convention nurtured a new ethos of participation among paysanos. In 1854, the elections for town council representatives (five per town) added vitality to this process. Neighbors actively participated in these elections, for they involved placing local government under the control of the local community.[38]

Wild Constitutionalism

In November 1852, after Alsina decided to prevent the meeting of the National Constitutional Assembly, Colonel Lagos received orders to summon the National Guard to attack Entre Ríos (J. Lagos 1972, especially chaps. 14, 15). Fearing that this action would trigger a civil war, Lagos refused to obey the order and, on December 1, issued a pronouncement calling paysanos of Luján to take arms against Alsina to save the constitutional process. Lagos's proclamation was directed against the isolationist position of the Buenos Aires government; he wanted the province to participate in the Santa Fe Constitutional Convention. Against the expectations of most upper-class urbanites, Lagos's propositions turned out to be enormously popular in the countryside. Town after town signed manifestos (proclamas) answering the colonel's call. Middling paysano supporters of constitutionalism gathered a superb army and held the city under siege for five months.

To the middling paysanos who gathered in local meetings, argued about the political situation, and drafted the manifestos, two essential questions were at stake: democracy and national organization.[39] Their "wild constitutionalism" combined demands for popular representation, free elections, and participation in the National Constitutional Convention. Paz, confraternidad, and organización were the watchwords of the rebellion. After twenty years of recurrent warfare, paysanos longed for peace; another civil war could rapidly erase the gains obtained under Caseros. So they favored a negotiated solution between Buenos Aires and the other provinces. The organization of the nation under a constitution was now a real possibility. In the past, Rosas had postponed the constitutional process with all kinds of excuses; now it was time for the People to resume their sovereignty and resolve the issue.

Although the language used in the manifestos contained elements of the rhetoric of Rosismo, the rural rebels presented radical demands unimagined by Rosas or the liberal leadership.[40] The neighbors (not "federalist neighbors" but simply "neighbors") raised their voices to demand their right to elect provincial representatives to the National Constitutional Convention. Their demands for free elections ("majority suffrage") and participation in the constitutional process were predicated on a radical notion of popular sovereignty. Rural towns began to "recall" their own delegates to the Buenos Aires legislature, reclaiming the direct exercise of popular sovereignty.[41] Three sections of the countryside, reads the Monsalvo manifesto, had taken back the powers granted to their deputies, hence rendering the Buenos Aires government illegitimate.[42]

An intense demand for political participation animated the rebellion. To the Guardia de Luján neighbors, 1810–1852 had been a period in which the country missed its opportunity to join the progress of other nations—all seemed "humiliation, destruction, and backwardness."[43] At the root of this unfortunate history of the nation was the lack of political participation by producers. Since 1810, rural neighbors had been absent from all the important decisions in the life of the province and, consequently, their resources had been employed and wasted in activities that did not help producers.[44] Now that the Dictator was gone, neighbors expected to build a producers' democracy, one in which the opinion of rural inhabitants mattered.

In the opinion of those who signed the manifestos, Caseros had brought new hope to the countryside. Urquiza's "happy revolution" promised the organization of the nation under a representative, federalist, republican system. Paysanos agreed enthusiastically with this proposal that could bring peace, union, and fraternity. The news of the San Nicolás agreement awakened dormant political energies in many rural communities. In town after town neighbors gathered and proclaimed their adherence to the call for a constitutional convention.[45] As General Flores made clear, the rebellion was a free decision by the paysanos. Lagos's pronouncement was "voted on" by the thousands of paysanos who refused to join the Buenos Aires militias and armies when Governor Alsina intended to invade Entre Ríos.

The Lagos rebellion brought to the surface a conception of political representation that did not contemplate the permanent delegation of power to elected authorities. The neighbors' manifestos affirmed the principle of "retroversion" of popular sovereignty. "Free from influence and coercion," reads the Guardia de Luján proclama, the neighbors of Guardia de Luján had retaken their sovereignty, suspended their representatives to the Buenos Aires assembly, and delegated power to the Constitutional Convention and its provisional director. Evidently, rural neighbors supported notions of political sovereignty and constitutionalism that were too radical for the city's liberal elite to accept.

Undoubtedly, peons and poor peasants manned the militias that maintained Buenos Aires under siege. But, as in other moments of the post-Caseros scenario, their voices were drowned out by the voices of more prominent neighbors. Those who signed the proclamas called themselves the "healthiest part of the neighbors" in the rural towns. Who were they? Among the lists of names supporting these manifestos I found not a single man belonging to the *peon class*. Big ranchers also seem to be excluded from the rosters. Apparently, small property owners were the most enthusiastic supporters of the rebellion. Peasants who, during the Rosas period, had gained their share in the trinity of property (land, cattle, and family) raised their arms in defense of property, peace, and confederation.

The fate of this movement is well-known. Despite the initial resignation of Governor Alsina, Lagos's siege of the capital was unsuccessful. Urbanites, organized into militias with a strong immigrant presence, posed a formidable resistance against the besieging army. Betrayed by his generals and old friends, Lagos finally dissolved his peasant army and went into exile. The effects of this rebellion proved enduring. Long after the rebellion, urban liberals continued to distrust the peasantry and the ranchers, whom they saw as the social force behind this "barbarous" attack on the center of "civilization." And, despite all the power of the forces of progress and all the energy invested in leaving the Tyranny behind, city politicians continued to suspect that a Rosista backlash was still possible.

Immigrants and the Police: Ethnic Tensions

Meanwhile, in the city, dramatic changes in the composition of the working population transformed the relationship between the police and the people. Encouraged by a renewed discourse on citizen's rights and freedom, immigrant residents accused the police of corruption, challenged their unbounded authority, and demanded respect and equal treatment. Due to their participation in the defense of the city, immigrant workers and merchants felt entitled to voice their discontent through the press or in the streets. Their protest—another moment in the democratic revival— triggered a series of ethnic tensions between immigrants and natives.

After 1856, mutual aggression and insults characterized the relationship between native policemen and immigrants.[46] In February 1859, Rafael Rabelo, an Italian sailor resident in La Boca, was arrested for instigating violence against the police. Offended by the corruption of police officers, Italians of La Boca had already started enforcing their own justice, having recently killed a vigilante. Though police corruption was not new, the visibility of Rabelo's protest grabbed the authorities' attention. He had visited Italians in jail, had alerted fellow immigrants against the police ploy—arresting immigrants on false charges to collect bribes—and had organized nocturnal vigils in front of the police station. Shouting death threats, complaining about the hypocrisy of the country's legal system, persuading other Italians to walk around the jail, he managed to preoccupy the police.[47]

Immigrants' vociferous demands could awaken the police's antiforeign sentiments. Another incident between the police and the neighbors of La Boca proves this point. On a hot January afternoon in 1864 a young creole policeman, Villarino, ran over a child with his horse. Two French immigrants (a doctor and a woodworker) who came to assist the child started an argument and were violently arrested by policeman Antonio Bono (both the doctor and the turner received bruises). In a moment, a group of Italian neighbors came to the rescue of the two Frenchmen and together they managed to subdue the policeman. When other policemen came to impose order, Bono was held down on the ground by a group of immigrants. The police interpreted this incident as an immigrant-orchestrated resistance against the city's legal authorities. In the weeks following the incident the police tried to take revenge, intimidating La Boca residents. Through different means, creole policemen made explicit their antiforeigner sentiments. One of the neighbors, Bernardo Facio, reported that after the incident a native policeman visited him and threatened his life. The policeman said that "he would take revenge the day [the next] war broke out; he would join the war and return to La Boca to kill some [of them]." According to neighbor Santiago Ferro, another policeman rode along Brown Street shouting that "he was Santafesino and he wanted to kill gringos" (immigrants). Another resident saw a drunken policeman wielding his sword and yelling that "he wanted to stab his sword into a gringo up to the hilt." After these incidents, the residents of La Boca submitted a formal protest and, as a result, an inquiry was ordered. The petition was signed by 130 neighbors, most of them Italian, who presented themselves as members of an "honest and industrious neighborhood." Their complaint was directed against the "habitual debauchery and libertinism" of the police, whose behavior had reached intolerable limits.[48]

What was new in this case was the organized resistance of immigrant neighbors against police brutality and arbitrariness. Not all encounters between immigrants and the police resulted in violent outcomes. In a context of increased ethnic tensions, immigrants used the press to ventilate cases of abuse of authority. The pages of the newspapers started to carry ads and reports in which private individuals, most of them immigrants, incriminated members of the police force in cases of corruption and abuse of authority, discredited politicians running for office, and accused other individuals of unethical behavior. This new weapon—the press—was quite threatening to traditional state functionaries, for it subjected their conduct to the tribunal of public opinion, something that could affect their reputation and honor.

The police's extortion of money for nonexistent misdemeanors was a thorny issue of dispute. An article published in Las Novedades on July 21, 1859, "Tropelía Inaudita" ("Unheard of Abuse"), denounced policeman Viedma for charging a "foreign and industrious worker," Domingo Durquet, a fine of 100 pesos for carrying a knife to a billiard hall. Durquet complained that he did not commit such a misdemeanor, suggesting that the police imposed fines on all butchers who patronized billiards, pocketing the revenue.[49] Underlying this publication was the assumption that by publicly exposing improper or illegal acts, authorities could be made responsible to the people. Encouraged by the same conviction, Italian Ignacio Vergara published in La Nueva Generación in 1860 an advertisement attacking his compatriot Rodolfo Venzano's credibility and honor. The advertisement congratulated electors for not having chosen Venzano for the position of port collector. Venzano, the ad claimed, was a drunken guardsman who pocketed the port fees.[50]

Underlying the ethnic tensions of 1856–1864 was a dual conception of authority. On one side were creole policemen, who defended the right to punish with severity for the preservation of order. On the other side were immigrant workers, who demanded personal autonomy, freedom of movement, and respectful treatment. To the latter, the creole police were the emblem of barbarism and abusive power, the opposite of personal civil liberty. Political differences were also part of the equation. Some immigrants (Italians and French) were more sympathetic to the cause of liberty than to the cause of federation, a fact that irritated many lower-class creoles. The sympathy Italians felt for Garibaldi necessarily associated them with the unitarios. Tired of hearing threats against foreigners and against Garibaldi by the natives, Cesareo Assaretto published a pamphlet in 1863 encouraging Italians to take revenge for the abuses of the creole "savages."[51]

Echoes from the Past?

In the era of progress the itinerant proletarian of the Rosas period disappeared from the sphere of state legibility. Displaced by more visible and vociferous social actors (middling rural producers, immigrant workers and farmers, middle-class politicians and publicists), their trace disappeared from the official records. Had poor paysanos become part of the past? A figure posing in the landscape of a harmonious and promising future? A mere number subsumed under the new statistical vision? A residuum of "natural violence" processed by the reconstituted judiciary? Though we search for signs of subaltern agency after the fall of Rosas, very little remains about peons and poor peasants in the official transcript.

The Difficulties of Demobilization

After Caseros, efforts to demobilize and disarm the federalist armies proved disappointingly slow. In March 1852, the justice of Dolores worried that "the numerous armed parties" belonging to the defeated Rosista army could detain and sack shipments of weapons, munitions, and uniforms dispatched by the allied army. A month later, the justice of Pilar, concerned about dispersed soldiers from the Rosista army, ordered their registration. On the promise of giving passes to all those who surrendered their weapons, he managed to register thirty-seven dispersed soldiers and to recover some weapons (12 spears, 6 swords, 4 *tercerolas*, and 3 *fusiles*).[52] This was, of course, a drop in the bucket, for many soldiers continued to wander through the territory of the province with their weapons and horses.

Deserters roaming the countryside continued to be perceived as a menace to property and a symptom of the difficulties of imposing order. Dispersed soldiers spread confusion among the population. As federalist soldiers refused to part with their blue ponchos and scarlet chiripás and jackets, people took them for legal soldiers. After the Lagos rebellion the fear of political persecution moved many ex-soldiers to retain their weapons and uniforms. In areas where the government knew that paysanos had supported the rebellion, special instructions were issued so that justices could persuade paysanos to deliver their weapons and return to their homes. The justices of San Fernando, Pilar, and San Vicente managed to collect the weapons without much resistance. In other districts the process was much more conflictive, and demobilization proceeded slowly.[53] In some cases the old authorities that had supported the siege of Buenos

Aires and Lagos's rebellion delayed the transmission of office, offering all sorts of excuses. In Patagones, for example, the local commander refused the authority of the new justice of the peace, and for four days resisted relinquishing his post.[54]

Resisting Military Service

After Caseros, forced recruitment and arbitrary arrest returned with a vengeance, generating much resentment and discontent. A state without sufficient fiscal resources and in a tug of war against two enemies (Indian tribes and the Confederation) could raise a strong army only by means of coercion. In this context, middling paysanos took over the resistance previously carried out by peons and soldiers and began to express openly and effectively their opposition to recruitment policies.

Burdened with greater obligations after the dismissal of regular soldiers, militiamen started to withdraw contributions of service. Some simply did not respond to the justice's or commander's call, arguing that they were busy with the wheat harvest. Those registered in the reserve militias (driving cattle for the army) had to be reassured by local authorities that they would not be drafted. The resistance against forced military service, though incipient early in the post-Caseros period, became widespread in 1856. That year, the request of the new minister of war Bartolomé Mitre for additional *contingentes* (quotas of forced draftees) produced more excuses than draftees. Local justices argued that the population, recently resettled after a major Indian "invasion," would not tolerate any new forced levie. Others argued that there simply were not enough vagrants and men of disorderly conduct in the countryside. The argument articulated by the justice of San José de Flores was quite persuasive: if all those asked to contribute military service were citizens, it was only fair to pay them a salary and upkeep. Rural opinion on this point was so powerful that the government was forced to change its policy regarding the Guard's service. Militiamen started to be paid by the day, just like day laborers. To provide for the help the justices needed, the authorities preferred to pay for services rather than risk the massive flight of paysanos.[55]

Local communities also resisted the call to capture and deliver "vagrants" to the military. In some cases, the ineffectiveness of local commissions entrusted with apprehending vagrants was such that the Ministry of Government felt it necessary to ask for the assistance of the local priest.[56] Some justices refused to draft vagrants for public works in spite of repeated orders from the ministry. The justice of Federación argued that minor felonies should not be punished with forced military service and that persecuting vagrants would only increase peons' emigration to neighboring provinces.[57] Paysanos' tactic of voting with their feet to resist forced recruitment began to show impressive results. If local communities did not cooperate with the Buenos Aires government in producing enough vagrants as forced draftees, the defense of the province would rest on a paid regular army, recruited with economic incentives.[58]

Continuity of Federalist Sentiments

The fall of Rosas did not banish overnight the loyalties and values on which Rosismo was based. In 1900 Cunningham Graham pointed out the resilience of Rosismo as a system of loyalties. In an often quoted passage, he recalled that in his youth, in a rural tavern of southern Buenos Aires, an old gaucho, to provoke the younger patrons of the place, stuck his knife into the counter and shouted "*Viva Rosas!*" twenty-five years after Rosas's fall (1876–1877) (Lynch 1998, 114). Sarmiento shared the anxieties of many city residents when he stated that the ongoing tensions between Buenos Aires and the littoral provinces could only result in the resurgence of Rosismo.[59] This fear preoccupied the liberal elite for at least a decade after Caseros. Everywhere contemporaries observed the presence of this phantasmal force. Soon after Urquiza's withdrawal, politicians started to call each other *rosines* (Rosista sympathizers) or *mazorqueros* (ex-members of the SPR), reminding voters of their personal or family collaboration with the recent Tyranny. Hilario Lagos's rebellion helped to magnify these fears. As town after town in the countryside held assemblies of neighbors and joined the rebellion, the liberal leadership faced its greatest nightmare. For the rebels not only resurrected the political imaginary of federalism, but their troops were dressed in the same colors as the federal army.

The new "democratic" environment failed to dispel public suspicion that in the countryside Rosas was still respected and admired. In 1852 an anonymous report indicated that Rosista sentiments were quite alive:

> In the town of Lobos the ex–justice of the peace, the colonel *Rosin* Arébalo's son-in-law has Rosas's portrait in the hall of his house, where anybody walking along the street can see it. Besides, he has Sa. Encarnación's portrait, to which he offers a wake every Saturday. . . . Commander Pío Sosa, another commander Tello, and Captain Andrada are the leaders of these infamous acts; the priest and policeman Miranda are advising paysanos to keep the scarlet ribbon in their pockets. . . . In San Isidro all police officers (alcaldes and tenientes) are the same as during the time of Rosas, they are proclaiming the old system and are well-known in their perversity.[60]

In December 1853, in faraway Patagones, the symptoms of federalist politics were still quite visible. The newly appointed functionaries had trouble establishing their authority. Neighbors resisted the abolition of the *divisa punzó* (scarlet emblem) and, guided by members of the Federalist Party, renewed their campaign against unitarios. The new authorities faced intimidation and disdain. The old Rosista commander and his friends gathered poor residents at balls, horse races, street walks, and barbecues and used these occasions to discredit the new authorities.[61]

Rosismo, as a style of politics, was alive and well. Was this true in towns closer to the influence of Buenos Aires? If so, was this related to the transformations brought about by progress? Unfortunately, not much of peons' and peasants' reactions is known after 1854. We know that in the city liberal publicists and politicians kept the memory of the dictatorship alive, but as the voices of peons and poor peasants disappeared from the public record, we do not know how they experienced the transition.

Where Have the Gauchos Gone?

Richard Slatta (1983), following a well-established interpretative tradition, contended that the expansion of railways fragmented the space in which gauchos lived, drastically reducing their geographic mobility. Deprived of their freedom to move, gauchos were forced to settle on cattle ranches as peons. Others were arrested and sent to the frontier. Immigrants displaced them from available rural jobs. In the end, gauchos disappeared as an identifiable social group, becoming a useful myth for the modernizing intelligentsia of the turn of the century. Although some of the symptoms pointed out by Slatta are valid, the thesis of the "disappearance" of gauchos demands reconsideration.

Paysanos had entered the civil wars as political subjects. They had fought wars that demanded political commitment. Their "armed opinion" mattered to their commanding officers. Most of them peasants and peons, they had joined the civil wars out of coercion, economic incentives, or factionalist patriotism. But once in the regiments, they became conscious of the importance of federalism, acquired a sense of the nation's history, and learned to distinguish their enemies. After 1852 these political interpellations came to an end. The most important closure experience for poor paysanos occurred in the terrain of politics. Hence, their "disappearance" could not be the result of technological or economic displacement. It was their political personas that ceased to be relevant to the new configuration of power.

Railroads, European immigrants, and land surveyors did much to change the overall appearance of the countryside, but nothing had such a profound impact on poor paysanos' lives as the end of the foundational contract between the peasantry and the state. The Rosista state had actualized this contract, making peons and peasants the defenders of a collective (imagined) community: the federation. In exchange, the state provided them with lands, food rations for their families, and the preservation of political rights. The new "liberal" leadership ceased to consider the rural poor as part of the political community. The municipal reform was the best confirmation that a local "democracy" could be built without the participation or votes of the majority of the population. In addition, the new government withdrew most state transfers to the working poor. Native workers "disappeared" from the records mainly because their political importance waned.

So, where have poor paysanos gone? The proposition that, broken by the railroad and more coercive legislation, they resigned themselves to be mere "labor" cannot be accepted without further consideration, for every exercise in social discipline breeds its own resistance. More important, if the "settling" or "subjugation" consisted in longer residence on the ranch and less mobility, this was part of a long process that can hardly be attributed to the change in political regime. Nor can the economic displacement of poor paysanos be taken as a purely occupational phenomenon resulting from the increased immigrant population. We need to consider other possibilities to respond to the question posed in this section.

During the Rosas period, poor paysanos suffering police persecution faced the problem of social reinsertion. To solve this problem they changed names, moved to a different town, and built a network of social connections that allowed them to pass unnoticed. Hence, it should not be surprising if, after 1852, poor paysanos, facing a new and unfavorable configuration of power, resorted again to multiple "arts of deception" to secure new social identities (as rural producers, as settlers in frontier lands). They had to disguise themselves in costumes more fitting to "progress" and "civilization"; consequently, we should not expect that changes in the attire of the rural poor tell us much about paysanos' identity—even assuming that the representations of Palliere and Pueyrredón faithfully reflect a process of social integration. Before and after Caseros, the working rural poor faced the state by vanishing into civil society.

It is possible also that, as new economic possibilities arose, they turned their itinerancy to new purposes. The claims of property owners about the emergence of mobile squatters may be pointing to the existence of new economic practices.[62] The numerous clusters of huts surrounding the large estancias could be one of the answers to the riddle of the "disappearance" of the gaucho. Mobile peons and day laborers settled in the lands of small property owners or along the borders between adjacent properties. When the owner presented a legal claim they restarted the migratory process. An old subsistence strategy adapted to new circumstances (the consolidation of statutory property rights and the surveying and fencing of the land), this could have been the fate of many of the members of the "peon class."

But this line of reasoning draws us away from the main argument. For, more than a question of economic reinsertion, the question of the displacement of the wandering working class centers on the closure of a type of politics, on the end of a form of engagement between peasants and the state. More than anything else the fall of the Rosas regime meant a redirection in the gaze of the state. No longer the basis of support of a factionalist politics, the peon soldier ceased to be an object of inquiry. As the danger shifted toward other subalterns (immigrants, women, indigenous peoples), the voices of native peons and laborers disappeared from the official script. The new form of governance reduced the visibility of the rural poor. No longer do we find in police archives long questionnaires addressed to rural peons or poor travelers. Instead, we encounter well-formatted contracts with immigrant soldiers, police reports of urban crimes, sketchy profiles of rural misdemeanors and felonies, and statistical reports on the population in general. The documents produced by the new "liberal" state seem to have lost the inquisitorial obsession to identify and describe the "peon class" that was characteristic of the Rosas era. In this way, the government of progress and middle-class public opinion entailed a relief and opened the way for the rearticulation of identity. But they also produced a silencing. After Caseros, the voices of the native rural subalterns were rarely recorded. We hear instead the voices of middling paysanos, of immigrant workers in Buenos Aires, of colonists of Chivilcoy, and of southern ranchers. The peon soldier, the itinerant worker, the poor paysano no longer speak to the state. Their personal stories are no longer relevant to state authorities. Itinerant rural workers disappeared from official visibility, in part because the state wanted to look elsewhere. When being unitario or federal no longer mattered, there was no need to interrogate paysanos about their individual military experience.

Locating native rural workers in the past became central to the reconstitution of subaltern alterity. Peons and poor paysanos not only vanished from sight, they also became residue from the Rosas era—a phantasmagoric force ready to reemerge as long as caudillo politics remained active.

If the wandering "peon class" was marked for extinction and treated as such—as the fodder for frontier armies, as bodies displaced to the outskirts of "civilization"—it was because of its association with the past dictatorship. Even before the liberal regime consolidated, the rural masses came to be associated with the political machinery of Rosismo and, for that reason, indistinguishable from the legacy of the Tyranny. Judicial discourse naturalized the construction of the rural poor as barbarians accustomed to violence. Yet it was in the political sense that the rural poor lost their visibility before the state. The whole machinery of progress (elected municipal councils, statistical reports, the measurement of land, the pampas crossed by railroads) reduced the peon soldier of the Rosas era into a relic of the past, into a symbolic, generic figure of discourse—the gaucho—with little bearing on the future of the republic. Avellaneda was not mistaken when he anticipated the displacement of gauchos by the power of progress, for he no longer needed the support of the rural poor to get elected or to secure territory.

To be sure, the "disappearance" of the wandering working class was marked by fragments of presence, by residues of subjectivity that still bothered those in power. They reappeared under various forms: the dispersed ex-soldiers after Caseros, the militias who followed Colonel Lagos, the Rosista plebe secretly plotting against the new authorities, the "vagrants" now sought by the neighbors' commissions, the criminals executed in public squares, the cattle rustlers who threatened ranchers' profits, the native policemen who expressed antiforeign sentiments. But this was a vanishing presence, placed at a greater distance from state power and the battles of the new era: progress, civilization, democracy. Their traces reaffirmed a lesson of history, a political experience not to be repeated. They all pointed to the sediment of a barbarism inherited from the era of Tyranny threatening the march of progress. Under a form of governance no longer concerned with the details of subaltern rural life, the wandering poor reached a closure of visibility. Fragments of evidence, little utterances, and minor occurrences still revealed the presence of the subaltern, but they were no longer personal stories criss-crossed with the history of the nation. They were only echoes of the past, particularities of a picture that presents itself as opaque, many times undecipherable.

The new actors and voices that emerged in this period added new modalities to an older contestation against state coercion, which in the postindependence period centered on the figure of the peon soldier. After all, immigrant residents were defending an anti-authoritarian perspective that was part of the mental universe and experience of itinerant workers. And the Chivilcoy immigrant settlers just like the native working class, were able to affirm rights sanctioned by custom through direct negotiation with ranchers and authorities. The same could be said of propertied ranchers and farmers; their rejection of unpaid services could be seen as a continuity of the rough bargaining of peon soldiers in the garrisons.

The machinery of progress—its aesthetics of market integration and peace, its dissemination of property rights, its statistical representation, its mechanical threat to the "desert" and its inhabitants, its promises of social mobility through education—managed to disarm the basic contract that united, in tension, the state and the rural poor. This figure, this subaltern would reappear in history as the agent of future rebellions against the central state, so as to make historians reconsider the identification of this agency with the past. To be sure, they would be interpellated again and again, but their presence and opinion would no longer be central to politics. Their "experience," fixed in a poetic narrative (*Martín Fierro*) and stylized into the idiom of lamentation and defiance, would soon become a reading sensation. But, for the moment, they disappeared from state visibility (and from the historians' gaze), taking with them the memories of a time that the new authorities claimed "would never return."

Conclusion

The main contributions of this study revolve around issues of state coercion, social conflict, markets, and subaltern experience. This book fills in some of the most evident oversights of existing historiography about the Rosas period. By presenting subalterns' political awareness, economic sagacity, linguistic competence, and relentless contestation of state policies, this study challenges notions of passivity and ignorance on the part of the subaltern sectors that, apparently, supported Rosista federalism.

First, the book recuperates a multiplicity of voices uttered from subaltern positions about issues of paramount importance for the history of the postindependence period: markets, legal authority, politics, and public memory. These fragments of subaltern experience—this accumulation of lamentations, opinions, and tactics—call into question several prior assumptions about the Rosas period. The fragments of life condensed in the *filiaciones* and *clasificaciones* present us with a subjectivity that defies conventional wisdom as to its position vis-à-vis the powerful. Rather than perennial passive victims of injustice, these agents "talk back" to the state, reminding authorities of the promises made about personal freedom, social equality, political incorporation, and economic well-being. Deserters' lamentations about the rigors of war and military discipline, veterans' recollections of the civil wars, women's active pursuit of "welfare" benefits, parents' defense of their sons against arbitrary arrest and recruitment all speak of a defiant and assertive "agency." In the face of a regime that was systematic in the use of force to achieve its notions of political stability and social order, these subaltern interventions are remarkable. They confront us with the negotiated nature of rule under caudillismo, something denied by the existing historiography.

Second, the study displaces the problem of domination and resistance from the private ranch to its rightful place: the recently expanded provincial state. The contestation between peasant-peons and state authorities over questions of military service, crime, and punishment constituted the most important source of social protest during this period. In military barracks the conflicts between officers and soldiers reveal the importance of concepts of individual autonomy, respect, and freedom in the discourse of subalterns. Outside the barracks, the contestation continued under different forms. Desertion, draft dodging, forging documents, and the denunciation of corruption and arbitrary exercise of authority were the ways peasants and peons challenged the powers of the newly formed provincial state.

Moreover, subaltern voices question the very notion of a landowning ruling class. In the "stories" of subalterns, the cattle ranchers are always out of focus (when not altogether out of the picture), their power obfuscated by the presence of local justices, military commanders, and commissioners. Subalterns' lamentations and grievances refer to a modern problematic: the unwritten contract between peasants and the postindependence state for the provision of military services in exchange for citizen rights. This contract and its contestation belong not to a semifeudal order or to a postindependence restoration of a colonial order, but to a republican (though not liberal) political culture.

Third, the book locates paysanos' interventions and voices in the context of an expanding and competitive market economy operating under conditions of labor scarcity. Subalterns' rejection of coercion (state and private) would have been more difficult in an economy with a surplus labor force. The prevalence of short-term contracts in the private economy and the relatively free entry and exit of workers into and from their employment contributed to the persistence of paysanos' itinerant habits. It is clear that the coercive powers of the law did not force the rural poor onto the private confinement of "feudal" cattle ranches. Quite the contrary: it promoted a continuous circulation of workers in and out of military quarters and across the dispersed geography of the labor market. The continued wanderings of peons and peasants during the Rosas period had much to do with the opportunities opened by an expanding export economy, in the context of an intensified enforcement of passport controls and enlistment papers.

Markets meant more for paysanos than historians have been ready to concede. Markets were essential not only for the reproduction of their labor capacities and life but also for the deployment of certain forms of sociability and identity. Many of these laborers' journeys were connected to the transportation of goods (via oxcart caravans) or cattle on the hoof. Their destination was often a market. In these markets, paysanos gathered useful information to search for a job, moving rapidly to the next destination. Markets mediated their circulation through space, no doubt influencing the way they behaved in front of the powerful. Frequent entry and exit into and out of the labor market produced, in addition to a bargaining predisposition, an awareness of the value of their labor for producers and state authorities.

The existence of wage differentials for skill, the importance attributed to earning one's own living, and the recognition by employers of peons' preference for mobility speak of the engagement of the subaltern in market society and culture. Peons and peasants were also consumers and as such participated in the general bonanza that the expansion of cattle ranching brought about. Not only did their physical stature increase—a sign of better nutrition and health—their attire also showed minor but significant improvements. Clothes and fabrics served paysanos to create enduring social connections and also to present themselves socially as free men, bearers of rights. This study shows how, in the context of an enforced uniformity of appearances and of a state gaze ready to identify poor clothes with a future of forced military service, paysanos engaged in true skirmishes for social distinction. Their remarkable skills in the arts of deception aided their transition from positions of ex-soldiers or fugitives from justice to a more secure position of residence and citizenship.

Fourth, concerning the question of the formation of a legal culture, this study recuperates the Rosista pedagogical enterprise of disseminating the Law among the lower classes. The restoration of the law was not a mere rhetorical pretense of a dictatorial regime; it was an experiment in social discipline that had enormous implications for the formation of civil and political identities. These communicational and disciplinary interactions demarcated the boundaries of subaltern possibilities for challenging authority, negotiating service, and exercising rights attributed to citizens. Though there was no "rule of law," the laws governed a vast subset of social interactions. In fact, the procedures of the justice system continued with changes that deepened the postindependence commitment to abolish privilege. More important, the pedagogic power of laws penetrated deep into subalterns' language and consciousness, altering the ways they addressed state authorities.

Fifth, in the terrain of political culture, this study reaffirms features traditionally associated with Rosismo. The unanimity of opinion, the mandated uniformity of colors, and the rhetoric of a holy war against unitarios were certainly there and cannot be denied. But in addition to this, the regime articulated a language of republicanism and social egalitarianism and attempted to recreate the nation's history (its origins and narrative, its heroes, its patriotic calendar). These significant transformations had an effect on the formation of a collective memory about the fatherland.

Rosista federalism was no doubt a repressive political order, but one that required cooperation and compliance from both middling paysanos and poor peons. The war machinery of federalism could not operate without their support. This made politics a fertile terrain for the interventions of subalterns. Deserters politically negotiating their reincorporation into the federalist army, ritualistically shouting *"Viva Rosas!"* after their demands had been met, represent the best example of how even the most hardened of ideological divides had to be negotiated on the ground.

My interpretation of political rituals during this period confirms Myers's (1995) findings about the republican nature of Rosas's political rhetoric. This insight is key to understanding the relations between the governor and the rural masses. In the public, ritual space, the regime presented itself as the inheritor of the ideals of May, adapted to the circumstances of a republic threatened from within and without. Rosismo's ideal political model involved a combination of force and consent. In practice, it depended on the contributions that many middling paysanos made in horses, cattle, and money. The regime could not have survived as long as it did relying only on the use of political terror or preying on the property of a minority. When one examines the importance of rumor in the political culture of the period and the anxiety of state authorities to contain this force, one is forced to recognize that this type of caudillismo had a more fragile structure than generally granted. The negotiated nature of rule was written all over the state archive. Military anxieties about soldiers' lack of loyalty and patriotism and the ever-present possibilities of mass desertions forced the regime to negotiate with the subaltern.

Finally, the study recuperates mobility as a type of infrapolitics and shows the extent to which this "weapon" was felt as a threat by state authorities. True, peons' and peasants' movements in and out of these institutions and across the geography of the nation betrayed a lack of panoramic vision. Yet they did not lack political significance. While moving insecurely over a terrain they did not know (provinces they had never visited before), soldiers made fundamental decisions: whether or not to join a passing regiment, whether to stay in the area or return to Buenos Aires. These decisions were, in the aggregate, crucial for the success of federalism in the civil war. Apparently, paysanos moved across the territory "tactically," without a fixed destination or route, as if testing the itinerary along their way. I call these movements across the territory "perambulations" or "wanderings," in a vein similar to Thompson (1993: 98–119). Moving about, ordinary folks in England were able to momentarily reappropriate the common forests and alleviate the devastating effects of enclosures. By passing along certain paths, they reaffirmed old, customary rights, even though in the end the capitalist would have the last word in reorganizing the space. Riding on horseback, Buenos Aires paysanos traveled longer distances than the restorers of England's forests, constructing on their way an altogether different set of "stories," affirming a different set of rights.

Notes

Introduction

Unless otherwise noted, all translations are mine.

1 I stress the scare quotes around this word, for the "peon class" was neither a class in itself—not a sociological group defined by its position with regard to the ownership of the means of production—nor a class for itself, aware of its position vis-à-vis (and opposed to) the other dominant class. It was a "class" imagined and created from above.

2 Though the study concentrates on the Rosas period, recurrently subalterns' stories and the state's history take the narration back into the 1820s, a period recalled as a foundational era of both "freedom" and "anarchy." The Rosas era, with regard to this period of rupture, appears as a time of order in the midst of a fratricidal political struggle and (at least for a part of the population) as a reversion of an earlier experiment in "democracy" into "tyranny."

3 All this information is what we would expect from a police report, except that the first part of the interrogation concludes with a "classification": the person is classified as fit or not for service, according to his "type" or "class." If he is unequivocally a member of the peon class, there is little doubt that he will be drafted.

4 Perhaps the inquisitor left out important details of the life story of those under interrogation and, quite likely, suppressed all verbal abuse directed against him or the governor. But what was left is rich enough. Moreover, this latter part of the stories did not seem to have been significantly corrected or manipulated.

5 Other records permitted me to complement and understand the issues referred to in these stories: reports on arrests sent quarterly by the justices of the peace (*Partes de Novedades*), letters and petitions addressed to Rosas, judicial records of military and civilian criminal cases, and the copious correspondence of local justices of the peace.

6 Subaltern demands translated elite republican rhetoric (equality, freedom, fraternity, and independence) into a more mundane, everyday idiom of necessities, commitments, and reciprocities. Their demands are proper to an epoch in which the subaltern became a political subject whose "armed opinion" was crucial for the resolution of factional conflicts among the elites. I borrow the allegory of "armed opinion" from González Bernaldo (1994).

7 Two important collections of the group's work are Guha and Spivak (1988)

and Guha (1997). The group received both enthusiastic reception and scathing criticism. See Prakash (1994), Bayly (1988), and O'Hanlon (1988). For Gramsci's use of the concept of subaltern, see Aschcroft, Griffiths, and Tiffin (1998, 214–19). For subalternists' use and adaptation of Gramsci's concepts, see Chatterjee (1989) and Patnaik (1988).

8 By translating poststructuralist concerns to the problems of writing the history of lower-class peoples in postcolonial situations, the works of the ISS group contributed to make historians aware of the problem of representation. For the impact of subaltern studies in Latin American historiography and cultural criticism, see LASSG (1993), Mallon (1994), Moraña (1997), Rabasa, Sanjinés, and Carr (1994), and Beverley (1999). Recently, a collection of articles of the Indian subalternists has been translated into Spanish; see Rivera, Silvia and Barragán (1998).

9 Guha's *Elementary Aspects* (1983) is full of references to Hobsbawm, Rudé, Thompson, Tilly, and other historians of collective action. In fact, the text could be read as a counterpoint between European and colonial Indian (peasant) unrest.

10 By that time (the mid-1980s), the Thompsonian project was already challenged from a number of positions. Stedman Jones (1983), Joyce (1991), and others had called into question the notion of an autonomous working-class culture, noting the embeddedness of notions of class in (elite) discourse of social and political reform. Joan W. Scott (1988) went even further, arguing that the Thompsonian notion of class was framed by the ordering of cognitive dichotomies of gender. On the American side, a labor historiography built around the notion of community (Herbert Gutman and David Montgomery) also went in the direction of political discourse. Culture was taken as a resource for building "working-class communities." See Arnesen, Greene, and Laurie (1998).

11 To my understanding, the subalternist perspective implies a double awareness: awareness of the representational nature of all "evidence" about subaltern subjects and awareness of the subalternity of the voice and claims of these subjects in relation to dominant figures and dominant discourse. Also, this perspective presupposes a more humble research/authorial position for the historian, to the extent that it recognizes the impossibility of reconstructing in a linear, homogeneous, and coherent fashion the life experience of the subaltern.

12 My understanding of questions of class, domination, and resistance also benefited from the work of the British Marxist historians. Reading *Albions' Fatal Tree* (Hay et al. 1975) encouraged me to look in the judicial archives for expressions, actions, and possibly arguments by workers and lower-class subjects. Linebaugh's work (1977; 1992) guided my search into the prison system. If someone had recorded the "confessions" of people impressed and sent to Rosas's army, none better than the very inquisitors at the military headquarters of Santos Lugares. This hindsight proved correct. At the state's center of military discipline and political torture were the documents necessary to unravel the subalterns' past.

13 In particular during the Rosas period, the absence of recognition of workers' presence and culture was all the more evident, given the insistence of liberal historiography that there lay the roots of the period's barbarism and fratricidal strife. One of the most important social histories supposedly dealing with itinerant laborers (Rodríguez Molas 1968) skipped the period as if rural workers had not been affected by the transformations brought about by Rosismo.

14 In industrializing England the working-classes reacted to the modernity produced by machines, the capitalist organization of production, the enclosure of communal lands, and the criminalization of custom. In Buenos Aires province, peons and peasants responded to a different sort of modernity: political and social.

15 No single event, such as the English Reform Act of 1832, brought together radical initiatives. The parallel reform of the River Plate took place eleven years earlier (1821) and entailed an unprecedented extension of suffrage to all males between 18 and 60.

16 In this regard, Foucault's work on the history of disciplinary institutions and discourse provided important insights. For if the Rosista armies and militias were not "total institutions," at least they helped to instill respect for state authority and "the law." Work by D. Hay et al. (1975) and others on the hegemony of the law also proved useful for thinking about the location and possibilities of the subaltern. The *juzgados* of the Rosas era bore little resemblance to eighteenth-century English courts; nonetheless, they constituted places of frequent interaction between state authorities and the rural poor.

17 For a comprehensive view of the historiographical debates around the Rosas period, see Etchepareborda (1972) and Jauretche (1959). The confrontations between revisionist and liberal historiography is examined in Halperin Donghi (1971) and Quattrocchi-Woisson (1995). Two recent books (Svampa 1994; Shumway 1991) present these tensions within historiography as moments of a cultural (and class) divide that survived the passage of time.

18 A fourth motif, the formation of a *saladerista* monopoly that stifled the forces of market competition, also colored the period, though with much less resonance and fewer repercussions.

19 As evidence, he reproduced the unitarios' story that Rosas employed deserters, fugitives, and criminals in his estancias (Ingenieros 1920, 102–104). There is documentary evidence that this was the case in the 1820s, when Rosas was administering the Anchorenas' ranches. In the mid-1830s and 1840s, a different picture emerges. Rosas as governor was able to dispatch soldiers and militias to particular *puestos* or ranches suffering from labor shortages, something other ranchers were unable to do.

20 This had some similarity with contemporary (1830s) developments in Europe, but along the Río de la Plata its premodernity was more evident. Here, the autocrat and the landowner class, in collusion, were recreating not aristocratic rule, but a "feudal" society.

21 Writing in the late 1930s, Manuel Gálvez (1942, 43–46) offered a more favorable view of Rosas's relationship to his peons. Rosas's generosity, equanimity, rigor, and identification with gauchos' lives explained the respect he inspired among the rural poor. Still, the estancia was a closed unit, a personal fief, away from the reach of the state and the general law. "In the fief that is his estancia, he imparts justice. The authorities do not enter there for any purpose nor does anybody dare to call on them." Similarly, Ricardo Levene (1937) in his textbook of Argentine history took for granted that Rosas was and acted as a "feudal lord": "A species of lord of the manor, exercising both civil and criminal jurisdiction, Rosas punished drunkenness, idleness, and theft, either expelling from his states or delivering to the authorities persons who indulged in those vices which he abominated" (392). Enrique de Gandía (1946), the director of the National Archives, shared the same opinion: "He was, in fact, a truly feudal lord" (clxvii).

22 Peña (1969, 63–64) attributed the proletarianization of gauchos to the Rosista state's criminalization of their customs and practices of sociability. Gori (1951) viewed vagrancy laws as the creation of a hacendado class preoccupied with defending their property rights. To Rodríguez Molas (1968) the enforcers of Rosas's laws acted as the midwives of peons' servitude. In his opinion, Sarmiento was right: "The land prevails, the defense of fief and cattle constitute the reason of the laws" (238). Giberti (1961) reached a similar conclusion: "The obstacles built against the wandering life of gauchos impelled them to work in estancias and gave the hacendados weapons to exercise effective command over peons and non-owning neighbors" (87).

23 With some variations, the idea that landowners designed and benefited from the coercive legislation that kept the rural poor in "wage servitude" has reappeared again and again. See, for instance, Sebreli (1972, chap. 11).

24 "The gaucho lost his freedom and anonymity in exchange for a wage, roof, food, and clothing. He became virtually the property of his patron; if the estate was his sanctuary, it was also his prison" (Lynch 1981, 107–108).

25 Though the scenario was displaced in time to encompass the post-Caseros period, Slatta's conclusion did not differ much from Ingenieros's. The landowning class created the legislative and judicial apparatus that in the end served to subordinate the wandering population of the pampas to the rancher class. The gauchos turned into peons. "Vagrancy and work laws, as well as the threat of military conscription, coerced the gaucho into becoming a wage earner, a soldier, or an outlaw" (Slatta, 1983, 93).

26 Because this perspective assumes a symbiosis or, at least, a communality of interests between large landowners and the autocratic state, I call it the "collusion thesis." For a more extended discussion and criticism of this thesis, see Salvatore (1991a).

27 Levene (1954, 204–206), trying to keep some distance from this extreme view, recognized nonetheless that a very reduced group of landowners had

benefited from Rosas's land policies. The explanation was simple: Rosas was the largest of these great landowners.

28 To Oddone (1967), Rosas's greatest sin was to have distributed large tracts of land among a few recipients, creating by this means a unified and powerful *clase terrateniente*. Burgin (1946, 30, 256) lamented that the Federalist Party's failure to implement a progressive agrarian policy revealed its "failure to rise above the limited scope of class interest." Rosas was, after all the representative of the estanciero class, a social group that had taken the leading role in the economic and political affairs of the province since the mid-1820s. Trias (1970) repeated Ingenieros's indictment: the cattle ranching and meat-salting "trust," having monopolized the supply of meat, proceeded to use this influence to colonize the state, thus obtaining important economic benefits. Rosas "expressed" the desire and interests of the rancher class, while "dragging along" the inert mass of the rural poor.

29 The ferocity of some of their attacks knew no limits: Rosas was accused of having sexual relations with his own daughter, of playing perverse sexual pranks on his servants, of suffering from nervous seizures. Later historians legitimized the vision of this generation, arguing that Alberdi and others had proposed a republic based on the "fusion" of existing parties (Romero 1969, chap. 5). To the subalterns contemporaneous with Alberdi, this made little sense, for it was obvious that the anti-Rosas activists and writers were allied with the Unitario Party. Recent studies (Schvartzman 1996; Iglesia 1998) recuperated this perspective, emphasizing the militant, political perspective of this literature.

30 As to the power of Rosas to attract the support of poor rural laborers, butchers, and black women, all was pure flattery and deceit (Varela 1975, 25, 28, 31). See also Lamas (1877) and Rivera Indarte (1946).

31 This situation could lead to further deterioration into "barbarism and banditry" (a "democracy without law," the Rosista alternative) or be transformed into a project of civilization and republican government (the post-Caseros alternative; Mitre 1947, 4:73–74).

32 They were elevated with his promises, only to be humiliated minutes later by his tyrannical caprice (De Gandía 1946).

33 Though the interpretations about the nature of the Rosas regime varied substantially, they shared the view that the special relationship between Rosas and the subalterns had engendered and sustained his dictatorship and that the "barbarism" of rural culture had facilitated Rosas's ascent to power. Sarmiento's *Facundo* (1974; orig. 1845) attributed the peculiarities of caudillo governments, and of the Rosas regime in particular, to the brutality and uncivilized nature of the "desert" and its inhabitants. Rosas himself was a social and cultural product engendered and sustained by a particular system of beliefs, sentiments, and sociability. On Sarmiento's social ideas, see Katra (1996) and Botana (1984); see also Halperin Donghi et al. (1994). Levene (1937) repeated later, almost word for word, Sar-

miento's position: Rosas was a social product and, consequently, not totally responsible for the brutality of his own actions; his concentration of power resulted from society's reaction to the consequences of "anarchy," his use of terror was part of a tradition inaugurated by the postindependent regimes, and his personal psychological structure was founded on the sentiments of an "uncivilized people," most of them blacks or suburban poor (415).

34   Mayo (1984); Salvatore and Brown (1987); Whigham (1988); Azcuy Ameghino (1990).

35   While agreeing on the increasing commercialization of production in the pampas and about the transitory nature of employment, these studies have rekindled the debate about the nature of gauchos. Some authors see Buenos Aires as a peasant society where rural inhabitants shared their time between tilling their own lands and tending cattle for estancieros; others view gauchos as itinerant, temporary laborers complementing wage income with direct appropriation. See "Polémica" (1987); Gelman (1989); Salvatore and Brown (1989).

36   See Mayo (1991) and Brown (1979). For a summary of recent literature, see Garavaglia and Gelman (1995).

37   I have criticized the "fear-protection" thesis in Salvatore (1991a; 1991b). See also Mateo (1993b) and Farberman (1997).

38   Ingenieros's interpretation collapsed the difference between Rosas the rancher (before 1829) and Rosas the governor, identified Rosas's recruitment and disciplinary policies with that of the "estanciero class," and, more important, equated peons' temporary refuge with the condition of servitude.

39   Current work on Rosas's land grants revised down previous estimates by Oddone. Although the Dictator quickened the pace of land appropriation, his contribution to the formation of a class of large landowners was more modest than previously believed (Infesta and Valencia 1987).

40   Though Rosas's notions of ranch administration could easily be endorsed by many cattle ranchers, his vision of social and political order remained controversial. Due to acute labor shortages, Rosas's policy of total militarization of the countryside found staunch opposition among ranchers. His Indian policy—pacification through bribes in kind—generated good business for many of his allies but did not solve the problem of frontier insecurity. Rosas's disciplinarians, many of them estancieros, did not necessarily share their landowning neighbors' opinions concerning forced recruitment and crime control. Halperin Donghi (1995) gives an interesting twist to this question, arguing that it was the Rosista state that held the landowning class captive to its polices and not the other way round.

41   Mitre's (1947) notion of a "savage democracy," reproduced many times in subsequent representations, relegated subalterns to a position of primitivism and barbarity. Ignorant and inarticulate, subalterns were to blame for the violence and brutality of the era of "tyranny." The Rosas regime turned into a "tyranny" (a deformation of an earlier experiment in republican democracy) precisely because of the "uncivilized" nature of the lower

classes. Rosas's terror was only the channeling of popular discontent and frustration against the upper classes (the *gente decente*) and their liberal-minded intelligentsia. Instead of construing favorable views of rural life, the Romantic generation blamed Nature ("the desert") for the production of an indolent, ignorant, and brutal rural population that, in turn, begat the Dictator.

42 More recent renderings of this interpretive tradition can be found in Trías (1988) and Sebreli (1972).

43 Roseberry (1998) uses the term in a similar fashion. Originally, the idea of a "social field" as a bounded but contested terrain was articulated by anthropologist Max Gluckman (1963, 297). Eric Wolf has used the metaphor of "fields of force" to refer to the attraction of two societies/cultures into mutual interaction (see Krech 1991).

44 I use the concept of hegemony in the traditional Gramscian sense. See Femia (1981), especially chapter 2.

45 At times, the overlapping of jurisdictions and duties produced intense disputes between authorities—for example, between local justices of the peace and military commanders—but, in general, these were spheres of power more or less clearly defined.

46 This is the formula used by Guha (1997) to refer to British rule in colonial India.

47 With a small demonstration of force, justices of the peace were able to extract some truth from the subjects they interrogated. Undoubtedly, the prospect of corporal punishment and estrangement from family acted as powerful stimuli to make subalterns talk. But they did not extract conformity from them.

48 According to Dipesh Chakrabarty (1992), our postcolonial histories generally inscribe themselves into a reduced number of "transition narratives" about the attainment of economic, political, or cultural modernity. Quite often, these national histories narrate the failure of marginal regions of the world economy to achieve any of the three forms of modernity (capitalist market economies, liberal republican government, or mass culture).

49 See Bhabha (1990), who ponders the instability and lack of fixity of colonial discourse when interpellating the subaltern. I use the word "story" as synonymous with a limited or micronarrative of experience. Other authors have used this term to refer to the basic story line, plot, or moral contained in a narration (see Cronon 1992).

50 Historians have come full circle around the issue of narrativity. Whereas they welcomed its return in the 1980s, recently there is a challenge to disarm the metanarratives on which history is built. See Cox and Stromquist (1998).

51 According to some authors (Amaral 1998; Sábato 1989; Sábato and Romero 1992), the main transition refers to the emergence of a capitalist market economy in Argentina, more specifically in Buenos Aires. To other historians, the postindependence transition implied a rupture in political governance, the creation of a regionally fragmented polity, and a long delay in

the construction of the nation-state, a phenomenon usually associated with the period 1863–1890 (Chiaramonte 1986). Only recently have some historians of Argentina begun to recognize in this rupture some modern forms of political identity and culture (Goldman 1980; Myers 1995). None to my knowledge have located in this period any consistent argument for the emergence of cultural modernity. The contrary is often the case. A diversity of authors, starting with the Generation of 1837, consistently criticized the stagnation and backwardness of "culture" in the postindependence period.

52 Implicitly, a suspicion of "vagrancy" was projected onto those of poor appearance and no fixed residence. But the state was less interested in spreading the "work ethic"; its overriding preoccupation was to raise large contingents of loyal federalists. For a different view, see Garavaglia (1997a).

53 Contemporary discussions about working-class formation in Britain had little to contribute to the problematic of postindependence Argentina. The absence of workers associations, the lack of indication that a language of class solidarity was replacing colonial forms of sociability, and the illiteracy of peons and peasants made the enterprise of recuperating the "sense of class" demanded by Asa Briggs nearly impossible. Signs of a European-style modern "working-class culture" were nowhere to be seen, and this posed an important obstacle to the investigation.

54 Though this book deals with conspiracies, attempted rebellions, and mass desertions, collective action was the exception rather than the norm.

55 The words of Miguel Anso find resonance in the way blacks, mulattos, and other individuals of "mixed blood" dealt with the categories of race during the colonial regime. Colonial subalterns never took the state's mandated racial categories as a permanent attribute of their social personas; on the contrary, they knew they could manipulate them and "pass" from one category to the other.

56 Concepts of disciplinary power and state visibility became crucial for my investigation of subaltern life. On the classificatory obsession of states, see J. C. Scott (1998) and Burchell, Gordon, and Miller (1991).

57 Probably there were other markers of social difference, but none transpired so markedly in the documents I examined. To my surprise, I found few signs of regionalism or localism in the language of these subalterns. To a certain extent, written sources tend to hide differences in intonation and rhythm that distinguish the speech of a tucumano from that of a cordobés or a puntano. Still, it is curious that in the interior of disciplinary spaces such as military garrisons, prisons, or militias tensions among different groups of provincianos never captured the attention of contemporary observers.

1 The Ways of the Market

1 Employment opportunities diversified as the export sector changed to a somewhat more ample product mix, including hides, tallow, grease, horse-

hair, wool, and jerky beef. More generous credit expanded the sphere of consumption and, in particular, that of popular consumption. The provincial state, with its demands of weapons, uniforms, horses, and military equipment, contributed to expand income and employment.

2 Foreign travelers found the gauchos lacking for the enterprise of modernity: though hospitable and skillful in equestrian feats, they carried with them the burden of indolence, ignorance, and brutal sociability. So did the intellectuals of the Generation of 1837, whose socially, geographically, and historically rooted literary and political essays produced a scornful view of the lower classes.

3 Overlooked by many travelers, the markets for grain seem to have been very active during this period, contradicting the notion that North American flour pushed competitors out of the market. The market for wheat, which operated at the same site as the market for *frutos del país* (national produce), registered daily sales of 300 to 350 *fanegas* (1.6 bushels) per day. *La Gaceta Mercantil*, no. 7014, March 3, 1847.

4 Accounts as separate in time of those of Samuel Haigh (1831) and Hinchliff (1863) replicate the same tropos of abundance and economy.

5 In fact, it could be argued that this mixture of races, social classes, and sensibilities in the marketplace separated the narratives prior to ca. 1865 from those that came afterward. Armaignac, a traveler of the late 1860s, found much elegance and good taste in the shops of Buenos Aires. Liberated from the constraints of federalist egalitarianism, the porteño upper class was able to express their sense of distinctiveness (Armaignac 1961, especially 10–12).

6 Brabazon (1981, 81) reported loaning $300 to a paisano whose wife was going to buy flour and make *tortas fritas*. The woman took her products in an oxcart to the nearby ranch, where peons and pobladores were engaged in branding cattle, and transformed the $300 into $1,000 in less than a day.

7 With one exception, indigenous peoples (not their commodities) had all but disappeared from the market by the 1850s. Azara, writing in the 1790s, reported that Indian groups traded their lassos, harnesses, buckles, pelts, ostrich feathers, and salt in the Buenos Aires market (in Mandrini 1993, 64).

8 For MacCann, traveling in 1851–1852, the marketplace of Buenos Aires was like Babel's tower, "a confusing place where different races interacted and different languages were spoken. The class element of people's attire added diversity to an already confused panorama" (qtd. in Trifilo 1959, 65).

9 "Remate. Frco. L de la Barra," *La Gaceta Mercantil*, no. 1647, July 1, 1829.

10 "Fábrica Americana," *La Gaceta Mercantil*, no. 7031, March 24, 1847.

11 *La Gaceta Mercantil*, no. 6973, January 13, 1847.

12 *La Gaceta Mercantil*, no. 6973, January 13 and 14, 1847.

13 For instance, a young clerk offers his services for a meat-salting plant or grocery shop; artisans and servants offer good references to whoever wants to hire them.

14 *La Gaceta Mercantil*, no. 3782, January 8, 1836.

15 Any informed resident of the city could have noticed the news about auctions posted by foreign brokers and commercial agents, local merchants, and judicial authorities.

16 "Expte seguido sobre el remate de la Loteria de Cartones," 1837, AGN X 31-10-2.

17 Depto de Policía, Buenos Aires, April 14, 1830, AGN X 36-3-6.

18 These petitions can be found in AGN X 31-10-2.

19 These *cédulillas* or *cartones*, made of paper or cardboard, were handprinted with ink. Some of them presented elaborate arabesques to make them appear more reliable. See "Boletos devueltos de la rifa de la casa de Da Maria Eugenia del Castillo," and "Boletos devueltos de un caballo y varias alhajas de D Santiado Whilde," AGN X 36-3-6.

20 This was the procedure followed by the Police Department when auctioning off a push-cart in September 1831. Lorenzo Laguna, Ensenada, September 2, 1831, AGN X 36-3-6.

21 On the history of gambling in Río de la Plata, see Mayo (1998).

22 On June 9, 1850, Rodolgo de Winterfedl put his farm (*chacra*) on the lottery; he started the operation at 10 A.M. and at 3 P.M., not having reached a winner, continued the next day.

23 *La Gaceta Mercantil*, no. 6670, December 31, 1845; *La Gaceta Mercantil*, no. 6663, December 22, 1845.

24 On July 23, 1849, the justice of the peace of Morón fined seven men for playing cards: the head of the household and six *hijos de familia*; the former was charged $500 in fines, the latter paid $50 each. JP of Morón to Chief of Police, Morón, July 23, 1849, AGN X 31-10-2. Around 1831 the fines imposed for this misdemeanor were $25 and $50, respectively. Sección 1a de Policia to Chief of Police, Buenos Aires, September 9, 1831, AGN X 36-3-6.

25 Opponents of the regime presented these auctions as occasions on which a few mazorqueros enriched themselves by means of corrupt and intimidating tactics. See, for example, Avila (1847, 32–33). Surely, justices, commissars, local notables, and men close to government had an advantage in these procedures, but it is unlikely that they cornered all auctions.

26 JP Cañuelas, December 28, 1840, AGN X 20-10-5.

27 Although the branding of cattle predated the revolution, the registration and control of these marks of property became more systematically enforced during the Rosas administration.

28 "Indagatoria," JP of Morón, July 22, 1831, AGN X 36-3-6.

29 If within eight days their legitimate owners did not come to claim their brands, the police sold the hides in public auction. March 23, 1830, Policía, AGN X 36-3-6.

30 *La Gaceta Mercantil*, no. 6987, January 29, 1847.

31 JP of Azul to Minister of Finance, Fuerte Azul, February 3, 1845, AGN X 17-6-4.

32 In 1849, the lack of half an ounce in a piece of bread was punished with a fine of 500 pesos. "Relación de las multas impuestas por este Depto," *La Gaceta Mercantil*, no. 7686, July 3, 1849.

33 "Cuaderno de las Cantidades Depositadas por los Repartidores de Panadería," AGN 31-10-2.

34 The maximum price fixed in 1842 (3 pesos per arroba) was four times greater than the one Rivadavia had established in 1827 (6 reales per arroba).

35 Secretaría de Rosas to J P Monsalvo, Buenos Aires, April 9, 1832, AGN X 21-4-3.

36 Bakers and bread peddlers, unsatisfied with this arrangement, continued to probe the limits of regulation, changing the quality of bread to satisfy new demands. In 1829 a group of bakers petitioned the government for permission to manufacture "privileged bread" (*pan de privilegio*), a product with better ingredients, deserving a better price (lower weight per piece) than that allowed in the official *arancel*. Buenos Aires, March 16, 1829, AGN X 15-2-3.

37 The maximum price for beef, for example, increased four times from 1827 to 1842.

38 "Contra José Castilla, José Ibañez, Felipe Coronel, José Portuguez, Toribio Aguirre por robo de cueros," AHPBA, Juzgado del Crimen, 41-2-148-36 (1850).

39 In 1853, the government acknowledged its inability to control such a proliferation of brands in the market and prohibited sales of cattle not conducted by their owners.

40 Curiously, on this point Rivadavia and Rosas agreed: only free markets could solve the problem of food supply (Giberti 1961, 101).

41 The rest of the cattle came from a region to the south of Buenos Aires and north of the Salado River. No herds came from the other regions—the northwest corridor or the Buenos Aires hinterland. This was the result of the displacement to the south of the cattle frontier as sheep farms occupied the better pastures of the central areas.

42 Free fixing of prices at the farm level was also the norm for sheepskins and wool.

43 On that day (February 27, 1847) 3,967 head of cattle were destined for consumption and 15,106 were earmarked for the meat-salting plants.

44 J P of Lobos to Rosas, Lobos, March 15, 1841, AGN X 21-2-1.

45 Gral Edecán de S E. to J P of Vecino, June 14, 1841, AHPBA, Juzg. de Paz Zona Sur, 34-4-40.

46 Mariano Flores, Agustin Reinoso, Villa de Luján, April 28, 1841, AGN X 21-7-5.

47 "Criminal contra Dn. Pascual Taborda," (1839), expte 910, AGN X 30-3-1.

48 When asked what motivated him to act in this fashion, he gave two reasons: Díaz Vélez was a unitario and the previous patrol had done the same.

49 Ramos Mejia (1907, 1:233–234). Captain Orillana, a *federal neto* holding a low clerical position, wrote to the governor in 1842 asking for the usufruct of the house left by unitario José Zorrilla. Buenos Aires, August 12, 1842, Bienes Embargados, Solicitudes, AGN X 17-3-6.

50 By 1845, the government was renting at subsidized prices numerous prop-

erties confiscated from the unitarios. JP Catedral Norte, July 28, 1845, AGN X 17-6-4.

51 See, for instance, the auction of the confiscated properties of unitarios Ulpiano Barredes y Pascual Costa. JP Cañuelas, December 28, 1840, AGN X 20-10-5.

52 JP of Lobos to Rosas, Lobos, March 5, 1841, AGN X 21-2-1; General Edecán de SE. to JP of Lobos, Santos Lugares, May 29, 1841, AGN X 21-2-1.

53 Comandante Dep. Norte to Manuel Corvalán, San Nicolás, July 5, 1845, AGN X 26-5-3.

54 "Cuaderno de los auxilios de reses que se sacan del Partido para consumo de la Division Fuerte de Mayo, y familias de federales en Campaña," AHPBA, Juzgado de Paz, 39-4-37.

55 In Fort Azul, for example, the army included among the fuerza consumidora veteran soldiers, militiamen, and their families. "Relación de la Fuerza que tiene esta división," Fuerte Azul, March 1, 1838, AGN X 43-1-5.

56 In September 1843, for example, the total number of beneficiaries at Villa Luján had increased to 86 (36 mothers, 42 wives, 4 daughters, 3 widows, and 1 father). AHPBA, Juzgados de Paz, Zona Centro, 39-4-36.

57 Edecán de SE to JP Cañuelas, Santos Lugares, April 24, 1841, AGN X-20-10-5.

58 Contemporary with this petition is the request by officers' wives at Baradero demanding some subsidies in hides. JP Baradero to Rosas, Baradero, March 25, 1841, AGN X 20-9-7.

59 JP of Quilmes to General Edecan M Corvalan, Quilmes, October 12, 1841, AGN X 21-4-6.

60 Long after Caseros, garrisons continued paying "meat bills" that helped to sustain the families of soldiers as well as the poor families of the neighborhood.

61 Petitorio, Abastecedores de los Corrales del Sud, January 12, 1834, AGN X 17-7-2.

62 Chief of Police Lucio Mansilla, supported the demands of cattle owners and so did prominent military and political federalists.

63 Among those signing the January 1834 petition were Badía and Cuitiño, two famous mazorqueros. Among the members of the commission appointed by the government were Santa Coloma, Hidaldo, and Videla, important commanders in the federal army.

64 "Reglamento de Corrales de Abasto," Departamento Gral. de Policía, Buenos Aires, January 31, 1834, AGTN X 17-7-2.

65 "Petitorio," Buenos Aires, November 22, 1834, AGN X 17-7-2. Some of these peons were slaves or ex-slaves having the last name of their masters.

66 "La precedente consideración no será menos perjudicial al público, desde qe es un principio universalmente reconocido, qe la mayor concurrencia de vendedores en todo ramo es el medio más eficaz de evitar qe complotada la codicia de unos pocos, sea su voluntad la ley qe tiranice a la comunidad consumidora" ("The preceding consideration will not be less harmful to the public, since it is a principle universally recognized that the greater

competition among sellers in all trades is the most efficacious means to avoid that the greed of the few becomes the will that tyranizes the consumer community") (ibid).

67 Art. 2, chapter 3: "todo abastecedor o amo de ganado será libre de pagar lo qe fuese al peon qe ocupa" ("Every cattle supplier or master will be free to pay whatever [sum] to the peon he employs").

68 " . . . esa libertad de pagar cada uno de los abastecedores lo que fuese de su agrado, trae las consecuencias del soborno de peones, las amenazas continuas de éstos a sus patrones en suspender sus trabajos sino se les abona tanto como otro les ofresca" (" . . . the suppliers' freedom to pay whatever they wish, brings about bribes to the peons, recurrent peons' threats to their employers of suspending their labors if they are not paid as much as others . . .") (ibid).

69 Pascual Aguilera, petition, Buenos Aires, December 7, 1839, AGN X 31-9-5.

70 The second time, the governor ordered the JP of Monsalvo to grant him a license. "Mateo Quinquela, peticion," Buenos Aires, July 19, 1832, AGN X 21-4-3.

71 Burgin (1946) maintains that, except for the protectionist concessions of 1835–1836 and the question of river navigation, Rosas's policies were consistent with the principles of economic liberalism.

2 Cash Nexus and Conflict

1 Thompson (1967), Montgomery (1979), Burawoy (1979), Pollard (1968), and others have shown that the imposition of "real subsumption" ("industrial discipline") in countries undergoing industrialization entailed a protracted struggle between workers and managers.

2 For a more extensive discussion of different forms of coercion, see Salvatore (2000).

3 A full criticism of the historiography can be found in Salvatore (1991a).

4 Joaquín F. Campana to Chief of Police, Capilla del Carmen, May 8, 1825, AGN X 31-9-5.

5 Martín Zaramiñana to Chief of Police, Ranchos, May 21, 1825, AGN X 31-9-5.

6 In October 1826, one of the Anchorenas' foremen complained that the recruiting parties had taken most peons, leaving only those who passed as slaves. Tala de los Anchorena, October 19, 1826, AGN VII, col. Ruiz Guiñazú, 16-4-7, 1334.

7 The complaints by a rancher in June 1824 captures well the mood: "Son los peones de ordinario altaneros, insubsistentes en los trabajos, y gozan de la perjudicialísima licencia de abandonar sin motivo justo una casa" ("Usually peons are haughty, unstable in their jobs, and they take joy in the harmful habit of abandoning the employment without a cause") (qtd. in Bagú 1966, 17–18).

8 In 1829 an advertisement offering a slave at a low price alerted prospective

buyers of the slave's limited remaining years in bondage. Another slave owner was candid about his offer: his young criado knows how to cook and to drive a carriage but "does not want to serve." A black *lavandera* was offered at a bargain price because she had refused to follow her masters to the countryside. See *La Gaceta Mercantil* 1829: "Venta de un Criado" (December 28); "Criado en Venta" (July 1); "Criado en Venta" (July 2); "Lavandera" (December 28).

9   Other important activities where wage relations prevailed were not recorded, probably due to the reluctance of proprietors to regularize their payroll; among them were slaughterhouse and meat-salting plant workers, peons of tallow workshops, and clerks of pulperías.

10 Of the 127 employers registered, 63 percent had only one worker, 28 percent had two to four workers, and only 8 percent had five to ten workers.

11 On early attempts to form artisan guilds and their failures, see Johnson (1976a, 1980, and 1995). See also Levene (1961, 365–371).

12 There were *lazoers*, watchers, feeders, butchers, salters, carriers, cleaners, drovers, and more. "Lista de los peones que existen en este establecimiento de mi mando . . . ," AGN X 43-2-8.

13 "Relación de Jornales de los operarios . . . en la obra del Muelle de Barracas," AGN X 23-8-4.

14 Parque de Artillería, "Relación de las Conducciones" (1836), AGN X 43-4-4.

15 "Lista de Peones al servicio del Cementerio," Buenos Aires, January 10, 1838, AGN X 43-1-5; "Relación de los sueldos de la tropa," San Isidro, February 1, 1828, AGN X 43-1-5; "Relacion de los gastos en la obra del cementerio," AHPBA, Juzgado de Paz Azul, 39-1-2; Criminal c/Antonio Sierra y Bernardo Repetto, AHPBA, Juzg. Crimen, 41-2-148-4 (1850).

16 Pedro Calderón to Rosas, June 4, 1845, AGN X 43-2-8.

17 Written labor contracts, like the ones distributed by Rivadavia's commissars in the 1820s, were the simplest of documents, containing only two promises: the worker promised to work during a certain period of time and the employer promised to pay a given wage rate. To acquire legal force, the document had to be signed in front of a police authority.

18 J. J. Anchorena to Saavedra, Buenos Aires, July 27, 1831, AGN VII 4-4-3.

19 This, rather than his "penalty codes" or his appealing personality, was the reason behind Rosas's success in recruiting peons (Aráoz de Lamadrid 1921, 273–274).

20 Rosas to Décima, Buenos Aires, March 20, 1832, AGN VII 16-4-8, no 1452.

21 J. Décima to J. J. Anchorena, Camarones, April 26, 1830, AGN VII 4-4-3.

22 In 1842 Rosas advised one of his foremen, Don Basilio, that he could use the help of the local justice to locate potential workers and that he should hire those peons "for their fair price, paying them by the day according to custom" (in Carretero 1970, 17).

23 Rosas advised his foremen to protect peons by extending them letters of conduct, by making dark peons pass for slaves, or simply by hiding them

from militia recruiters. Rosas to Morillo, October 24, 1826, AGN VII 16-4-7.

24 M. Morillo to Saavedra, Camarones, July 25, 1827, AGN VII 16-4-7.

25 Maria Herrera to Rosas, Las Flores, September 30, 1843, AGN X 26-4-2; Nicolás Anchorena to Morillo, Buenos Aires, December 28, 1834, AGN VII 16-4-8, no. 1542.

26 Ramírez to Rosas, Chacabuco, May 29, 1845; Rosario, August 11, 1845, AGN X 43-2-8.

27 Rosas's administrators replicated in the 1830s and 1840s almost the same complaints voiced by Santiago Sagasta to his boss, Pedro Aguirre, in the mid-1820s.

28 Amaral (1998, 170) has argued, based on estimates of aggregate labor supply and demand for the period 1787–1791, that labor shortages were mostly seasonal (winter).

29 Aggregate calculations of labor availability and requirements are, in this regard, of dubious utility, in addition to being imprecise and crude, for it is in relation to prevailing wage rates that labor shortages should be examined. The fact that activity rates were quite low is to be expected in a society experiencing a process of incomplete proletarianization.

30 Schoó to Rosas, San Martín, November 13, 1849; Ramirez to Rosas, Chacabuco, November 9, 1849, AGN X 26-8-4.

31 In the traditional method of daily roundups, lack of peons translated into a direct increase in the number of strays. Ramírez to Rosas, Chacabuco, May 26, 1847, AGN X-26-5-4.

32 Pedro R. Rodríguez to Ramírez, Buenos Aires, September 20, 1844, AGN X 43-2-8.

33 To make two drives (tropas) a month (an activity that required a team of thirty workers), the administrator had to gather peons from four or five puestos (settlements within the ranch). Ramírez to Rosas, Chacabuco, May 26, 1847, AGN X-26-5-4.

34 Sixto Casanova to Angel Pacheco, Estancia El Talar, May 29, 1844, AGN VII 1-3-1.

35 Ramírez to Rosas, Chacabuco, January 1, 1847, AGN X-26-5-4.

36 "At two of Rosas' estates in San José de las Flores ('Rosario' and 'San Benito'), the quarterly turnover rate for peons ran from 40 to 50 percent during the early 1840s" (Slatta 1983, 32).

37 Cmte Regto 3 to Rosas, Campamento Saladillo, Rosario, June 28, 1845, AGN X 26-5-3.

38 Laureano Ramírez to Pedro Calderón, March 20, 1845, AGN X 43-2-8.

39 Limited information about wages, contributed by draftees in their filiaciones shows important cross-regional differences.

40 The myth of the south as a refuge for runaways served to compensate for the uncertainty generated by the lack of information about wages in the southern districts.

41 Payments were made in periods that varied between one and three months.

Peons received the net value after deductions were taken for their *fallas* (absences). Less frequently, deductions included goods taken on credit at the local tavern.

42 Santiago Sagasta to J P Aguirre, January 29, 1827, A B C O P B A, Juan Pedro de Aguirre, 031-6-8.

43 Forms of sharecropping developed as a means to distribute risk between landowners and producers, yet seasonal activities continued to be paid in wages. See Sábato (1989, 79–125).

44 In 1844 a peon ran away from a ranch in Azul, leaving its owner with an outstanding debt equivalent to 1.3 times the peon's wage. In addition to a money advance, the rancher had authorized the peon to take goods on credit from the local tavern. Miguel Ibáñez, Loma Verde, June 5, 1844, A H P B A, Juzg Paz Azul, 39-1-2.

45 An account of June 1845 shows that peons were granted $300 in advance as a reward for their good service. Most of them had been at the slaughter-house for more than a year and showed a clean credit record. Pedro Calderón to Rosas, June 3, 1845, A G N X 43-2-8.

46 Peon of the *partidas acarreadoras* Jose María Tisera asked for an advance of $400, a sum larger than his salary. Pedro Calderón to Rosas, May 31, 1845, A G N X 43-2-8.

47 "Peones de la Casa de Gobierno," A H P B A, Contaduría, Cuerpo 34, doc. 2231.

48 "Gastos echos de peones y Capatases delos Establecimtos del Sor Cnel Dn Pablo Muñoz," Piedra, November 5, 1841, A G N X-21-2-4.

49 Peons employed by Anchorena earned 5 pesos a day if they worked during the day and 6 pesos if they worked during the night. Manuel Morillo to J. J. Anchorena, October 22, 1830.

50 Brown (1979, 189) has noted that loyalty and literacy were rewarded among ranch administrators and foremen. Mayo (1997a) has shown how a black slave could rapidly become principal foreman (*capataz mayor*) in a late colonial ranch.

51 Owing large debts to the ranch (Rosas had advanced their overseas tickets), Spanish peons could cause great damage if they left.

52 Laureano Ramírez to Rosas, Chacabuco, November 24, 1846, A G N X 26-5-4.

53 Schoó to Rosas, San Martin, April 5, 1846, A G N X 26-5-4.

54 "Estado qe manifiesta el debe y haber de los peones," Rincón del Rosario, September 2, 1838, A G N 25-6-6.

55 The ranch never discounted wages on Sundays; as for Saturday, it was a workday the same as the rest of the week. Schoo to Rosas, April 5, 1846, A G N X 26-5-4.

56 Instructions to foremen and administrators allowing them to punish criados (slave peons) with the stocks (*cepo*) and the lash are of this period. The famous letter in which Rosas instructs foreman Morillo to give three hundred lashes to a slave dates from March 8, 1833. In 1844, when Ramírez

asks for an escaped peon to be punished if found at Palermo, it is the government who has to deliver the punishment.

57 D. Schoó to Rosas, San Martin, March 22, 1846, AGN X 25-5-4.

58 Gelman (1998) has shown that Rosas, unable to control the settlement of new pobladores, ended up negotiating with them. Squatters were permitted to stay in part because they provided a crucial service to the estanciero: vigilance over the ranch's unfenced borders.

59 An 1849 advertisement offered six leagues of good land in Chivilcoy, including the thirty labradores who lived on the land. La Gaceta Mercantil, July 3, 1849.

60 Toribio Barrionuevo, filiación, Dolores 1845, AGN X 21-7-7.

61 José Rosas, filiación, Cañuelas 1842, AGN X 20-10-5.

62 Gregorio Rea, filiación, Santos Lugares 1851, AGN III 59-2-3.

63 Pedro Chávez, filiación, Villa de Luján, 1844, AGN X 21-7-6.

64 José María Olguín, filiación, Navarro 1849, AGN X 17-10-5.

65 When interrogated, Giménez declared that "he knew well that it was theft what they were doing, but since his patron consented and authorized this, he had no inconvenience or scruples in carrying on with it." Saturnino Maldonado, filiación, Fortín de Areco 1849, AGN X 20-9-6.

66 Sumario c/Juan de Dios Troncoso, Monsalvo, December 23, 1836, AGN X 21-4-3.

67 Sumario, San Lorenzo de Navarro, July 2, 1838, AGN X 21-4-4.

68 Juan de Dios Córdoba, filiación, Chivilcoy 1851, AGN III 59-1-3.

69 Juan Gutiérrez, filiación, Quilmes 1844, AGN X 21-5-1.

70 I borrow these terms from Hirschman (1970).

71 "Cuenta del peon Macedonio Britos," Loma Verde, June 5, 1844, AHPBA, 39-1-2.

72 Judicial records only marginally capture this phenomenon, for this type of offense was not considered important by the Rosista state.

73 Domingo Lescano escaped after stealing four horses, a mare, a branding instrument, and some clothes. JP of San Nicolás, Partes de Novedades, January–February 1839. Pedro Pablo Andrade left his employment immediately after getting an advance from his boss taking a pair of silver hoops (for the reins). JP of Dolores, Partes de Novedades, July–August 1837.

74 José Barbosa, filiación, Dolores 1844, AGN X 21-2-1. Others left quietly, like farm laborer Daniel Ceballos, who ran away leaving his patrón (a Guardia de Luján farmer) a debt of $187. Daniel Ceballos, filiación, Guardia de Luján 1845, AGN X 21-2-3; Marcos Costilla, filiación, Buenos Aires 1846, AHPBA, Cámara de Apelaciones, 9.1.3.134.

75 JP of Lobos (1840), AGN X 21-1-7; JP of Navarro, Partes de Novedades, May–August 1840.

76 On July 25, 1836, Gerónimo Caballero was arrested in Dolores for "having slaughtered two calves belonging to his patrón D. Silverio Ponce de León without the prior knowledge of the person in charge of the establishment." JP of Dolores, Partes de Novedades, January–February 1836.

77   JP of Dolores, *Partes de Novedades*, January–April 1839.

78   José Prado, an ex-soldier of Quiroga, was arrested in 1844 for *raterías* (small thefts) committed at a San Nicolas *barraca*. Filiación, San Nicolás 1844, AGN X 21-7-1. Rosarino Santiago Carballo was arrested for stealing hides and horsehair from the *barraca* in which he was employed. JP of San Nicolás, *Partes de Novedades*, January–April 1844.

79   "Portillo, Esteban y Domingo," AHPBA, Cámara de Apelaciones, 7.2104.8 (1827).

80   Francisco Suárez, filiación, Quilmes 1842, AGN X 21-4-6; Sumario c/Angel Pueblas, Estancia Fontezuelas, July 14, 1837, AGN X 43-8-8; Sumario indagatorio contra Guillermo Agüero, 1838, Lobos, AGN X 21-1-7. Considering that this was an "involuntary murder," Rosas pardoned Agüero, charging him with a fine of 500 pesos to be paid to Mosquito's widow.

81   Though this way of settling work disputes seems a bit extreme, situations like these existed in other trades. Violent labor relations plagued the business of oxcart transportation, leather tanning, and the slaughterhouses.

82   Jose Martínez to Chief of Police, San José de Flores, September 12, 1833, AGN X 33-4-1; D. Schoo to Rosas, San Martín, March 22, 1846, AGN X 25-5-4.

83   Later, a dispute broke out as Crisóstomo came to claim some clothes left at Mária's rancho. This time, Mária accused Crisóstomo of sexual assault and had him arrested. Crisóstomo González, filiación, Santos Lugares, 1851, AGN III 59-1-6.

84   Gómez worked for three months as a monthly peon, then during the wheat harvest. Afterward, he stayed on for twelve months without a clear work relationship with the estate. Manuel Gómez, filiación, Quilmes, 1842, AGN X 21-4-6.

85   In 1825 foreman Pedro Zabala presented to the courts a claim against his patrón, Don José López, for 16 pesos in unpaid wages. Lopez initially resisted the call of justice but was later arrested and forced to pay the debt. Morón, April 25, 1825, AGN X 31-9-5. In 1823, foreman Hilario Corvalán filed a complaint against his employer, Don Ramón Carmona, for refusing to pay past wages and for reacting violently to the peon's demand for payment. Criminal c/Ramón Carmona, AHPBA, Cámara de Apelaciones, 7.2.99.16 (1823).

86   "Sumario c/Agustín Pereyra," January 16, 1837, AGN X 20-9-7.

87   JP of Lobos, *Partes de Novedades*, January–April 1840; Comisaría de Villa Luján y su Guardia, *Parte de Novedades*, January–April 1843; JP of San Nicolás, *Partes de Novedades*, May–August 1838.

88   "Sumario por la muerte de Alvino Suárez," Quilmes, October 18, 1837, AGN X 21-4-6. Similarly, Felipe Frete, a veteran employed as an oxcart driver on a trip from Córdoba to Buenos Aires, took his knife and cut his boss's hat as a result of an argument at their arrival at Arrecifes. But we do not know the full discussion that preceded the fight. Felipe Frete, filiación, May 15, 1842, AGN X 20-9-7.

89   Inocencio Molina, filiación, Guardia de Luján 1845, AGN X 21-2-3.

90 In December 1839 a 14-year-old santiagueño peon, Miguel Gerónimo Toloza, was accused of the murder of his patrón's son. He had hit the boy in the head with an axe in revenge for the corporal punishment he had received from his employer. Toloza was reported as saying: "You will be paid for the floggings your father had inflicted upon me." Miguel Gerónimo Toloza, filiación, Guardia de Luján, December 7, 1839, AGN X 21-2-2.

91 Bernabé Coronel (16 years old) left his job at a meat-salting plant in Balvanera on account of a wage dispute. He told the police that "he did not want to work for his patrón because of the low daily wage the latter paid him." Filiación, Buenos Aires, 1841, AGN X 31-10-5.

92 The justice of the peace of Lobería, for instance, informed Rosas in August 1841 that "peons and foremen were not content with the salaries they earned." JP Lobería to M. Corvalán, August 23, 1841, AGN X 21-2-4.

93 In February 1862, Brabazon (1981, 179) experienced in person the bargaining spirit of paysanos. Some of the sheep shearers who had gathered at estancia La Felicidad (near Azul) approached and asked him for a raise; if he did not comply, they threatened, they would stop working altogether. When Brabazon refused, the whole group walked out.

3 Provincianos' Paths to Work

1 Rosas's Edecán to Comisario of Villa Luján, September 10, 1832, AGN X 21-7-5.

2 JP of Luján to Rosas's Edecán, March 12, 1838, AGN X 21-2-2.

3 Rosas's Edecán to Justice of Chivilcoy, Santos Lugares, November 2, 1851, AGN X 21-1-1.

4 Rosas's Edecán to JP of Chivilcoy, Santos Lugares, November 2, 1851, AGN X 21-1-1.

5 In addition to wages, both groups could expect meat rations, vicios, and, in some cases, clothes, knives, and other perks.

6 This could indicate that the rural police targeted single males or that they constituted the most mobile part of the rural workforce and thus attracted the attention of military recruiters and the guardians of order. Quite likely, the proportions of married males among the arrested (30 percent for provincianos, 23 percent for porteños) underestimated the degree to which women accompanied these migratory workers. As Socolow (1998) has shown, women were an important proportion of the workforce and the population of frontier towns.

7 The difference in age, on average, was not significant, provincianos being on average 29 years (SD = 8.9), porteños 26 (SD = 9.4).

8 Perhaps provincianos were classified as fit for infantry in disproportion to their riding skills (18 percent vs. 8 percent), but this was compensated by a larger share of young porteños considered fit for the music band, an equally despised assignment.

9 "Today, the works are in its greatest strength of activity, and . . . now, more than ever, peons are needed. Many of those who now serve on a monthly basis will stop working in order to travel to their countries [*país*]. Some are provincianos who had complied with the term of their contracts, others (who have no debts with the ranch) settle their accounts and leave. The same happens with the peons of the driving gangs (*partidas acarreadoras*], their diminishing numbers are already noticeable. At the end of January we shall see a reduction of the third of our peons" (Laureano Ramírez to Rosas, Chacabuco, January 1, 1847, AGN X 26-5-4).

10 Dataset Provincianos (a subset of dataset Filiaciones) with 161 observations.

11 Of the total number of provincianos in the sample, 60 percent had arrived in Buenos Aires province between 1841 and 1845.

12 Garavaglia (1999, 45) calls these "swallow-type migrations."

13 Information about the month provincianos were arrested confirms these findings. Of 248 migrants from the upper provinces, 15 percent were arrested in December–January, 22 percent in February–March, 13 percent in April–May, 14 percent in June–July, 18 percent in August–September, and 17 percent in October–November. Monthly peaks occurred in November (13.3%), March (12.9%), July (11.7%), and August (10.9%). This pattern does not support the view of migration as predominantly seasonal.

14 Guardia de Luján, March 1, 1838, AGN X 21-2-2.

15 Manuel Aguirre, filiación; and Florencio Almarás, filiación, Santos Lugares, March 3, 1851, AGN III 59-1-1; José Pio Miranda, filiación, Santos Lugares, April 20, 1849, AGN X 17-10-5.

16 Manuel Sánchez, filiación, Lobos, November 25, 1851, AGN X 18-2-6; Avelino Luna, filiación, Santos Lugares, March 30, 1846, AGN X 21-2-3.

17 Francisco Suárez, filiación, Quilmes, August 23, 1842, AGN X 21-4-6.

18 Andreś Montenegro, filiación, Quilmes, July 25, 1845, AGN X 21-4-6.

19 For Domingo Noriega we have three documents: a clasificación dated September 1845, a *media-filiación* dated February 1846, and a filiación dated August 1850.

20 Quilmes, February 16, 1844, AGN X 21-5-1.

21 "These periodical emigrations (usually for a determinate period) . . . respond to the preservation of a custom, to a certain spirit of adventure that we find in santiagueños' moral character, and to the numerous populations disseminated in the province" (Fazio 1889, 252).

22 Words from Gálvez reproduced by Farberman (1997, 10).

23 Farberman (1997) traces the migration of individuals and families to Buenos Aires as they tried to cope with impoverishment and the repression of new military bosses.

24 Few of the provincianos arrested (35 out of 161) made explicit the motive for their trip. Of these, 18 said they came searching for a job, 9 were members of military units returning to Buenos Aires or soldiers hired in the interior provinces, 4 came to purchase cattle, 3 came searching for a relative, and 2 were transported felons.

25 "Before thinking of moving his troop [train] the santiagueño traveler col-

lected all the most exact information [*noticias*] he could get about the country he had to go through: he needed to know if it had rained in the Southern regions, if there was good grass at a short distance from the road, if the surroundings of those places chosen to rest were open, if there was abundant water in the ponds [*represas*], if the more difficult points on the road were in good condition, if a creek or a *bañado* could pose new difficulties along the road" (Fazio 1889, 243).

26 Blas Ponce recounted his decision to migrate to Buenos Aires in these terms: he waited until the country was quiet (*cuando el País se tranquilizó*) before asking his commander permission to go down to Buenos Aires to work.

27 Usually, they had to choose between two roads. One went directly from Santiago to Sunchales (north of Santa Fé) to Córdoba or Rosario; the other passed through the towns of Loreto, Atamisqui, Salavina, and Sumampa and thence to the north of Córdoba (Ojo de Agua, Jesús María) before turning east in the direction of Rosario. At Sunchales, troops coming in the northward direction gathered to graze the animals (Fazio 1889, 242–243).

28 Martín Coronel was dismissed at El Tala by his patron after a long journey from Santiago. His brother Justiniano continued with the same oxcart troop to Buenos Aires, later settling in Tuyú.

29 Quilmes, June 22, 1843, AGN X 21-5-1; Santos Lugares, April 20, 1849, AGN X 17-10-5.

30 This tendency to move on was more pronounced among those who went directly to the city: of the twenty, only one mentioned the city as his residence at the time of his arrest.

31 Of 134 cases, 89 mentioned only one job, 32 mentioned two jobs, 11 mentioned three jobs, and 2 mentioned four jobs. Of 121 cases, 53 reported having been in one locality, 41 in two localities, 16 in three localities, and 11 in four localities.

32 Filiación, Ranchos, July 24, 1845, AGN X 21-5-2. When they were arrested, they were riding stolen horses, traveling southeast. They were trying to reach Don Arana's cattle ranch, where Aguirre's uncle worked as a foreman and could probably find them conchavos.

33 These filiaciones are located in AGN X 21-5-1. Though they lived in the same area, they had found different employments. The Argüello brothers had remained two months in the region. The older brother, Pablo, had been employed as a horse breaker for the local teniente alcalde. Abelardo had worked at Don Pedro Amaro's ranch earning $50 a month; his brother Lorenzo had worked for Maciel as a day laborer receiving $15 a day. Montenegro, the apparent leader of the group, had been at Maciel's farm for over twenty months earning $60 a month. Verón had stayed only one month working for D. F. Torres for $40 a month.

34 At their arrival, 90 percent were under 30; 40 percent came at age 21–25.

35 On the importance of family structure in determining migration, see Farberman (1995).

36 Members of the elite who reminisced about labor migrations liked to think of previous employers as the best aids for migrants. As they returned

annually to the same farms or ranches, santiagueños were said to reclaim the patronage of the old boss (*patrón viejo*) (see Fazio 1889, 251).

37 If they do, the relationship portrayed emphasizes the same origin of peons and employers as the basis for the support and protection dispensed.

38 "Up to April 10, 1848, we have earned, in two months, 2,500 pesos. . . . For that task we charged 600, in total we had already 3,100 pesos." Much later, when he had become an independent sheep farmer, he wrote: "[February 10, 1855] And after paying 830 pesos to the man who gathered the sheep, 4,150 to the shearers, and 830 pesos for fastening the wool-bales, it left me a profit of 1,890 pesos" (Brabazon 1981, 70, 145).

39 The word *beneficio* often referred to the procreation or multiplication of cattle.

40 To Brabazon, native-born sheep shearers "did not take things seriously" and were not very productive, being mainly interested in "drinking mate and eating meat in abundance" (1981, 49).

41 On the notion of citizenship in this transitional period, see Chiaramonte (1997, 117–118, 146–147). See also Cansanello (1994, 1995).

42 On the dichotomous social perception of migrants (transients vs. residents), see Cansanello (1994).

43 Chiaramonte has examined the ambivalence of political identities in the postindependence era, noting that terms such as *americanos, rioplatenses,* and *argentinos* were used interchangeably. See Chiaramonte (1989; 1997, 63–67, 120–124).

44 Military addresses of the period tend to support this view. A *proclama* addressed by General Paz in 1829 alerted the population of Córdoba of an incoming invasion of "foreign troops," referring to the federalist troops mostly composed of porteños.

4 Class by Appearance

1 The space of lifestyles, argues Bourdieu, is a social field constituted by two capacities: the capacity to produce classifiable practices and works, and the capacity to differentiate and appreciate these practices and products. Agents acquire competence to "read" the social significance of fashions, styles, and colors, and institutions define the "classes" of objects relevant as markers of social difference (1984, especially chap. 3).

2 Basic to the generation and reproduction of social difference is Bourdieu's concept of "habitus": the perdurable dispositions that generate classifications of objects according to class criteria and the ability to appreciate those differences (cultural competence). It is habitus that generates "taste," the system of significations that translates bundles of goods or possessions into meaningful indicators of class (1984, 177, 200–202).

3 Other authors have also focused on the social meaning of things. See Appadurai (1991), Douglas and Isherwood (1990), and Mukerji and Schudson (1991, especially the essays by R. Barthes and R. Williams).

4   Because Rosas expected the federal color *punzó* (scarlet) to be close to the heart of all soldiers, he designed military ponchos with scarlet inside (*forro*) as well as jackets and *camisetas* (knitted shirts) of the same color (Udaondo 1922, 199).

5   "En mi pago hay un pulpero/Que es hombre de mucho honor/Pero dicen que en su tierra/Era el mejor saltiador./Ahora anda de bota juerte/tiene capote y relós/Así es que con la lujuria/Gasta más pesos que arroz./Yo también conozco algunos/Que han sido de chiripá/Y ahora que tienen fraques/Se han pasado a la unidá./Quisiera que me digieran/Si se han pensado ser más/Por media vara de paño/Que llevan colgando atrás./Así es que por despreciarnos/A los que usamos chaqueta/Nos han puesto compadritos,/Mire si serán trompetas./Y luego se ande enojar/Si en saliendo a las orillas/Algún paisano les dice/Pintores y cagetillas" ("In my town, there is a tavern owner/Who is a man of great honor/But in his homeland, they say/He was the best highwayman./Now he wears 'strong boots'/He owns cape and watch/Thus, lavishly/He spends pesos as rice/I also know others/Who had worn chiripás/And now wear frock coats/They had changed to the Unidad [party]./I wish they told me/If they think they are superior/Due to one foot of cloth/That hangs from their behinds./Because they despise us/Those who wear jacket/They have labelled us *compadritos*/What a deceitful bunch!/And they later feel annoyed/If going to the [city] outskirts/A paysano calls them painters and pretentious snobs") *El Torito de los Muchachos*, no. 2, Ago 22, 1830.

6   "Paqueteria," *La Moda*, no. 9, January 13, 1838.

7   Unitario poets (as imagined by a federalist newspaper) encouraged ladies to continue using light blue and white, the colors of union and fatherland.

8   "Modas de Señoras," *La Moda*, no. 2, November 25, 1837.

9   The romantic disposition of the Generation of 1837 also associated clothes with social and political virtues. Although they praised the modesty and asceticism of Jacksonian democracy and encouraged their fellow citizens to wear more sober, less pretentious clothes, they despised the leveling of social distinction effected by the Rosas tyranny. *La Moda*, no. 2, November 25, 1837.

10 A model filiación can be found among the papers of the Juzgado de Paz de Giles, undated, AHPBA, 39-2-22.

11 Other clothes (shirts, jackets, and camisetas) were not as clear a mark of class as trousers/chiripás, waistcoats/ponchos, or boots/bota de potro.

12 To demonstrate this principle, Rosas himself dressed in ways that resembled the style of gauchos (Sebreli 1972, 193).

13 See, for example, *El Gato, baile campestre* (lithograph), in Palliere (1864, no. 149). Pellegrini's *Media Caña* (1841) shows paysanos dancing outside a pulpería. Here, some paysanos, without renouncing their traditional attire, have adopted high hats and military jackets resembling *paletós*. See also no. 155.

14 The iconography of the period invested this combination of affluence and restraint in the figure of the hacendado federal, a wealthy person dressed in

paysano style, carrying the emblems of federalism. See R. Monvoisin, *Gaucho federal—Buenos Aires*, oil on canvas, 1842. Reproduced from B. del Carril, *Monumenta Iconográphica* (1964).

15 In many cases, the classification of peon de campo coincided with that of *vago*, indicating that itinerant peons were placed in the same category as those allegedly without occupation or not willing to work.

16 Eighty-five percent of the filiaciones were dated between 1840 and 1849 and another 24 percent in the following decade.

17 A small minority did not seem to belong to this group. Meat suppliers (*abastecedores*), boat owners (*boteros*), and peons, disguised among the city gentry, were probably trying to get the same resguardo (safeguard paper) or exemption from service.

18 Even in the city, rural culture dominated among the lower strata of the population. Only artisans, servants, clerks, and, quite exceptionally, dealers in cattle might wear the clothes of resguardo.

19 I have selected only those cases with sufficient information about clothes to allow an in-depth analysis of the subject.

20 Codes of "urbanity" and good customs considered clothes an essential conveyor of difference, emphasizing the gender and class nature of styles (Diez de Bonilla 1874).

21 Scenes of arriving passengers at the port show the contrast between the traveler, dressed in European style (frock coats for men, and long and bell-shaped dresses for women), and the boaters and carters who carried them, dressed a lo paysano.

22 "Sumario por el suicidio de José Aguirre," AHPBA, Juzgado del Crimen (1850), 41-2-148-17.

23 Pictorial representations of the period coincide with this view: the middling hacendado federal differed little in his appearance from the small-scale criador or labrador, and the latter showed few marks of distinction over the dress of poor laborers.

24 Some of them selectively adopted a few items of town clothes as a job requirement (servants, military men, and clerks), but by and large, most avoided adopting the entire pueblero outfit. Only tavern owners dressed differently: their wardrobe included waistcoats, trousers, and ties, items hardly ever worn by other paysanos.

25 Those wearing the clothes of town residents (puebleros) were suspected of unitario leanings and also of lacking the degree of manliness and patriotism attributed to paysanos. Being in fashion was close to being an *afrancesado*, a word that evokes foreign sympathies, effeminate manners, and artistic predispositions.

26 Unfortunately, the information contained in filiaciones is insufficient to examine market preferences for woolens and cottons, an important distinction reflecting the market penetration of two manufactures in different stages of technological development.

27 "Criminal contra Antonio de los Santos," AHPBA, Juzgado del Crimen

(1829), 34-4-85-16; "Presentación de Juan Vázquez," Buenos Aires, March 28, 1838, AGN X-21-2-2.

28 By the same token, military officers tried to distinguish their group (the *clase de oficiales*) from the lower ranks, usually made up of illiterate men.

29 In the city, the difference between a free man and a slave was evident in their attire; not so in the countryside, where anyone who wanted to pass unnoticed wore paysano clothes. Advertisements for runaway slaves during 1836 show that black servants were better dressed than paysanos, wearing Nankin jackets, cloth trousers, and coconut shirts.

30 At the time of the southern rebellion of 1839, Rosas insisted on providing uniforms and "vices" to the federalist troops as quickly as possible.

31 Bejaramo to Lagos, Arroyo Grande, May 19, 1846, AGN VII (Hilario Lagos), Leg. 1; Aguilar to Chilabert, Batallón Patricios no. 3, Buenos Aires, October 8, 1849, AGN X 17-10-5. In February 1852, the minimum uniform of a Rosista soldier (cloth jacket, linen shirt, linen drawers, and cloth chiripá) cost 9 pesos 4 reales. Twelve years later, the cost of a uniform went up to 221 pesos. The cost of the uniform of an officer could be quite expensive; the jacket, a golden *galón*, and a velvet tie were worth 365 pesos in 1841. Rosas rewarded the soldiers of the successful campaign against the unitarios in 1839 with a set of clothes: a camiseta, a *ponchillo* of red *bayeta*, and a cap for each soldier. Rosas to Pacheco, Buenos Aires, November 14, 1839, AGN VII 1-2-10; A Pacheco a J. M. Rosas, Salto, November 27, 1829, AGN VII 1-2-5.

32 Officers' uniforms included silk kerchiefs, linen drawers and shifts, and woolen trousers. Those of common soldiers did not include trousers; their shirts, drawers, and kerchiefs were made of cotton. J. M. Rosas to Cmte. del Parque, Palermo, November 9, 1842, AGN VII 1-3-5.

33 Comando en Jefe del Ejército 1972, del Carril 1964, Udaondo 1922, Policía Federal Argentina 1974, and Fernández Rivas 1972.

34 A regular provision of uniforms to the regiment in Luján included 1,119 caps, 1,122 ponchos, 1,126 jackets, 1,134 chiripaes, 1,132 shirts, 1,132 calzoncillos, 1,128 neckerchiefs, and 2,250 divisas federales. Guardia de Luján, October 5, 1846, AGN VII 1-3-2.

35 "Sumario levantado en el pueblo de Ranchos sobre el Judas que hizo quemar D Gregorio Casales," AGN X 21-5-2.

36 Carlos Morel's oil *Payada en la pulpería* (1839) shows a dozen men in a tavern singing, listening, and chatting. Except for the tavern keeper, all wear a combination of dark hats with scarlet ribbons, scarlet gorras de manga, scarlet chiripáes, and blue ponchos with red inside. Although they are all federales united in song and in celebration, we cannot ascertain from the painting who is a soldier and who a civilian. Reproduced in F. Chávez, 1970, vol. 2, 279.

37 Peon Ciriaco Gómez had escaped twice, first from the regiment at Palermo and then from Rosas's saladero. Against him charges pended that "some people had seen him in the city dressed as a military." Ciriaco Gómez,

filiación, AGN III 59-1-6; Edecán to JP of San Nicolás, Santos Lugares, November 17, 1849, AGN X 21-7-1; Manuel G. López, Quilmes, September 1841, AGN X 21-4-6.

38 "Director de la Coalición Argentina del Norte," Mendoza, September 6, 1841, AGN VII 1-2-11.

39 On April 14, 1830, José M. Cortina wrote to Gral. A. Pacheco from Arrecifes: "I am sending you . . . the person of paysano Ferreira in whose possession was found carabinier Gorosito's trousers, by the seams and bottom holes you will see they are the same, for they have been closed on the front and opened on the sides. This paysano deserves an exemplary punishment in this town, he not only has purchased [the trousers] but is also protecting the thief, or perhaps he himself is the thief since he lives behind the quarters where the losses of *carabineros'* uniforms have been continuous." AGN VII 1-2-5.

40 See "Inventario del Sgto. Mayor D. Molina," Fuerte Azul, April 4, 1843, AHPBA, Juzgado de Paz de Azul, 39-1-2; "Inventario y tasación realizado . . . sobre los bienes que dejó al morir el teniente Jorge Cano," AHPBA, Juzgago de Paz Zona Norte, 39-4-39.

41 Anacleto Gómez filiación, AGN III 59-1-6. In November 1843 militiaman Zoilo Suárez, who was wearing the federal uniform, mocked paysano Adolfo Rodríguez for using a yellow galoon and not being an officer (the rest of his attire was that of a paysano; this triggered a dispute and later a knife fight. R. Millán to A. Reyes, Cañuelas, December 20, 1843, AGN X 20-10-5.

42 As the justice of Quilmes complained in March 1852, groups of uniformed men (not all of them soldiers) were pillaging the neighborhood under the protection of their "disguise" (stolen uniforms). Martín de la Serna to Minister of War, March 24, 1852, AGN X 18-5-8.

43 In 1837, Rosas's edecan wrote to country judges recommending they "try to abolish the fashion that the *logistas unitarios* had established lately which is to make paysanos starch their clothes with blue water, so that clothes turn a color close to light blue; this is a complete wickedness of the impious unitarios, a fashion in which paysanos entered out of innocence." Buenos Aires, June 20, 1837, AGN X 21-4-6.

44 Pacheco, "Relaciones exteriores," October 16, 1846; and Pacheco to M. Corvalán, Salto, September 3, 1839, AGN VII 1-3-1 and 1-2-8.

45 "Notes of goods recommended from Mrs Owen Owens & Sons" (Montevideo 1841), John Owens Papers, JRL. Shipments to Río de Janeiro instead showed a greater variety and intensity of colors.

46 Information about the origin of clothes is limited: we know about the origin of only 43 percent of the chiripás and 19 percent of the ponchos recorded.

47 Since the beginning of the century, Lancashire manufactures copied the designs, textures, and colors of these "domestic" pieces, offering pampa and arribeño-like ponchos at lower prices.

48 "Declaraciones de Toribio González," AHPBA, Juzgado del Crimen (1835), 41-1-117-10.

49 Having done this, González returned to the place where they hid the rest of the booty and was arrested by a police patrol advised of his movements.

50 Perhaps it was all a matter of timing: while the "holy war" lasted, the display of class distinction would be suspended and the egalitarian order of appearance would prevail.

51 Besides the repeated stories of their unwilling participation in the unitario army, unitario prisoners tried to hide their urbanite appearance by dressing in paysano garments.

5 The Power of Laws

1 The debate flourished during the 1930s and 1940s, as revisionism challenged the very foundations of liberal historiography. But the reinterpretation of Rosismo started much earlier, in the period 1880–1920, when amateur historians (Adolfo Saldías, Ernesto Quesada), ex-functionaries of the regime (Antonino Reyes), and positivist interpreters (Ingenieros, Ramos Mejía, Ayarragaray) posed serious questions to the conventional wisdom. See Quattrocchi-Woisson (1995); Etchepareborda (1972); and Halperin Donghi (1971). The paradigmatic interpretations contributed by Ramos Mejía (1907), Ibarguren (1930), and Lynch (1981) coincided on the point that the Rosas government had no credible judicial structure.

2 The title of *Ilustre Restaurador de las Leyes* was granted to Rosas by law in January 1830. It was a reward for his campaign against the rebels of December 1828. Others who participated in these campaigns were named "Worthy [citizens] of the Fatherland."

3 According to Lynch (1981, 210–211), summary proceedings, arbitrary executions, and almost no police evidence characterized the Rosista system of justice.

4 Even foreign observers who considered Rosas's rhetoric of republicanism a sham had to concede that the governor was responsible for undoing "anarchy" and restoring the authority of government (Molinari 1962, 75–76). In a strict sense, the critics of the Rosas regime pointed to the lack of legitimacy of the legal order. Contemporary legal theorists differ with regard to the proper definition of the "rule of law." To some, this term refers to a government subject to rules; to others, it is a system of rules governed by the principles of due process and ordered liberty (Fletcher 1996, chap. 1).

5 Rosas's proclama is reproduced in Zinny (1879, 143).

6 These two functions seemed indispensable for the reconstruction of a viable republic (Myers 1995, 78–81).

7 "Los sucesos de Octubre de 1833" (1834), qtd. in Myers (1995, 238–239). In actuality, Fiscal Agrelo had promoted a criminal case against five political newspapers: *Restaurador de las Leyes*, *El Defensor de los Derechos del Pueblo*, *El*

Relámpago, El Rayo, and *Dime con Quien Andas.* October 11 was the scheduled date for the meeting of the jury that would consider the case.

8 In the titles of the reprinted documents the terms Restaurador de las Leyes was used thirty-six times, more frequently than any other attribute ("Brigadier General," "Gobernador," "Héroe del Desierto").

9 About the organization and rhetoric of the 1829 rural movement that catapulted Rosas, see González Bernaldo (1994).

10 The 1830 law spelled out the three meanings of the "restoration": the reestablishment of a deposed political authority; the restitution of political, religious, and moral order; and the provision of peace and security to the inhabitants.

11 Scrutinized with the benefit of historical perspective, Garcia's words seem also deceptive, hiding the fact that unitarios had been expelled from the political community and indigenous peoples were considered "naturales" and, for that reason, not covered by the *derecho de gentes.*

12 The play was announced in *La Gaceta Mercantil,* no. 3781, January 7, 1836.

13 See, for instance, *El soldado federal* (Córdoba), no. 2, December 3, 1842.

14 Actually, the laws of the Rosas era were a combination of quite ancient legislation (some reaching back to the seventeenth century) and the laws and decrees passed by the postrevolutionary governments.

15 The poem, entitled "Federales y patrióticos sentimientos del Libre Pueblo Argentino . . . ," was written by Bernardo Echevarria, an officer in the federalist army and later justice of Tapalqué (see Chávez 1975).

16 "Agora no es aquel tiempo/En que unitarios mandaban/Que por su mal proceder/Todo lo desconcertaban./Cuando algún pobre solía/Dir a ver un figurón/Sin oirle le decían/"Retírese so gauchón." En tiempos tan desgraciados/Le asiguro, amigo Antonio,/Que el mirar hombres letrados/Era mirar al Demonio./Hoy, en fin, gracias a Dios,/Y a D. Juan Manuel de Rosas,/Ya se han compuesto las cosas,/Ningún guacho alza la voz;/ . . . /A todo hombre se respeta/En siendo de guenas prendas,/Si es de malas se le aprieta/Y se sujeta en las riendas./*Hoy se castiga el delito/Donde quiera que se encuentre*" ("Now it is different from those times/When unitarios ruled over/When, due to their ill conduct/all was confusion./When some poor man/went to see a figurón [pretentious nobody]/Without hearing him, they told him/'Go back, you peasant scum'/Those were unhappy times/I assure you, my friend Antonio,/That to look at a lettered man/Was to look at the Devil/Today, thanks to God,/and to D. Juan Manuel de Rosas,/ Things are now arranged,/No orphan raises his voice. . . ./Every man is respected if he has legally obtained clothes/otherwise, he is tightened/His reins fastened/Today crime is punished/Wherever found,/ . . . (Chávez 1975, 57).

17 See Salvatore (1994b). In a recent article, Garavaglia (1997a) agrees with this view, concluding that the difference in the Rosas administration was one of greater efficacy, a point already established by Díaz in his well-known 1952 study.

18 Barreneche (1997, 103–105) noted the reluctance of postindependence judges to introduce comprehensive reforms.

19 Among these additions, none was more important than the 1840 Bando, which extended the death penalty to felonies such as theft and woundings (Ibañez Frocham 1938, 219, 213–214).

20 The southern partidos included Tordillo, Mar Chiquita, Lobería, Vecino, Chapaleufú, Las Flores, Saladillo, Tapalquén, Bahía Blanca, and Patagones.

21 As Benito Díaz put it, "He was the most perfect instrument of control that the government had. Through him, the government knew of the inhabitants' political affiliations, of their numbers, wealth and power" (1952, 137–138).

22 Justices serving older towns possessed greater resources and manpower. In 1851 San Antonio de Areco had nine alcaldes and tenientes alcaldes, three policemen, and two scribes, in addition to a force of forty-four active and thirty reserve militiamen (Garavaglia 1997a, 245).

23 Rosas had to intervene in the tug of war between Colonel Garretón and Justice Juan Figueredo of San Nicolás. Figueredo to Rosas, June 18, 1839, AGN X 21-7-1.

24 JP of Mar Chiquita to M. Corvalán, San Pedro, July 25, 1845, AGN X 21-4-3; JP of Navarro to Rosas, October 10, 1830, AGN X 21-4-4; JP of Navarro to Rosas, October 10 and November 10, 1830, AGN X 21-4-4. In 1836, Justice Casimiro Villegas from Cañuelas threatened to resign due to the outrages of Commander Pedro Lorea, who tried to protect militiamen from judicial prosecution. Casimiro Villegas to Rosas, Cañuelas, February 13, 1836, AGN X 20-10-5.

25 In 1830, the police of the city lost their power to substantiate sumarios in criminal cases, a power that was conferred on lower-court judges.

26 Some justices argued that decision, claiming that the military law of 1823 granted them the responsibility of sending "vagrants" to the army. JP de Salto to Rosas, August 4, 1831, AGN X 21-2-2.

27 Selection procedures implemented by Rosas ensured that all JPs were committed federalists. Appointments were made by the governors from ternas prepared by the incumbent JP. Commonly, the candidates were local men having "medium to important wealth" and, of course, federales netos.

28 JP of San Nicolás to Ministry of Government, March 13, 1838, AGN X 21-7-1.

29 Tomás de Ciesa to Bernardo Victorica, Morón, March 1, 1839, AGN X 33-4-1.

30 AHPBA, Juzgado de Paz Zona Este, 39-4-37.

31 "Causa Criminal c/D. Mariano Tunes" (1841), Expte 920, AGN X 30-3-1.

32 In November 1832, the JP of Lobos sent the governor the sumario of Sandalio Carrizo, a prisoner accused of kidnapping, theft, desertion, and assault. The justice, taking the culpability of the accused as self-evident, excused himself for bypassing normal procedures. "Sumario a Sandalio Perez o Carrizo" (1832), Expte 1004, AGN X 30-3-5.

33 Antonino Reyes to Manuel Corvalán, Santos Lugares, November 14, 1846, AGN X 17-7-2.

34 "En el Pueblo de San Pablo de Salto . . . ," July 13, 1847, AGN X 17-8-1. A washerwoman had kept a shirt and a pair of drawers (or leggings) belonging to Sergeant Videla, still with stains of blood. The commander of the garrison, after confiscating Videla's trunk of clothes, sequestered another piece of incriminating evidence: the poncho without buttons or ribbons.

35 The evaluation of such evidence was left to Rosas (or to the professional judge appointed to examine the case).

36 Elsewhere (Salvatore 1994b), I have argued that another dichotomy—the division between central and local justice—was an integral part of the program of restoring the laws. Each type of justice aimed at quite different objectives: central justice was motivated by the recurrent demands of new recruits for the army; local justice was concerned instead with the "pacification" or "good order" of the countryside.

37 "Sumaria Información que ha lebantado Don Ildefonso Arias," January 1839, AGN X 29-10-3, expte. 182.

38 To determine what penalty corresponded to a given military crime, the comptroller examined the evidence, consulted the punishments prescribed in ordinary laws, and finally suggested a sentence adequate to the case.

39 The confusion between the two spheres was evident in the substantiation of a murder case in 1840. A militia officer had killed a civilian (a "good federal") in charge of a farm confiscated from the unitarios. After the usual discussion about which court was more appropriate, Rosas ordered the constitution of a mixed tribunal composed of Judge Baldomero García and the war comptroller. Together, they were to preside over the sumario process and afterward take the case to Rosas for a decision. "Causa Criminal contra el Tte de Milicias D. Mariano Tunes" (1841), Expte 920, AGN X 30-3-1.

40 Recent work on the relations between ranchers and pobladores (settlers tolerated by ranchers) shows that negotiation rather than domination was the characteristic mode of interaction (see Gelman 1998).

41 JP del Tuyu to Rosas, Tala de los Anchorena, January 8, 1840, AGN X 21-8-1. Deserters' confessions tended to be very precise about the name and location of the rancher who assisted them in their escape. For example, deserter Ramón Maldonado implicated rancher Don Gregorio Rodríguez in his declaration. Rosas ordered a sumario against Rodríguez. Santos Lugares, July 17, 1841, AGN X 21-2-1.

42 Don Francisco Rapallo, interrogated by the justice of the peace of Navarro in relation to the case of illicit refuge given to a deserter, was compelled to explain why he allowed the traveler to spend the night at his home. San Lorenzo de Navarro, November 12, 1842, AGN X 21-4-4.

43 Nicolás Anchorena to Antonino Reyes, Buenos Aires, February 9, 1844, AGN X 21-4-3; JP Saavedra to Roque Baudrix, San Pedro, September 13, 1843, AGN X 21-4-3.

44 Deserter Fernando Robledo claimed that the JP of Tordillo, knowing about

his desertion, gave him employment as ranch foreman, promising that he would not be bothered by the authorities. Edecan to JP of Tordillo, Santos Lugares, May 27, 1846, AGN X 21-7-7.

45 Opposition newspapers printed in exile usually presented the family relationship between Rosas and the Anchorenas as constitutive of the regime.

46 "Oficio de Justicia sobre la Desobediencia, Resistencia y Falta de respeto del Ciudadano D. Felipe Ma. de Escurra . . . ," Chivilcoy, April 10, 1848, AGN X 21-1-1.

47 "Inventario del Juzgado de Paz de Navarro," March 13, 1832, AGN X 21-4-4.

48 Rosas to JP of Baradero, Santos Lugares, May 22, 1842, AG X 20-1-3; A. Reyes to JP Lobería, Santos Lugares, October 18, 1851, AGN X 21-2-4.

49 In 1851, Rosas's military secretary sent a serious reprimand to the justice of Las Flores for having let a deserter enter his district and remain undisturbed (neither interrogated nor arrested). Santos Lugares, October 7, 1851, AGN X 21-2-4.

50 An often-quoted passage of the Rosas legend presents the governor ordering a black ranch peon to flog him (Rosas) for having violated a minor regulation at the estancia (Mansilla 1994, 30–31).

51 The inventories taken by the justices of their own offices reveal the existence of important collections of periodicals and legal texts. The justice house of Monte, for example, in 1832 had a collection of 379 issues of El Lucero (going back to 1830), 21 issues of La Gaceta Mercantil, 34 issues of El Gaucho (from 1830), and 8 issues of El Clasificador and 4 of El Federal, both from 1831.

52 In 1832, the JP of Ensenada informed Rosas that the newspapers had been distributed among several neighbors, who had read them with the enthusiasm proper to good federales. Parte de Novedades, JP de Ensenada, October 30, 1832, AGN X 21-1-5.

53 JP Ranchos to Edecan M. Corvalán, Ranchos, July 1, 1841, AGN X 21-5-2. According to the British envoy, the "Gaceta Mercantil . . . was read in all the corners of the country by the authorities of each district; the justice of the peace reading to the civilian, the military commander [reading] to the members of the army" (qtd. in Molinari 1962, 76).

54 Justo Calandria (the fictional paysano of B. Echevarria's poem) knew about the political demonstrations in Buenos Aires because the corporal at the justice office read the newspaper to him. Drinking mate in the kitchen, Calandria listened with visible emotion to the wonderful words that appeared to come out from printed writing ("una escritura imprensada") (Chávez 1975, 36–37).

55 "Sumaria . . . sobre el uso de Caballos Patrios," AGN X 29-11-7, exp. 462.

56 "Petición de Da. Nicolasa Sáenz de Cortina," October 31, 1831, AGN X 36-3-6.

57 Another ritual question posed to military witnesses is important in this regard: military men were asked whether they were covered under the rules of ordinary law (si les comprende las generales de la ley).

58 Professional efforts to disseminate legal information were rare. In 1834 *El Correo Judicial* tried to inform the reading public about new sentences and their rationale. The publication lasted less than a year.

59 Rosas to Dionisio Schoo, Buenos Aires, August 6, 1845, AGN X 43-2-8.

60 JP de Navarro to Rosas, Navarro, August 16, 1839, AGN X 21-4-4.

61 María Isabel Arriola (petition), Buenos Aires, December 14, 1837, AGN X 21-2-2.

62 Criminal c/Ramón Carmona, AHPBA, Cámara de Apelaciones, 7.2.99.16 (1823); Mariano Lima to Rosas, Fortín Areco, May 20, 1846, AGN 17-7-2.

63 See, for example, Carmen Borches (petition), Bue As, September 10, 1834, AGN X 16-6-1.

64 Sgto Escribiente (Fuerte Argentino), Bahía Blanca, November 3, 1846, AGN X 17-7-2. Though the package was going to the inspector of arms, the letter accompanying the report was addressed to Manuel Corvalán, Rosas's secretary.

65 JP of Mar Chiquita to M. Corvalan, San Pedro Indep., January 1, 1844, AGN X 21-4-3. When one of the libertas working at his ranch escaped with a peon and took refuge in a nearby regiment, Anchorena asked Rosas to order the restitution of "his" servant and indicated that the police should liberate the presumed kidnapper after he was properly admonished. Nicolás Anchorena to Rosas, November 29, 1840, AGN VII 16-4-10.

66 "Sumario contra pedro Antonio Cardoso" (1834), AHPBA, Juzg Paz, Z. Este, 39-4-37.

67 JP Juan Magallanes to Rosas, Baradero, August 13, 1841, AGN X 20-1-3; JP of Ensenada to Minister of Government, Ensenada, February 19, 1833, AGN X 21-1-5.

68 JP of Monsalvo a Rosas, Dolores, December 8, 1836, AGN X 21-1-2.

69 JP Navarro to Rosas, October 10, 1830, AGN X 21-4-4; Julián González Salomón to Chief of Police, Buenos Aires, July 10, 1836, AGN X 43-8-8.

70 Luis Noriega, clasificación, Vivoras (El Tordillo), December 24, 1846, AGN X 21-7-7.

71 Manuel Riquelme to Juan A. Linares, Arrecifes, September 6, 1837, AGN X 20-9-7. Riquelme's letter stated unequivocally that he was a miliciano, hence a citizen, and that the justice tried to make him work as a regular soldier. Juan A. Linares to Rosas, Bue As, September 10, 1837, AGN X 20-9-7.

72 Antonio del Valle a Rosas, Buenos Aires, March 3, 1837, AGN X 21-4-6.

73 Manuel José Vila to Gral M. Corvalán, San Nicolás, September 18, 1841, AGN X 21-7-1.

74 "Carta de Lector," *El Lucero*, no. 231, July 1, 1830.

75 "Roque Carranza, Cañuelas," AGN X 20-10-5.

76 JP Navarro to Rosas, October 10, 1830, AGN X 21-4-4.

77 Other authors, including Sowell (1992), Mallon (1995), and Barman (1988), have called this "popular republicanism."

78 See, for instance, petitions by Doña Máxima Zamudio, February 3, 1847, and Doña Josefa Vibanco, February 5, 1847, AGN X 17-8-1. In all cases,

Rosas directed the petitioners "to the judge of the case." The creation in 1838 of a special tribunal for treating cases of "notorious injustice" did nothing to disarm the public belief that Rosas was the only guarantor of justice.

79 "Era el señor Juez, venía . . ./Yo en cuanto al hombre lo vi/Ya me puse derechito,/Y él me dijo, Paisanito,/Que anda buscando pu aquí;/Le dije a lo que venía/Y lo que me había pasao/Y que si en algo había errao/Me perdonase pedia" ("It was the Judge, he was coming/ . . ./No sooner I saw the man/I straightened myself up,/And he told me, *Paisanito* [little peasant]/ What are you looking for, here;/I told him what I was coming for/And what had happened to me/And, if in some way I have failed/I asked him to forgive me . . .") (Chávez 1975, 38).

6 The Making of Crime

1 See Wiener (1990, especially introduction and chap. 1). For the relationship between class and crime, see Emsley (1987).

2 Recent historiography of the region has defied the traditional view of a two-class society in the pampas, estancieros and gauchos, pointing out the existence of an important segment of small-scale producers controlling a great deal of the cattle and sheep stock. See in particular Gelman (1996) and Garavaglia and Gelman (1995). To this we should add a sizable group of merchants, retailers, and transport entrepreneurs. Prior to these findings, however, Brown (1979, 1994) had sustained that small and medium-size producers were key to the economic revival of the region in the postindependence period.

3 About the "moral economy" of middle paysanos we know very little. Fradkin (1995) has shown the importance of custom in shaping informal property relations at the local level. Neighbors deferred to the authority of general opinion and local customary practices instead of taking the issue to the courts.

4 This fear, says Wiener (1990, 35), emerged more clearly in the 1830s and 1840s.

5 On the Generation of 1837, see Weinberg (1977), Katra (1996), and Myers (1998). On the relationship between the emerging national literature and travel narratives, see Prieto (1996).

6 Though intellectually committed to a discovery of the "real country," romantic writers failed to produce true ethnographies of lower-class life, as was the case in England.

7 Svampa (1994, 35–37) notes that the term "barbarism" emerged in Argentina as the result of the disenchantment with the "inorganic democracy" in the immediate postindependence.

8 For a critical analysis of El Matadero, see Salessi (1995, 55–74). On *Facundo*, see González Echevarría (1994). On *Amalia*, see Sommer (1991, chap. 3).

9 To capture the customs and mentality of gauchos Sarmiento created four

ideal types: the Pathfinder, the Native Guide, the Bad Gaucho, and the Singer. Of these, only the Gaucho Malo embodied the typical attributes of the outlaw.

10 For a history of this myth, see Iglesia and Schvartzman (1987).

11 State terror had left its mark on the habits of sociability of the gente decente, on the language of everyday conversation, even on children's games (Mansilla 1994, 69–77).

12 Alberdi, "De la anarquía y de sus causes," in Terán (1996, 183–228, 197).

13 Constant conflicts between farmers and ranchers over damage to crops and the dispersal of cattle were the symptoms. See Gelman (1997, especially 54, 79–81, 173–174).

14 The ranchers who discussed the best means to combat cattle rustling (ca. 1865) returned to the same motif (Sábato, 1989, 94–96). See also Halperin Donghi (1980, 1985).

15 Street disturbances caused by youngsters, newly arrived migrants, and free blacks became sources of concern. Szuchman (1988, chap. 4) found the greater mobility of men caused by the war to be a major force behind these new social anxieties.

16 Urbanites' sense of insecurity translated immediately into increases in the price of gold, the temporary closing of pulperías and barbershops, and the meeting of neighbors around the Fortaleza.

17 See, for example, "Inquietud entre los Extranjeros" (April 11, 1829); "Alarma en la Ciudad" (May 23, 1829); "Rumores" (August 8, 1829); "Fin de la Guerra" (June 27, 1829); "Rumores de Disturbios" (September 5, 1829), in the British Packet (1976).

18 It was at this time that vecinos became more assertive, claiming for their towns some of the benefits of "progress." Principal neighbors became crusaders of a "civilizing mission" that included initiatives such as hiring a teacher, getting a priest, or attracting a doctor to the town (Monsma 1992, chap. 5).

19 Embodying two distinct forms of political representation (the neighbor and the citizen), neighbor-citizens had both political rights (voting) and military duties (service in the local militias). See Cansanello (1994, 1995).

20 Military drills on Sundays added a militaristic dimension to the life of the community, its time now marked by bugle calls and cannon shots.

21 The political culture of these rural towns is examined in chapter 11. For an analysis of political repression and political festivities in a rural town, see Garavaglia (1998).

22 The threat of Indian invasions produced ambiguous effects in the construction of criminality. Being outside of the legal sphere, Indians were not considered criminals but "savages," their acts combining doses of economic acumen and uncontrolled violence.

23 In 1832 the justice of San Nicolás made 70 arrests, 37 of them for major crimes such as desertion, theft, or murder, and 33 for lesser offenses. Among the latter were 13 arrested for carrying knives, 5 for picking fights,

5 for provoking quarrels with their wives, 5 for engaging in illicit love, 2 for drunkenness, 2 for petty larceny, and 1 for unpaid debts.

24 On May 29, 1832 the justice of Cañuelas arrested an old neighbor of regular wealth, José Correa, for failing to pay a debt for which he had already been reprimanded.

25 In 1837 the justice of Chascomús sent eleven people to work on the construction of the new church as punishment for various misdemeanors (fights without consequence, insults, scandal, and unpaid debts). The felons (with food rations and no salary) were to work from six to ten days in this community endeavor. Chascomús, *Parte de Novedades*, 1837, AGN X 20-10-7.

26 For an analysis of the practice of kidnapping women as a means to form families, see Mayo (1985).

27 In many cases, justices did not report the origin of these offenders; they were all well-known to the local community.

28 JP of San Nicolás, *Partes de Novedades* (May–June 1837).

29 JP of Arrecifes, *Partes de Novedades* (May–August 1837 and January–April 1840).

30 Although he failed to pay his debt, Pedro Burnes, one of the town's tailors, was released two days after his arrest because of his profession.

31 Five of the outsiders arrested were travelers who lacked proper identification when approached by the local police. Two were deserters from the nearby garrison; the JP was only returning them to their unit.

32 JP of San Antonio de Areca, *Parte de Novedades* (January–April 1841), AGN X 21-5-7.

33 Take the case of the JP of San Nicolás in 1837. Seven of the 84 individuals arrested during that year were released after a few days due to lack of evidence. Most had been suspected of cattle or horse theft, probably accused by one of their neighbors.

34 Typically, the arrested traveled to Rosas's headquarters on horseback, their hands (and sometimes their feet) in shackles, accompanied by one or two guards. Before departing, they were subjected to an interrogation by the JP or the local police chief.

35 JP of San Nicolás, *Partes de Novedades* (January–February 1837), AGN X 21-7-1. Though Governor Rosas insisted on the standardization of the *Partes de Novedades*, the reporting of crimes varied from one district to the other. On occasion, justices made clear to Rosas that they were not recording those detained *por causas leves* (petty offenses).

36 The JP of Chascomús, for example, chose not to include in his reports those prisoners placed in his custody by other authorities as well as people arrested by "superior orders" to satisfy a request for a recruitment quota. JP of Chascomús, *Partes de Novedades*, AGN X 20-10-7.

37 Quite likely, what justices meant by the phrase *sin novedad* was that there had been only minor offenses not worthy of reporting to the governor.

38 Slatta and Robinson (1990) based their estimates on data on prisoners held

during 1822 in the city's jails and prisons, and on a second sample drawn from 657 cases taken from Trelles's summary index of police reports from 1827 to 1850. Szuchman (1984) used data on urban arrests taken from the newspaper El Lucero, the only rural statistics being those of San Antonio de Areco, ca. 1825.

39 Data generated from another source (a database of 1,364 soldiers drafted between 1810 and 1860) put registered desertions at 25 percent of recruitment. Although most assignments (destinos) included the obligation to serve three, four, or more years, the actual time of service was much shorter. Almost 60 percent of the recruits left the army before the end of the first year, the average term of service being close to ten months.

40 Unfortunately, we cannot extrapolate this estimate to account for all districts and the whole period. Hence, it is impossible to produce something like a "murder rate."

41 On September 27, 1832, the JP of Cañuelas reported two unsolved murders: that of Gda. del Monte merchant Joaquín Duarte, and that of santiagueño Francisco Padilla. JP Cañuelas, Parte de Novedades, AGN X 20-10-5.

42 One case reveals that wives of veterans got together to fight against male predators. Alcalde del cuartel 5 to J. M. López, Quilmes, June 2, 1842, AGN X 21-4-6.

43 Doña Florentina Amaya (San Nicolás) presented charges of rape against ex-policeman Tomás Gómez, Victorica to Rosas, Buenos Aires, January 28, 1837, AGN X 21-7-1. In 1848 the priest Bernardo Meléndez was arrested on charges of attempted rape of a poor woman. JP Tiburcio Lima, San Antonio de Areco, October 16, 1848, AGN X 21-6-1. Sandalio Carrizo, was executed in Lobos in November 1832 for, among other charges, kidnapping a young woman. JP of Lobos, November 26, 1832, AGN X 21-1-7.

44 "Sumario c/Guillermo Walter," Cañuelas, 1836, AGN X 20-10-5.

45 Though peons had the obligation to carry a contrata or employment paper, fewer than 1 percent actually did.

46 Available information about the fate of the arrested underscores the state's use of the criminal system for recruitment purposes.

47 This compares with a proportion of provincianos and foreigners of 31 percent for Lobos in 1854 (males only; Mateo 1993a, 179).

48 According to Slatta and Robinson (1990, 25), 4 percent of those in prison in 1822 belonged to this category.

49 The proportion was actually larger, to the extent that many soldiers and people without occupation also belonged to this "class." The middling sectors (merchants and clerks, ranchers, administrators, and farmers, etc.) were a true minority, constituting only 10 percent of the arrests.

50 Contrasted with statistics collected by Slatta and Robinson (1990, 28, table 2) for the city's prisons in 1822 (trigueños 21 percent, whites 53 percent, blacks 14 percent, mulatto 9 percent, Indian 2 percent, and Zambo less than 1 percent), the racial composition of the arrested in rural areas shows a greater presence of trigueños and a smaller proportion of whites and blacks.

51 Only indigenous people appear underrepresented in this sample. Clearly,

this is related to the fact that most non-Christian indigenous peoples kept their distance from *cristiano* civilization. Indian invasions (or raids) were dealt with by the army and not by the justice system. They were generally subject to retribution in kind (i.e., punitive expeditions).

52 In the 1869 census, 74 percent of the population living in the Buenos Aires countryside were younger than 30; 84 percent were younger than 40 (Sábato and Romero 1992, 293, table 5).

53 Garavaglia (1997a) reads a comparable set of data as a relaxation of local social control. The increased bureaucratization and central control of the JP's work tends to support a different conclusion. JPs improved the enforcement of regulations concerning public order precisely to contribute to the consolidation of the political order.

54 Notice the important reduction in the proportion of crimes against property (35 to 22 percent) and against the public order (10 to 6 percent) and the contemporary rise in crimes against the state (35 to 54 percent).

55 Based on a peculiar processing of sources, Garavaglia (1997a, 252–253) finds that southern districts were more violent than those of the north and that they prosecuted less frequently incidents of vagrancy and desertion. Garavaglia classifies as vagrancy most arrests resulting from lack of identification papers as well as those cases of petty larceny (*raterías*). Clearly, this method overestimates the incidence of vagrancy.

56 The paucity of information for the southern districts (Tandil, Chapaleufú, Azul, Las Flores, Dolores, etc.) makes comparisons between north and south less reliable than one would desire.

57 This issue is more fully developed in Salvatore (1991a).

58 Estimates by Slatta and Robinson (1990, 33) taken from the police summary index for 1822–1850 show the following breakdown: crimes against persons 39 percent, crimes against property 32 percent, crimes against the social order 18 percent, gambling 6 percent, fugitives 5 percent.

7 The Experience of Punishment

1 Gutiérrez (1944, 69–80). The episode actually took place on July 8, 1834 (Dellepiane 1956, 73).

2 Gutiérrez (1944, 79) writes: "Rosas había conseguido su objeto. El pánico más tocante se había apoderado de la población, y sobre todo de las familias unitarias, que pensaban, con razón, que al asesinato de los salvajes de la pampa seguiría el de los salvajes unitarios" ("Rosas had reached his objective. The most touching fear had taken hold of the population, particularly among the unitario families who thought, with reason, that the assassination of the savages from the pampa will be followed by that of unitario savages").

3 See Lamas (1877) and Cernadas de Bulnes (1993). Later, memorialists such as Gálvez (1942), Somellera (1962), and Calzadilla (1944) added verisimilitude to these portraits.

4   So much so that being numbed by fear and unable to react became a common argument used by lawyers to avoid the prosecution of political criminals during this period. This was called the "doctrine of uncontrollable fear" and was used in several court cases involving actions by mazorqueros. See Salvatore (2001).

5   To Ramos Mejía (1932, 150–169), the Dictator's violence was motivated by a neurosis that numbed his moral sensibility. His orders of execution, like all the violent pranks inflicted on peons, black soldiers, and house staff, were simply an expression of cruelty and perversity. Criminologist A. Dellepiane (1956, 249–253) found Rosas impassive to pain or remorse. He ordered executions with absolute tranquility of conscience, like a surgeon who removes a gangrened limb.

6   Similar to what Frank Graziano (1992) has found for the 1976–1983 military dictatorship, the unbounded nature of the violence carried out by the Mazorca had its support in a religious conception of a holy war between the pure and the impure.

7   To Avila (1847), this was the unleashing of class hatred against the men of frock coats and their culture, authorized by Rosas to punish those who had supported in words or thought the Lavalle invasion.

8   A large number of floggings applied over time would teach the recruit obedience, reducing the need to use harsher penalties later.

9   Only by stretching our imagination can we assimilate (as many opponents and liberal historians did) the Rosista regime of punishment with Foucault's "spectacle of the scaffold," in which an unbounded violence on the body of the condemned represents the arbitrary and absolute power of the monarch.

10 Vagrancy was a grave felony and thus punished by the central justice. This was so, not because the condition of unemployment was of great concern to the Rosista state, but because underneath any vagrant or unknown authorities could find a deserter.

11 This penalty, like imprisonment, was quite malleable; it could be regulated in terms of time.

12 In the countryside, justices were strict, sending most of the prisoners to the army headquarters at Palermo or to the Police Department in Buenos Aires. Few prisoners were executed, in spite of the existence of many recidivist deserters.

13 "Rufino Bitancor, por homicidio (1836)," AGN X 30-3-5, no. 1006.

14 "José Maria Cardoso, por deserción" (1840), AGN X 29-1-3, no. 188.

15 In February 1850, of the 125 inmates at the Police Depositary, 86 were put at the "disposition" of the governor and 30 were under the care of Judges Torres and Cárcova. The rest were not yet "classified." Buenos Aires, February 28, 1850, AGN X 43-7-7.

16 "Al Depósito," Buenos Aires, 1835, AGN X 31-9-5.

17 "Relación de los presos," Cuartel de Serenos, Buenos Aires, March 1, 1844, AGN X 26-4-2.

18 "En libertad y que vengan al Exto," 1840, AGN X 25-8-1.

19 Libros "Archivo del Cabildo," 1824–1850, APN.

20 Gregorio Roldán, clasificación, Santos Lugares, May 12, 1847, AGN X 21-7-7.

21 For rural towns, this presented the problem of having enough shackles for the detainees. As more felons were transported (in shackles) to the capital than the other way around, these instruments of detention tended to pile up in the central Police Department.

22 A. Reyes to Juan Coello, Santos Lugares, August 1849, AGN X 17-10-5.

23 Thanks to the work of historian Manuel Bilbao, we have access to some key information about the use of these instruments at Santos Lugares, Rosas's army headquarters and detention camp. Trying to make public information about key events of violence that had remained obscure, Bilbao interviewed Reyes thirty years after Caseros (1883, 116, 117).

24 Rosas to Laureano Ramírez, Palermo, March 11, 1845, AGN X 43-2-8.

25 In 1832 a 17-year-old paysano, José Castro, was given one hundred lashes and four years of forced service for horse theft. "Contra el paysano José Castro (1832)," AGN X 30-3-5, no. 1003. In the case of José Otamendi, his condition of ex-slave and second-time deserter made his punishment abnormally high: five hundred strokes. José María Flores, pardoned from a death sentence for assault followed by murder, was given ten years of military service.

26 In some cases, the floggings given to the slaves at the public jail were ordered by the criminal courts at the request of their masters. In other cases, the slaveholder negotiated directly with the prison's alcaide (director) the punishment he wanted to inflict on his or her slave. In an investigation carried out in 1818 it was established that corporals were allowed to give soldiers up to four lashes, sergeants a bit more, and captains up to twelve lashes. "Información indagatoria sobre castigos hechos a la tropa . . . ," Chascomús, 1818, AGN X 29-10-4, no. 236.

27 Neighbors' petitions to government and cases taken to the courts show that the authority of military officers to inflict pain on private individuals was contested, even when the subjects of punishment were blacks, Indians, or mestizo peons.

28 This was the case of a musician belonging to the Regiment Patricios's band, who was killed by the (sword) strokes given by his superior, Captain Mariano Bermúdez. "Sumario seguido contra el Sargento Ciudadano y Músico del Regimiento Patricios Julian Caré . . ." (1835), AGN X 29-10-3, no. 191 (sumarios militares).

29 JP of Quilmes to Rosas, April 23, 1841, AGN X 21-4-6.

30 Generally, Rosas reserved to himself decisions involving the death sentence. Only on rare occasions did he delegate that decision to local military commanders or other authorities.

31 The mere accumulation of offenses did not add up to a death sentence. "Incorrigible" delinquents were treated with long terms in the military—this was Rosas's main "reformatory."

32 La Gaceta Mercantil, January 29, 1844, qtd. in Myers (1995, 233).

33 In addition to executing prisoners, commanders assassinated key political figures in the towns, later parading their heads on pikes. The murder of Marco Avellaneda in Tucumán in vengeance for the death of Governor Heredia in October 1841 was one of these atrocities (Saldías 1968, 2:253).

34 In addition to the 1,393 *fusilados* (executed), Rivera Indarte included in his summary 3,765 *degollados* (beheaded), 722 murdered (probably with knife or pistol), and 4 poisoned.

35 In addition to the 83 executions "without reason" and the 3 executed for political motives, the attorney general included individuals executed in prison for their sympathies with the unitario cause.

36 JP Lobos to J. R. Balcarce, Lobos, November 26, 1832, AGN X 21-1-7. In May 1846 Lefil, an Indian of Catriel's tribe, was executed in Santos Lugares on charges of homicide and theft.

37 Gral Edecán de SE to JP de Gda de Lujan, Santos Lugares, October 9, 1845, AGN X 21-2-3; "Sumario por la muerte del joven Ignacio González," San Nicolás, April 27, 1838, AGN X 21-7-1.

38 On occasion, two out of three of those sentenced to death would be shot. In 1837 three deserters of the Sixth Regiment were sentenced to death in Azul. The local commander sent Goroso and Perez to the firing squad and made Ramírez watch the execution. Jefe del Regto 6 to Edecan M Corvalán, Hacienda de Sta Catalina de Azul, March 21, 1837, AGN X 20-10-1.

39 If the shooting was done between 9 and 10 A.M., the cadaver would be hung for a good eight hours.

40 General Pacheco said: "This spectacle will serve, hence, as exemplary so that such crimes are not repeated." Choele-Choel, September 30, 1833, AGN X 30-3-5, Expte 981. Earlier in that year, in June, Pacheco had presided over a case in which twelve soldiers and a corporal were involved in a plan of desertion. Soldier Antonio Abalos, who confessed to being one of the organizers, was sentenced to death and executed on June 30, 1833. The rest received extensions in their service (one to four years) and from two hundred to four hundred lashes each. "Antonio Abalos, sumario por deserción en masa" (1833), expte 1, AGN X 29-9-6.

41 "Declaratoria indagatoria contra los Carabineros Prudencio Guerreros, Hilario Avellaneda, Mariano Ponce, Juan Francisco Medina, y José Antonio García por deserción" (1836), Expte 387, AGN X 29-11-5 (sumarios militares).

42 "Relación de los Piquetes qe. han formado en cuadro en la Plaza del Retiro, en la ejecución del reo *Félix Oguendo* hoy 20 de marzo de 1849," AGN X 17-10-5.

43 Saldías (1968, 2:255) reproduces an 1841 letter by Colonel Maza (dated in Catamarca) explicitly acknowledging that he executed all unitario prisoners.

44 *La Gaceta Mercantil*, no. 7032, March 26, 1847.

45 The relevant part of the song is: "¡Sombras de Heredia y Dorrego,/Si es que ya en el cielo estáis,/Os rogamos por la Patria/Que estas tierras prote-

jáis! . . . A esta tierra en que con gloria/la fama de ustedes vive,/¡No dejéis que la profanen/Las tropas que trae Oribe! . . . ¡No dejéis que en mil hogares/Se sufran negros dolores!/¡No dejéis que aqui la paguen/Los justos por pecadores!" ("Specters of Heredia and Dorrego!/If you are in the heavens/We pray for the Fatherland/That you protect these lands! . . ./These lands in which the glory/of your fame lives,/Do not permit that it be profaned/By the troops of Oribe! . . ./Do not allow that thousands of homes/Suffer dark pains/Do not permit that/the just pay for the sinners' ") "Avellaneda y Lavalle," reproduced in Lanuza (1941, 19).

46 "Muerte del Gobernador Cubas" (in ibid., 57–60).

47 *Partes de Batalla de las Guerras Civiles* (1976, 284–287).

48 El *Lucero* published information about the executions ordered by Governor Javier López in Tucumán, including gruesome details about their deaths. El *Lucero*, no. 238, July 10, 1830.

49 Those who had entered the campaign as milicianos were citizens-in-arms. They resented being associated with the condemned and longed to be freed from that condition.

50 "Desertores del Campamento de la Barrancosa (1839)," AGN X 29-11-2, no. 293 (sumarios militares). Instead of being sent to Santos Lugares, as was customary, they were kept in prison at Zárate for a while. The governor wished the whole division to observe their sanctions.

51 In 1849, black militiaman Antonio Ferreyra was jailed for four months for assaulting a corporal. According to his account, the corporal had tried to punish him with a stick (*vara*) and he defended himself, hurting the corporal. Inspección General de Armas, May 22, 1849, AGN X 17-10-5.

52 I have found no account by a soldier that asserts having witnessed an execution at a federalist army garrison, or by peasants or peons in relation to the execution of a common criminal.

53 Both situations affected soldiers' perspectives. These were threshold conditions that demanded from them important decisions. In the former situation, they could either run away or denounce the unfair treatment to superiors. In the latter case, they had to decide whether to join another regiment or to return home.

8 Regiments: Negotiation and Protest

1 His strategy for restructuring social relations is best summarized in a memorandum he addressed to the government in 1820 (Saldías 1968, 1: 347–355).

2 "All those who are recruited," wrote Rosas, "must learn what is legal to do and must stop doing what is illegal" (qtd. in Saldías 1968, 1:35). Religious instruction would serve as auxiliary in this transformation. Rosas wanted to bring priests into the pampas who would "preach and fix in [gauchos] minds the maxims of subordination and adherence to order and to the true religion" (Ingenieros 1920, 2:162–163).

3 The Provisional Rules of 1817 made all men over 15 responsible for enlisting in the militias.

4 There were exceptions for illness, certain professions, and special family conditions, but the decisions made by the jury of neighbors were final (Dóminguez 1898, 1:334–337).

5 "Why, nobody is to be superior./The law is just one,/And gives its protection/To all who respect it. . . . Without asking whether he is porteño/Or is salteño or puntano,/That who offended the law,/Nor if he has a bad color;/The law is the same against crime/and never makes a distinction/ between creeks and lagoons,/between the rich and the poor" (qtd. in Shumway 1993, p. 92; my translation).

6 In his 1820 address to the people of Buenos Aires, Rosas explained that the militias of the southern division had come to save the city, not to destroy it; to protect the citizens, not to offend them. They had assembled by consent because of the need to restore order. Having achieved their goal, the militias respectfully withdrew, leaving the legitimate authorities in command (Bilbao 1961, 108–112).

7 "Contra el Cmte. del Esquadrón de San Borombón," AGN X 29-11-7, Expte. 466.

8 Captain of the local militias, auditor of the army in Perú, ex-governor of Salta, and ex-secretary of the Directorio, Campana was very offended by this debasing act.

9 Olivares, the alcalde temporarily chosen to conduct the elections of the towns' representatives, stubbornly defended legitimate civilian authorities against military abuse.

10 "Funes, Pedro, por abuso de autoridad," AGN X 29-11-4, Expte. 360; Martín Domato c/Pedro Olmos, AHPBA, Cámara de Apelaciones, Leg. 5, 5.1.5.3 (1823); "Rodríguez, Gaspar . . . por escándalo en su pulpería," AHPBA, Cámara de Apelaciones, 7.2.107.7 (1819).

11 "Tte. Mariano Cabrera y soldado Tiburcio Carreras," AGN X 29-10-3, Expte. 172 (1819). The beaten militiaman, a 15-year-old carpenter described as a chinito or a little Indian, said he felt insulted when the white militia officers mockingly commented: "Ayba el lobo [There goes the wolf]" in an obvious reference to his color. He responded, "El lobo de su madrina [Your godmother's wolf]," a sexually charged insult that moved the white officers to assault him.

12 "c/Martín Herrera, soldado," AGN X 29-11-7. The words that led to the fight illustrate the blending of egalitarianism and machismo. The soldier (Herrera) respectfully asked the corporal why he was beating him. Díaz responded: "Out of these damn'd [silver] braids nobody is more Man than I." To which Herrera replied: "Then [without galons] nobody is more than I."

13 At dances and on city streets, where the uniforms and braids of the participants were less visible, these conflicts were common. At times, their fights stemmed from confusions of this type; at other times, they related to the conflict of jurisdiction as perceived by the contenders. At a private party in

Fort Federación (1837), army Captain Hernández started a fight by commenting that militiamen "were good for nothing," that "none of them knew anything." "Sumario formado . . . contra el Cap. José María Hernández . . . ," AGN X 21-11-7. Lieutenant Colonel Manuel Delgado was accused in 1832 of striking a neighbor suspected of stealing horses from the Indians. JP of Navarro to Rosas, April 17, 1832, AGN X 21-4-4. Commander Pedro Lorea (from Cañuelas) insulted the JP, abducted witnesses, and obstructed justice. Casimiro Villegas to Rosas, Cañuelas, February 13, 1836, AGN X 20-10-5.

14 Bernardino Acosta served only eight to ten days of each month, after which he was licensed to work in the district. Filiación, Las Flores, December 24, 1845, AGN X 21-2-4.

15 JP of San José de Flores to Minister of War, January 14, 1856, AGN X 19-6-1. The militiamen of Guardia Patricia (Bue As), received $2 a day in 1829 for training, besides the expenses in food, "vices," and firewood. In 1849, their prest amounted to 20 pesos a month. Pedro Rosas y Belgrano, Tapalqué, May 1, 1849, AGN X 20-10-2. In 1845 the commander of the Fifth Regiment of Militias ordered each militiaman to bring three healthy horses, two halters (bozales), a lasso, a pair of bolas, and a mancador. Gen. Edecán to JP of Chapaleufú, Santos Lugares, August 6, 1845, AGN X 21-1-1.

16 An extant list for the militias of Fort Azul shows their social composition. Of the first company comprising 124 milicianos: 29 (23 percent) were owners, 29 (23 percent) foremen, 26 (21 percent) peons, 8 (6 percent) residents or family members of owners, 10 (8 percent) postillones, 15 (13 percent) military men. Milicia de Caballería, Fuerte Azul, ca. 1840, AHPBA 31-1-9.

17 Rosas himself had milicianos working on his estates. He complained that these militiamen took more from the ranches than they contributed in services (Carretero 1970, 17).

18 Edecán de S.E. to JP of Azul, Buenos Aires, October 20, 1837, AGN X 20-10-1.

19 Foreigners were exempted from active service, but it was not clear whether they could be called to assist in the mechanical or "passive" services.

20 This was not a novelty of the Rosas period. In 1824 Luján's police chief found it hard to recruit new members to the police patrols. The neighbors, busy harvesting their own grain, failed to volunteer their services. Juan Perichón, January 8, 1824, AGN X 31-8-5.

21 Benito Sosa to Rosas, February 22, 1831, AGN X 21-4-4; Francisco Elía to Minister of Government, Ensenada, February 19, 1833, AGN X 21-1-5; Juan Magallanes to Rosas, Baradero, August 13, 1841, AGN X 10-1-3.

22 At the ranches of Duraznillo and Carralauquén the JP confronted strong resistance. His postman was denied a fresh horse to continue the journey, and his policemen had been escorted off the ranch at knife point. J. M. Saavedra to Roque Baudrix, September 13, 1843, AGN X 21-4-3. Filiación, Monsalvo, January 15, 1847, AGN X 20-9-5.

23 Bernardo Echagüe to Rosas, Tapalqué, November 21, 1845, AGN X 26-5-3.

24 Some repented of their earlier attitude and asked to be incorporated. Francisco Bustamante, filiación, Guardia de Luján, November 14, 1845, AGN X 21-2-3.

25 Juan Luis Leguizamón, a porteño enlisted in the San Fernando militias, used an artful trick to avoid the draft: he took a temporary license to work in the neighboring district of Monte and then went elsewhere. After some wandering, he decided to start anew in El Tigre. Juan Leguizamón, filiación, San Fernando, January 30, 1839, AGN III 59-1-8.

26 "Con el mayor rendimiento," anonymous poem, qtd. in Canal Feijó (1942, 70–71).

27 Agustín Acosta to Rosas, Monsalvo, July 25, 1832, AGN X 21-4-3.

28 In 1836 the justice of Monsalvo received complaints from two neighbors that the comisionados had detained their foreman and peons even though they were carrying proper documents. JP of Monsalvo to Rosas, Dolores, December 8, 1836, AGN X 21-1-2.

29 Juan Magallanes to Rosas, Baradero, June 18, 1837, AGN X-20-10-3. Rosas's anger had to do with the justice's bargaining people's duties at the local level. If this behavior was consented to, parents' petitions would inundate the justices' offices. So he instructed Magallanes not to hear any more of these cases, forcing parents to address their complaints directly to him, in writing.

30 Doña Carmen de Borches, petition, Buenos Aires, September 10, 1834, AGN X 16-6-1.

31 Doña María de la Cruz Velázquez, petition, Buenos Aires, September 12, 1834, AGN X 16-6-1; Cisnona Quiroga, petition, September 26, 1834, AGN X 16-6-1; Nicolasa Machuca, petition, September 20, 1834, AGN X 16-6-1.

32 Comte. Batallón Restaurador to Inspector General de Armas, Buenos Aires, April 12, 1849, AGN 17-10-5.

33 Elías Galván, April 3, 1832, AGN X 29-10-3.

34 The decree of September 16, 1829 fixed $50 as the sum offered to each soldier who wanted to reenlist.

35 Rosas to Balcarce, Cerrillos, September 6, 1820, AGN VII 16-4-7, no. 1249.

36 Pascual Escalante, filiación, Campamento Pavón, March 10, 1845, AGN X 26-5-3.

37 Another possibility was to keep silent and later tell their stories to a superior officer or to the governor. As extant filiaciones make clear, deserters did present to Rosas or his edecanes at Santos Lugares a rosary of complaints about the injustices they witnessed.

38 Mainly because of its similarities with Hobsbawm's concept of "bargaining by riot."

39 Pascual Escalante did not; he continued his journey and presented himself to Colonel González as planned.

40 "Dragoniantes de Río Negro," AGN X 30-3-5, expte. 998 (1839), sumarios militares.

41 Fulgencio Iturres had been involved in another incident of protest in 1837 when he was a sergeant. In this incident he had been deprived of his rank and sentenced to six years in prison. Later, he managed to have this sentence commuted to service in a frontier garrison, Patagones.

42 "Sgto. Iturres y otros acusados de motín," AGN X 29-11-7, expte. 467 (sumarios militares).

43 His "duty as sergeant of brigade" did not consist in "hauling manure, thistle, and cheese in a cart." This was not only "private work," it was also humiliating work.

44 Villa Luján, November 30, 1845, AGN X 21-7-6.

45 Juan Romero, filiación, San Pedro, 1845, AGN III 59-2-3.

46 Escalante was a threat because he could voice his complaints against the officers; he knew how to use irony and lamentation; and a long military experience had empowered him to represent other soldiers.

47 Rosas's wife, Encarnación, used defamatory letters and rumors to prepare the popular "restoration" of October 1833 (Sáenz Quesada 1991, 77–88). González Bernaldo (1994) posits rumors as a major factor in the spread of the 1829 revolt.

48 He was reported saying: "It was a disgrace for this Country to be governed by Gauchos and highwayman/robbers [salteadores], while the men of light who could elevate it to the peak of its grandeur, had had to abandon it." Julián Solveyra, Guardia de Luján, March 12, 1831, AGN X 21-2-2.

49 Juzgado de Paz y Comisaría de Monsalvo, August 31, 1838, AGN X 21-4-3.

50 "Sumario a D. Antonio Delgado," Fortín de Areco, February 5, 1839, AGN X 20-9-6.

51 J P of Lobos to Rosas, February 10, 1840, AGN X 21-1-7; Antonino Reyes to J P of Azul, Santos Lugares, January 12, 1852, AGN X 27-1-5.

52 Campamento Pavón, March 10, 1845, AGN X 26-5-3; Comte. B. Echevarría to Rosas, Tapalqué, July 30, 1845, AGN X 26-5-3.

53 Liut. Francisco Romero to J P of Azul, November 7, 1839, AGN X 20-10-1.

54 Arrecifes, February 10, 1844, AGN X 20-9-7; "Relación de los presos," Cuartel de Serenos, March 1, 1844, AGN X 26-4-2; J P of Ranchos to Rosas, July 5, 1832, AGN X 21-5-2. This uprising was initiated by the rumor that Rosas had deceived Indians into a peace treaty, when his true intentions were to kill them all. M. Capdevila to Rosas, Fuerte Azul, October 4, 1836, AGN X 20-10-1.

55 To keep prisoners from returning to the federalist side, unitario chiefs in Montevideo spread the rumor that the federal army beheaded those who had joined the unitarios.

56 Santos Lugares, January 11, 1842, AGN X 21-1-1; Roque Carranza (o Ulloa), filiación, Cañuelas, AGN X 20-10-5.

57 "Declaraciones de Pedro Gómez," Arrecifes, December 29, 1851, AGN X 27-1-5.

58 Rumors reached Rosas's headquarters about the unpopularity of the governor of Santa Fé. There was widespread dissatisfaction regarding his military skills and administrative honesty.

9 Deserters' Reasons

1 I am borrowing here from Ludmer (1988) the idea that defiance and lament were the most salient tones of gauchos' voices, as constructed by gauchesco poetry.

2 I use the concept of "moral economy" in a more ample sense than that attributed to Thompson (1971, 1978) and J. C. Scott (1976). Here, it refers not only to popular or plebeian conceptions of the "ought to be" of the economy, but also to peasants' and peons' perceptions of what the state owed them.

3 Of the 541 filiaciones, I selected 178 cases of desertion with enough information about the reasons for desertion or about the itinerary followed by deserters after their escape. Seventy percent of the deserters explained to their captors the motivations behind their illegal acts; some gave more than one reason.

4 Recruits tended to avoid armed confrontations by escaping before their battalions marched to the front.

5 According to de Certeau (1984, 35–37), the powerful design and deploy "strategies," and the subaltern essays "tactics," mere maneuvers within the powerful's field of vision and territory.

6 Filiación 1845, AGN X 20-1-5; Filiación, 1851, AGN X 43-7-7; Filiación, 1844, AGN III 59-1-9. Pio Caraballo, a deserter from the Escolta Battalion, gave an almost identical explanation. Filiación, Ensenada, AGN X 21-1-5. Similarly, Pascual Quiroga justified his escape from Santos Lugares by stating that he had no uniform for the May 25 parade and was afraid of his superior officer's reaction. Filiación 1846, AGN X 21-3-4.

7 Filiación 1844, AGN III 59-2-4; Filiación 1846, AGN X 21-2-4.

8 AHPBA, Camara de Apelaciones, 9.1.3.133 (1848).

9 Juan Romero, filiación 1845, AGN III 59-2-3; and Andrés Payllaquén, *filiación*, 1852, AGN X 26-2-6.

10 Filiación 1844, AGN X 26-5-3. This is also true of nondeserters. José González, arrested in 1845 near Quilmes for carrying an expired passport and defying the police patrol, confessed that he had ridden to Magdalena to escort his sister back to Buenos Aires. Separated from his parents at the age of 20 (four years before) to take employment as a cattle driver, he remained in contact with his family in San Isidro. AHPBA, Camara de Apelaciones, 9.1.3.133.

11 José Diaz, 1844, AGN X 26-5-3; Francisco Coria, *filiación*, 1842, AGN X 20-10-5; Genaro Alvarez, filiación, 1845, AGN X 21-2-3; Pantaleón Ibarra (Navarro), filiación, 1845, AGN X 20-10-2.

12 Francisco Trivino, filiación, Cañuelas, July 5, 1843, AGN X 20-10-5; Vicente Pérez, filiación, May 2, 1845, AHPBA, Cámara de Apelaciones, 9.1.3.133. Manuel Sánchez escaped recruitment at Lobos to join his cousins serving in a cavalry division at Santa Fe. Filiación 1851, AGN X 18-2-6.

13 This is clear from Felipe Acuña's narration of his escape: after serving two months in the invernada and upset with his superior for not finding a

replacement, he asked for an ordinary leave to get vicios. Filiación, 1847, AGN X 20-9-6. See also Calixto Aguilera, *filiación*, 1846, AGN X 21-2-1; and Nemecio Coronel, *filiación*, 1845, AGN X 21-10-2.

14 Women contributed to create an informal system of meat distribution in rural towns that kept nutrition levels high, despite drastic fluctuations in the export economy.

15 Business and family governed Bustamante's decision to go to the countryside. After deserting the frontier garrison at Bahia Blanca, he resided in the city for over a year working as a butcher. Quite secure in this job, given his connections with the police, he risked all to provide beef to his family. Filiación 1846, AGN X 21-5-1 (Bustamante). Filiación 1844, AGN III 59-1-3 (Cufré).

16 AHPBA, Juzgados de Paz (Ranchos), 39.4.7.

17 Apolinario Gómez, 1845, *filiación*, AGN X 21-7-1; and Manuel Gómez, 1842, *filiación*, AGN X 21-4-6. Juan P. Rocha, filiación AGN X 21-5-1.

18 Filiación 1844, AGN X 21-5-1.

19 This was neither a capricious nor a new interpretation. Early in 1818 soldiers had appealed to the courts arguing that the lack of provision of the *prest* (subsistence salary) was sufficient reason to abandon the service. The government, to avoid the spread of desertions, passed a law on March 26, 1818 making the provision of food, clothes, and money (socorros) equivalent to the daily allowances (prest).

20 Filiación 1849, AGN III 59-1-4; Filiacion 1845, AGN X 21-4-5; Filiación 1849, AGN X 17-10-5; Filiación 1844, AGN X 26-5-3.

21 Raymundo Ramallo, 1844, Filiación, AGN X 20-10-2; Filiación, 1845, AGN X 20-1-5; Filiación 1840, AGN X 21-7-1.

22 Filiación, Santos Lugares, 1844, AGN X 20-1-2; Filiación 1845, AGN X 20-10-2.

23 Dr. Martinez, for example, found deserter Julian Tebes fit for cavalry service even though he claimed to have a dislocated shoulder (*sacado del cuadril*). Filiación 1846, AGN X 21-1-5. Deserter José Manuel Quintin, who had a limp and a "cloudy eye," was also found physically fit and was sentenced to provide fifteen more years of service. Filiación 1849, AGN III 59-2-2. The report written by Dr. Martínez about Jose Diaz's badly damaged arms is shocking: "This individual presents various scars on his left upper arm, dividing all muscular tissue until the Cubitus bone, his last three fingers lack movement, but despite his efforts to appear useless [*inutil*], the undersigned believes that he is able to continue his services to the fatherland." Jose Díaz, filiación, AGN X 26-5-3.

24 Manuel Candiota, while recounting his participation in the war against the Borogano Indians, showed his limp as evidence of the *lanzaso* (spear wound) he received in one of these encounters. Filiación, 1845, AGN X 21-7-1. Domingo Moyano, a 50-year-old veteran from Pilar, referred to his "rheumatic pains" and to "other *dolencias* [sufferings] proper to his age"; this time justice of the peace Besabe added: "He is an ailing [*achacoso*] man." AGN III 59-1-9 (1844).

25 Francisco Sejas, arrested in 1843 for deserting, stated "that he obtained a leave for 20 days to go to Guardia de Navarro and, because he was ill of the chest as a result of a *rodada*, he stayed on." Filiación, 1843, AGN X 21-2-3.

26 Sergeant Juan Rosas Migas lost his arm in one of these exercises. "Pertenecientes al Ejército de Vanguardia," January 1843, AGN X 31-10-5.

27 Filiación 1846, AGN X 21-3-7. Those who remained longer under similar situations probably took advantage of the protection offered by the authorities while entering into a wage-contract relationship.

28 Though often seen as a burden, the freedom to work also has a positive connotation: the negation of any form of unpaid or involuntary work.

29 While in service at Martín García Island, soldier Anacleto Fredes used to play cards. In 1845, playing with an officer, he won two ponchos and a *muda* (change of clothes). When the officer resisted delivering the garments, Fredes took them by force. AHPBA, Cámara de Apelaciones, 9.1.3.133 (1845).

30 Lucas Ferreyra, filiación, 1845, AGN X 21-6-1; Bruno Pérez, filiación, 1845, AGN X 21-6-1.

31 Sayago had gambled away 10 *pesos fuertes* belonging to a friend. To find someone who would lend him that amount, he went to the city; he was arrested before reaching his destination. Norberto Sayago, filiación, Villa Lujan, December 1850, AGN X 21-7-6. Filiación 1844, AGN X 20-10-7.

32 Jose Salinas, for example, escaped from the city's police and headed for the area where he knew Rosas had an estancia. A fellow prisoner had assured him that "reaching one of His Excellency's estancias nobody could take him away any more." Unfortunately, he never reached Rosas's estancia; he was arrested in Navarro in May 1842. Jose Salinas, filiación, Navarro, 1842, AGN X 21-4-4.

33 Valerio Leguizamón, filiación, Morón, 1847, AGN X 21-3-45.

34 Reluctance to return to their provinces (almost half of the deserters were provincianos) related to Buenos Aires's higher wages and greater political stability.

35 Twelve percent of deserters in the sample claimed to have visited their relatives (fathers, mothers, aunts, uncles, brothers, and sisters) after they deserted.

36 Gral Edecán to JP Gda Luján, Stos Lugares, August 30, 1841, AGN X 21-2-2; Gral Edecán to JP of Guardia de Luján, Santos Lugares, January 23, 1842, AGN X 21-2-3; Gral Edecán to JP Navarro, Santos Lugares, October 8, 1842, AGN X 21-4-4.

37 He had sent his young and rebellious son with his older brother to learn discipline and country work, but Cosme could not tolerate the punishment and came back. He then searched for another conchavo near town. JP of Cañuelas, September 14, 1844, AGN X 20-10-5. As Don Acosta later explained to the justice of the peace, he had known Cosme since he was a child and his father had worked for him as a peon. Hence, he did not see the need to report Cosme's return to the authorities.

38 These figures are consistent with my findings for the larger database of arrestees (*presos*).

39 Gral Edecán de SE, Santos Lugares, September 4, 1841, AGN X 21-4-6; JP of Areco to Rosas, San Antonio de Areco, April 24, 1841, AGN X 21-5-7; Feliciano Ferreyra, filiación, Chivilcoy, 1847, AGN X 21-1-1.

40 Ranchers provided limited accommodations to temporary laborers (a *quincho*, *alero*, or the kitchen); itinerant peons tried to avoid nocturnal raids by the partidas (patrols).

41 Juez de Paz de Ajó, Real Viejo, March 5, 1850, AGN X 20-9-5. Faustino Vera, after deserting from the invernada of Navarro, moved to Chivilcoy (a neighboring district), where he worked as a day laborer for Don Antonio Benavidez. His shelter, however, was elsewhere: first in Don Pedro Gonzalez's house and then in Francisco Repallo's. Filiación, Navarro, 1842, AGN X 21-4-4. Employer Jose Laurea was accused of hiding a deserter in the water well. Mar Chiquita, 1848, X 21-4-3.

42 Gral Edecán to JP of Lobos, Santos Lugares, July 19, 1841, AGN X 21-2-1. Sisterna's second employer in Lobos, Don Roque Espíndola, justified hiring a person without documents by stating that he knew Sisterna had worked for a neighbor. Gral Edecán to JP of Lobos, Santos Lugares, October 30, 1841, AGN X 21-2-1. Pressed by the officer, Marchant responded: "Being a widow, living by myself, how do you think I could ask men for passports who came to help in my labors, all well-known men." Gral Edecán to JP of Lobos, Santos Lugares, August 2, 1841, AGN X 21-2-1.

43 Gral Edecán de SE to JP of Las Flores, Santos Lugares, July 31, 1841, AGN X 21-2-4. Deserters' stories implicating JPs in protection deals, though frequent, need to be taken with caution, for some were simply made up.

44 Gral Edecan to JP of Las Flores, Santos Lugares, August 7, 1841, AGN X 21-2-4.

45 Gral Edecan to JP of Quilmes, Santos Lugares, August 16, 1841, AGN X 21-4-6. From jail, Ullúa spread rumors that a higher authority would come to his rescue. The JP, confused, gave him a passport to go to another county. "Roque Carranza," AGN X 20-10-5.

46 Juan José Flores, filiación, AHPBA, Camara de Apelaciones, 9.1.3.133.

47 After the desertion, the three ran to the forest, reached Bajada del Paraná, and tried to offer their services to different commanders: in Bajada to Captain Espindola, in Santa Fe to General Echagüe, in Salto to General Pacheco, in Santos Lugares to General Reyes. They managed to obtain a passport from each of these officers to go to the general headquarters. Their goal was to negotiate their reincorporation with Governor Rosas.

48 Some rural peons differentiated well between the two spheres. Valerio Leguizamón told his inquisitor that "when he was a paysano he served in the militias of Lujan's justice of the peace," but as soon as he was destined (commissioned) to a regiment he became a regular soldier (soldado de linea). Valerio Leguizamón, filiación, Morón 1847, AGN X 21-3-4.

49 Gral Edecán to Cmte Fuerte de Mayo, Santos Lugares, August 4, 1845, AGN X 26-5-3.

50 J. M. Plaza, Mulitas, July 31, 1845, AGN X 26-5-3.

51 Nicolás Bustos, filiación, Lobería, 1845, AGN X 21-2-4.

52 Filiación, Lobos, 1846, AGN X 21-2-1.

53 Inocencio Monsalvo, filiación, Santos Lugares, 1849, AGN III 59-1-9.

54 Deserter Pastor Leguizamón turned up at Rosas's headquarters after hearing news of Rosas's indulto in 1845. Marcos Rubio to Antonino Reyes, May 31, 1845, AGN X 26-5-3.

55 Gral Edecan to JP of Quilmes, Santos Lugares, March 2, 1841, AGN X 21-4-6. Miguel Sánchez Celis, a captain of the militias at Quilmes, got into trouble for interceding in favor of deserter A. Leiva: "Leiva came to see him and asked him to be his Godfather in order to obtain an indulto for a misdemeanor he committed." Celis then wrote a letter interesting Colonel Cáceres in the matter. JP Quilmes to M. Corvalán, Quilmes, July 28, 1846, AGN X 21-5-1. Francisco Funes, filiación, Santos Lugares, 1849, AGN III 59-1-5. Edecán de SE to JP of Lobos, Santos Lugares, July 7, 1841, AGN X 21-2-1.

56 Filiación, Buenos Aires, 1846, AGN X 21-1-5. This barrage of arguments failed to persuade Rosas, who knew that Etchegaray had already changed his name once and was not particularly truthful. He was charged with four additional years of military service.

57 Canto 33 reads: "Sin ninguna intención mala/lo hicieron, no tengo duda;/pero es la verdá desnuda,/siempre suele suceder:/aquel que su nombre muda/tiene culpas que esconder" ("With no evil intent/did they do this, I am sure/but it is the naked truth,/and it is always the case: that/he who changes his name/has some faults to hide") J. Hernández, *Martín Fierro* (1948), 185 (translated by H. A. Holmes).

10 Memories of War

1 Recollections of World War I, a war that left innumerable written memoirs by combatants, has prompted a vivid scholarly debate about the effects of war on the identity of soldiers. The myths, the neologisms, the metaphors, and the clinical cases provide the materials for studying the ways soldiers understood and lived this war—what Leed (1979) calls the "structure of experience," a distant possibility in the events of the Argentine civil war, with so few memoirs left, and most written by officers.

2 The "genre" of these stories is not easy to pinpoint. The stories contained in the filiaciones of civil war veterans lack the degree of narrative detail and symbolic power found in written literary memoirs of war. On literary narratives of WWI, see Fussell (1975). To some extent, these narratives participate in some of the traits of what Pratt (1992, 86–87) calls "survival literature," in which a survivor narrated his or her experience in a liminal situation (war, captivity, shipwreck, mutiny) and, in so doing, sought reintegration in the home society. Stories of experience in the civil wars, how-

ever, being prompted by the question-answer framework, lacked the embellishments characteristic of these types of narratives. On the implications for narratives of a question-answer framework, see Jauss (1989, 51–94).

3 Peter Brooks's definition of plot: "Plot is not a matter of typology or of fixed structures but rather a structuring operation peculiar to those messages that are developed through temporal succession, the instrumental logic of a specific mode of human understanding" (qtd. in Phelan 1989, 108).

4 See Feliciano A. Chiclana's petition in Solicitudes y Carpetas, 1826, AGN X 25-5-2.

5 Argüero served twenty-three years. He entered the Spanish army in 1803 and in 1810 "joined the Cause of Liberty" and had worked for it ever since. Buenos Aires, April 10, 1826, Solicitudes y carpetas, 1826, AGN X 25-5-2.

6 In actuality, the period 1822–1824 saw the most drastic reforms in the army, reforms that produced a shrinkage in the total number of commissioned officers and the general demobilization of the regiments (see Halperin Donghi 1972).

7 Benito Correa said he had served the republic for twenty years, having participated in ten campaigns.

8 "Documentos de Servicios . . . del Capn. retirado Dn Antonio Segovia," 1822, AGN VII, Colección Ruiz Guiñazú, 16-4-8, no. 1507; D. Justo Barbosa, August 5, 1826, AGN X 25-5-2; Celestino Balmaceda, August 16, 1826, AGN X 25-5-2.

9 See petitions by Juan Argüero, Pedro Castelli, Manuel Castro, and Victor Güiraldes in Solicitudes y Carpetas, AGN X 25-5-2.

10 In the early period of the revolution, "purity of blood" was an important element for obtaining an officer's commission. In 1810 Martín José de Segovia, a vecino and alcalde e barrio, petitioned for his son to be incorporated into the Patricios Battalion. He accompanied the petition with a baptismal record showing his son's limpieza de sangre.

11 Juan Fernández to Rosas, February 22, 1832, AGN X 24-7-3.

12 The French Revolution changed the calendar to underscore a total break with the past (Ozouf 1988, 158–196; Le Goff 1991, 189–193).

13 In 1844, on the anniversary of the declaration of independence, Don Adeodato de Gondra told the people of Tucumán that it was the responsibility of the men of his generation to preserve the independence gained by their parents (Archivo Americano 1947, 13–17).

14 Raymundo Ramallo, filiación, Santos Lugares, November 21, 1844, AGN X 20-10-2.

15 José Antonio Villasante, filiación, Ranchos, February 8, 1844, AGN X 21-5-2; Rafael Rojas, filiación, Santos Lugares, February 26, 1849, AGN III 59-2-3.

16 He was rewarded with the rank of sergeant major. Afterward, he remained in the city helping to train the cívicos of Catedral Sur. Agustín Delgado, filiación, Dolores, November 25, 1850, AGN X 21-1-2.

17 Antonio Cabrera, filiación, Santos Lugares, April 14, 1844, AGN X 21-2-3.

18 Pascual Escalante, filiación, Campamento Pavón, March 10, 1845, AGN X 26-5-3; Francisco Medina, filiación, Navarro, December 13, 1843, AGN X 21-4-4.

19 See Fentress and Wickham (1992), Goody (1977), and Burke and Porter (1987). On the literary character of peasants' narrations, see Zemon Davis (1987). On the ability of indigenous peoples to construct their own forms of historical consciousness, see Hill (1988) and Rappaport (1990).

20 "From the smallest poetic units to the largest, from the basic auditory structure to the syntax to the structure of meaning, the form of poetry in oral societies is ordered so as continually to provide the reciting poet with signposts showing him the way to proceed" (Fentress and Wickham 1992, 43).

21 Becco (1960, 62) reproduces one of these songs, entitled "Las doce palabras retornadas."

22 In another poem ("The Three Marías are Four") the same mnemotecnic device is used to descredit official religious belief: "The Three Marias are Four,/The Four elements are Five/The Seven Little Goats are Eight/The Ten Commandments are Eleven . . ." (Becco 1960).

23 Rosas's campaign to the desert was in 1833 (he departed in late March 1833 and returned in late May 1834). The disturbances between the *apostólico* and the *cismático* factions that led to Balcarce's resignation occurred in October and early November 1833. "Baldéz" refers to Captain Vicente Valdez, who marched in November 1839 from Dolores to extend the rebellion to Tandil. The names of federalist commanders (Esquiros, Rodríguez, Reynoso, and Aguilera) are also correct.

24 I am referring here to works such as Beverina (1974) and Quesada (1926b, 1927, 1965).

25 Often, the rain took care of them (paysanos carried these documents under their saddle or underneath their belts) or the military or judicial authorities retained them after interrogating the suspect. Many times, they were stolen by other paysanos in desperate need of a new identity.

26 Rosas's official "history," *Rasgos de la vida pública* (1842) also divided the past according to climatic moments: December 1, 1828, the year of the "tremendous explosion" of Lavalle's mutiny; 1833, the year in which "the government forgot its mission and succumbed to the unitarios"; March 7, 1835, the year of the granting of "extraordinary faculties" to Governor Rosas; October 29, 1840, the date of the agreement between Rosas and the King of France.

27 Cirilo Medina said that in "the last insurrection" (1840) he fell ill and had to remain in Ranchos. In the next campaign (1841), his brother died in the battle of Quebracho. Cirilo Medina, filiación, Ranchos, April 22, 1844, AHPBA, Juzgado de Paz, 39-4-37.

28 Soldiers' understanding of federalism might have been incorrect, but it was consonant with the official rhetoric about the civil war. The federation, a political entity of unclear territoriality and dubious organization, was a reality only in the mythical history of Rosismo. To the unitario

dissidents, the Confederation was itself a rhetorical invention (see Weinberg 1970, 139).

29 Some soldiers referred to May as the *mes de América* following the Rosista revolutionary calendar. None, however, renamed the year starting with 1830; when they recalled the "year 33" they were referring to 1833.

30 See, for example, *Calendario* (1849). See also *Almanaque Federal* (1845, 1848). This ordering of time was not peculiar to the Rosas period. In the *Nuevo e Interesante Alamanak* (1824) one can read: "Año bisiesto de la creación del mundo 7023, del Diluvio Universal 4781, de la Encarnación de Nuestro Sr. Jesus Cristo 1824, de la Corrección Gregoriana 242 . . . de la reconquista de la ciudad 19, de la defensa de Montevideo 18, de Nuestra Regeneración Política 15, de la Emancipación de la América del Sud 9" (" . . . 7023d leap year (*año bisiesto*) of the creation of the world, 4781st year of the Universal Deluge, 1824th year of Our Lord Jesus Christ's incarnation, 242th year of the Gregorian Correction; . . . 19th year of the reconquest of the city; 18th year of the defense of Montevideo; 15th year of our Political Regeneration; 9th year of the Emancipation of South America").

31 According to Halbwachs (1992), the capacity for telling accurate narratives about the past derives from the interaction between social environment and individual experience, that is, from the stimulation that society or groups generate for the process of retrieving personal memoirs.

32 Juan Camaña designed a pack of cards intended to impress in the memory of the popular classes the basic calendar of federalism. The cards had the dates of all the major events that good federales had to commemorate, from the birth of Rosas to the declaration of war that preceded Caseros (see Chávez 1970, 240).

33 Norberto Sosa, filiación, February 13, 1847, AGN X 20-10-2; Sandalio Fuentes, filiación, San Nicolás, February 18, 1841, AGN X 21-7-1.

34 Communicating the events of war and activating the memory of the *Patria Grande* was the purpose and function of the *cielitos patrióticos*, one of the earliest forms of gauchesco literature.

35 The poem "Batalla de Tucumán," reported by Zeballos, states: "Now, Jujuy is ours/so is Tupisa and Salta/all the province/is left vacant/they leave us/Fortunes, rifles, cannons, and lances/Taking only/their tied hands" (1905, vol. 1, 331). See also this allegorical poem to the battle of Tucumán: "Sobre èl en el veinticuatro/De Septiembre, el año Doce,/La Dulce Pátria salvóse/En los brazos del valor" (334–345).

36 The unitarios are identified with "that treacherous and mournful mob" that had "burdened the peoples with opprobrium/and offended the Federation."

37 They are named without titles and without first names, leveling them all as equals to the soldiers.

38 "De balde en otras aiciones/los dimos contra los cardos,/y, si no, que le pregunten/a Posadas, el mentao,/cómo le jué, allá en las Piedras,/y después, allá en los barcos./Diga Tristán . . . más no quiero/gastar pólvora en chimangos,/porque era Tristán más triste/que hombre pobre enamorao;/ Muesas, en la del Cerrito; Marcó, flojo y sanguinario/en la aición de Chaca-

buco;/en la pendencia de Maipo/habla Quimpe, y ese O'Relly,/yo otros muchos que áhura callo./" ("In vain, in other actions/we pushed them against the thistles/and, if not, let them ask/Posadas, the renowned/how he fared there, in Las Piedras/and afterwards there, in the ships/Let Tristán tell [you]/ . . . but it is not my intention/to waste time and energy,/because Tristán was sadder [in Spanish Tristán works with *triste*]/than a poor man in love;/Muesas, in the [battle] of Cerrito; Marcó, weak and blood-thirsty/ in the action of Chacabuco;/in the fight at Maipo/Quimple, please speak, and that O'Reilly,/and many others that now I do not mention/") (Bartolomé Hidalgo, "Nuevo Diálogo, Entre Ramón Contreras, gaucho de la Guardia del Monte y Chano, capataz de una estancia en las islas del Tordillo," in Tiscornia 1974, 62–64).

39 Sometimes the names of General Paz and of Santa Cruz were added to the *mueras* shouted in federal festivities, but hardly ever the name of General LaMadrid, a unitario respected for his valor and sacrifice.

40 Patriotic poems composed during the wars of independence initiated a practice of naming the enemy with a short name or *apodo*. Spanish General Tristán was often referred to as "Cuico." See "Batatalla de Tucumán (poem)," in Zeballos (1905, 330–332).

41 Ramón Cejas, filiación, Santos Lugares, October 3, 1845, AGN X 26-5-3; Julián Mercado, filiación, Santos Lugares, March 11, 1844, AGN X 20-10-7; Juan José Flores, filiación, August 1, 1842, AHPBA, Cámara de Apelaciones, 9.1.3.133; Estanislao Cufré, filiación, Santos Lugares, March 21, 1844, AGN III 591-1-3.

42 The JP of Mar Chiquita called Rivera an "incendiary," in addition to the usual "savage, unitario, and *Pardejón*." The same type of language can be read in a proclama prepared by General Urquiza before launching a major attack against Rivera. (Urquiza called Rivera an "incendiary, an invader, an assassin, and a vagrant"; 1924, 89–90). Urbanite federales celebrating their victory over the southern rebels in 1839 used all kinds of apellatives for the unitarios: "renegades," "bandits," "infamous," "traitors," "assassins." *Gaceta Mercantil*, August 10, 1839.

43 Anacleto Galván, filiación, Santos Lugares, February 7, 1843, AGN X 21-2-3.

44 Juan Ferreyra, *filiación*, Santos Lugares, March 9, 1845, AGN X 20-10-2.

45 Nicasio Mendoza, filiación, Santos Lugares, September 25, 1845, AGN X 26-5-3.

46 Blas Ponce, filiación, Chascomús, April 25, 1844, AGN X 20-10-7.

47 Francisco Iturrieta, filiación, Villa Luján, November 30, 1845, AGN X 21-7-6.

48 Pedro Salomón, filiación, Ranchos, January 26, 1845, AGN X 21-5-2.

49 Fermín Lares, filiación, San Nicolás, January 14, 1840, AGN X 21-7-1; Eugenio Flores, filiacíon, Lobos, March 16, 1844, AGN X 21-2-1; Facundo Cantero (or Juan Islas), filiación, Fortín Areco, October 19, 1845, AGN X 20-9-6; José Ignacio Saagarra, filiación, Villa Luján, July 27, 1845, AGN X 21-7-6.

50 José María Mendez reported his participation in the chase of caciques Maulí and Chocorí in June 1833 and in the campaign against the *indios chilenos* in Cerrito in October 1834. Later that year and again in 1835, his battalion attacked the Ranqueles. During March–April 1836 he joined the fight against Boroga chief Cañuquir. He participated in August of that year in the suppression of the Indian rebellion at Bahía Blanca, and in 1837 he repelled the invasion of Borogas and Ranqueles against Fort Argentino. José María Méndez, filiación, Fuerte Argentino, May 7, 1839, AGN III 59-1-9.

51 José Díaz, filiación, Santos Lugares, June 20, 1844, AGN X 26-5-3; Manuel Candiota, filiación, San Nicolás, November 11, 1845, AGN X 21-7-1; José Manuel Correa, filiación, Guardia de Luján, February 3, 1843, AGN X 21-2-3; Pedro Jerez, filiación, Fortín de Areco, May 30, 1842, AGN X 20-9-6.

52 Eulogio Zamudio, filiación, Lobos, March 28, 1845, AGN X 21-2-1; Eugenio Molina, filiación, Palermo de San Benito, August 20, 1851, AGN X 18-2-6; Juan Crisóstomo Alvarez, filiación, Santos Lugares, April 7, 1847, AGN III 59-1-1.

53 Sandalio Fuentes received a medal for his attacks against the Indians of Bahía Blanca. Filiación, San Nicolás, February 18, 1841, AGN X 21-7-1.

54 According to Benedict Anderson (1983, especially 47–65), pilgrimage assisted the process of imagining a new nation at a time when few or none of the requisites of nationhood (territoriality, commonality of customs, language) existed. American-born colonial bureaucrats, in their pilgrimages to the center of Spanish power, discovered the common elements that defined their identity (*americanos*) vis-à-vis Spaniards. Pilgrimage also served to define the national identity of lower-class subjects. The long march from country towns to Paris during the festivals of the Federation (1790) acted as a rite of passage where peasant soldiers could overcome their provincialism and imagine a national brotherhood (Ozouf 1988, 55–58).

55 To Angel Córdoba, it was not contradictory to claim that he had never served his homeland (patria) while, at the same time, giving an extensive account of his participation in the civil war. Angel Córdoba, filiación, Campamento Pavón, March 10, 1845, AGN X 26-5-3.

56 Genaro Alvarez, filiación, Guardia de Luján, October 17, 1845, AGN X 21-2-3.

57 Though his commitment to the Federal Cause lacks continuity—he changed commanding officers four times and deserted on three occasions—his account stresses a long life of military service.

58 Gregorio Carpio, filiación, Lobos, April 20, 1846, AGN X 21-2-1.

59 Félix Montenegro, filiación, Fortín Areco, June 9, 1844, AGN X 20-9-6.

11 Rituals of Federalism

1 On the nation as imagined community, see Anderson (1983); on ritual practices as a profusion of symbols, see Turner (1974).

2 In *Negara*, Geertz (1980) presents the Balinese state as a theater represent-

ing a model of politics, the "exemplary center" around which the life of many "composite villages" revolves. Though Geertz's view of rituals has been challenged recently for its exaggerated concern with order and cohesion, his conception of ritual politics as a "dense reality" is useful for reexamining the Rosista state in its ideal form. See Dirks (1994), Roseberry (1989), and Bell (1992).

3 For a summary of the debates surrounding the historiography of the Rosas period, see Etchepareborda (1972). Among the works that deal with the regime only a few can be mentioned here: Bilbao (1961); Saldías (1968); Ramos Mejía (1907); Ibarguren (1930); Irazusta (1941–1949); Dellepiane (1956); Arana (1954); Ravignani (1970); Astesano (1960); Carretero (1970); Lynch (1981); and Myers (1995).

4 Ansaldi and Moreno (1989, 77). A similar view is maintained by Lynch (1981), Burgin (1946), and Alvarez (1961).

5 For a criticism of this view, see Mayo (1997b).

6 In the squares of La Victoria, Monserrat, Lorea, Plaza Nueva, and Concepción, in front of the police department, in the Alameda near the port, and at Santos Lugares. Cmte. del Parque to Rosas, Buenos Aires, February 20, 1845, AGN X 43-4-5.

7 "Light blue jacket—light blue tights—large black shoes—monkey leather cap with a light blue ribbon—light blue tie . . ." (ibid.). Federal policemen were moustaches.

8 Quoted by Ingenieros (1920), vol. 2, 276. On the ceremonies of Rosas's taking office as governor, see Lynch (1981, 165).

9 Roger Chartier (1991) uses this term, "transfer of sacrality," to refer to the rechanneling of popular sentiments and rituals from religiosity to the public, political sphere.

10 JP José Nuñez to Rosas, San Nicolás, May 30, 1832, AGN X 21-7-1.

11 I use the term "Rabelaisian" to refer to the carnivalesque and festive components of popular rituals, though I am aware of the lack of some important ingredients of the festivities represented by Rabelais. See Bakhtin (1984).

12 The flag raised in the JP's house showed the sun on one side, on the other Rosas's portrait.

13 JP of Ranchos to Rosas, June 6, 1842, AGN X 21-5-2.

14 After the burning of the effigies, the crowd was divided into three groups to attend the ball. The multitude could not be assembled into a single ballroom.

15 A description of these festivities appeared in La Gaceta Mercantil, August 10, 1839.

16 What follows is based on the description made by the JP of Dolores. See JP of Dolores to Manuel Corvalán, Dolores, August 10, 1841, AGN X 21-1-2.

17 "Costo de las Fiestas Cívicas del año de 1828," Buenos Aires, July 18, 1828, AGN X 36-2-2.

18 Among the prescribed rituals were the cannon volleys, the fireworks, the

music band, and the aerostatic balloon (the latter was probably difficult to afford in the towns). "Programa de las Fiestas Mayas del año de 1828," in ibid., same folder.

19 Rosas, the poem reads, has defended with success "Our Independence" and has lavished gifts and exceptions to widows, military men, and hacendados. Other military authorities receive credit for "the preservation of Liberty." The names on the placards are General Pacheco, General Prudencio Ortiz de Rosas, Edecán Manuel Corvalán, Colonel Narciso del Valle, Colonel Vicente Gonzáles, Colonel Juan Aguilera, Commander Pedro Rosas y Belgrano, and the JP of Dolores.

20 The victories against "the tyrant Santa Cruz" were probably celebrated in many other towns. I have references of similar festivities in Villa de Luján.

21 JP of Arrecifes to Gen. Edecán, Arrecifes, May 10, 1839, AGN X 20-9-7.

22 "With the children of the Square, Sublieutenant Don José Ma. Obregón formed two Divisions, one were the federales, and the other the Savage unitarios. They formed into combat and the federales resulted the winners . . . they punished their prisoners with whips, afterwards retiring to my House, where I gave them a few coppers." JP of Areco to Rosas, San Antonio de Areco, October 16, 1840, AGN X 21-5-7.

23 JP of Dolores to Rosas, Dolores, May 1, 1839, AGN X 21-1-2.

24 The benemérito was usually an old veteran of the wars of independence or a figure in the two federal "restorations." JP of Areco to Rosas, San Antonio de Areco, April 24, 1837, AGN X 21-5-7. A similar welcome was offered to General Echagüe in 1842.

25 Gen. Edecán to JP of Areco, Buenos Aires, March 7, 1838, AGN X 21-5-7. The town of Luján offered a similar welcome to a minister of Chile who visited the town in 1839.

26 JP of Ranchos to Rosas, Ranchos, January 28, 1840, AGN X 21-5-2.

27 The 1831 campaigns were highly successful for the federalists. That year unitario General Paz was taken prisoner, General Pacheco defeated General Pedernera, and General Quiroga obtained a smashing victory over the unitarios at Ciudadela.

28 Proclama, JP José Núñez, San Nicolás, November 26, 1831, AGN X 21-7-1.

29 H. A. Cordero (1978, 265–270) describes the festivities of San Ignacio in 1610. See also Torre Revello (1929).

30 For a description of the festivities of May 24–26, 1822 and their cost, see Vogel (1991).

31 No longer do we see the granting of prizes to orphan girls, subsidies to widows, veterans, and invalids, and freedom to slaves. The practice of liberating prisoners, however, continued throughout the Rosas period.

32 In Mexico, for example, the colonized peoples dressed up as Turkish or Aztec warriors and faced the invading armies in *juegos de cañas* (cane combats). They fought over castles made of mats, engaged in naval combat on lagoons, persecuted Moorish cattle rustlers, or enacted apostle Santiago's victorious entry into Jerusalem. See Warman (1972, 56–84).

33 Representations like this were usually replicated on the night of May 25 in more formal plays, such as *Siripo* ("drama americano") or other adaptations of Greek or Roman dramas.

34 The Festival of the Federation was established July 1790 as an attempt to constrain the violence of village festivals and consolidate the achievements of the Revolution.

35 The festivals of the federation revealed the differences in concerns and mentalities between villagers and urban dwellers. In the Champs-des-Mars, an assortment of icons borrowed from different traditions (Egyptian and Greek antiquity, Christianity, Chinese, neoclassicism) gave the festival the quality of a bazaar that bedazzled observers. In the villages, fewer icons served to unify the population around the themes of liberty and equality. Planting a liberty tree became a reason for assembling and celebrating freedom.

36 In 1810 the revolution, 1816 the declaration of independence, 1828 the first restoration, 1831 the signing of the federal pact, 1833 the second restoration.

37 In the 1841 festivities of May 25 in Buenos Aires, as painted by Albérico Isola, a double column of infantry and cavalry protects the square.

38 Part of an ancient funerary theme, the pyramid represented the altar of the fatherland.

39 It would be a mistake, G. Koziol (1992, 293–295) warns us, to set them apart from the values and conflicts that pervade popular culture. A similar argument can be found in Bell (1992, 3–9).

40 The analogy among these communicative interactions may not in itself constitute a proof of popular receptions and understandings of federalism, but it does point to the ubiquity of certain representations in public spaces.

41 *La Gaceta Mercantil*, August 12, 1839.

42 Interestingly, Napoleon "the Codifier" was also perceived as a savior.

43 Rosas, División Izquierda, Río Colorado, June 26, 1833, AGN VII 16-4-8, no. 1492.

44 Rosas made mandatory the use of the federal *divisa* and *cintillo* (red ribbons attached to the jacket and to the hat) and gave preference to a simpler paysano dress style.

45 Public subscriptions to support the war effort, expressions in court in favor of the cause of order, generalized used of federal badges, etc.

46 JP of Tuyú to Rosas, January 8, 1840, AGN X 21-8-1.

47 Another possible interpretation hinges on the notion of independence: paysanos might be celebrating and imitating the resistance of Algerian bedouins to the French invasion.

48 See Montagnon (1986, chaps. 9, 10). Significantly, Abed el-Kader had been proclaimed a sultan in elections of a confederate type, had promised to govern with the Book of the Law in his hand, and had launched a holy war against the French. See Heggoy (1986).

49 JP of Bahía Blanca to Manuel Corvalán, Fort Argentino, September 28, 1838, AGN X 20-10-4.

50 JPS reported with pride how rich and poor attended the balls in the same type of clothes, abandoning all the pretense of city fashion.

51 This collective condemnation of the merchant/unitario had real consequences. It anticipated the actual expatriation of unitarios or the confiscation of their assets.

52 Mockery and laughter, elements that in Rabelais represent the triumph of life over death in a world of hunger, appear here as a political catharsis that reinforces the spectators' confidence in the final triumph of federalism. The fear of war is momentarily suspended.

53 Outraged, Ramos Mejía (1907, 256) called this poetry "octaves of a knife in the garter."

54 On the change of identity of paysanos persecuted as deserters, see chapter 9.

55 The Rosista state used a system of shifting alliances with the so-called friendly Indians to make war on tribes that resisted incorporation. See Ratto (1994, 1996).

56 Here a caveat is necessary: on occasion, when a major military campaign was launched, the militias would also be summoned as a backup force to the regular army.

57 During the French Revolution men imagined themselves as a family of (orphan) brothers united by the loss of the "father" (Hunt 1992).

58 On the discourse of independence, see Goldman (1980, 1989).

59 The former meaning was that utilized by the urban Jacobins to emphasize the need to eliminate the racial and status distinctions that constituted the foundation of the colonial state.

60 J. C. Chiaramonte (1997) calls attention to the ambiguity of these terms. The word "federation" obscures the true "confederal" organization of the provinces and misrepresents their juridical status as independent states.

61 More research about political representations (poetry, paintings, theater) is essential to elucidate this question.

62 For a full criticism of available notions of caudillismo, see the introduction to Goldman and Salvatore (1998).

12 Subalterns and Progress

1 I borrow the concept from J. C. Scott (1998).

2 *Album de Señoritas*, February 17, 1854, qtd. in Masiello (1994, 64).

3 Irigoin (1995) attributes the greater confidence of investors to monetary and financial reforms that eventually led to stabilization of the currency.

4 Daguerrotypes of the main sites of the city taken in 1852–1858 show little change. The Recova, Retiro, the port area, the Fort, the Alameda still retained their colonial design and general outlook. *Los años del daguerrotipo* (1995).

5 Aside from the appointment of the Immigration Commission (1854) and the facilities granted to a private philanthropic association for housing immigrants (1857), little else was done.

6 Transportation time dropped significantly. There was also greater reliability of travel along existing tracks. But tracks were quite limited before 1865 (Lewis 1983, 36, 41).

7 Between 1852 and 1860 the number of public schools rose from 16 to 37, while the number of pupils increased from 1,400 to 4,700. Between 1856 and 1860 private schools increased from 58 to 139 and the students attending these schools rose from 3,000 to 6,400 (Newland 1992, 149–150, 165, 155–56).

8 In January 1852, the lands confiscated in 1840 were restituted to their original owners. A law of October 1858 reclaimed as public domain all land donated between 1829 and 1852. In 1857, a law converted into small-scale tenancies all lands subject to *enfiteusis* (long-term tenancy). Rosas's lands were confiscated in 1857 and sold at public auction in 1859 (Cárcano 1972, chap. 10).

9 From Rosario to Tucumán, he wrote, "the road is traversed daily by vehicles with all types of productions and by passenger coaches full of industrious foreigners" (qtd. in Cárcano 1933, 276).

10 To Ferns (1968, 293) this was mainly the result of a change in the mentality of porteños, no longer opposed to free trade, foreign capital, and European immigrants.

11 Sarmiento wrote in 1853: "Mingling among the multitude attending the fireworks these days, who filled the plaza de la Victoria, I have not found the people, the rabble (*chusma*), the plebe, the ragged man. The place of Chile's rotos had been taken by thousands of Basques, Italians, Spaniards, French, etc. The dress is the same for all classes or, more properly speaking, *there are no classes* [my emphasis]. The gaucho abandons his poncho and the city invades the countryside, in the same way as Europe invades the city" (qtd. in Botana 1984, 329).

12 "We are here to declare that the land does not belong to the bull, to the savage, to the barbarian of the intermediate stage, and that we wish, on a day like this, to give it peacefully to civilization, to industry and to freedom. The act of possession has already been accomplished; *there it is* [pointing to the locomotive], the new conqueror that penetrates [the desert], dragging people along its way, marking the land with its iron feet, and drawing in the sky a column of smoke and fire as a revealing banner of human progress" (Avellaneda 1928, 35).

13 During his short period in office, Urquiza produced an avalanche of reforms: the abolition of the death penalty for political crimes, the banning of confiscation, the creation of the municipality of Buenos Aires, the appointment of commissions for drafting civil and commercial codes, the establishment of a Statistical Department, and more (Macchi 1981, 30–79).

14 The 1853 translation of W. Parish's *Buenos Ayres and the Provinces of the Rio de la Plata* marked the emergence of a statistical apparatus preoccupied with the international recognition of the region's economic potential (González Bollo 1999).

15 Their emergence in eighteenth-century Europe coincided with the recon-
ceptualization of government as the art of managing large populations and
their wealth. See Burchell, Gordon, and Miller (1991).

16 JP of Junín to Chief of Mesa Estadística, Junín, December 12, 1855, AGN X
43-8-9.

17 Decree of September 2, 1852, in *Recopilación de los debates* (1938, 17–23).

18 Law of October 11, 1854, reproduced in *Recopilación de los debates* (1938, 63–
65).

19 JP of Pilar, February 26, 1856, AGN X 19-6-1.

20 He even eliminated the soldiers' rations for *vicios y entretenimientos* (Macchi
1981, 71).

21 J. J. Urquiza to Cnel. E. Frías, Buenos Aires, September 2, 1852, AGN X
27-1-5.

22 The order to register for military service served as a good excuse for re-
introducing forced recruitment; those who failed to register were punished
with service in frontier garrisons.

23 Fortín Areco, August 3, 1852, AHPBA, Juzgado de Paz de Giles, 39-2-22.

24 Increased enforcement of the conchavo law turned vagrancy into the most
common cause for arresting poor paysanos. Province of Buenos Aires,
Decree of July 17, 1853.

25 During the siege of Buenos Aires, Mitre rediscovered the efficacy of a
citizens militia. To him the National Guard were at the "service of civilization and freedom" (Rottjer 1937, 56).

26 In 1853, Sergeant Major Muslera traveled through the central and northern
departments picking up draftees among those accused of vagrancy. Minister of Government to JP of Giles, Buenos Aires, December 28, 1853,
AHPBA, Juzgado de Paz de Giles, 39-2-22.

27 El Nacional, October 18, 1853; *Los Debates*, November 11, 1857.

28 Even Antonino Reyes, Rosas's faithful secretary for many years, was absolved of all wrongdoing in 1855, after having been sentenced to death a
year earlier.

29 According to the information provided by El Judicial the number of death
sentences passed between 1855 and 1864 amounted to thirty-six. This figure is probably an underestimation, as some judges failed to report information to the journal.

30 Most executions took place near the site where the murder had been committed. Of 34 sentences recorded, 23 were carried out in small rural towns
such as Salto, Arrecifes, Tandil, Dolores, or Azul, generally at the central
square. See Salvatore (2001).

31 El Judicial (May 1, 1855) found various factors responsible for the new crime
wave: violent habits acquired during the dictatorship, the increase in the
number of rural taverns, the generalized use of knives, and the lack of
religious instruction among the lower classes.

32 In 1856, two hacendados from San Isidro demanded retribution for the
damage caused by the army's horses to their wheat fields. They provided an

exact measure of the wheat lost and expected to be compensated in equal value. J P of San Isidro to A. Romero, San Isidro, October 14, 1856, AG N X 19-6-1.

33   The J P of Rojas reported that he could no longer give proper rations to policemen and militiamen due to the refusal of local proprietors to give auxilios in cattle. J P of Rojas to Minister of War, Rojas, November 1, 1853, AG N X 18-9-1. J P of Fuerte Federación to Minister of War, October 15 and 18, 1853, AG N X 18-9-1. Gerónimo Morales to Minister of Hacienda, Las Flores, March 14, 1852, AG N X 27-1-5A.

34   Gatherings of hacendados in Azul (August 26, 1856), Bahía Blanca (October 10, 1856), and Patagones (October 6, 1856) produced petitions to the Ministry of War that amounted to a rejection of the government's Indian policy.

35   The petition contained 214 signatures, 118 of them by the immigrants themselves and 95 by literate persons who signed for the illiterate members of the community. Their adversaries, the enfiteutas owning forty leagues of land, were only 12 (Birabent 1941, 66–67).

36   J P of San Fernando to Minister of War, October 24, 1853, AG N X 18-9-1.

37   From each partido a representative was chosen almost unanimously. J P of San Vicente to President of the Administrative Council, San Vicente, June 7, 1853, AG N X 18-9-1.

38   Municipal commissions were to take over the responsibilities and power previously granted to J P s, repairing public buildings, procuring funds for local improvements, overseeing the safety of food and markets, preventing scandals and riots, and identifying vagrants.

39   To city inhabitants who lived through the three-month siege, Lagos's followers were nothing short of "rural barbarians," still dressed in their Rosista uniforms.

40   Despite these similarities, the rebellions did not constitute another Rosista "restoration." Nowhere did the signers of these manifestos pay any tribute to the deposed Dictator. On the contrary, they showed strong sympathy for Urquiza, the leader who was to realize the dream of national organization.

41   Ironically, the signers were happy to grant General Lagos extraordinary authority to preserve the right to vote and the province's participation in the constitutional process.

42   J P of Monsalvo to Chief of Police, Miraflores, March 8, 1853, AG N X 18-9-1.

43   Acta, Guardia de Luján, February 19, 1853, AG N X 18-9-1.

44   "Never, until this moment, has any inhabitant of this partido had the option or invitation to deliberate on issues of public interest [convenience], not even for the purpose of employing our own resources for [our] improvement" reads one of the proclamas.

45   They interpreted the "revolution" of September 11 as a step backward. Here was a decision taken by a minority against the Will of the People.

46   In 1856, Italian Casimiro Bonello called a native sergeant "mercenary rabble" (Canalla Enganchada) implying that creoles were only good for the

socially inferior regular army. Chief of 5th Grenadiers Regiment to Chief of Police, Buenos Aires, May 12, 1856, libro 279, AGN X 33-10-10.

47 Finally Rabelo was sentenced to two years of military service for "fomenting meetings and riots" against the authorities. "Criminal contra Rafael Pascual Rabelo," AHPBA, Juzgado del Crimen, 41-4-194-45 (1859).

48 The accused, alcalde Bono, was reported as saying: "I shit on the braids, on the French, on Queen Victoria, and all gringos can be assured that I will kick them." Sumario, Buenos Aires, January 15, 1864, AGN X 32-1-5 (Policía).

49 This article, like others, gave rise to a legal demand for injurias (libel). "Don Juan J. Viedma contra Don Domingo Durquet," AHPBA, Juzgado del Crimen, 41-4-194-19 (1859).

50 "Dn. Rodolfo Venzano contra Ignacio Vergara por injurias," AHPBA, Juzgado del Crimen, 41-1-197-5 (1860).

51 The pamphlet was entitled "Proclama: Invitación a Todos los Ofendidos Amantes de la Verdadera Causa de la Libertad." See "Contra Cesareo Assaretto por publicación de proclamas sediciosas," AHPBA, Juzgado del Crimen, 38-1-222-20 (1863).

52 JP of Dolores to Governor Vicente López, Dolores, February 10, 1852, AGN X 18-5-8; JP of Pilar, Camarones, March 5, 1852, AGN X 18-5-8.

53 JP of Azul to Minister of Government, Azul, August 20, 1856, AGN X 19-6-1; M. de la Serna to Minister of War, Puente Barracas, March 24, 1852, AGN X 18-5-8; Minister of War to JP of Giles, Buenos Aires, July 17, 1853, AHPBA, Giles, 39-2-22; JP of San Fernando to Minister of War, August 17, 1853, AGN X 18-9-1.

54 Once out of office, he plotted with the federalists against the new authorities. JP of Patagones to Minister of War, Patagones, December 17, 1853, AGN X 18-9-1.

55 JP of Salto to Minister V. Alsina, Salto, January 2, 1856, AGN X 19-6-1; Circular, July 24, 1861, AHPBA, Juzgado de Paz de Bragado, 39-1-10; JP of Pila to Minister of War, Camarones, July 30, 1856; JP of Lobería to idem, San Agustín, August 28, 1856; JP of Vecino to Valentín Alsina, January 21, 1856, AGN X 19-6-1. JP of San José de Flores to Minister of War, January 14, 1856, AGN X 19-6-1; JP of San Nicolás to Minister of War, December 7, 1853, AGN X 18-9-1.

56 Minister of Government to JP of Giles, Buenos Aires, November 22, 1856, AHPBA, Juzgado de Paz de Giles, 29-2-22.

57 Only theft and murder, stated the justice, should be punished, not minor offenses considered part of paysanos' way of life. JP of Federación to Minister of Government, November 12, 1853, AGN X 18-9-1.

58 The Lagos rebellion gave paysanos a special point of contrast to judge recruitment policies. The rebels had appealed to the patriotism and federalism of paysanos—not to coercion—to recruit soldiers.

59 He wrote: "Mi temor era que, de reacción en reacción, volviesen, o a los hombres de Rosas, o a Rosas mismo. . . . Los hechos respondieron luego a la teoría: hubo revolución. Véase quienes formaron la Legislatura. Se nombro gobernador unitario (Alsina) y vino la reacción federal; hubo sitio.

Fueron naturalmente al poder Anchorena, don Lorenzo Torres, el general Pacheco al ejército. Era, pues, patente la reacción. Si Flores triunfa, teníamos a los de Rosas" (He wrote: "My fear is that, from one reaction to the other, the men of Rosas or even Rosas himself will return. . . . The facts responded later to the theory: there was a revolution. Look at those who formed the Legislature. [As soon as] a unitario governor was appointed (Alsina), the federalist reaction came upon us: there was a siege [to the city]. Anchorena Don Lorenzo Torres went naturally into office, and General Pacheco was appointed to the army. The reaction was, then, evident. If Flores would have triumphed, the men of Rosas would have returned") (Sarmiento 1954, 205).

60 Anonymous, 1852, AGN X 27-1-5A.

61 JP of Patagones to Minister of War, Patagones, December 17, 1853, AGN X 18-9-1.

62 Small property owners of Ramallo "tolerated" one to four agregado families on their lands, causing economic damage to neighbors' properties. JP of San Nicolás to Vélez Sársfield, San Nicolás, September 24, 1856, AGN X 19-6-1.

Glossary

abastecedores Suppliers of commodities (cattle, bread), either wholesale merchants or retail distributors.

Abasto (Mercado de Abasto) Place where cattle provisions for the city are concentrated and sold under the scrutiny of "corral judges."

agregados Squatters on ranchers' lands, their presence tolerated by the ranchers in exchange for some services (vigilance and occasional help in seasonal tasks).

alcaldes Rural policemen. Assistants to the police chief or to the justice of the peace.

bota de potro Leather sock or "boot" made from the skin of a mare's leg.

capataz Foreman, usually in charge of a small crew of laborers.

caudillismo Political order based upon the dominium of a strong man, the "caudillo." Generally, the caudillo exercises power without many institutional constraints, facilitated in part by the support he enjoys from the subaltern classes. There is an intense debate today about the meaning of "caudillismo," particularly as it relates to clientelism, feudalism, hegemony of country over city, and the informal nature of governance.

chiripá Rectangular piece of cloth (usually a poncho) crossed to cover the legs (to the knees) and tied to the waist. Used by paysanos in lieu of trousers.

cintillo Scarlet ribbon used by federalists around their hats.

clasificaciones Same as filiaciones.

conocido A person well known in the local community.

contratas Vouchers stating the basic conditions of a work contract (employer and worker, term of contract, and work to be performed). Used as protection against vagrancy laws.

cordobés Native of Córdoba province.

correntino Native of Corrientes province.

criadores Raisers of livestock (cattle and sheep) owning small herds. They may or may not own the land where their livestock grazes.

divisa Scarlet ribbon used by federalists on their jackets, ponchos, waistcoats, or shirts.

entrerriano Native of Entre Ríos province.

estancia A large extension of land devoted to livestock raising.

estancieros Owners of large estancias, or cattle ranches.

federales Followers or sympathizers of federalism, a doctrine that privileges the organization of the nation as a federation of provinces. In practice, federalism represented a cluster of values, including social equality, political unanimity, national independence, fraternity among federalist provinces, and opposition to the unitario party.

filiaciones Personal files or records filled out by justices of the peace, military chiefs, and police officers while interrogating soldiers, deserters, and suspected delinquents.

gaucho Rural inhabitant of the pampas: term usually used in a derogatory fashion.

gente decente Urban gentry, upper crust, or high brow. Literally "decent people." People whose upbringing and education made them feel superior to the urban plebe or to the country folk.

guía Voucher or document indicating commodities (cattle, horses, grain) being transported from one place to another. The document must specify the names of buyer and seller, the name of the driver, and the brands of the livestock.

jornalero Day laborer who is paid by the day.

labradores Peasant farmers, not necessarily owners of the land they till.

leva Forceful recruitment, usually in time of war.

mayordomo Ranch administrator or general overseer.

Mazorca Secret, parapolice society, renowned for its acts of intimidation and political violence against unitario suspects. The association's name was "Sociedad Popular Restauradora" (SPR).

mazorqueros Members of the Mazorca (SPR) or, in general, any sympathizer of Rosista federalism, disposed to inflict violence against a unitario suspect.

mendocino Native of Mendoza province.

miliciano Militiaman. Any resident neighbor registered in the local militias (active or reserve).

Partes de Novedades Documents through which justices informed Governor Rosas about felonies committed in their counties, staff of policemen under duty, and the compliance with Rosas's orders and decrees.

patria Fatherland. Refers also to the place (town or province) where the subject was born.

paysanos Country man or country folk. Refers to people of rural origins. Lacks the derogative connotations associated with the word "gaucho."

peones-vendedores Butchers and sellers of meat, working at the Abasto or Meat Provision.

porteños In the mid-nineteenth century, natives of Buenos Aires province (county and city). Today the term applies exclusively to residents of Buenos Aires city.

provincianos People born in provinces other than Buenos Aires. Migrants from the interior provinces residing in Buenos Aires province.

puestos Grazing lands with a work station or settlement within the ranch, where a foreman and a work crew (usually of cattle tenders) reside.

pulpería Tavern and general store, usually located in towns or in rural areas.

puntano Native of San Luis province.

ranchos Thatched-roof huts, the dwelling of most paysanos.

repartidores Distributors, retailers,

or peddlers of basic commodities (bread, beef, water, milk).

restauración Popular movement or revolt intended to restore or put back into office a "truly federalist" government.

Rosista The administration of Juan Manuel de Rosas, governor of Buenos Aires province. Otherwise used to indicate the sympathy of a person for Governor Rosas, his ideology or political regime.

saladero Meat-salting plant. Usually a small workshop where cattle is slaughtered, beef cut in strips and then dried in the sun.

santafesino Native of Santa Fé province.

santiagueño Native of Santiago del Estero province.

santos-y-señas Three-word slogans about federalism and its achievements.

sumarios Initial phase of a criminal legal case, including the first interrogations to witnesses and the accused. Also used to indicate the folder (or bundle of papers) containing such information.

tenientes alcaldes Rural policemen, assistants to the alcaldes. They were appointed by the local police chief or justice of the peace.

tertulia Afternoon soireé offered by elite families that included conversation, music, poetry recitation, and, on occasion, dancing.

transeúnte Transient; a person with no established place of residence.

trigueño Racial term. Refers to sunburned mestizos, people of mixed blood whose skin was lighter than mulattos, pardos, or achinados.

tucumano Native of Tucumán province.

Unanimismo Ideal situation imagined by federalists in which all citizens are of the same political opinion.

unitarios Followers or sympathizers of the Unidad, a doctrine that privileges the organization of the nation as a single, centralized republic. In practice, being a unitario meant holding a particular set of political, social, and cultural values (empathy with European culture and values, defense of individual freedom against Rosas's "tyranny," belief in material progress, and dislike for the Rosista plebe).

vecinos Permanent residents of a certain town and, for that reason, holders of political rights (to vote, for example).

vicios (vices) Rations of tobacco, yerba mate, and sugar distributed among peons or soldiers.

viscachas Hare-like or mole-like rodent.

yerba (mate) Infusion similar to tea, from Paraguay.

References

Archives

ABCOPBA   Archivo del Banco de la Provincia de Buenos Aires
AGN   Archivo General de la Nación (Buenos Aires)
AHPBA   Archivo Histórico de la Provincia de Buenos Aires (La Plata)
APN   Archivo Penitenciario Argentino (Buenos Aires)
JRL   John Rylands Library (Manchester, England)

Published Primary Sources

Academia Nacional de Historia. 1938. *La Moda. Gacetín Semanal de Música, Poesía, de Literatura y de Costumbres 1838.* Buenos Aires: A.N.H.

Almanaque Federal para el año bisiesto del señor de 1848. 1848. Buenos Aires: Imprenta del Estado.

Almanaque Federal para el Año del Señor de 1845. 1845. Buenos Aires: Imprenta Argentina.

Aráoz de Lamadrid, Gregorio. 1921. *Memorias del general Gregorio Aráoz de La Madrid.* Madrid: Ed. América.

Archivo Americano y Espíritu de la Prensa del Mundo. 1947. vol. 2. Buenos Aires: Ed. Americana.

Armaignac, Henry. 1961. *Viaje por las pampas de la Republica Argentina.* La Plata: Ministerio de Educación.

Aslina, Juan A. 1898. *La inmigración europea en la República Argentina.* Buenos Aires: Imprenta Calle México.

Avellaneda, Nicolás. 1928. *Discursos de Nicolás Avellaneda.* Buenos Aires: Lib. La Facultad.

Avila, Pedro C. 1847. *Ordenes privadas del general D. Juan Manuel Rosas en la Revolución de 1840 y abril de 1842.* Lima: Imprenta y Litografia de Justo Montoya.

Baudizzone, Luis M., comp. 1941. *Buenos Aires visto por viajeros ingleses 1800–1825.* Buenos Aires: Emecé.

Becco, Horacio J. 1960. *Cancionero Tradicional Argentino.* Buenos Aires: Hachette.

Bilbao, Manuel. 1883. *Vindicación y memorias de Don Antonino Reyes, arregladas y redactadas por Manuel Bilbao.* Buenos Aires: Imp. El Porvenir.

Brabazon, John. 1981. *Andanzas de un irlandés en el campo porteño (1845–1864).* Tran. E. A. Coghlan. Buenos Aires: Minist Cultura y Educación.

The British Packet. De Rivadavia a Rosas, 1826–1832. 1976. Buenos Aires: Solar/Hachette.

Calendario para el año del Señor 1849. 1849. Buenos Aires: Imprenta Oficial.

Calzadilla, Santiago. 1944. *Las beldades de mi tiempo.* Buenos Aires: A Estrada.

Canal Feijó, Bernardo. 1942. *El Norte.* Buenos Aires: Emecé.

Causa Criminal seguida contral el ex-gobernador Juan Manuel de Rosas. 1864. Buenos Aires: La Tribuna.

Chávez, Fermín. 1970. *Juan Manuel de Rosas. Su iconografía.* 3 vols. Buenos Aires: Oriente.

———. 1975. *Un nuevo diálogo gauchesco sobre Rosas.* Buenos Aires: Theoria.

Comando en Jefe del Ejército. 1972. *Reseña Histórica y Orgánica del Ejército. Uniformes de la Patria.* Buenos Aires: Círculo Militar.

Cruz Varela, Juan. 1838. In Kurlat and Minutolo 1965.

Del Carril, Bonifacio. 1964. *Monumenta Iconográphica. Paisajes, ciudades, tipos, usos y costumbres de la Argentina, 1536–1860.* Buenos Aires: Emecé.

Diez de Bonilla, Manuel. 1874. *Código completo de urbanidad y buenas maneras; según los usos y costumbres de las naciones más cultas.* Paris. Librería de A. Bouret.

Dóminguez, Ercilio. 1898. *Colección de leyes y decretos militares.* Buenos Aires: Cía. Sud-Americana de Billetes de Banco.

Echeverría, Esteban. 1997. *El matadero/La cautiva.* Madrid: Cátedra.

Efemérides sangrientas de la dictadura de Juan Manuel de Rosas. 1911. Buenos Aires: Talleres Gráficos de Rafael Palumbo.

El Correo Judicial. Edición Fascimilar 1834. 1946. Buenos Aires: Facultad de Derecho y Ciencias Sociales.

Esteves Saguí, Miguel. 1980. *Apuntes históricos. Recuerdos para mis hijos al correr de la pluma.* Buenos Aires: Academia Nacional de Historia.

Fazio, Lorenzo. 1889. *Memoria descriptiva de la provincia de Santiago del Estero.* Buenos Aires: Cia. Sud-Americana de Billetes de Banco.

Franco, Luis L. 1946. *Rosas entre anécdotas.* Buenos Aires: Claridad.

Gálvez, Victor (Vicente G. Quesada). 1942. *Memorias de un viejo.* Buenos Aires: Solar.

Gelman, Jorge, ed. 1997. *Un funcionario en busca del estado. Pedro Andrés García y la cuestión agraria bonaerense.* Quilmes: Universidad Nacional del Quilmes.

Gutiérrez, Eduardo. 1944. *Juan Manuel de Rosas. Los dramas del terror.* Buenos Aires: Harpón.

Haigh, Samuel. 1831. *Sketches of Buenos Ayres, Chile, and Peru.* London: E. Wilson.

Hinchliff, Thomas Woodbine. 1863. *South American Sketches; or a visit to Rio Janeiro, the Organ Mountains, La Plata and the Parana.* London: Longman, Green, and Roberts.

King, J. Anthony. 1846. *Twenty-Four Years in the Argentine Republic.* New York: Appleton and Co.

Lamas, Andrés. 1877. *Escritos políticos y literarios de D. Andrés Lamas durante la guerra contra la tiranía de D. Juan Manuel Rosas.* Buenos Aires: Casa editora calle Cangallo.

Lanuza, José L. comp. 1941. *Cancionero del tiempo de Rosas.* Buenos Aires: Emecé.

La Rosa de marzo. 1843. Ed. facsimilar. (1941). Buenos Aires, Ediciones Augusta.

Los años del daguerrotipo. Primeras fotografías argentinas 1843–1870. 1995. Buenos Aires: Fundación Antorchas.

MacCann, William. 1969. *Viaje a Caballo por las provincias argentinas*. Buenos Aires: Solar/Hachette. First published in London, 1853.

Mansilla, Lucio V. 1994. *Rozas. Ensayo Histórico-Psicológico*. Buenos Aires: AZ editora. Originally published in 1852.

Mármol, José. 1991. *Amalia*. Buenos Aires: Porrúa. Originally published in 1851.

Masiello, Francine, comp. 1994. *La mujer y el espacio público: el periodismo femenino en la Argentina el siglo XIX*. Buenos Aires: Feminaria.

Moure, Amédée. 1957. *Montevideo y Buenos Aires a mediados del siglo XIX*. Buenos Aires: Ed. Perrot.

Nieves, Manuel María. 1861. *Los mártires de Buenos Aires o el tirano Juan Manuel de Rosas*. 2d ed. Buenos Aires: Authors'.

Nuevo e Interesante Almanak de Buenos Ayres para el año de 1824. 1824. Buenos Aires: Impr. de los Expósitos.

Palliere, León. 1864. *Escenas Americanas. Reproducción de Cuadros, Aquarelles y Bosquejos*. Buenos Aires: Litografía Pelvilain.

Parish, Woodbine. 1852. *Buenos Ayres and the Provinces of the Rio de la Plata*. London: John Murray.

Partes de Batalla de las Guerras Civiles, 1822–1840. 1976. vol. 2. Buenos Aires: Academia Nacional de Historia.

Policía Federal Argentina. 1974. *Antiguos uniformes policiales 1812–1936*. Buenos Aires: Museo Policial.

Rasgos de la vida pública de S.E. el Sr. Brigadier General D. Juan Manuel de Rosas. 1842. Buenos Aires: Imprenta del Estado.

Recopilación de los debates de leyes orgánicas municipales. 1938. vol. 1, 1821–1876. Buenos Aires: Consejo Deliberante.

Relación de las fiestas . . . del fausto matrimonio del Rey Nuestro Señor Don Fernando VII. 1830. Habana: Imprenta Fraternal del Real Cuerpo de Artillería.

Rivera Indarte, José. 1946. *Tablas de Sangre. Es acción santa matar a Rosas*. Buenos Aires: Antonio Dos Santos. First published in Montevideo 1843.

Rodríguez Molas, Ricardo, ed. 1957. *Luis Pérez y la biografía de Rosas escrita en verso en 1830*. Buenos Aires: Clio.

Rosas, Juan Manuel de. 1968. *Instrucciones a los mayordomos de estancias*. Buenos Aires: Plus Ultra.

Rosas en las láminas de "El Grito." 1974. Buenos Aires: Peña Lillo y Monte Chué.

Sarmiento, Domingo F. 1950. *Campaña en el Ejército Grande*. In *Obras Completas de Sarmiento*, vol. 14. Buenos Aires: Luz del Día.

———. 1954. *Memorias*. In *Obras Completas de Sarmiento*, vol. 49. Buenos Aires: Luz del Día.

———. 1974. *Facundo*. 6th ed. Buenos Aires: Losada. Originally published in 1845.

Scarlett, Peter Campbell. 1957. *Viajes por América a través de las Pampas y los Andes*. Buenos Aires: Claridad. First published in London, 1838.

Somellera, Andrés. 1962. *La tiranía de Rosas. Recuerdos de una víctima de la mazorca*. Buenos Aires: Nuevo Cabildo.

Terán, Oscar Terán, comp. 1996. *Escritos de Juan Bautista Alberdi. El redactor de la ley*. Quilmes: Universidad Nacional de Quilmes.

Tiscornia, Eleuterio, comp. 1974. *Poetas Gauchescos.* Buenos Aires: Losada.

Trifilo, S. Samuel. 1959. *La Argentina vista por viajeros ingleses: 1810–1860.* Buenos Aires: Gure.

Varela, Florencio. 1975. *Rosas y su gobierno. Escritos políticos, económicos y literarios.* Buenos Aires: Ed. Freeland.

Weinberg, Félix. 1970. *Florencio Varela y el "Comercio del Plata."* Bahía Blanca: Universidad Nacional del Sur.

Zeballos, Estanislao S. 1905. *Cancionero popular de la Revista de Derecho, Historia y Letras.* Buenos Aires: Impr. de J. Peuser.

Secondary Sources

Agulhon, Maurice. 1981. *Marianne into battle: Republican imagery and symbolism in France, 1789–1880.* Cambridge, England: Cambridge University Press.

Alvarez, Juan. 1961. *Las guerras civiles argentinas.* Buenos Aires: Coyoacán.

Amaral, Samuel. 1987. "Rural production and labour in late colonial Buenos Aires." *Journal of Latin American Studies* 19(2): 235–78.

——. 1998. *The rise of capitalism on the pampas: The estancias of Buenos Aires, 1785–1870.* Cambridge, England: Cambridge University Press.

Amin, Shahid. 1995. *Event, metaphor, memory: Chauri Chaura, 1922–1992.* Berkeley: University of California Press.

Anderson, Benedict. 1983. *Imagined communities: Reflections on the origin and spread of nationalism.* New York: Verso.

Ansaldi, Waldo, and José L. Moreno, eds. 1989. *Estado y sociedad en el pensamiento nacional.* Buenos Aires: Cántaro.

Appadurai, Arjun, ed. 1991. *La vida social de las cosas.* Mexico: Grijalbo.

Arana, Enrique. 1954. *Rosas en la evolución política argentina.* Buenos Aires: Instituto Panamericano de Cultura.

Arnesen, Eric, Julie Greene, and Bruce Laurie. 1998. *Labor histories: Class, politics, and the working-class experience.* Urbana: University of Illinois Press.

Arrieta, Rafael. 1944. *Centuria Porteña. Buenos Aires según los viajeros extranjeros del siglo XIX.* Buenos Aires: Espasa-Calpe.

Aschcroft, Bill, Gareth Griffiths, and Helen Tiffin. 1998. *Key concepts in post-colonial studies.* London: Routledge.

Assadourian, Carlos Sempat. 1983. *El sistema de la economía colonial: el mercado interior, regiones y espacio económico.* Mexico: Editorial Nueva Imagen.

Astesano, Eduardo. 1960. *Rosas, bases del nacionalismo popular.* Buenos Aires: A. Peña Lillo.

Ayarragaray, Lucas. 1904. *La anarquía argentina y el caudillismo.* Buenos Aires: F. Lajouane.

Azcuy Ameghino, Eduardo. 1990. *Economía y sociedad colonial en el ámbito rural bonaerense.* In M. Rapoport, ed., *Economía e historia.* Buenos Aires: Tesis.

Baczko, Bronislaw. 1991. *Los imaginarios sociales. Memorias y esperanzas colectivas.* Buenos Aires: Nueva Visión.

Bagú, Sergio. 1966. *El plan económico del grupo rivadaviano (1811–1827)*. Rosario: Universidad Nacional del Litoral.

Bajarlia, Juan-Jacobo. 1969. *Rosas y los asesinatos de su época*. Buenos Aires: Ed. Dos.

Baker, Keith Michael. 1981. Enlightenment and revolution in France: Old problems, renewed approaches. *Journal of Modern History* 53 (June): 281–303.

Bakhtin, Mikhail. 1984. *Rabelais and his world*. Bloomington: Indiana University Press.

Barba, Enrique. 1962a. Las reacciones contra Rosas. In R. Levene, ed., *Historia de la nación Argentina*, vol. 7. Buenos Aires: El Ateneo.

——. 1962b. Formación de la tiranía. In Academia Nacional de Historia, ed., *Historia de la nación Argentina*, vol. 7. Buenos Aires: El Ateneo.

Barman, Roderick. 1988. *Brazil: The forging of a nation, 1798–1852*. Stanford: Stanford University Press.

Barreneche, Osvaldo. 1993. Esos torpes dezeos: delitos y desviaciones sexuales en Buenos Aires, 1760–1810. *Estudios de historia colonial* (La Plata): 29–45.

——. 1997. Crime and the administration of criminal justice in Buenos Aires, Argentina, 1785–1853. Ph.D. diss., University of Arizona.

Bayly, C. A. 1988. Rallying around the subaltern. *Journal of Peasant Studies* 16(1): 110–120.

Bell, Catherine. 1992. *Ritual theory, ritual practice*. New York: Oxford University Press.

Beverina, Juan. 1974. *Las campañas de los ejércitos libertadores*. Buenos Aires: Ed. Rioplatense.

Beverley, John. 1999. *Subalternity and representation: Arguments in cultural theory*. Durham, N.C.: Duke University Press.

Bhabha, Homi, ed. 1990. *Nation and narration*. London: Routledge.

Bilbao, Manuel. 1961. *Historia de Rosas*. Buenos Aires: Orientación Cultural.

Birabent, Mauricio. 1941. *Chivilcoy: la región y las chacras*. La Plata: Impresiones Oficiales.

Blackwelder, Julia K., and Lyman L. Johnson. 1982. Changing criminal patterns in Buenos Aires: 1890 to 1914. *Journal of Latin American Studies* 14(2): 359–379.

Bosio, Jorge A. 1972. *Historia de las pulperías*. Buenos Aires: Plus Ultra.

Botana, Natalio R. 1984. *La tradición republicana: Alberdi, Sarmiento y las ideas políticas de su tiempo*. Buenos Aires: Sudamericana.

Bourdieu, Pierre. 1984. *Distinction: A social critique of the judgement of taste*. Cambridge, Mass.: Harvard University Press.

Brown, Jonathan C. 1976. Dynamics and autonomy of a traditional marketing system: Buenos Aires: *Hispanic American Historical Review* 56(4): 605–629.

——. 1979. *A socioeconomic history of Argentina, 1776–1860*. Cambridge, England: Cambridge University Press.

——. 1986. The bondage of old habits in nineteenth-century Argentina. *Latin American Research Review* 21(2): 3–31.

——. 1994. Revival of the rural economy and society in Buenos Aires. In M. D. Szuchman and J. C. Brown, eds., *Revolution and restoration*. Lincoln: University of Nebraska Press.

Brunet, Michel. 1986. *Le Roussillon: Une societé contra l'etat 1780–1820*. Toulouse: Association des Publications de l'Université Toulouse-Le Mirail.

Burawoy, Michael. 1979. *Manufacturing consent: Changes in the labor process under monopoly capitalism*. Chicago: University of Chicago Press.

Burchell, Graham, Collin Gordon, and Peter Miller, eds. 1991. *The Foucault effect: Studies in governmentality*. Chicago: University of Chicago Press.

Burgin, Miron. 1946. *Aspectos económicos del federalismo argentino*. Buenos Aires: Hachette.

Burke, Peter, and Roy Porter. 1987. *The social history of language*. Cambridge, England: Cambridge University Press.

Calhoum, Craig. 1993. Habitus, field, and capital: The question of historical specificity. In C. Calhoum et al., eds. *Bourdieu: Critical perspectives*. Chicago: University of Chicago Press.

Calvert, Susan, and Peter Calvert. 1989. *Argentina: Political culture and instability*. Pittsburgh: University of Pittsburgh Press.

Cansanello, Oreste C. 1994. Domiciliados y transeúntes en el proceso de formación estatal bonaerense, 1820–1832. *Entrepasados* 4(6): 7–22.

——. 1995. De súbditos a ciudadanos: los pobladores rurales bonaerenses entre el antiguo régimen y la modernidad. *Boletín del Instituto Ravignani* 11: 113–139.

Cárcano, Miguel A. 1972. *Evolución histórica del régimen de la tierra pública, 1810–1916*. 3d. ed. Buenos Aires: Eudeba.

Cárcano, Ramón J. 1933. *De Caseros al 11 de setiembre*. Buenos Aires: Roldán.

Carretero, Andrés. 1970. *El pensamiento político de Juan M de Rosas*. Buenos Aires: Platero.

——. 1972. *La propiedad de la tierra en la época de Rosas*. Buenos Aires: El Coloquio.

Carvajal y Robles, Rodrigo de. 1950. *Fiestas de Lima por el nacimiento del Príncipe Baltasar Carlos, Lima 1632*. Sevilla: Consejo Superior de Investigaciones Científicas.

Cernadas de Bulnes, Mabel. 1993. *El pensamiento de Valentín Alsina en el exilio (1835–1852)*. Bahia Blanca: Universidad Nacional del Sur.

Certeau, Michel de. 1984. *The practice of everyday life*. Trans. S. Rendall. Berkeley: University of California Press.

——. 1986. *Heterologies: The discourse on the other*. Manchester, England: Manchester University Press.

Chakrabarty, Dipesh. 1992. Postcoloniality and the artifice of history: Who speaks for Indian pasts? *Representations* 37 (winter): 1–26.

Chapman, Stanley D. 1979. British marketing enterprise: The changing role of merchants, manufacturers, and financiers, 1700–1860. *Business History Review* 53: 2.

Chartier, Roger. 1991. *The cultural origins of the French revolution*. Durham, N.C.: Duke University Press.

Chatterjee, Partha. 1989. Caste and subaltern consciousness. In *Subaltern Studies VI*. New Delhi: Oxford University Press India.

Chiaramonte, José Carlos. 1986. Legalidad constitucional o caudillismo: El problema del orden social en el surgimiento de los estados autónomos del litoral argentino en la primera mitad del siglo XIX. *Desarrollo Económico* 26: 102.

———. 1989. Formas de identidad en el Río de la Plata luego de 1810. *Boletín del Instituto de Historia Argentina y Americana "Dr. Emilio Ravignani"* 3(1): 71–92.

———. 1995. Acerca del orígen del estado en el Río de la Plata. *Anuario IEHS* (Tandil) 10: 27–50.

———. 1997. *Ciudades, provincias, Estados: Orígenes de la Nación Argentina (1800–1846).* Buenos Aires: Ariel.

Chiaramonte, José Carlos, and Pablo Buchbinder. 1992. Provincias, caudillos, nación y la historiografía constitucionalista argentina, 1853–1930. *Anuario IEHS* (Tandil) 7: 93–120.

Chiaramonte, José Carlos, Marcela Ternavasio, and Fabián Herrero. 1995. Vieja y nueva representación: los procesos electorales en Buenos Aires, 1810–1820. In A. Annino, comp. *Historia de las elecciones en Iberoamérica, siglo XIX.* Buenos Aires: Fondo de Cultural Económica.

Clementi, Hebe. 1984. *Las fiestas patrias.* Buenos Aires: Leviatán.

Cobb, Richard C. 1987. *The people's armies: The armees revolutionaires: Instrument of the terror in the departments.* New Haven, Conn.: Yale University Press.

Cordero, Héctor A. 1978. *El primitivo Buenos Aires.* Buenos Aires: Plus Ultra.

Cox, Jeffrey, and Shelton Stromquist, eds. 1998. *Contesting the master narrative: Essays in social history.* Iowa City: University of Iowa Press.

Crespi, Liliana. 1995. La condición jurídica de los libertos en Buenos Aires 1810–1850. *Jornadas Inter-Escuelas de Departamentos de Historia*, Montevideo.

Cronon, William. 1992. A place for stories: Nature, history, and narrative. *Journal of American History* 78(4): 1347–1376.

Cuarterolo, Miguel A. 1995. Las primeras fotografías del país. In *Los Años del Daguerrotipo. Pimeras fotografías argentinas, 1843–1870.* Buenos Aires: Fundación Antorchas.

Cutter, Charles. 1995. *The legal culture of northern New Spain, 1700–1810.* Albuquerque: University of New Mexico Press.

Danzelot, Jacques. 1979. *The policing of families.* Trans. R. Hurley. New York: Pantheon Books.

Darnton, Robert. 1984. *The great cat massacre and other episodes in French cultural history.* London: Penguin.

De Gandía, Enrique. 1946. Estudio preliminar. In Tomas de Iriarte, ed. *Memorias,* vol. 4. Buenos Aires: Edic. Argentinas SIA.

Dellepiane, Antonio. 1956. *Rosas.* Buenos Aires: Obrerón.

Deppelier, Nestor R. 1936. *Los embargos en la época de Rosas.* Buenos Aires: Bernabe y Cia.

Devoto, Fernando. 1989. Los orígenes de un barrio italiano en Buenos Aires a mediados del siglo XIX. *Boletín del Instituto Ravignani* 3(1): 93–114.

Díaz, Benito. 1952. *Juzgados de paz de campaña de la provincia de Buenos Aires (1821–1854).* La Plata: Universidad Nacional de La Plata.

Dirks, Nicholas B. 1994. Ritual and resistance: Subversion as a social fact. In N. B. Dirks, G. Eley, and S. B. Ortner, eds. *Culture/power/history: A reader in contemporary social theory.* Princeton, N.J.: Princeton University Press.

Douglas, Mary, and B. Isherwood. 1990. *El mundo de los bienes*. Mexico City, Grijalbo.

Duarte, Carlos F. 1987. Las fiestas de Corpus Christi en la Caracas hispánica. *Boletín de La Academia Nacional de la Historia* (Caracas) 70 (279): 675–692.

Elías, Norbert. 1982. *The civilizing process*. Trans. Edmund Jephcott. New York: Pantheon.

Emsley, Clive. 1987. *Crime and society in England, 1750–1900*. London: Longman.

Etchepareborda, Roberto. 1972. *Rosas: controvertida historiografía*. Buenos Aires: Pleamar.

Farberman, Judith. 1995. Familia, ciclo de vida y economía doméstica: el caso de Salavina, Santiago del Estero en 1819. *Boletín del Instituto Ravignani* 12: 33–59.

——. 1997. Los que se van y los que se quedan: familia y migraciones en Santiago del Estero a fines del período colonial. *Quinto Sol* 1(1): 7–40.

Femia, Joseph V. 1981. *Gramsci's political thought: Hegemony, consciousness, and the revolutionary process*. Oxford: Clarendon Press.

Fentress, James, and Chris Wickham. 1992. *Social memory*. Oxford: Blackwell.

Fernández Rivas, Jorge. 1972. *Uniformes del ejercito argentino 1810–1820*. Buenos Aires: All-cop.

Ferns, Henry S. 1968. *Gran Bretaña y Argentina en el siglo XIX*. Buenos Aires: Solar/Hachette.

Fletcher, George P. 1996. *Basic concepts of legal thought*. New York: Oxford University Press.

Forrest, Alan. 1989. *Conscripts and deserters: The army and French society during the revolution and empire*. New York: Oxford University Press.

Foucault, Michel. 1979. *Discipline and punish: The birth of the prison*. Trans. A. Sheridan. New York: Vintage Books.

Fradkin, Raúk O. 1995. Según le costumbre del pays: Costumbre y arriendo en Buenos Aires durante el siglo XVIII. *Boletín del Instituto Ravignani* 11: 39–64.

Fussell, Paul. 1975. *The great war and modern memory*. Oxford: Oxford University Press.

Gálvez, Manuel. 1942. *Vida de don Juan Manuel de Rosas*. Buenos Aires: El Ateneo.

Garavaglia, Juan C. 1993. Migraciones, estructuras familiares y vida campesina. Areco arriba en 1815. In Garavaglia and Moreno, eds. *Población, sociedad, familia y migraciones*.

——. 1997a. Paz, orden y trabajo en la campaña: la justicia rural y los juzgados de paz en Buenos Aires, 1830–1852. *Desarrollo Económico* 37 (146): 241–260.

——. 1997b. De "mingas" y "convites": la reciprocidad campesina entre los paisanos rioplatenses. *Anuario IEHS* 12: 131–139.

——. 1998. Escenas de la vida política en la campaña: San Antonio de Areco en una crisis del rosismo. *Estudios Sociales* (Santa Fé) 8 (15): 9–30.

——. 1999. *Pastores y labradores de Buenos Aires*. Buenos Aires: Ediciones de la Flor.

Garavaglia, Juan C., and Claudia Wentzel. 1989. Un neuvo aporte a la historia del textil colonia: los ponchos frente al mercado porteño (1750/1850). *Amario del IEHS* (Tandil): 4.

Garavaglia, Juan C., and Jorge Gelman. 1995. Rural history of the Río de la Plata, 1600–1850: Results of a historiographical renaissance. *Latin American Research Review* 30 (3): 75–105.

Garavaglia, Juan C., and José Luis Moreno, eds. 1993. *Población, sociedad, familia y migraciones en el espacio rioplatense*. Buenos Aires: Cántaro.

Gatrell, V. A. C., and T. B. Hadden. 1972. Criminal statistics and their interpretation. In E. A. Wrigley, ed. *Nineteenth-century society: Essays in the use of quantitative methods for the study of social data*. New York: Cambridge University Press.

Gayol, Sandra. 2000. *Sociabilidad en Buenos Aires. Hombres, honor y cafés 1862–1910*. Buenos Aires: Ediciones del Signo.

Geertz, Clifford. 1980. *Negara: The theater state in nineteenth-century Bali*. Princeton, N.J.: Princeton University Press.

Gelman, Jorge. 1989. New perspectives on an old problem and the same source. *Hispanic American Historical Review* 69: 4.

———. 1996. Unos números sorprendentes. Cambio y continuidad en el mundo agrario bonaerense durante la primera mitad del siglo XIX. *Anuario IEHS* 11: 123–145.

———. 1998. Un gigante con pies de barro: Rosas y los pobladores de la campaña. In Goldman and Salvatore, *Caudillismos rioplatenses*.

Giberti, Horacio. 1961. *Historia económica de la ganadería argentina*. Buenos Aires: Solar.

Gluckman, Max. 1963. *Order and rebellion in tribal Africa*. London: Choen and West.

Goldberg, Marta B. 1976. La población negra y mulata de la ciudad Buenos Aires: 1810–1840. *Desarrollo Económico* 16 (61): 75–99.

Goldman, Noemí. 1980. Iluminismo e independencia: Monteagudo y Pasos Silva (Kanki) en la prensa revolucionaria de 1811–1812. In *El discurso político: lenguaje y acontecimientos*. Buenos Aires: Hachette.

———. 1989. Los "Jacobinos" en el Río de la Plata: modelo, discursos y prácticas (1810–1815). *Cuadernos Americanos* (17): 157–178.

Goldman, Noemí, and Ricardo Salvatore, eds. 1998. *Caudillismos rioplatenses. Nuevas miradas a un viejo problema*. Buenos Aires: Eudeba.

Gonzalez Bernaldo, Pilar. 1989. Producción de una nueva legitimidad: ejército y sociedades patrióticas en Buenos Aires entre 1810 y 1813. *Cuadernos Americanos* 3 (5): 134–156.

———. 1992. La création d'une nation. Histoire politique des nouvelles appartenances culturelles dans la ville de Buenos Aires entre 1829 et 1862. Ph.D. diss., Universite de Paris I, Pantheon-Sorbonne.

———. 1994. Social imagery and its political implications in a rural conflict. In M. D. Szuchman and J. C. Brown, eds. *Revolution and restoration*. Lincoln: University of Nebraska Press.

González Bollo, Hernán. 1999. Estado, ciencia y sociedad: los manuales estadísticos y geográficos en los orígenes de la Argentina moderna, 1852–76. *Final Report CONICET grant*. Buenos Aires, 1999.

González Echevarría, Roberto. 1994. A lost world rediscovered: Sarmiento's

facundo. In T. Halperin Donghi et al., eds. *Sarmiento: Author of a nation.*
Berkeley: University of California Press.

Goodwin, Paul B. 1977. The Central Argentine Railway and the economic development of Argentina, 1854–1881. *Hispanic American Historical Review* 57 (4): 613–632.

Goody, Jack. 1977. *The domestication of the savage mind.* Cambridge, England: Cambridge University Press.

Gori, Gaston. 1951. *Vagos y mal entretenidos: Aporte al tema hernandiano.* Santa Fe: Colmegna.

Gradenigo, Gaio. 1987. *Italianos entre Rosas y Mitre.* Buenos Aires: Ediciones Ediliba.

Graziano, Frank. 1992. *Divine violence.* Boulder, Colo.: Westview.

Guastavino Gallent, Guillermo. 1969. *Las fiestas de moros y cristianos y su problemática.* Madrid: Consejo Superior de Investigaciones Científicas.

Guha, Ranajit. 1983. *Elementary aspects of peasant insurgency in colonial India.* Delhi: Oxford University Press India.

———. 1997. *Domination without hegemony: History and power in colonial India.* Cambridge, MA: Harvard University Press.

Guha, Ranajit, and Gayatri Chakravorty Spivak, eds. 1988. *Selected subaltern studies.* New York: Oxford University Press.

Halbwachs, Maurice. 1992. *On collective memory.* Trans. L. A. Coser. Chicago: University of Chicago Press.

Halperin Donghi, Tulio. 1963. La expansión ganadera en la campaña de Buenos Aires, 1810–1852. *Desarrollo Económico* 3 (12): 57–110.

———. 1968. Revolutionary militarization in Buenos Aires, 1806–1815. *Past & Present* 40 (July): 84–107.

———. 1971. *El revisionismo histórico argentino.* Mexico: Siglo Veintiuno.

———. 1972. *Revolución y guerra. Formación de una elite dirigente en la Argentina criolla.* Buenos Aires: Siglo Veintiuno.

———. 1980. *Proyecto y constucción de una nación: Argentina 1846–1880.* Caracas: Biblioteca Ayacucho.

———. 1982. *Guerra y finanzas en los orígenes del estado argentino, 1791–1850.* Buenos Aires: Editorial de Belgrano.

———. 1985. *José Hernández y sus mundos.* Buenos Aires: Editorial Sudamericana/ Instituto Torcuato Di Tella.

———. 1988. Argentina as a born-liberal nation. In Joseph Love and Nils Jacobsen, eds. *Guiding the invisible hand.* New York: Praeger.

———. 1995. The Buenos Aires landed class and the shape of Argentine politics, 1820–1930. In E. Huber and J. D. Stephens, eds. *Agrarian structure and political power: Landlord and peasant in the making of Latin America.* Pittsburgh: University of Pittsburgh Press.

Halperin Donghi, Tulio, et al., eds. 1994. *Sarmiento: Author of a nation.* Berkeley: University of California Press.

Hay, Douglas et al., eds. 1975. *Albions' Fatal Tree: Crime and Society in Eighteenth-Century England.* New York: Pantheon Books.

Heggoy, Alf Andrew. 1986. *The French conquest of Algiers, 1830: An Algerian oral tradition.* Athens: Ohio University Press.

Hill, Jonathan D., ed. 1988. *Rethinking history and myth: Indigenous South American perspectives on the past.* Urbana: University of Illinois Press.

Hirschman, Albert O. 1970. *Exit, voice, and loyalty: Responses to decline in firms, organizations, and states.* Cambridge, MA: Harvard University Press.

Hobsbawm, Eric J. 1971. *Primitive rebels.* Manchester, England: Manchester University Press.

———. 1975. *Captain swing.* New York: Norton.

Hunt, Lynn A. 1992. *The family romance of the French revolution.* Berkeley: University of California Press.

Ibañez Frocham, Manuel. 1938. *La organización judicial argentina.* Buenos Aires: Ed. La Falcultad.

Ibarguren, Carlos. 1930. *Juan Manuel de Rosas: su vida, su tiempo, su drama.* Buenos Aires: Librería "La Facultad."

Iglesia, Cristina, comp. 1998. *Letras y divisas: Ensayos sobre literatura y rosismo.* Buenos Aires: Eudeba/Instituto de Literatura Hispanoamericana.

Iglesia, Cristina, and Julio Schvartzman. 1987. *Cautivas y misioneros. Mitos blancos de la conquista.* Buenos Aires: Catálogos.

Infesta, María Elena. 1999. La enfiteusis en Buenos Aires, 1920–1850. In S. Amaral and M. Valencia, comps. *Argentina: El país nuevo.* La Plata: Editorial de la UNLP.

Infesta, María E., and Marta E. Valencia. 1987. Tierras, premios y donaciones. Buenos Aires, 1830–1860. *Anuario IEHS* (Tandil) 2: 177–213.

Ingenieros, José. 1910. *La evolución sociológica argentina: De la barbarie al imperialismo.* Buenos Aires: Libr. J. Menéndez.

———. 1920. *La restauración,* vol. 2 of *La evolución de las ideas argentinas.* Buenos Aires: L. J. Rosso y Cia.

Instituto de Investigaciones Históricas. 1951. *Descripción de las fiestas cívicas celebradas en Montevideo en Mayo de 1816.* Montevideo: Universidad de la República.

Irazusta, Julio. 1941–1949. *Vida política de Juan Manuel de Rosas.* 3 vols. Buenos Aires: Albatros.

Irigoin, María Alejandra. 1995. Moneda, impuestos e instituciones: la estabilización de la moneda corriente en el estado de Buenos Aires durante las décadas de 1850 y 1860. *Anuario IEHS* (Tandil) 10: 189–218.

———. 2000. Finance, politics and economics in Buenos Aires, 1820s–1860s: The political economy of currency stabilisation. Ph.D. diss., London School of Economics.

Jauretche, Arturo. 1959. *Política nacional y revisionismo histórico.* Buenos Aires: Peña Lillo.

Jauss, Hans Robert. 1989. *Question and answer: Forms of dialogic understanding.* Minneapolis: University of Minnesota Press.

Johnson, Lyman L. 1976a. The silversmiths of Buenos Aires: A case study in the failure of corporate social organization. *Journal of Latin American Studies* 8 (2): 181–213.

———. 1976b. La manumisión de esclavos en Buenos Aires durante el virreinato. *Desarrollo Económico* 16 (63): 333–348.

———. 1980. The entrepreneurial reorganization of an artisan trade: The bakers of Buenos Aires, 1770–1820. *The Americas* 37 (2): 139–160.

———. 1981. The impact of racial discrimination on black artisans in colonial Buenos Aires. *Social History* 6 (3): 301–316.

———, ed. 1990. *The problem of order in changing societies.* Albuquerque: University of New Mexico Press.

———. 1995. The competition of slave and free labor in artisanal production: Buenos Aires, 1770–1815. *International Review of Social History* 40: 409–424.

Joyce, Patrick. 1991. *Visions of the people.* Cambridge, England: Cambridge University Press.

Katra, William H. 1996. *The Argentine generation of 1837.* London: Associated University Presses.

Korol, Juan Carlos, and Hilda Sabato. 1979. *"The camps": Inmigrantes irlandeses en la provincia de Buenos Aires, 1840–1890.* Buenos Aires: CISEA.

Koziol, Geoffrey. 1992. *Begging pardon and favor: Ritual and political order in early medieval France.* Ithaca, N.Y.: Cornell University Press.

Krech, Shepard. 1991. The state of ethnohistory. *Annual Review of Anthropology* 20: 345–75.

Kurlat de Korin, Itta, and Cristina Minutolo. 1965. *La revolución del sur.* Chascomús: Secretaría de Cultura de la Municipalidad de Chascomús.

Lagos, Juan. 1972. *General H. Lagos. De los últimos virreyes a los primeros presidentes.* vol. 2. Buenos Aires: Círculo Miltar.

Latin American Subaltern Studies Group (LASSG). 1993. Founding statement. *boundary 2* 20 (2): 110–21.

Leed, Eric J. 1979. *No man's land: Combat and identity in World War I.* Cambridge, England: Cambridge University Press.

Le Goff, Jacques. 1991. *El orden de la memoria.* Buenos Aires: Paidós.

Lettieri, Alberto R. 1999. *La república de la opinión.* Buenos Aires: Biblos.

Levene, Ricardo. 1937. *A history of Argentina.* Chapel Hill: University of North Carolina Press.

———. 1954. *La anarquía de 1820 y la iniciación de la vida pública de Rosas.* Buenos Aires: Union de Editores Latinos.

———. 1961. Investigaciones acerca de la historia económica del Virreinato del Plata. In *Obras de Ricardo Levene,* vol. 2. Buenos Aires: Academia Nacional de Historia.

Lewis, Colin M. 1983. *British Railways in Argentina, 1857–1914.* London: Athlone.

Linebaugh, Peter. 1977. The ordinary of Newgate and his account. In J. S. Cockburn, ed. *Crime in England 1550–1800.* Princeton, N.J.: Princeton University Press.

———. 1992. *The London hanged: crime and civil society in the eighteenth century.* Cambridge, England: Cambridge University Press.

Ludmer, Josefina. 1988. *El género gauchesco: Un tratado sobre la patria.* Buenos Aires: Editorial Sudamericana.

Lynch, John. 1981. *Argentine dictator: Juan Manuel de Rosas, 1829–1852.* Oxford: Clarendon Press.

——. 1998. *Massacre in the pampas, 1872. Britain and Argentina in the age of migration*. Norman: University of Oklahoma Press.

Macchi, Manuel E. 1981. *El breve gobierno de Urquiza en Buenos Aires*. Concepción del Uruguay: Offset Yusty.

Mallon, Florencia E. 1994. The problem and dilemma of Latin American subaltern studies: Perspectives from Latin American history. *American Historical Review* 99 (5): 1491–1515.

——. 1995. *Peasant and nation: The making of postcolonial Mexico and Peru*. Berkeley: University of California Press.

Mandrini, Raúl J. 1993. Las transformaciones de la economía indígena bonaerense (c. 1600–1820). In R. Mandrini and A. Requera, eds. *Huellas en la tierra*. Tandil: IEHS.

Mariluz Urquijo, José M. 1968. La comercialización de la producción sombrera porteña. *Investigaciones y Ensayos* 5 (July–December): 103–129.

Mateo, José. 1993a. Población y producción en un ecosistema agrario de la frontera de Salado, 1815–1869. in R. Mandrini and A. Requera, eds. *Huellas en la tierra*. Tandil: IEHS.

——. 1993b. Migrar y volver a migrar. Los campesinos agricultores de la frontera bonaerense a principios del siglo XIX. In Garavaglia and Moreno, eds. *Población, sociedad, familia y migraciones*.

Mayo, Carlos A. 1984. Estancia y peonaje en la región pampeana en la segunda mitad del siglo XVIII. *Desarrollo Económico* 23 (92): 609–16.

——. 1985. Amistades ilícitas: las relaciones extramatrimoniales en la campaña bonaerense, 1750–1810. *Cuadernos de Historia Regional* 1 (2): 3–9.

——. 1991. Landed but not powerful: The colonial estancieros of Buenos Aires (1750–1810). *Hispanic American Historical Review* 71 (4): 761–779.

——. 1995. *Estancia y sociedad en la pampa, 1740–1820*. Buenos Aires: Biblos.

——. 1997a. Patricio de Belén: nada menos que un capataz. *Hispanic American Historical Review* 77 (4): 597–617.

——. 1997b. Juan Manuel de Rosas, el estanciero. In F. E. Barba and C. A. Mayo, eds. *Argentina y Chile en época de Rosas y Portales*. La Plata: Editorial UNLP.

——, comp. 1997c. *Pulperos y pulperías de Buenos Aires, 1740–1830*. Mar del Plata: UNMP.

——, comp. 1998. *Juego, sociedad y estado en Buenos Aires, 1730–1830*. La Plata: Editorial de la Universidad Nacional de La Plata.

Mayo, Carlos A., and Amalia Latrubesse. 1986. *Terratenientes, soldados y cautivos: La frontera, 1736–1815*. Mar del Plata: Universidad Nacional de Mar del Plata.

Mazzeo, Victoria. 1988. Migración internacional en la ciudad de Buenos Aires, 1855–1980. *Dirección de Estadística y Censos*. Pamphlet. November.

Mendoza, Prudencio. 1928. *Historia de la ganadería argentina*. Buenos Aires: Talleres Graf. L. J. Rosso.

Mitre, Bartolomé. 1947. *Historia de Belgrano y de la Independencia Argentina*. vol. 4. Buenos Aires: Ed. Estrada.

Molinari, Diego L. 1962. *Prolegómenos de Caseros*. Buenos Aires: Devenir.

Moncaut, Carlos A. 1977. *Estancias bonaerenses*. City Bell, Argentina: El Aljibe.

Monsma, Karl M. 1992. Ranchers, rural people, and the state in post-colonial Argentina. Ph.D. diss., University of Michigan, Ann Arbor.

Montagnon, Pierre. 1986. *La conquete de l'Algérie, 1830–1871.* Paris: Pygmalion.

Montgomery, David. 1979. *Workers' control in America: Studies in the history of work, technology, and labor struggles.* Cambridge, England: Cambridge University Press.

Montoya, Alfredo. 1956. *Historia de los saladeros argentinos.* Buenos Aires: Raigal.

Moraña, Mabel. 1997. El boom del subalterno. *Revista de Crítica Cultural* 14: 48–53.

Mukerji, Chandra. 1983. *From graven images: Patterns of modern materialism.* New York: Columbia University Press.

Mukerji, Chandra, and M. Schudson, eds. 1991. *Rethinking popular culture.* Berkeley: University of California Press.

Myers, Jorge. 1995. *Orden y virtud. El discurso republicano en el régimen rosista.* Buenos Aires: Universidad Nacional de Quilmes.

———. 1998. La revolución de las ideas: la generación romántica de 1837 en la cultura y en la política argentinas. In N. Goldman, ed. *Nueva Historia Argentina,* vol. 3. Buenos Aires: Sudamericana.

Newland, Carlos. 1992. *Buenos Aires no es pampa.* Buenos Aires: Grupo Editor Latinoamericano.

Oddone, Jacinto. 1967. *La burguesía terrateniente argentina.* Buenos Aires: Libera.

O'Hanlon, Rosalind. 1988. Recovering the subject: Subaltern studies and histories of resistance in colonial South Asia. *Modern Asian Studies* 22 (1): 189–224.

Ortiz, Ricardo M. 1974. *Historia económica de la Argentina.* Buenos Aires: Plus Ultra.

Ozouf, Mona. 1988. *Festivals and the French revolution.* Cambridge, MA: Harvard University Press.

Pandey, Gyanendra. 1992. In defense of the fragment: Writing about Hindu-Muslim riots in India today. *Representations,* no. 37, Special Issue: Imperial Fantasies and Postcolonial Histories (winter): 27–55.

Patnaik, Arun K. 1988. Gramsci's concept of common sense: Towards a theory of subaltern consciousness in hegemonic processes. *Economic and Political Weekly* 23 (5): 2–10.

Peña, Milcíades. 1969. *El paraíso terrateniente: Federales y unitarios forjan la civilizacion del cuero.* Buenos Aires: Ediciones Fichas.

Phelan, James. 1989. *Reading people, reading plots.* Chicago: University of Chicago Press.

Polémica: Gauchos, campesinos y fuerza de trabajo en la campaña rioplatense colonial. 1987. *Anuario IHES* 2: 23–70.

Pollard, Sidney. 1968. *The genesis of modern management.* Harmondsworth, England: Penguin.

Prakash, Gyan. 1994. Subaltern studies as postcolonial criticism. *American Historical Review* 99 (4–5): 1475–1490.

Pratt, Mary Louise. 1992. *Imperial eyes: Travel writing and transculturation.* London: Verso.

Prieto, Adolfo. 1996. *Los viajeros ingleses y la emergencia de la literatur argentina, 1820–1850*. Buenos Aires: Sudamericana.

Quattrocchi-Woisson, Diana. 1995. *Los males de la memoria*. Buenos Aires: Emecé Editores.

Quesada, Ernesto (1926a). *La época de Rosas*. Buenos Aires: A Moén.

——. 1926b. *Lamadrid y la Coalición del Norte*. Buenos Aires: Artes y Letras.

——. 1927. *Lavalle y la batalla de Quebracho Herrado*. Buenos Aires: Artes y Letras.

——. 1965. *Acha y la batalla de Angaco*. Buenos Aires: Pampa y Cielo.

——. 1975. *Pacheco y la Campaña de Cuyo*. Buenos Aires: Plus Ultra.

Rabasa, José, Javier Sanjinés, and Robert Carr, eds. 1994. Subaltern studies in the Americas. Special issue of *dispositio/n* 19 (46).

Ramos Mejía, José María. 1907. *Rosas y su tiempo*. Buenos Aires: F. Lajouane.

——. 1932. *Las neurosis de los hombres célebres en la historia argentina*. Buenos Aires: Talleres Gráficos L. J. Rosso.

Rappaport, Joanne. 1990. *The politics of memory: Native historical interpretation in the Colombian Andes*. Cambridge, England: Cambridge University Press.

Ratto, Silvia. 1994. *Indios amigos e indios aliados: orígenes del "Negocio Pacífico" en la provincia de Buenos Aires (1829–1832)*. Buenos Aires: Instituto de Historia Argentina y Americana Dr. Emilio Ravignani.

——. 1996. Conflictos y armonías en la frontera bonaerense, 1834–1840. *Entrepasados* 6 (11): 21–34.

Ravignani, Emilio. 1970. *Rosas: interpretación real y moderna*. Buenos Aires: Editorial Pleamar.

Reber, Vera Blinn. 1972. British mercantile houses in Buenos Aires, 1810–1880. Ph.D. Diss. University of Wisconsin, Madison.

Richelet, Juan E. 1928. *La Ganadería argentina y su comercio de carnes*. Buenos Aires: J. Lajouane and Cia.

Rivera Cusicanqui, Silvia, and Rossana Barragán, comps. 1998. *Debates post coloniales: Una introducción a los estudios de la subalternidad*. La Paz: SIERPE.

Rodríguez Molas, Ricardo. 1968. *Historia social del gaucho*. Buenos Aires: Edic. Marú.

Romero, José Luis. 1969. *Las ideas políticas en Argentina*. Buenos Aires: Fondo de Cultura Economica.

Rosa, José Maria. 1962. *Defensa y pérdida de nuestra independencia económica*. 3d ed. Buenos Aires: Librería Huemul.

Roseberry, William. 1989. Balinese cockfights and the seduction of anthropology. In *Anthropologies and histories*. New Brunswick, N.J.: Rutgers University Press.

——. 1998. Social fields and cultural encounters. In G. Joseph, C. LeGrand, and R. Salvatore, eds. *Close encounters of empire: Writing the cultural history of U.S.–Latin American relations*. Durham, N.C.: Duke University Press.

Rottjer, Enrique I. 1937. *Mitre militar*. Buenos Aires: Institución Mitre.

Sábato, Hilda. 1985a. "La formación del mercado de trabajo en Buenos Aires, 1850–1880. *Desarrollo Económico* 24 (96): 561–592.

——. 1985b. Trabajar para vivir o vivir para trabajar: empleo ocasional y escasez de mano de obra en Buenos Aires, ciudad y campaña, 1850–1880. In N. Sánchez Albornoz, ed. *Población y mano de obra en América Latina*. Madrid: Alianza Editorial.

——. 1989. *Capitalismo y gandería en Buenos Aires: La fiebre del lanar, 1850–1890*. Buenos Aires: Sudamericana.

Sábato, Hilda, and Luis Alberto Romero. 1992. *Los trabajadores de Buenos Aires: la experiencia del mercado, 1850–1880*. Buenos Aires: Editorial Sudamericana.

Sáenz, Jimena. 1969. Las fiestas mayas en Buenos Aires. *Todo es Historia* 3 (25): 54–59.

Sáenz Quesada, María. 1980. *Los estancieros*. Buenos Aires: Editorial de Belgrano.

——. 1982. *El estado rebelde: Buenos Aires entre 1850–1860*. Buenos Aires: Editorial de Belgrano.

——. 1991. *Mujeres de Rosas*. Buenos Aires: Planeta.

Saguier, Eduardo. 1993. *Mercado inmobiliario y estructura social*. Buenos Aires: Centro Editor de América Latina.

Sahlins, Marshall. 1994. Cosmologies of capitalism: The trans-Pacific sector of "The world system." In N. B. Dirks et al., eds. *Culture/Power/History*.

Saldías, Adolfo. 1968. *Historia de la Confederación Argentina*. Buenos Aires: Eudeba.

Salessi, Jorge. 1995. *Médicos, maleantes y maricas*. Rosario: Beatriz Viterbo.

Salvatore, Ricardo D. 1991a. Autocratic state and labor control in the Argentine pampas: Buenos Aires, 1829–1852. *Peasant Studies* 18 (4): 251–78.

——. 1991b. Modes of labor control in cattle-ranching economies: California, southern Brazil, and Argentina, 1800–1870. *Journal of Economic History* 51 (2): 441–51.

——. 1994a. The breakdown of social discipline in the Banda Oriental and the Littoral, 1790–1820. In M. D. Szuchman and J. C. Brown, eds. *Revolution and restoration*.

——. 1994b. El Imperio de la Ley: Delito, estado y sociedad en la era Rosista. *Delito y Sociedad* 4/5 (August): 93–118.

——. 1996a. Fiestas federales: Representaciones de la República en el Buenos Aires rosista. *Entrepasados* 6 (11): 45–68.

——. 1996b. Invitación violenta: Indios, Estado y Representación durante la época de Rosas. In E. Reichel and I. Gutfreind, eds. *America platina e historiografia*. Sao Leopoldo: UNISINOS.

——. 1996c. Stories of proletarianization in rural Argentina, 1820–1860. *Dispositio/n* 19 (46): 197–216.

——. 1996d. North American travel narratives and the ordering/othering of South America (c. 1810–1860). *Journal of Historical Sociology* 9 (1): 85–110.

——. 1998a. Expresiones federales: formas políticas del federalismo rosista. In N. Goldman and R. Salvatore, eds. *Caudillismos rioplatenses*.

——. 1998b. Heights and welfare in late-colonial and post-independence Argentina. In J. Komlos and J. Baten, eds. *The biological standard of living in comparative perspective*. Stuttgart: Steiner Verlag.

——. 2000. Repertoires of coercion and market culture in nineteenth-century Buenos Aires province. *International Review of Social History* 45 (3): 409–448.

———. 2001. Death and liberalism: Capital punishment after the fall of Rosas. In R. Salvatore, C. Aguirre, and G. Joseph, eds. *Crime and punishment in Latin America*. Durham, N.C.: Duke University Press.

Salvatore, Ricardo D., and Jonathan C. Brown. 1987. Trade and proletarianization in late colonial Banda Oriental: Evidence from the Estancia de Las Vacas. *Hispanic American Historical Review* 67 (3): 431–459.

———. 1989. The old problem of gauchos and rural society. *Hispanic American Historical Review* 69 (4): 733–745.

Schvartzman, Julio. 1996. *Micro-crítica. Lecturas argentinas (cuestiones de detalle)*. Buenos Aires: Biblos.

Scott, James C. 1976. *The moral economy of the peasant: Rebellion and subsistence in Southeast Asia*. New Haven, Conn.: Yale University Press.

———. 1985. *Weapons of the weak: Everyday forms of peasant resistance*. New Haven, Conn.: Yale University Press.

———. 1990. *Domination and the arts of resistance: Hidden transcripts*. New Haven, Conn.: Yale University Press.

———. 1998. *Seeing like a state: How certain schemes to improve the human condition have failed*. New Haven, Conn.: Yale University Press.

Scott, Joan W. 1988. *Gender and the politics of history*. New York: Columbia University Press.

Sebreli, Juan José. 1972. *Apogeo y ocaso de los Anchorena*. Buenos Aires: Siglo Veinte.

Shumway, Nicolas. 1991. *The invention of Argentina*. Berkeley: University of California Press.

———. 1993. *La invención de la Argentina*. Buenos Aires: Emecé.

Slatta, Richard W. 1982. Pulperías and contraband capitalism in nineteenth-century Buenos Aires province. *The Americas* 38 (3): 347–362.

———. 1983. *Gauchos and the vanishing frontier*. Lincoln: University of Nebraska Press.

———. 1989. Civilization battles barbarism: Argentine frontier strategies, 1516–1880. *Review of Interamerican Bibliography* 39 (2): 177–194.

Slatta, Richard W., and Karla Robinson. 1990. Continuities in crime and punishment, Buenos Aires, 1820–1850. In L. L. Johnson, ed. *The problem of order in changing societies*. Albuquerque: University of New Mexico Press.

Socolow, Susan Migden. 1990. Women and crime: Buenos Aires, 1757–1797. In L. L. Johnson, ed. *The problem of order in changing societies*. Albuquerque: University of New Mexico Press.

———. 1998. Women of the Buenos Aires frontier, 1740–1810: Or the gaucho turned upside down. In D. J. Guy and T. E. Sheridan, eds. *Contested Ground*. Tucson: University of Arizona Press.

Sommer, Doris. 1991. *Foundational fictions*. Berkeley: University of California Press.

Sorensen Goodrich, Diana. 1996. *Facundo and the construction of Argentine culture*. Austin: University of Texas Press.

Sowell, David. 1992. *The early Colombian labor movement: Artisans and politics in Bogota, 1832–1919*. Philadelphia: Temple University Press.

Stedman Jones, Gareth. 1983. *Languages of class.* Cambridge, England: Cambridge University Press.

Svampa, Maristella. 1994. *El dilema argentino: Civilización o barbarie.* Buenos Aires: El Cielo por Asalto.

Szuchman, Mark D. 1984. Disorder and social control in Buenos Aires, 1810–1860. *Journal of Interdisciplinary History* 15 (1): 83–110.

——. 1986. Household structure and political crisis: Buenos Aires, 1810–1860. *Latin American Research Review* 21 (3): 55–93.

——. 1988. *Order, family, and community in Buenos Aires, 1810–1860.* Stanford: Stanford University Press.

——. 1990. Childhood education and politics in nineteenth-century Argentina: The case of Buenos Aires. *Hispanic American Historical Review* 70 (1): 109–138.

Ternavasio, Marcela. 1995. Nuevo régimen representativo y expansión de la frontera política: Las elecciones en el estado de Buenos Aires, 1820–1840. In A. Annino, comp. *Historia de las elecciones en Iberoamérica, siglo XIX.* Buenos Aires: Fondo de Cultura Económica.

Thompson, Edward P. 1967. Time, work-discipline and industrial capitalism. *Past & Present:* 38.

——. 1971. The moral economy of the English crowd in the 18th century. *Past & Present:* 50.

——. 1978. Eighteenth-century English society: Class struggle without class? *Social History* 3 (2).

——. 1993. *Customs in common: Studies in traditional popular culture.* New York: New Press.

Torre Revello, José. 1929. *Del Montevideo del siglo XVIII: fiestas y costumbres.* Montevideo: Siglo Ilustrado.

Trias, Vivián. 1970. *Juan Manuel de Rosas.* Montevideo: Ediciones de la Banda Oriental.

——. 1988. *Los caudillos, las clases sociales y el imperio.* Montevideo: Edic. de la Banda Oriental.

Turner, Victor. 1974. *Dramas, fields, and metaphors: Symbolic action in human society.* Ithaca, N.Y.: Cornell University Press.

Udaondo, Enrique. 1922. *Uniformes militares usados en la Argentina desde el s. XVI hasta nuestros días.* Buenos Aires: Pegoraro.

Urquiza, Alfredo F. de. 1924. *Campañas de Urquiza.* Buenos Aires: Lajouane.

Vogel, Hans. 1991. Fiestas patrias y nuevas lealtades. *Todo es Historia* 25 (287): 42–50.

Warman, Arturo. 1972. *La danza de moros y cristianos.* Mexico: Instituto Nacional de Antropología e Historia.

Weber, Eugen J. 1976. *Peasants into Frenchmen: The modernization of rural France, 1870–1914.* Stanford: Stanford University Press.

Weinberg, Félix. 1977. *El salón literario de 1837.* 2d ed. Buenos Aires: Hachette.

Whigham, Thomas. 1988. Cattle raising in the Argentine northeast: Corrientes, c. 1780–1870. *Journal of Latin American Studies* 20 (November): 313–35.

Wiener, Martin J. 1990. *Reconstructing the criminal*. New York: Cambridge University Press.

Zemon Davis, Natalie. 1987. *Fiction in the archives*. Stanford: Stanford University Press.

Zinny, Antonio. 1879. *Historia de los gobernadores de las provincias argentinas*. vol. 1. Buenos Aires: Imprenta Mayo.

Index

Halperin Donghi, Tulio, 31
Hegemony: belief in justice, 181–83; lack in regiments of, 17; of laws, 181–84, 195–96
Hidalgo, Bartolome, 343
Historical memory, 357

Immigrants: land redistribution claims and, 408; native police and, 411–14; political demands and, 408–9; progress and, 396
Indian peoples: attack against Ranqueles, 348; fighting the Indians, 348–49; Indians in revolutionary festivals, 379; Indian soldier insulted, 300; rumors of Indian attacks, 290
Ingenieros, Jose, 10, 41–42

Justice: local vs. central, 239; swiftness of, 255
Justices of the peace: as central figures, 2; conflicts with military chiefs, 166–67; ideological affinity, 167–68; increased number of, 165; leniency toward local residents, 206; moral policing, 205; order in countryside, 168; powers of, 166, 204; religious observance, 205; search for evidence, 170; supervised by professional judges, 169

Labor force: advertising services, 68–69; African workers, 29; as commodity, 33; Palermo workshops, 67; provincianos, 95–128; shortages, 70–74; state as employer, 67–68
Labor relations: absenteeism, 80; conflicts at workplace, 85–90; incentives and penalties, 76–81; lack of deference, 83; misconceptions about, 61; sujetados, 84; violent interactions, 90–92
Lagos rebellion, 409–11
Law: social equality and, 267
Legal order: archives on the pampas, 177; belief in justice, 181–83; centrality of law, 164, 425; colonial laws, 165; cooperation from neighbors, 183–85; correctional justice, 204; defiance of justice, 189–90; discretionary justice, 207; enforcement of

laws, 165–68; equality before law, 171–75, 374; expectation of justice, 188–89; legal literacy, 194; military fueros, 171–72; nepotism, 174–75; pedagogy of laws, 175–80, 237; private justice, 172–74; procedural rules, 169–71; protecting fugitives, 173–74; resguardos, 190; role of neighbors, 207; Rosista rhetoric, 161–65; subalterns and, 16; swift justice, 168–69. See also Justices of the peace
Liberalism, 26
Lopez, Estanislao, 375

Macro-narratives, 18–19, 21
Markets: advertisements, 31, 34; bread, 39–40; cattle, 30–31, 34, 39–40, 41–42; competition, 35, 41–45, 59; diversity of, 34; domestic production, 32; European commodities, 28; export bonanza, 25; flourishing of labor and commodity markets, 16; food abundance, 27, 32; incentives and penalties, 76; labor, 61–76; logic of, 76, 80; market culture, 27; market spectacles, 26–27, 34; new goods, 33; paysanos and, 424; provincianos vs. portenos, 100–104; public auctions, 31, 34–37, 46; pulperias volantes, 57; regulation of, 30–31, 38–40, 42, 57, 59; wage imperfections in, 75–76. See also Consumption; Labor Force
Marmol, Jose, 199–200
Massacres (1840, 1842), 233; public trial, 405
Mazorca, 200
Mazorquero, 233
Meat rations, 76–77
Militarization: importance for paysanos of, 20; of rural life, 9, 203; resistance against draft, 266
Military life: conspiracy to desert, 282–83; contract at entry, 278; disease, 259; economic contract, 303; fighting Indians, 348; heroism in combat, 346–47; lack of medical services, 307; oaths, 180; passive services, 222, 266; pilgrimage across fatherland, 350; "private services," 308–9; reforming power of, 240; santos (pass-

RICARDO D. SALVATORE is Professor of Modern History at Universidad Torcuato di Tella in Buenos Aires, Argentina. He edited (with Carlos Aguirre and Gilbert M. Joseph) *Crime and Punishment in Latin America: Law and Society Since Late Colonial Times* (Duke, 2001); (with Gilbert M. Joseph and Catherine LeGrand) *Close Encounters of Empire: Writing the Cultural History of U.S.–Latin American Relations* (Duke, 1998); (with Noemí Goldman) *Caudillismos Rioplatenses: Nuevas miradas a un viejo problema* (Eudeba, 1998); and (with Carlos Aguirre) *The Birth of the Penitentiary in Latin America* (University of Texas Press, 1996).

Library of Congress Cataloging-in-Publication Data
Salvatore, Ricardo D.
Wandering paysanos : state order and subaltern experience in Buenos Aires during the Rosas era / Ricardo D. Salvatore.
p. cm.
Includes bibliographical references and index.
ISBN 0-8223-3086-5 (cloth : alk. paper)
1. Peasantry—Argentina—Buenos Aires (Province)—History—19th century. 2. Buenos Aires (Argentina : Province)—Politics and government—19th century. I. Title.
HD1339.A7 S25 2003
982'.1204—dc21   2002153876